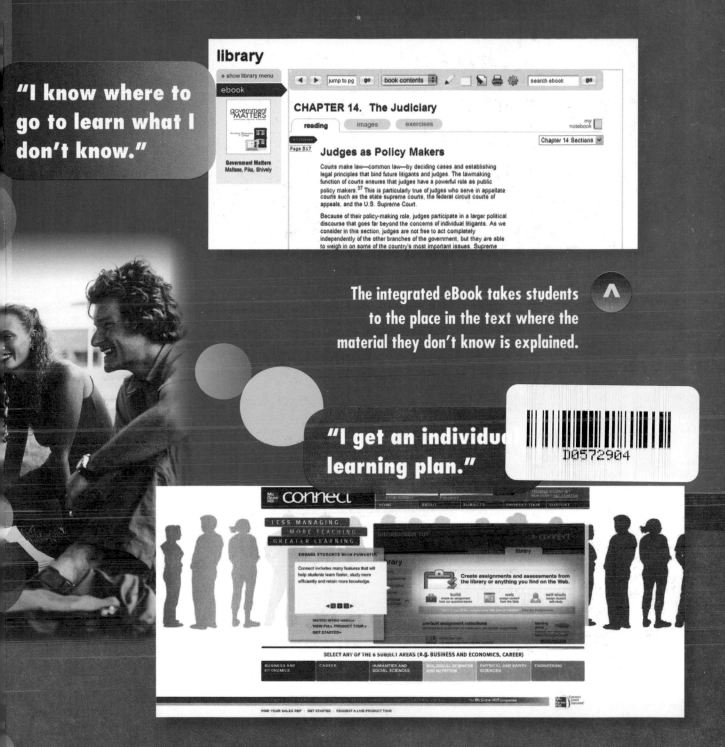

"I know where to go to learn what I don't know."

The integrated eBook takes students to the place in the text where the material they don't know is explained.

"I get an individual learning plan."

rich reporting tools give students instructors detailed views of how a student is performing during semester.

LearnSmart generates an individualized learning plan so students study most what they understand least.

Contents
★ ★ ★

Brief Contents

* * *

GOVERNMENT MATTERS: AMERICAN DEMOCRACY IN CONTEXT

Published by McGraw-Hill, a business unit of The McGraw-Hill Companies, Inc., 1221 Avenue of the Americas, New York, NY 10020. Copyright © 2013 by The McGraw-Hill Companies, Inc. All rights reserved. Printed in the United States of America. No part of this publication may be reproduced or distributed in any form or by any means, or stored in a database or retrieval system, without the prior written consent of The McGraw-Hill Companies, Inc., including, but not limited to, in any network or other electronic storage or transmission, or broadcast for distance learning.

Some ancillaries, including electronic and print components, may not be available to customers outside the United States.

This book is printed on acid-free paper.

1 2 3 4 5 6 7 8 9 0 DOW/DOW 1 0 9 8 7 6 5 4 3 2

ISBN: 978-0-07-337894-7
MHID: 0-07-337894-1

Senior Vice President, Products & Markets: Kurt L. Strand
Vice President, General Manager: Michael Ryan
Vice President, Content Production & Technology Services: Kimberly Meriwether David
Managing Director/Director: Gina Boedeker/Matthew Busbridge
Brand Manager: Meredith Grant
Senior Director of Development: Dawn Groundwater
Senior Development Editor: Lui T. Moy
Editorial Coordinator: Nikki Weissman
Marketing Manager: Patrick Brown
Director, Content Production: Terri Schiesl

Content Project Manager: Robin Reed
Buyer: Susan K. Culbertson
Designer: Tara McDermott
Cover/Interior Designer: Maureen McCutcheon
Cover Image: (front cover) © iStockphoto/Michael Brown; (back cover) © plainpicture/apply pictures
Senior Content Licensing Specialist: John C. Leland
Art Editor: Ayelet Arbel
Photo Researcher: Deborah Bull
Media Project Manager: Jodi Banowetz
Typeface: 10.5/13 Minion Pro
Compositor: Laserwords Private Limited
Printer: R.R. Donnelley—Willard

All credits appearing on page or at the end of the book are considered to be an extension of the copyright page.

Library of Congress Cataloging-in-Publication Data

Maltese, John Anthony.
　　Government matters : American democracy in context / John Maltese, Joseph A. Pika, W. Phillips Shively. — 1st ed.
　　　　p. cm.
　　Includes index.
　　ISBN 978-0-07-337894-7—ISBN-10: 0-07-337894-1 (hard copy : alk. paper)
　　1. United States—Politics and government—Textbooks. 2. Democracy—United States—Textbooks. I. Pika, Joseph August, 1947- II. Shively, W. Phillips, 1942- III. Title.
JK276.M34 2013
320.473—dc23
　　　　　　　　　　　　　　　　　　　　　　　　　　　　　　　　　　　2012009894

The Internet addresses listed in the text were accurate at the time of publication. The inclusion of a website does not indicate an endorsement by the authors or McGraw-Hill, and McGraw-Hill does not guarantee the accuracy of the information presented at these sites.

www.mhhe.com

GOVERNMENT MATTERS

* * *

AMERICAN DEMOCRACY IN CONTEXT

JOHN ANTHONY MALTESE
University of Georgia

JOSEPH A. PIKA
University of Delaware

W. PHILLIPS SHIVELY
University of Minnesota

Mc
Graw
Hill

Connect
Learn
Succeed™

GOVERNMENT MATTERS

CHAPTER 3

FEDERALISM ★

CHAPTER **4**

★ CIVIL LIBERTIES

CHAPTER **5**

★ CIVIL RIGHTS

PUBLIC OPINION AND POLITICAL SOCIALIZATION ★

PART 3 PEOPLE AND POLITICS

CHAPTER 7

★ POLITICAL PARTIES

CHAPTER 8

★ NOMINATIONS AND ELECTIONS

PARTICIPATION, VOTING BEHAVIOR, AND CAMPAIGNS ★

CHAPTER 10

★ INTEREST GROUPS

MEDIA AND POLITICS ★

CONGRESS ★

PART 4 INSTITUTIONS OF AMERICAN DEMOCRACY

CHAPTER 13

★ THE PRESIDENCY

CHAPTER 14

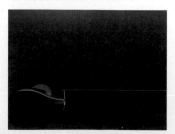

★ BUREAUCRACY

CHAPTER **16**

★ THE ECONOMY AND NATIONAL BUDGET

CHAPTER **17**

★ DOMESTIC POLICY

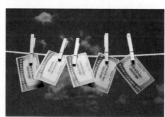

CHAPTER 18

FOREIGN AND NATIONAL SECURITY POLICY ★

APPENDICES ★

GOVERNMENT MATTERS:

* * *

AMERICAN DEMOCRACY IN CONTEXT

| THIS MAY BE THE ONLY COURSE YOUR STUDENTS TAKE IN POLITICAL SCIENCE. MAKE IT MATTER. |

CONTEXT **MATTERS**

| MAKE AMERICAN GOVERNMENT MATTER BY PUTTING IT IN CONTEXT FOR YOUR STUDENTS. | *Government Matters: American Democracy in Context* is a first edition that tells the story of the making and development of our distinctly American democracy. It not only inspires students to ask, "Why are we the way we are?" but also gives them the knowledge and context they need to answer for themselves, "Why does it matter?"

WHY ARE WE THE WAY WE ARE . . . AND WHY DOES IT MATTER?

Why Are We the Way We Are? pulls together the historical and comparative explanations that address the introductory questions regarding the distinctive features of American politics, while . . . *And Why Does It Matter?* analyzes why these distinctive features are relevant to students. For example, U.S. political parties are more decentralized than those in many other nations—partly because of our electoral system and partly because of a long history of party reform starting with the Progressive Movement—making it more difficult for Congress to take action on social and economic problems.

Why Are We THE WAY WE ARE?

This chapter highlighted aspects of American political parties that require special explanation:

- the fact that there are only two major parties
- their relatively loose and decentralized structure
- the fact that in recent decades the two parties have become much more deeply divided than they once were

THE TWO-PARTY SYSTEM

The two-party system can probably best be explained by our winner-take-all electoral system. As discussed earlier in the chapter, two-party systems are much more common in countries with winner-take-all electoral systems. Other contributing factors are probably our elected preside[...] winner-take-all effect, and also the many state laws [...] parties to get access to the ballot and gain public [...]

LOOSE AND DECENTRALIZED PART[...]

The second notable characteristic of American [...]

. . . AND WHY DOES IT Matter?

Parties matter to us because they are the most effective device available to bring together policy makers and politically concerned citizens throughout the country. If we want to address problems through government policy, political parties are indispensable to the effort.

Having just two parties seems to work satisfactorily for this purpose because our parties have proved themselves able to evolve in response to changing policy needs, especially with help from the periodic rise of third parties that push them to evolve.

The loose and decentralized structure of our parties, however, is another story. In combination with the division of our government into competing units that "check and balance" each other, the loose organization of our parties [...]

PERSPECTIVE

These chapter-opening vignettes set the stage for the rest of the chapter discussion, as well as help students see political connections, by comparing a historical moment, current event, or policy in the United States to that of another country. For instance, students can examine the lives of rural farmers in Bangladesh and witness how the absence of groups that represent their interests affects their daily survival.

PERSPECTIVE
What Is the Value of a Well-Developed Interest Group System?

When the Obama administration proposed a national health plan in 2008 and 2009, organizations such as the American Association of Retired Persons (AARP), the American Medical Association (AMA), trade unions, and activist organizations like MoveOn.org fueled pressure to pass the plan. But as the proposals developed, groups representing the pharmaceutical industry, health insurance companies, and others questioned the proposal, and groups representing taxpayers pushed to prevent tax increases. A wide array of groups was involved in making final decisions on the bill.

PICTURE YOURSELF . . .

Students are invited to consider what it would be like to experience some aspect of the political system of another country in order to fully understand and appreciate that same aspect of government in the United States. Students can imagine being a tourist in Kenya, for example, and then understand the implications of daily life without the benefits of a bureaucracy.

picture YOURSELF . . .
AS A TOURIST IN KENYA

readily available.) Making international calls to family and friends back home is frustrating. In most areas of the country you can't use an international calling card or even reach 800 numbers. When you are able to find a way to get through, the long-distance rates are outrageously high. At the other extreme, Internet cafes in Nairobi, the nation's capital, now provide ready access to such things as exquisitely detailed maps that help guide your travels.

Because English is the official

frequently blocked by goats or people, and the local drivers have never finished a driver's education course. For example, when confronted by a traffic jam, Kenyan drivers routinely cross the median and force oncoming traffic to make way for them. Driving conditions are even worse during the rainy seasons, which occur in November and again from late March into May.

Only after you've been in Kenya for a while do you realize how many of the services provided by government

You are enjoying your vis

PRACTICE MATTERS

| MAKE AMERICAN GOVERNMENT MATTER BY GIVING YOUR STUDENTS A CHANCE TO PRACTICE WHAT THEY LEARN. | Reading about government is one thing; but being able to *apply* what is learned during lectures or from the page is another. When students get hands-on, they learn more.

GOVERNMENT IN ACTION

Give your students a chance to practice American government by allowing them to compete against a computer or each other in a first-of-its kind virtual world in which students learn by doing. In *Government in Action* students run for re-election and pass legislation, touching on every aspect of the course in their attempt to gain political capital.

POLITICS IN PRACTICE

Students have the opportunity to apply content knowledge and critical thinking skills through Politics in Practice. In these online interactive exercises, students analyze primary sources, public opinion, statistical research, and videos in order to respond to a critical question about American politics. For example, why is voter turnout among the millennial generation so low, and how do groups mobilize these voters to go to the polls? Find out in the role of Junior Assistant of Media Programs assigned to propose a media-based action plan to help "Get Out the Vote!"

CONNECT

McGraw-Hill's Connect® American Government offers a wealth of assignable and assessable interactive course materials. Detailed reporting helps students and instructors gauge comprehension and retention—without adding administrative load. A fully searchable, web-optimized eBook provides instructors and students with a reliable source of course content.

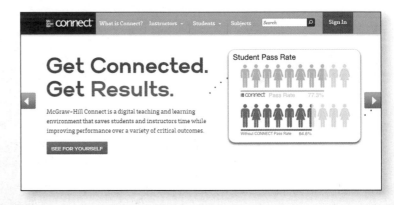

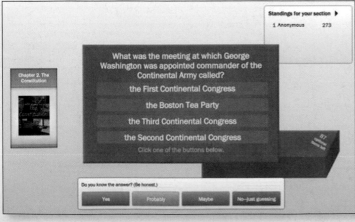

LEARNSMART

McGraw-Hill LearnSmart™ assesses a student's knowledge of course content through a series of adaptive questions, intelligently pinpointing concepts students do not understand and mapping out a personalized study plan for success. LearnSmart assists students in absorbing foundational concepts, allowing instructors to focus valuable class time introducing higher-level concepts.

FLEXIBILITY **MATTERS**

| MAKE AMERICAN GOVERNMENT MATTER BY GIVING YOUR STUDENTS MULTIPLE OPTIONS FOR ACCESSING COURSE CONTENT. | You can choose how you want your students to receive their course materials via the following tools:

Craft your teaching resources to match the way you teach! With McGraw-Hill Create™, you can personalize your book's appearance by selecting the cover and adding your name, school, and course information. Order a Create book and you'll receive a complimentary print review copy in three to five business days or a complimentary electronic review copy (eComp) via e-mail in about one hour. To get started, go to **www.mcgrawhillcreate.com** and register today.

Introducing McGraw-Hill Create *ExpressBooks*! ExpressBooks contain a combination of pre-selected chapters, articles, cases, or readings that serve as a starting point to help you quickly and easily build your own text through McGraw-Hill's self-service custom publishing website, Create. These helpful templates are built using content available on Create and organized in ways that match various course outlines across all disciplines. We understand that you have a unique perspective. Use McGraw-Hill Create ExpressBooks to build the book you've only imagined! **www.mcgrawhillcreate.com**

This text is available as an eTextbook at **www.CourseSmart.com**. At CourseSmart your students can take advantage of significant savings off the cost of a print textbook, reduce their impact on the environment, and gain access to powerful web tools for learning. CourseSmart eTextbooks can be viewed online or downloaded to a computer. The eTextbooks allow students to do full text searches, add highlighting and notes, and share notes with classmates. CourseSmart has the largest selection of eTextbooks available anywhere. Visit **www.CourseSmart.com** to learn more and to examine a sample chapter.

McGraw-Hill Tegrity Campus® is a service that makes class time available all the time by automatically capturing every lecture in a searchable format for students to review when they study and complete assignments. With a simple one-click start and stop process, you capture all computer screens and corresponding audio. Students replay any part of any class with easy-to-use browser-based viewing on a PC or Mac. Educators know that the more students can see, hear, and experience class resources, the better they learn. With Tegrity Campus, students quickly recall key moments by using Tegrity Campus's unique search feature. This search helps students efficiently find *what* they need *when* they need it across an entire semester of class recordings. Help turn all your students' study time into learning moments immediately supported by your lecture.

BLACKBOARD

McGraw-Hill Higher Education and Blackboard® have teamed up.
What does this mean for you?

1. **Your life, simplifed.** Now you and our students can access McGraw-Hill's Connect and Create from within your Blackboard course—all with one single sign-on. Say goodbye to the days of logging in to multiple applications.

2. **Deep integration of content and tools.** Not only do you get single sign-on with Connect and Create you also get deep integration of McGraw-Hill content and content engines right in Blackboard. Whether you're choosing a book for your course or building Connect assignments all the tools you need are right where you want them inside of Blackboard.

3. **Seamless gradebooks.** Are you tired of keeping multiple gradebooks and manually synchronizing grades into Blackboard? We thought so. When a student completes an integrated Connect assignment, the grade for that assignment automatically (and instantly) feeds your Blackboard grade center.

4. **A solution for everyone.** Whether your institution is already using Blackboard or you just want to try Blackboard on your own, we have a solution for you. McGraw-Hill and Blackboard can now offer you easy access to industry-leading technology and content, whether your campus hosts it, or we do. Be sure to ask your local McGraw-Hill representative for details.

ONLINE LEARNING CENTER

The password-protected instructor side of the Online Learning Center (**www.mhhe.com/maltese1e**) offers an **Instructor's Manual, Test Bank,** and **PowerPoints** to accompany *Government Matters.*

The Instructor's Manual includes chapter summaries, chapter outlines, lecture outlines, and abundant class activities. Our dynamic PowerPoints include figures from the textbook, and the Test Bank includes more than 1,000 multiple-choice and short-answer questions.

Ask your local McGraw-Hill representative for password information.

This may be the only course your students take in political science.

MAKE IT **MATTER!**

ACKNOWLEDGMENTS

To all of the people who contributed their insights, suggestions, and thoughts to the development of *Government Matters*, we are deeply indebted.

Randall E. Adkins, *University of Nebraska, Omaha*
Philip Ardoin, *Appalachian State University*
Robert Ballinger, *South Texas College*
Yan Bai, *Grand Rapids Community College*
Nancy Bednar, *Antelope Valley College*
Brian A. Bearry, *University of Texas at Dallas*
Felecia Bennett-Clark, *Henry Ford Community College*
Curtis R. Berry, *Shippensburg University*
David Birch, *Lone Star College, Tomball*
Paul Blakelock, *Lone Star College, Kingwood*
Patricia Bodelson, *St. Cloud University*
Scott Boyklin, *Georgia Gwinnett College*
Gary Brown, *Lone Star College-Montgomery*
Ronald Brown, *Wayne County Community College District*
Jennifer Byrne, *James Madison University*
John P. Burke, *University of Vermont*
Brian Robert Calfano, *Missouri State University*
Jamie Carson, *University of Georgia*
Dina D. Castillo, *San Jacinto College, Central Campus*
Anita Chadha, *University of Houston, Downtown*
Jennifer Bryson Clark, *South Texas College*
Rosalind Blanco Cook, *Tulane University*
John Crosby, *California State University, Chico*
Jim Davis, *Oklahoma State University*
Kevin T. Davis, *North Central College*
Vida Davoudi, *Lone Star College, Kingwood*
Alexander Dawoody, *University of Maryland*
Nelson C. Dometrius, *Texas Tech University*
Amy Dreussi, *University of Akron*
Walle Engedayehu, *Prairie View A & M University*
Matthew Eshbaugh-Soha, *University of North Texas*
Henry Esparza, *University of Texas at San Antonio*
Brandon Franke, *Blinn College, Bryan*
Scott A. Frisch, *California State University Channel Islands*
Yolanda Garza Hake, *South Texas College*
Michael Gattis, *Gulf Coast Community College*
Alan Gibson, *California State University, Chico*
Larry Gonzalez, *Houston Community College, Stafford Campus*
Griffin Hathaway, *Illinois Central College*
Audrey Haynes, *University of Georgia*
Eric Heberling, *University of North Carolina, Charlotte*
Wanda Lee Hill, *Tarrant County Community College, South*
John E. Hitt, *North Lake College*
Steven Holmes, *Bakersfield College*
Gregory Hudspeth, *St. Philip's College*
Frank Ibe, *Wayne County Community College District*
Sarbjit Johal, *Fresno City College*
U. Lynn Jones, *Collin College*
Julie Lantrip, *Tarrant County College*
Dedric Todd Lee, *Jefferson College*
B. J. Martinez, *Northwest Vista College*
Thomas Masterson, *Butte College, Chico Center*
Dene McArthur, *South Texas College*
Michael McConachie, *Collin College*
Clay McFaden, *University of Houston, Houston Stan Mendenhall – Illinois Central College*
Eric Miller, *Blinn College, Bryan*
Kent Miller, *Weatherford College*
Will Miller, *Southeast Missouri State University*
Kay Murnan, *Ozarks Technical Community College*
Jalal Nejad, *Northwest Vista College*
Timothy Nokken, *Texas Tech University*

Michael Nojeim, *Prairie View A & M University*
Sunday P. Obazuaye, *Cerritos College*
John Osterman, *San Jacinto College*
Fernando Pinon, *San Antonio College*
Jerry Polinard, *University of Texas, Pan American*
Donald Ranish, *Antelope Valley College*
Steven Reti, *College of the Canyons*
Tim Reynolds, *Alvin Community College*
Beth A. Rosenson, *University of Florida*
Joanna Sabo, *Monroe County Community College*
Mario Salas, *Northwest Vista College*
Shad Satterthwaite, *University of Oklahoma, Norman*
Gilbert Schorlemmer, *Blinn College, Bryan*
Scot Schraufnagel, *Northern Illinois University*
James M. Scott, *Oklahoma State University, Stillwater*
John F. Shively, *Longview Community College*
Mark Shomaker, *Blinn College, Bryan*
Susan Siemens, *Ozarks Technical Community College*
Brian Smentkowski, *Southeast Missouri State University*
John G. Speer, *Houston Community College*
Matt Stellges, *Blinn College—Bryan*
Robert Sterken, *University of Texas, Tyler*
Beatrice Talpos, *Wayne County Community College District*
John J. Theis, *Lone Star College, Kingwood*
Judy Tobler, *Northwest Arkansas Community College*
Stanley Tylman, *Lincoln Land Community College*
Sarah Velasquez, *Fresno City College*
John Vento, *Antelope Valley College*
Tiffiny Vincent, *Blinn College*
Al Waite, *Central Texas College*
Bruce Wilson, *University of Central Florida*
Van Allen Wigginton, *San Jacinto College*
Tony E. Wohlers, *Cameron University*
Robert Wood, *University of North Dakota*
Kevin Wooten, *Angelina College*

PERSONAL ACKNOWLEDGMENTS

The authors are grateful to the many people at McGraw-Hill who have worked with us on this project. Monica Eckman lured us in, and Beth Mejia, Mark Georgiev, Carla Samodulski, and Briana Porco saw us through the early stages of this project. Meredith Grant, Lai Moy, Naomi Friedman, Nikki Weissman, Dawn Groundwater, Mike Sugarman, Lisa Pinto, Patrick Brown, and Matthew Busbridge on the Editorial and Marketing side; Holly Paulsen, Robin Reed, Ayelet Arbel, Judy Waller, Mary Rostad, Iara McDermott, Maureen McCutcheon, John Leland, and Deborah Bull on the Production side; and Andrea Helmbolt, Jodi Banowetz, Meghan Campbell, Jocelyn Spielberger, Nathan Benjamin, and Southern Editorial on the Digital side helped us bring it to completion. Special thanks to Lai for the countless hours she spent helping us revise text. Thanks also to Janet Tilden for her able copyediting. We are also grateful to the staff members at our respective universities, and especially to Logan Dancy who assisted us ably with data analysis. Above all, we are grateful to our families who tolerated our long and erratic periods of work on this project. *Government Matters* has been more work than any of us imagined when Monica signed us up, but we are proud of the results—written through sickness and health—and grateful to those who prodded us to make it better, even though we sometimes resisted. Most of all, we are grateful to our students whose curiosity remains contagious.

John Maltese, Joe Pika, and Phil Shively

Understanding American politics involves much more than "knowing the facts." It also requires an understanding of the causal connections in politics. From these connections, students can see how and why the decisions and actions of government officials matter to them. We have tried in this text to help students understand why politics has developed as it has in the United States, and to see the effects of our politics in things that they care about.

The three of us have been teaching American politics for more years than we want to count, and we have found that students want very much to see the connections between things. They especially want to see why policies they care about have or have not been put in place. Our twin strategies to help students understand American politics are analysis of its historical development, and comparisons with the politics of other countries. Beyond understanding causes, we also try to help students understand the *effects* of politics by showing them how our politics brings about distinctive policies that matter to them.

Causal connections run throughout the book. We use comparison, historical development, and the implications for policy as ways to meet students' needs and to motivate them—not to fill a niche for comparativists, specialists in American political development, or policy wonks. This is, at heart, a straight-ahead introduction to American politics, but one that adds essential context. In other words, we take seriously students' desire to understand why our system operates the way it does and how its operation matters to them.

Our experience is that many introductory American government texts are cluttered with boxes and features. We have minimized all but the most important. We integrate most of our features—notably the capstones of each chapter: "Why Are We the Way We Are? . . . And Why Does It Matter?"—into the text itself because they are so central to our presentation. In each chapter, "Why Are We the Way We Are?" presents historical and comparative explanations for the distinctive characteristics of American politics discussed in that chapter. ". . . And Why Does It Matter?" helps students to understand why these distinctive features matter to them as citizens.

Students appreciate course materials that help them learn and truly understand difficult concepts. We have been animated by the desire to write a book worth reading and not just "cover the basics." We have challenged ourselves in writing *Government Matters: Democracy in Context* and we want to challenge students, in the best sense of that word, to arrive at a better appreciation and a deeper understanding of how and why American politics matters. We have enjoyed working together on this project. We hope that you and your students will find similar pleasure from using it.

John Maltese, Joe Pika, and Phil Shively

Phil Shively, John Maltese, Joe Pika

JOHN ANTHONY MALTESE is the Albert B. Saye Professor and head of the Department of Political Science at the University of Georgia. His books include *The Selling of Supreme Court Nominees* (winner of the C. Herman Pritchett Award), *Spin Control: The White House Office of Communications and the Management of Presidential News,* and, with Joseph A. Pika, *The Politics of the Presidency,* now in its eighth edition. He is a Josiah Meigs Distinguished Teaching Professor and was named the Georgia Professor of the Year by the Carnegie Foundation and the Council for Advancement and Support of Education (CASE). He writes about classical music in his spare time, for which he has won a Grammy Award from the National Academy of Recording Arts and Sciences.

JOSEPH A. PIKA is the James R. Soles Professor of Political Science and International Relations at the University of Delaware where he has been recognized for excellence in teaching, advising, and service, the latter for his seven years on the State Board of Education. Professor Pika's areas of research include the American presidency and vice presidency, Delaware politics, and education policy. He has published multiple editions of *Politics of the Presidency* (the eighth edition, coauthored with John Maltese, was published by CQ Press in February 2012), *Confrontation and Compromise: Presidential and Congressional Leadership, 2001–2006* (with Jason Mycoff—Rowman & Littlefield, 2007), and *The Presidential Contest* (with Richard Watson, CQ Press, 1996). He is an avid sports fan and political activist.

W. PHILLIPS SHIVELY is Professor of Political Science at the University of Minnesota and has also served on the faculties of Yale University, the University of Oregon, and Oslo University, Norway. He has served as editor of the *American Journal of Political Science,* as Program Chair for the national meetings of the American Political Science Association, and as principal investigator and chair of the Comparative Study of Electoral Systems project (CSES). At the University of Minnesota, he has been inducted into the Academy of Distinguished Teachers for his work with students. His research centers on the comparative study of elections and statistical methods of research. Besides political science, Professor Shively's other main loves are natural history and classical music.

DEMOCRACY AND
AMERICAN POLITICS

- Understand the nature of politics, government, and citizenship.
- Differentiate among the types of democracies that exist in the world, and identify the qualities that make a government truly democratic.
- Examine the functions of government, as well as some of the challenges and controversies that affect its ability to perform each function effectively.
- Identify the four basic American values and describe how these values help to define the character of American politics.
- Explore the primary political ideologies that have helped to inform contemporary political discourse in the United States.
- Understand how comparison and historical analysis can deepen our understanding of American politics.

PERSPECTIVE
What Difference Does Democracy Make?

In the United States, trains covered with bright, fanciful graffiti are often seen rolling down the tracks. The graffiti constitutes vandalism, but while vandalizing property by painting graffiti is illegal in most states and cities, authorities do not usually enforce the laws against it very strictly. In fact, some Americans admire graffiti as an elevated art form, romanticizing graffiti artists as individuals who thumb their noses at the government.

It is different in Singapore. In 1994, 18-year-old American student Michael Fay ran afoul of Singapore's stringent laws protecting order and cleanliness. Singaporean police arrested Fay for stealing highway signs and vandalizing a car by scratching its paint. His court sentence: four months in jail, a fine of over $2,000, and four strokes with a cane. The caning—a common punishment in Singapore—was administered with a six-foot long, one-inch thick cane that can cause serious injury. Other acts that are not necessarily considered crimes in the United States but can draw similarly serious punishments in Singapore include spitting in public, littering, or selling chewing gum.

Singapore was a British colony until it became independent in 1965. Today, it is a prosperous financial center and technology exporter. Average incomes in Singapore are somewhat higher than those in the United States; crime rates are low; and the country is very clean, partly because of its stringent punishments for littering and similar offenses that other countries would consider minor. Its government is one of the least corrupt in the world.

Although efficient and prosperous, however, Singapore is not a democracy. Its government regulates citizens' behavior tightly. Elections are held regularly, but the People's Action Party, which has governed without interruption since it led the country to independence more than 45 years ago, does not allow a significant opposition party to develop or function. Rather, it requires all organizations to register with the government. In the 2011 election, for instance, the Party got 60 percent of the vote, winning 81 of the 87 seats in Singapore's Parliament. Additionally, organizers of any public gathering of more than five people must obtain a special permit. The Party also controls the media, all of which are owned by government-linked companies. Such control includes the banning of all political films and political television programs.

By contrast, the United States is less efficient and less tightly organized than Singapore, but it is a democracy. The media are not controlled by the government. The right of groups to organize and gather publicly is guaranteed in the First Amendment of the Constitution. And citizens who criticize public officials are protected against harassment. Such a democracy implies that the government is not as free as a government like Singapore's to put laws in place that lack broad support. This means that harsh anti-littering laws with physical punishment and jail time would not be tolerated by the public, even though such laws might produce a very clean country.

Actually, Singapore probably presents the most attractive instance of a non-democracy we can come up with, since most non-democracies are not particularly well organized or well run. Singapore's government avoids corrupt practices, it runs efficiently, and it has helped the country to prosper economically. But the lack of political freedom in Singapore has its costs. The people of Singapore, perhaps in self-defense, are much more passive than Americans. While 17 percent of Americans discuss politics frequently, only 4 percent of Singaporeans do. Forty-one percent of them say that they never discuss politics at all. As far as political participation is concerned, 76 percent of Americans say that they would be willing to attend a lawful demonstration, whereas only 24 percent of Singaporeans would.[1]

WE BEGIN THIS CHAPTER by laying out the nature and functions of government in general. We then clarify just what "democracy" is, placing it in the context of various forms of government and discussing how American democracy influences the development of democracies worldwide. We examine how American values and ideologies shape Americans' views on what government should or should not be doing. Throughout this book, we demonstrate how to use comparison and historical analysis as tools to deepen our understanding of the American system. As you read this chapter, keep in mind our two core questions:

WHY ARE WE THE WAY WE ARE?
WHY DOES IT MATTER TO YOU?

In particular, how has the way government functions in America helped to shape basic American values?

GOVERNMENT AND POLITICS

When the people in a country need to consider changing the way things are done, they engage in **politics,** the process by which collective decisions—decisions that are binding for everyone in the country—are made for a country.[2] Collective decisions include such things as a law, a system of taxes, or a social program. We use "process" in this definition very broadly to include not only the actions of government officials, but also all of the considerations that influence them, such as elections, public opinion, and the media. Politics consists of all the factors that contribute to collective decisions.

For example, in 2009, after President Obama called for a major overhaul of the nation's health care systems, many voices contributed to that debate and to the political process that followed:

- policy schools, which provided scholarly assessments of various sorts of health care delivery systems
- the American Association of Retired Persons (AARP) and labor unions, which ran advertisements favoring reform
- insurance groups and business organizations, which ran counter-advertisements opposing reform
- corporations like 3M, which encouraged their employees to write their member of Congress opposing the reforms
- the cable news channel MSNBC, which provided pro-reform press coverage, while Fox News, another cable channel, offered anti-reform coverage
- opponents of reform, who conducted raucous protests at town hall meetings held by members of Congress
- ordinary citizens, who talked to one another about the merits of the proposals
- members of Congress, who engaged in arm-twisting, deals, and bargaining as they attempted to craft and pass the legislation

All of these voices were part of the politics associated with the decisions about whether, and how, to reform the U.S. health care system.

To facilitate the decision-making process, regardless of who participates (or is allowed to participate), every country has a **government.** A government helps a country to maintain internal order, to interact with other countries, and to develop laws and policies. What sets government apart from any other group is that only the government has the right to make decisions that are binding on everyone within the nation's borders.

The government has the right to use force (the threat of fines or jail) to ensure that the laws are followed and to implement decisions that are binding on everyone.[3] Other groups can make more limited decisions, but they are prohibited from using force to implement them. A corporation like Microsoft, for instance, can decide to design

Politics consists of making collective decisions. Many parts of society contribute to political debates, but governments alone have the power to make and enforce collective decisions that bind everyone in the country—citizens and non-citizens alike. While this section introduces various forms of government, the rest of the book will focus on democratic government.

politics
The process by which decisions that are binding for everyone in the country are made, such as a law, a system of taxes, or a social program.

★ The Washington state-based advocacy group, United for National Health Care, publicizes their support of healthcare reform. In this way, they added their voice to the national debate.

the Windows operating system for personal computers in a particular way, but that decision is binding only on those who voluntarily buy its product. Furthermore, Microsoft cannot use force to implement its decision. By contrast, the government of the United States can pass a law outlawing child pornography for everyone in the country and can use force to make sure everyone follows it.

Every person living in a country, then, is required to obey its laws—citizens and noncitizens alike. **Citizens** are people who are fully qualified and legally recognized as members of a country. However, not everyone living in a country at a given time is considered a citizen. Citizens of other countries who are visiting briefly or who are in the country to work or pursue their education for a long or indefinite period of time are not citizens. Also, several million illegal aliens live and work in the United States. But whether they are citizens or not, all who reside within a country's borders are both protected by the country's laws and required to obey them.

Various types of governments exist, and political scientists distinguish between them according to the basis of their power—in other words, where they get their right to rule. Many countries throughout the world have some form of nondemocratic government, in which a small group of people govern and the rest of the citizens of the country have no direct voice in what the government does. Important types of non-democracy include government by army officers, government by a hereditary monarch, government by a single party that allows no other parties to operate (Singapore, for instance), and government by religious leaders (Iran, for example). In this chapter, however, we will focus on democratic government because that is the form of government in the United States.

DEMOCRACY AS A FORM OF GOVERNMENT

In a **democracy,** all citizens can participate in the making of governmental policy at least to some extent, even if indirectly. Though democracy is generally defined as "rule by citizens," this definition is more an ideal than a concrete, observable phenomenon. As we will see in this section, a variety of factors influence how fully and how directly citizens in a democracy share in the rule of the country. In fact, there is no country in the world where all citizens have precisely equal roles in making the decisions of the country. However, a number of countries approximate the ideal well enough that we call them democracies. As shown in Figure 1.1, 116 countries—more than half of all countries in the world—are democracies.

DIRECT DEMOCRACY

The closest approximation to rule by all citizens is **direct democracy,** in which all of the citizens of a community gather to decide policies for that community. It was the mode of government in some ancient Greek city-states, and it still exists today in New England town meetings where all citizens come together to discuss and decide issues.[4]

ARCTIC OCEAN

ATLANTIC OCEAN

PACIFIC OCEAN

PACIFIC OCEAN

INDIAN OCEAN

◼ Democracy

FIGURE 1.1

★ DEMOCRACIES OF THE WORLD

Which regions of the world are especially likely to have democratic governments?

Source: Freedom House, Electoral Democracies 2009.

Direct democracy is possible only in a small community with relatively simple issues to decide. Even a direct democracy does not exactly accomplish "rule by the citizens," at least in the sense that all citizens contribute equally to the decision-making process. As in any group formed to accomplish assigned tasks, some people are more experienced or articulate than others, so not everyone is able to contribute equally. In fact, a direct democracy may actually express the will of only a fairly small group of leaders.

INDIRECT DEMOCRACY

Direct democracy is impossible in a complex, modern country such as the United States. How could millions of U.S. citizens come together to make decisions? Faced with thousands of complex, detailed issues each year, how could all citizens participate adequately and still do anything else with their lives? Accordingly, almost all democracies today, with a few exceptions (such as the town meetings mentioned previously), are **indirect democracies,** also called *representative democracies*. In an indirect democracy, all citizens vote to choose, from among alternative candidates, the people who will be in charge of making decisions and implementing policies. In the United States, for example, the people of a city may elect a mayor and members of a city council; residents of each state elect a governor and other statewide officials as well as members of the state's legislature. Every eligible U.S. citizen can vote to elect the president and members of Congress to represent them.

What is needed for indirect democracy to work well? Obviously, elections are a basic requirement. But are elections enough? Earlier in the chapter, we explained that Singapore holds elections regularly, but we noted that in the 2011 election, the People's Action Party, which has ruled the country since 1965, got 60 percent of the vote, winning 81 of the 87 seats in Singapore's Parliament, and that the government achieved

indirect democracy
Democracy in which the people do not decide policies for the community themselves, but elect representatives to decide the policies.

★ Attendees of the Republican Party's National Convention voice their values to party leadership.

this result by suppressing opposition. Such outcomes show that elections alone do not a democracy make. Thus, effective indirect democracy goes beyond just holding elections; a number of other pieces must also be in place to ensure that the elections offer citizens a chance to affect decisions through their vote:

- free elections with real choice
- broad participation in the elections
- freedom of speech and media
- the right to organize and to seek access to officials
- majority rule . . .
- . . . but with protection for minority rights

The first four requirements are discussed in this section. The twin requirements of majority rule and protection of minority rights are discussed later in this chapter in the section titled "The Challenges of Democracy."

Elections, of course, are the first requirement of indirect democracy, but between elections the full population of citizens should also be actively engaged in debate over broad policy alternatives, even if they do not know every detail of a given proposal. Elected officials, in turn, need to pay attention to those public debates. In an indirect democracy, at least in principle, citizens control policy making through their representatives. If these citizens feel issues have not been resolved as they wish, they can remove their representatives from office.

Another basic requirement of democracy, beyond the formal arrangements of voting and elections, is sufficient individual freedom to allow open debate. This in turn requires freedom of speech and a free, uncontrolled media. A country might hold regular elections and yet not be a democracy. Singapore is such a country. Another good example is Russia, which holds regular elections with alternative candidates but maintains such stringent governmental control over the media that the country cannot be considered a full democracy.

Citizens of a democracy also need to be able to organize independently into political parties and other organizations to pool their political efforts. Again, countries may hold elections yet fail to meet this requirement. For instance, China, which is ruled tightly by its Communist Party, holds elections in which individuals are allowed to run for office freely and sometimes can even win against the official candidate. But these independents are not allowed to form an organization to coordinate their efforts, which prevents them from having an effective voice. The Chinese system is not a democracy because it is impossible for isolated individuals to challenge the sole legal political organization, the Communist Party, in any effective way.

For a democracy to function effectively, therefore, it needs more than just elections. A true democracy allows those with competing points of view to present their ideas in a lively and effective way through the following principles and structures:

- competing political parties
- freedom of speech and association
- equal access of voters to the process of selecting public officials
- equal access to those officials once they are elected

These requirements or *principles of democracy,* as they apply to the United States, are a central focus of this book. The United States was the world's first modern democracy, and over the years aspiring democracies have measured themselves against the U.S. system, treating it as a standard. The extent to which the principles of democracy are realized in countries of the world today varies greatly, however. How does the United States' democracy compare with that of other governments around the world? Of the 116 democracies shown in the map in Figure 1.1, Freedom House, an organization that researches and promotes democracy, places the United States, along with only 47 other countries, in the highest category of democracies that meet most fully the requirements of a democracy.

Since the first modern democracy was established in the United States at the end of the eighteenth century, the spread of this form of government has been very gradual. In a sudden spurt starting in the mid-1970s, however, many countries shifted from nondemocratic forms of government to democracy. As you can see in Figure 1.2, democracies represented just 31 percent of the world's states in 1977, but by the mid-1990s, about 62 percent of the world's states had become democratic, with the sharpest increase occurring between 1989 and 1995.[5]

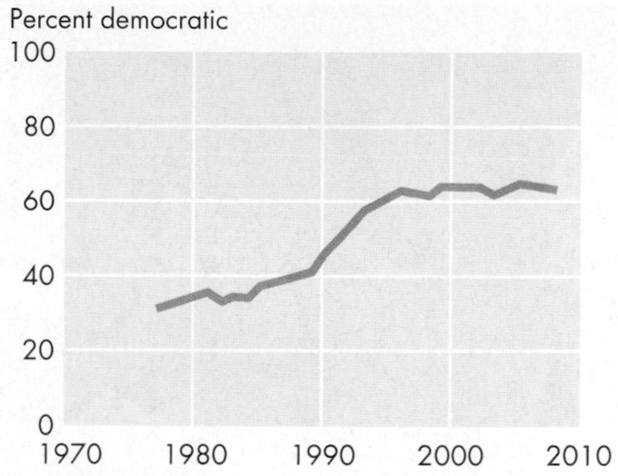

Since the 1990s, however, there has been essentially no growth in the number of democracies, and recently the number has declined somewhat. Indeed, the period since 1999, when a coup in Pakistan overturned that country's democratic government and growth in the overall number of democracies slowed, has been dubbed a "democratic recession."[6]

Percent democratic

FIGURE 1.2

★ GROWTH OF DEMOCRACY
   IN THE WORLD

What was unusual (or not) about the rapid growth of democracies between the mid-1970s and mid-1990s? Why didn't democracy continue to spread after the mid-1990s at the same rate?

THE CHALLENGES OF DEMOCRACY

Perhaps the widespread adoption of democracy shown in Figure 1.2 stems ultimately from a basic human need for respect. Even if democracy is imperfect as practiced, the aspiration toward a more democratic form of government implies that all people are of equal worth and, at least in principle, have a right to be heard. Certainly, this aspiration has been present throughout American history and has led to a perception of the United States as a moral leader of the world. Translating the aspiration into practice, however, presents obvious difficulties. Democracies face two difficulties in particular— the problem of ensuring majority rule, and the problem of protecting minority rights.

Ensuring Majority Rule

Representative democracy embodies the principle of **majority rule**—the idea that 50 percent plus one of the people should be able to choose a majority of the elected officials in a country and thereby determine its direction. The first challenge of democracy is that of ensuring majority rule. Aside from many questions about the mechanics of elections (which we will explore in greater depth in Chapter 8), the fact that representative democracy makes people equal only in their right to vote also limits majority rule. The vote is a powerful resource in democratic politics, but other resources that are unequally distributed—for example, money, education, and social position (being a newspaper editor, for instance)—give some citizens more access to decision making than others. To the extent that these other resources affect the decisions that elected

majority rule
The principle that 50 percent plus one of the people should be able to elect a majority of elected officials and thereby determine the direction of policy.

★ A baseball game in San Francisco, CA captures a cross section of American society, which comprises many types of minorities and majorities.

minority rights
Basic human rights that are considered important to guarantee for minorities in a democracy.

republic
A country that is not ruled by a monarch but by the people through its representatives.

officials make, 50 percent plus one of the votes may not be the determining factor. According to surveys, most of the post-war era strong majorities in the United States, for instance, have favored prayer in the schools and stricter control of handguns, but neither practice has become national law.[7]

Protecting Minority Rights

Even if majority rule always prevailed, democracies would still face a second challenge—protecting **minority rights,** or the basic freedoms of smaller groups within the general population. These may be racial, ethnic, or religious groups or individuals whose opinions differ from those of the majority. For example, what if a majority wanted to take away from a minority group such basic human rights as the right to equal treatment by the government or the right to speak freely? The principle of majority rule would seem to validate this decision, but most people would not agree that it would be the right thing to do. In a telling example, in the late nineteenth and early twentieth centuries, white majorities in the Southern states passed many laws pushing African Americans minorities into inferior, segregated schools and other public facilities, and denying them the right to vote. Overcoming the activities of these majorities did not occur until the 1950s and 1960s, and doing so took rulings from the Supreme Court, as well as congressional and presidential action. In the late twentieth and early twenty-first centuries, majorities of voters in many states voted to bar same-sex marriage—yet another example of the tension between majority rule and minority aspirations.

When studying a democracy like the United States, we need to examine how the country deals with these two basic problems: How, and to what degree, is majority rule ensured? And how are minority rights protected under majority rule? These two questions will figure prominently in the succeeding chapters of this book.

REPUBLICS

A concept that is often contrasted with democracy, and sometimes confused with it, is the *republic*. In the study of politics in general, a *republic* is simply a country not ruled by a monarch. But in the study specifically of American politics, we add another layer of meaning to the term. As you will see in Chapter 2, as the original founders of the United States considered how to design the new democracy and write its constitution, they used the term *republic* to denote government by the people's elected representatives, who—while they are ultimately responsible to the people—rule primarily on the basis of their own intelligence and experience. So, for them, a republic was distinguished from direct democracy as well as from monarchy. We will use the term **republic** to mean an indirect democracy that particularly emphasizes insulation of its representatives and officials from direct popular pressure. In political rhetoric today, the term "republic" is often chosen by people who favor democracy but do not favor intense and direct popular involvement in democratic government.

FUNCTIONS OF GOVERNMENT

As we have seen, in the division of labor required by representative democracy, some people serve as the elected representatives of the citizens and rule on their behalf. These people are the government, and they make decisions that are binding for all people in the country. Since most people, all other things being equal, would prefer not to be bound by rules, our views of government and its functions are generally characterized by some ambivalence: On the one hand, we do not enjoy being ruled; on the other hand, the alternative would result in chaos.

More precisely, what sorts of functions do governments perform? As a first answer to this question, consider the Preamble to the United States Constitution, in which the authors laid out their reasons for establishing a central government:

Some things can only be done effectively by governments: maintaining order and safety, and providing "public goods" (a term we will define in this section). Beyond those two functions, of course, governments can choose to do many other things. There is always controversy about how active government should be. Overall in the United States the government is less involved in people's lives than in many other prosperous countries—why is this so?

> We the People of the United States, in Order to form a more perfect Union, establish Justice, insure domestic Tranquility, provide for the common defense, promote the general Welfare, and secure the Blessings of Liberty to ourselves and our Posterity, do ordain and establish this Constitution for the United States of America.

This Preamble alludes to two basic kinds of services that cannot easily be accomplished without government, and their provision accounts for two functions of every government of the world. The first function, captured by the phrase "[to] insure domestic Tranquility," is to provide basic security for people to live together and to deal with each other in financial transactions. The second function, exemplified by the phrase "[to] provide for the common defense," is to provide certain services called "public goods," among them national defense, that can only be provided effectively by government. In addition to providing these two basic kinds of services, governments can and do perform a range of additional functions, as expressed by the phrase "[to] promote the general welfare."[8]

In other words, governments *have* to exist in order to provide a secure social and financial environment and public goods, but they can do other things as well. And governments often end up doing a variety of "other things" since, once a government exists, citizens often want it to perform additional services. Thus, government can shape the context of our lives in all sorts of ways. Let's look more closely at these functions of government.

MAINTAINING ORDER AND SAFETY

Since the government is the sole entity with the right to use force and coercion to implement its choices, it is able to enact and enforce rules against crimes such as murder, burglary, and assault, thus ensuring our security. It can also provide a common currency for—and regulate—financial transactions and guarantee that contracts will be enforced, ensuring the security of our property. To ensure enforcement of the relevant laws, the government maintains agencies such as the police, the FBI, and the Treasury Department. In effect, government provides the basic social and financial network within which people can carry on their lives securely, functioning in the society and in the economy. This is true of every government in the world.

PROVIDING PUBLIC GOODS

public good
Something that benefits all members of the community and that no one can possibly be prevented from using.

A *public good* is a very specific term. **Public goods** are more than just "goods for the public"; they are, precisely, policies that cannot possibly be given to some people while being withheld from others.[9] Public goods include national defense, space exploration, basic medical research, and public health programs to control the spread of disease. It is physically impossible to prevent any member of the community from using these goods. For instance, the U.S. government cannot defend its entire country's borders without also defending Phil Shively in Minneapolis, Minnesota. Most importantly, the use of public goods cannot be restricted just to those who have helped to pay for them.

free riders
Those who take advantage of the fact that a public good cannot possibly be denied to anyone, by refusing to pay their share of the cost of providing the public good.

Thus public goods are dogged by the problem of **free riders,** who reason that since they will obtain the good in any case, they can get away without paying for its cost: "If I don't pay my share, the army will still be there, and I'll get all the benefits of it. Why should I pay?" Everyone could reason like this, so if a public good such as defense were left to private corporations or to organizations accepting voluntary donations, it would end up inadequately financed, and everyone would lose out.[10] That is where government comes in. Since a government has the right to use force to implement its choices, it can require people to pay taxes, and then use that tax money to pay for the public good. Mandating shared payment of a public good eliminates free riders.

Let's consider the case of public television, a public good that is not provided by the government in the United States and therefore suffers a serious free rider problem. Television signals that are broadcast on the air waves are a public good because no one in the community can physically be prevented from picking them up with a receiver, so public television stations are faced with the problem of free riders. For this reason, every few months, the station's staff finds itself forced to run on in a staccato patter in the hopes of encouraging viewers to help defray the costs of running the station. They appeal to guilt: "Only one in ten of you who watch this station is a member; the rest of you are free riders." They appeal to acquisitiveness: "For the basic $35 membership, we offer this lovely ceramic mug, embossed with the station's logo." Perhaps the most effective pitch occurred a few years ago in Minneapolis, Minnesota, when the station staff promised that if they reached their goal early, they would cut off the fund drive at that point. Contributions flooded in![11]

In short, through such actions as providing for the defense of the country, exploring space, protecting the environment, and developing public health programs such as immunization, the government is fulfilling its function of providing public goods. If the air quality is preserved, it is preserved for all of us and cannot be preserved for just some of us. And so preserving the air quality, a public good, raises the problem of free riders and is undertaken by government.

PROMOTING THE GENERAL WELFARE

Beyond these two essential functions of providing a basic network of protective laws and security and providing public goods, however, government can also do more. Recall that in addition to establishing justice, insuring domestic tranquility, and providing for the common defense (things only a government can do), the authors of the Constitution wanted the government to "promote the general welfare." The general welfare can be promoted through various government services, and almost all governments do provide some benefits beyond the basic requirements. The American government performs each of the following services:

- providing infrastructure
- regulating the economy to ensure that it operates fairly
- providing support to people in vulnerable positions
- redistributing income to improve the lives of citizens with less wealth
- regulating behavior

Providing Infrastructure

Many other services that people feel are important as a basis for the economy and society, such as education, highways, and parks, are not public goods; in principle, they could be provided just to those who were willing to pay for them and withheld from those who don't. For example, all education could be offered by private schools and all highways could be offered to users on a toll basis (essentially the way railroads are). However, these are basic and important services that most people think government should provide because they constitute the underlying infrastructure for everything else; certainly, in the United States, government provides such services.

Regulating the Economy to Ensure It Operates Fairly

This function of government goes beyond just maintaining order by enforcing contracts. As part of ensuring the fair regulation of the economy, the government regulates many financial transactions to make sure that everyone involved has enough information to make intelligent choices. The sale of stocks is regulated, for instance, to require companies offering stock to disclose full information so that those buying the stock know what they are getting. Drug companies must submit potential drugs to the U.S. Food and Drug Administration to make sure they are safe before they are offered for sale.

★ In 2008, some people blamed the federal government for the stock market crash and the economic decline. They argued that the government's lifting of regulations on lenders had caused a crisis in the housing market.

Providing Support to People in Vulnerable Positions

By providing money and services, government can make sure that members of the society who are in an economically vulnerable position have reasonable support. The government provides support through the Social Security system to retirees, children who have lost a parent, and disabled people. The government also provides unemployment insurance, offers disaster relief, and in many other ways tries to help those who are either temporarily or permanently in a vulnerable position.

Redistributing Income to Improve the Lives of Citizens with Less Wealth

Through the federal income tax system, and through the design of certain programs like the pension system in Social Security, the government tries to lessen income inequalities in American society.

Regulating Behavior

Beyond the need to maintain public order, the government also passes laws to regulate people's behavior (examples include laws against obscenity, public nudity, and the use of various drugs) and uses its police to enforce those laws.

CONTROVERSIES ABOUT GOVERNMENT FUNCTIONS

We organized the discussion of government functions in the previous sections according to how much public consensus exists for government action in each. Few dispute that the government should maintain social and economic order, though of course there are often lively disputes over *how* the government does this. (No one disputes the need for police forces, for instance, but people often disagree about how the policing should be done.) Certain public goods, such as national defense and diplomacy, are similarly uncontroversial, at least in the sense that the people agree that the government should provide them. There is a good deal of consensus around the need for government to provide for infrastructure, as well—especially for elements such as education and highways. However, as we go down the list of functions, there is less consensus for a government-regulated economy.

Furthermore, within any of the areas of government function, people often disagree about just *how* active the government should be, even if they generally concur that the government should be involved to some extent. How much is the right amount to spend on national defense? And what about environmental protection? Although considered a public good, it is surrounded by controversy: Should the government take actions to reduce human contributions to the warming of the earth's atmosphere? And of course, in areas such as redistribution of income or regulation of behaviors, the extent and nature of government activity are also often quite controversial, leading to questions such as whether the government should eliminate the tax on inherited wealth (the estate tax or "death tax").

Governments around the world differ in how active they are. In general, the United States government provides fewer goods and services, and spends less on them, than most other wealthy countries. National and local governments account for 37 percent of all expenditures in the United States each year, evidence of a large and active government, it is true. But governments in Britain and Sweden account for more of their countries' expenditures than this—45 percent in the case of Britain and 54 percent in the case of Sweden.[12]

The scope of American government is much greater today than it was at an earlier time in its history. In 1936, for instance, national and local governments accounted for only 16 percent of all expenditures, much less than the current level of 37 percent. And as another indication of the increased scope of government, the United States *Federal*

Register, which lists all the rules and regulations of the federal government, has grown from 2,335 pages long in 1936 to 82,419 in 2011. Thus, the scope of American government has grown steadily since the mid-twentieth century, though it is still smaller than that of most other wealthy countries. As we see in Figure 1.3, the United States, Britain, and Sweden all had relatively small government presences at the beginning of the twentieth century. In all three countries government grew as a result of the two world wars and the depression in the first half of the twentieth century, but the United States has continued, despite substantial growth, to have a smaller presence of government than the other two countries.

Governments also differ in how relatively active they are in the different areas of government functioning. Although the United States spends more on national defense than most other wealthy countries, many of these other countries spend much more than the United States on social services and on protecting the vulnerable. For instance, in 2007 just 2 percent of all government spending in Germany went to national defense, compared with 62 percent for social programs and health; the figures were very different for the United States: 12 percent for defense, but only 42 percent for social programs and health.[13]

The proper scope of government, and the choices it should make, are always controversial. Differences in the size of the government's presence, and in what sorts of functions and policies the government emphasizes, are due largely to differences in what the people of the country value. We explore Americans' values in the next section.

FIGURE 1.3

★ GROWTH OF GOVERNMENTAL ACTIVITY IN THE U.S., BRITAIN, AND SWEDEN

Government's expenditures as a percentage of all economic activity grew in all three countries, but less in the United States than in Sweden or Great Britain. What would account for the sudden spike in U.S. government spending around 1940?

AMERICAN VALUES

People derive their values from the general culture they inherit from past generations and also from their personal experiences. We will deal with Americans' "political culture" in detail in Chapter 6. For our purposes here, we can note that the Europeans who first settled the thirteen original colonies, most of whom came from England, brought with them from their home country many ideas about how government should operate. These ideas—passed from generation to generation and gradually modified by the ideas of newer cultures and immigrant groups as well—have helped to shape the values of Americans today. Historical experiences have also helped to shape these values. As we will explore in further detail in this chapter, the original migration from Europe, the continuing lure of an open frontier for much of the nineteenth century, and the modification of our values by newer cultures and ethnic groups, have profoundly influenced Americans' ideas about the proper role of government.

Four basic American values have played a prominent role in determining the extent of government's involvement in people's lives and what the government does:

1. fairness based on contributions
2. freedom and individualism
3. support for the rule of law
4. religion

Let us look at each of these values separately.

FAIRNESS BASED ON CONTRIBUTIONS

fairness
The belief that everyone should be treated in the way that they deserve.

Fairness—treating people in the way they deserve—is a universal value found in all societies. Societies differ, however, in what they see as the basis for determining what people deserve. In the United States, fairness is often interpreted as getting what one deserves on the basis of what one has accomplished or contributed. In many other countries, fairness may more likely be interpreted in terms of equality—that is, as getting the equal treatment one deserves based simply on being a member of the society.

In a recent survey, people in 52 countries were asked a series of questions including the following:

> Imagine two secretaries, of the same age, doing practically the same job. One finds out that the other earns considerably more than she does. The better paid secretary, however, is quicker, more efficient and more reliable at her job. In your opinion, is it fair or not fair that one secretary is paid more than the other?[14]

In almost all of the countries, a majority thought it was fair to pay the more efficient secretary the higher wage, but the size of the majority that believed this varied greatly. Fully 89 percent of Americans thought the difference in pay was fair—a higher percentage than in all but 4 of the 52 countries and a higher percentage than in any Western European country. Only 11 percent of Americans thought the difference was *un*fair, while about a quarter of the Italian and Spanish respondents felt it was unfair, as did about a third of the Indian and Brazilian respondents.

It's not that Americans don't believe strongly that they and others should be treated

fairly—they do, as reflected by the public outcry over the government's decision to distribute "bail out" aid to bank executives in 2009. But what these survey results demonstrate is that Americans base fairness on one's level of effort and one's contributions to society, rather than on everyone being treated equally. Because of this view, government programs that are intended to help the vulnerable and make income distribution more equal tend to be controversial in the United States and usually face an uphill fight. When such proposals *are* made, arguments in favor of them tend to emphasize what the vulnerable or the poor have contributed through their own efforts, rather than their neediness or the importance of treating everyone equally. Americans are much more likely to support programs for retired workers than for other at-risk populations, in large part because retired workers are thought to deserve support as a result of their earlier contributions.

This is not to say that the definition of fairness as treating everyone equally or according to their need lacks any support at all. In another part of the survey cited earlier, almost half of the Americans stated that they believe in general that incomes should be made more equal. But overall, there is more emphasis on fairness as equal reward for equal accomplishment than in most countries.

FREEDOM AND INDIVIDUALISM

In addition to fairness, Americans also regard freedom and individualism as important values. **Individualism** is the belief that people should be able to rely on themselves and be free to make decisions and act, subject to as little governmental or other societal control as possible. We value highly those who think for themselves. In 2008, for example, John McCain presented himself in the presidential campaign as an independent thinker and toured in a bus called the "Maverick Express." When John F. Kennedy wrote a book titled *Profiles in Courage,* he featured public officials who had taken stands that went against their party or the opinions of their constituents, doing instead what they thought was right. Generally, Americans have always liked rebels and nonconformists, those who "march to a different drummer" or "color outside the lines."

The value of individualism has its roots in colonial times. Many of the early settlers from Britain—Catholics in Maryland, Quakers in Pennsylvania, and Puritans in New England—had fled to the colonies to escape from religious persecution and religious discrimination. Other colonists, such as convicted criminals and poor farmers, had emigrated to escape punishment and to start over after having their land taken away from them. On some level, all of these colonists had sought freedom from government control.

individualism
The belief that people should have freedom to make decisions and act, with as little government intervention or other control as possible.

★ Obama administration policies that empowered the federal government led some to accuse the president of socialist tendencies. The Libertarian Party's "Don't Tread on Me" slogan expresses a deep-seated suspicion of powerful government shared by individualists.

Over the last two centuries many waves of immigrants, including but not limited to Asians, Eastern Europeans, and Latin Americans, arrived in this country with little except their self-sufficiency and their willingness to work. Their primary goal was to build good lives for themselves and their children. Their experience of relying on their own labor and on their own determination to succeed reinforced the traditional American values of individualism and self-reliance.

For many years, America was considered a "frontier society," and this status encouraged the nation's disposition toward individualism.[15] Until the twentieth century, open land always beckoned. On the frontier, government ruled with a relatively loose hand and individuals had a good deal of independence. Indeed, this independence was one of the appeals of the frontier.

Finally, an important current in political thought that emerged around the time of the American Revolution and the founding of the new nation further contributed to this affinity for individualism: classical liberalism. According to **classical liberalism,** a country's highest goal should be to allow all individuals in the nation to develop their intellectual and moral capacities to the fullest by making decisions for themselves rather than having decisions made for them by others. From this goal, it followed that the right of individuals to make their own decisions should be a basic principle of good societies and proper government.[16] Classical liberalism is obviously different from what we call "liberalism" today. As we will see later in this chapter, today's liberalism

classical liberalism
The doctrine that a society is good only to the extent that all of its members are able to develop their capacities to the fullest, and that to encourage this result, government should intervene as little as possible in people's lives.

argues for considerable central control in some areas such as the economy, while arguing for individual freedom in others, such as abortion and free speech.

A major voice in classical liberalism at the time was John Locke; his writings influenced both the Declaration of Independence and the American Constitution (see Chapter 2).[17] The Bill of Rights, as the first ten amendments of the Constitution are collectively called, enshrines a number of protections for individual choice against government control—protections for freedom of speech, religion, press, and free association, as well as protections against abuse by the government in criminal prosecutions.

The strong individualism and emphasis on freedom promoted by these various influences has persisted in the United States to the present. In a study in which people from 40 countries were asked whether they would choose freedom or equality, if they were forced to make a choice, Americans ranked third in the percentage choosing freedom. Seventy-one percent of Americans chose freedom compared, for instance, with only 45 percent of Italians, 41 percent of Brazilians, and 21 percent of Chinese.[18] In a different study, comparing IBM employees in 40 countries, Americans ranked above workers in all of the other countries on how much they valued freedom and challenge in their work.[19]

THE RULE OF LAW

rule of law
The idea that laws, rather than the whims or personal interests of officials, should determine the government's actions.

The **rule of law,** another basic American value, is the principle that laws, rather than the whims or personal interests of officials, should determine the government's actions. The Preamble to the Constitution refers to the rule of law in the phrase "[to] establish Justice." This principle deals not with what the government should do, but rather with how the government should comport itself. According to the rule of law, government should be guided by basic principles and should follow fair procedures, as summarized in the statement, "Ours should be a government of laws, not of men."

The rule of law embodies the idea that everyone should be treated the same way; thus, it is related to the value of fairness. It goes beyond simple fairness, however, in that it also maintains that careful procedures should be set up to limit what government can do. Remember that the government is the one entity in a country with the right to use force to implement its decisions; the rule of law limits government so that it cannot abuse its power by treating people unfairly. For example, consider the many protections—some of which are stated in the Bill of Rights—that are designed to preserve the rights of accused persons in U.S. criminal trials. These include the right against unreasonable searches for evidence; the assumption that a defendant is considered innocent until proven guilty; and *habeas corpus,* the right to not be held in prison for more than a short time without being charged with a crime.

The Bill of Rights was included in the Constitution in order to guarantee to Americans the same rights that English citizens had traditionally enjoyed. Thus, the United States established traditions of the rule of law earlier than most countries. It was not until after World War II, for instance, that France honored the right of *habeas corpus* or instituted the requirement that the accused is presumed innocent until proven guilty. In general, Britain and its former colonies such as the United States, Canada, Australia, and India established strong traditions of the rule of law earlier than continental European countries and their former colonies.

RELIGION

Americans are unusually religious. In one study 58 percent of Americans—a far greater percentage than in any other prosperous country in the world—indicated that God is very important in their lives. Thirty-seven percent of Canadians responded in kind, but very few did from Great Britain, Japan, Sweden, France, or other prosperous countries (see Figure 6.7 on page 203).[20]

Moral values rooted in religion have figured strongly throughout U.S. history, influencing both conservatives and liberals. For example, Christian denominations were partially responsible for the nineteenth-century Abolitionist Movement. Many churches also supported a powerful temperance movement in the late nineteenth and early twentieth centuries; this movement led ultimately to a constitutional amendment banning the sale of alcoholic beverages (the Eighteenth Amendment, which was passed in 1920). The Civil Rights Movement in the 1950s and 1960s drew strong support from both African American and white churches. Today, conflicts over abortion, same-sex marriage, proposals to ban pornography, and the teaching of creationism in public schools have strongly moral religious roots.

VARIATIONS AND CONFLICTS IN VALUES

Fairness, individualism, belief in the rule of law, and religion are all basic American values, but this does not mean that every American holds these four values equally, nor does it mean that every American views each of the values in the same way. For instance, as discussed earlier, though Americans are more likely than citizens of other countries to envision fairness in terms of equal treatment for equal accomplishment, many Americans do also envision it at least partly in terms of treating everyone equally or according to their need.

★ Not all Americans agree on the role of religion in public life or what the separation of church and state should mean for American governments.

Sometimes the values conflict with each other. Should the government set limits to executives' pay (fairness), or should they leave each executive free to earn whatever the market will bear (individualism)? Should homeowners have to build structures pleasing to their neighbors (fairness), or should they be free to build whatever they want, no matter how bizarre (individualism)? Should prayer be required in the schools (religion) despite the Constitution's ban on the government establishing a religion (rule of law)? Such conflicts between values form the underlying basis of American ideologies.

AMERICAN IDEOLOGIES

KEY to understanding ★

How do conflicts about values form the basis for American ideologies? Americans organize their ideas about politics into two main ideologies: conservatism and liberalism. Because individualism is such a strong value in America, there has never been an ideology in America that supported governmental intervention in both economic matters and social/religious matters, even though such ideologies are found in some other countries. Liberalism and conservatism have helped to inform contemporary political discourse in America.

ideology
An interconnected set of ideas.

An **ideology** is an interconnected set of ideas that forms and organizes our ideas and attitudes about politics. Our attitudes on gun control, on same-sex marriage, on appropriate levels of taxes, and on many other issues cluster and connect with each other. If we know whether individuals support gun control, for instance, that information may often help us to surmise whether they favor allowing same-sex marriage. Thus, our ideas about politics form an interconnected structure, which we term an ideology. An ideology organizes our ideas and attitudes for us. It also adds emotional intensity to our views on issues, as our attitude on each issue is reinforced and strengthened for us by the issue's connection to the other attitudes in the ideological cluster.

In this chapter, we will present a brief overview of and framework for understanding American ideologies. As indicated earlier, the four basic American values can sometimes conflict with one another. Not surprisingly, Americans' ideologies relate to different combinations of these basic values. Two particular lines of conflict between values form the primary basis of Americans' ideologies: the conflict between individualism and fairness and the conflict between individualism and moral beliefs.

The conflict between individualism and fairness, especially the broader interpretations of fairness, yields an economic left–right dimension or basis for ideology, with support for economic free choice at one end (the right), and support for government interventions (through regulations, taxes, and programs) to ensure economic fairness and equality at the other end (the left). Examples would include the dispute in

★ A demonstration against regulating abortions. Which of the three American ideologies—liberalism, conservatism, and libertarianism—might have been represented among these demonstrators?

2012 over whether to provide tax cuts to people with large incomes, and recurring disputes over whether to impose rules on banks to limit the fees they may charge customers.

The conflict between individualism and moral beliefs yields what is sometimes called a "social issues" dimension or basis for ideology, with support for free choice in such issues as abortion, sexually explicit entertainment, and drug or alcohol use at one end and support for government interventions to enforce moral values in such issues at the other. Moral issues do not only figure on the political right, of course. Those on the left have also sometimes favored moral imperatives over individual freedom of choice, as in liberals' desire to regulate hate speech. Currently in the United States, however, a constellation of moral values on the right is a major factor defining the political landscape.

As you can see in Figure 1.4, when we put these two dimensions together, we have a two-way grid of possible ideologies. Individual Americans' ideologies can be located on the grid, depending on how they feel about government intervention to ensure economic fairness and how they feel about government intervention to enforce policies based on religious views. For instance, a person who opposes intervention in either case would be located in the lower-left part of the grid (low on economic intervention, and low on social intervention). Similarly, we can use location on the grid as the basis for describing the major American ideologies.

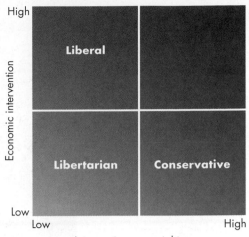

FIGURE 1.4

★ VALUE CONFLICT AND IDEOLOGY
We have divided the grid into four quadrants here for the sake of simplicity. In reality both dimensions are gradients, so that one person can be located higher than another or farther to the left, even though both are located in the same quadrant. Each dimension is a matter of degree. Where do you think you would fall on the grid?

CONSERVATISM

Conservatism is located in the lower-right part of the grid. It combines a desire for government intervention on behalf of moral views such as support for prayer in the schools and opposition to same-sex marriage, with a desire *not* to have the government intervene in the economic realm to bring about fairness through regulation of business, taxes, programs, and other policies. Conservatives argue that fairness in all such settings is better accomplished by allowing free markets to work without government intervention.

conservatism
In the United States, the ideology that supports government intervention on behalf of religious values but opposes intervention in the economic sphere.

LIBERALISM

Liberalism is located in the upper-left part of the grid. It combines a desire for governmental intervention to reduce economic inequality and inequalities between groups, especially between the majority and minority groups, with a desire *not* to have the government intervene to enforce policies based on religious views by regulating personal behaviors. Thus, liberals tend to favor higher tax rates for the wealthy than for the middle class and the poor, and programs and policies to ensure equal treatment of women, members of ethnic and racial minorities, and gays and lesbians, but tend to oppose, for example, having the government ban pornography or require prayer in the schools.

liberalism
In the United States, the ideology that opposes government intervention on behalf of religious values but supports intervention in the economic sphere to reduce inequality.

★ A protester in the "Occupy Philly" movement. How does her ideology pull all of these issues together into one interconnected set of ideas?

OTHER IDEOLOGIES

libertarianism
In the United States, the ideology that opposes government intervention in any area of people's lives.

Libertarianism opposes government intervention of any sort so that people will have the maximum individual freedom to make their own decisions, and so it falls in the lower-left part of the grid. It is a minor ideology in terms of its numbers of supporters (the Libertarian Party received just one percent of the votes in the 2012 presidential election), but it has played a more significant role in our political discourse than those numbers suggest. Ron Paul, a libertarian, ran fairly strongly in the Republican presidential primary elections in 2012, getting as much as 30 percent of the vote in some states; his appearances on college campuses, especially, drew large and lively crowds. His son, Rand Paul, also a libertarian, was elected to the United States Senate in 2010 on the Republican ticket.

The libertarian ideology is simple: On the economic issues dimension, libertarianism coincides with conservatism, opposing the use of government programs to promote economic equality, but on the social issues dimension, it coincides with liberalism, opposing government restrictions on personal behaviors. Libertarianism is in fact the survival of classical liberalism, discussed on page 17, and as such, is deeply rooted in the history of American thought.

The upper-right part of the grid, characterized by support for government intervention in both dimensions, is left unlabelled because there is no well-organized American ideology that falls in that part of the grid. In many European and Latin American countries, this part of the grid is filled by Christian-Democratic ideology; for instance, Angela Merkel, the chancellor of Germany, heads a Christian-Democratic party (see this chapter's "Picture Yourself" feature for more on values and ideology in Germany). Christian Democrats favor government intervention in support of religious values and also favor governmental economic and regulatory intervention to ensure fairness.

This combination of positions has never caught on strongly in the United States. There are, of course, some Americans who fall into this part of the grid; they often describe themselves ideologically as "economically liberal but culturally conservative." However, no single term captures this combination of positions, and no structured organizations, think-tanks, or political parties represent it. It may be that such an ideology has had difficulty taking full hold in the United States because of Americans' strong predisposition to individualism.

Two ideologies that originated in Europe but that never took a strong enough hold in the United States to become significant are socialism and fascism. Because some American political figures are occasionally mislabeled as "socialist" or "fascist," we will briefly introduce these ideologies here for the sake of clarification and to help you better understand how they are used in American political rhetoric.

Socialism developed out of conflicts between workers and employers in Europe in the nineteenth and early twentieth centuries—conflicts that were much more intense than similar conflicts in the United States. The socialist ideology at that time called for workers to take over the power of the state (either through elections or by revolution) and then use the state to control the economy by taking over and running all major industries. The end result was to be a society of equal citizens, with no economic or social distinctions among them. Socialism was a minor political force in the United States in the early twentieth century, reaching its high point in 1912 when its presidential candidate, Eugene V. Debs, received 6 percent of the vote nationally. Today, "Socialist" parties in Europe have largely abandoned the goal of having governments take over industry, but rather are democratic, free-market parties that favor policies to reduce economic inequalities.

It has always been puzzling why there never was a large socialist party in the United States, given that through much of the twentieth century socialism was a major political force in many other parts of the world. Perhaps the most succinct analysis was offered by Friedrich Engels, one of the founders of the international socialist movement, in a letter to an American friend. Engels attributed socialism's weakness in the United States to (1) the system of elections, which makes it harder to succeed with a new party than in most countries (we will look at this topic in detail in Chapter 8); (2) immigration and slavery, which had established a patchwork quilt of Irish, Germans, Czechs, African Americans, and others in which politics was dominated by disputes between ethnic groups rather than between workers and capitalists; and (3) the prosperity of the country, which gave workers a living standard better than anywhere else.[21]

Fascism was a nationalist, often racist ideology that flourished in Europe in the 1930s, in the midst of the Great Depression and the devastation of World War I. Leaders like Hitler in Germany and Mussolini in Italy adopted a showy, militaristic style of politics centered on a single, charismatic leader (themselves). A credible fascist movement in the United States has never come about, although some small white power movements have adopted many of the symbols of fascism, such as the lightning bolt or the Nazi swastika.

socialism
An ideology that favors having the government take over most businesses and run them in the interest of social and economic equality.

fascism
A nationalist, racist ideology of the 1930s that centered power on a single charismatic leader.

picture YOURSELF ...

AS A GERMAN CITIZEN

As a German, how would your values compare with those of an American? In a survey conducted in 2006, both Americans and Germans were asked whether people should take more responsibility for themselves or whether the government should take more responsibility to see that everyone is provided for. The response gap was telling: 51 percent of Germans thought that the government should take more responsibility; only 28 percent of Americans agreed with this sentiment.* Why?

Classical liberalism, with its doctrine of giving individuals as much room for independent decision making as possible, never caught on as strongly in Germany as it did in Great Britain and its former colonies. As a result, as a German citizen, you are less suspicious of government activity and less anxious about wanting to preserve your own individual sphere of choice

from government regulation. You are neither bothered by very detailed governmental supervision of people's lives, nor by rules such as barring stores from opening on Sunday or requiring that all trash must be sorted into multiple categories.

Another value that is fairly distinctive comes from Germany's experience with Hitler and the Second World War in the 1930s and 1940s. Tired of tumult and defeat, and knowing that many neighboring countries have blamed Germany for committing terrible crimes during that war, you are suspicious of military action. You are also wary of emotional nationalism, which was a hallmark of the Nazi regime.

This reluctance to pursue military options and suspicion of nationalism

shows up in opinion surveys. Only 22 percent of you said you were "very proud" of your nationality, compared with 63 percent of U.S. citizens who were asked the same question. When asked whether you would be willing to fight for your country in the event of war, only 37 percent of you said "yes," compared with 63 percent of Americans.**

As you look across the Atlantic, you realize that though you have many things in common with the people of the United States, there are also differences, which sometimes condition the relations between your country and theirs. You find that Americans often do not understand why Germany will not contribute as much as the United States would like to common

* World Values Survey, fifth wave, 2006 (accessed February 1, 2010).
** Ibid., fifth wave, 2006 (accessed February 1, 2010).

military efforts in Afghanistan, for instance. But on the other hand, you yourself find it hard to understand why Americans are reluctant to be regulated by governments and international organizations in the cause of helping to slow down global warming.

questions to consider

1. Free speech and other individual political rights are well protected in Germany, yet Germans are also very willing to allow the government to intervene in economic decisions. Is there any contradiction in this? Do you think support of economic intervention by the government makes it harder to ensure general freedom for people? Explain your response.

2. As noted in the discussion of ideologies, no well-organized political movement in the United States has ever supported high governmental intervention in *both* economic matters and social issues. (The upper-right quadrant of Figure 1.4 is empty, in other words.) In Germany, however, many religious citizens who want the government to reflect religious values in its policies also favor economic intervention. How might politics in the United States be different if that part of the political landscape were equally well populated?

THE ROLE OF IDEOLOGICAL CONFLICT IN AMERICAN POLITICS

Conservatism and liberalism are the two major ideologies in the United States, with many Americans calling themselves conservatives or liberals and with numerous organizations espousing their positions. Think tanks and organizations such as the Cato Institute and the Tea Party Movement feed conservatism, while groups such as People for the American Way and the Progressive Change Campaign Committee feed liberalism; conservatives find a media home in Fox News while liberals prefer to watch MSNBC. Conservatism and liberalism are loosely associated with the two major American parties, with conservatives gravitating to the Republican Party and liberals to the Democratic Party. The ideologies both shape and are shaped by parties, in a mutual relationship that we will explore in Chapter 6.

Conflict between differing ideologies—in which people's values influence their views on the role of government, those views crystallize as ideologies, and conflict between adherents of the different ideologies shapes political debate—lies at the heart of American politics. All of the succeeding chapters of this book will explore aspects of how this process works out—for example, through elections, through the activities of interest groups, and through the organization of the presidency.

For instance, many Americans oppose same-sex marriage on religious grounds and do not want the government to extend the benefits of marriage to same-sex couples. Other Americans believe that all couples should have the same access to the benefits and legal protections the government provides to married couples (such as favorable tax rates) and believe that legalizing same-sex marriage would be the only fair course of action. Once the issue arose in the 1990s, these two value-positions came to be quickly identified with liberalism and conservatism, since each position fit well with other positions already supported by the two ideologies. Republicans and Democrats have brought the issue into electoral politics, and it is thought to have had an impact on many contests, especially the 2004 presidential election. This issue has fueled many recent struggles between liberals and conservatives, including the choice of justices for the Supreme Court and amendments to many state constitutions.

HOW TO UNDERSTAND AMERICAN DEMOCRACY

★ **KEY** TO understanding

How can we understand why our system of government works as it does? We employ two key tools to help deepen your understanding of how American democracy functions—and why it functions as it does: historical analysis and comparisons with other countries.

comparison
Comparing aspects of a country's government and politics to those aspects in other countries, to better understand their causes.

historical analysis
Examining the way politics has developed over time in a country, in order to understand how its development has helped to shape its current form.

Our fundamental goal in writing this text is to give you insight into how our particular form of democracy works and how it came to be. Earlier in your studies, you may have learned a good many facts about American politics—for example, about the separation of powers or the process by which a bill becomes a law. You will learn such facts from this book as well, but beyond learning what makes up American politics and government, you will also explore *causes*—what makes the U.S. system work as it does, and *effects*—what difference does that make, and why should we care?

To further this goal of comprehending causes and effects, we use two main tools to help you gain a fuller understanding of American government and politics: comparison and historical analysis. When we use **comparison,** we compare aspects of U.S. government and politics to those same aspects in the governments and politics of other countries. This comparative tool exposes us to possibilities beyond what we observe in the United States, while offering insights into why various aspects of U.S. government and politics operate as they do. A second tool, **historical analysis,** allows us to investigate the roots and evolution of the U.S. system, allowing us to more knowledgeably evaluate how and why the U.S. system came to exist in its current form. The goal of both is to help you gain a more in-depth understanding of American democracy than you could acquire from a simple description of our politics.

As an example of how comparison and historical analysis may help us to understand one aspect of American politics, we focus on one facet of American life—the fact that Americans volunteer more for public purposes than people in most countries do (see Figure 1.5). Americans are distinctly more likely than citizens of other countries to do volunteer work in their communities. In a survey of the citizens of 40 countries, U.S. citizens ranked first in volunteerism. Asked, for example, if in the last month they had volunteered to do charitable activities such as giving money or time or helping strangers, 60 percent of Americans responded in the affirmative. By contrast, in France, a prosperous European country, only 31 percent of respondents said they had done volunteer work of this sort.[22]

Why do Americans volunteer so much more readily than citizens of many other countries? Comparison may help us to some extent in answering this question. One possible explanation, for instance, might be that countries such as France have a much more thorough and inclusive welfare state than the United States—that is, a system in which the government assumes relatively full responsibility for ensuring its citizens' well-being. Thus, in France, health care is provided universally through the government, and the vast majority of colleges and universities are run by the government. Since their government assumes this greater responsibility, the French might not feel as much need as Americans to contribute their time volunteering to help others. Another possible explanation from comparison would take note of Americans' unusually high religiosity and suggest that this might lead to an unusual level of voluntary efforts to help others.

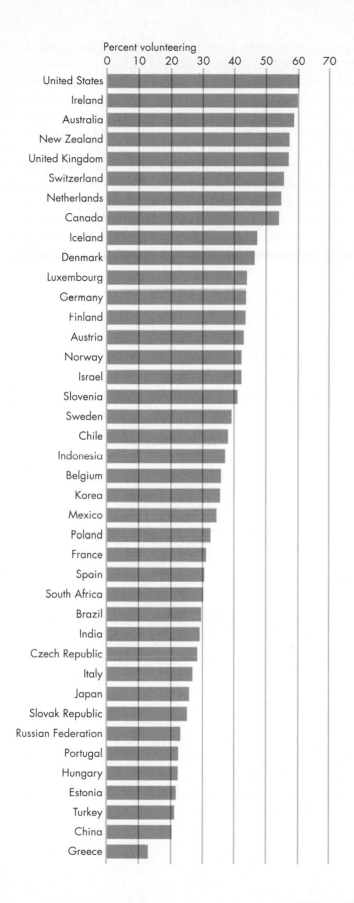

Percent volunteering

United States	
Ireland	
Australia	
New Zealand	
United Kingdom	
Switzerland	
Netherlands	
Canada	
Iceland	
Denmark	
Luxembourg	
Germany	
Finland	
Austria	
Norway	
Israel	
Slovenia	
Sweden	
Chile	
Indonesia	
Belgium	
Korea	
Mexico	
Poland	
France	
Spain	
South Africa	
Brazil	
India	
Czech Republic	
Italy	
Japan	
Slovak Republic	
Russian Federation	
Portugal	
Hungary	
Estonia	
Turkey	
China	
Greece	

FIGURE 1.5

★ AMERICANS VOLUNTEER AT A HIGH RATE

Sixty percent of Americans volunteered time, gave money, or helped strangers in a given month—more than the citizens of any other country. In general, citizens of prosperous European and North American countries were more generous in this way than citizens of other countries, but Americans top even this group. Why is this so?

Source: OECD, "Society at a Glance 2011" at http://www.oecd.org/document/24/0,3746,en_2649_37419_2671576_1_1_1_37419,00.html#publications

On this particular question, however, historical analysis is probably more helpful than comparison. In the United States, volunteering has established a long tradition. As early as 1832, Alexis de Tocqueville, a young French aristocrat who journeyed to the United States to study how the new democracy worked, commented on how willing Americans were to work voluntarily for the common good. American society at that time was made up mostly of farming communities with a great deal of social equality, in which neighbors helped each other more or less as a matter of course. On the frontier, in fact, neighbors *had* to rely on each other, because the government had little presence there. The evolution of American society from these roots may have had a good deal to do with the high incidence of volunteering today.

These comparative and historical explanations work together to give us a richer understanding of volunteering in America than we could gain simply from an observation that Americans volunteer a great deal. We hope this example has offered a taste of how you can use comparison and historical analysis to better understand American politics and American democracy as it exists today.

Why Are We
THE WAY WE ARE ?

In the chapter-opening vignette, we saw that the United States is a more complete democracy than Singapore. How has the United States maintained a democracy in which opposition can function freely, a strong rule of law exists, and government power is limited in order to protect individuals' freedom? And how did the American values that go with our democracy develop?

AMERICA'S LONG PROSPERITY

As the world's oldest electoral democracy, the United States has had a long time to establish the tradition by which two major parties alternate in power. Singapore, however, has only been an independent country since 1965 and thus is still finding its way politically. Unlike in the United States, the rights of opposition leaders and the government's ability to restrict debate remain open questions in Singapore.

The United States' long prosperity has also helped it to maintain and develop its democratic institutions. Being prosperous helps a country to maintain democracy; in fact, the average per capita income of democracies is almost twice that of non-democracies.[23] There are some exceptions—poor democracies like Ghana in Africa or India in Asia and wealthy non-democracies like the Arab oil states in the Mideast—but by and large, countries that are well-off economically are much more likely than poor countries to have well-established

democracies. The reasons why this is so are not fully understood, but it may simply be that people find it easier to work out their differences peaceably when they are reasonably well-off economically. The United States has been one of the world's most prosperous countries for two centuries.[24] This has helped it to cement its democratic form of government even during trying times like the nineteenth-century Civil War when that government was severely tested.

TRADITIONS AND THE FRONTIER EXPERIENCE

Americans' values have also helped to strengthen its commitment to democracy and contributed to its strong emphasis on the rule of law and individual freedom. Traditions involving the rule of law came from England, where a strong rule of law had developed over several centuries before the American Revolution. The stress on individual freedom also initially came from English traditions, but it is stronger in the United States today than it is in England or in any other major, established country. It is likely that the long experience of an open frontier in America, where the reach of government was necessarily limited and settlers had to provide for themselves, helped to accentuate an already strong sense of individualism and desire for freedom. The end result of all these factors has been a well-established democracy with a firm commitment to the rule of law, where citizens continue to highly value individualism and freedom.

. . . AND WHY DOES IT Matter?

It may seem strange to ask why it matters that the United States is a democracy with a strong emphasis on individual self-reliance and freedom. It is hard to imagine the United States being anything else, and the word "democracy" so purrs with respectability that it is a little hard to take the question seriously. Nonetheless, it is worth raising the question. After all, relatively few countries in the world have been democracies consistently for even the last few decades. We saw in Figure 1.2, for instance, that fewer than a third of the world's countries were democracies in 1977.

What would be different about the United States if it were *not* a democracy? Though it is difficult to speculate about such a broad question, there are some things we can probably conclude from comparisons with other countries. First of all, the United States would probably be just as prosperous if it were not a democracy. Most analyses of democracy and economic growth have concluded that it does not make much difference to the prospects for economic growth whether a country is democratic or not.[25] And we can see from many examples such as China or Singapore that a country can grow and prosper even though it is not a democracy.

Though democracy is not the source of countries' prosperity, however, it does affect how the fruits of that prosperity are distributed. In general, democracies are better than non-democracies at responding to the broad needs of their people. This makes sense, since in a democracy the government is accountable to all of the people for its policies. A review of the well-being of people in democracies and non-democracies concluded that democratic governments' policies in health and other areas were sufficiently better for people than those of nondemocratic governments to make a difference of three or four years in life expectancy.[26] We can assume from this that if the United States were not a democracy, various policies of the government would be significantly less helpful to the broad range of people in the country.

Even a few extra years of life expectancy, though, are probably not enough reason to choose democracy. In country after country around the world in the 1970s and 1980s, as people established democracy in their countries, they did not do it to improve their living standard or their health, but because of deep aspirations for human dignity. The basic appeal of democracy is the individual dignity it confers on each citizen by giving him or her a small share of the power of government, and the protection its rule of law offers against arbitrary acts by the government. These are the values behind the movements to democracy in other countries in the twenty-first century. And as we have seen, they are values deeply rooted in the American culture. Probably the greatest difference democracy makes to Americans is that it fulfills those values.

critical thinking questions

1. In the introductory comparison of Singapore and the United States, we saw that Singapore is cleaner, has less crime, and enjoys a slightly higher average income than the United States, but Singapore does not allow open competition between opposing values in its limited democracy. Which do you think would be the better country to live in? Why?

2. We introduced the concept of "public goods" on page 12, and along with defense spending, we used the space program and basic medical research as examples of public goods. To check on your understanding of the concept, explain why the space program and basic medical research, for example, are public goods.

3. Germans are less willing than Americans to sacrifice (pay taxes, accept a lower income) to help prevent environmental pollution.[27] And yet Germans are much more active in recycling than Americans; they divide their recycling into several different categories, and Germany has drastically reduced its production of garbage and trash. How might you explain this paradox?

4. Can you think of reasons why Americans might be unusually religious, compared with people in other prosperous countries?

key terms

A Note from the Authors

We are glad you have chosen to study American politics. All three of us have found government and politics to be engaging, exciting, and personally rewarding—both as an academic subject for study, and in practice. Politics sometimes suffers from popular distaste in America. Most people love "national leaders" but hate "politicians." To lead the nation absolutely requires politics, however, and we hope that as you study American politics you will come to recognize what skillful politicians can do to make people's lives better. After all, Abraham Lincoln and Franklin Delano Roosevelt, two of our most successful and revered presidents, were also two of the most skillful politicians to have ever operated in American politics. Politics is important and good, and fortunately (as you will know if you have ever been involved in a campaign), it can also be great fun. We hope you enjoy this course.

THE FOUNDING AND
THE CONSTITUTION

- Explain how the American colonies came into being, and describe the influence of British tradition on the rights that the colonists came to expect.
- Describe the factors that led to the American Revolution, and explain how the basic principles of the revolution shaped the governments that followed.
- Outline the structure and power of government under the Articles of Confederation, and describe the weaknesses that ultimately led to their failure as a form of government.
- Describe the delegates to the Constitutional Convention, including the issues that united and divided them, and the compromises among them that led to the final document.
- Identify the four core principles and major provisions of the U.S. Constitution, as well as the ways in which it was undemocratic.
- Evaluate the arguments of those on both sides of the ratification battle, and the roles of the Federalist Papers and the Bill of Rights in helping to secure ratification.
- Describe the formal process of amending the U.S. Constitution as well as the informal process of amendment through interpretation.

PERSPECTIVE
What Compromises Are Necessary for Ratifying a National Constitution?

It had been a long, hot summer, and the framers of the Constitution were growing weary. The process of drafting a constitution had led to passionate debates about issues ranging from the role of religion in government to the extent of federalism, which is the sharing of power between the national government and local governments. Since convening in May, the framers had agreed that the national government would consist of three branches: legislative, executive, and judicial. The executive branch would be led by a president. A Supreme Court would enforce the Constitution, which provided for a representative government elected by the people. Now, as the end of August approached, the framers remained deadlocked on several key issues. Nevertheless, they were determined to find compromises that would allow them to finish their work and send the Constitution on for ratification. Did this scenario take place in Philadelphia during the summer of 1787? No—Baghdad, summer of 2005.

Indeed, there are some significant similarities between the experiences of the framers in 1787 America and 2005 Iraq. Both were engaged in writing what scholars refer to as "post-conflict constitutions"—that is, constitutions written after winning a struggle for independence or overthrowing an existing government. Both the Constitutional Convention in Philadelphia and the Constitutional Drafting Committee in Baghdad (each with fifty-five delegates) were attempting to solve what appeared to be insoluble political problems. In 1787 Philadelphia, the framers, concerned with the weakness of the central government under the Articles of Confederation, were attempting to create a national government strong enough to coerce compliance with national law at a time when the core principles of the American Revolution had produced "an instinctive aversion to coercive power of any sort and a thoroughgoing dread of the inevitable corruptions that result when unseen rulers congregate in distant places."[1] How could they create a national government strong enough to keep the nation together but not so strong as to undermine core principles such as liberty or to excessively infringe on the autonomy of states? In 2005 Baghdad, the framers were similarly trying to balance a strong central government with regional autonomy. And both sets of framers consisted of rival factions that disagreed fundamentally about core issues. Could consensus be built under such circumstances?

Let's also consider the significant differences between 1787 Philadelphia and 2005 Baghdad. For one, the American framers were working in uncharted territory. Individual states had created constitutions in the wake of the Declaration of Independence, but the concept of a written constitution governing an entire nation was new and untested. Moreover, there had never before been a republican (that is, representative) government on the scale of the United States. In contrast, constitution writing had become something of a cottage industry by 2005. In just the past 50 years, some 200 new constitutions have been drafted for nations ranging from Albania to Zambia.[2] This has allowed observers to analyze which processes work best when creating a new constitution.[3] Another difference was that the Iraqi framers faced a nation much more deeply divided along lines of ethnicity, language, religious sect, and region than did the American framers. Moreover, the post-conflict situations were different: Whereas the American colonists had fought to win their independence from a colonial power, a tyrannical Iraqi government had been overthrown as a result of an invasion by outside forces, and the Iraqis drafted their constitution under the watchful eye of an occupying force.

That fact that there are similarities between the U.S. and Iraq constitutions themselves is no accident. The U.S. Constitution has endured and become a model for many constitutions around the world. We now take for granted the success of the U.S. Constitution, but that success is really quite amazing. The American colonies were, as historian Joseph J. Ellis put it, "generally regarded as a provincial and wholly peripheral outpost of Western Civilization." Nonetheless, they "somehow managed to establish a set of ideas and institutions that, over the stretch of time, became the blueprint for political and economic success for the nation-state in the modern world."[4]

THIS CHAPTER BEGINS with a discussion of the American colonies—of why people settled in them and what divided and what united these colonists. The colonies enjoyed considerable autonomy until the 1760s. We examine why and then discuss the factors that set the colonists on the path to revolution. Following the Declaration of Independence in 1776, the colonists went about establishing a new government. We see why their first attempt, the Articles of Confederation, ended in failure and then discuss the drafting and ratification of the U.S. Constitution, including the compromises that made passage possible. We conclude by looking at the core principles and specific articles of the Constitution and at how the Constitution is formally amended and otherwise changed. As you read this chapter, keep in mind our two core questions:

WHY ARE WE THE WAY WE ARE?
WHY DOES IT MATTER TO YOU?

In particular, how did the British tradition—things like the Magna Carta, the English Bill of Rights, and the writings of British philosophers such as John Locke—influence not only the American Revolution itself, but the subsequent system of government established in the United States?

THE AMERICAN COLONIES

In order to understand the factors that eventually led to the American Revolution, it is first necessary to understand how the colonies came into being and why they endured for so long. Europeans "discovered" America through Christopher Columbus in 1492. By then, North America had been populated for as long as forty thousand years and was already home to as many as ten million aboriginal or native people. France, Holland, and England led some explorations of the eastern seaboard of North America in the 1500s, but the road to English settlement did not really begin until 1606, when King James I issued charters to establish American colonies.

How and why did the American colonies come into being? Who populated them, how were they governed, and what rights did colonists come to expect from the British tradition? Understanding the influence of the British tradition is especially important. The violation of perceived rights led directly to the American Revolution. Ironically, reliance on British thought provided the justification for independence from Britain. The principles derived from the British tradition matter because they subsequently influenced the formation of the new American government. ★

MOTIVATIONS FOR COMING TO THE COLONIES

Several factors led to the migration of people from England and other European countries to North America. One factor was religion. As early as the 1560s French Protestants (known as Huguenots) came to what is now South Carolina and Florida to escape religious persecution, and the New England colonies, in particular, were settled by people seeking religious freedom for themselves. Religious beliefs across the colonies varied considerably. The Pilgrims—a group of religious *separatists* (those who advocated a complete break with, or separation from, the Church of England)—sailed on the *Mayflower* in 1620 and settled the Plymouth colony in Massachusetts. The Puritans—a group of *nonseparatists* (those who sought to reform the Church of England rather than break away from it)—settled the Massachusetts Bay colony, soon outnumbering the Pilgrims. The Maryland colony was originally envisioned as a haven for English Catholics, though in the end few Catholics settled there. And Huguenots settled the Dutch colony of New Netherland, which later became the English colonies of New York and New Jersey.

In addition to religion, economic incentives drew people to the colonies. This was especially true in colonies from Maryland south, where the draw for colonists was the opportunity to make money by growing tobacco. Whereas Massachusetts was viewed initially as a religious colony, Virginia began as a corporate colony financed by a joint-stock company. The emphasis on growing crops for profit in the south led to the development of large plantations and inhibited urban development. Initially, these plantations lured young men from England and other European countries to work on them as indentured servants—laborers who entered a contract to work for no wages for a fixed period of time (usually three to seven years) in return for food, clothing, shelter, and their transportation to the colony. Some have suggested that as many as half of all white immigrants to the colonies during the seventeen and eighteenth centuries may have come as indentured servants. Later, white servitude gave way to slavery when plantation owners resorted to buying slaves from Africa instead of

★ Tobacco farming continues today in the United States. However, with the decline in domestic demand, U.S. farmers are hoping to sell their production overseas to countries like China.

utilizing indentured servants. Since economic incentives rather than religious freedom tended to draw people to the southern colonies, they were more religiously and ethnically diverse than their northern counterparts.[5]

DIFFERENCES AND COMMONALITIES AMONG THE COLONISTS

The historian Edmund S. Morgan characterized the colonists as "a quarrelsome, litigious, divisive lot." There were sectional quarrels both within colonies and between colonies. For example, tensions were so rife between western North Carolina and eastern North Carolina that civil war erupted in 1771. Morgan noted that the "hostility which every American seemed to feel for every other American" was such that in 1765 James Otis, who became a leader in the movement for independence, commented that "were these colonies left to themselves tomorrow, America would be a shambles of blood and confusion."[6]

How, then, Morgan asks, did these same people unite to create one of the most influential and long-lasting governments in Western civilization? He suggests that the answer may lie in the fact that, despite their differences, the colonists shared a number of fundamental similarities. They were predominantly of English descent, overwhelmingly Protestant, and mostly farmers. In addition, property ownership was relatively common. Since ownership of property was a requirement for voting, widespread ownership meant greater political engagement.[7] The squabbling, then, was mostly among "family," and the factors that led to revolution, factors we discuss in the following sections, brought that family together against a common enemy.

EARLY COLONIAL GOVERNMENT AND EVENTS IN BRITAIN

At first, the American colonies enjoyed a considerable degree of autonomy from Britain. The king appointed governors in most colonies, and these royal governors appeared to have great power; but in practice, they served as "paper tigers."[8] Colonies had their own elected assemblies, and, since governors ultimately depended on those assemblies for funding, they generally avoided antagonizing them by opposing their legislation. And the governors were so far removed from the king that the colonists usually did pretty much as they pleased. Moreover, events in Britain during the 1600s reinforced the power of the colonial assemblies, undermined the influence of the king, and preoccupied the British, distracting their attention from the colonies.

Familiarity with a few key elements of British history, starting with the Magna Carta from the 1200s, is essential to understanding our own political development. The Magna Carta spelled out certain fundamental principles that the American colonists later embraced as a basis for revolution and as essential building blocks of the new government they would create—hence its significance. Along with other subsequent events in England that we will also discuss, it helped to create the "stew" of British political thought and action that influenced the American experience and the thinking of our constitution-makers.

The Magna Carta

The *Magna Carta* (which means "great charter" in Latin, the language in which it is written) is one of the great documents in Western civilization, and its articulation of rights strongly influenced the framers of the U.S. Constitution. The Magna Carta dates to 1215, when King John (ruler of England from 1199 to 1216) was forced to sign it by English barons who had renounced their allegiance to the king and revolted after John had imposed heavy taxes, waged an unsuccessful war with France, and quarreled with the Pope.

The Magna Carta was a practical document designed to remedy specific abuses of the king. Many of the 63 chapters into which it was later divided are unimportant to us today, but some stand as a fundamental basis for the rule of law—the idea that even the most powerful leader of government is bound by the law. These important chapters focus especially on courts and the administration of justice, which the barons believed John had undermined. Chapter 39, probably the greatest part of the Magna Carta, emphatically states the requirement of *due process of law,* or of fair procedures:

> No free man shall be seized or imprisoned, or stripped of his rights or possessions, or outlawed or exiled, or deprived of his standing in any other way, nor will we proceed with force against him, or send others to do so, except by the lawful judgment of his equals or by the law of the land.[9]

This provision of the Magna Carta limited the power of kings and later served as the basis for the guarantees in the fifth and fourteenth amendments of the U.S. Constitution that government shall not take a person's life, liberty, or property without due process of law. Modern-day Miranda warnings are an outgrowth of this (see Figure 2.1).

The fact that King John was forced to sign this document set an important precedent of free men standing up to the king. In 1297, the Magna Carta was placed in the statute books of England, where it remains to this day. By the end of the fourteenth century, the Magna Carta had come to be viewed not just as any ordinary statute, but as the fundamental law of the realm. It was invoked again to justify rebellion against King Charles I in 1642.

Civil War, the Glorious Revolution, and the English Bill of Rights

In 1642, just 36 years after King James I had issued the first charters establishing American colonies, civil war erupted in England. James I (who ruled from 1602 to 1625) and his son and successor, Charles I, believed in the divine right of kings—that is, the idea that kings derived their right to rule from God and were not accountable to their subjects. They thus believed that they had absolute control over Parliament (the legislature in England) and could, for example, impose taxes without its consent. Charles I took

---

MIRANDA WARNING

1. YOU HAVE THE RIGHT TO REMAIN SILENT.
2. ANYTHING YOU SAY CAN AND WILL BE USED AGAINST YOU IN A COURT OF LAW.
3. YOU HAVE THE RIGHT TO TALK TO A LAWYER AND HAVE HIM PRESENT WITH YOU WHILE YOU ARE BEING QUESTIONED.
4. IF YOU CANNOT AFFORD TO HIRE A LAWYER, ONE WILL BE APPOINTED TO REPRESENT YOU BEFORE ANY QUESTIONING IF YOU WISH.
5. YOU CAN DECIDE AT ANY TIME TO EXERCISE THESE RIGHTS AND NOT ANSWER ANY QUESTIONS OR MAKE ANY STATEMENTS.

WAIVER

DO YOU UNDERSTAND EACH OF THESE RIGHTS I HAVE EXPLAINED TO YOU?
HAVING THESE RIGHTS IN MIND, DO YOU WISH TO TALK TO US NOW?

FIGURE 2.1

★ MIRANDA WARNING

The Miranda warning card, carried by police officers, exemplifies a modern example of Americans' due process rights.

other unilateral steps as well, including arbitrary arrests and detentions, quartering troops in private homes, and even imposing martial law. He summoned and dissolved Parliament at will, and claimed an absolute right to veto any legislation it passed. Increasingly angered, Parliament and its supporters waged a civil war against the king and his supporters.

In rising up against Charles I, Parliament invoked the Magna Carta and argued that the king was violating the rights of individuals. Opponents of the king argued that if he could tax without the consent of Parliament, then the English people and Parliament, their representative assembly, were in a state of servitude to the king. As we will see, concern about taxation without representation later became a key issue in the road to revolution in the American colonies. Parliamentary servitude was also seen as resulting from the king's claim to the power to summon and dissolve Parliament at will and to veto any legislation.

The decades that followed were rocky times in England. Suffice it to say here that Charles I was eventually beheaded. When his son, Charles II, tried to succeed him another civil war ensued. Charles II fled to France, and Parliament declared England a "free state" to be governed as a commonwealth without a king. That commonwealth lasted from 1651 until 1659. Charles II returned to England and was restored to the throne in 1660. King Charles II was now careful not to oppose Parliament, but his brother, James II, who succeeded him in 1685, tried to reassert the divine right of kings and to rule without Parliament. As a result, he was run out of the country in what became known as the Glorious Revolution of 1688.

The action of James II led Parliament to enact the English Bill of Rights, a statute that spelled out the basic rights of Englishmen and that limited the power of future kings and queens. Among other things, the Bill of Rights declared freedom from taxation by royal prerogative: only Parliament, the representative of the people, could impose taxes. The English philosopher John Locke (1632–1704) echoed this basic tenet in his *Two Treatises of Government* published that same year: Life, liberty, and property are natural rights of man; therefore, property cannot be taken without the consent of its owners or their representatives. Together, the Magna Carta and the Bill of Rights were considered to be part of England's "unwritten" constitution, which came to be seen by British citizens as containing fundamental, inviolable principles.

Implications for the Colonies

These events in England set the stage for parliamentary sovereignty—the idea that Parliament was superior to all other parts of government. But by the 1700s, parliamentary sovereignty would become a bone of contention for the American colonies as Parliament increasingly attempted to impose its will on them. The Magna Carta and the English Bill of Rights, which Parliament had used to fight absolute monarchy in the 1600s, now served to delineate rights that the colonists felt they deserved, too. The difference for the colonists in the 1700s was that they used the Magna Carta and the Bill of Rights to fight against parliamentary sovereignty rather than absolute monarchy.

"NO TAXATION WITHOUT REPRESENTATION"

Some things never change: People hate taxes, or at least taxes that seem excessive or otherwise unfair. The colonists seethed at taxes imposed on them by Parliament because they considered them not only unfair but a flagrant violation of parliamentary power. Since the colonists had no elected representatives in Parliament, they believed that these taxes violated a fundamental principle of the English Bill of Rights: no taxation without representation. (You will recall that the Bill of Rights declared freedom from taxation by royal prerogative and instead gave Parliament the power to tax *because that body represented the people.*) Anger over taxation without representation is, in no small measure, what led to the American Revolution.

The Sugar Act and Stamp Act

The first seeds of revolution were planted in 1764 when Parliament enacted the American Revenue Act, better known as the Sugar Act. People in England had been complaining of too many taxes, and so Parliament used the act to shift some of the tax burden to the American colonists. The Sugar Act imposed duties on certain foreign goods imported into the American colonies—sugar and other goods including coffee, some wines, and pimiento. The timing could not have been worse, as the colonies were facing a bad economy. Not only did the new duties on imported goods increase prices for the colonists, but they also hurt American manufacturers of rum by making ingredients more expensive. As a result, the American rum trade was threatened to be priced out of the market; foreign buyers who had previously imported American rum now turned to other sources.

Colonists reacted harshly to the Sugar Act. They quickly took up the rallying cry of "no taxation without representation." New England was hit especially hard by the Sugar Act. The Massachusetts assembly adopted a proclamation stating that it looked upon the duties imposed by the act as a tax, one "which we humbly apprehend ought not to be laid without the Representatives of the People affected by them." Such taxation without representation deprived the colonists of "the most essential Rights of Britons."[10]

Parliament made matters even worse for the colonists by imposing the Stamp Act the following March. From 1756 to 1763, the British had fought the French and Indian War in Canada and on the western frontier of the colonies, part of a larger struggle among a number of countries, including Britain and France, which transpired in Europe and elsewhere. British victory in the French and Indian War had been expensive, and the Stamp Act was a move by Parliament to raise money, ostensibly to pay for England's continued military presence in North America after the war. The act imposed a direct tax on a wide array of printed materials in the colonies, including everything from legal documents to newspapers and playing cards. Such materials had to either be printed on specially marked paper or have tax stamps affixed to them to indicate that the tax had been paid.

The Stamp Act galvanized the colonies. Several colonial assemblies adopted resolutions denouncing the tax. The first and most famous was a series of resolutions passed by the Virginia House of Burgesses on May 29, 1765, at the urging of Patrick Henry (famous for his cry "Give me liberty or give me death!"). These Virginia Stamp Act Resolutions (also known as the "Virginia Resolves") stated that "the taxation of the people by themselves, or by persons chosen by themselves to represent them, . . . is the distinguishing characteristic of British freedom. . . ."[11] In so doing, the Virginia Resolves invoked the spirit of the Magna Carta and the English Bill of Rights.

The Stamp Act also provoked representatives from nine of the thirteen colonies to gather at Federal Hall in New York in October 1765.[12] This so-called **Stamp Act Congress** was the first official meeting of colonial representatives, and it resulted in a Declaration of Rights. The declaration rejected the claim by the British Prime Minister,

★ American newspapers bitterly opposed the Stamp Act.

Stamp Act Congress
The first national meeting of representatives from the colonies in 1765. In response to duties (taxes) imposed by Parliament on the colonies through the Stamp Act, this Congress passed a Declaration of Rights that denounced taxation without representation—an important step toward the American Revolution.

★ **THE BOSTON MASSACRE AS DEPICTED BY PAUL REVERE.** Is Revere's depiction of the Boston Massacre—British soldiers firing point blank into a small crowd of un-armed colonists and their dog—an accurate portrayal of the event? If not, what is inaccurate about it?

George Grenville, that as British subjects, the colonists enjoyed "virtual representation" in Parliament even if they did not formally elect representatives to Parliament. In direct defiance of Grenville, the declaration made it clear that "the only representatives of these colonies are persons chosen therein," adding that "no taxes can be constitutionally imposed on [the colonies] but by their respective legislatures."[13]

Representative bodies were not the only ones motivated by the Stamp Act to take action. Throughout the colonies, individuals formed associations known as the Sons of Liberty to attack British authority and resist taxation without representation by whatever means necessary. In some places, violent protests erupted. Those who distributed the hated stamps were hung in effigy, and in some cases their homes were attacked. Defiant colonists refused to use the stamps, and they also boycotted British goods.

The British Response

The reaction of the colonists to the Stamp Act alarmed the British, and in February 1766 Parliament repealed the act. But, in March, it also passed the Declaratory Act, stating that colonial bodies had "against law" claimed "the sole and exclusive right of imposing duties and taxes" in the colonies. Noting that "all [colonial] resolutions, votes, orders, and proceedings" that denied Parliament's power to tax (including the Virginia Resolves and the Stamp Act Congress's Declaration of Rights) were "utterly null and void," the act reiterated that the colonies were "subordinate unto, and dependent upon the imperial crown and Parliament of Great Britain."[14]

Then, the next year, Parliament enacted the Revenue Act of 1767, the first of the so-called Townshend Acts, named after Charles Townshend, the chancellor of exchequer (treasury), who advocated them. Whereas the Stamp Act was a direct tax on goods in the colonies, the Revenue Act (like the earlier Sugar Act) was an indirect tax that placed duties on imported goods, including the paper, paint, glass, and tea the colonies imported from England. Townshend assumed that indirect taxes would be more palatable to the colonists than direct taxes, but his assumption was wrong. The Massachusetts House of Representatives reiterated the now-familiar protest: no taxation without representation.

This time, England's response was harsh. It ordered the royal governor to dissolve the Massachusetts legislature. Soon thereafter it sent regiments of British troops to Boston. The Redcoats became a hated fixture there. One cold night in March 1770, a group of several hundred men and boys pelted a small band of nine Redcoats with rocks, snowballs, chunks of ice, and oyster shells. Alarmed, the soldiers fired back, killing five men. The British soldiers had been provoked, but the incident was quickly dubbed the "Boston Massacre" and used to rally opposition to the oppressive force of the British.[15] Nonetheless, John Adams—a future president of the United States—defended the British soldiers when they were tried for murder. He secured a verdict of "innocent" for the captain, who was tried first. In a subsequent trial of the remaining eight soldiers, six were acquitted and two were found guilty of the lesser charge of manslaughter.

The Boston Tea Party

As it had done with the Stamp Act, England backed down in the face of the colonial reaction to the Revenue Act. The colonists boycotted the imported goods that were subject to duties, and in 1770 England rescinded the duties for all goods except tea. Colonists evaded the remaining tea tax by buying smuggled tea from Holland, but Parliament foreclosed that option in 1773 when it passed the Tea Act. The primary purpose of that act was to save the nearly bankrupt East India Company by giving it a monopoly to sell tea in the colonies. Parliament lowered the price of tea so much that the tea from the East India Company—even after the tea tax—was cheaper than smuggled tea. Parliament assumed that the colonists would welcome the cheap tea. Instead, the colonists viewed the cheap tea as a trick to get them to accept British taxation. Americans tried to block British ships bringing the tea from the East India Company. In many cases this blockade worked, but in Boston a British ship refused to leave the harbor without unloading its cargo of tea and collecting the duty on it. The showdown led, on December 16, 1773, to the Boston Tea Party, in which a group of colonists disguised as Mohawk Indians boarded the ship and dumped all 342 chests of tea into the harbor. This act of defiance marked an important step toward revolution.[16]

Parliament responded to the Boston Tea Party by passing a series of measures in 1774 known as the Coercive Acts (or, as the colonists liked to call them, the Intolerable Acts). These acts were designed to punish Massachusetts. Among other things, the Coercive Acts closed Boston Harbor to all commerce until England received payment for the destroyed tea, brought the Massachusetts government under full British control, forbade most town meetings, and allowed British troops to be quartered in private buildings and homes in Boston.

★ Shown here, members of the modern Tea Party movement expressing their concerns about taxes.

THE FIRST CONTINENTAL CONGRESS

Though aimed at Massachusetts, the Coercive Acts had potential ramifications for all of the colonies. As a result, representatives from all of the colonies except Georgia met in Philadelphia in September and October 1774 to decide how to respond. The delegates at these meetings of the First Continental Congress in essence represented twelve different nations. Although they came together in response to the common threat to their liberties posed by Great Britain, the colonies remained deeply divided on many issues. As historian Merrill Jensen put it, "The large colonies were pitted against small ones; colonies with many slaves were in opposition to those with fewer; colonies that had no western lines contended with those that did."[17] Despite these differences, the First Continental Congress resulted in an agreement by the colonies to engage in a total boycott of British goods.

The First Continental Congress also produced a declaration of rights and grievances. Among other things, the declaration asserted the right to "life, liberty, and property," denounced the keeping of British troops in the colonies in times of peace as "against law," and reiterated that "the foundation of English liberty, and of all free government, is a right in the people to participate in their legislative council." Since the colonists were not represented in Parliament, they claimed the right to a "free and exclusive power of legislation" in their own colonial assemblies, subject only to veto by the king.[18]

The rallying cry of "no taxation without representation" had evolved into something far more significant: All legislation produced by a parliament in which the colonists were not represented was now considered suspect. And colonies with disparate interests and outlooks were uniting against Great Britain and around the cause of liberty. As our review of historical events makes clear, the liberty that the colonists sought was a direct outgrowth of rights espoused by the British tradition. England's failure to enforce those rights precipitated revolution.

REVOLUTION AND INDEPENDENCE

★ **KEY** to understanding

What factors led to the American Revolution, and how did the basic principles of the revolution shape the governments that followed? For many colonists, breaking ties with Great Britain was a difficult step. However, *Common Sense,* an enormously successful publication, did much to justify the break and rationalize revolution. The Declaration of Independence framed the revolution as a defense of "unalienable rights" that Great Britain denied its citizens in the colonies. Britain had, in other words, broken its "social contract." This concept of a social contract led directly to our written constitution—a sharp break from Britain's less formal "unwritten" constitution.

Although some members of the First Continental Congress still hoped for reconciliation with Britain, war was looming. In anticipation of rebellion, British troops fortified Boston. Colonists also prepared for conflict by organizing small groups of armed militia known as Minutemen. On April 19, 1775, fighting broke out in Massachusetts in the towns of Lexington and Concord.

THE SECOND CONTINENTAL CONGRESS

Once fighting broke out in Lexington and Concord, the colonies quickly sent representatives to the Second Continental Congress to oversee steps toward independence and manage the impending war. By the time the Second Continental Congress convened in Philadelphia on May 10, 1775, full-fledged war had already erupted. The Congress officially created the Continental Army and appointed George Washington to command it. But more than a year was to pass before the Second Continental Congress voted to approve the Declaration of Independence. The Congress then turned to writing the first, ill-fated, U.S. Constitution: the Articles of Confederation.

The delay in formally declaring independence occurred because many colonists, who came predominantly from England, remained reluctant to make a full break with their homeland. Breaking their allegiance to the king—a powerful symbolic figure—proved especially difficult. Then, in January 1776, Thomas Paine anonymously published his 48-page pamphlet, *Common Sense.* Saying, "I offer nothing more than simple facts, plain arguments, and common sense," Paine provided a compelling justification for independence, and did so—as historian Joseph J. Ellis put it—"in language that was simultaneously simple and dazzling."[19] Paine took aim at King George III himself and sharply dismissed the institution of monarchy. The pamphlet's timing could not have been better. Colonists had just learned that the king had rejected any effort to resolve the dispute with them diplomatically and would instead seek to smash the rebellion with military force.[20] Breaking allegiance to the crown no longer seemed so difficult. And even though Parliament had been the source of the legislation that had prompted the dispute between Britain and the colonies, the king now became the symbolic enemy.

Wha WANTS ME

★ Thomas Paine is shown here holding the scrolls depicting the "rights of man." His best-selling pamphlet, *Common Sense,* helped fuel the quest for independence.

Common Sense was an instant best seller, with some 120,000 copies sold in the first three months alone and 500,000 copies sold within a year. This was at a time when the official population count of the colonies (excluding slaves and Native Americans) was only about 2.5 million.[21] Compare this to the nearly *62 million* copies that would need to be sold to reach a proportionate number of Americans today.[22] Clearly, Paine's rallying cry for independence had hit a nerve.

THE DECLARATION OF INDEPENDENCE

In May 1776, just four months after the publication of *Common Sense,* the Virginia House of Burgesses instructed its delegates to the Second Continental Congress to propose independence—making Virginia the first of the colonies to call for such a resolution. That same month, the Continental Congress urged colonies to adopt constitutions in anticipation of impending independence and statehood. New Hampshire had already adopted a constitution on January 6, 1776, and South Carolina had followed suit on March 26.[23] Then, on June 7, Virginia's Richard Henry Lee proposed before the Continental Congress, "that these United Colonies are, and of right ought to be, free and independent States. . . ."[24] To implement Lee's resolution, the Congress created a committee consisting of John Adams, Benjamin Franklin, Thomas Jefferson, Robert Livingston, and Roger Sherman to prepare what would eventually become the American **Declaration of Independence.**

The committee delegated the task of writing the declaration to Adams and Jefferson, and Adams deferred to Jefferson. Jefferson then proceeded in a matter of days to write

Declaration of Independence
A statement written by Thomas Jefferson and approved by the Second Continental Congress on July 4, 1776, that asserted the independence of the American colonies from Great Britain.

the Declaration of Independence, which includes what are now some of the most famous words in the English language:

> We hold these truths to be self-evident, that all men are created equal, that they are endowed by their Creator with certain unalienable Rights,[25] that among these are Life, Liberty, and the pursuit of Happiness. That to secure these rights, Governments are instituted among Men, deriving their just powers from the consent of the governed, – That whenever any Form of Government becomes destructive of these ends, it is the Right of the People to alter or to abolish it, and to institute new Government. . . .

In writing these words, Jefferson drew upon John Locke's *Two Treatises of Government.* As mentioned earlier, Locke believed that people enjoy certain natural rights, including "life, liberty, and property," that cannot be taken away without their consent. Through a **social contract,** people come together in a society under a government whose authority they agree to obey. If, however, a government deprives them of their natural rights without their consent, the social contract is broken and the people have a right to rebel and replace that government with one that would adhere to the terms of the social contract. This concept of a social contract led the newly independent states, and eventually the new federal government, to adopt written constitutions. These constitutions served as contracts spelling out the powers of government and the rights of the people.

In making his case for rebellion in the Declaration of Independence, Jefferson listed a specific set of grievances against Britain. In expressing these grievances, he did not even mention Parliament but rather took aim exclusively at King George III: "The history

social contract
The idea, drawn from the writings of John Locke and others, that government is accountable to the people and bound to protect the natural rights of its citizens. If government breaks this contract, the people have the right to rebel and replace the government with one that will enforce it.

★ Popular uprisings, such as this one in Egypt, depict ramifications of a broken social contract in the contemporary world.

of the present King of Great Britain is a history of repeated injuries and usurpations, all having in direct object the establishment of an absolute Tyranny over these States." Jefferson listed 27 specific grievances and, finally, declared that "these Colonies are, and of Right ought to be Free and Independent States, that they are Absolved from all Allegiance to the British Crown, and that all political connection between them and the State of Great Britain, is and ought to be totally dissolved. . . ."

Meanwhile, some delegates to the Continental Congress thought it premature to declare independence. A preliminary vote on July 1 showed that two of the thirteen colonies (South Carolina and Pennsylvania) opposed independence. Another, New York, abstained because its delegates did not have clear instructions from home about how to vote. (Each colony had a single vote in Congress determined by a majority vote of the delegates from that colony.) In an attempt to secure unanimity among the colonies, Congress delayed the final vote on Lee's resolution until the next day. The tactic worked. South Carolina reversed its vote and, as the result of strategic abstentions by two of its delegates, Pennsylvania now voted 3-2 in favor of independence instead of 4-3 against it. New York still abstained, but the New York Provincial Congress formally voted to support independence a few days later. Congress approved the final language of the Declaration of Independence on July 4, 1776, and the first public reading of the Declaration took place four days later in Philadelphia. The next day, July 9, George Washington ordered that the Declaration be read to members of the Continental Army in New York.

Independence had been declared, but the Revolutionary War dragged on until 1781. The official peace accord, in which Great Britain recognized the independence of the United States, was not signed until 1782.

THE ARTICLES OF CONFEDERATION

With the Declaration, the colonies asserted their independence but still mostly lacked a formal government. As already mentioned, in the months preceding the Declaration, would-be states had begun drafting their own written constitutions. By the end of 1776, all but three of the states had drafted and ratified constitutions. Georgia and New York followed suit in 1777, as did Massachusetts in 1780. These constitutions created state governments. However, a new national government to oversee the 13 states was also needed. The problem—similar to the one faced in Iraq in 2005—was how to balance regional autonomy with national power.

In the short run, the Second Continental Congress operated as the national government. The Continental Congress also took responsibility for writing a national constitution and, in fact, had appointed a committee for this purpose even before voting to approve the Declaration of Independence. But the process of drafting the constitution proved to be slow. The problem, above all, was that the new states were understandably wary of central authority. Furthermore, differences among the states led to heated debates. Large states wanted proportional representation in the national government, while small states wanted equal representation. Similarly, there was debate about whether states should supply funds to the national government in proportion to their population. If so, did the slave

KEY TO understanding ★

The Articles of Confederation were a failed post-conflict constitution. Drafting them was a contentious process that took over a year, and ratification of the document took much longer. Once in place, the Articles proved to have many flaws. These weaknesses and certain other key events led to the decision to replace the Articles with a new Constitution. What accounted for the Articles' failure, and what accounts for the success of the subsequent U.S. Constitution?

population count? Southern states, with large slave populations, said no. Later, during the Constitutional Convention of 1787, southern states would take a contradictory stance and argue that their slave population should count for purposes of representation in Congress. At this juncture, however, the issue did not arise because all states had equal representation in the Continental Congress and the states assumed that this practice would continue.

Debate also revolved around control of the land west of the colonies. The western boundaries for some states were not yet established. Should the new national government have the power to set those boundaries?[26] As a result of such debates, the drafting of the first national constitution, known as the **Articles of Confederation,** took well over a year; on November 17, 1777, the Continental Congress finally voted to approve the Articles. Ratification by the states was an even slower process, and the Articles of Confederation did not officially take effect until March 1, 1781.[27]

As its title indicates, the relationship that the Articles of Confederation established among the states was that of a **confederation,** or a union of independent, sovereign states. In a confederation, the primary power, especially with regard to domestic affairs, rests with the individual states; the central government is limited to such functions as leading the nation's defense and foreign affairs. Confederations are relatively rare. A recent example is the State Union of Serbia and Montenegro, a confederated union of two former republics of Yugoslavia. Serbia and Montenegro maintained autonomous governments; they were united only for the purpose of defense. Their confederation lasted only from 2003 to 2006, when it was dissolved as the result of a referendum. Switzerland is a rare example of a successfully functioning confederation.

THE STRUCTURE AND POWER OF GOVERNMENT UNDER THE ARTICLES OF CONFEDERATION

The Articles of Confederation were designed to protect state sovereignty—the power and autonomy of the states coming together in this confederation. The national government consisted solely of a weak *unicameral* (one-house) legislature; there was no executive or judicial branch. It had only those powers expressly delegated to it by the states, such as appointing army officers, waging war, controlling the post office, coining money, and negotiating with Indian tribes. Other powers not specifically given to the national government by the Articles of Confederation were reserved to the states.

Delegates to the Confederation Congress were appointed by state legislatures (see Figure 2.2). To ensure equality among the states, each state—regardless of its size or the number of delegates it sent—had a single vote in Congress (as had been the practice in the First and Second Continental Congresses). A state cast its vote in accordance with the votes of the majority of its delegates; if a state could not achieve a majority among its delegates on a particular vote, it would abstain from voting.[28] Passage of legislation required at least nine of the thirteen votes, and amendment of the Articles of Confederation required a unanimous vote.

Articles of Confederation
The first constitution of the United States (1781–1788), under which states retained sovereignty over all issues not specifically delegated to the weak central government, comprising a unicameral (one-house) legislature and no independent executive or judiciary.

confederation
A union of independent, sovereign states whose central government is charged with defense and foreign affairs, but where the primary power—especially with regard to domestic politics—rests with the individual states.

FIGURE 2.2

★ THE STRUCTURE OF THE CONFEDERAL GOVERNMENT

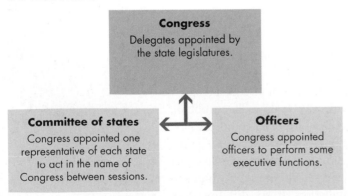

Congress
Delegates appointed by the state legislatures.

Committee of states
Congress appointed one representative of each state to act in the name of Congress between sessions.

Officers
Congress appointed officers to perform some executive functions.

WEAKNESSES OF THE ARTICLES OF CONFEDERATION

When drafting the Articles of Confederation, the delegates to the second Continental Congress focused more on the potential threats posed by a national government than on the benefits such a government might provide. After all, their bitter experience with England was fresh on their minds. Therefore, they were more concerned with limiting government than empowering it.[29] Moreover, people still thought of themselves as citizens of their particular state: They were Virginians or New Yorkers rather than Americans. Worse, states fundamentally mistrusted each other. They also had widely divergent economic interests and often saw each other as competitors. All of these factors proved to be sources of the following weaknesses of the Articles of Confederation:

- The national government had too little power (for example, no power to tax or to regulate commerce among the states) and no permanent home.
- The new nation had no common currency.
- No separation of powers existed at the national level: limited powers rested solely in a weak legislative branch, with no separate executive or judicial branches.

The most obvious weakness of the Articles was that *the national government had too little power.* For example, Congress had *no power to tax.* This severely limited the ability of the national government to raise money to pay for debts incurred during the Revolutionary War. Congress issued requisitions to the states for funds (that is, requests for money), but payment was voluntary and compliance was poor.[30] To modern eyes, not giving Congress the power to tax seems strange, but if you remember that the American Revolution was a revolt against taxation by a distant government, then withholding of this power from the unfamiliar and distant national government (as opposed to familiar and near state governments) becomes more understandable.[31]

Congress also *lacked the power to regulate commerce among the states.* As a result, states jostled for economic advantage, routinely using protective tariffs (taxes imposed on imported goods) against one another as well as against foreign nations. Free trade was further hindered by the fact that the new nation had *no common currency.* Although the new national government could, and did, print money to pay war debts, each state produced its own currency. Since some states printed more money than others, currency from different states had different values. This further complicated trade among the states and also hurt the economy.

Significantly, Congress did not even have a permanent home. It originally sat in Philadelphia, but the delegates fled to Princeton, New Jersey in June 1783 when a mutinous group of hundreds of Revolutionary War veterans mobbed Independence Hall, where the Confederation Congress was then meeting, to demand pay for their war service. After a little more than four months in Princeton, the Confederation Congress then moved to Annapolis, Maryland, before proceeding to Trenton, New Jersey in 1784, and finally to New York City in 1785. Historian David O. Stewart has noted that Congress's homelessness was a potent symbol of its frailty, adding "Vagabondage is not the hallmark of a great government."[32]

★ Rhode Island's $3 bill came to be worth no more than the paper it was printed on.

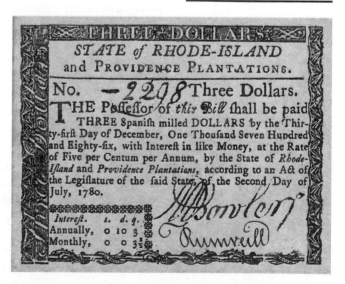

Another notable weakness was the fact that there was *no separation of powers* at the national level: All power, such as it was, lay in the legislature, and the national government had no judicial or executive branch. The lack of a federal judiciary compounded the problems associated with trade wars among the states. For example, some states passed legislation cancelling their debts to other states. With no federal judiciary to turn to, those affected by such legislation sometimes had no legal recourse. Likewise, the lack of a federal judiciary made it difficult to resolve boundary disputes among the states. The lack of an executive branch meant that the national government had no real ability to execute its laws. Early attempts to administer laws through ad hoc committees, councils, and conventions were unsuccessful. Congress did create several permanent departments in 1781 (including treasury, foreign affairs, and war), but they remained mere appendages of a weak legislature.[33]

In short, the new national government had no power to lead, and often did not even have enough power to do what little it was supposed to. The national government seemed to be little more than a "rope of sand" holding the confederation together.[34] The states did not help the situation. They encroached on the authority of the national government by raising their own military, ignoring the nation's treaties with foreign powers, and waging war with Native Americans. Sometimes states did not even bother to send delegates to Congress, making it difficult to muster the necessary quorum for passing legislation.[35]

SHAYS' REBELLION

By the mid 1780s, the new nation was in the midst of an economic depression. Farmers, in particular, had gone into debt to rebuild their farms after the Revolutionary War, in which many of them had served as soldiers. The combination of a bad growing season, high interest rates, and high state taxes to pay off the war debt made it impossible for many farmers to pay their bills. Foreclosures (losing one's property due to failure to pay a loan) skyrocketed, and imprisonment for debt was common. In Massachusetts, desperate farmers facing foreclosure and imprisonment turned to the state for help. When help did not come, the farmers—led by Daniel Shays, who had been a captain in the Continental Army—banded together and tried, by force, to shut down the courthouses where foreclosures were issued. This armed rebellion by more than 2,000 farmers came to be known as **Shays' Rebellion.** It began in August 1786 and continued into 1787.

Shays' Rebellion
An armed rebellion by farmers in Massachusetts who, facing foreclosure, tried using force to shut down courthouses where the foreclosures were issued. The national government's inability to quell the rebellion made the event a potent symbol of the weakness of the Articles of Confederation.

Massachusetts appealed to the national government for help in restoring order. Congress requisitioned states for money to fund a national militia to quell the rebellion, but only one state, Virginia, complied. Without money, Congress was powerless to act. Massachusetts did not have enough money in its own state treasury to fund a state militia, and therefore had to rely on money from private donors. The whole event was unsettling and it proved to be an important turning point. By highlighting the impotence of the national government, Shays' Rebellion galvanized the nation. Those who had long feared that the Articles of Confederation were deficient now had a dramatic example of Congress's inability to maintain order and protect the safety of the people.

Virginia had already called for a convention to discuss a uniform regulation of commerce to remedy one of the primary defects of the Articles of Confederation. Only five states sent delegates to the convention, which convened in Annapolis, Maryland in the fall of 1786, but the timing—with Shays' Rebellion as a backdrop—was propitious. One of the delegates was Alexander Hamilton, who had previously served in the

Confederation Congress; frustrated by the weakness of the national government, he had resigned in 1783. Long opposed to the Articles of Confederation, Hamilton now drafted a resolution that called on Congress to authorize a convention to examine the need either to amend the Articles of Confederation or replace them altogether. Shays' Rebellion provided the impetus for the Annapolis Convention to support Hamilton's resolution. Congress now felt pressure to act. On February 21, 1787, it passed a resolution to convene a Constitutional Convention in Philadelphia for "the sole and express purpose of revising the Articles of Confederation." Convinced that the Articles needed to be replaced altogether, James Madison on May 7, 1787, issued a detailed critique of the Articles of Confederation called "The Vices of the Political System of the United States." At the end of that month the Constitutional Convention convened.[36] History was about to be made.

STARTING OVER: THE CONSTITUTIONAL CONVENTION

Philadelphia, deemed the largest, wealthiest, and (some said) the most beautiful city in British America, remained so throughout the Revolutionary period. Though New York would soon overtake it in population, Philadelphia was still considered the most populous U.S. city in 1787, and its port on the Delaware River continued to be the nation's busiest. Epidemics of yellow fever had, however, left the city with a reputation for disease, leading at least two delegates to refuse to attend the convention.[37] Yet, rooms were hard to find because other groups met in the city that summer in addition to the Constitutional Convention, so some delegates had to share quarters. It was a hot summer, but there were plenty of taverns in which to quench one's thirst.

KEY To understanding ★

This section focuses on the efforts of the Constitutional Convention to draft a document to replace the Articles of Confederation. The resulting Constitution was the product of consensus, conflict, compromise, and creativity among the 55 delegates (all white males) who attended the convention during the hot summer of 1787. We examine these delegates, their motives, the issues that united and divided them, and ultimately the compromises among them that led to the final document.

THE DELEGATES AND THEIR MOTIVES

All of the states except Rhode Island (which opposed changing the Articles of Confederation) sent delegates to the Constitutional Convention. Of the 74 delegates the states had appointed, only 55 actually attended the convention, and far fewer attended the entire convention. The attendees included two of the most famous men in America, George Washington and Benjamin Franklin, and other luminaries such as James Madison and Alexander Hamilton. Notably absent were John Adams and Thomas Jefferson, who were abroad serving as ambassadors to Great Britain and France, respectively. Some passionate advocates of states' rights, such as Patrick Henry, also stayed away.

In 1913, an influential political scientist and historian named Charles A. Beard published a book called *An Economic Interpretation of the Constitution* in which he proposed a controversial thesis: in writing the constitution, the framers' primary goal had been to protect their property holdings and financial self-interest.[38] Beard argued that the framers were a group of wealthy elites who had been adversely affected by the type of government created under the Articles of Confederation (see Table 2.1 for an overview of the delegates' characteristics).[39] Beard argued that in establishing property rights and protecting the economic interests of elites, the framers had purposely limited the ability of the majority to exercise real power—essentially at the expense of the middle

TABLE 2.1
characteristics of the delegates to the constitutional convention

All were white and male.

Thirty-five were lawyers.

Almost three-fourths of them had served in the Confederation Congress.

Twenty-five had served in the Continental Congress during the Revolution.

Fifteen had participated in drafting their own state's constitution.

Eight had signed the Declaration of Independence.

At least one-third owned slaves (12 owned or managed plantations with slave labor).

Most were young, with many still in their twenties and thirties (Franklin, at 81, was a notable exception).

and lower classes (debtors and small farmers). Beard also noted that the right to vote was limited to white males—and, in many states, to white males who owned property.

Beard published his book at a time when a majority of the Supreme Court interpreted the Constitution as protecting economic rights at the expense of individual rights (see Chapter 3). Critics of that interpretation (including progressives who wanted more government regulation of business to protect workers) were quick to embrace Beard's thesis. But do the data bear out Beard's hypothesis? Did a "consolidated economic group whose property interests were immediately at stake" really frame the Constitution to their benefit? And was ratification really driven, as Beard suggested, by propertied elites?

In the 1950s, historians such as Robert E. Brown and Forrest McDonald suggested that a rigorous analysis of the data debunked Beard's thesis. They pointed out that the framers were not as monolithic in their interests as Beard suggested (for example, some *opponents* of the Constitution also came from the privileged wealthy class, and not all supporters were wealthy creditors), and that a broader array of interests than Beard recognized had influenced the framers.[40]

Nonetheless, debate continues. Reality may rest somewhere between Beard's clearcut assumptions and the views of critics like Brown and McDonald. The framers, after all, were politicians influenced by a range of factors. Economics was undoubtedly one of them, but not the only one—or even, necessarily, the most significant one.

A bare quorum of delegates attended the opening session of the Constitutional Convention on May 25 in what is now called Independence Hall (the room where the members of the Second Continental Congress signed the Declaration of Independence). Thirteen tables—one for each state's delegation—were arranged in a semicircle. Rhode Island's table always remained vacant, and the New Hampshire delegates arrived two months late. No more than 11 state delegations were ever in attendance at any one time. As had been the practice in Congress, each state delegation had one vote. The group deliberated in absolute secrecy so that delegates could express their views without fear of outside retaliation or pressure. Despite the heat, they kept the large windows closed and posted sentries outside to ward off eavesdroppers.[41]

picture YOURSELF ...

AS A ZIMBABWEAN CITIZEN

ZAMBIA

Zambezi R.

HARARE ★

ZIMBABWE

BOTSWANA

MOZAMBIQUE

SOUTH
AFRICA

Zimbabwe, a country located in southeast Africa, is currently poised to vote on a new constitution. The existing regime has been accused of widespread human rights violations, and the country has been plagued by economic and food crises. In 2006 a United Nations report concluded that Zimbabwe's life expectancy rates were the lowest in the world (37 for males and 34 for females).* In an effort to provide a better government, Zimbabwe's Minister for Constitutional Affairs, Eric Matinenga, was determined to produce a constitution based on a great deal of input from the people, rather than one drafted by isolated elites.

As we have seen, Charles Beard argued that the U.S. Constitution was drafted by an isolated group of wealthy elites eager to protect their economic self-interest. In contrast, Zimbabwe hoped to secure widespread

* "Zimbabwe Life Expectancy Lowest in the World,"
  Public Health, April 10, 2006 (http://www.
  medicalnewstoday.com/articles/41339.php).

popular input into the writing of its constitution. Whether or not Beard's economic interpretation is correct, the Constitutional Convention in Philadelphia did take place behind closed doors, with no direct input at that phase from the people. There was no popular referendum (vote by the people) on whether the Constitutional Convention should be held. Likewise, ratification of the final document came through the votes of ratifying conventions in the individual states, rather than a popular referendum. As we have seen, Beard emphasized the undemocratic aspects of the ensuing Constitution. The process that was attempted in Zimbabwe offers an interesting contrast.

Imagine that you are one of the 1,750 Zimbabwe citizens who trained for weeks to be part of one of the 70 teams of 25 people each who fanned out across the country as part of the constitution-drafting process. Your mission was to educate the people about this process and to seek their input on how to shape the document. As a member of one of those teams, you were supposed to canvass people for their views on how the constitution should deal with a wide range of specific issues such as human rights, elections, and the justice system. Lack of funding delayed these efforts, and political squabbles disrupted the process—which did not go completely according to plan. Nonetheless, the goal was for

continued

your team to report your findings to those drafting the constitution. Unlike the U.S. Constitution, the final document will be submitted to the people in a referendum, which was originally scheduled for June 2011 but then delayed.**

** "Drafting of New Constitution to Begin in Zimbabwe," *Turkish Weekly,* January 6, 2010 (http://www.turkishweekly.net/news/95098/drafting-of-new-constitution-to-begin-in-zimbabwe.html)..A draft constitution was likely to be ready by March 2012 at the earliest, but it appeared unlikely as of December 2011 that a referendum would take place in 2012 (http://allafrica.com/stories/201111290088.html).

questions to consider

1. What are the strengths and weaknesses of Zimbabwe's approach to drafting a constitution?

2. What effect might this type of popular input have had on the drafting of the U.S. Constitution? How might the U.S. Constitution have been different if there had been such input?

3. Would a popular referendum have been a better way to ratify the U.S. Constitution, rather than reliance on state ratifying conventions? Some have suggested that the Constitution might not have been ratified if the decision had been left to a popular referendum. As you read further in this chapter, consider why that might have been the case.

LARGE STATES VERSUS SMALL STATES: THE VIRGINIA AND NEW JERSEY PLANS

James Madison of Virginia was the first out-of-state delegate to arrive in Philadelphia on May 3. By May 17, all seven Virginia delegates had arrived. The group included George Washington, Edmund Randolph, and George Mason. The Virginia delegation quickly took the lead. Madison issued his "Vices of the Political System of the United States." He had also prepared a historical study of republics and confederations through the ages. By examining previous confederations, Madison tried to show that confederations were, by their very nature, doomed to failure.[42] Most significantly, the group of Virginia delegates met every morning at a local boarding house to plot strategy for how to convince the delegates to construct a new constitution rather than merely amend the Articles of Confederation, as some preferred. They also met each afternoon to greet arriving delegates.

This reminds us that the drafting of the Constitution was a distinctly political process, which involved consensus on some issues (such as the need for a limited, republican form of government) and conflict on others (such as what system of representation to adopt). Ultimately, compromise (on issues such as slavery, representation, presidential selection, and the court system) and creativity among the delegates (their embrace of federalism, for example) led to success. Keep these "4 C's" in mind—consensus, conflict, compromise, and creativity—as you read the remaining Constitution sections.

Once the convention formally assembled on May 25, Virginia's power became immediately evident. The delegates unanimously chose George Washington as its presiding officer. He sat facing the rest of the delegates; Madison sat next to him taking notes and never missed a day of the proceedings. After establishing the rules of the convention, Edmund Randolph, the head of the Virginia delegation, rose and introduced his delegation's proposal for a new constitution, the result of the daily strategy sessions they had held. This so-called **Virginia Plan,** primarily authored by James Madison and consisting of 15 draft resolutions, was designed to replace rather than amend the Articles of Confederation and to establish a strong central government consisting of three branches: a *bicameral* legislative branch, an executive branch, and a judicial branch (see Figure 2.3).

Virginia Plan
A plan, favored by large states, to replace (rather than amend) the Articles of Confederation and create a strong national government consisting of three branches. It also called for replacing the one-state/one-vote system used under the Articles of Confederation with proportional voting power in the legislature.

Popular election of one of the two houses of the legislature—an important innovation—would allow power to flow more directly from the people than from the states. Another important—and very contentious—innovation dealt with the voting power of states in the legislature. The Virginia Plan called for the replacement of the one-state/one-vote system with proportional voting power in both houses of the legislature: the number of representatives from each state would be based on the state's population and each of their representatives would have one vote. This new voting plan would increase the power of large, more populated states at the expense of small, less populated states. It therefore prompted major debate at the convention. The proposal to base representation on population also raised a nasty question: Were slaves to be included when counting the population of a state? Bluntly put, were they to be counted as people or property?[43]

Small states strongly opposed the Virginia Plan. On June 9, William Patterson of New Jersey stood and proclaimed that he was "astonished" and "alarmed" at the Virginia Plan's proposal to base a state's voting strength on its population.[44] He then introduced an alternative set of proposals that came to be known as the **New Jersey Plan,** aimed at merely amending (rather than replacing) the Articles of Confederation. It, too, called for three branches, but unlike the proposals under the Virginia Plan, the New Jersey Plan called for maintaining a *unicameral* legislature, a weak executive branch comprising *multiple* officers (elected by Congress and subject to removal only upon majority vote of the state governors) rather than a single president, and a Supreme Court whose members would be elected by the executive officers (see Figure 2.4). Representatives to the legislature would continue to be chosen by state legislatures rather than being elected by the people. The New Jersey plan also retained the one-state/one-vote system (rather than the proportional voting plan introduced by the Virginia Plan). As a result, small states initially supported the New Jersey Plan.

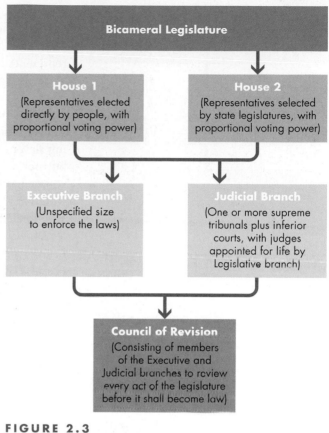

FIGURE 2.3

★ CENTRAL GOVERNMENT UNDER THE VIRGINIA PLAN

New Jersey Plan
A plan, favored by small states, to amend (rather than replace) the Articles of Confederation. It would have retained the one-state/one-vote system of voting in the national legislature, with representatives chosen by state legislatures.

THE THREE-FIFTHS COMPROMISE AND THE GREAT COMPROMISE

The two questions of state representation dominated the next few weeks of discussion at the convention: (1) Should there be proportional representation in Congress, as called for in the Virginia Plan, or equal representation (one-state/one-vote), as called for in the New Jersey Plan? (2) In the event that proportional representation was chosen, who would be counted as representative? The Virginia Plan called for representation in Congress to be based on the "numbers of free inhabitants" in a state. This concerned other, smaller, southern states because slaves made up such a large

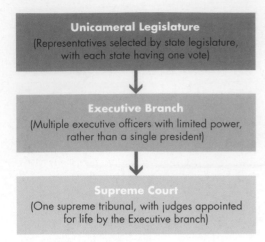

FIGURE 2.4

★ CENTRAL GOVERNMENT UNDER THE NEW JERSEY PLAN

Three-Fifths Compromise
The decision by the Constitutional Convention to count slaves as three-fifths of a person for purposes of representation.

proportion of their population (see Figure 2.5); if slaves were not counted, those states' power in Congress would be diminished.

To lure small southern states to accept the idea of proportional representation, James Wilson of Pennsylvania, a supporter of the Virginia Plan, introduced the so-called **Three-Fifths Compromise:** Each slave would count as three-fifths of a person for purposes of representation. This obviously deplorable solution would give southern states strong enough influence in Congress to prevent it from abolishing slavery (a possibility that was already a concern to these states), but not as much influence as they would have if slaves were fully counted. (Of course, slaves did not have the right to vote and therefore would not be represented in Congress. Women did not have the constitutional right to vote either, but white women *did* count as full persons toward determining the number of representatives a state would have.) On June 11, the convention endorsed the Three-Fifths Compromise by a vote of 9–2, with only Delaware and New Jersey voting against it.[45]

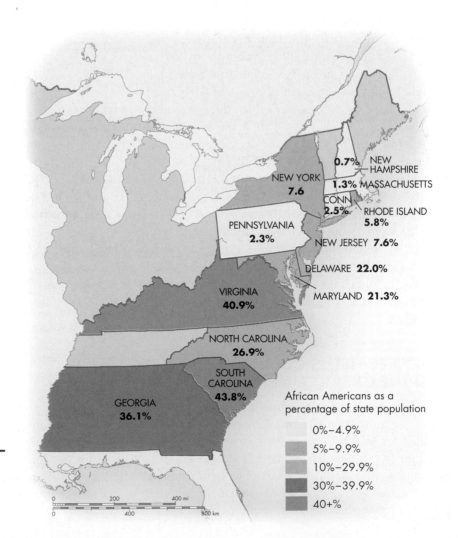

FIGURE 2.5

★ AFRICAN AMERICANS AS A PERCENTAGE OF STATE POPULATIONS, 1790

Source: U.S. Census Bureau (http://www.census.gov/population/www/documentation/twps0056.html).

It soon became clear, however, that even with the Three-Fifths Compromise, proportional representation was not a done deal. Quite to the contrary, that issue continued to dominate discussion for weeks and threatened to deadlock the convention. Finally, another compromise ended the impasse. Devised by Roger Sherman and Oliver Ellsworth of Connecticut, this so-called **Great Compromise** (sometimes referred to as the *Connecticut Compromise*) called for a bicameral legislature, as in the Virginia Plan, with a different method for determining representation in each house and different procedures for selecting representatives in each house. In the lower house (which eventually became the House of Representatives), the Virginia Plan would prevail:

- Representation would be proportional.
- Representatives would be elected by the people.

In the upper house (which eventually became the Senate), the New Jersey Plan would prevail:

- Representation would be equal (each state would have two representatives).
- Representatives would be selected by state legislatures.

In keeping with the principle of "no taxation without representation," all legislation dealing with raising and spending money would originate in the lower house.

The Convention debated the Great Compromise for 11 days, and, on June 29, the compromise finally passed. The compromise ended the deadlock and resolved the fundamental question of representation in the legislature. Now the delegates shifted their attention to the other two branches of government.

Great Compromise
The decision by the Constitutional Convention to resolve the debate over equal versus proportional representation by establishing a bicameral (two-house) legislature with proportional representation in the lower house, equal representation in the upper house, and different methods of selecting representatives for each house.

CREATING THE EXECUTIVE AND JUDICIAL BRANCHES

You will recall that the Articles of Confederation did not provide for an independent executive branch. Furthermore, most state governors were selected by the legislature, had little or no veto power over legislation, and served short terms.[46] By the time the Constitutional Convention met in 1787, some believed the pendulum had swung too far in the direction of limiting executive power. For example, Thomas Jefferson had served as governor of Virginia for two years and experienced firsthand the powerlessness of that position. Though still wary of executive power, Jefferson wrote that his experience with the 173 members of the Virginia legislature had convinced him that "173 despots would surely be as oppressive as one."[47] This concentration of power ran counter to the idea of separation of powers and resulted in unchecked legislative power. With mounting concerns about this issue, arguing for a strong executive at the Constitutional Convention was easier than it would have been immediately after finalizing the Declaration of Independence.

When introduced, the Virginia Plan called for an executive branch to be selected by Congress, without specifying its size or tenure or its specific powers. The New Jersey Plan called for a plural, rather than a single, chief executive to be selected by Congress. In discussions, some individual delegates, such as James Wilson and Gouverneur Morris, both of Pennsylvania, led the charge for a stronger, more independent executive than that contemplated by either the New Jersey Plan or the original Virginia Plan, but the delegates remained divided on the issue of executive power through August.

The delegates eventually agreed to a single chief executive, to be called the "president"—a strategic choice to diffuse concerns about a strong executive. A derivation of the Latin word *praesidere*, "president" means "to sit at the head of" and "to defend." "President" therefore implied passive guardianship rather than aggressive leadership. George Washington, who served a mostly passive, ceremonial function at the Constitutional Convention, had been its "president." Despite agreement on what to call the chief executive, the delegates remained divided over what powers to give to, and how to select, the president.[48]

In a compromise that helped to establish our current system of checks and balances, the convention agreed to split a number of traditionally executive powers, such as declaring war, making treaties, and appointing officials, and allow the president and Congress to *share* them. Thus, Congress would declare war, but the president would wage it. Presidents would negotiate treaties, but those treaties were subject to ratification by the Senate. The president would nominate ambassadors and other officials, but they could serve only if the Senate confirmed them. Nonetheless, the question remained: Who would select the president?

James Wilson noted that no issue perplexed the delegates more than determining "the mode of choosing the President of the United States."[49] Additionally, how long should the president serve? Should he be eligible for reelection? Selection by Congress had been the default position throughout the summer. Advocates of a more powerful executive feared that this method of selection would perpetuate a model of executive subservience to the legislature. Popular election—a natural alternative—posed its own problems. First, it would give the large states an advantage over the small ones. The three most populous states had nearly as many eligible voters as the remaining ten states combined.[50] Small states thus feared that they would have little influence in the selection of a president. Second, the Framers feared the masses and assumed that voters would be ill-informed and motivated more by local interests than the common good (an example of consensus among the delegates). George Mason scoffed that letting the people choose the president would be "as un-natural" as referring "a trial of colours to a blind man."[51]

The Committee on Postponed Matters finally proposed a compromise that won the support of the delegates: the president (and vice president—the first time this post had been recommended) would be chosen by an *Electoral College* consisting of electors from each of the states. The number of electors from each state would be equal to the combined total of that state's representatives and senators in the U.S. Congress. Each state would select these electors according to rules established by its own state legislature.

Similar debates ensued about the federal judiciary. Most delegates agreed that some sort of federal judiciary was necessary. But should it consist of just one court of last resort or a broader system of federal courts? How should judges be selected—by Congress or the president? If Congress had the power to select, should both houses of Congress participate or just one house? If just one of them participated, which one should it be?

Answers to these questions, as to others, came in the form of compromises and creative solutions. The Constitution created one Supreme Court but left it to Congress to decide whether to create other, lower federal courts. Judges for the court were to be nominated by the president, but the nomination was to be subject to confirmation by the Senate. (See Chapter 15 for more details about both the selection process and the creation by Congress of a lower federal judiciary.) The framers also embraced federalism (discussed in more detail in Chapter 3)—a creative solution that gave some powers to the national government and others to the states. Federalism allowed proponents of a strong national government as well as proponents of states' rights to feel that they had won on some issues.

THE CONSTITUTION

After almost three months of debate and much compromise, the Convention completed a final draft of the Constitution. It consisted of a preamble followed by seven articles. When the Constitution came to a vote, 39 of the 55 delegates voted to support it. However, the supporters constituted a majority of each of the 12 state delegations in attendance and each state had one vote, so the final vote in favor of the Constitution was 12–0.[52] Thirty-nine delegates signed the document on September 17, 1787—the last day of the convention. Of those delegates in attendance, only three refused to sign the Constitution.

CORE PRINCIPLES

The establishment of the Constitution represented a significant break from the past. This break is evident from the first three words of the Preamble to the Constitution, "*We the people*," which stood in marked contrast with the Articles of Confederation's "We the undersigned delegates of the states," signifying that America was now one people rather than 13 individual states. No one could predict just how successful and influential the Constitution would be, but more immediately apparent was how path-breaking it was.

The governmental design created by the Constitution can be understood in terms of four core principles (see Table 2.2). **Republicanism,** the first of these principles, stands in contrast with both direct democracy and monarchy. A *republican form of government* is one in which power rests with the people (as opposed to a monarch or, as under the Articles of Confederation, the states), but where the people rule only indirectly: through elected representatives bound by the rule of law. Rule by representatives would presumably temper the passions of public opinion associated with a direct democracy, while elections would assure that those representatives remained accountable to the people for their actions. Republicanism had never been tried in a country as vast as the United States, and some feared that elected representatives would be tempted to act tyrannically rather than according to the rule of law. When Benjamin Franklin was asked what kind of government the Constitution provided, he responded: "A republic, if you can keep it."

republicanism
A form of government in which power rests with the people, but where the people rule only indirectly through elected representatives bound by the rule of law.

TABLE 2.2
four core principles of the U.S. constitution

Republicanism: Power rests with the people, but the people rule indirectly.

Federalism: Power is divided between the central and state governments.

Separation of powers: Power is divided across all three co-equal branches of government.

Checks and balances: Power is both divided and shared among the three branches, with each branch having some control over the other two.

Second, the Constitution instituted a system of *federalism*. In contrast with both a confederation, where the primary power is left to the states, and a *unitary system*, where all areas of power belong to the central government, a *federation* is a system in which power is divided between the central government and the state, or other regional, governments. The Constitution listed the powers of the national government, and it also listed the powers denied to the states, implying that all other powers were retained by the states. The Tenth Amendment (part of the American *Bill of Rights*, ratified in 1791) clarified this further, stating: "The powers not delegated to the United States by the Constitution, nor prohibited by it to the States, are reserved to the States respectively, or to the people." Dividing powers between the national government and the states was another check designed to prevent tyranny.

As we will see in Chapter 3, debate continued even after the ratification of the Tenth Amendment about precisely what powers were reserved to the states and when, if ever, Congress could interfere with those powers. It was clear, however, that when it was exercising its constitutionally enumerated powers, the national government was supreme: If conflicts arose between national and state law in such cases, national law would always prevail. As the **supremacy clause** of Article VI, Clause 2 put it, the Constitution, as well as acts of Congress and federal treaties passed pursuant to the Constitution, were "the supreme Law of the Land; and the judges in every State shall be bound thereby, any Thing in the Constitution or Laws of any State to the Contrary notwithstanding."

Third, the Constitution instituted **separation of powers** across branches of the national government. Like federalism, this was designed to prevent the concentration of power in any one part of government. Thus, the framers divided the national government into three coequal branches and gave each a separate function. The legislative branch was given the power to make the laws, the executive branch the power to enforce (or execute) the laws, and the judicial branch the power to interpret the laws. This stands in contrast with parliamentary systems such as England, where the prime minister and the cabinet, who together perform the executive function, are drawn from the legislature.

Finally, to further ensure that power would not become concentrated, the Constitution set up a system of **checks and balances** in which each of the three branches among which power was divided would have some degree of control over the other two. In other words, power is both divided and shared, as shown in Figure 2.6. We have already discussed how war powers, appointment power, and treaty power are each shared between the president and Congress. There are also other checks. For example, the president is given the power to veto legislation. Moreover, that veto can be overridden only by a two-thirds majority of both houses of Congress (as opposed to simply getting the most votes, which is required for passing legislation in the first place). Thus, the president has a check on Congress, but this check is itself limited. Similarly, courts have a check through their power to interpret laws passed by Congress, and—by means of judicial review—to strike down laws and executive actions that violate the Constitution. Though not specifically enumerated in the Constitution, judicial review—as discussed below—has become an accepted part of our constitutional system.

THE ARTICLES OF THE CONSTITUTION

The Constitution has just seven articles, preceded by a preamble and followed by the 27 amendments that have been made since its ratification. The preamble spelled out the justification for the Constitution ("to form a more perfect Union"), its

supremacy clause
Article VI, Clause 2 of the Constitution specifying that federal laws and treaties passed pursuant to the Constitution trump contradictory state laws dealing with the same topic.

separation of powers
The division of governmental powers among three separate and co-equal branches: legislative, executive, and judicial.

checks and balances
A method to protect against unrestrained governmental power by dividing and sharing powers among the legislative, executive, and judicial branches.

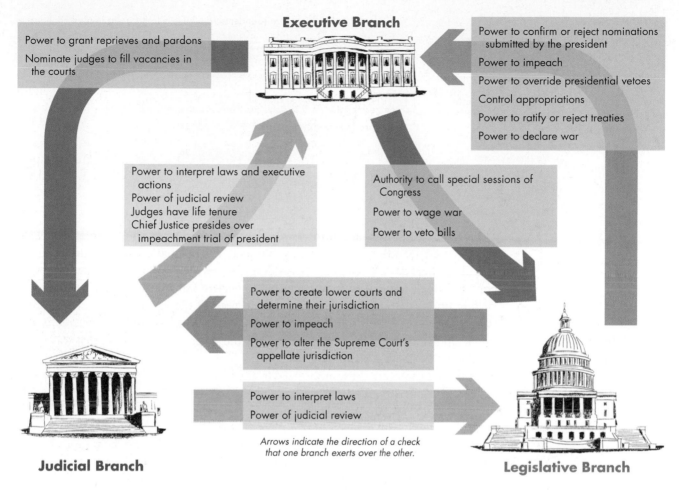

Executive Branch

Power to grant reprieves and pardons

Nominate judges to fill vacancies in the courts

Power to confirm or reject nominations submitted by the president

Power to impeach

Power to override presidential vetoes

Control appropriations

Power to ratify or reject treaties

Power to declare war

Power to interpret laws and executive actions
Power of judicial review
Judges have life tenure
Chief Justice presides over impeachment trial of president

Authority to call special sessions of Congress

Power to wage war

Power to veto bills

Power to create lower courts and determine their jurisdiction

Power to impeach

Power to alter the Supreme Court's appellate jurisdiction

Power to interpret laws

Power of judicial review

Arrows indicate the direction of a check that one branch exerts over the other.

Judicial Branch

Legislative Branch

FIGURE 2.6

★ SYSTEM OF CHECKS AND BALANCES IN THE U.S. FEDERAL GOVERNMENT

fundamental goals (which included establishing justice and "securing the blessings of Liberty"), and made clear that the new Constitution and the government established by it were created by "We the people" (as opposed to being created by the states, as had been the case previously). The first three articles that follow the preamble each spell out the power of one of the three branches of government. The remaining articles are concerned with federal–state relations as well as with the relations among the states, and provide procedures for ratifying the Constitution and amending it.

Article I: The Legislative Branch

Because legislators are the representatives of the people, the framers thought of the legislative branch as being the most important and presented it first. What does current public opinion, as shown in Figure 2.7, suggest about that assumption? Article I opens by stating, "All legislative powers *herein granted* shall be vested in a Congress of the United States, which shall consist of a Senate and House of Representatives" [emphasis added]. In other words, Congress is limited to those powers given to it by the Constitution. Those powers fall into two broad categories: *enumerated* powers and *implied* powers.

FIGURE 2.7

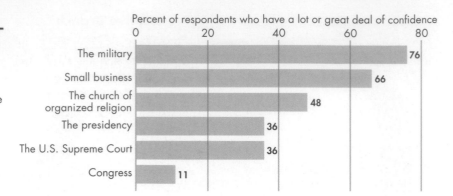

★ CONFIDENCE IN GOVERNMENT AND AMERICAN INSTITUTIONS

The framers thought that Congress would be the most important governmental institution. How do people feel about it today, based on the findings shown here?

Source: Gallup Poll, July 2011 (http://www.pollingreport.com/institut.htm).

enumerated powers
Powers specifically listed in the Constitution, such as congressional powers outlined in Article I, Section 8.

Enumerated powers are those powers specifically listed. Most enumerated powers are in Article I, Section 8, where you will find 17 clauses that contain a laundry list of specific powers given to Congress, including the power to impose and collect taxes, to borrow money, to regulate commerce, and to declare war. Some of these powers were lacking under the Articles of Confederation, notably the power to collect taxes and regulate commerce. Legislative powers not given to Congress, and not covered under implied powers, were presumably retained by the states, a presumption that was made explicit by the Tenth Amendment.

implied powers
Powers not specifically enumerated in the Constitution, but which are considered "necessary and proper" to carry out the enumerated powers.

Implied powers are those authorized by the *necessary and proper clause* of Article I, Section 8, Clause 18. The *necessary and proper clause* (discussed in Chapter 3) expands the enumerated powers by saying that Congress has the power to "make all Laws which shall be necessary and proper for carrying into Execution the foregoing Powers, and all other Powers vested by this Constitution in the Government of the United States, or in any Department or Officer thereof." This clause is sometimes also referred to as the "elastic clause," because it serves to expand Congress's power. The question is, by how much?

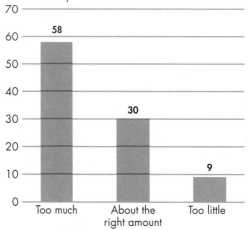

FIGURE 2.8

★ GALLUP POLL: DOES THE FEDERAL GOVERNMENT HAVE TOO MUCH POWER, JUST ENOUGH, OR TOO LITTLE POWER?

What does this figure tell us about how Americans view the power of the central government today? Are the concerns expressed in this poll valid?

Source: Gallup Poll, March 2011 (http://www.pollingreport.com/institut.htm).

The answer to that question depends on the meaning of the phrase "necessary and proper." Does it mean that Congress only has the power to make those laws absolutely *essential* to carrying out the enumerated powers? Or does it mean that Congress has the power to make any law that might be *useful* to carrying out the enumerated powers? Defenders of a strong central government, such as Alexander Hamilton, preferred the latter (broad) interpretation of the necessary and proper clause, because it would further expand Congress's power at the expense of the states. In contrast, those who wanted the states to retain as much power as possible, such as Thomas Jefferson, preferred the first (narrow) interpretation, because it gave Congress less opportunity to expand its power. As we shall see in the next chapter, this debate played out in arguments before the U.S. Supreme Court and remains a matter of contention to this day (see Figure 2.8).

The final section of Article I lists the powers that are withheld from the states. For example, states are forbidden to enter into treaties with foreign nations, coin money, or impose duties on imports and exports without the consent of Congress. (For more on Congress's constitutional powers, see Chapter 12.)

Article II: The Executive Branch

Article II vests the executive authority in the president. In other words, it gives the president the power to carry out the laws. However, the ambiguity of the opening sentence of Article II has led to considerable debate about the precise scope of executive power. Unlike the opening of Article I, the opening of Article II does not limit powers to those "herein granted," even though Article II does contain enumerated powers. It simply says, "The executive Power shall be vested in a President of the United States of America." Does the omission of the words "herein granted" give presidents greater leeway than Congress? People disagree about the answer to this question. As we shall see in Chapter 13, three quite different interpretations of the scope of presidential power have emerged.

Article II, Section 2 enumerates specific powers of the president, such as serving as commander-in-chief of the armed forces, granting pardons, negotiating treaties, and appointing specified officials with the advice and consent of the Senate. In addition, Article II spells out the way in which presidents will be elected and eligibility requirements for the office (Section 1); it requires that the president give information to Congress about the state of the union and recommend for its consideration such measures as he deems necessary and expedient, and that he "take Care that the Laws be faithfully executed" (Section 3); and it provides guidelines for the president's impeachment and removal from office (Section 4).

Article III: The Judicial Branch

Article III is the shortest of the articles delineating the three branches of government. It creates a Supreme Court and says that the judges will hold office "during good Behaviour"—in other words, unless they are impeached, they will have life tenure (the method for selecting Supreme Court justices was spelled out in Article II). Life tenure was designed to promote judicial independence, as was a guarantee that justices receive a compensation for their services that would not be reduced during their tenure. No federal courts existed under the Articles of Confederation, and some members of the Constitutional Convention feared that a large federal judiciary with expanded jurisdiction would interfere with decisions that they felt should be left to the states. Therefore, Article III postponed the decision about creating federal courts in addition to the Supreme Court by giving Congress the authority to establish lower federal courts if it chose to do so (which it quickly did, in the Judiciary Act of 1789, as discussed in Chapter 15).

Articles IV–VII

The remaining four articles of the Constitution cover a wide range of issues. Article IV deals with the states and their relations. It requires states to give "full faith and credit" to the laws and judicial proceedings of other states, prohibits discrimination by one state against citizens of another state, guarantees a republican form of government in every state, and delineates procedures for admitting new states. Article V spells out the processes by which the Constitution can be amended. Article VI contains the supremacy clause, forbids the use of any religious test as a qualification for holding any office (in other words, candidates could not be disqualified because of their religious views, or lack thereof), and guaranteed that debts incurred by the Confederation would be honored under the Constitution. Finally, Article VII spelled out the procedure for ratifying the Constitution.

RATIFYING THE CONSTITUTION

The ratification of the Constitution by the states was a very political process, and by no means certain; fierce debates ensued. Federalists argued in favor of ratification, and Anti-Federalists argued against it. But, unlike the highly secretive Constitutional Convention, the state ratifying conventions were open to public scrutiny. The Constitution's lack of a bill of rights proved to be a significant obstacle. Anti-Federalists feared that this omission would allow the new central government to infringe upon the rights of the people. Ratification only came when the Federalists compromised and signaled that they would support the addition of a bill of rights through the amendment process.

The vote to approve the Constitution at the Convention was only the beginning of the battle. The document still had to be ratified by the states. Article VII of the Constitution spelled out the procedure: Each state would hold a ratifying convention. For the Constitution to take effect, at least nine of the thirteen conventions would have to vote in favor of approval. Once nine states voted to approve the Constitution, the failure of remaining states to vote for approval would leave them as independent nations. The process ended up lasting more than two and a half years, during which time the Articles of Confederation remained in place. Unlike the debates at the Constitutional Convention, which were shrouded in secrecy, debate over the ratification of the Constitution was a distinctly public affair and the conventions were widely covered by the press.

FEDERALISTS VERSUS ANTI-FEDERALISTS

Federalists
Those who supported ratification of the Constitution and the stronger national government that it created.

Anti-Federalists
States' rights advocates who opposed the ratification of the Constitution.

Supporters of the Constitution, and of the stronger national government it created, quickly dubbed themselves **Federalists.** Opponents, who feared that the proposed national government would be too strong and who preferred that more power remain with the states, came to be known as **Anti-Federalists.** As historian Joseph J. Ellis has noted, however, both sides were really "federalists," which literally meant favoring a federal system wherein power would be shared between a central government and state governments. The two sides simply disagreed over how power should be allocated in that system.[53]

Federalists started out with the upper hand in the debate. Their opponents lacked any substantive alternative to the Constitution except the Articles of Confederation, which were tainted with the stench of failure. Federalists were also aided by the fact that early ratifying conventions were in states that supported the Constitution; this would help to build momentum for ratification. Nonetheless, the Anti-Federalists probably reflected the sentiments of a majority of the American people, who remained deeply distrustful of a new and unfamiliar central authority and of its power to tax. Furthermore, many people still thought of themselves as citizens of their particular state rather than citizens of the United States. Indeed, ratification of the Constitution might well have failed had it depended on a national referendum (the method used by a number of countries in recent years, including Iraq in 2005), as suggested by the map in Figure 2.9.

Federalist Papers
Essays by James Madison, Alexander Hamilton, and John Jay. supporting ratification of the Constitution. Originally published in newspapers under the pseudonym "Publius" (Latin for "the people"), they were gathered together in 1788 and published in two volumes as *The Federalist*.

A month after the Constitutional Convention ended, Federalists began publishing pro-Constitution articles in newspapers in New York, where ratification was in doubt. The articles appeared under the pseudonym "Publius" (Latin for "the people"), and in 1788 they were gathered together and published in two volumes as *The Federalist*. Now commonly known as the **Federalist Papers,** these 85 articles, written by James Madison, Alexander Hamilton, and (to a lesser extent) John Jay, provided not only a vigorous defense of the Constitution but also rich theoretical insights that still serve as a basis for understanding the Constitution today. In contrast with the populist tract *Common Sense,* which in 1776 helped to galvanize mass support for independence, the

Federalist Papers failed to have the same mobilizing effect among the general populace because they proved to be too dense and erudite for the average reader. They did influence and mobilize elites—Federalist delegates at the ratification conventions—but their greatest impact has been on subsequent generations who have used them as guides for interpreting the Constitution.

Those opposed to the Constitution penned their own articles under pseudonyms like "Brutus" and "Cato" (the names of Ancient Roman senators who decried tyranny when Julius Caesar took control away from the Senate and assumed power over the Roman Republic). The Anti-Federalist critique focused on the dangers of centralized power, which they worried would become despotic and infringe not only upon states' rights but also upon individual liberties. The fact that the Constitution lacked a bill of rights fueled their concern.

Having so recently fought a war of independence to secure liberty, many readers shared these penmen's wariness of a strong national government. Less familiar today

FIGURE 2.9

★ REGIONAL SUPPORT FOR FEDERALISTS AND ANTI-FEDERALISTS

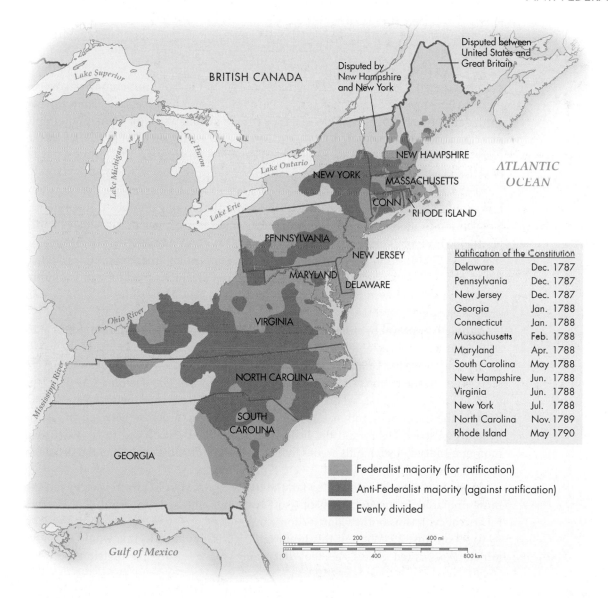

Ratification of the Constitution

Delaware	Dec. 1787
Pennsylvania	Dec. 1787
New Jersey	Dec. 1787
Georgia	Jan. 1788
Connecticut	Jan. 1788
Massachusetts	Feb. 1788
Maryland	Apr. 1788
South Carolina	May 1788
New Hampshire	Jun. 1788
Virginia	Jun. 1788
New York	Jul. 1788
North Carolina	Nov. 1789
Rhode Island	May 1790

Federalist majority (for ratification)

Anti-Federalist majority (against ratification)

Evenly divided

than the Federalist Papers (and written by a broader range of people), these opposition articles and speeches have, in recent years, been collected together and published.[54] Among the leaders of the Anti-Federalists were three Virginians: Patrick Henry, one of the most famous orators in America; George Mason, a passionate advocate for a bill of rights; and Richard Henry Lee, who, on June 7, 1776, had introduced the resolution calling for independence from Britain (see page 45). As this list suggests, Anti-Federalists included prominent individuals who had played important roles in the creation of the United States.

ANOTHER COMPROMISE: A POST-RATIFICATION BILL OF RIGHTS

Delaware was the first state to ratify the Constitution in December 1787. Pennsylvania, New Jersey, Georgia, and Connecticut quickly followed suit. Massachusetts, however, derailed this momentum with a chief Anti-Federalist concern: that the new central government would run roughshod over the rights of the people.

During the Constitutional Convention, George Mason, a delegate from Virginia, had proposed that the Constitution include a bill of rights. The majority of the framers rejected this proposal, however, indicating that since government was limited to those powers granted by the Constitution, and the Constitution did not empower government to infringe upon those rights, a bill of rights was unnecessary. They further argued the potential danger of such a list: Failure to include a specific right might imply that that right was unprotected. These arguments did not convince Mason, who was so upset at the omission that he refused to sign the Constitution. Mason went on to become a leading opponent of its ratification.

As the debates played out, it became clear that without a bill of rights, the Constitution would not be ratified. But Federalists feared that calling another Constitutional Convention to modify the existing document would lead to new debates about issues far afield from a bill of rights. Therefore, Federalists conceded the issue by promising that if the Constitution was ratified, they would support an amendment to provide a bill of rights. This broke the logjam in Massachusetts, which voted for ratification in February 1788, followed by the required ninth state, New Hampshire, in June of that same year,

Although approval by nine states led to ratification of the Constitution, four states still remained opposed and thus not part of the new nation. Not only would their failure to ratify leave the United States geographically split, but two of the four states were seen as key to the nation's success: Virginia and New York. The outcome was not clear in either state. Virginia, whose ratifying convention convened before New York's, became the focus of attention. At Virginia's convention, a debate between the Anti-Federalist Patrick Henry and the Federalist James Madison proved to be a defining moment. Indeed, Joseph Ellis argues that it might be "the most consequential debate in American history."[55]

Of the two men, Henry was, by far, the better orator. But Madison was, by far, the more prepared. In the end, Madison's soft-spoken, point-by-point rebuttal of Henry's theatrical criticisms of the Constitution won out. Virginia voted to ratify by a vote of 89 to 79 on June 25. Without this important turning point, Virginia would not have joined the United States—a step that would have assured a division between northern and southern states (North Carolina, the last potential barrier between north and south, did not ratify the Constitution until November 1789, after George Washington had already been sworn in as president). Had the Anti-Federalists won in Virginia, the confidence of other states in the new national government might well have been shaken. Still, it is worth remembering that although Madison's position prevailed in the vote to ratify the Constitution, Henry's passionate defense of liberty strongly influenced the eventual decision to amend that Constitution to add a bill of rights.

AMENDING THE CONSTITUTION

The Articles of Confederation had all but precluded amendments by requiring that they receive unanimous support from all the states. The framers now made the process easier, but not so easy that amendments would overwhelm the Constitution. Indeed, the U.S. Constitution stands out not only for its longevity but also for its relatively few amendments as compared with state constitutions and those of many other countries. Plenty of amendments have been suggested (well over 10,000), but only 33 amendments have been formally proposed to the states and only 27 of those have been ratified—10 of which make up the Bill of Rights.[56] (See Table 2.3 for descriptions of the six formally proposed amendments that were never ratified.[57])

As a stark contrast, consider France, which has had 15 different constitutions since 1789 and has existed under monarchy and dictatorship as well as under various republics. France's current constitution was introduced in 1958 and, as of 2011, had already been amended 18 times. Or take an example from within the United States: The state of Alabama has had six constitutions since becoming the twenty-second

---

TABLE 2.3
the six failed amendments

Congressional Apportionment Amendment (1789). More specifically delineated the number of people to be represented by each member of the U.S. House of Representatives. Ratified by 11 states.

Anti-Title Amendment (1810). Any U.S. citizen who received a title of nobility from a foreign power, or who—without the consent of Congress—accepted any gift from a foreign power, would be stripped of citizenship. Ratified by 12 states.

Slavery Amendment (1861). Prohibited Congress from passing laws that would abolish or interfere with slavery or other "domestic institutions" of the states. Ratified by 3 states.

Child Labor Amendment (1926). Granted Congress the power to regulate the labor of children under the age of 18. Ratified by 28 states.

Equal Rights Amendment (1972). Prohibited both the national government and the states from denying or abridging any rights on the basis of sex, thereby establishing the equality of men and women. Ratified by 35 states.

District of Columbia Voting Rights Amendment (1978). Granted the residents of the District of Columbia full representation in both houses of the U.S. Congress, as well as full participation in the Electoral College. Ratified by 16 states.

state in 1819, and its current one—adopted in 1901—has been amended 827 times as of 2011. The stability of the U.S. Constitution is partly attributable to its ambiguity. That ambiguity has allowed flexibility in interpreting the Constitution, and flexibility of interpretation in turn has helped to ward off frequent amendment.

THE FORMAL AMENDMENT PROCESS

As specified by Article V, the process of amending the Constitution consists of two stages: proposal and ratification. As shown in Figure 2.10, proposals can be made in either of two ways:

- by a two-thirds vote of both houses of Congress, or
- by a request to Congress from two-thirds of the state legislatures to call a convention to propose amendments.

To date, all 33 amendments were proposed by Congress. The alternative route—a convention convened by a vote of the state legislatures—poses several problems. The Constitution does not specify how delegates to the convention should be chosen, how many delegates there should be, or what rules such delegates should follow. In addition, such a convention could presumably introduce as many amendments as it wanted. The last time we had a convention, in 1787, we ended up with an entirely new constitution. Fears that another convention could lead to similarly radical change, together with uncertainty about the mechanics of such a convention, make amendment proposals by Congress a safer and easier option.

Whether proposed by Congress or a convention, amendments must by ratified by the states. Like proposals, ratification can come about in either of two ways (with Congress specifying the method for each amendment proposed):

- by a vote of three-fourths of the state legislatures, or
- by a vote of three-fourths of specially convened state-ratifying conventions.

FIGURE 2.10

★ THE CONSTITUTIONAL AMENDMENT PROCESS

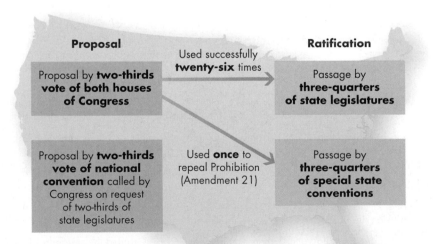

As of 2012, only one of the 27 amendments ratified—the Twenty-First, repealing prohibition—was ratified by state conventions. In that case, Congress predicted that passage by state conventions was more likely than passage by conservative state legislatures.

INFORMAL METHODS OF CONSTITUTIONAL CHANGE

In addition to changes to the Constitution through formal amendment, changes—subtle and not so subtle—have come about as a result of interpretation by the other branches of government. We usually think that such interpretation is done by federal courts, particularly the Supreme Court, but Congress and the president also share a role in interpreting the Constitution. The ambiguity of so much important constitutional language makes interpretation essential. Since individual clauses of the Constitution can often be interpreted in different ways, the Constitution has been changed not only through formal amendment but also through shifting interpretations of such clauses.

Judicial Interpretation

The Supreme Court engages in judicial interpretation in the course of exercising its power of judicial review—that is, its power to strike down acts of government that violate the Constitution, the supreme law of the land. To decide what specific acts violate the Constitution, the Court must of course interpret relevant constitutional language. For example, weighing the constitutionality of a law providing for the death penalty in serious criminal cases requires the Court to determine what is meant by the Eighth Amendment's ban on "cruel and unusual" punishment. Even if the Court determines that the death penalty itself is not cruel and unusual, other questions may arise: Is it cruel and unusual to execute children or the mentally disabled? Answers to such questions require interpretation of the Eighth Amendment. Such answers may change over time as membership of the Court changes, even though the Constitution itself is not formally amended.

Judicial review is an important way of enforcing the rule of law—the idea that government is limited in its actions by the nation's constitution. Despite this vital function, judicial review was not a power specifically granted by the Constitution. Rather, it was established by the Supreme Court in the 1803 case *Marbury v. Madison*.[58] (See Chapter 15 for a more complete discussion of *Marbury v. Madison* and of the roots of judicial review.)

Ambiguous constitutional language complicates the task of judicial interpretation. For example, the Fourth Amendment bans "unreasonable searches and seizures," but what exactly does that mean? Judges disagree not only about what the word "unreasonable" means, but also about what constitutes a "search" (for instance, is a wiretap a search?). Similar difficulties extend to many of the most important clauses of the Constitution.

Even seemingly straightforward clauses, like the First Amendment command that Congress shall make no law abridging freedom of speech, can lead to widely divergent interpretations. What, exactly, does constitutionally protected "speech" entail? Is every verbal utterance protected (including libel, obscenity, false advertising, and verbal threats to assassinate the president or overthrow the government)? Is speech even limited to verbal utterances, or does the First Amendment also protect symbolic speech, such as burning an American flag? And if it protects symbolic speech, what does *that* entail? Answers to such questions about the meaning of "speech" affect the outcome of cases decided by the Court. (For a more in-depth analysis of interpretations of protected speech, see Chapter 4).

Since a simple majority of the Court has the power to determine what an ambiguous clause of the Constitution means, and since such meaning is—to a certain extent—in the eye of the beholder, changes in the membership of the Court can lead to changing interpretations of such clauses. For example, the Equal Protection Clause of the Fourteenth Amendment, which guarantees that no state shall deny to any person the equal protection of the laws, was long interpreted by the Supreme Court to allow "separate but equal" public schools for black and white students. But then the Supreme Court overturned its previous interpretation of the clause, declared separate but equal schools to be a violation of equal protection, and paved the way for school desegregation with its landmark ruling in the 1954 case *Brown v. Board of Education*.[59] No formal amendment altered the language of the Constitution, but the change in the Constitution's meaning was no less profound.

This ability of the Court to adjust its interpretation without the long and difficult process of constitutional amendment can be a good thing. The ambiguity—and therefore the flexibility—of the Constitution has its advantages: Clauses like "cruel and unusual punishment" and "equal protection" are interpreted according to contemporary values that can evolve over time. Some say this flexibility has helped the Constitution to endure. Others, however, fear that judges sometimes take advantage of this flexibility to "legislate from the bench." Why, they ask, should unelected judges pick which interpretation is correct based on their own value judgments and ideological predilections? Shouldn't such answers be left for majorities to decide through the democratic process? Those who favor judicial interpretation say no because they fear the "tyranny of the majority" and believe unelected judges will be more dispassionate than the whims of temporary majorities. This debate will be discussed in more detail in Chapter 15.

Congressional Interpretation

Members of all three branches of government take an oath to uphold the Constitution. Even though neither Congress nor the president has the power of judicial review, both must—like the Court—interpret the Constitution. Such interpretation by Congress and the president is known as **coordinate construction**.[60]

coordinate construction
Refers to constitutional interpretation by Congress or the president. Proponents of coordinate construction believe that all three branches of government (not just the judiciary) have the power and duty to interpret the Constitution.

Whenever Congress passes any law it must be mindful of constitutional limitations on its power. Consider, for example, the First Amendment command that Congress shall make no law abridging the freedom of speech. Congress must interpret that language before enacting a law dealing with speech. The Supreme Court, of course, may disagree with that interpretation and strike the law down using its power of judicial review, but since so few laws make their way to the Supreme Court, these initial determinations by Congress are important and can influence prevailing understandings of what constitutional clauses mean.

Sometimes the Supreme Court fails to nullify a law that others believe to be unconstitutional. A notable early example of this was the Sedition Act of 1798, which made it a crime to criticize the government. This law was passed when the

Federalist Party controlled Congress and the White House, and it targeted members of the opposition Democratic-Republican Party led by Thomas Jefferson. Jefferson and his followers were convinced that this law was an unconstitutional violation of free speech. Today, courts would no doubt agree, but when Jefferson became president in 1801 the law was still in effect. Even though federal courts had not struck it down, Jefferson wrote that he believed "that law to be a nullity, as absolute and as palpable as if Congress had ordered us to fall down and worship a golden image; and that it was as much my duty to arrest its execution at every stage, as it would have been to have rescued from the fiery furnace those who should have been cast into it for refusing to worship the image."[61] Therefore, Jefferson pardoned those convicted for violating the act, and Congress, now controlled by Democratic-Republicans, passed legislation that repealed it. In this case, Congress and the president took it upon themselves to reverse what they believed to be an unconstitutional law.

Presidential Interpretation

Article II, Section 1, Clause 8 of the Constitution directs the president to "preserve, protect and defend the Constitution of the United States." Article II, Section 3 directs the president to "take Care that the Laws be faithfully executed." Some argue that these clauses require coordinate construction: the president must interpret the Constitution to make sure that it is upheld and faithfully executed, just as Jefferson did when he pardoned those convicted of violating the Sedition Act.

In recent years, such coordinate construction has taken the form of *presidential signing statements*. These are statements issued by the president when he signs a bill into law. Presidents since James Monroe have issued such statements. Traditionally, they were ceremonial in nature: a statement celebrating the passage of the law. More recently, presidents such as Ronald Reagan used signing statements to clarify how they believed executive branch officials should interpret ambiguous parts of the law.

Increasingly, however, signing statements came to be used by presidents to identify portions of the law that they believed to be unconstitutional. Some laws passed by Congress are hundreds, even thousands, of pages long. The president does not have the power of a *line item veto;* he cannot, in other words, strike a particular line or clause from a bill before signing it. If he uses his veto power, he must reject the bill in its entirety. A signing statement allows the president to sign the bill but express his belief that one or more parts of it are unconstitutional. In using signing statements in such a way, most presidents, such as Bill Clinton (1993–2001), would note the portion they believed to be constitutionally suspect, but would enforce the law in its entirety unless the Supreme Court struck down that portion of the law.

George W. Bush used signing statements in a more controversial manner. He routinely used signing statements to express his intent *not to enforce* certain provisions of the law he was signing. In one famous example, Bush signed with much fanfare the so-called McCain Amendment banning the use of torture by U.S. officials, but quietly issued a signing statement claiming the power to disregard the law when he, as commander in chief, deemed it necessary to do so. The general public, as well as most members of Congress, were unaware of Bush's extensive use of signing statements until the practice was publicized by an April 2006 article in the *Boston Globe*.[62]

★ Unbeknownst to Senator John McCain, who sponsored the Detainee Treatment Act, President Bush, after signing the Act into law, claimed the right not to enforce it.

Subsequently, an August 2006 report by a Task Force of the American Bar Association found that Bush had used signing statements to challenge more than 800 specific provisions of laws he had signed. In one signing statement alone, Bush raised 116 specific objections involving almost every part of the Consolidated Appropriations Act of 2005 that he had just signed.[63] In short, Bush claimed the power to disobey portions of laws he had signed whenever he felt that those provisions conflicted with *his* interpretation of the Constitution. Critics claimed the president had exceeded his powers by imposing his own interpretation of the Constitution without waiting for a ruling from the courts.

Shortly after taking office, Barack Obama instructed government officials not to enforce Bush's signing statements without first getting clearance to do so from the attorney general. However, Obama indicated that he might use signing statements himself in some instances.[64] For example, in June 2009, President Obama issued a signing statement accompanying a war spending bill. In it, he said that he could ignore restrictions that Congress had placed on U.S. aid provided to the World Bank and International Monetary Fund. Some Democrats in Congress expressed concern that President Obama had used a tool that he and fellow Democrats had criticized President Bush for using.[65] However, Obama's use of signing statements has been less frequent and less controversial than Bush's had been.

ENFORCING THE CONSTITUTION

At the end of the day it is important to remember that the words of the Constitution are not enough to guarantee either liberty or the rule of law. Those words must be enforced. Many governments—including dictatorial communist regimes—have had constitutions with lofty but often meaningless language protecting basic rights. Even in our own country, African Americans were denied fundamental rights, such as the ability to vote, long after the Thirteenth Amendment to the Constitution had abolished slavery and the Fourteenth Amendment guaranteed the equal protection of the laws. As the great twentieth-century American judge Learned Hand once wrote: "Liberty lies in the hearts of men and women; when it dies there, no constitution, no law, no court can save it; no constitution, no law, no court can even do much to help it."[66]

Why Are We
THE WAY WE ARE ?

The American Revolution is obviously a pivotal event in determining why we are the way we are. By now, you should be able to delineate the factors that led to the American Revolution. Chief among these factors are the historical development and political thought of England, which influenced the colonists' views of their rights as citizens. These, in turn, have had an enduring influence on our system of government.

INFLUENCES FROM ENGLISH DOCUMENTS

We are the way we are partly because of the influence of two great documents from England: the Magna Carta and the English Bill of Rights. The Magna Carta serves as a fundamental basis for the rule of law, which guarantees that everyone—including the most powerful leader of government—is bound by law. It also protects citizens by guaranteeing due process of law. These concepts continue to be cornerstones of our governmental system—ones that we will encounter again and again throughout this book. So, too, is the principle, derived from the English Bill of Rights, that government must be accountable to the people.

In the days leading up to the American Revolution, colonists used these documents to justify their rights and highlight abuses by the English government. The colonists' desire to make government accountable and to protect the rights of individuals also led them to re-think how government should be constituted. Thus, these documents eventually influenced the language used in the U.S. Constitution and established basic principles that we still expect government to abide by.

JOHN LOCKE AND THE PRINCIPLE OF A WRITTEN CONSTITUTION

Likewise, the writings of John Locke not only influenced the language of the Declaration of Independence but helped to establish enduring principles. Drawing on Locke's idea of the social contract, Americans embraced written constitutions when creating governments at the state and national levels.

In contrast, England had an "unwritten" constitution that consisted of some written documents (such as the English Bill of Rights and Acts of Parliament), but also unwritten parliamentary conventions and royal prerogatives. Americans did not believe England's more amorphous constitution had done enough to protect the rights of its citizens, in part because Parliament could alter the constitution through simple legislation. The fact that we have a written constitution embodying a republican form of government designed to protect individual liberty and to prevent concentrations of power in government is, in no small measure, a direct outgrowth of the history and influences discussed in this chapter.

Today, written constitutions (largely based on the U.S. example) are the norm. Unwritten constitutions, such as those in the United Kingdom, Israel, and New Zealand are now the exception. Yet the success of our Constitution depends not only on the strength and flexibility of its own structure, but also on the convergence of other less definable factors, including timing and luck, coupled with an underlying commitment to the rule of law. This makes it more difficult to determine how, when, or even whether the success of the U.S. Constitution can be duplicated in other countries, such as Iraq.

. . . AND WHY DOES IT Matter?

Understanding why we are the way we are is important. But why does it matter? We tend to take our system of government for granted and forget that its structure was not preordained. As we have seen, the Framers of the Constitution had fundamentally different views on many specific issues. Many aspects of our government could have been different if competing arguments had won at the Constitutional Convention, state ratifying conventions, or at any number of other points in our history.

For example, think of how things might have been different if the United States had not approved a written Constitution and embraced judicial review as a mechanism to enforce it. We could have survived—and probably survived quite well—without either of them (England has), but the consequences to you would have been quite profound. We will see in future chapters how much judicial review touches all of our lives. School desegregation, abortion rights, and free speech protections—to name just a few things shaped by judicial review—would have had to come from political action rather than the courts. That means that some of the rights you now expect might have been delayed or never even granted. But it also means that politicians would have had to confront some issues on which they now defer to courts. The result would have been a system worse in some ways and perhaps better in others, but the result would have had a direct impact on your life.

critical thinking questions

1. Some scholars have noted that constitution-making often takes place in crisis-laden, post-conflict situations that provide disincentives to cooperation and make the creation of a successful constitution difficult. In reviewing our own constitutional development, it is important to remember that the first attempt to create a constitution for the United States—the Articles of Confederation—failed. What factors account for the successful drafting and ratification of the subsequent U.S. Constitution?

2. Imagine if round-the-clock cable news networks, attack ads, and the Internet had existed when our Constitution was written and ratified. How might they have changed the process? Consider the discussion of the Virginia ratifying convention in the section titled "Another Compromise: A Post-Ratification Bill of Rights." Would it have been harder for James Madison to prevail over Patrick Henry in today's media environment? Why or why not?

3. Identify ways in which the original Constitution was undemocratic. Assess the strengths and weaknesses of those provisions. How have amendments made the Constitution more democratic? What undemocratic features remain? Should any of these remaining features be altered or abolished? If so, which ones, and how?

4. Think about the four core principles of the Constitution discussed in this chapter: republicanism, federalism, separation of powers, and checks and balances. Each of these principles influences the way government operates and the policies it enacts. Now think about a policy issue that is important to you—for example, education, health care reform, balancing the budget, same-sex marriage, or the legalization of marijuana—and assess how each of these principles affects the development and implementation of that policy.

key terms

FEDERALISM

★ ★ ★

- Define federalism and explore the roots and functions, as well as the strengths and weaknesses, of the U.S. federal system.
- Differentiate between powers allocated to the national government and to the states as outlined by the U.S. Constitution.
- Compare two divergent ways of interpreting the U.S. Constitution, and discuss how each affects the balance of power between the national government and the states.
- Explain how two landmark cases under the Marshall Court helped to establish a balance of power between the federal and state governments.
- Analyze the resurgence of states' rights in the period leading up to the Civil War.
- Discuss the evolution of federalism during the New Deal era.
- Understand the continuing evolution of federalism during the last half of the twentieth century and into the twenty-first century.

PERSPECTIVE
Should the National Government Centralize Education?

The U.S. governing system of *federalism* allows states and localities to retain broad powers over a range of issues involving health, safety, public welfare, morality—and education. So, it was somewhat surprising that President George W. Bush, who had embraced states' rights during the 2000 election campaign, proposed and signed into law the "No Child Left Behind Act" of 2001, which gave the national government greater control over education.

Bush modeled "No Child Left Behind" on reforms he had initiated as governor of Texas. The program, which initially enjoyed broad bipartisan support, requires states that receive federal funds for education to test public school students in reading and math every year from third to eighth grade, and at least once in high school. Schools must not only make these test scores public but also report how certain groups within the school, such as blacks, Hispanics, and learning-disabled students, fared. With this law, President Bush hoped in part to narrow the gap between the scores achieved by different student groups and end what he called "the soft bigotry of low expectations."[1]

Despite initial support for No Child Left Behind, the actual implementation of the 670-page law has generated great controversy. For example, critics claim that schools have become so concerned with boosting test scores in order to secure funding that they "teach to the test" at the expense of a broader education. Additionally, critics note that some individual states—responsible for creating their own tests—have lowered standards in an attempt to boost their test scores.[2] As a result, some now call for even greater centralization: Rather than allowing each state to design and administer its own test, these critics suggest that a uniform national test be designed and administered instead. Others take an opposite approach: they believe that No Child Left Behind took centralization too far and argue that control of educational policy should be returned to the hands of local officials rather than a "faraway bureaucracy"—that is, the federal government.

The U.S. federal system stands in stark contrast to the *unitary system* of government that exists in many other countries, such as France. A unitary system allows France to have a highly centralized educational system, unlike that of the United States. This means that rather than leaving curricular decisions and other education-related policies to localities, such decisions are made at the national level. So, too, are decisions about the recruitment and training of teachers and the examinations administered to students. Centralized control of education in France helps to foster a sense of French nationalism and minimize regional differences. Even the language taught in the schools is said to have broken down regional dialects.[3]

Whether or not this is a good thing is debatable. France has long been proud of its educational system, which sets high academic standards that are uniformly enforced across all schools. Some point to it as a model. But others, including an agency of the French government itself, have suggested that the French educational system has its weaknesses: student test scores have fallen, children from lower socioeconomic backgrounds seem to be left behind, schools largely ignore nonacademic activities (such as sports and music), and the whole system is administered by a lumbering bureaucracy.[4] Partly in response to such concerns, France has recently taken some small steps toward decentralizing education, at least at the margins. Yet, such changes— while minimal—have created great controversy, much in the same way No Child Left Behind did in the United States.

Although decentralization efforts in France began in the 1980s,[5] more recently, the conservative French president Nicolas Sarkozy—motivated in part by poor international rankings of French higher education—gave universities more autonomy with regard to budgets, recruitment, and salaries. Some feared these reforms marked a step toward the privatization of education (in France the best schools—unlike the United States—have been public rather than private). Students and teachers alike vehemently opposed the reforms and took to the streets in heated demonstrations.[6] Students feared that the costs of education would go up, and teachers feared that their salaries would go down.

In the United States, however, debates about who should control educational policy reflect a much broader debate between national supremacy and states' rights. Such debates are prompted by our system of federalism, which leaves unclear the precise division of power between the national and state governments.

THIS CHAPTER BEGINS with a comparison of federal and unitary systems and a discussion of why we have a federal system. It details how the Constitution allocates power between the national government and the states, and how ambiguity in the Constitution has sparked ongoing debate about where to draw the line. The chapter goes on to explore the debate between dual federalists, who believe in states' rights, and cooperative federalists, who believe in a strong national government. Their competing views about the nature of our union, how to read the Constitution, and the proper role of the United States Supreme Court lead to very different conclusions about the balance of power in this country. Both positions have prevailed at different points in our history, and much of this chapter focuses on the ebb and flow between dual federalism and cooperative federalism. As you read this chapter, keep in mind our two core questions:

WHY ARE WE THE WAY WE ARE?
WHY DOES IT MATTER TO YOU?

In particular, how can the tug-of-war between dual federalists and cooperative federalists affect the balance of power in the United States?

UNDER[...]

Issues involving federalism affect you daily, whether you realize it or not. They have provoked heated debate on everything from the constitutionality of educational reform under George W. Bush to the health care reform legislation enacted under the Obama administration to legalization of same-sex marriage and the call to repeal the Defense of Marriage Act (DOMA).

United States operates under a federal system, but what exactly is a federal system? What are the alternatives to a federal system, and what are their strengths and weaknesses? The extent to which power is concentrated in the national versus the regional governments has been the subject of enduring debate in the United States, as well as a characteristic that significantly distinguishes it from other countries.

Except for a few tiny nations, all countries have more than one layer of government; they have not only a central, national government but also regional governments (called "states" in the United States). *Federalism*—a defining characteristic of the U.S. Constitution—requires that power be divided between these two layers of government. In the United States, the duty of interpreting how the Constitution delineates these powers falls to the Supreme Court. Whether its members are cooperative federalists or dual federalists makes a huge difference. *Cooperative federalists* read constitutional clauses broadly to expand the power of Congress. *Dual federalists,* on the other hand, see such expansion as an invasion of states' rights. Congress's ability to enact Social Security, minimum wage laws, gun control legislation, child labor laws, and an "individual mandate" that requires everyone to purchase health care insurance are just some of the issues that hang in the balance of this debate. So, too, is the ability of states to pass more stringent environmental standards than the federal government, to allow the use of medical marijuana, and to determine minimum drinking ages. To understand these debates, we must first explore the roots and functions of the U.S. federal system.

THE FEDERAL SYSTEM

Unlike most other democracies in the world, the United States formally divides power between the national and state governments to form a **federal system** of government. The Constitution gives Congress the authority to legislate in certain specific areas while reserving other legislative powers to the states. Power is divided, with the national government having authority over some issues, and states having authority over others. As such, two layers of government control the same geographic area and group of people, but each layer is responsible for dealing with different political issues. However, the delineation between these two layers is not always clear. The resulting gray areas, where reasonable people disagree about whether the national government or the states have authority to act, can make federalism somewhat difficult to understand. In addition to dividing certain powers, our federal system ensures that some powers are shared. For example, both states and the national government have the power to tax.

The first American attempt at self-governance, the Articles of Confederation, employed a very different governing structure: a **confederal system.** In a confederal system, ultimate authority rests primarily with regional entities (such as states) that have banded together to form a league of independent governments. A central government may exist, as it did under the Articles of Confederation, but it is created by the regional governments and has only limited powers, usually associated with defense and foreign affairs.

At the opposite extreme of a confederal system is a **unitary system,** which characterizes the vast majority of governments in the world today. In unitary systems, such as those of England and France, the central government has ultimate control over all areas of policy. The central government may delegate some of its power to regional or local

KEY TO understanding ▲

federal system
A system in which power is formally divided between the national government and regional entities such as states.

confederal system
A system of government in which power rests primarily with regional entities that have banded together to form a league of independent governments.

unitary system
A system of government in which the national government has ultimate control over all areas of policy.

Unitary system

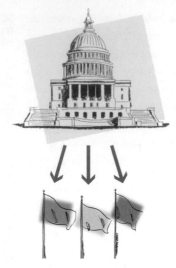

The central government is sovereign, with no legal superior. It may create state governments and delegate legal authority to them. It can also eliminate such governments.

Confederal system

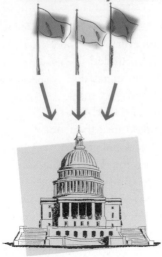

An alliance exists among independent sovereign governments, which delegate limited authority to a central government of their making. The independent sovereign governments retain sovereignty, with no legal superior, over all matters they do not delegate to the central government.

Federal system

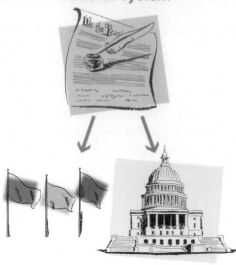

State governments are sovereign in specified matters, and a central government is sovereign in other specified matters. The matters over which each government is sovereign are set forth in a constitution, which is the supreme law of the land.

FIGURE 3.1

★ THREE SYSTEMS OF GOVERNMENT

Who is sovereign in each of these systems?

governments, but—unlike a federal system—a unitary system allows the central government to overrule any political decision made by local government. The central government is not, in other words, *obligated* to share power (as it is under a federal system); it can trump local action whenever it chooses to do so. (See Figure 3.1.)

After having fought and won a revolution to gain independence from England and its perceived tyranny, embracing a unitary system in America did not have much appeal. Therefore, the United States created a federal system, becoming the first nation to do so. Although a federal system now exists in a number of other countries including Australia, Brazil, Canada, Germany, India, and Mexico, countries with a federal system remain a distinct minority. Federal systems tend to be found in larger countries (with some notable exceptions, such as Belgium). Thus, while federal systems make up only 10 percent of the world's countries, they encompass 38 percent of the world's people and cover 49 percent of the world's land area (see Figure 3.2).

In the United States, a division of power exists not only between the national government and the states but also between the state and local governments. This division varies from state to state, as does the number of governmental units within a particular state. Today, power in the United States is divided among more than 89,000 governmental units at the national, state, and local levels, resulting in a very complicated system of decision making.

STRENGTHS AND WEAKNESSES OF A FEDERAL SYSTEM

The sharing of power between the national government and the states reflected the Framers' belief in limited government. They feared that concentrations of power would breed tyranny. Thus, through *separation of powers*, they divided power horizontally at

FIGURE 3.2

★ FEDERATIONS OF THE WORLD

According to this map, are large nations or small nations more likely to adopt federal systems? Why do you think this is the case?

Source: Minister of Public Works and Government Services Canada, 2012 (http://www.pco bcp.gc.ca/aia/index.asp?lang=ong&page=world mondo)

the national level between the three co-equal branches of government—legislative, executive, and judicial—and established a system of *checks and balances*. At the same time, they used federalism to divide power vertically between the national government and the states. The resulting division of power not only gives individual states autonomy to deal as they see fit with policy areas over which they have control (such as education), but also increases the number of opportunities for people to influence and control different units of government.

This dispersal of power is thought to be one of the great strengths of federalism. In addition to protecting against dangerous concentrations of power and allowing a degree of autonomy to the states, federalism gives individual states the opportunity to experiment with different types of policy responses to public problems. As U.S. Supreme Court Justice Louis Brandeis once put it, "It is one of the happy incidents

★ Following the BP oil spill of 2010, state and federal governments squabbled as they attempted to contain the damage. Decentralization can slow emergency responses to crises as the two levels of government attempt to coordinate their responses and determine whose responsibility it is to act.

of the federal system that a single courageous state may, if its citizens choose, serve as a laboratory; and try novel, social and economic experiments without risk to the rest of the country."[7] Thus, individual states have been able to experiment with everything from educational policy to the legalization of medical usage of marijuana (currently permitted in 16 states). Federalism has also allowed states to give greater protection than the national government to issues such as the environment.

Yet, as critics have noted, federalism also has its weaknesses. For instance, although dispersal of power may give citizens more opportunity to influence the political process, it also provides more veto points that can be used to stifle action on important issues. Likewise, state autonomy can translate into inaction; states may be unresponsive to policy problems that fall under their purview. And while federalism may allow states to experiment with different types of policy responses, variation among states can lead to inconsistencies in the way citizens are treated in different states. At its worst, states' rights can become a justification for policies that undermine social justice, such as racial segregation and Jim Crow laws (see Chapter 5).

THE CONSTITUTIONAL ALLOCATION OF THE POWERS OF GOVERNMENT

★ KEY TO understanding When the U.S. Constitution supplanted the Articles of Confederation, the powers of government shifted. Certain powers were allocated exclusively to the national government and others to the states. Still others were identified as powers to be shared between the two levels. What powers are specifically prohibited by the Constitution? And what provisions in the Constitution deal with relationships among the states? All of these constitutional provisions shape the ongoing debate about the balance of power in the United States.

Ever since the founding of the United States, a debate has persisted about how to divide power between the national government and the states. The Articles of Confederation came down decidedly in favor of the states. Then the U.S. Constitution created a federal system, with the national government and the states sharing power. However, the language of the Constitution leaves ambiguous the precise balance of power between the two. Such ambiguity was a compromise between those delegates who wanted a very strong national government and those who supported states' rights. Each side hoped their interpretation of this ambiguous language would prevail later on, but the result has been ongoing debate about the balance of power.

NATIONAL POWERS

When states entered into the Constitution, they specifically delegated certain powers to the new national government. Chief among these are those given to Congress. Article I, Section 8 of the Constitution includes a laundry list of specific congressional powers known as the enumerated powers (see Chapter 2 and Table 3.1).

In addition to these enumerated powers, the last clause of Article I, Section 8, known as the **necessary and proper clause,** gives Congress the *implied power* to "make all laws which shall be necessary and proper for carrying into Execution the foregoing Powers, and all other Powers vested by this Constitution in the Government of the United States, or in any Department or Officer thereof." The necessary and proper clause is sometimes also referred to as the **elastic clause** because it allows the powers of Congress to expand like an elastic band. Just how elastic this clause should be has long been the subject of intense debate.

necessary and proper (or "elastic") clause
The last clause of Article I, Section 8 of the Constitution, which authorizes Congress to make "all laws which shall be necessary and proper" for executing the Constitution's enumerated powers; sometimes called the elastic clause because it allows congressional powers to expand.

Starting with the Thirteenth Amendment, which abolished slavery, several constitutional amendments have included an *enabling clause*, which gives Congress the power to enforce the provisions of the amendment through appropriate legislation. Enabling clauses therefore allow Congress's power to expand. As with implied powers, however, determining what legislation is "appropriate" has been the focus of debate.

Article VI of the Constitution contains the so-called **supremacy clause.** This clause states that the U.S. Constitution, all "Laws of the United States which shall be made in Pursuance thereof" (in other words, laws constitutionally enacted under Congress's enumerated or implied powers, or as a result of power derived from enabling clauses), and "all Treaties made . . . under the authority of the United States" are "the supreme Law of the Land." This means that states must obey each of these, and that "the Judges in every State shall be bound thereby, any Thing in the Constitution or Laws of any State to the Contrary notwithstanding." At first glance, this seems very clear cut: Any time a state law or a provision of a state constitution conflicts with national power in the form of the U.S. Constitution, an act of Congress, or a Treaty, it must give way to "the supreme Law of the Land." Yet, the ongoing debate about how much power Congress can legitimately derive from either the necessary and proper clause or the enabling clauses raises persistent contention: Precisely which laws are made in pursuance of the Constitution and thus considered "supreme"?

STATE POWERS

Those who opposed ratification of the Constitution did so because they felt it gave the new national government too much power—power that could be used to infringe upon both individual liberties (such as freedom of speech) and states' rights. Ultimately, ratification came as the result of a promise to add a Bill of Rights through the process of amendment (see Chapter 2). Among the first 10 amendments that collectively form the Constitution's Bill of Rights, the **Tenth Amendment** serves as the major weapon in the arsenal of states' rights.

The Tenth Amendment says: "The powers not delegated to the United States by the Constitution, nor prohibited by it to the States, are reserved to the States respectively, or to the people." *Delegated powers* include the enumerated and implied powers of Congress. Once you subtract these delegated powers, plus any powers that the Constitution prohibits states from having, you are left with the *reserved powers* of the states. These reserved powers are commonly referred to as a state's **police powers.** States have these powers as well as others that are specifically listed (see Table 3.2).

The Founders allowed the states to manage and maintain public order by passing laws to protect (police) the health, safety, morals, and public welfare of their people. Police powers also permit state regulation of things like crime, education, marriage, and traffic. Since these powers are left to individual states, the resulting laws may vary from state to state. The ambiguity of constitutional language can make it difficult to draw a clear line between delegated powers and reserved powers. In fact, the exact parameters of the police powers have fluctuated across time due to the U.S. Supreme Court's changing interpretation of constitutional language.

TABLE 3.1
national powers

Congress's enumerated powers include but are not limited to the authority to:

- Tax, borrow and coin money
- Regulate interstate commerce
- Declare war
- Provide for an army and navy
- Make uniform naturalization laws
- Create a system of federal courts

supremacy clause
Article VI, Clause 2 of the Constitution specifying that federal laws and treaties passed pursuant to the Constitution trump contradictory state laws dealing with the same topic.

Tenth Amendment
The amendment to the Constitution that says: "The powers not delegated to the United States by the Constitution, nor prohibited by it to the States, are reserved to the States respectively, or to the people."

police powers
The powers reserved to the states under the Tenth Amendment dealing with health, safety, public welfare, and morality.

TABLE 3.2
state powers

Powers belonging to the states include the authority to:

- Provide for public health, safety, and morality
- Regulate commerce within the state
- Establish local governments
- Ratify amendments to the U.S. Constitution
- Determine voter qualifications
- Conduct elections

TABLE 3.3
concurrent powers

Concurrent powers include the authority to:

- Levy taxes
- Borrow money
- Charter banks and corporations
- Establish courts

For example, shifting interpretations of the commerce clause and the Tenth Amendment have allowed Congress to legislate in areas long thought to be the province of the states. Federal minimum wage laws were once routinely struck down by the Supreme Court as an unconstitutional infringement of state police powers under the Tenth Amendment. Now the Court upholds federal minimum wage laws as an acceptable exercise of Congress's commerce clause power. Neither the language of the Tenth Amendment nor the commerce clause changed—just the Court's interpretation of that language. We will examine concrete examples of such changes later in this chapter.

CONCURRENT POWERS

concurrent powers
Powers shared by the national government and the states (both, for example, have the power to tax).

Some powers belong exclusively to the national government (such as the power to declare war). Others belong exclusively to the states (such as the power to establish local governments within a state). However, there are also some powers that are *shared* between the national government and the states. These are known as the **concurrent powers** (see Table 3.3).

The power to tax is one example of a concurrent power. Although there are some limits on what types of tax each level can impose—states cannot impose a tariff (an import tax) without the consent of Congress, and the federal government cannot impose a tax on real estate—both the national government and the states can impose *excise taxes* (non-property taxes, such as taxes on payrolls, estates, gasoline, and cigarettes). For example, Congress raised the federal tax on a pack of cigarettes from 39 cents a pack to $1.01 a pack in 2009.[8] In addition to this federal tax, individual states are free to add their own tax on cigarettes. They are also free to choose their own tax rate. As of 2012, the state of New York had the highest rate ($4.35 per pack) and Missouri had the lowest (17 cents per pack), with an average tax of $1.45 per pack across all the states.[9] Thus, the cost of cigarettes can vary considerably from state to state.

Other concurrent powers include the ability to establish courts, borrow money, and charter banks and corporations. Once again, however, the precise line between exclusive powers and concurrent powers can change over time, largely because of changing interpretations of constitutional language by the U.S. Supreme Court.

PROHIBITED POWERS

In addition to granting powers to the national government and the states, the Constitution also prohibits certain specific powers. Article I, Section 9 of the Constitution lists powers denied to Congress. For example, Congress is prohibited from passing a *bill of attainder* (a law declaring a person or group of persons guilty of a crime without a trial) or an *ex post facto law* (a law that makes an act a criminal offense retroactively, even though the act was not a crime when committed). Among other things, Congress is also prohibited from granting titles of nobility, and from favoring one state over another when exercising its authority to regulate interstate commerce.

Article I, Section 10 of the Constitution lists powers denied to the states. States, for example, are prohibited from entering into treaties, coining money, altering obligations of contracts, or issuing a *Letter of Marquee and Reprisal* (a warrant authorizing what would otherwise be an act of piracy: the attack and capture of a ship). And, like Congress, states are prohibited from passing bills of attainder, ex post facto laws, and titles of nobility.

RELATIONSHIPS AMONG THE STATES

States, of course, have to get along with each other. Bitter rivalries had existed among the states during the Articles of Confederation as they jostled for economic advantage. Mindful of this, the Framers of the Constitution took effort to include provisions for states to resolve disputes and to assure that states recognize each other's contracts and judicial decrees. Article IV contains three clauses that focus on relationships among the states.

First, the **full faith and credit clause** requires each state to give "full Faith and Credit . . . to the public Acts, Records, and judicial Proceedings of every other State." As the Supreme Court has explained, each state existed under the Articles of Confederation as an "independent foreign entity" that was "free to ignore obligations created under the laws or by the judicial proceedings" of other states. The full faith and credit clause meant to change that by making states "integral parts of a single nation."[10] In particular, the clause ensures that things such as contracts and judicial decrees from one state are recognized and honored in every other state. A primary purpose of the clause was to protect commerce and trade. A question that the Supreme Court will likely soon resolve is whether the full faith and credit clause would require a state that prohibits same-sex marriage to recognize a same-sex marriage from another state that allows it.

Second, the **privileges and immunities clause** forbids a state from denying citizens of other states the rights it confers on its own citizens. Thus, a citizen of one state cannot be precluded from traveling through or residing in other states or, while there, be prohibited from purchasing property or denied the protection of the law.

Third, the **extradition clause** deals with someone who is charged with a crime in one state, but who flees justice. If that person is found in another state, the extradition clause requires that state to return (extradite), upon request, that person to the state where the crime was committed.

In addition, Article I allows states, with the consent of Congress, to enter into **interstate compacts.** Interstate compacts are contracts between two or more states that create an agreement on a particular policy issue. As described by the Council of State Governments, interstate compacts enable states "to act jointly and collectively, generally outside the confines of federal legislative or regulatory process while respecting the view of Congress on the appropriateness of joint action."[11]

Rarely used before the twentieth century, interstate compacts have become common since World War II. Over 200 such compacts are currently in operation, most of which have been created in the past 75 years. In general, there are three broad types of interstate contracts:

- *border compacts*, which establish or alter the boundaries of states.
- *advisory compacts,* which create a commission to study a problem and then issue a report offering advice to the respective states.
- *regulatory compacts,* which establish an administrative agency to develop rules and regulations governing a particular issue.[12]

Interstate compacts cover a broad range of policy issues, including conservation, resource management, transportation, education, mental health, civil defense, and emergency management. A famous example of a regulatory compact is the Port Authority of New York and New Jersey, created in 1921 to build, maintain, and operate bridges and tunnels between the two states. Over the next two decades, the Port Authority built, among others, the George Washington Bridge, the Goethals Bridge,

full faith and credit clause
The requirement of Article IV, Section 1 of the Constitution that requires states to recognize "the public Acts, Records, and judicial Proceedings of every other state."

privileges and immunities clause
A provision of Article IV, Section 2 of the Constitution that forbids a state from depriving citizens of other states the rights it confers upon its own citizens.

extradition clause
A provision of Article IV, Section 2 of the Constitution that requires states to return (extradite), upon request, a fugitive who has fled the law to the state that has jurisdiction over the crime.

interstate compacts
Contracts between two or more states that create an agreement on a particular policy issue.

★ The Bayonne Bridge, which spans the Kill Van Kull tidal strait to connect Bayonne, New Jersey, with Staten Island, New York, illustrates the work of the Port Authority of New York and New Jersey, an example of an interstate compact.

the Holland Tunnel, and the Lincoln Tunnel. The Port Authority was also charged with building terminals, piers, airports, and even the World Trade Center in Manhattan—all designed to improve commerce and trade.[13]

Finally, Article III, Section 2 of the Constitution gives the Supreme Court the authority to resolve disputes among states, such as those involving water rights (as depicted in Figure 3.3). Such disputes are among the few types of cases that can actually be initiated before the Supreme Court under its *original jurisdiction* (see Chapter 14), rather than coming to the Supreme Court on appeal.

COMPETING INTERPRETATIONS OF FEDERALISM

KEY to understanding

There are two widely divergent views about how to interpret the Constitution. Dual federalism supports states' rights, while cooperative federalism supports national supremacy. Why would the choice to embrace one of these interpretations over the other have such profound consequences for the balance of power in the United States? And how would the choice influence what policies Congress can pursue?

★

As we have already suggested, ambiguity in constitutional language dealing with federalism has led to much debate over the relative balance of power between the national government and the states. Before we turn to specific examples, it is important to explain two competing interpretations of federalism: dual federalism and cooperative federalism.

DUAL FEDERALISM

Dual federalism is an interpretation of federalism that favors states' rights. It views the Constitution as a contract among preexisting states. Under the Constitution, these states willingly delegated certain powers to the new national government, but dual federalists believe that states retain all powers not specifically delegated.

Dual federalists also believe that the Constitution is a fixed document (rather than a "living" document that is subject to changing interpretations). They emphasize the Constitution's clearly delineated express powers (such as Congress's enumerated

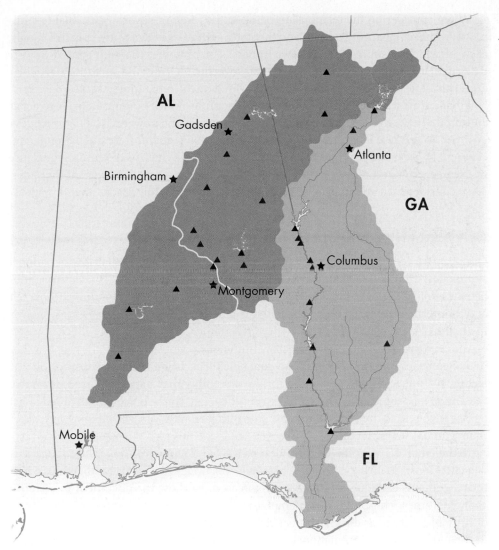

FIGURE 3.3

★ MAP OF THE APALACHICOLA-CHATTAHOOCHEE-FLINT RIVER BASIN

Georgia, Alabama, and Florida have been fighting over water rights in the Apalachicola-Chattahoochee-Flint River Basin. Article III, Section 2 of the Constitution allows the Supreme Court to settle such disputes under its original jurisdiction.

Source: http://www.lawrencevilleweather.com/blog/2007/10/where-exactly-is-the-lake-lanier-drainage-basin.html

powers), and believe that the Constitution should be interpreted consistently over time. They reject the idea that judges can use ambiguous language in the Constitution to augment the powers of the national government at the expense of the states. Therefore, they embrace a very narrow interpretation of Congress's implied powers. To them, the necessary and proper clause allows only a very limited expansion of congressional power to do those things *absolutely necessary* or *essential* to carrying out the enumerated powers. There must, in other words, be a very direct link between enumerated and implied powers.

Dual federalists also firmly embrace the Tenth Amendment, which they believe stands as a significant limit on the power of the national government and an important protector of states' rights. They believe that any actions of Congress that go beyond the enumerated powers and a very limited interpretation of the implied powers violate the Tenth Amendment. They further believe that the Supreme Court should employ the Tenth Amendment to rein in the national government and protect the prerogatives of the states.

dual federalism
An interpretation of federalism that favors states' rights and regards states and the national government as "dual sovereigns" (two relative equals).

When considering the relationship between the levels of government, dual federalists view the national government and the states as *dual sovereigns*—two relative equals, each of which is supreme in its own sphere. For example, the enumerated powers delegated to Congress make the national government supreme in those particular areas, but states remain supreme in areas covered by the remaining reserved powers.

Finally, dual federalists believe that the proper role of the Supreme Court is to act as an umpire between these two equals. It should uphold the power of the national government to exercise its express powers, but strike down attempts by the national government to use broad readings of constitutional language (such as the commerce clause or the necessary and proper clause) to intrude upon the reserved powers of the states. They consider such attempts to be power grabs that violate the Tenth Amendment.

COOPERATIVE FEDERALISM

Cooperative federalism is an interpretation of the Constitution that favors national supremacy. The term *cooperative federalism* was coined in the twentieth century and is usually applied to the period associated with the "New Deal" of Franklin D. Roosevelt and its aftermath. However, its basic tenets can be used to describe earlier eras, such as the national supremacy associated with the Supreme Court in the early 1800s.[14]

Cooperative federalism views the Constitution as a contract among the *people* rather than a contract among the states. The dual federalists' belief that the Constitution was a compact among the states allowed for the possibility that states could secede—leave the Union—as the Confederacy did during the Civil War. The cooperative federalist perspective rejects that possibility and puts ultimate authority with the people rather than with the states.

Rather than viewing the Constitution as a fixed document, cooperative federalists view the Constitution as an "organic"—living—document. They believe that the Constitution contains ambiguous language for a reason: to allow the document to adapt to changing times. Thus, rather than emphasizing the fixed nature of the express powers of the Constitution, as dual federalists do, cooperative federalists emphasize the ability to expand the power of the national government through a very broad interpretation of the necessary and proper clause. This broad interpretation allows Congress a wider range of implied powers than a dual federalist interpretation would allow: Congress can do anything that is *useful* or *helpful* to carry out its enumerated powers. There need only be, in other words, a very tangential link between the enumerated and implied powers.

In stark contrast with dual federalists, cooperative federalists minimize the significance of the Tenth Amendment. Rather than seeing it as a meaningful limit on the power of the national government, they dismiss the Tenth Amendment as a mere "truism."[15] In other words, the Tenth Amendment simply states the obvious: Powers that do not belong to the national government belong to the states or the people. Cooperative federalists do not believe that powers of the national government have to be expressly delegated, but instead assert that they can include implied and even *inherent* power (in other words, powers that any sovereign government must hold, whether or not they are expressly enumerated or implied, such as defending its borders or acquiring new territory).

Quite simply, the national government has whatever power it is able to derive—be it from narrowly defined enumerated powers or from broadly construed implied or inherent powers. Unlike the dual federalists, cooperative federalists do not believe the

Tenth Amendment can be used to prevent these broad interpretations of implied and inherent powers. This interpretation is what reduces the Tenth Amendment to the truism that states simply have whatever power is left over.

When considering the relationship between the levels of government, cooperative federalists view the national government as supreme. They see the relationship as strictly hierarchical (as opposed to the system of dual sovereignty that dual federalists espouse).

Finally, rather than viewing the Supreme Court as an umpire between two dual sovereigns, cooperative federalists consider the Supreme Court to be a player on the national team. Thus, the Supreme Court should uphold broad interpretations of constitutional language (such as the commerce clause or the necessary and proper clause) that can be used to expand the power of the national government at the expense of the states.

EARLY PRECEDENTS: NATIONAL SUPREMACY PREVAILS

John Marshall, appointed Chief Justice of the Supreme Court in 1801 by President John Adams, was the longest-serving Chief Justice in the history of the Supreme Court. He presided over several landmark cases that expanded the power of Congress at the expense of the states. Chief among these are *McCulloch v. Maryland* (1819) and *Gibbons v. Ogden* (1824), both of which reflected the views of cooperative federalism.

MCCULLOCH V. MARYLAND (1819)

At issue in *McCulloch v. Maryland* was whether Congress had the authority to create a national bank. The enumerated powers did not specifically give such authority to Congress. Those who said that Congress had the authority anyway, such as Alexander Hamilton, the first Secretary of the Treasury, embraced a broad cooperative federalist interpretation of the elastic clause and argued that creating a national bank was "necessary and proper" (that is, useful or helpful) to carrying out Congress's enumerated powers. After all, the Constitution specifically gave Congress the power to collect taxes, borrow money, coin money, and regulate the value of money. Surely, he argued, a national bank would help to facilitate these other enumerated powers.[16] Those who believed Congress did not have authority to create a national bank, such as Thomas Jefferson, employed a narrow dual federalist interpretation of the elastic clause and argued that a national bank was not absolutely necessary or essential for these enumerated powers to be carried out.

Congress embraced Hamilton's position and created the First Bank of the United States in 1791 and the Second Bank of the United States in 1816. To express its opposition, the state of Maryland then passed legislation to tax all banks operating in the state that were not chartered by the state. James McCulloch, the head of the Baltimore branch of the Second Bank, refused to pay the tax. This led to a lawsuit between McCulloch and Maryland that ended up in the Supreme Court.

The Court confronted two legal questions when deciding *McCulloch v. Maryland*: Did Congress have the authority to create a national bank? And if so, did the state of Maryland have the authority to tax the Baltimore branch of that bank? The Court unanimously decided that Congress did have the authority to create a national bank. It concluded that creating the bank was a legitimate exercise of Congress's implied powers. In so doing, the Court embraced Hamilton's broad, cooperative federalist interpretation of the necessary and proper clause. By assuming that the necessary and proper clause allows Congress to do those things that are appropriate (as opposed to essential) to carrying out its enumerated powers, and consistent with the spirit (as well as the letter) of the Constitution, the ruling paved the way for Congress to expand significantly its powers, and to do so at the expense of the states.

With regard to the second question, the Court concluded that the state of Maryland could not tax the Baltimore branch of the national bank without violating the supremacy clause. As Marshall stated, "the power to tax involves the power to destroy."[17] States "have no power, by taxation or otherwise, to retard, impede, burden or in any manner control the operations of the constitutional laws enacted by Congress. . . ."[18] Since Congress has the authority to create a national bank, a state cannot punish that bank, or discourage its operation within its borders, or seek to destroy it through taxation. To do so would violate the supremacy of national law.

The Supreme Court's answer to both of these legal questions had profound consequences. Its broad interpretation of the necessary and proper clause remains, to this day, an important source of congressional power. In addition, the limit on the power of states to tax the national bank became an important precedent that continues to prevent states from retaliating against or otherwise impeding other entities created by Congress, such as regulatory agencies, that operate within states.

GIBBONS V. OGDEN (1824)

In *Gibbons v. Ogden,* the Marshall Court again ruled in favor of broad national power, this time in relation to the **commerce clause** of the Constitution (Article I, Section 8). Now the debate focused on how broadly to read the enumerated powers of the commerce clause, which gives Congress the authority to regulate interstate commerce. But what, exactly, does this authority entail?

commerce clause
Article I, Section 8 of the Constitution, which gives Congress the authority to "regulate Commerce with foreign Nations, and among the several States, and with the Indian Tribes."

Dual federalists believe the commerce clause gives Congress only those powers essential to regulate the trade of actual goods and commodities among the states. Therefore, Congress's power is largely limited to regulating the *transportation* of these goods and commodities across state lines. Cooperative federalists believe the commerce clause gives Congress the authority to regulate anything that has even an incidental effect on interstate commerce. Thus, in the twentieth century, broad cooperative federalist interpretations of the commerce clause expanded Congress's power to include regulation of the *workplace* (including the passage of minimum wage laws and maximum hour laws), which dual federalists insist should fall to states under their police powers.

Gibbons v. Ogden set an early precedent for a broad reading of commerce clause power. The case dealt with whether navigation and the transportation of people (rather than of goods and commodities) across state lines were subject to regulation by Congress. Why did this become a question? Aaron Ogden operated a steam-powered ferryboat between New Jersey and New York. The state of New York controlled who could navigate in those waters, and Ogden operated his boat with a state-sanctioned license (part of a steamboat monopoly). Soon thereafter he faced competition from another ferryboat operated by Thomas Gibbons. Instead of a state-sanctioned license, Gibbons had a federal license granted to him by Congress. Unhappy with the competition, Ogden obtained an injunction from a New York state court to prevent Gibbons from operating his steamboat without a state-sanctioned license. Gibbons appealed, arguing that a license from Congress trumped a state-sanctioned one.

In an opinion again written by Chief Justice Marshall, the Court embraced the broad interpretation of Congress's commerce clause power and determined that Congress did have the power to issue the license. With this opinion, the Court rejected the dual federalist interpretation that "commerce" should be limited to the transportation of goods and commodities across state lines, and should not include navigation.[19]

Having concluded that Congress had the power to regulate navigation and issue the license to Gibbons, the Court then used the supremacy clause to conclude that New York State could not grant a steamboat monopoly that would render that license void. To do so would interfere with Congress's commerce clause power.

Again, this broad interpretation of the commerce clause has had profound long-term consequences. It paved the way for post-1937 rulings by the Supreme Court that allowed Congress to use the commerce clause to pass legislation dealing with everything from minimum wage laws to racial discrimination in restaurants.

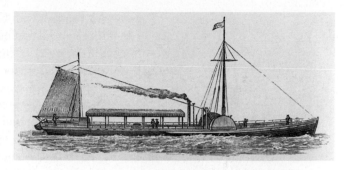

THE "CLERMONT," ★ 1807   The Supreme Court's conclusion in *Gibbons v. Ogden* that Congress could regulate interstate navigation under the commerce clause greatly expanded the power of Congress. Shown here is a steamboat of that era.

THE RESURGENCE OF STATES' RIGHTS

Although the Supreme Court under John Marshall solidly embraced the idea of national supremacy, the debate over federal power versus states' rights was far from settled. Indeed, it remained one of the most significant and divisive political issues of the 1800s. John Marshall's successor as Chief Justice, Roger Taney, moved the Supreme Court in a decidedly dual federalist direction. The most notorious ruling of the Taney Court—and possibly the most notorious Supreme Court ruling of all time—came in the infamous *Dred Scott* case of 1857 (see Chapter 5). Embracing dual federalism, the Court concluded that Congress had exceeded its powers when it abolished slavery in the territories. By insisting that the issue of slavery be left to individual states, the Court effectively ruled out a national legislative solution to the issue. In so doing, the ruling helped to precipitate the Civil War.

The years leading up to the Civil War (1861–1865) led to a rise in dual federalism. Southern states—unhappy with policies of the national government dealing with everything from tariffs to slavery—embraced states' rights as well as the doctrines of nullification and secession, which led to the Civil War. At the same time, the Supreme Court, under Marshall's successor, Roger Taney, favored states' rights in rulings such as *Dred Scott*. After the Civil War, another dual federalist era prevailed from 1895 to 1937.

KEY TO understanding ★

NULLIFICATION, SECESSION, AND THE CIVIL WAR

The debate over slavery was the overriding political issue in the days leading up to the Civil War, and states' rights came to be used as a justification to maintain it. Andrew Jackson's vice president, John C. Calhoun, was an outspoken proponent of states' rights. He proposed that states should be able to invalidate federal laws that they believed to be unconstitutional through the process of **nullification.**

nullification
The concept that states can invalidate federal laws that they believe to be unconstitutional.

★ In 2010, Idaho Governor C.L. "Butch" Otter (pictured here) proposed using the Doctrine of Nullification to invalidate the health care reform bill championed by President Obama. Several other states such as Texas, Maine, Oregon, and Nebraska also contemplated the use of nullification in response to health care reform.

secession
The act of withdrawing from membership in a federation.

In contrast with Calhoun, President Jackson—sympathetic to states' rights but convinced that nullification would destroy the Union—rejected the idea of nullification. Undeterred, Calhoun continued to advocate his nullification doctrine. As a result, South Carolina issued a formal Ordinance of Nullification in 1832.[20] Jackson's continued opposition to nullification led Calhoun to resign as his vice president the next month. Congress went on to pass legislation that authorized the use of military force against states that refused to enforce federal law.[21] Advocates of nullification lost the battle, but the seeds of Southern discontent had been sown.

In the decades that followed, slavery further inflamed relations between the national government and the Southern states. The election of Abraham Lincoln as president in 1860 proved to be the last straw. He had made it clear in the campaign that he supported efforts at the national level to prohibit slavery. Building on the concept of nullification, Southern states now claimed the right of **secession:** the ability to withdraw from the Union. South Carolina formally exercised that right on December 20, 1860. By February 1861, seven states had seceded, and after the outbreak of hostilities between the North and South in April, four more states followed suit. Together, the states that seceded formed the Confederate States of America.

The defeat of the Confederacy in the Civil War seemed to establish once and for all that states cannot secede, a view endorsed by the Supreme Court in *Texas v. White* (1869).[22] Nonetheless, fringe movements at both ends of the political spectrum continue to embrace the idea of secession. Today, the Texas Nationalist Movement calls for the secession of Texas.[23] As of 2009, it claimed that more than 250,000 Texans had signed up in support of that goal.[24] Vermont's secessionist party, called the Second Vermont Republic,[25] ran a slate of nine candidates in statewide elections in 2010. If you think such candidates never win, look to Alaska. There a candidate representing the Alaska Independence Party,[26] Walter Joseph Hickel, drew enough support to be elected governor of Alaska in 1990. That party's 2006 attempt to place an initiative on the ballot calling for Alaska to secede from the United States was blocked by a ruling of the Alaska Supreme Court, which held that any attempt at secession violated the U.S. Constitution.[27]

THE RISE AND FALL OF NATIONAL POWER IN THE WAKE OF THE CIVIL WAR

The so-called Civil War Amendments to the Constitution—the Thirteenth (1865), Fourteenth (1868), and Fifteenth

★ Invoking the memory of the Alamo, an important battle in the Texas War of Independence from Mexico in 1836, today's Texas Nationalist Movement depicts the federal government as an oppressive force and calls for the secession of Texas.

picture YOURSELF ...
AS AN ALBANIAN MUSLIM IN KOSOVO

SERBIA

MONTENEGRO

PRISTINA ★
KOSOVO

ALBANIA

MACEDONIA

In 1992, communism fell in eastern Europe and the six republics that had, since 1943, made up the Socialist Federal Republic of Yugoslavia (Bosnia-Herzegovina, Croatia, Macedonia, Montenegro, Serbia, and Slovenia) dissolved. Today, they are recognized as six separate countries.

One of these countries, Serbia, is predominantly Christian. As an Albanian Muslim living in Kosovo—a province in Serbia—you must deal with many challenges. Differences in language, ethnicity, and religion have long fueled conflict between your fellow residents in Kosovo and those in the rest of Serbia, as well as with the other former Yugoslavian republics. Therefore, you were not surprised when a series of wars broke out in the wake of Yugoslavia's dissolution. At the time, the president of Serbia, Slobodon Milošević, who had also been president of the once unified Yugoslavia, revoked Kosovo's autonomy and turned it into a police state.

When this happened, you were a university student in Pristina, the largest city in Kosovo. But Milošević cut your education short. He expelled you and 20,000 of your fellow students, and fired some 800 professors—all because the Serbs had perceived the university to be a breeding ground for Albanian nationalism. Even more shocking and horrifying to you were the reports of "ethnic cleansing"—the forcible removal of the civilian population of a specific ethnic group from a particular geographic location. In Bosnia, this led to genocide—the murder of more than 8,000 Muslims by Serbs and the expulsion of at least 25,000 more. Although Milošević stood accused of orchestrating the genocide, he was not arrested until 2001—almost 10 years later. He was sent to The Hague, Netherlands, to stand trial at the international war crimes tribunal, but he died before the trial ended.

The Kosovo resistance against Milošević and the Serbian aggression led to war in 1998–1999. Hushed accounts told of Albanian citizens being massacred, their villages burned, and tens of thousands forced out of their homes by Serb forces.* Unemployment soared to at least 40 percent—an incredible level, but described by some as an underestimate. You and your family found yourselves struggling to survive. Eventually, the United Nations intervened and authorized a NATO-led peacekeeping force to ensure Kosovo's autonomy within Serbia, but this and ensuing elections in Kosovo failed to keep you and your fellow Albanians from feeling marginalized. You remained impoverished; your culture and religion continued to be reviled. It is not surprising that a separatist movement gained strength.

Fast forward to February 17, 2008: the day that Kosovo declared independence from Serbia. It was a great, long overdue day for you. You celebrated with your friends in the streets of Pristina, where thousands gathered to cheer independence and wave the flag of Kosovo.

But today, more than four years later, many of the nations of the world still do not recognize Kosovo's independence. Although the International Court of Justice denies Serbia's claim that Kosovo's secession violated international law,[†] as of February 2012, only 87 out of 193 United Nations member states had recognized Kosovo's independence.

This example reminds us that separatist movements—like the one that led to the U.S. Civil War—exist in many

* Anthony Loyd, "Kosovo Deserves Its Independence," *The Times*, December 12, 2007 (http://www.timesonline.co.uk/tol/comment/columnists/guest_contributors/article3037002.ece).
† "Kosovo Independence Move Not Illegal, Says UN Court," *BBC News*, July 22, 2010 (http://www.bbc.co.uk/news/world-europe-10730573).

continued

other countries around the world. Yet the United States has avoided serious separatist movements since the Civil War. Why? A primary reason is that, despite their many differences, U.S. states do not have major religious or ethnic cleavages that turn them against each other. For example, a recent study by the Pew Forum on Religion and Public Life found that 78.4 percent of Americans identified themselves as Christian. Only 4.7 percent identified themselves as belonging to another religion: 1.7 percent identified themselves as Jewish, 0.7 percent as Buddhist, 0.6 percent as Muslim, 0.4 percent as Hindu, and so forth. Most of those who did not identify themselves as Christian identified themselves as unaffiliated (16.1 percent).[‡] This stands in stark contrast with the rest of the world, where more than half of the population is non-Christian.[§] The absence of religious cleavages is one reason that our system of federalism has lasted so long.

[‡] http://religions.pewforum.org/reports
[§] Gary Langer, "Poll: Most Americans Say They're Christian," July 18, 2001 (http://abcnews.go.com/US/story?id=90356&page=1).

questions to consider

1. How would you compare America's reasons for declaring independence in 1776 with Kosovo's in 2008?

2. Is it consistent for the United States to recognize Kosovo's right to secede from Serbia while denying the right of its own states to secede?

3. Can you imagine a serious separatist movement emerging in the United States? If so, what factors do you think would prompt it?

Amendments (1870)—greatly expanded the power of the national government. They prohibited slavery, prevented states from abridging the right to vote on account of race, and prohibited states from depriving any person of due process of the law or the equal protection of the laws. Each contained an enabling clause, which expanded Congress's power to enforce the provisions of these amendments.

Although it did not happen immediately, the Fourteenth Amendment also paved the way for the incorporation of the Bill of Rights—in other words, making the provisions of the Bill of Rights binding upon states as well as the federal government (see Chapter 4). Thus, the long-term effect of the Fourteenth Amendment has been to restrict the power of states by preventing them from passing legislation that would violate the First Amendment or other specific provisions of the Bill of Rights.

The Civil War also expanded the role of the national government in other ways. For example, the cost of the war led to the first federal income tax. The war also led the federal government to become involved in a form of social welfare: creating and maintaining a vast pension system for war veterans and war widows. Nonetheless, the debate between dual federalists and cooperative federalists was far from over, and dual federalists soon began to win important victories from the Supreme Court.

As early as 1873, the Supreme Court began to limit the scope of the Fourteenth Amendment.[28] Ten years later, the Court sharply limited the enabling clause power that Congress derived from the Fourteenth Amendment.[29] But the biggest boost to states' rights came in *Plessy v. Ferguson* (1896). By ruling that state-imposed "separate but equal" facilities (such as schools) for whites and blacks did not violate the equal protection clause of the Fourteenth Amendment, the Court gave great leeway to states to impose racial segregation.[30] This paved the way for a broad interpretation of states' rights that allowed states to pass Jim Crow laws and impose barriers to prevent blacks from voting (see Chapter 5).

The Court's narrow, dual federalist interpretation of the commerce clause from 1895 to 1937 also limited Congress's ability to regulate the workplace through such things as child labor laws and minimum wage laws. Starting in 1895, the Court embraced the

so-called *direct-indirect test* to delineate congressional power under the commerce clause.[31] According to this test, Congress could only use its commerce clause power to regulate those things that had a direct effect on interstate commerce (such as the actual *distribution* of goods and commodities across state lines). It could not regulate those things that had only an indirect effect on interstate commerce (such as the *production* of items shipped in interstate commerce). Thus, Congress could not regulate manufacturing, mining, and agriculture, which the Court considered to be the province of states under their police powers. Attempts by Congress to pass workplace regulations were mostly struck down by the Supreme Court as violations of the Tenth Amendment.[32] So, too, were attempts by Congress to regulate the economy.

THE NEW DEAL AND THE RISE OF COOPERATIVE FEDERALISM

The stock market crash of 1929 and the ensuing Great Depression transformed politics in the United States. The Republican Party had dominated national politics since the Civil War, but the Depression led to a *partisan realignment*—a lasting shift in voters' partisan identification. Republicans, who had controlled the White House and maintained solid control of both houses of Congress since 1921, lost control of all three branches of government in the 1932 elections when Franklin Delano Roosevelt won the White House and fellow Democrats took control of the House and the Senate. In contrast, the Supreme Court—given the lifetime tenure of its members—remained unchanged, standing as a dual federalist obstacle to the New Deal.

During the first four years of the presidency of Franklin D. Roosevelt (1933–1945), the Supreme Court used dual federalist principles to strike down major pieces of New Deal legislation passed by the Democrat-controlled Congress. The Supreme Court reversed course with its "switch in time that saved nine." How did its subsequent cooperative federalist rulings shift the balance of power between the national government and the states?

KEY TO understanding ★

THE SUPREME COURT THWARTS THE NEW DEAL

Roosevelt and his fellow New Deal Democrats greatly expanded the power of the national government. In stark contrast to the *laissez-faire* economic policies of their predecessors, which held that government should defer to the free market and intervene as little as possible in economic affairs, New Dealers believed government intervention in the economy was an essential step toward recovery.

A centerpiece of the New Deal was the National Industrial Recovery Act (1933), or NIRA, which authorized the federal government to regulate industry in order to spur recovery. The NIRA also established a national public works program to create jobs. In the process, the government created vast regulatory structures in the form of the National Recovery Administration and the Public Works Administration. Congress claimed that it had the authority to do this by embracing a broad cooperative federalist interpretation of its commerce clause powers. The Supreme Court, however, was still controlled by dual federalists, and it struck down the NIRA as unconstitutional in *Schechter Poultry Corp. v. U.S.* (1935).[33]

The Supreme Court struck down other major pieces of New Deal legislation, including legislation that gave government the authority to regulate wages, working hours, and production standards in the coal industry. Embracing a classic dual federalist interpretation of the direct-indirect test, the Court concluded that Congress did not have authority under the commerce clause to regulate production. The Court insisted that production had only an indirect effect on interstate commerce; even if that indirect effect was extensive, Congress was powerless to regulate because production was a purely local activity that fell under states' police powers.[34]

President Roosevelt was furious about the string of defeats handed to him by the Supreme Court. After the Supreme Court invalidated the NIRA in *Schechter,* FDR held a press conference in which he criticized the decision by equating it with the Court's infamous ruling in *Dred Scott.*[35] The press dubbed the four members of the Court who most consistently voted against the New Deal the "Four Horsemen of the Apocalypse."[36] In the battle between the Four Horsemen and Roosevelt, the electorate seemed to come down squarely on the

★ By 1936, the repudiation of the Republican Party was clear: Democrats won a 333-89 majority in the House and a 75-17 majority in the Senate, and FDR was reelected in a landslide (523 electoral votes to Republican Alf Landon's 8).

side of Roosevelt. While the Court continued to hand the New Deal more defeats, the president and his New Deal allies won landslide victories in the 1936 elections.

Emboldened, the newly reelected Roosevelt asked Congress to increase the size of the Supreme Court from nine to fifteen members. Several of the rulings against the New Deal had been by 5-to-4 or 6-to-3 votes, with dual federalists controlling the majority. Roosevelt assumed that expanding the size of the Court would allow him to appoint a new cooperative federalist majority that would uphold Congress's power to enact New Deal legislation.

THE SUPREME COURT EMBRACES COOPERATIVE FEDERALISM

In opposition to the dual federalist "Four Horsemen" of the Supreme Court were three cooperative federalist justices who usually voted to uphold New Deal legislation. The press dubbed them the "Three Musketeers."[37] In addition, there were two decisive "swing" justices on the nine-member Court.[38] In 1937, these two centrist justices joined the Three Musketeers to form a new 5-4 cooperative federalist majority.

Even though the votes that led to this majority took place before FDR announced his Court-packing plan, this has sometimes been called "the switch in time that saved nine" because it diffused the justification for expanding the size of the Court. Cooperative federalists won another victory at the end of the 1937 Supreme Court term when one of the Four Horsemen retired and Roosevelt had the opportunity to replace him. The remaining Four Horsemen soon retired as well. By the time President Roosevelt died in office in 1945, he had appointed all nine justices on the Court—the result of natural attrition.[39]

The results of these membership changes were striking. In a series of cases, the Court overturned earlier dual federalist precedents. In April 1937, the Court upheld the National Labor Relations Act in a broad cooperative federalist ruling that rejected the rigid interpretation of the direct-indirect test it had used the year before. Now Congress could use its commerce clause power to regulate the production of goods as well as the transportation of goods across state lines. The vote in that case was 5-to-4.[40] By 1941—just four years later—the transformation was complete. The Court unanimously overturned *Hammer v. Dagenhart,* a landmark 1918 dual federalist ruling that had held that Congress could not use its commerce clause power to regulate child labor by stopping the shipment of goods produced by children across state lines. In its new embrace of cooperative federalism the Court dismissed the Tenth Amendment as merely a "truism."[41]

★ Between 1935 and 1943, the WPA created almost 8 million jobs.

IMPLEMENTING COOPERATIVE FEDERALISM

The expansion of national power made possible by the "switch in time" led to a much more complex relationship between the national government and the states. The old dual federalist relationship has sometimes been described as "layer cake federalism," with each layer of government having clearly defined responsibilities. With the federal government becoming more active in telling states and localities what to do, the cooperative federalist relationship looked more like a marble cake. States now cooperated with the federal government (hence the term "cooperative federalism") by implementing its rules and regulations rather than having independent control as they did under dual federalism.

As Congress's power to regulate increased, it imposed more and more legal requirements on states (ranging from dictates to maintain the privacy of medical records to regulations designed to maintain clean air and drinking water). Money from the federal government to implement these requirements typically came in the form of

categorical grants. These are grants for states to do very specific, federally mandated things. Sometimes states are required to match a portion of that grant with their own money. Categorical grants are used to pay for such things as Medicaid and Food Stamps, programs that were part of President Lyndon Johnson's so-called "Great Society" in the 1960s—a federal expansion agenda that also included "War on Poverty" initiatives such as Head Start (which offers preschool education for poor children) and Upward Bound (which helps prepare poor high school students for college). The Great Society also expanded the federal government's role in the arts, environmental protection, and motor vehicle safety.

Such programs, of course, cost money. Not surprisingly, the federal budget steadily increased as the federal government took on more and more responsibilities. Sometimes Congress imposed a legal requirement on states to administer these programs but offered no money to pay for them. These requirements are called **unfunded mandates.** The 1990 Americans with Disabilities Act (ADA) is a good example. This law mandates that public transportation be accessible to people with disabilities, but it does not pay states or localities to retrofit trains and buses to comply with the law. Such unfunded mandates became a substantial portion of many states' budgets.

THE NEW FEDERALISM AND BEYOND

After the federal expansion of Lyndon Johnson's Great Society (1964–1969), Republican president Richard Nixon (1969–1974) sought to shift some of the balance of power back to the states. President Nixon coined the phrase *New Federalism* to describe this new approach.

THE NEW FEDERALISM

One of the ways New Federalism tried to restore power to the states was by implementing the use of **block grants** to states. Unlike specifically targeted categorical grants, where the federal government tells states precisely how and where to spend funds, block grants give states more flexibility. Block grants are meant to be spent on some general area, such as education or transportation, but states are relatively free to spend the money as they wish within that broad parameter.

President Nixon proposed consolidating 129 different categorical grants into six block grants. Congress stymied this initial proposal, but did begin to create some new block grants. President Ronald Reagan (1981–1989) had more success. At his urging, Congress consolidated 77 categorical grants into nine block grants in 1981. The move may have given more flexibility to the states in terms of how to spend the money, but states ended up with less money to spend as a result of the consolidation. Another expansion of block grants took place in 1996 when Democrat Bill Clinton held the White House and Republicans controlled Congress.[42]

In his 1996 State of the Union Address, President Clinton (1993–2001) famously stated "The era of big government is over." He added, however, that "we cannot go back to the time when citizens were left to fend for themselves." Instead, he envisioned a leaner federal government working in partnership with state and local governments, as well as with religious, charitable, and civic associations.[43] Toward this end, Clinton and the Republican Congress limited the ability of the federal government to impose

★ Head Start promotes school readiness by providing educational, nutritional, and other services to preschool children and their families. The Bush Administration's attempt to shift the funding source for Head Start from a categorical grant to a block grant created controversy because of the possibility that states might divert the funds to less successful programs.

unfunded mandates on states, reformed the federal welfare system, and abolished federally imposed speed limits.

Despite his stated belief in states' rights during the 2000 presidential campaign, President George W. Bush (2001–2009) actually presided over increases in national power. Much of this was related to the September 11, 2001, terrorist attacks on the World Trade Center and the Pentagon, which led to the creation of the Department of Homeland Security and the expansion of federal power to fight the "War on Terror." But Bush also increased federal involvement in other areas such as education (with his "No Child Left Behind" legislation) and entitlements (with his prescription drug plan for Medicare).

Appointments to the Supreme Court by Republican presidents starting with Nixon also had an effect on Supreme Court rulings dealing with federalism. In 1995, for the first time since 1936, the Court struck down a piece of legislation on the grounds that Congress had exceeded its commerce clause power. In *U.S. v. Lopez*, a 5-to-4 majority invalidated the Gun Free School Zones Act of 1990, in which Congress banned guns from "school zones": the grounds of a public, parochial, or private elementary or secondary school, and the area within 1,000 feet of those grounds. Congress used its commerce clause power to do this; specifically, it prohibited any firearm in these zones "that has moved in or affects interstate or foreign commerce." The Court majority, however, concluded that regulating guns fell under states' police powers.

Several other rulings have extended this shift back toward states' rights. For example, the Court, in *U.S. v. Morrison* (2000) struck down the provision of the federal Violence Against Women Act of 1994 that gave women the right to sue their attackers in federal court. Congress claimed that many states did not prosecute crimes against women as much as they did crimes against men. Arguing that violence against women affected commerce (such as workdays lost due to the violence), Congress used its commerce clause power to justify the law. At the time of its enactment, domestic abuse against women was estimated to cost between $5 and $10 billion a year.[44] But, once again, a 5-to-4 majority of the Supreme Court concluded that in so doing Congress had exceeded its commerce clause power and invaded the police powers of the states.

FEDERALISM IN THE TWENTY-FIRST CENTURY

Today, several hot-button issues relate to federalism. Despite its rulings in *Lopez* and *Morrison,* the Supreme Court ruled 6-to-3 in 2005 that the commerce clause gives Congress the power to pass the Controlled Substances Act which, among other things, prohibits the possession of home-grown marijuana for personal medical use. The George W. Bush administration supported this outcome and enforced the Controlled Substances Act, but the Obama administration announced that it would not seek to arrest those who use and supply marijuana for medical purposes, as long as they do not violate state law.[45] A subsequent administration, however, could reverse course and enforce the act.

Same-sex marriage also raises issues of federalism. In February 2011, President Obama instructed the Justice Department to stop enforcing the 1996 Defense of Marriage Act, which he believed to be unconstitutional. Although several states had legalized same-sex marriage, the Defense of Marriage Act meant that the federal government did not have to recognize those marriages.[46] Similarly, there are lingering questions about whether states that ban same-sex marriage could be forced to recognize a same-sex marriage from another state based on the full faith and credit clause of the Constitution. Public opinion increasingly supports same-sex marriage (see Figure 3.4).

Even health care reform raised issues of federalism. Congress's commerce clause power led to cases challenging the Patient Protection and Affordable Care Act of 2010—a major part of the health care reform package passed by Congress under President Barack Obama. A key provision of the act requires individuals, with a few exceptions, to purchase health insurance by 2014 or pay a tax penalty. This requirement is known as the "individual mandate."

Congress claimed it had the authority to enact the individual mandate under its commerce clause power because individuals who choose not to buy health insurance will affect the health care market, which is a form of commerce. Others, however, argued that in order for Congress to use its commerce clause power, there must be "economic activity" to regulate, and this requires voluntary action on the part of those being regulated. For example, those who grew medical marijuana voluntarily did so. It was that voluntary act that Congress could regulate. In comparison, the individual mandate compels an unwilling person to perform an involuntary act. The Supreme Court concluded that Congress could not use the commerce clause to impose the individual mandate, but upheld the mandate nonetheless as a valid exercise of Congress's power to tax.[47]

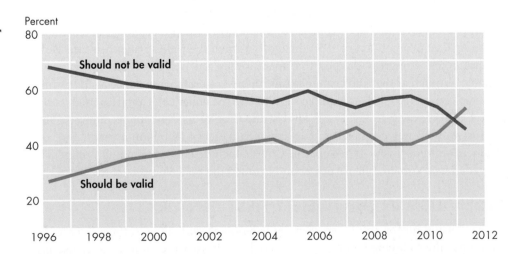

FIGURE 3.4

★ PUBLIC OPINION ON SAME-SEX MARRIAGE

How has public opinion about same-sex marriage changed since DOMA was passed?

Source: Gallup Poll, May 20, 2011.

Why Are We
THE WAY WE ARE ?

By now, we hope that you understand how significantly our system of federalism shapes the way we are. Before reading this chapter, for example, you may have assumed that Congress can legislate in pretty much any area it wants to. And yet, as we have seen, interpretations of federalism have profoundly influenced Congress's ability to pass laws in areas as wide-ranging as Social Security, gun control, minimum wages, highway speed limits, education policy, farm subsidies, violence against women, and discrimination in public accommodations such as restaurants and hotels.

THE FRAMERS' BELIEF IN LIMITED GOVERNMENT

Why we are the way we are is directly tied to the Framers' decision to abandon the confederal system used under the Articles of Confederation and to create instead a federal system of government when writing the Constitution. Their choice of a federal rather than a unitary system was partly a pragmatic (and innovative) compromise to win support for ratification of the Constitution, but it also appealed to their belief in limited government. This compromise led to a complicated system of power-sharing between the national government and the states. The resulting system has both strengths and weaknesses.

On the positive side, federalism—along with separation of powers and our system of checks of balances—helps to prevent concentrations of power in any one part of government. It also gives a degree of autonomy to individual states to pass laws that reflect local values, and allows individual states to experiment with different solutions to policy problems that fall within their purview. Experimenting with various approaches to education, such as charter schools, exemplifies the positive side of state autonomy. On the negative side, state autonomy can make policy implementation more difficult, resulting in inaction and/or unequal standards throughout the country.

For example, in 2010, the Texas State Board of Education revised the state's K-12 social studies and history curriculum, generating nationwide debate. Among other things, the new curriculum—passed by a 9-5 vote along party lines—required textbooks used in Texas schools to question the rationale for the separation of church and state, to examine the impact of the United Nations on U.S. sovereignty, and to stress the superiority of the American free market system as compared with other economic systems around the world.[48] Additionally, Kansas made it a requirement to challenge Darwin's theory of evolution in the classroom.[49] This and the Texas school board ruling are the direct result of our system of federalism.

A basic question—*should different states be able to set different standards for what is taught in their public schools?*—lies at the heart of debates surrounding No Child Left Behind. Again, the way these debates are resolved will affect your life. For example, the educational standards established by the state you came from likely affected your ability to pursue higher education at an institution of your choice. Do you think you would have been better or worse off without No Child Left Behind? And should No Child Left Behind be modified so that all states must administer the same test with the same standards? Should the federal government be given even greater power to ensure equality of education for all groups of students by establishing national curricular standards? Should our educational system follow the French model of centralization? Or did No Child Left Behind give the national government too much power?

Such questions are not limited to education. For example, several states have passed harsh anti-immigration laws because they believed that the national government was not doing enough to secure the nation's borders and stem the tide of illegal immigration (see Chapter 5). Is this permissible? Can different states have different standards on this issue? The Obama administration challenged such laws on the grounds that they exceeded the authority of the states; regulating immigration, it argued, is a power that belongs to the national government. The Supreme Court's answer to this question will not only influence the balance of power between the national government and the states, but will affect the lives of many people—perhaps even you.

SUPREME COURT INTERPRETATIONS OF CONSTITUTIONAL LANGUAGE

Understanding that we have a federal system is only the starting point for understanding why we are the way we are. Ambiguity in the language of the Constitution has led to significant, ongoing debates about precisely where to draw the line between the powers of the national government and the powers of the states.

At any given time in our history, the Supreme Court has been instrumental in establishing that line. Where the Court has chosen to draw it has largely been a reflection of whether a majority of justices embrace dual federalism or cooperative federalism. Quite simply, the scope of Congress's power (and conversely the power of the states) has ebbed and flowed depending upon which of these two positions prevailed at any particular point in time. As you know by now, part of what makes federalism so complicated is this fluctuation. Quite simply, federalism has meant different things at different times. That is why understanding the differences between dual federalism and cooperative federalism is so essential to understanding why we are the way we are.

We are the way we are today because of the 1937 "switch in time" that shifted the Court in a decidedly cooperative federalist direction. Although cooperative federalism has been tempered somewhat since the 1990s, the scope of national power is still largely a result of cooperative federalist rulings by the Marshall Court in the early 1800s that were expanded upon in the years since 1937.

. . . AND WHY DOES IT Matter?

Most people do not initially think that federalism will be the most engaging topic they will cover when studying American government. They may even think of it as boring, but first impressions can be deceiving. After all, federalism was one of the most contentious issues, if not *the* most contentious issue, from the Constitutional Convention through most of the 1800s. Debates about national supremacy versus states' rights permeated the Constitutional Convention, influenced the development of our political parties, led to the Civil War, and shaped subsequent civil rights policies.

Those debates have never gone away. They were at the forefront of whether Congress, during the Progressive Era of the 1890s to the 1920s, could pass legislation protecting employees in the workplace through laws regulating things like minimum wages, child labor, and maximum hours. Embracing dual federalism, the Supreme Court mostly said "no."

As the United States struggled to emerge from the depths of the Great Depression in the 1930s, the debate turned to whether the New Deal legislation implemented by President Franklin Roosevelt and his fellow Democrats in Congress was constitutional. Until 1936, the answer was again mostly "no." That changed with the "switch in time" in 1937. That switch not only meant that New Deal legislation designed to regulate the economy was upheld, but that workplace regulations that had been routinely struck down for decades were now deemed constitutional.

Today, many of the most controversial aspects of federalism deal with social issues such as same-sex marriage, gun control, health care reform, education, and the use of medical marijuana. Far from being uninteresting, we believe that federalism—throughout our history—has involved some of the most fascinating and relevant issues one can imagine. Certainly these policies relate to you on a daily basis: what you studied in high school, who you can marry, at what age you can drink alcohol, how fast you can drive, whether or not there is a minimum wage, and whether you can be discriminated against in a hotel because of your race, to name just a few. Just as profoundly, federalism will shape your future. After all, things like Social Security and Medicare would not have been possible without the "switch in time." Think about that the next time someone says that federalism is boring or unimportant. In fact, few aspects of our governmental system have a greater impact on your daily life.

critical thinking questions

1. As you follow current events, ask yourself: How do perspectives on federalism influence what policies can be implemented concerning those issues?

2. One's decision about whether to support states' rights or national supremacy sometimes varies according to the policy issue in question. For example, some conservatives who otherwise support states' rights balk at the idea of allowing states to recognize same-sex marriage or approve the use of medical marijuana. Can such discrepancies be reconciled?

3. Think back to the opening vignette of this chapter. Should the national government take more control of educational policy in this country? Why or why not?

4. Did the Framers make the right choice when they created a federal system in this country? Did the Supreme Court make the right choice with its "switch in time" in 1937?

key terms

CIVIL LIBERTIES

- Explain the purpose of the Bill of Rights and the process by which its provisions came to be "incorporated."
- Define prior restraint and examine the various free speech tests devised by the Supreme Court to distinguish between actions that are constitutionally protected and those that are not.
- Explore the debate over where to draw the line between constitutionally protected free exercise of religion and unprotected conduct.
- Discuss the arguments for and against the constitutional right of privacy, and recognize the types of issues to which it applies.
- Understand the concept of procedural due process and other rights of criminal defendants, and examine how judicial interpretation of constitutional language can affect those rights.

PERSPECTIVE
How Much Government Control of the Internet Is Too Much?

The Internet has transformed the way that people communicate. It has also vastly increased access to information. The governments of some countries, accustomed to censorship, regard the Internet as a threat and have tried to control their citizens' access to it. China, for example, has developed one of the most sophisticated Internet filtering systems in the world. E-mail, websites, blogs, chat rooms, and bulletin boards are all filtered for content by the government. Both Google and Yahoo! controversially agreed to alter their search engines in China in order to comply with government censorship, and the Chinese government blocked Facebook, Twitter, and YouTube in 2009 and cracked down on microblogs in 2011.[1]

At the time of the crackdown, China had a population of 1.3 billion, with roughly 485 million Internet users. The government requires Internet Service Providers (ISPs) to track precisely who is online and what sites users visit, and the government holds ISPs legally accountable if their users violate laws regulating Internet use. Likewise, the government requires Internet Content Providers (ICPs) to verify the identity of those logging onto their sites and to track their online activity. Failure to do so can lead to revocation of their business license and even arrest.

After signing up for Internet service, Chinese citizens are required to register with the local police within 30 days. Those using Internet cafés must present an identification card, which the café keeps on file for 60 days along with a detailed log of each patron's online activity. The café must cut off access to any patron who tries to access a forbidden website and must file a report with the government about such attempts. Forbidden websites have included Voice of America, foreign news outlets such as CNN and BBC News, and any site that deals with controversial topics ranging from Tibetan independence to democracy. Among the keywords that trigger filtering systems and block Internet access are "revolution," "equality," "freedom," "justice," "Taiwan," "Tibet," "democracy," "dissident," "STD," and "human rights."[2]

Many Westerners, including civil rights organizations, have criticized China's censorship.[3] But Chinese leaders have fought back, arguing that such criticism smacks of a double standard. Thus, Liu Zhengrong, deputy chief of the Internet Affairs Bureau in China, has pointed out that it is common practice around the world to remove "illegal and harmful" information from the Internet and claimed that China's Internet regulations were no different.[4]

U.S. citizens do not have to register with the police when they sign up for Internet service, of course. Nor does the U.S. government filter content the way the Chinese government does. There are, in short, huge differences between the United States and China when it comes to freedom of speech on the Internet. And yet, U.S. citizens do encounter some limits in their use of the Internet. For example, posting or downloading child pornography is a crime. And as part of the Bush administration's post–9/11 "War on Terror," the U.S. National Security Agency monitored, without court order, e-mails, text messages, and phone conversations involving communication with anyone believed to be outside the United States. The Obama administration continued such surveillance. With a court order, all Internet activity can be monitored by the government.

Perhaps as a result, the U.S.–based Electronic Privacy Information Center and the British-based organization Privacy International ranked the United States as having among the worst records in the world for protecting its citizens' privacy, along with China and Russia. The two organizations took several factors into account in arriving at this measure, including the level of government surveillance of each country's citizens. How do the conclusions of this report square with the presumption many Americans have that the protection of civil liberties is a fundamental part of their system of government? The protection of civil liberties is supposed to be one of the hallmarks of the U.S. system of government. Yet it is the role of the U.S. Supreme Court to interpret our liberties, and its changing interpretations of constitutional language have led to the expansion and contraction of specific rights over time. The actual language of the First Amendment has not changed, but as the membership of the Supreme Court shifts, and as American values and societal norms evolve over time, the justices apply different standards to interpret the provisions within the Bill of Rights.

Should federal agents be allowed to monitor how you use the Internet? How the justices and the American people answer this question might well depend on whether we perceive a substantial threat to national security. The nation has long struggled with the issue of when and how to balance liberty and authority. This is especially relevant when confronting how to combat the threat of terrorism. Are civil liberties inviolable, or can they be limited to protect national security? Is it possible, as Supreme Court Justice Robert Jackson once suggested, that too rigid an application of individual liberties, one not tempered by "a little practical wisdom," could—at least in extreme instances—"convert the constitutional Bill of Rights into a suicide pact"?[5] Reasonable people offer convincing arguments on both sides of this issue.

IN THIS CHAPTER, we analyze the evolving interpretation of the Bill of Rights. First, we examine how the reach of the Bill of Rights was expanded to limit state as well as federal action. We then explore the First Amendment rights: the freedoms of speech, press, assembly, and religion. Although the right of privacy is not mentioned explicitly in the Constitution, it now plays an important role in our political system. We evaluate its emergence and application to the right to choose abortion, the rights of homosexuals, and the right to die. Finally, we look at the rights of criminal defendants and the death penalty, returning eventually to the question of how to strike a balance between national security and civil liberties. As you read this chapter, keep in mind our two core questions:

WHY ARE WE THE WAY WE ARE?
WHY DOES IT MATTER TO YOU?

In particular, how has the U.S. system's fundamental commitment to the rule of law affected how the Supreme Court interprets those liberties?

THE BILL OF RIGHTS

Civil liberties consist of the basic rights and freedoms that citizens enjoy without governmental interference. These include not only the freedoms of speech, press, assembly, and religion, but also the guarantee that government will not take one's life, liberty, or property without due process of law. These liberties are spelled out in the first 10 amendments to the United States Constitution, collectively known as the **Bill of Rights.** In contrast with civil liberties, *civil rights* (discussed in Chapter 5) focus not on the freedoms from government interference found in the Bill of Rights, but rather on the guarantee of equal treatment by the government found in the equal protection clause of the Fourteenth Amendment. In other words, "civil rights" refers to *freedom from governmental discrimination* (unequal treatment) based on some individual characteristic such as race, gender, or disability. Thus, the right to peaceably assemble is a civil liberty guaranteed by the First Amendment, but if the government were to arbitrarily discriminate in the enforcement of that right—by determining that people with green eyes can peaceably assemble but that people with blue eyes cannot—we would call that discriminatory treatment a violation of civil rights.

The Bill of Rights is such a central part of the Constitution that it is hard to imagine the document without it. And yet, in the waning hours of the Constitutional Convention of 1787, the members of the convention—voting as state delegations—unanimously rejected a proposal for a Bill of Rights that was introduced by George Mason of Virginia, an ardent defender of individual rights who had drafted the famous Virginia Declaration of Rights in 1776.[6]

Many of the delegates, such as Alexander Hamilton, felt that a Bill of Rights was unnecessary. Seven of the states already had a bill of rights in their own state constitution.[7] Hamilton also believed that the Constitution limited the powers of the national government to those enumerated. Therefore, he believed that the national government would be powerless to abridge rights. As he put it in *Federalist 84*, "Why declare that

The Bill of Rights—the first ten amendments to the U.S. Constitution—spell out the civil liberties that citizens enjoy. Why were these guarantees omitted from the original Constitution? What led to their addition as amendments? Once ratified, the provisions of the Bill of Rights were understood to limit only the actions of the federal government, not the actions of states. Applying specific provisions to the states came only through the process of "incorporation." What constitutional language does incorporation rely on? What are the consequences of incorporation for states' rights?

civil liberties
The basic freedoms that citizens enjoy from governmental interference, such as the freedoms of speech, press, assembly, and religion, and the guarantees of due process and other specific protections accorded to criminal defendants.

Bill of Rights
The first 10 amendments of the U.S. Constitution, which form the basis of civil liberties.

things shall not be done which there is no power to do?"[8] Moreover, enumerating specific rights could easily lead to the omission of others. Would the implication be that the national government was free to infringe upon rights that were not enumerated? Finally, confronting the issue of a Bill of Rights at this late stage might lead to another long round of debate and undermine fragile compromises that were already in place.

Mason disagreed, believing that the Constitution gave too much power to the national government. The lack of a Bill of Rights intensified the fear that the national government might subvert states' rights as well as those of individuals. But Mason had not been able to convince delegates to the Constitutional Convention to accept his position. His personality did not help. He was an impatient man who disliked compromise. His verbal jousting tended to alienate opponents.[9] In the end, a frustrated Mason famously refused to sign the Constitution, saying that he would sooner chop off his right hand than do so.[10] He then became a leading critic of the Constitution during the ratification debate.

James Madison, another delegate from Virginia, had opposed a Bill of Rights—at least initially. Due in part to the persuasive efforts of Thomas Jefferson, however, Madison later became one of its strongest proponents.[11] His conversion was partly pragmatic. It came as he was running for Congress from a district in Virginia that strongly favored a Bill of Rights. But it also was a matter of timing and strategy. Before the ratification of the Constitution, its opponents were calling for a second Constitutional Convention to modify the proposed document. Madison knew that such a convention could lead to a radical transformation of the Constitution and undermine the goals of the Federalists. Therefore, the initial goal was to get the document ratified unscathed.

Once the Constitution was ratified, however, the dangers posed by amendments became less serious. At that point, a Bill of Rights could be used to defuse lingering opposition to the Constitution. As Madison put it in January 1789, "Circumstances are now changed: The Constitution is established . . . and amendments, if pursued with a proper moderation and in a proper mode, will not only be safe, but may serve the double purpose of satisfying the minds of well meaning opponents, and of providing additional safeguards in favour of liberty."[12]

Thus, acting on a proposal by Madison, the First Congress sent 12 amendments to the states for ratification. The first two, dealing with the size of the House of Representatives and the compensation of senators and representatives, were not ratified. As a result, the proposed Third Amendment, dealing with the freedoms of religion, speech, and the press, became the First when the amendments that make up the Bill of Rights were ratified in 1791.[13]

THE BILL OF RIGHTS AND THE STATES: THE ORIGINAL UNDERSTANDING

Just as it is hard to imagine our Constitution without a Bill of Rights, so it is hard to imagine our Bill of Rights not protecting individuals from state laws that infringe upon their liberties. And yet the Bill of Rights was originally thought to limit only the power of the *national* government—not the power of the states. States' rights advocates, in particular, had pushed for a Bill of Rights to prevent the new national government from encroaching not only on individual rights but also on the power of the states.

It is telling that James Madison's proposal that the Bill of Rights include an amendment that said "no *state* shall violate the equal rights of conscience, or the freedom of the press, or the trial by jury in criminal cases" was rejected.[14] Instead, the First Amendment clearly states, "*Congress* shall make no law. . . ." And even though the remaining amendments seemed more general (the Sixth, for example, says: "In *all* criminal prosecutions, the accused shall enjoy the right to a speedy and public trial, by an impartial jury. . . ."), the common understanding was that these guarantees applied only to actions by the *federal* government, such as federal criminal prosecutions.[15] Thus, after the ratification of language in the First Amendment that says "Congress shall make no law respecting an establishment of religion. . . .," seven states (Connecticut, Georgia, Maryland, Massachusetts, New Hampshire, South Carolina, and Vermont) continued to maintain some form of religious establishment.

In the 1833 case, *Barron v. Baltimore,* the U.S. Supreme Court reaffirmed the view that nothing in the Bill of Rights limited state action. Chief Justice John Marshall wrote the opinion in *Barron.* Given what we know about Marshall, his ruling might seem surprising. He was, after all, an ardent Federalist who did much in other cases to strengthen the national government at the expense of the states. Why would he write an opinion in this case that vindicated states' rights? It may simply be that the answer was so obvious and the intent of the Framers so clear that the outcome was preordained. As Marshall himself put it, the legal question presented was "of great importance, but not of much difficulty."[16] But there was another issue—one not directly raised in the case—that may have influenced the Court: slavery.

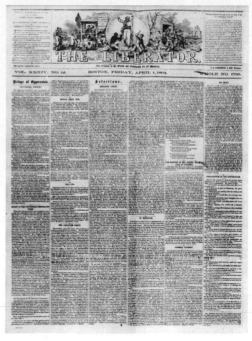

★ *The Liberator* was a newspaper that advocated the abolition of slavery.

The reality of slavery is impossible to reconcile with the concept of liberty espoused by the Framers. And yet many Framers, including James Madison and Thomas Jefferson, owned slaves. As discussed in Chapter 5, the Constitution did not use the word *slavery,* but it nonetheless endorsed it in several ways. Madison himself had reassured the Virginia ratifying convention that nothing in the proposed Constitution would interfere with slavery in the states.[17] Even George Mason, who went on to advocate the abolition of slavery and had been one of the earliest champions of a Bill of Rights, had owned slaves.

By the time the Supreme Court decided *Barron v. Baltimore,* slavery had become a hot-button issue. Abolitionists were mobilizing. *The Liberator,* an important antislavery newspaper, had begun publishing in 1831. Fearful that the rising tide of abolitionist literature might lead to slave rebellion, southern states began around 1830 to adopt laws that restricted freedom of speech and of the press.[18] Discrimination against blacks had been taken for granted. Now it was spreading to whites who spoke out on their behalf. Thus, *Barron* arguably "avoided troubling questions" by promoting "the stability of the Union at the expense of liberty."[19]

In the coming years, state restrictions on civil liberties intensified. For example, Virginia made it a felony for abolitionists to enter the state and speak in favor of abolishing slavery, or for anyone to circulate books that denied the right to own slaves. By 1859, Virginia even banned the *New York Tribune.* Missouri not only imposed severe penalties for expressing anti-slavery views, but required that state officeholders take a test oath to assure that they supported slavery. In North Carolina, a man was convicted and

★ In 2011, the Supreme Court struck down a California law outlawing the sale of violent video games to children under the age of 18, calling it an unconstitutional violation of free speech rights. Prior to incorporation, the First Amendment would not have applied to the state of California.

incorporation
The process by the which the Supreme Court has made specific provisions of the Bill of Rights applicable to state and local governments as well as the federal government.

sentenced to a year in prison for distributing to fellow whites an anti-slavery book that Republicans were using as a campaign document in 1858. Mob violence against abolitionists was also on the rise.[20] And through it all, the Bill of Rights of the United States Constitution offered no protection.

THE INCORPORATION OF THE BILL OF RIGHTS

In order for the specific provisions of the Bill of Rights to limit state action, they needed to be *incorporated*. **Incorporation** simply means applying the Bill of Rights to the states. If you say that the First Amendment guarantee of free speech has been incorporated, you mean that the free speech clause not only limits actions by the federal government (Congress shall make no law . . .), but it has also come to limit state action (so that no state government shall make any such law either).

Some people have called for "total" incorporation: making every specific provision of the Bill of Rights applicable to the states—nothing more, nothing less. Others have called for "selective" incorporation: making only the most essential provisions applicable to the states. Still others have argued that there may be fundamental rights that are not specifically enumerated in the Constitution but that are so important that the Supreme Court should recognize them and use them to limit the actions of both the federal government and the states. When the Court discovers one of these unenumerated rights (such as privacy) and applies it to the states, the result is called incorporation "plus." This could be either total incorporation plus (applying all the specifically enumerated provisions of the Bill of Rights to the states plus other rights deemed fundamental by the Court) or selective incorporation plus (applying only the most fundamental provisions of the Bill of Rights to the states plus other rights deemed fundamental by the Court).

But if the Bill of Rights was originally meant to limit only the actions of the national government, what justifies incorporation? Two clauses in the Fourteenth Amendment (ratified in 1868) provided opportunities for incorporation: the privileges or immunities clause and the due process clause. Using either of these clauses to apply the Bill of Rights to the states has proven to be controversial. Some argue strongly that these clauses were meant to incorporate the Bill of Rights and should be used to do so.[21] Others vehemently reject that contention.[22] This is yet another example of how reasonable people can disagree fundamentally over the meaning of the Constitution.

The privileges or immunities clause of the Fourteenth Amendment says: "No state shall make or enforce any law which shall abridge the privileges or immunities of citizens of the United States. . . ." Some, such as Rep. John Bingham (R-Ohio) who drafted this clause, used the words "privileges" and "immunities" as shorthand for the fundamental rights of citizens of the United States that states could not abridge: the Bill of Rights. After all, the words "rights," "liberties," "privileges," and "immunities" were all used pretty much interchangeably at that time.[23] The Supreme Court, however, rejected that interpretation in the so-called *Slaughterhouse Cases* of 1873 and embraced a cramped interpretation of privileges and immunities that basically reduced it to protecting a narrow range of rights of U.S. citizens, such as the ability to travel through states and purchase property.[24] As a result, the ability to use the clause to incorporate the Bill of Rights seemed to evaporate.

There the matter stood until the twentieth century, when a new set of Supreme Court justices turned to the Fourteenth Amendment's due process clause to accomplish what the privileges or immunities clause had not. Even though the due process clause is not as clear-cut a means of incorporating the Bill of Rights as was the privileges or immunities clause, eventually the Supreme Court used it to achieve incorporation.

The due process clause of the Fourteenth Amendment says, "No state shall . . . deprive any person of life, liberty, or property without due process of law." This **due process clause** (like the other due process clause in the Fifth Amendment limiting federal action) was meant to guarantee fairness. It does not prevent government from depriving someone of life, liberty, or property, but it does require that the government employ fair procedures before doing so. This notion of applying fair procedures is known as "procedural due process."

How, then, could the due process clause be used to incorporate provisions of the Bill of Rights? One way is to argue that states violate due process if they do not follow certain procedural guarantees in the Bill of Rights such as the protection against double jeopardy But it can also be argued that if the actual content or *substance* of a particular state law violates a basic right, such as the First Amendment right of free speech, then the law itself constitutes a violation of due process because it is fundamentally unfair. This latter approach is known as **substantive due process.**

Over time, the Supreme Court used the due process clause to incorporate most— but *not all*—of the provisions of the Bill of Rights through a long process of selective incorporation, and has done so one clause at a time. (See Table 4.1.) Justice Benjamin Cardozo's majority opinion in *Palko v. Connecticut* (1937) offered a justification for selective incorporation: Those rights that are "implicit in the concept of ordered liberty" should be incorporated, but other provisions of the Bill of Rights should not be.[25] In other words, some rights are more important than others. But deciding which provisions of the Bill of Rights to incorporate can be subjective. Justice Hugo Black tried to minimize that subjectivity by suggesting that *every* provision of the Bill of Rights be applied to the states through the process of total incorporation. To do otherwise, he argued, allowed Supreme Court justices to substitute "their own concepts of decency and fundamental justice for the language of the Bill of Rights."[26] Black's argument did not prevail. Thus, the Third and Seventh Amendments have not been incorporated, nor have portions of the Fifth and Eighth Amendments (see Table 4.2). But since the unenumerated right of privacy has been incorporated, it looks like the concept of selective incorporation *plus* ended up winning the incorporation battle.

The most recently incorporated provision of the Bill of Rights is the Second Amendment right to "keep and bear arms." This came in a 5-4 ruling in *McDonald v. Chicago* (2010).[27] Prior to that, the Supreme Court had long held that the right to keep and bear arms was limited by the introductory clause of the Second Amendment, which indicated that the right was "necessary to the security of a free State" and related to a "well regulated Militia." Thus, in rulings dating back to 1876, the Supreme Court held that the Second Amendment only limited the national government, not states, and that the limit on the national government only prevented it from abolishing state militias.[28] In other words, the amendment did not create an individual right of gun ownership.

By the late twentieth century, however, federal gun control legislation had become a controversial political issue. Polls showed that a solid majority believed that the Second Amendment protected private gun ownership (see Figure 4.1), and the National Rifle Association lobbied vigorously against gun control legislation, arguing that it violated the Second Amendment. Then, in 2008, the Supreme Court agreed, striking down a

due process clauses
Clauses in the Fifth and Fourteenth Amendments that prevent the federal government (in the case of the Fifth) and states (in the case of the Fourteenth) from depriving people of life, liberty, or property without fair proceedings.

substantive due process
A judicially created concept whereby the due process clauses of the Fifth and Fourteenth Amendments can be used to strike down laws that are deemed to be arbitrary or unfair.

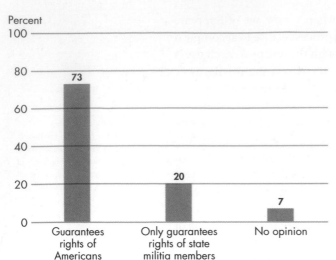

Percent

Source: *USA Today*/Gallup, Feb. 8–10, 2008.

FIGURE 4.1

★ GALLUP POLL ON THE RIGHT TO BEAR ARMS

Survey respondents were asked in 2008 whether they believe the Second Amendment guarantees the rights of individual Americans to own guns, or whether they believe it only guarantees members of state militias such as National Guard units the right to own guns. How did public opinion square with the Supreme Court's interpretation of the Second Amendment prior to 2008? Did the Court do the right thing when it incorporated the Second Amendment?

District of Columbia law that banned the ownership of handguns and regulated other firearms in the District.[29] Having recognized for the first time that the right to keep and bear arms is an individual right, the next step was incorporation—which came in the *McDonald* case. Nonetheless, the Court pointed out that gun ownership is not an absolute right. Like speech, it can still be regulated under certain circumstances.

This discussion illustrates how, as new issues become salient over time, Americans may expect the Supreme Court to reevaluate the incorporation of specific rights (see Tables 4.1 and 4.2). Whether the Court chooses to do so depends largely on an interchange between evolving American values and societal norms, past precedents set by the Supreme Court, and individual judgment of the Supreme Court justices currently sitting on the bench.

TABLE 4.1
chronology of provisions incorporated

PROVISION	AMENDMENT	YEAR	CASE
"Public use" and "just compensation" conditions in the taking of private property by government	V	1896 and 1897	*Missouri Pacific Railway Co. v. Nebraska*, 164 U.S. 403; *Chicago, Burlington & Quincy Railway Co. v. Chicago*, 166 U.S. 226
Freedom of speech	I	1927	*Fiske v. Kansas*, 274 U.S. 380; *Gitlow v. New York*, 268 U.S. 652, 625 (1925) (dictum only); *Gilbert v. Minnesota*, 254 U.S. 325 (1920) (dictum only)
Freedom of the press	I	1931	*Near v. Minnesota*, 283 U.S. 697
Fair trial and right to counsel in capital cases	VI	1932	*Powell v. Alabama*, 287 U.S. 45
Freedom of religion	I	1934	*Hamilton v. Regents of University of California*, 293 U.S. 245 (dictum only)
Freedom of assembly and, by implication, freedom to petition for redress of grievances	I	1937	*De Jonge v. Oregon*, 299 U.S. 353
Free exercise of religious belief	I	1940	*Cantwell v. Connecticut*, 310 U.S. 296
Separation of church and state; right against the establishment of religion	I	1947	*Everson v. Board of Education*, 330 U.S. 1

Continued

PROVISION	AMENDMENT	YEAR	CASE
Right to public trial	VI	1948	*In re Oliver*, 333 U.S. 257
Right against unreasonable search and seizures	IV	1949	*Wolf v. Colorado*, 338 U.S. 25
Right to travel as an aspect of "liberty"	V	1958	*Kent v. Dulles*, 357 U.S. 116 (right to travel internationally); *Crandall v. Nevada*, 73 U.S. (6 Wall.) 745 (1867) (right to interstate travel)
Freedom of association	I	1958	*NAACP v. Alabama*, 357 U.S. 449
Exclusionary rule as concomitant of unreasonable search and seizures	IV	1961	*Mapp v. Ohio*, 367 U.S. 643
Right against cruel and unusual punishments	VIII	1962	*Robinson v. California*, 370 U.S. 660
Right to counsel in all felony cases	VI	1963	*Gideon v. Wainwright*, 372 U.S. 335
Right to vote	XIV	1964	*Reynolds v. Sims*, 377 U.S. 533
Right against self-incrimination	V	1964	*Malloy v. Hogan*, 378 U.S. 1, 84 S.Ct. 1489; *Murphy v. Waterfront Commission*, 378 U.S. 52
Right to confront and cross-examine witnesses	VI	1965	*Pointer v. Texas*, 380 U.S. 400
Right of privacy	Implied by various	1965	*Griswold v. Connecticut*, 381 U.S. 479
Right to impartial jury	VI	1966	*Park v. Gladden*, 385 U.S. 363
Right to speedy trial	VI	1967	*Klopfer v. North Carolina*, 386 U.S. 213
Right to compulsory process for obtaining witnesses	VI	1967	*Washington v. Texas*, 388 U.S. 213
Right to jury trial in cases of serious crime	VI	1968	*Duncan v. Louisiana*, 391 U.S. 145
Right against double jeopardy	V	1969	*Benton v. Maryland*, 395 U.S. 784
Right to counsel in all criminal cases entailing a jail term	VI	1972	*Argersinger v. Hamlin*, 407 U.S. 25
Right to keep and bear arms	II	2010	*McDonald v. Chicago*, 561 U.S. 3025

OTHER INCORPORATED PROVISIONS		
Right of petition	I	Included by implication of other First Amendment incorporations
Right to be informed of the nature and cause of the accusation	VI	Included by implication of other Sixth Amendment incorporations

Source: Craig Ducat, *Constitutional Interpretation*, 9th ed. (Boston: Wadsworth, 2009).

TABLE 4.2
provisions of the first eight amendments not incorporated

AMENDMENT	PROVISION(S) NOT INCORPORATED
III	All
V	All
VII	Right to indictment by grand jury
VIII	Right against excessive bail; right against excessive fines

Source: Craig Ducat, *Constitutional Interpretation*, 9th ed. (Boston: Wadsworth, 2009).

THE FIRST AMENDMENT FREEDOMS OF SPEECH, PRESS, AND ASSEMBLY

★ **KEY** TO understanding

The freedoms of speech, press, and assembly are essential to the democratic process, but none were incorporated until the twentieth century. If these freedoms are not absolute, how and where should one draw the line between what is constitutionally protected and what is not? Answering that question has provoked debate. The Supreme Court has developed a series of (sometimes contradictory) tests designed to distinguish between actions that are constitutional and those that are not. Depending upon which test is used, First Amendment guarantees will be protected to varying degrees.

It is hard to imagine a democratic system working without the free exchange of ideas. The ability to report on the actions of government, to express support for or opposition to governmental policies, to engage in meaningful debate, and to be knowledgeable enough about current issues to cast an informed vote all presuppose freedom of speech and of the press. Americans rightly count these as some of their most precious freedoms. But how much freedom does the First Amendment really allow? How much *should* it?

The phrase "Congress shall make no law" sounds categorical, yet Congress has passed quite a few laws that restrict freedom of speech and of the press in one way or another, and the Court has upheld many of them. Indeed, the Supreme Court has consistently ruled that neither freedom of speech nor of the press is absolute.

FREEDOM OF THE PRESS AND PRIOR RESTRAINT

prior restraint
Censorship before publication (such as government prohibition against future publication).

In the common law tradition inherited from England, the principle of freedom of the press had a rather narrow meaning: no prior restraint on publication. A **prior restraint** means censorship before publication. Such censorship emerged very quickly after the invention of the printing press. England required prepublication licensing as early as 1534. To publish something, an author first had to submit the material to the government for approval. This meant that the government could squelch political criticism and control the content of what people read. Prior restraint provoked great opposition, and England abolished the practice in 1695. Thereafter, the principle of no prior restraint became a part of English common law.

The principle of no prior restraint may have been what the framers had in mind when they wrote the First Amendment, but it was not until 1931 that the Supreme Court, by a narrow 5-4 vote, held a prior restraint to be unconstitutional in *Near v. Minnesota.* In that case, Minnesota had imposed an injunction against a newspaper, *The Saturday Press,* on the grounds that it created a "public nuisance" because of its "malicious, scandalous, and defamatory" content.[30] There is no doubt that the newspaper was anti-Semitic, but the Court majority ruled that the injunction—which prohibited future publication—violated the First Amendment. Despite its ruling, the majority held that in "exceptional cases" the government could still prohibit publication in advance. For example, the Court suggested that the government could use prior restraint to prohibit a publication detailing troop movements in times of war. The Court also suggested that obscene material was subject to prior restraint. And, despite the general presumption against prior restraint, the majority still held that certain types of punishment *after* publication were constitutional.

Forty years later, the Nixon administration tried to use *Near v. Minnesota* to justify imposing a prior restraint on *The New York Times* to prevent it from publishing a series of articles based on classified government documents related to Vietnam known as the "Pentagon Papers." The government argued that publication of the documents would harm national security. However, the Supreme Court ruled against the government in *New York Times v. United States* (1971) in a splintered 6-3 vote.[31]

In addition to national security sometimes justifying prior restraint, some argue that the Sixth Amendment guarantee of a fair trial may sometimes justify prior restraint. "Gag orders" to prevent prejudicial publicity are commonplace in some countries. For example, the French Civil Code protects the presumption of innocence by restricting the media from depicting suspects in handcuffs or describing them as guilty prior to conviction.[32] There are no such constraints on the U.S. media, where courts protect even sensationalistic pre-trial coverage under the guise of freedom of the press.

WHAT DID THE FRAMERS MEAN BY "FREEDOM OF SPEECH"?

If the framers thought that "no prior restraint" was the principle behind freedom of the press, what principle did they have in mind for freedom of speech? It simply is not clear. When the First Amendment was ratified, Pennsylvania was the only state whose constitution specifically protected speech, but it did so by closely linking it to freedom of the press (other states, such as Massachusetts, protected only freedom of the press).[33]

The free speech clause of the First Amendment raises many questions. Does it guarantee more than prohibition against prior restraint? Is it limited to political speech? Did it simply mean that only states could regulate speech? The Supreme Court has consistently rejected the notion that freedom of speech is absolute. Still, the question remains: where should courts draw the line? Is obscenity constitutionally protected? False advertising? Threats to overthrow the government? For that matter, is "speech" limited to verbal utterances and written words? Or are symbolic expression and other forms of nonverbal communication also protected? In short, even though the First Amendment language dealing with freedom of speech and of the press may, at first glance, seem clear-cut, it is anything but.

THE ALIEN AND SEDITION ACTS OF 1798

James Madison expressed the fear that a Bill of Rights might serve merely as a "parchment barrier" against "overbearing majorities." There was justification for that fear. As the Pulitzer-Prize-winning historian Leonard Levy has noted, "any member of the Constitutional Convention could have cited examples of gross abridgments of civil liberties in states that had bills of rights."[34]

Arguably, this is what happened when Congress enacted the Alien and Sedition Acts just seven years after ratification of the Bill of Rights. These four separate laws were passed when the United States was under threat of war with France. One of them, the Sedition Act, allowed for the prosecution of anyone who "shall write, print, utter or publish" any "scandalous and malicious" statement against the government, or either house of Congress, or the president. Since the Federalist Party controlled both the White House and Congress, this act effectively meant that critics of the Federalists—notably opposition newspaper editors representing the views of the Democratic-Republican

★ To protect the presumption of innocence, French law prohibits the media from publishing images of defendants in handcuffs. Compare that with the United States. Here the publication of such images is permitted. For example, the *New York Post* published a front-page photo of Scott Peterson in handcuffs with the blaring headline "Monster in Chains" weeks before his trial for murdering his wife. Do such depictions interfere with the right to a fair trial? Or is freedom of the press more important?

Party—were subject to imprisonment for up to two years and a $2,000 fine if convicted.[35] Ten people, including a member of the U.S. House of Representatives, were convicted under the act before it expired in 1801.[36] The Supreme Court never ruled on the constitutionality of these laws, but President Thomas Jefferson later pardoned all of those who had been convicted. In fact, the Supreme Court did not rule on a free speech case until 1919. That case involved convictions under the Espionage Act of 1917 as amended by the Sedition Act of 1918.

THE SUPREME COURT CONFRONTS RESTRICTIONS ON SPEECH

One month after the United States entered World War I, Congress passed the Espionage Act of 1917. The Espionage Act made it illegal to "attempt to cause insubordination, disloyalty, mutiny, or refusal of duty in the military or naval forces."[37] A year later, Congress passed the Sedition Act of 1918 as an amendment to the Espionage Act. It kept the language quoted above but inserted "or incite or attempt to incite" after "willfully cause or attempt to cause." It also made it a crime to "willfully utter, print, write, or publish any disloyal, profane, scurrilous, or abusive language" about the government or Constitution of the United States or its military or naval forces or the flag of the United States or the uniform of the Army or Navy, or to "willfully advocate, teach, defend, or suggest the doing of any of the acts or things in this section enumerated" (such as obstructing the recruitment or enlistment of military personnel). Offenders were subject to a fine of up to $10,000, imprisonment for up to 20 years, or both.

These laws led to the arrest of more than 6,000 people. Among those convicted were members of the Socialist Party of America, whose leader, Eugene V. Debs, ran for president in each election from 1900 through 1912, winning over 900,000 votes—roughly 6 percent of the popular vote—in 1912. More than 70 socialists had been elected to the office of mayor in cities around the country, and two socialists had been elected to Congress.

The Socialist Party opposed U.S. entry into World War I. It believed that war in general amounted to government coercion of the working class by capitalist elites. As part of that opposition, Charles Schenck and other Socialist Party members prepared and mailed a leaflet to some 15,000 young men who had been drafted.[38] The leaflet did not directly encourage draft resistance, but it did argue that the draft violated the Thirteenth Amendment prohibition on "involuntary servitude" and it urged recipients to petition the government for repeal of the draft. Schenck was arrested and charged with violating the Espionage Act. Convicted and sentenced to 15 years in prison for distributing the leaflets, Schenck appealed to the United States Supreme Court, arguing that his First Amendment right to free speech had been violated. He lost: An unanimous Supreme Court upheld his conviction in *Schenck v. United States*.[39]

Justice Oliver Wendell Holmes wrote the decision for the Court. In it, he created the **clear and present danger test** to determine the limits of constitutionally protected speech. Over the years, that test has come to be associated with protecting free speech, but it was originally used to justify restricting speech. Holmes himself later came to be seen as a champion of free speech, but that stance is not so apparent in this initial case. The fact that the United States was at war influenced Holmes' decision. He admitted that "in many places and in ordinary times" the leaflet would have been constitutional. But, he added, "the character of every act depends upon the circumstances in which it

clear and present danger test
A free speech test that allows government to restrict only speech that poses a clear and present danger of substantive evil; over time it has become increasingly protective of speech.

is done." That reasoning led to one of the most famous lines in any Supreme Court decision: "The most stringent protection of free speech would not protect a man falsely shouting fire in a theatre and causing a panic." The question that the Court must answer is whether "the words are used in such circumstances and are of such a nature as to create a clear and present danger that they will bring about the substantive evils that Congress has a right to prevent."[40]

The unanimity of the Supreme Court began to fragment by the end of the year, although a 7-2 majority still upheld the convictions of Jacob Abrams and several other Russian immigrants in *Abrams v. United States*.[41] Once again the defendants— self-proclaimed anarchists and revolutionaries—were charged with violating the Espionage Act for distributing leaflets that called for workers to rise up against the "hypocritical," "cowardly," and "capitalistic" government of the United States by engaging in a general strike. Language in the leaflet specifically targeted munitions workers. Unlike the flyers at issue in *Schenck,* which were sent through the mail to young men who had been drafted, the flyers in this case were dumped out the windows of an apartment building in lower Manhattan. Although many factories in that area made clothes, shoes, buttons, and hats, none manufactured weapons of war. Abrams and his co-defendants were convicted and sentenced to 20 years in prison. The majority of the Court in *Abrams* used the clear and present danger test to uphold the convictions, but this time Holmes and Louis Brandeis dissented. Like the majority, Holmes and Brandeis used the clear and present danger test, but they reached the opposite conclusion.[42]

The split grew in the ensuing years, with Holmes and Brandeis remaining lonely dissenters. By 1925, in *Gitlow v. New York,* the majority no longer claimed to use the clear and present danger test. Instead, the justices in the majority used the so-called **bad tendency test** to argue that government cannot be expected to measure the danger of every utterance in a "jeweler's scale" to determine its threat. "A single revolutionary spark may kindle a fire that, smoldering for a time, may burst into a sweeping and destructive conflagration." Why wait for the clear and present danger of the roaring flame when the government could easily put out the spark? It should be able to "suppress the threatened danger in its incipiency."[43] In contrast, Holmes and Brandeis continued to embrace the clear and present danger test and made it more protective of speech. According to their new interpretation, only speech that posed a grave threat of "serious evil"—one in which the danger was not just possible but *imminent*—could be punished by the government.[44]

The degree to which the Supreme Court is willing to protect speech—or any other part of the Constitution—depends in part upon who is sitting on the Court. From the late 1930s through the 1950s, the membership of the Court was profoundly transformed. Until 1937, corporate lawyers appointed by Republican presidents dominated the Court. But President Franklin Roosevelt eventually had the opportunity to appoint a new majority. His imprint on the Court not only led to the rise of cooperative federalism (discussed in Chapter 3), but also helped to spur the rights revolution of the twentieth century.

The move to incorporate the Bill of Rights began in earnest during the 1930s. And, as new cases came before it, the Supreme Court began to protect free speech rights more vigorously. Nonetheless, it took time to overturn some of the old free speech precedents—especially when the speech in question advocated the violent overthrow of the government. The fear of communism in the 1940s and 1950s led to renewed restrictions on speech. For example, the Supreme Court upheld the convictions of

bad tendency test
The least protective free speech test, which allows government to restrict speech that merely poses a tendency or possibility to do harm (as opposed to a clear and present danger).

Eugene Dennis and other members of the Communist Party in 1951 even though some critics claimed that they were convicted for mere advocacy that posed no clear and present danger.[45]

Ironically, a Republican president, Dwight Eisenhower, helped to institutionalize the rights revolution by appointing Chief Justice Earl Warren and other liberals to the Supreme Court in the 1950s. Still, it was not until 1969 in *Brandenburg v. Ohio* that the Supreme Court finally overturned a precedent that still employed the old bad tendency test in cases advocating violence against the government. The Court now ruled that the government could only punish advocacy that incites or produces "imminent lawless action."[46]

Although the Court unanimously rejected the bad tendency test in *Brandenburg,* new fractures were already emerging. Both Hugo Black and William O. Douglas agreed with the rest of the Court that Brandenburg's conviction should be overturned, but they argued that the Court did not do *enough* to protect speech. Both believed that speech is absolutely protected by the Constitution—a view that the majority of the Supreme Court has never embraced. However, Justice Black believed that only *pure* speech was absolutely protected. He was among those who had read the free speech clause literally to protect just "speech"—not *conduct* that may accompany speech or *symbolic expression.* The fact that Black was unwilling to go as far as some of his non-absolutist colleagues in protecting these other forms of expression is a reminder of the difficulty of determining precisely what the First Amendment protects.

Symbolic Speech

symbolic speech
Communication that is neither spoken nor written but is nonetheless accorded free speech protection under the First Amendment.

The category of **symbolic speech** consists of forms of expression such as signs or symbols instead of pure speech. The Supreme Court first accorded First Amendment protection to symbolic speech in the 1931 case *Stromberg v. California.* In that case, the Court overturned the conviction of 19-year-old Yetta Stromberg for flying a red flag at a communist youth camp in California. In so doing, it struck down a California law that made it a felony to display a red flag "as a sign, symbol or emblem of opposition to organized government."[47]

Since the 1960s, the Supreme Court has applied First Amendment protection to a number of other forms of symbolic expression. For example, it upheld the right of high school students to wear black armbands to class as a form of protest against the Vietnam War in *Tinker v. Des Moines Independent Community School District* (1969).[48] The majority did not recognize an absolute right to wear the armbands, but it claimed that in this case there was no evidence that the armbands had disrupted classroom routine and therefore First Amendment rights should prevail.

The issue of student speech continues to be controversial. In 2002, high school students in Juneau, Alaska, were allowed to miss their regularly scheduled classes in order to watch the Olympic torch pass by at a school-sponsored event across the street. One of the students displayed a banner at the event that read "Bong Hits 4 Jesus." The school principal seized the banner (school policy prohibited the display of messages promoting drug use at school events) and suspended the student. Were the student's First Amendment rights violated? A 6-3 majority of the Supreme Court said "no" in *Morse v. Frederick* (2007).[49] Only one justice in the majority (Clarence Thomas) argued that students have *no* free speech rights and that *Tinker* should be overturned. The rest of the majority simply argued that the school's interest in deterring drug use by students justified its action in this case.

Symbolic speech cases often raise issues of "conduct," which consists of actions rather than words. Conduct (such as trespassing, disturbing the peace, or destroying property) may accompany speech and can be punished by the government. However, speech and conduct can be intertwined so closely that it may be difficult to determine where one ends and the other begins. For example, Justice Black dissented in the *Tinker* case, arguing that students wearing armbands amounted to constitutionally unprotected conduct rather than constitutionally protected speech. His concern focused on the potential disruption to the learning environment.

Another symbolic speech case that raised the issue of conduct is *Texas v. Johnson* (1989), which involved burning the American flag. The Supreme Court voted 5-4 to overturn the conviction of Gregory Johnson for burning an American flag to protest the policies of President Ronald Reagan.[50] Johnson burned the flag outside the 1984 Republican National Convention in Dallas, Texas. President George H.W. Bush responded to the Court's controversial ruling by calling (unsuccessfully) for a constitutional amendment to protect the flag. In *Texas v. Johnson,* the majority emphasized that the Supreme Court had consistently rejected the idea that an "apparently limitless variety of conduct can be labeled 'speech' whenever the person engaging in the conduct intends thereby to express an idea," but added that there are some types of conduct—such as the burning of the American flag in that case—that are "sufficiently imbued with elements of communication" to fall within the scope of First Amendment protection.[51] The challenge remains: How and where to draw that line?

Obscenity

A majority of the Supreme Court has never considered obscenity to be a form of constitutionally protected speech, and the Court has pointed to obscene publications as an exception to the general First Amendment rule of no prior restraint.[52] The problem has been *defining* obscenity. As Justice Potter Stewart famously proclaimed in 1964, "I know it when I see it," but defining it in concrete terms remains elusive.[53]

For many years, the Supreme Court used the *Hicklin* test to determine whether something is obscene. Derived from *Regina v. Hicklin,* an 1868 case from England, the test made it easy to restrict speech.[54] According to the *Hicklin* test, any material that had merely a *tendency* "to deprave or corrupt" a child could be outlawed. A publication, such as a book, did not have to be considered as a whole. A single, isolated passage could be taken out of context and used to suppress the book or punish its distributor.

For example, Congress passed the Comstock Act in 1873, which made it illegal to mail "obscene, lewd, or lascivious" material, including information about birth control or abortion that might be contained in any publication of any kind. The act also prohibited the mailing of birth control devices themselves. Those convicted of violating the act could be fined up to $2,000 and imprisoned for up to 10 years with hard labor. The Supreme Court used the *Hicklin* test to uphold that law in 1877.[55]

The Supreme Court abandoned the *Hicklin* test in *Roth v. United States* (1957). The new *Roth* test was much more protective of speech. It no longer allowed isolated passages to be taken out of context, and it no longer used children as the baseline for judging whether material was obscene. Now the question was whether an *average* person "applying contemporary community standards" would find that the "dominant theme of the material, taken as a whole, appeals to the prurient interest." Thus, a novel that could have been banned using the *Hicklin* test because of an isolated paragraph that a child might happen to read would now be judged in its entirety by the standards of an average adult.

Still, questions remained. Are "community standards" national or local? How does one measure the "dominant theme" of a work? And what exactly is a "prurient interest"? Justice William Brennan, who wrote the opinion in *Roth,* tried to answer those questions in subsequent cases, but a majority of the Court could not agree on any single interpretation of the test. To Brennan, "community standards" meant the standards of "society at large" (a national community standard), and material could be deemed obscene only if, taken as a whole, it was "utterly without redeeming social importance" and did not possess even a "modicum of social value."[56]

By the 1970s, the Supreme Court was moving in a more conservative direction. President Richard Nixon, who had criticized the Supreme Court's obscenity rulings during his 1968 presidential campaign, had the opportunity to replace four justices during his first three years in office, including Chief Justice Warren. The new Court, headed by Chief Justice Warren Burger, grappled with the issue of obscenity in *Miller v. California* (1973). The resulting *Miller* test kept some aspects of the *Roth* test: the relevant audience continued to be the average person, and the material in question still had to be considered as a whole. But community standards were now defined as local rather than national, and material had to lack "serious literary, artistic, political, or scientific value," thereby rejecting the contention that material had to be utterly without redeeming social importance.

Although the legal definition of obscenity now seems to be limited to hard-core pornography, the Supreme Court has ruled that the broadcast media can be regulated more stringently—partly to assure that scarce airwaves are used in the public interest. As a result, government can ban language and nudity on the broadcast media that

★ Richard Gere kisses Bollywood star Shilpa Shetty during an AIDS awareness event in New Delhi. Indian authorities issued arrest warrants against Gere and Shetty for public obscenity.

may be offensive but is not obscene. For a complete discussion of government regulation of the airwaves, as well as a discussion of government regulation of the Internet, see Chapter 11.

Libel and Slander

The First Amendment protects neither **libel** (written defamation of character) nor **slander** (spoken defamation of character), but the Supreme Court has set a high standard for government officials and other public figures who seek damages for defamation. In the landmark 1964 libel case, *New York Times v. Sullivan,* the Court held that public officials seeking damages for libel must prove not only that the statement is false and damaging, but that it was made with "actual malice," that is, "made with knowledge that it was false or with reckless disregard of whether it was false or not."[57] In the absence of malice, falsity of the claim is not enough. Subsequent Supreme Court cases extended the actual malice standard to other public figures besides government officials.

Why such an exacting standard for public figures? Other liberal democracies such as Canada and Germany have rejected such a high standard.[58] Justice Brennan, who wrote the opinion in *New York Times v. Sullivan,* attributed it to a "profound national commitment" in the United States "to the principle that debate on public issues should be uninhibited, robust, and wide-open, and that it may well include vehement, caustic, and sometimes unpleasantly sharp attacks on government and public officials."[59] To allow anything less would interfere with a basic principle of the First Amendment: the free flow of ideas and opinion on matters related to the public interest. It could also interfere with the media's ability to act as a government watchdog.

The actual malice standard makes it difficult but not impossible for public figures to win libel suits. Private figures who neither hold public office nor fall into the categories of celebrity that make an individual a public figure are not bound by the actual malice standard and may recover libel damages more easily. Whether one is a public or private figure, certain types of material are generally immune from libel charges. These include the publication of opinion as opposed to fact (such as a restaurant review) and parody (such as political cartoons).

libel
Written defamation of character, which is not accorded First Amendment protection.

slander
Spoken defamation of character, which is not accorded First Amendment protection.

False Advertising

In 1943, the Supreme Court ruled that the First Amendment does not protect commercial advertising.[60] But what happens when political speech is part of a commercial advertisement? Faced with such instances in the 1970s, the Supreme Court has accorded some degree of First Amendment protection to commercial speech. For example, it struck down state laws that prevented lawyers from advertising and that banned advertising for abortion services.[61] It also struck down a federal law that prohibited the mailing of unsolicited advertisements for contraceptives.[62] Nonetheless, the Court has made it clear that the First Amendment does not prevent government from passing laws to prevent false, misleading, or deceptive advertising. In addition, government can require that warning labels be printed on products such as tobacco, alcohol, and medicinal drugs.

CAMPUS SPEECH

In the 1980s and 1990s, many public colleges and universities implemented speech codes that were designed to combat discrimination and harassment on campus. These codes were intended to prohibit abusive language that attacks individuals because of characteristics such as their race, ethnic origin, religious beliefs, or sexual orientation.

Some argue that racist and sexist speech stifles intellectual exchange, and that such codes actually increase free speech by removing intimidation. Others denounce such codes as "political correctness" and argue that the codes reflect a political agenda. For example, some conservative Christians have complained that codes have been used to restrict their speech and vilify their views. When Roger Williams University in Rhode Island temporarily froze funding for a College Republican newspaper that ran a series of articles condemning homosexuality, Jason Mattera, the editor of the paper at the time, said, "You're not automatically a bigot if you don't agree with [homosexuality]. What they're essentially doing is silencing the only conservative voice here on campus."[63]

The Supreme Court has not directly ruled on the constitutionality of campus speech codes, but some lower courts have. For example, a federal court struck down a University of Michigan code in 1989 that banned "any behavior, verbal or physical, that stigmatizes or victimizes an individual on the basis of race, ethnicity, religion, sex, sexual orientation, creed, national origin, ancestry, age, marital status, handicap, or Vietnam-era veteran status."[64] An "interpretive guide" of the code issued by the University Office of Affirmative Action included examples of conduct that could be sanctioned. One example read: "A male student makes remarks in class like 'Women just aren't as good in this field as men,' thus creating a hostile learning environment." A graduate student in biopsychology, who was studying the biological bases of individual differences in personality traits and mental abilities, challenged the law. He feared that discussion of controversial theories about biologically based differences between the sexes and races might lead to sanctions against him. Although the court struck down the University of Michigan's code on the grounds that it was overly broad and too vague, other campus codes still stand.

FREEDOM OF ASSEMBLY

In addition to the freedoms of speech and of the press, the First Amendment guarantees "the right of the people peaceably to assemble. . . ." Such assembly is essential to the free exchange of ideas. It is at the basis of everything from political parties to protest marches. But like other First Amendment freedoms, it is not absolute. As with speech, there are certain **"time, place, and manner restrictions."** In other words, the freedoms of speech and assembly do not mean that people can assemble anytime, anywhere, and say whatever they want however they want. Just as students are not completely free to disrupt algebra class with political speech, the right of assembly must be balanced against other interests such as traffic safety, noise restrictions, and trespass laws.

For example, as part of the civil rights struggle of the 1960s, Harriet Adderly and other university students assembled outside a jail in Tallahassee, Florida, to protest racial segregation and the earlier arrest of fellow civil rights demonstrators. However, their assembly took place on restricted property. The county sheriff warned them to move their protest elsewhere, but the protesters refused and were arrested for trespassing. The Supreme Court upheld their subsequent convictions, noting that the trespass statute was designed to further the security of the jail. Moreover, the protesters had no lack of notice, the law was clear and uniformly applied, and the arrest took place not because of the *content* of the protesters' speech but because of their *conduct:* where they were saying it.[65]

In contrast, the Supreme Court overturned the convictions of civil rights protesters who were arrested on the grounds of the South Carolina state capitol. Unlike the jailhouse grounds, the area around the state capitol was open to the public and was considered a "public forum": a place where people traditionally gather to express their views. And in contrast with the trespass ordinance in Florida, the breach of the peace ordinance that police used to arrest the protesters in South Carolina was vague and randomly applied. In fact, the breach of the peace was caused more by agitated onlookers than by the protesters themselves, who were peacefully singing hymns and songs such as "We Shall Overcome." In this case, the arrest *did* appear to be based upon the content of the protesters' speech and therefore violated the First Amendment freedoms of speech and assembly.[66]

Once again, it is sometimes difficult to determine when assembly is permissible and when it is not, especially in trying to determine precisely which locales constitute a public forum. Balancing public safety concerns with First Amendment rights can also be tricky. For example, the Supreme Court ruled in 1978 that the Chicago suburb of Skokie, Illinois—home to a large Jewish population—could not deny a permit for a march by the American Nazi Party.[67] Many in Skokie viewed it differently. They equated the Nazi march with constitutionally unprotected "fighting words" that would provoke a riot. In a 1942 case the Supreme Court had suggested that some words are so inflammatory, so certain to provoke a violent response, that they are not deserving of free speech protection.[68] Others insisted that preventing the march would constitute a prior restraint; if a breach of the peace or riot ensued because of the march, the conduct should be punished after the fact. In the end, a federal court forced the City of Skokie to permit the Nazis to march.

Consider, too, the case of the Westboro Baptist Church, whose 75 members have staged hundreds of protests to highlight their belief that the ills of the United States— from the 9/11 terrorist attacks to Hurricane Katrina and other natural disasters—are

★ Aryan Nations demonstrators march through the streets of Coeur d'Alene, Idaho, with a Nazi flag. Are such marches by hate groups deserving of First Amendment protection?

God's punishment for a society that condones homosexuality. They first gained national attention by picketing the funeral of Matthew Shepard, a college student who was beaten to death in 1998 because he was gay. Their signs proclaimed that Shepard was in hell because "God Hates Fags." More recently the church targeted funerals and burials of American soldiers killed in Iraq—carrying signs such as "Thank God for Dead Soldiers" and "God Hates Your Tears"—because they believe that U.S. combat deaths are an example of God's just retribution for homosexuality in America.[69]

Such actions provoked the Southern Poverty Law Center to label the church a "hate group." Almost 30 states have passed laws restricting graveside demonstrations. Congress also entered the fray by passing the Respect for America's Fallen Heroes Act (Pub.L. 109-228) to establish buffer zones around military cemeteries during burials; President George W. Bush signed it into law on May 29, 2006. Only three members of the House of Representatives voted against the bill. One was Ron Paul, a Republican from Texas who sought the Republican presidential nomination in 2008 and 2012. Another was Barney Frank, an openly gay Democrat from Massachusetts. Both questioned the constitutionality of the law and argued that it violates civil liberties. The Supreme Court has not directly ruled on the constitutionality of the law, but in 2011 it did reject a lawsuit brought against the Westboro Baptist Church by the family of a soldier whose funeral was picketed. The picketers stayed outside a 1,000-foot buffer zone from the church, and the Court upheld the picketing on free speech grounds.[70]

THE FIRST AMENDMENT GUARANTEE OF FREEDOM OF RELIGION

★ KEY TO understanding

The First Amendment contains two religion clauses: the establishment clause and the free exercise clause. Both are subject to differing interpretations, and both were incorporated in the 1940s. The establishment clause prevents government from imposing religion upon citizens. But does it create an impenetrable wall of separation between church and state that prohibits any government support of or financial aid to religion, or does it only prevent government from giving preferential treatment to one religion over another? The free exercise clause is designed to protect the right of citizens to practice their religion. Both have raised questions in regard to what exactly constitutes government support for religious institutions and constitutionally protected conduct.

Much controversy has been generated by the two religion clauses in the First Amendment: the **establishment clause** and the **free exercise clause.** Incorporation has added fuel to the fire because it allowed the Supreme Court to use the First Amendment to strike down such customs as prayer in the public schools (which, if not for incorporation, would be a matter for individual states and localities to decide).

THE ESTABLISHMENT CLAUSE

What does it mean to "make no law respecting an establishment of religion?" Should the establishment clause do nothing more than prevent Congress from interfering with the ability of states to establish religions? Or was it intended, as Thomas Jefferson famously put it in 1802, to establish "a wall of separation between church and state"? Even the Framers disagreed about how to answer such questions.

The incorporation of the establishment clause in 1947 revived the debate. States were now prohibited from passing laws respecting an establishment of religion, but it remained unclear exactly what "establishment" means. At one extreme, so-called "separationists" argue that the establishment clause erects a high, impenetrable wall of separation between church and state that prohibits any governmental support of or financial aid to religion. At the other extreme, so-called "accommodationists" argue that the establishment clause only prevents the government from giving preferential treatment to one religion over another. Government aid or support to religion is acceptable as long as it is nondiscriminatory. In between are a variety of middle-ground approaches.

The battle between these two positions has played out in high-profile cases involving such issues as prayer in public schools and displays of religious symbols on public property. In *Engel v. Vitale* (1962), the Supreme Court ruled on a case involving a prayer written by the New York State Board of Regents to be recited aloud each morning by students in New York's public schools: "Almighty God, we acknowledge our dependence upon Thee, and we beg Thy blessings upon us, our parents, our teachers, and our country."[71] The majority of the Court embraced a separationist view and held that any state-sponsored prayer in public schools violated the establishment clause, even if the prayer was nondenominational and participation in its recitation was voluntary.

The decision left students free to pray privately in school, and many religious organizations such as the American Baptist Convention, the American Jewish Congress, the American Lutheran Church, the Episcopal Church, the National Council of Churches of Christ, and the United Presbyterian Church initially supported the ruling on the grounds that religious training should be left to families and churches. Others, such as Senator Barry Goldwater (R-Ariz.), declared that the Court had "ruled against God."[72] Later, President Ronald Reagan expressed his opposition to the ruling in the 1980s, and his attorney general, Edwin Meese III, went even further. In a July 1985 speech to the American Bar Association, Meese criticized the Supreme Court for ignoring the original intent of the establishment clause and called incorporation a "politically violent and constitutionally suspect" blow to federalism.[73] Over the years several attempts to overturn *Engel v. Vitale* by constitutional amendment have failed.

Most countries around the world have also rejected the type of state-sponsored prayer at issue in *Engel v. Vitale.* A study by the American Civil Liberties Union concluded that only 11 out of 72 countries surveyed permitted such prayer. The countries that do permit state-sponsored school prayer range from Saudi Arabia and Libya to Germany and Great Britain, and in the latter two countries, participation by students must be voluntary.[74]

Many establishment clause cases in the United States have involved disputes over some form of government funding. *Everson v. Board of Education* (1947), the case that incorporated the establishment clause, is an example.[75] Under New Jersey law, parents of schoolchildren were reimbursed for the cost of transportation to and from school, including parents of children who attended private religious schools. By a 5-4 vote, the Supreme Court ruled that such a reimbursement by the government did not violate the establishment clause.

In *Everson,* the money went to parents. What if government funds go directly to the religious schools? For instance, Pennsylvania had a program that reimbursed church-affiliated elementary and secondary schools for the cost of teacher salaries related to instruction in nonreligious subjects such as math and English. When the Supreme

establishment clause
First Amendment provision that prevents government from imposing religion on citizens and is used to justify the separation of church and state.

free exercise clause
First Amendment provision that protects the right of citizens to practice their religion without governmental interference.

★ Incorporation of the establishment clause allowed the Supreme Court to strike down state laws requiring prayer in the public schools. Do you believe the Court correctly interpreted the word "establishment" in cases such as *Engel v. Vitale?*

Court considered that program in *Lemon v. Kurtzman* (1971), it created a test to help determine when a law or program violates the establishment clause.[76] According to the three-part *Lemon* test, government laws and programs do not violate the establishment clause if the following conditions are satisfied:

1. They have a secular (nonreligious) purpose *[the intent prong]*.
2. Their primary effect is neither to advance nor inhibit religion *[the effect prong]*.
3. They do not lead to excessive government entanglement with religion *[the entanglement prong]*.

The Pennsylvania program failed the *Lemon* test because it failed the last prong. Only "excessive and enduring entanglement" could guarantee that teachers were not interjecting religious beliefs into secular classes. The Supreme Court subsequently used the *Lemon* test to strike down an Alabama law that provided for a one-minute moment of silence in all public schools "for meditation or voluntary prayer."[77] The Court said that the law failed the first prong of the *Lemon* test: its clear intent was to promote religion. The ruling implied that some moment of silence laws, if properly written and implemented, might pass the *Lemon* test. Likewise, the Supreme Court struck down a Louisiana law that required the teaching of "Creation Science" (a literal interpretation of the Biblical account of creation) alongside the teaching of evolution. The Court again said that the law violated the first prong of the *Lemon* test: the intent of the legislature was to promote religion.[78]

More recently, a lower federal court used the *Lemon* test when ruling on the constitutionality of a huge 5,280-pound granite monument to the Ten Commandments that Roy Moore, the Chief Justice of the Supreme Court of Alabama, commissioned and had installed in the central rotunda of the state judicial building in 2001. The Eleventh Circuit Court of Appeals ruled in 2003 that the monument violated the first two prongs of the *Lemon* test and had to be removed.[79] Moore refused to obey the ruling. Because of that, he was removed from office by a unanimous vote of the Alabama Court of the Judiciary.

The issue of separation of church and state is not unique to the United States. Article I of the French Constitution says that France shall be a "secular" republic, and since 1905 France has had a law requiring the separation of church and state.[80] In 2004, France passed a controversial law that banned the wearing of conspicuous religious symbols such as Muslim headscarves, Sikh turbans, Jewish skullcaps, and Christian crucifixes in government-operated primary and secondary schools.[81] Although the law was couched in the language of separation of church and state, many denounced it as a violation of religious freedom.

In the United States, the establishment clause and the free exercise clause are similarly apt to be at odds. The Supreme Court decided the *Everson* case the way it did partly

★ Muslim women in England protest outside the French Embassy in London. They were unhappy with the French law banning the wearing of Muslim headscarves and other religious symbols.

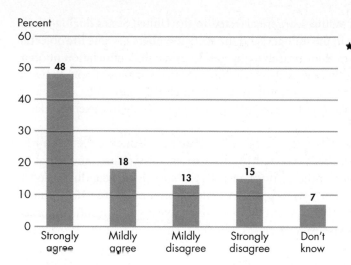

Percent

FIGURE 4.2

★ SEPARATION OF CHURCH AND STATE

How did those surveyed in this poll respond when asked whether they agreed that "The First Amendment requires a clear separation between church and state"? What do you think "a clear separation between church and state" means? Is the answer obvious?

Source: First Amendment Center, State of the First Amendment Survey, 2010.

because if the government had denied reimbursement of transportation costs to parents of children who went to religious schools while reimbursing parents of children who went to secular schools, the former group could feel that it was being penalized for its religious beliefs: a violation of the free exercise clause. Such tension between the establishment and free exercise clauses is not unusual. Whatever the tension, a majority seems to support the idea of a clear separation between church and state. (See Figure 4.2.)

THE FREE EXERCISE CLAUSE

We take our right to worship for granted, but many countries restrict the free exercise of religion—sometimes brutally. For example, Eritrea—a small country in the northeastern part of Africa—bars many religious groups from practicing their faith publicly. Those who do are subject to arbitrary arrest and detention. Thousands of religious prisoners have been tortured or otherwise ill-treated, sometimes resulting in death. Members of the armed forces face severe punishment for the possession of any religious material, including Bibles. The government is especially fearful of Protestant Evangelical, Pentecostal, and other Christian denominations not traditional to Eritrea.

Among those persecuted in Eritrea are Jehovah's Witnesses. They are denied government-issued identity cards and therefore cannot get legal recognition of marriages and land purchases. Jehovah's Witnesses who, on religious grounds, have refused to serve in the military have been summarily imprisoned—sometimes for over a decade—without a trial. Children of Jehovah's Witnesses have been expelled from their schools for refusing to salute the flag (Jehovah's Witnesses believe that such salutes are forbidden by the teaching of the book of Exodus in the Bible). And, like members of other unrecognized religious sects, Jehovah's Witnesses are regularly arrested without charge and imprisoned for varying amounts of time.[82]

Jehovah's Witnesses have also faced persecution in this country. Persecution of Witnesses was especially rampant during the Second World War because of their refusal to salute the American flag and their attempts to secure religious exemptions from military service—actions that led to charges that they were un-American. Some even claimed that Jehovah's Witnesses were Nazi sympathizers when in fact the Witnesses' campaign to do away with flag salutes had actually begun when Jehovah's Witnesses in Nazi Germany were sent to concentration camps for refusing to salute Hitler and the Nazi flag.[83]

Thousands of Jehovah's Witnesses were arrested in the United States during World War II for refusing to serve in the military, and the sect's members became the object of mob violence. Their door-to-door proselytizing and their harsh denunciation of organized religion, especially Catholicism, also fueled strong feelings against them. Between 1938 and 1946 alone, Jehovah's Witnesses were at the center of 23 Supreme Court cases. One of these cases, *Cantwell v. Connecticut* (1941), incorporated the free exercise clause of the First Amendment.[84]

Cantwell and many other free exercise cases illustrate the distinction between religious *belief,* which is absolutely protected by the free exercise clause, and religious *action,* which is not. Similar to the distinction between speech and conduct, the so-called "belief-action distinction" was recognized by the Supreme Court in 1879 when it unanimously upheld an act of Congress that outlawed polygamy.[85] Mormons claimed that the law violated their free exercise rights, but the Court said that the law applied equally to everyone and restricted only action, not belief.

The Court also grappled with the belief-action distinction in *Cantwell.* Newton Cantwell and his two teenage sons traveled from state to state spreading the word of Jehovah. In New Haven, Connecticut, an overwhelmingly Catholic city, their proselytizing met harsh resistance. After several people complained to the police, the Cantwells were arrested and convicted for violating a state law that prohibited individuals from soliciting money for any cause without a license. They were also convicted of the common law offense of breach of the peace.

The Court unanimously struck down the Connecticut law because it allowed the government to pick and choose what causes were eligible for solicitation. The Court reaffirmed the belief-action distinction but concluded that the law violated the First Amendment because it allowed the same action to be treated differently depending upon the beliefs of those carrying out the action. The Court also overturned the breach of the peace conviction on the grounds that the Cantwells' actions were not "noisy, truculent, overbearing or offensive," nor did they draw a crowd or impede traffic. However, the breach of the peace conviction could have been upheld under the belief-action distinction if the Cantwells' actions had done any of those things.

Two years later, the Supreme Court decided another important case involving Jehovah's Witnesses on free speech rather than free exercise grounds. *West Virginia State Board of Education v. Barnette* (1943) overturned a 1940 case called *Minersville School District v. Gobitis.*[86] Both cases dealt with whether mandatory flag salutes in public schools violated the rights of Jehovah's Witnesses. Twelve-year-old Lillian Gobitas (the name was misspelled in court records) and her younger brother, William, refused to obey the mandatory flag salute policy of Pennsylvania public schools and were expelled. The Supreme Court upheld the expulsion on the grounds that the flag salute had a legitimate secular purpose: fostering patriotism.

Reaction to the Court's ruling was swift and unexpected. Many erroneously believed that the ruling confirmed that Jehovah's Witnesses were un-American. It led to outbreaks of violence against Jehovah's Witnesses that only intensified when the United States entered World War II: "mobs throughout the United States stoned, kidnapped, beat, and even castrated Jehovah's Witnesses."[87] This reaction helped to convince a 6-3 majority in *Barnette* to overturn *Gobitis.* The majority in *Barnette* concluded that a flag salute was a form of symbolic expression and that for the government to compel such expression violated the free speech clause of the First Amendment.

Deciding when it is permissible for a generally applicable law to restrict free exercise rights can be tricky, as can deciding what exactly constitutes a protected religion. Do federal laws that criminalize drug use restrict the free exercise rights of Native Americans who use peyote as part of their religious worship services? Can a Muslim woman's driver's license be revoked if she refuses on religious grounds to remove her veil for a driver's license photo? Can localities use animal cruelty laws to prevent animal sacrifice when it is used as part of a religious worship service? The legal tests used to judge such cases have changed over time, but since 1990 the Court has held that generally applicable laws—those that apply equally to everyone, regardless of their religious beliefs—are presumed to be constitutional as long as they have a rational basis, even if they incidentally restrict some free exercise rights. (For a full discussion of the rational basis test, see Chapter 15.)[88]

THE RIGHT OF PRIVACY

In addition to the specific guarantees of the Bill of Rights, such as freedom of speech, the Supreme Court has recognized one of the most controversial constitutional rights: the unenumerated right of privacy. This recognition has raised a whole host of questions. What is the basis for this right? After all, the word "privacy" never appears anywhere in the Constitution. Is it permissible for the Court to "discover" new rights and use them to strike down laws? Or do such discoveries amount to the Court impermissibly "legislating from the bench"? The right of privacy is especially contentious because it often involves highly controversial practices such as birth control, abortion, and consensual sex among adults, as well as the right to die.

KEY TO understanding ★

Unlike other guarantees of the Bill of Rights, the right of privacy is not specifically enumerated. The Supreme Court came to recognize it even though the word "privacy" is never once mentioned in the Constitution. The result has been a series of controversial rulings by the Supreme Court on issues such as abortion, the rights of homosexuals, and the right to die. What are the arguments for and against the right of privacy?

THE NATURAL RIGHTS TRADITION

The United States has a long natural rights tradition. **Natural rights** are those basic, fundamental rights that all human beings are entitled to, whether government recognizes them or not. The English philosopher John Locke identified life, liberty, and property as the quintessential natural rights. Thomas Jefferson borrowed from Locke when he wrote the Declaration of Independence. Some of those who opposed the addition of a Bill of Rights to the Constitution were afraid that an enumeration of rights would suggest that no unenumerated rights existed. Thus, the Bill of Rights ended up including the Ninth Amendment: "The enumeration in the Constitution, of certain rights, shall not be construed to deny or disparage others retained by the people." Some people see this as a textual justification for the Supreme Court to recognize and enforce unenumerated rights. Others argue that the Ninth Amendment was only meant to allow states to go further in recognizing rights than the federal government: lack of an enumerated right in the Constitution did not mean that it could not be recognized by a state.

Still others have asked a more fundamental question: Do natural rights exist at all? Even if they do, should a simple majority of the Supreme Court be entrusted with discovering them? To do so might open the door to judicial policy making. For example,

natural rights
Basic rights that all human beings are entitled to, whether or not they are formally recognized by government.

in the early part of the twentieth century, a majority of the Supreme Court read economic rights into the Constitution and used them to strike down government regulations of business such as minimum wage laws, maximum hour laws, and child labor laws. Since 1937, when the Supreme Court overturned that line of decisions, the majority of the Court has viewed the decisions in those cases as misguided—an attempt by the Court majority to impose its policy judgments on everyone else.

Ultimately your enthusiasm (or disdain) for reading rights into the Constitution and then using them to strike down legislation may depend upon what you think about the legislation in question. If you like the legislation that is struck down, it is easy to accuse the Court of unjustifiable judicial activism. If you don't like the law, it is easy to praise the Court for vindicating natural rights.

DISCOVERING THE RIGHT OF PRIVACY

The Supreme Court first used a constitutional right of privacy to strike down a law in *Griswold v. Connecticut* (1965).[89] By a 7-2 vote, the Supreme Court struck down a Connecticut law that made it a crime for anyone, including married couples, to use any form of birth control. In his opinion for the Court, Justice Douglas argued that this law violated the right of privacy of married couples (it took a future case to extend this constitutional protection to unmarried couples).[90]

Where did this right of privacy come from? Douglas argued that it was implied by specific language in the Bill of Rights. He noted that the First Amendment's guarantee of free speech and assembly protects the freedom to associate and implies a right of privacy in one's associations. The Third Amendment's prohibition against quartering soldiers in any house in time of peace without the permission of the owner suggests a zone of privacy against government intrusion. So, too, does the Fourth Amendment's ban on unreasonable searches and seizures and the Fifth Amendment's ban on self-incrimination. The Ninth Amendment clearly states that the failure to enumerate a specific right does not mean that it does not exist. Finally, the Fourteenth Amendment allows for fundamental rights to be incorporated. Taken together, Douglas argued that these specific provisions imply a zone of privacy broad enough to protect the marital bedroom from government intrusion and fundamental enough so that it applies to the state of Connecticut.

Not all the justices agreed with Douglas. Some thought the right of privacy was even more expansive than Douglas admitted. Others strongly rejected any right of privacy. Hugo Black admitted that the Connecticut law was "every bit as offensive to me as it is to my Brethren of the majority."[91] But Black was a literalist, and he looked in vain for a specific constitutional clause that the law violated. "I like my privacy as well as the next one," Black wrote, "but I am nonetheless compelled to admit that government has a right to invade it unless prohibited by some specific constitutional provision."[92]

ABORTION

Griswold v. Connecticut paved the way for *Roe v. Wade* in 1973.[93] *Roe* is one of the most famous and one of the most controversial of all Supreme Court decisions. It involved a Texas law that criminalized abortions. Was that law constitutional? By a 7-2 vote, the Supreme Court said no. But in so doing, it tried to balance two competing constitutional rights: the privacy right of a woman to control her own body versus the state's interest in protecting the life of the fetus.

Justice Harry Blackmun's majority opinion assumed that the right of privacy is fundamental and that any law interfering with that right triggers strict scrutiny. (For a more complete discussion of the strict scrutiny test, see Chapter 15.) Since the Texas anti-abortion law interfered with a woman's right of privacy, the state of Texas had to demonstrate that it had a compelling reason to restrict that privacy right. The state claimed to have two compelling reasons: (1) protecting the health of the mother and (2) protecting the life of the fetus.

Blackmun assessed these claims in the light of medical technology as it existed in 1973. He relied on statistics showing that the abortion procedure was actually safer than childbirth until the end of the first trimester of pregnancy (each trimester represents three months of a pregnancy). Therefore, he concluded that the state did not have a compelling interest in regulating abortion procedures on safety grounds prior to that first "compelling point"—the end of the first trimester. However, he said that states did have a compelling interest in passing laws that regulated the abortion procedure in order to protect maternal health from that point forward.

Blackmun then asked: When does a state have a compelling interest in protecting the life of the fetus? At one extreme are those who argue that states have a compelling interest in doing so from the point of conception. Those at the other extreme argue that states do not have a compelling interest until childbirth because a fetus is not a "person" until then. Blackmun sought a compromise. When he was writing in 1973, a fetus could not survive outside of the mother's womb until the end of the second trimester, known as the point of "viability." Using that as his second "compelling point," Blackmun concluded that states have a compelling interest to regulate (and to ban completely, if they so choose) abortions in the last trimester.

This so-called "trimester framework" gave a woman's privacy right priority in the first three months of pregnancy, but gave the state's interest in protecting life priority in the last three months of pregnancy. In the second trimester, states could regulate abortions in order to protect maternal health but could not ban the procedure altogether. In contrast, the two dissenters argued that laws banning abortions are a reasonable exercise of state police powers.

Like any middle ground position, the trimester framework came under attack from both sides. As time went by, advances in medical technology also eroded it. The first compelling point moved closer toward childbirth, while the second compelling point moved closer to conception. In other words, late-term abortions became safer, and premature babies born at earlier stages in their mothers' pregnancies began to survive with greater frequency. That change affected the second trimester, in particular. This development led some, such as Justice Sandra Day O'Connor, to suggest that the trimester framework should be abandoned.[94]

By 1992, the composition of the Supreme Court had changed dramatically since the 1973 decision in *Roe*. Many predicted that a new majority existed that would be willing to overturn *Roe v. Wade*. The opportunity to do so came in *Planned Parenthood of Southeastern Pennsylvania v. Casey* (1992).[95] The resulting 5-4 decision abandoned the trimester framework but reaffirmed the "central tenet" of *Roe*. It also established a new "undue burden standard" (a middle ground between strict scrutiny and rational basis) that made it easier for some abortion restrictions to stand.

The availability of abortion varies across countries (see Figure 4.3). For example, a woman can go to prison for having an abortion in Chile. Abortion is illegal under all circumstances or permitted only to save the life of the mother in much of Africa and

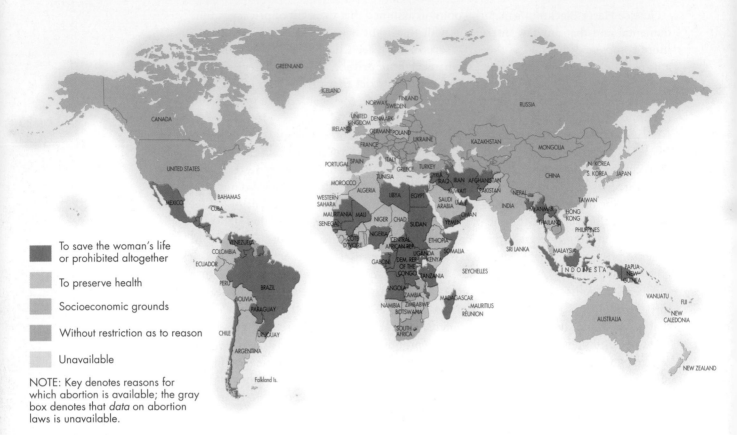

To save the woman's life or prohibited altogether

To preserve health

Socioeconomic grounds

Without restriction as to reason

Unavailable

NOTE: Key denotes reasons for which abortion is available; the gray box denotes that *data* on abortion laws is unavailable.

FIGURE 4.3

★ ABORTION LAWS AROUND THE WORLD, 2011

Source: The Center for Reproductive Rights

South America. On the other hand, it is legal in most European countries (Ireland is a notable exception). Some European countries, such as France, require a woman to undergo counseling before obtaining an abortion. Germany technically prohibits abortion, but under a law passed by the German Bundestag in June 1995, a woman will not be prosecuted for obtaining an abortion during the first trimester as long as she undergoes counseling that seeks to persuade her to carry the pregnancy to term. The law was a compromise brought about after the reunification of East and West Germany in 1989. Abortion was one of the great debates of reunification because the people of East Germany had been accustomed to very liberal abortion laws whereas the people of West Germany had not.

Despite such debates in other countries, abortion is an especially contentious issue in the United States. As the political theorist Ronald Dworkin has noted, the controversy over abortion is in part a result of the explosive mix of religiosity and progressive women's movements in this country. The United States, he notes, is not only "among the most religious of modern Western countries" (and "by far the most fundamentalist"), but also the home of a women's movement that has traditionally been more powerful than anywhere else.[96] Another important factor may be the way national abortion law came about in the United States. Instead of resulting from the normal process of political struggle and compromise worked out by Congress, it was established by the Supreme Court in *Roe v. Wade*. If *Roe* is ever overturned, each state legislature will need to decide whether or not to allow abortions, unless Congress chooses to enter the fray and establish a uniform policy for the entire country. Either way, political fights over the issue would be fierce.

THE RIGHTS OF HOMOSEXUALS

How far does the right of privacy extend? *Griswold* gave married couples a limited privacy right to use contraceptives free from government intrusion. *Roe* then extended that right to cover aspects of bodily autonomy in the abortion cases. But what about state laws that criminalize certain types of consensual sexual behavior among adults?

This issue came before the Supreme Court in *Bowers v. Hardwick* (1986).[97] The state of Georgia made it a felony, punishable by up to 20 years in prison, to engage in sodomy (defined by the law as oral or anal sex). The law applied equally to homosexual and heterosexual couples, including married partners. This case involved a gay Atlanta bartender named Michael Hardwick who was arrested for engaging in oral sex with another man in his own bedroom. A police officer accidentally discovered them when he came to serve Hardwick a warrant for not appearing in court for an open container violation. The District Attorney did not prosecute Hardwick, but he did not drop the charges either. Therefore, Hardwick brought a civil suit challenging the constitutionality of the Georgia law in federal court. He argued that it violated the right of privacy. By a narrow 5-4 vote, the Supreme Court rejected that claim and upheld the Georgia law, claiming that it had a rational basis. The dissenters used strict scrutiny to conclude that the law violated the right of privacy.

The Supreme Court overturned *Bowers v. Hardwick* in *Lawrence v. Texas* (2003).[98] This time the majority concluded that laws criminalizing private, consensual homosexual conduct have no rational basis. Justice Scalia criticized this conclusion in dissent. If states have no rational basis to proscribe homosexual conduct, he asked, "what justification could there possibly be for denying the benefits of marriage to homosexual couples exercising '[t]he liberty protected in the Constitution'?"[99] His prediction that the majority's reasoning would make it more difficult for courts to uphold laws banning same-sex marriage proved to be correct.

In 2003, the Supreme Judicial Court of Massachusetts ruled 4-3 in *Goodridge v. Department of Public Health* that "barring an individual from the protections, benefits, and obligations of civil marriage solely because that person would marry a person of the same sex violates the Massachusetts constitution."[100] Several other states plus the District of Columbia now either recognize same-sex marriage or recognize civil unions or domestic partnerships of same-sex couples. However, the vast majority of states explicitly ban same-sex marriage. The Supreme Court is expected to grapple soon with the constitutionality of the Defense of Marriage Act, which defines marriage as the union of one man and one woman for all federal purposes.

The Netherlands became the first nation in the world to recognize same-sex marriage in 2001. Since then, Argentina, Belgium, Canada, Iceland, the Netherlands, Norway, Portugal, South Africa, Spain, and Sweden have followed suit. Civil unions and domestic partnerships are allowed in more than 20 other countries, including the Czech Republic, Denmark, France, Germany, Portugal, and the United Kingdom. At the other extreme, homosexual conduct is punishable by death in such countries as Iran, Nigeria, Saudi Arabia, and Somalia.

THE RIGHT TO DIE

Courts have long recognized a common-law right of individuals to refuse most unwanted medical procedures. But does the right of privacy also extend a broader constitutional right—one that includes a right to die? May patients refuse invasive procedures that would extend their lives, such as the use of an artificial respirator, on privacy grounds? The issue is complicated because such patients are often incapacitated and are not able to express their wishes. Moreover, they may have left no written instructions, such as a living will. Can the patient's guardian make a substituted judgment for the patient in such a situation? This question is especially controversial because refusal of treatment under these circumstances often leads directly to the death of the patient.

Guardians sometimes argue that their loved one would not want to be kept alive with no hope of meaningful recovery—if for example, the patient were brain dead. They offer the legal argument that forcing artificial life support on patients violates a fundamental right of privacy. But others argue that decisions to withdraw life support violate the patient's right to life and may even constitute murder.

The Supreme Court first confronted the right to die issue in *Cruzan v. Director, Missouri Department of Health* (1990).[101] As in *Roe v. Wade,* the Court balanced competing interests. The majority noted that patients have a constitutionally protected right to refuse medical treatment, but argued that such a right must be balanced against the competing interests of states (such as their interest in protecting life). Thus, the Court upheld a Missouri law requiring "clear and convincing" evidence that a patient would want life support refused before granting a guardian's request to discontinue it.

Seven years later, the Court ruled that a patient's privacy right does not include a right to commit suicide. Individual states, using their police powers, are the ultimate arbiters of such decisions. Only one state—Oregon—has thus far chosen to allow doctor-assisted suicide. In 2006 the Supreme Court rejected an effort by the Bush administration to block that law.[102] Aside from Oregon, there are only three other places in the world where doctor-assisted suicide may be performed openly and legally: Belgium, Switzerland, and the Netherlands.[103]

THE RIGHTS OF CRIMINAL DEFENDANTS

KEY to understanding ★

The Constitution contains several provisions designed to protect the rights of those accused of committing a crime. Some are found in Article I, while others are found in the Bill of Rights. Some provisions of the Bill of Rights protect against specific actions (such as double jeopardy and self-incrimination). But the due process clauses of the Fifth and Fourteenth Amendments more generally require states and the federal government to follow fair procedures before taking away a person's life, liberty, or property. This leads to the question: Is it possible to achieve due process of law (a fair trial) if the other specific guarantees of the Bill of Rights have not been incorporated?

Article I of the Constitution contains several specific rights of the criminally accused. For example, it provides for the **writ of *habeas corpus,*** a court order that allows a judge to release a prisoner who is being detained illegally. It also prohibits *bills of attainder* (laws that allow someone to be punished without a trial) and *ex post facto laws* (laws that make an action illegal retroactively). But most of the rights that we associate with the criminally accused are found in the Bill of Rights. Originally, of course, guarantees contained in the Bill of Rights applied only to federal criminal prosecutions. Incorporation made most of these guarantees applicable to the states as well. Since most criminal trials take place at the state level, incorporation has had a profound effect on our criminal justice system.

DUE PROCESS RIGHTS OF THE ACCUSED

We spoke earlier in this chapter about the concept of *procedural due process:* the idea that the government must follow fair proceedings before taking away a person's life, liberty, or property. The due process clause of the Fifth Amendment limits the actions of the federal government ("No person shall be . . . deprived of life, liberty, or property, without due process of law"). The Fourteenth Amendment added another due process clause that specifically limits state action ("No state shall . . . deprive any person of life, liberty, or property, without due process of law").

The Bill of Rights contains other specific guarantees that deal with the rights of criminal defendants. For example, the Fourth Amendment protects against "unreasonable searches and seizures." The Fifth Amendment requires grand jury indictment in capital or otherwise infamous crimes and protects against double jeopardy (being tried twice in the same court for the same crime) and self-incrimination. The Sixth Amendment guarantees the right to a speedy and public trial by an impartial jury in which the accused has the opportunity to confront witnesses against him or her and has the right to a lawyer. The Eighth Amendment protects against "cruel and unusual punishment" as well as "excessive bail" and "excessive fines."

Can the Fourteenth Amendment's guarantee of due process be met without incorporating these specific guarantees? Until the middle of the twentieth century, the Supreme Court often said yes. Most of the provisions of the Bill of Rights dealing with criminal defendants have only recently been incorporated, the majority of them in the 1960s. Even today, some provisions—such as the Fifth Amendment right to grand jury indictment and the Eighth Amendment right against excessive bail—have not been incorporated. (See Table 4.2 on page 117.)

Before incorporation, states merely had to apply due process, and the Supreme Court often upheld convictions in cases where states did not follow other specific guarantees in the Bill of Rights—for example, convictions in cases where defendants were tried twice for the same crime or denied the right against self-incrimination.[104] As long as the overall criminal process seemed to be fair, a procedural error based on one of the specific guarantees of the Bill of Rights typically was not deemed serious enough to overturn a state court conviction.

Even after incorporation, the Supreme Court continues to recognize that there may be more than one way for states to prosecute accused criminals while still protecting their rights. Only those specific guarantees of the Bill of Rights that the Court has deemed "fundamental" have been incorporated. This has been done through the process of selective incorporation discussed earlier in this chapter. But some of the incorporated provisions are ambiguous, allowing the Court to give states some flexibility in the way they apply even some of the incorporated provisions.

A good example is the Sixth Amendment right to trial by jury in criminal cases. The Supreme Court incorporated that right in 1968.[105] But what exactly does a right to trial by jury mean? The Sixth Amendment says nothing about the specific size of the jury. Nonetheless, all federal juries consist of 12 people. Likewise, federal criminal cases require a unanimous verdict to convict (even though the specific language of the Sixth Amendment does not require unanimity). Does incorporation of the Sixth Amendment bind the states to juries of 12 people and unanimous jury verdicts? The Supreme Court has said no.[106] Nonetheless, the Court has held that juries that are *too* small (which it defines as any made up of fewer than six people) violate due process.[107] Likewise, it held that verdicts that are not unanimous may violate due process if the jury is too small: it ruled that even though 11-1 and 10-2 verdicts are constitutional, a 5-1 verdict violates due process.[108] These cases show some of the problems associated with incorporating a particular clause while still trying to give some deference to states to create rules governing the size of juries and how they reach a verdict.

picture YOURSELF ...
AS A PROSPECTIVE JUROR IN JAPAN

Throughout Japan, groups of people recently gathered to participate in more than 500 mock trials. Some took part in play-reading sessions of "Twelve Angry Men," a 1954 television play about tense jury deliberations that became a classic 1957 movie. All of these events were staged in order to prepare citizens for a radical change in Japan's criminal justice system: the adoption of a system of trial by jury.

We take jury trials for granted, but 80 percent of Japanese in a recent poll opposed the change and said that they did not want to serve as jurors. Why not? The jury system violates several deep-seated cultural norms shared by Japanese: "a reluctance to express opinions in public, to argue with one another and to question authority." * The mock trials and play-reading sessions attempted to overcome those obstacles.

The new Japanese jury system is quite different from the one used in the United States. In Japan, six jurors sit with three professional judges. When weighing guilt or innocence and determining sentences, the jurors must arrive at a majority decision and have the support of at least one of the three judges.[†] Unlike American jurors, they can question witnesses.

Potential jurors were not the only ones nervous about the change. Lawyers were not used to making closing arguments or having to speak in terms that ordinary people could understand.[‡] Experts expressed concern that randomly selected jurors would not be qualified enough to render verdicts in complicated criminal cases.[§] Prosecutors were afraid that conviction rates might fall.

In Japan, only those cases in which conviction is almost certain are brought to trial. The conviction rate for all prosecutions in Japan is over 99 percent, and failure to obtain a conviction can be a career setback. Jurors might also question the tools used by prosecutors, whose investigatory powers are largely unchecked. Unlike the United States, where *Miranda* warnings and other procedural guarantees protect criminal defendants, suspects in Japan can be held for up to 23 days without access to a lawyer. Confessions of guilt are common during that time.[**]

The first case utilizing the new system took place in August 2009. More than 2,000 people lined up to watch the proceedings. Katsuyoshi Fujii, age 72, had already confessed to stabbing a neighbor to death; the jury was charged with determining a sentence. They questioned Fujii and the victim's son, and heard from Fujii's lawyers, who sought

* Norimitsu Onishi, "Japan Learns Dreaded Task of Jury Duty," *The New York Times*, July 16, 2007.
† Justin McCurry, "Trial by Jury Returns to Japan," *Guardian*, August 3, 2009 (http://www.guardian.co.uk/world/2009/aug/03/japan-trial-by-jury-returns).
‡ Richard Lloyd Parry, "Trial by Jury Returns to Japan and the Lawyers Aren't Happy," *The Times*, February 28, 2009 (http://www.timesonline.co.uk/tol/news/world/asia/article5818123.ece).
§ "Japan's Landmark Jury Trial Ends," *BBC News*, August 6, 2009 (http://news.bbc.co.uk/2/hi/8188447.stm).
** Bennett Richardson, "In Reform Bid, Japan Opts for Trial by Jury," *Christian Science Monitor*, June 4, 2004 (http://www.csmonitor.com/2004/0604/p06s02-woap.html).

leniency. Prosecutors could have asked for the death penalty but suggested 16 years in jail; the jurors sentenced him to 15. This first case went smoothly, but a survey of potential jurors showed that one in four remained unwilling to serve—even though refusal would subject them to a fine of 100,000 yen (roughly $1,300). Additional play-reading sessions may be in order.

questions to consider

1. Might the use of jurors in Japan lead to greater protection of civil liberties? If so, how?

2. What do you think of the claim expressed by experts in Japan that randomly selected jurors are not qualified to decide complicated cases? Is that a valid concern for American juries?

3. The right to trial by jury in criminal cases is a guarantee of the Sixth Amendment of the U.S. Constitution. Why is that right so important?

JUDICIAL EXPANSION OF THE RIGHTS OF THE CRIMINALLY ACCUSED

In addition to specific guarantees in the Bill of Rights, the Supreme Court has used judicial opinions to expand the rights of the criminally accused. For example, it ruled in *Gideon v. Wainwright* (1963) that the Sixth Amendment right to legal representation applies to those who cannot afford a lawyer.[109] If the accused is too poor to hire one, the court must assign one. Many states have responded by creating a system of public defenders: lawyers whose full-time job is defending indigent criminal suspects.

The so-called **Miranda warnings** are another prime example of the Court expanding rights. After watching countless movies and television shows in which criminal defendants are read their rights, you can probably recite these warnings by heart:

> You have the right to remain silent. Anything you say can be used against you in court. You have the right to talk to a lawyer of your own choice before questioning. If you cannot afford to hire a lawyer, a lawyer will be provided without charge.

These warnings are the result of a 1966 case called *Miranda v. Arizona*.[110] Prior to this case, the admissibility of confessions in state criminal cases was judged on a case-by-case basis using the basic standard of due process, with the Fifth Amendment right against self-incrimination not applying to police interrogations. *Miranda* required police to warn suspects, prior to questioning, that they had the right to remain silent and to request a lawyer. Absent such warnings, information obtained from suspects may not be admitted as evidence in court. Although some criticized the *Miranda* warnings as an example of the liberal Warren Court affording too many rights to criminal defendants, the conservative Rehnquist Court upheld the central holding of *Miranda* by a 7-2 vote in *Dickerson v. United States* (2000).[111]

Yet another judicially created principle is the **exclusionary rule,** which prevents illegally seized evidence from being introduced in criminal trials. Created by the Supreme Court in *Weeks v. United States* (1914), the exclusionary rule was originally limited to federal cases.[112] Even when the Supreme Court incorporated the Fourth Amendment ban on unreasonable searches and seizures in 1949, it initially ruled that incorporation did not require states to apply the exclusionary rule.[113] That changed in 1961 with *Mapp v. Ohio,* which required states to enforce the exclusionary rule.[114] Like *Miranda* warnings, the exclusionary rule has generated controversy. Some argue that it goes too

Miranda warnings
The list of rights that police must read to suspects at the time of arrest, including the right to remain silent and the right to request a lawyer. Absent such warnings, information obtained from suspects is inadmissible in court.

exclusionary rule
Principle, created by the Supreme Court, that illegally seized evidence may not be introduced in criminal trials.

far in protecting the rights of criminal defendants because it might allow a guilty person to go free if a police officer violates search and seizure guidelines. Others argue that it is an essential element of due process and an important deterrent against police misbehavior.

In the years since *Mapp* was decided, the Supreme Court has made some exceptions to the exclusionary rule. One of the most significant came in *United States v. Leon* (1984).[115] In that case the Court ruled that evidence seized by police pursuant to an invalid warrant may be admissible because the error lies not with the police but the magistrate who issued the warrant. This is known as the "good faith exception."

THE DEATH PENALTY

Whether to administer the death penalty—and, if so, how—leads to great debate. The Eighth Amendment bans "cruel and unusual punishment." Does capital punishment violate that ban? If not, where does one draw the line between forms of execution that are constitutional and others that are not? In the United States, lethal injection is the most common form of execution, followed by electrocution, the gas chamber, hanging, and use of a firing squad.

Thirty years ago, lethal injections were introduced in the United States as a more humane alternative to other forms of execution. In 2008, the Supreme Court considered whether lethal injections cause unnecessary pain, thereby violating the Eighth Amendment. Typically, lethal injections consist of a three-drug cocktail administered intravenously. The first drug, an anesthetic, renders the condemned unconscious; the second drug paralyzes the body; the third drug causes cardiac arrest. Medical personnel do not administer lethal injections because to do so would violate the Hippocratic Oath, and critics charge that the prison employees who typically administer these drugs are often poorly trained. If the first drug is not administered correctly, the inmate can experience excruciating pain that may not be apparent to onlookers because of the paralysis caused by the second drug. By a 7-2 vote, the Court upheld the use of lethal injections.[116]

As of January 2012, 34 states administer the death penalty. The vast majority of executions take place in the South; the fewest take place in the Northeast (see Figure 4.4). More than half the countries in the world have abolished the death penalty in either law or practice. It has been abolished completely in Canada, Australia, Britain, most of Europe, and parts of South America and Europe. The United States is one of only five fully developed nations to retain the death penalty (the others are Japan, Singapore, South Korea, and Taiwan). According to Amnesty International, 23 countries carried out executions in 2010. The United States had the fifth highest rate of confirmed executions in the world, behind China, Iran, North Korea, and Yemen.[117] (See Figure 4.5.)

Since the late 1960s, a majority of Americans have consistently supported the death penalty (see Figures 4.6 and 4.7). Support for the death penalty reached a high of 80 percent in 1994 and declined to 61 percent in 2011.[118] Only two Supreme Court justices have argued that the death penalty itself constitutes cruel and unusual punishment. However, a majority of the Court did rule in 1972 that random and arbitrary imposition of the death penalty may constitute both cruel and unusual punishment and a violation of due process.[119] It also ruled in 1977 that the death penalty may be an excessive form of punishment for certain types of crimes (such as rape of an adult).[120]

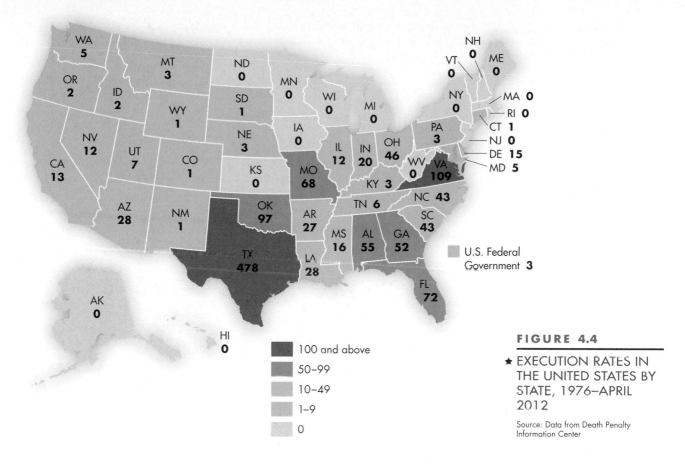

WA 5
OR 2
MT 3
ND 0
MN 0
WI 0
MI 0
NH 0
VT 0
ME 0
NY 0
MA 0
RI 0
CT 1
NJ 0
DE 15
MD 5
ID 2
WY 1
SD 1
IA 0
IL 12
IN 20
OH 46
PA 3
WV 0
VA 109
NV 12
UT 7
CO 1
NE 3
KS 0
MO 68
KY 3
NC 43
CA 13
AZ 28
NM 1
OK 97
AR 27
TN 6
SC 43
TX 478
LA 28
MS 16
AL 55
GA 52
AK 0
HI 0
FL 72

U.S. Federal Government 3

100 and above
50–99
10–49
1–9
0

FIGURE 4.4

★ EXECUTION RATES IN THE UNITED STATES BY STATE, 1976–APRIL 2012

Source: Data from Death Penalty Information Center

In 2002, the Court ruled that executing mentally retarded offenders was unconstitutional.[121] The Court extended that ruling in 2005 to offenders who were under the age of 18 when they committed their crime.[122]

TERRORISM AND CIVIL LIBERTIES

One issue the courts have confronted recently is whether combating terrorism justifies restrictions on civil liberties. Since the September 11, 2001, terrorist attacks on the World Trade Center and the Pentagon, both Congress and the president have taken actions that limit civil liberties. In October 2001, Congress passed the USA PATRIOT Act, which expanded the government's power to monitor e-mail communications and gather information from libraries and bookstores about what people were reading. It also contained "sneak and peek" provisions that allowed the government to seize information without informing the person involved. The government argued that such measures were necessary to combat the threat of terrorism.

At the same time, President Bush secretly authorized the use of warrantless wiretaps by the National Security Agency on telephone calls between the United States and foreign countries in cases where one of the parties was suspected of links to al-Qaeda. When *The New York Times* revealed the program in 2005, critics charged that the Bush administration had ignored civil liberties and violated the 1978 Federal Intelligence and Surveillance Act (FISA) which allowed such wiretaps only if a special court issued a warrant for the tap either before or up to 72 hours after the start of the surveillance.[123]

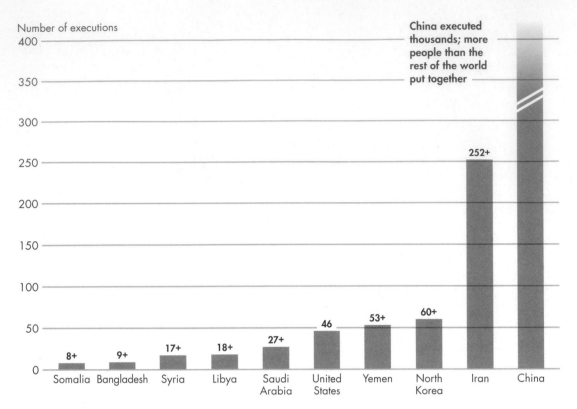

Number of executions

China executed thousands; more people than the rest of the world put together

Somalia	8+	
Bangladesh	9+	
Syria	17+	
Libya	18+	
Saudi Arabia	27+	
United States	46	
Yemen	53+	
North Korea	60+	
Iran	252+	

FIGURE 4.5

★ COUNTRIES WITH THE HIGHEST NUMBERS OF EXECUTIONS, 2010

Note: Plus signs indicate that the figure calculated by Amnesty International is a minimum.

Source: Data from Amnesty International

In the summer of 2007, Congress passed legislation that temporarily sanctioned the use of warrantless wiretaps. In May 2011, President Obama signed an extension of the USA PATRIOT Act that placed no new restrictions on the use of wiretaps.[124]

Critics raised particular concern about the Bush administration's treatment of suspected terrorists. The administration claimed the right to detain terror suspects, including U.S. citizens, indefinitely without charge and without access to a lawyer. Several Supreme Court decisions limited the powers claimed by the Bush administration.

FIGURE 4.6

★ THE DEATH PENALTY AND PUBLIC OPINION, 1936–2011

Survey respondents were asked, "Are you in favor of the death penalty for a person convicted of murder?"

Source: Gallup Poll, (http://www.gallup.com/poll/1606/death-penalty.aspx)

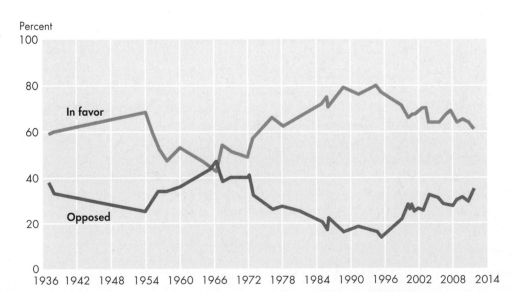

Percent

In favor

Opposed

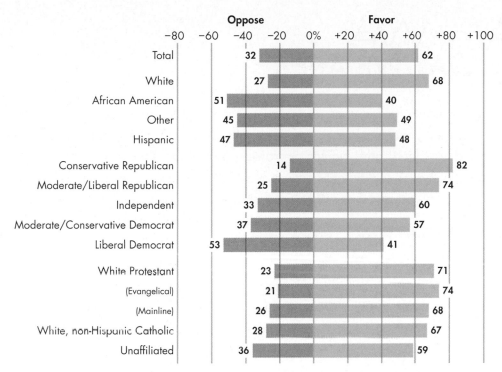

FIGURE 4.7

★ SUPPORT FOR THE DEATH PENALTY BY DEMOGRAPHIC GROUP, 2007

After reaching a high in the 1990s, support for the death penalty has dropped off. The graph illustrates support for the death penalty by demographic group. What might account for the differences in opinion across these groups?

Source: Data from Gallup, Inc. and Pew Research Center

For example, *Hamdi v. Rumsfeld* (2004) held that U.S. citizens, including terror suspects, have the constitutional right to consult a lawyer and to contest their detention before an independent tribunal.[125]

The Bush administration wanted any trials of these detainees to take place before a military commission rather than in federal court, and the president authorized the use of such military commissions by executive order. However, a 5-3 majority of the Supreme Court held in *Hamdan v. Rumsfeld* (2006) that military commissions were not authorized by Congress and violated international law.[126] The ruling was seen as a major setback for the Bush administration, but the Republican-controlled Congress subsequently passed the Military Commissions Act of 2006 at the urging of the White House. The Act authorized the use of military commissions. The Obama administration initially banned the use of military tribunals to try terror suspects, but rescinded that ban in 2011.

Civil libertarians also expressed concern about the use of "enhanced interrogation techniques," such as waterboarding, used against terror suspects by the Bush administration. The Bush administration denied that such techniques constituted torture, but critics disagreed and President Obama revoked the executive order issued by Bush that had authorized enhanced interrogation.[127]

In all of these instances, the Bush administration pointed to the broad prerogative powers claimed by presidents during war and other emergencies as a justification for their actions. Despite criticizing the Bush administration's use of such prerogative powers, Obama continued to employ at least some of them.[128] The result has been an erosion of civil liberties. Does warding off terrorism justify rescinding civil rights? In several cases, the Supreme Court has decided that it does not.

Why Are We
THE WAY WE ARE ?

Constitutional language provides a basis for civil liberties, but constitutional language alone is not enough. The constitutions of many other countries, including China, offer similar guarantees that ultimately prove to be hollow. The U.S. system is different because of its fundamental commitment to the rule of law—its willingness to hold the government accountable to the Constitution.

SUPREME COURT INTERPRETATION

The ambiguity of constitutional language dealing with civil liberties gives the Supreme Court great power to determine the actual scope of those liberties. Throughout this chapter, problems of interpretation have emerged again and again, whether the relevant constitutional clause deals with speech, obscenity, religious establishment, or the rights of criminal defendants.

We are the way we are because of how the Supreme Court interprets such clauses. The fact of the matter is that such interpretations can change—sometimes dramatically. Consider, for example, the difference between the standards established by the *Hicklin* test and the *Roth* test for determining what is obscene. Once again, constitutional language did not change, but judicial interpretations of it did. Ultimately, the Court determines what our civil liberties mean.

INCORPORATION

In addition to interpreting the meaning of specific guarantees, the Supreme Court has extended the reach of the Bill of Rights through incorporation. Our system would be very different if the Supreme Court had not selectively incorporated most of the guarantees of the Bill of Rights.

We are the way we are because the Supreme Court has chosen to limit state as well as national action. To measure the difference, think back to how states limited free speech in order to protect the institution of slavery prior to the Civil War. Incorporation forces states to be accountable to the First Amendment and the other provisions of the Bill of Rights that the Supreme Court has chosen to incorporate.

TERRORIST THREATS AND OTHER EMERGENCIES

Emergency situations are sometimes used to restrict civil liberties. For example, freedom of speech has been curtailed in time of war. Such curtailments prompted Supreme Court decisions in cases such as *Schenck v. United States* during World War I. Rightly or wrongly, government officials—including Congress, the president, and the Supreme Court—sometimes conclude that, in the short run, safety and security are more important than vigilant enforcement of at least some civil liberties. Such has been the case in the period since the September 11, 2001, terrorist attacks. To combat the ongoing threat of terrorism, government has eroded certain privacy rights and curtailed the due process rights of terrorist suspects.

. . . AND WHY DOES IT Matter?

The way that civil liberties are interpreted and enforced matters to you. Your ability to protest the government, worship as you please, use birth control, and decide whether to refuse medical treatment all depend not only on what the Constitution says but also on how the Supreme Court interprets it.

That is why so many Americans pay attention to who sits on the Court and what tests its majority uses to judge the constitutionality of laws. Being able to identify what kind of test the Supreme Court uses in particular cases may seem pedantic at first, but that choice affects everything from the regulation of your sexual behavior to whether an invocation is allowed at high school football games.

Incorporation matters, too. It matters to states, whose policy options are affected; to taxpayers, who may have to fund requirements like jury trials in criminal cases; and to you, whose rights are extended. At the end of the day, we think policies concerning things like prayer, guns, protest, sex, life, and death probably matter to you.

critical thinking questions

1. How would our system of government be different if the Supreme Court had not embraced incorporation, and how would that difference affect you?

2. When, if ever, would you be willing to allow government to curtail your civil liberties?

3. To what extent should the Supreme Court be able to recognize rights that have not been enumerated in the Constitution?

key terms

bad tendency test, *121*

Bill of Rights, *111*

civil liberties, *111*

clear and present
 danger test, *120*

due process clauses, *115*

establishment
 clause, *129*

exclusionary rule, *141*

free exercise clause, *129*

incorporation, *114*

libel, *125*

Miranda warnings, *141*

natural rights, *133*

prior restraint, *118*

slander, *125*

substantive due process, *115*

symbolic speech, *122*

time, place, and manner
 restrictions, *127*

writ of *habeas corpus*, *138*

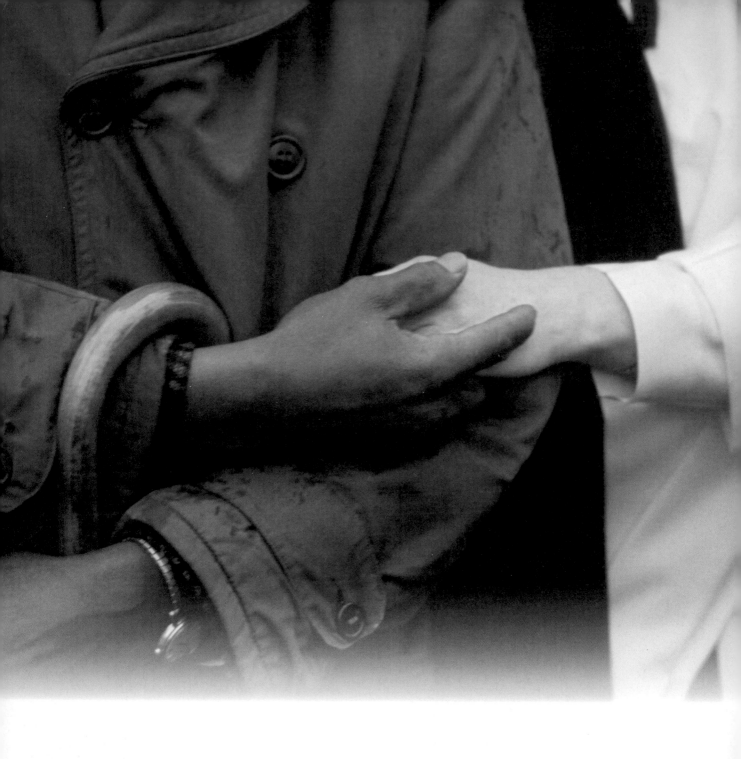

CIVIL RIGHTS

★ ★ ★

- Identify how the U.S. Constitution and the U.S. Supreme Court addressed slavery prior to the Civil War.
- Examine the history of discrimination against African Americans and their struggle for equal treatment after the Civil War.
- Evaluate the role of the courts in expanding African-American civil rights in the twentieth century.
- Review the history of gender inequality in the United States.
- Analyze the roots and ramifications of ethnic discrimination in the United States.
- Investigate how the fight for civil rights has moved beyond race, gender, and ethnic origins.
- Explain the actions the federal government has taken toward redressing past discrimination, and evaluate the effectiveness of these actions.

PERSPECTIVE
Should the United States Use Foreign Aid and Diplomacy to Promote the Human Rights of LGBT Communities in Other Countries?

In 2011, President Obama marked International Human Rights Day by announcing, "The struggle to end discrimination against lesbian, gay, bisexual, and transgender (LGBT) persons is a global challenge, and one that is central to the United States commitment to promoting human rights." President Obama directed all U.S. agencies engaged in foreign activity to "ensure that U.S. diplomacy and foreign assistance promote and protect the human rights of LGBT persons."[1] This pronouncement came on the heels of a warning from the conservative British Prime Minister, David Cameron, that the United Kingdom would reduce foreign aid to countries that refuse to recognize LGBT rights.[2]

The statements by President Obama and Prime Minister Cameron were aimed at countries such as Nigeria, which was considering a harsh crackdown on gay rights. The Nigerian Senate had already passed a bill that outlawed gay rights groups and made same-sex marriage or cohabitation a criminal offense, punishable by up to 14 years in prison. Those who helped to facilitate a same-sex marriage could be imprisoned for up to 10 years, and the bill allowed anyone who "directly or indirectly makes [a] public show of same-sex amorous relations" to be imprisoned for up to 10 years. To become law, the bill also had to be passed by the Nigerian House of Representatives, and some political and religious leaders in Nigeria used the statements by Obama and Cameron to rally support for the law.[3] As one lawmaker put it, if Western nations want to withhold their aid because of such a law, "to hell with them."[4] Homosexual conduct is illegal in most African countries. In some areas, including 12 of Nigeria's 36 states, same-sex sexual activity is punishable by death by stoning.

Nigeria's Anglican Archbishop Peter Akinola was at the forefront of the campaign against LGBT rights in Nigeria, as were conservative Muslims and U.S.–based Christian evangelical groups who were active in Africa. Nigerian Information Minister Labaran Maku said, "We live in a democracy, we live in a free country, we live in an independent country," adding, "some of the things that are considered fundamental rights abroad . . . can be very offensive to African culture."[5]

Nonetheless, Secretary of State Hillary Clinton declared that "gay rights are human rights, and human rights are gay rights," and emphasized the need for laws to protect equal rights in places such as Africa. "In many places, including my own country," she said, "legal protections have preceded, not followed, broader recognition of rights." Only when the change was implemented did many understand how "it strengthened our social fabric."[6]

As recently as 1986, the United States Supreme Court upheld the right of U.S. states to criminalize private, consensual homosexual conduct.[7] Not until 2003 did the Supreme Court reverse course and declare such laws unconstitutional.[8] That ruling paved the way for the legalization of same-sex marriage in several U.S. states plus the District of Columbia. Several other states recognize same-sex civil unions and grant same-sex partners the same state-level spousal rights as heterosexual married couples. Increasingly, judges and law makers have treated same-sex marriage as a civil rights issue. Almost 30 states, however, have reacted to these new laws by passing initiatives or constitutional amendments defining marriage as a union between a man and a woman. Social conservatives and some religious groups back such initiatives.

Is the United States promoting civil rights by using foreign aid as a tool to discourage laws that discriminate against homosexuals in other countries, or is the United States impermissibly meddling in other nation's business? What about here at home? Should same-sex marriage be treated as a civil right, or are prohibitions against same-sex marriage different from other types of discrimination encountered by members of the LGBT community?

THIS CHAPTER explores the evolution of civil rights for various groups. We focus first on the civil rights of African Americans, including the Civil War Amendments to the Constitution and their interpretation by the Supreme Court, the rise and fall of Jim Crow Laws and voting restrictions, and the modern civil rights movement and the legislation it has generated. Then we examine efforts by other groups to secure civil rights, including women, Native Americans, immigrants, the LGBT community, and people with disabilities. Finally, we focus on efforts to redress past discrimination, including affirmative action. As you read this chapter, keep in mind our two core questions:

WHY ARE WE THE WAY WE ARE?
WHY DOES IT MATTER TO YOU?

In particular, how has the U.S. government attempted to correct past discrimination? In what ways does the government continue to advance civil rights in this country?

SLAVERY IN AMERICA

The struggle for **civil rights** in the United States—freedom from governmental discrimination (unequal treatment) based on age, gender, race, or other personal characteristics—has affected many groups in the United States. Slavery—sanctioned, however discreetly, by the U.S. Constitution—paved the way for decades of racial discrimination in the United States, and so we start there.

SLAVERY AND THE CONSTITUTION

The U.S. Constitution did not contain the words "slave" or "slavery," but debates about slavery—by then a firmly entrenched (and legally recognized) practice—greatly influenced the framers. Slavery, of course, does not comport with the framers' lofty rhetoric of rights, but the hard truth is that several sections of the Constitution not only recognized, but indirectly sanctioned the practice of slavery.

For example, Article I, Section 9, in roundabout language, prohibited Congress from abolishing the importation of slaves until 1808, and empowered Congress to impose a tax or duty "on such Importation, not exceeding ten dollars for each Person." Article IV, Section 2 contained the so-called **fugitive slave clause,** which required the return of slaves (those "held to Service or Labour in one State under the Laws thereof") if they escaped to another state—even one where slavery was outlawed. And the so-called Three-Fifths Compromise of Article I, Section 2, discussed in Chapter 2, allowed each slave to be counted as three-fifths of one person for purposes of representation and taxation. Even the Bill of Rights originally did nothing to protect African Americans because the incorporation of the Bill of Rights—made possible by the ratification of the Fourteenth Amendment in 1868—is mostly a twentieth-century phenomenon (see Chapter 4).

Congress outlawed the importation of slaves in 1808, but the legality of slavery itself was a decision left to individual states. Early on, some states, such as Massachusetts (1780), New Hampshire (1784), and Vermont (1791), abolished slavery through their state constitutions. But slavery continued to be legal in many states and slaveholders in those states argued that slaves were property protected by the Fifth Amendment of the U.S. Constitution. Pro-slavery and anti-slavery forces in Congress agreed on the Missouri Compromise in 1820, which—with the exception of Missouri—banned slavery north of the 36° 30′ latitude line. But Congress repealed the Missouri Compromise through passage of the Kansas-Nebraska Act of 1854, thereby allowing each territory to decide for itself whether or not to allow slavery. Anti-slavery forces faced another blow in 1857, when the Supreme Court weighed in and declared that Congress had acted unconstitutionally by banning slavery in the Missouri Compromise (see Figure 5.1).

SLAVERY AND THE SUPREME COURT

Proponents of slavery generally embraced states' rights, but they did champion one aspect of national supremacy: the power of Congress to enforce the fugitive slave clause of the Constitution through legislation such as the Fugitive Slave Act of 1793. This, they argued, prevented states from passing laws, such as one enacted by Pennsylvania in 1826 to protect the due process rights of African Americans. The Supreme Court invalidated the Pennsylvania law in 1842, arguing that the federal government had exclusive power to regulate the return of fugitive slaves.[9]

civil rights
Freedom from governmental discrimination (unequal treatment) based on age, gender, race, or other personal characteristics.

fugitive slave clause
A provision of Article IV, Section 2 of the Constitution that required the return of escaped slaves to their owners even if they fled to a state where slavery was outlawed. Repealed by the Thirteenth Amendment (1865).

FIGURE 5.1

★ THE MISSOURI
COMROMISE

Source: http://teachingamericanhistory
.org/neh/interactives/sectionalism/
lesson1

Closed to slavery by Missouri Compromise

Open to slavery by Missouri Compromise

Free states and territories

Slave states and territories

A year earlier, the Supreme Court had ruled in favor of 53 Africans who, on the slave ship *Amistad* bound for Puerto Principe, Cuba, had revolted, killed the captain, and tried to return the ship to Africa but ended up in the United States instead. There, pro-slavery advocates deemed the men slaves and wanted them tried for mutiny, murder, and piracy. Abolitionists, on the other hand, viewed the men as victims: freemen who had been kidnapped and therefore had a right to resist their captors. The Supreme Court sided with the abolitionists. It freed the Africans and allowed them to return to Sierra Leone.[10]

DRED SCOTT.

The *Amistad* case was a rare Court victory for abolitionists, who suffered a stinging defeat in *Dred Scott v. Sandford* (1857), one of the most infamous decisions ever handed down by the Supreme Court. The case involved Dred Scott, who had been born a slave in Virginia and had been sold to an army surgeon, John Emerson, in 1832. Emerson's military career took him to Illinois and the Wisconsin territory, where slavery was banned. Eventually, while serving in the Seminole War, Emerson left Scott with his wife in St. Louis, Missouri. Emerson died in 1843, and Scott tried to purchase his freedom from Mrs. Emerson. She refused, and Scott subsequently sued for his freedom, citing precedents in Missouri case law holding that slaves brought to Missouri after having resided in free states or territories were entitled to their freedom.

The Missouri trial court ruled in favor of Scott, but the Missouri Supreme Court overturned the ruling and abandoned earlier "once free, always free" precedents. The U.S. Supreme Court affirmed that ruling. In so doing, it could have simply declared that the Missouri Supreme Court had the final word on Missouri law. Instead, in an opinion written by Chief Justice Roger B. Taney, the Supreme Court issued a sweeping ruling that deemed African Americans a "subordinate and inferior class of beings" who were—even if they were free blacks—disqualified from U.S. citizenship and therefore unable to sue in federal court.[11] Moreover, the Court ruled that Congress had exceeded its authority when it passed the Missouri Compromise, and explicitly held that slaves were property whose owners deserved constitutional protection.[12]

Reaction to the *Dred Scott* decision was fierce. It crystallized attitudes on both sides of the slavery issue and, many argue, made the Civil War inevitable. That war was largely, but not exclusively, a battle over slavery. President Abraham Lincoln issued the Emancipation Proclamation in September of 1862 freeing slaves in all Confederate states that did not return to Union control by January 1, 1863. Notably, the Emancipation Proclamation did not free slaves in Union states. The complete abolition of slavery did not come until after the Union victory in the Civil War, with the ratification of the Thirteenth Amendment to the Constitution on December 6, 1865.

CIVIL RIGHTS FOR AFRICAN AMERICANS AFTER THE CIVIL WAR

The Civil War amendments to the Constitution—the Thirteenth, Fourteenth, and Fifteenth Amendments—did much to lay the groundwork for equal rights, but many obstacles remained. The **Thirteenth Amendment (1865)** abolished slavery and other forms of involuntary servitude. The **Fourteenth Amendment (1868)** contained, among other things, the equal protection clause stating that no state shall "deny to any person within its jurisdiction the equal protection of the laws." It also, as discussed in Chapter 4, contained language that has made most provisions of the Bill of Rights applicable to the states through the process of incorporation. The **Fifteenth Amendment (1870)** guaranteed that the right to vote would not be "denied or abridged by the United States or by any State on account of race, color, or previous condition of servitude." Nonetheless, events conspired to prevent these provisions from having full effect for more than a century.

KEY TO understanding ★

Despite constitutional amendments abolishing legalized slavery, offering equal protection of the laws, and guaranteeing that the right to vote would not be denied or abridged on the basis of race, color, or previous condition of servitude, the rights of African Americans continued to be abridged for many years after the Civil War. How did states and the Supreme Court perpetuate unequal treatment after these amendments?

Thirteenth Amendment (1865)
Constitutional amendment that abolished slavery and other forms of involuntary servitude.

Fourteenth Amendment (1868)
Constitutional amendment containing the guarantee that no state shall deprive any person of the equal protection of the laws.

Fifteenth Amendment (1870)
Constitutional amendment guaranteeing that the right to vote will not be denied based on race, color, or previous condition of servitude.

Black Codes
Post-Civil War laws that perpetuated discrimination against African Americans.

THE BLACK CODES AND THE CIVIL RIGHTS ACTS OF THE 1860s AND 1870s

Although Southern states were required to ratify the Thirteenth Amendment before being readmitted to the Union, they proceeded to pass laws known as the **Black Codes** that replaced Slave Codes that had existed before the Civil War. These new Black Codes, which varied from state to state, perpetuated legal discrimination and effectively "preserved slavery in form after it had been abolished in fact."[13]

Thus, South Carolina law required that African Americans who contracted to work for white employers be known as "servants," and their employers be known as "masters." All the codes allowed unemployed blacks to be arrested for vagrancy and then hired out to pay off their fine. For example, the Louisiana code required that "every adult freed man or woman shall furnish themselves with a comfortable home and visible means of support within twenty days after the passage of this act." Those

★ Segregated drinking fountains are an example of Jim Crow laws. This one was in a streetcar terminal in Oklahoma City.

who did not meet that requirement—which was almost impossible to fulfill in such short time—were to be "immediately arrested by any sheriff or constable" and hired out to "the highest bidder, for the remainder of the year."[14] The various codes also prohibited blacks from pursuing certain occupations, living in certain areas, marrying whites, and owning firearms. They excluded blacks from voting and authorized whipping as a form of punishment for blacks.[15]

Congress quickly intervened to invalidate the Black Codes through passage—over the veto of President Andrew Johnson—of the Civil Rights Act of 1866. The Black Codes also helped to precipitate passage of the Fourteenth and Fifteenth Amendments to the Constitution, and Congress passed additional Civil Rights Acts in the 1870s that were the most sweeping national efforts to protect African Americans until the 1960s. The Civil Rights Act of 1875 was particularly important because Congress outlawed discrimination in businesses such as restaurants, hotels, and theaters from which African Americans were frequently barred. Each of the Civil War amendments contained an enabling clause—that is, a provision that gave Congress the power to enforce the amendment through legislation. In passing the Civil Rights Act of 1875, Congress relied on its enabling clause power to enforce the equal protection clause.

THE SUPREME COURT INTERVENES: THE *CIVIL RIGHTS CASES* AND *PLESSY V. FERGUSON*

Civil Rights Cases (1883)
Cases wherein the Supreme Court ruled that Congress did not have the authority to outlaw private discrimination in business establishments.

The flurry of protection accorded African Americans by Congress proved to be short-lived. Soon the Supreme Court turned back many of the advances brought about by the Civil War Amendments and the Civil Rights Acts. In the **Civil Rights Cases (1883),** the Court ruled 8 to 1 that Congress did not have the authority to outlaw private discrimination in hotels, restaurants, and other business establishments because the equal protection clause only limited *state* action: "No *state* shall . . . deny to any person within its jurisdiction the equal protection of the laws." Thus, the enabling clause only empowered Congress to pass laws preventing state-sanctioned discrimination.[16]

The lone dissent came from John Marshall Harlan, a southerner from Kentucky. Harlan had previously owned slaves and had originally opposed the Emancipation Proclamation and the Civil War Amendments, but he later changed his mind and become one of the great champions of civil rights. He had, in 1877, been the first southerner appointed to the Supreme Court after the Civil War and his nomination generated opposition because of that.[17]

Thirteen years after the *Civil Rights Cases,* the Supreme Court took an even more significant step in **Plessy v. Ferguson (1896).** An 1890 Louisiana law required railroad companies to provide "equal but separate accommodations for the white and colored business" and made it a criminal offense for a person of one race to insist on occupying a seat in a railroad car designated for another race. An organization of black and white citizens proceeded to challenge the law. They recruited 30-year-old Homer Plessy, who was one-eighth black, to purchase a seat on the railroad car for whites. Plessy was light-complexioned and could easily pass for a white man, but according to Louisiana law he was considered black. Once Plessy took his seat, he announced that he was one-eighth black, refused to move, and was arrested. As such, he was able to challenge the Louisiana law. In a 7-1 ruling, the Court upheld the Louisiana law. It embraced the view that the equal protection clause of the Fourteenth Amendment allowed segregation of the races, thus establishing the **separate but equal doctrine.** Justice Harlan was once again the lone dissenting voice. In passionate and eloquent language, he chastised the majority for its ruling. "Our Constitution is color blind," he insisted, "and neither knows nor tolerates classes among citizens. . . . The thin disguise of 'equal' accommodations for passengers in railroad coaches will not mislead any one, nor atone for the wrong this day has done."[18]

Plessy v. Ferguson (1896)
A Supreme Court ruling that established the "separate but equal" doctrine, upholding state segregation laws.

separate but equal doctrine
Based on the *Plessy v. Ferguson* ruling that claimed the equal protection clause of the Fourteenth Amendment allows the segregation of races.

THE RISE OF JIM CROW LAWS AND BARRIERS TO VOTING

The separate but equal doctrine embraced by the Supreme Court in *Plessy v. Ferguson* led to the proliferation of state and local laws requiring the segregation of the races. These came to be known as **Jim Crow laws**—named after a character in minstrel shows played by a white man in blackface. Laws such as those banning intermarriage among the races, requiring separate schools for black and white students, and preventing white female nurses from working in wards for black patients are all examples of Jim Crow laws. At the same time, states embraced a variety of discriminatory devices used to keep African Americans from voting. These included poll taxes, literacy tests, grandfather clauses, and white primaries.

Poll taxes required each voter to pay a tax in order to vote. Poll taxes had been common during the colonial period but had become rare by the mid-1800s. They were revived in the late nineteenth century as a way to prevent poor blacks from voting. The Supreme Court unanimously upheld the constitutionality of poll taxes in *Breedlove v. Suttles* (1937), but the Twenty-Fourth Amendment to the Constitution (1964) banned the use of poll taxes in federal elections, and the Supreme Court declared the use of poll taxes in state elections to be unconstitutional in *Harper v. Virginia State Board of Elections* (1966), thereby overruling *Breedlove.*[19]

Literacy tests were also administered as a precondition for voting. Although theoretically meant to determine whether a voter could read and write, complicated questions on literacy tests were really designed to prevent African Americans from voting. They frequently included arcane questions about the U.S. Constitution and state law. These tests prevented many literate blacks from voting, but they did not prevent illiterate whites from voting because **grandfather clauses** exempted voters from literacy tests and poll taxes if they could prove that their grandfathers had voted before a date that corresponded with the end of the Civil War. The Supreme Court struck down the use of grandfather clauses in *Guinn v. United States* in 1915.[20] Congress finally suspended the use of literacy tests through the Voting Rights Act of 1965.

Jim Crow laws
State and local laws requiring the segregation of the races, including prohibition of interracial marriage and mandating of racially segregated schools.

poll taxes
Tax payments required prior to voting; revived by states in the late nineteenth century as a way to prevent poor blacks from voting.

literacy tests
A precondition for voting in some states, purportedly to verify a voter's ability to read or write, but designed to prevent blacks from voting.

grandfather clauses
Exempted voters from literacy tests and poll taxes if they could prove that their grandfathers had voted before the end of the Civil War.

★ Members of the 2011 Congressional Black Caucus at a "For the People Jobs Initiative" town hall in Los Angeles. African-American members of Congress established the nonpartisan caucus in 1969. Today, African Americans make up approximately 10 percent of the membership of the House of Representative but none were represented in the Senate during the 112th Congress.

The Democrats were the dominant party in the "solid South" after the Civil War—so much so that whatever candidate won the primary election was all but guaranteed to win the general election. To further minimize the influence of black voters, southern states instituted **white primaries.** In other words, only white voters were allowed to vote in the primary election—the only one that really mattered because whichever Democratic candidate won the primary was assured of victory in the general election.

white primaries
A Southern strategy for minimizing black voter influence that allowed only white voters to vote in the primary elections (the only ones that really mattered).

AFRICAN-AMERICAN CIVIL RIGHTS IN THE TWENTIETH CENTURY

KEY TO understanding

Courts played a key role in expanding the civil rights of African Americans in the twentieth century. The NAACP initiated many of these cases. *Brown v. Board of Education,* in particular, served as a catalyst for the civil rights movement that eventually prompted Congress to pass the Civil Rights Act of 1964 and the Voting Rights Act of 1965. Would civil rights have expanded as quickly without judicial intervention? Why were courts able to accomplish what the political process could not?

★

The combination of Supreme Court rulings, Jim Crow laws, and voting restrictions had a devastating effect on the rights of African Americans. The Ku Klux Klan, a white supremacist vigilante group that had originally formed in the 1860s but mostly died out after Reconstruction ended, resurfaced with a vengeance in the twentieth century. By the 1920s, the Klan had become a major social and political force. Its symbol of intimidation was the burning cross, and over the years the Klan came to be associated with the lynching of African Americans and other mob violence.

The Ku Klux Klan gained strength during a period of massive immigration from Europe. In addition to white supremacy, it embraced harsh anti-immigrant, anti-Catholic, and anti-Semitic views. The Klan was so prevalent in some states, such as Alabama, that politicians felt they had to join it in order to win elections. This was true even of some progressive politicians, such as Hugo Black, who briefly joined the Klan in 1923, was elected to the U.S. Senate from Alabama in 1927, and went on to be appointed to the U.S. Supreme Court by Franklin Roosevelt in 1937.[21] Neither Black's tenure in the Senate nor his rulings on the Supreme Court reflected the views of the Klan; in fact, Black became a champion of civil rights.

THE NAACP AND THE FIGHT FOR CIVIL RIGHTS THROUGH THE COURTS

In 1909, a coalition of blacks and progressive whites formed the **NAACP** (the National Association for the Advancement of Colored People), an organization devoted to promoting the civil rights of African Americans. Early in its history, the NAACP turned to the courts to accomplish its goals. It played an important role in the above-mentioned *Guinn v. United States* (1915), which struck down the use of grandfather clauses. The NAACP also brought legal challenges to segregation. For example, a case brought by the NAACP led the Supreme Court in 1917 to strike down a Louisville, Kentucky, ordinance that required residential neighborhoods to be segregated by race.[22] Involvement in these early cases was piecemeal and largely unorganized.

NAACP
National Association for the Advancement of Colored People, an organization devoted to promoting the civil rights of African Americans.

By the 1920s, however, the NAACP began planning a more systematic strategy to use legal challenges to fight segregation. It hired full-time legal staff and, in 1939, created a separate group—the NAACP Legal Defense and Education Fund (the LDF)—to devote all of its energies to litigation. Thurgood Marshall, who had worked on the NAACP's legal staff since 1935, became the first director and chief counsel of the LDF. He went on, in 1967, to become the first African-American justice on the U.S. Supreme Court. The NAACP timed the creation of the LDF well. The Supreme Court's "switch in time" in 1937 (see Chapter 3) led the Court to become more receptive to cases involving individual rights. As a result, the LDF's systematic court challenges led to a series of court victories over the next decade, notably in the area of segregated education.

★ Today, the federal government is still fighting for equal protection. In 2011, the U.S. Department of Justice filed suit against Joliet, Illinois, on the grounds that the city was seeking to reduce its African-American population by seizing the federally subsidized housing development shown here and displacing its African-American residents through a legal procedure known as eminent domain.

Initially, the LDF won victories without directly overturning *Plessy v. Ferguson* and its separate but equal doctrine. *Sweatt v. Painter* (1950) is a good example. That case involved Heman Marion Sweatt, an African American who had applied to the University of Texas Law School in Austin. The school automatically rejected his application because Texas law prohibited integrated schools. When Sweatt sued, Texas hastily created a separate law school for blacks in Houston. The Supreme Court unanimously ordered the University of Texas to admit Sweatt to the Austin campus because the separate law school for blacks was clearly not its equal.

Although the Court did not overturn the separate but equal doctrine, its ruling was based on more than the physical inequities between the schools, such as the comparative sizes of their faculty and libraries. Significantly, it implied that separate law schools for blacks in Texas could never be equal to those for whites. A law school "cannot be effective in isolation from the individuals and institutions with which the law interacts," Chief Justice Vinson wrote, yet the separate law school for blacks excluded the 85 percent of the population that included most of the "lawyers, witnesses, jurors, judges and other officials" with whom Sweatt and other African American lawyers would inevitably deal.[23]

Based on that language, the NAACP decided that the time had come to challenge the separate but equal doctrine head-on. The LDF brought challenges to segregated primary and secondary schools in Delaware, Kansas, South Carolina, Virginia, and Washington, D.C., on the grounds that such segregation violated the equal protection clause of the Fourteenth Amendment. At the Supreme Court level, these challenges were consolidated into one case: ***Brown v. Board of Education*** (**1954**).

Brown v. Board of Education (1954)

Supreme Court decision that overturned the "separate but equal" doctrine and declared racially segregated schools to be unconstitutional.

BROWN V. BOARD OF EDUCATION

When *Brown v. Board of Education* was first argued before the Supreme Court in 1952, the justices were divided about how to rule. Even Chief Justice Vinson, who had written the opinion in *Sweatt v. Painter*, was reluctant to take the next step and explicitly overrule *Plessy v. Ferguson*.[24] The justices were still deadlocked in the summer of 1953 when Vinson unexpectedly died and was replaced by Earl Warren. Partly as a stalling tactic to bide time to gain greater consensus, the Court ordered the case to be reargued. An astute politician, Chief Justice Warren also convinced his colleagues to divide *Brown* into two cases. The first would focus on the merits of the case (whether segregated schools violated the equal protection clause), and the second would focus on the more difficult question of relief (how to implement school desegregation if they did).

Under Chief Justice Warren's leadership, the Court issued a unanimous decision in 1954 rejecting the application of the separate but equal doctrine to elementary and secondary schools. The decision effectively overturned *Plessy v. Ferguson*, although it technically applied only to segregated schools. Warren wrote the opinion in *Brown* himself and chose simple, non-accusatory language. He assumed, correctly, that the opinion would be printed in newspapers around the country, and he wanted average people to be able to read and understand it. He noted in the opinion that "education is perhaps the most important function of state and local governments" and that "it is doubtful that any child may reasonably be expected to succeed in life if . . . denied the opportunity of an education." Warren then turned to the central question: "[I]n the field of public education, the doctrine of 'separate but equal' has no place."[25] Having overturned the separate but equal doctrine, a more difficult problem remained: how to implement school desegregation. In *Brown v. Board of Education II* (1954), the Supreme Court unanimously ordered local school boards and the lower courts to handle the planning and implementation, but allowed them to do so "with all deliberate speed"— a phrase that seemed to invite delay and obstruction. Indeed, much of the South mobilized against enforcement of school desegregation.

In 1957, Governor Orval Faubus of Arkansas ordered the Arkansas National Guard to block the entry of African-American students at Little Rock Central High School, prompting a showdown with President Dwight D. Eisenhower. Eisenhower federalized the Arkansas National Guard, thereby taking control away from Faubus, and sent federal troops to Arkansas to enforce desegregation. In a measure of public sentiment at the time, Faubus was named one of the "Ten Most Admired Men in America" in a 1958 Gallup poll. As late as 1964—a decade after the initial ruling in *Brown v. Board of Education*—only about 2 percent of black children in the South attended elementary or secondary schools with white children.[26]

THE CIVIL RIGHTS MOVEMENT

Although *Brown v. Board of Education* did not immediately bring about school desegregation, it did serve as a major catalyst for the ensuing civil rights movement. Buoyed by its success in *Brown,* the NAACP continued to fight segregation in other venues. When Rosa Parks was arrested in Montgomery, Alabama, on December 1, 1955, for refusing to sit in the back of a city bus as Alabama law required, the NAACP not only helped with her successful legal battle but organized a boycott of the Montgomery bus system that lasted for 381 days. A 26-year-old black minister, **Martin Luther King, Jr.,** came to prominence during that boycott. King embraced the philosophy of nonviolent civil disobedience taught by India's Mahatma Gandhi (1869–1948) and formed the Southern Christian Leadership Conference (SCLC) in 1957.

Another group that embraced nonviolent resistance was the Congress of Racial Equality (CORE). Among CORE's activities were the Freedom Rides begun in 1961 to test a 1960 Supreme Court ruling in *Boynton v. Virginia* that struck down racial segregation in interstate passenger transportation (such as interstate buses and bus stations) on the grounds that it violated the federal Interstate Commerce Act.[27] Freedom Riders were groups of black and white civil rights activists who rode Greyhound and Trailways buses through the South. At least one black Freedom Rider on each bus would sit with a white counterpart at the front of the bus—the area traditionally reserved for white passengers only—and at least one black Freedom Rider would sit in the back of the bus to avoid arrest, report back to CORE, and arrange bail for those who were arrested.

Tensions rose as the buses traveled into the Deep South. The first—a Greyhound bus that was usually full—held only five regular passengers as it passed into Alabama, along with seven Freedom Riders and two journalists. When the bus pulled into the station at Anniston, Alabama, a mob of about 50 people led by the Ku Klux Klan attacked the bus, beating it with clubs, metal pipes, and chains, smashing its windows, and slashing its tires.

When the police arrived, they did not arrest anyone. Instead, they simply escorted the bus to the city limits. The police then turned back to town and let the bus go on its way, even though 30 or 40 cars carrying members of the mob had followed them.

Martin Luther King, Jr.
Prominent civil rights leader who embraced Gandhi's nonviolent civil protest and formed the Southern Christian Leadership Conference in 1957.

★ Martin Luther King, Jr. waving to the crowd that heard his famous "I Have a Dream" speech.

Finally unable to go any further because of its slashed tires, the bus stopped and the mob attacked the bus again. Someone threw a flaming bundle of rags into the bus that then exploded and started a fire in the bus. The mob held the door of the bus shut, shouting, "Burn them alive!" Only when the gas tank exploded did the startled mob retreat, allowing the Freedom Riders to escape.[28]

After mobs attacked other buses, Attorney General Robert Kennedy told Alabama governor John Patterson that he would call in federal troops if the state could not maintain law and order. Patterson dispatched the Alabama National Guard to help protect Freedom Riders traveling through the state. Over the next few months, some 300 Freedom Riders were arrested in Mississippi. The arrests and savage attacks shocked people around the nation, including many southerners, and drew national attention to ongoing civil rights abuses in the South.

In 1963, Martin Luther King and the SCLC used boycotts and nonviolent protests to bring attention to segregated businesses in Birmingham, Alabama. For example, they organized "sit-ins" where African Americans would peaceably occupy seats at a "whites only" restaurant. Police arrested hundreds of protesters including King. Then, at the direction of Police Commissioner "Bull" Connor, they used high-pressure water hoses, electric cattle prods, and police dogs to disperse a group of protest marchers that included women and children. Horrific images of police violence again shocked the nation and helped to propel the civil rights movement forward. That summer, King was among the organizers of the huge March on Washington for Jobs and Freedom.

CONGRESS TAKES ACTION

Public outcry over the violent reaction to desegregation in the South and attention focused on the civil rights movement by the March on Washington put pressure on Congress to act. Congress had already passed civil rights acts in 1957 and 1960, but these acts produced little or no change. President John F. Kennedy was assassinated in November 1963, just months after Martin Luther King's "I Have a Dream" speech, and his successor—Lyndon Johnson—urged Congress to pass sweeping civil rights legislation to honor the memory of President Kennedy. The **Civil Rights Act of 1964** was the most sweeping civil rights legislation since the 1870s. It contained six major provisions, shown in Table 5.1.

A year later, Congress passed another landmark piece of legislation: the **Voting Rights Act of 1965.** The act came as a response to ongoing efforts to keep blacks from voting in the South. In March 1965, Martin Luther King, who had joined a local voter registration campaign, helped to organize a 50-mile march from Selma, Alabama—where only 2 percent of eligible African Americans were registered to vote—to the state capital in Montgomery. The march was designed to draw attention to the struggle to achieve voting rights for blacks. Governor George C. Wallace ordered state troopers to stop the march. As the marchers approached the Edmund Pettus Bridge on Route 80, the troopers—some on horseback—used whips, nightsticks, and

Civil Rights Act of 1964
The most sweeping civil rights legislation since the 1870s, which expanded civil rights and increased protections against various forms of discrimination.

Voting Rights Act of 1965
Landmark legislation that outlawed literacy tests and took other steps to guarantee the voting rights of African Americans.

TABLE 5.1
major provisions of the civil rights act

1. It barred arbitrary discrimination in voter registration.
2. It outlawed discrimination in public accommodations associated with interstate commerce, such as motels, hotels, and restaurants.
3. It authorized the U.S. Justice Department to file lawsuits to force the desegregation of public schools.
4. It authorized, but did not require, federal funds to be withheld from programs that practiced discrimination.
5. It banned discrimination in employment based on race, color, religion, national origin, or sex, and created the Equal Employment Opportunities Commission (EEOC) to enforce that ban.
6. It expanded the power of the U.S. Commission on Civil Rights, a watchdog group charged with investigating civil rights abuses and making recommendations to remedy them.

tear gas to break up the march. Televised images of the brutal attack yet again shocked the nation and led President Johnson to call out the National Guard to protect the marchers. As the marchers continued toward Montgomery, President Johnson addressed a joint session of Congress on March 15, 1965, to urge passage of the Voting Rights Act. Congress moved quickly, and the president signed the Act into law on August 6, 1965.

The Voting Rights Act contained two major provisions. First, it outlawed literacy tests. Second, it provided federal oversight of state and local elections in areas where a pattern of discrimination had been established. Such areas could not make any changes to their election law or voting requirements without obtaining "preclearance"— approval in advance from the U.S. Department of Justice. The Voting Rights Act, coupled with voter registration drives in the South, led to an increase in the number of black voters registered to vote in the South from 29 percent of eligible black voters in 1960 to roughly double that by 1970.[29]

These laws did not end concerns about racial discrimination in voting. The contested presidential election in 2000 and subsequent recounts in Florida highlighted the fact that predominantly black counties in Florida tended to have the least accurate voting equipment and often provided poor instructions to voters at the polls. This led to concerns about possible discrimination. Some critics also allege that state laws requiring all voters to bring state-issued photo identification discriminate against minority voters. Proponents of such laws argue that they are needed to combat voter fraud. Critics argue that these laws disproportionately affect minority voters, who are less likely to possess state-issued photo IDs than their white counterparts. Thus, the Obama Justice Department rejected a South Carolina voter ID law because registered minority voters there were almost 20 percent less likely than registered white voters to have state-issued photo IDs (see Chapter 9).[30]

This recent controversy serves as a reminder that the landmark civil rights legislation of the 1960s did not resolve every aspect of discrimination. Despite great advances, race continues to be a source of contention. And, as we shall see later in this chapter, efforts to remedy past discrimination through affirmative action have raised allegations of "reverse discrimination."

WOMEN AND EQUAL RIGHTS

★ KEY to understanding

The civil rights of women were long denied in the United States. Not until 1920 did women have the constitutional right to vote, and still their social and economic rights continued to lag behind those of men. How does the Supreme Court's application of the equal protection clause to gender discrimination differ from its application to discrimination based on race or ethnicity, and why did the proposed Equal Rights Amendment to the Constitution fail?

African Americans and other minorities are not the only citizens who have struggled for equality and the right to vote in the United States. Throughout most of American history, cultural stereotypes perpetuated the widely held view that women were inferior to men. Like children and the feeble-minded, women were viewed as generally well-intentioned but, by nature, less capable and less responsible than men.[31] The men who drafted the U.S. Constitution debated the legal status of slaves in that document but never thought to discuss the legal status of women.[32] Women, after all, were not considered capable of engaging in politics. They were not only restricted from voting, serving on juries, and pursuing higher education, but were considered by common law to have no legal existence apart from their husbands. This meant that they could not sign contracts or even own or inherit property. Most states even allowed men to subject their wives to "reasonable" physical punishment.[33] When Arkansas extended property rights to women in 1835, it had nothing to do with women's rights. Instead, in a time of economic panic, it was designed to shelter the husband's property from creditors.[34]

Closed out of politics, women joined churches at higher rates than men and used religion as a pathway to social activism through charitable work, temperance societies, and abolitionism. Women of the nineteenth century were not expected to speak in public to audiences of men (middle-class Americans were shocked when the British radical Frances Wright dared to do so in the late 1820s), but some religious organizations—such as Quakers—encouraged women to give personal witness in church meetings. One Quaker, Lucretia Mott, became a leading figure in the women's rights movement.[35] Mott advocated the abolition of slavery, and—along with Elizabeth Cady Stanton—served as part of the American delegation to the World Anti-Slavery Convention in London in 1840. There, after much debate, the convention leaders barred women delegates from participating on the convention floor; they were only allowed to view the proceedings from the galleries. Furious at the slight, Mott and Stanton vowed to advocate for women's rights back home.[36]

THE FIGHT FOR WOMEN'S SUFFRAGE

The Seneca Falls Convention—organized by Mott and Stanton and held in Seneca Falls, New York, in July 1848—is often viewed as the birth of the organized women's rights movement in the United States. Spanning two days, the convention attracted some 300 participants, mostly women, but the abolitionist and African American leader Frederick Douglass also attended (the convention advocated the abolition of slavery as well as the advancement of women's rights). The convention issued a Declaration of Sentiments concerning the rights of women that was modeled on the Declaration of Independence. Borrowing language from Thomas Jefferson, this Declaration made an important addition: "We hold these truths to be self-evident: that all men *and women* are created equal. . . ." [emphasis added]. The document then went on to catalogue a long list of grievances. For example, women were denied their inalienable right to vote, forced to submit to laws in which they had no voice, denied property rights, and "if married, in the eye of the law, civilly dead." Men had oppressed women "on all sides," the Declaration proclaimed, and "withheld from her rights which are given to the most ignorant and degraded men. . . ." To rectify this, the Convention—after much debate—used the Declaration to make a then shocking vow: that it was "the duty of the women of this country to secure to themselves the sacred right of the elective franchise."[37]

In the years that followed, various groups were formed to fight for women's right to vote, including the National Woman Suffrage Association, founded in 1869. This fight became known as the **women's suffrage movement.** The Constitution originally left it up to states to determine voting requirements. Initially, no state allowed women to vote, and many states further restricted the franchise by requiring the ownership of property (a right typically withheld from women) in order to vote. Some sort of property qualification had existed in all of the colonies and were not abandoned by all of the states until 1856.[38] New Jersey briefly allowed women to vote, from 1790 to 1807, but not until 1890—two decades after the Fifteenth Amendment prohibited the abridgement of voting rights "on account of race, color, or previous condition of servitude"— did another state, Wyoming, extend the franchise to women. By 1900, only three more states had joined Wyoming in allowing women to vote: Colorado (1893), Idaho (1896), and Utah (1896). For a global view of women's suffrage, see Table 5.2.

By the turn of the twentieth century, an organization called the Women's Christian Temperance Union (WCTU) had gained tremendous power and influence. Formed in 1873 by a group of evangelical Christian women, the WCTU quickly developed into a mass organization of women fighting for social and moral reform. Often associated primarily with the abolition of alcohol, the WCTU also embraced other social reform issues including the advocacy of labor rights for women, fighting prostitution and poverty, and promoting public health and international peace. It also became a powerful engine in the fight for women's suffrage.

That fight gained momentum during the early twentieth century. Starting around 1908 and continuing for a decade, women took to the streets in huge parades and mass gatherings to advocate for their right to vote. Those calling for women's suffrage came from a variety of backgrounds and classes and races, and they wanted to be able to vote

women's suffrage movement
The drive to grant women the right to vote.

TABLE 5.2
years, by select countries, in which women gained the right to vote

1893: New Zealand	1902: Australia	1913: Norway
1918: United Kingdom	1918: Canada	1919: Germany
1920: United States	1930: South Africa	1932: Brazil
1944: France	1945: Italy	1945: Japan
1947: Argentina	1950: India	1952: Greece
1953: Mexico	1956: Egypt	1963: Kenya
1971: Switzerland	1984: Yemen	

Source: Data from Inter-Parliamentary Union, (http://www.ipu.org/wmn-e/suffrage.htm)

in order to accomplish different goals. Nonetheless, they stood united on the short-term goal of securing women's suffrage.

A constitutional amendment to guarantee women the right to vote had first been drafted by Susan B. Anthony and Elizabeth Cady Stanton and introduced in the U.S. Senate in 1878. Congress consistently failed to pass it in the years that followed, but President Woodrow Wilson (1913–1921) became a champion of the proposed amendment. After initial, unsuccessful appeals to Congress, President Wilson called Congress into special session in 1919 to consider the amendment again. This time it passed and Congress sent it to the states for ratification. After decades of hard work, women finally gained their constitutional right to vote through ratification of the **Nineteenth Amendment** in 1920.

Nineteenth Amendment (1920)
Constitutional amendment that guaranteed women the right to vote.

WOMEN'S RIGHTS IN THE WORKPLACE

Despite securing the constitutional right to vote, women's social and economic rights still lagged far behind those of men. Women continued to be precluded from engaging in a wide range of professional activities. By the turn of the twentieth century, many lower-class women worked for low wages as seamstresses in the garment industry. Well into the twentieth century, well-educated women were largely restricted to being elementary and high school teachers, nurses, or secretaries, and many colleges and universities continued to deny admission to women. Princeton and Yale did not admit women until 1969, and Harvard College did not admit women until 1972 (Harvard Medical School began admitting women in 1945 and Harvard Law School followed suit in 1953). As late as 1970, only about 8 percent of U.S. physicians were women, and only about 4 percent of lawyers were female. Careers in business and politics were also elusive.

Women had entered the workforce in large numbers during World War II because of the labor shortage created by men entering the military, but they were largely displaced after the war. By the 1960s, women still found it difficult to be hired for many occupations. When the Equal Employment Opportunity Commission or EEOC (created by the Civil Rights Act of 1964) failed to enforce the law against sex discrimination in hiring, a group of women's activists formed the National Organization for Women (NOW) to fight for women's rights.

THE EQUAL RIGHTS AMENDMENT (ERA)

Equal Rights Amendment (ERA)
A proposed constitutional amendment that would have guaranteed that the government could not deny or abridge the rights of women on account of their sex. It was not ratified.

The National Organization for Women lobbied for a constitutional amendment to guarantee equal rights to women. The **Equal Rights Amendment (ERA)** had first been introduced in Congress in 1923. The Republican Party included support for the ERA in its party platform beginning in 1940, followed by the Democrats in 1944, but Congress did not pass the ERA and submit it to the states for ratification until 1972.

The main text of the proposed Equal Rights Amendment was straightforward. Section 1 stated simply: "Equality of rights under the law shall not be denied or abridged by the United States or by any state on account of sex." Section 2 gave Congress the power to enforce the amendment through legislation, and Section 3 said it would take effect two years after ratification. But ratification never came. Congress stipulated a seven-year deadline for ratification, which required support from 38 of the 50 states. By 1979, only 35 states had ratified the ERA. Congress granted a 39-month extension, but no additional states ratified the amendment during that time, so it died.

Part of the opposition to the ERA came as a result of the 1973 Supreme Court decision *Roe v. Wade,* which struck down state anti-abortion laws (see Chapter 4). Although *Roe* was not directly related to the ERA, opponents managed to portray support of the ERA as equivalent to support for abortion. Several states that had initially voted to ratify the ERA subsequently voted to rescind their ratification. After the failure of the ERA, NOW and other women's groups followed the example of the NAACP and fought for women's rights through court cases.

However, courts still apply the equal protection clause somewhat differently when ruling on classifications based on gender as compared with how they apply it in cases involving racial or ethnic classifications. The Supreme Court uses *strict scrutiny* (see Chapter 15) when a law treats someone differently because of race or ethnicity. However, when dealing with classifications based on gender, it uses an intermediate standard between strict scrutiny and mere reasonableness associated with the *rational basis test* (see Chapter 15). In other words, government need only demonstrate an important justification for classifications based on gender.

This intermediate level of scrutiny came into effect in order to give women greater protection than they had previously enjoyed (when gender discrimination was subjected to the mere rational basis test). But gender-based discrimination still does not trigger strict scrutiny because gender-based classifications can be motivated by factors other than discrimination.[39] For example, state laws that restrict women from working in an area that may pose environmental hazards if they become pregnant are designed to protect women, not discriminate against them. But when do such protections cross the line and become outmoded paternalism? For example, should it be permissible for the U.S. Selective Service System to exclude women from the military draft? Is such exclusion a form of gender discrimination, or does the government have an important interest in protecting women from combat? Exclusion of African Americans from the draft would clearly be considered racial discrimination. But using the intermediate standard for classifications based on gender, the Supreme Court in 1981 upheld the restriction on drafting women.[40]

SEXUAL HARASSMENT IN THE WORKPLACE

Title VII of the Civil Rights Act of 1964 made it unlawful to discriminate in the workplace. This included discrimination with regard to hiring, firing, financial compensation, and other terms and conditions of employment. In addition, Congress passed Title IX of the Education Amendments of 1972 to eliminate discrimination on the basis of sex in any educational program that receives federal funding. Left unclear was whether sexual harassment constituted a form of sex discrimination in these contexts.

picture YOURSELF ...

AS A WOMAN IN ZAMBIA

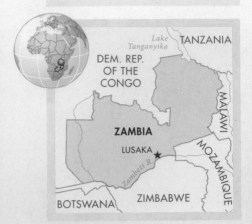

Zambia is a democratic republic and one of the most urbanized countries in sub-Saharan Africa. Its constitution guarantees the equality of men and women but contains an exception for laws governing adoption, marriage, divorce, the inheritance of property, and other matters of "personal law." Moreover, Zambia—like the United States—has a dual court system (see Chapter 15). Statutory law is supposed to take precedence over local customary law, but deep-seated tradition is

difficult to overcome—especially in rural areas.

In fact, discrimination against women is deeply rooted in Zambia's customary law. For example, adultery is lawful for men but not for women. The law

recognizes men as superior to women, giving men the authority to control the movements of their wives and daughters. Women are often viewed as property belonging to someone. Therefore, customary law often precludes women from owning or inheriting property.* Thus, when women are widowed or abandoned, they may be evicted from their homes.

Courts in Zambia have tried to extend property rights to women married under customary law (laws do exist to protect the property rights of women married under statutory law).† But even if a woman managed to retain land, she could not determine what crops to plant on it. That is considered to be a man's decision. Women are more apt to work in the fields. By one estimate, they make up 70 percent of unpaid labor on small-scale farms.**

* "Human Rights Violations in Zambia, Part II: Women's Rights," Shadow Report, UN Human Rights Commission, July 2007, pp. 5, 10, and 12 (http://www2.ohchr.org/english/bodies/hrc/docs/ngos/omct_zambia1.pdf).

† "Human Rights Violations in Zambia, Part II: Women's Rights," p. 28.

** Henry Machina, "Women's Land Rights in Zambia: Policy Provisions, Legal Framework, and Constraints." Paper presented at Regional Conference on Women's Land Rights, Harare, Zimbabwe, May 2002, p. 2 (http://www.oxfam.org.uk/resources/learning/landrights/downloads/womenzam.rtf).

questions to consider

1. **What are the consequences of a dual court system in Zambia for women's rights?**

2. **In a deeply patriarchal society, how effective can law be in changing behavior toward women?**

3. **How different is the plight of women in Zambia today from that of women in the United States during the nineteenth century?**

Until the late 1970s, most courts concluded that sexual harassment did not constitute discrimination under existing law. That changed in 1976 when a federal district court recognized that "quid pro quo" sexual harassment—that is, implicit or explicit requests for sexual favors in return for employment or advancement in the workplace—was a legitimate form of sex discrimination under Title VII.[41]

In addition to quid pro quo harassment, the Supreme Court ruled in 1986 that sexual harassment that creates a "hostile work environment" also violates Title VII. A hostile work environment was defined as unwelcome physical or verbal conduct of a sexual nature that is so persistent or severe that it causes an intimidating, hostile, or offensive work environment. In the case that established this precedent, Mechelle Vinson was hired by Sidney Taylor as a teller trainee at a bank. Vinson quickly rose to teller, head teller, and then assistant branch manager. Although these advancements were based on merit alone, Taylor—Vinson's supervisor—engaged in a persistent pattern of sexual harassment. He made sexual advances to her, exposed himself, and forcibly raped her on several occasions. Fearful of losing her job, Vinson engaged in sexual intercourse with him 40 or 50 times over the course of four years. A unanimous Supreme Court agreed that this persistent pattern of sexual harassment by Taylor amounted to a form of discrimination based on sex.[42]

Today, a hostile work environment need not consist of the level of abuse endured by Mechelle Vinson. It can be established by persistently leering (staring in a sexually suggestive manner), making offensive remarks about one's looks, clothes, or body parts, inappropriate touching (including patting or pinching), telling lewd or sexual jokes, or sending sexually suggestive notes, e-mails, or pictures. The Supreme Court extended protection to cases of same-sex harassment in 1998.[43]

EQUAL PAY FOR EQUAL WORK

Another issue related to the workplace is the concept of equal pay for equal work. Women have typically earned less than men, even when performing exactly the same job. In 1963, Congress took action to redress that inequity by passing the **Equal Pay Act.** At the time, women earned an average of 59 cents for every dollar earned by men. The Equal Pay Act prohibited wage discrimination based on sex. Thus, employers cannot pay one gender a lower wage for equal jobs requiring equal skill, effort, and responsibility that are performed under similar working conditions.

Equal Pay Act (1963)
Legislation that prohibits wage discrimination based on sex.

The Equal Pay Act allowed women to sue employers who did not comply with its provisions, but women's salaries continued to lag behind those of their male counterparts. According to the Institute for Women's Policy Research, women still earned only 81.2 cents for every dollar earned by men as of 2010 (see Figure 5.2). And a 2007 Supreme Court decision, *Ledbetter v. Goodyear Tire & Rubber Company,* made it more difficult for women to sue over discriminatory wages. In a 5-4 ruling, the Court interpreted the 180-day statute of limitations for filing claims as starting with the initial salary decision by an employer (rather than within 180 days of the most recent discriminatory paycheck). For example, a failure to give a raise to a woman performing the same job performed by a man could not be contested beyond 180 days of the salary decision itself—even if the female employee did not discover the discrepancy until after that 180-day period. Lilly Ledbetter found herself in just such a situation, but the Court ruled that since she had filed her claim after her 180-day window of opportunity, she could not sue.

Since the *Ledbetter* decision was based on an interpretation of statutory law (rather than constitutional law), Congress overturned the decision through passage of the Lilly Ledbetter Fair Pay Act, which President Obama signed into law in 2009. That Act clarified the statute of limitations and said that the 180-day statute of limitations resets with each discriminatory paycheck. The extended time period made it easier for women to file equal pay claims.

FIGURE 5.2

★ THE WAGE GAP, 2010

Despite passage of the Equal Pay Act in 1963, a wage gap still exists in the workplace today. How does it vary by ethnic group? How might you explain these variations?

	MEN'S MEDIAN WEEKLY EARNINGS	WOMEN'S MEDIAN WEEKLY EARNINGS	WOMEN'S EARNINGS AS PERCENT OF MEN'S	SHARE OF FEMALE WORKERS IN OCCUPATION	SHARE OF MALE WORKERS IN OCCUPATION AS PERCENT OF ALL MALE WORKERS	SHARE OF FEMALE WORKERS IN OCCUPATION AS PERCENT OF ALL FEMALE WORKERS
	$824	$669	81.2%	44.7%	100%	100%
10 most common occupations for women						
All female workers (44,472,000)						
Secretaries and administrative assistants	$725	$657	90.6%	95.7%	0.2%	5.2%
Registered nurses	$1,201	$1,039	86.5%	90.5%	0.4%	4.4%
Elementary and middle school teachers	$1,024	$931	90.9%	80.9%	0.8%	4.4%
Nursing, psychiatric, and home health aides	$488	$427	87.5%	87.0%	0.3%	2.6%
Customer service representatives	$614	$586	95.4%	66.2%	0.9%	2.3%
First-line supervisors/managers of retail sales workers	$782	$578	73.9%	45.5%	2.1%	2.2%
Cashiers	$400	$366	91.5%	71.5%	0.7%	2.1%
First-line supervisors/managers of office and administrative workers	$890	$726	81.6%	66.9%	0.8%	2.0%
Receptionists and information clerks	$547	$529	96.7%	92.5%	0.1%	1.8%
Accountants and auditors	$1,273	$953	74.9%	59.1	1.0%	1.8%
Sum					7.4%	28.8%
10 most common occupations for men						
All male workers (55,059,000)						
Driver sales workers and truck drivers	$691	$492	71.2%	3.3%	4.2%	0.2%
Managers, all other	$1,395	$1,045	74.9%	36.6%	2.2%	1.6%
First-line supervisors/managers of retail sales workers	$782	$578	73.9%	45.5%	2.1%	2.2%
Janitors and building cleaners	$494	$400	81.0%	28.5%	2.0%	1.0%
Retail salespersons	$651	$421	64.7%	42.1%	1.8%	1.7%
Laborers and freight, stock, and material movers, hand	$508	$419	82.5%	15.8%	1.8%	0.4%
Construction laborers	$569	*	*	2.2%	1.6%	0.0%
Sales representatives, wholesale and manufacturing	$983	$842	85.7%	24.0%	1.5%	0.6%
Computer software engineers	$1,590	$1,445	90.9%	20.6%	1.4%	0.4%
Chief executives	$2,217	$1,598	72.1%	25.6%	1.4%	0.6%
Sum					20.0%	8.7%

Notes: * Earnings data are made available only where there are an estimated minimum of 50,000 workers in an occupation.

Source: IWPR compilation of data from the U.S. Department of Labor, Bureau of Labor Statistics, 2010. "Household Data Annual Averages, Table 39." <http://www.bls.gov/pub/special.requests/lf/aar39.txt> (retrieved February 2011).

In 2011, the Supreme Court also made it more difficult for women to use a class action lawsuit to sue for discriminatory wages, promotions, and job assignments. In 2000, a 54-year-old employee filed a sex discrimination suit against Wal-Mart. This eventually turned into a class action lawsuit on behalf of 1.6 million women who had worked for the company since 1998. Women made up 70 percent of Wal-Mart's hourly workers but only 33 percent of management. In a 5-4 ruling, the Supreme Court concluded that those bringing the class action did not have enough in common to constitute a class because they had not provided convincing proof of a company-wide pattern of discrimination. The dissenters, including all three of the Court's female justices, disagreed and criticized the majority for disqualifying the class action suit at the starting gate.[44] The standard set by the Court will make large class action suits more difficult in the future. Some observers, including House Minority Leader Nancy Pelosi (D-Calif.), called the ruling a setback for the cause of women's equality.[45]

★ Supporters of the class action suit against Wal-Mart rally outside the Supreme Court building. The Court's subsequent ruling has been criticized by some as a setback for women's rights in the workplace.

TITLE IX

The above-mentioned **Title IX** of the Education Amendments of 1972 was intended to abolish all forms of sex discrimination in public education. Title IX led to more women attending institutions of higher education. For example, the percentage of female law school students rose from about 8 percent in 1970 to 33 percent in 1980.[46] Passage of Title IX also led to women being admitted to previously all-male public institutions, including the four U.S. military academies (Air Force, Coast Guard, Military, and Naval) in 1976. The Virginia Military Institute, a publicly funded school, continued to deny admission to women until the Supreme Court ruled in 1996 that its exclusion of women violated the equal protection clause.[47]

Despite its broader impact, Title IX is best known to the public for the effect it has had on high school and collegiate athletics. In 1979, the Department of Health, Education and Welfare under President Jimmy Carter established a three-pronged test to be applied specifically to athletic programs. An institution was deemed to be in compliance if it satisfied any one of the three prongs:

1. Student participation in athletics is proportional to the number of male and female students enrolled at the institution.

2. The institution is expanding opportunities for the underrepresented sex in athletics.

3. The institution is accommodating the interests and abilities of the underrepresented sex.

As a result, the number of female sports at high schools and institutes of higher education increased dramatically, with women's basketball leading the way. At the same time, many institutions dropped some men's sports such as wrestling.

Title IX
One of the Education Amendments of 1972 designed to abolish all forms of sex discrimination in public education.

DISCRIMINATION BASED ON ETHNICITY

KEY to understanding ★

Numerous ethnic groups have fought to end discrimination, including Native Americans, immigrants, and Hispanics (the largest minority group in the United States today). What kind of discrimination have these groups faced? What are the origins of this discrimination?

The fight for civil rights has certainly not been confined to blacks and women. Many ethnic groups have faced discrimination at various points in the history of the United States. Often such discrimination has been similar to that faced by African Americans.

NATIVE AMERICANS

As we saw in Chapter 2, North America was already home to as many as 10 million indigenous people when Christopher Columbus "discovered" America in 1492. These Native Americans were deeply affected by European colonization. Their population fell prey to epidemic diseases brought from Europe (such as smallpox, measles, influenza, and cholera), warfare with white settlers, and forced migration. Early on, tens of thousands of Native Americans were enslaved by colonists, but the Native American slave trade mostly died out by 1730 when the African slave trade expanded.

As population expanded in the United States, settlers began to move to the lower South where land was occupied by Native Americans. To facilitate this expansion, Congress passed the Indian Removal Act in 1830. The Act called for the relocation of Native American tribes in the southeastern United States, including the Cherokee, Chickasaw, Choctaw, Creek, and Seminole. The first to be moved was the Choctaw tribe, which was resettled from what are now the states of Alabama, Mississippi, and Louisiana to "Indian Territory" (present-day Oklahoma). Some 17,000 Choctaws embarked on the journey, but harsh weather and lack of food led to the death of as many as 6,000 of them en route—a journey that came to be known as the "trail of tears." In Florida, the Seminoles refused to leave, resulting in a bloody war that lasted from 1835 to 1842.

Manifest Destiny—the nineteenth-century belief that the United States was destined to expand westward across the continent—had a particularly devastating effect on Native Americans. Again, the westward move was largely the result of population growth, but it was also spurred by the search for new farmland. As Americans moved westward, more Native Americans were displaced and killed in battles. The Indian Appropriations Act of 1851 authorized the creation of Indian reservations where Native Americans could be relocated. Enforcement of the policy by the U.S. Army led to a series of conflicts including the Sioux Wars, which culminated in the massacre of women and children at Wounded Knee, South Dakota, in 1890.

Starting with passage of the Dawes Act in 1887, U.S. policy toward Native Americans began to shift toward assimilation rather than separation—part of an effort to convert Native Americans to Christianity. This included coercing children from Indian reservations to attend boarding schools such as the Carlisle Indian Industrial School in Pennsylvania (which the Native American athlete Jim Thorpe attended). The clear purpose of relocating children to these boarding schools was assimilation. This practice, however, led to a weakening of the identity and culture of Native Americans. Reservations continued to exist, but under the Dawes Act only those Native Americans who left their tribes were allowed to become U.S. citizens and vote. Not until 1924 did the Indian Citizenship Act grant citizenship to all Native Americans born within the United States, including those born on reservations. Despite their citizenship, many Native Americans were denied the right to vote by states and continued to face other forms of discrimination.

A coordinated civil rights movement for Native Americans has emerged only in the past 50 years, perhaps because tribes were small and scattered. The American Indian Movement (AIM), a radical Native American activist movement, formed in 1968. It drew publicity through organized protests, including the occupation of Mount Rushmore (which is on land that once belonged to Native Americans) and protests at World Series and Super Bowl games in which participating teams used figures of Native Americans as mascots or team names (such as the Cleveland Indians or Washington Redskins). While AIM tried to generate publicity, the Native American Rights Fund (NARF), founded in 1970, followed in the tradition of the NAACP's Legal Defense Fund and the National Organization for Women by using court cases to secure rights for Native Americans. This included efforts to recognize tribal sovereignty, guarantee the religious freedom of Native Americans, uphold voting rights, and protect sacred places such as Native American burial grounds. These efforts have had mixed results. For example, the Supreme Court held that government could restrict the use of peyote as a sacramental element in Native American religious ceremonies.[48]

After several years of effort by two U.S. senators—Sam Brownbeck (R-KS) and Byron Dorgan (D-ND)—Congress passed a formal apology to Native Americans in 2009. The apology was buried in the 2010 Defense Appropriations Bill. Little noticed at the time of its passage, the bill apologized "on behalf of the people of the United States to all Native Peoples for the many instances of violence, maltreatment, and neglect inflicted on Native Peoples by citizens of the United States." President Obama signed the bill into law on December 21, 2009.[49]

IMMIGRANTS

The United States is a nation of immigrants, but at various times during its history, segments of the population have embraced *nativism*—that is, opposition to immigration. For example, the immigration of large numbers of Irish and German Catholics starting in the 1830s led to the so-called Know Nothing Movement in the 1840s and 1850s, an anti-Catholic group that opposed immigration. The organization formed a national political party, formally known as the American Party, and scored some electoral victories—especially in Massachusetts—but quickly faded.

Later in the 1800s, large numbers of Chinese came to the United States in search of gold in California and jobs building the transcontinental railroad. Some labor organizations, such as the Knights of Labor, led opposition to the cheap labor provided by Chinese immigrants and called for their expulsion. Some of this opposition led to riots against Chinese laborers. Even Congress became involved. For the first and only time in its history, Congress passed legislation banning immigration on the basis of race: the Chinese Exclusion Act in 1882 banned further immigration of Chinese for 10 years. Many people spoke openly of the so-called "Yellow Peril" posed by this supposedly "inferior race." Congress extended the Chinese Exclusion Act in 1892 and made it permanent in 1902. Not until 1943, when China was an ally of the United States in World War II, did Congress allow limited immigration of Chinese.

Despite the easing of immigration restrictions, widespread racism toward people of Asian descent continued. This was compounded by racist portrayals of the Japanese—an enemy of the United States during World War II. Fearing a Japanese invasion of the West Coast after Pearl Harbor, President Franklin Roosevelt ordered the forced relocation of some 117,000 people of Japanese descent who lived in that area—two-thirds of them native-born U.S. citizens—to concentration camps.

★ Once the only immigrant group to be excluded from entering the United States, there are now 4.0 million Chinese residing within the country's borders, according to the 2010 U.S. Census.

One such citizen, Fred Korematsu, was arrested when he refused to leave his home in San Leandro, California. The Supreme Court, in a 6-3 decision, upheld the conviction. In his dissent, Justice Murphy wrote that the policy that allowed Korematsu's arrest went over the brink of constitutional power and fell into "the ugly abyss of racism."[50]

In 1988, President Ronald Reagan signed congressional legislation that extended a formal apology to Japanese Americans who had been affected by the relocation policy, and authorized reparations (monetary compensation) of $20,000 to each of the surviving detainees. Since those who were relocated had lost homes, businesses, and most of their property as well as their liberty, many considered this to be paltry compensation, and many of the survivors died before payment could be made. In January 1998, President Bill Clinton awarded Fred Korematsu a Presidential Medal of Freedom—the highest civilian award in the United States.

Immigration from Eastern and Southern Europe in the late nineteenth and early twentieth centuries also led to nativist movements. Immigrants from places such as Italy and Poland provided cheap labor but provoked fears that they were flooding the market and taking jobs away from Americans. Negative stereotypes were commonplace, as were extreme prejudice and even violence. In New Orleans, a mob of some 10,000 people lynched eleven Italians in 1891—one of the largest mass lynchings in U.S. history.[51] During this period, the Ku Klux Klan embraced anti-immigrant and anti-Catholic views, as well as white supremacy.

THE CURRENT CONTROVERSY OVER ILLEGAL IMMIGRANTS

It is estimated that there are some 12 million illegal immigrants in the United States.[52] Many of these are Hispanics who have crossed the border from Mexico. How to deal with illegal immigration has become a divisive issue. So far, calls for immigration reform by George W. Bush and Barack Obama have gone nowhere.

Some states—such as Alabama, Arizona, Georgia, Indiana, and Utah—have responded by enacting tough immigration laws. These laws have raised civil rights concerns. For example, the Arizona law required police "when practicable" to detain people they suspect are in the U.S. illegally and verify their status (raising the fear of racial profiling—that is, using race or ethnicity as the primary reason to suspect that an individual has broken the law). The Alabama law—the toughest in the nation when it was enacted—made it a crime for immigrants not to carry their registration documents with them at all times. It also required schools to determine the immigration status of children who are enrolling, as well as their parents.

The Justice Department filed suit against the Arizona law in 2010 on the grounds that it interfered with the authority of the federal government to patrol the borders and could lead to police harassment. The Supreme Court agreed to hear the case during its 2011–2012 term.[53] Civil rights groups also have filed challenges. Litigation is ongoing, but opponents have won some victories. In October 2011, the 11th Circuit Court of Appeals struck down the above-mentioned provisions of the Alabama law, although it also allowed other controversial provisions—such as those making it a felony for illegal immigrants to enter into "business transactions" with the state (such as applying for a driver's license) and invalidating all contracts knowingly entered into with illegal immigrants.[54]

HISPANICS

Hispanics are the largest and fastest-growing minority group in the United States. They made up 16 percent of the nation's total population according to the 2010 census. The U.S. Census Bureau has estimated that Hispanics will make up 30 percent of the nation's population by 2050.

Hispanics have also faced discrimination. Mexican Americans in the Southeastern United States and California confronted discriminatory laws and practices similar to those faced by African Americans. These included segregated schools, the use of poll taxes and other devices to discourage voting, and exclusion from service on juries. In 1928, the League of United Latin American Citizens (LULAC) formed to combat discrimination. It also engaged in voter registration drives, community education campaigns, and litigation to further the rights of Hispanic Americans. It successfully sued in 1945 to integrate the Orange County School System in California, where Hispanics had been compelled to attend segregated schools. The Federal District Court decision in *Mendez v. Westminster,* an important precursor to *Brown v. Board of Education,* concluded that requiring separate schools for children of Mexican ancestry violated the equal protection clause of the U.S. Constitution.[55] The subsequent ruling by the Ninth Circuit Court of Appeals in *Mendez v. Westminister* decided the case on narrower grounds but still struck down the segregation.[56] LULAC also brought an end to the exclusion of Hispanic Americans from juries through a landmark Supreme Court case, *Hernandez v. Texas.*[57] Another group, the Mexican American Legal Defense and Education Fund (MALDEF), was organized in 1968 to fight for civil rights through a combination of advocacy, educational outreach, and litigation. Since then it has brought successful legal challenges to attempts by public school districts to charge tuition to children of undocumented immigrant parents and to redistricting plans that discriminated against Latino voters.[58]

Hispanics are now a significant voting bloc nationwide, with especially high populations in important swing states such as California, Texas, and Florida, which have a large number of electoral votes in presidential elections (see Figure 5.3). Despite

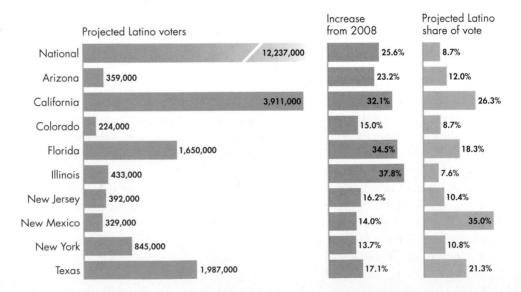

FIGURE 5.3

★ THE HISPANIC VOTE

What do these numbers indicate about the significance of the Hispanic vote in the United States?

Source: Data from "Latino Voters Will Come Out in Record Numbers in 2012," News Taco, The Latino Daily. (http://www.newstaco.com/2011/06/23/latino-voters-will-come-out-in-record-numbers-in-2012/)

	Projected Latino voters	Increase from 2008	Projected Latino share of vote
National	12,237,000	25.6%	8.7%
Arizona	359,000	23.2%	12.0%
California	3,911,000	32.1%	26.3%
Colorado	224,000	15.0%	8.7%
Florida	1,650,000	34.5%	18.3%
Illinois	433,000	37.8%	7.6%
New Jersey	392,000	16.2%	10.4%
New Mexico	329,000	14.0%	35.0%
New York	845,000	13.7%	10.8%
Texas	1,987,000	17.1%	21.3%

their increasing numbers, Hispanics made up only 3 percent of the Senate and 5 percent of the House of Representatives in the 111th Congress. Barack Obama appointed the first Hispanic justice to the Supreme Court in 2009, and presidents since Jimmy Carter have focused in varying degrees on appointing Hispanic judges to the lower federal courts.

The growing use of Spanish in the United States as a result of the rising Hispanic population has led to debate. The United States has no "official" language at the national level, but some have pushed to make English the country's official language. In contrast to the federal government, 31 states have designated English as the official language (see Figure 5.4). The actual scope of these state laws varies from one state to another. While some simply declare English to be the official language, others prohibit or limit government from offering non-English language assistance or services (such as courtroom translation, multilingual emergency police lines, and multilingual election ballots). Is there anything wrong with that? At what point, if any, does insistence on "English-only" violate individual rights? So far, the Supreme Court has not struck down such laws. Should it? Some groups, such as MALDEF and the American Civil Liberties Union, think so.

★ Sonia Sotomayor is the first Hispanic justice on the Supreme Court. She is of Puerto Rican descent.

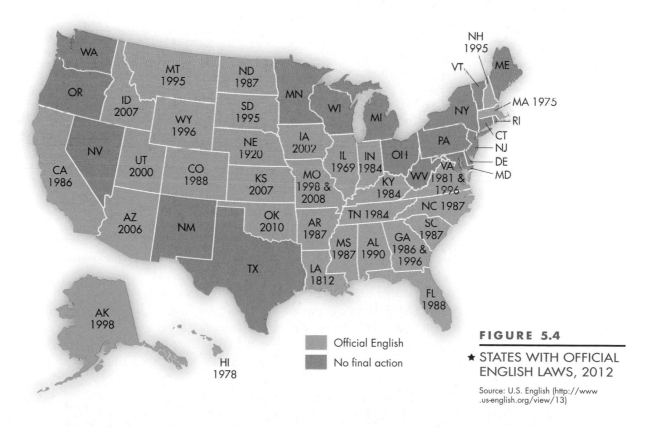

Official English

No final action

FIGURE 5.4

★ STATES WITH OFFICIAL ENGLISH LAWS, 2012

Source: U.S. English (http://www.us-english.org/view/13)

NEW FRONTIERS IN CIVIL RIGHTS

KEY TO understanding ★

Civil rights battles are no longer confined to groups claiming discrimination based on race, gender, or ethnic origin. Today incidents of discrimination based on sexual orientation and physical disabilities are also being framed as civil rights issues. Is access to public transportation for the disabled a civil right? What about same-sex marriage?

The civil rights movement for blacks, women, and ethnic minorities has a long history, even if success has been recent and incomplete. Within the government, civil rights advocates have made great strides toward the equal treatment of individuals regardless of race and gender, and they have begun to work to achieve similar gains for other groups, such as members of the LGBT community and individuals with disabilities.

LESBIANS, GAYS, BISEXUALS, AND TRANSGENDERED (LGBT) RIGHTS

Advocating the rights of lesbians, gays, bisexuals, and the transgendered (LGBT) is a recent phenomenon. As we saw in Chapter 4, laws criminalizing private homosexual conduct between consenting adults were commonplace through much of U.S. history. Laws sentenced people to jail and hard labor for homosexual conduct. Illinois became the first state to decriminalize such conduct in 1962, but the U.S. Supreme Court did not strike down such laws until 2003.

The 1964 Civil Rights Act banned discrimination in employment based on race, color, religion, national origin, or sex, but it did not ban discrimination based on sexual orientation. As a result, lesbians and gay men continued to face routine discrimination in getting and retaining jobs, in securing housing, and in gaining custody of their children. Same-sex partners were denied privileges that were routinely granted to heterosexual partners, ranging from hospital visitation rights to employment benefits. Change has come slowly. Wisconsin, in 1982, became the first state to ban employment discrimination based on sexual orientation, and since then 21 other states and the District of Columbia have followed suit. Efforts to enact federal legislation in the form of an Employment Non-Discrimination Act have so far been unsuccessful, as has passage of federal legislation to prevent housing discrimination.

Homosexuals were long banned from serving in the U.S. military. During his 1992 presidential campaign, Bill Clinton pledged to allow all people to serve in the military regardless of their sexual orientation. Once elected, he faced strong opposition from the military to enacting such a policy. The compromise solution, "Don't Ask, Don't Tell," prohibited the military from asking service members or applicants about their sexual preferences. But the compromise only protected closeted homosexuals, not those who were openly gay, lesbian, or bisexual. As a presidential candidate, Barack Obama promised to bring an end to "Don't Ask, Don't Tell," and as president he succeeded. Congress passed the "Don't Ask, Don't Tell Repeal Act" in 2010. By a vote of 250 to 175, the House of Representative voted to repeal the law in December 2010, but the real hurdle was the vote in the Senate where Republicans initially filibustered the repeal. Eight moderate Republicans ended the impasse by breaking ranks with their party to achieve a filibuster-proof majority: 63-33. The law took effect in September 2011. For the first time in America's military history, service members could reveal their sexual orientation without fear of reprisal. While 67 percent of those surveyed in a Gallup poll approved of the repeal, opposition still exists among some.[59] In another step to promote LGBT rights, President Obama ordered hospitals that receive Medicare or Medicaid payments to grant visitation rights for same-sex couples.[60]

Courts have also played a major role in extending gay rights. For example, the Supreme Court, in a 6-3 vote in 1996, struck down Amendment 2 to Colorado's state constitution. Amendment 2 had been enacted by voter initiative as a response to local ordinances that banned discrimination based on sexual orientation in housing, employment, education, public accommodations, health and welfare services, and other transactions and activities. The amendment precluded any action by any part of state government to enforce those ordinances or to protect individuals based on their "homosexual, lesbian, or bisexual orientation, conduct, practices, or relationships."

In his majority opinion, Justice Anthony Kennedy noted that Amendment 2 violated the equal protection clause because it classified "homosexuals not to further a legitimate legislative end but to make them unequal to everyone else. This Colorado cannot do. A state cannot so deem a class of persons a stranger to its laws." He also noted that Amendment 2 seemed "inexplicable by anything but animus toward the class it affects."[61] Nonetheless, some forms of discrimination remain legal. For example, in 2000, the Supreme Court upheld the Boy Scout's ban on homosexuals being scoutmasters.[62] Most recently, attention has focused on the issue of same-sex marriage (see Chapter 4), asking whether laws banning it violate equal protection. The Supreme Court has yet to rule on that issue, but it almost certainly will do so at some point in the relatively near future.

★ George Takei, the actor who played Sulu in the original *Star Trek* television series, was among the first to take advantage of the legalization of same-sex marriage in California.

DISABILITY RIGHTS

Efforts to protect the rights of the disabled are also relatively recent. Through much of our history, people with disabilities were shunned and discriminated against. Parents often hid their children with disabilities and sometimes even killed them. Perspectives began to change in the wake of World War II when many disabled veterans returned home. But even as social stereotypes began to recede, physical barriers remained. Few buildings or modes of mass transit were handicap accessible, and disability was not deemed a protected category in the Civil Rights Act of 1964.

The first legislation directly protecting the disabled came in 1973 with the Rehabilitation Act, which prohibited disability discrimination by the federal government in the hiring of federal employees and in programs that received federal aid. The act was amended in 1978 to require handicap access to federal buildings.

In 1990, Congress passed the Americans with Disabilities Act (ADA). The ADA defines disability as "a physical or mental impairment that substantially limits a major

life activity." That definition has been subject to interpretation. The Supreme Court, for example, has ruled that conditions that can be corrected with medication or other corrective devices are not covered. Thus, blindness is covered but nearsightedness is not. Still, there are gray areas.

Most significantly, the ADA requires both public and private employers to make "reasonable accommodations" for employees with disabilities, and it requires that public buildings and services be accessible to people with disabilities. Thus, buses and trains have been made wheelchair accessible, and buildings have added ramps, handrails, and other accommodations for the disabled. Private businesses are covered; for example, rental car companies must provide vehicles with hand controls for disabled drivers. Telecommunications companies are also required to accommodate the deaf and hard of hearing. For example, captions are provided on television shows and telecommunications devices for the deaf are provided by telephone companies. Such accommodations required by the ADA can be expensive. As a result, the ADA was opposed by many members of the business community.

REDRESSING PAST DISCRIMINATION

★ KEY TO understanding

For decades, discrimination stood as a barrier to success for many Americans. Is it enough to end discrimination, or should steps be taken to redress past discrimination? The most notable effort to redress past discrimination has been affirmative action. Some have called for other forms of governmental action, such as apologies and even the payment of reparations.

What should government do to remedy and atone for violations of civil liberties, such as slavery and other forms of past discrimination? This is a difficult and often politically charged question. Are apologies appropriate? Are they enough? Should the government pay reparations, as it did to Japanese Americans who were interned during World War II? Many of the formal vestiges of discrimination have been removed in this country, but does anything more need to be done? For example, should policies be enacted to remedy past discrimination by insuring that certain groups are represented in college admissions and hiring? If so, how long should such policies stay in place?

AFFIRMATIVE ACTION

affirmative action
A policy intended to promote equal opportunities for members of previously disadvantaged groups in education and employment.

President Lyndon Johnson introduced the idea of **affirmative action**—a policy intended to promote equal opportunities for members of previously disadvantaged groups in education and employment—at a commencement speech at historically black Howard University on June 6, 1965. Three months later, he signed an executive order that implemented affirmative action for the first time. Executive Order 11246 not only prohibited federal contractors from discriminating in employment on the basis of race, but also required them to "take affirmative action to ensure that applicants are employed . . . without regard to their race, color, religion, sex, or national origin." The actual implementation of affirmative action has caused heated debate (see Figure 5.5). Opponents argue that it amounts to preferential treatment of minorities and women—"reverse discrimination"—which should be considered a violation of the equal protection clause.

In its first major ruling on affirmative action in *University of California v. Bakke* (1978), the Supreme Court, in a complicated 5-4 decision, struck down race-based quotas in the admissions process at the University of California Medical School, arguing that quotas in this instance—where race was the only criterion used by the University to fill its "minority" positions—were not the least intrusive means of achieving racial diversity among the student body. At the same time, the Court did not completely rule out the use of quotas in all circumstances. It recognized that achieving racial diversity is a legitimate goal and that race or sex can be one of many factors considered in the admissions process.

In the 1980s and 1990s, several Supreme Court decisions limited, but did not abolish, affirmative action. Most notably, the Court began to apply strict scrutiny to affirmative action cases. In early cases, the majority of the Court did not treat affirmative action as a violation of equal protection, but by 1995 it did.[63] This meant that the government had to demonstrate a compelling justification for a racial classification rather than just a rational basis, and that any necessary interference with a fundamental right to achieve that compelling interest be the least restrictive means of achieving the end. Thus, it became more difficult for specific instances of affirmative action to withstand judicial scrutiny.

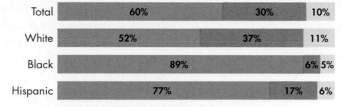

To help blacks get better jobs/education?

	Favor	Oppose	Don't know
Total	60%	30%	10%
White	52%	37%	11%
Black	89%	6%	5%
Hispanic	77%	17%	6%

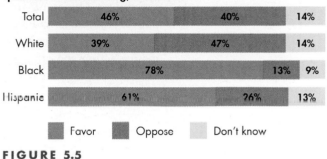

Which give special preferences to qualified blacks in hiring/education?

	Favor	Oppose	Don't know
Total	46%	40%	14%
White	39%	47%	14%
Black	78%	13%	9%
Hispanic	61%	26%	13%

  ■ Favor   ■ Oppose   ■ Don't know

FIGURE 5.5

★ PUBLIC VIEWS ON AFFIRMATIVE ACTION

The graph reflects data collected in response to the question, "To overcome past discrimination, do you favor affirmative action programs?"

Source: © 2007 Pew Research Center, Social & Demographic Trends Project. Blacks See Growing Values Gap Between Poor and Middle Class, http://www.pewsocialtrends.org/2007/11/13/blacks-see-growing-values-gap-between-poor-and-middle-class/

Nonetheless, the Supreme Court continues to uphold limited forms of affirmative action in areas such as law school admissions. In a 5-4 decision in *Grutter v. Bolinger* (2003), the Court—using a strict scrutiny test—concluded that the University of Michigan had a compelling interest in obtaining a "critical mass" of minority students, and that its consideration of race in the admissions process was narrowly tailored to achieve that interest. Nonetheless, the opinion for the Court by Justice Sandra Day O'Connor suggested that affirmative action was a temporary solution: "We expect that 25 years from now, the use of racial preferences will no longer be necessary to further the interest approved today."[64] In 2012, the Supreme Court agreed to revisit the issue of affirmative action in higher education. A ruling in the case, involving the University of Texas, is expected in 2013 and it will likely reverse or cut back on existing affirmative action policies.[65]

APOLOGIES AND REPARATIONS

The U.S. House and Senate (but not the U.S. president) have formally apologized for slavery, President Obama signed a law in 2009 that included an apology to Native Americans, President Reagan signed a law apologizing to Japanese Americans for their internment during World War II, and in 2012 the House passed a resolution apologizing for the Chinese Exclusion Act.

Some argue that apologies are not enough and that more tangible action needs to be taken to atone for past discrimination, such as reparations paid to Japanese Americans who had been placed in relocation camps during World War II. In that case, money was paid only to those who had been sent to the relocation camps, not to their descendants. Why has the government paid reparations to Japanese Americans and not to former slaves or Native Americans?

Various arguments have been made in support of reparations. The most obvious is atonement for past injustices. For example, thousands of slaves were subjected to forced, unpaid labor in the years before the Civil War, and some argue that their descendants should be compensated for that. Others see reparations as a way to redistribute wealth and political power. Still others see reparations as primarily a symbolic gesture—even a teaching moment.[66] Various arguments have also been made against reparations. One argument raised by opponents of reparations is that those who would pay for reparations had nothing to do with the injustices that took place. Another argument is that reparations have already been effectively paid through such things as affirmative action and other social services programs. Yet another is that administering reparations programs would be impracticable, divisive, and hugely expensive.[67]

Why Are We
THE WAY WE ARE?

Despite the Founders' assertions of liberty and equality, large segments of our population have found both to be elusive during much of our history. During that time, government often played an active role in restricting civil rights, or at least in condoning such restrictions. However, in the last half century, in particular, government has taken actions to advance civil rights and correct past discrimination through legislation, court cases, affirmative action policies, and other measures. How have these efforts helped to shape why we are the way we are?

RACE

Race continues to be a defining issue in American politics. American political and economic development has been deeply influenced both by slavery and by later forms of racial discrimination, often sanctioned by those in power. We are the way we are in part because of—and in part despite of—this "stain on our soul."

In 2008, Americans elected the country's first African-American president. The next day, President George W. Bush said: "No matter how they cast their ballot, all Americans can be proud of the history that was made yesterday." Obama's election came less than 50 years after the brutal attacks on the Freedom Riders for defying segregation. Not only did Obama's election demonstrate remarkable strides in race relations, but—as political commentator Juan Williams wrote—it highlighted a unique fact: "There is no other nation in the world where a 75 percent majority electorate has selected as their supreme leader a man who identifies as one of that nation's historically oppressed minorities." Williams added that Obama's election did not end discrimination in America, nor did it minimize the fact that "inside black America, there is still disproportionate poverty, school dropouts, criminal activity, incarceration and single motherhood." But it did shift the discussion, so that now the discussion is "how the child of even the most oppressed of racial minorities can maximize his or her strengths and overcome negative stereotypes through achievement."[68]

JUDICIAL AND CONGRESSIONAL ACTION

Courts have profoundly influenced civil rights in this country. Early Supreme Court decisions in the wake of the Civil War, such as *Plessy v. Ferguson* and the *Civil Rights Cases,* set back the cause of civil rights for many decades. But, more recently, many advances in civil rights have been brought about by federal courts. Judicial independence has allowed judges to take actions that legislators could not or would not dare to take. Interest groups such as the NAACP, the Native American Rights Fund, and the Mexican American Legal Defense and Education Fund have also played an important role in bringing litigation to spur judicial action. More recently, courts have been at the forefront of protecting individuals from discrimination on the basis of sexual orientation. Congress has played an important role, too, with legislation ranging from the Civil Rights Act of 1964 to the Don't Ask, Don't Tell Repeal Act of 2010.

CITIZEN MOBILIZATION

Citizen mobilization is an important part of the civil rights movement—not only for African Americans but for other groups, as well. Boycotts, nonviolent resistance, public gatherings, and dynamic leaders have helped to promote civil rights. From the Seneca Falls Convention in 1848, to the 1963 March on Washington and Martin Luther King's galvanizing "I Have a Dream" speech, to more recent marches for immigrant rights, citizen mobilization draws publicity and can be used to exert political pressure. We are the way we are because people like you took action. That is what has made civil rights movements possible.

. . . AND WHY DOES IT Matter?

The advances discussed in this chapter affect you directly. You are protected from many forms of discrimination that were routine for previous generations of Americans. You are not compelled to attend segregated schools or sit at the back of the bus because you are black; denied the right to vote because you are a woman; kept off a jury because you are Hispanic; precluded from serving in the military because you are gay; or unable to access public facilities because you are handicapped.

Nonetheless, past discrimination continues to affect our national identity, citizen discourse, and the way Americans view each other today. Opposition to social welfare programs often has racial overtones, as do views about immigration. And social and religious values weigh heavily in debates about emerging civil rights issues such as same-sex marriage. Indeed, efforts to extend civil rights in such areas contribute to the so-called "culture war," and differing views about whether issues such as same-sex marriage constitute a civil right sharpen the edge of polarized politics.

During the 2012 election, there was renewed debate about whether some voting registration systems and state election laws were still designed to discourage minority voting. For example, Florida banned early voting on the Sunday before Election Day, when black churches typically encouraged voting. Attorney General Eric Holder promised renewed federal oversight of such laws, including state laws requiring a photo ID to vote (which some view as a move to discourage minority voting).[69] These laws matter, as does your ability to assess whether they do, in fact, discriminate.

critical thinking questions

1. **What types of discrimination have African Americans faced? How and to what extent have they overcome this discrimination?**

2. **How have women in the United States earned rights in the workplace? Where do women still face challenges?**

3. **How should the United States deal with the issue of illegal immigration? Do state laws that restrict the rights of illegal immigrants raise civil rights issues?**

key terms

affirmative action, *180*

Black Codes, *155*

Brown v. Board of Education (1954), *160*

civil rights, *153*

Civil Rights Act of 1964, *162*

Civil Rights Cases (1883), *156*

Equal Pay Act (1963), *169*

Equal Rights Amendment (ERA), *166*

Fifteenth Amendment (1870), *155*

Fourteenth Amendment (1868), *155*

fugitive slave clause, *153*

grandfather clauses, *157*

Jim Crow laws, *157*

literacy tests, *157*

Martin Luther King, Jr., *161*

NAACP, *159*

Nineteenth Amendment (1920), *166*

Plessy v. Ferguson (1896), *157*

poll taxes, *157*

separate but equal doctrine, *157*

women's suffrage movement, *165*

Thirteenth Amendment (1865), *155*

Title IX, *171*

Voting Rights Act of 1965, *162*

white primaries, *158*

PUBLIC OPINION AND POLITICAL SOCIALIZATION

- Define public opinion and explain its role in political decision making.
- Describe American political culture and explain how it has evolved over time.
- Define American exceptionalism and consider the factors that have contributed to this perspective.
- Understand political socialization and the sources through which Americans learn their values.
- Identify the ways in which different groups affect public opinion and politics in general.
- Evaluate the factors that bring about changes in public opinion.
- Explain how ideologies acquire their structure.
- Explore the different methods by which public opinion can be measured.

PERSPECTIVE
What Difference Does Public Opinion Make?

The United States spends less than most prosperous countries to provide basic welfare to its people. In 2008 the government spent less than one-fourth of our gross domestic product on housing, health, recreation, education, and social programs. ("Gross domestic product" is the total amount spent in a country in a year on all goods and services.) In that same year Sweden spent 37 percent of its gross domestic product on such programs.[1] Sweden is known to be a "welfare state" whose government spends a great deal to meet basic human needs. It provides several hundred dollars a month of basic support to all families with children, provides full health care for everyone in the country, and provides free university education for all.

We might expect from this that Swedes are especially supportive of government programs to provide for people. But ironically, when Americans and Swedes are asked whether the government should ensure that everyone is provided for, or whether people should take more responsibility to provide for themselves, only 33 percent of Swedes thought the government should provide for people. Americans actually supported welfare state programs somewhat more than the Swedes, with 45 percent in favor.[2]

Why is it that countries' policies do not match the wishes of their citizens more closely? How is it that Swedes, who believe less in government intervention than Americans, spend so much more on government support for their citizens than we do? What role does public opinion play in determining a country's policies?

IN THIS CHAPTER, we start by defining public opinion, and then we analyze how it is informed by political culture and political knowledge. Next, we evaluate what the role of public opinion should be in a democracy. We then turn to how public opinion is formed—what agents influence the development of values and formation of views within a society. We explore whether and how public opinion changes over time, and we examine trends among different groups within society. We look at how Americans have measured public opinion in the past and how we measure it now. Finally, we turn to the important issue of when and how public opinion determines policy making. As you read this chapter, keep in mind our two core questions:

WHY ARE WE THE WAY WE ARE?
WHY DOES IT MATTER TO YOU?

In particular, how is public opinion formed, and how does it affect policy?

PUBLIC OPINION

KEY TO understanding

What is public opinion, and what role should it play in a democracy? Public opinion is the overall opinion of citizens on political issues. Some people have stronger voices than others and therefore have a greater impact. Public opinion was originally thought of as the opinion of those who write or speak about politics. In recent years, however, the concept has broadened to encompass the accumulation of everyone's opinions, measured by opinion polls and weighted equally.

public opinion
The collective opinion of citizens on a policy issue or a principle of politics

Public opinion consists of the combined voices of all the people in a society on political issues. Today, to measure public opinion we usually ask people in a poll or survey how they feel about an issue and then add up their opinions; we treat this as "public opinion" on the issue. However, public opinion as it actually enters political decision making is not a simple sum of everyone's opinions on an issue. Some people are heard more in politics than others. Bloggers, newspaper columnists, citizens who write or e-mail their representatives in Congress, those who are active in electoral campaigns—all of these individuals add more than other people to public opinion as it is actually heard by government officials. Think of a choir in which some people have especially strong voices. What decision makers hear is determined more by the strong voices than by other members of the choir. It is very difficult to come up with a full picture of public opinion in this sense, because it would mean taking into account thousands of variations in how much impact different individuals have. As a general rule, political scientists look at the simpler version of public opinion as the sum of all individual opinions, and that is how we will present it in this chapter.

In a sense, public opinion was born at the Founding of the Republic. Although some of his colleagues—including Alexander Hamilton—were less enthusiastic about its role in the new country, James Madison argued for a strong role for public opinion. Along with Thomas Jefferson, he argued that the social and intellectual elites could not be assumed to have a monopoly on truth, and he encouraged the growth of newspapers to facilitate a "general intercourse of sentiments."[3] Ever since that time, public opinion has been recognized as an important factor in American democracy.

Until the 1940s, public opinion was thought of solely as the more complex entity composed of writers, lecturers, party activists, and others whose voices were heard publicly. After polling and survey analysis were invented in the 1940s, however, it became possible to measure how all people in the country felt about an issue, and from then on, "public opinion" more and more began to mean the average of all individual opinions.

POLITICAL CULTURE

Public opinion is in part a product of a country's political culture. The **political culture** of a country consists of the political attitudes and beliefs held broadly among its citizens, which form the basis for their political behavior. These attitudes are not so much about specific policy issues as about the basic underlying political system.

Political culture varies a good deal from one country to another, and it is in good part responsible for major differences in how politics is conducted. We can sometimes detect differences in culture by looking at popular behaviors and sayings. For instance, the Japanese tend to emphasize consensus and dislike conflict to a greater extent than Americans, as illustrated by two popular sayings:

- The nail that sticks out gets hammered down. (Japan)
- The squeaky wheel gets the grease. (United States)

The basic differences reflected in these two sayings must surely have something to do with the fact that political decisions are more likely in Japan than in the United States to be made on the basis of unanimous consent, rather than by a vote in which one side wins and the other side loses. Individualistic assertion and challenges are highly valued in the United States, less so in Japan.

Political culture usually changes slowly. French political thinker Alexis de Tocqueville visited the United States in the early nineteenth century to examine the workings of U.S. democracy. In his seminal work, *Democracy in America,*[4] he outlined the American approach to politics—its emphasis on individuality and freedom, reliance on local politics and voluntary organizations, restlessness and desire for progress. These attitudes still guide American politics today. This is stunning when we consider the fact that the America he saw was an almost totally agricultural society, without modern means of communication or a preeminent role in world politics. Since that time, American society has absorbed many waves of immigrants who initially came to the United States with very different cultures. Our country and society have changed immensely since de Tocqueville wrote his book, yet the underlying political culture has remained almost unchanged.

The basic American values of fairness, individualism, religion, and the rule of law that we introduced in Chapter 1 are an important part of America's political culture. In addition, four other aspects of any political culture are especially important if democracy is to work well:

- *Tolerance of those advocating unpopular ideas.* If those who dissent are not allowed to present their positions publicly,

political culture
A people's attitudes, beliefs, and factual assumptions about the basic nature of society and basic principles of politics.

★ The crowd at a "cheering section" at a Nippon League baseball game in Japan. Members of the cheering section do not spread out, but sit close together in an agreed-upon formation, leaving large sections of the stadium empty. They do everything in unison throughout the game.

★ The idealized American cowboy has long conveyed the American ideal of independence and self-sufficiency.

there will be no opportunities to debate new ideas and no possibility for change.

- *Trust in the system of government.* Although citizens in a democracy must be willing to criticize individual officeholders, they need to trust that the overall system will be fair.

- *Political efficacy.* People must believe that what they do can make a difference in government policies.

- *Political knowledge and attention to policies.* People must know enough about politicians and their policy positions to choose between them.

Let us see how well Americans' attitudes fit with these four cornerstones of democracy.

POLITICAL TOLERANCE

Americans' level of tolerance for dissent is disappointingly low, but it is not worse than that of other democracies around the world. In 2010, 38 percent of Americans thought that someone who is opposed to churches and religion should be barred from teaching in a college, and 22 percent thought that such a person should not be allowed to give a public speech. Similarly, 24 percent thought that speeches offensive to ethnic groups should not be allowed.[5] Intolerance of this sort is not uncommon in democracies around the world. Levels of tolerance in Israel, Great Britain, and New Zealand are fairly similar to those in the United States.[6]

Over the last few decades, Americans appear to have become increasingly tolerant of dissent. In 1954, as seen in Figure 6.1, a surprising 88 percent of Americans thought that someone opposed to religion should not be allowed to teach in a college, but the proportion of people who hold this viewpoint has declined steadily since then.[7] There have been similar declines in intolerance for other forms of dissenting speech and action.

FIGURE 6.1

★ IS INTOLERANCE DECREASING IN AMERICA?

Shown here is the percent of Americans believing that a person who is against churches and religion should be barred from teaching in college. What may have brought about the decrease in such intolerance since the 1950s?

Source: Data from Samuel Stouffer, *Communism, Conformity, and Civil Liberties* (New York: Doubleday, 1995) and James Davis, et al, *General Social Surveys, 1972–2010,* National Opinion Research Center, 2010.

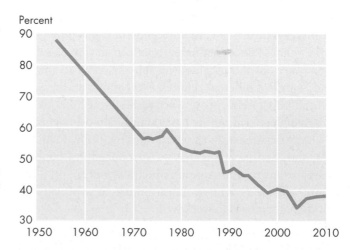

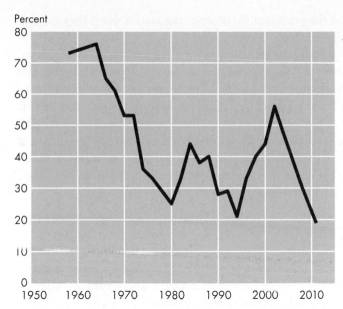

Percent

FIGURE 6.2

★ TRUST IN GOVERNMENT ALL OR MOST OF THE TIME

Shown here is the percent of Americans who trust government "all or most of the time," measured at two-year intervals. What might explain the rise and fall of people's trust in the government?

Source: Gallup polls (www.gallup.com/poll/5392/trust-government.aspx).

TRUST IN GOVERNMENT

Democracy requires that citizens must be skeptical about individual officeholders and be prepared to vote them out of office. However, citizens also need to have a general, overall sense of trust that the system is fair. A general distrust of the government breeds corrosive cynicism and apathy.

As Figure 6.2 shows, trust in government has fluctuated widely over the last several decades.[8] Overall, the level of trust has dropped significantly since the 1950s and early 1960s, although the movement has not been continuously downward. Trust seemed to reach a nadir in the early 1990s. It recovered somewhat after that, but dropped sharply again after 2002.

To some extent, trust in government responds to events. Trust dropped sharply following the divisive Vietnam War in the mid 1960s. Patriotism surged following the destruction of the World Trade Center in 2001, and the level of trust in government increased along with it. However, the general drop in trust that has occurred since the late 1950s and early 1960s goes beyond any particular set of events, and opinion just cannot seem to bounce back to pre-1968 levels. What happened? It might be argued, of course, that the events associated with the Vietnam War from 1963 to 1975 seared the American psyche so deeply that we have never recovered from them. But over half of the American electorate in 2011 were small children, or not yet born, when the war ended in 1975.

Another possibility is that the way the media reports on government officials changed in the early 1970s when reporters learned during the Watergate affair in 1974 that investigating unpleasant stories about officials could be a virtuous act that served democracy. In the past, the press had been deferential to officials, collaborating to mask unpleasant facts about them. President John F. Kennedy, for example, was often unfaithful to his wife, but there was no mention of that character flaw in the press during the 1960s. But after Watergate, in the late 1990s, the press feasted on the story of President Bill Clinton's sexual relationship with Monica Lewinsky, and the U.S. House of Representatives impeached the president for obstructing justice when they claimed that he had lied about this relationship.

We do not want to overemphasize the role of the media as an explanation for declining trust in government, however. The truth is that nobody really knows for certain why trust has declined. Furthermore, the decline of trust may not be an entirely bad thing. *Some* level of popular trust in government is needed for democracy, but there is no magic number that is the "right amount" of trust. Too much trust can leave officials unchallenged, and a deferential press may allow corruption to flourish. On the other hand, too little trust can lead to ineffective cynicism and an urge to throw out all politicians, good or bad. Are current levels of trust too low? About right? How would one find the answer to this question?

POLITICAL EFFICACY

Like trust in government, Americans' sense of political efficacy—their belief that they can affect what the government does—has declined over the last several decades. In 1960 just 27 percent of Americans believed that people have no say in what the government does, but by 2008 this figure had risen to 49 percent.[9] This change is probably related to the decline in trust, but it also reflects what citizens think is possible for them in the American democracy.

Although efficacy has declined somewhat over the years, United States citizens generally rank highly on this factor in comparison with citizens of other countries. In one study comparing 38 different countries, the United States ranked first in the number of its citizens who believed that if the government passed an unjust law, they would be able to do something to get the law changed.[10]

POLITICAL KNOWLEDGE AND ATTENTION TO ISSUES

How well do Americans follow politics, and how much do they know about political issues? Americans are uncomfortable with politics, especially if it involves conflict. We love "leaders," for instance, but dislike "politicians." Sometimes to devalue a proposal Americans will say, "Oh, that's just politics." This attitude goes back a long way. In 1863 Henry David Thoreau called politics "the gizzard of society."[11]

Similarly, Americans do not like political conflict. They regularly tell interviewers that they wish the political parties would not spend so much time quarreling but would just sit down and work out good policies everyone could agree on. (Whether this kind of solution is actually possible on most issues is, of course, another question.) In fact, it appears that most Americans are more concerned about the style of politics than about which policies are put in place. Their main concern is that the process should be civil and fair.[12]

With their relative interest in style over the substance of policies, Americans are often not well informed about policy issues. In a study of the 2000 election, for instance, citizens were asked to identify where George W. Bush or Al Gore stood on the single key issue that each had made most prominent in his campaign.[13] Only 52% knew that Bush favored large cuts in income taxes (his signature issue), and only 58% knew that Gore proposed providing free prescription drugs for the elderly.[14]

AMERICAN EXCEPTIONALISM

People often speak of **American exceptionalism,** the idea that the United States is different from the rest of the world and therefore is very special. In general, this idea stems from the history of the United States as a revolutionary country, the first modern democracy. The phrase "American exceptionalism" actually is used in a number of different ways:

Political figures and others often cite "American exceptionalism"—the idea that Americans hold unique values that give them a special role in history. A comparison of Americans' and Iranians' values suggests, however, that differences between the two cultures are not that basic.

- To some, it refers to a uniquely American ideology, based on freedom, equality, and individualism. We noted in Chapter 1 that these are important values for Americans.

- To some, it has to do with our immigrant history. More than most countries, we are a nation of immigrants and our society has served as a "melting pot" for many cultures, sending a message of openness and tolerance.

- To some, it embodies the idea that America is a shining city on the hill, ". . . that we Americans are a special people with a special destiny, to lead the world toward liberty and democracy."[15]

- And often, the concept is just used to convey a sense that Americans are different from the rest of the world and the United States is better than other countries.

American exceptionalism
The idea that the political culture of the United States is distinctive in the world and that the United States has a special role to build democracy in the world.

One setting in which American exceptionalism has been cited in recent years is the Mideast, where Americans led in opposing Islamic fundamentalism after the attacks of September 11, 2001. The United States began occupying Afghanistan in 2002 in an attempt to establish a democratic government there, then invaded Iraq in 2003 to depose dictator Saddam Hussein and establish democracy. In these efforts there was a strong sense of fulfilling a mission to bring democracy to the Mideast, but there was also a concern that America's democratic values might be perceived as too alien to be assimilated by Islamic political culture. Many Americans have expressed the view that American democratic values are antithetical to fundamentalist Islam: "The reaffirmation of Islam, whatever its specific sectarian form, means the repudiation of European and American influence upon local society, politics, and morals."[16] In 2001 President George W. Bush said of the 9/11 Islamic terrorists: "They hate our freedoms—our freedom of religion, our freedom of speech, our freedom to vote and assemble and disagree with each other."[17]

The Mideast provides a good test of just how "exceptional" American values are. Does American exceptionalism truly set the United States apart from the Islamic world? Certainly, the United States has been in conflict with various Islamic entities, most notably Iran, and Islamic terrorists have attacked U.S. citizens. Table 6.1 compares the values of Americans and citizens of Iran. On social issues such as homosexuality, abortion, and equal treatment of women and men, there are indeed significant differences between the two cultures. But on basic ideas about how politics should operate, the two are very close. Support for democracy is about the same, and Iranians are about as likely as Americans to believe that religious leaders should not be involved in politics. These results do not indicate basic cultural differences on the question of democracy.

TABLE 6.1
values of americans and iranians

	USA	IRAN
Attitudes on Democracy		
Agree: It is important to live in a democracy.	88%	82%
Agree: Religious leaders should not influence how people vote.	61%	60%
Social Values		
Agree: Homosexuality is never justified.	32%	82%
Agree: Abortion is never justified.	26%	61%
Agree: University is more important for a boy than for a girl.	8%	56%

Source: World Values Surveys, 2005–2008 Wave.

POLITICAL SOCIALIZATION

★ **KEY** to understanding

How are values learned in the United States and other nations? Political socialization is the process in which political values and attitudes are transferred from one generation to another and imparted to immigrants from other countries. In general, political values and attitudes are learned most intensely during the teen and young adult years. The various sources of learning are called agents of political socialization. To be effective, an agent must be (1) credible, and (2) seen as relevant to politics. Some important agents of political socialization are family, friends, school (especially college), media, and events.

political socialization
The process of learning political values and factual assumptions about politics.

political identity
An image of who you are, to the extent that your identity carries political content, such as your religion or your membership in a political party.

party identification
A sense of belonging to one or another of the political parties.

Individuals form political beliefs through **political socialization:** the learning of political values and factual assumptions about politics. In principle, this process can occur at any age and under any circumstances, but it tends to be concentrated at certain points in our lives.

Like most learning, political socialization occurs most readily in childhood and diminishes as people grow older. However, young people tend not to pick up explicit and detailed information about politics much before their teen years. Children learn in their families many basic social attitudes, such as trust in people and attitudes toward authority, which will be important in shaping their later response to politics. But most children acquire only rather primitive ideas about what government is and how politics works ("the president runs things," for instance). It is only later, in adolescence and early adulthood, that people form more concrete ideas about politics. They can also continue to learn and change throughout their adult lives, especially if they are exposed to extraordinary events.

The basic understandings of politics that constitute political culture are a large part of what is passed on to new generations through political socialization. But in addition, people also learn the **political identities** that will form the basis of their political lives: their religion (to the extent that it has political content), and their identification with a political party. Initially, most Americans identify with their parents' religion, although new experiences later in their lives may cause their beliefs to evolve. Similarly, many Americans identify in a fairly basic way with one of the two major political parties ("I'm a Democrat" or "I'm a Republican"). We call this **party identification,** and like any other self-identification it can color and shape the way we approach politics. We will examine party identification in detail in Chapter 9.

A variety of sources influence the political learning process. These sources are called **agents of political socialization.** In order to have a strong impact on socialization, an agent must meet two conditions:

- The agent must be *credible.*
- The agent must be seen as *relevant* to politics.

As we will see, some potential agents meet only one of these conditions and therefore fall short of the influence they otherwise would wield. Among important agents are families, peer groups (friends), schools, college, the media, and political events.

FAMILIES

Families are the most important agents of socialization. Parents have great credibility with their children, especially when children are young. Parents instill basic, underlying values in young children, such as respect (or disrespect) for authority, definitions of fairness, and obligations to others, that provide much of the basis for their later political beliefs. In adolescence and young adulthood, children often adopt their parents' specific beliefs or views, even though they are apt to challenge and question their parents' views on everything from proper dress to politics as they establish an independent identity. Studies find that parents' attitudes still play a significant role at this age in areas such as party identification, beliefs about how the economy should function, and understandings of how foreign relations work. For example, one study that followed children as they grew to adulthood found that the children of Democratic parents were three times more likely to identify themselves as Democrats than as Republicans by their mid-30s, while children of Republican parents were more than twice as likely to be Republicans as Democrats.[18] Parents also influence how their children view specific policy issues, although not as strongly as they influence party identification.[19]

PEER GROUPS

Young people find **peer groups**—friends, acquaintances, and others in the same social circumstances—highly credible. However, friends often have little connection to politics. They may strongly influence your choice in clothes, your economic habits, and your understanding of sexual morality, but unless they themselves are interested in and informed about politics (which many are not) they will have little influence on your political views. The exception to this rule, of course, would be groups of

★ Parents sometimes involve their children in political activities such as taking them to meet local politicians.

agents of political socialization
The people and institutions from whom we learn about politics.

peer groups
Groups of friends and acquaintances that can strongly influence our choices and values.

friends who form precisely because all of the members are interested in politics. A group of friends who met at an Obama rally are going to be very strong agents in molding one another's views on politics.

SCHOOLS

Schools are the one place where the government can deliberately try to reshape a country's political culture by controlling part of the political socialization process. Revolutionary governments that have made it a major part of their mission to remake their population—governments like those of Nazi Germany, the Soviet Union, or North Korea—have devoted extensive resources to political socialization in their schools. But all countries attempt to socialize children to some extent. Schools in the United States try to develop patriotic, informed citizens both directly, through such devices as a daily pledge of allegiance to the flag, and indirectly through the distribution of class materials in courses such as civics or government. Projects such as "Kids Voting" encourage civic participation, holding mock elections on the same day as regular elections.

In general, the impact of schools on political socialization appears to be limited. Schools meet the relevancy test—they obviously are relevant to politics when they teach politics. But unless what they are teaching is consistent with what parents and friends are already saying, their *credibility* on the subject is weak. The Nazis in Germany, for instance, replaced large numbers of teachers in German schools in an attempt to create the "new German man," and many feared that after World War II a horrid generation of young adults would have emerged from those schools. It never happened. Parents—not the Nazis' educational programs—had shaped students' views about politics.

In the United States, schools also have a limited impact on children's political knowledge and beliefs. In a national assessment of high school students, the U.S. Department of Education found that whether or not their high school had offered a course on civics and government had only a small effect on how well students understood American politics.[20]

COLLEGE

Attending college appears to be a stronger formative influence than the elementary and secondary schools. When students attend college they are often living apart from their parents for the first time. Furthermore, American college instruction generally encourages students to question accepted truths and think critically about issues.

We might expect from this openness to new thinking that college students would often be in the forefront in new directions in politics. A survey of students across the country in 1976—a fairly liberal period in American history during the aftermath of the Vietnam War—showed that at that time many more students were liberal than conservative. But when the same survey was repeated in 1984 at the height of Reagan's new conservative era, a majority were conservatives.[21] Students often gravitate to new movements. In 2008, students were one of the major bulwarks of Barack Obama's "change" candidacy, and in 2012 they were disproportionately active in Ron Paul's libertarian challenge within the Republican Party.

These surveys and examples do not suggest that students gravitate ideologically toward one extreme or the other. The research simply suggests that college students are more willing than most citizens to adopt different ideas. One common misconception is that colleges make students more politically liberal. A nationwide study that followed incoming freshmen to graduation found that they did become slightly more liberal over their time in college, but the shift was not large. Twenty-five percent were liberal when they entered college, and 33 percent were liberal when they graduated. And at the time they graduated, they were no more liberal than the population of 18 to 24 year olds generally.[22] Probably the greatest impact of a college education is an increase in political interest and the ability to comprehend information about politics.

MEDIA

As we will see in Chapter 11, the media functions as a source of political information for the public as well as a filter that identifies which political issues are important enough to cover, investigate, or debate. The mass media are becoming increasingly important as an agent of socialization. Up until the 1990s the media consisted of newspapers, magazines, network television, and radio. None of these sources of information had great credibility with citizens when they dealt with politics, because people thought the media should be neutral politically and resisted any overt attempts at persuasion.

In recent decades, with the advent of the Internet and the rising popularity of talk radio, people have increasingly turned to new media sources that are accepted as more partisan. Talk radio personalities such as Rush Limbaugh, TV figures like Ed Schultz, and bloggers of all persuasions are viewed as appropriately political because they make no claims to neutrality or objectivity. Oddly enough, TV comedians such as Jon Stewart, Stephen Colbert, David Letterman, or Jay Leno are trusted precisely because they do not *look* as though they are about politics; their primary job is to get laughs, not to drive a political agenda.

How much impact do the media have as providers of information? A study of beliefs about the Iraq War found that of those who relied mainly on print media for their news, about 17 percent believed (mistakenly) that weapons of mass destruction (WMD) had been found in Iraq after American forces had deposed Saddam Hussein's government in 2003. Of those who relied primarily on CNN or the established national television networks— NBC, ABC, and CBS—about 20 percent believed WMD had been found. Of those who relied primarily on the Fox

★ Stephen Colbert and Jon Stewart at the Rally to Restore Sanity and/or Fear, dubbed the "Million Moderate March," October 30, 2010.

network for their news, about 33 percent shared this belief.[23] Clearly media can make a real difference in what you believe.

The media can also have more indirect effects. Television, in particular, is better suited to short sound bites and dramatic, tension-inducing messages than to lengthy explanations. The shift in focus from print media to television and the Internet has

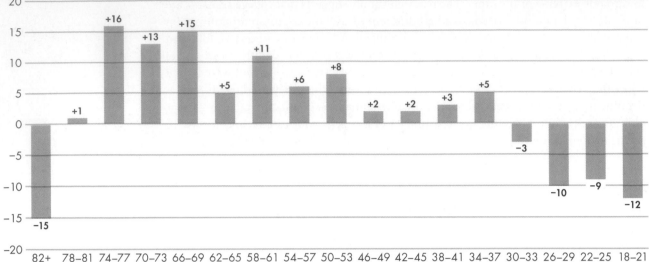

Percent Democratic minus percent Republican

Age in 1990

FIGURE 6.3

★ EMERGENCE OF THE NEW DEAL GENERATION

The partisan direction for age groups is calculated here by subtracting the percent who identified with the Republican Party in 1990 from the percentage who identified with the Democratic Party. Which group appears to have been most affected by the Depression and the New Deal?

Source: Data from Robert S. Erikson and Kent L.Tedin, *American Public Opinion*, updated 7th ed.

generational effect
A change in a whole generation's political viewpoint brought about by an event.

changed the very nature of political discussion and campaigns. In one study, an experiment in which subjects watched various sorts of televised debates demonstrated that when the debates involved impolite behavior (for example, the type showcased in negative advertisements), this behavior lessened the viewers' overall trust in government.[24]

POLITICAL EVENTS

Not only can people, as individuals or organized into institutions, serve as agents of socialization, but major life-changing events can as well. Events like the Great Depression, the Vietnam War, or the terrorist attacks of 9/11 can affect political perspectives of an entire generation, in a process often called the **generational effect.** For example, in 1964 Democratic President Lyndon Johnson spearheaded the passage of the Civil Rights Act of 1964, which outlawed racial segregation of restaurants and other facilities. During the presidential election that came later in that year, Republican presidential candidate Barry Goldwater argued against the bill. The conflict permanently shifted the positions of both African Americans and Southern Whites. From 1952 through 1962, 58 percent of African Americans had identified themselves as Democrats; in 1964, this figure jumped to 80 percent Democrat and has remained at that high level ever since. In the decades following 1964, white Southerners, who largely opposed the civil rights legislation, gradually migrated to the Republican Party.

Figure 6.3 provides a dramatic illustration of another event that had clear socializing effects on a generation of young people: the Great Depression of the 1930s and Democratic President Franklin Roosevelt's New Deal. The figure shows the partisan direction for different age groups 50 years later. The oldest age group, those 82 years old and older at the time of the study, had come of age before the Depression hit in 1930. As befit the Republican era of Calvin Coolidge (1923–1929) and Herbert Hoover (1929–1933), the members of this group were distinctly Republican in their sympathies. But starting with the group who were 16 to 19 years old in 1932, the year Americans elected Roosevelt, a strongly Democratic generation emerged.[25]

picture YOURSELF ...
AS A YOUNG PERSON IN CHINA

As a young person who was born and raised in China, what was your political socialization like? Probably the two strongest agents of socialization in your life were your family and the schools you attended. Both emphasized values from a political culture (going back thousands of years) that especially values political stability and fears chaos. The old Confucian culture of China viewed all parts of the universe, right down to the family, as being in harmony under the strong leadership of a benign head (the emperor, the father, and so on) who was expected to work selflessly for the general good. Any threat to this authority ran the risk of chaos, a fear that was borne out often in chaotic periods in the history of China. After the communist revolution in 1949, the communist government, fearing challenges to its authority, adapted the old Confucian values to meet its own needs.

Your parents and teachers have drilled into you the view that challenges to authority invite social breakdown. Note, by the way, that the schools have been so effective because they reinforced, rather than challenging, what you had already learned in your family. In school, your teachers have also emphasized in two semester-long courses that Britain, France, Germany, Japan, Russia, and the United States have repeatedly humiliated and exploited China. By the time you reached the university, you and your friends had become strongly nationalistic, and you regard foreign criticism of China as a continuation of this humiliation. You are not challenged by great diversity in society; 92 percent of Chinese belong to a single ethnic group, the Han, and most non-Han are concentrated in Tibet and southwestern China.*

You and your friends are very optimistic. After all, China's economy has grown by 10 percent every year for the last quarter-century. You live in a way your parents only dreamed of. Because of China's rule of one child per family, enforced strictly (at least in the cities), you are probably an only child and are perhaps a bit spoiled.

You and your friends are also very idealistic—one of your most attractive characteristics. You want to change the world for the better and are not at all cynical about this ambition. Again, this quality fits with long-established Confucian values, which have a strongly positive view of human possibilities. In the Chinese tradition, both people and nature are seen as innately good, a view that contrasts sharply with the Western tradition, which considers people to be innately sinful and in need of divine forgiveness, and perceives nature as an adversary and a danger. This ancient view of people is alive and present in your perception of what you should do in the world, leading you to expect the best of yourself and of others.

Now you find yourself in a time of turmoil brought on by the very economic progress that makes you proud of your country. The growth of the economy, fueled by entrepreneurs willing to

* CIA World Factbook.

continued

make huge speculative bets, has created a society that has upended the Chinese ideal of harmony in the world. Some people have become fabulously rich without respecting the old rules for how people deal with each other, while peasants remain poor and are often exploited by the new rich. All of these changes have left you about two parts optimistic and one part confused.

questions to consider

1. What is the value of dissent? The political culture of the United States, emphasizing individualism and freedom from control, does not stress the dangers of social breakdown as much as Chinese political culture. Could that be a danger for the United States? Or is the Chinese emphasis on the dangers of breakdown a problem for them because it stultifies dissent?

2. When a culture is confronted with rapid economic change, as in China, how can it adapt? Has the political culture of the United States changed as a result of the economic turmoil and decline of the period since 2001?

GROUP DIFFERENCES IN THE UNITED STATES

KEY TO understanding

How do group identities affect public opinion and politics in general? Groups that often differ politically are racial and ethnic groups, religious groups, people from different social classes, men and women, and regions of the country. These groups vary in their values and in how they respond to issues and candidates.

Demographic, social, economic, and religious groups in American politics often share common political values, views, and experiences. As members of a group interact, they may share information or misinformation about events or candidates. They often tend to respond similarly to particular candidates or immediate issues. Politics often consists of marshalling a coalition of groups in the population either to win an election or to build support for a particular policy, so groups' opinions may serve as important building blocks for politics.

AGE

The American population is growing older, as we see in Figure 6.4. How will this affect American politics? On some issues, younger and older Americans might be expected to differ because of their self-interest. For example, we might expect older Americans to want higher Social Security retirement benefits and younger Americans to be more concerned about help for first-time homebuyers. Surprisingly, however, there is little evidence that these sorts of issues divide younger and older Americans.

FIGURE 6.4

★ AMERICA, AN AGING NATION

The percentage of adults over 65 has been steadily increasing while the percentage under 30 has decreased. At what point will there be more adults over 65 than under 30? How do you think that shift will affect politics?

Source: Data from U.S. Census Bureau.

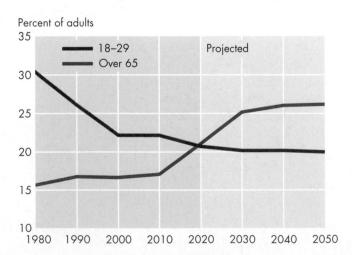

Differences between younger and older Americans do show up, however, when new issues or candidates arise. When views on an issue are changing, older generations often hold to the accepted view on the emerging issue, while the younger generations are more willing to embrace the newer view. When an insurgent candidate appears, younger voters are more likely to support the new face. For example, during the Republican presidential primary race in 2012, young voters in the Republican primaries flocked to Ron Paul, an insurgent face in national politics, while older voters were more likely to support Mitt Romney, former governor of Massachusetts. In the New Hampshire primary 46 percent of voters under 29 supported Paul but only 12 percent supported Romney; of voters over 65, 26 percent supported Paul, but 42 percent supported Romney.[26]

RACE AND ETHNIC GROUPS

America is becoming increasingly diverse in its racial and ethnic makeup; the Census Bureau estimates that by 2050 only about half of the population will consist of non-Hispanic whites. Most of the increase in population is among Hispanics and Asian Americans. The percentage of African Americans has remained steady and is projected to do so in the future, while the percentage of non-Hispanic whites has declined sharply and is projected to decline more. Figure 6.5 shows these shifts in the major ethnic groups.[27] As we will see in Chapter 9, these shifts are likely to have important effects on American politics.

Differences in opinion between racial and ethnic groups are due partly to economic disparities between the groups. African Americans, for example, have lower average incomes than whites and not surprisingly, are much more in favor of government programs for the poor than are whites. In a survey, 54 percent of African Americans but only 20 percent of whites thought that the government should see to it that every person has a job and a good standard of living.[28] And 52 percent of African Americans but only 37 percent of whites thought that the government should provide more services, even if that means an increase in government spending.

Although differences such as these between the races are due partly to the fact that whites' average incomes are higher than those of other groups, there is something more at work as well. In a survey comparing whites and non-whites, non-whites were distinctly more likely than whites to favor governmental action to make incomes more equal, even taking into account differences in the groups' income levels.[29]

Racial and ethnic groups often have strong feelings on specific issues that affect them directly. For example, African Americans support affirmative action more strongly than other groups, while Hispanics favor pro-immigrant policies such as bilingual education in public schools and amnesty for illegal aliens. Some issues can be so important that they determine long-term partisan loyalties. In 2012, almost half a century after the Civil Rights Acts, 91 percent of African Americans still voted for Democratic candidates in House races.[30]

Common experience and frequent interaction within ethnic and racial groups can also shape more general political attitudes. Trust in government is lower among African Americans, for instance, than among other groups—an attitude that may be reinforced

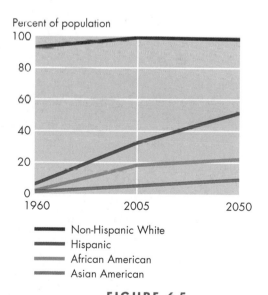

Percent of population

Non-Hispanic White
Hispanic
African American
Asian American

FIGURE 6.5

★ POPULATION SHIFTS AMONG MAJOR ETHNIC GROUPS

by a general sense among African Americans that the police single them out for stops and searches and for prosecution. When African American athlete O. J. Simpson was tried for murdering his wife in a widely watched, televised trial in the early 1990s, whites generally believed he was guilty but African Americans generally believed that the Los Angeles police had planted fake evidence to falsely convict him. In a survey taken at the time, 72 percent of white respondents thought Simpson was guilty, while 71 percent of African Americans thought he was innocent.[31]

Voting patterns have historically been more evenly divided among Hispanics than among African Americans. On the one hand, Hispanics tend to back Democratic economic policies. On the other hand, as a group with many devout Catholics, Hispanics tend to identify with Republicans' socially conservative values. However, the emergence of controversial immigration policies in recent years had the potential to move Hispanics solidly into the Democratic camp, since on the whole Republican members of Congress have taken a much harder line against illegal immigration than Democrats. In 2012, 68 percent of Hispanics voted for Democratic candidates in House races.[32]

RELIGION

As shown in Figure 6.6, Americans are more religious than citizens of other economically well-off countries. Only the populations of less-developed countries are more

FIGURE 6.6

★ IMPORTANCE OF RELIGION IN AMERICA

This figure shows the percent of the population for whom God is very important in their lives. In general, religion is more important in poorer countries. Why might this be? Why might religion be more important in the United States than in other rich countries?

Source: Data from World Values Study, 2005–2008 sample.

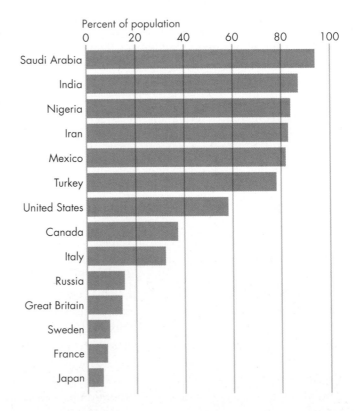

religious than Americans.[33] What impact does religion have on political opinions? What role does religion play in American politics?

Religion is an important determinant of voting behavior. Shared values can lead a religious group toward or away from a political party. Catholics were a core part of Franklin Delano Roosevelt's New Deal coalition in the 1930s and continued to be a solid part of the Democratic Party until the 1970s, held largely by economic issues and general party loyalty. The rise to prominence of the abortion issue, however, led to a gradual movement of Catholics away from the Democratic Party as Catholic doctrine conflicted with what became the Democratic position favoring freedom of choice. Today, as evidenced by the 2012 election (see Figure 6.7), Catholic voters are almost evenly divided between the two parties.[34]

Protestants are divided between "mainline" denominations and Evangelicals. About 40 percent of white Protestants are members of mainline denominations such as Presbyterian, Episcopal, Methodist, and the United Church of Christ. As we see in the figure, members of these denominations tend to be split fairly evenly between the parties, although there is a slight tilt toward the Republicans. Evangelicals, who make up about 60 percent of white Protestants, are growing in number. Evangelicals hold conservative moral values that are central to their politics, and thus they have become a mainstay of the Republican Party, which tends to voice their views in such matters as abortion and gay rights. As indicated in Figure 6.7, this group voted strongly Republican in 2012.

The "Other" category in the figure encompasses an amalgam of Orthodox Christians, Jews (about 2 percent of the U.S. population), Muslims (0.6 percent), smaller numbers of Buddhists, Hindus, Sikhs, and other sects, and those with no specific religion. Of these, Jews tend to be liberal on most economic and social issues. Much more than any of the major Christian groups, they support higher taxes, governmental help for the poor and minorities, international engagement by the United States, freedom of choice on abortion, and legalization of same-sex marriage. Of Jews in the United States, 68 percent identify themselves as Democrats and only 21 percent as Republican.[35] On average, Jews are relatively well-off economically and might be expected therefore to be conservative at least on economic issues. However, their shared historical experience as an oppressed minority appears to have led most Jews to hold a solidly liberal position on political issues across the board.

Muslims are a small but growing minority in the American religious landscape. They identify as strongly with the Democratic Party as Jews do, possibly because of the Iraq War and their personal experiences during the War on Terror, which has often caused them to encounter a fairly generalized suspicion of all Muslims.[36] Their incomes tend to be a bit above the average for the overall population. However, they strongly favor generous government services for the poor. Their position on this issue may reflect the strong emphasis in the Islamic religion on caring for the needy. At the same time, they are conservative on moral issues: 61 percent think homosexuality should be discouraged, and 59 percent think the government should do more to protect morality.

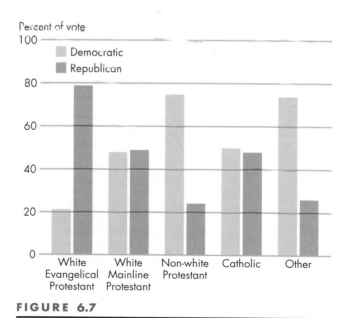

FIGURE 6.7

★ 2012 PRESIDENTIAL VOTE BY RELIGIOUS GROUP

These positions, too, are consistent with general Islamic principles. Overall, America's Muslims tend to be economically liberal but socially conservative.[37]

On one obviously interesting question, 76 percent of American Muslims state that they are concerned about the rise of Islamic extremism around the world. This opinion compares favorably with the response of many other Muslim populations around the world. In Germany, for instance, only 58 percent of Muslims express such a concern; in Egypt, 52 percent; and in Jordan, 61 percent.[38]

SOCIAL CLASS

Income differences in America are greater than they are in most of the world, and they are increasing, as shown in Figure 6.8. The United States ranked eighty-first among 127 countries in the gap between the incomes of the richest 10 percent of the population and the poorest 10 percent. (Ranking number 1 meant a country had the smallest gap between rich and poor; ranking 127 meant it had the largest gap.) And among prosperous, fully developed economies, the United States ranked right at the bottom.[39] How will the expanding gap between rich and poor affect politics?

Social class became a dividing line in American politics starting with Franklin D. Roosevelt's New Deal in the 1930s, which transformed the Democratic Party into a liberal party committed to policies that benefit the poor.[40] Low-income Americans continue to be strong supporters of economic programs like those of the New Deal that promote economic equality and opportunities for the poor, but as shown in Figure 6.9, they are more conservative when it comes to the social and religious positions that also characterize liberalism today.[41] Thus, low-income Americans are torn. Economic issues pull them toward the Democratic Party, while social and religious issues pull them toward the Republican Party. Overall, they tend to be Democrats.

High-income Americans include business executives as well as professionals such as lawyers and doctors. Those associated with business strongly favor the Republican Party, as they have since the 1930s. But the growing population of well-paid professionals tends to provide fertile ground for the Democrats because these professionals tend to side with the liberals on social issues. The conflicting influences of the economic and social issues shown in Figure 6.9 often pose a special problem for the Democratic

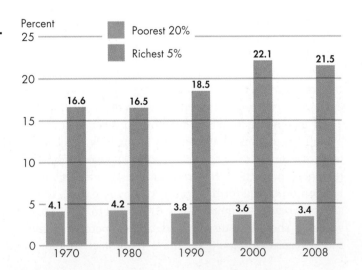

FIGURE 6.8

★ **WIDENING INCOME DIFFERENCES**

From 1970 to 2008 the share of all income going to the richest 5 percent of Americans increased, while the share going to the poorest 20 percent declined. What are the likely political effects of this trend?

Source: United Nations, Human Development Report 2010.

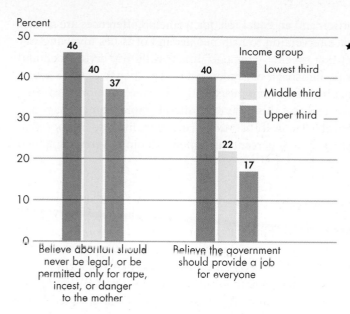

Percent

FIGURE 6.9

★ ATTITUDE DIFFERENCES BY SOCIAL CLASS

The less well-off favor government creation of jobs but oppose abortion. Is politics made more complicated because the social classes break down differently with regard to social and economic issues, or does this serve to make politics more moderate?

Source: Data from National Elections Study, 2008, Presidential Election Study.

Party. A Democratic candidate who focuses on issues of special interest to professionals, such as gun control, freedom of choice, or an internationalist foreign policy, runs the risk of alienating lower-income members of the party.

GENDER

Before the 1980s, men and women voted alike and held similar views on political issues. Over the last few decades, however, a **gender gap** has opened up, in which women usually vote in greater numbers for Democratic candidates than men do. (Or men vote in greater numbers for Republican candidates than women do—you can describe the gender gap either way.) In 2012 the gap was 10 percentage points.

At the same time, as Figure 6.10 shows, modest differences have opened up on numerous issues. Perhaps surprisingly, men and women do not differ greatly on major

gender gap
The difference between the percent of women and the percent of men voting for a candidate, which has been significant since about 1980.

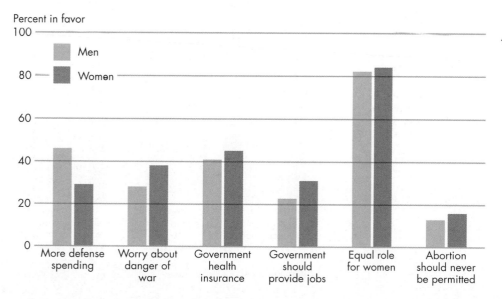

FIGURE 6.10

★ GENDER DIFFERENCES ON ISSUES

Source: Data from National Elections Study, 2008, Presidential Election Study.

feminist issues such as abortion and an equal role for women. Differences are greater on questions of government intervention to help people, and of issues involving war and foreign policy. The fact that specific "women's" interests do not divide men and women suggests that there may be aspects of gender that lead women to espouse liberal positions. One argument that has often been raised is that women are more nurturing and men are more aggressive, and that this difference attracts more women than men to liberal causes. Another possible factor is that women are more likely to be poor than men are; in the most recent census, 15 percent of women lived in poverty, compared with 11 percent of men.[42]

REGIONS OF THE COUNTRY

Despite all the talk of "red states" and "blue states," the various regions of the United States do not differ as much as we might expect on political issues. People who live in the South are more conservative in their views on social issues such as abortion (featured in Figure 6.11) or same-sex marriage than those who live on the West Coast. But the regions do not really vary much in their views on economic issues such as aid to the poor, or in their views on internationalist issues such as increased spending on foreign aid.

There are, however, significant differences in the ways regions of the country line up in support for the Democratic and Republican Parties. The Democrats can generally count on the West Coast and the Northeast, while the Republicans can generally count on the South and the Mountain states. This means that most presidential elections for the past 30 years have been decided in the Midwest. Even in the extremely strong Barack Obama victory of 2008, this pattern was evident. Obama made notable incursions into the Republican heartland, winning Colorado, New Mexico, Virginia, North Carolina, and Florida, but the key to his victory lay in winning solidly in the Midwest.

FIGURE 6.11

★ ATTITUDE DIFFERENCES BY REGION

Attitudes on abortion, aid to the poor, and the war on terror, broken down by region. Why are the differences by region no greater than what we see here?

Source: Data from National Elections Study, 2008, Presidential Election Study.

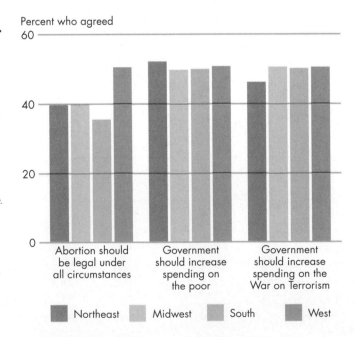

HOW PUBLIC OPINION CHANGES

On many issues, public opinion remains fairly stable over time. Figure 6.12, for example, shows that support for a government-provided health insurance program has been rather stable over the last four decades. Attitudes on many other social programs such as aid to children or support for the disabled have shown similar patterns. However, over the same period the United States has been going through a period of great social change. Different groups in society relate to one another differently from the way they did in the past, and attitudes toward these groups have changed. In the last few decades of the twentieth century, for example, many wives and mothers moved into the workforce instead of being homemakers. As shown in Figure 6.12, attitudes on whether women should have an "equal role with men in running business, industry, and government" have shown steady, evolutionary change.

Opinion can change in the population in two main ways. First, political events or leaders may sway people to shift their opinions. In 1992, there was an upward jog in the otherwise rather stable support for government health insurance, as shown in Figure 6.12, after Bill Clinton campaigned for this policy during the presidential election. In 2008, the figure again rose slightly as presidential candidates debated national health insurance during the 2008 campaign.

The terrorist attacks on the World Trade Center and the Pentagon on September 11, 2001, brought about a swift transformation of public opinion. In a survey administered just before the attacks, 53 percent thought that "the world is more dangerous now compared to ten years ago." When the same survey was repeated just two years later in 2003, 73 percent had this opinion.[43] Similarly, in the wake of the botched relief effort in 2005 after Hurricane Katrina struck New Orleans, what had been a gradual decline over a decade in perceptions that the government "is almost always wasteful and inefficient" was suddenly reversed, with a jump from 47 percent agreeing with the statement before Katrina to 56 percent after Katrina.[44]

GENERATIONAL REPLACEMENT

In contrast to quick changes like these, large-scale, steady changes in public opinion usually come about by a different process: **generational replacement.** The change in opinions about the role of women shown in Figure 6.12 is an example of generational change. Sometimes a change in the overall attitude of Americans occurs not because everyone's opinions change at the same time but because younger Americans take a new position, while older Americans do not change, or at least do not change as much as the younger ones do. As time passes and the oldest Americans gradually pass from the scene and are replaced by younger ones, the overall state of American opinion on the issue transforms gradually and steadily. It takes about 30 to 50 years for generational replacement to happen.

generational replacement
Change in overall attitudes caused by differences of opinion between young and old that gradually lead to a shift in overall opinion as older citizens pass from the scene.

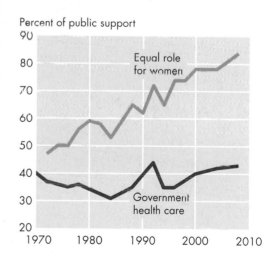

Percent of public support

FIGURE 6.12

★ EVOLUTION OF OPINION ON TWO ISSUES

Change over time in support for an equal role for women and for a government health insurance plan for everyone. What are the implications for politics of these two patterns of change?

Source: Data from National Elections Study, 2008, Presidential Election Study.

★ Pillars of light form a memorial to the fallen World Trade Center.

Figure 6.13 shows how generational replacement contributed to Americans' gradual acceptance of an equal role for women in business and government. Reading down the right-hand column of the figure we see that support for an equal role of women among the total electorate grew from 47 percent in 1972 to 84 percent in 2008. The other three columns of the figure show the contributions of three generational cohorts. The width of each bar shows the size of the cohort. In 1972 the youngest generation, born after 1958, had not yet entered the electorate and is absent from the figure. The other two generations are about equally large, with the middle generation (born between 1927 and 1958) a bit larger than the oldest one; the right-hand column is the sum of these two. Moving down each column, we see the oldest generation gradually disappear from the electorate by 2008, while the youngest generation appears for the first time in 1984 and dominates the electorate by 2008.

The shaded area of each bar shows the proportion of each generation supporting an equal role for women. At no point is more than a bare majority of the oldest generation supportive, while the youngest generation is always strongly supportive. As we go down the figure from 1972 to 2008 the oldest generation disappears and the youngest generation takes over. This shift is what largely drives the overall rise in support (the right-hand column).

CHANGES IN PARTY IDENTIFICATION

Over the last few decades, a particularly important change in public opinion in the United States has been a slow decline in party identification. Party identification is fairly stable. It can shift in response to events, as shown in Figure 6.14 where Democratic identification increased in 2008 in response to the unpopular presidency of George W. Bush and Republican identification grew from 1980 to 1988 in response to the popular presidency of Ronald Reagan.[45] Such shifts are usually fairly small.

A long-term evolution of party identifications has occurred over the past 50 years, however. First, the gap between Democrats and Republicans created by the New Deal has narrowed, probably by a process of generational replacement as the New Deal generation passes from the scene. Secondly, the number of independents—voters who do not identify with either party—has increased. From 23 percent in 1952 this figure grew to 40 percent in 2008, with most of the growth occurring in the 1960s and early 1970s. That timing would suggest that the decline resulted from disenchantment with political parties after the Vietnam War. But if that was the cause, why has the number of independents remained high, even as the Vietnam era fades ever further in our rear-view mirror?

A key to understanding the trend may lie in the fact that similar increases in the numbers of independents have occurred in most industrialized democracies, even those that were not involved in Vietnam. Is this growth in political independence caused by increased levels of education, which might make citizens less dependent on the parties for leadership and guidance on policies? Or could the increasingly aggressive investigative press, by criticizing politicians and revealing scandals, have led to a diminished faith in all political institutions, including the parties? Or could the increase in the number of independents be related to the overall decrease in trust in government? Political scientists do not have a clear, agreed-upon explanation for the rise of independence.

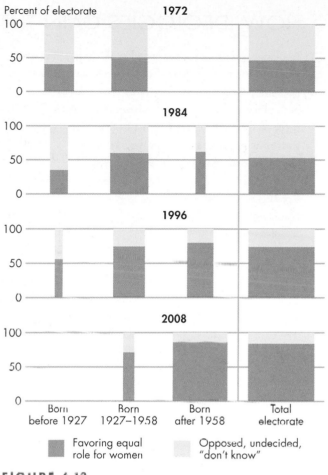

FIGURE 6.13

★ ATTITUDE EVOLUTION BY GENERATIONAL REPLACEMENT, 1972–2008

How much of the total change shown here was a result of generational replacement, and how much a result of changes across time within each generation?

Source: Data from National Election Studies.

FIGURE 6.14

★ CHANGES IN PARTY IDENTIFICATION

Change in the percent identifying as Democrats, Republicans, and independents from 1952 to 2008. Which has been more important—the narrowing of the Democratic advantage over Republicans, or the increase in the percent identifying themselves as independents?

Source: Data from National Election Studies.

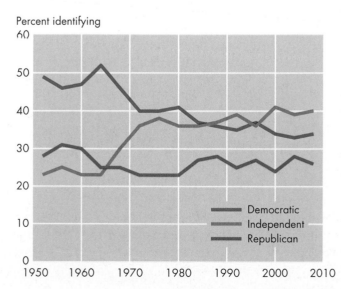

HOW IDEOLOGIES GAIN THEIR STRUCTURE

KEY TO understanding ★

Ideologies group our ideas together in clusters that are interconnected and reinforce each other; these interconnections provide mental structures that help us to understand politics. Ideologies often are based on a set of core ideas from which all others flow. Libertarianism is formed in this way, but while liberalism and conservatism are structured partly in this way, they are also structured significantly by their connections to the Democratic and Republican parties.

We introduced and described American ideologies in Chapter 1. Ideologies are clusters of ideas that relate to each other and bolster each other. No belief or value you hold exists in isolation from your other beliefs and values. Here's a simple example: If you thought that the Republican Party was good, and you knew that Mitt Romney was the presidential candidate of the Republican Party, the odds are that you thought in 2012 that Romney would make a good president. Our ideas are interconnected and bolster each other, although the connections are not always as obvious as this one.

Ideologies help structure public opinion. But how do ideologies develop? How does a particular cluster of ideas form into an ideology, and why does that set of ideas, rather than another, cohere?

Every ideology has a structuring principle that causes its parts to relate to each other. A central, organizing idea may play this role. Most European ideologies, such as socialism or Christian democracy, are structured in this way. In the United States, libertarianism is similarly organized around a central idea: that government should intervene as little as possible in people's lives in order to maximize individuals' freedom to make their own decisions. From this one idea, positions follow on a wide range of policies: opposition to using taxes to make people more equal, opposition to gun control, legalization of recreational drugs, and freedom of choice on abortion. Libertarianism, because it is organized strictly around the core idea of maximizing individual freedom, holds together tightly. Each position its adherents take can be deduced logically from this central core principle.

However, ideologies can be structured in other ways as well. Liberalism and conservatism have central ideas that help to determine their structure, but to some extent their structure also comes from the long-running competition between the Democratic and Republican parties. Liberals share a central goal of caring for the weaker members of society and accordingly welcome an active role for government in the economy. Conservatives share two central goals: maintaining traditional values and societal structures, and minimizing governmental intervention in the economy. These general goals help to determine liberals' and conservatives' positions on many issues of the day. But unlike libertarianism, liberalism and conservatism have also been strongly influenced by the evolution of the Democratic and Republican parties.

How have the parties shaped liberalism and conservatism? Abortion policy provides an example. Today opposition to abortion is an important belief of conservatives, and liberals support freedom of choice on abortion. However, at the time of the 1973 *Roe* v. *Wade* Supreme Court decision that kicked off the modern conflict over abortion, many liberals opposed abortion. By accidents of immigration history, large numbers of Italians, Poles, and other Catholic immigrant groups were part of the Democratic Party's liberal coalition at that time, and most members of these groups opposed abortion because of their Catholic faith. However, another important part of the liberal coalition in the Democratic Party—the feminist movement—insisted on a woman's right to choose an abortion, a position known as "pro-choice." Over the 1970s and 1980s bitter fights took place within the Democratic Party between pro-life forces and pro-choice feminists. As the pro-life side gradually lost these intra-party debates, large numbers of its adherents moved over to the Republican Party and became conservative, while others shifted their position to blend feminism with the other facets of their liberalism. A striking example is the evolution of Senator Ted Kennedy of Massachusetts, a leader of liberals nationally. In 1971, two years before the Supreme Court decision, Kennedy said in a speech that the Democratic Party would always defend the rights of the unborn; by the mid-1970s he was a leading pro-choice figure.[46] It was not that Kennedy had shifted from being conservative on abortion to being liberal on abortion. Rather, his liberalism was consistent with opposing abortion in 1971, but by the mid-1970s freedom of choice had become part of liberalism.[47]

This outcome was not inevitable. If the pro-life wing had won the debate in the Democratic Party, the freedom-of-choice position might have become part of conservatism, with its general opposition to government regulation. And opposition to abortion (remember liberalism's central concern of caring for the weak) could have been a part of liberalism. This alternative path only seems strange to us because events worked out the other way historically, and we are used to what we have today.*

HOW PUBLIC OPINION IS MEASURED

To get a sense of how public opinion may be shifting, researchers need to be able to measure it accurately. The most frequently used tool to measure public opinion is the **poll,** a set of questions asked of a carefully drawn sampling of some population (for instance, the population of a state, a city, or the whole country), selected in such a way that the respondents are likely to mirror the total population fairly accurately. The best way to construct this sample—and polling today always involves some variation of this method—is to draw a random sample of the population. A **random sample** is a sample drawn from the full population so that every member of the population has an equal probability of being picked to be in the sample. One way of thinking about it is to imagine that everyone in the country is assigned a different, randomly chosen number, that those numbers are put in a hat, and that a certain number of them are then drawn from the hat to make up the sample. This is, in fact, approximately how a random sample is drawn, except that the selection is done by computer instead of from a hat.

Polling organizations draw a sample for the obvious reason that for a large population it would be too expensive and time-consuming to ask everybody in the population to answer a question. If a random sample includes a large enough number of people, it will provide an accurate estimate because if everyone in a population has an equal probability of being in the sample, then the sample will not be biased toward one viewpoint or another. Any single person would of course be an inaccurate predictor of the views of the

KEY TO understanding ★

Can public opinion be measured reliably, and if so, how? The method used most often today is a survey of questions asked of a random sample drawn from the full population. Early polls did not always accurately gauge the views of the public, but over time pollsters learned how to predict election outcomes with a small margin of error. Even the best of methods has some problems, however. The exact wording of a question can affect a polling result, and a poll question puts the respondent in an inherently artificial situation.

poll
A set of questions asked of a carefully constructed sampling of a population, selected in such a way that the people in the sample are likely to mirror the total population fairly accurately.

random sample
A sample drawn from the full population in such a way that every member of the population has an equal probability of belonging to the sample.

---

* AUTHORS' NOTE: The question of whether parties structure ideology—or whether ideologies are more central to people, and people therefore identify with the party that best fits their ideology—is difficult to answer definitively. We observe that conservatives tend to be Republicans, and Republicans tend to be conservative. But which causes which? When two phenomena are intertwined this tightly it is difficult, but not impossible, to assess definitively which is the original cause. The interpretation we have given here (that ideologies take their structure in the United States largely on the basis of parties' positions) is our best judgment based on the evidence. But we must note for you that whereas at some points in this book we are giving you well established and agreed-upon facts, in this case we are giving you our best call on a question of interpretation and judgment.

whole population, but as you add another person and then another and another, people who differ greatly will tend to cancel each other out so that the average of all of the people you have drawn will come to be fairly close to the average of the whole population.

A simple test can help show how this system works. If you choose one member of your class randomly by drawing names from a hat, and you measure her height, that result will obviously not be an accurate measure of the average height of members of your class. But if you now add nine more class members, similarly pulled from the hat at random, the average of their heights will probably be fairly close to that of the class as a whole.

It turns out, somewhat surprisingly, that a random sample of just a few thousand Americans is large enough to provide a fairly accurate estimate of anything you wish to measure for the full population—anything from their average height to their opinion of the president's performance. The estimate is not perfect, of course; the only way to get a perfect measure would be to ask everyone. Polling agencies accordingly measure, and report, their **margin of error** in the estimate. The margin of error is a measure of how close the sample estimate is likely to be to the true value, based on statistical theory and given the size of a sample. A poll result showing that 55 percent of a state's likely voters support candidate X, for example, with a margin of error of plus or minus 3 percent, means that 95 percent of the time, the actual support for candidate X should be somewhere between 52 and 58 percent. A margin of error of plus or minus 3 percentage points is usually considered satisfactory for public opinion estimates.

margin of error (in polling)
Statistical measure of how much the sample estimate from a poll is likely to deviate from the true amount in the full population.

EARLY ATTEMPTS AT POLLING

Social scientists have been trying to estimate public opinion since the early twentieth century, but it took some time before they established a reliable scientific process. Along the way, they made several famous goofs.

It wasn't until the 1930s, for instance, that the importance of random sampling was understood. Before that time, many people simply thought that the *bigger* the sample, the more accurate it would be. A comic case of sampling mistakes from the early days of opinion polls is the *Literary Digest* poll. The *Literary Digest* was a popular magazine with a huge circulation in the United States in the early part of the century. Starting in 1924, the *Digest* ran an ambitious poll in presidential election years. The poll reached virtually everyone who owned a car or a telephone because it was sent out to a mailing list obtained from telephone directories and state automobile registration lists, as well as to all of the *Digest*'s subscribers. Only about 20 percent of the sample ballots mailed out were returned, but even at that, the *Digest* had over 2 million respondents each time the poll was taken.

The *Digest*'s sample was huge, but it was not random: different types of people had different probabilities of being included in it. And so it distorted the U.S. population in two ways. First, the *Digest* essentially sampled only the upper and middle classes, inasmuch as those who did not have a car or a telephone—at a time when cars and telephones were far less universally owned than today—did not get onto the mailing list. Also, the *Digest* sampled only those who were interested enough and energetic enough to return the sample ballot. Because only 20 percent of those who received the ballot returned it, this seems to have been a rather select sample.

In 1924, 1928, and again in 1932, the *Digest* poll was very successful, but only by accident. It came within a few percentage points of the actual outcome in each of those elections. Apparently, the interested middle class sample the *Digest* drew upon did not vote much differently from the rest of the country from 1924 through 1932, so its sympathies matched the way the country was going to vote in those elections. Between

1932 and 1936, however, President Franklin Roosevelt initiated the New Deal, which broadened his support among the poor and drove many members of the middle class to the Republicans. By 1936, the New Deal had opened up a gap between the middle class and the rest of the country. Based on its largely middle-class sample, the *Digest* predicted a landslide victory in that year for Roosevelt's opponent, Alf Landon. Landon, however, ended up with just 37 percent of the vote and carried only Vermont and Maine. The *Literary Digest* went out of business the next year.

Another famous goof occurred in 1948 when all the polls predicted a victory for Thomas Dewey over Harry S. Truman. They had all stopped their polling operations a couple of weeks before Election Day and missed a late surge of support for Truman. Some papers, based on these polls and a few early returns, famously headlined Truman's defeat (which obviously did not happen). Needless to say, those who administer polls have now learned to continue polling right up to the election.

Even today, although polling has become much more accurate, there are occasional miscalls, especially in primary elections where, unlike in a general election, voters' preferences are not anchored by the more stable attitude of party identification. In a primary election, all candidates are of the same party, and so voters may move easily from one to another. In the general election, party loyalties solidly anchor voters to candidates, and only independents tend to move easily back and forth. A dramatic primary miscall occurred in the New Hampshire Democratic primary in 2008 in which polls showed Hillary Clinton behind, and in fact on the eve of the primary she and her staffers were discussing how to handle her impending defeat. To everyone's surprise, including her own, a very late surge brought her the victory.

POLLS TODAY

Today, no one uses a classic random sample of the entire population because it simply costs too much. Picking one person in Twin Falls, Idaho, and sending an interviewer to ask her questions, then picking another person on a remote farm in Arkansas, and so on, would be impossibly expensive. Some sort of compromise is necessary.

Cluster Sampling

In **cluster sampling,** a random selection of perhaps a hundred locations in the country is made, an interviewer is sent to each, and a small random sample of perhaps 20 or 30 people are interviewed at each site. When the interviews from all the sites are added together, they approximate a true random sample.

Random Digit Dialing

Even easier to administer than cluster sampling is a **random digit dialing** telephone poll (RDD). In this method, telephone numbers are dialed randomly, drawing something like a true random sample. This system is faster and cheaper than sending interviewers out to cluster sample localities, but it has some serious drawbacks. Since about 95 percent of American homes have telephones, randomly selecting numbers from the phone book would seem to be a good way to approximate a true random sample. Unfortunately, though, different sorts of people have very different patterns of phone access. People working two jobs are rarely at home

cluster sample
An approximation of a true random sample, in which a sample of localities is randomly drawn and then a small random sample of individuals are interviewed in each locality.

random digit dialing
Drawing a roughly random sample by randomly dialing telephone numbers.

★ Faulty polls had made the *Chicago Tribune* so certain Harry Truman would lose that they brought out this edition reporting his defeat. Truman loved it!

to answer the phone. To further complicate matters, cell phones are not accessible in this way. And some people whose phones are equipped with caller identification will simply never answer the phone unless they know the caller. Nonetheless, this method of sampling is used a great deal because of its convenience. For instance, if a campaign or news organization wants to ascertain overnight what the effect of a presidential debate has been, there is no other way to reach a roughly random sample as quickly.

Internet Polling

Internet polling

Drawing a truly random sample and getting the people in the sample to agree (in return for an incentive) to take part in surveys administered online.

A recently developed alternative is **Internet polling,** in which a genuinely random sample of Americans agree to fill out a certain number of survey questionnaires online. In order to avoid the problem that not everyone has a computer, those who have been picked for the sample but do not have computers are often given a free one. Because all people in the sample can be reached and they can respond to the questionnaires at a time that fits their own inclinations and convenience, Internet polling approximates a random sample better than RDD sampling and gives more accurate results. Because of its accuracy and flexibility, Internet polling is becoming very popular in social scientific research. It is important to distinguish scientific Internet polls of this sort from the many "straw polls" on the Internet or television that people voluntarily respond to; those straw polls are as unreliable as the old *Literary Digest* poll. In true Internet polling, the investigators pick their sample of people so that it will be random; people cannot simply volunteer to participate.

POLLS IN POLITICAL CAMPAIGNS

As political campaigns, and the media coverage of them, have become more sophisticated, various polls have developed to serve special purposes for either the media or candidates in an election campaign. Some examples follow.

Tracking Polls

tracking polls

Short, simple polls that are repeated day after day to allow a candidate to track exactly how a campaign is going on a daily basis.

Candidates use **tracking polls** throughout their campaigns. These are short, simple polls—often the pollster just asks whom the respondent will vote for or how he or she responds on a particular issue. These polls are repeated day after day to allow a candidate to track exactly how the campaign is going on a daily basis. These polls are always done by phone, to provide instant turnaround.

Exit Polls

exit polls

Polls conducted on Election Day at the voting places to provide television news stations with instantaneous analysis of what was moving the voters on that day.

News networks use **exit polls** to enable them to call the results of an election as quickly as possible after the polling stations close. News networks also use these results to provide some simple analysis for their viewers, such as how women voted, how many people were concerned about the economy, and so on. They poll people throughout Election Day by stopping them as they leave the voting place and asking them for information about how they voted and how they feel about various issues. Because they have drawn a random sample of voting places and a random sample of people at each voting place, their poll is based on a cluster sample that approximates a true random sample. And because it occurs during the voting, it provides an instantaneous read on what was moving the voters that day.

Push Polls

push polls

Sets of questions used by political campaigns to present negative information about an opposing candidate by taking advantage of the trust people feel for pollsters.

These are not true polls at all, but a perversion of polling. A **push poll** consists of questions posed to voters in such a way that they present negative information about a candidate. The purpose of a push poll is not to find out what the voter thinks but to communicate a negative message by taking advantage of the trust people feel for pollsters. Push poll questions are not used by pollsters, but by political campaigns masquerading as pollsters in order to hurt their opponent. The purported pollster does not even bother to write down the answer. A famous example was the question asked of many thousands of South Carolina voters before the 2000 Republican presidential primary: "Would you be more likely or less likely to vote for John McCain for President if you knew he had fathered an illegitimate black child?" McCain and his wife had in fact adopted a dark-skinned girl from Bangladesh.[48]

LIMITATIONS OF POLLS

Polls are not a perfect measure of public opinion. They have several limitations. First of all, as we have noted, a poll result is an approximation based on a sample of the overall population. There is some margin of error around any poll result.

A more serious problem, however, is that how a question is phrased can change the outcome of the poll. When a survey asked people in 2011 whether "global warming" is real, 44 percent of Republicans and 87 percent of Democrats said yes. But when it asked whether "climate change" is real, the number of Republican saying yes climbed to 60 percent while Democrats stayed the same, at 87 percent.[49] Apparently Republicans responded differently to the two wordings of the question, so depending on how the question was worded, you would find either a deep divide between the parties or a less striking difference between them.

Another difficulty with polls is that asking the public about policy questions puts them in an artificial situation; responding to hypothetical questions cannot substitute for actual law making. For instance, each of the following statements would probably attract a solid majority of support in a poll: "Taxes should be lowered." "Government services should be increased." "The budget should be balanced." But it is impossible to achieve these three objectives simultaneously. Respondents in a survey have the luxury of saying yes to all three at once, but the government is limited to doing what is actually possible. Obviously, this particular problem with polls limits the extent to which they should serve as a mandate for policy makers.

★ Cindy McCain, wife of 2008 presidential candidate John McCain, with their adopted daughter, Bridget, at the Republican National Convention.

These limitations do not mean that polls are useless. They just mean that pollsters must be skillful and must operate with care, both in constructing their surveys and in interpreting the results for candidates, officials, and the media. And they mean that you should read poll results with care.

When you see results from a poll, you should first note how large the sample size is and how large a range of error the pollster reports. A sample of a couple of thousand people is usually adequate nationally, and this would yield a range of error of something like plus or minus 3 percent. Then, you should note how people were contacted—if it was a telephone poll, for example, you should bear in mind that the pollsters will have missed certain types of people. And finally, you should read the question that people were asked, and see whether it looks to you as though the question was subject to misunderstanding or seemed intended to yield a biased result. With these precautions, you can become a good critic of polling data.

Why Are We
THE WAY WE ARE ?

The nature of public opinion, and the ways opinion changes, vary less from one country to another than many of the other aspects of politics. There are basic cultural differences from one country to another, of course. But overall, people are people, and they have similar needs and desires wherever they live. Many of the things we looked at in this chapter—Americans' levels of tolerance, the ways Americans are socialized, and the ways public opinion changes—are much the same in most countries of the world.

STABILITY

Despite these overall similarities, American public opinion differs from that of many other countries in two particularly interesting ways. First, in new democracies like Poland or Nigeria mass attitudes are unstable. No one in these democracies has had a long time to build firm political beliefs based on experience in the democracy, and they have also not had an opportunity to learn about democracy from an earlier generation through political socialization since the earlier generation did not live in a democracy. Accordingly, party loyalties fluctuate rapidly, with parties often appearing at one election only to disappear at the next. Views on policies may also fluctuate widely. As a long-established democracy, the United States has rather stable patterns of opinion, as you have seen in this chapter. That is not to say that opinions do not change but that change occurs on a fairly stable base.

PRAGMATISM

Second, Americans' tradition of pragmatism, carried over initially from England in the eighteenth century, has led us to rely much less than people in most other countries on basic first principles as our structuring principle in forming

ideologies. Like our original British forebears, we tend to prefer dealing with each particular problem as it comes along, rather than applying a broad, abstract principle to each problem. It may be partly because of this heritage of pragmatism that liberalism and conservatism are based as much on the constellation of issues adhering within each of the two major parties as on logical derivation from first principles.

Our two-party system probably also contributes to the looser logical structure of our ideologies. In a multiparty system there would not be so much of a tendency to match up the parties to two dominant ideologies, with each adjusting to the other.

These important variations help to define what is unique in American public opinion, as compared with opinion in other countries. The fact remains, however, that across the world patterns of public opinion vary less than do many other aspects of politics.

. . . AND WHY DOES IT Matter?

We began this chapter with a puzzle: Americans believe about as much as the citizens of Sweden and many other prosperous democracies that people should provide for themselves, as opposed to the government providing for people's welfare. But there is a big difference between how much the United States government does for people's welfare and how much the Swedish government and the governments of other countries do. This incongruity raises a very basic question: How much difference does public opinion make to what the U.S. government does? If opinion is about the same in Sweden and the United States, why is it that the Swedish government does so much more in providing for people's welfare than the government of the United States?

The answer, obviously, must be that public opinion is only part of what goes into governmental policy making. The "public" does not make laws; government makes laws. And as we will see in succeeding chapters, this process involves interest groups, political parties, courts, and a variety of elected entities. We probably should not expect a one-to-one relationship between opinions and policy. But on the other hand, in a democracy there should be *some* sort of relationship.

Clearly something else about American politics limits governmental involvement in social programs to a degree below what public opinion seemingly would tolerate, as indicated by the comparison with Sweden. We can also point to other areas in which policy departs fairly markedly from public opinion. For instance, in repeated polls over a decade, a majority of Americans have said they favor stricter gun control laws.[50] And yet there is little national regulation of gun ownership; and outside of large cities, advocating gun control is an unpopular stand for candidates to take in elections.

We should not conclude, though, that public opinion has no impact on policy. Public opinion certainly does not always *determine* public policy; we have shown examples in which it does not, and more are available. But in both direct and indirect ways public opinion often does affect policy.

For example, public opinion did contribute in various ways to the massive increase in defense spending under President Ronald Reagan after 1980.[51] Starting in 1978, Congressional Republicans led a strong campaign charging that under Democratic President Jimmy Carter, the United States was falling behind the Soviet Union in military power. At the time, public opinion was very responsive to this charge; in 1978, for the first time in a decade, more Americans thought defense spending should be increased than thought it should be reduced. Over the next two years, support for defense spending surged, so that by 1980 about 45 percent more Americans thought defense spending should be increased than thought it should be reduced. The new president, Ronald Reagan, came into office in 1980 on a wave of support for increased defense spending, and he promptly proposed a large military buildup. Social scientists have estimated that the issue of defense spending contributed about 8 percentage points to Reagan's share of the vote in 1980, providing most of the margin by which he won.[52]

Thus, public opinion on defense spending helped put in place a president who was pledged to an increase in spending. At the level of individual congressional districts as well, variations in opinion from one district to another led to marked differences in how much spending members of Congress voted for in 1981.[53] Members from districts where opinion most strongly favored the buildup voted on average for about $45 billion more in defense spending than members from districts where the public was least supportive of the buildup, raising the eventual appropriation to a bit under $200 billion. Both at the overall national level and at the level of individual congressional districts, public opinion played a significant role in the decision to increase defense spending.

The Reagan defense buildup is just a single example of the effect of public opinion on policy. But a broader study of almost 2,000 policy proposals, drawn from across all areas of policy for the period from 1981 to 2002, showed the following:

- If only 10 percent of the public supported a change, the change occurred an estimated 19 percent of the time.
- If support for a change was overwhelming, with 90 percent of the public in favor, the change occurred an estimated 46 percent of the time.[54]

The study shows both the substantial impact of public opinion and its limitations. Proposals with broad public support were more likely to be enacted than those the public opposed. But even when the public overwhelmingly supported a proposed change, it only happened about half the time. And when the public was wholeheartedly against a proposed change, 19 percent of the time the change occurred. Most of the 19 percent had to do with proposed tax increases, aid to foreign countries, or sending U.S. troops overseas.

How does public opinion exercise its influence? Public opinion can operate by so many paths that it is difficult to pin down its effects on any given policy very precisely. It may work through electoral change, as voters put in place officials whose views are closer to theirs. We saw this in the case of Ronald Reagan's 1980 election bid.

It may work via the media, as opinions from the public work their way into the pronouncements of the elite and from there into policy making. For example, popular concerns about free trade worked in this way across the last two decades to gradually reduce many officeholders' commitment to expand free trade.

It may work by strengthening the hand of a president, who can point to public opinion favoring a policy in getting Congress to act. In 2011, for instance, President Obama campaigned for an extension of payroll tax reductions, using public opinion polls that showed strong support for the extension.

Or it may not work at all, as in the question of gun control.

In short, public opinion has a significant, but not determinative, role in the making of policy. Certainly, it is an important part of the democratic process.

critical thinking questions

1. In an election environment dominated by 30-second television commercials, how much confidence can we have in the people's ability to make wise decisions about candidates' fitness for office?

2. How much impact do you think parents have on Americans' approaches to politics? What attitudes do you think parents help to shape in their children? What has your own experience been?

3. We saw that poorer Americans are more liberal on economic issues than better-off Americans, but the differences are not huge. Is it surprising that social class differences in attitudes are no larger than this, given the high degree of economic inequality in America? What might lead to such small differences across social classes?

4. Americans generally value independence and appear to shun strict partisanship. Yet, party identification is an important determinant of how they vote, and it adds stability and predictability to U.S. politics. Do you think, on balance, that the impact of strong party identifications on American politics is a good thing or a bad thing? Why?

key terms

POLITICAL PARTIES

* ★ ★

- Define *political party,* identifying key players and how they function in the party.
- Understand the significance of political parties in different forms of government, and describe what distinguishes them from each other.
- Examine the history of political party development in the United States, and explore the two waves of political reform that weakened party organization.
- Describe how American parties are organized and the impact of party structure on political processes in the United States.
- Understand the causes and effects of a two-party system.
- Explore how third parties survive and operate within a two-party system, and examine the impact of third parties on American politics.
- Define *responsible party government* and explain why parties in the United States have been successful or unsuccessful in fulfilling this governing doctrine.

PERSPECTIVE
How Centralized Can Political Parties Be?

The American comedian Will Rogers once quipped, "I am not a member of an organized party. I am a Democrat." Democratic and Republican Parties in the United States are loosely organized, evolving political groups that have no formal enrollment or membership process; those who wish to work for the party can just show up. Most importantly, no one person or office controls the entire organization. Although Barack Obama is often correctly referred to as the leader of the Democratic Party, he cannot tell Democratic Senators or members of the House of Representatives what to do; he must negotiate—sometimes even plead—with them. Additionally, he cannot tell a state party leader what to do.

In contrast, Mao Zedong, the former chairman of China's Communist Party, rejected all forms of negotiation and pleading. On May 16, 1966, he unleashed the "Cultural Revolution," a decade of upheaval and violence within the party that he hoped would bring it back to its original revolutionary roots. Mao had headed the Communist Party since it began as a revolutionary movement in pre-war China, and he had led it to national victory in 1949. Since then the party had ruled China as a one-party state, allowing no political opposition. By the 1960s, though, Mao thought that many newer members of the party, those who had not shared in the long revolutionary struggle before 1949, were simply opportunists who saw that the only route to a good government job was through the party. Many were well-educated children of the middle class.

In an effort to bring the party back to its working-class roots, Mao's Cultural Revolution mobilized large groups of young Chinese called "Red Guards" to terrorize landowners, intellectuals, and established leaders such as teachers, university presidents, and government officials. Hundreds of thousands were killed or committed suicide. The son of Deng Xiaoping, who would later succeed Mao as chairman of the Party, was thrown from a three-story window during an interrogation and permanently crippled.

After Mao's death in 1976, the Cultural Revolution ended and new leadership in the Party reversed many of Mao's actions. The Party today still rules the state, allowing no organized political opposition, but it presides over a partially free-market economy that is the exact opposite of Mao's socialist doctrine. It continues to be a tightly controlled, centralized organization. The Party is huge, with 78 million enrolled members as of the last National Party Congress.[1] Becoming a member is not easy. Aspiring members must first be recommended by an existing Party member and then must pass a one-year probationary period; many who apply to join the Party are rejected.

The point of this comparison is that no one person or group within an American party could direct the party as Mao did or his successors have done. It is impossible to imagine an event like the Cultural Revolution—organized violence orchestrated for the purpose of reshaping a party's membership or ideology—taking place in the United States.

IN THIS CHAPTER we consider just what a political party is and why the Chinese Communists and the U.S. Democrats or Republicans—while obviously very different from each other—are all indeed examples of political parties. Along the way, we examine the history of American parties and the two-party system, focusing on what parties do, how they are organized, and how smaller parties operate within the basic two-party system. Additionally, we explore how effective American parties are at bringing political issues to the fore and finding solutions for them. As you read this chapter, keep in mind our two core questions:

WHY ARE WE THE WAY WE ARE?
WHY DOES IT MATTER TO YOU?

In particular, why are political parties in the United States so loosely organized, and what effect does this have on American politics?

DEFINING POLITICAL PARTIES

Political parties are found in almost all countries, democracies and non-democracies alike, although they may fulfill varying purposes depending on the country. As we saw in the "Perspective" vignette, the Democratic and Republican parties of the United States and the Communist Party of China are very different organizations, but all three are political parties. A **political party** is an organization comprising officeholders or would-be officeholders and activist supporters spread throughout the population; its primary purpose is to put its members into government office. It can accomplish this purpose either by competing with other parties for government office in democratic elections as in the United States, or by banning all other parties and appointing its own leaders to office as in a non-democracy like China. Political parties should not be confused with interest groups. An interest group, like a party, is a group of people with shared policy goals; but while the primary purpose of a party is to help determine who holds political office, the primary goal of an interest group is to influence what policy choices those officeholders make.[2]

> A political party is made up of officeholders, would-be officeholders, and their supporters. As an organization, its main purpose is to help its members gain public office. Political parties are an integral part of politics in almost all countries—in non-democracies as well as democracies. They also vary around the world in how tightly they are organized; American parties are relatively loosely structured and decentralized.

KEY TO understanding ★

political party
An organization combining activists and potential officeholders, whose purpose is to determine who will hold office.

Political parties were invented for a specific purpose by politicians in the United States and (a little later) in Great Britain. Before democracy was developed in these two countries during the late eighteenth and early nineteenth centuries, there were many ways to attain office, but none involved appealing simultaneously to large numbers of people. You might be born into a hereditary office, you might be appointed, or you might actually buy the office. Once Britain and the United States became democracies, however, these positions were filled by election; this system required prospective officials to seek the votes of a thousand or more people. Politicians soon realized that organizing voters into a single, nationwide club—that is, a party—would help to mobilize them to support the party's candidates. It could also help to retain voters for the party, even as they moved from one place to another. A popular official could travel from place to place, helping to convince voters to choose other like-party candidates, and eventually raise enough money to hire professional staff who could help with the job of organizing thousands of voters. And so, the political party was created.

But what kind of an organization *is* a political party? In many countries, political parties are formal organizations that people apply to join; if they are accepted, they pay dues to the party. Parties in many democracies are organized in this way. For example, the Conservative Party of Great Britain has 300,000 enrolled members, and unless you pay your dues you cannot consider yourself a member. (To get a sense of what this is like, see "Picture Yourself as a Member of Great Britain's Conservative Party" in this chapter.)

In the United States, political parties are constructed more loosely. There is no single list of all the people who are members of either of the two main parties; in fact it is hard to state just what set of people makes up the Democratic Party or the Republican Party. Does the Republican Party consist of all those in the United States who voted for the Republican presidential candidate in the last election? Or does it consist of all those who have registered to vote as Republicans? (Such a registration list might answer our question, except that almost half the states do not require a voter to designate a party when registering.) Does the party consist only of Republican officeholders? What about the office that calls itself the "Republican National Committee"? There is no clear boundary to indicate which people belong to the party and which ones do not.

What difference does it make whether parties are centralized? Because parties are so loosely organized in the United States, politics plays out differently in this country than in most other democracies. A tight, formal party organization can exert much more control over what its officials do than can the loosely organized American parties. In Argentina, for instance, party officials control who can be on the ballot for a congressional election, and they use this power to punish any members of Congress who vote differently from their party's position. Members who do this regularly are usually expelled from the party and taken off its list on the ballot. As a result, members of Argentina's Congress are very obedient to party leaders.[3]

In the United States, candidates essentially make their own way to Congress. They get on the ballot by their own efforts, usually through a primary election, and although they then receive some help from their party in getting elected, they are in Congress primarily because of their own initiative and funds they have raised for themselves. As a result, their party's leaders in Congress have only limited power over what they do. Members sometimes vote differently from how their party's leaders have asked them to vote.

picture YOURSELF ...

AS A MEMBER OF GREAT BRITAIN'S CONSERVATIVE PARTY

You have been interested in politics for a long time, and recently you decided to join the Conservative Party. You had hesitated before because the party seemed stodgy and stuck in the past,

but you have been impressed by its new leader, David Cameron, a young and energetic man who became prime minister in 2010. So you joined up, paying the annual dues (about $40.00 U.S. a year, but $8.00 a year if you are under 23). By joining, you became one of about 300,000 members of the party, most of whom are over 65. (The predominance of older members was one of the reasons the party had always seemed to you to be covered in cobwebs.) It is a party that favors free enterprise but is socially moderate, with policy positions ranging from keeping taxes low, to combating global warming, to saving local British pubs.

Unlike a political party in the United States, the Conservative Party in Great Britain has a single, unified organizational structure. The key position is the leader of the party, a member of the House of Commons who leads the party both in the House and in the country. David Cameron has been party leader since 2005. He was chosen as leader through a two-step process in which his fellow Conservative members of the House first narrowed the choice to two candidates (both of them members of the House), and then the party's 300,000 dues-paying members around the country voted to choose one of the two. (As a member, you'll vote in this process from now on.)

All other parts of the party serve as a supporting structure for Cameron and the party's elected members in the House of Commons. Cameron, as leader, dominates the party. He controls the other members of his party in the House because the only way to advance to positions of greater power is through appointment by the leader; as a result, it is very rare for House members to vote against the wishes of their party leader. Cameron controls a large national staff that hires regional and local party agents, conducts research on policy, and publishes propaganda. He also appoints a majority of the members of a Management Committee that oversees the party's day-to-day operations. Ordinary party members are organized in constituency associations, one for each parliamentary district in the country. Each association chooses the party's candidate for its district, but the associations have little influence otherwise in national party policies.

You are optimistic about the future of the party, and because you are fascinated by politics and are ambitious, you may well try to stand as a candidate for the House of Commons yourself at some point within the next several years. To do this, you will need to convince a selection committee in one of the constituency associations to nominate you for that district, and then you will of course need to win the election. But you have high hopes.

questions to consider

1. **What are some disadvantages of a tightly organized party? Advantages?**

2. **Why do you think British citizens pay money to join a party and work actively in it, when members of the House of Commons control most of what happens in the party and therefore ordinary members have little say over its decisions?**

3. **What sorts of incentives might draw people into joining a party like this?**

PURPOSES OF A POLITICAL PARTY

One of the wonders of modern politics is that the political party, originally devised in order to help some officeholders attain and keep their jobs, has proved to be useful for many other purposes as well. Because it is uniquely an organization that combines government officials and a network of activists around the country, the political party has become the central organizing force linking the government to the people in almost all countries of the world—democracies and non-democracies alike. It has performed a variety of functions beyond its original role as a campaign machine:

- campaigning
- mobilization

The political party was invented as a way to organize voters in democratic elections, but its unique nature—joining government officials and supporters in one organization—has made it useful to all kinds of governments for a variety of purposes: campaigning, mobilization, recruitment and socialization of leaders, providing identity, and providing a channel for control. The section that follows discusses and exemplifies these purposes.

- recruitment and socialization of leaders
- providing identity
- providing a channel for control

CAMPAIGNING

Obviously, parties are useful for their original purpose: to campaign and build support for the candidates of the party. They help to identify candidates, raise money to help support their campaigns, provide policy research and advice on presenting issues, and conduct get-out-the-vote drives to bring their supporters to the polls.

MOBILIZATION

mobilization
Energizing of large numbers of people to act together.

Parties, which join together leaders and a geographically dispersed membership, are an ideal tool for mobilization. **Mobilization** involves systematically energizing large numbers of people to act together, in a demonstration, an election, or any other combined action. Instances of such mobilization by parties occur in many nations around the world. For example, when Syria came under intense international pressure in 2005 to withdraw its troops from the neighboring state of Lebanon, its allies in the Lebanese Hezbollah Party mobilized a demonstration of 500,000 supporters (out of the total Lebanese population of 3.7 million people) to support Syria's role there. This example reveals the potential of parties to mobilize populations at critical moments in a nation's history.

American political parties are less united on political issues than many parties in other countries, so they do not often sponsor large, issue-oriented demonstrations. But they do mobilize their supporters at each election to get them to the polls.

★ Mitt Romney poses with young supporters. Parties depend on grass-roots members like these to energize campaigns and get their supporters to the polls.

RECRUITMENT AND SOCIALIZATION OF LEADERS

Recruitment—identifying promising young people and bringing them into positions of public leadership—is a vital function for any country. Once recruited, leaders and officials also need to be socialized into their political roles. *Socialization* is the process, discussed in Chapter 6, by which people learn political values and factual assumptions about politics. In addition to what most people learn, newly recruited future leaders need to acquire an additional body of lore, responsibilities, and leadership skills in order to perform well. Because a political party brings together within its organization both seasoned political leaders and young activists, it is well placed to seek out promising young people, give them experience at relatively small jobs, and gradually move those who do well to more important jobs, while imbuing them with the values that the political leadership wishes to encourage.

PROVIDING IDENTITY

For active members, the political party can become a vital, central part of their identity. *Party identification* (which we examined in Chapter 6 and will discuss later under "Party in the Electorate") can be a strong feeling. As a source of identity, parties provide continuity and a political community in a political world that is otherwise quite fluid. If party connections are passed on from parents to children or if local party organizations continue their activity across generations, political continuity can extend even beyond a single lifetime.

The three maps of Tennessee in Figure 7.1 exemplify this tendency. At the time of the Civil War the state was divided over the issue of secession. The shaded counties in Map A were most strongly opposed to secession, as indicated by the vote for the Constitutional Union candidate in 1860. Two areas of opposition stand out: eastern Tennessee, and a pocket of opposition in the west. After the War, opposition to secession translated into support for the Republican Party, which had held the Union together. This made sense at the time, but the pattern continued to hold in election after election, long after the issues of the Civil War had receded into the depths of history. In Map B we see that the areas in which Republican Richard Nixon ran most strongly in 1960 are approximately the same areas that opposed secession in 1860. And in Map C we continue to see the same two main areas of strength in the vote for Republican John McCain in 2008.[4]

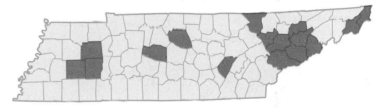

A. Counties >60% for Bell (anti-secession) in 1860

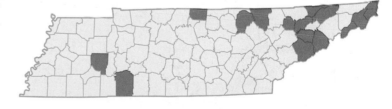

B. Counties >70% for Nixon (Republican) in 1960

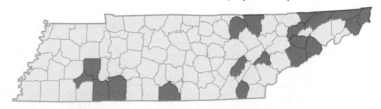

C. Counties >70% for McCain (Republican) in 2008

FIGURE 7.1

★ CONTINUITY OF REPUBLICAN STRENGTH IN TENNESSEE

The regions of the state that opposed secession in 1860 became areas of strength for the Republican Party, even 150 years after the Civil War. Is it good or bad to have such partisan continuity?

PROVIDING A CHANNEL FOR CONTROL

Sam Rayburn, who was for many years the leader of the Democratic Party in the U.S. House of Representatives, used to caution new members, "To get along, go along." In other words, to advance within the House hierarchy, obey orders.

Rayburn's advice points to another characteristic of a party: It brings together a group of officeholders in an overarching organization, providing a means by which some of the officeholders can control what others do. In other words, the party does not exercise control directly but provides a channel within which control can be exercised. This function helps to make governmental decision making possible. The leaders of a party have many rewards and punishments at their disposal—nominations for various offices, support in passing favored legislation, and so on, or the withholding of such support. Leaders use these inducements to force obedience on lesser party figures in legislative votes and in campaign activity.

THE DEVELOPMENT OF AMERICAN POLITICAL PARTIES

★ **KEY** to understanding

American parties developed as a way to mobilize support for members of Congress in the early years of the Republic, and they have evolved over time in response to changing problems. Two waves of political reform in the twentieth century weakened the parties organizationally and made them more decentralized. An in-depth exploration of the factors that led up to this reform follows.

As we have seen, the United States, as the first electoral democracy in the world, was the country that originally invented political parties. The process took only a few decades (see Figure 7.2), and by the late 1820s these parties were well organized. The Democratic Party, which can trace its roots back to that time, is the oldest political party in the world.

EARLY PARTY FORMATION

The Founders did not envision political parties contesting elections. Indeed, they set it up so that the president and senators would not be elected directly at all. An *Electoral College* of distinguished citizens selected by the states would choose the president, and each state's legislature would appoint the senators. Although elections were to be held for members of the House of Representatives, the

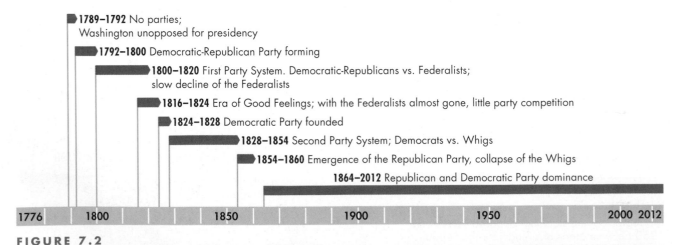

FIGURE 7.2

★ TIMELINE OF PARTY DEVELOPMENT IN THE UNITED STATES

Founders expected that men of local standing and reputation would usually be elevated to the House of Representatives in a quiet, dignified fashion and not in hotly contested campaigns. George Washington, for instance, ran unopposed in the presidential elections of 1789 and 1792.

However, after a few years, serious conflicts began to develop in the House. A Federalist group centering on the Treasury Secretary, Alexander Hamilton, favored the creation of a centralized national bank to control the economy and was suspicious of extending democracy. A loosely knit group dubbed the "Anti-Federalists" crystallized around Thomas Jefferson in opposition to Hamilton's proposals. On most issues Hamilton's supporters prevailed, but although many members voted for him some of the time, they opposed him some of the time as well. Stability did not characterize either the Federalists or their opposition.

★ Statue in Washington, D.C. of Thomas Jefferson, founder of the Democratic-Republican Party—the world's first political party.

By the middle of the 1790s the anti-Federalists opposing Hamilton were losing steadily in Congress. They began to develop an organization to try to change the situation by getting more of their own sympathizers into the House and the Senate, in the latter case by winning elections in state legislatures. The impetus for this strategy came from Jefferson and other congressional leaders, as well as from supporters in the electorate.[5] Thomas Jefferson and James Madison vacationed in New York in 1791, ostensibly to conduct botanical studies, but instead they are thought in fact to have met with Aaron Burr and George Clinton from that state. Their goal: to arrange an alliance in the Congress between opponents of Hamilton in the North, and the planters of Virginia and others in the South.

Eventually, this alliance took the name "Democratic-Republican Party." At about the same time, activist clubs supporting democratic policies began to form around the country, with the first two Democratic clubs forming in Philadelphia in 1793. Eventually 40 to 50 Democratic clubs developed, an impressive number considering that only 65 congressional districts existed in the country at the time.[6] Between politicians seeking alliances and active citizens in the electorate, the first American political party was born.

The First Party System, 1800–1820

The new party proved immediately successful, winning a majority of the seats in the House of Representatives in the election of 1800. This period between 1800 and 1820, marked by conflict between the Democratic-Republicans and the Federalists, is called the **First Party System.** Federalist power gradually declined, and the group became in effect a regional New England party; it did not even offer a presidential candidate to oppose James Monroe in the election of 1820. This election marked the "**Era of Good Feelings.**" With the Federalists on the verge of disappearing, there was no opposition to the Democratic-Republican Party and thus no partisan conflict.

The Era of Good Feelings could not last, however. In a large society, there are simply too many sources of conflict to allow government to proceed for long without organized political conflict. John Quincy Adams succeeded Monroe in 1824. From then until the election of 1828, Senator Martin Van Buren of New York, who had become upset with Monroe for cooperating too much with former Federalists and who disagreed with many of Adams' policies, launched a successful effort to nominate and

First Party System
The period from 1800 to 1820, which was marked by the appearance of the new Democratic-Republican Party and the gradual decline of their opponents, the Federalists.

Era of Good Feelings
A brief period centering on the election of 1820 when the Federalists were in sharp decline and there was no organized opposition to the dominant Democratic-Republican Party.

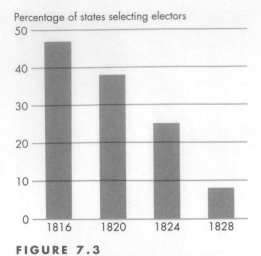

Percentage of states selecting electors

FIGURE 7.3

★ PERCENTAGE OF STATES SELECTING
PRESIDENTIAL ELECTORS IN THE STATE
LEGISLATURE

By 1828 almost all states held elections at
which the voters–rather than the state
legislature–chose the state's presidential
electors. How did this affect the development
of political parties?

Whig Party
A party active from 1830 to the
verge of the Civil War; it opposed
the extension of presidential power
and supported development of
transportation and infrastructure.

Second Party System
The period from the early 1830s
until just before the Civil War,
which was marked by rivalry
between the Democratic Party and
the Whigs.

elect as president Andrew Jackson, a military hero of the War of 1812, who had been the losing presidential candidate in the 1824 election. To do this, Van Buren invented a new kind of party, focused on attracting and mobilizing mass support among voters. This was the Democratic Party, today the oldest political party in the world.

A change at that time in the selection of presidential electors made it possible to organize a large political party to contest elections. From 1789 to 1820, in about half the states, the legislature had chosen presidential electors through a bargaining process among the legislators; voters were not involved in these decisions, so it would not have made sense to organize them through a party. Starting with the 1820 election, however, the system rapidly evolved into one in which voters chose the electors in almost all states, as shown in Figure 7.3.

By 1828, in almost all states the voters chose the president. Van Buren realized that a coordinated campaign across the country could be very effective under these circumstances, and he worked for three years to build such an organization around the 1828 candidacy of Andrew Jackson. The new Democratic Party (actually a revamping of the old Democratic-Republican Party) raised money and established a network of newspapers around the country. It held campaign rallies and parades, especially at Fourth of July celebrations all over the country, and introduced campaign paraphernalia—including hickory sticks, to play off of Jackson's nickname, "Old Hickory." This new party was successful. Jackson won with 56 percent of the vote.

The Second Party System, 1828–1854

Gradually over the next decade the Democratic Party expanded its reach, and eventually it had some sort of organization in every state. At the same time, its opponents— the remnants of the old Federalist Party, plus Democratic-Republicans who were opposed to Jackson's policies—formed a rival party, the **Whig Party.** Thus was born the **Second Party System,** a system of party alliances and conflicts that characterized American politics from the early 1830s until just before the Civil War. The Whigs differed from the Democrats mainly in opposing extensions of the president's authority and in pushing for policies to build up the nation's infrastructure and support the development of manufacturing.

Along with the emergence of the Democrats and Whigs, the Second Party System was also marked by an abundance of smaller parties, many of which were active for only a few elections. During this time Americans experimented with a variety of different policy-based parties, including the Anti-Masonic Party and the American Party (also known as the "Know-Nothing Party"), which opposed immigration. Many of these, including the Liberty Party and the Free Soil Party, represented early manifestations of the growing debate over slavery that would eventually tear the Second Party System apart.

150 YEARS OF DEMOCRATS AND REPUBLICANS

In 1854 a new anti-slavery party was formed: the Republican Party. It rapidly replaced the Whig Party as the main opposition to the Democratic Party, gaining power for the first time in 1860 with the election of Abraham Lincoln. This election ignited the Civil War. After the Civil War, the American party system settled into two main parties: the Democratic Party and the Republican Party. This two-party system continues today, although the parties have changed dramatically over the intervening century and a half.

The Golden Age of Parties, 1860–1900

Two characteristics defined the political period between 1860 and 1900: (1) a fairly close division between the Democratic and Republican parties, and (2) intensely partisan voters lined up in well-organized, strong parties. It is for the latter of these characteristics that the period is often dubbed the "Golden Age" of parties.

The election of 1860, and the ensuing Civil War, resulted in a Republican North arrayed against a Democratic South. For about 40 years voters primarily replayed the Civil War with each election. After the Civil War, or at least after the end of the Reconstruction period during which southern African Americans had been able to vote, the Democrats held a bastion of electoral strength in the South and Republicans held a similar regional lock on the North. The Golden Age represented a period of intense partisanship and high voter turnout—perhaps a reflection of the passion of the Civil War. Between 1876 and 1892, although Republicans won most national elections, the parties were actually fairly evenly matched. During this period the largest margin any presidential candidate won by was just three percentage points.

At this time, local party organizations were well organized and active, and local party "bosses" with **political machines** wielded great power. In both rural areas and cities, local organizations of both parties established networks of supporters whom they rewarded with **patronage**—jobs on the public payroll given in return for their loyalty to the party. In large cities especially, party bosses took advantage of the floods of immigrants arriving in the United States from Europe. These groups, who mainly populated large cities, needed help finding a way to thrive in the new country. Parties helped immigrants get city jobs, gave them packets of food when times were especially hard, and provided other favors; in return, the party machine expected the immigrants to vote for its candidates and organize their friends to vote for them. In 1905, George Washington Plunkitt, an officer of the Tammany Hall machine of New York City, described his operations in this way:

> What tells in holdin' your grip on your district is to go right down among the poor families and help them in the different ways they need help. I've got a regular system for this. If there's a fire in Ninth, Tenth, or Eleventh Avenue, for example, any hour of the day or night, I'm usually there with some of my election district captains as soon as the fire-engines. If a family is burned out I don't ask whether they are Republicans or Democrats, and I don't refer them to the Charity Organization Society, which would investigate their case in a month or two and decide they were worthy of help about the time they are dead from starvation. I just get quarters for them, buy clothes for them if their clothes were burned up, and fix them up till they get things runnin' again. It's philanthropy, but it's politics, too—mighty good politics. . . .
>
> And the children–the little roses of the district! Do I forget them? Oh no! They know me, every one of them, and they know that a sight of Uncle George and

political machine
A party organization providing its supporters with benefits such as city jobs and other favors, and in return controlling them politically.

patronage
Financial rewards (especially public jobs) given to people in return for their political support.

candy means the same thing. Some of them are the best kind of vote-getters. I'll tell you a case. Last year a little Eleventh Avenue rosebud whose father is a Republican, caught hold of his whiskers on election day and said she wouldn't let go till he'd promise to vote for me. And she didn't.[7]

There is probably more than a little exaggeration in Plunkitt's account. Whether the little rosebud really grabbed her father's whiskers we will never know. However, his description explains in a general way the relationship between a political machine and its supporters in the Golden Age.

Even as Plunkitt was saying these words, however, the Golden Age was coming to a close. As we will see in the next section, reformers were working to weaken the hold of political bosses on the voters. The static, fairly even division of the two parties nationally was being shaken up by new political forces. By the 1890s, the Populist Party was campaigning for free trade and a weaker currency that would help small farmers in the South and West pay off their debts to eastern banks. In 1896 the Democratic Party took up this cause, effectively absorbing the Populist Party, and nominating a Populist, William Jennings Bryan, as its presidential candidate. In an election that would have lasting ramifications, the Republican Party beat back this challenge and strengthened their hold in the Northeast and Midwest in a way that ensured their general dominance of national politics until the coming of the New Deal in the 1930s.

Progressive movement
A movement of mostly middle-class reformers in the early twentieth century who worked to eliminate machine politics.

★ A few days prior to his 2004 senate win, Barack Obama had lunch with Chicago's Mayor Richard M. Daley, son of the earlier Mayor Daley. The Chicago Democratic organization is still a potent force in elections.

Republican Dominance and Progressive Reform, 1900–1932

Two characteristics defined the political period between 1900 and 1932. After the election of 1896, the Republican Party enjoyed a long era of electoral dominance. They had held the edge in the close contestation of the Golden Age, but from 1896 to 1928 the average margin of victory for Republicans in presidential elections was 15 percent. The only Democrat elected president during this period was Woodrow Wilson (1913–1921), whose victory in 1912 was made possible because the Republicans temporarily split into two parties. During this period, a regionally based Republican Party dominated all states in the Northeast and Midwest; it faced a Democratic Party with primarily rural roots, considerable support in the West, and a strong base among white Southerners. People's economic status had little to do with whether they voted for the Republicans or the Democrats; instead, voters' support for one party or the other was determined primarily by the region in which they lived.[8]

Another important development of this period was the rise of the **Progressive movement,** a loose collection of reformers who brought to an end the "Golden Age." The Progressives' goals were to make politics more open and issue-oriented by eliminating many of the means that machines had used to reward their supporters.[9] The rising middle class did not need help from the parties as poor immigrants had. They resented the domination of machines and thought (often with reason) that they were corrupt—that they used government money and public jobs to enrich themselves and get people to vote for them. Reform candidates challenged the older politicians, and in 1905, Plunkitt himself lost his position as party district leader to a reformer. Eventually, machines gradually lost influence in American politics, although as late as 1968, Mayor Richard Daley still ran Chicago politics through a successful, old-style machine.[10]

Running candidates against the old-style politicians, however, was just one tactic used by the Progressives. They also worked to change the political rules that had allowed bosses to rule. Under Progressive influence, many states took the power to nominate candidates for office away from party officials and gave it to voters by adopting **direct primaries** in which voters choose in a preliminary election each party's candidates for the general election. The Progressives also made it more difficult for machines to provide public jobs to their workers through new **civil service laws,** which required job-seekers to take competitive examinations. (The civil service system is analyzed in detail in Chapter 14.) In the end, the party bosses did not have enough power over elections or enough rewards to offer their troops to continue the kind of domination they had enjoyed. As an indirect result of the reforms, not only the city bosses, but *all* party organizations became looser and more decentralized because they had fewer tools with which to reward or punish their members.

Other Progressive reforms were intended to weaken party leaders in the state government. Three measures allowed voters to insert themselves directly into governmental decision making, bypassing the party leadership: the referendum and the initiative, which allow voters to vote yes or no on policy proposals rather than having the legislature decide them; and the recall, a rare type of election that allows voters to remove an official at any time—not just at regularly scheduled elections. These reforms (which are discussed in greater detail in Chapter 9) were not introduced at the national level. But many states, especially in the West, adopted one or another of them during the early twentieth century. Today many states use these ballots, at least to some extent, in lawmaking.

The New Deal and Democratic Dominance, 1932–1964

Throughout the period from 1900 to 1932, various smaller parties had tried to raise issues related to the problems of the poor, such as the right of workers to form unions and strike, and income redistribution through taxation. None, however, were able to shake up the basic regional alignment of the two major parties. Eugene Debs ran as a socialist candidate for president in every election from 1900 to 1920, receiving as much as 6 percent of the national vote. And in 1924 Robert LaFollette, running as the candidate of the Progressive Party, received 17 percent of the vote. So change was in the air even before the Depression broke.

Then the disastrous Depression hit in 1929, with massive unemployment and bankruptcies across the country. Franklin Roosevelt and the Democrats swept the Republicans away and initiated a new era of Democratic dominance based on a new set of political alignments. With Roosevelt's election in 1932 and his reelection in 1936, the parties reshaped themselves quickly into a business-oriented Republican Party with strong support from the upper middle class and lingering regional support in rural

direct primary
An election to determine a party's nominee for a general election.

civil service laws
Laws requiring that public jobs be filled on the basis of competitive examinations.

areas of the Northeast and Midwest, and a labor-oriented Democratic Party that drew support from labor unions, liberals, and northern African Americans while maintaining a stronghold in the white South.

The new orientation of the two parties ushered in a period of Democratic dominance. Democratic candidates won six of the eight next presidential elections with an average margin of 4.7 percentage points. The transformation of the Democrats nationally into a liberal party during the New Deal created a basic tension within the organization. While the party increasingly emphasized extending rights to members of labor unions and other disadvantaged groups, its southern branch continued to defend a harsh system of segregation that denied rights to African Americans. For many years the party existed as an uneasy coalition between these two very different impulses. The palpable strain within the party threatened to explode at certain moments, such as when President Harry Truman (1946–1953) desegregated the nation's military in 1948, but the party held its unlikely coalition together until the 1960s.

Republican Recovery, 1964–Present

With the rise of the Civil Rights movement in the 1960s, it became impossible to hold the two incompatible parts of the Democratic Party together. Things came to a head when Democratic presidents John F. Kennedy (1961–1963) and Lyndon Johnson (1963–1968) developed laws in 1964 and 1965 to end racial segregation. With the signing of these laws, the South began a shift from the Democrats to the Republicans that reshaped electoral politics for decades.

The sound of President Johnson's soft southern voice quoting from the civil rights anthem "We Shall Overcome" in the middle of his address on the Voting Rights Act of 1965 was—at that time—a shock to the nation. As a white southerner himself, Johnson had earlier worked closely with segregationist leaders, but he pushed hard for these bills. He is said to have told an aide as he signed the 1964 bill, "We have lost the South for a generation." As you see in Figure 7.4, he was right.

Each bar in the graph shows the Democrats' percent of the electoral vote in the South, minus their percent of the electoral vote in that year outside the South. Until 1964 the Democrats did better in the South than in other states, often dramatically so. But in 1964, the Democrats' historical advantage in the South suddenly turned negative.[11] Today the Republicans, not the Democrats, have a solid stronghold of electoral support in the South.[12] The Civil Rights Act of 1964 marks a rare moment when a single act changed the shape of the political landscape.

Absorbing the South brought a large number of more conservative voters into the Republican Party and pulled the party to the right. As a result, the party lost strength in many areas where its members had traditionally been more liberal. The Democrats picked up strength not only where there were large minority populations, but also where Republicans had traditionally been more liberal. The Northeast and the West Coast, where the Democrats and Republicans had previously been evenly matched, moved strongly to the Democrats. In 1960, 57 Republicans and 55 Democrats had been elected to the House of Representatives from the Northeast and the West Coast; by 2012, in a fairly typical election year, only 24 Republicans were elected, compared with 90 Democrats.[13] But in nationwide elections these gains did not make up for the Democrats' loss of their Southern bastion. From 1932

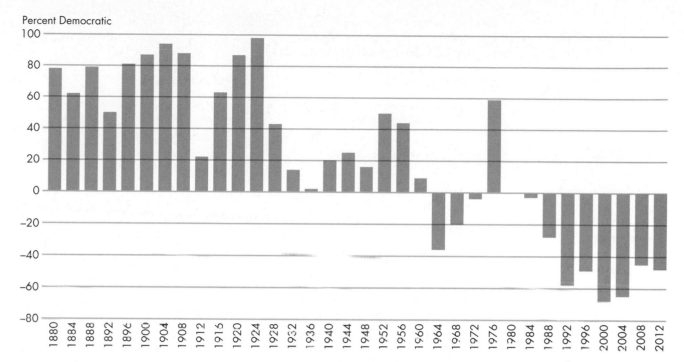

Percent Democratic

FIGURE 7.4

to 1960, Democrats won 6 of 8 presidential elections. From 1964 to 2012, they won only 6 of 13.

Other shifts over the period have also contributed to changes in the makeup of the parties. The most important have been the rise of the religious right in the Republican Party and of feminism and environmentalism in the Democratic Party. Today the Republican Party includes many business interests, the religious right (especially with regard to the abortion issue), people who are especially concerned about national defense and security, and higher income groups; the Democratic Party includes racial and ethnic minorities, labor, environmentalists, feminists, and those with lower incomes. In an important development in 2010, the Tea Party—not actually a party, but a movement of people concerned about the growth of government and the national debt—overturned a number of established Republican figures in primary elections and shifted the center of gravity of the party to lean in favor of reducing the size of government. This leaning had always been part of the Republican program, but the Tea Party made it a more central part of the agenda.

★ THE LOSS OF THE DEMOCRATIC ADVANTAGE IN THE SOUTH, 1880–2012

What may have accounted for the temporary return to a Democratic advantage in 1976? (Jimmy Carter of Georgia ran against Gerald Ford of Michigan in that year.)

THE PARTIES TODAY

What do the parties look like today? We can view them by looking at two different snapshots: a comparison of their core beliefs, and a comparison of their bases of support in the population. First, we will look at their beliefs by examining the two parties' platforms at the 2012 election (see Table 7.1). In every election year, each party holds a national convention at which it nominates candidates and writes a platform laying out its positions on political issues.[14] The platforms are long and comprehensive (the Democrats' platform in 2012 was 32 pages long, the Republicans' 54 pages).

TABLE 7.1
the democratic and republican platforms in 2012

	DEMOCRATIC PLATFORM	REPUBLICAN PLATFORM
Taxes	Raise taxes on those making over $250,000 a year; leave taxes unchanged for those making less.	Reduce income taxes by 20% for all taxpayers, and eliminate the estate tax.
Abortion	Guarantee women's right to choose.	Guarantee "individual right to life which cannot be infringed."
Same-sex marriage	Support marriage equality and the movement to secure equal treatment for same-sex couples.	Pass a constitutional amendment defining marriage as the union of one man and one woman.
Medicare	Reform Medicare through cost savings without cutting benefits; oppose privatizing it.	Open Medicare to competition by giving recipients subsidies for insurance and letting them choose policies.
Health care	Obama's Affordable Care Act has expanded coverage, broadened services, and brought insurance to those with pre-existing conditions.	Repeal the Affordable Care Act; develop responsible healthcare reform through the free market.
Immigration	Pass comprehensive immigration reform, and the DREAM act that would allow young undocumented immigrants to stay in the country for college or military service.	Do not provide any form of amnesty for undocumented immigrants.
Energy	Encourage all forms of energy, through government subsidies and rules.	Do not pick winners and losers, but instead let the free market and the public's preferences determine industry outcomes.
Defense	Agree with the Republicans and argue for a strong defense.	Agree with the Democrats and argue for a strong defense.

As a second snapshot of the parties, Table 7.2 shows how different parts of the population voted in elections for the House of Representatives in 2010.[15] No election is "typical," but off-year elections (ones when there is no presidential contest) give a fairly good picture of a party's base of support; in these elections voters are focusing on the parties rather than a particular national candidate. We see in Table 7.2 that the base support for the Republican Party includes men, whites, born-again Evangelical Christians, those with higher incomes, and the South and the Midwest. The Democrats' base of support is the opposite.

Another important difference between the parties is that Republicans are more strictly ideological than Democrats, perhaps because of the importance of religion to party members and the party's emphasis on adherence to central principles. In a 2011 poll, 68 percent of Republicans said that they would rather have a representative in Congress who stuck to his or her principles, no matter what; only 32 percent wanted a representative who compromised to get things done. The numbers were exactly reversed for Democrats—only 32 percent wanted a representative who stuck to principles no matter what, while 68 percent preferred one who would compromise to get things done.[16]

TABLE 7.2
party support by different groups, 2010

	VOTED DEMOCRATIC	VOTED REPUBLICAN
Gender		
Men	41%	55%
Women	48	49
Ethnicity		
White	37	60
African American	89	9
Hispanic/Latino	60	38
Asian	58	40
Family income		
Less than $30,000	57	40
$30,000–$49,999	51	46
$50,000–$99,999	44	53
$100,000–$199,999	43	56
$200,000+	34	64
Religious right		
White Evangelical/Born-again Christians	19	77
All others	55	42
Region		
East	54	44
West	49	48
Midwest	44	53
South	37	61

Reforms Weaken the Parties: Round Two

We described earlier how the reforms of the Progressive movement ended the "Golden Age" of strong party organizations. In the 1970s a second wave of reform further weakened party organizations. A broad movement in opposition to the Vietnam War had appealed to the Democratic Party at its 1968 convention to nominate Eugene McCarthy. McCarthy, however, lost to Hubert Humphrey, who was nominated primarily on the strength of his connection to party officials. Humphrey had not run in a single primary that year, while McCarthy and Robert Kennedy (who was assassinated during the campaign) had energized large numbers of supporters in the primaries. At the time, most state delegations were controlled by their state party organizations; only 14 states and the District of Columbia held presidential primaries. And so Humphrey was able to garner a majority of delegates without having had to run in any primaries.

In reaction to this "back-room deal," the Democratic Party set up the McGovern-Fraser Commission to recommend reform. The commission proposed rules that would lead to the selection of a broader and more diverse range of delegates, with a better representation of women, different age groups, and racial and ethnic minorities. As a side effect, however, most states shifted to primary elections as their way of selecting delegates, since they thought this would be the easiest way to comply with the new rules. This move to widespread primary elections took away one of the remaining powers of many state party organizations.

At about the same time, Congress enacted the Federal Election Campaign Act of 1971, a reform that regulated party expenditures and decreased state party activities in federal elections. The act caused state parties to concentrate more on state elections and to be less active in congressional and presidential elections. It also led to a proliferation of Political Action Committees, which contribute to candidates independently of the parties.[17] We discuss this act in more detail in Chapter 8.

Along with these reforms, technological changes during this period hurt the parties by making it possible for candidates to campaign more independently. In the Golden Age, candidates depended on their parties for large numbers of foot soldiers to distribute campaign literature, gather names of supporters, and get voters to the polls on Election Day. With the advent of television, candidates could raise contributions and conduct their campaigns mainly through television advertisements and direct mailings, without depending on the party apparatus.

As party organizations became less important, candidates became more central to the campaigns, with their own personal campaign groups, their own money, and their own television advertisements and campaign flyers urging a vote for them, rather than for the party generally. With this increased emphasis on the characteristics of individual candidates, **split-ticket voting,** in which voters cast their ballot for a mix of Democratic and Republican candidates rather than voting for the candidates of just one party, increased markedly during the early 1970s. None of this means that parties disappeared; they did not. But state and city party organizations became less important in national politics than they had once been.

split-ticket voting
When several candidates for different offices appear on a ballot, the practice of voting for a candidate of one party for one office and a candidate of another party for another office.

critical election
An election that causes the bases of support for the two main parties to change fairly suddenly.

★ CANDIDATE MITT ROMNEY COURTED PARTY ACTIVISTS IN 2012

Electoral Realignments and Partisan Change

It is vital that parties be able to change, especially since introducing new ideas by establishing new parties appears so difficult. No new party has succeeded in displacing the Democrats and Republicans since 1860, but the two parties have evolved dramatically during that time. This capacity for evolutionary change is one advantage of the loose organizational connection between the party organization and its members that we described earlier. A tightly organized party with close control by its leaders and a large, entrenched central staff might find it more difficult to absorb new policy directions and to respond to new sources of conflict.

An election that causes the two parties to change and realign themselves in response to new issues is called a **critical election.** As we saw in Figure 7.1, party support in different segments of the population and different parts of the country, such as in Tennessee, usually remains stable over time. American electoral politics since 1860 has been marked by long periods of such stability. After each such period, however, a critical election occurs during which major parts of the population switch their party support and a new period of stability ensues. The lasting change produced by a critical election is called an **electoral realignment.** We have described three such realignments: one that centered on the election of 1896; the New Deal realignment; and the realignment of the 1960s and 1970s in which the South shifted to the Republicans and the Democrats strengthened their position in the Northeast.

electoral realignment
A new and lasting rearrangement of the geographic and social bases of support for the parties, ushered in by a critical election.

It is a little misleading to call the changes that bring about realignment "critical elections," because change has usually extended over more than one election. Critical elections have often been preceded by a series of abortive attempts at change by new third parties who have raised new issues that eventually help to bring about the critical change; one example is the unsuccessful presidential candidacy of Robert LaFollette in 1924, which prefigured many of the issues that would make up the New Deal realignment a few years later. Also, the critical change itself, in which the Democratic and Republican parties reorient themselves around the new issues, may in fact take more than a single election to occur. For instance, the shift of the South to the Republicans, which started in 1964, was only completed at the presidential level in the 1980s. And in the House of Representatives, whose seats are slower to change because of personal and local ties, it was only in 1994 that the Republicans gained a majority of House seats in the South. The basic outline of this process is clear, however: Republican and Democratic support remains stable over a long period of time, even as new issues arise that are not consistent with the orientation of the two parties; and then, finally, an election or series of elections occurs in which the two main parties reorient themselves along the new issue lines.

party in the electorate
The party's supporters in the electorate, including those who identify with the party and vote for it and activists who campaign for it.

THE STRUCTURE OF AMERICAN PARTIES

Since American parties are not well-defined formal organizations with clearly drawn boundaries, we usually analyze them by looking at three broad groups of people who are loosely joined by their shared ideology and goals: the party in the electorate, the party organization, and the party in government. The **party in the electorate** consists of all citizens who have a tie to the party and participate in elections. To a large extent, these are simply citizens who identify with the party and vote for it, but the party in the electorate also includes activists who work to elect the party's candidates. A party also needs a **party organization,** a formal structure of party officers and committees to conduct conventions, handle the legal paperwork of campaign laws, raise money, and perform other necessary functions. Finally, the **party in government** consists of a party's elected officials in Congress, state legislatures, and executive offices like governors or the president; these officials share common party ties and organize themselves along party lines.

American parties consist of three groups: the party in the electorate (voters and supporters); the party organization (a formal structure that carries out daily housekeeping and organizes the national nominating convention); and the party in government (officeholders of the party). None of these groups fully controls the direction of the party. What impact do these three groups have on the parties?

KEY TO understanding ★

These three parts exist independently of each other in the sense that they are not combined within a single organizational structure. Each part supports and influences the other two, however. The members of the party in government are only in government, for instance, because the party in the electorate voted for them; and the party organization supports the party's elected officials and new candidates in elections. This

party organization
A formal structure that conducts managerial and legal tasks for the party.

party in government
The elected officials of a party, who organize themselves along party lines.

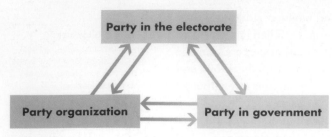

FIGURE 7.5

★ This diagram shows the mutual influence and support among the three components of a party.

pattern of mutual support and influence among the three parts is illustrated in Figure 7.5.

Some other democracies such as Brazil have loosely organized parties, but most countries' parties are clearly defined organizations. As we have seen, the loose organization of American parties may have some advantages in that it allows them to be flexible and adapt to changing times and circumstances.

THE PARTY IN THE ELECTORATE

As Chapter 6 explains, many Americans identify with one of the American parties, and this *party identification* is not casual. Once a person decides that he or she is a Democrat or a Republican, it is unusual for that identity to change. Party identification strongly affects which candidate people will vote for, and it also colors how they view political issues. About 60 percent of Americans, when asked, identify themselves as either a Democrat or a Republican.

As the parties became less influential in the 1960s and 1970s, the party in the electorate also decreased in size. The number of Americans identifying with one of the parties dropped steadily during that period, and the percentage of independents increased from about 20 percent in the early 1960s to about 40 percent in the mid-1970s.[18] The number of party identifiers has remained roughly stable since then, however.

Another way to look at the party in the electorate is to note those who vote Democratic and those who vote Republican, as we did in Table 7.2. These are not exactly the same people as the Democratic and Republican party identifiers, since independents vote, and identifiers frequently vote a split ticket or even desert their preferred party entirely in a given election. As we noted at the beginning of this chapter, the outlines of an American party are fairly blurred. We can think of the party in the electorate as either the party's voters, or its party identifiers, or some blend of the two.

Party identifiers and voters form the broad base of each party. Over the last several decades, there has almost always been a larger number of Democratic identifiers than Republican identifiers in the population, but the Republicans generally turn out in larger numbers to vote, which helps to even out the electoral strength of the two parties.

Some party supporters do more for their party than just vote. They surf the Internet, contribute money to candidates, work in campaigns, wear campaign buttons or put bumper stickers on their cars in an effort to convince their friends, neighbors, and family to vote for their favored candidate. They provide a significant source of campaign funds and do much of the campaign work. These activists' opinions have a greater impact on the party's leaders than those of supporters who merely vote for them. This is partly because activists are more likely to involve themselves in the nomination process by voting in primary elections or attending party nominating conventions—so politicians need to pay attention to them to get their support for nomination—and partly because the party needs activists to work enthusiastically during campaigns.

In any church, club, or other type of organization, those who are most active tend to believe most strongly in the group's goals. This general rule holds true for political

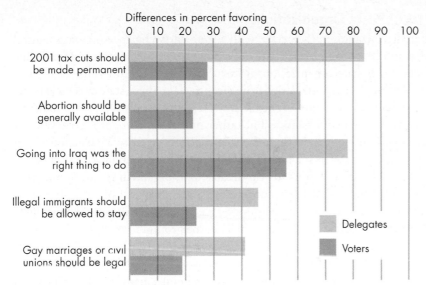

Differences in percent favoring

2001 tax cuts should be made permanent	
Abortion should be generally available	
Going into Iraq was the right thing to do	
Illegal immigrants should be allowed to stay	
Gay marriages or civil unions should be legal	

Delegates

Voters

FIGURE 7.6

★ DIFFERENCES BETWEEN DEMOCRATIC AND REPUBLICAN DELEGATES AND VOTERS

Why are convention delegates more widely separated on every issue than their parties' voters?

Source: Based on New York Times / CBS News "2008 Republican National Delegate Survey" and "2008 Democratic National Delegate Survey": http://graphics8 .nytimes.com/packages/pdf/politics/20080901-poll.pdf and http://graphics8.nytimes.com/packages/pdf/politics/ demdel20080824.pdf.

parties as well and has been observed to be true in many democracies around the world: those who are most active in a political party usually adhere more strongly to its ideology than those who are less active. This means that most parties are controlled by members who are more unified ideologically than the general membership. American parties are no exception to this rule. Figure 7.6 shows that the differences on issues between delegates to the national Democratic and Republican conventions (a good representative group of activists) are greater than the differences between Democratic voters and Republican voters as a whole.

The difference between delegates to the two conventions was especially pronounced regarding the question of whether the tax cuts of 2001 should be made permanent. Of the Republican delegates, 91 percent thought the tax cuts should be made permanent, but only 7 percent of the Democratic delegates agreed with that position, for a difference of 84 percentage points. The difference between Republican and Democratic voters was not as sharp; 62 percent of Republican voters thought the cuts should be made permanent, compared with 34 percent of Democratic voters, for a difference of 28 percentage points. Although voters for the two parties were divided on this and other issues, the party activists were even more deeply divided. As a result, the conventions were run by people who held stronger views than most of the voters for their party.

THE PARTY ORGANIZATION

To mobilize the party's supporters and to coordinate the efforts of activists, a party needs something beyond the personal commitment of its activists. It also needs a permanent organization. Today each party is organized into three types of structures that—as befits our loosely organized parties—operate independently of each other:

- state and local party organizations
- a national committee
- congressional campaign committees

State and Local Party Organizations

Parties have an organization in each state, with a state party chairperson and a central committee that concerns itself primarily with helping candidates in statewide and state legislative races. Each state organization, in turn, is based on numerous local party organizations. Although their role varies from state to state, these state and local organizations are not like the machines of the old days. They generally do not try to determine who will be nominated for office, but rather operate as a support structure for those who achieve nomination through their own efforts in primary elections or at state conventions. The work of state and local parties primarily involves fundraising, conducting issue research and polls for candidates, and organizing state nominating conventions in those states that use a convention. State and local organizations also provide the troops for grassroots campaigning in elections. Neighborhood campaigning for local and state candidates requires people on the ground to canvass voters door-to-door, distribute lawn signs, staff booths at fairs, and so on. It is the state and local party organizations that identify and mobilize these workers.

State and local organizations vary widely, so any general statement about them will have exceptions. Some organizations involve themselves at least to some extent in trying to determine who the party's candidates will be, but in general they confine themselves to providing services to candidates.[19]

National Committees

Each party has a **national committee** that oversees the day-to-day business of the party, raises money to support candidates and to assist state party organizations, and organizes the national nominating convention every four years. Organizing the convention is one of the most important things a national committee does. The **national nominating convention** consists of several hundred delegates from around the country, who have either been elected in their state's primary election or chosen at a state convention. These delegates choose the party's presidential and vice-presidential candidate for that year, and write a **party platform** that lays out the party's principles and party positions. The platform reflects the judgment of the convention's delegates and is usually influenced strongly by the likely nominee. In keeping with the decentralized nature of American parties, however, it is not binding on any of the party's candidates; many candidates will ignore important points of the platform if they disagree with the points or think the points would not work well politically in their races.

The Democratic National Committee, which has about 500 members in all, includes all state party chairs and vice-chairs, plus two hundred additional members who are either elected in primary elections or at state conventions, and a variety of members representing affiliated groups. The Republican National Committee is smaller, with about 150 members. It is made up of a committeeman and committeewoman from each state and territory, plus the state chair of any state that the Republicans carried in the preceding presidential election or that has a significant Republican presence in other ways.

The chair of each national committee is chosen by the party's presidential nominee and then elected by the National Committee. If the nominee loses, the National Committee usually chooses a new chair to replace the nominee's pick. National Committee chairs are not supposed to try to determine the ideological direction of the party, and are expected to be neutral in races among potential presidential nominees.

When the party does not hold the presidency, usually no one person speaks for its members, and in this case the chair of the National Committee may emerge as a

spokesperson. Even then, however, the party's congressional leaders are usually the primary focus of attention in the national media.

A good example of the limited role of a national committee in determining its party's direction is an attempt by the Republican National Committee in 2010 to adopt a "Purity Pledge." This pledge consisted of a set of conservative principles that all its candidates either had to agree to or else be denied party endorsements and campaign money. The attempt failed badly. Fierce opposition to the pledge led to its being watered down to a resolution that "urged" the leadership of all Republican organizations to withhold support from candidates who did not support the list of conservative principles. Bob Tiernan, the Republican chair from Oregon, who had opposed the resolution, said of it: "Read the resolution. It says what it says; it's a suggestion. There's nothing mandatory there. There's nothing required. I am a chairman: I am not going to take that back and make my candidates sign it."[20]

Congressional Campaign Committees

Each party has a committee in the Senate and a committee in the House of Representatives whose purpose is to raise money for candidates for Senate or House seats and to recruit able candidates. These **congressional campaign committees** focus their support on candidates who have a chance to win and thereby increase the size of their party's delegation in the Senate or House.

The Resurgence of National Party Organizations

Although the three national organizations for each party—the national committee and the two congressional campaign committees—operate independently of each other, all have thrived in recent years. As the power of state party organizations declined in the 1960s and 1970s, the size and activities of the national party organizations, ironically, increased. Many of the same technological changes that have

congressional campaign committees
Four committees, two for each party in the Senate and the House of Representatives, that recruit able candidates for Senate or House seats and raise money for congressional campaigns.

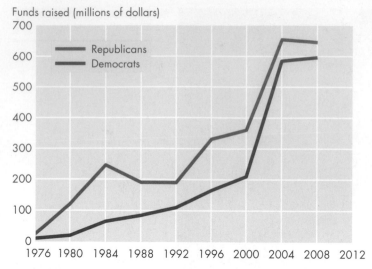

Funds raised (millions of dollars)

— Republicans
— Democrats

FIGURE 7.7

★ MONEY RAISED BY
NATIONAL PARTY
COMMITTEES IN
INDIVIDUAL
CONTRIBUTIONS

The Republican Committees
raised more than the
Democrats each year, but is
the difference between
them constant or
narrowing?

made candidates more independent of state organizations—television advertising, polling, direct marketing, and Internet campaigning—have also meant that candidates need large sums of money, as well as support and tutoring in the technical aspects of campaigning. The national organizations help to provide these. Figure 7.7 shows the amount of money raised by national party committees. For each party the National Committee, the Senate Campaign Committee, and the House Campaign Committee are combined in the figure; in most years the majority of the money was raised by the National Committees of the two parties.[21]

Over the last 20 years, as shown in Figure 7.7, the six national committees have grown enormously, with combined budgets in 2008 of over a billion dollars. During this period, they grew from small operations with a few staff members who worked out of rented offices, to organizations with several hundred employees housed in their own dedicated buildings near the Capitol. In an earlier era, the state party organizations sent money to the national organizations to help keep them going, but now the flow has reversed, with the two parties' national committees helping to subsidize the operations of the state party organizations.

THE PARTY IN GOVERNMENT

As noted earlier in the chapter, parties provide leading government officials with a means of influencing, and often controlling, what other officials of their party do. The party in government provides the structure through which officials exercise this control. All of a party's elected officials share a common partisan identity, and they are tied together organizationally as well; to some extent at least, all of them rely on the party organization for help with their campaigns. They also share a common ideology. The party's structure enables them to work together, and also allows their leaders to guide them in this collective effort. The party in government most clearly provides structure and coherence to policy making within each of the houses of Congress and in the relations of Congress with the president.

Parties in Congress

Members of both houses of Congress are organized by party and do much of their most important business through their party organizations. House members actually spend a considerable amount of their time working only with the other members of their own party. Republicans are members of the House Republican Conference, and Democrats are members of the House Democratic Caucus. During meetings of these two groups, which happen at least once a week, party leaders communicate the party's positions on issues as well as the party's legislative strategy—and the rank-and-file members raise issues and push back if they disagree with their leaders.

★ Even former presidents sometimes play a prominent role in the party. Here former president Bill Clinton helps campaign for Democratic presidential hopeful Barack Obama in Florida in 2008.

The two parties in the Senate are organized into a Senate Republican Conference and a Senate Democratic Conference, with an internal structure similar to the Conference and Caucus in the House of Representatives. In contrast with the House, however, individual senators have traditionally been more powerful in their own right than House members have been. If nothing else, each senator is 1 in 100, while each House member is 1 in 435. Party leaders in the Senate have to tolerate more defections from their ranks than leaders in the House do, and they also have to negotiate more often with members of the opposite party to get bills passed.

Presidents and Parties

Presidents are recognized as the leader of their party nationally. A sitting president is the public face of his or her party, and the party's fortunes rise or fall with the popularity of the president. The president appoints the chair of the party's national committee and is invaluable to the party as a fundraiser. In addition, presidents use their importance to their party to help them govern. Party ties are especially important in the president's relations with Congress. When the president's party also controls the two houses of Congress—admittedly not a particularly common situation—the party in Congress normally supports the president by adopting his program as its own general agenda. When the president's party does not control one or both houses of Congress, the situation is not as helpful for him. However, even then presidents use their ties to their party to help monitor legislation, despite their party being in the minority.

Parties in State Government

Governmental structures in the states are similar to those of the national government—with a governor and a legislature rather than a president and Congress—but parties generally affect decision making even more strongly at the state level than they do nationally. In many states, the division of powers between the governor and the legislature is less strict than it is at the national level, so a governor can work more directly with the legislators of his or her party. (For instance, governors in some states help to name the party leaders in the legislature and join in the regular meetings of their party's legislators.) Also, many state legislatures meet only on a part-time basis, and members have other jobs at the same time, so that leadership by the governor or by other party leaders meets with less resistance; part-time legislators do not usually have the time or resources to build up an independent, individual position in the legislature. In addition, because seniority is not as much a factor in committee assignments as it is in Congress, party leaders in state legislatures often have more discretion in appointing members to committees, which gives them more rewards with which to shape legislators' behavior. As a result, state legislatures often have a very high degree of party unity, and the legislative parties work more closely with governors in most states than congressional parties do with the president.

THE TWO-PARTY SYSTEM

The United States has two major parties, and it is very difficult for other parties to gain office. The main reason is probably our winner-take-all system of elections. In this section we learn what this system entails and how it helps to sustain a two-party dominance that strongly influences American politics.

two-party system
A party system with two, and only two, parties that regularly nominate candidates with a serious chance of winning office.

multiparty system
A party system in which three or more parties regularly have a significant chance of gaining office.

Since 1864 the Democratic and Republican parties have had a virtual monopoly on elected office in the United States. In that period every president has been either a Democrat or a Republican, and 99 percent of all members of the House of Representatives have belonged to one of these two parties. Many other parties have tried to enter government, but no other party has been able to establish itself as a serious contender for power on a continuing basis. The Greenback Party, Populists, Prohibition Party, Socialists, Progressives, and others, as well as independent candidates like Ross Perot (who ran for president in 1992) have all tried, but none have been able to break the hold of the Republicans and Democrats.

The United States, in other words, has a **two-party system** in which two—and only two—parties are regular contenders for governmental office. Some countries are one-party systems where only a single party is allowed to nominate candidates for office. (China, whose politics we examined at the opening of this chapter, is an example of a one-party system.) Many other countries have **multiparty systems** in which three or more parties regularly contend for office with a significant chance of success. Brazil, for instance, has four major parties—the Workers' Party, the Brazilian Democratic Movement, the Social Democrats, and the Democrats—and many smaller parties that nonetheless regularly win some seats in Congress. Twenty-two different parties hold at least one seat in Brazil's Congress.

Unlike the United States, most of the world's democracies are multiparty systems, as shown in Figure 7.8. Having a two-party system affects United States politics in at least two important ways. For one, compared with most multiparty countries, the range of policy options offered by parties in the United States is narrower. Neither of the two major parties in the United States has argued that the government should nationalize major industries, for instance, or that it should establish a national religion or halt immigration. Individuals *within* one of the parties may have argued for these or other radical proposals, but because each party must appeal to a broad range of people in order to be large enough to win in a two-party system, it cannot adopt a distinctively radical position like one of these and still gain the 50 percent of the votes it needs to win an election. In contrast, Norway, with its multiparty system, has a moderately socialist Labor Party; a more socialist Left Socialist Party; an environmentalist Green Party; an anti-immigrant, anti-tax Progress party; a free-enterprise

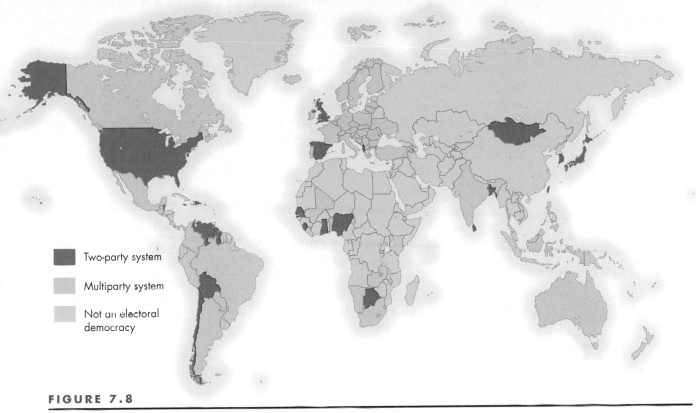

FIGURE 7.8

★ PARTY SYSTEMS OF THE WORLD'S DEMOCRACIES

Note: Calculated from information in the CIA World Factbook, accessed online April 5, 2011. A cutoff point always has to be set between two-party systems and multiparty systems. In this case, we have defined two-party systems to be electoral democracies in which the two largest parties hold at least 85 percent of the seats in the lower house of the congress or parliament. A few of the two-party systems under this definition (Botswana, for example) are systems in which a single very large party competes with a number of parties that are far smaller than it is; these do not allow for the sort of lively competition between parties that we normally associate with two-party systems.

Conservative Party; a Christian Party; and more—all with representation in the Norwegian parliament.

Secondly, the fact that each party in a two-party system must be large enough to include a range of differing opinions is probably one reason for the loose organization of American political parties. If a party is a "big tent," it is harder for it to enforce uniform political views on its members or its candidates. As we have seen, when some members of the Republican National Committee tried to establish a code of policy positions that all Republican candidates must adhere to, they failed.

THE U.S. ELECTORAL SYSTEM AND THE TWO-PARTY SYSTEM

Why does the United States have a two-party system when most democracies in the world are multiparty systems? A diverse country like the United States certainly would have a wide enough range of opinions to sustain a variety of parties, so there must be something that regularly forces American politics to fit into just two parties. That "something" is our winner-take-all system of elections, in which candidates run in a district (or a state, or the country as a whole), and the one candidate who does best in the district takes office.

We will look at the U.S. electoral system in detail in Chapter 8 and will also see that elections can be organized in other ways. For our purposes in this chapter, the important thing is to realize that winner-take-all systems like that in the United States generally help large parties and hurt small ones, and for this reason they have a strong tendency over time to produce two-party systems. To see why this would be so, consider congressional elections. Congressional elections pose a steep challenge for a significant but small party, such as the Green Party. With the support (let us say) of no more than a tenth of the population, spread fairly evenly across the country, it is difficult for the Greens to win congressional seats. In a three-way race, even if the Democratic and Republican candidates were exactly tied, the Green candidate would have to get over 33 percent of the vote to win, which would be more than three times its national average. An even higher percentage would be necessary if the two major parties were not tied.

In a presidential race, the odds are even starker. At least the Greens might have a few local pockets of strength in which they could get three, four, or five times their national average and win a few congressional districts. But in the national vote for president, winning with 10 percent would be impossible. The Greens would have to get at least 34 percent of the entire national vote, and even that number would work only if the Democratic and Republican candidates split the rest of the vote evenly. In this way, our winner-take-all electoral system punishes small parties and rewards large parties. As a result, over time small parties disappear and a two-party system emerges.

THIRD PARTIES IN AMERICAN POLITICS

KEY TO understanding

Other parties ("third" parties) have always operated within the two-party system. While they vary in ideology and type, their greatest impact has been their ability to raise new issues. In order to neutralize the challenge from the third party, one or the other of the two main parties has often been forced to address these issues. In this way third parties have sometimes been key factors in the evolution of the two major parties.

★

third parties
Small political parties that are so greatly handicapped by the single-member, plurality electoral system in the United States and other obstacles that they have a low probability of winning office.

Even with our basic two-party system, there have always been additional, smaller parties such as the Libertarian Party in American politics. They are commonly called **third parties,** even though they might more properly be called minor parties since there are often fourth, fifth, and even more parties running candidates in an election. In the 2012 presidential election there were actually 25 candidates for president on the ballot in at least some states: Democrat Barack Obama and Republican Mitt Romney, of course, but also candidates of significant parties like Gary Johnson of the Libertarian Party (on the ballot in 48 states) and less significant ones like Tom Stevens of the Objectivist Party (on the ballot in only 2 states). None of the other 23 candidates had much chance to win. Aside from egotism, or eternal hope, what leads small parties to contest elections in which their chances of success are so small?

Not only are third parties handicapped by the winner-take-all electoral system, but they also face other barriers. Most states have special rules designed to limit "nuisance" candidacies; these rules generally require candidates of any party but the two major ones to gather large numbers of signatures before they can appear on the ballot. This process is costly and time-consuming, and it helps explain why the Libertarian Party was on the ballot in 48 rather than all 50 states, and the Objectivist Party in only 2.

Also, public funding of campaigns, where it is available, is usually based on the size of the vote a party gained at the preceding election. Because their share of the vote is generally slight, third parties get only a small subsidy, or none, for their campaign.

In a national presidential campaign, third-party candidates can get public funds only *after* the election—not during the campaign, when they need it—and then only if they appeared on the ballot in at least 10 states and received at least 5 percent of the total national vote. Most third parties, in most years, would not qualify for this subsidy.

Despite all of these handicaps, however, third parties have been active throughout American history. Third parties come in many varieties, including three major types:

- offshoots from a major party
- ideological or single-issue parties
- vehicles for independent candidates

OFFSHOOTS FROM A MAJOR PARTY

Some third parties arise when there is a split in a major party. Party splits can occur for a variety of reasons. In 1912, for instance, followers of Theodore Roosevelt left the Republican Party to form the Progressive Party, with Roosevelt as its presidential candidate. Roosevelt broke from the Republicans for personal reasons and also to pursue the goals of the Progressive movement. In 1948 southerners bolted from the Democratic Party and formed the States' Rights Democratic Party, with Strom Thurmond as their candidate. Their break from the Democrats was made in an effort to try to maintain racial segregation in the South.

IDEOLOGICAL OR SINGLE-ISSUE PARTIES

Some long-term third parties promote a single issue or a broad ideology. Especially in the nineteenth and early twentieth centuries, ideological parties like the Populist Party and the Socialist Party ran candidates in a number of elections and enjoyed some success, at least at the congressional level. And single-issue parties like the Free Silver party and the Prohibition Party likewise were stable fixtures for at least a period of time, with some successes. Enduring parties of this sort in contemporary politics include the Green Party and the Libertarian Party. The Green Party supports sustainable environmental policies, local involvement in politics and the economy, and social justice. The Libertarian Party supports limited government and individual freedom.

VEHICLES FOR INDEPENDENT CANDIDATES

Since the middle of the twentieth century, the most prominent third parties have formed to serve the needs of independent candidates, who used them to get access to the national stage. In 1968 George Wallace, the segregationist governor of Alabama, formed the American Independent Party to run for president as a gadfly. Maintaining that there wasn't "a dime's worth of difference" between the two main parties, he asked voters to "send them a message" and received 13 percent of the national vote. In 1992 Ross Perot, a wealthy businessman, financed his own campaign and ran as an independent but with a national organization of supporters he called United We Stand America. With a platform that emphasized balancing the budget, he received 19 percent of the vote. In 2008 billionaire (and mayor of New York) Michael Bloomberg for some time prepared for a possible campaign for president as an independent, but eventually decided against it.

THIRD PARTIES CAN MAKE A DIFFERENCE

Can third parties accomplish anything politically, beyond giving their candidates the thrill of the campaign? One effect of third parties, for which they draw criticism, is that they sometimes act as "spoilers," drawing most of their supporters from one of the two major parties and causing that party to lose the election. In 1912 Theodore Roosevelt's Progressive Party drew its voters mainly from the Republican Party and ensured the election of Democrat Woodrow Wilson (1913–1921). In the very close election of 2000 it is likely that Democrat Al Gore would have won instead of Republican George W. Bush (2001–2009) if Ralph Nader had not run as the Green Party's candidate. Bush carried Florida by only 307 votes, while Nader got 97,488 votes in Florida. Since Nader's Green Party supporters were more likely to have voted Democratic than Republican were he not in the race, Gore would probably have carried Florida if Nader had not been on the ballot. And if Gore had carried Florida, he would have won the election.[22]

More importantly, however, third parties have often been able to bring issues to national attention and force the two major parties to deal with them. Several times in American history, third parties have successfully promoted an issue or an ideology, even if they themselves have not been able to gain office to implement their ideas. The Democratic and Republican parties are constantly evolving in their ideologies and policy positions, and third-party campaigns have often influenced that evolution.

The Populist Party, for instance, which received 9 percent of the national vote and carried five states in 1892 with its "free silver" program of inflationary policies to help farmers and debtors, succeeded in taking over the Democratic Party in 1896, and William Jennings Bryan, a Populist figure, was nominated for president by the Democrats. The Prohibition Party never achieved more than local success in electing candidates, but it did succeed in its goal of national prohibition when the Eighteenth Amendment to the Constitution, outlawing the sale and consumption of alcoholic beverages in the United States, was passed in 1919. (The policy proved unpopular, however, and was reversed by the Twenty-first Amendment. This amendment passed in 1933 and made alcohol legal again.)

In 1924 Robert LaFollette, running as the candidate of the newly reconstituted Progressive Party, garnered 17 percent of the national vote with trade-union support; his platform included nationalizing railroads and providing help for distressed farmers. His candidacy is often seen as a forerunner to Franklin Roosevelt's New Deal, as for instance in his campaign to ban child labor, which Roosevelt later accomplished in 1938.

The Green Party today has seen its environmental concerns incorporated into many public policies, and the Libertarian Party's concern for limited government has been adopted strongly by the Republican Party. Third-party efforts, then, are not necessarily in vain. They can lead to policy successes even if the third party rarely wins an election.

RESPONSIBLE PARTY GOVERNMENT

As we have seen, parties are formed with the purpose of helping to determine who holds office. There are two general views on *how* American parties might do this.[23] One view is that because our two major parties are necessarily large, they therefore need to be broad and inclusive. The fact that a party, if it is to succeed in the United States, must embrace at least half the population means that each will probably be a coalition of various interests. From this perspective, parties bring together diverse groups of interests and shape them into an organization capable of acting in government. Parties are seen as holding companies for evolving, changing groups of interests. To the extent that they have programs, the programs are a blend of the various interests that make up the party. A party that attains office should run the government by making compromises and putting together policies based on its supporters' interests and the needs of the nation. In other words, parties should *reflect* and *coordinate* public opinion.

According to the alternative view, a party should articulate a clear program, offer it to the electorate, and if it wins an election, put that program into effect. If it is out of office, it should offer an alternative program that it would put into effect if it could displace the governing party. In other words, parties should *lead* public opinion and offer the public distinct choices. This is the doctrine of **responsible party government,** under which parties should:

1. present policies to the electorate
2. carry them out if elected
3. develop alternatives to the government's policies when out of office
4. differ sufficiently between each other to offer voters a choice[24]

This doctrine is attractive because it provides clear accountability. Before an election, voters consider parties offering two alternative programs. They choose one of the parties, with its program, and once in office the party implements that program. If voters are pleased with the result, they keep the party in office. If not, they vote in the alternative party with its program.

responsible party government
Doctrine stating that parties should present clear alternative programs and enact them faithfully once in office.

The Tea Party wing of the Republican Party sees the role of the party in this way; in their view, the party should offer a clear policy vision—cutting spending to reduce the national debt—and should pursue it without compromise, letting the voters decide whether that is what they want. "Tea Party" Republicans have shown less desire to blend the various interests of different parts of the party, than to have the party speak with a clear voice.

As party unity increases and the division between the Democrats and Republicans widens, American parties appear to have evolved over the last few decades to become more like responsible parties. Although the parties are still rather broad and diverse, each party more and more has developed a unified core of ideas that makes it distinguishable on the political party landscape. As we have seen, each party in Congress is increasingly unified, and more distinct from the other party in its voting on bills. The Contract with America, developed by House Republicans under the leadership of Newt Gingrich in the 1994 election, is an example of a strong attempt at making a party "responsible" in the sense used here. This Contract laid out a set of 10 bills that Republicans promised to bring to a vote if they acquired a majority of the House in the election. They did win the election and did introduce the bills they had promised, but their bills largely failed in the Senate and did not become law. The Republicans controlled the Senate as well as the House, but they were not able to get all of their members to vote for the Contract bills.

Even though the parties have become more distinct from each other, however, it is not clear that the accountability that should in theory go with responsible parties has materialized. The parties do present competing programs, but our system of government, with its divided powers and numerous checks and balances, makes it difficult for a victorious party to put its program into place after it has been elected. And our decentralized parties do not offer a vehicle for disciplining officials and making them unite behind the party's policies. In 2009, the victorious Democrats—who in 2008 had achieved the presidency and control of both the House of Representatives and the Senate—endured a year of frustration as major parts of their program failed in Congress. Of President Obama's significant campaign planks, the Democrats passed their "race to the top" educational reform and—after a long, agonizing struggle—they passed a major health plan. But they failed to enact new rules for union elections, a plan to reduce global warming, and immigration reform. Similarly, in 2004 with Republican control of both the House and Senate, and fresh from reelection, Republican President George W. Bush was unable to enact either immigration reform or Social Security reform. With the parties in their current form, we may have gained the less pleasant part of responsible party government—heightened conflict and tension between the parties—without reaping the benefit of increased accountability.

Why Are We THE WAY WE ARE ?

This chapter highlighted aspects of American political parties that require special explanation:

- the fact that there are only two major parties
- their relatively loose and decentralized structure
- the fact that in recent decades the two parties have become much more deeply divided than they once were

THE TWO-PARTY SYSTEM

The two-party system can probably best be explained by our winner-take-all electoral system. As discussed earlier in the chapter, two-party systems are much more common in countries with winner-take-all electoral systems. Other contributing factors are probably our elected presidency, which exaggerates the winner-take-all effect, and also the many state laws that make it difficult for third parties to get access to the ballot and gain public funding for their campaigns.

LOOSE AND DECENTRALIZED PARTIES

The second notable characteristic of American parties, their decentralized organization, might also result partly from the electoral system, which probably encourages their loose, decentralized structure because two large parties necessarily must each include a number of diverse viewpoints. After all, it is difficult to impose a tight, centralized organization on supporters holding a variety of views. However, the electoral system cannot be the sole reason because many countries with winner-take-all electoral systems have parties with strong central organization. In Great Britain, for example, a country that has a winner-take-all system, parties are formal organizations, and they exert close control over their members in parliament.

Something else must be at work as well, then. Other factors that may also contribute to American parties' decentralized, less formal organization include:

- the relatively slow development of the parties as new inventions in the world's first democracy, which meant that they evolved gradually rather than being founded directly as organizations
- the individualistic political culture of the United States, which makes Americans reluctant to take orders and shape their behavior to fit a collective mold
- the federal system, with many governmental functions located in the states, that requires parties to have separate organizations in each of the 50 states and adapt their organization and tactics to the elected offices they want to win

DEEP PARTISAN DIVISIONS

The third aspect that we noted—the increased division and rancor between the parties—is harder to explain. This level of animosity does not appear to be happening simultaneously in other countries, so the explanation probably lies in events peculiar to the United States. Several political scientists have suggested that the movement of Southern conservatives away from the Democratic Party in the 1960s and 1970s, and the rise of the religious right in the Republican Party that led some liberal Republicans to leave that party, has sorted conservatives and liberals more definitively into the two parties, with the Democratic Party more purely liberal than it was when it still had many Southern members, and the Republican Party more purely conservative than it was before a number of moderate Republicans left the party.[25] With the two parties now less torn internally, but more united against each other, partisan conflict has intensified.

. . . AND WHY DOES IT Matter?

Parties matter to us because they are the most effective device available to bring together policy makers and politically concerned citizens throughout the country. If we want to address problems through government policy, political parties are indispensable to the effort.

Having just two parties seems to work satisfactorily for this purpose because our parties have proved themselves able to evolve in response to changing policy needs, especially with help from the periodic rise of third parties that push them to evolve.

The loose and decentralized structure of our parties, however, is another story. In combination with the division of our government into competing units that "check and balance" each other, the loose organization of our parties makes it difficult to address national policy issues. As Madison foresaw, compromise is required to bridge the divisions of government. But in an increasingly ideological, polarized party system "compromise" has become a dirty word.

The parties' contribution to policy making is mixed. Compromise across the two parties is difficult because the parties are so polarized ideologically, but because of their loose internal structure and the division of powers in government, it is also difficult for either party acting alone to drive its proposals to become actual policy. Often, the end result is paralysis.

critical thinking questions

1. Should American parties be more like coalitions of interests, or should they act like "responsible parties"? Why?

2. What do you think American politics would be like if political parties were eliminated? (A few cities in the United States have "nonpartisan" elections, for example, in which the candidates' political party affiliations are not listed on the ballot.) Would elected officials view their responsibilities in the same way if we had no political parties? How might campaigns and elections change without political parties? Do you think the influence of special interests would decrease or increase? Explain your answer.

3. If the Progressive movement had not made changes in the early twentieth century to weaken state and city party organizations, how would American politics look today? In what ways would politics be different? In what ways would politics probably be similar?

4. As illustrated in Figure 7.1, political parties provide structure and continuity to elections by establishing long-lasting identities among voters. Is the sort of continuity illustrated in the figure a good thing? Why or why not? What are its benefits and its drawbacks?

5. Given the increasing ideological unity of the two parties, could the two parties become so far apart ideologically that there would be an opening for a new, more moderate party that was situated somewhere between the other two? Consider the difficulties of breaking into the two-party system of the United States. What would need to happen to allow a new party to establish itself and become permanently competitive?

key terms

civil service laws, *235*

congressional campaign committee, *245*

critical election, *240*

direct primary, *235*

electoral realignment, *241*

Era of Good Feelings, *231*

First Party System, *231*

mobilization, *228*

multiparty system, *248*

national committee, *244*

national nominating convention, *244*

party in government, *241*

party in the electorate, *241*

party organization, *241*

party platform, *244*

patronage, *233*

political machine, *233*

political party, *225*

Progressive movement, *234*

responsible party government, *253*

Second Party System, *232*

split-ticket voting, *240*

third parties, *250*

two-party system, *248*

Whig Party, *232*

NOMINATIONS
AND ELECTIONS

★ ★ ★

- Analyze the factors that contributed to the development of U.S. elections.
- Understand how elections make officials accountable to citizens.
- Describe each phase of the presidential campaign and the strategies that determine candidates' success.
- Examine the congressional election process and understand what makes it so difficult to unseat incumbent members.
- Identify the different types of electoral systems, the characteristics of the SMDP system, and the effects of this system on U.S. parties and voting.
- Analyze how the U.S. electoral system affects the representation of women and minorities in government.
- Understand why it is difficult to regulate campaign expenditures.

PERSPECTIVE
How Do Different Nations Respond to a Close Election?

The 2000 presidential election between Democrat Al Gore and Republican George W. Bush came down almost to a tie. The outcome hinged on who had won in Florida, a state where about six million votes were cast and Bush led by only 537. A long vote recount followed in that state, sometimes in a circus-like atmosphere. Outside Gore's official residence, a group of young Bush enthusiasts chanted, "We won. You lost. Get over it." Meanwhile, Gore supporters seethed. They knew that no matter what happened in the counting of the electoral votes by state, Gore had still received half a million more individual votes than Bush across the country as a whole. The long recount period ended dramatically on December 12, when the Supreme Court, in a close 5-4 decision, ordered the counting to stop; this decision effectively made Bush the president-elect.[1] Al Gore accepted the outcome and urged his supporters not to challenge it. The 2000 election was historic—one of a handful where one candidate won the most individual citizen votes, but the geographic distribution allowed the other candidate to win more of the states' electoral votes and ultimately, the election.

Six years later, on July 2, 2006, Mexico experienced a similarly close presidential election. Felipe Calderon of the National Action Party received 35.8 percent of the votes, only 150,000 votes more than Andrés Manuel López Obrador of the Party of the Democratic Revolution. Since this was only the second fully democratic presidential election in Mexican history, dealing with the close result proved difficult for the new democracy. As in the United States, a long recount ensued; it did not end until September 5. More than 100,000 supporters of the losing party engaged in huge demonstrations in Mexico City to protest the election outcome. One protest closed several miles of the city's main thoroughfare, and in another demonstration protestors took over the tollbooths on four major national highways and prevented the collectors from taking tolls. Even after Calderon became president, the protests continued. At one massive rally, López Obrador declared himself "Legitimate President" and tried to establish a parallel presidency, but this action went too far for most people. Demonstrations gradually petered out over the next several months.

The reactions of Americans and Mexicans to similarly close elections were strikingly different. In general, Americans simply felt it important to get a result. The American tradition of a peaceful transfer of power trumped the seemingly complex and counterintuitive election process. In the Mexican experience, even though the outcome had resulted from a simpler and more straightforward election process, large segments of the population did not accept it as legitimate.

Elections are important as a way to give citizens a voice in the government's decisions, but also as a way to provide peaceful transitions of power at regular intervals. The longstanding system of elections in the United States allows this to happen with broad general acceptance.

IN THIS CHAPTER we explore the development and establishment of elections in the United States—elections that can command broad acceptance even in circumstances as difficult as the 2000 election. We then consider how presidential candidates are nominated and elected. We see how citizens can use elections effectively to control what politicians do in office, and evaluate whether elections produce officeholders who accurately represent the broad population in terms of gender and ethnicity. Finally, we look at how campaigns are conducted and financed. As you read this chapter, keep in mind our two core questions:

WHY ARE WE THE WAY WE ARE?
WHY DOES IT MATTER TO YOU?

In particular, what factors determine how well elections succeed in allowing voters to hold politicians responsible for their actions?

THE DEVELOPMENT OF ELECTIONS IN THE UNITED STATES

★ **KEY** to understanding

The current system of elections in the United States underwent a fairly lengthy evolution before becoming the complicated system that it is today. Voting, for instance, started out as a privilege granted only to a select few, but it was eventually extended to all Americans, regardless of their race, gender, or ethnicity.

Elections are meant to ensure one of the fundamental qualities of a democracy: a government responsive to the people's wishes. This sounds so easy, but it is far from automatic. In fact, elections in the United States have evolved dramatically from the original constitutional design. The Founders were not anxious to establish direct democratic control of the government by citizens. Initially only the House of Representatives was directly elected, and because most states required voters to meet property requirements, participation was severely restricted. Over time, however, selection of the president came to be closely tied to the votes of citizens in the states; the Senate became directly elected (1913); and voting rights were extended to former male slaves (1870), women (1920), and 18- to 20-year-olds (1971). In 1965 the Voting Rights Act gave the Attorney General the authority to bar discrimination in voting rights by race in states with a pattern of discrimination; this effectively ended widespread informal disenfranchisement of African Americans in the South. As a result of these changes, national elections today include a far larger proportion of the population and are far more significant in the U.S. system of government.

Historically, the United States has generally been a leader, rather than a follower, in extending voting rights to its citizens. The United States was one of the first democracies in the world, at least in the sense of establishing general manhood suffrage by the middle of the nineteenth century, and it was the fourteenth country in the world to extend suffrage fully to women (see Figure 8.1).[2] In this regard it compares favorably with other countries of the time, such as Britain or France.

The march toward universal suffrage has not necessarily ended. Not all adult Americans can vote, even today. The most notable exclusion is of felons—people who have been convicted of crimes ranging in seriousness from shoplifting to murder. States determine exactly who can vote, within limits set by the U.S. Constitution. Today 48 states bar incarcerated prisoners from voting (Maine and Vermont are the exceptions). But 12 states deny the vote—in some cases permanently—even to ex-felons who have done their time.

The election process also has evolved over time. In the 1880s and 1890s, as we saw in Chapter 7, major reforms introduced several procedures we now take for granted:

- the government, not the political parties, now prints the official ballots
- ballots include the names of candidates from all parties

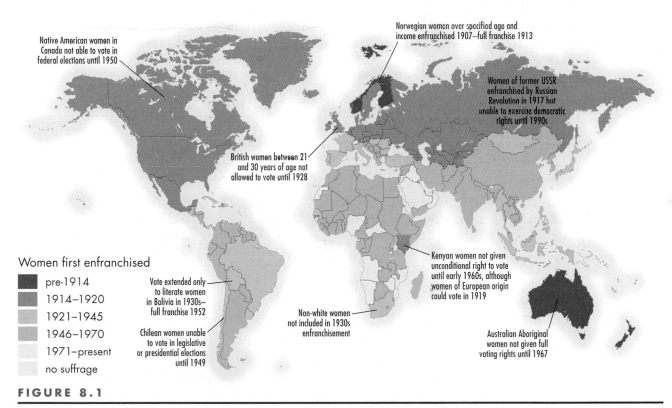

Native American women in Canada not able to vote in federal elections until 1950

Norwegian women over specified age and income enfranchised 1907—full franchise 1913

Women of former USSR enfranchised by Russian Revolution in 1917 but unable to exercise democratic rights until 1990s

British women between 21 and 30 years of age not allowed to vote until 1928

Kenyan women not given unconditional right to vote until early 1960s, although women of European origin could vote in 1919

Women first enfranchised

- pre-1914
- 1914–1920
- 1921–1945
- 1946–1970
- 1971–present
- no suffrage

Vote extended only to literate women in Bolivia in 1930s— full franchise 1952

Chilean women unable to vote in legislative or presidential elections until 1949

Non-white women not included in 1930s enfranchisement

Australian Aboriginal women not given full voting rights until 1967

FIGURE 8.1

★ WOMEN'S SUFFRAGE AROUND THE WORLD

Women won the right to vote in the United States in 1920. How does this compare with other countries?

Source: From *Phillip's Atlas of World History.* (http://qed.princeton.edu/index.php/User:Student/Women_and_the_right_to_vote,_20th_Century).

- ballots are distributed only at polling places
- ballots are cast secretly, not openly

Together, these provisions are referred to as the **Australian ballot** because they were first adopted in Australia. They are intended to ensure that elections are fair and secret.

This evolution continues today. In the uproar over the 2000 presidential election, many people realized for the first time that voting procedures vary greatly from one state to another and even from one county to another within the same state. This awareness sensitized politicians to develop clearer rules regarding voter registration and to instill in the people greater confidence that a vote cast will be a vote counted, regardless of the type of voting machine being used. Accordingly, Congress adopted the Help America Vote Act in 2002,[3] which provided money to replace punch-cards and paper ballots with electronic voting machines; it also established a national commission to help the states administer elections fairly.

Over the last several years, but especially in 2011 and 2012, a somewhat different set of initiatives to change election procedures emerged. Legislators in 23 states, primarily Republicans, pushed for bills to make it more difficult for people to vote. These proposals involved a mix of requirements, including photo identification at the polls, a reduced period for early voting, and longer periods of residence in the district before registering to vote. Proponents of the bills argued that they would eliminate fraud, while opponents argued that fraud has not been a real problem and that the real motivation was to make voting more difficult for ethnic minorities, the elderly, students, and other groups that often vote Democratic.

ELECTIONS AS TOOLS FOR ACCOUNTABILITY

The chief purpose of elections in the United States and all other democracies is to provide **accountability**—the ability of voters to impose consequences on officials for their actions, including removal from office. Accountability allows citizens to ensure, through their votes, that the government enacts policies with which they agree. Voting is of course not the only way citizens can influence officials, but it *is* the one tool by which they can directly hold officials responsible for their policies.[4] The U.S. system includes three types of elections to select officials: primary elections, general elections, and recall elections. (As noted in Chapter 7, primary elections and recall elections were added during the Progressive era.)

In a primary election, all those who wish to be nominated by a party appear on the ballot, and the party's supporters vote on who will represent the party in the subsequent general election. In the **general election,** voters make their final choices of public officials. In addition to primary and general elections, a number of states also offer recall elections—the ultimate accountability, by which citizens may petition to have state officials removed from office before they have even completed their terms. Recall elections are not used frequently, but from time to time, they figure importantly in political conflicts; in 2011, for instance, several Wisconsin state legislators were forced into recall elections following a fight over Governor Scott Walker's proposal to limit collective bargaining by public employees.

Elections in the United States are unusually complex. Voters elect national officials—the president, members of the House of Representatives, and members of the Senate—as well as an often bewildering array of choices for state and local offices. At the local level, court clerks, school board members, judges, water district members, and others are often elected along with major state and national officials. This "long ballot" originated in the 1830s with the expansion of popular control during the presidency of Andrew Jackson; the idea was that citizens should control as many officials as possible through elections.

The long ballot contrasts sharply with the more limited number of offices filled through elections in most other countries. In Britain, for example, the only officials elected nationally are the members of the House of Commons, their parliament. Primary elections do not take place because local party organizations nominate candidates for the 650 districts that need to be filled. The formal campaign lasts just 17 days from the time the election date is announced.

America's numerous and varied elections, carried out across long campaign periods, give citizens ample opportunity to compare candidates and many chances to exercise influence. It is exciting to be involved in them. However, they can also bewilder citizens and discourage participation. In the rest of this chapter we will consider how these elections proceed and to what extent they ensure accountability.

★ In 2011 Wisconsin voters organized recall elections against Governor Scott Walker.

THE PRESIDENTIAL CAMPAIGN

KEY to understanding

★ The presidential campaign starts with the nomination, which is contested state by state in primary elections or caucuses. The states with the earliest primaries or caucuses have the greatest influence on nominations. Each party then convenes a national convention to name its presidential candidate and write the party platform. Conventions and candidate debates provide important turning points for the general election campaign, which increasingly involves strategic use of technology and specialized consultants. Unlike the citizens of most other countries, Americans are involved throughout the election process rather than only during its final stage.

nomination
The designation of candidates among whom voters will choose in an election.

The first step in determining who will hold any office, from the presidency on down, is determining who will be the candidates. This process of **nomination** is a critical part of the election. Voters can exercise much more influence by helping to nominate candidates than by just choosing between the nominated candidates on Election Day, since there is typically greater scope for choice in primaries. In the early 2012 presidential primaries there was no contest on the Democratic side because no one ran against Barack Obama. This is usually the case when a party has a sitting president. On the Republican side, however, voters could choose among seven candidates, ranging from Herman Cain, a successful pizza company CEO, to Rick Santorum, a former United States Senator, to Mitt Romney, a business leader and former governor of Massachusetts. It is true that the general election still offered voters a genuine choice in the final two candidates, Mitt Romney and Barack Obama. But it can be argued that the presorting of the primaries, where at least for Republicans a wider range of alternatives was available, actually offered voters greater influence on the outcome than the choice in the general election between just two candidates.

What is involved in winning the presidential nomination? Narrowing the list of hopefuls down to one candidate from each party is a long, grueling, exciting, and expensive process. Parties nominate their presidential candidates at national conventions, where the convention delegates vote to choose the party's candidate. The trick for a candidate is to have won enough delegates by the time of the convention to ensure receiving a majority of the votes. The delegates are the key. How, then, are they selected?

SELECTING THE DELEGATES

Most delegates are chosen in the states, with the national parties designating how many delegates each state will be allocated.[5] For the two main parties, the number of delegates per state is based not only on the state's population but also on how much support the voters of that state have historically given to the party's candidates. Therefore, the geographic makeup of the two conventions will differ. Figure 8.2 compares a map of the United States as it looks according to the Democratic convention with a map of the United States as it looks according to the Republican convention. The "Democratic" version of the United States has a swollen Northeast and West Coast, reflecting the party's strength in those regions, whereas the "Republican" version has a swollen South and mountain region.

★ Mitt Romney and Newt Gingrich competed for the Republican presidential nomination in 2012. Here they share a friendly—or at least polite—moment after a debate during the campaign for the nomination.

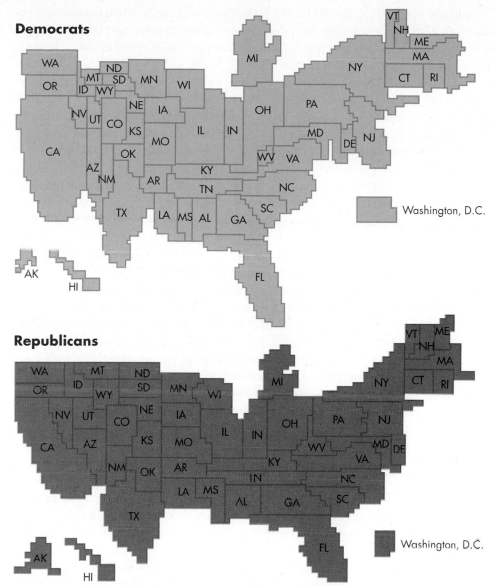

Democrats

Republicans

FIGURE 8.2

★ BATTLE FOR
   THE DELEGATES

The United States, as represented in the Democratic and Republican Conventions. Each state is magnified or shrunken to reflect that state's share of the convention's delegates, and thus reflects areas of core strength for each party.

Source: *Wall Street Journal*, January 30, 2008, p. A4.

Each state government decides by law how the delegates for that state will be chosen. Two main devices are used to choose delegates: primary elections or caucuses followed by state conventions. In addition to delegates chosen by primary elections and by caucuses, each party also has a relatively small number of delegates who are called **superdelegates** in the Democratic Party and **unpledged delegates** in the Republican Party. These are elected officials and members of the parties' National Committees whose roles in the parties nationally automatically afford them seats at the conventions. But the overwhelming majority of delegates for both parties are chosen through primary elections or caucuses.

PRIMARIES AND CAUCUSES

Since 1972 most states have used primary elections to choose the parties' convention delegates. In 2012, for instance, 39 states held presidential primary elections for the

superdelegates
Delegates to the Democratic Party's national nominating convention who are not selected through a primary or caucus procedure but go to the convention because of the office they hold in the party or the government.

unpledged delegates
Delegates to the Republican Party's national nominating convention who are not selected through a primary or caucus procedure but go to the convention by right of the office they hold in the party or the government.

Republican nomination, and 37 for the Democratic nomination. In a presidential primary, all who aspire to be the party's candidate submit to the voters lists of delegates who support them. Voters in the 2012 Republican primaries chose among a Romney list, a Paul list, a Santorum list, and so on.

States and localities use primary elections not only to choose delegates to the parties' presidential nominating conventions but also to determine who the candidates will be in many other political races—for instance, congressional elections and elections for local offices such as mayor. The two main types of primary election are the closed primary and the open primary: In a **closed primary,** voters register as affiliated with a specific party or as an "independent." Those affiliated with a party may vote in that party's primary; independents do not vote. In an **open primary,** all voters including independents may vote in whatever party primary they choose, regardless of how they are registered.[6]

Open primaries have two key effects. First, voters who really support one party may choose to vote in the other party's primary. Often, this happens because there is a more important choice in the other party's primary than in their own. (In 2012, for instance, with Obama unopposed in the Democratic primaries, some Democratic voters may have decided to vote in the Republican primary—where there was some choice—rather than in their own where there was no choice.) This is called **crossover voting.** There has always been some worry about crossover voting, because of another possibility—that a party's supporters might cross over in an attempt to hurt the other party by getting a weak candidate nominated. There is little evidence that this ever happens in a big way; voters do not usually respond in large numbers when candidates or others try to organize a mischievous cross-over of this sort. In Michigan's open primary in 2012, conservative Republican Rick Santorum sponsored phone calls to Democrats urging them to vote in the Republican primary to help defeat Mitt Romney, and he was joined in this effort by liberal Democrats who urged a cross-over vote for Santorum because they thought he would be the easier candidate to beat in the general election. The tactic worked to some extent—of the small number of Democrats voting in the primary, 53 percent voted for Santorum. But Democratic participation in the primary only rose to 9 percent from its level in 2008 of 7 percent, so apparently not many Democrats responded to the call.

A second, even more important effect of open primaries is that "independents"— those who have registered to vote but have not declared for either party—can vote in the primary. Independents often play a major role in these contests. In the 2008 presidential primary in New Hampshire—an open primary—independents made the difference in John McCain's victory over Mitt Romney.

Instead of primaries, some states—including Iowa, Minnesota, and Nevada—use party **caucuses** and state conventions to select convention delegates. Legislatures of caucus states set a date on which state party organizations hold their "caucuses," or meetings. Caucuses come in waves. First, each party organizes precinct caucuses— neighborhood meetings of party supporters. All people living in the neighborhood can attend, whether or not they are active in politics. At the meeting, which usually takes a few hours, those who attend vote to send some of their fellow attendees on as delegates to the next round of the party's caucuses. In the next round, held a few weeks later, these delegates attend a convention covering a larger geographic area—usually a county or congressional district—to choose delegates to the party's state convention. The state convention then selects the state's delegates to the party's national convention. At every

closed primary
A primary election in which only those who have registered with a party designation may vote; they may vote only in that party's primary.

open primary
A primary election in which all voters may participate and may choose which party's primary they wish to vote in.

crossover voting
Voting in a primary election for a party other than the one with which you are registered.

caucus
A gathering of party supporters at the neighborhood level who select delegates to a state nominating convention, which in turn selects delegates to the national nominating convention.

level, candidates' advocates compete to send to the next level delegates who are pledged to support their candidate. This process is depicted in Figure 8.3.

Primary elections involve more formal campaigning and advertising than caucuses, while caucuses consist more of grassroots conversations among neighbors and active party supporters. Another difference between the two is that more people usually participate in a primary election than in caucuses, since showing up to vote in a primary takes less time than attending a caucus meeting. In 2012, for instance, 7 percent of those eligible to vote in Iowa attended a party caucus, but 31 percent of those eligible to vote in New Hampshire voted in that state's presidential primary.[7]

THE ROAD TO NOMINATION

For the candidates, the hectic schedule of primaries and caucuses determines a great deal of their strategy. Typically a large number of candidates jockey for a party's nomination, unless a sitting president or vice president is running (which usually results in no contest for that party's nomination). In order to win in the many state primaries and caucuses, candidates must make themselves known to the voters. Four factors can help with this:

- prior fame (in 2012, for instance, Mitt Romney was already well-known because he had run in 2008)
- media coverage
- volunteers
- money for advertising

Candidates cannot do much about the first factor—they are either well known at the start, or they are not. What they *can* control is how much media attention they get, how effective their campaign organization is, and how much money they raise. Both media attention and fundraising can be helped by success in early contests, so candidates focus a great deal of their effort on them.

The Early Contests: The Importance of Timing

Traditionally, the Iowa caucuses open the nomination contest for both parties and are then followed by the primary election in New Hampshire. In 2008, two other early contests were added: the Nevada caucuses and the South Carolina primary. Candidates have learned to invest a huge effort in these early contests because success at this stage convinces pundits and activists that the candidate has a genuine chance to win the nomination. More extensive attention in the news, and increased cash contributions, follow.

The 2012 Republican nomination race illustrates how Iowa and New Hampshire, the two earliest contests, can affect candidates' fates. A year before these contests, the Republican field was crowded, with nine candidates. The situation was fluid; at one time or another five different candidates led in national polls during the year running up to the Iowa caucuses. Mitt Romney stood out from the pack somewhat, as he had run in 2008, had plenty of money, and had a large organization of supporters. But another candidate, Rick Santorum, decided to stake everything he had on Iowa. He had little money and practically no staff, but he spent most of a year going back and forth across the state in an old Dodge Ram pickup, eventually visiting every one of Iowa's 99 counties. Up to that point he had never figured largely in national polls, but he scored an upset victory in Iowa, beating Romney by just 34 votes.

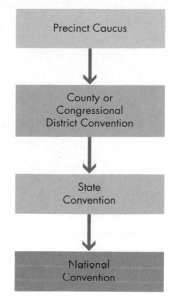

FIGURE 8.3

★ CAUCUS-BASED SELECTION OF DELEGATES

Santorum's success in Iowa brought him contributions and made him a nationally known candidate. He did not campaign heavily in New Hampshire, where Romney won, but he resurfaced in early February when he won three states in one night. By the time of the Michigan and Arizona primaries in late February, only four candidates remained—Mitt Romney, Rick Santorum, Ron Paul, and Newt Gingrich—yet, most observers characterized the race as now being between just two of them: Romney and Santorum. Romney went on to eventually win the nomination. This result is typical. Since 1976, no candidate of either party who lost both in Iowa and New Hampshire has received the party's nomination.[9] Candidates who have won only one of the two contests have received their party's nomination half the time. And *every* candidate who has won in both states has gone on to get the party's nomination. The impact of these two small states on national nominations is astounding.

Frontloading and the Schedule of Contests

States know that candidates pay attention to the early contests. An early date pays off for a state financially—Republican candidates spent about $15,000,000 in South Carolina in 2011–2012 leading up to the primary—and it also means that candidates emphasize political issues that matter to the state. Primary and caucus dates are set by the states' legislatures, and many states try to push their primaries and caucuses forward as much as they can to take advantage of this candidate attention. In the run-up to the 2012 conventions, states engaged in a scramble to **frontload** their delegate selection, getting it as close to the front of the lineup as possible. In an attempt to limit this contest among the states, both parties stated that they would penalize delegates who were selected before March 6, with the exception of the traditional early states: Iowa, New Hampshire, Nevada, and South Carolina. As we see in the timeline in Figure 8.4, however, several states defied the national party and moved their primaries or caucuses up in spite of the penalties.

As you can see from Figure 8.4, these rules resulted in a massive bunching of primaries and caucuses on March 6, dubbed **Super Tuesday** because a number of states select their delegates on that day. Because of this frontloading, 811 delegates out of a total of 2,286 delegates had been chosen for the Republican convention by March 6. After Super Tuesday, the remaining primaries and caucuses were spread out through late June.

Mitt Romney, who had won in New Hampshire and several other states, won over half the delegates on Super Tuesday and became the clear front-runner. No one was able to gain on him after that, and by May 1 all of his significant rivals had dropped out. This left him the clear winner.

Once all delegates have been chosen, they come together in each party's national convention. At the convention the delegates choose the party's candidates for president and vice-president and write the party's platform.

The National Convention

The role of the national convention has changed dramatically over the last 50 years. Before 1972, only a few states relied on presidential primaries or used caucus/convention systems to choose their delegates. Most states' delegations were appointed by the state's party leaders and included large numbers of hard-boiled political pros. When these delegations got together for bargaining and horse-trading, the conventions were filled with suspense and drama. Often balloting would run through the night—sometimes even longer. The 1924 Democratic convention, for instance, required 103 ballots, over a period of 17 days, to produce a nominee.

frontload
To move a state's primary or caucuses to the earliest date that the party's rules will permit.

Super Tuesday
The first Tuesday in a primary season on which parties allow states (except for early contests like New Hampshire or Iowa) to schedule primaries or caucuses; large numbers of states usually schedule their contests for this day, which makes it "super."

FIGURE 8.4

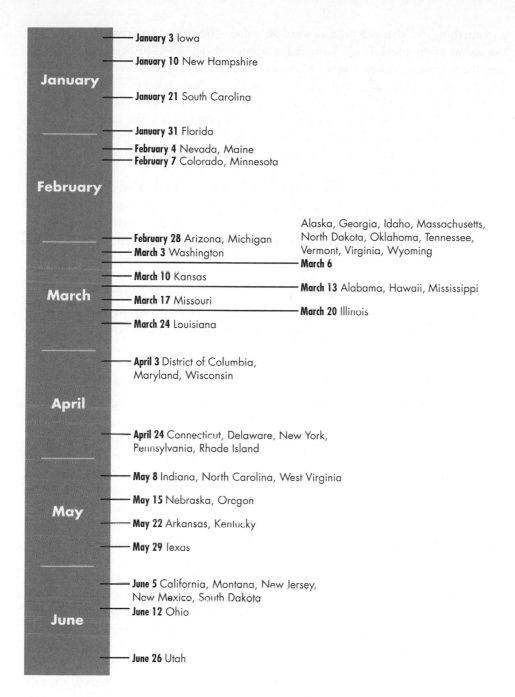

January

— January 3 Iowa

— January 10 New Hampshire

— January 21 South Carolina

— January 31 Florida

— February 4 Nevada, Maine
— February 7 Colorado, Minnesota

February

— February 28 Arizona, Michigan
— March 3 Washington

Alaska, Georgia, Idaho, Massachusetts,
North Dakota, Oklahoma, Tennessee,
Vermont, Virginia, Wyoming
— March 6

— March 10 Kansas

— March 13 Alabama, Hawaii, Mississippi

March
— March 17 Missouri

— March 20 Illinois

— March 24 Louisiana

— April 3 District of Columbia,
Maryland, Wisconsin

April

— April 24 Connecticut, Delaware, New York,
Pennsylvania, Rhode Island

— May 8 Indiana, North Carolina, West Virginia

— May 15 Nebraska, Oregon

May
— May 22 Arkansas, Kentucky

— May 29 Texas

— June 5 California, Montana, New Jersey,
New Mexico, South Dakota
— June 12 Ohio

June

— June 26 Utah

All of this changed in 1972. The troubled 1968 Democratic convention led to a series of rule changes that caused states to move to primary elections and caucuses for their delegate selection. Since 1972, with all but a few delegates chosen through primaries or caucuses, it has almost always been the case that one candidate shows up with enough delegates to win the nomination outright on the first ballot. No major party convention has opened with any doubt about who was going to be nominated since 1976.

Today, conventions are managed affairs, with music and entertainment, videos about the soon-to-be-candidate's life, testimonials from ordinary citizens, funny hats, and anything else that will hold viewers' attention. The party platform, which lays out the vision of the party, is still written and approved. The soon-to-be-candidate manages the writing, to ensure that the platform will be consistent with his or her positions. Usually some minor but heated conflict about the platform takes place, and television commentators use such disputes to keep viewers interested. The party also helps to stimulate interest about the convention with suspense about the candidate-to-be's choice for a vice-presidential running mate—a decision usually made a few days before the convention opens. In effect, though, the convention serves as a weeklong infomercial for the candidate-to-be.

Actually, the shift to primaries and caucuses after the 1972 reforms would not in itself have been enough to turn the nominating conventions into foregone conclusions. After all, if many candidates vied for the nomination in dozens of primaries and state conventions, in theory four or five candidates could each do well, in different states, and no one candidate would arrive at the convention with a majority of the delegates. Balloting could still run through the night. The crucial added ingredient, as we have seen, is that the initial primaries in states like Iowa and New Hampshire winnow the field by concentrating resources and media attention on one or two early winners. The extended wave of contests in other states takes it from there, almost always leaving one clear winner by the eve of the convention.

HOW REPRESENTATIVE ARE PRIMARIES AND CAUCUSES?

In either a primary or a caucus, participation is low compared with the general election. In 2012, 70 percent of eligible Iowans voted in the general election, but only 7 percent attended caucus meetings. In New Hampshire, 72 percent of those who were eligible voted in the general election, and only 31 percent in the primary. We saw in Chapter 7 that activists usually hold stronger, more ideological views than the general electorate, and we might expect from this that those who make the extra effort to vote in primaries or attend caucuses would be more extreme in their views than ordinary voters of their parties. If this were so, then our system of primaries and caucuses might be an important source of the current polarization of American politics, since candidates would have to appeal to ideologues to get the nomination. Indeed, many commentators and political scientists have in the past thought that the system of caucuses and primaries contributes to political polarization in this way.

Apparently, however, even though primaries and caucuses do not draw as broadly from among the party's supporters as the general election does, they draw broadly enough that those who participate in them are not very different from the full base of party supporters. We see in Figure 8.5 that in 2008, Iowans who planned to attend their parties' caucuses were more polarized than registered voters of the two parties, but only by a little bit. The difference between those planning to attend the two caucuses on whether immigration was an important issue was only slightly greater than the difference among registered Democrats and Republicans as a whole. On other issues as well (not shown in the figure), caucus attendees were only slightly more polarized than their parties' registered voters.[10]

We find the same thing in primary elections. Alan Abramowitz has found that Democratic primary voters are about as liberal as Democrats voting in the general election, and Republican primary voters are about as conservative as Republicans voting in the general election.[11] The fact that caucus attendees and primary voters are reasonably representative of their parties' voters is reassuring.

But even if primaries and caucuses are fairly representative of their parties' voters, those voters are not representative of the full electorate. And that sometimes causes a problem for the parties, when the ideological partisans who vote in the primaries or go to caucuses produce candidates who are so ideologically oriented that they do not do well in the general election (where more moderate independents are often the swing vote). For instance, in the Republican primary election for a U.S. Senate seat in 2010 Christine O'Donnell, a very conservative candidate with little experience, defeated an experienced but moderate member of the House, Mike Castle, who had had the backing of party leaders. She went on to lose in the general election by 17 percentage points—in a state the party had been sure it was going to carry.

NOMINATIONS IN OTHER COUNTRIES

The U.S. system of nominations is more spontaneous and unpredictable than systems in other parts of the world. This can be both good and bad. Political parties in most other democracies are more tightly organized than ours, and they control their nominations carefully, not involving the broad population as is done in the United States. This usually means that candidates are nominated by people who have worked with them personally or know them well in other ways. The Labor Party candidate for prime minister in Australia, for instance, is always a member of the House of Representatives, elected by the other Labor members of the House. The current prime minister, Julia Gilliard, was chosen in 2010 by a vote just of the 72 Labor members of the House of Representatives. No one else participated in the choice.

Note that this selection was made by fellow members of the House who had worked with her on a daily basis and knew her strengths and weaknesses well. While systems like this have the obvious advantage that those choosing the nominee know what they are doing, it also means that nominees tend to be of a predictable type—experienced, not a maverick in the House of Representatives, able to get along within the organization. That profile sounds good, but perhaps Australians might yearn sometimes for someone a little less predictable.

The looser selection system in the United States provides a wider range of candidates, which can have both disadvantages and advantages. Primary voters, who have little direct knowledge of any of the candidates, may respond to fame, name recognition, or unusual approaches to the issues. In the 2008 and 2012 elections, serious presidential candidates in the United States included a charismatic lawyer and community organizer who had served part of a term in the Senate (Barack Obama); a lawyer and wife of a former president, starting her second term in the Senate (Hillary Clinton); a former CEO of Godfather's Pizza and articulate columnist (Herman Cain); a third-term member of the House of Representatives (Michele Bachmann); and a lobbyist who had retired from the Senate after just one term but who had the advantage of being a well-known actor (Fred Thompson). Although candidates like these have sometimes been criticized for lacking experience, the more spontaneous U.S. system has also helped to bring forward unusual talents such as Harry S. Truman, a clothing store owner and senator, and Ronald Reagan, a former actor and governor of California.

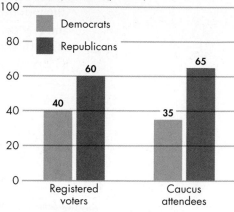

Degree of importance (percent)

FIGURE 8.5

★ IMPORTANCE OF IMMIGRATION

This graph shows how important the immigration issue was to registered voters and caucus attendees in Iowa. How big is the difference between Democrats and Republicans in the two groups? What does this indicate about how well the caucuses represented the parties' voters in general?

Source: Data from David P. Redlawsk, Caroline J. Tolbert, and Todd Donovan, *Why Iowa?* (Chicago: University of Chicago Press, 2011), p. 131.

As a result of America's unusual system of nominations, American leaders are different from leaders of most other democracies.[12] They vary more than other leaders and are less experienced, so there is often a greater change when a new person takes office than is seen in other countries. And America's leaders more often bring unusual backgrounds or perspectives to their office.

picture YOURSELF . . .
AS A SUPPORTER OF THE NDC IN GHANA

Ghana, a country of 24 million people, is located on the west coast of Africa and reestablished a democratic government in 1991 after a series of dictatorships over the preceding decades. In December 2008 Ghana held elections for president and for the members of its parliament. During this election, you were a supporter of the National Democratic Congress (NDC), one of the two main parties in Ghana. The other main party is the New Patriotic Party (NPP).

Your party and the NPP are very evenly matched across the country. The NDC draws a bit more of its support from the poorer parts of the country than the NPP does, but from a policy standpoint it really does not make much difference which party rules. Both are centrist and support free markets. The ornate new presidential palace built by the outgoing NPP president caused a bit of a stir in this year's election, but the importance of this "issue" simply serves as a good example of the absence of serious policy differences between your party and the NPP. However, members of parties can feel passionately about their organization even if there are no big policy differences between parties. The fact is, you and your fellow NDC supporters have resented the fact that the NPP has ruled for the last eight years, and you feel that it is your turn.

The 2008 campaign is lively, featuring huge party rallies of supporters who have painted themselves in their party colors. Participation in the election is high, with turnout by 70 percent of those eligible to vote. The final outcome is very close, as your NDC candidate John Atta Mills wins by only 23,000 votes out of almost 9 million cast. The slim margin concerns the Electoral Commission, which feels it cannot certify a winner until it re-runs the election in one

district where ballot distribution has supposedly been compromised. As rumors circulate that this special election is a plot by the military and the NPP to steal the close election, you and several hundred of your friends demonstrate outside the Electoral Commission offices—a protest that is repelled by the police with water cannons—demanding that they certify Mills as president immediately. Fortunately, following the re-vote in the district a week later, Mills is declared the winner without incident. Ghana successfully changes power from one party to another, even in an excruciatingly close election.

Though you admit to partisan feelings, you acknowledge that the real hero of the election is opposition candidate Mr. Akufo-Addo of the NPP (shown making his vote in the inset photo). He promptly conceded the election, despite his and his supporters' suspicions that the NDC had used intimidation tactics and fueled irregularities in the Volta region. (Meanwhile, you and your fellow NDC supporters suspect that similar irregularities and violence had been perpetrated against citizens in the Ashanti region.) Despite his misgivings, Mr. Akufo-Addo declared that it was important to respect the outcome of the election and not to prolong the partisan contest. The election was close and at times nerve-wracking, but it ended up as a success for democracy.

questions to consider

1. How much sense does it make to have such strong partisan feelings about two parties that differ very little in terms of policy?

2. In the United States, parties differ more on policy issues than the Ghanaian parties do, and yet Ghana's election campaign, and people's behavior in the election, are reminiscent of an American election. Is there no difference between elections that involve strong policy positions and those that do not? If there are differences, what might they be?

3. Can you see any aspects of this description of Ghana's election that help to explain why Ghana is a successful democracy?

THE GENERAL ELECTION

Presidential campaigns for the general election do not really start until it becomes clear who the Democratic and Republican nominees will be. At that point, the candidates must pivot from appealing to the partisans who voted in primaries or attended caucuses to appeal instead to the full electorate, including independents. To get the nomination, the candidates had to engage in highly partisan rhetoric. But in the general election they must move more to the political center, where the majority of the votes lie.

The conventions, and then the candidate debates, provide noteworthy points in the campaign that can shift candidates' chances. Though today conventions do not attract the television audience they had when they were wide-open contests, they still command a large audience. As a result, conventions always provide a bump up in the polls for their candidate. In 2012 the bumps were rather small, possibly because the campaigns had started their advertising early and many voters had already solidified their positions. The Republican convention (which many thought was staged ineffectively) lifted Mitt Romney by only 1.5 percentage points relative to Barack Obama. Obama got a better bump from his convention, raising his standing by 4.4 percentage points.[13]

Debates are major events for the campaign because they allow the candidates to argue their positions and share their platforms with an engaged audience. Three presidential debates were held in 2012: on October 3, October 16, and October 22.[14] Debates usually do not shift campaigns greatly, but 2012 was an exception. Until the debates the Obama campaign had successfully sowed distrust of Romney among the public, and

Obama had consistently led Romney by 4 or 5 percentage points in the polls. But at the first debate Obama seemed tired and not engaged, while Romney was energetic and shifted away from the conservative positions Obama had been attacking him for. Overnight, Romney moved to approximately a tie in the polls, which held from then until the election. Obama was better prepared for the second and third debates, but neither of those debates changed things much.[15]

CONGRESSIONAL ELECTIONS

KEY To understanding

Incumbent members of Congress are difficult to defeat: The boundaries of districts for the House of Representatives can be manipulated to help get them reelected, and both Senators and House members enjoy several other advantages as well. More so today than in the past, however, voters appear to be judging members by their party rather than as individuals. In order to change which party controls Congress, they may vote out even established incumbents. Parties may thus serve as better vehicles for electoral accountability than individual members.

Congressional elections determine who will sit in the Senate and the House of Representatives. In presidential election years, the party that wins the presidency usually gains seats in the Senate and House as well, although the president still may face a Congress with one or more of the houses controlled by the opposite party. In midterm elections—conducted two years later, when the president is not on the ballot—congressional races may offer the electorate a chance to react to the president's program two years into his term in office. Often midterm elections bring only minor changes in the Congress, but sometimes they can change politics dramatically—as happened in 2010. A Republican landslide left President Obama facing a House of Representatives controlled by Republicans, and many of the new members, who had been supported by the Tea Party, were very conservative.

Congressional elections play out much like presidential elections, with one important difference: presidential elections are competitive, with two or more candidates vying in closely fought general election contests. But in congressional races, as we will see below, it is usually difficult to oust incumbent members of Congress—those who already hold a seat—when they run for reelection (see Figure 8.6). The basic nomination process for congressional candidates is similar to that for presidents. In caucus states, congressional district conventions nominate the candidate for each district, and senators are nominated by statewide conventions. In primary states, the voters simply choose the House and Senate candidates in the primary election.

FIGURE 8.6

★ HOUSE INCUMBENT SUCCESS, 1964–2010

Why are people so reluctant to challenge an incumbent? Being an incumbent brings real advantages, and the overwhelming majority of House incumbents seeking reelection over the past four decades have been successful.

Source: Data from Center for Responsive Politics, http://www.opensecrets.org/bigpicture/reelect_img.php?chamb=H

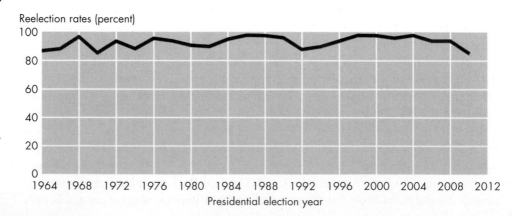

Usually few or no candidates from either party challenge a sitting member of Congress, because incumbent members hold many advantages in elections and are difficult to dislodge. Since often no one of real substance steps up to challenge the incumbent, it is unusual to have a real contest for nomination. A party may consider itself lucky if it has even one serious candidate to run against an incumbent of the other party, and in many districts, party leaders have to work hard to convince any promising person to run. In 2012, for instance, of the 377 members of the House of Representatives who ran for reelection, 40 ran unopposed by the other party.

The big exception to this situation occurs when there is an **open seat,** which happens when a sitting member retires, runs for some other office, or dies. When a seat opens up, both parties engage in spirited contests. Now all those who would like to try for a seat in Congress go for it, because they see their best chance. In 2012, there were 58 open House seats, about 13 percent of all seats.

How big an advantage do incumbents enjoy? From 1994 to 2000, new members, having now achieved incumbency, improved their vote by about 6 percent the first time they ran for reelection.[16] This bonus was significant; it meant that having already won one election, incumbents now had an added cushion of about one voter out of twenty to ward off opponents.

MANIPULATION OF DISTRICT BOUNDARIES

One source of incumbents' advantage, at least for House members, is that their district boundaries are sometimes manipulated to help them gain reelection. Senators are elected from states, whose boundaries are fixed. But every 10 years House district boundaries undergo **redistricting** after the national census.[17] Some areas lose population and others grow, so district boundaries need to be redrawn in order to keep the geographic size of the districts approximately equal—as required by rulings of the Supreme Court.[18]

State governments are responsible for setting the boundaries of congressional districts. Some states, including California (since 2008), have given bipartisan commissions responsibility for doing this. But in most states governors and state legislatures are in charge. And as might be expected, district boundaries are often manipulated to benefit powerful individual politicians or a political party. Setting boundaries in this way is called **gerrymandering,** a term coined when Governor Elbridge Gerry signed a law setting up a distorted district in Massachusetts in 1812 (see Figure 8.7).

Gerrymandering relies on making your opponents waste votes. It works like this: Suppose you are in a state that is split roughly 50-50 in party allegiance and has four House seats. A fair election would generally result in two seats for each party. If you can control how the boundaries for the four districts are drawn, however, you can construct one district that is made up of places where the opposing party is traditionally strong and can expect to get about 80 percent of the vote. (You may have to pull together some areas that aren't right next to each other, which is why Governor Gerry's "Gerrymander" stretches out in ungainly ways.) Since you have shoehorned so many of your opponent's supporters into this one vote-heavy district, the rest of the state now has more of your voters than of your opponent's. If you spread these remaining voters evenly across the other three districts, all three should be safe for your party. As a result, your gerrymandering has transformed a state that is evenly divided into one with a 3 to 1 advantage in congressional representation for your party. This process is illustrated in Figure 8.7, where each D stands for 10,000 voters for party D, each R stands

FIGURE 8.7

★ THE FAMOUS GERRYMANDER MAP CARTOON

In 1812 Governor Elbridge Gerry created an ungainly district in northeastern Massachusetts, designed to help an incumbent of his Democratic-Republican party. Elkanah Tisdale drew this cartoon for *The Boston Gazette* depicting the district as a reptilian monster. It looked to some like a salamander, so an editor said, "Let's call it a Gerry-mander." And so a new word was born.

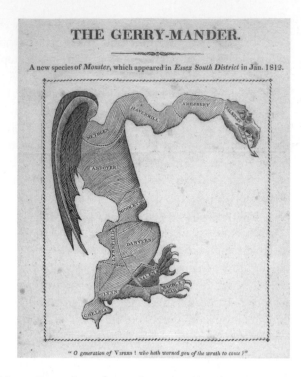

THE GERRY-MANDER.

A new species of *Monster*, which appeared in *Essex South District* in Jan. 1812.

"*O generation of Vipers! who hath warned you of the wrath to come?*"

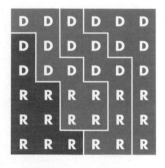

FIGURE 8.8

★ HOW THE Ds TURNED 50 PERCENT OF THE VOTE INTO THREE SEATS OUT OF FOUR

It would also be possible to create two 65 percent R seats and two 65 percent D seats, thus creating four very safe seats for incumbents. Do you see what you would need to do to accomplish this?

for 10,000 voters for party R, and boundaries have been drawn within the square to divide it into four districts with equal populations. Gerrymanders would be funny, as in Figure 8.8, if they did not represent such a distortion of democratic representation.

The redistricting of Texas in 2003 is a good example of gerrymandering in action. Republicans gained control of both houses of the legislature in Texas in 2002 and redrew the boundaries of the state's congressional districts, which the Democrats had drawn earlier in the year to give themselves an advantage. With the new boundaries, the Texas congressional delegation shifted in 2004 from 17 Democrats and 15 Republicans to 11 Democrats and 21 Republicans—a net gain for the Republicans of 6 seats.

A variant of gerrymandering can occur if neither party fully controls the state government. In that case, the two parties sometimes cooperate to rig the boundaries so that the incumbent members of Congress from both parties get safe seats. This compromise makes both parties happy because their members of Congress are less vulnerable. Only the public loses. An incumbent gerrymander does not distort party strengths the way a party-line gerrymander does, but it does reduce competition by creating a large number of safely Republican and safely Democratic seats.

Gerrymandering is not solely an American phenomenon, but the United States is one of only a few countries where it is common. Most countries that base their elections on districts—Great Britain, Australia, and Canada, for instance—use nonpartisan commissions to draw district boundaries.

INCUMBENTS' OTHER ADVANTAGES

Although gerrymandering contributes to the lack of competition in congressional elections, so do a variety of other advantages that incumbents enjoy after they have first been elected, namely:

- control of the news
- staff to support constituents

- ability to add "pork" to legislation
- easier access to campaign contributions
- experience

Control of the News

In general, the news media do not follow closely what any individual member of the House of Representatives does. They do not even follow closely what senators do, except for a few with star appeal like Charles Schumer or John McCain. This leaves members of Congress free to fill the void by providing their own news about what they have been doing, putting all of their activities in a positive light. They send glowing newsletters to their constituents (they receive free postage, called "franking," for the newsletters). They spend time in their districts, where they give speeches, appear at state fairs, visit churches, and attend other events. And they send press releases about their activities to newspapers and television stations; since the media generally do not have reporters shadowing a member, the member gets to be his or her own "reporter."

Staff to Support Constituents

Citizens have long been encouraged to "call your member of Congress" when they run into trouble with government procedures. Members maintain skilled staffs to help their constituents make their way through the federal bureaucracy. (Often, this is a job student interns get to help with.) In 2012, for instance, staff for Steve Chabot (R), who represents Ohio's 1st Congressional District, assisted more than 700 constituents; the most common problems involved Social Security, Medicare, and the Veterans Administration.[19]

Ability to Add "Pork" to Legislation

Members of Congress are often able to insert into more general laws specific items that benefit just a particular city, school, or business in their district. In principle, adding such "pork" is a bad way to make laws, since policy should address general problems in uniform ways. However, most members love adding "pork" because it allows them to provide special favors to groups in their district. Special projects can range from undeniably good ones (aid to Joplin, Missouri, after it was devastated by a tornado) to at least apparently bad ones ($250,000 to support the National Mule and Packers Museum in Bishop, California).

Easier Access to Campaign Contributions

Congressional and senatorial campaigns are expensive, and all candidates have to raise money to pay for them. This is easier for incumbents than for challengers, because lobbyists, businesses, and political groups are eager to get access to sitting members and will contribute as a way to get in to talk to a member of Congress. In 2008, for instance, incumbent House members were able to raise an average of $1,430,000 for their campaigns, compared with an average of $489,000 raised by their challengers.[20] (See Figure 8.9.)

Experience

Not all of the advantages enjoyed by incumbents are bad. Incumbents have gained experience in office, after all, and have learned how to do their jobs. They have

FIGURE 8.9

★ CAMPAIGN CONTRIBUTIONS TO HOUSE INCUMBENTS AND THEIR CHALLENGERS

Average contributions to incumbents and those challenging them. Is the gap between incumbents and their challengers narrowing or stable?

Source: Data from Federal Election Commission press release, December 29, 2009, table "Historical Comparison for General Election Campaigns 1992–2008".

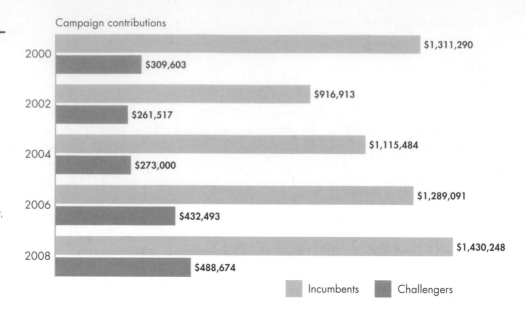

Campaign contributions

Year	Incumbents	Challengers
2000	$1,311,290	$309,603
2002	$916,913	$261,517
2004	$1,115,484	$273,000
2006	$1,289,091	$432,493
2008	$1,430,248	$488,674

Incumbents   Challengers

mastered policy issues. They have learned a lot about the district they represent. In short, to some extent their service in Congress has made them better prepared to serve again. This advantage shows up in head-to-head debates with challengers, where the incumbent often seems more articulate and better informed. It is likely that some portion of the 6 percent advantage incumbents enjoy simply consists of true value added.

PARTY ACCOUNTABILITY

Because of gerrymandering and the special advantages described in the previous section, voters have a difficult time holding members individually accountable for what they do in office. It almost seems to take a well-publicized scandal to make an incumbent vulnerable enough to be ousted. As an alternative to holding members individually accountable, however, voters can instead use elections to hold the two *parties* accountable, as governing teams. This would fit with the idea of "responsible party government" that we introduced in Chapter 7. To hold parties accountable as teams, voters who did not like the policies that had been passed by a party could punish the party by voting against its candidates at the next election.

Congressional elections in recent years have in fact begun to hinge more on support for the two parties than for individual candidates, though it is also true that voters still vote to a significant extent for the individual member regardless of party. This trend toward voting by party has happened partly because the anomaly of a conservative— but Democratic—South, which endured from the Civil War into the 1970s, has gradually been replaced by the more natural conservative, Republican South. It has also occurred because activists of both parties have become more polarized. Since the parties now offer the voters a clearer choice than they have in the past, voters have responded by using party affiliation as a stronger basis for deciding how they will vote in a given election.

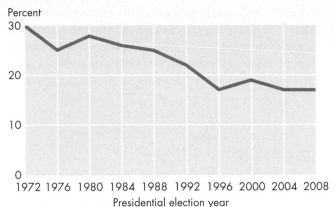

FIGURE 8.10

★ PERCENT OF VOTERS SPLITTING THEIR TICKET, 1972 TO 2008

How steady has the decline in split-ticket voting been over this period? Does this indicate anything about the rise in party-based voting?

Source: Data from National Election Studies, ANES Guide to Public Opinion and Voting Behavior.

split-ticket voting
When several candidates for different offices appear on a ballot, the practice of voting for a candidate of one party for one office and a candidate of another party for another office.

Clear evidence for a closer coupling of incumbents' races to their parties is seen in the decline of **split-ticket voting** (Figure 8.10), in which people vote for a presidential candidate of one party while simultaneously voting for a congressional candidate of the other party. The percentage of voters voting for a member of Congress of a different party from their presidential choice has declined fairly steadily from 30 percent in 1972 to 17 percent in 2008. Today the fate of members of Congress is more closely tied to their party than it used to be.

Elections that change Congress significantly, such as we might expect with party accountability, have increased since the 1970s. As shown in Figure 8.11, since 1972 only seven congressional elections led to a net shift of 20 or more seats, but three of these were the elections of 2006, 2008, and 2010. The 2010 shift was the largest since 1948. As you will see in Chapter 12, members of Congress now vote more uniformly along party lines than they used to, presenting two clear alternative policy visions to the voters. And, as we would expect, voters are responding by using elections as tools to choose which party will govern. Party accountability is increasing.

So, taken as a whole, how well does our system of congressional elections—with its mix of a certain amount of sheltered incumbency and a certain amount of party accountability—work? One way to answer this question is to compare the U.S. system with one where gerrymandering does not take place (because a nonpolitical commission draws district boundaries), and where incumbents do not enjoy many individual advantages. This can provide a baseline of how much accountability we might expect of congressional elections. Great Britain, which fits these criteria, provides a good comparison.

Even in Britain we should still expect to see some districts that are safe for one party or another. Just as in the United States, British people tend to live in areas with others who agree with them politically, so many districts naturally will be heavily Conservative or heavily Labour. But that is the only thing that should give incumbents any safety. Under these circumstances, how much incumbent turnover is there in

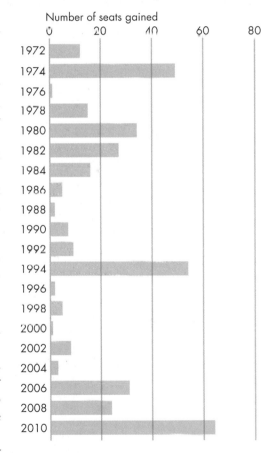

FIGURE 8.11

★ ELECTIONS THAT CHANGE CONGRESS

The figure shows the number of seats gained by the winning party at each election to the House of Representatives since 1972. Do the large changes in 2006, 2008, and 2010 represent a new trend in congressional elections, or might they be just a coincidental cluster of "change elections"?

Source: Data from Office of the Clerk of the U.S. House of Representatives

British elections? In the 2005 and 2010 elections, 12 percent of incumbents who stood for election each year were defeated.[21] This is nearly twice as much turnover as typically happens in the United States where even at a time of unusual turnover in Congress, from 2004 through 2010 an average of only 7 percent of incumbents were defeated. This suggests that gerrymandering and incumbents' other advantages reduce turnover by about half in the United States.

ELECTORAL SYSTEMS AND THEIR EFFECTS

electoral system
A set of rules to determine, based on the outcome of an election, which individuals will hold office.

single-member-district, plurality (SMDP) electoral system
An electoral system in which the country is divided into districts, each of which elects a single member to the Congress or parliament. The candidate receiving a plurality of votes wins the seat.

An **electoral system** is a set of rules that determine, from the votes cast in an election, which individuals will hold power in the government. We shall look here at the two major types of electoral systems, starting with the system used in the United States.

THE UNITED STATES: WINNER-TAKE-ALL

The United States uses the **single-member-district, plurality** system (**SMDP**) for its congressional elections and also for its presidential elections (except for the intervening step of the Electoral College). In an SMDP system, a country is divided into districts, usually with roughly equal populations.[22] Each district elects a single official—a member of Congress, for instance. Parties nominate candidates to run in the district, and the candidate who wins a *plurality* of the votes—the largest number of votes, though not necessarily a majority—wins the seat. For obvious reasons, SMDP systems are often called "winner-take-all."

For a presidential election the whole country makes up one big single "district," with the candidate who gets a plurality of the votes usually winning the election. As noted, the Electoral College complicates this situation, but it only rarely changes the outcome of the election from what the simple SMDP result would be.

The use of the SMDP system has affected politics in the United States profoundly because of one very important side effect: *SMDP systems generally help large parties and hurt small ones, and for this reason they tend to produce two-party systems.* In other words, it is almost certainly true that because we have an SMDP electoral system, including an elected president, we have a two-party system.

To see why SMDP has this effect, think of the challenge congressional elections would represent under our system for a hypothetical small party, the Revolutionary Inaction Party (RIP). With the support (let us say) of no more than a tenth of the population, spread fairly evenly across the country, it would be difficult for the RIP to win many seats, and in fact the RIP likely would win none at all. In a three-way race, even if the Democratic and Republican candidates were exactly tied, the RIP candidate would have to get over 33 percent of the vote to win, which would be more than three times its national average. An even higher percentage would be necessary if the two major parties were not tied.

In a presidential race, the odds are even starker. At least the RIP might have local pockets of strength in which it could get three, four, or five times its national average and thus win a few congressional districts. But in the national vote for president, winning with 10 percent would be impossible.[23] The RIP would have to get at least

34 percent of the entire national vote, and even that number would work only if the Democratic and Republican candidates split the rest of the vote evenly. In this way, SMDP electoral systems punish small parties and reward large parties. And as a result, over time small parties disappear or are short-lived, and a two-party system emerges.

PROPORTIONAL REPRESENTATION

Many other democracies around the world use a different electoral system, **proportional representation** or **PR.** Most European and Latin American countries use PR, as well as many other democracies, including Israel, South Africa, and Indonesia. Though there are a number of variants of PR, at its heart it is simple: Each party registers a ranked list of candidates with a commission prior to the election; the people vote, and the commission calculates the percentage of the vote each party received; the commission then allots to each party that percentage of seats in the parliament, counting down from the top of the ranked list.

> **proportional representation (PR) electoral system**
> An electoral system in which seats are allocated to parties in proportion to their shares of the vote.

For example, there are 435 members of the House of Representatives in the United States. If the United States had a PR system, our hypothetical RIP would submit in advance a list of candidates ranked in order by how much the party wants them to be in Congress. The names at the top of the list would be party leaders; promising young figures would come a bit further down, and willing drudges would appear near the bottom. After the election, if the RIP candidates received 10 percent of the vote, the electoral commission would assign them 10 percent of the House seats (43 or 44, depending on rounding); the commission would count down from the top of the list, and the first 43 or 44 names would become members of the House. The RIP, who got practically no seats under the SMDP system, would get their proportional share under PR.

Since PR systems do not hurt small parties as SMDP does, countries using PR systems tend to have multiple parties involved in their politics. Norway has 7 parties sitting in its parliament; Germany has 5; Israel has 12, and Brazil has 22. As Table 8.1 shows, the great majority of countries with SMDP systems have just two major parties, while very few countries with PR systems are limited to two.[24]

Given the many diverse interests in American politics, if the United States had proportional representation in its congressional elections and did not have an elected president, we would almost certainly have more than two major parties engaged in our government. At the very least, there would probably be a labor party, a party representing middle-class and business interests, an African American party, a conservative

TABLE 8.1
the prevalence of two-party systems in SMDP electoral systems

Most countries using proportional representation have multiparty systems, and most countries using SMDP systems have two-party systems. Of the 71 PR countries in the table, only 9 have two-party systems, while of the 14 SMDP countries, all but 3 have two-party systems.

	PR	SMDP
Two-party systems	9	11
Multiparty systems	62	3

Source: Data from International IDEA Table of Electoral Systems Worldwide (www.idea.int); Elections Worldwide Project.

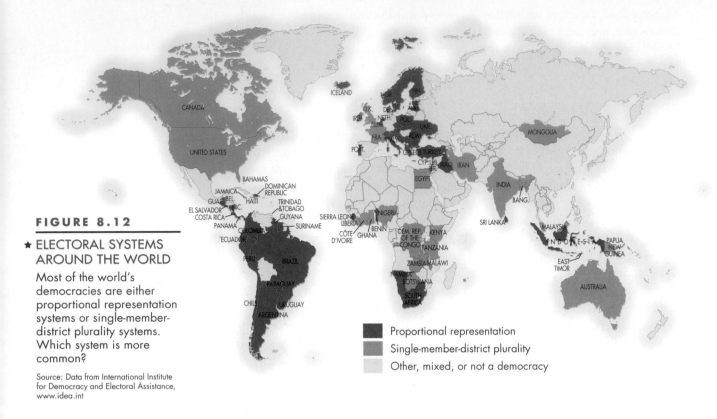

FIGURE 8.12

★ ELECTORAL SYSTEMS AROUND THE WORLD

Most of the world's democracies are either proportional representation systems or single-member-district plurality systems. Which system is more common?

Source: Data from International Institute for Democracy and Electoral Assistance, www.idea.int

■ Proportional representation
■ Single-member-district plurality
■ Other, mixed, or not a democracy

Electoral College
The system by which presidents are elected in the United States. Voters vote for a set of electors, and the set that wins casts its vote for the candidate to which it is pledged.

religious party, a farmers' party, and an environmentalist party. Under proportional representation, the nature of American politics would be markedly different. The map in Figure 8.12 shows the countries around the world that use winner-take-all systems, PR, a mixture of the two, or some other electoral system.

THE ELECTORAL COLLEGE AND PRESIDENTIAL ELECTIONS

We have written so far as if Americans simply vote for a presidential candidate, and the candidate with the most votes (a plurality) wins. This is almost true, but the **Electoral College** provides a twist that occasionally changes the outcome from what a simple plurality vote would give. It also modifies candidates' strategies in the campaign. Given how infrequently it actually changes the outcome of an election, the way it modifies candidates' strategies may actually be its most significant effect.

The writers of the Constitution devised the Electoral College because they did not want a direct electoral connection between citizens and the president. They decided instead to base the selection of a president on the states. Each state was to select a group of electors, equal to the number of representatives and senators the state had in Congress. These electors would then meet to cast votes to determine who should be president. The state tallies would be added up, and the person with the most votes would become president.

The Constitution did not specify how the electors were to be chosen, and indeed until 1816 most states' electors were appointed by the states' legislatures. But during the early nineteenth century, with the development of national political parties and the growing popularity of electoral democracy, the system as we see it today took shape.

The parties' presidential nominees conduct a national campaign, and each party in each state names a set of electors pledged to vote for its candidate. On Election Day, when you step inside the voting booth and choose your candidate, you are not in fact choosing that candidate directly. Instead, you are choosing the slate of electors that represent him or her. Although you see your candidates' names on the ballot, Candidate A or Candidate B, when you cast your vote, you're choosing the electors on behalf of A or the electors on behalf of B.

In most states the slate that gets the plurality of votes wins, so in effect each state is "winner-take-all." The two exceptions to this pattern are Maine and Nebraska, which have decided to choose their electors partly by congressional district and partly state-wide, so that it is possible for some of the state's electors to be for one candidate, others for another candidate. In 2008, for instance, Nebraska split its electoral votes, with one going to Barack Obama and four going to John McCain; all four of Maine's votes that year went to Obama. The chosen state electors gather in the state capital to cast their votes for president and vice-president. Thus the Electoral College never actually meets as a body but consists of the sum of 51 separate meetings in the states and the District of Columbia.

The Electoral College affects the presidential election in four ways:

- A candidate with the most popular votes will not necessarily win the election.
- Candidates' campaign strategies are affected.
- States with small populations have a slightly exaggerated impact on the outcome.
- Many states do not legally require electors to vote as they had originally pledged to do before the election.

Popular vs. Electoral Votes

The most obvious effect of the Electoral College—and the one that draws people's attention to it—is the possibility that the candidate with the higher total popular vote can lose if the opposing candidate comes out ahead in electoral votes. This outcome is most likely to happen if one candidate's support is concentrated geographically so that the candidate rolls up huge majorities in the relatively small number of states he or she does win. If one of the candidates has won in a number of such states, that candidate might in the end have received more votes than the opposing candidate, while still failing to win in enough states to get a plurality of electors in the Electoral College. This scenario has happened in the United States in only two presidential elections—1888 and 2000—and in both elections the popular vote was very close, functionally almost a tie.[25] Even though the situation is rare, when it does happen it feels very wrong to many people.

Strategic Campaigning

A second significant impact of the Electoral College, and one that probably matters more year in and year out than the rare overturning of popular majorities, is its effect on candidates' strategies. Since all states except Maine and Nebraska vote as unitary blocs, with all of a state's electoral votes going to the candidate who wins a plurality in that state, it makes sense for candidates to pay little attention to states where they already know they are very strong (that is, they will win that state even if they don't show up often during the campaign), or very weak (they could show up every day and still never carry the state). Instead, candidates spend a lot of time and money on close states, and they also focus their campaign messages on those states.

In 2012, just 11 states were considered "not safe" for one party or the other, and so the candidates focused almost solely on those battleground states: Colorado, Florida, Iowa, Michigan, Nevada, New Hampshire, North Carolina, Ohio, Pennsylvania, Virginia, and Wisconsin. (In contrast, for instance, Massachusetts is always safely Democratic and Utah safely Republican.) In the twelve months leading up to November, 2012, over half of President (and candidate) Obama's trips within the United States went to just the eleven battleground states. He traveled 33 times to North Carolina, Virginia, and Florida, for instance, but only 7 times to any other Southern state.[26] Voters in Ohio became sick of political ads on TV, while viewers in Utah may have considered them occasional, almost refreshing, breaks in the routine. This discrepancy happens only because the Electoral College system packages voters into states, some of which are worth competing for and some of which are not. If the elections were a straight popular plurality vote, candidates would troll just as hard for additional votes in Massachusetts or Utah as in Ohio. Any vote, anywhere, would count equally.

Small-Population vs. Large-Population States

A third effect of the Electoral College, less important than the first two, is that states with small populations have a slightly exaggerated impact on the election. House seats are divided proportionally to a state's population, but each state also gets two senators, no matter what its population is. As a result, although a small state with just one House seat might have a population that is one-third that of a neighbor that has three House seats, it would have 3 electors (1 + 2), compared with its neighbor's 5 electors (3 + 2).

Casting Pledged Votes

A final minor quirk of the Electoral College is that many states do not have any legal provision requiring electors to vote in the end as they had originally pledged to do before the election. This type of incident is rare and has never happened in a situation when it could have changed an outcome. Usually it occurs by accident or is done to make a point. In 2000, for instance, Barbara Lett-Simmons, a Democratic elector for the District of Columbia, abstained rather than cast her vote for Al Gore in order to protest the lack of congressional representation for the District of Columbia. Her vote would not have changed the outcome of the election had she cast it as she was pledged to do.

Positive Effects

There are also several possible advantages to having an Electoral College. The system emphasizes the federal nature of the country, based as it is on states. It also forces a candidate to have a reasonably broad appeal across the different regions of the country, since under the Electoral College one cannot win with 90 or 100 percent of the vote in one region but little or no support elsewhere. And finally, minorities may benefit from the Electoral College since they are often concentrated in battleground states like Ohio, Florida, and Pennsylvania.

PROPOSALS FOR CHANGING THE ELECTORAL COLLEGE

Many changes have been suggested for the Electoral College, mainly because of the possibility that the winner of the popular vote could lose in electoral votes, but also to some extent because of the Electoral College's exaggeration of the effects of battleground states, and its overrepresentation of small states.

The three main proposals are

- replace the Electoral College with a simple, straight popular vote
- retain the Electoral College structure but have each state allot its electors by congressional district, as is done in Maine and Nebraska
- have most or all states pledge to cast their electoral votes for whichever candidate wins the national popular vote

The first proposal would be hard to accomplish since a constitutional amendment requires the consent of three-fourths of the states, and many small states would be reluctant to give up the minor advantage they enjoy under the current system.

The second proposal would not eliminate the advantage enjoyed by small states, but it would eliminate the emphasis on battleground states, since states would not vote as units. And because the outcome would be based on a larger number of smaller units, it would probably make it less likely that the winner of the popular vote could lose the election in the Electoral College. One problem with this proposal is that presidential candidates' success would be based on congressional districts, which are often gerrymandered. There have been recent attempts to introduce the method in California, North Carolina, Wisconsin, and Pennsylvania, but all four proposals failed.

The third proposal is intriguing. Without amending the constitution at all, states could achieve the same effect as if the Electoral College had been abolished. The winner of the national popular vote would get a majority of electoral votes no matter what happened in which states. Nine states have pledged to take this step if enough other states will adopt a similar rule.[27]

ELECTIONS AND THE REPRESENTATION OF WOMEN AND MINORITIES

Women and members of minority groups have unique experiences, and if these are not fully represented in the government, officials will be limited in the ways they understand and respond to issues. As shown in Figure 8.13, however, women and minority groups are represented in Congress at less than their proportion in the population. And they are even more underrepresented in the presidency. Until Barack Obama, there had never been a president who was anything other than white and male.

Only 17 percent of the members of the U.S. Congress are women, but women are underrepresented in almost all democracies. The average representation of women in parliaments worldwide is 19 percent; Sweden and the central African country of Rwanda are the champions at women's representation, with 56 percent of the seats in Rwanda's lower house and 46 percent of the seats in Sweden's lower house held by women.[28]

A country's electoral system affects how easily the country can accomplish more equal representation of women and minorities. In a proportional representation system where each party submits a ranked list of candidates to the electoral commission in advance of the election, it is fairly easy to require that the lists be balanced by gender and ethnicity. By law, for instance, 50 percent of the candidates on party lists in Italy must be women, and 30 percent in Argentina.[29]

KEY TO understanding ★

The United States falls slightly below the world average in terms of the number of women and minority members elected to office. The SMDP electoral system makes it difficult to set rules that will increase such representation; "majority-minority" districts provide one way (though awkward) to alleviate the disparity.

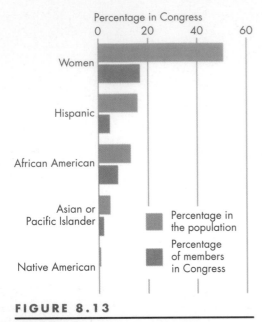

Percentage in Congress

FIGURE 8.13

★ REPRESENTATION OF WOMEN
AND MINORITIES IN CONGRESS

Which groups are closest to having
representation equal to their share of the
population? Why do you think that might be so?

Source: Data from www.house.gov

SMDP systems, such as the one used in the United States, offer fewer ways to encourage female or minority representation. Because just one candidate can run for office in each district, parties cannot provide a balanced mix of candidates in any single district. And in the United States, parties have little control over who is nominated across the various districts, since this decision is up to the primary voters in each district.

A special device has been developed to help ensure minority representation in some House districts. The Supreme Court, which otherwise tries to minimize extreme gerrymandering, has in several cases allowed states to create very strange-looking gerrymandered districts—**majority-minority districts,** in which a majority of the district's voters belong to an ethnic minority. This makes it likely that the district will elect a minority member.[30] Figure 8.14 shows Illinois's 4th Congressional District, which was specially tailored to produce a Hispanic majority.

Majority-minority districts usually succeed in their goal of assuring added minority representation. A good example is the 6th District of South Carolina, which was created in 1992 to ensure an African-American representative for parts of Charleston and Columbia. James Clyburn won the seat and has held it ever since, going on to become a member of the Democratic Party leadership in the House of Representatives.

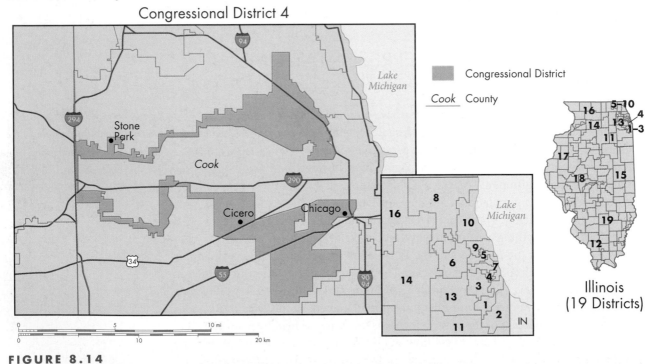

Congressional District 4

FIGURE 8.14

★ ILLINOIS'S 4TH CONGRESSIONAL DISTRICT

This majority-minority district was constructed to produce a Hispanic majority. Would a member of Congress find it difficult to represent such a strung-out district?

Source: www.nationalatlas.gov

Majority-minority districts have a serious drawback, however. By concentrating minority voters in one district, they make it possible for the party that is less supported by minority voters to do well in a number of other districts. African Americans tend strongly to vote Democratic, for instance, so a majority-minority African-American district would do just what a Republican gerrymander might aim for—concentrate a large number of Democratic voters in one district. In fact, the 6th District of South Carolina was originally created by a coalition of African-American legislators (who wanted to be sure of electing an African-American member of Congress) and Republican legislators (who wanted to gerrymander the district to help Republican candidates in all of the surrounding districts). Creating a special district to help an ethnic minority may end up simultaneously hurting the minority's partisan interests elsewhere.

majority-minority district
A congressional district in which a majority of the electorate are of an ethnic minority. Sometimes these are deliberately created through gerrymandering.

CAMPAIGN FINANCE

American political campaigns are expensive affairs. In the United States in 2012, candidates for the presidency, for seats in the Senate and the House of Representatives, and for state and local offices—along with advocacy groups working from outside the candidates' campaigns ("SuperPacs," which are discussed on page 290)—spent about $6 billion on the campaigns. To truly appreciate how much money this is, consider the amount of money spent during Great Britain's 2010 national election, where candidates and parties spent a total of only $88 *million* on their campaigns.[31]

The United States is not the only expensive country in the world. In Japan in 2000 parties reported expenditures of $3.1 billion.[32] But there are only a few countries with campaigns as expensive as those in the United States.

Obviously, nothing is free in this world, and assembling effective campaigns to challenge incumbent officials can require a great deal of time and money. Expensive campaigns have two bad side effects, however. First, officials spend too much time soliciting contributions. In what has come to be called the "permanent campaign," elected officials have to start almost the day after they take office calling potential donors for their next campaign. United States senators must collect $9,000 every single day they are in office, including weekends and holidays, to prepare for the next election.[33]

Second, elected officials incur obligations to those who have given them contributions. Groups like automobile dealers, trial lawyers, and investment bankers can influence legislation with contributions of just a few hundred thousand dollars. The fine print of such legislation may make a difference to them of many millions of dollars.

KEY TO understanding ★

American campaigns are expensive. While some other aspects of campaigns have been regulated, it has proved impossible to put direct limits on campaign expenditure because it is protected from regulation by the First Amendment. "Independent" groups outside of the parties and the formal campaigns are free even of the limited regulation to which parties and candidates are subject.

THE DILEMMA OF LIMITING CAMPAIGN SPENDING

Numerous efforts have been made to limit the role of money in electoral politics. Attempts to put caps on campaign spending raise a basic dilemma, however, since the First Amendment of the Constitution guarantees freedom of speech, and the Supreme Court has ruled that to limit campaign expenditures is to limit free speech.[34] Accordingly, past laws that attempted to limit the role of money in politics by capping candidates' expenditures have been struck down by the Court. Reformers have sought other ways to accomplish the same goal, but these attempts have never been fully successful. No matter how Congress tries to regulate campaign finance, concerns about free speech have always forced reformers to leave open some avenues for finance and expression, which then become loopholes through which campaigns can draw finance indirectly. Today there are regulations attempting to limit large contributions to candidates, to require that contributions be reported, and to regulate the format of campaign advertisements. But there is no limit on what candidates or other groups may spend in campaigns.

REGULATING CAMPAIGN FINANCE FOR PARTIES AND CANDIDATES

Over the years Congress has passed several laws to regulate campaign finance, most recently the Bipartisan Campaign Reform Act of 2002, better known as the McCain-Feingold Act. As a result of these laws, and modifications made in them by Supreme Court decisions, campaign finance is now regulated in the following ways:

- Compliance and disclosure
- Limits to contributions
- Public financing for presidential candidates
- "Stand by your ad"

Compliance and Disclosure

The Federal Election Commission (FEC) was created in 1974 to oversee compliance with election laws, and publish information on candidates' spending. Candidates are required to report to the FEC who contributed to the campaign and how the campaign's funds were spent.

Limits to Contributions

Individuals' contributions to candidates and parties are limited. In 2012 these limits were $2,500 to any candidate, $5,000 to any Political Action Committee (see below), $10,000 to any local party committee, and $30,800 to national party committees. The total of all the individual's contributions could not exceed $117,000 a year.

Groups such as the National Association of Realtors, the Sierra Club, and the Pro-Life Campaign Committee can form **political action committees** (**PAC**s) to gather and coordinate their members' contributions. PACs are special organizations set up by groups to make contributions to candidates. They are allowed to contribute up to $5,000 per candidate. There are now about 4,000 PACs, so they make up a significant part of the political landscape.

political action committee (PAC)
An organization that donates money to political candidates and officeholders.

Public Financing for Presidential Candidates

In an attempt to persuade presidential candidates to voluntarily accept limits on their expenditure, the government provides public financing for presidential candidates, both for primary elections and for the general election—but with a string attached. Any candidate who accepts the subsidy must also voluntarily agree to a limit on expenditures. In 2012 the limits if a candidate accepted the public funding were approximately $46 million for the primary season and $91 million for the general election.

This subsidy usually succeeded in the past in limiting candidates' direct spending in presidential elections. But in 2008 Barack Obama became the first presidential candidate ever to refuse the subsidy and limits for the general election campaign. John McCain did accept the subsidy and its accompanying limits for the general election.

Obama gambled that with his sophisticated Internet operation, he could raise enough in individual contributions to justify turning down the public subsidy. His gamble was spectacularly successful, as he raised $657 million in individual contributions.[35] It may be that the ease of raising money over the Internet is making the carrot of public subsidies less effective as a way to regulate spending. In fact, some have called 2008 the "death knell" of public financing. In 2012 both Romney and Obama decided not to accept public financing for the general election.

"Stand by Your Ad"

The McCain-Feingold Act added a new provision, presumably to improve the tone of campaigning, that requires candidates to take public responsibility for their advertisements. Every ad in a campaign has to include a statement by the candidate: "I'm Representative Dottard, and I approve this ad."

INDEPENDENT EXPENDITURES

All of the provisions we have reviewed here apply to political parties and candidates for office. However, a huge loophole in the regulation of campaign finance arose in the 2004 election in the form of **527 committees** (named after the provision of the tax law that applies to them)—nonprofit political organizations that are formally independent from the parties or any candidate's campaign. Because 527 committees are not formally part of any campaign, they do not fall under the regulation of the Federal Election Commission. They can run even very nasty television ads attacking a candidate, as long as they are formally set up as issue advocacy ads rather than as campaign ads. An ad might conclude with the line "So, please call Representative Dottard and ask him to stop supporting international terrorism" instead of "So, please vote against Representative Dottard." This makes the 527 committee technically not part of a campaign.

Since they are not subject to the FEC's regulation, 527 committees may accept contributions of any size and do not need to disclose their sources. They can have a substantial impact on a campaign. In the first presidential election under the new rules, "independent" groups spent about one-third of the total amount spent on the campaign that year from all sources.

In 2010 the Supreme Court expanded the possibilities of independent expenditure in the important "Citizens United" decision.[36] Citizens United is a nonprofit organization that "seeks to reassert the traditional American values of limited government, freedom of enterprise, strong families, and national sovereignty." It had released a film in 2008, *Hillary: The Movie,* a very unflattering portrait of Democratic candidate Hillary Clinton. A lower court had ruled that the movie could not be aired within 30 days of a primary because the McCain-Feingold Act prohibited all organizations from broadcasting "electioneering communications" close to elections. The Supreme Court stated that this provision of the Act violated the First Amendment, and ruled therefore that corporations and unions could not be limited

527 committees
Advocacy groups that are allowed to advertise on political issues and are not subject to regulation by the Federal Election Commission.

★ A conservative group called Citizens United produced *Hillary: The Movie,* which portrayed 2008 presidential candidate Hillary Clinton in an unflattering light.

Super PAC
Independent campaign organization that may raise unlimited funds, and spend them on overt attacks or support for candidates; it may not directly coordinate its strategy with campaigns.

in their funding of independent political broadcasts during elections.

In light of the Citizens United decision and a related appeals court decision, the Federal Election Commission established an additional type of independent campaign organization, the **Super PAC.**[37] A Super PAC may raise unlimited amounts of money from corporations, unions, and individuals. And, unlike 527 committees, Super PACs may spend money on overt attacks or support for candidates. However, they must report their donors' contributions to the FEC, which 527 committees do not need to do. Like 527 committees, they may not donate money to candidates, and they may not coordinate their activities with the campaign.[38]

The advent of 527 committees and Super PACS is rapidly changing the political terrain. In 2012, just one Super PAC, "Make Us Great Again," which supported Rick Perry, raised $55 million to support his campaign.[39]

Four aspects of Super PACs are especially notable:

- *Flexibility.* Thanks to their flexibility, Super PACs dominated advertising in the 2012 primaries. In the run-up to Super Tuesday, for instance, Mitt Romney's campaign spent $1.2 million on advertising, while his associated Super PAC, "Restore Our Future," spent $7 million.[40]

- *Degree of dependence.* Super PACs are usually not truly independent of the candidate's campaign, although the two must stay technically unconnected. The Romney national campaign office and the "Restore Our Future" Super PAC both were located in one suite of offices, and they shared many consultants; many officers of Restore Our Future were former Romney campaign aides.[41]

- *Large donors.* Since there are no limits on individual contributions, Super PACs are usually dominated by large donors. Republicans have especially benefited from large gifts—more than two dozen gifts of over $1 million during the primary race alone—but Obama also attracted multimillion gifts to his Super PAC "Priorities USA Action."

- *Prolonged nomination contests.* An unforeseen consequence of Super PACs has been that they have the potential to prolong nomination contests. Newt Gingrich would have probably felt he had to quit the race after New Hampshire in 2012, but was kept alive by just one family's $10 million gift to his Super PAC.

The presence of 527 committees and numerous Super PACs has had at least two probably bad side effects on elections. First, because their contributors tend to be ideological, they often take harsh stances to the far left or right, increasing the polarization of politics. Second, candidates lose some control over their own campaigns, since the rhetoric of "independent" ads is removed from their direct control. The ads may be largely welcome to the campaign, but they also carry a risk of backfiring.

Why Are We
THE WAY WE ARE ?

Our discussion of elections in this chapter suggests several important characteristics of elections in the United States. Americans exercise a wider range of electoral choices than citizens of many other countries—not only in general elections, but also in primary elections and occasional special elections like recalls. Our campaigns are long, complex, and expensive, involving many offices over a long campaign season. We elect our candidates in particular ways, using an SMDP electoral system to elect members of Congress, and an Electoral College to elect presidents. And while citizens exercise limited accountability through elections, especially elections to Congress, the level of accountability appears to be increasing. How can we explain these characteristics of American elections?

LONG, COMPLEX CAMPAIGNS

We can understand our long and complex campaigns partly as a result of the Jacksonian push for broad democratic control of government in the early nineteenth century, which put a wide range of offices on the ballot. Also, unlike other countries in the world, our Constitution allows state governments to determine how national elections are administered, and this means that rules vary

from place to place. Add primaries and caucuses to these factors, and the result is a campaign season that involves many candidates, at many levels of government, over many months.

DIRECT INPUT OF CITIZENS

The unusual degree to which citizens are drawn into the electoral process—through primaries and caucuses, but also from time to time through the referendum or recall—is a direct legacy of the Progressive movement and its efforts to weaken the central leadership of parties, which we discussed in Chapter 7. And the reform push in the Democratic Party after 1972 produced rules that led all states to use primaries or caucuses to select convention delegates. As a result, American citizens participate in a wide range of electoral choices.

EXPENSIVE ELECTIONS

Why are our elections so expensive? One reason, of course, may be our long campaigns, which cost more money than short ones would. But another reason may be the decentralized structure of American parties, which means that candidates are largely on their own. This has brought about the "permanent campaign," in which officials start raising money for the next campaign almost from the day they are sworn into office.

ELECTORAL SYSTEMS

Our use of the SMDP electoral system for congressional elections, and the Electoral College for presidential elections, may in part be due to the fact that the United States was the first electoral democracy. Proportional representation had not yet been invented when elections started in the United States, and SMDP seemed the natural way to provide representation to towns and localities. In a self-reinforcing circle following the introduction of SMDP, the system resulted in just two major parties, which in turn have favored maintaining the SMDP system that benefits them. There have been sporadic efforts to change to some other electoral system, but the major parties have always supported maintaining the old system.

The Electoral College originated in the Founders' desire to shield presidential selection from direct democracy. Why does it continue today, even though the original reason for an Electoral College has disappeared? It has survived partly because it is difficult to change the Constitution and partly because its obvious disadvantages are balanced by some advantages.

ACCOUNTABILITY

American presidential elections produce a high degree of accountability, but congressional elections have in the past produced relatively little individual accountability because of gerrymandering and the advantages of incumbency. However, it appears that accountability of parties (as compared to individuals) is increasing in congressional elections. This may be due to the increased party polarization of American politics.

. . . AND WHY DOES IT Matter?

How does the way we elect officials affect government policies? First, we can judge elections partly by how well they produce accountability. It is not entirely clear whether America's long and complex campaigns strengthen citizen control or weaken it. On the one hand, voters' participation in the nomination process through primaries or caucuses gives them greater influence than simply voting in elections. But on the other hand, weakening the parties by giving voters this power makes it less easy for parties to operate in a unified way and present themselves as "teams" for party accountability. We have seen that the key to accountability in congressional elections may be for parties to be accountable as teams. So it may be that providing more voter impact on the choice of individual candidates, at the expense of parties' organizational strength, actually lessens overall accountability.

We can also judge elections by their effect on public policies we care about. Many aspects of our elections—our system of nominating presidents (especially the emphasis on early primaries and caucuses), the SMDP system, and the Electoral College—lead politicians to emphasize the needs of pivotal states or districts, and distract them from broader social needs. Just as one example, presidential candidates generally feel a need to support subsidies for corn ethanol because of the many corn growers in Iowa, which is a pivotal state for nomination.

Candidates are led not only to focus on particular localities, but also, in another way, to focus on particular economic interests. The importance of money in our elections makes candidates dependent on those who contribute to their campaigns, and this often competes with the wishes of the voters as a whole.

All of these aspects of our electoral system—the Electoral College, the SMDP system, the long series of primaries and caucuses, and the importance of campaign funds—lead politicians away from attending to the broader needs of the population, motivating them to focus instead on narrow geographic or economic interests.

Looking just at electoral systems, this may be why countries with proportional representation tend to spend more on broad social security, health, and similar policies (by about 8 percent of their gross domestic product) than countries with SMDP systems do.[42] It is important to keep in mind, however, that the direction of causation is not entirely clear on this. It is at least possible that the difference comes about not because proportional representation leads to more social spending, but because countries where social spending is popular (Sweden, for instance) have been more likely to adopt proportional representation in the first place.

Accountability, and politicians' focus in policy making, provide two very strong reasons why elections matter.

critical thinking questions

1. Should the Electoral College be changed, and if so, in what way? How would you accomplish the changes you suggest, and what would be their effects?

2. How could American elections be changed to reduce the effect of large campaign contributions on officeholders' decisions? (Remember that any changes must be consistent with the Constitution's guarantees of free speech.)

3. It has been suggested that all states should hold their presidential primaries on the same day, rather than stretching out the nomination process over many months. How would this affect U.S. politics? Consider all of the varied effects of our current system—the nature of campaigning in early states, the effect on campaign costs, and so on.

4. Do you think individual accountability or party accountability is a better way for voters to hold Congress accountable? Why?

5. Are majority-minority districts a good thing for politics? Why or why not?

key terms

PARTICIPATION, VOTING
BEHAVIOR, AND CAMPAIGNS

- Define the different ways in which citizens can participate in the political process.
- Analyze the dynamics of voter turnout and explore its impact on the party system and political decision making.
- Summarize the key factors that influence people's voting decisions.
- Understand how campaigns influence citizens' choices, and examine the strategic decisions campaigns face.
- Evaluate the causes of party polarization and its impact on U.S. politics.

PERSPECTIVE
Why Is Voter Turnout Lower in the United States than in Many Countries?

The day after the 2008 presidential election, Americans celebrated the fact that the 62 percent turnout for the election was the highest in more than 20 years. By contrast, after their 2009 parliamentary election, Norwegians expressed deep concern that their turnout had been only 76 percent, down from their usual levels. Norwegians are used to a higher level of voter turnout than Americans are, and they are not alone in this. In the second half of the twentieth century, more than 100 countries experienced a higher average turnout in elections than did the United States.[1]

Turnout matters. The flip side of the relatively high turnout for the U.S. election in 2008 is that while 62 percent voted, fully 38 percent of Americans who were eligible to vote neglected to do so. And as we will see later in this chapter, that figure has real consequences for U.S. politics.

Figure 9.1 traces voter turnout for the United States and Norway over more than a century. As you can see, the low turnout rate in the United States is not a simple story. From the 1870s to 1900, turnout in the United States was in the 70 to 80 percent range, but then it dropped sharply over the next 20 years, settling in at a range of about 55 to 65 percent. Norway's path was just the opposite. Starting from Norway's first election in 1900, turnout grew steadily over about 40 years and settled into a range of 75 to 85 percent.

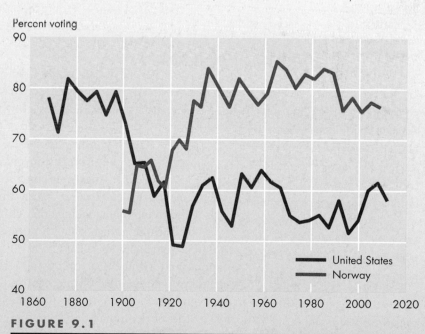

FIGURE 9.1

★ VOTER TURNOUT IN THE UNITED STATES AND NORWAY, 1860–2012

Source: Data from U.S. Census Bureau, Historical Statistics of the United States and Statistical Central Bureau, Statistics Norway.

It is not that Americans are less interested in politics than Norwegians are. In surveys, Americans are a bit more likely than Norwegians to report that politics is important in their lives (55 percent in the United States, 52 percent in Norway).[2] People in the two countries appear to be fairly evenly matched when it comes to political interest.

Instead, the discrepancy in voter turnout between the United States and Norway suggests a more complex story. What caused turnout in the United States to drop, just as turnout was rising in Norway? Since general interest in politics is comparable in the two countries, we must look to other factors to explain this puzzle.

IN THIS CHAPTER, we examine how Americans participate in politics and what impact this has on our democratic system. First, we explore various types of political participation—both conventional and unconventional. Then we grapple with the puzzle of low voter turnout in the United States and analyze why turnout declined in the last century. Next, we look specifically at which demographic groups are more likely to vote and what factors affect voters' decisions. We also evaluate how election campaigns are organized to take advantage of the factors that are known to have the greatest influence on voters' decisions. Finally, we discover how election campaigns have contributed in part to the growing party polarization in this country. As you read this chapter, keep in mind our two core questions:

WHY ARE WE THE WAY WE ARE?
WHY DOES IT MATTER TO YOU?

In particular, why do Americans vote in relatively small numbers, and why have they become increasingly polarized by party?

POLITICAL PARTICIPATION

KEY to understanding

★

Citizens can take part in politics through unconventional participation such as demonstrations, or through conventional participation like voting. Both types of activities play important roles in political systems—whether they are democracies or authoritarian forms of government. As you read this section, consider why Americans participate in the ways they do, both conventionally and unconventionally. What is the effect on politics of the mix of types of participation in the United States?

political participation
All of the various ways that citizens can influence the government.

Voting is the most basic way citizens participate in democracies, but it is not the only way. We call citizens' varied political actions—all of the various ways that citizens attempt to exert influence on the government—**political participation.** It may be either unconventional or conventional.

People engage in **unconventional participation** when they seek to publicize a cause through dramatically confrontational behavior, often making other citizens uncomfortable in the process, or by disrupting the normal workings of government. Unconventional participation includes such acts as joining boycotts, attending demonstrations and sit-ins, and occupying government offices. In the twentieth century, Mahatma Gandhi popularized the use of civil disobedience in his campaign to rid India of its colonial rule. Gandhi's movement shamed Britain, advertising to the world India's desire for independence. In the 1960s, Dr. Martin Luther King, Jr., adopted these same techniques as a leader of the civil rights movement in the United States.

Conventional participation is routine behavior that occurs within the regularly instituted processes of democracy. People engage in conventional participation by voting in elections, working for a candidate or party, joining an interest group, contributing to a campaign or a political cause, displaying a bumper sticker on their cars, signing a petition, writing a letter to a member of Congress, or pursuing a constitutional case in the courts. Conventional participation is necessary for the proper functioning of a democracy, providing ordinary citizens with a voice in government.

UNCONVENTIONAL PARTICIPATION

Citizens resort to unconventional participation for two reasons: because normal democratic participation is closed to them, or because they believe unconventional tactics will be more effective than conventional ones. If citizens are barred from conventional participation in politics, they may use unconventional participation to draw attention to this failure of democracy. But even when conventional participation is freely available to them, they may choose to use unconventional participation as a tactic, simply because they believe they are more likely to influence events by unconventional participation than by conventional participation.

Unconventional Participation as a Necessity

In many nondemocratic countries, citizens participate unconventionally because such means are the only avenue open to them. After a disastrous earthquake in China in 2008, for instance, when children died because shoddily constructed schools collapsed, their parents took the step—unusual and risky under China's authoritarian government—of circulating a petition to ask the government to punish those who had built the schools. The government responded first by harassing the parents, then by threatening to put them in jail, and finally by offering them cash payments. The government eventually quieted the protest, but the protestors had made their point in the only way that was available to them.

In 2011, large demonstrations occurred in many countries across the Mideast and North Africa, as citizens tried to overturn nondemocratic regimes. The demonstrators prevailed in Egypt and Tunisia, but in other countries they were put down by brutal retaliation.

Sometimes, even in what are nominally democracies, large groups of people are shut off from the workings of the democratic process, and they may then turn to unconventional participation to make their voices heard. In the 1960s in the United States, African Americans were effectively barred from voting throughout most of the South, and the civil rights movement used unconventional participation—boycotts, demonstrations, and sit-ins—to build sympathy and force change. (The civil rights movement and its tactics are analyzed in detail in Chapter 10 as part of our discussion of social movements.)

unconventional participation
Behavior that challenges the normal workings of government by disrupting it or by making people uncomfortable.

conventional participation
Routine behavior that occurs within the formal governmental process of a democracy, such as voting in elections, working for a candidate or party, putting a bumper sticker on your car, or contacting a member of Congress.

★ Parents of children who died in the collapse of an elementary school during the 2008 earthquake in China march to demand an investigation of the school's collapse.

★ Facebook helped play a huge role in toppling non-democratic regimes in the Middle East in 2011. Pictured here is Arab Spring in Egypt.

Unconventional Participation as a Tactic

In a democracy like the United States, even if a group in the population has full access to the normal processes of democratic government, it may decide that it cannot marshal enough influence through those processes to win the change it is seeking. Groups with few financial resources or without an established organization may choose unconventional participation to publicize their cause in a way that does not require either. The demonstrations in the late 1960s against the Vietnam War, which contributed to the United States' withdrawal from that country in 1975, are an example of how unconventional participation can succeed in effecting policy change.

But unconventional participation has limitations. Unless a group can build sympathy by appealing to a basic value such as fairness or equality, it may simply generate a backlash by those who are made uncomfortable by the confrontation. Pro-life groups picketing Planned Parenthood clinics have not appeared to generate broader support for their position, for example. Angry faces berating young women entering the clinics have probably generated more negative backlash than positive responses from the general public.

The "Occupy Wall Street" demonstrations in 2011 took great pains to make sure that their members did not harass officials or engage in violence of any sort, because they were worried about provoking a backlash.

Unconventional participation is nothing new in American experience. The famous "Boston Tea Party," which helped to initiate the American Revolution, was an exercise in unconventional participation. During that incident, Bostonians threw crates of British tea into the harbor waters to protest favorable treatment for the British East India Company, which was undercutting colonial merchants. In 1863, during the Civil War, protests against the military draft by New Yorkers—mostly poor Irish immigrants—developed into six days of general riots that left more than 100 dead.

Americans have been at least as active in unconventional participation as citizens of other countries. In a study of 55 countries, Americans ranked fourth in frequency of joining boycotts and ranked near the middle (thirty-fourth) in their participation in peaceful demonstrations.[3]

CONVENTIONAL PARTICIPATION

Most participation in democracies is conventional. Table 9.1 shows how often Americans participated politically in various ways during the 2008 election.[4] Some people simply voted and did not participate in any other way, but many others went beyond that to try other ways of influencing the outcome of the election.

Participation that goes beyond voting appears to be increasing. While 10 percent of Americans displayed a button, bumper sticker, or sign in 2000, this number rose to 18 percent in 2008; and while 9 percent gave money to a campaign in 2000, this number climbed to 13 percent in 2008. These increases may be due in part to the influence of the Internet, which makes it very easy for people to communicate with others and to donate money to causes.

Compared with other countries, conventional forms of participation (other than voting) are relatively common in the United States. For instance, in the study of 55 countries that we referred to earlier, Americans ranked sixth in how often they signed petitions.[5] The big puzzle about Americans is their low voting turnout relative to other countries, given how active they are in other ways. Why do Americans, who established the first modern democracy, choose to exercise their voting rights less frequently than citizens of other countries? What factors affect voting decisions? It is to these issues that we now turn.

TABLE 9.1

conventional participation in the 2008 election

PERCENT OF ELIGIBLE VOTERS WHO . . .	
Voted in the 2008 election	62%
Tried to influence vote of others by talking to them	45%
Displayed a button, sticker, or sign	18%
Contributed money	13%
Attended a meeting, rally, speech, etc.	9%
Worked for a party or candidate	4%

Source: Data from U.S. Census Bureau

VOTER TURNOUT

Americans vote in smaller numbers than the citizens of many other countries, as shown in Figure 9.2.[6] Political scientists have no single explanation for why voter turnout is low in the United States, but they believe a variety of factors may play a role. Part of the explanation may be sought in the factors that caused voter turnout to drop so sharply in the early twentieth century. But part of the explanation also must be sought in conditions today that affect how likely citizens are to vote.

THE DECLINE OF VOTER TURNOUT IN THE TWENTIETH CENTURY

The right to vote was progressively extended to almost all adults during the nineteenth and twentieth centuries, but actual voter turnout declined significantly in the early twentieth century. As is often the case with groups that have newly received the right to vote, women did not fully exercise this right immediately after they won it in 1920. As late as the 1950s, women turned out to vote at rates that were about 10 percentage points behind those of men, and it was not until 1984 that women for the first time matched men's voting turnout.

This was probably one cause of the general decline of voter turnout in the twentieth century, but that decline was not just a matter of women having been added to the mix. The decline in turnout had actually started well before 1920.

A second partial cause for the general decline was the adoption of a number of devices by Southern states starting in the 1890s to discourage voting—among others, a "poll tax" that had to be paid in order to vote, primary elections that were restricted to whites, and special barriers to registration such as literacy tests. These devices were put in place to prevent African-American citizens from voting, but they tended to discourage voting by everyone. However, these special policies in the South are also not a complete explanation for the general drop in turnout, because the 1890 turnout also dropped outside the South, in states that had not implemented any of these devices to discourage voting. It did not drop as much elsewhere as it did in the South, but clearly something else was happening at the same time that led to decreased turnout.

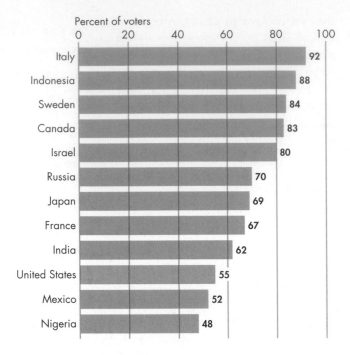

FIGURE 9.2

★ AVERAGE VOTER TURNOUT IN SELECTED COUNTRIES, 2009–2011

Note that the United States ranks near the bottom in voter turnout. Why do you think this is the case?

Source: Data from IDEA, (http://www.idea.int/vt/)

Finally, the introduction of the Australian ballot in the late nineteenth century may have played a role. (See Chapter 8 for an explanation of the Australian ballot.) The ballot was now secret, and parties could not oversee how their supporters voted. This may have decreased their efforts at mobilization, thus contributing to the drop in turnout.[7]

All of these were probably part of the cause, but political scientists still have not fully explained the early drop in voting turnout. We also wonder why turnout never recovered fully after its decline, but continues today at levels lower than in the nineteenth century and at lower levels than in many other countries. There are many puzzling aspects of voter turnout today.

For instance, as Figure 9.3 shows, the percentage of the population that is high school and college educated grew steadily after the Second World War, but this increase in education levels had no impact on turnout.[8] We would have expected it to raise turnout, because in general the more highly educated people are, the more likely they

FIGURE 9.3

★ TURNOUT AND THE RISE OF EDUCATION

As Americans became more highly educated, they did not participate at higher levels. How might you explain the fact that participation did not rise with increased education?

Source: Data from U.S. Census Bureau

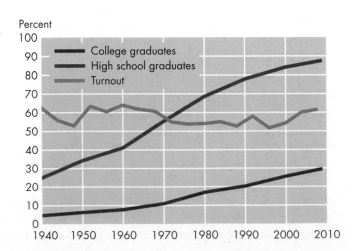

are to vote. (In the 2008 presidential election, 79 percent of college graduates voted, 55 percent of high school graduates did so, and only 39 percent of those with less than a high school education went to the polls.)[9] This puzzle is just one of many posed by the decline of voter turnout in the twentieth century.

The decline of voter turnout over the early twentieth century helps us to some extent to understand the current level of turnout, but it also leaves us with additional questions. What other factors affect voter turnout today?

CONVENIENCE AND MOTIVATION AS FACTORS AFFECTING TURNOUT

Why don't more people who are eligible to vote do so? Why is turnout lower in the United States than in countries like Indonesia and Israel, where more than 80 percent of eligible voters go to the polls? What brings people to the polls, or encourages them to stay home?

Convenience

One obstacle to voting is the difficulty of getting out to vote. Voting is easier in most countries than it is in the United States, which is part of the reason for the relatively low turnout in the United States shown in Figure 9.2. As you no doubt realize if you have voted, almost all states in the United States require prior **registration** by voters before they can vote, which is not the case in most countries. In most states this procedure must have been completed at least a few weeks before the election itself.[10] Thus not one, but two, actions are required to vote. In a study comparing the United States with 20 other democracies, all but a few of the other countries entered citizens automatically on the voting rolls, without requiring any extra action by the individual, in a process known as **automatic registration.** The study estimated that if the United States used automatic registration, it would have raised voting participation by about 14 percentage points.[11] This difference alone would have been enough to close much of the gap between the United States and Norway shown in Figure 9.1. On the other hand, in the nineteenth century the United States had Norway-like levels of voting turnout without automatic registration. So clearly other factors must be at work as well.

Another, probably more minor, inconvenience for American voters is that the Election Day always falls on a Tuesday, which means that many people who work during the day must either vote during their lunch break or before or after work. Most other countries hold their elections on a Sunday or declare Election Day a national holiday so that few people are working and it is more convenient for them to go to the polls. In recent years, a number of state governments have enacted early voting reforms that minimize the inconvenience of voting on a workday by allowing registered voters to cast their ballot by mail at any time they wish during the weeks leading up to the election. In 1992, only 7 percent of all votes were cast before Election Day, but this figure increased to 20 percent in 2004 and 30 percent in 2008.[12] The growth of early voting almost surely will help to raise levels of participation.

The complexity of the ballot creates an additional obstacle for American voters to overcome. We saw in Chapter 8 that United States

registration
A requirement by almost all states that citizens who wish to vote enroll prior to the election.

automatic registration
Enrollment of voters done by the government automatically, without requiring the individual to take any particular action to be eligible to vote.

★ Reasons for low voter turnout in the United States include complexity of the ballot and confusion about the mechanics of voting itself.

TABLE 9.2
offices on the ballot in one county, 2012

President
United States senator
Member of the U.S. House of Representatives
Governor
Secretary of State (West Virginia)
State attorney general
State treasurer
State auditor
State commissioner of agriculture
Member of the state Senate
Member of the state House of Delegates
Justice of the Supreme Court of Appeals
Circuit judge
County commissioner
Prosecuting attorney
Sheriff
Assessor
Magistrate
Surveyor
Conservation district supervisor
Member of the board of education

paradox of voting
The fact that one person's vote is highly unlikely to change the outcome of an election, so there is no concrete benefit for an individual who chooses to vote.

elections are typified by the "long ballot" with many offices open to election. Table 9.2 lists the number of offices for which voters in Marion County, West Virginia, had to choose their preferred candidate in 2012. In Great Britain, by contrast, in a national election voters face a ballot with just one office: member of the House of Commons. There is no other office elected in Britain, except for separate town and city elections for mayor and city council. The amount of information American voters must seek out and digest in order to make an educated choice during an election is undoubtedly a further deterrent to turnout.

Motivation

Aside from the question of whether voting is easy or difficult to do, people must want to vote in the first place. A famous paradox in political science, the **paradox of voting,** suggests that it should actually make no sense to vote. The argument goes like this: If a person is seeking to accomplish a policy goal by voting in a national election, the probability that his or her single vote will change the outcome of that election is so low as to be effectively zero. In order for the person to change policy by his or her vote, the election would have to be decided by a single vote—but in an election in which 100,000,000 votes are cast, the probability is near zero that the result will be exactly a tie except for that one vote. As psychologist B. F. Skinner once wrote, "The chance that one man's vote will decide the issue in a national election is less than the chance that he will be killed on his way to the polls. We pay no attention to chances of that magnitude in our daily affairs. We should call a man a fool who bought a sweepstakes ticket with similar odds against him."[13] This argument ultimately does not make sense, of course, since if everybody else followed the advice not to vote, the one person left voting would control everything. But it does leave open the reasonable question, why *do* people want to vote?

A few people only get out and vote if they think an election will be close. In 2004, for example, 78 percent of those who thought the election between George W. Bush and John Kerry was close turned out to vote, compared with a turnout of 74 percent among those who thought the election was not close.[14] This is why turnout in presidential elections is usually higher in close "battleground states" than in states that are safely in one candidate's column. In 2012, across the battleground states of Colorado, Florida, Iowa, Michigan, Nevada, New Hampshire, North Carolina, Ohio, Pennsylvania, Virginia, and Wisconsin, 65 percent of eligible citizens voted; in the rest of the states,

50 percent voted.[15] These are not huge differences, though. Why do so many people vote even when the election is not close and their vote cannot be the determining one? There must be something else that leads them to vote.

A much more important motivating factor is an individual's sense that voting is part of his or her role and duty as a citizen. It is this sense of civic responsibility that resolves the paradox of voting by suggesting that voters do not vote to benefit themselves as individuals, but because of a sense of obligation as a citizen and a member of the community to participate in elections. People feel fulfilled when they vote, similarly to how they feel when they volunteer in their communities. In fact, as we see in Figure 9.4, states that have high levels of volunteering have high voter turnout, and vice-versa.[16]

Each dot in the figure represents a state of the United States. Its vertical height in the chart indicates the percent of its population voting in the 2006 congressional election, while the dot's distance from the left indicates the percent of its population that volunteered in community organizations between 2005 and 2007.[17] For instance, Kansas, with a volunteer rate of 36.2 percent and voting turnout in the congressional election of 40.9 percent, is located 36.2 units across the graph from left to right, and up 40.9 units from the bottom. Its dot is circled on the graph. Most states whose citizens volunteered at high rates also had a high turnout in the election.

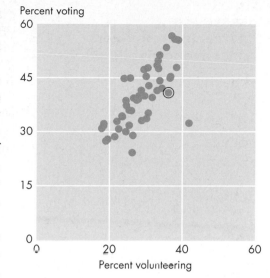

FIGURE 9.4

★ VOLUNTEERING AND TURNOUT IN STATES

States (the blue dots in the figure) with high levels of volunteering also have high voter turnout.

Source: Data from U.S. Census Bureau, (http://www.census.gov/hhes/www/socdemo/voting/publications/p20/2010/tables.htm)

WHO VOTES?

Different groups in the population are affected differently by the factors that make people more or less likely to vote. In this section, we look specifically at the relationship between voting and age, voting and ethnic identification, and voting and socioeconomic status.

Age

Young voters participate less in American elections than older voters. Figure 9.5 shows how different age groups voted in the 2010 election.[18]

Voting participation only reaches its full stride when Americans are in their fifties or sixties. After that age, it grows slowly until advanced old age, when it declines because of general frailty and increased difficulty in getting to the polls. Lower participation by younger citizens has been fairly constant over the period in which polling allows us to examine it. In 1948 the youngest group of potential voters was a full 20 percentage points behind the next age group, and similar differences have held in almost every election since then.[19] In almost every democracy in the world young people participate less than older people. The United States is not alone in this.

A likely explanation for the lower participation of younger people is that they do not appear to engage fully in their role as citizens until they are older. In 2008, different age groups were asked whether they follow politics and public affairs "most of the time."[20] As we see from Table 9.3, the percentage that were attentive to public affairs increased with age.

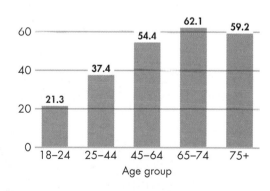

FIGURE 9.5

★ VOTER TURNOUT AND AGE, 2010

What might account for the lower turnout of young voters?

Source: U.S. Census Bureau, Current Population Statistics.

TABLE 9.3

percentage of voters attentive to public affairs

Under 18	14%
18–33	25%
34–49	32%
50–65	38%
Over 65	29%

FIGURE 9.6

★ VOTER TURNOUT AMONG MAJOR ETHNIC GROUPS

Source: U.S. Census Bureau, (http://www.census.gov/hhes/www/socdemo/voting/publications/p20/2010/tables.htm)

TABLE 9.4

voting turnout by income level, 2010 midterm elections

Income under $20,000	30% voted
$20,000 to $49,999	44% voted
$50,000 to $99,999	54% voted
Income over $100,000	61% voted

Like the relationship between age and voting, this age-based relationship has also been constant for as long as it has been measured.

Major efforts to increase participation by young voters had some success in the 2008 presidential election. For instance, the New Voters Project, associated with the Student Public Interest Research Groups (PIRGs), used a combination of door knocking and phone calls to register students to vote, and then to remind them on Election Day to get to the polls. On the average, in precincts they targeted, they increased young voter turnout by 157 percent.[21]

Ethnicity

Asians, Hispanics and African Americans do not vote as regularly as non-Hispanic whites. (Figure 9.6 shows the general voter turnout among different ethnic groups.)[22] The reasons for this pattern are unclear. Their lower participation may result from the difficulty of voting in minority neighborhoods, lower education levels, or the absence of specific organizations to mobilize them politically. African Americans have the highest turnout of the minority ethnic groups; in the 2008 election, in fact, they turned out to vote at higher levels even than whites. Barack Obama's candidacy meant that in that election there was a mobilizing organization with a special appeal to African-American voters.

Income

People of different income levels also vary markedly in their propensity to vote. The higher an individual's income, the more likely he or she is to vote, as Table 9.4 indicates.[23] As was true of age and ethnicity, differences like these have held consistently for as long as they have been measured.

In many countries of the world, there is not as great a difference between how much people of different income levels vote as there is in the United States. As we see in Table 9.5, the differences are much less in France, Italy, and India.[24]

In all three countries, there is at least one political party that represents the interests of the poor more explicitly than either party does in the United States, making special efforts to mobilize them and get them to the polls.[25] This shows up in a much lower difference between turnout of the well-off and the poor in these countries than in the United States. Additionally, voting is compulsory in Italy, which further helps to decrease differences in turnout between different groups.[26] These countries show that it is possible to reduce the gap between high and low income groups.

WHAT DIFFERENCE DOES IT MAKE WHO VOTES?

One reason nonvoting is a serious problem for democracy is that when different groups participate at different rates, the outcome of the election no longer mirrors the overall population's interests accurately. Although an individual voter does not change the outcome of an election, when a *group* of people with shared interests do not vote as much as other groups, the impact of their individual decisions not to vote is multiplied by the number of members in the group. Group differences in participation can change the election outcome, and as a result, political officials will probably not consider all groups in the population equally when they frame policies. They are more likely to pay attention to those groups whose members vote regularly—those on whom their jobs depend.

Since older, well-off white citizens are more likely to vote than those who are young, poor, and/or members of minority groups, most public officials who wish to be reelected are especially attentive to their needs. It is surely no coincidence that Social Security is one of the hardest programs to change in American politics. In 2010 citizens over 65 made up 24 percent of those who actually voted, though they made up only 18 percent of eligible voters.[27] Similarly, the fact that those with incomes under $20,000 a year in 2010 made up only 6 percent of those who voted, although they were 10 percent of those eligible to vote, probably makes it more difficult for Congress to pass legislation that would help poor people.

The group differences we have seen here pose a recurring problem for the Democratic Party. Because Democratic supporters tend to be poor and members of ethnic minorities, in general they are less likely to vote than supporters of the Republican Party. In the 2008 election, 86 percent who said they identified with the Republican Party reported voting, but only 78 percent of those who said they identified with the Democratic Party did so.[28] These differences in turnout by their supporters make it harder for Democratic Party candidates to win elections.

TABLE 9.5
differences in income and voting turnout

	PERCENT VOTING, OF THE POOREST 20% OF THE POPULATION	PERCENT VOTING, OF THE RICHEST 20% OF THE POPULATION	DIFFERENCE
France	73	84	11
Italy	86	92	6
India	57	47	−10
United States	55	83	28

TURNOUT IN CONGRESSIONAL ELECTIONS

Because presidential elections involve a longer and more intense campaign and the single most powerful governmental office in the United States, there is almost always higher turnout for presidential elections than for so-called **"midterm" elections.** Presidents are elected every four years, but members of the House of Representatives are elected every two years. Senators serve six-year terms and are not all elected in the same year, so every two years one-third of senate seats are up for election. In between presidential elections, therefore, there is always a midterm election at which voters choose members of the House of Representatives, a third of the senators, and a number of state officials.

Without the greater visibility of presidential candidates on the ballot, turnout drops in midterm elections as compared with presidential elections. Over time, this produces a "sawtooth" pattern in turnout, as shown in Figure 9.7.[29]

Because many presidential-year voters drop out two years later, those who vote in the off-year are different from those who vote in the presidential election. First of all,

midterm election
Elections held two years after a presidential election, in which all members of the House of Representatives and one-third of Senators are elected, and many states hold elections for governor and other state offices.

Percent of voting-age population who voted

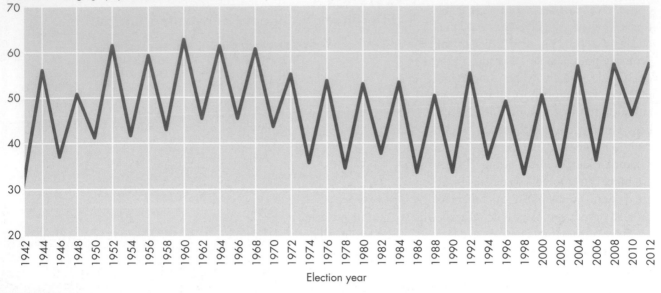

Election year

FIGURE 9.7

★ VOTER TURNOUT IN
PRESIDENTIAL AND
MIDTERM ELECTIONS

The graph shows turnout in
elections since 1942. With
such lower turnout in off-
year elections, do these
elections mean something
different from presidential
elections?

Source: U.S. Census Bureau, Statistical
Abstract of the United States.

referendum
A provision of elections allowing
citizens to vote directly on
constitutional amendments or
changes in law.

initiative
A procedure by which a sufficient
number of voters, by petition, can
place a proposition on the ballot to
be decided in a referendum.

they are less likely to be supporters of the president's party. In the 2008 presidential election, turnout was swollen by voters who were drawn to the winner, Barack Obama. This surge of support for the winner's party is true of any presidential election; with that candidate off the ballot two years later, the president's supporters lose their special motivation to vote and the president's party almost always loses some seats in the off-year election.

Also, any groups that are underrepresented among those who vote become even more underrepresented in the less exciting midterm elections. For instance, those who were under 45 years old dropped from being 42 percent of all voters in 2008 to 34 percent of all voters in 2010.[30]

VOTING IN REFERENDUMS

Up to this point we have looked at elections in which voters choose among candidates to decide who should hold office. As we saw in Chapter 7, however, during the Progressive era a number of states established provisions for citizens to vote directly on policies rather than just elect representatives to decide on policy. A **referendum** puts on the ballot a proposed policy or an amendment to the state's constitution. Voters vote "yes" or "no" on whether the proposal should become law. The **initiative** is a related reform. It allows a sufficient number of voters, by petition, to require that a proposal be voted on by the legislature or submitted to voters as a referendum.

A referendum places a large burden on the voter. As we will see in the next section, most Americans have limited information even about the positions candidates have taken on major issues in well-publicized presidential campaigns. A referendum demands even more effort on the part of the voter. Before each election, for instance, California's Secretary of State mails every voter a book listing the various propositions, analyzing them and giving arguments pro and con. How likely is it that voters who have demonstrated an inability to seek out and absorb presidential candidates' positions on issues will study this book well enough to be informed about the propositions they are voting on? In most election years one or two propositions get a great deal of publicity and are probably well understood by most voters. In 2012, for example, a referendum in North Carolina to define marriage as between one man and one woman generated broad interest. But most propositions involve narrow, sometimes technical questions that do not attract a great deal of news coverage or advertising.

Turnout in referendums is surprisingly high, considering the challenge they pose to voters. Of course, the voters are usually in the voting booth anyway to vote for candidates, but most of them also cast votes on all of the propositions on the ballot. In 2010, for instance, the lowest total vote for any proposition on the California ballot (on a proposition regarding legislative redistricting) was fully 90 percent of the number of votes cast for governor.

Most states in the United States use referendums from time to time; but only a few, like California, make it a regular and prominent procedure for law making. Internationally, only Switzerland and a few other countries use the referendum routinely for law making, but many countries use it occasionally on matters of great moment. In these cases, the question of whether or not voters are informed does not really arise because the issues are so important and widely publicized that all voters are probably very familiar with them. Spain, for instance, has used the referendum three times: in 1976, to approve the new constitution establishing Spain as a democracy; in 1986, on the question of whether to join the NATO military alliance with the United States; and in 2005, to approve the new constitution for the European Union. Since the United States has no provision for national referendums, this kind of referendum, on a dramatic national issue, has never happened.

HOW PEOPLE MAKE VOTING DECISIONS

So far we have looked at how citizens participate in politics in the United States and what factors affect whether they turn out to vote in elections. But how do they decide whom to vote for when they do vote? This is, after all, the determining event in democratic politics: citizens control policies and candidates through their use of the vote. Four factors shape voters' decisions when they vote: what they think personally of the candidates; how they view the state of the nation and the economy; the candidates' party; and policy issues. How they evaluate these things, however, is conditioned by their generally rather low level of knowledge about the candidates and issues.

KEY TO understanding ★

People decide how to cast their vote based partly on the characteristics and qualifications of the candidates; partly on how they view the state of the nation and the economy (voting against incumbents if times are bad); partly on party; and partly on policy issues. Various groups in the population have traditional patterns of party support. What happens to the balance between parties when groups like Hispanics, which historically have had Democratic ties, increase in the population?

LOW LEVELS OF INFORMATION

Voters obviously cannot spend their entire lives gathering facts on which to make an intelligent choice, so we would expect them to base their decisions on information that is at least to some extent limited. However, by any standard, voters in the United States are under-informed—though voters in most other democracies are no better. A study conducted after the 2010 election showed that fewer than half knew the Republicans had won the House and the Democrats had won the Senate, and only three-quarters knew that the federal budget deficit was larger than it had been in the 1990s.

TABLE 9.6
percentage of voters accurately stating candidate's position

	CORRECT ANSWER (YES)	INCORRECT ANSWER (NO)	DON'T KNOW
Gore: favor free prescription drugs for the elderly?	58%	8%	36%
Bush: favor large cuts in income taxes?	52%	11%	37%

Only one-sixth knew that the majority of the government loans made to banks in 2009 had been repaid.[31] These facts had been widely presented in the media, yet they had eluded many voters.

Often even the most important policy positions of candidates do not penetrate deeply into the electorate's consciousness. In a study of the 2000 election, for instance, citizens were asked to identify where George W. Bush or Al Gore stood on the issue positions that had figured prominently in the campaign.[32] Even on the single most central issue for each candidate, as we see in Table 9.6, only a narrow majority of citizens were able to say correctly what the candidate stood for.[33]

Some voters are well informed, of course, but many are not. As a result, as we will see in the following sections, they must often make their decisions based on limited evidence.

THE CANDIDATES

Voters look for two main qualities when they choose a candidate for office. First, they consider how well the candidate can perform the job. Second, they seek a candidate who is honest.[34]

Voters judge competence from a candidate's track record when holding other positions, and also from how intelligent and well-informed the candidate appears to be in debates and interviews. Vice-presidential candidate Sarah Palin hurt her chances (and those of her running mate John McCain) in the 2008 campaign when she seemed to be uninformed about the issues during a televised interview with Katie Couric. It did not help when Saturday Night Live reproduced the interview verbatim, with Tina Fey playing Palin.

Honesty is not as easy to assess as performance, except in rare and dramatic instances where officials are caught committing illegal acts, as in the case of Representative William J. Jefferson (D-Louisiana). Jefferson was indicted in 2007 on charges of receiving bribes. Included in the evidence was a film showing him receiving a briefcase containing a $100,000 bribe, along with $90,000 that investigators found in his freezer. The indictment and the scandal led to his defeat in the next election.

Such cases *are* rare, however, and therefore voters need to assess a more normal version of honesty: not whether an official is corrupt

★ Comedian Tina Fey produced an eerily accurate caricature of Sarah Palin during the 2008 presidential election. She reinforced public doubts about Palin's competence, but Palin retained a substantial base of support among those who identified with her values.

and will take a bribe, but whether his or her word can be trusted. Such judgments can be difficult to make because there is usually not much evidence to go on, so voters look for indirect indicators of honesty. Designers of attack ads seek out inconsistencies in the candidate's past behavior or statements, which may suggest to voters a lack of integrity. In 2004, the chief Republican attack ad against presidential candidate John Kerry was a video of Kerry explaining his vote against support of the war in Iraq by saying, "I actually did vote for the $87 billion [in war funding] before I voted against it."

Other characteristics that can attract voters are a lively speaking style, a voice that carries well on radio and television, and the ability to connect with listeners and to project a feeling of empathy. In 2000, Vice President Al Gore came across as patronizing and rude when he sighed audibly several times during his debate with George W. Bush. In 2012, Mitt Romney had several gaffes suggesting he was out of touch with ordinary people, including offering in a debate to bet Rick Perry $10,000 in a disagreement about health insurance, and telling a group of unemployed workers "I'm unemployed too." Both men lost their elections.

In presidential elections, although we can point to occasional gaffes like these, the two candidates are usually quite well matched. The grueling series of primary elections candidates must survive mean that the eventual nominee almost has to be a superior candidate. How else would he or she have won dozens of primary races? It is precisely because the two candidates are usually evenly matched that small lapses can make a difference.

In races for House or Senate seats, or state and local government positions, the candidates often differ more noticeably in their appeal. One reason that many House members coast to reelection is that it is difficult for the challenging party to find a candidate with broad experience and proven performance to run successfully against the incumbent. Often a member of Congress is opposed by someone with only a limited background in public service, not enough to demonstrate to the voters an ability to perform the job well.

THE STATE OF THE NATION AND THE ECONOMY

If voters are satisfied with the state of the nation and believe the economy is doing well, they tend to reelect a sitting president or to vote for the nominee of a retiring president's party. Conversely, if they feel things are going badly, they punish the incumbent party by voting against the sitting president or the president's designated successor. The punishment or reward is most dramatic in the presidential race because voters view presidents more than any other elected official as responsible for the overall state of the nation and economy. Nevertheless, voter satisfaction influences their views of all candidates, including those running for state and local offices.

Two especially notable examples of economic voting were the elections of 2008 and 2012. In 2008, an unpopular war in Iraq, a severe economic downturn, and some instances of poor performance by the national government, such as lingering memories of the failure to bring relief to the victims of Hurricane Katrina in 2005, led to a wave of Democratic successes at all levels. Republicans lost the presidential race, lost 10 percent of their seats in the House of Representatives and lost 14 percent of their Senate seats. They lost seats in 33 state legislatures while gaining seats in only 8.

By 2010 the parties' positions had reversed. The Great Recession that started in 2007 had barely ended, and unemployment was still high. Since the Democrats controlled the White House and both houses of Congress, it was now their turn to be punished for

bad economic times. They lost 25 percent of their House seats and 10 percent of their Senate seats; in the states, they lost seats in 44 legislatures while gaining seats in only 2.

Economic well-being influences voters' choices more than any other issue except war. Political scientist Robert Erikson has estimated that an annual average change of 1 percent in people's disposable income over a president's four years results in an expected change in his party's vote at the next presidential election of 2.8 percentage points, a powerful effect.[35] Similarly strong effects of the state of the economy on elections have been observed in many other countries.[36]

Beyond the state of the economy, changes in any aspect of the quality of people's lives can help or hurt candidates. In fact, political scientists Christopher H. Achen and Larry M. Bartels have shown that voters punish incumbents if bad things happen, even if the government could not have done anything about them.[37] Achen and Bartels have investigated droughts and other such adverse events, including voter reaction to a rash of deadly shark attacks on the southern New Jersey coast in July 1916. In the presidential election that November, support for President Woodrow Wilson, who was running for reelection, dropped by about 3 percentage points in the coastal counties. The president could not have prevented the shark attacks, but he was nonetheless punished at the polls for them.

Voting behavior like this is called **retrospective voting.** Voters look back at the years an official has been in office and vote to reelect the official if their lives and the lives of those around them have gone well over those years. While voters may sometimes be moved by odd issues like shark attacks, by far the most important retrospective voting occurs when voters respond to national conditions such as wars or the state of the economy.

Retrospective voting helps to overcome one challenge democracies face. In a democracy, voters are supposed to choose candidates whose actions and policies will best

retrospective voting
Voting to reelect an official if your life and the lives of those around you have gone well over the years that the person has been in office; if not, voting to oust the official.

meet their needs. But we have seen that many voters are uninformed or wrongly informed about public issues and candidates' specific policy positions. Retrospective voting allows voters who may not be familiar with public policy debates to select candidates who serve them well. They may not know the candidates' economic proposals in detail, but they know how well-off they have been for the past four years. Retrospective voting is a blunt instrument, but it does allow even the most uninformed citizens to hold their government accountable.

PARTY IDENTIFICATION

As we saw in Chapter 6, many voters develop *party identification*, a sense of belonging to one of the political parties: "I am a Democrat," or "I am a Republican," or—for those who are not attached to a party—"I am an independent." Unlike candidate characteristics and the state of the nation, party identification does not vary greatly from election to election. Hence it has a stabilizing impact on voter choice.

It is true that party identification can change in response to events. Many African Americans changed their identification from Republican ("the party of Lincoln") to Democrat in the 1960s when the Democratic Party pushed through desegregation measures under Presidents Kennedy and Johnson. Identification can also shift by small amounts in response to less monumental events. From 2004 to 2008, for instance, the number of people identifying themselves as Democratic increased by a few percentage points in response to the unpopularity of the Bush administration. From 2008 to 2010 Democratic identification dropped back again in response to the state of the economy and the uproar over President Obama's health care plan.[38]

Overall, however, party identification tends to be stable. A person who is a Republican at age 30 is likely to be a Republican at age 50. Once people develop an identification with the Democratic or Republican Party, they begin to interpret events and evaluate candidates in a way that is consistent with that identity. For instance, by January 2006 about 80 percent of Republicans supported the war in Iraq that had been initiated by Republican George W. Bush. In contrast, only about 20 percent of Democrats did so, as party identification helped to shape voters' view of the war.[39] In this way, party identification is self-reinforcing. Attachment to the party leads a voter to adopt attitudes on issues and candidates that in turn strengthen further the voter's attachment to the party.

Partly as a result of this process of continual reinforcement, voters generally become stronger partisans as they grow older. We see in Figure 9.8 that as they get older, party identifiers steadily become more likely to describe themselves as identifying "strongly" with the party rather than identifying "weakly" with it.[40]

Party identification determines strongly how people vote. Look at how party identifiers and non-identifiers voted in 2012:

- 92 percent of Democratic identifiers voted for Barack Obama
- 45 percent of independents voted for Barack Obama
- 6 percent of Republican identifiers voted for Barack Obama

FIGURE 9.8

★ AGE AND STRENGTH OF PARTY IDENTIFICATION

The graph shows percentages of party identifiers of various ages who identify "strongly." What factors might lead partisans to strengthen their identification as they get older?

Source: Michael S. Lewis-Beck, William G. Jacoby, Helmut Norpoth, and Herbert F. Weisberg, *The American Voter Revisited* (Ann Arbor: University of Michigan Press, 2008), Table 7.6.

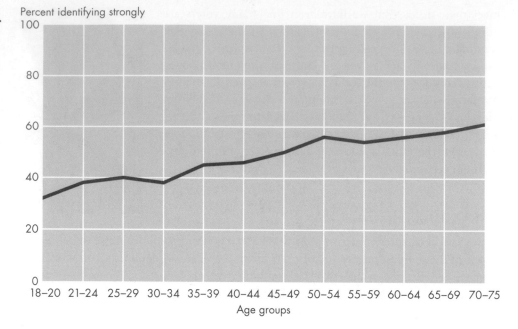

Percent identifying strongly

Age groups

The stability of voters' party identifications affects campaign strategies. Consider, for example, that in 2012 media pundits and the nominees' strategists were clearly able to identify early in the campaign "battleground states" such as Ohio and Nevada where the race would be close. They could also predict that other states such as Utah and Massachusetts would vote so one-sidedly for one party or the other that they could be safely ignored. The only reason they could make such predictions about the states was the voters' party identifications. Mitt Romney was new to the scene, never having been nominated for president before, and the state of the nation had changed in important ways since 2008. But because everyone knew that a state whose voters had voted heavily Democratic in 2008 was likely to vote heavily Democratic again in 2012, analysts could confidently predict which states would be close in 2012 and which would not.

Party identification adds structure to elections in another way that has profound effects on government. Because Republican identifiers are likely to vote for the Republican candidate for president, for members of Congress, for governor, and for local officials, the outcome of one race becomes closely tied to the outcomes of the others. As a result, all sorts of officeholders find that they have a stake in the success or failure of other officials from their party. As we saw in Chapter 7, these relationships provide a central party structure that strongly affects how the different parts of the government work with each other.

POLICY ISSUES

To a lesser extent than candidates' qualifications or party connection, particular policy issues such as lowering or raising taxes, abortion rights, gun control, or health care play some role

TABLE 9.7
Issues and Voting in 2012

(a) Keep abortion legal

	FAVORED	OPPOSED
% Voted for Obama	67	21
% Voted for Romney	31	77

(b) Keep or expand the 2010 health care law

	FAVORED	OPPOSED
% Voted for Obama	87	15
% Voted for Romney	11	83

(c) Offer illegal immigrants a chance to apply for citizenship

	FAVORED	OPPOSED
% Voted for Obama	61	24
% Voted for Romney	37	73

Source: Exit polls

in voters' decisions. It is true, as in Table 9.7, that voters' answers when they were asked about abortion, health care, or amnesty all affected their choices in the election.[41] Most who favored abortion, health care, or amnesty voted for Barack Obama. Most who opposed abortion, health care, or amnesty voted for Mitt Romney. However, plenty of voters chose a candidate who did not fit with their own preference on all issues.

The issue positions expressed by voters in Table 9.7 may be partly just a reflection of their party identification, so issues probably have even less direct effect on voters' choices than the table would suggest. In some ways the limited impact of issues on voting should not be a great surprise. We have seen that many voters are simply unaware of candidates' positions on issues. Further, one issue may cancel out another one. For instance, what is a voter to do if she favors restricting abortion (a Republican position) but also favors national health care (a Democratic position)? Unavoidably, she will have to vote for a candidate who disagrees with her on one of these two issues.

WHO VOTES FOR WHOM?

What do all of the factors involved in people's voting choice mean for different groups in the population? We know that because of their historical experiences, some groups have very distinctive party identifications. African Americans overwhelmingly identify themselves as Democrats, and Hispanics are also strongly pulled in that direction.

Also, candidates often have personal attributes that allow them to appeal to specific groups in the population. George W. Bush, a born-again Christian, had a special appeal for born-again Christians in 2000 and 2004. Barack Obama won a larger number of votes from African Americans in 2012 while receiving fewer votes than most Democratic candidates would usually have received from Southern whites.

picture YOURSELF ...

AS A VOTER IN ISRAEL

Israel has had full electoral democracy since its founding in 1948. With a proportional election system that can accommodate small political parties, it has a lot of parties. In the 2009 election, for example, you could choose among 31 different parties, of which 12 garnered enough votes to win seats in the Knesset (the parliament of Israel). As an Israeli citizen, you probably voted. Israel generally has a high turnout; its turnout of 65 percent in 2009 was unusually low. Turnout was lower among the Arab minority but still respectable.

Because Israel has a proportional representation electoral system, when you walked into the voting booth you did not vote to choose a particular candidate, nor a particular member of the Knesset to represent your locality. Instead, you simply voted for one of the parties. The more people who voted for a party, the more members that party would have in the Knesset.

Your choice of which party to vote for was largely determined by security issues and your ethnic group. The huge,

dominant issue in Israeli politics is security—how to relate to your country's Arab neighbors—and this issue was emphasized especially in the 2009 election because Israel had recently invaded the Gaza Strip in response to rockets fired into southern Israel by Hamas, the governing force in Gaza. Voters in Israel are so absorbed by questions of whether (and how) to pursue peace initiatives with their neighbors, what to do about Israeli outposts in neighboring Palestinian areas, and how to ensure that their armed forces are strong, that economic and social issues tend to play a less important role than they do in other countries.

Beyond that one big issue, politics is also occupied by sparring between different linguistic and ethnic groups within the population. Arabs, who comprise 20 percent of Israel's population and who divide themselves further as either Bedouin or Druze Arabs, vote primarily

for a few Arab parties. As for the Jewish population, some parties appeal especially to the large population of Russian immigrants, some appeal especially to North African immigrants, and some appeal especially to the older immigrant population from Europe.

Of course, other issues also play a role. Some parties appeal to strictly religious Jews and others to secular Jews. These groups conflict on social issues such as what public services should operate on the Sabbath. And to some extent economic issues also influence your party choice. But at the end of the day, the security issue and ethnic divisions dominate Israeli politics.

More than in most established democracies, the parties remain very fluid, and voting does not appear to be strongly anchored by party identification. For instance, the party that got the biggest share of the vote in the 2009 election was Kadima, a new centrist

party that did not even exist two elections ago. In its first election in 2006,
Gil—a new party devoted entirely to
the interests of retired people—won an
impressive 7 seats out of a total of 120
in the parliament.

To sum up, as an Israeli voter you
voted in an issue-rich election, with many
political parties to choose from. Your
vote was more strongly influenced by ethnic identity than by party identification.

questions to consider

1. **What would it be like to choose among 31 different parties, if our electoral system were like Israel's and we had perhaps a dozen significant parties vying for congressional seats?**

2. **What do you think electoral politics would be like in the United States if our elections were as dominated by security issues as they are in Israel? Since the terrorist attack on September 11, 2001, have elections in the United States had some of this character?**

Of those who showed up at the polls in 2012, different groups in the United States voted as shown in Figure 9.9.[42] Major sources of Obama's victory were non-whites, young voters, voters with low incomes, and of course, Democratic party identifiers. Two important contributing factors were the *gender gap*, with 55 percent of women voting for Obama compared with 45 percent of men, and the fact that 45 percent of independents voted for Obama. Education also played a role. Oddly, Obama drew support among those with the lowest and those with the highest levels of education, reflecting the fact that the Democratic Party pulls together a coalition of poor people and professionals.

The groups in the population among whom Democratic candidates have done well in recent years are mostly those whose numbers are increasing: racial and ethnic minorities and college-educated whites. In fact, if in 2012 these groups had been present in the population in the same proportions they were in 2000, the year that George W. Bush was first elected president, Barack Obama probably would have lost.[43] In a sense, demographic change defeated Mitt Romney in 2012.

That the Democrats' demographic bases of support are all growing poses a potential problem for the Republican Party. Non-Hispanic whites made up two-thirds of the population in 2012, but they are projected to shrink to about

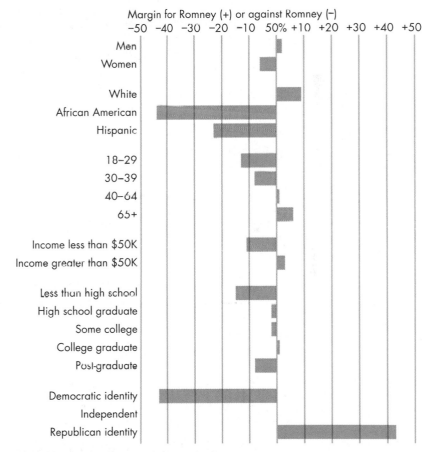

FIGURE 9.9

★ HOW VARIOUS GROUPS VOTED IN 2012

The bars show how far groups' votes exceeded or fell below 50 percent for the Republican candidate, Mitt Romney. A bar to the left indicates that a group voted against him, a bar to the right that they voted for him. Which groups differed most sharply from each other?

Source: Exit polls

half of the population by 2040. And the proportion of the population that has not graduated from college will continue to shrink as well.

Does this situation mean that the Republican Party is doomed? Hardly. The American two-party system has a way of keeping itself competitive. Over the last 150 years, neither the Democratic Party nor the Republican Party has ever received more than two-thirds of the two-party vote in a presidential election, and over that period the longest string of successive wins by one party in presidential elections has been five in a row.[44] Apparently, when one party becomes disadvantaged, either it tries harder or the party that is on top becomes complacent, and the tables turn. If history is a guide, it is likely that the demographic shifts of coming decades will not result in Democratic Party hegemony. But in order for this not to happen, the Republican Party will need to increase its support from among minorities and/or college-educated whites.

POLITICAL CAMPAIGNS AND THE VOTERS' CHOICES

political campaign
The period during which candidates try to convince voters to support them.

political consultant
Professional political strategist who advises candidates on broad strategy as well as specific logistics.

All of the factors that affect voters' choices come together in the **political campaign.** Campaigns are carefully designed by professional strategists, right down to what color of jacket a candidate should wear, what states should be contested or written off, and what social groups the candidate should reach out to. The **political consultant** is an expert who advises the candidate on all such matters. There are about 7,000 professional political consultants in the United States, and they sometimes acquire star power in their own right.[45]

A good example is Stuart Stevens, a Republican consultant who managed Mitt Romney's presidential campaign in 2012. He has worked for Republican gubernatorial candidates like Haley Barbour and Chris Christie, and has served as a media adviser to most Republican presidential candidates since 1996. He is known as a cocky, sharp-elbowed operator who enjoys the blood-sport aspect of politics, but he has much wider interests as well. He is a triathlon competitor, has skied the last 100 miles to the North Pole, and has written a book on fine restaurants in Europe. His general strategy with Romney was to bring out his candidate's natural strengths, which is why the campaign kept a relentless focus on Romney's business background and success as a manager. But his campaign experience allowed him to reach down even into specific tactics of timing—when Romney felt he needed to release his income tax returns, the campaign chose the day of Barack Obama's State of the Union speech, when reporters would be busy covering the president.[46]

TECHNOLOGY AND THE TOOLS OF THE CAMPAIGN

The technology available to consultants—and their candidates—has exploded in recent years. Tools available to campaigns include the following:

- polls
- focus groups
- television advertisements

- free media
- websites and social networking sites
- targeted marketing

Polls

Presidential candidates get daily tracking polls to follow every up-tick and down-tick of the campaign so that they can adjust quickly to shifts. (See the discussion of polling and public opinion surveys in Chapter 6.)

Focus Groups

A **focus group** is a small group of 10 or 20 people who discuss issues and the candidate in a meeting led and monitored by a professional from the campaign. They may be shown trial advertisements, for instance, to see how they react to them. Or the leader may just ask the participants what they like or dislike about the candidates. A focus group offers a nuanced and in-depth look at what voters think, what they are feeling, and what appeals to them.

focus group
A small group of people who meet with campaign workers to discuss issues and a candidate.

Television Advertisements

These are a basic workhorse for candidates and are also, because they cost so much, one of the great money-soaks of campaigns. Early in campaigns, candidates tend to use feel-good **"introduce" ads,** which attempt to familiarize voters with the candidate, who is often pictured surrounded by children and puppies, or—with sleeves carefully rolled up above the elbow—talking with voters.

Later in the campaign, candidates often spar back and forth with **attack ads** that try to portray the opponent in a bad light. These include more content on issues than the earlier ads, since in attack ads the candidates—and "independent" groups that back them—try to tag their opponents as supporting unpopular issue positions: "Representative Rascal *says* she will not raise your taxes, but she voted 20 times over the last 16 years to raise taxes." Attack ads are unpopular, probably because of the sarcastic tone they often adopt and their use of unfair, unflattering photographs of the opponent. In fact, however, they deal much more with political issues than other advertisements do.[47]

"introduce" ads
Upbeat television ads, usually appearing early in a campaign, that are designed to create a positive first impression of a candidate.

attack ads
Television ads criticizing the opponent, usually in terms of the opponent's positions on issues and his or her record in office.

Free Media

Specialized media consultants have developed many ways to get the public media to spread the word about a candidate, saving the candidate precious advertising dollars and possibly also adding credibility to the candidate's message. For instance, if an ad is controversial or clever, the ad itself may become a news story and be broadcast over and over for free, or it may go viral on YouTube. The famous "Swift-boat" ads of the 2004 presidential campaign falsely accusing Democratic presidential candidate John Kerry of lying about his military record were shown more often for free than as paid ads because of the controversy they generated.

Websites and Social Networking Sites

All campaigns now build and maintain elaborate websites. A website provides an incredibly efficient way to reach millions of people at once with a political message or

fundraising pitch. Barack Obama's 2008 campaign pioneered the use of Web technology, with a website that was compared favorably to Apple's website.[48] In January 2008 alone, Obama generated $32 million in new contributions, enrolling 224,000 donors who had never given to him before and setting a new monthly record for campaign donations. Websites also include chat rooms where supporters can compare notes and encourage one another, a sign-up page to recruit volunteers, daily blogs from campaign staff, and other features.

The possibilities for social networking on the Internet have also opened up new ways of reaching out to potential voters for campaigns. The 2012 Obama campaign had 12 million Twitter subscribers and 25 million followers on its Facebook page. Republicans, too, largely caught up with the new possibilities of the Internet in 2012, so both parties were fully engaged online.[49]

The advent of the Internet and multiple forms of social media such as Facebook and Twitter has significantly altered the way candidates run their campaigns. Because the Internet allows for anonymity, community, and immediacy, it has introduced a new kind of energy and creativity to campaigns, which was dramatically demonstrated during the YouTube presidential primary debates in 2007. Instead of responding to questions posed by reporters, candidates responded to questions on citizen-created YouTube videos. These debates were largely deemed the best, most revealing candidate debates that had been staged up to that time. They were not repeated in 2012, but YouTube clips figured prominently in the 2012 campaign.

The Internet has changed the overall nature of campaign discussion and expanded the mix of people involved. In addition to the regular media, an informal and mostly amateur universe of political blogs now keeps a running commentary on the campaign. Every statement a candidate makes is immediately fact-checked and analyzed by hundreds of political junkies. Before the days of YouTube, a candidate could misspeak or trip over a chair in Dallas without the incident having any impact beyond Dallas, but now, with viral media, that image will spread over the Internet and land on Facebook walls, in Twitter posts, or in text messages in a matter of seconds.

Targeted Marketing

targeted marketing
Using consumer research to divide voters into tiny segments based on a wide variety of indicators so that different messages can be sent to various groups of voters.

In 2004 the Republicans introduced a new technique into politics, **targeted marketing.** A technique that had been used for a decade in business, the process works like this:

1. Analyze public opinion surveys to see how groups of people with different patterns of consumption vote (research the model of car they own, the magazines they subscribe to, whether they have cable TV, and so on).

2. Gather voluminous, publicly available information about individuals in the electorate—the model of their car, their income, their magazine subscriptions, their street address, and so on.

3. Put the two together to predict how each citizen will vote. In 2008 the Republican Party had such a list, which included almost all households in the United States; with this list they could identify individually every voter who was likely to support a Republican candidate. By 2012 both parties were using the technique.

Before the advent of targeted marketing, a party that wanted to get its supporters out to vote would target neighborhoods where, because of past election returns, it knew it had a lot of supporters. But this strategy meant that the party would accidentally approach many of its opponents (who lived in neighborhoods that in general supported the party), and would miss many of its supporters (who lived in neighborhoods with lots of its opponents). Targeted marketing allows a party to go into all neighborhoods, even those where its opponents are strong, and target just its supporters in each location. Working from its list of potential supporters, a campaign can contact them on Election Day to make sure they vote.

In 2012 targeted marketing became even more effective with the development of online *retargeting*. Retargeting identifies Web-surfers interested in a candidate by the sites they click on, and then targets them for ads that follow them from site to site. For instance, if a person clicked on Mitt Romney's or Barack Obama's website, popup ads for that candidate appeared on the next sites the person went to, whether they were political sites or not.

THE FLOW OF FACTORS IN THE CAMPAIGN

The four factors that affect voters' choices—the candidates, the state of the nation and the economy, voters' party identification, and specific issues—play out somewhat differently over the course of the campaign.

The Candidates

Except for well-known incumbents, the candidates are often new. To raise their profile, candidates tend to start their campaigns with feel-good introduce ads to define themselves positively. At this stage, then, issues do not figure prominently in the campaign. Most of the attention that issues do receive comes in the lengthy and little-read **position papers** in which candidates detail their positions on various sets of issues. Later in the campaign, attack ads predominate, and since these usually include more information about issues, the end of the campaign is usually marked by more discussion of issues than the beginning.

position papers
Documents prepared by candidates describing in detail their stands on various issues.

State of the Nation and the Economy

These provide a basic context for the campaign, potentially posing problems for an incumbent and opportunities for a challenger throughout the campaign. Both candidates are likely to expend some effort in trying to shape or reshape people's impression of how things are going with the economy, but there are limits to what candidates can do to spin the voter's perception of economic conditions.

Party Identification

Similarly, there is not much candidates can do to affect voters' party identification. However, party identification helps to determine campaign strategies. A candidate in a district where most voters identify with the other party is likely to minimize his association with the party. His lawn signs, for instance, may not have any indication of party affiliation: "Representative Piffle—Fighting for You!" His opponent is likely to feature her party affiliation prominently: "Reelect Representative Whiffle to Ensure a Republican Majority!"

The outcome of a campaign often will hinge on the ebb and flow of these factors that shape voter choice, due at least in part to how successful the candidates have been in manipulating them. In 2012, for instance, party identification helped Barack Obama. Democratic party identifiers led Republicans by about 7 percentage points, although Obama's advantage in party identifications was partly balanced by the fact that Republicans usually are more likely to vote than Democrats.

The economy was a huge problem for Obama. By 2012 there were finally signs that the Great Recession was easing, but the recovery was slow. Accordingly, the Romney campaign focused sharply on the economy, asking voters to consider whether they were better off now than they had been in 2008. The Obama campaign tried to shift the focus away from the economy by emphasizing a new specific issue—women's reproductive rights—and by asking voters to focus on the two candidates. Obama had an advantage in candidate evaluations partly because he was well-liked, and partly because Romney was not widely known before the start of the campaign, which made it easier to paint a picture of him for the voters. Romney had had to pull back sharply for the general election from very conservative positions he had adopted during his fight for the Republican nomination, and this allowed Obama's campaign to paint him as untrustworthy. They also added attacks on his record as a businessman, claiming that he had unfeelingly closed factories and fired workers. In the end, the election turned primarily on the state of the economy, and on voters' evaluations of the candidates.

ELECTORAL MOBILIZATION VERSUS CHANGING MINDS

We have dealt with two aspects of voting in this chapter, and campaigns have to deal with both of them: voter turnout (whether potential voters get to the polls at all), and the choices voters make once they are ready to cast their vote. Two broad strategies are available to a campaign: it may try to change the minds of those who support the other candidate, and/or it may rely on **electoral mobilization** of its own supporters—making sure they actually get out and vote.

electoral mobilization
An election strategy that relies on getting a candidate's supporters to the polls.

Some campaign tools are more useful for one of these strategies than for the other. For instance, television ads and political debates are effective for changing people's minds because an ad or a candidate's arguments in the debate can be persuasive. They are poor devices for mobilizing a candidate's supporters, however, because the entire television audience sees the ad or debate; a candidate's supporters see it and are presumably motivated to vote, but so are the opponent's supporters.

By contrast, targeted marketing is a great tool for mobilization but not a tool for changing minds; its whole point is to focus on a candidate's supporters. Similarly, the Internet allows the campaign to mobilize its supporters by writing instantaneously to a list of email addresses consisting only of supporters or likely supporters, and Google can allow a candidate's ad to follow a voter from site to site, based on the voter's searches.

Over the years the relative weight that campaigns have placed on mobilization versus changing voters' minds has changed more than once. From 1864 up to approximately the 1950s, most elections were determined not by voters shifting from one party to another but by one party being more successful than the other at getting its supporters out to vote. From the 1950s until very recently, most elections were determined primarily by voters switching their support between one election and the next.[50] But since about 2000, the tide seems to have partially turned, with parties' success at mobilization once again becoming part of a winning strategy.

For instance, in North Carolina in 2008, the centerpiece of the Obama campaign was a huge drive to register African Americans. The goal was to increase the percentage of African Americans who were registered voters from 19 percent of the electorate, which it had been in 2004, to 23 percent, and then to get them to the polls on Election Day. The campaign calculated that if Obama raised the African-American proportion of the vote to 23 percent and gained the votes of 35 percent of white voters, he would carry North Carolina. To accomplish these twin goals, he employed approximately 150 campaign workers in the state.[51] In the end, the campaign met both goals exactly: 23 percent of voters in North Carolina were African Americans in 2008, and Obama got exactly 35 percent of the white vote.[52] True to his campaign's strategic prediction, Obama narrowly carried the state.

It is likely that changing technology has had much to do with the renewed emphasis on mobilization in recent elections. The emphasis on changing voters' minds from the 1950s to the 1990s was probably due to the arrival of television, which first began to figure in presidential elections in the 1950s, and to presidential debates, which were first held in 1960. In the 1990s, however, cable television arrived with its more specialized channels, which allow a party to target particular kinds of voters, and the Internet also developed. Targeted marketing was first used in 2004. At about this time campaign strategy shifted back toward mobilization.

Whatever its cause, the shift to a greater reliance on mobilization is significant because these two strategies correspond to differing approaches to politics. When candidates are trying to change voters' minds, they focus on the voters who are in the middle and are uncertain which of the two candidates to support, because these are the easiest voters to convince. This means that the candidate must aim for the moderate center of public opinion. However, when the strategy is to get your supporters out to vote, that means the candidate must excite supporters. This strategy requires a partisan, not a moderate, approach. So the renewed emphasis on mobilization has probably helped to encourage a more partisan, less centrist form of politics. This may be one contributing factor in the heightened partisan tone of politics that we examine in the next section.

party polarization
Increased feelings among partisans that their party is right and the other is wrong.

PARTY POLARIZATION AMONG VOTERS

Starting roughly in the late 1970s, American voters have become increasingly divided by **party polarization**.[53] That is, those who identify with each party have felt more strongly that their party is right and the other is wrong, and those party identifiers have voted increasingly along straight party lines. As you see in Figure 9.10, the average percentage of Democrats or Republicans willing to vote for the other party's presidential candidate has decreased gradually from 19 percent in 1964 to 9 percent in 2008.[54]

Democrats and Republicans have also become more ideologically distinct over this period, with Democrats more consistently liberal and Republicans more consistently conservative. Republicans are increasingly likely to describe themselves as "conservative" and Democrats increasingly unlikely to do so, as shown in Figure 9.11.[55]

KEY TO understanding ★

Parties have become more polarized in recent decades, partly because many conservatives have left the Democratic Party while liberals have left the Republican Party, and partly because Americans increasingly isolate themselves in communities where they rarely meet people with political views opposed to theirs. As you read this section, consider the effects of polarization on American politics. Is it bad for voters to be polarized? Are there any possible advantages?

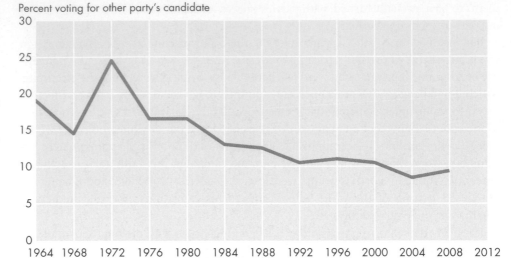

Percent voting for other party's candidate

FIGURE 9.10

★ VOTING FOR THE OTHER PARTY

Fewer voters select the other party's candidate today than in the past. What might be the effect on politics of this decline?

Source: Data from National Election Studies, Guide to Public Opinion, (http://www.electionstudies.org/nesguide/nesguide.htm)

Party polarization promotes bad feelings about the candidates and those serving in government. Survey respondents' average ratings of presidential candidates on a scale of 0 to 100 have declined fairly steadily from an average rating of 62 in 1976 to 55 in 2008, and almost all of this decline has resulted from partisans thinking less of the opposing party's candidate.[56] Party polarization accentuates negative aspect of the opposing candidate. And most importantly, party polarization makes it difficult for officials to compromise with each other.

On the other hand, strong partisan feelings also appear to energize the electorate and make them more engaged in politics. We see in Figure 9.12 a sharp increase from 1976 to 2008 in the percent of voters who say they care a lot who wins the presidential election.[57] This increase follows closely the growth of party polarization. The increase in voting turnout in 2004 and 2008 that we saw for the United States in Figure 9.1 may have resulted partly from the passions aroused by party polarization.

What has caused the increased polarization along party lines in the United States over the last few decades? This is not the first time in American history that voters have been sharply polarized along party lines. From the Civil War until the 1930s, Americans were deeply divided by party. With the exception of occasional distractions like Teddy Roosevelt's third-party candidacy in the 1912 election, the country was deeply divided into "red" states (most of the Northeast and Midwest) and "blue" states (the South)—even more than it is today. In essence, voters refought the Civil War at every election. The South and several regions within northern states that had been sympathetic to the Confederacy (such as southern Indiana and parts of northeastern Pennsylvania) voted for the Democrats, while the rest of the country mostly voted for the Republicans.

As we saw in Chapter 7, however, this clear geographic division by party was shaken up by Roosevelt's New Deal realignment, which created an uneasy alliance of conservative white, segregationist Democrats from the South, liberal northern Democrats, and African

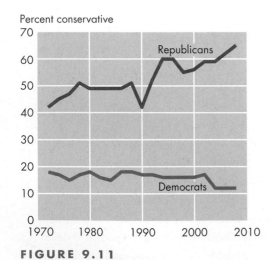

Percent conservative

FIGURE 9.11

★ PARTY AND IDEOLOGY

Democrats and Republicans have been drawing away from each other ideologically since 1970. Which party has shifted the most in ideology over this period?

Source: Data from National Election Studies, Guide to Public Opinion, (http://www.electionstudies.org/nesguide/nesguide.htm)

Americans—opposed by a basically northern and western Republican Party that was predominantly conservative but itself had a liberal minority. As a result of these alliances, the voters of the two major parties did not line up cleanly on opposite sides of important issues. Conservative southern Democrats actually agreed more with Republicans on issues than with their northern cousins, but they remained Democrats. And liberal Republicans often found that they shared many interests with Democrats, although they belonged to opposing parties. Consequently, the hostility between the parties diminished.

Party differences remained muted until the 1960s. When the Democratic Party began to advocate racial desegregation in the South, white Southerners began to move in large numbers from the Democratic to the Republican Party. At the same time, as conservatives began to dominate the Republican Party, many liberal northern Republicans left their party. These twin moves, which eliminated much of the ideological overlap between the parties, sharpened party polarization.

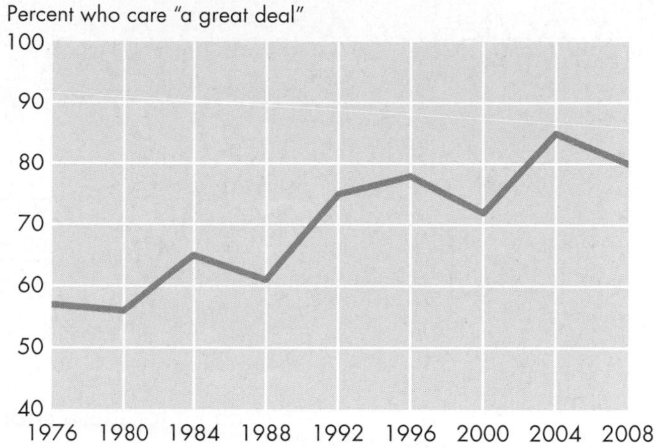

In addition to the reduction in ideological overlap, new patterns of residential migration seem also to have reinforced party polarization over the last several decades. Increasingly, when Americans move they relocate to communities where people share their lifestyle and often their broad beliefs about politics and society. Hip young people move to Seattle or to Cambridge, Massachusetts. Well-off retirees move to golf resorts. Others move to communities where they will find people who share their religious beliefs.

Communities have always been politically distinctive, but it appears that the increasing mobility of Americans has resulted in a population that is increasingly segregated in terms of values. In the very close presidential race in 1976, for instance, only 27 percent of Americans lived in "landslide" counties that Jimmy Carter either won or lost by more than 20 percentage points. But by 2000, in a similarly close presidential election, 43 percent lived in "landslide" counties.[58]

Thus it appears that the rise of party polarization in recent decades is not so much a new development in American politics as it is a return to a normal state of affairs that was interrupted for 60 years or so by the unstable, moderating coalitions that followed the New Deal. And, it appears to have been further reinforced by the increasing homogenization of our communities.

Percent who care "a great deal"

FIGURE 9.12

★ INCREASINGLY, VOTERS CARE WHO WINS

The flip side of polarization is that Americans are more engaged in elections. Is our greater engagement worth the polarization that seems to have caused it?

Source: Data from National Election Studies, Guide to Public Opinion, (http://www.electionstudies.org/nesguide/nesguide.htm)

Why Are We
THE WAY WE ARE?

American voters do not turn out to vote as much as citizens do in most democracies, and since this is particularly true of poor Americans, there is a significant difference between the turnout of the poor and the well-off. As to *how* they vote, Americans' voting decisions are particularly influenced by their party identification and by the state of the nation and the economy. How can we account for these characteristics of America's voters?

LOW VOTER TURNOUT

As we saw at the beginning of the chapter, voter turnout in the United States was once as high as it is in Norway today, but in the early twentieth century it dropped substantially and eventually settled at a level 10 to 15 percentage points below the normal turnout rate in Norway. How did such a difference arise?

Americans' low turnout is not due to a lack of interest. They are just as interested as Norwegians or citizens of other countries, and they rank highly in forms of participation other than voting.

So what *does* cause it? Our low voter turnout probably has multiple causes. First of all, our national institutions are more complex than those of many countries. Because the U. S. Constitution divides power between the president, House of Representatives, and Senate, voters have to vote for up to three offices at every presidential election. Add to these the many offices that would be appointed

in other countries but are elected in the United States, such as judge, county commissioner, and even the members of a university's board of regents, and the American voter is often faced with a daunting ballot. Further, administration of elections was constitutionally delegated to the states, and therefore rules inevitably vary from one place to another. Finally, with prior registration required in many states and voting occurring on a weekday rather than on a weekend or holiday, our system works in many ways to make voting difficult.

LOWER TURNOUT AMONG THE POOR THAN THE WELL-OFF

Why is there greater inequality of participation between the poor and the well-off in the United States than in most countries? One reason may be that there is not a party in the United States that distinctly serves the interests of the poor and tries to mobilize them for elections. Another cause, however, is that all of the difficulties of voting that explain low turnout in general have an even greater effect on the poor. Complex elections that force the voter to gather information about many candidates are especially difficult for those with less education. And inconvenient elections, with requirements for prior registration and voting on a workday, are more difficult for those working two jobs than for those who are retired or working one job. Simply eliminating separate registration might eliminate a large part of the difference in turnout between the poor and the well-off.

PARTY IDENTIFICATION

Another notable feature of American voting behavior is the importance of party identification in shaping the way many voters interpret news and political campaigns and in determining how they vote. Voters in many other countries also rely on party identification in their voting, of course, but this is not true everywhere. As we saw in the "Picture Yourself . . ." box, for instance, Israelis do not rely on party identification to determine their voting behavior as much as Americans do, possibly because the security issue dominates all choices in Israeli elections.

Why is party identification so strong in America? In part, generations of citizens have had time to develop strong partisan identities because the United States has had a stable democracy for centuries. Further, our single-member-district electoral system, which makes it difficult for new parties to displace older ones (see Chapter 8), has helped to ensure that voters are faced repeatedly with the same parties, with which they can gradually form an identification. And finally, the many offices that are generally up for election also probably help to build voters' party identification. With up to 20 choices on a ballot, many involving little-known figures, voters may feel they need some help in sorting through all of the choices. If voters identify with one or the other of the parties, the political party designation opposite a candidate's name gives them a helpful cue, so over the years they may develop the habit of relying on parties for guidance.

STATE OF THE NATION AND THE ECONOMY

American voters are no different from voters in most countries in basing their vote to a large extent on the state of the nation and how the economy is doing. This seems to be almost universal in democracies, although the degree to which voters use this to decide their vote varies by how much they believe the government can actually do about the economy.[59] Probably voters depend on retrospective voting like this because information on specific issues is often difficult to come by and is difficult for them to process.

. . . AND WHY DOES IT Matter?

We would expect that since the turnout of some groups is low, political leaders would not take their preferences into account as much as groups that do turn out to vote. In other words, we can expect inequality in participation to translate into inequality in policies. A study by Martin Gilens provides some evidence that this is true.[60]

Gilens shows that when poor people and the affluent differ in their views on policy, government policies tend to fit the views of the affluent more closely than those of the poor. Now, this obviously may not be just because of the low turnout of poor people on Election Day. The affluent affect policy in many ways, such as contributing to campaigns; and officials may share the world view of the affluent more than the world view of the poor. But elected officials' responsiveness to the affluent does suggest strongly that failing to vote hurts the poor.

In Gilens' study the greater participation of the affluent sometimes made policy more conservative than it would have been if it reflected the views of the poor. For instance, the poor were more willing to see increases in income taxes than in gasoline taxes, because they do not pay much income tax but gasoline represents a major part of their budget. The affluent were more interested in seeing a cut in income taxes and were willing to see gasoline taxes rise. What happened? The government cut income taxes and increased gasoline taxes.

On social and religious issues, however, the government's responsiveness to the affluent made policy more liberal. The affluent were more likely than the poor to support liberal abortion policy, stem cell research, and bans on school prayer. And during the period of the study, federal policy tended to support all of these positions.

The way government responds to different groups in the population provides a strong reason to make sure that you, and those who agree with you, vote.

critical thinking questions

1. What roles do conventional and unconventional participation play in a democratic society?

2. A number of countries make voting mandatory. For instance, a number of years ago Australia made nonvoting a misdemeanor, issuing a ticket comparable to that for a traffic violation for failing to vote. Generally, mandatory voting increases turnout sharply—in Australia, turnout rose immediately from under 60 percent to 91 percent. Would mandatory voting be a good solution for the low turnout in American elections? What would be its possible drawbacks?

3. How does party polarization benefit and harm American politics?

4. Does retrospective voting provide a good corrective to the problem of ill-informed voters? Explain your answer.

key terms

attack ads, *319*

automatic registration, *303*

conventional participation, *299*

electoral mobilization, *322*

focus group, *319*

initiative, *308*

"introduce" ads, *319*

midterm election, *307*

paradox of voting, *304*

party polarization, *323*

political campaign, *318*

political consultant, *318*

political participation, *298*

position papers, *321*

referendum, *308*

registration, *303*

retrospective voting, *312*

targeted marketing, *320*

unconventional participation, *298*

INTEREST GROUPS

- Differentiate between interest groups and political parties, and understand the role each type of group plays in American politics.
- Describe the key historical events that led to the development of national interest groups, and identify the factors that contributed to their rise.
- Explain how the problem of free riders can complicate an interest group's efforts to organize, recruit, and maintain membership.
- Identify the types of resources interest groups use to influence policy and explain how the availability of each resource can determine a group's tactical decision making.
- Describe the two broad categories of tactics that interest groups employ to influence officials, as well as what makes each set of tactics effective or ineffective.
- Identify the factors that determine whether an interest group will succeed or fail in accomplishing its policy goals.
- Examine the issues that affect how accurately and equally interest groups represent the concerns of all segments of American society.
- Understand the roots of interest group reform and examine whether such efforts can effectively transform interest group behavior.
- Define the social movement and discuss what distinguishes it from other types of interest groups.

PERSPECTIVE
What Is the Value of a Well-Developed Interest Group System?

When the Obama administration proposed a national health plan in 2008 and 2009, organizations such as the American Association of Retired Persons (AARP), the American Medical Association (AMA), trade unions, and activist organizations like MoveOn.org fueled pressure to pass the plan. But as the proposals developed, groups representing the pharmaceutical industry, health insurance companies, and others questioned the proposal, and groups representing taxpayers pushed to prevent tax increases. A wide array of groups was involved in making final decisions on the bill.

Such is the way policy develops in the United States, where thousands of organizations advocate on behalf of groups in society. Even if many of these groups serve good purposes in the end, it is not pretty to see a large number of groups all pursuing their self-interests. Interest groups, often denigrated as "special interests," are unpopular in the United States, with people often commenting that Americans "have the best democracy money can buy." But what would American politics be without interest groups? Without interest groups, policy makers might never see the need for policy changes, and they might never learn how proposed changes will affect different groups of citizens. Interest groups are an important part of the political process, but they are largely absent in many poor countries. Consider, for example, the contrast between Bangladesh and the United States.

Bangladesh is a poor, densely populated country adjoining India in South Asia. It has a population of 158 million people (about half the population of the United States) squeezed into a land mass about the size of Iowa. Only half of adult Bangladeshis can read and write. Since Bangladesh gained its independence, its politics has been dominated by the army and two major political parties: the Awami League and the Bangladesh Nationalist Party. Control of the government has gone back and forth between the two parties, with intervals in which the army has seized control and governed by itself. The two parties devote most of their energy to settling old grudges and historical grievances, or to creating disadvantages for the other party through constitutional change. As a result, the parties offer few solutions to people's daily problems.

To deal with government or economic problems, especially in rural regions, Bangladeshis rely primarily on a patron who provides them with emergency help when needed and helps to intercede with the government on their behalf. In return, they offer their patron loyalty and support. The population consists of innumerable networks of this sort, some based on one or another of the parties, some based on families or alliances of families, and some based on rural villages and their leaders. These patron networks function in much the way big-city party machines did in the United States in the late nineteenth and early twentieth centuries; George Washington Plunkitt of Tammany Hall (see Chapter 7, pp. 233–234) would have felt at home in Bangladeshi politics.

Bangladeshis' reliance on these local networks makes it difficult to form national interest groups centered around a shared idea or occupation. As a result, interest groups are found almost solely among the one-quarter of the Bangladeshi population that live in large cities. These interest groups comprise mostly the urban elites who agitate to protect their own interests in government. The three strongest organized interests in all of Bangladesh are the Bangladesh Civil Service (Administration) Cadre Association, which represents highly ranked civil servants in the capital; the Bangladesh Supreme Court Bar Association, representing elite lawyers; and the army.[1] Aside from these, there are organizations representing businesses of Dhaka, the capital city; a variety of unions for workers in the cities; and foreign aid organizations that lobby the government. Many other possible interests are left unrepresented. For instance, there is not a well-organized interest group for agriculture, even though Bangladesh is a predominantly agricultural country.

What does this mean for the country? The political elite live in a world of their own, where the problems of the country's people rarely intrude. For instance, when a hurricane struck southwestern Bangladesh in June 2009, killing 200 people and leaving hundreds of thousands homeless, the prime minister never visited the site, nor did the government do much to help those who were affected. With no political organizations representing the rural populations of southwestern Bangladesh, the government felt free to ignore the problem.

IN THIS CHAPTER we examine interest groups in the United States, exploring how they use the resources available to them to accomplish their political goals. We look especially at whether all sorts of citizens are equally well represented by interest groups. We note that interest groups in the United States have become what they are today partly because of the general expansion of the U.S. government since the Second World War—an expansion that the United States shared with all highly developed economies. Partly too, decentralized and relatively non-programmatic political parties left a vacuum in American politics that interest groups have filled. By comparing the United States' system of interest groups to the rudimentary systems of countries like Bangladesh or the highly developed systems of countries like Denmark, one can see how a well-developed system of interest groups aids democracy and society. As you read this chapter, keep in mind our two core questions:

WHY ARE WE THE WAY WE ARE?
WHY DOES IT MATTER TO YOU?

In particular, how well do interest groups represent all interests and bring them to the government's attention?

INTEREST GROUPS IN AMERICAN POLITICS

Organized interest groups are necessary for politics. Without them, as we saw in looking at Bangladesh, the government might ignore the needs of many people. Americans have long been ambivalent about such groups, however. In 1787, James Madison wrote in *The Federalist No. 10* that the ability of interests to organize is the essence of freedom—but he also complained of the "mischief of factions." Today people often refer to interest groups as "pressure groups" or "special interests," reflecting the prevailing view that they are often too strident and that they pursue their own interests at the expense of the common good.

An **interest group** is a group of people who put forth a coordinated effort to influence the government's policies. This purpose distinguishes it from a political party, which aims primarily to determine who will hold office in government. Although political parties sometimes promote policies in order to get their candidates into office, and interest groups will often work to get representatives into office who are sympathetic to their policy proposals, the difference is one of emphasis. Parties' *central* concern is getting their candidates elected, and interest groups' *central* concern is achieving their policy objectives. This difference in emphasis leads to differences in what they do politically. Interest groups emphasize two broad activities: organizing and mobilizing supporters, and lobbying to persuade officials to enact a policy. We will look closely at each type of activity later in this chapter.

There are several distinct types of interest groups in the United States, as seen in Table 10.1.

CITIZEN GROUPS

Citizen groups are membership organizations open to all who agree with the policy goals of the organization. Since members are brought together by a shared idea rather than by a material interest, citizen groups tend to be ideological and idealistic. Examples include the environmental group Clean Water Action, which works to keep water

KEY TO understanding ★

The United States has a very diverse set of interest groups. Interest groups are distinct from political parties, but what exactly is an interest group? What role does an interest group play in American politics? Interest groups in America vary in number and type, and each has specific sets of resources available to it.

interest group
A group of people organized to influence government policies.

citizen group
A membership organization based on a shared set of policy goals; the group is open to all who agree with the policy goals of the organization.

TABLE 10.1
types of interest groups

- Citizen groups
- Corporations
- Labor unions
- Agricultural associations
- Professional associations
- Trade associations
- Governmental and nonprofit groups
- Foreign governments
- Social movements

in drinking supplies and in the environment clean and safe; National Right to Life, which works to limit or eliminate abortion; the National Council of La Raza (NCLR), which works to further the interests of Hispanic-Americans; and the National Rifle Association (NRA), which works to ensure that Americans may own guns with minimal restrictions.

CORPORATIONS

Corporations often operate directly in the political arena to help shape policy that will enhance their profits. Most large corporations have an official with a title like "Vice President for Public Affairs" who is responsible for coordinating the corporation's relations with government and trying to influence how laws and regulations are written. Over 750 corporations maintain special offices in Washington, D.C., to manage their relations with the government. Microsoft, for instance, has four vice-presidents or assistants in its home office who deal with government relations, and a staff of 24 in a special office in Washington, D.C.[2]

LABOR UNIONS

Most unions are active in elections and maintain political staff in Washington to represent them. Their goals are often broader than the goals of a corporation, embracing many issues such as health care, workplace safety, or tax policies that affect their members. Unions also lobby to protect and expand their ability to bargain collectively with employers. In 2011 unions around the country were forced into great activity to defend themselves when Republican governors and legislatures elected in 2010 tried to pass a number of laws making it more difficult to unionize workers. Wisconsin, in particular, saw huge demonstrations and sharp conflicts over the governor's proposal to make it illegal for public employees to bargain collectively through a union.

AGRICULTURAL ASSOCIATIONS

Agricultural associations are organizations either of farmers in general, or of particular kinds of farmers, such as the Southern Peanut Growers. They tend to focus fairly narrowly on issues important to their members' farming activities, such as trade policy, environmental regulations, and price supports. For instance, in 2010 the Corn Refiners Association (CRA) ran a major advertising campaign and lobbied the Food and Drug Administration to change the term "high fructose corn syrup" to "corn sugar." Since health concerns have been raised about high fructose corn syrup, the CRA thought consumers would be less put off by the new term.

agricultural association
An organization either of farmers in general, or of a particular kind of farmer.

professional association
An organization of members of a profession.

PROFESSIONAL ASSOCIATIONS

Professional associations are organizations of members of a profession, such as the American Medical Association (AMA) or the National Society of Accountants. They may lobby for benefits for their members or on behalf of issues in which their members are experts by virtue of their profession. For instance, the AMA lobbies to improve Medicare reimbursements to doctors, but also lobbies to influence how the government responds to epidemics. Even lobbyists are represented by a professional association, the American League of Lobbyists!

TRADE ASSOCIATIONS

Trade associations are organizations of businesses who share the same trade, such as Printing Industries of America or the National Automobile Dealers Association. There are also broader organizations that represent larger groups of businesses, such as the National Association of Manufacturers, which represents all manufacturing businesses, and the U.S. Chamber of Commerce, which represents all businesses of any sort. Where individual corporations generally work to influence narrow regulatory or tax issues that will make a specific difference to them, trade associations lobby on broader issues such as general tax policies or trade policies that affect all their members.

★ MoveOn.org supporters rally in California to support Wisconsin's public employee unions.

trade association
An organization of businesses who share the same trade.

OTHER GROUPS THAT LOBBY OFFICIALS

Some groups that do not represent a broad-based membership nonetheless maintain an active lobbying presence in Washington. Governmental and nonprofit institutions such as the armed forces, the Red Cross, and many universities maintain a lobbying presence to advance the interests of their offices. Also, foreign governments often hire Washington lobbying and public relations firms to represent their interests, set up contacts with members of Congress and the executive branch, and advise them on how to relate to the broad public.

SOCIAL MOVEMENTS

Social movements are informally organized, often temporary groups that spring up around an issue or an event. They usually emphasize demonstrations rather than regular lobbying. Examples include the many groups in the civil rights movement of the 1960s, the Tea Party movement, the Occupy Wall Street movement that sprang up in 2011, and local groups opposed to the construction of an airport or highway. A social movement is more a network of activists than an organization. Typically it consists of a number of people who engage in political activities such as demonstrations more or less spontaneously, and it has a number of competing leaders rather than a single structure with one leader.

social movement
An informally organized, often temporary group that springs up around an issue or an event to advance a specific point of view.

WASHINGTON'S INTEREST GROUP UNIVERSE

How numerous is each of type of interest group in Washington? Table 10.2 provides two ways to answer this question. The first column shows the distribution of all organizations that exist, and the second column indicates the degree to which organizations show up as major players in shaping policies. Though there are far fewer citizen

groups in Washington than there are offices of corporations and trade associations (see the first column), the citizen groups involve themselves more often and more actively than one would expect based on their numbers alone (second column). This makes sense, since corporations and governmental institutions usually are concerned about a few narrow issues, whereas citizens' groups are usually concerned about a broad set of issues such as protection of the environment, opposition to abortion, and so forth.

TABLE 10.2
the washington universe of interest groups

The first column shows the distribution of groups with a lobbying office in Washington, based on a directory of registered lobbyists.[3] The second column shows the distribution of groups that were identified as major participants across a number of issues in a set of 98 congressional bills studied by a group of political scientists.[4]

	REGISTERED LOBBYISTS	MAJOR PARTICIPANTS ON ISSUES
Corporations	43%	17%
Trade, agricultural, and professional associations	24	39
Unions	2	7
Citizen groups and nonprofit organizations	14	31
Governmental institutions	17	6

Source: United Nations Development Programme. *Human Development Report* 2009. (http://hdr.undp.org/)d Table M of Statistical Annex.

THE RISE OF INTEREST GROUPS

Groups with shared interests have always organized in America. As early as 1832, French essayist Alexis de Tocqueville commented on how willing Americans were to work voluntarily for common goals:

> In no country in the world has the principle of association been more successfully used or applied to a greater multitude of objects than in America. Besides the permanent associations which are established by law under the names of townships, cities, and counties, a vast number of others are formed and maintained by the agency of private individuals.[5]

KEY TO understanding ★

The United States has had a long tradition of cooperative group activity, but it took two key events to develop national interest groups—the Civil War and the onset of the Progressive movement. Beyond these two events, the expansion of government activity after World War II brought forth a proliferation of interest groups, which continues today. What factors contributed to their rise, and what historical events moved these groups from representing local to national levels of interest?

Alexander Hamilton and James Madison in the *Federalist Papers,* and George Washington in his farewell address on retiring from the presidency, all noted the prevalence of groups. They worried about the power of "factions," a term that embraced both political parties and particular interests.

In the early years of the republic most interest groups were local, focusing on issues such as getting a canal constructed or establishing a school. Two formative experiences in American history helped to expand this system of representation from a local to a *national* level: the Civil War and the Progressive movement of the early twentieth century.

In the run-up to the Civil War, abolitionists expressed their opposition to slavery by organizing nationally. Also, in both the South and the North, groups were formed to encourage settlement in new states in attempts to tip the balance between free states and slave states. During the Civil War, volunteer groups on both sides played a large role in providing military supplies and bringing aid to the wounded. These experiences of organizing on a large scale both before and during the war led to a flowering of national interest groups after the war: the Grange, a national organization to further the interests of farmers; the Grand Army of the Republic, an organization of Union war veterans; and the Women's Christian Temperance Union, which pushed for the prohibition of alcohol.[6]

The Progressive movement led to a further expansion of interest groups in the first two decades of the twentieth century. This movement was not a single organization but rather a loosely connected group of people calling for a variety of reforms, including such things as regulation of railroads, anti-trust

★ **WOMEN'S CRUSADE AGAINST INTEMPERANCE** The Women's Christian Temperance Union, one of the first national interest groups to organize on a large scale after the Civil War, supported the legislation that established Prohibition—a period of time when sale and possession of alcoholic beverages were outlawed in the United States. Many women believed that liquor often led to poverty and spousal abuse.

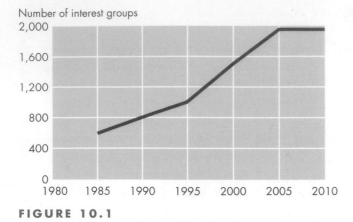

Number of interest groups

FIGURE 10.1

★ THE GROWTH OF THE INTEREST GROUP UNIVERSE

The number of interest groups operating in Washington has tripled since the mid-1980s. What difference would it make to an interest group's work in the capital if it was one of 2,000, compared with being one of a few hundred?

Source: Data from *Washington Representatives,* serial (Washington, D.C.: Columbia Books), various annual volumes.

legislation, an end to child labor, and electoral reforms to reduce corruption. Multiple interest groups arose to pursue each of these varied goals.

The burgeoning success of these groups led to new forms of business regulation. For example, the establishment of the Food and Drug Administration (FDA) in 1906 involved the government in regulating the purity of food products for the first time. As regulation increased, businesses intensified their own lobbying of the government by forming new trade associations to defend their interests. Thus, both as a result of the new impetus for reform and because of corporations' response to new regulations, interest group activity grew rapidly during the early twentieth century. Between 1900 and 1920 alone, more than 1,500 new interest groups testified before congressional committees. During the entire nineteenth century, by contrast, fewer than 400 had done so.[7]

The rest of the twentieth century saw further growth of the interest group universe, especially as government expanded its role in people's lives after World War II. This growth in government led to a corresponding expansion of interest groups, including new environmental groups and civil rights groups as well as increasing numbers of business associations and specialized groups. The growth of interest groups continues today. As illustrated in Figure 10.1, from 1985 to 2010 *Washington Representatives,* a publication that lists interest groups and their lobbying staffs in Washington, grew from 638 pages to 1,943 pages.

THE PROBLEM OF FREE RIDERS

★ KEY TO understanding

This section continues the discussion that began in Chapter 1, where we presented the problematic relationship between public goods and free riders. An interest group produces a public good for its members when it successfully campaigns for a government policy from which everyone in the group benefits, even those who did nothing to push for it. How can free riders complicate an interest group's ability to form and to maintain membership?

How do interest groups form, and how do they maintain themselves? This question might at first glance seem silly. Why shouldn't an interest group start if enough people agree on a policy they want enacted? Unfortunately, the problem of public goods complicates interest group formation. When a public good is produced, it is impossible to withhold it from some people while giving it to others. If anyone receives a public good, everyone receives it; if it exists at all, it cannot be denied to anyone. Thus, as we saw in Chapter 1, a public good always brings with it the problem of *free riders*—individuals who decide not to help produce the good, knowing that if is produced at all, they cannot be prevented from sharing in it. They can have their cake without helping to bake it.

Consider again the example of air quality cited in Chapter 1. If a city's air quality is improved, everyone in the city benefits, regardless of whether they actively participated in the clean-up effort. In the same way, the fruits of an interest group's efforts are a public good for all of its potential members. If an interest group gets a new bill passed—an improvement in veterans' benefits, for instance—the bill benefits all veterans in the same way. Veterans can choose to be free riders, reasoning that no matter whether they join the interest group, they will still get the same benefits if it wins. Why should they pay dues, or travel to Washington, or do any of the other things the interest group might ask of them, if they will enjoy the fruits of its labors in any case?

How can an interest group form and maintain itself despite the problem of free riders? It turns out that this question has somewhat different answers for different types of groups. A corporation does not have the problem since it does not need to attract members, but let us consider the other three main types of groups: trade, agricultural, and professional associations; unions; and citizen groups.

TRADE, AGRICULTURAL, AND PROFESSIONAL ASSOCIATIONS

For a trade association like the National Automobile Dealers Association (NADA) or a professional association like the American Medical Association (AMA), any single automobile dealer or doctor can easily decide to be a free rider, since dealers and doctors enjoy any policy gains by the groups even if they have not joined. How, then, do trade, agricultural, and professional associations manage to maintain their memberships? One thing that helps them is that even though potential members might think that they could not make much difference by joining, the economic stakes for each of them are often very high. They may decide to join even though they think they can make only a small difference.

Most of these groups, however, do not count on their members' public spirit. They have also devised a wide array of **selective benefits,** which (unlike public goods) can be given to members but withheld from non-members. Besides its lobbying work, the NADA offers its members advice and information on laws and regulations, develops research data on the industry and distributes it to members, runs training programs for dealers and their staff, provides employee benefits plans for dealers, and offers discounts on PCs and other IT equipment. These added benefits can be restricted to members, so many dealers who might otherwise decide to be free riders choose to join in order to receive the selective benefits. Fully 91 percent of United States new-vehicle dealers are members of NADA.

In a study of the importance of selective benefits, members of several trade associations were asked if they would continue as members of the association if it did no lobbying at all. Although the lobbying efforts of the associations were important to their members, an average of about 70 percent of the members of each association said that selective benefits alone would be enough to keep them in the association.[8]

TRADE UNIONS

Unions also face a public goods problem, because the contract they bargain for with an employer is a public good. If the union negotiates a raise with the employer, all employees of the firm receive the same raise, whether or not they have joined the union and supported it with their dues. As a result, in states where it is permitted, unions often try to require that all employees pay dues if the union is bargaining on their behalf. When this is allowed, it eliminates the free rider problem.[9] Unions also offer a variety of selective benefits to their members, such as group insurance policies and discount vacation packages. Figure 10.2 shows how union strength varies among the states.

selective benefits
Benefits that can be given to some people but withheld from others; they are the opposite of public goods.

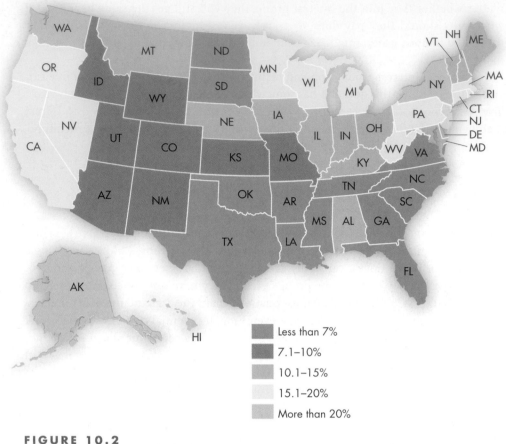

	Less than 7%
	7.1–10%
	10.1–15%
	15.1–20%
	More than 20%

FIGURE 10.2

★ UNIONIZED LABOR IN THE UNITED STATES

Which regions have especially strong union organization, and in which are unions weakest? How does the regional distribution of union strength compare with the regional bases of Democratic Party strength?

Source: Data from Bureau of Labor Statistics, http://www.bls.gov/news.release/union2.t05.htm.

CITIZEN GROUPS

Citizen groups generally organize around an idea or around support for an ethnic group or community, and so they do not face as difficult a problem with free riders as other groups. The satisfaction of joining a collective effort for something you believe in is its own reward. Membership is not just a tool that one uses to get other rewards, but is itself the pleasure and the prize, so it is easy to join instead of being a free rider. Many citizen groups are able to flourish with large memberships. The NRA has 4.3 million members; Amnesty International has 2.2 million members worldwide, and The Nature Conservancy claims over 1 million members in the United States.

Nonetheless, the public goods problem does exist for citizen groups, even though it is not as intense as for other groups. A person who is interested in the environment but has many other demands on his or her time might still decide not to join the Environmental Defense Fund, leaving others to take care of that problem. In order to encourage membership many citizen groups offer small selective benefits, such as glossy magazines for members or tote bags adorned with the organization's logo.

SOURCES OF INFLUENCE FOR INTEREST GROUPS

Interest groups have various resources available to them to help influence officials. The most obvious is money, but other possible resources include a large and committed body of supporters, technical expertise, access to important information, and the group's reputation.

Interest groups use multiple resources to influence officials—from money to technical expertise to political information. To what degree does the availability of certain types of resources affect the tactical decisions an interest group makes?

MONEY

If they have sufficient money, interest groups can hire lobbying firms to help them present their case in Washington, can contribute to candidates' campaigns, and can run advertising campaigns publicizing their stance on issues. (For more discussion of these tactics, see the next section, "Interest Group Tactics.") Citizen groups have the fewest financial resources, as Table 10.3 shows. Most of the money lies with corporations, trade and professional associations, and unions.

Note that the groups vary not only in how much money they have, but also in what they choose to spend their money on. Unions spend less money on Washington lobbying, for instance, partly because they have their own officials who perform this task skillfully; instead, they allocate more of their funds to campaign contributions. The most basic finding from Table 10.3, however, is that citizen groups have much less of all the things that money can buy.[10]

MEMBERS

A broad and active body of supporters in the population can be a potent resource for a group, both as a pool of potential voters and as a source of e-mails and calls to members of Congress. The National Rifle Association (NRA), for instance, has an estimated 4.3 million members, and many of those members are sufficiently committed that they will vote for candidates based on the endorsements of the association.[11] Its members are potent tools that make the NRA one of the most powerful lobbying groups in the United States.

TABLE 10.3
average financial resources of interest groups

The average resources listed in this table are of those groups identified as "major participants" in Table 10.2.[12] Thus, although the table does not include all groups of each sort that exist, what it features is more interesting and useful: It highlights the groups that have a major influence on congressional decision making.

	PERCENTAGE WITH HIRED LOBBYISTS	AVERAGE SPENDING ON LOBBYING	AVERAGE PAC CAMPAIGN CONTRIBUTIONS
Corporations	79	$1,051,985	$965,132
Trade associations	69	$1,274,502	$439,204
Professional associations	44	$973,333	$884,844
Unions	45	$475,559	$4,265,099
Citizen groups	25	$177,814	$187,354

Source: Frank R. Baumgartner, Jeffrey M. Berry, Marie Hojnacki, David C. Kimball, and Beth L. Leech, *Lobbying and Policy Change: Who Wins, Who Loses, and Why*, table 10.3, p.199.

Trade associations and even corporations can also often mobilize grassroots support for a position they wish the government to take. For example, the 18,000 members of the NADA managed to get automobile dealers exempted from the Dodd-Frank Wall Street Reform and Consumer Protection Act of 2010, which initiated significant new government regulation of those lending money. They achieved this victory to some degree by raising and spending money from their members ($3.5 million spent on lobbying in 2009 and the first half of 2010, and $10 million in campaign contributions for the 2008 election), but also by mobilizing their members, who were strategically spread across all congressional districts in the country, to contact their members of Congress.[13] Corporations often will ask their stockholders and workers to contact members of Congress on behalf of a bill that will affect the corporation.

Although all sorts of groups can mobilize grassroots support, this is a resource in which citizens' groups and unions are especially strong. Citizen groups like the Audubon Society, National Right to Life, the American Association of Retired Persons (AARP), and the NRA are able to count on large numbers of committed supporters, as are trade unions. It is partly through this resource that many citizen groups are able to make up for relatively weak financial assets. Unions, of course, have considerable financial strength as well.

TECHNICAL EXPERTISE

Lobbying often involves having the technical knowledge to answer such questions as, "How quickly might we expect cheap electric cars to be developed?" "How much lithium is likely to be available worldwide 20 years from now?" "How can we define brain death?" Interest groups, especially professional associations, often have that knowledge as well as the expertise to draft legislation or provide expert testimony in congressional hearings. For instance, experts from the American Medical Association would be able to speak about the most cost-effective way to treat terminal illnesses. Government bureaucracies and congressional committees need such expertise, and if an interest group can provide it, that helps the group to influence the decisions that are made.

Aside from a group's own members, many interest groups receive help with technical information from *think tanks,* independent foundations that specialize in research on public policy. Though these operate independently of any interest group, they often have a clear leaning to the left or the right. Many corporations and business groups look to conservative think tanks like the American Enterprise Institute or the Heritage Foundation, while unions and liberal groups look to liberal think tanks like the Economic Policy Institute and Institute for Policy Studies.

POLITICAL INFORMATION

Interest groups often gather political information that is important to members of Congress in a number of ways: They may put the members in touch with experts who can advise them on technical matters; they may help to find out how other members will be voting; they may help to identify who will oppose a bill; and they can assist in organizing alliances among members.

As one senior member of Congress said of the information that lobbyists shared with him about expected opposition on a bill he was proposing:

> They tell you who is for it and who is against it; they don't send you out there thinking it's all just apple pie. They let you know the Heart Association is against it, and so are some of your best friends in the House. Then you know where you stand. Surprises are nice for parties, but not for legislating.[14]

★ Images such as this one of BP workers cleaning an oil-soaked pelican furthered the company's uphill battle to regain its reputation after the oil spill in 2010.

GROUP REPUTATION AND SYMPATHY

Finally, groups may benefit (or lose) from an intangible resource—their general reputation and the sympathy people feel for them. The Red Cross, churches, veterans, and family farms, for instance, are all groups that people respect and for whom they feel sympathy. This helps them both in appeals to public opinion and in the reception they get from officials when they lobby them. Reputation can also be a negative factor. After the oil spill in the Gulf of Mexico in 2010, BP Oil Company had an uphill fight in any lobbying efforts because of its loss of general reputation.

Corporations, business groups, and unions usually do not benefit greatly from group reputation and sympathy, since they are seen as economic interests that are out for their own advantage. Many citizen groups, however, are seen more as campaigning for the general good rather than their own interest. Amnesty International, which works to free political prisoners around the world, is a good example of this.

inside tactics
Tactics that involve working directly with government officials.

outside tactics
Tactics that seek to influence officials indirectly, such as working in elections and mobilizing supporters to bring pressure on decision makers.

INTEREST GROUP TACTICS

Interest groups employ two types of tactics to influence officials: **inside tactics,** in which they work directly with officials; and **outside tactics,** in which they influence officials indirectly by working in elections and by mobilizing supporters to put pressure on the officials.

Interest groups' tactics can be classified in two broad categories: inside tactics, which include lobbying and litigation, and outside tactics, which include campaign contributions and advocacy ads. Individual groups that stand on the same side of an issue can also form coalitions as a way to support each other and pool their resources. What does it take to make each of these tactics succeed?

KEY TO understanding ★

INSIDE TACTICS

Most organizations spend the majority of their time employing inside tactics, since many of the policies that engage them involve narrow rules and regulations that are best addressed through direct contact with members of Congress and executive offices, or through litigation in the courts.

Lobbying

When representatives of the group meet with officials regarding a law or regulation, this is known as **lobbying.** It is the quintessential "inside" tactic. Originating in

lobbying
Attempting to persuade officials to enact a policy.

England in the seventeenth century, the term "lobby" referred to the anteroom of the House of Commons. People would seek out members of the House in this lobby to plead special issues; as such, they came to be known as "lobby-agents" ("lobbyists" today).[15]

Lobbyists who are experienced in Washington decision making can help a group influence national decisions. Lobbying firms often employ former members of Congress, cabinet officials, or congressional staffers to help present their positions to Congress and the administration. These former players know how to frame arguments in a way that will influence government officials; they know how decisions are made; and they are often intimately familiar with the details of the types of policies in which they specialized. While former members of Congress and cabinet officials can help to arrange contact with current officials whom they knew when they served, former staffers often have more thorough knowledge of policies and procedures than former officials do.

Figure 10.3 shows how the business of lobbying has grown in recent years.

The public's picture of lobbying generally involves a lobbyist persuading a member of Congress to do what the member otherwise would not do—often because of a large campaign contribution from the lobbyist's group. Contributions certainly play a role in lobbying, but the reality of lobbying is more subtle than that picture. Most of the time lobbyists approach legislators who already agree with them or probably will do so. They are less likely to approach a Congress member who is known to be opposed to the group, since the odds of changing that member's mind are probably low.[16] Perhaps the member has longstanding, close ties to the other side. Or perhaps the member represents a district that would be hurt by the lobbyist's proposal. The member may also have a strong, well-known ideological position that is inconsistent with the proposal.

FIGURE 10.3

★ GROWTH IN LOBBYING SPENDING AND REGISTERED LOBBYISTS IN WASHINGTON

In 2007 new regulations went into effect that required stricter reporting of registered lobbyist activities. According to the figure, the number of registered lobbyists increased steadily until after 2007, when the number started to decline. Yet lobbying spending continues to go up steadily. How might those regulations have produced the odd divergence here in the growth of registered lobbyists and lobbying expenditures? (You'll see one possible answer later in this chapter in the section titled "Interest Group Reform.")

Source: Calculations by the Center for Responsive Politics, based on data from the Senate Office of Public Records.

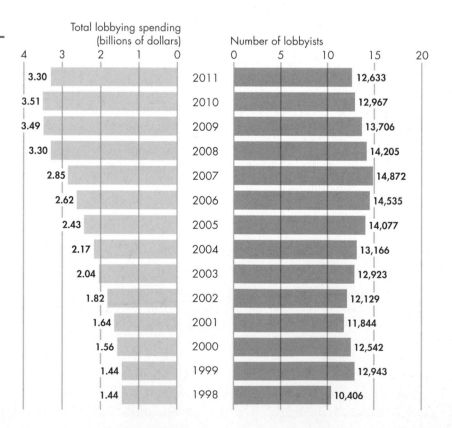

Total lobbying spending (billions of dollars) / Number of lobbyists

Year	Total lobbying spending (billions of dollars)	Number of lobbyists
2011	3.30	12,633
2010	3.51	12,967
2009	3.49	13,706
2008	3.30	14,205
2007	2.85	14,872
2006	2.62	14,535
2005	2.43	14,077
2004	2.17	13,166
2003	2.04	12,923
2002	1.82	12,129
2001	1.64	11,844
2000	1.56	12,542
1999	1.44	12,943
1998	1.44	10,406

If lobbyists are not typically trying to persuade a member of Congress to change his or her position on an issue, what do they talk about when they meet? To a large extent, lobbyists view the member as a potential ally on their proposal. In their visit they extend an invitation to collaborate on the proposal. They draw on their own technical expertise and present the member with in-depth policy analyses and sound arguments to use in debate. Sometimes they will even offer the member special studies that show the impact their proposal would have on a particular group (hog farmers, auto dealers, all of the people in the member's district, and so on). Lobbyists may assist in crafting legislative language for a bill. They may report on how other members feel about the issue, and recommend which officials they've identified as key people with whom they can bargain. They can offer a head-count of how many members are already committed on either side of the proposal. All of these strategies help a member who is already inclined to support the group, and thus they increase the group's chances of success.

Members of Congress face many demands on their time, and as generalists, they must deal with a wide range of bills. Lobbyists do just one job—lobbying—and they work on one policy area, mastering it in depth. This allows them to offer members of Congress detailed policy information and valuable political advice on an issue, which members simply do not have time to gather for themselves.[17]

Lobbying members of the executive branch and civil service regulators also fit this general picture, except that in this case technical expertise becomes more important relative to other things the lobbyist can offer. In lobbying regulators, raw political power is less important than it is in lobbying members of Congress, since regulators are not elected and do not need the many services interest groups might offer them if they had to run a campaign. As a result, groups that are particularly strong in technical expertise (and weaker in other resources such as broad membership or reputation) will especially emphasize working with regulators. For example, financial firms were unhappy with the Dodd-Frank Wall Street Reform and Consumer Protection Act of 2010, which restricted in various ways what financial firms could do. But the firms took comfort from the fact that many of the details of the bill were left to be worked out later by regulators. They felt they could be more successful in lobbying regulators than they had been with Congress, because the resources important in working with regulators played to their strengths.

Litigation

Litigation is another inside tactic, in which interest groups work through the courts—either bringing cases in court themselves or offering *amicus* briefs in cases that others have initiated. In an ***amicus* brief,** lawyers for the group present complementary arguments to strengthen the case of the lawyers on the side they favor, even though the group is not directly involved as a litigant. Bringing a case or submitting an *amicus* brief can be an effective tactic, but because it requires relatively few resources, it is a tactic especially emphasized by groups that do not have broad support, abundant

***amicus* brief**
A formal document filed in a court case by a group not involved as a direct participant in the case, arguing a position on one side or another of the case.

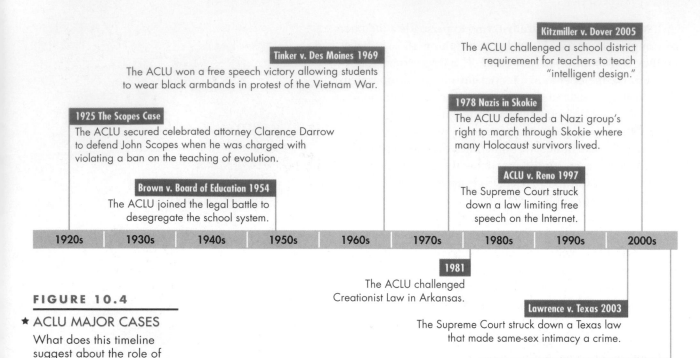

Tinker v. Des Moines 1969
The ACLU won a free speech victory allowing students to wear black armbands in protest of the Vietnam War.

Kitzmiller v. Dover 2005
The ACLU challenged a school district requirement for teachers to teach "intelligent design."

1925 The Scopes Case
The ACLU secured celebrated attorney Clarence Darrow to defend John Scopes when he was charged with violating a ban on the teaching of evolution.

1978 Nazis in Skokie
The ACLU defended a Nazi group's right to march through Skokie where many Holocaust survivors lived.

Brown v. Board of Education 1954
The ACLU joined the legal battle to desegregate the school system.

ACLU v. Reno 1997
The Supreme Court struck down a law limiting free speech on the Internet.

| 1920s | 1930s | 1940s | 1950s | 1960s | 1970s | 1980s | 1990s | 2000s |

1981
The ACLU challenged Creationist Law in Arkansas.

Lawrence v. Texas 2003
The Supreme Court struck down a Texas law that made same-sex intimacy a crime.

Safford Unified School District v. Redding 2009
The ACLU protected the right to privacy of a 13-year-old Arizona girl.

FIGURE 10.4

★ **ACLU MAJOR CASES**

What does this timeline suggest about the role of interest group litigation in U.S. politics?

Source: Text from ACLU: www.aclu.org/aclu-history

funds, or other political tools. (While anything involving lawyers sounds as though it would be expensive, a court case, even one involving a team of several lawyers, is in fact far less expensive than an advertising campaign or a major PAC. It also does not require a broad national organization.)

The American Civil Liberties Union (ACLU), which defends free speech and the separation of church and state, relies primarily on litigation for two reasons: (1) the first amendment of the Constitution offers it a strong basis for arguments in court, and (2) it does not have the sorts of political resources that would make it effective in lobbying Congress or the executive branch. (See Figure 10.4 for a timeline of major ACLU cases.) Corporations often rely on litigation as one of their tools to influence public policy because they already maintain large legal staffs for other purposes, and because many of the questions they are interested in are fine technical points that lend themselves to resolution in court.

OUTSIDE TACTICS

Outside tactics vary quite a bit and range from working with the organization's members in ways that support the lobbyists' inside approaches, to broad activities among the general public.

Grassroots Lobbying

One tactic that groups use to supplement their lobbying is **grassroots lobbying,** in which an interest group uses its members to help its Washington lobbyists influence a bill. Obviously, for this tactic to be effective, the group needs a large membership that is committed enough to write, send emails, phone, or visit Washington for a "lobbying

grassroots lobbying
Activities by an interest group to influence a decision by a member of Congress indirectly by mobilizing their supporters in the member's district to bring pressure to bear on the member.

day" with their members of Congress. Groups like the NRA or Planned Parenthood can rely on members and supporters to help in such efforts. As one congressional staff member described his boss's vote to repeal catastrophic health insurance a year after having voted in favor of it:

> It was a no-brainer. He got over five thousand letters for the repeal of the insurance, and literally eight letters in favor of the current insurance. He didn't have much choice really. He had to vote for repeal.[18]

In 2012 a group of Internet companies including Reddit, Wikipedia, and Google opposed a bill called the Stop Online Piracy Act. The bill had been pushed by the entertainment industry to help close sites that distribute stolen copies of music and films, but the Internet companies argued that it would limit free speech. Several of them shut down their operations for a day, with a note asking their users to ask Congress to reject the bill. In the most dramatic example of grassroots lobbying to date, emails poured in to Congress, and within two days the bill was dead after most of its sponsors had reversed themselves.

Campaign Contributions

Campaign contributions are important to congressional and presidential candidates. Interest groups often give large sums of money to support candidates. These contributions serve two purposes: to help get sympathetic candidates into elected positions, and to put officials, once elected, in a group's debt. Groups do not expect that officials will do what they want simply because they have given them money. For one thing, groups on the other side of an issue are also likely to have given the official contributions, so the groups tend to cancel each other out. But they do expect that their contribution will get them "access." That is, they expect that they will not find it difficult to get in to talk to officials if they have contributed to their campaigns.

Most interest groups use political action committees (PACs) to organize their campaign contributions. The amounts involved can be large. The National Beer Wholesalers Association donated over $15 million to candidates between 2000 and 2011.[19] Because PACs often give to all sorts of members in order to obtain access, they often give even to members who are not especially supportive of the group. The business PACs in Figure 10.5, for instance, gave about equally to Democrats and Republicans even though the Republican members were generally more supportive of business interests. The labor PACs followed a different strategy, giving almost solely to Democratic candidates.

Campaign Assistance

In addition to monetary campaign help, a group with a large and devoted membership may also help candidates in other ways. They can endorse the incumbent or, less frequently, the challenger; provide favorable stories about the candidate in the group's newsletter; encourage members to vote; and assist the campaign by having members make phone calls, drop literature, or perform other volunteer tasks. Unions are especially active in this aspect of elections, but most groups with a large membership do some of these things.

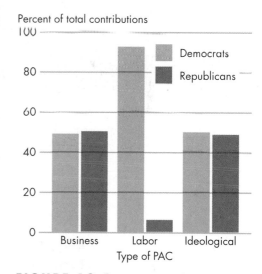

FIGURE 10.5

★ PAC CONTRIBUTIONS TO MAJOR PARTY CANDIDATES, 2009–2010

Business and labor are often opposed to each other on major policies, but their patterns of contributions are very different.

Source: Data from Open Secrets website, http://www.opensecrets.org/bigpicture/blio.php

Groups may also assign **group ratings** to help elect members who are friends of the group and defeat those who are enemies. Many groups analyze how members of Congress have voted and publish scores indicating how favorably the members voted on issues of its concern. The ratings typically range from 0 for no support to 100 for the highest support. The ratings help voters who support the group to vote for or against members, depending on how they have been rated by the group.

Advocacy Advertisements

Interest groups may run ads to try to frame the public debate about an issue. In 2009, for instance, labor unions and business groups targeted select states and congressional districts with television advertisements arguing for (unions) and against (business) the proposed "Card Check" bill that would make it possible to unionize workplaces without a secret-ballot election if a majority of the workers signed a card asking to have a union represent them. The groups chose states and districts where they thought senators or representatives might be led to change their vote if public opinion shifted.

★ ONE OF THE FAMOUS HARRY AND LOUISE ADS One of the Louise quotes from the original ads was "Having choices we don't like is no choice at all."

The most famous use of advocacy ads, which in fact introduced the technique for the first time, came in 1993, when President Bill Clinton introduced a plan for universal health care for all Americans, a plan that had been developed by his wife Hillary's task force on health policy. The Health Insurance Association of America, a health insurance industry lobby group, ran a series of advocacy advertisements opposing the Clinton proposal, which are widely credited with having been a major factor in its failure. The multimillion dollar series of 14 ads featured two actors, "Harry" and "Louise," sitting at their kitchen table worrying about whether health care would be bureaucratic under the Clinton plan, whether they would be able to choose their own doctor, and whether specialized services would be available. By the time the ad series had been completed, Senate Majority Leader George Mitchell declared that the health care reform bill was dead. It would be 16 years until another president, Barack Obama, would try to bring about a comprehensive reform of health care—this time with success.

In an ironic postlude, the actors who played Harry and Louise came back to their kitchen table in 2009 in an advertisement (this time sponsored by *supporters* of comprehensive health care reform) urging support for President Obama's health care proposals.

Demonstrations, Protests, and Boycotts

Interest groups occasionally utilize unconventional forms of participation, including demonstrations, protests, and boycotts. These tactics are highly visible and meant to help sway broad public opinion. They can be very effective under some circumstances—the civil rights movement in the 1960s was built on demonstrations, marches, and boycotts—but often they do not have much effect. They are most effective when a group strikes a sympathetic chord with the public that might have been difficult to tap except by showing the determination of its members. Civil rights demonstrations and Gay Pride parades have both been successful in this way. Antiwar demonstrations can be effective if a war is unpopular, but do not have much effect unless there is a broad underlying uneasiness about the war.

In general, groups emphasize demonstrations and protests if they have a devoted membership and broad support in the population, but lack other resources. Most well-organized interest groups that have significant resources do not use demonstrations and protests as a tactic. The one type of interest group that uses unconventional participation as its primary tactic is the social movement, which is discussed in detail later in the chapter.

COALITION FORMATION

A frequent tactic of interest groups, whether they are using inside *or* outside tactics, is to form a coalition with other groups that are on the same side of an issue. Members of a coalition pool their resources and help each other out. Almost every major bill involves coalitions of groups on both sides of the bill. Occasionally coalitions can create strange bedfellows. Some conservative evangelical Christian groups worked with labor unions and immigrant groups in 2010 to try to pass a bill making it easier for illegal immigrants to become citizens.[20] The evangelical groups would not usually be on the same side of the issues as liberal groups, but they were drawn into the coalition by their concern for Hispanic church members and by Christian doctrine.

CHOICE OF TACTICS

How often do organizations use these various tactics? Table 10.4 shows the results of a survey of tactics used by interest groups operating in state government.[21]

Note that fewer groups engage in litigation, electoral activity, or protests than engage in lobbying and grassroots lobbying. Most of the time, most interest groups are focused on specific decisions being made in government, rather than on the broader principles usually addressed by electoral activity or demonstrations.

Not all groups do the same things, however. Different interest groups have different mixes of resources, and in the preceding section we made the point that a group often chooses tactics that take advantage of the resources with which they are most well endowed. Unions, for example, usually have a large number of committed members and considerable financial resources, which may steer them toward tactics like campaign assistance and advocacy advertisements, as well as lobbying. Immigrant groups often have large numbers of supporters but not much money; they may rely more on demonstrations and on grassroots lobbying than on other tactics. Corporations have ample money but rather limited bases of supporters available to them; they may rely especially on campaign contributions and on technical expertise.

The history of the civil rights movement in the United States provides a good example of how the resources available to a group help to determine its tactics. In the 1940s and 1950s the movement for civil rights for African Americans was relatively weak. The majority of African Americans were still barred from voting in the South; they were poor and did not have much money to contribute; and the movement did not have many white allies, either in or outside of public office. The chief civil rights organization at this time was the National Association for the Advancement of Colored People (NAACP), and its chief tactic was litigation. As discussed in Chapter 5, the NAACP's court challenges resulted in a series of civil rights victories including *Brown v. Board of Education*.

TABLE 10.4

tactics used by state government interest groups

TACTIC	% OF GROUPS USING EACH TACTIC
Lobbying	
Testifying at legislative hearings	99
Contacting government officials directly	97
Helping to draft legislation	88
Litigation	
Filing suit or *amicus* briefs	40
Grassroots lobbying	
Having influential constituent contact legislators	92
Mounting grassroots lobbying effort	86
Letter-writing or e-mail campaigns	83
Electoral activity	
Campaign contributions	45
Working on election campaign	29
Endorsing candidates	24
Running advertisements	21
Protests, demonstrations, and boycotts	
Engaging in protests or demonstrations	21
Coalition formation	
Entering coalitions with other groups	93

Source: Adapted from Anthony J. Nownes and Patricia Freeman, "Interest Group Activity in the States", *The Journal of Politics* 60:1 (February, 1998), p. 92.

These successes inspired increasingly broad financial and political support for civil rights in the 1960s. African Americans became bolder politically; many more were willing to march in demonstrations to help draw attention to their cause and they began to acquire significant numbers of white allies. At this time, new rival organizations using different tactics appeared, including the Congress on Racial Equality (CORE) and Martin Luther King, Jr.'s Southern Christian Leadership Conference (SCLC). Drawing on the growing public support for civil rights, which gave them new and greater resources, the new organizations emphasized nonviolent demonstrations, the use of economic power through boycotts, and provocation of segregationists into violence that increased popular sympathy for the demonstrators.

At this time, groups did not emphasize electoral activity. During the 1960s many southern African Americans still could not vote or were just acquiring the vote, and in any case, demonstrations were proving to be powerful tools. By the 1970s and 1980s, however, demonstrations began to be less effective. The public had become more used to them, and police had learned not to respond in the picturesquely violent ways that demonstrators once counted on. At the same time, the electoral importance of African Americans had grown. The African-American percentage of the electorate in many northern cities had reached a point at which African Americans could often determine the outcome of mayoral and other elections. In the South, thanks to the gains of the

1960s, most African Americans were now free to vote and could determine the outcome of many elections. Accordingly, the activity of African-American civil rights groups shifted to emphasize elections. One payoff of this strategy was the development of the Congressional Black Caucus as a strong player in the House of Representatives.

Litigation and demonstrations remain tools of the civil rights movement, but the movement has broadened its repertoire over time. At all points in its history, the availability of resources strongly conditioned the movement's choice of tactics.

DETERMINANTS OF GROUPS' SUCCESS OR FAILURE

How do the various resources available to interest groups help to determine how successful they will be in accomplishing their policy goals? Clearly resources count. A group that has a large and devoted membership or the financial strength to marshal a strong lobbying effort, to contribute to campaigns, and to conduct advertising programs is more likely to get what it wants than a group with fewer resources. In 2010, for instance, the House of Representatives passed the DISCLOSE (Democracy Is Strengthened by Casting Light on Spending in Elections) Act, which required sponsors of political advertisements to identify themselves in the ad and disclose the source of their funds.[22] The NRA, which is very active in advocacy advertising, did not want to be subject to such regulation. Drawing upon the strength of its large and devoted membership, it persuaded Congress to provide an amendment exempting them from disclosure.

The success or failure of an interest group's efforts in enacting a policy proposal depends on the group's resources and tactics, as well as the situation it faces in Congress or with the executive branch. To what degree can these resources and tactics help interest groups accomplish their policy goals—or not—and how can the situation a group faces in Congress affect its success or failure?

KEY To understanding ★

Often, in a complicated bill of 2,000 or so pages, an interest group with significant financial or other resources can succeed in getting a detail inserted that appears minor but could make a difference to the group of millions of dollars. For instance, in a tax bill titled the American Jobs Creation Act of 2004, many interest groups succeeded in getting riders inserted—small, special exemptions—with little attention from anyone. The Professional Golfers Association (PGA) was one of those groups. A "golfers" rider exempted from new, tighter pension rules any organization that had been incorporated on July 2, 1974—curiously, the precise date on which the PGA was incorporated. The golfers' success followed a special event in which members of Congress were invited to play golf with professionals, while simultaneously being lobbied by PGA staff. In the same bill a rider allowed shipbuilders such as Northrop Grumman to use a special accounting procedure that reduced their tax bills by $495 million.[23] Many interest group successes are of this sort—seemingly small details that pass under the radar but are critically important to the group. Thus, much of the time resources may determine a group's success or failure.

However, even a group with many resources can face an uncertain situation in its quest to influence legislation. Often a group on the other side of the issue has just as many resources—and one of them will have to lose. Additionally, some aspects of the congressional legislative process are not affected very much by a group's resources. There are a number of such factors, but two especially important ones are:

• having (or lacking) a "champion" within the legislature or Congress;
• being able to garner attention in a crowded legislative agenda.

CHAMPIONS WITHIN THE LEGISLATURE OR CONGRESS

A **champion** is a legislator who believes strongly in the goals of the group, often because of personal experience. A champion frequently makes the difference between a group succeeding or losing. A sitting member of the body can lobby his or her colleagues in a very credible way and can bargain with them, trading votes on other issues for support on this issue. Consider, for instance, Senators Paul Wellstone and Peter Domenici, and House member James Ramstad, all of whom had a personal or family connection with mental illness or addiction. For many years, they worked with groups advocating for the mentally ill to pass a law requiring insurance companies to pay for treatment of mental illness or addiction in the same way they would pay for other illnesses. The effort finally succeeded when Ramstad was able to get the Mental Health Parity and Addiction Equity Act passed in 2008. He apparently held out on a refusal to vote for the emergency financial bailout that year until he was promised passage of the bill he had long championed.

THE ABILITY TO GARNER ATTENTION

Congress deals each year with a thousand or more potential bills, so it is hard to attract members' attention to any one bill.[24] As noted, each individual member of Congress is pulled simultaneously in many directions. Often a lobbyist will have only a few minutes with a member to make a complicated, technical argument. As one lobbyist related:

> It's not easy to explain what clinical social workers do, how they differ from other social workers, and why this bill needs to be passed—in two sentences or two minutes. Often you don't have any more time than that. There's a huge education problem.[25]

Perhaps one reason a champion can be so important is that the group can at least count on that one member to sit still long enough to absorb a complicated argument!

The congressional calendar also poses a problem. Many proposals, even those pursued by groups with ample resources, fail because they are just not able to break into the relatively small number of issues that can be dealt with in a session of Congress. To quote another lobbyist, who was working to get an accelerated tax depreciation schedule for computer equipment:

> The only tax bills getting serious attention [in this session] are the estate tax and the "marriage penalty," which affect lots more people than our issue. It's hard to get people in Congress to pay attention to our issue and get involved in passing it.[26]

Because the problem of getting attention and committee time for a proposal is so critical for its success, frequently those who oppose a proposal may find that the best way to kill it is to make sure that it does not get dealt with. Rather than make a frontal assault on the merits of an issue, they may succeed simply by allowing inertia to work, or by arguing that other issues have to be considered first.

Trying to get your proposal considered is an uphill fight, but it is not an impossible one. Resources can help to get a bill onto the crowded calendar, especially a large and devoted membership willing to write letters or e-mails urging Congress members to make sure the bill is considered. An advertising campaign may also be effective.

Or, a champion can help from the inside. However, even groups with many resources often fail to break through the legislative logjam.

An example of how a policy proposal can fail, even though the interest groups proposing it had ample resources and faced little opposition, is the attempt by the telecommunications industry in 2000 to end a 3 percent excise tax on telecommunications.[27] The tax, which applied to all phone bills and cable television, was originally an excise tax on telephone service dating back to 1898. It had been repealed and reinstated several times since then, usually when the government felt the need to raise some additional cash. With the budget in surplus in 2000, the telecommunications companies thought this would be a good time to repeal the tax. A repeal would allow them to reduce the charges to their customers, and possibly raise their rates at the same time to increase their profits.

picture YOURSELF ...

AS A DANISH CITIZEN

Denmark is a society awash in interest groups, but their role differs greatly from the role of interest groups in the United States. Denmark and other Scandinavian countries have traditionally involved interest groups directly in government decision making, in a way that makes them almost part of the government rather than a set of interests pressing the government from outside.* As a Danish citizen, you can see how deeply your nation's interest groups influence policy making.

In this kind of system, the government assumes as a matter of course that all interest groups will be involved in any discussion, so the groups do not have to work very hard to get the government's attention. When an issue comes up for consideration, for instance, your government constructs a commission of civil servants, members of parliament, and representatives of all interest groups in order to discuss it and frame a proposed bill to deal with it. As the considered bill passes through all its stages, interest group representatives participate formally in the hearings and legislative debates. Once a bill passes, sometimes the interest groups, rather than the governmental bureaucracy, run whatever program has been established. For instance, the Danish unemployment

continued

compensation system is administered jointly by the national trade unions and the national employers association—not the government.

The significance of interest groups in government activities and policy making leads groups to be impressively organized. About 70 percent of Danish workers belong to unions (compared with 12 percent in the United States), and there is a wide range of unions, including the Danish Association of Managers and Executives, the Danish Union of Journalists, and the Danish Union of Church Workers. As a student, you are likely to be a member of the National Association of Students. Membership is voluntary, but more than half of all students are members. This association has served as a powerful force in shaping universities' internal policies and in shaping national policy, where it meets with other stakeholders such as the Danish Rectors' Conference in committees of the Ministry of Education.

Since essentially all groups are organized, business groups and corporations make up a smaller part of the universe of interest groups in Denmark than they do in the United States. Of the registered lobbyists in the United States, 67 percent represent corporations, trade associations, or professional associations (refer back to Table 10.2). In a survey of Danish interest groups, 40 percent are business or professional interests, 21 percent trade unions, and 34 percent citizen groups.[**]

Interest groups in Denmark are not as controversial as they tend to be in many other countries, because they are seen more as working cooperatively with other stakeholders to reach consensual decisions than as engaged in combat to win their particular point.

* Such a system is often called "neocorporatism." The chief examples of neocorporatism are the Scandinavian countries, plus Germany and Austria.

** Anne Binderkrantz, "Different Groups, Different Strategies: How Interest Groups Pursue Their Political Ambitions," *Scandinavian Political Studies, 31*(2), (2008), Table A1.

questions to consider

1. An advantage of a system like Denmark's is that it helps to ensure that all interests are represented in any decision. What might be disadvantages of such a system?

2. The Danish system emphasizes those with a stake in decisions, usually an economic stake, though it might also be a stake based on religion or ethnicity. Might there be problems with bringing into the process citizen groups, whose members are unified by a shared idea rather than by a shared economic or social position?

3. Could the U.S. system be changed to work like Denmark's? What would be required to make such a change?

The companies hired a major lobbying firm to press their case, and garnered favorable press treatment. They formed good alliances with other groups, including Mexican Americans who as frequent users of long-distance favored the bill. Nobody actively opposed the change, and the bill passed the House of Representatives in May with an almost unanimous vote. However, the bill languished in the Senate while the leadership dealt with other bills they considered more pressing. Just before the end of the session supporters made an effort to pass it by attaching it to the general Treasury appropriations bill, but the president vetoed that bill for other reasons. By the next session of Congress the budget surplus had disappeared, and there was no chance to get the bill passed. Despite all sorts of advantages, the bill failed in Congress, as often happens with proposals for change in a crowded docket.

Its supporters later succeeded partially, via a totally different tactic—litigation. In 2005, a Court of Appeals ruled that long-distance calls could not be taxed by the government. The IRS therefore issued new regulations that exempted long-distance calls and cable television from the excise tax. Local telephone service, however, continues to be taxed.

REPRESENTATION AND THE ORGANIZATION OF PUBLIC OPINION

Interest groups are the one part of the political system that can best represent public opinion and bring it to bear in an organized way on governmental authorities. Political parties cannot do this very well, because they are involved in trying to acquire governmental power for themselves. This quest for power compels parties to incorporate many compromises in their programs to appeal to the broadest spectrum of support, especially in a two-party system like the United States. Thus a political party, by virtue of its most basic goal, cannot usually serve to articulate and represent any single group's needs. It has a different task: to blend various needs into a larger organization. A party seeks to blend differences, but an interest group seeks to represent its members' wishes clearly and precisely.

This works well if all parts of society are represented by well-organized groups. The United States is something of a half-filled glass in this regard. Despite its well-developed interest group system, how accurately does it reflect American society? As we will see, the parts of society that are well represented by organized interest groups diverge from the overall society in various ways:

- First, interest groups tend to represent those who are financially well off more than those who are not so well-off.
- Secondly, producer interests—those involved in making a product—are easier to organize than consumer interests—those who purchase the product. Accordingly, producers are more thoroughly organized than consumers. Finally, some groups enjoy other special advantages that make it easier for them to organize themselves and influence officials.

ORGANIZATION OF THE WELL-OFF

In general, interest groups tend to represent the concerns of those who are relatively well-off. The prominence of corporations and trade associations in the interest group universe guarantees this, but even citizen groups have a tendency to over-represent the well-off.

Because joining a citizen group is a voluntary act that is not based primarily on economic incentives, the sorts of people who tend to join citizen groups are the same as those who volunteer or turn out to vote in elections: older, better-educated, more economically prosperous Americans. As a result, citizen groups tend to organize around issues that reflect the interests of such segments of society—issues like the preservation of historic buildings, protection of the environment, and protection of animals' rights.

Another reason why the well-off are more strongly represented in the interest group universe is that those who enjoy greater financial comfort are likely to have acquired, either from their education or from their jobs, the sorts of organizational and technical skills that interest groups need. As a result, groups representing the well-off are more likely than others to be effectively organized. For all of these reasons, those in the society who are well-off are better represented than those who are not. There are relatively few interest groups seeking to help poor, rural Americans or other disadvantaged groups.

PRODUCER INTERESTS AND CONSUMER INTERESTS

producer interest
A group of people involved in producing a product.

consumer interest
A group of people consuming a product.

Another distortion in the interest group universe is caused by the difference between "producer" interests and "consumer" interests. A **producer interest** is any group of people involved in making a product. Any product may involve a number of producer interests: a corporation, a trade union, and one or more professional organizations. Examples of producer interests are Microsoft Corporation, the United Auto Workers union, the American Medical Association, and the National Farmers' Union—any economic entity made up of those who produce something. A **consumer interest** is any group of people who use or purchase the producers' goods or services. Most groups of consumers are not formally organized, so it is harder to provide examples of them. But

some examples include the National Association of Homebuyers, the American Automobile Association (AAA), and Public Citizen, Ralph Nader's consumer advocacy organization.

Note that the producer/consumer distinction differs from the "well-off"/"not so well-off" distinction. Groups of consumers may be relatively well-off—those who buy cruise vacations, for instance, or upscale clothing—or they may be less well-off. And producer groups, while they include corporations and well-paid professionals, also include trade unions representing workers who are not very well-off.

Producer interests are always easier than consumer interests to organize due to the higher concentration of producer interests. To take one example, every family in the United States pays about $40 more for food each year because of import restrictions on sugar, which the powerful American Sugar Alliance of sugar growers defends.[28] The higher cost of sugar shows up not only in candies and soft drinks but also influences the cost of many other food items containing sugar, such as mayonnaise and bread. Although the added expense for a family is significant, it is not large enough that they will give up evenings and weekends to organize for a change in the restrictions. However, the money accumulates across the country to $1.9 billion—all concentrated on sugar cane growers in Florida, Louisiana, and Hawaii; beet sugar growers in a few states in the northern plains; and a small number of sugar-processing plants. This is enough money to make a difference of 10 or 20 percent in the profits of the companies and the earnings of their workers, and that is something for which people *will* give up their evenings and weekends. Washington is saturated with letters, campaign contributions, and lobbying visits from the affected companies and their workers—but Washington hears almost nothing from the people who bear the extra costs. The producers' strong organization supports the restrictions and faces very little organized opposition.

The bias of interest group activity toward producer groups pervades a wide range of policies—from regulations on telecommunications, finance, and other areas to product safety and the prices paid by consumers. This difference between producers and consumers is found in all countries, not just the United States. In a survey of German interest groups, for example, 61 percent of all interest groups consisted of corporate groups, unions, or professional associations. Only 3 percent represented "other" economic groups, mostly consumer groups.[29]

SPECIAL CIRCUMSTANCES AFFECTING GROUP ORGANIZATION

A variety of special circumstances also make it easier to organize some groups than others. For instance, it is easier to organize people who live or work closely together, it is easier to organize older people than younger people, and some groups are located in ways that heighten their significance to elected officials.

Contiguous Residence

It is easier to organize a group of people if they live close together and communicate with each other frequently than if they are spread throughout society and have only sporadic contact with each other. In the early days of the labor movement, the first groups to organize were groups like lumberjacks (who lived together in lumber camps in the forest) and miners (who lived together in company towns built near the mine). It was harder at that time to organize live-in servants, who by definition, lived separately from each other in the houses that they served. Today, contiguity continues to have its advantages: Church groups are relatively easy to organize, for instance, because they congregate once a week for worship services, and this makes it easy to organize them for political action.

Age

Just as citizens under 30 tend not to vote as regularly as older citizens, they are also more difficult to organize in interest groups. This is due in part to the same reasons that make them less likely to vote. For instance, younger citizens are often not as fully engaged with their role as citizens as they will be when they are older. Young people also typically do not have great resources, nor do they have a great deal of free time. They may be transient, serving in the military or studying in a state or city that they do not regard as their long-term residence, and thus less likely to commit time and money to improving the local situation there. As a result of all these factors, many students and other young people are not active in interest groups, and their needs tend to receive relatively little attention in public policies involving health care, transportation, and housing.[30]

Strategic Location

Some groups are strategically located and thus important to elected officials. For instance, while there are only about 1.25 million Cuban Americans in the United States, most of them are concentrated in Florida. With Florida wielding 27 electoral votes and so evenly divided politically that it is very difficult for a presidential candidate to win there without the Cuban American vote, the approximately one million Cuban Americans in the state get close attention from presidential candidates. This has helped Cuban-American interest groups like the Cuban-American National Foundation to exert a strong influence on American policy toward Cuba.

Given the difficulty of organizing those who are less well-off, the challenges involved in organizing consumer interests, and the variety of circumstances that give some groups special advantages in organizing and lobbying, we can conclude that the interest group universe in the United States does not reflect fully the concerns of all segments of society. Yet while the universe of interest groups does not represent all American interests as well as it might, if there were no interest groups at all,

★ MIGRANT WORKERS PICKING GRAPES Only 1 percent of agricultural workers are enrolled in labor organizations. What aspects of migrant workers' lives might make it difficult to organize them as an interest group?

government would probably be dominated by a truly small set of very powerful interests, as we saw in the introductory sketch of politics in Bangladesh. Although the universe of interest groups in the United States does not mirror society perfectly, it still serves to inject citizens' interests into the political process in a way that is crucial for democracy.

INTEREST GROUP REFORM

KEY TO understanding Efforts to reform the American system of interest groups have usually been set off by a scandal in lobbying. Just how much can these reforms actually help to solve problems associated with interest-group activity? Are they potent strategies that might transform interest groups' behavior? What are the problems they are trying to solve?

Just as we saw with political parties, interest groups are viewed with suspicion by many Americans, even though they are an integral part of the country's politics. As noted at the beginning of this chapter, interest groups are often referred to as "special interests," a term that underscores the concern of many Americans that interest groups, by seeking to promote the well-being of one part of society, work against the common good. Also, many people feel that the playing field is uneven, with some interest groups wielding large sums of money and using powerful connections in government. Although interest groups are the main vehicle by which politicians can become aware of the need for changes in policy and learn how those proposed changes will affect different groups of citizens, they are often regarded as a necessary evil.

INTEREST GROUP SCANDALS

Periodically in American history, scandals associated with interest groups have led to attempts to regulate lobbying and interest-group behavior. One of the factors that led to the rise of the Progressive movement in the early years of the twentieth century, for instance, was widespread reportage of bribery and corruption in the U.S. Senate.

More recently, in 2004, allegations of corruption and fraud arose in connection with Washington super-lobbyist Jack Abramoff. Abramoff was a well-connected Washington insider who represented a number of Indian tribes, foreign governments, and telecommunications firms. As a lobbyist he spent freely, organizing golf trips to Scotland for government officials and entertaining them in expensive boxes at professional sporting events. In highly publicized cases he was convicted in 2004 of defrauding his Native American clients of millions of dollars, and in 2006 he was convicted of trading favors for officials' votes.

There have been a number of attempts to regulate interest groups since the 1990s, and the Abramoff case proved the catalyst for yet another attempt in 2007. In general, these attempts have focused either on restricting group actions that are seen as particularly inappropriate, or on bringing greater transparency to the groups' activities. Transparency involves making sure that the activities of interest groups are carried out openly, with disclosure of whom the groups represent, how much they are spending, and who the recipients of their expenditures are.

RESTRICTION OF ACTIVITIES

Efforts to restrict the actions of interest groups have dealt both with their campaign activities (especially advocacy advertisements), and with the nature of their lobbying activities. The most important recent effort to restrict groups' activities in campaigns is the McCain-Feingold law, which we discussed in Chapter 8. However, as noted there, the *Citizens United v. Federal Election Commission* Supreme Court decision in 2010 eliminated portions of the bill.

Regarding lobbying activities, the main limitation on how lobbyists may contact government officials is found in the 2007 **Honest Leadership and Open Government Act,** passed in reaction to the Abramoff scandal to strengthen an earlier 1995 act known as the Lobbying Disclosure Act. The 2007 act:

Honest Leadership and Open Government Act
A bill regulating and limiting contacts between lobbyists and members of Congress

- Bars former members of Congress, officials of the executive, and staff members from engaging in lobbying activities for from one to two years after leaving office, to prevent a lobbying firm from unduly influencing them by holding out the possibility of employment immediately once they have left office.
- Makes it a federal crime for a lobbyist to provide gifts or meals to officials or their staff.
- Bars former senators who are now lobbyists from walking onto the Senate floor or going to the Senate gym.

Beyond the provisions of these laws, when President Barack Obama entered office he limited his administration's contacts with lobbyists in a number of ways. He did not allow lobbyists to participate in his transition team as he entered office, or to take jobs in his administration. And he did not allow members of his administration to talk with any lobbyists when they were designing projects that would be part of his economic stimulus package of 2009. All of these laws, and President Obama's restrictions, attempted to limit the extent to which lobbyists could use their personal connections or financial enticements to help influence decisions.

INCREASING TRANSPARENCY

Provisions to increase transparency by requiring lobbyists to register and to disclose their activities are found in the 1995 and 2007 acts. The 1995 act had required anyone serving as a lobbyist to register with the government so that there would be a clear list of who was lobbying. The 2007 act strengthened this requirement in a number of ways. Lobbyists now must submit a report of their activities four times a year, detailing all campaign contributions and all meetings with officials.

EFFECTS OF THE REFORMS

The direct effect of the reforms has been rather modest, as lobbyists and officials generally have been able to find other ways to communicate. For instance, a lobbying group that is connected to a PAC may refrain from buying a member of Congress a meal during business hours, but then can join the member, courtesy of the PAC, at a fundraising meal in the evening. At least some lobbyists have also been able to evade the 2007 act entirely. After the passage of the act the number of registered lobbyists dropped by about 15 percent.[31] No one thinks that the actual number of federal lobbyists declined during that time, but because of the more stringent reporting rules and the possibility of criminal penalties, many who could squeeze through loopholes in the definition of "lobbyist" chose to do so in order to avoid being subject to the rules.

There is a more serious problem with the reforms, however, than the fact that they have not been very effective. A common thread running through the reform efforts is a suspicion of moneyed interest groups. The reforms seek to limit lobbyists' use of gifts, meals, and employment offers to influence members of Congress. They seek to limit advertisements by groups that have a great deal of money. They seek to identify those who are providing a group with funds.

However, these efforts may simply be attacking symptoms of a deeper problem that is not addressed by the reforms—the fact that the interest group universe does not represent all parts of society equally well. Reformers are addressing a symptom of the problem—the fact that moneyed interests use their money—but they find it difficult to address the core problem.

SOCIAL MOVEMENTS

KEY TO understanding ★ A social movement is a unique kind of interest group that is loosely coordinated rather than formally organized. This loose organization offers both advantages and disadvantages over traditional interest groups. What sets them apart especially is that their activity requires few resources; thus they often express the concerns of those who would not otherwise have an articulate voice in politics. How can social movements influence political decisions?

In our introduction to interest groups we included the social movement as one type of interest group, but social movements have not figured largely in the rest of the chapter so far. This is because they do not act like other groups. They do not lobby, and they are not organized into formal structures. As mentioned earlier in this chapter, *social movements* are informal networks with minimal structure that deal with politics outside of normal governmental decision-making. Take a look at Figure 10.6 for one way to understand what a social movement is and how it compares to a political party or a traditional interest group.

As you see in Figure 10.6, a political party seeks primarily to determine who will occupy governmental positions, and is formally organized in a permanent structure. A traditional interest group is also formally organized in a permanent structure but seeks primarily to determine policy on some issue or issues. A social movement may be concerned either about issues or about who holds office; what sets it apart from either a party or a traditional interest group is its loose, informal, flexible structure.

MOVEMENTS THAT HAVE MADE A MAJOR IMPACT

Social movements have often had a major impact on politics. The most famous example is the success of the civil rights movement in the 1960s in desegregating public facilities and gaining the right to vote for African Americans. Another important social movement in American politics is Gay Pride. Gay Pride parades started in commemoration of the Stonewall Riots in New York City in 1969 but have developed into an annual event occurring simultaneously in many cities around the country. Gay, lesbian, bisexual, and transgender (GLBT) mobilization, and the gradual shift in Americans' views about rights of GLBT individuals, have been greatly strengthened by the movement.

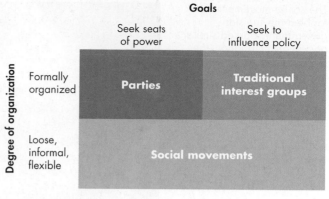

FIGURE 10.6

★ PARTIES, TRADITIONAL INTEREST GROUPS, AND SOCIAL MOVEMENTS

Source: W. Shively, *Power and Choice: An Introduction to Political Science*, 12e.

The feminist movement of the 1960s was another successful social movement. Partly in response to Betty Friedan's influential book *The Feminist Mystique,* and partly because of the generally heightened political activity at the time, many groups of women joined together to discuss common problems and define those problems as political (involving government policies or general practices in society) rather than as the personal fault of women. From these groups sprung a general, loosely coordinated campaign for changes in reproductive policy, workplace practices, and government regulations based on gender.

The massive anti-globalization protests against the World Trade Organization (WTO) meetings in Seattle in 1999 were another important social movement. The demonstrations against the WTO represented a joint effort by many disparate groups, ranging from anarchists to trade unionists, and filled the streets with tens of thousands of demonstrators who successfully disrupted Seattle and upstaged the meeting of WTO ministers. Most of the participants in this and later anti-globalization demonstrations have been young.

The most recent successful social movement is the Tea Party movement, which started in 2009 as a series of protests against taxes and the Obama administration's health care bill. The Tea Party is not a party and in fact has no unified central leadership. It is a disparate group, but the core beliefs of its members suggest a distrust of elected officials and a desire to remove most of them from office, a belief that the constitutional order of the country has been undermined by extra-constitutional actions of government, and a desire to lessen the impact of government in people's lives—especially by lowering taxes. It is a strongly anti-elite movement of people who have historically felt scorned by what they view as the political and media elites. The fact that the movement has managed to engage individuals who had previously been unengaged in politics is a testament to the Tea Party's success and popularity.

All of these movements have in common the fact that they were based on underrepresented groups in society that did not have many political resources: African Americans, gays and lesbians, women in the 1960s, young people, and nonpolitical, anti-elite members of the middle class. U.S. social movements typically are a last resort for the under-represented, but in poor countries like Bangladesh or in nondemocracies that do not have regular avenues for participation, they may be the main or only outlet available for most citizens. In 2011, for instance, after 23 years of

dictatorial rule in Tunisia, a social movement arose that toppled the government and led to a new, democratic regime; from there, social movements spread to Egypt and the rest of the Middle East. In China, where organized opposition is illegal, thousands of loosely organized social movements arise to protest local issues each year.

DISADVANTAGES AND ADVANTAGES

A social movement has both disadvantages and advantages. First, because by definition it is not well organized and does not have an established staff and structure, it is difficult for a social movement to amass many of the sorts of resources to which political leaders respond. Social movements typically do not have much money. They do not normally have specialized expertise to offer governments. They do not have ongoing staffs capable of doing long-term, tedious organizational jobs like amassing databases of voters and getting them to the polls.

Second, because social movements usually are temporary, counting their organizational life not in decades but in months or years, they cannot easily monitor an ongoing policy the way that an established interest group such as a union or a corporation can. They can respond explosively to a single event or cause, and either block an action of the government or bring about a new program, but they are not good at sifting through the thousands of pages of regulations that will follow annually from an established governmental program.

What they *can* do, though, is draw lively media attention to their cause via demonstrations, all of which provide dramatic material for television news. Consider the memorable, sometimes outrageous signs seen at Tea Party rallies, or the anti-globalization demonstrators in 1999 who dressed up as turtles, or the resolute civil rights demonstrators in the 1960s who risked being attacked by police dogs for the sake of their cause. Additionally, while a social movement may lack some of the advantages of an established interest group, it also lacks the inertia and inhibitions of an established

★ Anti-WTO protesters in Seattle, Washington, dressed as sea turtles to dramatize the effects of free trade on the environment. Does dramatic action of this sort help to accomplish the group's aims, or does it hurt? Why?

interest group. It does not have permanent staff who might worry that behaving in outrageous ways might hurt them later in their careers, or lobbyists who want to be able to speak calmly with government officials.

If social movements are successful, they often eventually morph into established interest groups. The civil rights movement after its successes of the 1960s settled into a group of national and local interest groups, including the NAACP, the Urban League, and others. The women's movement of the late 1960s evolved into a set of established interest groups, including the National Organization for Women (NOW) and Emily's List.[32] Social movements are ultimately not as effective on a day-to-day basis as traditional interest groups, but they do offer opportunities to groups that are not well represented by traditional interest groups to bring issues to the attention of the government in a sudden and explosive way. They can offer a voice for those who might otherwise remain unheard.

Why Are We
THE WAY WE ARE ?

Our discussion of interest groups in this chapter suggests two important characteristics of interest groups in the United States. First, we have a vibrant, active system of interest groups that use a wide array of tactics. This stands in stark contrast to the interest group systems—or lack thereof—of countries like Bangladesh, whose reliance on patrons and local networks makes it difficult for citizens to formally mobilize around a shared idea or occupation. Second, however, the face of the interest group universe differs significantly from the face of American society overall. How can we account for these two characteristics of American interest groups?

VARIED, ACTIVE INTEREST GROUPS

How did the United States develop such active interest groups? The main cause, undoubtedly, is the large role that government plays in our lives, both in regulating businesses and in providing benefits directly to people. Where there are many rules and regulations, there are many reasons to influence the government. All other countries with a large governmental presence in people's lives—Japan, Australia, Canada, the countries of Western Europe, and others—have a similarly large number of interest groups. In contrast, in Bangladesh as well as in all other poor countries that have small, weak governments, interest groups are few and weak.

However, American interest groups go beyond even what a large government role might explain. They are more active and more assertive than those in other countries, even countries with a large government presence in people's lives. This is probably because they have more varied opportunities to influence policy than are available in other countries. Since our political parties are relatively weak organizations, without much ability to force legislators to shape their votes to fit party doctrine, interest groups are able to fill a power vacuum, trying through a variety of means to shape members' votes. In countries with strong, disciplined parties like Great Britain or Argentina, lobbyists do not pay much attention to members of the parliament, because they know they cannot sway votes. Interest groups are active in these countries, but they tend to focus just on the executive and the bureaucracy, since a major focus of American interest groups—the Congress—is irrelevant for them.

A further reason for our active, assertive groups is that our divided system of government, with a separate and independent president, House of Representatives, Senate, and Supreme Court, opens up many avenues for interest groups to pursue advantages or to block others' efforts. So does our federal system, which gives considerable power not just to the national government but to 50 state governments as well. The American lobbying industry is one of the largest and most active in the world. The large role of government in Americans' lives, our weak political parties and our divided institutions of government offer interest groups many more opportunities for influence than they have elsewhere, and interest groups have developed ways to take advantage of those opportunities.

UNEQUAL REPRESENTATION OF AMERICAN SOCIETY

Another noteworthy aspect of American interest groups is that the universe of interest groups does not reflect all interests in American society equally well. As we saw, this is due at least in part to the natural advantages of organizing some kinds of groups. For instance, in almost every country of the world producer interests are more fully organized than consumer interests.

There are two ways in which the interest group universe might be reshaped to reflect all the interests in society more adequately. First, if we could lessen the role of money in American campaigns some of the advantages of the well-off would be reduced.

A second strategy might be for the government to bring interest groups deliberately into the process of government as entitled players, as we saw in the "Picture Yourself" example of Denmark. A guaranteed, automatic place at the conference table is a strong stimulus for a group to organize; the Danish government will even organize an interest group if none exists already for a recognizable interest. As a result, the interest group universe in Denmark is more representative of Danish society as a whole, at least in the realm of economic concerns, than is the case in the United States. This is probably not a likely strategy for making the playing field more level for American interest groups, however, since it would require changing many aspects of American politics simultaneously.

. . . AND WHY DOES IT Matter?

The United States falls somewhere between Bangladesh, which has only a few interest groups, and Denmark, where the interest group system is especially extensive. Essentially, all countries with well-developed economies have interest group systems that are extensively developed, as the United States and Denmark do. But what difference might it make if the United States had a system like Denmark's? Even assuming it would be possible to do this in the United States, a comparison of the two countries suggests that there are trade-offs in such a system.

One obvious advantage of Denmark's system is that with a more even playing field among all interest groups, there should be greater economic equality, as the advantages of the better-off parts of society are reduced. That certainly is true of the United States and Denmark. The richest 10 percent of Americans have incomes on the average that are 16 times as great as those of the poorest 10 percent, but in Denmark the richest 10 percent have incomes only 8 times as great as the poorest 10 percent.[33] And this is not just a matter of peculiarities of the United States or Denmark. When we look more generally at a group of countries that work with their interest groups in this way (the Scandinavian countries plus Germany and Austria) and compare them with a group whose interest groups have few formal ties with government (Ireland, Canada, the Netherlands, Switzerland, Great Britain, and the United States), the average ratio of rich incomes to poor incomes in the first group is just 7, while the average ratio in the second group is 11.[34]

In terms of economic equality, there seem to be advantages to an arrangement like that of Denmark. However, we must remember that bringing the interest groups directly into government makes them part of the system rather than allowing them to function as critics and gadflies. As we have seen, it leads them to have a relatively subdued public presence. It is possible that the lack of a vibrant link between populace and government leaves Danes feeling disconnected from government. In a survey, 56 percent of Danes, but only 31 percent of Americans, said that they thought there was nothing they could do about a law they might think to be unjust.[35]

We see, then, that how interest groups function in a country can make a real difference in policy outcomes and in people's lives. It matters, first of all, whether interest groups are abundant and well organized, but it also matters who these interest groups represent and what their role is in politics.

critical thinking questions

1. Given all of the advantages of money and concentrated producer interest on the part of business interests, it is not surprising that business interest groups often achieve their goals politically. But citizen groups that do not have these advantages are able to win reasonably often in head-to-head conflicts with business interests. How is it that citizen groups can often prevail, even though they usually lack the business interest's advantages? What are their countervailing advantages?

2. If the United States adopted a policy like that of Denmark, legally requiring the government to consult at all stages of bills with representatives of all affected interests, how do you think it would affect decision making?

3. Why is it that even though interest groups are widely derided, efforts to reform lobbying in Washington have had relatively little effect?

key terms

agricultural association, *334*

amicus brief, *345*

champion, *352*

citizen group, *333*

consumer interest, *356*

grassroots lobbying, *346*

group ratings, *348*

Honest Leadership and Open Government Act, *359*

inside tactics, *343*

interest group, *333*

lobbying, *343*

outside tactics, *343*

producer interest, *356*

professional association, *334*

selective benefits, *339*

social movement, *335*

trade association, *335*

MEDIA AND POLITICS

★ ★ ★

- Discuss the role and responsibility of the media in a democratic system.
- Examine new advances in media dissemination and explore their influence on the democratic process in the United States.
- Explain why the federal government has more power to regulate broadcast media than print media.
- Analyze the relationship between the government and media reporters.
- Assess the way the media report the news and consider how such reporting can lead to certain types of media bias.

PERSPECTIVE
How Have the Internet and Social Media Affected Politics?

Mohamed Bouazizi, like many people in Tunisia, could not find a job. He was 26 years old and had a university degree in computer science, but he was a victim of his country's soaring unemployment. In desperation, he began to sell fruit from a cart in his rural home town of Sidi Bouzid to support himself and his family. However, he did so without a license, and on December 17, 2010, a government official ordered him to stop. She confiscated the scale he used to weigh his fruit, an expensive item for him. This had happened before, and he knew he would have to pay a bribe to get his scale back. He complained, but the official just slapped him in the face. When Bouazizi went to the government office to retrieve his scale, officials would not let him in. Outraged, Bouazizi doused himself with gasoline in the middle of the street outside the government office. Shouting, "How do you expect me to make a living?" he lit himself on fire. He initially survived, but finally died on January 4, 2011.[1] This extraordinary act of defiance sparked a revolution in Tunisia that soon spread to other countries in the Middle East.

Not so long ago, Tunisia's state-controlled media could have suppressed news about Bouazizi's rebellious act. But word of his act spread among Tunisian citizens by way of Twitter and other social media. The news led to a mass uprising that was, in turn, publicized on blogs, social networking sites, and YouTube. With his security forces unable to put down the uprising, the authoritarian President Zine El Abidine Ben Ali fled the country. The result has been dubbed a "Twitter Revolution." Pundits had similarly dubbed earlier uprisings in Iran and Moldavia as Twitter revolts, and unrest in Tunisia soon spread to Egypt and beyond, with transformative results.

In the United States, the Internet and social media have helped to fuel a revolution of a different kind: the Tea Party movement. The movement brought together like-minded individuals to promote events and sponsor protests demanding reductions in government spending, the national debt, and the federal budget deficit. The Tea Party had no single leader; instead, its grassroots activists used the Internet to organize and to mobilize, as well as to publicize its causes to others. Millions of Americans took notice and joined the movement with great fervor. Then, in the 2010 midterm congressional elections, the Tea Party celebrated several victories. It used Twitter and Facebook to great effect, developing a presence on these sites that in many cases dwarfed that of the movement's opponents.[2] Tea Party candidates went on to win Republican primary elections in Colorado, Delaware, Florida, Kentucky, and Nevada.[3]

Throughout the world, interactive digital media are influencing politics and altering the way news is consumed and reported. Mainstream media are no longer the sole, or even the primary, source of news access and delivery. Smart phones and touch pads have made the news more mobile, and YouTube, Facebook, Twitter, and blogs have allowed anyone with access to the Internet to post anything they want.

THIS CHAPTER PROVIDES AN OVERVIEW of the media and its relationship to government. It begins with a discussion of the functions of the media. Although these functions have remained steady over time, the media themselves have changed considerably. The second section explains *how* these changes have happened by tracing the historical development of the media from the colonial era to the present and by examining the technological developments that have helped to spur change. The latter part of this chapter explores the relationship between reporters and officials. We look at the impact of the media, especially television, on political campaigns. Finally, we assess the way the media report the news and study three types of bias they might exhibit: ideological, corporate, and structural. In reading this chapter, keep in mind our two core questions:

WHY ARE WE THE WAY WE ARE?
WHY DOES IT MATTER TO YOU?

In particular, how does access to information contribute to a healthy democracy?

THE FUNCTIONS OF THE MEDIA

Throughout our history, the media have played a central role in providing information to the people. Elements of the **mass media**—the wide array of organizations and outlets that collect and distribute that information—have changed considerably over time, but their basic functions have remained largely the same. These functions include:

- reporting and interpreting the news,
- helping to set the public agenda,
- serving as agents of socialization,
- providing a public forum, and of course,
- providing entertainment.

In this section, we analyze these functions to assess the significant impact of the mass media on our political system.

mass media
The wide array of organizations and outlets that collect and distribute information to the people.

REPORTING AND INTERPRETING THE NEWS

An informed citizenry is an essential part of democracy: voting, taking stances on issues of public policy, and ensuring governmental accountability all depend upon it. As a result, one of the most important functions of the media is to convey information: *to report the news.* Media outlets from local newspapers to network news broadcasts and political blogs provide vital information on public policy and government performance that citizens in a democracy need. Reporters evaluate how government responds to natural disasters and notify the public of legislative initiatives. They inform their audience of crime and poverty rates, of the environmental and economic consequences of new industries in local areas, and of the deeds and misdeeds of public officials. In a democracy, we use all of this information to guide our decisions as we participate in public affairs—whether through posting a comment below an online article, forwarding that article to a friend, or casting a vote based on the information in that article.

filtering
The process by which the media decide what constitutes "news"— what to cover and what not to cover.

framing
The way the media interpret, or present, the news that they have decided to cover.

HELPING TO SET THE PUBLIC AGENDA

The media confront important decisions when reporting the news. First they must decide what, exactly, constitutes "news." Much more happens every day than we learn about through the news. Reporters must decide which events and issues to cover. This decision about what to cover and what not to cover is known as **filtering.** As we shall see later, factors ranging from the routines of reporters to profit motives influence such decisions.

Deciding *what* to cover is only the first step. Next, reporters must decide *how to interpret* what they report. The way that the media interpret a story—how they present it—is often referred to as **framing.** News stories provide us with a window on reality, but what we see depends upon on how the window

is framed. Framing involves choosing certain organizing themes that highlight particular aspects of a story at the expense of others. That frame, intentional or not, promotes a particular perspective.[4]

By choosing what to report and how to report it, the media play an important role in setting the public agenda. Coverage of a particular issue may, for example, influence whether or not legislation is enacted and how public figures react to particular issues. For example, articles by Samuel Hopkins Adams were published in *Collier's Weekly* in 1905 highlighting the false claims of and dangers posed by "patent medicines" (liniments, tonics, and pills peddled to consumers as a cure for everything from venereal disease to cancer), creating a public furor that led Congress to pass the Pure Food and Drug Act in 1906. More recently, on *The Daily Show,* Jon Stewart urged Congress to enact a health care bill for first responders to the September 11, 2001, terrorist attacks; his advocacy raised public awareness of the issue and has been credited as an important factor that convinced Congress to pass such legislation in December 2010.[5]

For many years, a Gallup poll has asked, "What is the most important issue facing the country?" Studies suggest that on some issues, such as crime, the level of concern expressed by respondents has more to do with the amount of media coverage the issue has received than with objective standards such as the crime rate.[6] It goes without saying that the public will not consider an issue to be important if they have never heard about it.

In the 1980s, for example, the media brought American attention to the famine in Ethiopia, but an international media watchdog group criticized that coverage: It noted that international media first ignored the famine; then, when they focused attention on it, they promoted short-term humanitarian relief rather than publicizing structural solutions that might have prevented another famine from occurring in the future.[7] Media attention prompted Michael Jackson and Lionel Richie to write the song, "We Are the World." Together with fellow pop stars they raised more than $250 million through a globally televised LiveAid concert in 1985 to benefit victims of the famine, but the absence of structural reform has made Ethiopia increasingly dependent on food aid from other countries.[8] Thus, the media helped to set the agenda by publicizing the situation in Ethiopia, but its decision to frame the famine as a humanitarian relief story rather than a structural reform story meant that the activism of the 1980s did not prevent the recurrence of famine, which erupted again in the Ethiopia in 1999.

SERVING AS AGENTS OF SOCIALIZATION

The media serve as important agents of political socialization. As discussed in Chapter 6, socialization refers to the process by which people form beliefs: the shaping of norms, customs, values, traditions, and social roles. The media socialize audiences not only through news reporting but also through entertainment programming. Thus, television dramas and comedy shows teach viewers about the values and standards that Americans apply to life, about the roles played by various groups in society (such as minorities, immigrants, women, and the LGBT community), and about government institutions (such as the criminal justice system). Even sporting events reinforce political values: competition (a hallmark of our capitalist system), the importance of rules, the regulation of behavior by authorities such as referees and umpires, and—through international events such as the Olympics—nationalism. Studies have suggested that young people who watch sports on television have higher levels of national loyalty and are more likely than their peers to view authority figures as legitimate.[9]

SERVING AS A PUBLIC FORUM

The media provide an opportunity for the exchange of views on political issues. Candidates and public figures use the media to publicize their differing views on public policy and to promote their agendas. The media also give citizens an opportunity to express their views through letters to the editor in newspapers and call-in shows on radio and television. The rise of the Internet and social media has exponentially increased such opportunities. Blogs, YouTube, Facebook, Twitter, and other social media make it possible for anyone to share his or her views. As a result, the line between news consumer and news producer has blurred.

This democratization of the news is both good and bad. On the positive side, the amount of information available to us from many different points of view has vastly increased. We can access news from the *Drudge Report*, the *Daily Kos*, the *Huffington Post*, *Little Green Footballs*, and *WorldNet Daily*—not to mention many less reputable sites. But this democratization of the news has undermined the **gatekeeping** role that mainstream media used to play. Professional reporters are supposed to vet the information they write, verifying facts and sources before publication. As gatekeepers, they are expected to avoid publishing rumors and outright falsehoods. Now that anyone can post a story, those safeguards have been undermined. Yet many people consider even fly-by-night blogs to have the same legitimacy as the *Wall Street Journal* or *The New York Times*.

In addition to using technology to express one's views, devices such as cell phone and Flip video cameras have allowed individuals to provide coverage of breaking news. Thus, even when the mainstream media are not present, officials now run the risk of having any statement they make in public recorded and uploaded for worldwide consumption. In 2011, protesters of Occupy University of California, Davis took cell phone video of campus police officer Lieutenant John Pike casually pepper spraying a seated line of students. Protesters uploaded that video to YouTube and received more than a million views within the first few hours. The video triggered a national debate over the use of

gatekeeping
The role played by reporters in vetting and verifying information and news sources in order to prevent publication of inaccurate information.

★ Onlookers use cell phone cameras and video to capture images of a police officer casually pepper spraying a seated line of students during an Occupy protest at UC–Davis.

force against student protesters and called attention to the issues raised by the Occupy movement. Hence, new technology raises public scrutiny of our democratic system.

Yet, to what extent did the protesters exploit the event to suit their purposes? To what extent are other individuals and groups using amateur media channels to manipulate the public? Conservative activist James O'Keefe—a self-described **citizen journalist** (a non-professional who nonetheless sets out to report news via alternative outlets such as the Internet)—has used undercover videos to embarrass a variety of organizations, including the community action group ACORN (the Association of Community Organizations for Reform Now). In 2009 he and a sidekick posed as a pimp and a prostitute and secretly recorded the conversations they shared with low-level workers from ACORN. Selectively edited videos of the pair seeking advice for how to secure a low-interest federal loan to buy a house were uploaded to the Internet and then eventually leaked to the mainstream media. The pair indicated the house would be used as a brothel populated by underage Salvadoran girls. The videos portrayed ACORN employees as apparently condoning illegal activity (prostitution) and offering advice for how to evade federal tax laws.[10] The videos were widely criticized for being purposely misleading, but they helped to put ACORN out of business.

The Internet has also made it easier to expose government secrets. In 2010, WikiLeaks—a nonprofit website launched in 2006 as a whistle-blowing site to bring "important news and information to the public"—published more than 250,000 leaked U.S. diplomatic cables, some of which were classified.[11] *The New York Times* and other news organizations subsequently published excerpts from those cables.[12] This monumental leak led to denunciations by government officials and to debates about whether WikiLeaks' editor-in-chief, Julian Assange, should be treated as a journalist and be forced to reveal his sources. Unlike conventional media, Assange's organization is not transparent. Except for Assange, the names of WikiLeaks personnel are mostly not known to the public. And there is no way for the public to know how WikiLeaks chooses what to leak. Is its selection designed to promote some sort of agenda? The answer is not clear.

PROVIDING ENTERTAINMENT

Of course, another important function of the media is entertainment. Not surprisingly, even news programs and talk shows are designed, in part, to entertain their audiences. Media outlets pick stories and decide how much coverage to allot to specific issues with this goal in mind. In the United States, most media outlets are for-profit corporations who are motivated to increase the size of their audience in order to make more money. Making news entertaining furthers this goal. The profit motive leads to the reduction of complex issues to simple narratives with an emphasis on drama, conflict, personalities, and brevity. Crime, scandal, partisan battles, unsolved mysteries, the rise and fall of celebrities, and titillation attract audiences. Elite media outlets such as *The New York Times* and *Wall Street Journal* may provide more in-depth coverage in a less flamboyant style than, say, the *New York Daily News,* but profit is just as much of a motive for them.

Unlike the media in many countries, media in the United States are mostly independently owned and operated enterprises that exist to make money. Thus, much of what appears in American media is pure entertainment. Indeed, news constitutes a small fraction of the schedule on network television, which people are most likely to turn to for dramas, sporting events, reality shows, and comedies. Even newspapers devote a great deal of space to entertainment: style, food, sports, music, and movie reviews.

citizen journalist
A non-professional who reports news via alternative outlets such as the Internet or other social media.

★ While television programs such as *Law and Order: Criminal Intent* may help to educate the public about the criminal justice system, they can also create misconceptions among viewers.

On television, people learn about the criminal justice system from *Law and Order,* about lawyers and politicians from *The Good Wife,* and about current events from *Saturday Night Live, The Daily Show,* and *The Colbert Report.* On the one hand, these programs raise public awareness of important issues, as we saw with *The Daily Show* and public health care for first responders. On the other hand, these programs can create misconceptions among the public. Do police regularly use brutality to elicit confessions from persons accused of crimes? Is blood splatter analysis or DNA evidence as reliable as shows like *Dexter* and *CSI* would have you believe? In recent years, legal analysts and law journals have tracked what they call the CSI effect—the tendencies of juries to acquit a suspect when they believe prosecutors did not produce sufficient forensic evidence. Jurors ask questions about "mitochondrial DNA" or "latent prints" when no such terms had been introduced during the court case.[13] The Ohio State Bar Association has even crafted instructions that can be issued to juries warning of the CSI effect, and individual judges have issued warnings to juries.

TRACING THE DEVELOPMENT OF MEDIA IN THE UNITED STATES

The mass media in America began with the opening of the first commercial press in 1638. By the 1800s, improvements in the printing press and the manufacture of paper made it quicker and easier to print newspapers. In 1837, Samuel Morse patented the telegraph, which allowed information to be transmitted long distances using Morse code. Several newspapers created the New York Associated Press in 1848 to share the cost of transmitting news via telegraph.[14] By 1861, telegraph cables linked the east and west coasts of North America, and by 1866 a successful trans-Atlantic cable—an amazing feat at the time—facilitated continuous communication among continents.[15]

The twentieth century saw the advent of radio and television, and the twenty-first century experienced the rise of social media. Each of these developments has radically altered the way news is delivered and given public figures new ways to communicate with the people.

KEY TO understanding ★

How have the media changed over time, and what impact have these changes had on the democratic process? Newspapers played a significant role in instigating revolutionary sentiment in colonial America. By the nineteenth century, technological advances made newspapers affordable to the lower economic classes who were now enfranchised. With the rise of radio and television, news from afar could be broadcast directly into viewers' living rooms—making issues more immediate. The proliferation of social media has ushered in a new age of information dissemination in which more people not only have access to information but take part in creating it.

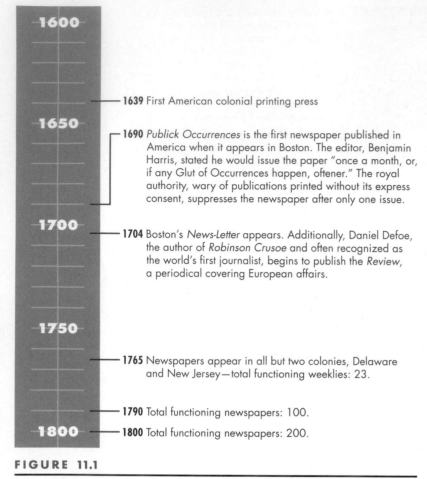

1600

1650

1639 First American colonial printing press

1690 *Publick Occurrences* is the first newspaper published in America when it appears in Boston. The editor, Benjamin Harris, stated he would issue the paper "once a month, or, if any Glut of Occurrences happen, oftener." The royal authority, wary of publications printed without its express consent, suppresses the newspaper after only one issue.

1700

1704 Boston's *News-Letter* appears. Additionally, Daniel Defoe, the author of *Robinson Crusoe* and often recognized as the world's first journalist, begins to publish the *Review,* a periodical covering European affairs.

1750

1765 Newspapers appear in all but two colonies, Delaware and New Jersey—total functioning weeklies: 23.

1790 Total functioning newspapers: 100.

1800   1800 Total functioning newspapers: 200.

FIGURE 11.1

★ THE STEADY RISE OF NEWSPAPERS IN AMERICA, 1639–1800

BEGINNINGS

When the first commercial press opened in Cambridge, Massachusetts, in 1638, it churned out almanacs, sermons, and religious tracts as well as books for the fledgling Harvard College, but newspapers did not become a fixture until the 1700s. The first colonial newspaper, *Publick Occurrences Both Forreign and Domestick,* published its one and only monthly edition in Boston in 1690. The paper was full of sensational stories and salacious rumors (including a report that the King of France had slept with his son's wife). The entertainment value of these stories intrigued readers but shocked Boston's Puritan clergy. Royal authorities banned further publication.[16] Fourteen years passed before another colonial newspaper, the Boston *News-Letter,* appeared. By 1765 there were newspapers in all but two of the colonies.[17] Then, concurrent with the American Revolution and its aftermath, came an information explosion: 100 newspapers by 1790, a number that doubled in the next decade alone.[18] Figure 11.1 offers a brief timeline of this steady rise of newspapers.

The media played an important role in the period leading up to the American Revolution. Although newspapers fanned the flames of revolution, the real catalyst proved to be the pamphlet *Common Sense,* anonymously published by Thomas Paine in January 1776. This pamphlet became a runaway bestseller and a potent rallying cry for revolution (see Chapter 2). American patriots recognized the power of the printed word to further their cause, and by the time the colonies declared independence, newspapers were passed from household to household and read aloud at meetings in coffee houses and inns. The press thus gained a prestige that made it an important player in the creation of the United States.[19]

THE PARTISAN PRESS

partisan press
A type of journalism associated with the late 1700s through the early 1800s when newspapers were affiliated with and controlled by a particular political party or emerging political party.

Newspapers became an important venue for debating the merits of the proposed U.S. Constitution during the ratification debates of 1787–1788. These debates helped to set the stage for the era of the **partisan press** that emerged when the new federal government created by the Constitution began to operate in New York, the nation's first capital. Political leaders sought to use newspapers to mold public opinion in support of their positions. Alexander Hamilton created the *Gazette of the United States* in 1789 to serve as the official mouthpiece of the incumbent Federalists.[20] In return, the

Federalist-controlled government awarded the paper patronage. Hamilton, who was Secretary of the Treasury, arranged for printing orders from the Treasury Department to go its way, and also anonymously wrote many *Gazette* articles. For a time the paper also printed the nation's laws, and its masthead carried the words "By Authority," thereby indicating its status with the government.[21]

When the nation's capitol moved to Philadelphia in 1791, Secretary of State Thomas Jefferson created an opposition newspaper, the *National Gazette,* to criticize Federalist policy. These rival newspapers reflected the breach between Hamilton and Jefferson, and helped to foster the development of political parties in the United States. The rival newspapers' polarized positions on matters of public policy, coupled with their frequent editorial attacks on each other, drew attention from around the nation. As a result, other newspapers followed their lead, aligning themselves with one party or the other.[22]

THE PENNY PRESS AND YELLOW JOURNALISM

Technological developments transformed newspapers in the 1800s. Instead of making paper by hand, as had been done for eighteenth-century newspapers, newly developed machines made paper quickly and easily. Before these developments, a printer could only produce about a thousand copies of a newspaper per day.[23] Advances in printing presses allowed publishers to print newspapers cheaply and rapidly, leading to the emergence in 1830 of the **penny press**— newspapers that literally sold for a penny (rather than the six cents that was typical at that time). The sharp reduction in price made newspapers accessible to people of every economic class and led to a dramatic increase in sales. Economic incentives spurred newspapers to focus on issues other than politics, such as style and entertainment. As a result, the era of the partisan press came to an end. By the 1850s, members of Congress were using their *franking privilege* (their ability to send mail to constituents free of charge) as an alternate means of communicating directly with the people.

The large daily circulation of the penny press spurred advertising—another important source of revenue for newspapers. More money allowed newspapers to hire more reporters, and the telegraph allowed reporters around the nation to transmit information quickly to newspapers. This helped give rise to Washington correspondents who covered political news in the nation's capital.

Competition for readership—epitomized by the heated rivalry between publishing giants William Randolph Hearst and Joseph Pulitzer—led to the rise of **yellow journalism** in the late 1800s. Marked by scandal-mongering, sensational reporting with blaring headlines, and the introduction of pages of comics printed in color in the Sunday edition, the phrase "yellow journalism" originally referred to a hugely popular comic strip that first appeared in Pulitzer's *New York World.* That comic depicted a goofy-looking "Yellow Kid"

penny press
Newspapers that emerged in 1830 and that, due to technological advances, sold for one penny—a sixth of what papers had previously sold for. This development made newspapers accessible to a wide array of people from all economic classes.

yellow journalism
A type of journalism that emerged in the late 1800s, characterized by scandal-mongering and sensationalistic reporting.

★ The development of hand-cranked, flatbed presses, and eventually steam-driven rotary presses made the printing process even faster.

wearing a brightly colored yellow dress, shown in situations connected with the news of the day. Hearst later lured the Yellow Kid to the rival *New York Journal,* and the image of the Kid became an advertising gimmick, plastered on walls through New York City. Critics began to derisively refer to these newspapers as the "yellow press," and the term *yellow journalism* became a pejorative term denoting poorly researched and exaggerated reporting. Whatever its merits, yellow journalism led to soaring circulation. By 1898, the *New York Journal's* Sunday edition consisted of as many as 52 pages and reached more than 600,000 readers.[24]

THE RISE OF OBJECTIVE JOURNALISM AND THE FOURTH ESTATE

objective journalism
A type of journalism that embraces the idea that newspapers should report news in a fair and neutral manner, devoid of partisanship and sensationalism (as opposed to yellow journalism).

A backlash against yellow journalism led to the rise of **objective journalism:** the idea that newspapers should report "facts" in a fair and neutral manner that was devoid of partisanship and sensationalism. Arthur Ochs, who bought *The New York Times* in 1896, embraced this view, and the *Times*—in contrast with Hearst's *New York Journal* and Pulitzer's *New York World*—tried to exemplify this new approach.

Objective journalism is the antithesis of the partisan press, and it was promoted by another early twentieth century development: journalism schools. Joseph Pulitzer served as the catalyst for this development. The University of Missouri opened the first journalism school at his urging in 1908, and when Pulitzer died in 1911 he left two million dollars to Columbia University. As a result of this bequest, Columbia opened a School of Journalism in 1912 and created the Pulitzer Prizes, which included awards for outstanding journalism. Thus, many people today associate Pulitzer with journalistic excellence rather than yellow journalism.

Fourth Estate
A term used to describe the press as a social and political force independent of government.

muckraking
A type of journalism prevalent in the early part of the twentieth century that exposed corruption in business and government in order to promote reform.

The rise of objective journalism helped to make newspapers watchdogs for government accountability. The term **Fourth Estate** is often used to describe the press as a force independent of government. During the Progressive Era of the 1890s through the 1920s, reporters and other authors began to publish articles focusing on corruption in government and business, and on social issues such as child labor and working conditions. This early investigative reporting came to be known as **muckraking** and it often prompted governmental action, such as the enactment of the Pure Food and Drug Act discussed earlier.

The term "muckraking" is associated with early twentieth century reporting, but investigative journalism and book-length exposés continued beyond that point. Ralph Nader's 1965 book *Unsafe at Any Speed* exposed the dangers of automobiles, prompted the passage of legislation to promote auto safety—including seat belt laws—and fostered a consumer rights movement in the United States. The reporting of Carl Bernstein and Bob Woodward for the *Washington Post* in the 1970s helped to expose the Watergate scandal that led to the resignation of President Richard Nixon in 1974.

RADIO

Wireless communication of telegraph signals began in the late 1890s, and experiments in transmitting the human voice soon followed. Commercial radio emerged in the 1920s, with the number of licensed radio stations in the United States rising from 30 in January 1922 to almost 500 just a year later.[25] With the development of commercial broadcasting came expanded coverage of news and politics. Print media allowed for the widespread distribution of news, but the development of radio in the twentieth century provided an intimacy and immediacy that the print media could never have achieved. Edward R. Murrow's reports on the German bombing of London in 1940 transmitted the sounds of war to a spellbound radio audience in the United States.

Although politicians had long used print media to communicate with their constituents, radio allowed political leaders to bypass the critical filter of reporters and bring their messages, in their own voices, directly into the living rooms of Americans. President Franklin D. Roosevelt used radio as a new way to interact with the American people. Starting on March 12, 1933—just days after his inauguration—FDR gave the first of 31 radio speeches called "Fireside Chats." His relaxed tone and friendly voice calmed an anxious nation in the grips of the Great Depression and later, World War II. He used simple language, stories, and analogies to justify his policies, and he addressed his audience as "you" and "we"—thereby forging an intimate bond with the people and building a sense of shared purpose. Millions wrote to the president to express their appreciation.[26]

Radio continues to play an important role in politics today. This is largely because of **talk radio,** a media forum that opens the lines to listeners to discuss various topics of interest; talk radio became a major political force in the 1990s. Americans who felt that mainstream television and newspaper media outlets articulated liberal viewpoints found an outlet in these talk shows. Hosts with a clear-cut conservative viewpoint, such as Rush Limbaugh, Laura Ingraham, and Sean Hannity, not only voiced their own opinions but interacted with callers on the air. This allowed for a direct (and sometimes emotional) form of public discourse. By 1997, news/talk had become the most popular radio format in America. Figure 11.2 shows the trends in talk radio listenership between 1995 and 2008.[27]

talk radio
A radio forum that opens the lines to listeners to discuss various topics of interest.

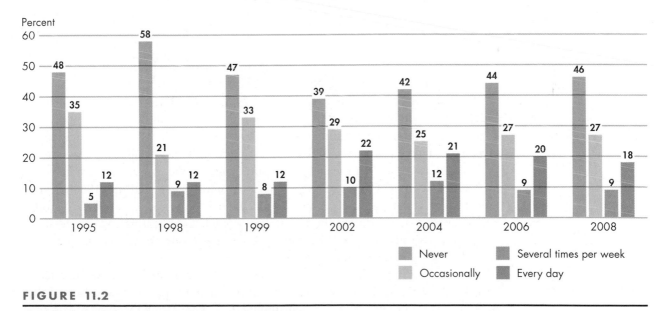

FIGURE 11.2

★ TRENDS IN RADIO TALK SHOW LISTENERSHIP

What do these numbers suggest about the popularity of talk show radio? What factors do you think have contributed to this trend?

Source: From Harrison, *American Democracy Now*, 2/e, figure. 10.3, p. 317. Data from The Gallup Poll. *Media Use and Evaluation.* http://www.gallup.com/poll/1663/media-use-evaluation.aspx Copyright © 2010 McGraw-Hill Companies, Inc.

Today, nationally syndicated hosts such as Limbaugh and Hannity reach some 15 million listeners a week.[28] Efforts by liberals to break into the talk radio market have had only limited success. Air America, a network designed to promote talk show programming with a liberal viewpoint, lasted only six years—from 2004 to 2010.

TELEVISION

Bell Laboratories first demonstrated television in the United States in 1927, telecasting the image and voice of Commerce Secretary Herbert Hoover (elected President of the United States the next year) from Washington, D.C., to New York City, but commercial broadcasting did not begin until the late 1940s. Like radio before it, television exploded onto the national scene, as Figure 11.3 depicts, bringing an even greater immediacy than radio, for the obvious reason that it allowed people to watch as well as listen to events.[29]

By 1982, a government report concluded that more Americans owned televisions than refrigerators or indoor plumbing.[30] Since viewing was then primarily limited to the three broadcast networks (ABC, CBS, and NBC), Americans watched events together. The assassination of President John F. Kennedy on November 22, 1963, demonstrated the power of the new medium. Over the next three days, Americans were glued to their television screens as they watched, live, the shooting of the alleged assassin Lee Harvey Oswald by Jack Ruby, the return of the president's body to Washington, and the state funeral. NBC alone aired over 71 hours of coverage. Some 166 million Americans in more than 51 million homes watched the events unfold, often for hours on end, with an average of 93 percent of all households with a television set tuned in.[31] Television thus created a national community with shared political experiences.

By the 1960s, the nightly newscasts of the three major television networks became a staple of American television. Newspapers had been Americans' primary source of news through the early 1960s, but by 1967 Americans cited television as their primary source of news. Walter Cronkite, the anchorman of the "CBS Nightly News" and a major on-screen presence during the Kennedy assassination, earned the moniker "the most trusted man in America."[32] Television strongly influenced public perceptions. For example, many argue that the daily television images of the war in Vietnam helped to turn public sentiment against the war. When Cronkite concluded in a 1968 televised report that the war was likely to end in stalemate, it sent "shock waves" through the White House.[33] Later, during the 1970s, dramatic televised hearings by congressional committees investigating the Watergate affair helped to convince the nation that President Nixon should resign or be impeached.

Such changes in public opinion based on the influence of news sources are referred to as **media effects.** These changes can lead to volatility in everything from policy stances to voting preferences. Those without strong preexisting views on a particular topic are most susceptible to media effects. Stories about events in faraway countries may have greater media effects because such stories often involve topics far removed from our ordinary experiences.

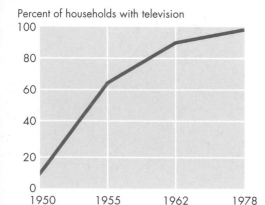

Percent of households with television

FIGURE 11.3

★ THE EXPLOSION OF TELEVISION ONTO THE NATIONAL SCENE

Only about 9 percent of U.S. households had television in 1950, but in just 30 years that figure rose to almost 100 percent.

Source: Data from Steve M. Barkin, *American Television News: The Media Marketplace and the Public Interest* (Armonk, NY: M. E. Sharpe, 2003), p. 37.

media effects
Changes in public opinion based on the influence of the media.

Television was transformed by the development of satellite technology and cable television in the 1970s and '80s. Satellites allowed for the instant transmission of video images around the world. For example, images of President Nixon's path-breaking visit to China in 1972 allowed Americans to watch in real time as he met with Chinese leaders and visited historic sites such as the Great Wall. Satellite technology spurred the proliferation of cable television networks, which gave television viewers a huge array of programming to choose from. Cable television had long existed to provide access to the broadcast networks in remote areas but only became a venue for separate cable networks in the 1970s. By 1980 there were 28 cable television networks, but only a little over 10 percent of American households had cable service. By the end of the decade, there were 79 cable networks and more than half the homes in the United States were connected.[34]

The creation of the 24-hour Cable News Network (CNN) in 1980 fundamentally altered the nature of television news by helping to create a never-ending news cycle. Fox News and MSNBC joined the fray in 1996. Political scientists and other analysts have studied the impact of these 24-hour news channels on politics, sometimes referred to as the CNN effect. Cable news created an even greater immediacy to the news, focusing public attention on crises as soon as they occurred. Instantaneous reporting forced politicians and public officials to respond publicly to crises more quickly than they used to, giving them less time to reflect on their decisions. Figure 11.4 provides an overview of where on television most Americans get their news since the advent of cable news.

In addition, cable news relied heavily on talk shows because they were cheap, easy to produce, and appealed to viewers. However, the heated rhetoric of such shows sometimes blurs the line between news and entertainment. That line has become even

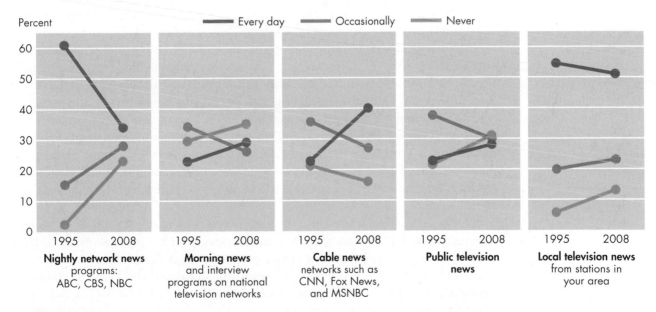

FIGURE 11.4

★ SOURCES OF TELEVISION NEWS FOR AMERICANS

Where have most Americans gotten their television news once cable news came onto the scene?

Source: From Harrison, *American Democracy Now*, 2/e, figure. 10.4, p. 318. Data from The Gallup Poll. *Media Use and Evaluation.* http://www.gallup.com/poll/1663/media-use-evaluation.aspx. Copyright © 2010 McGraw-Hill Companies, Inc.

more complicated with satirical programs such as *The Daily Show with Jon Stewart* and the *Colbert Report*. A 2004 poll by the Pew Research Center for the People and the Press found that 21 percent of people age 18 to 29 said that they regularly learned news about that year's presidential campaign from *The Daily Show* and *Saturday Night Live*.[35]

Prior to cable and satellite television, ABC, CBS, and NBC had truly been *broadcast* networks—each appealing to as wide an audience as possible. The proliferation of channels provided by cable and satellite services led to **narrowcasting,** which is designed to target a particular niche in the market. This has led to channels that focus on specialized programming dealing with everything from sports to food; target a particular demographic group such as Spanish-speaking viewers (TeleMundo), African Americans (Black Entertainment Television), or young people (MTV); or appeal to people with particular ideological views. Fox News, for instance, appeals to more conservative viewers, while MSNBC appeals to more liberal viewers. Narrowcasting thus polarizes the American public along both demographic and partisan lines, rather than uniting them as the three networks used to do.

THE NEW MEDIA

The media were transformed yet again by a series of technological developments in the late twentieth and early twenty-first centuries. Satellite technology and cable were early examples of the so-called **new media.** They paved the way for the Internet and smart phones, which created unparalleled opportunities for direct communication with the American people. At the same time, **social media** outlets such as blogs, Twitter, YouTube, and Facebook democratized the process by giving ordinary citizens an easy opportunity to express and share their views, as discussed earlier.

The Internet—with its many opportunities for specialized websites and blogs—is also an ideal venue for narrowcasting. Conservatives turn to blogs such as Hit and Run, Little Green Footballs, and Redstate, while liberals turn to blogs such as the Daily Kos, Crooks and Liars, and Think Progress. By allowing consumers to rely on news sources that merely reinforce their preexisting views, narrowcasting may increase partisanship, polarize public opinion, and make political compromise by policy makers more difficult. From blogs to online editions of traditional newspapers and magazines, news increasingly reaches the public from the Web. Tweets and smart phone apps have made online access even easier. Cable television has been hurt by this trend, as indicated by Figure 11.5.

Newspapers have also been hurt. In 1999, only 6 percent of people polled claimed to get most of their national and international news from the Internet. By 2009, that number was up to 42 percent—a higher percentage than those who claimed to get most of their national and international news from newspapers, as Figure 11.6 shows. Between 2009 and 2010 newspaper circulation rates continued to fall, as did their advertising revenue. Indeed, newspapers were the only major media outlet to see a decline in advertising revenue. (To compare the change in revenue across various media, see Figure 11.7.)

narrowcasting
Programming designed to appeal to a particular segment of the population (as opposed to broadcasting, which is designed to appeal to as many people as possible).

new media
Media, such as cable television and the Internet, that that led to a vast increase in the amount of information available to the people and allowed targeting of particular segments of the population via specialized channels and Web pages.

social media
Technologies such as blogs, texting, video file sharing, and other Internet resources that enable people to exchange information. These technologies have helped to blur the line between news consumer and news producer.

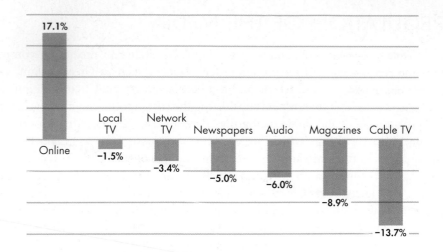

FIGURE 11.5

★ AUDIENCES TURN TO THE WEB

Bars show the percentage change in audience from 2009 to 2010.

Source: Pew Research Center.

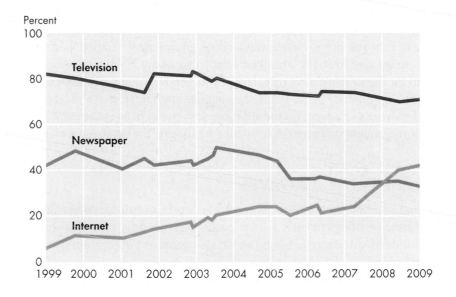

FIGURE 11.6

★ COMMON SOURCES OF NEWS IN THE UNITED STATES

This figure shows where Americans got most of their national and international news from 1999 to 2009.

Source: Pew Research Center.

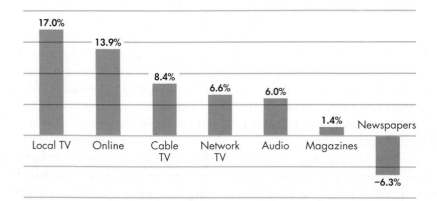

FIGURE 11.7

★ ADVERTISING REVENUES FOR U.S. MEDIA OUTLETS

Bars show the percentage change in revenue for U.S. media outlets from 2009 to 2010. What do Figures 11.5, 11.6, and 11.7 suggest about the changing role of newspapers in the United States? Are these changes any cause for concern?

Source: Pew Research Center.

GOVERNMENT REGULATION OF THE MEDIA

★ KEY to understanding

The broadcast media helped to precipitate government regulation of scarce airwaves in order to promote the public interest. The emergence of cable and satellite technology diminished the scarcity of airwaves but raised questions of whether and how to regulate new technology such as the Internet. Why does the government have greater power to regulate the broadcast media than the print media? Is it appropriate for the government to regulate the content of broadcasts? What about content on the Internet?

In many other countries, state-run media are common. Even in some democracies, such as Great Britain, radio and television have been run as a public corporation, with government subsidizing the cost of technological development and news gathering. The British Broadcasting Corporation (BBC), which began radio transmissions in 1922 and television transmissions in 1936, is an example of such a *public service broadcaster*. In other words, it was designed to provide high-quality, balanced coverage without the economic pressures associated with private ownership. However, state-run media in many other countries—ranging from China to Iran—are a far cry from the BBC. There, state-run media are used to tout the "party line" and squelch news that might put the government in an unfavorable light. Indeed, much of the world enjoys little freedom of the press (see Figure 11.8).

By contrast, the media in the United States are mostly privately owned and operated for profit. Moreover, the First Amendment of the Constitution guarantees extraordinary freedom of the press. Nonetheless, some government regulation of the media does exist in the United States. This is especially true of the broadcast media (radio and television) for the simple reason that airwaves are limited. When commercial radio stations began to proliferate in the 1920s, their signals often interfered with each other. As more and more stations went on the air, more and more chaos ensued. As a result, the radio industry sought government regulation to allocate the scarce airwaves.

REGULATING THE AIRWAVES

Federal Communications Commission (FCC)

An independent U.S. government agency created by the Communications Act of 1934 to oversee and regulate the broadcast industry.

The Communications Act of 1934 created the **Federal Communications Commission (FCC)** to issue broadcast licenses (which could be revoked for failure to abide by FCC rules), allocate broadcast frequencies (which are treated as public property to be leased by the government), and regulate broadcasters to ensure that their use of scarce airwaves is in the public interest.[36] The FCC's power extends over radio, television, wire, and cable communications.

The FCC has considerable power to determine who can broadcast. It has the authority to issue, revoke, or deny renewal of broadcast licenses to radio and television stations. The FCC also has the ability to regulate private ownership of the broadcast media by limiting the number of broadcast stations a single entity can own. Regulation of ownership is designed to prevent a monopoly of scarce airwaves by a small number of broadcasters. The emergence of cable and satellite technologies diminished the scarcity argument and led Congress to pass the Telecommunications Act of 1996 which abolished many of the cross-market barriers that had previously prevented telephone companies, cable systems, and broadcasters from offering similar services.[37]

This deregulation allowed single companies to offer a wide array of services, such as telephone, cable, satellite, and Internet. Critics have complained that this has led to too much concentration of ownership in a few large corporations such as Comcast and Time Warner. The Telecommunications Act still barred a single entity from owning stations with an aggregate national audience of more than 35 percent, but the FCC—which reviews ownership rules every four years—subsequently took steps to allow

Free

Partly free

Not free

FIGURE 11.8

★ MAP OF PRESS
FREEDOM

Based on this map, which
countries possess the
greatest press freedom?
Can you identify any
characteristics of these
countries that may help to
account for that freedom?

Source: Freedom House. (http://www
.newseum.org/exhibits-and-theaters/
permanent-exhibits/world-news/
press-freedom-map.html)

greater concentration of ownership. In 2003, it proposed increasing the aggregate national audience cap from 35 to 45 percent. The proposal generated strong opposition, but Congress agreed to increase the cap from 35 to 39 percent. Subsequent attempts by the FCC to relax the existing ban on cross-ownership of newspapers and broadcast stations in a single market have been challenged in court, where they remain in limbo.[38]

With cell phone signals and wireless Internet connections taking up more and more of the airwaves, dropped calls and slow connections are becoming more common. To counter these problems, the FCC has proposed reclaiming airwaves from "inefficient" users, such as broadcast television, and auctioning them off to the highest bidder. This has spurred a battle between the old media, who do not want to relinquish airwaves, and the new media who would benefit from the move.[39]

Yet another battle rages over so-called **net neutrality**—the unhindered flow of information over the Internet without interference by those that run or own the service providers. The FCC has rules pending that would prevent Internet providers from blocking access to particular websites or applications or from giving preferential treatment to content providers who pay for faster transmission. The rules face court challenges and opposition from Republicans in Congress.[40] In general, Europe has maintained a more hands-off approach to the issue. There, mobile providers have considerable discretion to manage and prioritize data. It is common, for example, to block the use of Skype because it would take away from the revenue that could be generated by an operator's own calling services. However, the European Union is planning a review of the issue.[41]

net neutrality
The unhindered flow of information over the Internet without interference by those who run or own the service providers.

REGULATING BROADCAST CONTENT

The FCC's interest in assuring that scarce airwaves are used in the public interest has led to content regulation of the broadcast media. From early in its history, the FCC sought to assure that broadcasters offer fair, balanced coverage of public issues and political campaigns.

One example of content regulation is the **equal time rule.** If stations sell air time for a political advertisement for one candidate, they must provide equal time to any other candidate who wishes to purchase it. From 1949 to 1987, the FCC also tried to promote balanced coverage of public issues more generally through the so-called **Fairness Doctrine.** As described by the FCC, the Fairness Doctrine required licensees to

> . . . devote a reasonable percentage of their broadcasting time to the discussion of public issues of interest to the community served by their stations and [to ensure] that such programs be designed so that the public has a reasonable opportunity to hear different opposing positions on the public issues of interest and importance to the community.[42]

The wording of the Fairness Doctrine was vague. What exactly is a "reasonable percentage" of broadcasting time? How does one determine which issues are "of interest and importance to the community"? Nonetheless, the FCC continued to enforce the doctrine, and the U.S. Supreme Court unanimously upheld its constitutionality in 1969.[43] Some, however, believed that the Fairness Doctrine actually inhibited the discussion of competing viewpoints rather than promoting it because stations found it easier to avoid discussing certain topics altogether than to broadcast competing viewpoints. In addition, cable and satellite technology undermined the scarcity argument that had been used to justify the Fairness Doctrine.

The FCC stopped enforcing the Fairness Doctrine in 1987. This had an unexpected consequence: It led to the emergence of political talk radio. Rush Limbaugh began his nationally syndicated radio talk show in 1988. When the Fairness Doctrine was enforced, a radio station airing a conservative talk show also had to air a liberal talk show or otherwise provide balanced coverage of issues in a single show. This mostly prevented stations from airing political talk radio. Without the Fairness Doctrine, political talk radio—often vitriolic in tone—exploded onto the scene and has expanded to cable television.

In the wake of the bombing of the Alfred P. Murrah Federal Building in Oklahoma City in 1995, President Bill Clinton denounced "promoters of paranoia" who spread hatred on the public airwaves, noting that "bitter words can have consequences."[44] Clinton

★ Rush Limbaugh talks politics on his radio program.

claimed that he was not targeting conservative talk radio with that comment, but such programs dominated the airwaves. In 2009, Clinton, though no longer president, suggested reinstating the Fairness Doctrine to provide public exposure for countervailing points of view and ensure a more balanced coverage of issues on the air, and he is not alone in making this suggestion.[45]

In its effort to promote "the public interest," the FCC also has the power to issue fines to stations that broadcast indecent or obscene material, and to revoke or deny renewal of such a station's license. As discussed in Chapter 4, obscene material is not protected by the First Amendment. "Indecent" material that would otherwise pass constitutional muster may still be punished if broadcast. The FCC cited the following reasons for this lower threshold for punishing indecent broadcast material: access to broadcasts by unsupervised children, the need to protect nonconsenting adults who may inadvertently tune into offensive broadcasts, protection of the privacy of households that broadcast signals invade, and the scarcity of spectrum argument that allows government to regulate airwaves in the public interest.[46]

The Supreme Court ruled in favor of the FCC position in a landmark 1978 case involving a New York radio station that aired comedian George Carlin's "Seven Dirty Words" monologue.[47] More recently, the FCC fined television stations for broadcasting the infamous "wardrobe malfunction" during the halftime of the 2004 Super Bowl when Justin Timberlake tore off part of Janet Jackson's costume, briefly exposing her breast on national television. The Supreme Court heard another challenge to FCC regulation of the airwaves in 2012, but ultimately declined to rule on whether FCC regulations violate the First Amendment.[48]

Cable and satellite transmissions are not subject to the same restrictions as the traditional broadcast media (since the scarce spectrum argument does not apply and people pay to receive these transmissions). Thus, shock jock Howard Stern abandoned FM radio as the broadcast medium for his sexually provocative show and moved to satellite radio in 2006 in order to avoid FCC regulations.

picture YOURSELF ...

AS A MEDIA CONSUMER IN ITALY

Italy is a parliamentary, democratic republic in Europe—a region of the world that boasts a very high level of press freedom. Yet, despite freedom of speech and of the press being constitutionally guaranteed in Italy, its media are not so free. In fact, the map of press freedom around the world in Figure 11.8 shows Italy's press as only "partly free." Why this discrepancy? In large measure, the culprit is Silvio Berlusconi, the former prime minister of

Italy. As his tenure as prime minister drew to a close, he gained worldwide notoriety for his "bunga-bunga" sex parties and his subsequent trial on charges of abuse of power and having sex with an underage prostitute He finally resigned not because of these scandals but because of the European economic crisis and the fear that Italy might default on its debts.

Berlusconi continues to be notorious for the control he exerts over the Italian

continued

media. For some 30 years, he and his family have controlled the top three commercial television channels in Italy, and as prime minister, he was able to control the state-run RAI television. As a result, he was in a position to dictate what is broadcast to about 90 percent of the national audience. He also owns print media. Through a combination of personal threats and political and corporate pressure, he used the media to build and maintain his own political power and to fend off charges of corruption.

After earning a fortune in the real estate market, Berlusconi founded the cable television station Telemilano in 1974 and soon began to expand his acquisitions to broadcast television, newspaper and magazine publishing, and online services, not to mention a soccer team and other investments. In the process he broke the monopoly of RAI, the state-run television service, and introduced such innovative television programming as Italy's first nude game show. He then created a political party, Forza Italia (cleverly named after the soccer chant, "Go, Italy!"), and used his media empire to catapult the party and himself to power. He first served as Italy's prime minister from 1994 to 1995, then again from 2004 to 2006, and finally from 2008 to 2011.

To view this situation from an American perspective, the author of a book on Berlusconi's media empire put it this way:

> Imagine if Bill Gates of Microsoft were also the owner of the three largest national TV networks and then became president and took over public television as well. Imagine that he also owned Time Warner, HBO, the *Los Angeles Times,* the New York Yankees, Aetna insurance, Fidelity Investments, and Loews theaters, and you begin to get a sense of how large a shadow Silvio Berlusconi casts over Italian life.*

Such an extreme concentration of ownership—which the U.S. government has sought to prevent—has the potential to limit the marketplace of ideas. By squelching competing points of view, it would undermine the public good that FCC regulations have sought to instill. Italy's media monopoly serves as a warning about what could happen in the United States if ownership of the media were allowed to become even more concentrated, and it reminds us of the important role that the media should play as a Fourth Estate—a role largely ceded when Berlusconi was in power because of his tight grip on the supposedly "free" media.

In his last three years in office, Berlusconi publicly urged businesses not to advertise in newspapers that were critical of his handling of the economy; created a task force to examine ways to control not only the reporting of Italian media but also foreign media reporting in Italy in order to stamp out "bad news;" sued *La Repubblica* for libel over its coverage of his alleged hiring of an underage prostitute; tried to criminalize the publication of wiretapped conversations by law enforcement officials (such as one in which he threatened a commissioner); and supported an unsuccessful bill to license and regulate the content of any website carrying video content, such as YouTube (something no other Western democracy has attempted).** How does this square with freedom of the press?

* Alexander Stille, *The Sack of Rome* (New York: Penguin, 2007), p. 10.
** Darian Pauli, "Berlusconi's Chilling Effect on Italian Media," *Open Society Foundations,* March 30, 2010 (http://blog.soros.org/2010/03/berlusconis-chilling-effect-on-italian-media/).

questions to consider

1. **How would you describe the relationship between government and the media in Italy?**

2. **What threats to freedom of the press do you see there?**

3. **What cautionary notes does this Italian example raise for the American system? Could something similar happen here?**

REGULATING THE INTERNET

Congress has made several attempts to regulate the Internet. Many of these efforts have been designed to protect children from access to sexually oriented material. In 1996, Congress passed the Communications Decency Act (CDA), which criminalized posting of indecent or obscene material on the Internet. The Supreme Court struck down the law in 1997 on the grounds that it was overly broad.[49] By criminalizing not only "obscene" material but also "indecent" and "patently offensive" material, the act could have held someone criminally liable for posting material that otherwise had First Amendment protection, such as novels that contained adult themes like J. D. Salinger's *The Catcher in the Rye* and James Joyce's *Ulysses*.

The next year, Congress passed the Child Online Protection Act (COPA). Unlike the CDA, which criminalized postings by anyone (including participants in chat groups), COPA targeted commercial distributors. It imposed a $50,000 fine and six months in prison for any commercial distributor who knowingly posted "material harmful to minors" without restricting their site to those who could prove that they were adults. Federal courts again struck down the law on the grounds that it was too broad.[50] For example, the law considered any nudity, whether or not it met the legal definition of obscenity, to constitute "material harmful to minors."

Most recently, Congress passed the Children's Internet Protection Act (CIPA) in 2000. CIPA requires schools and libraries whose computers and Internet access are subsidized by the government to install filters to block images that are pornographic or harmful to minors. The library may temporarily disable filters for adults who need access to such sites for "bona fide research or other lawful purposes." This time, the Supreme Court upheld the law.[51]

GOVERNMENT AND THE MEDIA

Most of what we know about government and current events comes from the news media. Yet, as political scientist W. Lance Bennett has pointed out, "the typical news fare covers only a narrow range of issues, from the viewpoints of an even narrower range of sources, with emphasis placed on drama over depth, human interest over social significance, and formula reporting over perceptive analysis."[52]

Not surprisingly, government officials try to influence what the media will and will not report. They also try to influence—or **spin**—how that news will be reported. As a result, government officials have established public relations infrastructures through which they provide information and access to reporters. Such infrastructures organize and provide "routine channels" of information for the media. These include things like press briefings, press releases, and access to official proceedings (such as congressional hearings and court trials) and other non-spontaneous events (such as speeches and staged ceremonies).[53]

Large groups of reporters, often referred to as "packs," are assigned to cover these routine channels. A good example is the White House press corps, which gathers much of its information from the White House Press Office and its briefings. This so-called

KEY TO understanding

How do the media cover government and public officials? Despite freedom of the press, these officials interact with the media as part of their goal to elicit public support for their policies. The media also play a major role in election campaigns. Candidates and public officials attempt to control the information that the public receives about them, but the media act as a filter and interpreter of that information. Who wins in this interaction, reporters or politicians? How does it affect U.S. citizens?

★

spin
Attempts by government officials to influence how the media will report an event by suggesting how a story should be framed.

pack journalism has consequences. Studies have found that a substantial majority of news stories are based on these routine channels. Stories based on "enterprise" (independent research by reporters, including interviews conducted at the reporter's own initiative) are less common because they require more work. In a landmark study, Leon V. Sigal studied a sample of stories printed in *The New York Times* and *Washington Post* between 1949 and 1969. He found that 58.2 percent of those stories were based on routine channels and only 25.8 percent were based on enterprise.[54]

PRESIDENTS AND THE PRESS

Public support is a president's most visible source of political power. Presidents and their surrogates routinely take messages directly to the people in an effort to mold mandates for policy initiatives. This process of **going public** was largely a twentieth-century phenomenon.[55] Nineteenth-century presidents made few public speeches.[56] They also had limited interactions with the press.

Theodore Roosevelt (1901–1909) began the practice of meeting regularly with reporters (often during his late-afternoon shave), and he was the first president to provide a room for them in the White House.[57] Woodrow Wilson (1913–1921) was the first president to hold regularly scheduled press conferences. He was also the first president since John Adams (1797–1801) to deliver the State of the Union address orally (instead of sending a written message to Congress), thus establishing a tradition that continues to this day. Not until 1933 did Franklin Roosevelt create the White House Press Office, a quintessential public relations infrastructure. Today, the president communicates far more directly and far more often with the public than ever before. During his first year in office, President Obama gave 411 public speeches, comments, and remarks; held 23 town hall meetings and 42 news conferences (five of which were formal, solo White House sessions); and gave 158 interviews (90 of which were televised).[58]

The Press Office is the most visible White House staff unit that deals with the media. The Press Office, under the direction of the White House Press Secretary, distributes the news of the day and responds to questions from the White House press corps. In 1969, Richard Nixon created an additional White House Office of Communications to target the presidential messages to local media, coordinate the flow of information from the entire executive branch, and plot long-term communications strategy. In subsequent administrations, some of these functions have been carried out by other staff units, but all three functions are now commonplace.[59]

Radio and television gave presidents the opportunity to communicate directly with the American people, often in very personal terms. Since the three major networks dominated television until the rise of cable television in the 1980s, and since those networks typically cancelled regularly scheduled programming for "newsworthy" events such as a presidential speech or news conference, presidents could command a huge audience that had nowhere else on television to turn.

President John F. Kennedy (1961–1963) mastered the art of the televised press conference. Witty, quick, and telegenic, he turned press conferences into an opportunity for the president to speak to the people as well as the press. With more and more Americans getting their news from television, presidents also became adept at creating **photo opportunities** to reinforce themes they were trying to convey. The Reagan White House (1980–1989) perfected the art of staging events so as to guarantee compelling images for use on the evening newscasts of the three major networks.

★ President Obama's presence during a live webcast town hall at Facebook headquarters earned him access to voters he might not have otherwise been able to reach.

The explosion in the number of channels on cable and satellite television diminished the ability of presidents to monopolize the airwaves when they gave a speech or news conference. Nonetheless, these channels opened up other opportunities for politicians to transmit direct, targeted messages to particular constituencies. Presidential candidate Bill Clinton used MTV in 1992 to target young voters, a then novel practice that is now commonplace. As president, Barack Obama has appeared on everything from ESPN, where he filled out his brackets for the NCAA Men's Basketball Championship, to a music awards show on Spanish-language Univision. The Internet and other new media have made it even easier for the president to target messages. The White House under the Obama administration now regularly communicates via Twitter (over 3 million followers), Facebook (some 1.5 million fans), and YouTube (where its channel averages 250,000 visits per month). It also has a blog, a Flickr photo stream, and a variety of online programs encouraging participants to offer "advice, opinions, and feedback on important issues."[60]

CONGRESS AND THE PRESS

The sheer size of Congress and the diversity of its membership make it much more difficult for the media to cover Congress as an institution than to cover the president. At the national level, media tend to focus on congressional leaders and key committee chairs. Congressional hearings are also ideally suited for media coverage, especially those covering dramatic issues.

Congress built press galleries in the 1850s for the emerging Washington press corps. Even more reporters came to Washington, D.C., during the Civil War (1861–1865). Competition among newspapers also led them to send high-profile individual correspondents to Washington to report for their paper with a distinctive voice, rather than relying on pool reporting via wire services as they might from more remote locales.[61] By the 1870s, such correspondents were a fixture in Washington.

In the twentieth century, efforts to broadcast public sessions of the House and Senate long faced resistance. The first bill to allow radio coverage of the House of Representatives was introduced in 1922 but failed. Finally in 1947, Congress allowed various committee hearings from both houses to be televised. Television coverage of two Senate hearings in the 1950s created a sensation—one investigating organized crime, and another (chaired by Senator Joseph McCarthy) investigating alleged communist infiltration of the U.S. military. Later, in 1973, televised hearings of a Senate committee investigating Watergate also created a sensation. Nonetheless, the House did not allow regular television coverage of its proceedings until 1979 (experimental broadcasts had taken place in 1977). The Senate did not allow television coverage until 1986. Today, C-SPAN provides gavel-to-gavel coverage of both, along with many committee hearings.[62]

In England, televising the proceedings of the House of Lords began in 1985, followed by the proceedings of the House of Commons in 1989. Such broadcasts have spread to many other legislative bodies around the world. C-SPAN now provides access to broadcasts of many countries' legislative debates.[63]

The media are especially important to individual members of Congress. Members use the media to communicate with their constituents. In his landmark 1974 study, political scientist David Mayhew argued that members of Congress engage in three primary activities: advertising, credit-claiming, and position taking.[64] The media immeasurably aid all three. In this age of polarized politics, the media aid another activity, as noted by political scientist Gary King: taunting opponents. King found that between 2005 and 2007, about 27 percent of congressional press releases were devoted to taunting.[65]

Republicans have been more active than Democrats in utilizing social media to communicate with their constituents. They have about 1.3 million followers on their Twitter accounts, compared with about 600,000 followers for Democrats. Keenly aware of how important social media had been in the 2008 presidential election, the House Republican caucus established a team in 2009 to respond almost immediately on Twitter to announcements or comments from the White House or from Democrats on the floors of Congress. A staff member for House Speaker John Boehner sat at a desk with several television sets showing different stations as well as action on the floor of the House and Senate. When a Democrat made a comment meriting a response, he did some rapid research, often including a check with Republican officials to make sure that the response would be consistent with party policy, and sent off a response within minutes. Boehner's response did not miss the news cycle in which the original statement appeared and addressed a wide audience through Twitter.[66]

THE SUPREME COURT AND THE PRESS

The Supreme Court is covered far less by the media than Congress or the president. This is largely because of the nature of the institution. Supreme Court justices are appointed for life and perform most of their duties behind closed doors. The expectation that they remain "objective" precludes public scrutiny. And even though oral arguments are open to the public, they are not allowed to be televised. When decisions are handed down, they are often lengthy and complicated. Expert analysts interpret the decision for broadcast and online media outlets.

The Supreme Court does have a public information office that distributes copies of decisions when they are handed down and provides reporters with access to oral arguments, but there are no press briefings. The rare press releases that are issued are usually confined to bland announcements related to personnel. Media coverage is limited mainly to coverage of decisions in highly charged cases. Lack of coverage of the many other cases before the Court is coupled with misrepresentation of what the Court does. For example, the media frequently misinterpret the Court's refusal to review an action by a lower court (which simply means that the Court has chosen not to intervene and will let the lower court ruling stand) as a decision on the merits of the case (as if the Court were actually embracing the ruling of the lower court that they have left untouched).[67]

Starting with *Bush v. Gore,* which decided the outcome of the 2000 presidential election, the Supreme Court has issued live audio recordings of oral arguments in a few high-profile cases on the same day as oral arguments. Since October 1955, the Court has made audio recordings of all oral arguments. They are now made available to the public on the Supreme Court's website the Friday after the oral arguments take place.

ELECTIONS

The media play an important role in elections. Television, in particular, has affected the way political candidates campaign for public office. Style, image, and the ability to communicate well in front of television cameras all became more important. News values also influence campaigns. Television news, which usually devotes, at most, two or three minutes to any given story, thrives on drama and conflict. It tends to treat politics like a sporting event. Strategy, momentum, competition, and error often receive more coverage than a candidate's stance on policy, which may be complicated and difficult to explain accurately in a short news report.

Candidates, of course, try to get their messages to the voters through a combination of free media coverage and paid political advertising. Sometimes the two converge. For example, a controversial negative television advertisement may be repeated free of charge on news shows that are reporting about it. Campaign speeches, photo opportunities, media interviews, and debates are all vehicles for free media exposure, although the media have a considerable amount of control over what they present and how they present it. For example, television news programs may air snippets from a speech, but reporters choose which snippets to air and also add their interpretation of the speech. Such news reports of candidate activities are sometimes referred to as "mostly mediated" messages, because candidates do not appear to exercise much control over them. However, precisely because they appear to be out of the candidate's control, such coverage can have the most influence over the public.[68]

"Partially mediated" messages include things like television interviews, debates, and press conferences where candidates have considerable leeway to say what they want. Nonetheless, they are partially mediated because members of the media are asking questions. Such questions act as a constraint on what the candidate can talk about, and reporters can also challenge what the candidates say. Nonetheless, candidates who respond well to tough questioning can win over swing voters.[69] Live coverage of presidential nominating conventions is another example of a partially mediated event.

Paid advertising is yet another way that candidates communicate their messages. Such advertisements are called "unmediated" messages because the media are mere conduits for their distribution. Although candidates control the content of these messages, the public know that they are meant to be self-serving and may be more apt to discount them than other types of messages.[70] Negative advertising has emerged as an especially common form of campaign advertising. The public claims to dislike such ads, but when they strike a chord with what voters already think or crystallize a perception, they can be very effective.

Today, candidates use social media and the Internet to target messages to particular segments of the electorate and to raise money. The Republican primary races in 2012 saw heavy use of social media, which fit well with the candidates' attempts to reach small, focused audiences of Republican activists.[71] Both Barack Obama and Mitt Romney used social media extensively in the general election, and their first debate became the most Tweeted event in U.S. political history.

ASSESSING THE MEDIA

★ **KEY** TO understanding

How well do the media actually perform? Filtering and framing inevitably lead to choices about how to present the news. Does that mean that the media are biased? If so, how?

Building upon what we have learned in the rest of this chapter, we now turn to an assessment of the media. In particular, we examine media bias and explore how journalistic norms structure the news and influence what we know (and don't know) about politics. Many factors can potentially create bias—including the personal political views of reporters, ownership patterns, and even the norms, values, and routines involved in the gathering and delivering of the news.

BIASED NEWS

As we have already seen, the media engage in filtering and framing whenever they report the news. A frame may be consciously chosen to promote a particular agenda (such as an ideological bias). But the choice of a frame is sometimes just a reflection of shared journalistic norms and conventions. For example, norms of "objective journalism" often lead to stories depicting two sides of an issue when, in reality, there may be *many* sides to that issue. In such a case, the frame oversimplifies the issue and provides a false sense of "either-or." Attempts to create balanced coverage may also give a false impression that "both" sides of an issue are equally valid.

Consider a story on gun control. One possibility would be to frame it as a constitutional issue: Does gun control legislation violate your Second Amendment rights? Another would be to frame it as an issue of public safety: Does gun control legislation protect your children? Such choices are inevitable. It is impossible to report the news without framing it. But the choice of a frame may alter the way the public interprets the issue. This leads to a persistent question: Are the media biased? And, if so, *how* are they biased? Is it an ideological bias? A corporate bias? Or is it a structural bias—one influenced by journalistic values and norms?

The media are often accused of ideological bias. President Nixon, for example, accused the media of a liberal bias. Studies have found that few journalists identify themselves as conservative. For example, a 2008 poll by the Pew Research Center found that only 8 percent of national journalists identified themselves as conservative, as opposed to 53 percent who identified themselves as moderate and 32 percent who identified themselves as liberal.[72]

A 2009 Pew poll found that 60 percent of those surveyed believed that news organizations had a partisan bias (up from 45 percent in 1985). Of those, 50 percent believed that news organizations had a liberal bias, while 22 percent believed that they had a conservative bias. The same poll also found a sharp drop in the public's assessment of press accuracy and fairness. In 1985, 55 percent of respondents felt that the press "get the facts straight;" by 2009, only 29 percent felt that they did. In 1985, 34 percent of respondents felt that the media "deal fairly with all sides;" by 2009, only 18 percent felt that they did.[73] As Figure 11.9 shows, over half of those polled since 2002 consistently believe that the media has some sort of an ideological bias.

Some observers say that ideology is less important in influencing news stories than the corporate interests of those who own the media, and that concentration of media ownership may make this corporate bias even worse. For example, reporters for daily newspapers may tend to be liberal, but those who own the newspapers tend to be conservative. How does this affect media coverage? On the editorial pages, at least, newspapers are more apt to support conservative candidates.

Michael Parenti is a proponent of the view that owners, often out of the fear of offending corporate advertisers, dictate what can and (probably more importantly) what *cannot* be covered. Thus, Parenti points to efforts to squelch stories that would harm corporate interests. For example, *New York Times* publisher Arthur Sulzberger urged editors in the 1970s not to write stories about automobile safety and pollution that might offend the auto industry, which happened to be one of the paper's biggest advertisers.[74]

In short, private ownership of the media creates a commercial bias. These media are in business to make money, and that purpose influences the way they market themselves. In addition to avoiding stories that may offend corporate sponsors, they may frame stories in such a way as to generate the largest possible audience. Concentration of media ownership fuels this concern. Six corporate conglomerates now dominate the industry. As Figure 11.10 indicates, these six conglomerates make billions of dollars every year.

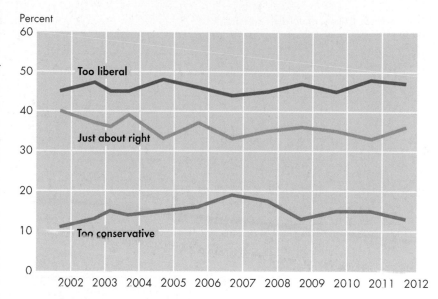

FIGURE 11.9

★ MEDIA BIAS AS PERCEIVED BY THE AMERICAN PUBLIC

Do most Americans feel that the media have an ideological bias? What type of bias do they perceive?

Source: Gallup Poll (http://www.gallup.com/poll/149624/majority-continue-distrust-media-perceive-bias.aspx)

FORMULAIC NEWS

While some critics point to ideological or corporate bias in the news, others—such as political scientist Lance Bennett—argue that journalistic values, norms, and routines may be more influential in structuring what the media report and how they report it. This structural bias results in the use of news formulas that shape the information we

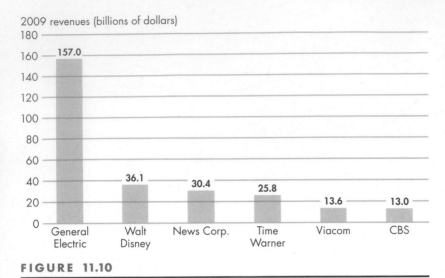

2009 revenues (billions of dollars)

FIGURE 11.10

★ MEDIA OWNERSHIP

To what extent do you think the concentration of media ownership affects media bias?

Source: Data from Susan Holmberg, (http://www.freepress.net/ownership/chart/main)

receive, but which may not advance the cause of democracy. These formulas include personalization, dramatization, fragmentation, and what Bennett calls the "authority-disorder bias."

Personalization refers to "the overwhelming tendency to downplay the big social, economic, or political picture in favor of the human trials, tragedies, and triumphs that sit at the surface of events."[75] An emphasis on *dramatization* means that issues are presented as simple narratives that "emphasize crisis over continuity, the present over the past or future, and the personalities at their center."[76]

Personalization and dramatization go hand in hand to squelch in-depth analysis of complex policy issues such as health care reform. Instead, the media tend to offer dramatic narratives that emphasize conflicts between sharply drawn characters at the center of policy debates. Thus, instead of educating the public so that they can become informed, active participants in the political process, the media tend to treat politics as a spectator sport to be watched from the sidelines.

The emphasis on individual actors over the broader political context and on self-contained dramatic narratives at the expense of in-depth analysis promotes *fragmentation*: short, isolated stories presented as "dramatic capsules that make it difficult to see the causes of problems, their significance, or the connections across issues."[77] Moreover, an issue that receives a great deal of attention one day may be displaced by another issue the next, making it difficult to trace the development of policy over time.

Finally, the so-called *authority-disorder bias* refers to the tendency of the news media to be preoccupied with stories about disorder—occasions when the normal world is called into question—framed by the questions of how, when, and whether authorities can establish or restore order. Natural disasters, economic crises, terrorist attacks, killers on the loose, and scandals perpetrated by supposedly trustworthy officials all inflict disorder in various ways. Bennett notes that the generic plot device of authorities attempting to restore order "can be combined endlessly within personalized, dramatized, and fragmented news episodes."[78] Thus, stories about the BP oil leak in the Gulf of Mexico were less likely to focus on the broader policy issues associated with offshore drilling and its safety, and more likely to focus on the short-term success or failure of BP executives and government officials to stop the leak. The story largely went away when the oil leak was plugged, even though the policy issues involved were as important as ever.

Why Are We
THE WAY WE ARE **?**

Clearly, the media play a very important role in a democracy: they provide information about government and politics to the people. Our system of government depends upon free and open lines of communication. How well the media actually perform this function is affected by technological changes, government regulation, and the relationship between reporters and public officials. Thus, it is worth recapping each of these influences in order to better understand why we are the way we are.

TECHNOLOGICAL DEVELOPMENTS

Today's media are the product of a long series of technological advances. Each advance has improved our access to information. The creation and proliferation of newspapers in the 1700s provided a new and important source of information for the people—one that unified around certain themes that helped to precipitate the American Revolution. The ability to mass-produce newspapers quickly and cheaply in the early 1800s made information more accessible to a broader segment of the population. Access to information by the lower economic class through the new penny press allowed them to become more informed and engaged citizens. But more people buying more newspapers spurred publishers to try to make greater and greater profits. This, in turn, led to the rise in yellow journalism at the end of the 1800s and eventually to a backlash that promoted "objective" journalism in the early 1900s. Radio, television, satellites, cable television, the Internet, and social media have all expanded the range of information we receive and the immediacy with which we receive it—thereby allowing Americans to hold political representatives more fully accountable.

GOVERNMENT REGULATION

The broadcast industry, stymied by a limited number of airwaves and stations that interfered with each other's broadcast signals, sought government regulation and got it in the 1930s. The resulting regulations have had a significant impact on the evolution of broadcast media in the United States. Not only did the government grant broadcast licenses at specific frequencies and take steps to prevent broadcast monopolies, but it sought to regulate scarce airwaves to provide for the public good. This meant that the government began to regulate the content of broadcasts. Although content distributed by print media would have First Amendment protection under the Constitution, it was subject to government regulation when distributed by the broadcast media. This is largely because of the government's interest in regulating scarce airwaves in the public interest (there is no such scarcity argument for other sorts of publications). It is also because broadcasts invade people's homes and thus can reach unsupervised children and nonconsenting adults who might otherwise be bombarded with offensive broadcasts when flipping the dial.

The advent of satellite and cable technology, along with the rise of the Internet, complicated the issue. These technologies also invade the home, but they do not compete for scarce airwaves in the same way that radio and television did. As a result, attempts to regulate the content of the Internet have been less successful than efforts to regulate radio and television, but many people remain concerned about children's access to offensive material online.

REPORTERS AND OFFICIALS

Reporters act as gatekeepers of information—filtering and framing the news— but they must rely on government officials for much of the news that they report. Officials attempt to spin the news to their advantage, and they have established public relations infrastructures through which they provide information and access to reporters. The ensuing pack journalism affects the type of news we get: rather than independent analysis and hard-hitting reports, pack journalism promotes uniform coverage of information that is spoon-fed to reporters by officials. More broadly, the way news is reported affects the body politic. Media helped to foment the American Revolution in the 1700s, just as it helped to unite a nation against foreign enemies during World War II. Today, narrowcasting, talk radio, cable news rants, and anonymous blogs exacerbate polarized politics even as the new media offer us unprecedented amounts of information and an unprecedented ability to share our views. In the flood of information now available, accuracy may be a casualty.

Think about how news coverage affects the government's response to events and the types of leaders we have. Twenty-four-hour news coverage of catastrophes such as Hurricane Katrina or the BP oil spill in the Gulf of Mexico, coupled with the authority-disorder bias that news formulas perpetuate, created an unrealistic expectation that government should immediately solve the problem. Fulfilling such expectations is often difficult, if not impossible. Dashed expectations can, in turn, promote cynicism and undermine trust in government.

Radio, television, and the new media have all given officials opportunities to bypass the critical filter of reporters by taking messages directly to the people via speeches and targeted messages on Twitter, Facebook, and other venues. Social media have also led to the rise of citizen journalism, which allows almost anyone armed with a Flip camera or a smart phone to become a media producer. But citizen journalists lack a gatekeeper, so it is difficult for news consumers to assess whether the information they provide is accurate. The ability of anyone to post whatever they want can also fuel unsubstantiated rumors and promote conspiracy theories.

. . . AND WHY DOES IT Matter?

All of this matters to you. First and foremost, your ability to influence government decisions that affect you is diminished if you do not understand the basis of those decisions, the consequences of those decisions, and how to affect those decisions. Knowledge is power—power that allows you to make political decisions that are in your best interest. The media provide access to that knowledge.

Many people in many parts of the world lack that access. State-run media, censorship, and harsh government crackdowns on critical reporters stifle freedom of the press. But social media matter. They are making it harder for governments to restrict people's access to information. Social media helped to spur the Arab Spring uprisings in the Middle East. They have also made it easier for social and political movements to mobilize in the United States. The Tea Party and Occupy Wall Street are just two examples.

The way news is presented also matters, as does your ability to view news outlets and their accounts with a critical eye. Understanding how and why stories are framed; being aware of ideological, corporate, and structural bias in the way news is reported; knowing that social media have undermined—for good and bad—the gatekeeping function of reporters; and recognizing the formulas that reporters use to report the news all help you to develop a critical lens to better assess the information you receive. The media's emphasis on personalities over substance and on fragmentation over sustained analysis may make news more entertaining, but it also diminishes your ability to understand issues and your ability to influence the direction of public policies that directly affect you.

Awareness of how the media work—their strengths and shortcomings—should empower you to assess the news more critically and use it more astutely. As Sherlock Holmes told his trusty sidekick Watson: "The Press, Watson, is a most valuable institution, if you only know how to use it."[79]

critical thinking questions

1. As you read the news and watch reports on television, can you identify examples of personalization, dramatization, and fragmentation in the news? The "authority-disorder bias"? Are these a problem?

2. Is it bad that so many media reports come from routine channels of information? Is it practical to move away from such dependence?

3. Do the media do a good job of socializing our young people?

4. Are the new media good or bad for democracy? Why?

key terms

citizen journalist, 374

equal time rule, 386

Fairness Doctrine, 386

Federal Communications Commission (FCC), 384

filtering, 371

Fourth Estate, 378

framing, 371

gatekeeping, 373

going public, 390

mass media, 371

media effects, 380

muckraking, 378

narrowcasting, 382

net neutrality, 385

new media, 382

objective journalism, 378

pack journalism, 390

partisan press, 376

penny press, 377

photo opportunity (or "photo-op"), 390

social media, 382

spin, 389

talk radio, 379

yellow journalism, 377

CONGRESS

- Explain the responsibilities of Congress to the American people and its relationship with the other institutions of government.
- Describe the powers granted to Congress by the Constitution, how Congress uses these powers, and the situations in which Congress would carry out or extend these powers.
- Examine the historical context that produced the current congressional structure, and explain how this structure creates a complex law-making process.
- Identify the key players and the critical building blocks that allow Congress to function effectively.
- Understand how Congress builds enough agreement among members to ensure coherent action.
- Explain how a bill becomes a law.

PERSPECTIVE
How Can Legislative Bodies React Effectively During Times of Economic Crisis?

Congress seldom acts quickly. It usually deliberates carefully so that by the time proposed legislation becomes law, it has survived many hurdles—in a deliberate process that presumably strengthens the final product. It was surprising, therefore, how rapidly the U.S. Congress responded to the financial crisis of September and October 2008, especially because Democrats controlled Congress and Republicans the presidency. The Swedish parliament had to overcome party divisions in 1992 to craft a similar program of action during a banking crisis, but this was less surprising than the successful U.S. effort.

Evidence of a global financial crisis had mounted over the prior 18 months but accelerated rapidly in September 2008. The U.S. real estate market began a sharp decline in late 2006. As a result, investment firms, banks, mutual funds, and individual investors suffered major setbacks. And the problem spread to other countries with American investments. President Bush propped up two government agencies critical to the mortgage markets and helped several private investment banks avoid going bankrupt, but these efforts were too little too late. Financial doubt gripped foreign and domestic investors, driving down global stock markets. By October 2008, the worldwide losses linked to these bad debts in the United States totaled approximately $1.4 trillion.

Amidst the turmoil and despair, Treasury Secretary Henry Paulson and Federal Reserve Board Chairman Ben Bernanke proposed a rescue plan, recommending that Congress approve $700 billion in assistance to failing banks to prevent further damage to the stock market and the larger economy.[1] Paulson's proposal was breathtakingly brief—only three pages long—and allowed for little congressional or judicial oversight of the Treasury Department's future actions. The vagueness was intended to reduce wrangling with Congress over details.[2] President Bush urged Congress to approve the legislation, but many citizens expressed outrage at the thought of saving the careers of greedy bankers who had made bad decisions. Mail from constituents to

Congress ran 9-1 against the "bailout" plan (as it was termed by the media), and there were public protests in many cities. Heated negotiations produced a compromise proposal that was expected to pass both chambers of Congress.

On September 23, 2008, in a dramatic vote, the House rejected the proposed plan 228–205. Democrats voted 140–95 in favor of the plan, but Republicans voted 65–133 against it, soundly rejecting the recommendations of their own party's president. Opponents among liberal Democrats felt that the plan should have helped homeowners rather than bankers. Opponents among conservative Republicans thought the plan would have moved the nation toward socialism. Many opponents cited the overwhelmingly negative phone calls and mail from their constituents. Partisan recriminations filled the air, and on the day of the House defeat, the Dow Jones Industrial Average, a widely used index of stock market activity, fell 777 points in its largest single-day decline in history.

Two days later, the Senate turned the tide when it voted 74–25 to approve a modified rescue proposal. Several "sweeteners" were added to the bill (now more than 400 pages long) in an effort to win votes from both reluctant Democrats and Republicans. Tax breaks for the middle class and tax credits to subsidize solar, wind, and alternative energy production added another $100 billion to the projected cost of the plan. Congress also established ways to oversee the program and released only half the funding upfront and the rest as needed. Forty Senate Democrats and 34 Republicans, a broad bipartisan base, approved the plan. Two days later, the House reversed its earlier position and voted yes, 263–171.

Within two weeks the governmental system had produced a remarkably wide-ranging change in the operations of the American economy. This had happened despite strong opposition from the public and nervous members of the president's party who faced elections in less than two weeks. Crisis had prompted action by legislators who concluded that the danger to the economy justified going against constituents' wishes.

How did a government with a multiparty parliamentary system handle a similar crisis? Sweden's parliament faced a severe banking crisis in 1992. Much as had happened in the United States, years of unregulated lending practices had produced frenzied commercial (business) and home loan markets in Sweden with soaring prices, and as the economy began to slow, borrowers could not repay their loans. Sweden's coalition government of four conservative parties was five votes short of being able to pass an emergency proposal on its own, and center-left parties would only support the plan if taxpayers' interests were put ahead of investors'. Sweden's long tradition of interparty cooperation aided the negotiations. Most disagreements were kept behind the scenes, not fought out in highly publicized encounters. Unlike U.S. House Republicans who saw little to be gained by supporting an unpopular president with an unpopular plan just a few weeks before the next election, Sweden's party members loyally voted to support the compromise. Power in parliamentary systems usually lies in the hands of party leaders who are confident that members will follow their lead. Bargaining is therefore simpler if negotiators want to find common ground.

IN THIS CHAPTER, we examine the functions of Congress and the many powers it exercises, chief among them being its control over the federal budget, the so-called *power of the purse,* as illustrated in the opening Perspective. We then examine the structure of Congress and explore how it operates. We analyze Congress's frequent problems in establishing agreement within each chamber, then between the House and Senate, and finally with the president. Many centers of decision making must resolve their differences. Party leaders in each chamber must win the support of powerful members who chair important committees as well as outspoken segments of the majority party. In this sense, the opening story about 2008 illustrates an exception to Congress's usual operations. We also take a look at internal and external influences on the decision-making process. Finally, we outline the legislative process, looking at how a bill becomes a law. As you read this chapter, keep in mind our two core questions:

WHY ARE WE THE WAY WE ARE?
WHY DOES IT MATTER TO YOU?

In particular, why is it so difficult for legislators to reach collective decisions?

power of the purse
Congressional authority to set the national budget, which provides legislators with enormous influence in the checks and balances system.

THE FUNCTIONS OF CONGRESS

Congress is the branch of government charged with making laws and representing the people. In this section we will first consider how citizens can use Congress to guide government. Then we will look closely at services provided to constituents and mechanisms for overseeing the executive branch.

As the government branch designed to be most responsive to the public, Congress serves multiple functions. Like legislatures around the world, Congress legitimizes government, partly because it represents the people's interests and responds to constituents' distinctive needs. Legislators can act independently or reflect the views of their constituents. Although Congress is primarily a lawmaking institution, in the American system it also oversees the activities of the executive branch, serving as an important check on executive branch powers.

LEGITIMACY

Legislatures arose in history as a way for monarchs to placate their subjects' demand to participate in governing and to voice their views on public affairs. In this way, legislatures provide government with **popular legitimacy,** the sense that because citizens help shape the government's decisions, these decisions will be accepted by the people. Even in nations where legislatures are overshadowed by powerful executives, legislatures can provide an element of popular representation and influence. Although they may only indirectly shape government policies, legislatures in these nations can still help constituents navigate the bureaucracy and ministries and represent local interests much as an American congressional representative would.[3]

popular legitimacy
Belief among the citizens of a political system that the government's actions deserve to be obeyed because they reflect the will of the people.

REPRESENTATION

Judging from its leading place in the Constitution—as the subject of Article I—Congress was intended to be "the people's branch" and the principal means for the people to control the government. From the outset, voters directly elected members of the House

★ Democratic Senator John Tester from Montana farms and hunts like most members of his constituency. He fought to allow hunting of the endangered gray wolf, which preys on livestock. His positions riled up Montana environmentalists but pleased Tester's constituency.

of Representatives. Although senators were originally chosen by state legislatures, the nation established popular election of senators in 1917 when states ratified the Seventeenth Amendment.[4] Because legislators expect to be held accountable by voters in their states or districts, members of Congress are likely to translate the people's will into programs and policies.

There is a strong tradition in the United States for legislators to represent the local interests of their constituents, which are not always in line with those of the nation as a whole. Local representation was paramount under the Articles of Confederation when members of Congress represented the interests of their states. After the House of Representatives was created, members of the House linked the national government to even smaller areas within states, and representatives were attentive to the particular needs of their districts' residents. Instead of readily articulating a single vision, it is therefore the job of Congress to construct a common vision out of the 435 House and 100 Senate views of what the nation's interest really is.

U.S. election rules heighten this constituency-first perspective. By using single-member districts as discussed in Chapter 8—one representative chosen for a specific area rather than several from a large district—it is virtually certain that members of Congress working in Washington will be attentive to the top priorities of the folks who elected them back home. In contrast, the proportional voting systems found in many parliamentary democracies deemphasize ties to a constituency, making it easier to adopt a more general party perspective.[5]

Models of Representation

Members of Congress are expected to represent their constituencies' interests and ideals. But do they? Do they vote in line with what their constituents want? Or do they rise above these needs to serve what they see as the greater interests of the nation? Congress does sometimes choose a course contrary to public opinion, as we saw in the Congressional response to the financial crisis of 2008. To explain this behavior, political scientists have identified three different models of representation: the trustee model, the delegate model, and the politico model.

The **trustee model** of representation conflicts with widely held beliefs in the United States. In this view, elected representatives should follow their own convictions in making decisions on behalf of their constituents; constituents chose them to use their judgment in making decisions, and elections will later determine whether they continue to enjoy that confidence. Under this model, legislators have been elected for their skills, good character, and judgment. Once in office they are not obliged to respond to the preferences of their constituents, which are seldom clear enough to use as a guide in making decisions.

The contrary position, the **delegate model** of representation, contends that representatives should consult their constituents on pending issues and follow the views of their district's voters even if it goes against their own personal preferences or best judgment. Toward this end, many legislators now use district polls—mail or phone—to determine their constituents' views on pending policy issues. Visits back home allow

trustee model
A form of representation in which legislators are not required to reflect the preferences and opinions of their constituents because voters expect them to use their own knowledge and good judgment.

delegate model
A form of representation in which legislators closely reflect the preferences and opinions of constituents in discharging their representative responsibilities—for example, voting the way constituents prefer on an issue.

legislators to hear constituents' views in person, and town hall meetings are one way to ensure that those views reflect a cross-section rather than only the legislator's closest supporters.

It is unlikely that any one legislator is always a trustee or always a delegate. Instead, a legislator's approach to representation is likely to be located along a sliding scale with trustee and delegate at opposite poles. The **politico model** of representation recognizes that legislators are likely to respond to their constituents' views differently at different times. Politicos will be sensitive to the needs of their constituents some of the time but also follow their own judgment at others.[6] In fact, adept politicians will strike a balance between relying on their own judgment and following the apparent wishes of their constituency, particularly when these are strongly expressed. However, it would be difficult to determine constituents' wishes on every issue, and we know that public opinion often shifts. At a minimum, legislators will not want to follow every whim of constituency opinion, but they also realize they must have an explanation for going against strongly held views on important issues.

To make sure legislators are representing their values and interests, citizens can scrutinize the activities of their representatives. Since 1979, the House has televised its proceedings on the floor; the Senate began to televise its proceedings in 1986. Even more complete is the *Congressional Record,* a nearly verbatim account, corrected for grammatical errors and with extended comments supplied by the members, that has been published overnight since 1873. The *Congressional Record* includes a digest of congressional activities for that day—bills introduced, votes taken, and committee meetings held—and full versions of amendments and bills. The Library of Congress maintains a computerized database of these materials dubbed *THOMAS* in honor of Thomas Jefferson. Gavel-to-gavel coverage of House and Senate proceedings is available on C-SPAN, the Cable-Satellite Public Affairs Network, as are many committee hearings.

Pork Barrel Projects and Earmarks

Legislators are not only sensitive to their constituency's political interests but have also historically served local economic needs. Until late in the nineteenth century, serving in Congress was largely a part-time job while farming, operating a business, or practicing law was a full-time job back home. Having a part-time legislature ensured that representatives would remain closely tied to their constituents' lives. Local representatives traveled to Washington to encourage support for westward expansion and economic growth by bringing benefits back home—public money for the construction of roads, canals, and railroads came from the federal government, as well as jobs and contracts for services and supplies purchased by the federal government. By the last half of the nineteenth century, it was widely expected that legislators would deliver a share of this public **pork barrel** to their districts' residents, a share of the benefits funded by the national treasury and distributed throughout the nation. Today, federal dollars for weapons systems, highway construction, government research and education are pieces of pork that legislators are expected to deliver back home. When serving in Congress became a full-time job, legislators spent most of their time in Washington rather than in their districts. Yet pork barrel spending has expanded.

With the ballooning federal budget deficit, there has been growing pressure to reduce the amount of federal pork returned to constituents. Controversy has especially focused on **earmarks,** spending on projects authorized by Congress without undergoing the usual process of review. As documented by Citizens Against Government

politico model
A form of representation in which legislators play different roles depending on whether constituents have strong views on an issue and the nature of that issue.

pork barrel
The traditional way to preserve pork for gradual consumption, it refers more recently to public money used to meet local needs that lack a sound public purpose.

earmark
Provision in a bill that provides a benefit to a specific organization or for a specific project, either through direct spending or a tax break.

★ Critics called the proposed Gravina Island Bridge in Ketchikan, Alaska "the Bridge to Nowhere," the symbol of wasteful earmarks. It would have spent nearly $400 million from the federal budget to connect the mainland to an island with 50 residents and an airport that receives year-round ferry service.

Waste, an advocacy group opposed to wasteful spending, the number of earmarks peaked at 14,000 in 2005 (see Figure 12.1) and their dollar value at $29 billion in 2008. Although spending on any one project that supports a park, an arts center, a bridge, a summer camp, or jobs in a local factory may be modest, the cumulative effect is significant. Since 1991, CAGW has identified 109,978 projects worth $306 billion.[7]

While it is easy to denounce earmarks as examples of wasteful spending, they also reflect legislators responding to local needs by committing a small percentage of the federal budget (one-half of one percent in 2009). Some students of Congress defend earmarks, while others condemn them.[8] Under pressure from Tea Party members, House Republicans adopted a two-year ban on earmarks in 2010. Senate Democrats did the same for 2011, and individual Republican Senators have followed suit. President Obama pledged to veto bills with earmarks. But Congress is now debating just what qualifies as an earmark and which ones might really be necessary. In short, the nuances remain to be sorted out.

FIGURE 12.1

★ THE RISE IN EARMARKS, 1991–2006

Over nearly 20 years, the number of earmarks grew dramatically. Do you think one party was responsible for this growth or Congress in general?

Source: Citizens Against Government Waste. *2006 Congressional Pig Book* (http://www.cagw.org/reports/pig-book/#trends);*CQ Researcher*, June 16, 2006, 16(23).

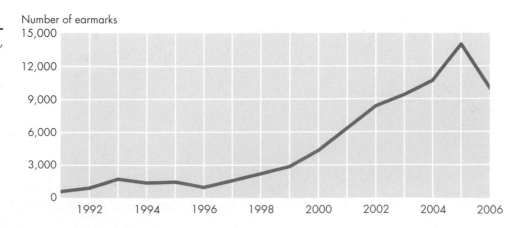

Number of earmarks

DEMOGRAPHIC REPRESENTATION

Although members of Congress are expected to represent the people who elected them to office, they do not reflect the demographic composition of the larger population. In other words, Congress is not a microcosm of American society (see Table 12.1). Consistently, the proportion of women in Congress is lower than in the general population, and the same is true for African Americans and Hispanics. In fact, most members in both chambers are older, white, Protestant males. Likewise, they are far better educated and drawn from a rather narrow range of professional careers.

Although minority representation remains disproportionately low, there has been a gradual increase in the number of women and persons of color in Congress over the past 30 years, as shown in Figure 12.2. Moreover, African Americans and women have

---

TABLE 12.1

selected comparisons of the 112th congress and U.S. national population

What do these statistics tell us about the composition of Congress? Was the situation any different more than two centuries ago for the delegates to the constitutional convention?

CHARACTERISTIC	112TH CONGRESS	NATIONAL POPULATION
Age	56 years (Republican) 60.8 years (Democrat)	37.2
Completed bachelor's (four-year) degree	92% (House) 99% (Senate)	27.5%
Law degree	38% (House) 55% (Senate)	0.36% (practicing attorneys)
Women	16.8%	50.8%
African American	8.1%	12.6%
Hispanic	5.7%	16.3%

Sources: All statistical data on the composition of Congress and the population is gathered from the 2010 U.S. Census Data and the CRS Report for Congress authored by Jennifer E. Manning, "Membership of the 112th Congress: A Profile," March 1, 2011 (http://www.senate.gov/reference/resources/pdf/R41647.pdf)

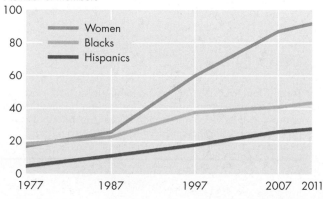

Number of members

- Women
- Blacks
- Hispanics

1977 1987 1997 2007 2011

FIGURE 12.2

★ MINORITIES AND WOMEN IN CONGRESS

How do their shares of congressional membership compare with these groups' standing in the general population? Why has the number of women grown faster than that of the other groups?

Sources: Greg Giroux, "An Old Boys' Club with New Twists." *CQ Weekly Online* (February 26, 2007), 604–608; Jennifer E. Manning, "Membership of the 112th Congress: A Profile," CRS Report, June 1, 2011 (R41647).

★ Three Kennedys (from top to bottom)—John, Ted, and Robert—were strong advocates for racial equality and for improving the lives of the nation's poor, despite their own privileged upbringing and family wealth, providing examples of substantive representation.

become more influential in Congress.[9] Nancy Pelosi's selection as Speaker of the House in January 2007 demonstrates how women have become part of the congressional power structure. Six women chaired congressional committees in the 112th Congress—one in the House and five in the Senate. Despite long-term improvements, however, the United States still trails many other nations in terms of the percentage of women in the lower house of the legislature, ranking 69th among the 187 nations on whom data is collected by the Inter-Parliamentary Union.[10]

If you believe that only someone with your own demographic characteristics can accurately reflect your views, a position known as **descriptive representation,** Congress will inevitably perform its representation function poorly for most of us. The other possibility is for a legislator to advocate for a group's interests even without sharing that group's demographic characteristics, an example of **substantive representation,** shifting the emphasis from who representatives are to what they do. John, Teddy, and Robert Kennedy provide classic examples of politicians who came from a wealthy Massachusetts family but championed the interests of minorities and the poor. Lawyers—of whom there are many in Congress—are trained to represent clients' interests regardless of their background, perhaps helping them to understand the needs of people unlike themselves.

Members of Congress tend to be wealthier, older, whiter, and more often male than the average American, yet not all members of Congress vote in line with the interests of their demographic group. Senator John Kerry, a member of the wealthy Forbes family and married to the heiress of the Heinz fortune, is one of the most liberal Democrats in the Senate, strongly supporting initiatives that help low-income families.

CONSTITUENCY SERVICE

Many scholars argue that above all else, modern legislators who make a career of public service are concerned with reelection.[11] To ensure reelection, they must go beyond the responsibilities of legislating in D.C. to serve their constituents. Through their offices at home and on Capitol Hill, representatives and senators have staffs to provide **constituency service** to their voters—to forward information about federal programs, intercede on the citizens' behalf in their dealings with government bureaucrats, assist in applying for benefits or federal jobs, and convey the political concerns of constituents to their legislator. District-based staffs help constituents with numerous concerns such as contacting federal agencies to resolve problems; assisting with passports; dealing with Social Security and veterans' benefits; obtaining federal grants; flying flags over the Capitol that can be presented as keepsakes; and arranging tours of the U.S. Capitol. A list of services offered by a given representative can be found on his or her website, usually under a paragraph explaining how important constituency service is to the legislator.

Legislators meet regularly with constituents in Washington and back in their home districts. Members of Congress have breakfast at their neighborhood restaurants and attend Rotary Club meetings, religious gatherings, and other community events; all of these activities provide opportunities to connect with constituents and make their presence known in the community.[12] In Chapter 8 we discussed the advantages incumbents have over challengers. Research has shown that representatives serving their first terms (freshmen) are most vulnerable to being defeated for reelection and are therefore more likely to make frequent home visits than colleagues with more years of seniority. This reinforces the notion that home service is particularly valuable for those seeking reelection.

LAWMAKING

Lawmaking is perhaps the most important activity of Congress, and the process is always complex and often unappealing. Otto von Bismarck, a nineteenth-century German prime minister, supposedly remarked: "Laws are like sausages; it is better not to see them being made." Regardless whether this statement is real or apocryphal, its meaning is clear—the process is not pretty.

Nonetheless, as Figure 12.3 shows, Congress devotes tremendous amounts of time and attention to lawmaking—the process of considering and passing bills. A **bill** is a proposal for a government program or action, originating in either the House or Senate, that applies to the entire nation. Over a period of 10 Congresses—each Congress consists of a two-year period—the number of bills introduced into Congress rose from just under 6,000 to 11,000. And Congress approved a much smaller percentage of those measures, ranging from a high of nearly 11 percent to a low of 4 percent. Winnowing down the volume of proposed bills usually falls to congressional committees who ignore some requests, combine others, or simply cannot muster sufficient support to act on still others. In other words, the steep drop-off between bills introduced and enacted could well reflect a great deal of work, not a failure to act. Moreover, Congress is in session much of the year: over this same 20-year period, the number of days the House was in session ranged from 241 to 290, while the Senate ranged from 274 to 343 days in session annually.

descriptive representation
Belief that the extent to which a legislature reflects the demographic composition of the larger population is vitally important in determining the legislature's responsiveness to group needs.

substantive representation
The capacity of a legislator or a legislature to represent the interests of groups despite not sharing the demographic characteristics of that group.

constituency service
Assistance provided by representatives and senators to help residents of their districts or states resolve problems involving government programs and agencies.

bill
Proposal for government action that is introduced in either the House or Senate and may result in a law.

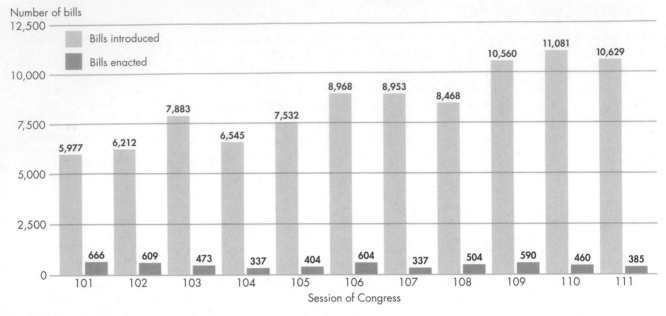

Number of bills

Bills introduced

Bills enacted

Session of Congress	Bills introduced	Bills enacted
101	5,977	666
102	6,212	609
103	7,883	473
104	6,545	337
105	7,532	404
106	8,968	604
107	8,953	337
108	8,468	504
109	10,560	590
110	11,081	460
111	10,629	385

FIGURE 12.3

★ BILLS INTRODUCED AND ENACTED BY CONGRESS, 1989–2010

The number of bills enacted is always dramatically lower than the number introduced. What are some reasons for this gap?

Source: Table 395, "U.S. Congress—Measures Introduced and Enacted and Time in Session: 1989–2006," and Table 414, "U.S. Congress—Measures Introduced and Enacted and Time in Session, 1993–2010." *Statistical Abstract of the United States: 2012.*

EXECUTIVE OVERSIGHT

Under the U.S. system of separate institutions sharing powers, Congress checks the actions of the executive branch, including both presidents and bureaucrats. Congress investigates actions of the president and the bureaucracy in multiple ways. Individual members of Congress can write letters to federal officials launching an inquiry into problems encountered by constituents. But such efforts are likely to bear greater fruit if a committee or subcommittee initiates the investigation by holding formal hearings where agency officials and non-governmental experts provide testimony on key questions. Committee staff might also conduct extensive research or ask a research arm of Congress—the Congressional Research Service or the Government Accountability Office—to conduct an evaluation. Executive officials, of course, frequently view such oversight efforts as intrusive, interfering with the discharge of their duties.

This function differs from the operations of a parliamentary system where there is little distinction between executive and legislative powers—ministers in the government also hold seats in parliament, and the government's actions are aligned with the parliament's preferences. Rather than a system of legislative powers checking the executive, the two branches usually cooperate with one another.

The many functions served by Congress are derived from a broad interpretation of the powers granted under the Constitution, which we turn to next.

TABLE 12.2

abridged version of the enumerated powers of congress, found in article I, section 8 of the constitution

- Provide for national revenues—taxes, import and export duties, and special fees—as long as they apply equally across the nation.
- Borrow money to meet national expenses.
- Regulate international as well as interstate trade.
- Regulate bankruptcies, establishing laws that apply across the nation.
- Coin money, regulate its value relative to foreign currencies, and establish a uniform system of weights and measures.
- Establish and enforce laws against counterfeiting.
- Establish a system of post offices and highways.
- Oversee copyrights and patents for new inventions.
- Establish uniform rules about becoming a citizen.
- Create a system of federal courts below the Supreme Court.
- Define and punish piracy and violations of international law.
- Declare war as well as establish, maintain and govern land and naval forces.
- Organize, arm, oversee and call out the national guard ("the militia") to enforce national law, suppress rebellions and repel invasions.
- Make all laws which shall be necessary and proper for carrying into Execution the foregoing Powers, and all other powers vested by the Constitution in the Government of the United States.

CONSTITUTIONAL POWERS

In Chapter 2 we learned that Congress exercises both *enumerated and implied powers* (see Table 12.2). In this section, we explore some of these powers in greater depth.

NECESSARY AND PROPER CLAUSE

Congress has used its final power, found in the necessary and proper clause, to expand its influence beyond the enumerated powers. Because of its catch-all character, the necessary and proper clause provides Congress with enormous flexibility, giving it another name—the **elastic clause**—because it has allowed Congress to stretch its institutional power to include responsibilities the founders did not originally envision. The clause has given rise to countless actions by Congress that have expanded its reach. For example, while federal criminal laws probably numbered about 100 in 1900, they now are estimated at more than 3,000, many dealing with drugs but some dealing with areas of law traditionally reserved to the states. In a recent Supreme Court case, Carol Bond of Pennsylvania appealed a six-year sentence for violating a federal chemical weapons law. Her case arose when she spread some chemicals on the car, front-door handle, and mailbox of a woman having an affair with her husband. The court ruled unanimously that she could challenge the federal law as impinging on state jurisdiction where she would have received a much lighter sentence if any punishment at all.[13] Thus, the court was challenging the tendency of Congress to expand the powers of the federal government and, at the same time, its own.

KEY TO understanding ★

The U.S. Constitution grants Congress specific powers that it needs to carry out its functions. How does Congress use its powers involving treaties, appointments, and impeachment to check the executive branch? In addition, the Constitution assigns significant powers to Congress and gives Congress the right to expand these powers, so that it can safeguard the interests of the people. As a result, the U.S. Congress is arguably the most powerful branch of the federal government.

elastic clause (necessary and proper clause)
This constitutional provision provided Congress with flexibility, allowing it to determine which new areas of national need it would address and which areas of government activity it would move into to fulfill its responsibilities.

IMPEACHMENT

Although the two congressional chambers must exercise many powers jointly, the Constitution also enumerates different powers for each chamber. The House is authorized to initiate all revenue bills (Art. I Sect. 7) and to initiate impeachment of government officials, including the president (Art. I Sect. 2). Because each chamber must approve any law for passage, the question of who initiates revenue bills may be less critical than who initiates impeachment proceedings.

Since 1789, the House has initiated impeachment proceedings 17 times, twice against a president—Andrew Johnson in 1868 and Bill Clinton in 1998—with the House effectively serving as a prosecutor. (The House came close to taking action against John Tyler in 1842, and in 1974 the House Judiciary Committee approved charges against Richard Nixon, but the president resigned before the entire House voted on articles of impeachment.) The other cases involved the impeachment of federal judges. The Senate, serving as judge and jury in impeachment trials (the Chief Justice of the Supreme Court presides in cases against presidents), votes on the charges with a two-thirds majority required for removal. The Senate has removed eight federal judges from office, acquitted six judges, and acquitted the two presidents. Most recently, the Senate removed G. Thomas Porteous, Jr., from the U.S. District Court for the Eastern District of Louisiana, who had been impeached by the U.S. House of Representatives on March 11, 2010, on charges of accepting bribes and making false statements under penalty of perjury. He was convicted by the U.S. Senate and removed from office on December 8, 2010.

★ U.S. District Court Judge G. Thomas Porteous, Jr., was impeached and removed from office for taking cash bribes and filing for bankruptcy under a false name.

TREATIES

The Senate also has a distinctive charge to provide "advice and consent" on treaties as well as presidential appointments (Art. II Sec. 2). Treaties require a two-thirds vote for approval. Few have been rejected outright (only 21 of several thousand submitted), but some treaties have died in committee, others have been withdrawn by the president in the face of certain defeat, and still others have been amended by a simple majority vote before being approved.

A continuing example of Senate delay is the Convention on the Elimination of All Forms of Discrimination Against Women (CEDAW), what is commonly described as a universal bill of rights for women. The United States is one of only seven nations in the world that have not yet ratified this treaty signed in July 1980 and approved by 186 nations. The Senate Foreign Relations Committee favorably recommended the treaty in 1994 and 2002, but opponents have blocked action on the floor. Opponents are concerned about workplace rights—mandating paid maternity leave and equal pay for work of equal value, abortion rights and military service.[14] Changes made in treaties can create problems because either the president or the foreign nation in question may reject the modifications; across history, 43 such amended treaties failed to go into force.

APPOINTMENTS

Given the large number of appointments subject to Senate approval, the chamber seldom rejects presidential nominations. According to an official estimate, roughly 4,000 civilian and 65,000 military nominations are submitted to the Senate during each two-year session of Congress.[15] Most government appointees subject to Senate confirmation leave office when the president departs, but federal judges hold office for life (unless they are removed for misbehavior) giving the Senate considerable influence over the judiciary. Throughout its entire history, the Senate has voted down only nine presidential nominees for cabinet positions, though additional nominees have withdrawn during the process. For example, Tom Daschle, a former senator nominated by President Obama to serve as Secretary of Health and Human Services, withdrew from consideration in 2009. The Senate has also rejected 12 nominees for Supreme Court vacancies, although another 11 withdrew their nominations and the Senate took no action on 10 more. See the discussions in Chapters 13 and 15.

THE STRUCTURE OF CONGRESS

Globally, legislatures arose in different historical contexts and developed differently. Although Canada and the United States share a common history as colonies of Great Britain, Canada remained a colony longer and adopted British practices drawn from a later period in British constitutional development. Hence, Canada's prime minister heads a government supported by a majority in the House of Commons and leads a cabinet with collective responsibility for executive policies. Both of these were developments in British politics that followed American independence. (See Chapter 13 for more on the parliamentary model.) In the same way, many African and Asian nations adopted legislative systems closely resembling those of their colonizers; often those systems were established by the colonizing countries prior to withdrawing from the nation.

BICAMERALISM

As we discussed in Chapter 2, congressional representation was a major issue at the constitutional convention in 1787 and ultimately resulted in a **bicameral legislature** with proportional representation in the House and equal representation in the Senate. The House of Representatives, with directly elected representatives, was intended to be more responsive to the wishes of the people. Senators, chosen by the state legislatures and serving for longer terms, were expected to be less responsive to the opinions of the day. Representatives must seek the public's continued support every two years and senators every six years, with one-third standing for election each two-year cycle.

Congress is divided into two equal chambers, the House and the Senate. Worldwide, about one-third of national legislatures have some degree of bicameralism (see Figure 12.4), and 49 of the 50 states have legislatures with two chambers—Nebraska is the only state with a unicameral legislature. Most legislative bodies in the world are unicameral, or function as though they are unicameral because one branch is substantially stronger than the other. For example, the British House of Lords can delay action on legislation, but the House of Commons may take action without the Lords' approval. Sometimes the two chambers of a legislature reflect different interests in society, while other times they are largely redundant, representing the same social interests. In both the United States and Germany, the constituent states of the federal republic exercise important powers and are represented in the upper chambers. In the

bicameral legislature
A legislature that has two chambers, with each chamber typically reflecting a different part of society or political grouping.

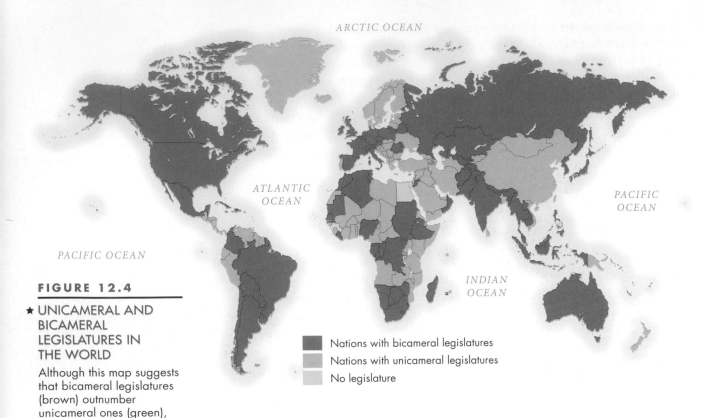

ARCTIC OCEAN

ATLANTIC
OCEAN

PACIFIC
OCEAN

PACIFIC OCEAN

INDIAN
OCEAN

■ Nations with bicameral legislatures
■ Nations with unicameral legislatures
□ No legislature

FIGURE 12.4

★ UNICAMERAL AND
BICAMERAL
LEGISLATURES IN
THE WORLD

Although this map suggests
that bicameral legislatures
(brown) outnumber
unicameral ones (green),
few bicameral systems have
two chambers that are
equally powerful, as in the
United States.

U.S. Senate, however, California has the same weight as Delaware—while in the
German Bundesrat, the upper chamber, state representation is proportional to population and larger states have more seats.

Having two constitutionally equal chambers, as the United States does, makes policy making more complex and often more time-consuming, as we saw in the opening
example involving the emergency legislation passed in response to the economic crisis
in the fall of 2008. And, as we noted above, their powers differ. Some differences
between the chambers can be surprising. For example, staff members in the House
have employee benefits and privileges that differ from those of staff members in the
Senate. Loyalty to a chamber can sometimes get in the way of legislative work; House
members will seek to defend their turf from encroachment by senators and vice versa.
Even members of the same party may find themselves feuding because the dynamics
within the two houses are different and the party structures separate. For example,
although the Republicans controlled both chambers of Congress from 2003 to 2007,
House Republicans were more conservative than Senate Republicans, who were in turn
more likely to compromise with their Democratic colleagues. The result was a family
feud—Republicans from the two chambers openly criticized each other.

Thus, the effects of bicameralism are wide-ranging and pervasive, adding a level of
complexity absent in many other political systems. In the case of the bank crisis in
2008, the House reversed its original opposition to the administration's plan only after
the Senate approved a more acceptable compromise. This sequence was altered in 2009
when Congress adopted a sweeping economic stimulus package proposed by the newly
elected Obama administration. The House approved an initial version of the stimulus
bill, and the Senate approved a different version, carefully crafted to address the concerns of three moderate Republican senators whose votes were needed for passage.

Bicameralism increases the number of politically important figures in the decision-making process. American legislators first must find enough votes to pass proposals inside their own chamber and then must resolve differences with the second chamber. Negotiations and bargaining are also important in unicameral legislatures, but decision making is usually more streamlined.

CONGRESSIONAL SESSIONS

Based on the election cycle of House members, each session of Congress is numbered according to the two-year term when a new Congress is elected. Thus, the 112th Congress ran from January 2011 to January 2013, when a new class of members—435 Representatives and one-third of the Senate—will be sworn in. These two-year periods are therefore distinct. Membership changes from one Congress to the next. The 87 new members of the House sworn in on January 6, 2011, included a large number of Tea Party Republicans who wanted less government and lower spending than the members they replaced. Thus, action on any legislation introduced during the previous two years must have been completed or else the process begins again, a reasonable rule since the new Congress may disagree with the decisions of its predecessor. Yet this too, like the bicameral nature of Congress, makes the legislative process more complex than in most parliamentary systems.

★ Utah's freshman Republican senator Mike Lee is sworn into office. The 2010 midterm elections swept Lee and other candidates supported by the Tea Party Movement into Congress.

HOW CONGRESS OPERATES

Congress employs thousands of people in addition to its elected members. To understand how this complex institution functions, we start by examining its critical building blocks and then ask whether Congress can act in a coherent manner.

INFLUENCE IN CONGRESS

We can think of Congress as having multiple centers of power and decision making. Jockeying for power are the rank-and-file members, the party leaders, and the committee chairs. Assisting these legislators in their efforts to influence decisions are the congressional staff and support agencies.

Rank-and-File Members

The 535 members of Congress are constitutional equals. Each has an independent claim to fulfill a role established by the constitution to represent the interests of the people who elected him or her. Consequently, members realize constituents will evaluate their

KEY TO understanding

Rank-and-file members, party leaders, committees, sub-committees, and congressional staff members are important to congressional operations. Congress needs internal expertise to confront the executive, a role that is less important in parliamentary systems. But the internal divisions in Congress makes checking the executive more difficult. As you read through this section, ask yourself why the House follows more rigid rules than the Senate.

★

performance and therefore they are motivated to be responsive to constituents' concerns and interests between elections; at least, this is what the theory of democracy expects.

Members of Congress often coordinate their efforts with those of other members. Representatives from the same state will work together on projects that produce common benefits. Members work with legislators in other states who hail from districts with similar economic interests. They form groups based on shared interests, known as *congressional member organizations,* which meet regularly to share information and coordinate strategy. There were 645 such informal organizations in 2009, with each House member belonging to 26 and each senator to 12.[16] For example, members from districts with steel factories compose a steel caucus. Sometimes ideology or identity forms the basis of shared interests. The Tea Party Caucus became highly influential in the House after the 2010 elections swelled its ranks to 52 members. In contrast, the Blue Dog Coalition, a group of moderate to conservative Democrats, shrank from 54 to 26 members after the 2010 mid-term elections. The Black Caucus, a group of 41 African-American members in the 112th House (no Blacks served in the Senate), promotes legislation favorable to African Americans and has grown in importance as their membership has expanded. Republican and Democratic Hispanic members of Congress now meet in separate groups after having once met together.

Almost all rank-and-file members have a party label that influences how they behave and how they vote. (There were two Independents in the 112th Senate who met with the Democrats.) Being in the majority party has important advantages for all party members; therefore, cooperating on a common agenda and developing shared strategies are ways to accomplish mutual goals. During most of the twentieth century, party leaders had few ways to force members to toe the party line, so leaders appealed to loyalty and emphasized how standing together would help them get reelected. But the influence of party on rank-and-file members is growing.

★ Members of the Congressional Black Caucus use their collective voting power to influence legislation. Here they are shown in December 2010 criticizing President Obama's agreement with congressional Republicans to extend tax cuts adopted early in the Bush administration.

As we saw in Chapter 10, a candidate's party label has become increasingly important in guiding how voters choose among candidates. There is still a great deal of candidate-centered campaigning, a focus on the candidate's personality, community roots, and responsiveness to the district. But since the 1970s, national influences have grown. Parties have increased the financial support they provide to candidates and also pay for independent advertising that touts the party's positions on high-profile issues or attacks the opponent.

Inside Congress, party has also become more important, as shown by how often voting follows party lines. *Congressional Quarterly* has tracked **party unity** in Congress for decades, a measure of how often a majority of Democrats are aligned against a majority of Republicans on votes with recorded positions, so-called roll call votes. The pattern is clear. Around 1970, party majorities faced off only 50 to 60 percent of the time. By the 1990s, this happened 85 to 90 percent of the time in both the House and the Senate. Thus, partisanship has grown and bipartisanship has declined, as Figure 12.5 illustrates.

Today, members who abandon party loyalty stand out like sore thumbs. Dan Boren (D, OK) voted with the majority of other House Democrats only 35 percent of the time before deciding to leave Congress in 2011. The previous record low among House Democrats was Ralph Hall (D, TX) whose support dipped below 30 percent three times during the period from 1995 to 2004 before he changed parties and became a Republican. Zell Miller (D, GA) held the Senate record low party unity score in 2004 when he voted with the majority of other Senate Democrats only 2 percent of the time before retiring![17]

In some respects, the influence of parties in Congress is becoming more like that found in parliamentary systems. We used to say that party leaders in Congress were weaker than those elsewhere because the U.S. leaders could not control the choice of

party unity
A measure of how often a majority of Republican legislators vote against a majority of Democrat legislators.

FIGURE 12.5

★ PARTY UNITY, 1956–2010

Over the past four decades there have been dramatic changes in party unity in both the House and Senate. What factors do you think have contributed to this rise, and what are some of its consequences?

Source: Shawn Zeller, "2010 Vote Studies: Party Unity." *CQ Weekly* (January 3, 2011), pp. 30–35 (http://library.cqpress.com/cqweekly/weeklyreport112-000003788817).

Percent of total House membership

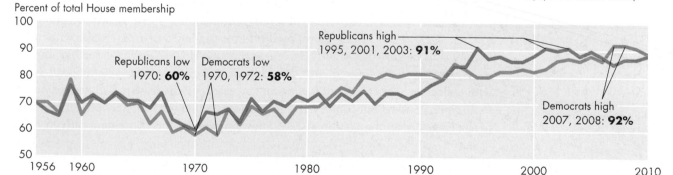

Percent of total Senate membership

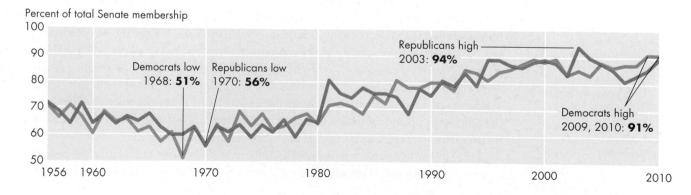

nominees for election—voters did so in primaries—whereas parliamentary leaders could deny the nomination to disloyal members. But pressure from party leaders is not the only means of enforcing party unity. In 2010, for example, the Tea Party Movement in the Republican Party challenged a number of incumbents who were criticized for being RINOs, Republicans In Name Only, because their voting records were not conservative enough. One example is Mike Castle, House member from Delaware who, instead of seeking reelection to the House, sought a Senate seat. Castle had voted with his Republican colleagues only 70 percent of the time, the second lowest level in the 111th Congress, but the state and national Republican Party organizations backed the popular Castle who was expected to win against the Democrat. But Castle lost in the primary to a Tea Party-backed candidate, Christine O'Donnell, who later went on to lose the general election. Just as forces from the Republicans' conservative wing have sought to remove moderates, liberals in the Democratic Party have targeted their own moderates; for example, Connecticut liberal Democrats denied Senator Joe Lieberman the party's nomination in 2006 because of his support for the Iraq war. Lieberman won his reelection bid by running as an Independent, something Castle declined to do. Thus, pressure has grown within parties to enforce greater party loyalty.

★ Senator Joseph Lieberman served Connecticut for many years as a moderate Democrat, often supporting bipartisan initiatives. His support for the war in Iraq eventually caused his state's Democrats to deny him their nomination during a primary election. He ran as an independent and won in the 2006 general election. In 2008, he campaigned for John McCain, not the Democratic party's nominee for president.

Today, there is less tolerance for rank-and-file members who vote their conscience or support bipartisan solutions. Senator Olympia Snowe, a moderate Republican from Maine, voted with the Democrats on health care reform and economic stimulus programs in the 111th Congress, and then voted against Republican-proposed reforms to Medicare in 2011. She voted with Republicans on key votes only 49 percent of the time in 2009 but increased her support to 73 percent of the time in 2010. By contrast, the average Senate Republican voted with colleagues 89 percent of the time on key votes.[18] Party leaders had limited power to discipline Snowe, but conservative Republicans, unhappy with her votes, threatened to challenge her re-nomination in 2012. Snowe announced her retirement early in 2012.

Party Leaders

Despite sharing an equal constitutional status, not all members of Congress have equal influence. Among the most influential are party leaders. Congress has four major party organizations: Democrats and Republicans in the House and in the Senate. When the party's members meet together, they constitute a **party conference** (Republicans) or **party caucus** (Democrats). Each party group follows different rules in selecting its leadership, in creating specific party committees that develop policy positions, and in appointing members to committees. The leader of the majority party becomes the leading figure in the chamber: the **Speaker of the House** is a position established in the Constitution, while the **Senate Majority Leader,** with far fewer powers, has emerged as the leading figure in the Senate.

Today's House Speaker wields wide-ranging powers over the legislative process, determining who serves on which committees, when legislation is scheduled for a vote,

party conference
Term used by House Republicans and both Democrats and Republicans in the Senate referring to the meeting of all party members.

party caucus
Term used by House Democrats referring to the meeting of all party members.

Speaker of the House of Representatives
Constitutionally prescribed position of the presiding officer in the House, which became more partisan and more program-focused in the nineteenth century.

Senate Majority Leader
Leader of the majority party in the Senate, who plays an important role in managing the business of the chamber.

who can speak on the floor, and how votes are taken. The Speaker is also a strategist who seeks to keep the majority party in power by articulating an agenda and working toward its achievement. By comparison, the Senate Majority Leader has far fewer powers but is also responsible for scheduling the work of the Senate. Most of the Majority Leader's influence resides in convincing others to cooperate, a task likened to "herding cats" because of Senators' deep independence.

The leaders of the 112th Congress are listed in Table 12.3. The vice president presides over the Senate when he attends its sessions, voting only in the event of a tie. When the vice president is absent, the chair is taken by the *president pro tempore*, a position specified in the Constitution, but junior members of the majority party often fill the chair, a largely powerless position. The Speaker of the House presides only on the most important occasions, typically asking another member of the majority party to preside the rest of the time.

★ Harry Reid, Democrat from Nevada, became the Senate Majority Leader in January 2007.

There are also subordinate party leadership positions, members who are principally responsible for ensuring that their colleagues work together when necessary. Because they enforce party discipline, they are known as **whips,** a term derived from fox hunting when one member of the hunting group was responsible for keeping the dogs from straying, an apt image for the party whip's job.[19] Party whips inform members of the work schedule, party strategies, and preferred positions on issues, and they make sure members are present for important votes. They also seek to determine members' preferences beforehand so they will know how the vote is likely to turn out. As we have suggested, party discipline is difficult to enforce in the U.S. Congress. Ultimately, members usually win or lose nomination in their home states because of their own campaign efforts, and the party plays a limited role. This ordinarily gives members greater independence from the party than is found in most other democracies.

whip
The member of the party leadership team charged with keeping the members in line—that is, getting them to cast votes in the way the party leaders would like.

TABLE 12.3
party leaders in the 112th congress

HOUSE	SENATE
Majority (Republican)	*Majority (Democrat)*
Speaker—John Boehner (OH)	Majority Leader—Harry Reid (NV)
Majority Leader—Eric Cantor (VA)	Asst. Maj. Leader—Richard Durbin (IL)
Majority Whip—Kevin McCarthy (CA)	Caucus Vice Chair—Charles Schumer (NY)
Conference Chair—Jeb Hensarling (TX)	Conference Secretary—Patty Murray (WA)
Minority (Democrat)	*Minority (Republican)*
Minority Leader—Nancy Pelosi (CA)	Minority Leader—Mitch McConnell (TN)
Minority Whip—Steny Hoyer (MD)	Asst. Min. Leader—John Kyl (AZ)
Asst. Minority Leader—Jim Clyburn (SC)	Conf. Chair—Lamar Alexander (TN)
Caucus Chair—John Larson (CT)	Policy Comm. Chr.—John Thune (SD)

Political parties play a fundamental role in organizing Congress. Not only do they organize the proposed legislation that comes to the floor for the entire chamber to consider, but they also exercise pervasive influence through the committees. The chair of *every* standing committee in both the House and Senate is a member of the majority party in that chamber. And the majority party in the chamber also has a majority of members on every committee. That means that in the 112th Congress, Republicans chaired and held a majority on every House committee and Democrats on every Senate committee. In the 111th Congress, Democrats held majorities in both chambers, just as the Republicans did in five of the six Congresses from 1995 to 2007. As shown in Figure 12.6, Democrats controlled both the House and Senate from 1955 to 1981; even more impressively, Democrats held an uninterrupted majority in the House from 1955 to 1995.

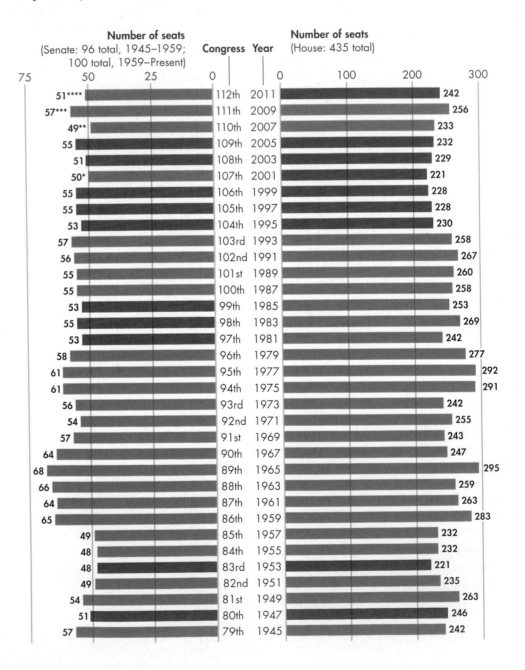

FIGURE 12.6

★ PARTY CONTROL OF CONGRESS, 1949–2011

Based on what you know about parties and elections, how do you explain the long period of Democratic domination in the House and the more recent party control changes in both the House and Senate?

* There were 50 Ds and 50 Rs until May 24, 2001, when Sen. James Jeffords (R-VT) switched to Independent status, effective June 6, 2001; he announced that he would caucus with the Democrats, giving the Democrats a one-seat advantage.

** Independent Sen. Bernard Sanders (VT) and Independent Democrat Sen. Joseph Lieberman (CT) gave the Democrats a one-seat majority.

*** Senators Sanders and Lieberman voted with the Democrats. Republican Senator Arlen Specter (PA) became a Democrat in April 2009.

**** Senators Sanders and Lieberman voted with the Democrats.

Source: http://artandhistory.house.gov/house_history/partyDiv.aspx; http://www.senate.gov/pagelayout/history/one_item_and_teasers/partydiv.htm

Number of seats (Senate: 96 total, 1945–1959; 100 total, 1959–Present)

Number of seats (House: 435 total)

Congress	Year	Senate	House
112th	2011	51****	242
111th	2009	57***	256
110th	2007	49**	233
109th	2005	55	232
108th	2003	51	229
107th	2001	50*	221
106th	1999	55	228
105th	1997	55	228
104th	1995	53	230
103rd	1993	57	258
102nd	1991	56	267
101st	1989	55	260
100th	1987	55	258
99th	1985	53	253
98th	1983	55	269
97th	1981	53	242
96th	1979	58	277
95th	1977	61	292
94th	1975	61	291
93rd	1973	56	242
92nd	1971	54	255
91st	1969	57	243
90th	1967	64	247
89th	1965	68	295
88th	1963	66	259
87th	1961	64	263
86th	1959	65	283
85th	1957	49	232
84th	1955	48	232
83rd	1953	48	221
82nd	1951	49	235
81st	1949	54	263
80th	1947	51	246
79th	1945	57	242

Parties help members make decisions on pending policy issues, both in the committees and on the floor of the chambers. Similar to the voting cues that citizens receive from party identification (see Chapter 9), legislators' party identification guides them in making voting decisions. On issues that are particularly complex or outside of the legislator's area of expertise, the member is likely to defer to the party's position or that of a trusted colleague to make the required decision.[20]

Legislators weigh the benefits and drawbacks when deciding whether to vote for or against the party's position. Party leaders consider a member's party loyalty when placing bills on the legislative calendar, distributing valued legislative benefits, such as committee assignments, and determining which members' bills may be considered on the floor. Along with ways to reward loyalty inside the chamber, party leaders can help loyal members by providing campaign help.[21]

Thus, members can benefit from party loyalty or be punished for too much independence. Tom DeLay (R-TX), who served House Republicans as Majority Whip for eight years and then as Majority Leader for two and a half, earned the nickname "The Hammer" for his tough enforcement of party loyalty. He proudly displayed a long leather bull whip in his office to symbolize this reputation. One example of DeLay's toughness involved Connecticut Republican Christopher Shays, who defied the party's leadership and forced action on a campaign finance reform bill that the Republican leaders opposed. In the next Congress, when Shays sought to become chair of the Government Reform Committee, party leaders punished him by refusing to give him the job, a position he was next in line to hold.[22] The message was clear to fellow Republicans: if you oppose the leadership there will be consequences. Democrats can also play rough: Nancy Pelosi refused to appoint the senior Democrat, Jane Harman (D-CA), as chair of the House Intelligence Committee in 2007, possibly because Harman had supported the U.S. invasion of Iraq while Pelosi and most other Democrats had opposed it.[23]

Committees and Subcommittees

Congressional committees are not expressly mentioned in the Constitution, yet they are vital for the legislature's daily operations. When legislative bodies deal with public problems, they seldom work effectively as a **committee of the whole,** the entire group meeting together to gather information, discuss possible solutions, and craft legislative language. Instead, Congress creates subgroups to develop recommendations for the larger body to consider. As legislators become knowledgeable about specific areas of public policy, the collective ability of Congress to make better policies grows. Nonetheless, this specialization becomes a source of internal division and differential influence.

Early in their history both the House and Senate began to rely on committees to help complete their work. These early committees were *ad hoc* or **select committees;** that is, they were temporary groups appointed to work on specific problems. After hearing a debate on the floor of the House, committees would assemble to draft legislation. The House, however, moved quickly toward adopting more permanent committee structures, or **standing committees,** whose members continued working throughout a full session of Congress and even across sessions on the same policy problems, their **committee jurisdictions.** One of the most influential House committees, Ways and Means, which is responsible for overseeing the government's sources of revenue, was created as a select committee in 1789 and became a standing committee in 1795. It remains even today one of the most powerful committees in the House but was even more influential until 1865, when the House created a separate Appropriations Committee and shifted

committee of the whole
Situation in which the whole House or whole Senate considers business rather than delegating work to committees.

select committee
Congressional committee formed for a specific purpose and limited period of time.

standing committee
A permanent committee in the House or Senate whose responsibilities carry over from one Congress to the next, as does much of its membership.

committee jurisdiction
Defined areas of standing committee responsibilities, comprising the policy areas, programs, and agencies that each committee oversees.

TABLE 12.4

standing committees in the 112th congress

HOUSE COMMITTEES	SENATE COMMITTEES
Agriculture	Agriculture, Nutrition, and Forestry
Appropriations	Appropriations
Armed Services	Armed Services
Budget	Banking, Housing, and Urban Affairs
Education and Workforce	Budget
Energy and Commerce	Commerce, Science, and Transportation
Ethics	Energy and Natural Resources
Financial Services	Environment and Public Works
Foreign Affairs	Finance
Homeland Security	Foreign Relations
House Administration	Health, Education, Labor, and Pensions
Judiciary	Homeland Security and Governmental Affairs
Natural Resources	Judiciary
Oversight and Government Reform	Rules and Administration
Rules	Small Business
Science, Space, and Technology	Veterans' Affairs
Small Business	
Transportation and Infrastructure	
Veterans' Affairs	
Ways and Means	

Sources: http://www.house.gov/committees/; http://www.senate.gov/pagelayout/reference/e_one_section_no_teasers/org_chart.htm

responsibility for government spending away from Ways and Means. The Senate did not create select committees until 1816, when it created 11 standing committees. Table 12.4 lists the House and Senate standing committees of the 112th Congress.

Today there are 16 standing Senate committees, four Special or Select Committees, and four **joint committees** with members from both the House and Senate. In the House, there are 20 standing committees, two select committees, and of course the four joint committees—the Joint Economic Committee, the Joint Committee on the Library, the Joint Committee on Printing, and the Joint Committee on Taxation.

Most committees also maintain subcommittees that focus members' efforts on an even narrower range of policies. The House and Senate Appropriations committees have the most subcommittees in Congress, with 12 in each chamber.

The chairs of committees and subcommittees can wield great power, including the ability to move a bill forward in the law-making process or let it die in committee. Thus, members seek to serve on committees dealing with issues that have a direct bearing on their constituency or committees that deal with policies of personal interest. Committees are often described as the "work horses" of Congress, and without them, Congress would face an even greater challenge: every legislator would have to gain the knowledge and specialization needed to decide on the thousands of pieces of legislation introduced every year.

joint committee
Congressional committee that includes members from both the Senate and House.

Richard Fenno, an expert on Congress, identified three goals sought by every member of Congress: reelection, power within the chamber, and good public policy.[21] The committee system advances all three goals. By serving on committees with a direct bearing on their constituency, legislators increase the likelihood of benefitting their district and thereby increasing their chances of reelection. For example, virtually all the members of the House Committee on Agriculture come from districts with major farming interests, including several from California, Georgia, Iowa, Illinois, Minnesota, and Texas, important farming states. Frank Lucas (R-OK), the committee chair, represents 32 counties—largely agricultural—in northern and western Oklahoma. Lucas holds a degree in Agricultural Economics and owns a farm and cattle ranch in a district that ranks high in receiving agricultural subsidies from the federal government. Rising to the role of subcommittee or committee chair substantially increases an individual's power in the chamber. Committees also provide the best opportunity to shape public policy.[25]

Not all committees are created equal. Those considered more prestigious deal with important areas of government action such as taxes, spending, business and banking policies, and foreign and defense policy. In the House, the Rules, Appropriations, Ways and Means, Energy and Commerce, and Financial Services committees are top assignments.[26] For the Senate, the Appropriations, Foreign Relations, Finance, Judiciary, and Armed Services committees are the top five.[27] Freshmen—first-year members of Congress—tend to serve on committees with lower prestige, but they hope to move up the pecking order in the future as party leaders balance seniority, party loyalty, and geographic representation in making committee appointments.

Congressional Staff

Members of Congress rely heavily on the efforts of personal and committee staff members, whose positions were created to help them discharge their many responsibilities and to achieve Fenno's three goals. Many congressional aides, particularly those working back home in the district or state, are engaged primarily in constituency service. Committee staffers tend to be policy specialists who assist with law making and oversight. Each House member is allowed to employ up to 18 full-time staff members and as many as 4 part-time assistants; there is no limit on the number of aides a senator may employ although there is a limited budget.[28] Members of Congress can decide how to distribute their staff between their Washington, D.C., and district offices.

Both the majority and minority members of committees and subcommittees receive support from committee staff; the majority staff is always larger. These aides work to draft legislation, write committee reports, and oversee executive agencies within the committee's jurisdiction. They also maintain committee records, manage funds, maintain schedules, and respond to public inquiries about committee activities. Party leaders' staffs help steer the caucus or conference's activities. Staff who work for the entire House and Senate keep the chambers operating efficiently. There are an estimated 16,000 legislative staff members—most working for members rather than committees—and another 13,000 aides working in the support agencies discussed below.[29]

Congressional Support Agencies

Early in the twentieth century, Congress recognized that it required far more extensive information to make well-informed policies than its members and modest personal and committee staffs could provide. As a result, it created several research agencies to

TABLE 12.5
support agencies of the U.S. congress

AGENCY	YEAR CREATED	EMPLOYEES	PURPOSE
Government Accountability Office	1921	3,000+	Audit agency operations, investigate illegal activities, analyze options
Congressional Research Service	1914	650	Provide background on policy, interpret constitutional issues, report on legislative issues
Congressional Budget Office	1974	230	Provide accurate, nonpartisan economic analyses and projections

assist its policy making. Policy experts in these agencies analyze problems and make recommendations. Critical features of the three staff support agencies are summarized in Table 12.5.

DISTINCTIVE FEATURES OF HOUSE AND SENATE RULES

Life in the Senate and House is very different. Not only are senators under less immediate pressure to defend their positions in reelection campaigns, but many also aspire to move to the White House. As the saying goes, each morning senators see a future president in the mirror. In addition, senators represent larger and more diverse statewide constituencies and receive more media attention than members of the House; the media cover Senate floor debates more widely, and the additional visibility fuels personal ambition. Debates in the House are rarely covered because discussion must be more structured and is subject to many more rules and constraints.

In fact, because of its larger size, the House generally follows more structured procedures than the Senate. To get anything accomplished, the House cannot allow all 435 members to have their say on a bill. In contrast, the tradition in the Senate is to allow any Senator to speak for as long as the member deems necessary on any issue, allowing unlimited discussion that might last for days or even weeks. The classic example is the **filibuster,** a delay tactic developed in the Senate during the mid-nineteenth century to prevent a bill from going to a vote on the floor. (Originally, unlimited debate was also allowed in the House, but this practice was phased out in 1841 when member comments were limited to a maximum of one hour but now seldom exceed five minutes.) In the event of a filibuster, one senator or a group of senators may talk for an unlimited amount of time, monopolizing the floor and preventing a vote on an issue. This tradition gives minorities in the chamber enormous power to frustrate a majority.

In 1917, the Senate adopted a rule that empowered two-thirds of its members to end a filibuster with a vote on **cloture,** closing discussion and

filibuster
Delay tactic used in the Senate that rests on members' right to speak as long as they desire on a topic, thereby preventing a vote from being taken.

cloture
Senate rules provision that allows 60 votes to conclude debate on a bill and bring it to a vote on the floor.

clearing the way for a vote on the issue. This rule was used for the first time to end debate on the proposed Treaty of Versailles in 1919. In 1975, the rule was changed to require a three-fifths vote, or the support of 60 senators, to limit debate. Senator Strom Thurmond (R-SC) holds the record for the longest filibuster ever conducted by a single senator (24 hours and 18 minutes), in opposition to the Civil Rights Act of 1957. The use of a filibuster or even the threat of one is often enough to deter a bill from ever reaching the floor for a vote because a filibuster would hold up all the other business before the Senate, as discussed later in this chapter.[30]

Committees and political parties are more important in the operations of the House than the Senate, again due to differences in the chambers' size. Although the House has more committees and subcommittees, committees in the Senate typically have more members. The Senate conducts more work in full committee than in subcommittees and spends more time dealing with legislation as a committee of the whole. As a result, an individual senator is probably more consequential in the lawmaking process than a rank-and-file representative.[31]

Political parties are also more prominent in the House, providing a critical structure to organize the work of the body. The majority party in the House determines the rules under which a bill may be debated and voted upon by the full membership on the floor. Historically, senators operated in a more "clubby" atmosphere where cross-party friendships and bipartisan coalitions were more readily formed than in the House, although the rise of partisan conflict has threatened that tradition. The Senate's majority and minority party leaders normally negotiate about the scheduling of bills and operate, of course, within the tradition of full debate. House party leaders are forced to exercise greater control in order to get work accomplished.

COMPARISONS WITH OTHER LEGISLATURES

In a system that relies on a strong legislature to check the power of the executive, such as that found in the United States, it makes sense that committees and specialized staffs have powerful roles. In contrast, parliamentary systems have different needs. Depending on the political system, parliamentary committees exercise some powers but are less involved in policy making than their U.S. counterparts. Instead, policy making is centered in the hands of the government, led by the cabinet, which in turn is supported by a majority in parliament. In Italy, for example, parliamentary committees can exercise discretion over minor legislation, but they have little power to shape significant legislation, which is dominated by the government and its parliamentary majority.

In fact, there is little reason for parliaments to develop strong centers of policy specialization. Department ministers, who are also members of parliament (MPs), function as the legislature's policy experts, making it unnecessary for MPs to develop broad and comparable expertise. The cabinet—acting individually as ministers and collectively as the government—performs many of the same functions as American legislative committees, shaping policy that reflects the views of the larger legislature. Ministers, appointed by the prime minister to oversee a part of the government, in turn rely on career government officials to provide them with expert guidance. Thus, under the U.S. Constitution, a strong committee system, coupled with the independent professional staffs created by Congress, creates a legislature capable of overseeing the bureaucracy and challenging the executive.[32]

picture YOURSELF . . .

VISITING PARLIAMENT HOUSE IN NEW DELHI, INDIA

The Parliament House is an imposing circular building ringed by 144 columns. Completed in 1927, it is known commonly as Sansad Bhawan. You hear the sound of fountains as you gaze at the extensive lawns and ponds that dot the surrounding estate. And all this is within a city with nearly 12 million residents. Inside Parliament House are the 555 members of the Lok Sabha, the directly elected representatives of India's 1.1 billion citizens, and the members of the Rajya Sabha, not to exceed 250, who are chosen by the legislatures of India's 29 states and 6 union territories.

When India, the world's largest democracy, conducted elections in 2009, more than 700 million registered voters were eligible to choose among 4,617 candidates running in 543 single-member districts. The process was complex and colorful, and the result was not always pretty. *The Economist* reported that nearly a quarter of

the Lok Sabha's members had faced criminal charges, including rape, murder, and kidnapping.* But overall India's experiment in democracy has been unusually successful. With only a few exceptions, stable democracies are prosperous, industrialized countries. India is one of those exceptions, however. Today, after a decade of rapid economic growth, it ranks in the upper third internationally in per capita income, and for most of its history as an independent nation it has been much worse off than that, with crushing levels of poverty. Yet it has sustained a democratic government since gaining its independence from Britain in 1947.

Getting inside the Sansad Bhawan is not easy. Like many other nations, India must deal with terrorists targeting major national symbols, in this case activity by separatist groups from

several regions of the country. Five terrorists died during a suicide attack on the parliament in December 2001; the exchange of fire killed 7 guards and injured 22 bystanders. Once you are past security and able to observe parliament's operations, you see a curious combination of practices derived from both Britain, India's long-time colonial ruler, and the United States. As in Britain, the Indian prime minister and members of the Council of Ministers (the cabinet) are accountable to the lower, elected house of parliament and subject to close interrogation during Question Hour—the regular opportunity for members of the legislature to pose direct questions to the prime minister and members of the cabinet. Reformers of the American system of government often advocate introducing this practice in the United States.

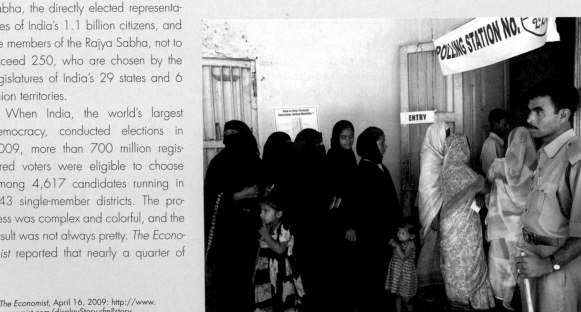

* *The Economist*, April 16, 2009: http://www.economist.com/displayStory.cfm?story_id=13492427 and http://www.economist.com/displayStory.cfm?story_id=13497128

Behind the scenes, though, you would find several practices that are more similar to the U.S. Congress than to the British parliament. Foremost among these is the system of relatively powerful standing committees, 17 groups that correspond to the principal departments of the government. Through these committees, the Indian parliament exercises oversight of the government's administration—ministers are not eligible to serve on the committees, which means that their investigations are likely to be more searching and critical, with a level of scrutiny that is more typical of the United States than Britain.

You would also notice the great diversity among delegates to India's parliament; 79 seats are reserved for "scheduled castes" (members of the economically depressed "untouchable" class) and 40 seats for "scheduled tribes" (indigenous peoples). Delegates also come from speakers of India's 30 main languages and members of six major religions. As one might expect, India's political parties are diverse as well—nearly two dozen parties had representatives in the parliament, and 300 ran candidates in the 2009 election.

questions to consider

1. Should members of the United States Congress have the opportunity to question the president in public as members of the Indian parliament can quiz their prime minister?

2. Should the Indian parliament become more like the U.S. government and exclude government ministers not just from the work of standing committees but from all parliamentary activities?

3. What advantages does the U.S. system, which precludes executive branch officials from serving in Congress, have over the Indian system, which excludes government ministers from serving on standing committees but not from participating in other parliamentary activities?

ASSEMBLING COALITIONS TO MAKE ACTION POSSIBLE

As a multi-member body with many centers of decision making, Congress faces an especially daunting challenge: how to build enough agreement among members to act on pressing public problems. Countervailing forces are at work in Congress: powerful decentralizing forces pull members in different directions while centralizing forces, mainly party leaders, attempt to overcome the decentralizing influences and coordinate action. Over time, Congress has sometimes strengthened party leaders' ability to provide central coordination but later reacted against an excessive consolidation of power. These pushes and pulls are a permanent feature of congressional life.

KEY TO understanding ★

Congress often struggles to take coherent action, particularly in the House, whose larger membership presents problems. Responding to this challenge, party leaders centralized control over their colleagues at the turn of the twentieth century, triggering rebellions by the rank-and-file members. Committee chairs dominated for much of the century, but power once again shifted back to party leaders under both Democrats and Republicans. Most recently, decentralization again prevails. Why do legislators periodically want to decentralize decision making?

DECENTRALIZING FORCES

Imagine yourself as a member of Congress. As a constitutional equal to 534 others, you have no reason to defer to other members' ideas or preferences, and there are many incentives to prefer your own views. In your desire to be reelected, you seek greater visibility. Voters back home will want to know how you helped them during the previous two or six years. Serving your personal interests and those of the constituency easily take priority over serving the common interest of the party. And only in extraordinary circumstances, similar to the financial crisis of 2008 or following the terrorist attacks of 9/11, will the residents of diverse districts scattered across the nation demand the same action from government.

Similarly, legislative committees make coordinated action more difficult. By dividing a chamber's collective labor into specialized groups, committees make it possible for the House and Senate to consider more problems and to examine them in greater detail than could be accomplished by the committee of the whole, but committees also serve to divide the chamber. Each standing committee has a committee jurisdiction— perhaps 10 to 15 areas of government policy and programs over which it exercises authority. Sometimes bills that fit in several jurisdictions are referred to more than one committee as a way to avoid arguments between committees determined to defend their turf.[33] But committees and subcommittees exercise considerable autonomy as they make policy decisions, and this can fragment efforts to coordinate action.

When the Bush administration asked Congress to consolidate 22 existing organizations to create the Department of Homeland Security, lawmakers had to reconcile many overlapping jurisdictions. Researchers for the 9/11 Commission discovered that 88 congressional committees and subcommittees held some share of jurisdiction over the proposed department, creating a tangled web of what could be considered *too much* congressional oversight. Inevitably, the committees and subcommittees would provide the department with contradictory guidance, and department employees would need to respond to questions and probes from 88 different centers of congressional decision making, as shown in Figure 12.7, unless Congress simplified its own structure.[34]

FIGURE 12.7

★ COMMITTEE OVERSIGHT OF THE DEPARTMENT OF HOMELAND SECURITY

Figuring out which congressional committees had oversight responsibility for the new Department of Homeland Security was virtually impossible.

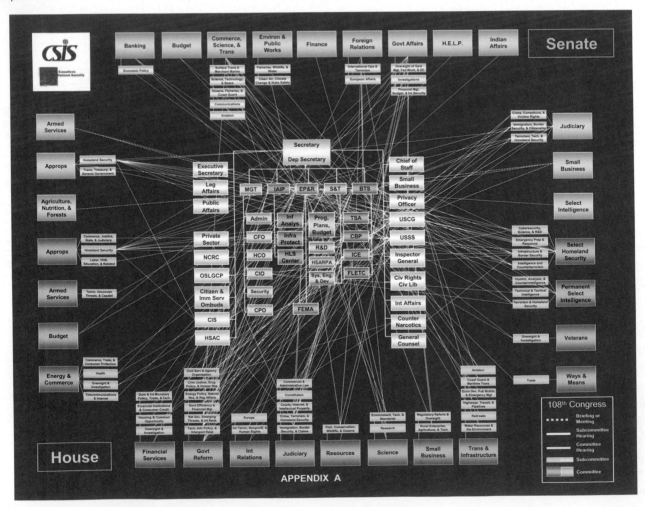

By January 2005, the total number of committees sharing jurisdiction over the department was down to 79, and by mid-2006 that total stood at 65, still very high. Congress apparently considered consolidation good medicine for the executive branch but not for itself as powerful committee chairs fought to retain control over important pieces of Homeland Security that they had overseen for years. The result was a drain on department time and energy. During the first three and one-half years of its existence, the department participated in 601 congressional hearings and presented nearly 6,000 congressional briefings; the two department secretaries had appeared before Congress 38 times.[35]

We said earlier that the Senate had created 11 standing committees by 1816 and there are only 16 today. You might conclude that fragmentation must not be a serious problem, but you would be mistaken. In the 112th Congress, the Senate had 16 standing committees and 73 subcommittees; the House had 20 standing committees and 98 subcommittees for a combined total of 207 legislative bodies.[36] The committee system extends the institution's legislative capacity at the same time that it fragments the chambers' ability to act.

CENTRALIZING FORCES

In the United States, parties have the greatest potential to mold the many pieces of Congress together into a coherent whole. The same is true of parliaments around the world, where parties assume responsibility to form a government and then must retain sufficient cohesion to remain in power. There are different ways to amass enough support behind policy initiatives to make action possible. In models based on the British system, parties develop policy proposals before an election and compete to determine which party will receive the public mandate to govern. We saw this in 2010 when the Conservative Party led by David Cameron won the most seats in the British House of Commons and replaced Labour as the party forming a government. The alternative model—prominent on the European continent—is for parties to compete in elections for shares of power in the legislature and after the election develop policies as a way to build a governing coalition. Thus, policies precede elections in the British model and follow elections in the continental model. In both cases, parties are more powerful than in the United States, although that may be changing as the influence of party grows.

Although elements of the British model are present in the United States—loose party platforms serve as the basis for election appeals—there is also the need to build coalitions following elections, much like the continental European systems. But in the United States, those coalitions can shift from one issue to the next. Only political parties are capable of providing policy coherence, but that potential is often unrealized—thwarted by resistant committee chairs, by factions within the parties, and by individual members who choose not to support the party on votes that conflict with their district's or state's interests or threaten their chances for reelection. The story has been repeated throughout U.S. history: Strong party leaders establish discipline over a balky membership who then rebel against leaders who are viewed as dictatorial. This pattern is most dramatic in the House of Representatives.

Originally, the Speaker of the House functioned much as the Speaker in the House of Commons in England does today—as a neutral moderator of debate expected to preside over the chamber impartially. Henry Clay, selected as Speaker in 1811 during his first term in the House (something that would never happen today), is credited

★ Henry Clay, depicted (left) in 1850 speaking on the Senate floor, had earlier revolutionized the job of Speaker of the House of Representatives. His service was recognized at a symposium in 2011 by Speaker John Boehner and former Speakers Nancy Pelosi and Dennis Hastert (right).

with transforming the Speakership into a position that guides action by the majority party. Clay participated in debates, insisted on exercising the right to vote, and used his power to appoint committee members in a way to advantage his own party.[37]

Rise and Fall of the Czars

Senate party leaders guide their colleagues mostly through bargaining and personal persuasion, but House party leaders have relied more heavily on a set of formal powers wielded by strong individuals who control their members and the chamber. At the end of the nineteenth century, Thomas B. Reed (R-Me) imposed order on a highly disorderly chamber when, as Speaker of the House, he introduced a new set of rules that gave him control over the chamber's business and dramatically reduced the minority party's influence. For this, Speaker Reed earned the title of "czar." Reed and his successor Joseph G. Cannon punished party members who failed to follow their lead— denying them support for legislation that might help the member's constituency and help them get reelected, much as Tom DeLay did more recently. In 1910, the House membership revolted against the overly powerful Speaker. Thirty rebellious progressive Republicans joined with Democrats to remove the Speaker as chair of the powerful **Rules Committee,** the key to the Speaker's power.

The Era of Committee Government

The 1910 revolt democratized decision making in the House and gave rise to an era of **committee government** that lasted for half a century, when committee chairs were the principal centers of congressional power. For a while, party members tried to govern themselves by reaching consensus during their meetings, but that effort was short-lived, leaving a leadership vacuum into which stepped the chairs of the standing committees. The key to the power of these congressional barons was their automatic selection through the **seniority rule**—choosing the member of the majority party with the longest continuous service on a committee to serve as its chair. Thus, chairs owed their power to neither the party leader nor the chamber's party majority but to their own ability to get reelected year after year and decade after decade. Members from **safe seats** where they were unlikely to face serious challenges rose to power because of their political longevity, not their personal ability or their responsiveness to their colleagues. As a result, committee chairs were able to resist control from presidents, party leaders, and the conference or caucus until 1975 when Democrats refused the reappointment of three senior members who had expected to continue serving as committee

Rules Committee
Powerful committee in the House of Representatives that reviews all bills to determine the guidelines for debate and amendment under which they will be considered on the floor.

committee government
Period during the mid-twentieth century when chairs of the standing committees were the most powerful figures in the Congress.

seniority rule
Long-running practice followed in Congress in which the member of the majority party with the longest continuous service on a standing committee automatically becomes its chair.

safe seats
Members of Congress who, election after election, win by large margins.

chairs—the first violation of seniority in 50 years. During the period from 1925 to 1975, parties were unable to provide coherence or direction without the cooperation of powerful chairs. When chairs disagreed with the party's leaders or the party majority on policy matters before their committees, they effectively exercised a personal veto.

Two Directions of Reform

Congressional reformers in the last quarter of the twentieth century had to make a strategic choice. Should they further democratize and diffuse power within Congress by strengthening the subcommittees in order to overcome the power of the committee chairs? Or should they risk consolidating power once again into the hands of a party leader who would be accountable to the full membership of the party? In essence, Democrats in the House (the majority) tried both strategies. Empowering subcommittees did not help parties coordinate action, but rebuilding the power of party leaders during the 1980s did.

When Republicans gained control in 1994, they followed the reverse sequence, first consolidating power in the hands of a charismatic leader, Newt Gingrich (R-GA), but then reducing the leader's power during the 1990s and 2000s. Gingrich constructed a common policy agenda—the Contract with America—for the 1994 elections; most Republican candidates for the House swore to support the party on 10 policies. The strategy worked, and Republicans triggered a political earthquake.

With a unified party at his back, Gingrich personally selected committee chairs, pointedly ignoring seniority, limited them to a maximum six-year term, eliminated three committees, renamed others, and realigned committee jurisdictions. Committee members had to pledge to follow the leadership's guidelines, and Gingrich sometimes bypassed committees altogether by using task forces to rewrite legislation the committees had produced. Eventually, Gingrich's actions grated on his Republican colleagues, who were increasingly upset by his impulsive, confrontational style. After Republicans lost seats in the 1996 and 1998 elections, his colleagues pressured Gingrich to resign from Congress when he was charged with ethical misconduct. After Gingrich, House Republicans chose a consensus-building leader in Dennis Hastert, the next Speaker.

When Democrats won a majority in 2006, Nancy Pelosi mobilized House Democrats into a coherent force to confront President Bush on budget and foreign policy issues during his final two years in office. Her tactics—criticized by Republicans as dictatorial—made it impossible for the minority party to influence business and forced Democrats to toe the leadership's line. That did not change following Barack Obama's presidential victory in 2008. Republicans regained a House majority in the 2010 midterm elections, making John Boehner the Speaker with many new Republican members anxious to assert their influence. Boehner loosened the reins that Gingrich had tightened 16 years earlier, expanding the role of committees and subcommittees and permitting members to propose far more amendments during final debates on legislation.[38] But when Boehner found it difficult to coax House Republicans to follow his lead in negotiating a solution to raising the debt ceiling limit in 2011, some observers pointed precisely to the Speaker's less-demanding style as the source of the problem.[39]

PRESIDENTS AND INTEREST GROUPS

In assembling coalitions, Congress responds not only to pressures arising from within the House and Senate but also to important outside forces, including the president and lobbyists representing interest groups.

Although presidents cannot directly introduce bills, they do influence congressional action. Presidents since Franklin D. Roosevelt have had an impact on the operation of Congress in the following ways:

- Presidents identify the agenda of national issues. This happens especially through the annual State of the Union Address and the budget message. (See Chapter 13)
- Presidents propose specific solutions to national problems. Rather than simply point to issues and wait for Congress to act, presidents craft recommendations that their allies in Congress will push forward.
- Presidents actively lobby members of Congress for their support. In fact, the executive branch has many **legislative liaisons** who serve as lobbyists for agency and presidential proposals.
- Presidents ask the public to pressure Congress. When Congress is reluctant to follow the president's lead, the chief executive may enlist the public to urge their representatives to support his proposals.

legislative liaison
White House and agency officials whose job is to lobby Congress on behalf of the president or an agency.

Congressional members of the president's party share a common outlook on government and have common electoral interests—helping a president from your own party can help you get elected if the president is popular in your state or district. But any single vote against the president's proposals will not change the government, unlike a parliamentary system where the government's very existence might be at stake if it loses party support on a key issue. American presidents serve for fixed terms, and a vote on any single issue is unlikely to affect the party's control of the presidency in the next election. Thus, support from members of the president's own party is not guaranteed, and members will desert their colleagues if they disagree on ideological grounds or because of how a program is likely to affect their constituency.

To succeed, presidents often need votes from members of the opposition party. Sometimes they appeal to groups within the party whose policy views are closer to the president's than to those of their colleagues. For example, a group of Southern Democrats voted frequently with Republican presidents and Republican members of Congress to form the **conservative coalition** from 1940 to 1964, and for another two decades, that same coalition reassembled on spending and defense issues. At other times, presidents seek support from a few members of the opposition party who share their views on a specific policy (like Senator Snowe, as noted earlier), or from representatives who need something for their district—funding for a bridge, a water project, or a new building. In short, presidents construct shifting coalitions to help them achieve their goals.

conservative coalition
The voting alliance of a majority of Republicans with conservative Southern Democrats (a minority of Democrats) that frequently frustrated the efforts of liberal reformers from 1940 to 1964 and after.

President Barack Obama won crucial support from Republicans at the end of 2010 during the lame duck session of Congress—the period when the outgoing Congress conducts business after the midterm elections but before the new members have been sworn in. Obama agreed to continue the Bush income tax cuts for two more years if Republicans agreed to extend unemployment insurance and reduce Social Security taxes, steps that he believed would ease the lives of middle-class voters. Liberal Democrats wanted the second half of the deal but were adamantly opposed to extending the tax cuts, and large numbers voted against the president. In this instance, a Democratic president won the votes he needed from Republicans rather than from his own base, which had been enormously loyal to the party and the president during the previous two years.[40]

Thousands of lobbyists visit and phone Congress every day. According to the Center for Responsive Politics, a nonpartisan public watchdog group in Washington, more than 10,000 persons registered to lobby Congress during the first three months of 2011. This total included roughly 200 former members of the House and Senate who assumed lucrative lobbying jobs after they retired or were defeated. The number of lobbyists has varied over the past decade but has remained high.

Lobbyists seek to protect and promote the central concerns of the group that hired them. To achieve these goals, lobbyists communicate favorable information to the legislators, share reports based on technical research or circulate surveys of their members' opinions. They even draft legislative language that can be introduced by congressional "champions."[41] Lobbyists also host legislators and important staff members at receptions or golf outings, pay for trips and speaking engagements at conventions, and participate in electioneering, as discussed in Chapter 10.

Members of Congress deny that they trade their votes for campaign support, but campaign contributions might have more subtle effects. Considerable research shows that a group that contributed to a member of Congress finds it easier to get onto that legislator's schedule for a meeting than do groups that helped the member's opponent. Interest groups expect that legislators they have helped will in turn be more receptive to the groups' pleas for help. We also know that legislators give priority to issues that attract higher levels of campaign contributions than to those that do not. On the other hand, some evidence also indicates that legislators dedicate more effort to mastering details of these policies, thereby building Congress's capacity to make better decisions.[42]

Government watchdog groups like the Center for Responsive Politics, Common Cause, and Center for Public Integrity carefully monitor campaign contributions and highlight instances where high levels of campaign support correlate with favorable legislative votes. There are, in addition, examples of outright bribery. Take Randy "Duke" Cunningham (R-CA) who resigned from Congress in November 2005 after admitting that he had received more than $2 million in bribes and gifts from defense firms in return for helping them to obtain lucrative contracts. Cunningham, a highly decorated Navy veteran who had been elected eight times to the House, was a member of the Defense Appropriations Subcommittee and therefore able to influence both Pentagon and congressional decisions. On the Democratic side, William J. Jefferson (D-LA), a nine-term representative with a seat on the powerful Ways and Means Committee, was videotaped accepting a $100,000 bribe from a defense contractor. The FBI later recovered most of the "cold cash" hidden in Jefferson's home freezer. Are Cunningham and Jefferson the exceptions or the rule? That uncertainty has led some reformers to advocate public financing plans for federal elections to remove the appearance and reality of improper behavior, as well as the temptations.

THE LEGISLATIVE PROCESS

How do all the pieces we have reviewed—inside and outside of Congress—come together? Lawmaking is one of the most complex processes in American government. Typically legislators introduce a bill with the support of co-sponsors, and then Congress subjects it to a grueling review. Before it can become law, the bill must be reviewed, potentially modified, and win support in both the House and Senate.

There is no single path by which bills become laws. While there is a general pattern for how proposals can become law (which we discuss later), the actual procedure varies from case to case. Indeed, there are so many possible variations that the official explanation in a congressional publication requires 55 pages and includes no diagrams to help the puzzled public track the process.[43] And increasingly, Congress has turned to using

KEY TO understanding

To become law, proposals must survive a complex, multi-step process that takes them through subcommittees and committees in both the House and Senate. Opponents have many opportunities to kill proposals, and if unsuccessful in one chamber, they can turn to the other. Differences between House and Senate versions must be resolved before they can be sent to the president for action. Given the required two-year time frame, is it surprising that proposals often do not survive this grueling process?

★

atypical procedures that do not follow the generic stages. This, of course, flies in the face of what school children have learned for decades when they memorized a process. We have presented such a diagram in Figure 12.8, largely as a way to orient readers to the idealized process. In reality, the passage of statutes is almost always different from the sterile diagram: full of bargaining, contending with the unexpected, overcoming opposition—the elements of politics.

The idealized process includes the following steps:

- **Introduction.** Bills must be introduced by one or more representatives or senators—presidents cannot do so.
- **Committee action.** Most proposals are referred to committees where subcommittees might take action, as well as the full committee. But there is no necessity that a proposal move forward, and most bills die in committee. When considered by the full committee, a proposal undergoes **mark up,** where it is read line-by-line and word-by-word while members consider changes. If a proposal is stuck in committee, an absolute majority of House members can bypass the blockage by using a **discharge petition,** signed by a majority of House members, that releases a proposal from a committee's control so that it may be considered by the full house.
- **Scheduling.** To receive a vote on the floor of the House or Senate, proposals must be scheduled for action, which again makes them susceptible to delay or inaction. In the House, this critical stage is controlled by the Rules Committee, which in turn is dominated by the Speaker. In the Senate, the Majority Leader negotiates the schedule of business with the Minority Leader. The House and Senate control their own schedules, so the chamber that finishes first on a proposal may have to wait months or indefinitely for the other to act.
- **Floor action.** Floor action varies. The House Rules Committee recommends to the full chamber the terms under which a proposal will be considered on the floor— the length of debate and whether amendments will be considered. Rules place strict time limits on debate and may severely limit or preclude amendments from the floor. A **closed rule** forbids amendments, thereby ensuring that the committee's work will prevail or fail. By contrast, an **open rule** provides the opportunity for members to amend the bill on the floor, usually regarded as an indication that the originating committee produces lower-quality legislation or could not resolve the key disagreements on policies within its jurisdiction. Amendments offered in the House must be germane to the bill. **Riders,** or unrelated amendments and provisions, are seldom attached to House bills but allowed in the Senate where debate is unlimited unless three-fifths of the full Senate invokes cloture, which limits further debate to 30 hours. Sponsors of Senate bills must be prepared to fend off unwanted riders and deal with the potential for freewheeling debate.
- **Conference.** The House and Senate must adopt the same version of a bill, which often requires that they form a **conference committee** with members from both chambers to resolve differences. Negotiators with strongly held views about the legislation in question represent the House and Senate versions and may take months to iron out differences or fail to reach a compromise at all. The new version must then be approved by both chambers.
- **Presidential action.** Presidents must take action on **enrolled bills,** those sent for their consideration, within 10 working days. The president may sign the bill into

mark up
A committee's line-by-line, word-by-word review of a bill's text prior to a final vote on the modified version.

discharge petition
Parliamentary maneuver that allows a majority of House members to bring a bill up for a vote on the floor even though the responsible committee has not provided a final report.

closed rule
Restrictive guidelines provided by the House Rules Committee that preclude amendments made from the floor during consideration of a bill.

open rule
Guidelines provided by the House Rules Committee that allow germane amendments to be made from the floor during consideration of a bill.

rider
Amendment to a bill that is usually unrelated to the central subject of the bill; allowed in the Senate but usually not allowed in the House.

conference committee
Temporary committee, consisting of both House and Senate members, formed to resolve differences in versions of a bill approved by both chambers before it can be sent to the president.

enrolled bill
Final version of a bill that has survived the legislative process and is sent to the president for his signature or veto.

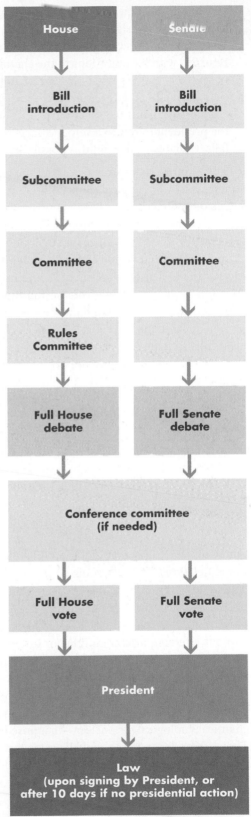

FIGURE 12.8

★ HOW A BILL BECOMES A LAW

Congress

To become law, legislation must pass both the House and Senate in the same form.

Bill introduction

Bill is introduced by a member and assigned to a committee, which usually refers it to a subcommittee.

Committee action

Subcommittee conducts studies, holds hearings, and makes revisions. If approved, the bill goes to the full committee.

Full committee may amend or rewrite the bill, before deciding whether to send it to the floor, recommending its approval, or to kill it. If approved, the bill is reported to the full House or Senate and placed on the calendar.

House only: Rules Committee issues a rule governing the debate on the floor and sends the bill to the full House.

Floor action

Time for debate and opportunity to amend proposals are highly structured in the House. Senate procedures are more unstructured and allow for a filibuster.

Conference action

If necessary, a conference committee composed of members of both House and Senate meet to iron out the differences between the bills. The compromise bill is returned to both the House and Senate for a vote by the full chamber.

Each chamber votes on conference committee version. If it passes, the bill is sent to the president.

Presidential decision

President signs or vetoes the bill or takes no action. Congress may override a veto by a two-thirds vote in both the House and the Senate.

House → Bill introduction → Subcommittee → Committee → Rules Committee → Full House debate → Conference committee (if needed) → Full House vote → President

Senate → Bill introduction → Subcommittee → Committee → Full Senate debate → Conference committee (if needed) → Full Senate vote → President

President → Law (upon signing by President, or after 10 days if no presidential action)

law, veto it, or allow the time limit to expire without taking action. A bill becomes a law if a president signs the bill or if he neither signs nor vetoes the bill during the 10-day period and Congress is still in session. If the president vetoes the bill, it is returned with his objections to the chamber in which it originated, where Congress has the opportunity to override the veto by a two-thirds vote in each chamber, thereby making it law despite the president's opposition. If the president takes no action during the 10 days but Congress adjourns, thereby making it impossible for the president to return a veto message, he has exercised a **pocket veto** and the bill fails. Congress can avoid this possibility by not officially adjourning.

This summary, however, leaves out the real drama of law making. Supporters devise strategies to win support from indifferent committee chairs or to counter the arguments of opponents who have many opportunities to kill proposals they do not want. Party leaders may make a proposal a priority and bypass reluctant committees altogether. Advocates may realize that their best hope for success is to sidestep the standing committees and add provisions to another bill more likely to pass—for example, funding for the Defense Department. Sometimes proposals become part of an omnibus spending package, a single vote on funding many different government activities for another year, thereby making most proposals invisible within the larger package.

Defenders of the laborious legislative process insist that thorough review of proposals results in better laws and ensures that they enjoy broad political support. Because the process provides many opportunities where opponents can block action, it also helps explains why negotiation and compromise are so essential in American politics.

But slow is not always possible or desirable, as we saw in the Perspective vignette that opened this chapter. Presidents and party leaders sometimes circumvent the time-consuming legislative process through **fast-track legislation,** usually sidestepping the standing committees and bringing legislation more directly to the House or Senate floor. Fast-track strategies come at the cost of deliberation and place greater control in the hands of party leaders.[44] Here's an example of rapid action.

House Joint Resolution 114, better known as the Authorization for the Use of United States Armed Forces in Iraq, was introduced in the second session of the 107th Congress to justify President Bush's use of force against Iraq as part of the War on Terror. On October 2, 2002, the resolution was referred to the House Committee on International Relations. Three working days later, the bill moved to the House floor for a vote. The Rules Committee limited debate on the resolution to 17 hours, longer than usual but shorter than critics of the action had wanted. On October 10, the bill passed the House and went to the Senate. The following day, the Senate also passed the resolution without referring it to committee or proposing any amendments. After the weekend, the bill went to President Bush, who signed it the following day. From House introduction to formal law, the process took two weeks, proving that a bill *can* move through the process quickly. Critics of U.S. forces moving into Iraq (see Chapter 18) did not believe Bush administration claims that Iraq possessed weapons of mass destruction—chemical, biological, or nuclear—that posed a threat to the United States and its allies. They believed Congress should have taken a longer time to debate and deliberate. Supporters of the administration's proposal believed that Congress had been fully briefed by intelligence officials, that the evidence was compelling, and that congressional deliberation had been adequate.

Congress elevates the basic logic of the American Constitution into an organizational principle: *fragment power to prevent its abuse.* But adherence to this principle comes at a high cost. Bicameralism divides Congress and there are many centers of congressional decision making and power within the chambers, challenging the collective capacity of Congress to produce coherent policies. Assembling the support needed for action is almost always a tedious process. Emergencies sometimes trigger a more rapid institutional response, as with the financial recovery decision of 2008 and the decision in 2002 about the use of force in Iraq. Why is it usually so difficult for Congress to take concerted action?

CONSTITUENCY PRESSURES

The tradition of serving one's constituency is deeply engrained in the U.S. Congress, the product of constitutional design, election rules, and historical development. Members of Congress serve their constituents in practical matters and represent their constituency politically as they craft and pass laws. Even under conditions of unified government when the same party controls Congress and the White House, legislators are expected to represent the people who sent them to Washington. When local interests conflict with demands from the president, party leaders, or the party's members in Congress, legislators often abandon the common effort and vote according to local interests. In 2008, as we saw in the Perspective story at the beginning of the chapter, Republican House members initially opposed President Bush's financial rescue plan when they received overwhelmingly negative responses from constituents. Through

negotiation, the president and party leaders were finally able to fashion a compromise bailout package that could be defended against voters' grassroots anger. Yet this task was much more difficult to accomplish in the United States than in parliamentary systems where party discipline is greater.

ELECTION SEPARATE FROM THE EXECUTIVE

The U.S. election system helps explain much about Congress's difficulties in taking collective action and its relationship to presidents. Members of Congress come from single-member districts and have won primary and general elections largely because of their own efforts. It takes enormous time and effort to determine what Congress wants to do about public problems as party leaders try to resolve differences among rank-and-file members. Even presidents from the majority party in Congress cannot be certain that legislators will support their initiatives. By contrast, in a parliamentary system members of the majority party risk losing their seats if they oppose their party's leader, the prime minister. In both types of systems, parties provide a potential bridge to link executive and legislative action. In contrast with parliamentary systems, in the United States there is no guarantee that the same party will control Congress and the presidency, and party leaders have limited leverage over individual legislators.

INTERNAL DIVISIONS

Congress is a complex institution. Finding common ground between opposing positions entails working through an elaborate decision-making system that has grown over time. Committees, subcommittees, and their chairs play critical roles in the law-making process, far greater than one finds in parliamentary systems. Political parties, their leaders, and the subgroups that exist within them play important roles in the United States and in parliamentary systems, but party, despite its recent prominence in the United States, has historically been less important than elsewhere. Pulling **all** these pieces together into a unified whole almost never happens. Assembling **enough** pieces in order to take action is the more common goal. Over time, Congress has followed different strategies to enable it to take action—centralizing power during some periods and decentralizing it during others. That pattern of action and reaction is likely to continue into the future.

CHECKING THE EXECUTIVE BRANCH

Ultimately, Congress has a separate constitutional responsibility to address national problems that is no less legitimate than the president's. And instead of working together as happens in parliamentary systems, the U.S. executive and legislative branches often work at cross-purposes. Sometimes that independence is needed to check runaway presidents. There can also be runaway Congresses. Congress offers a deliberate approach to fashioning public policy, providing ample opportunity for multiple interests to be heard, for minorities to protect their interests, and for compromises to be negotiated. But this classic process can also produce flawed products—slow responses, laden with deals needed to secure approval, more or less addressing the issues confronting the nation. If the public is primarily looking for quick responses and rapid solutions to major problems, Congress will appear to be the source of frustrating delay. Presidential decisiveness trumps congressional deliberation in emergencies where quick action is required.

. . . AND WHY DOES IT Matter?

Congressional decisions determine whether college loans are available, strategies to improve education, when to deploy new weapons systems for defense, whether Social Security benefits are adequate and health care available, how much individuals and corporations pay in taxes, and the quality of interstate highways. The public wants many things from Congress, frequently contradictory—solutions to local problems, as well as laws and policies that meet the entire nation's needs; carefully and deliberately crafted legislation, and timely responses to crises; a check on excessive executive power, and less bickering within the chambers and with the president; partisan coherence and bipartisan cooperation. All of these objectives cannot be achieved at the same time!

The U.S. election system helps explain much about Congress's difficulties in taking collective action. Members of Congress come from single-member districts and have won primary and general elections largely through their own efforts. They are motivated by factors that will win them reelection, such as responding to the needs and desires of their constituency and supporters. They also need to respond to powerful individuals within Congress who can thwart their efforts to be responsive to these groups. By contrast, in a parliamentary system members of the majority party risk losing their seats if they oppose their party's leader, the prime minister. If reformers succeeded in making party organizations and leadership as powerful in the U.S. electoral process as they are elsewhere, members of Congress would become less responsive to their own constituencies. These changes might make Congress more efficient in adopting legislation but would weaken its ability to represent the populace and thereby make government actions less legitimate.

In contrast with parliamentary systems, the U.S. system has no guarantee that the same party will control Congress and the presidency. At worst, lame duck sessions can paralyze the government, making it unable to respond to the needs of the people. But in those systems where cooperation between the two elected branches of government prevails, the legislature provides less of a check on the executive. What is more valuable to the nation? Again, in gaining one advantage we sacrifice another.

History demonstrates that Congress is an evolving institution with the capacity to adopt internal reforms needed to enhance its effectiveness. It has created and expanded the technical expertise needed to confront presidents and adopted reforms needed to reduce internal fragmentation. Institutional change is possible and likely. And the most powerful force likely to motivate change is the public's demand that its legislators start doing business differently. Consequently, as the needs of the nation evolve, so does the legislative branch—without even requiring an amended Constitution.

critical thinking questions

1. Many members of Congress relocate to Washington, weakening their ties to the constituents who elected them. Other candidates, such as Hillary Clinton, move to a district or state in order to run for office and start with weak ties to the area they represent. Should Americans rethink the relationship between constituency and representation so that the quality of representation counts more than the strength of the representative's local roots?

2. Should members of Congress give greater priority to the demands of their constituency or the demands of their party? Placing emphasis on the constituency fulfills the legislator's representational function but sacrifices the law-making function, which requires that members work together in a coordinated way. Where should the balance lie?

3. Legislative committees perform valuable services for Congress as a whole, but they tend to be dominated by their leaders. How can Congress derive the maximum benefit from standing committees while avoiding the tendency for leaders to dictate their work? Is the Gingrich reform of limiting committee chairs to six years of service the right answer?

4. Congressional staff members have become a powerful force on Capitol Hill. They are experts on politics and policy and are important advisors to the elected officials. How much assistance should U.S. legislators have? Are congressional aides the key to helping Congress play a co-equal role to the executive or simply a way to help legislators get reelected?

key terms

bicameral legislature, *415*

bill, *411*

closed rule, *436*

cloture, *426*

committee government, *432*

committee jurisdiction, *423*

committee of the whole, *423*

conference committee, *436*

conservative coalition, *434*

constituency service, *411*

delegate model, *406*

descriptive representation, *411*

discharge petition, *436*

earmark, *407*

elastic clause (necessary and proper clause), *413*

enrolled bill, *436*

fast-track legislation, *438*

filibuster, *426*

joint committee, *424*

legislative liaison, *434*

mark up, *436*

open rule, *436*

party caucus, *420*

party conference, *420*

party unity, *419*

pocket veto, *438*

politico model, *407*

popular legitimacy, *405*

pork barrel, *407*

power of the purse, *405*

rider, *436*

Rules Committee, *432*

safe seats, *432*

select committee, *423*

Senate Majority Leader, *420*

seniority rule, *432*

Speaker of the House of Representatives, *420*

standing committee, *423*

substantive representation, *411*

trustee model, *406*

whip, *421*

THE PRESIDENCY

* ★ *

- Explain the features that distinguish presidential from parliamentary systems.
- Describe the five principal roles of the president as laid out in the Constitution, new roles not found in the Constitution, and the reasons those roles have changed over time.
- Analyze the factors that affect a president's approval ratings.
- Describe the staff support that allows the president to manage and fulfill the responsibilities of his role.
- List the formal qualifications for president outlined by the U.S. Constitution, as well as the personal and psychological characteristics an individual needs to serve successfully in this role.
- Describe the president's primary goals and the strategies the president employs to achieve these goals.

PERSPECTIVE
What Are the Consequences of Leaders Making Unpopular Decisions?

On March 20, 2003, U.S. President George W. Bush and British Prime Minister Tony Blair ordered their nations' armies to invade Iraq. The leaders believed that Iraq was developing weapons of mass destruction (biological, chemical, and potentially nuclear weapons) and supporting terrorist activities. After dramatic military successes at the outset, the operation faltered. Modest levels of Iraqi resistance escalated into a large-scale insurgency that produced heavy casualties and rising costs. Despite mounting domestic and international criticism, Bush and Blair led their parties to election victories after the initial invasion. Bush narrowly won a second presidential term in November 2004, and Republicans strengthened majorities in both the House and Senate. Blair led his party to a third consecutive election victory in May 2005. But there the similarity ended.

Bush's Republican Party colleagues suffered a crushing defeat in the November 2006 congressional midterm elections, losing their majority in the House of Representatives (originally secured in 1994) and their majority in the Senate (that dated to 2002). The 2006 election was widely viewed as a referendum on the administration's Iraq policy, and the public's verdict was decisively negative. Bush remained in office for two more years as a "lame duck"—a term applied to presidents serving out their final years in office without much prospect of exercising leadership over Congress. Then in 2008, Democratic candidate Barack Obama won the presidency and Democrats won solid Democratic majorities in both houses of Congress with a promise to get the United States out of Iraq.

On the other side of the Atlantic, Blair's party remained the majority for four more years, but Blair was forced to leave office on June 27, 2007, by critics within his own party who recognized the public's growing disenchantment with him and a political style that emphasized image rather than substance even on matters as important as Iraq.[1] The Labour Members of Parliament (MPs) in the House of Commons chose to replace Blair with Gordon Brown, a long-time member of the British cabinet. There was no campaign, no general election, and not even a vote among the members of Brown's party outside of the House of Commons. Nor was Brown a lame duck. Instead, he continued to enjoy a majority in the House of Commons and had time to establish himself as the new party leader before the next general election, held in May 2010, when the Labour Party lost its majority in Parliament and lost control of the prime ministry.

Bush, Blair and their respective parties suffered similar fates but on very different timetables. Despite growing discontent, Blair and Brown held onto power with a majority in Parliament because British general elections are not conducted on a fixed schedule as they are in the United States. British governments may serve for up to five years between elections, and the prime minister can determine when to call a general election, thereby giving the ruling party the opportunity to time the election at a point of maximum popularity. The British took longer to register growing unhappiness with their political representatives and in the meantime, the prime minister was still able to be effective.

IN THIS CHAPTER, we examine executive power in the United States. We first seek to learn more about the presidency by contrasting it with parliamentary systems. We analyze how the job of the president has evolved over time and determine what factors triggered these changes. In doing so, we explore how different presidents have perceived and altered presidential power. We investigate institutions that support the president, such as the Executive Office of the President, the cabinet, and the vice president. Finally, we assess the personal qualities and strategies presidents need to be successful. As you read this chapter, keep in mind our two core questions:

WHY ARE WE THE WAY WE ARE?
WHY DOES IT MATTER?

In particular, why has the presidency evolved into the office it is today, and what does that mean for you?

PRESIDENTIAL AND PARLIAMENTARY SYSTEMS

★ KEY TO understanding

The presidential form of government used in numerous political systems around the world was invented in the United States. Its fundamental features become clearer when contrasted with parliamentary government. What advantages does a presidential system have over a parliamentary system, and vice versa?

The different fates of Bush and Blair—heavily but not fully determined by the war in Iraq—reflect the structural differences between presidential and parliamentary systems of government. Presidents are elected to four-year terms separately from Congress and cannot be dismissed from office by the legislature except for extraordinary reasons. **Impeachment,** the constitutional process for removing a president from office before a term has expired, triggers such a major constitutional crisis that it has never been successfully used. **Prime ministers** are elected members of parliament who serve as the leader of the legislative majority as long as they enjoy the support of their party colleagues—an uncertain length of time. When Blair's colleagues lost confidence in him, he was replaced by Brown in a relatively smooth transfer of power.

In addition, presidents direct the bureaucratic agencies of government, sharing with senators the power to select members of the cabinet (principal heads of the departments) but enjoying exclusive power to fire them. In parliamentary systems, the cabinet is a collective body of MPs who, at least in theory, stand or fall together and therefore reach positions on policy with which they all agree.

The designers of the American Constitution invented the **presidential system.** Unhappy with the ineffective government that operated under the Articles of Confederation, they created a strong executive to provide energy for the central government. But they also did not want a king, an option that some members of the Constitutional Convention proposed.

★ President Bush and Prime Minister Blair coordinated their foreign policies.

Although some analysts have suggested that the United States has an "elected king," that suggestion underestimates the extensive limits placed on presidential power, which we will review.

Some democracies have followed the American model. When Mexico and the South American countries won their independence from Spain and Portugal in the nineteenth century, they tended to set up presidential systems in imitation of the United States, and those systems have continued as the traditional design in the region.[2] In the 1980s and 1990s, aspiring democracies in Asia (South Korea, Philippines) and Eastern Europe chose to establish presidential systems.[3] In other parts of the world, as nations gained independence in the period from 1945 to 1975, most emerging democracies adopted a **parliamentary system** along the lines of their colonial powers.[4]

Not all nations stick with their original design for executive power. Countries that have encountered problems with parliamentary government have sometimes adopted a presidential or a hybrid system that has both a directly elected president and a prime minister who enjoys a parliamentary majority. So, for instance, France set up a blend of parliamentary and presidential government in 1958 after a military mutiny and near civil war had thrown the parliamentary government into chaos, giving rise to a new system with firmer leadership at the top. Nigeria established a presidential system in 1975 after an ineffective, squabbling parliamentary system had been succeeded by a series of military governments. Worldwide, presidential systems offer a clear focus for leadership—someone to hold accountable for the successes and failures of governments. Frequently, however, presidents have refused to give up power and have become dominant political leaders far beyond their original term of office (see the "Picture Yourself" feature in this chapter).

As we saw in the example that opens this chapter, while President Bush had to deal with a divided government, prime ministers seldom face that problem. Prime ministers and their cabinets usually remain in office only as long as they have the support of a majority in the parliament. A parliamentary majority may consist of a single party or a

impeachment
Power of the Congress to remove a president from office before the elected term has expired. Technically, the House impeaches ("charges") a president with "high crimes and misdemeanors" and the Senate may find the president guilty or not guilty of the charges.

prime minister
Executive officer in a parliamentary system who is supported in the legislature by a majority of his or her own party or a majority based on a coalition.

presidential system
Political system distinguished by having an executive selected separately by the public rather than by the legislature; frequently characterized by fewer parties but higher levels of legislative-executive conflict.

parliamentary system
Political system in which the legislature (parliament) selects the executive either through a single party majority or a majority coalition, providing for closer institutional coordination.

★ **LAME DUCKS**   Political commentators—especially critics—are quick to point out the problems encountered by presidents as they approach the end of their term in office. The public is less approving and Congress is less cooperative as presidents come to the end of their first four-year term or approach year eight. Political cartoonists love to portray them as lame ducks, and both President Bush and President Obama received their share of razzing.

coalition of parties. When struggles among coalition members produce internal divisions, coalition governments can resemble a divided U.S. government with Congress and the president, controlled by different parties, warring with one another, but that is the exception. Minority party governments also can occur when the prime minister does not have a firm majority in parliament, but minority governments are inherently unstable and short-lived. Thus, it almost never happens that prime ministers are faced with a legislature that is controlled by a party or parties other than their own—as is frequently the case for presidents.[5]

lame duck
Description of presidents nearing the end of their fixed term in office who have little remaining leverage to accomplish their policy goals.

Parliamentary systems largely avoid the problem of **lame ducks,** second-term presidents approaching the end of their service and unable to accomplish much because everyone expects them soon to be gone. Even first-term presidents can quickly become irrelevant if their public approval declines or their party loses the midterm election. In a parliamentary system, majority parties will replace prime ministers as soon as they lose the ability to command majority support in parliament, though that change might take some time in coalition governments.

The constitutional design of a government is a powerful influence on those holding official positions, but other factors also determine the role the president plays in our political system.

THE EVOLVING JOB OF PRESIDENT

When the Founders invented this new job, what did they anticipate the president would do? Five core presidential responsibilities are suggested in the Constitution. Although the Constitution does little more than outline the president's responsibilities, these roles have gained detail over the years as presidents interpreted their powers and took actions that then became precedents for their successors. Congress also helped shape the office by assigning new responsibilities for policy leadership to help the nation meet emerging national needs. As a result, today's presidency is far more robust and varied than the original outline of the job found in the Constitution.

CONSTITUTIONAL ROLES

Foremost in the Constitution are the two roles played by presidents in dealing with international affairs; presidents provide a unitary voice in dealing with security threats from abroad and in managing relations with the international community. These responsibilities were traditionally held by monarchs, and the writers of the Constitution placed them primarily, though not exclusively, in the president's hands. Congress jealously guarded its prerogatives on the home front, and the president's domestic roles were relatively minor until the twentieth century when they expanded rapidly.

Commander-in-Chief of the Armed Forces

On March 19, 2011, U.S. President Barack Obama ordered U.S. planes to enforce a United Nations-declared "no fly zone" over Libya. U.S. missiles attacked air defense systems and the navy established a blockade of the Libyan coastline. President Obama explained these actions as an effort to avert a large-scale humanitarian crisis during a Libyan civil war. But the NATO-based coalition also supported the democratic forces opposed to the Libyan dictator. Although Congress later criticized the president for exceeding his legal powers in Libya, President Obama argued that he was acting entirely within his role as commander-in-chief. Article II, Sections 2 and 3, of the U.S. Constitution specifies that the president "shall be commander in chief of the Army and Navy of the United States, and of the militia of the several states, when called into the actual service of the United States."

Commander-in-Chief
Role established in Article II of the Constitution regarding the president's oversight of the nation's military forces.

Chief Diplomat

In 2011, the Senate approved three trade treaties originally submitted by President Bush and supported by Obama. These followed on the heels of eight free trade agreements negotiated by George W. Bush and approved by the Senate during his two terms in office, including agreements with Australia, Chile, Singapore, and Ukraine. This means that Americans shopping for reasonably priced wine and fresh grapes can buy those produced in Chile at lower prices than they otherwise could. In turn, Chileans can buy American-made machinery and cars at better prices. Under the U.S. Constitution, presidents take the lead in helping the American economy by making treaties and agreements that expand the flow of goods. Presidents can "make treaties, provided two

chief diplomat
Role established in Article II of the Constitution regarding the president's powers to conduct foreign affairs.

★ Soldiers watch President Obama announce that the head of the Al Qaeda terrorist network, Osama bin Laden, is dead, after the president authorized a raid on bin Laden's compound.

chief legislator
Role established in Article II of the Constitution that outlines the president's checks on Congress.

thirds of the Senators present concur; . . . appoint ambassadors, other public ministers and consuls; [and] . . . receive ambassadors and other public ministers." In interpreting these powers, the Supreme Court has given the president wide powers to serve as the sole voice of the nation in international affairs, but still the connections with Congress are blurred. Will Congress approve treaties? Will the House, lacking a vote on the treaty itself, provide the money needed to implement the treaty agreements? Just how independently can Congress act in international relations? In order to curtail the congressional role, administrations have increasingly shifted from using treaties toward using executive agreements, commitments that are made by presidents alone but are just as binding as treaties.

Chief Legislator

As you will see in Chapter 17, multiple presidents have proposed solutions to the nation's health care problems, starting with Teddy Roosevelt early in the twentieth century. Lyndon Johnson succeeded in establishing Medicare, a health care program for the elderly, but other efforts failed, most recently the reforms proposed by Bill Clinton. It was therefore historic when Congress narrowly approved the health care plan presented by President Obama in March 2010. After a long process, Obama was able to exercise the president's principal role in legislation—the prerogative to sign bills before they become law or veto them subject to an override by two-thirds of the members of both houses of Congress, found in Article I, Section 7. (Presidents can also ignore a bill and it will become law without his signature after 10 days.) There is a brief elaboration of these legislative powers in Article II, which specifies that "He shall from time to time give to the Congress information of the state of the union, and recommend to their consideration such measures as he shall judge necessary and expedient," as well as the power to convene and adjourn Congress, now largely moot because Congress is in session year-round.

Chief Administrator

Remarkably, supervising the civilian federal bureaucracy, now including approximately 2 million employees, is barely suggested in the constitution's job description. As the central government assumed more power over time, the federal bureaucracy grew (see

★ President Lyndon B. Johnson signs the bill creating Medicare with former president Harry Truman looking on. Since the administration of Franklin D. Roosevelt, Congress has often turned to presidents for recommendations on necessary legislation.

Chapter 14). Most of the federal establishment consists of career civil servants, but presidents appoint a group of persons to senior positions to guide policy and program decisions. Through these appointments, presidents can make a significant impact on policy.

In 1981, President Ronald Reagan nominated Anne Gorsuch Burford head of the Environmental Protection Agency (EPA). Burford shared Reagan's view that federal environmental policies were too restrictive and should be regulated more by state than by federal governments. She therefore slashed the EPA's budget by 22 percent and stopped enforcing many EPA restrictions on polluters.[6] As a result, Reagan was able to curtail the implementation of environmental policies and reduce what he felt was their negative impact on the nation's economy. In a similar way, President Obama advanced his education agenda by sidestepping a deadlocked Congress and authorizing his Secretary of Education, Arne Duncan, to allow states to avoid meeting deadlines under the law passed in 2002, known as No Child Left Behind.

Chief Magistrate

During the 40 years between 1972 and 2012, there were 11 different directors of the FBI. For the 48 years between 1924 and 1972 there had been just one—J. Edgar Hoover. Hoover had been reappointed by president after president, Republicans and Democrats, to this sensitive position that helps presidents "take care that the laws be faithfully executed," bringing violators of more than 200 categories of federal law to court. This provision in the Constitution establishes the charge that the president be the nation's chief law enforcer. This task is also associated with the president's responsibility to nominate federal judges. Because Americans rely heavily on the courts as a means to resolve disputes (not true in all political systems), the selection of federal judges is particularly important and has become increasingly politicized over the past three decades at the federal level. Through the nomination of judges, presidents can exercise a major influence on the general direction of the federal judiciary, but

chief administrator
Role established in Article II of the Constitution, the wording of which suggests the president's responsibilities to direct the national administrative apparatus.

chief magistrate
Implied role established in Article II of the Constitution dealing with the president's responsibilities in enforcing the laws and ensuring effective operation of the courts.

there is no guarantee how many vacancies they will be able to fill during their service in office. Finally, the Constitution provides presidents with the exclusive power to issue pardons to violators of federal laws unchecked by Congress.

EXPANDED CONSTITUTIONAL ROLES

In general, there are two broad categories of presidential responsibilities: those included in the Constitution and those that have developed over time through practice and precedent. Because the constitutional provisions were so vague, the president's roles in foreign and domestic policy have grown as a result of struggles with Congress over how much power the president would be able to exercise over these policies.

Commander-in-Chief

Although Congress has the power to declare war, presidents order U.S. forces into action. Over time, members of Congress struck working understandings with executives of just how much power presidents could exercise over the armed forces. At times, however, Congress has resorted to legislation and relied on its control of the purse strings to curtail the president's activities.

Since early in U.S. history, presidents have expanded their role in national security policy. In response to pirate attacks on American merchant vessels, Thomas Jefferson (1801–1809) built ships to provide coastal defense without obtaining prior congressional approval. Seeking to promote Western expansion, Andrew Jackson (1829–1837) used the military to forcibly drive Native Americans out of Mississippi, Florida, and Georgia despite widespread political opposition. In order to save the Union, Abraham Lincoln (1861–1865) took a series of steps—including calling the state militias into federal service without congressional authority or funding—at the outset of the Civil War that significantly stretched the boundaries of presidential powers. Teddy Roosevelt (1901–1909) famously deployed the navy on a round-the-world display of power that Congress had specifically prohibited, and Franklin Roosevelt (1933–1945) established new precedents for coordinating war policy in a global conflict. In a nuclear world where the United States confronted a hostile power, presidential actions took on enormous significance—wrong steps could trigger showdowns with the Soviet Union, believed by Americans to be an implacable enemy. As a result, even greater latitude was given to presidents to deploy forces around the world to deal with regional problems in Korea, the Middle East, and Vietnam.

Angered by President Richard Nixon's actions during the Vietnam War, however, Congress passed the **War Powers Resolution** in 1973. This resolution limited the circumstances under which the president could commit troops, required the president to report promptly to Congress, limited the involvement of U.S. forces to 60 days unless Congress approved the military action, and gave Congress the authority to terminate the commitment of U.S. troops. In 2011, President Obama came under harsh criticism from Republicans in Congress for not seeking legislative authorization of U.S. involvement in Libya after the initial 60 days had run out. The administration argued that the United States had turned over control of the operation to NATO and that American forces were not being placed in a hostile combat situation—they were providing logistical support and all attacks were being conducted by unmanned drones rather than by manned aircraft. As this case illustrates, new situations and technological advances force Congress and the president to develop new interpretations of their powers.

War Powers Resolution
Passed by Congress over Nixon's veto in 1973, this law establishes a framework for Congress to participate in presidential decisions to use force—short of a formal declaration of war—and to halt such a military deployment.

Authors of the Constitution may have dreamed of the United States becoming a power comparable to England, France, and Spain, but it was not until the eve of the twentieth century that the nation first became *a* world power and then the world's *only* superpower with forces stationed around the globe (see Chapter 18). This new status brought new questions: When can the president initiate the use of force without securing a congressional declaration of war? Who can halt the use of that force when it seems to have been a mistake? Emergency situations might require action at any time—and in cases where speed and secrecy is required, is it not best for the president to take the lead? In April 2009, President Obama launched a daring operation in which U.S. Navy SEAL snipers rescued an American sea captain held captive by Somali pirates. Could the operation have been successful if the president had waited for congressional approval? Yet just how much authority should the president have to determine military strategy? The political situation faced by each president does more to answer this question than a final interpretation of constitutional authority.

Chief Legislator

The annual **State of the Union Address** has evolved into one of the central rituals of American government. In January of each year, presidents deliver a prime-time televised address to a joint session of Congress also attended by members of the cabinet, the Supreme Court, the Joint Chiefs of Staff, and the ambassadorial corps. This setting is all the more dramatic for occurring so infrequently, unlike in Britain where the prime minister answers questions from members of Parliament on a weekly basis.

George Washington and his successor, John Adams, had met with Congress personally to deliver this message, but Thomas Jefferson discontinued the personal presentation, thinking it resembled too closely the monarch's opening of parliament in Britain. A century later, President Woodrow Wilson (1913–1921) reestablished the practice, seizing upon the mass-circulation newspapers to project the president's message, a development carried to new heights with the introduction of radio and television. In his pre-presidential writings, Wilson, considered one of the first political scientists, had developed a model of national leadership that emphasized an energetic, solution-generating president whose direct link with the people led to voicing their needs. By renewing the president's personal appearance before the joint session of Congress, Wilson embodied this new model of presidential leadership. Today Americans expect presidents to direct the nation's attention to the agenda of issues and policy answers.

Presidents since Franklin Delano Roosevelt (FDR) have set the national agenda not only through the annual State of the Union Address but also through the president's budget message and high-profile public appeals. Presidents today also take agenda setting a step further by crafting legislative initiatives and by actively lobbying individual members of Congress to support these initiatives, as discussed in Chapter 12.

State of the Union Address
Annual address delivered by the president in person to a joint session of Congress and other government leaders. Today this address is broadcast to a primetime television audience.

EXTRA-CONSTITUTIONAL ROLES

Over time, presidents' domestic roles have proliferated even though these additional responsibilities have not been added officially to the Constitution. Given the difficulty of amending the Constitution, Congress has passed laws that add explicit responsibilities to the president's job description. Congress delegates to presidents responsibility for overseeing a policy area and for submitting information or issuing a periodic report, such as AIDS relief—an emergency plan for helping people around the world suffering from HIV/AIDS. Sometimes Congress arranges staff support to assist the president in meeting these requirements. In 1969, for example, in response to rising public awareness of environmental hazards, Congress created the Council on Environmental Quality to coordinate federal environmental efforts.

In addition, presidents might decide to initiate actions in areas not specifically forbidden in the Constitution or assigned elsewhere in the federal government. In this way, presidents establish precedents that their successors can follow. The 12 years of Franklin D. Roosevelt's presidency (1933–1945) proved to be a watershed for the office. Roosevelt confronted major crises at home and abroad—the Great Depression and World War II—and the country needed strong leadership. Congress came to depend upon the president to set its agenda. The media began to follow national politics by primarily reporting on the president, a practice encouraged by FDR giving frequent briefings to reporters with White House assignments. Finally, the president and a growing group of staff assistants made more systematic efforts to manage the burgeoning federal bureaucracy needed to implement a wide range of programs designed to combat unemployment and poverty, including Social Security, and to regulate economic practices that were seen as contributing to the Depression, trading in stocks and bonds through the Securities and Exchange Commission. Not only did the federal government grow by leaps and bounds, but the nature of its activities changed. FDR thus set the precedent not only for the expansion of the president's role as chief legislator, but also in developing new roles. Taken as a whole, FDR's actions created the **modern presidency,** a combination of expanded activities, a larger staff to provide help, and higher expectations than earlier presidents had faced.

Chief Budgeter

During World War I, government officials recognized how inefficiently the normal budget process operated in Washington; each department and agency went directly to Congress with its requests for the next year while the president watched from the sidelines even though he was nominally the chief administrator. Both Presidents William Howard Taft (1909–1913) and Wilson sought broader authority.

In 1921 Congress passed a law requiring the president to be the **chief budgeter,** assembling a single, unified budget that is presented to Congress each year. This action triggered the famous aphorism that "the president proposes and Congress disposes." Presidential budgets are never adopted unchanged, but all provide the starting point for the annual discussion about the budget for the next *fiscal year,* the 12-month period from October 1 of the current year through September 30 of the next calendar year. Subsequent presidents have introduced new budgeting techniques (Lyndon Johnson, Jimmy Carter) or expanded either the policy or management roles of their budgeting aides (FDR, Richard Nixon).

Chief Economist

After the Great Depression and World War II, as the nation returned to normal conditions, Congress charged the president with responsibility for maintaining full employment and a healthy economy. In essence, the country was affirming the expanded responsibilities that FDR had exercised at the height of the national crisis. The president performs the role of **chief economist** with the help of the Council of

modern presidency
Shaped heavily by FDR's 12 years in office, modern presidents are distinguished from earlier executives by the expanded roles they play, the additional staffs they have to help them, and the greater expectations held by the public.

chief budgeter
Presidential role established by the Budget and Accounting Act of 1921, which instituted more regular procedures for creating and overseeing a unified federal budget.

chief economist
Presidential role that emerged from the aggressive economic leadership of Franklin D. Roosevelt during the Great Depression of the 1930s and was codified by the Employment Act of 1946, which requires that the president submit an annual economic report dealing with macroeconomic policy (employment, production, and investment).

Economic Advisers, a group of professional economists, and the Federal Reserve Board and its Chair, who is nominated by the president to an independent term. (See the discussion in Chapter 16.)

Chief Communicator

On the night of Sunday, May 1, 2011, President Obama spoke to the nation, announcing the death of Osama bin Laden. This was a recent example of a role that has expanded greatly in the twentieth and twenty-first centuries. In times of crisis, national sorrow, or particular significance, presidents capture the public's attention, helping them sort out and understand the significant developments from the bewildering array of information and current events that unfold on 24-hour television news channels. Teddy Roosevelt pioneered techniques to communicate broadly with the public through newspapers in the late nineteenth century. F.D.R. spoke directly to the nation through "fireside chats" delivered by radio, making him a presence in every American's living room. In 1960, John F. Kennedy and then Vice-President Richard Nixon held the first

chief communicator
Informal role that presidents have come to play by being the focal point of media coverage and the public's attention on major matters of national policy.

★ Clockwise from the left, (1) Teddy Roosevelt uses the "bully pulpit" to address a crowd about his programs and without a microphone. (2) F.D.R. speaks to the nation through a fireside chat. (3) Barack Obama communicates his policies through the White House website.

televised debate during that year's presidential campaign, and Kennedy went on to conduct live press conferences. More recently, George W. Bush and Barack Obama expanded communications on the Internet and through social media.

Political Leader and Head of State

Virtually all political systems find a way to fill two critical roles. A **political leader** is able to mobilize action directed at solving the nation's common problems, a position likely to trigger conflict over both means and ends. At the same time, each system needs a **head of state** who symbolizes the unity of the nation, the sense of common identity and purpose that binds together its citizens. In many nations, these responsibilities are vested in different people. For example, the British prime minister is the political figure while the Queen of England is the symbolic unifier. Britons can revel in the joy of watching a future king get married without reference to their political preferences, as happened in 2011 when Prince William married Catherine Middleton. In systems without a monarch, the president often functions as the head of state (as in France and Germany), operating largely outside the political realm while the prime minister or premier leads the government.

In the United States and a few other systems (see Table 13.1), the two roles are combined into one. Presidents are both the central political figure in the nation and the symbolic head of state. Some presidents, such as Dwight D. Eisenhower,[7] may deemphasize the more political activities that adhere to the job, but all presidents must balance these two potentially conflicting roles. If in the midst of a political scandal a president puts the nation's military forces on alert because of an international crisis, for example, in which capacity is he or she acting? When just such an alert occurred during Richard M. Nixon's term (1969–1973), many people questioned whether Nixon used the crisis as a way to reduce the political pressures that were mounting on him during investigations into crimes committed during the 1972 election. Similar questions surrounded Bill Clinton's decision to bomb Iraq in December 1998 while the House of Representatives was considering the president's impeachment.

Heads of state usually serve as moral beacons for and representatives of the entire nation. Thus, when scandal rocks a monarchy, many people become concerned about losing the image of rectitude that the royal family is expected to maintain. For this reason, a number of highly publicized scandals involving royal children have alarmed people in Britain and Monaco over the past several decades. Similar concerns were raised about Bill Clinton's marital infidelity with White House intern Monica Lewinsky; George W. Bush not so subtly promised in 2000 to return trust and morality to the White House.

By contrast, political leaders are expected to represent and advocate for only a portion of the nation, members of their own party. As an integral member of their party's leadership team, the president triggers conflict but is expected to manage it productively.

TABLE 13.1
nations combining and separating political leader from head of state

COMBINED	SEPARATE
United States	United Kingdom (monarch)
Mexico	Israel (elected president)
Brazil	Germany (elected president)
Nigeria	France (elected president)
Philippines	Russia (elected president)
Kenya	South Africa (elected president)

THEORIES OF PRESIDENTIAL POWER

Not all presidents approach the job in the same way. Although the range of roles the president must fulfill is extensive, presidents have substantial flexibility in determining how to allocate their time and which roles to emphasize. Some responsibilities are probably inescapable. Defense, foreign, and economic policies seem to be permanent fixtures of the modern presidency, but even those areas can vary from one president to another. In the post–Cold War world that Bill Clinton confronted in the 1990s, foreign and defense policy seemed substantially less important than the economy. In the post–9/11 world, however, George W. Bush emphasized international security. So presidents will vary in *what* they do, depending on the situations they confront.

Moreover, presidents have considerable flexibility in *how* they perform the job. Some have enlarged the office by expanding the president's powers beyond a narrow interpretation of the Constitution while others have felt more constrained by the letter of the constitutional provisions. The Constitution's language is unclear: "The executive Power shall be vested in a President of the United States of America." What does that mean? Unlike the language found in the Constitution on Congress, there is no enumeration of presidential powers or limiting clauses. As a result, presidential power has been open to interpretation.

Teddy Roosevelt and William Howard Taft engaged in the classic debate over the boundaries of presidential power. Although Taft had been Roosevelt's secretary of war and was his immediate successor (Taft also later became Chief Justice of the Supreme Court), he differed greatly in his interpretation of the president's role.

Roosevelt had helped to fashion a new definition of the president as the people's champion; he articulated what is now called the **stewardship theory** of presidential power. In Roosevelt's view, the only powers that were off-limits for presidents were those expressly forbidden by the Constitution (as we have seen, virtually none) or in congressional statutes. Taft, following on Roosevelt's heels, regarded the job in narrow terms, believing that Roosevelt had taken excessive freedoms in the position. Taft articulated the **constitutional theory** of presidential power which denied that any president could call upon inherent powers to act in the interests of the people. Most expansively, the **prerogative theory** would allow presidents to engage in even those activities that are expressly forbidden in the Constitution if they are in the national interest, such as Lincoln's suspension of the writ of *habeas corpus* during the Civil War. Over time, Americans have generally had a higher regard for presidents who approached the job aggressively—seizing opportunities and stretching powers to meet new challenges. Thus, Jackson, Lincoln, and the two Roosevelts get high marks, though there are potential limits to how far a president can go.

Aggressive interpretations are not always praised, however. Richard Nixon's assertion of presidential power and prerogative at the time of Watergate in the 1970s produced widespread concern and a severe backlash from both Congress and the public. **Watergate** refers to a collection of political scandals that Congress revealed during the investigation into an illegal break-in at the Democratic National Committee Headquarters at the Watergate complex in Washington, D.C., on June 17, 1972. The probe uncovered political dirty tricks played on the Democrats, illegal campaign contributions made to Nixon's campaign, an "enemies list" maintained by the president and populated by his political critics, illegal wire-taps, and secret bombings in Laos and Cambodia.

stewardship theory
View of the president's role as a "steward" of the people who serves their interests because of the president's unique role as the representative of the entire nation and who is therefore empowered to define the position as broadly as necessary.

constitutional theory
View of the president's powers, elaborated by William Howard Taft, as strictly limited to those enumerated in the Constitution or conferred by congressional statutes.

prerogative theory
View that justifies an executive using discretionary power to act in areas without congressional approval or even to violate the law if such action is in the public good and consistent with the national interest.

Watergate
The political scandals associated with Richard Nixon, triggered by the judicial, congressional, and media investigations into the illegal break-in at the Democratic National Committee's offices in the Watergate office complex in Washington, D.C.

picture YOURSELF ...
AMONG EGYPTIANS TOPPLING A REPRESSIVE PRESIDENT

Imagine yourself participating in the movement to unseat Egypt's undemocratic leader that started on January 25, 2011. Thousands of Egyptians took to the streets to protest three decades of repressive rule suffered under Hosni Mubarak, the former air force officer who became president in 1981 and used a declared state of emergency to suppress opposition, censor the media, arrest critics, rig elections, and maintain power. It was certain that the 83-year-old president would engineer another reelection in September and then find a way to install his son as his successor. Instead of the handful of youthful protesters who turned out in past demonstrations, large numbers took to the streets in many Egyptian cities and kept doing so day after day in marches, acts of civil disobedience, and labor strikes. Tens of thousands grew to hundreds of thousands and then to millions in this most populous Arab country of 80 million. Police crackdowns produced hundreds of deaths, but the number of protesters overwhelmed Mubarak's police loyalists, and military officers refused to order their troops to open fire on civilians.

Tahrir Square (which means "Liberty Square") in downtown Cairo became the focal point of this revolution where hundreds of thousands gathered in support of change. Young Egyptians led the way, demanding "democracy, social justice, and an end to corruption, torture and police brutality."* Youthful organizers pioneered novel political tactics on the Internet, using Facebook, Twitter, and video blogging to maintain contact, plan, and launch protests. Pictures of a brutal police killing spread like wildfire on the Web in late 2010. Tunisians blazed the trail when they successfully ousted their president of 24 years in mid-January after a month of often violent actions. At that point, tens of thousands of Egyptians started the campaign to do the same in Egypt where prices were rising rapidly, jobs were scarce, and political freedom nonexistent. Mubarak tried to defuse the protests—promising reforms, pledging not to run for reelection, appointing a new vice president, and trying to maintain support among the military, but in the end he resigned, setting off joyous celebrations. But change was not only about one man. Egypt's military, fearing the influence of Islamists and domestic strife, kept a firm grip on the timing of parliamentary elections, the writing of a new constitution, and subsequent presidential elections. The tyrant was gone, but the struggle for democracy remained unfinished.

* Heba Saleh, "Egyptian Youth Mobilise Via the Internet," *Financial Times*, January 25, 2011; also see Roula Khalaf, "At Hand, an Arab Awakening," *Financial Times*, February 4, 2011.

questions to consider

1. Have the actions of any American president been so repressive that they called for a response of mass civil disobedience?

2. Should the United States have actively intervened to help Egyptians overthrow their repressive government sooner?

In short, a host of embarrassments came to light that went well beyond a simple campaign burglary. For Nixon, however, the problem grew. A secret, voice-activated taping system in the Oval Office documented the president's involvement in a conspiracy to cover up White House involvement in the break-in. This evidence implicated the president in an illegal act and led the House Judiciary Committee to approve three articles of impeachment for obstruction of justice, abuse of power, and contempt of Congress. Nixon resigned rather than face the almost certain fate of impeachment by the House of Representatives and then trial and conviction in the Senate. Throughout this prolonged political crisis, Nixon's legal claims were often seen as assertions that presidents are "above the law" rather than subject to the "rule of law." As Nixon once told a television interviewer, "When the president does it, that means it is not illegal."[8]

The debate over the limits of presidential power is not purely historical. During George W. Bush's term, a major controversy arose in response to an aggressive assertion of presidential power—the **unitary executive doctrine**—advanced by Bush and his vice president. After 9/11, President Bush and Vice President Cheney tried to prevent another terrorist attack by pushing such measures as the use of wiretaps without court warrants; harsh means of interrogating terrorist suspects, regarded by human rights activists as torture; and holding terrorist detainees "without charge, without access to a lawyer and without regard to the laws of armed conflict."[9] The Bush administration also refused to share information with Congress and claimed that it would not obey specific provisions of laws the president disagreed with even though he had signed them, so-called signing statements. Taken together, these actions suggested to some that the administration's true goal was aggressive expansion of presidential power.[10] This debate carried over to the current administration when President Obama continued to use signing statements even after having criticized them during his campaign for president.

unitary executive doctrine
Controversial view of the president's constitutional authority, espoused by the George W. Bush administration, that rejects congressional or judicial encroachments on executive authority and asserts the right of presidents to take actions that might even violate the law.

PUBLIC APPROVAL OF PRESIDENTS

Presidents govern relatively alone, not as part of the political team one finds in parliamentary systems. It should not be surprising, then, that American history frequently portrays "great" presidents as wielding so much power that they can shape events and deliver both peace and prosperity to the nation. Washington, Lincoln, and Teddy and Franklin Roosevelt often are portrayed as having mastered events. Washington led American forces to victory over the Redcoats and then created a new government; Lincoln preserved the Union by defeating the Confederates; Teddy Roosevelt took on the forces of unrestrained economic greed and his cousin Franklin led the nation out of economic depression and to victory in World War II. These thumbnail descriptions simplify what really happened and give too much credit to the leaders. The opposite is also true. Those presidents who fall short of lofty expectations are largely ignored or considered failures. James Buchanan, usually depicted as ineffective on the eve of the Civil War, and Warren G. Harding, who brought a new low to White House morality, usually head this dubious list.

Many Americans have an exaggerated sense of the president's influence in shaping events. But many presidents have not been able to deliver the expected peace and prosperity. Patterns of public approval reveal how the public grows disappointed during each administration.

KEY TO understanding ★

Americans also want to believe that the votes they cast in presidential elections have meaning. They expect winners to solve global warming, find a way to fund Social Security well into the future while keeping taxes low, and protect the nation from international terrorists and economic disruption. In truth, presidents confront severe limits to their power even if the public's expectations seem to know no limits.

As we noted in comparing parliamentary and presidential systems, political and economic power in the United States is fragmented. To be successful, presidents must find ways to convince those who control that power to work with them. This is the reality identified in 1960 by Richard Neustadt in his highly influential book *Presidential Power,* where he famously argued that "Presidential power is the power to persuade."[11] In other words, although they may seem to command others, presidents are simply one among many influential figures in American political and economic life and must use bargaining as the way to achieve their goals. Subsequent studies have suggested that Neustadt understated the extent to which presidents truly can act without winning the support of others and that presidents also derive great influence from their modern role of chief communicator.[12] But most scholars agree that U.S. presidents enjoy very constrained powers.

Congress, bureaucrats, judges, the public, the media, interest groups, state and local officials, business executives, and union officials all exercise a measure of political power. Presidents need to work with them to achieve their goals. Moreover, presidents cannot simply choose which problems to address. The issues they confront are dictated by real or potential emergencies (think terrorist attacks or global warming), the decisions of other nations (North Korea's and Iran's pursuit of nuclear weapons), or natural and manmade disasters (Hurricane Katrina and massive oil spills at home, and the AIDS epidemic in Africa). While presidents may enter the office with an agenda of issues they want to address, their attention and energies are inevitably redirected toward unexpected problems.

George W. Bush encountered the unexpected on September 11, 2001. The nation's agenda suddenly shifted to strengthening homeland security and finding ways both to bring the terrorists to justice and to prevent future attacks. Immediately after 9/11, public approval of George W. Bush soared to an all-time high, exceeding even that expressed for his father during the opening days of the Persian Gulf War in 1991 and for Harry S. Truman when he unexpectedly assumed the presidency upon the death of Franklin D. Roosevelt in 1945. Inevitably, Bush's approval rating declined from that unnaturally high level. But there is a striking pattern: nearly all presidents since Truman have left the Oval Office with lower approval ratings than when they entered (see Figure 13.1). Even when he was reelected, only about half of the public approved of G. W. Bush's performance in office. By July 2007, about two-thirds of the public disapproved of the president's performance and one-third approved. Bush also encountered problems with foreign perceptions of his leadership, receiving high disapproval ratings abroad.

As the Pew Global Attitudes Project has documented, international opinions of Obama were considerably more favorable than those of Bush, but not everywhere. In Pakistan, for example, surveys found Obama was regarded as only modestly better than Bush had been. Pakistani confidence in American leaders "to do the right thing regarding world affairs" doubled, from 7 percent to 13 percent under Obama, but that was still the lowest level among the six Muslim nations surveyed. And confidence slipped to 10 percent in 2011 even before the raid that killed Osama bin Laden, which is almost sure to have made it fall still further.[13]

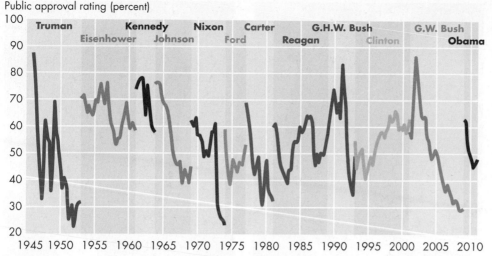

Public approval rating (percent)

FIGURE 13.1

★ PUBLIC APPROVAL
OF PRESIDENTS:
TRUMAN-OBAMA

Why does almost every
president leave office with
lower public approval than
when he began? How do
you think Clinton avoided
this fate?

Source: *Wall Street Journal*, (http://online
.wsj.com/public/resources/documents/
info-presapp0605-31.html)

George W. Bush is only the latest in a line of presidents who have been seen as failures when they left office—only Bill Clinton left the job with higher public approval than when he entered, partly because expectations were low at the outset of his service. Given this historical record of declines in presidential support, some observers have wondered if the presidency is such an impossible job that no one is likely to succeed. Does the job exceed the capacity of any individual?

THE INSTITUTIONAL PRESIDENCY

The president's job is large and seems to always be growing—too large for one person. Consequently, since the administration of Franklin D. Roosevelt, presidents have received help from a staff of political and policy experts working in the White House and in the larger Executive Office of the President (EOP). Collectively, these staffs are referred to as the **institutional presidency.**

The institutional presidency protects presidents from the danger of overload. The president's time, energy, and knowledge are finite, but the demands of the job seem infinite, and the potential for exhaustion is high. Surrounding the president with policy experts and persons who can provide assistance is one way to avoid the rapid aging and burnout that is apparent in photographs of presidents early and late in their terms.

KEY TO understanding

Given presidents' extensive responsibilities, they need help, and since 1939 that assistance has been provided through the Executive Office of the President. The vice president and cabinet are additional sources of assistance, but managing all these staffs poses special challenges.

★

institutional presidency
Term applied to the staff support enjoyed by modern presidents, especially those staff units with relatively continuous operation such as the Office of Management and Budget, the National Security Council, and the cabinet.

THE EXECUTIVE OFFICE OF THE PRESIDENT

From a relatively small group that never exceeded 60 even at the height of World War II, the number of people working in the White House grew to more than 600 during the Nixon years and has leveled off at 400 to 500 in subsequent administrations. President Obama requested funding for 465 for 2012. Some write speeches, some work with Congress, others give presidents political advice and maintain their extensive

★ President Bill Clinton early in his term in 1993 (left) and again in the latter part of his presidency in 2001 (right). By the end of his term, the demands of the job are visible.

Executive Office of the President
Bureaucratic structure created in 1939 to house the personal staff and professional staff units created to help the president discharge a growing range of responsibilities.

National Security Council
Group created in 1947 to coordinate foreign, defense, financial, and intelligence policies for the president.

schedule of meetings and public appearances. This staff makes up the **Executive Office of the President** (EOP). In addition, a collection of policy experts toil in the EOP with a total workforce of about 1,400 over and above those in the White House. Some staff units are well known:

- NSC—Since 1947, presidents have assembled a group of senior cabinet advisors—the secretaries of state, defense, and the treasury as well as the vice president, chairman of the Joint Chiefs of Staff and CIA director—to coordinate foreign policy advice through the **National Security Council** (NSC). A group of policy specialists also provide the president with advice on the full range of international and security issues independent of the cabinet departments who are sometimes suspected of having an organizational bias.

- OMB—The Office of Management and Budget (preceded from 1921 to 1971 by the Bureau of the Budget) assists the president in overseeing the annual budget process and managing the bureaucracy.

- CEA—The Council of Economic Advisers helps the president develop policies to combat inflation and maintain full employment and a healthy economy.

Less well-known components of the EOP include the Office of National Drug Control Policy and the Office of Science and Technology Policy. Over time, more than 50 staff units have been housed in the EOP, some for a year or less, until other organizational arrangements were made (see Table 13.2).

How do presidents use all this help? Staff members provide information for the president to use in making decisions and serve as the president's eyes and ears in Washington and throughout the world. As the public demands that the president address increasingly complex problems, the president requires additional staff to furnish expertise.

As political parties and Congress have become increasingly fragmented, for example, presidents need full-time liaisons who know the ins and outs of politics in different parts of the country and on Capitol Hill.[14]

The president's most senior advisors enjoy regular access to the Oval Office and become Washington power brokers operating in the shadow of the president. The roster shifts with each administration and during the administration. White House chiefs of staff are frequently the most powerful figures because they coordinate the president's schedule, control the flow of paper into the Oval Office, defend the president's interests in negotiations with Congress and the bureaucracy, and explain the administration's policies. Some have also been controversial. Rahm Emanuel, Obama's first chief of staff, was notorious for his sailor-like vocabulary and renowned for his aggressive, often abrasive style in advancing the president's priorities. As a former member of the House, he understood how to engineer passage of Obama's legislative agenda, including health care reform. However, he made few friends in doing so.

TABLE 13.2

staff units in the EOP and white house of president Barack Obama

- Council of Economic Advisers
- Council on Environmental Quality
- National Security Council
- Office of Administration
- Office of Management and Budget
- Office of National Drug Control Policy
- Office of Science and Technology Policy
- Office of the United States Trade Representative
- Office of the Vice President
- Executive Residence
- The White House

Source: http://www.whitehouse.gov/administration/eop

THE VICE PRESIDENT

Since the presidency of Jimmy Carter (1977–1981), presidents have had another influential advisor—the vice president. One of Carter's most lasting legacies as president was revamping the vice presidency so that Walter (Fritz) Mondale became a partner in office. Previously, vice presidents were the forgotten men of American government, occupying a job frequently derided by its own occupants.

Under the Constitution, the VP's only responsibility is to preside over the Senate, voting only in the event of a tie. They also succeed to the presidency in the event of a vacancy resulting from death, resignation, or removal through impeachment. Lyndon Johnson described this part of the job rather like being a vulture hovering in the wings of the White House and unlikely to endear himself to the president or his closest advisors. Thus, the Mondale changes were an important break with the past, and most subsequent presidents have given vice presidents important tasks to complete. Arguably, Dick Cheney, VP for George W. Bush's two terms in office, became the most powerful vice president in American history by overseeing the administration's intelligence and counterterrorism activities. Both Cheney and his successor, Vice President Joe Biden, were general advisors to the president, drawing on their extensive experience with Congress and foreign policy.[15]

The original selection procedure made the person receiving the second highest number of electoral votes the VP, theoretically the second most qualified person in the land to be president. But this procedure made it possible for presidents and vice presidents to be political enemies rather than allies. Thomas Jefferson, Vice President to John Adams from 1797 to 1801, was regarded as Adams' principal political opponent

★ Except when they determine presidential disability, cabinet meetings have no decision-making authority independent of the president. President Lincoln once famously asked for a vote of the cabinet on which all others present voted "no," and the president announced "the ayes have it."

cabinet
Group of senior advisors to either a president or prime minister who head a major department and meet collectively to discuss policy and political issues.

and was not invited to cabinet meetings. The Twelfth Amendment, adopted in 1804, partly solved this problem by establishing separate balloting for president and vice president in the Electoral College. The rise of political parties during the nineteenth century meant that presidents and vice presidents ran on a common ballot. Once the vice presidency became a way to balance a party's national ticket, it was filled by a parade of "also-rans" who gained their position because of the electoral votes they could deliver in the election.

THE CABINET

For most of American history, presidents relied primarily on **cabinet** members to help them discharge their responsibilities. The president appoints the heads of the major departments of the federal government. There are currently 15 such positions: Secretaries of Agriculture, Commerce, Defense, Education, Energy, Health and Human Services, Homeland Security, Housing and Urban Development, Interior, Labor, State, Transportation, Treasury, Veterans Affairs, and the Attorney General (Justice). When most of these positions were created, there was no White House staff or EOP. Now, however, most cabinet secretaries are overshadowed by personal advisors as president after president has centralized policymaking in the White House. For example, with 240 staffers, Obama's National Security Council rivals both the Department of Defense and the State Department for guiding foreign and national security policy. In practice, many analysts divide the cabinet into two groups, an *inner* and *outer* cabinet. The Secretaries of State, Treasury, and Defense and the Attorney General are usually close advisors to the president. Secretaries of the other departments—less critical areas of policy—usually have significantly less influence in the White House.

In parliamentary systems, cabinet members share the political executive's burdens in a system of collective responsibility. The members of the cabinet reach decisions together and the government stands and falls as a group. But no such tradition exists in the United States. The cabinet consists of 15 persons selected by the president and confirmed by the Senate who are charged with overseeing bureaucracies also created by and often heavily influenced by Congress as well as the clientele groups they serve (see Chapter 14). Whereas the cabinet may once have been an important instrument for developing and advancing policy ideas, it has never developed a tradition of collective responsibility in the United States.

Finding ways to lighten the president's burden has been an ongoing concern since Franklin D. Roosevelt's administration. Ironically, this large collection of advisors poses its own challenges: court politics[16] can become rampant with advisors maneuvering for influence; **groupthink**[17] poses the opposite danger if aides become more eager to agree with one another than to assess issues critically. Presidents might be isolated from reality and function in an echo chamber established by aides who tell them only what they believe the leader wants to hear. Or aides might use the reflected power from close proximity to the president for their own ends, leading to personal or political scandals that damage the administration. Staffing, then, is a two-edged sword, with the capacity to help or to damage a president.

groupthink
The tendency within a small group of presidential advisors to agree with one another because finding consensus on policy matters and maintaining group loyalty is more important to them than critically evaluating policy options.

PERSONAL QUALITIES NEEDED TO SUCCEED

To serve as president of the United States, a person must be at least 35 years old, a natural-born citizen, and a resident of the United States for at least 14 years. Yet the qualities needed for success in the presidency go far beyond these formal requirements. Which personal traits of presidents seem most important to carrying out their responsibilities? According to presidential scholar Fred Greenstein, six personal traits matter most:[18]

KEY To understanding ★

The U.S. Constitution names the formal qualifications that candidates must possess to serve as president. However, it is often the personal and even psychological characteristics of an individual that determine how successful they will be in office.

- *Effectiveness as a public communicator.* Until Teddy Roosevelt burst onto the scene at the beginning of the twentieth century, this ability resided almost exclusively in written rather than oral communication. With the rise of radio and television, presidents need to have oral communication skills that enable them to impress audiences in both formal speeches and extemporaneous settings.

- *Organizational capacity.* To what degree can presidents design an information processing and decision-making system that serves their needs? This skill has become critical with the rise of the institutionalized presidency.

- *Political skill.* Classically, presidents need to bargain with numerous skilled players, calculating their advantages, demonstrating their prowess, and creating a record of rewarding friends and punishing opponents.

- *Vision.* Presidents need to inspire others—the general public as well as the fellow partisans and civil servants they lead. Insight into current problems and future challenges is just as important as rhetorical ability in developing a compelling vision.

- *Cognitive style.* Presidents who can cut to the heart of a problem are preferred over those who become swamped in minutiae. The ability to process and analyze large volumes of ideas and information is more important than the specific knowledge they have already mastered.

- *Emotional intelligence.* "Character" is sometimes used as the shorthand term for a solid emotional foundation unlikely to fall victim to personal insecurity, suspicion, unwarranted anger, or irrational behavior.

In addition, Richard Neustadt argued that a successful president must have extensive political experience; an "amateur" in the ways of Washington is likely to fail. Nonetheless, Americans have seemed willing in the last quarter of the twentieth century and beginning of the twenty-first to ask "Washington outsiders" to serve as president. Presidents Carter, Reagan, Clinton, and George W. Bush came to Washington after serving as state governors. Barack Obama was still a first-term senator when he solidly beat long-time senator John McCain in the 2008 presidential election. Very few candidates who lacked experience in elected political office have won either party's presidential nomination, with the exception of military heroes, most recently Eisenhower in 1952 and 1956.

Yet experience does not always produce a candidate who is psychologically fit for the presidency. Even with all the assistance they now receive, presidents must have the capacity to deal with severe on-the-job pressures, especially with the many defeats they will suffer in Washington's contentious political atmosphere. What kind of temperament should the president have? Ronald Reagan's sunny outlook seemed unshakeable even in the darkest moments of his presidency as he recovered from an assassin's bullet in 1981, combated a severe economic recession in 1982, and suffered through a lingering foreign policy scandal that brought into question his own competence in 1986–1987. By contrast, Richard Nixon brooded in response to criticism and believed that he was the victim of a conspiracy triggered by the liberal media.

Nixon rose to national prominence in Congress and then as vice president. Nixon's experience, instead of equipping him for the job of president, seemed to reinforce deep insecurities grounded in his pre-political life. Inheriting the Vietnam War from Johnson, Nixon felt besieged at home and authorized a variety of tactics to silence his critics: conducting government surveillance of student groups demonstrating against involvement in Vietnam; creating a special White House staff dubbed "the plumbers" who used illegal wiretaps and break-ins to plug leaks to the media; using Internal Revenue Service audits to harass critics; and undermining his opponents with dirty tricks during the 1972 presidential campaign. After Nixon tried to cover up his own involvement in the Watergate break-in, he became the first president to resign from office on August 9, 1974.[19]

President William J. Clinton's problems—both their manifestation and origin—were different from Nixon's. Bill Clinton dedicated himself to becoming president after meeting President Kennedy on the White House grounds as a

★ President Nixon bids farewell to his staff prior to leaving the White House.

★ Young Bill Clinton attending Boys Nation in Washington, D.C., positioned himself to shake the hand of President John F. Kennedy.

17-year-old participant in Boys Nation. Clinton overcame a dysfunctional family background to excel academically and socially at prestigious colleges—Georgetown University, Oxford University (as a Rhodes Scholar), and Yale Law School. After serving as governor of Arkansas for 14 years, he successfully ran for president. Clinton's personal problems became a political issue in January 1998 when he publicly denied having had an extramarital affair with Monica Lewinsky, a former White House intern. Independent Counsel Kenneth Starr sought to prove that the president had lied under oath about his relationship with Lewinsky, and Starr's report became the basis for the House's action on December 19, 1998. For only the second time in U.S. history, the House voted to approve two articles of impeachment against a sitting president—in this instance, for perjury to a grand jury and obstruction of justice. The vote in the Senate fell well short of the two-thirds majority required for removal from office and Clinton was found "not guilty." Hence, for both Nixon and Clinton, long service in government did not provide the kinds of coping mechanisms and temperamental resources needed for office.

GOALS AND STRATEGIES FOR SUCCESS

First-term presidents have three major goals: reelection, good policy, and creating a legacy. Presidents turn to the task of seeking reelection early in their third year, shortly after the congressional midterm elections. If they have not scored important policy accomplishments by the end of year two, they are unlikely to do so as the presidential election approaches. Criticism of the president's record rises as challengers compete for the opposition party's nomination, and challenges can be mounted within the president's party as well. From the perspective of the White House, then, good policy and good politics coincide: early policy success strengthens the president's chances for reelection.

Second-term presidents, no longer eligible for reelection, still push for policy success but largely as a way to fashion their legacies, hoping to make an even deeper mark on the nation's history. But second-term presidents face an even briefer window of opportunity before they become lame ducks serving out the duration of a term. Franklin Roosevelt avoided lame duck status by winning four national elections in 1932, 1936, 1940 and 1944. By breaking the unwritten two-term limit, self-imposed by George Washington and then honored by his successors, Roosevelt ultimately triggered adoption of the **Twenty-Second Amendment,** advanced in 1946 by the first Republican-controlled Congress since 1930, which limits presidents to two terms and ensures that their final months or years in office will be less productive.

Ironically, presidents have the best chance of gaining congressional approval of their principal proposals when they first arrive in office, before they really know much about their new position. Later in the administration, political appointees are in place and able to formulate more thoughtful solutions to the nation's problems, but by then the administration has usually experienced a decline in influence and is less able to get them accepted.[20]

A "honeymoon period" follows the president's inauguration, when public approval is strong and disapproval normally low. Members of Congress are still evaluating the

KEY TO understanding ★

Presidents pursue three general goals: reelection, good public policy, and a favorable legacy. To achieve success, they can choose a mixture of three broad strategies—legislative, administrative, and judicial. No single strategy is guaranteed to be successful.

Twenty-Second Amendment
Advanced in 1946 by the first Republican-controlled Congress since 1930, limits presidents to two terms and ensures that their final months or years in office will be less productive.

new leader in the White House and eager to make a good first impression. Media discussions are largely positive. Unfortunately for the incumbent, the honeymoon cannot last forever. The president's party typically loses seats in the midterm elections, especially in the House. Media treatment becomes more critical. Public opinion shifts with events but generally moves in a negative direction, registering lower approval and greater disapproval of how the president is handling the job. As a result, presidents are advised to "hit the ground running" by concentrating on a focused list of goals that will not overwhelm Congress and trying to achieve the greatest amount of change in the first year. To achieve their goals of reelection, good policy, and a legacy for their successors, presidents have developed three strategies for success: legislative, administrative, and judicial.

LEGISLATIVE STRATEGY: PRESIDENTS AND CONGRESS

Most Americans think of presidents pursuing their policy goals by proposing legislation to Congress, much like Franklin Roosevelt's **New Deal** or Lyndon Johnson's **Great Society.** Both FDR and LBJ won congressional support for impressive lists of legislation that expanded the range of services that government provides to citizens, including Social Security and Medicare, programs that changed the lives of millions of American seniors. Most major initiatives require presidents to secure congressional agreement—that is, pursue a **legislative strategy.** This is particularly true if presidents want policies to endure beyond their own years in office. Broad, bipartisan support in Congress makes it less likely that the opposition party will reverse major policies as soon as it regains power on Capitol Hill or in the White House. Thus, presidents are wise to let members of Congress from both sides of the aisle shape major federal programs such as retirement benefits for the elderly (Social Security), health care for the elderly (Medicare), financial assistance for the needy (welfare), and federal aid to education (No Child Left Behind). By contrast, when Republicans felt excluded from shaping the new national health care policy passed by Democrats in 2010, they quickly set about trying to dismantle "Obamacare," as they called it. After Republicans gained a House majority, they voted more than thirty times to defund or scrap the law.

Cooperation between the president and Congress is not limited to major programs, however. In a system of "separated institutions sharing and competing for powers,"[21] government action on questions both large and small needs to be coordinated rather than independent. In many situations—for example, the annual appropriations needed to pay for next year's programs—government can take action only through coordinated efforts.

Party

The president's party frequently serves as a bridge to build institutional cooperation. As we saw in Chapter 12, legislators do not always vote on the basis of party. But party members share a set of beliefs that binds a president to many like-minded legislators. Thus, a critical factor for presidents is how many members of their own party are serving in Congress. If you are a Republican president, it is in your interest to help members of your own party get elected in order to maximize the support you will have in Congress. George W. Bush, for example, campaigned aggressively for his party's candidates in 2002, traveling widely to generate publicity, to raise campaign funds, and to win voter support. The effort paid off when Republicans regained control of the Senate

New Deal

The title given by Franklin D. Roosevelt to characterize the many reform proposals offered during the 1930s to move the United States out of the Great Depression. Teddy Roosevelt had proposed a "Square Deal" and Harry Truman later offered a "Fair Deal"—additional examples of slogans used by presidents to characterize their programs.

Great Society

Name given to the comprehensive program of action proposed and enacted under the leadership of Lyndon B. Johnson in the mid-1960s, which focused on eliminating poverty and racial injustice in areas such as employment, health care, and education.

legislative strategy

Presidential strategy to achieve goals based on proposals presented to Congress for statutory action.

and expanded their majority in the House. Barack Obama tried the same approach in 2010 but without the success; Democrats lost the majority in the House and saw their majority in the Senate shrink.

Over the previous 50 years, Republican presidents had seldom enjoyed Bush's success in winning control of Congress. As a result, Republican presidents Eisenhower, Nixon, Ford, Reagan, and George H. W. Bush served during periods of **divided government,** confronting either one or two houses of Congress controlled by the Democrats (see Figure 13.2). With the exception of Eisenhower's first two years in office, **unified government** was a Democratic phenomenon for half a century until the presidency of George W. Bush. At the outset of Bush's term, the Senate was divided 50/50, with Vice President Cheney casting the tie-breaking vote. When halfway through 2001 Senator James Jeffords (VT) changed his allegiance from the Republican Party to become an Independent who voted with the Democrats, the Republicans lost control of the Senate. The Republicans regained control in the midterm elections of 2002, and Bush once again enjoyed unified party control for four years until it was lost in 2006. Obama enjoyed it for two years but then also faced divided party control.

Of course, presidents can also work with members of the opposition party. **Bipartisanship**—broad cooperation between members of both parties—was a staple of American foreign policy in the early post–World War II era (see Chapter 18) but has declined in recent decades. **Competitive bipartisanship** is a different pattern wherein presidents of one party find some areas of common agreement with the opposition party's congressional leaders while agreeing to disagree in other areas. Eisenhower famously sought to identify areas of compromise during private chats (lubricated by "bourbon and branch water") with the two fellow Texans who led the Democrats in Congress: Speaker of the House Sam Rayburn and Senate Majority Leader Lyndon B. Johnson. Finally, under **cross-partisanship** a segment of the opposition party's legislators cross party lines to vote with the president's party in open opposition to their own party's leadership.[22] Southern Democrats in Congress, for example, have often voted with Republicans rather than with Northern Democrats because their own party's majority is too liberal for their taste on defense and social issues.

Many studies suggest that Capitol Hill itself has shifted dramatically. Partisan conflict has grown and cross-aisle friendships, let alone legislative partnerships between Democrats and Republicans, are less common than in the past. When Bill Clinton allied himself with Republicans and moderate Democrats to pass legislation like the North American Free Trade Agreement (NAFTA) in 1993 and welfare reform in 1996, he outraged liberal Democrats who opposed both proposals. George W. Bush received critical support from congressional Democrats in passing his solutions to the economic crisis of 2008. Obama was fully aligned with liberal members of his party during his first two years in office but adopted more moderate positions after Republicans gained control of the House in 2011. For example, many progressives were upset that the president reached an agreement with Republicans in the summer of 2011 on raising the debt ceiling through spending cuts but without raising taxes. They thought he had gone too far in accepting the Republican terms.

Of course, all presidents are happy to solicit support from individual legislators in the opposition party who are willing to break with the majority of their party based on

divided government
When political systems elect the president and legislature independently, conflict can easily arise if Congress is controlled by a party other than that of the presidency.

unified government
Distinct from divided government, a situation in which the presidency and the two houses of Congress are controlled by the same political party, providing the basis for joint action.

bipartisanship
Broad agreement on policy across the membership of both major U.S. parties, as in the containment of Soviet expansion following World War II.

competitive bipartisanship
Agreement between the president and the opposing party's congressional leaders in selected policy areas while they continue to disagree in others.

cross-partisanship
A president's efforts to find selected members of the opposing party who will vote for certain policy proposals, often in exchange for the president's support for a goal of their own.

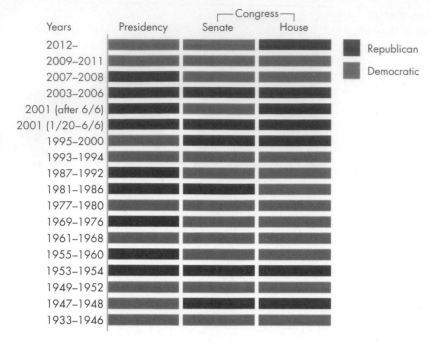

Years	Presidency	Congress	
		Senate	House
2012–			
2009–2011			
2007–2008			
2003–2006			
2001 (after 6/6)			
2001 (1/20–6/6)			
1995–2000			
1993–1994			
1987–1992			
1981–1986			
1977–1980			
1969–1976			
1961–1968			
1955–1960			
1953–1954			
1949–1952			
1947–1948			
1933–1946			

Republican
Democratic

FIGURE 13.2

★ DIVIDED AND UNIFIED CONTROL OF GOVERNMENT, 1933–2012

As this table shows, periods of unified party control of Congress and the White House are not all that frequent. Since 1933, how many years has the United States had unified party control and how many years has there been divided party control?

principle or in exchange for presidential support of an important government project in the legislator's state or district. Unlike parliamentary systems, there are few ways to compel American legislators to vote with their party, and that opens the possibility of crossover support for an opposition president.

Setting the Legislative Agenda

It is not unusual for presidential proposals and budgets to be declared "dead on arrival," without even a ghost of a chance at approval. This was frequently the case for Republican presidents like Ronald Reagan who annually proposed deep budget cuts in programs that the Democratic majority in Congress had created. Thus, presidents can fashion the content of the agenda in an effort to trigger bargaining and compromise or can choose instead to take stands that are likely to produce confrontation. Although it may sound strange, confrontation is sometimes preferred in order to dramatize programmatic and budgetary differences that will be highlighted in upcoming elections. This was true for Harry Truman in 1948 and for Barack Obama in 2011 and 2012.

Vetoes

veto

Constitutional power of a president to reject legislation passed by the legislature. In the United States, presidents have 10 days to act on legislation, which may be signed or returned with objections to the house in which it originated. Congress may override the veto and pass the bill by means of a two-thirds majority in both houses.

Presidential vetoes can be a powerful influence on policy. Often the mere threat of a **veto** is sufficient to force legislative opponents to bargain and negotiate over matters of presidential concern in order to salvage other things the opponents want. Some presidents have relied more heavily on this constitutionally based power than others.

As shown in Figure 13.3, among modern presidents since FDR, President Gerald R. Ford relied heavily on his veto power. Confronted by predominantly assertive Democratic Congresses, President Ford cast 66 vetoes in slightly over two years. (After the 1974 elections, Democrats controlled the Senate 61–39 and the House 291–144, a veto-proof margin in the House if all Democrats voted together.) Although Congress overrode Ford more frequently than any other modern president, he prevailed on more than 80 percent of the vetoes he cast. This illustrates the power of a veto—they work most of the time. Assembling the two-thirds majority required to override a veto in *both* houses of Congress is a difficult task.

pocket veto

A bill does not become law if the president fails to sign it within the required 10-day period and Congress has adjourned during that time.

Jimmy Carter and Bill Clinton discovered that their Democratic allies in Congress often disagreed with their policy preferences. Carter actually relied more heavily on the **pocket veto**—a president's capacity to kill a bill by taking no action when Congress has adjourned—than he did on the regular veto.

Leaders in other presidential systems also exercise veto powers, but there is nothing similar in parliamentary systems, where the legislature's support is virtually automatic. Boris Yeltsin, Russia's first president after the fall of the Soviet Union, exercised his veto power 219 times in five years in a series of high-visibility showdowns with the Federal Assembly (the legislature), a rate so high that he was charged with abusing his powers and acting arbitrarily—he even vetoed one bill a second time, after it had been passed over his initial veto. Russia's Constitutional Court was called upon to mediate the conflict.[23] Some Latin American systems provide the president with an "amendatory" veto through which the executive can make additions, deletions, and substitutions to vetoed bills. Only three Latin American countries (Honduras, Guatemala, and the Dominican Republic) empower their presidents to issue vetoes like those in the United States.

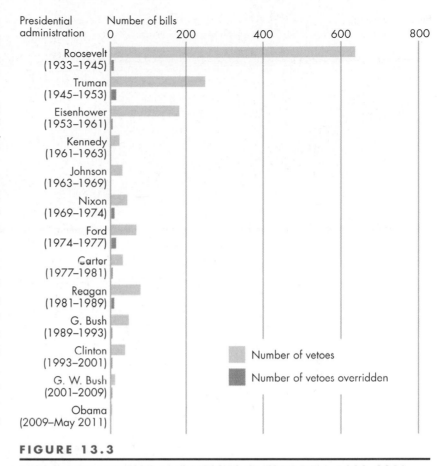

Presidential administration — Number of bills (0, 200, 400, 600, 800)

Roosevelt (1933–1945)
Truman (1945–1953)
Eisenhower (1953–1961)
Kennedy (1961–1963)
Johnson (1963–1969)
Nixon (1969–1974)
Ford (1974–1977)
Carter (1977–1981)
Reagan (1981–1989)
G. Bush (1989–1993)
Clinton (1993–2001)
G. W. Bush (2001–2009)
Obama (2009–May 2011)

Number of vetoes
Number of vetoes overridden

FIGURE 13.3

★ PRESIDENTIAL VETOES AND VETOES OVERRIDDEN, 1933–2011

Congress seldom overrides presidential vetoes. Why do you think Gerald Ford suffered the largest percentage of overrides?

Source: Office of the Clerk, (http://clerk.house.gov/art_history/house_history/vetoes.html)

Going Public

Not all presidents are willing to bargain. Following the example of Teddy Roosevelt, some presidents prefer to appeal for public support over the heads of Congress—they do this by **going public.** Relying on techniques that resemble those used in campaigns, presidents who choose this route place pressure on legislators to support their initiatives or suffer the electoral consequences of blocking a popular president's proposals. Although the tactic of going public has been successful in some instances, it also has limits. Eighteenth and nineteenth century views of leadership precluded presidents from addressing the public, let alone going over the heads of Congress to win the public's support.[24] Now presidents employ advisors to help them devise photo opportunities—newsworthy activities to form the basis of reporters' stories. Radio and television give presidents regular opportunities to make their case directly to the nation rather than through journalists' interpretations of what the president said. Charles DeGaulle, France's World War II leader and president of the Fifth Republic from 1959 to 1969, also brought major issues directly to the nation's citizens, relying heavily on his

going public
A presidential strategy designed to influence Congress by appealing directly to the public, asking them to pressure legislators for passage of the president's proposals.

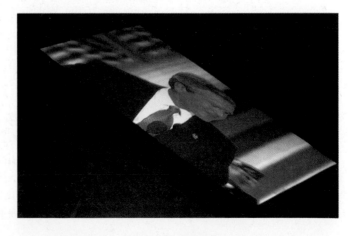

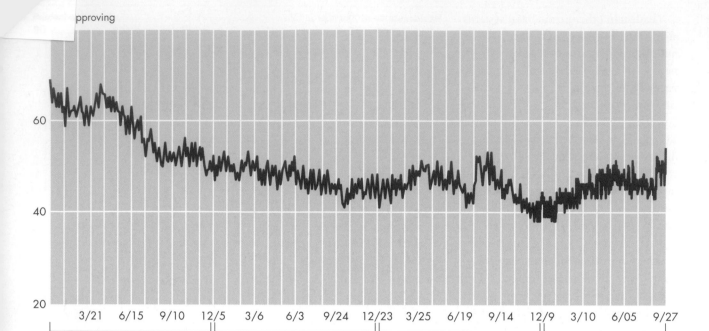

60

40

20

| 3/21 | 6/15 | 9/10 | 12/5 | 3/6 | 6/3 | 9/24 | 12/23 | 3/25 | 6/19 | 9/14 | 12/9 | 3/10 | 6/05 | 9/27 |

2009 2010 2011 2012

FIGURE 13.4

★ PRESIDENT OBAMA'S
APPROVAL RATING

Although President
Obama's approval rating
has ups and downs, the
overall trend is downward,
as with most modern
presidents. What happened
in April 2011 to cause the
sudden jump in Obama's
approval?

Source: Gerhard Peters and John T.
Woolley. "Presidential Job Approval."
The American Presidency Project,
(http://www.presidency.ucsb.edu/data/
popularity.php)

standing as a national hero to rally their support. Thus, going public is not a strategy used exclusively by American leaders.

More recently, the public pays less attention to presidents. Fewer people watch the president's speeches on TV or follow his actions in the daily news. In the early 1970s, President Nixon could expect 50 percent of the TV-watching public to tune into a speech on Vietnam policy. Seventy percent of the public would read about the speech in the next day's newspaper, and 60 percent would watch reports on the evening news. By the early twenty-first century, however, George W. Bush was able to garner only 20 percent of the viewing public for a speech on Iraq, and news consumption habits had changed dramatically so that only 40 percent of the public read newspapers, trailed by a third who watched the evening news.[25] Going public may not be as powerful a presidential strategy today as it once was. We are still unsure whether using social media will help presidents communicate their message with greater effectiveness. The decline in Obama's public approval ratings (Figure 13.4) continued despite introducing the new strategy.

However, if the Washington elite *believe* that a president's oratorical gifts could influence the public, they may still be intimidated. Ronald Reagan's reputation may have exceeded his skills as the "great communicator," but others believed in his ability to move public opinion.[26] Thus, rhetorically gifted and media-savvy presidents may continue to rely on this strategy.

ADMINISTRATIVE STRATEGY: PRESIDENTS AND THE BUREAUCRACY

When Congress resists presidents' appeals, chief executives sometimes use unilateral means to accomplish their goals. They can develop regulations or issue executive orders that advance the administration's goals. Such actions can be reversed by the next administration, but they have the force of law for a period of time.

What happens when a "chief executive" of the national government gives an order? Harry Truman once predicted that Dwight Eisenhower, his successor, would be frustrated as president. "Poor Ike," in Truman's view, would expect obedience as a lifelong member of the military who had climbed the ranks to become Supreme Allied Commander during World War II, but in Truman's experience, presidents seldom issue orders that others obey.

Truman, of course, was exaggerating, but only a little. Presidents do not *control* the executive branch. Congress determines the organization of the federal bureaucracy, ultimately establishes the budgets that support its operations, reserves to itself the right to control personnel, and is highly assertive in guiding federal programs and influencing agency decision making. For many reasons, presidents are described as "reigning but not ruling"—that is, holding office without exercising real control over the executive branch. Nonetheless, presidents can advance their programs using an **administrative strategy.** Presidents can use a wide range of resources, reviewed in Chapter 14, to control the federal bureaucracy, including the oversight of personnel and budgets. Presidents also can develop regulations and issue unilateral edicts, discussed in the following section.

administrative strategy
Strategy to achieve the administration's goals by using the president's budget, personnel, reorganization, and regulatory powers.

Regulations

One of the oldest aphorisms in politics is that "the devil's in the details." Political parties, interest groups, and policy advocates can agree on general goals while disagreeing on how to achieve those goals. No political institution is more concerned with details than the bureaucracy, whose specialists thoroughly understand the ins and outs of policies and programs—their politics, histories, limitations, and funding. Such details lie at the heart of regulations that translate broad legislative goals into concrete programs of action, and bureaucrats play the central role in developing federal regulations.

For presidents, regulations provide an opportunity to shape programs while bypassing extensive bargaining. Anticipating that his party would lose the 2006 congressional elections, George W. Bush surveyed his cabinet for initiatives that could be accomplished through regulations.[27] The resulting list was long, including potential action in environmental, health, and labor policies. The administration even figured out a way that regulations could reduce health care spending—an area of rapid growth—in ways that Congress had already rejected.

Bush was by no means the first president to pursue such a strategy. As a longtime employee of the Office of Management and Budget explained to a journalist, "'At the end of the presidency, the administration generally has a number of policies it wants to implement before exiting the White House. . . . They want to push things through because, among other reasons, there is no long-term political downside to doing things, since everyone will be gone.'"[28] *CQ Weekly* charted the total number of pages in the *Federal Register,* the government publication in which proposed and final regulations must appear, for each year of the past five administrations. Although multiple factors influence the *Register's* page totals, it is noteworthy that the totals increased in the final two years of each administration (see Figure 13.5). Presidents realize the need to act before the administration's time in office expires.[29]

Industries and interest groups that are affected by government regulations closely monitor the regulatory process, and Congress may vote against rules through a resolution of disapproval or refuse to provide funding for their enforcement. But when administrations, such as Clinton's, adopt large numbers of regulations late in their final

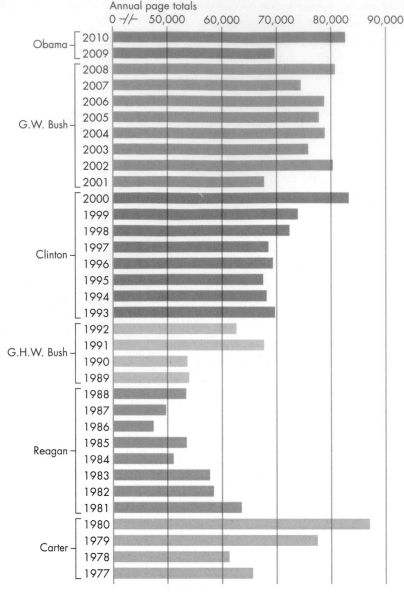

FIGURE 13.5

★ ANNUAL PAGE TOTALS IN THE *FEDERAL REGISTER*, 1977–2010

Most presidents eventually turn to using regulations as a way to accomplish their goals. How might party control of Congress, public approval, administration policy goals, and year in office influence the patterns found in this figure?

Source: Data from Office of the Federal Register, (http://www.llsdc.org/attachments/wysiwyg/544/fed-reg-pages.pdf)

executive orders
Unilateral decrees issued by presidents to deal with policy or procedural matters that fall under their authority.

year, neither Congress nor the affected stakeholders are able to halt all the objectionable ones. Those who are affected by a regulation can also challenge its legality in the courts.

Unilateral Actions

Legislation and vetoes attract enormous media attention, but some presidential actions remain outside journalists' usual coverage. **Executive orders,** presidential proclamations, and presidential memoranda help presidents accomplish goals unilaterally rather than through bargaining with Congress. Like regulations, executive orders must be published in the *Federal Register,* but memoranda are not. Both are examples of the president's ability to govern by decree rather than by persuading—to take direct, unilateral action over some aspect of administration or policy in order to modify laws or even take action in areas not covered by the Constitution or statute.[30] As shown in Figure 13.6, some presidents rely more heavily on executive orders as their term in office winds down. Many executive orders have had important policy implications. For example, Franklin Roosevelt used an executive order in 1942 to authorize the forced relocation of Pacific Coast residents of Japanese heritage (including 70,000 American citizens) to internment camps during World War II. Harry S. Truman used an executive order to integrate America's armed forces in 1948. In the 1960s, Lyndon Johnson used an executive order to create the first government affirmative action program designed to open employment opportunities to minorities who formerly had been blocked from some professions.

Presidents have often used executive orders as a way to respond to national emergencies, both economic and international. During World Wars I and II, both Presidents Wilson and Roosevelt used executive orders to mobilize the nation for war, and FDR used them to take direct action to combat the Great Depression. But even under crisis conditions, executive orders can be challenged and reversed. Harry S. Truman authorized the military through an executive order to seize U.S. steel mills in the midst

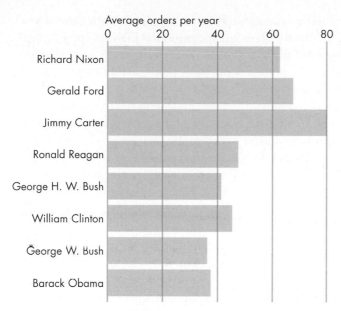

Average orders per year

FIGURE 13.6

★ EXECUTIVE ORDERS PER YEAR

George Washington issued the first executive order, and the government began to number them in 1862. More than 13,600 had been issued through early 2012. Why do some presidents issue more executive orders than others?

Source: National Archives, (http://www.archives.gov/federal-register/executive-orders/disposition.html)

of the Korean War when a strike was about to close them. When mill owners went to the courts, the president was ordered to rescind his command. FDR's order to remove American citizens of Japanese descent from their homes in four western states and detain them in government camps to prevent sabotage was originally upheld by the courts but declared unconstitutional in December 1944. Congress later apologized and provided compensation for the victims in 1988.

When presidents use regulations to pursue their goals, they must meet procedural requirements set forth in the Administrative Procedures Act. By contrast, executive orders, presidential proclamations, and memoranda need not follow a process that allows for systematic review and comment by those directly affected.[31] But rapid response comes at potential cost: without full review, there is the risk of presidents making an error or triggering political controversy.

JUDICIAL STRATEGY: PRESIDENTS AND THE COURTS

Since the 1970s, presidents have pursued their policy goals using a **judicial strategy**, selecting like-minded nominees for the federal judiciary. Similarly, in guiding the enforcement activities of the Department of Justice, administrations have made choices about priorities and areas to emphasize or deemphasize. For presidents who are able to nominate many federal judges, their most enduring legacy is likely to be the federal judiciary they have helped to shape. Serving for terms of life or good behavior, federal judges have the potential to influence policy for years to come through the decisions they make in cases that come before them. To the extent that a president carefully selects nominees on the basis of ideology or judicial philosophy, the president can have a major impact on public policy for decades after leaving office.

Judicial Selection

Presidents make a conscious effort to select federal judges who share their political values and judicial philosophy. Although the media highlight battles over Supreme

judicial strategy

A presidential strategy designed to achieve the administration's goals through the appointment of like-minded judges to the federal judiciary and the establishment of clear priorities for federal law enforcement.

Court vacancies, there are far more vacancies that arise on federal district and appeals courts where more than 850 federal judges sit. Judges enjoy lifetime appointments unless they are impeached or until they leave office because of death or resignation. Thus, in selecting federal judges, the president can potentially have an impact on public policy for decades into the future.

Beginning with Jimmy Carter and Ronald Reagan, presidents have used selection as a means to achieve specific goals. For Carter, diversifying the demographics of the federal judiciary was most important. Carter significantly increased the number of African-American, Hispanic, and female judges, groups that were severely underrepresented on the bench. President Reagan injected another note: judges' judicial philosophy and ideology. The White House Counsel's office, a component of the White House staff, took the lead in identifying and investigating potential nominees. Reagan's staff conducted extensive interviews with potential candidates for all vacancies, not just those for the Supreme Court. Staff members asked about policy views and judicial philosophy so that a nominee's views would be consistent with that of the administration.[32] Presidents since Reagan have followed similar procedures.

Depending on the number of vacancies that develop and whether Congress establishes new judgeships to deal with the growing caseload that burdens the federal courts, presidents have the potential to nominate a large number of judges. Reagan and Clinton, in particular, nominated large percentages of the total federal judiciary during their double terms in office. Not all nominees are confirmed. Moreover, the nomination process has become particularly contentious in recent decades, as is also reflected in the time required for action by the Senate (see Figure 13.7). Under Carter, the average number of days required for the Senate to move from nomination to a confirmation vote was 78 days. For Obama's first two years the average time had stretched to 214 days by mid-2011.[33] As presidents have become more explicit about the policy goals they hope to pursue, the Senate has become more assertive in exercising its confirmation powers, especially opponents who freely use delay tactics.

Presidential nominations to the Supreme Court receive special attention from the media. Across U.S. history, 152 people have been nominated to serve on the nation's

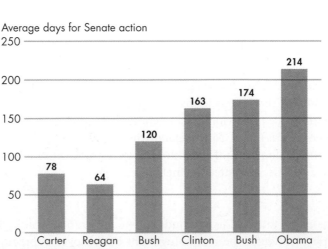

Average days for Senate action

FIGURE 13.7

★ TIME REQUIRED FOR PRESIDENTIAL JUDICIAL NOMINATIONS TO BE CONFIRMED, 1977–2010

Why does it take longer and longer for presidents' judicial nominees to win Senate confirmation?

Source: Data drawn from Table 1, page 13 of *Justice Held Hostage: Politics and Selecting Federal Judges*, updated 2006, The Constitution Project, (http://www.constitutionproject.org/pdf/JusticeHeldHostageUpdated.pdf) and from Russell Wheeler, *Judicial Nominations and Confirmations in the 111th Senate and What to Look for in the 112th*, Brookings Governance Studies, January 4, 2011.

highest court.[34] Twenty-six nominations "failed," four of which were withdrawn by the president in anticipation of a Senate defeat. Not all presidents have the chance to name a Supreme Court Justice. President Obama has had the opportunity to nominate two successful candidates, Sonia Sotomayor and Elena Kagan. Although presidents invest enormous amounts of time and effort in selecting Supreme Court nominees, they do not always get what they had expected. President Eisenhower was surprised at the activism of Chief Justice Earl Warren and had strong reservations about the Warren Court's decision to integrate public schools.

Enforcement

Presidents have the responsibility of enforcing federal laws, which they delegate to the Department of Justice. Currently, the department's six major enforcement divisions reflect the major categories of federal law that might be violated: criminal, civil, tax, antitrust, environment and natural resources, and civil rights. Major operational subdivisions include the Federal Bureau of Investigation (FBI), the Drug Enforcement Administration (DEA), and the U.S. Marshals Service.

In addition to apprehending violators of federal laws and bringing them to the courts for trial, the department can choose to be more or less aggressive in pursuing certain types of lawbreakers and launch special efforts in one or more areas. These shifting priorities reflect administration priorities. For example, detecting and preventing terrorism now stands as the number-one priority in the DOJ's strategic plan, along with combating violent crime, identifying and stopping computer crime (especially child pornography and intellectual property theft), stemming the flow of illegal drugs, penalizing corporate and civic corruption, and promoting civil rights and civil liberties.[35]

Administrations exercise *prosecutorial discretion* by choosing to stress certain areas of law enforcement.[36] An administration might hire additional staff, appoint more aggressive leaders, increase budgets, and so on. Thus, the Kennedy administration launched a concerted effort against organized crime, and Johnson's Justice Department placed a heavy emphasis on enforcing civil rights. Presidents Ford and Carter stressed antitrust regulations, while Presidents Nixon and Reagan did not. Members of the Washington community battle over especially strategic decisions, such as appointments, and might praise or criticize nominees expected to be more or less aggressive in enforcing some area of the law.

Why Are We
THE WAY WE ARE?

Today's presidency dramatically differs from the one invented in 1789. Congressional demands and the actions of presidents themselves have fleshed out the original constitutional roles presidents were to play and created entirely new ones. More than ever before, the nation relies on the ability of presidents to act with secrecy, unity, and dispatch—institutional advantages that the Founders expected presidents to have over Congress—in addressing international and economic problems. Nonetheless, American presidents are far from omnipotent. In fact, they spend much of their time assembling support for the policies they propose, whereas prime ministers can be assured of much more consistent cooperation. Why has the presidency evolved into the office it is today?

THE DESIGN OF PRESIDENTIAL GOVERNMENT

The challenges that presidents confront in doing their job are heavily determined by the basic constitutional design. Unlike a parliamentary system, in which the prime minister is also an elected member of the legislature and the leader of the majority party, presidential systems elect the executive separately from the legislature, which (as Republican presidents frequently discovered over six decades) may be under the control of the opposite party. The design of the government is important in other ways as well. In the United States, although the presidential election is divided into 51 separate contests waged for Electoral College votes, it is national in scope, giving modern presidents an *individual* claim to representing the interests of *all the people*. In a parliamentary system, the majority party makes a *collective* claim to hold a mandate from the public, but only as long as the party remains united. No comparable "glue" holds together the president's congressional supporters. National elections in a parliamentary system are also called at the leader's discretion, representing a powerful source of leverage; in a presidential system elections are held at fixed intervals and can occur at a time when the president's popularity and that of the party are at low ebb. As a result, presidents are always scurrying to generate support.

Presidential systems also diffuse power—the responsibility for policy making is divided between legislative and executive branches. Presidents, then, are frequently isolated in their pursuit of legislative and bureaucratic support. By contrast, prime ministers can expect the legislature to support the government's policy goals. Cabinet members in a parliamentary system also serve as members of parliament, providing a direct link with the legislative majority, whereas cabinet members in a presidential system can come from a variety of careers in business and academia, and if they are drawn from the legislature, they must resign their positions.

CHANGES IN CONTEXT

Changes in political, social, and technological conditions have altered the presidency in important ways. The president's economic responsibilities—nowhere to be found in the Constitution—became a critical part of the job as 13 very separate states evolved into an economically integrated nation. FDR's economic leadership at the time of the Great Depression made economic policies a permanent feature of the political system. New twentieth-century technologies made presidents the darlings of the mass media, encouraging journalists to provide personalized stories that capture the public's attention whether delivered electronically or in print. And today's presidents are encouraged rather than discouraged, as they were in the past, to speak directly to the nation's citizens. President Obama can send text messages to Americans or choose to communicate through television and radio. This accessibility makes modern presidents a real presence in the lives of Americans, heightening the personalized nature of the office.

EXCESSIVE EXPECTATIONS

Have presidents lived up to the tasks they are expected to perform? Some have, but many have not. And it may have become increasingly difficult for presidents to succeed regardless of the help they receive and the strategies they pursue. Compared with executives in other political systems, presidents seem to confront higher expectations of individual performance while they are at the same time unable to command as much political support. Public expectations may have become so high that all presidents run a high risk of being perceived as failures.

Presidents have become more adept at mixing strategies—legislative, administrative, and judicial—to pursue the programmatic goals they set.

And since the watershed administration of FDR, the nation has found new ways to help presidents succeed—providing them with more help and investing ever greater time and effort in finding a person with the right blend of skills and character. Nonetheless, pressure remains high to perform.

. . . AND WHY DOES IT Matter?

Where once presidents were given expanded powers when the nation faced extraordinary problems, presidents are now powerful even in ordinary times. Others in the government lean on them in dealing with even the most routine matters.

Today's world is far more complex than it was in the eighteenth century. Economic relationships, both domestic and international, are far more difficult to understand and control. Around the world, weapons are more dangerous, ideologies more threatening, and U.S. interests far more extensive. Most presidential elections find one or more candidates running televised ads that build on citizens' insecurities—impulsive opponents should not be trusted with nuclear weapons, and those with limited experience are unprepared to deal with crises that arise in the middle of the night. As these issues became more prominent in the twentieth century, presidential power grew. Two world wars, a cold war, and a global depression led the nation to lean ever more heavily on presidents to define problems and solutions; presidents are also better able to coordinate complex government actions than Congress. Nor is this an exclusively U.S. phenomenon, as observers have noted the shift of influence toward executives around the world.

How strong does the president need to be? This question was posed at the Constitutional Convention and has echoed throughout American history. Advocates for a more powerful president have argued that a highly decentralized nation—with power divided between federal and state governments as well as among separate branches within the federal government—needs a strong force at the center to pull the pieces together in times of national need, particularly in times of crisis. Thus, Congress and the courts have given presidents more power during wartime and during periods of economic crisis. And today that power does not recede significantly during non-crisis periods. The opposite argument has also been consistent over time: powerful executives pose a threat to citizens' rights and liberties; only by checking presidential power can the nation hope to preserve its hard-won rights. Can we afford a powerful presidency? Can we afford *not* to have a powerful president? Although questions still arise, the United States seems to have accepted a greatly expanded role for its chief executive.

critical thinking questions

1. In comparison with other presidents in U.S. history, how do you evaluate the performance of George W. Bush and Barack Obama as president? How might those evaluations be different in 20 years?

2. The argument is usually made that presidents are better able than Congress to respond rapidly to crises and to maintain secrecy in delicate situations. Do you agree? What advantages might Congress have over the presidency in such situations?

3. Are there ways to ensure that presidential candidates have the personal qualifications needed to be a successful president?

4. If you were president, how would you deal with the challenges posed by divided government?

key terms

administrative strategy, 473

bipartisanship, 469

cabinet, 464 ✓

chief administrator, 451

chief budgeter, 454 ✓

chief communicator, 455

chief diplomat, 449

chief economist, 454

chief legislator, 450

chief magistrate, 451

Commander-in-Chief, 449 ✓

competitive bipartisanship, 469

constitutional theory, 457

cross-partisanship, 469

divided government, 469

Executive Office of the President, 462

executive order, 474 ✓

going public, 471

Great Society, 468

groupthink, 465

head of state, 456

impeachment, 447

institutional presidency, 461

judicial strategy, 475

lame duck, 448

legislative strategy, 468

modern presidency, 454

National Security Council, 462

New Deal, 468

parliamentary system, 447

pocket veto, 470

political leader, 456

prerogative theory, 457

presidential system, 447

prime minister, 447

State of the Union Address, 453

stewardship theory, 457

Twenty-Second Amendment, 467

unified government, 469

unitary executive doctrine, 459

veto, 470

War Powers Resolution, 452

Watergate, 457

BUREAUCRACY

★ ★ ★

- Explore the importance of bureaucracy in American government and understand the tensions between bureaucratic power and democratic ideals.
- Discuss how Weber's model reflects the development of modern bureaucracy, and describe the features that distinguish the U.S. federal bureaucracy from other public bureaucracies around the world.
- Examine the growth of federal bureaucratic power in the United States.
- Identify the numerous organizational structures that make up the federal bureaucracy and describe the unique role that each one plays.
- Analyze the factors that determine the true size of the U.S. federal bureaucracy.
- Understand the means by which the public holds government administrators and their actions accountable.

PERSPECTIVE
How Do Governments Respond during Natural Disasters?

The worst natural disaster in American history occurred in August 2005 when Hurricane Katrina overwhelmed New Orleans, flooding sections of the city to depths of up to 15 feet, forcing hundreds of thousands of residents to flee their homes, and killing nearly 2,000. In the aftermath, public officials sought answers. How could this destruction have happened? Who failed to do his or her job? Why didn't the thousands of victims (most of them elderly or young and poor) who were jammed into the Louisiana Superdome or rescued from the rooftops of their houses receive help more quickly? Media and political attention immediately turned to FEMA, the Federal Emergency Management Agency, a part of the newly created Department of Homeland Security (DHS) and a small part of the federal bureaucracy.

President Jimmy Carter created FEMA in the 1970s, consolidating emergency relief programs scattered throughout the government. Under President Bill Clinton, FEMA made significant improvements. The agency pre positioned workers and supplies in anticipated disaster locations, worked closely with state and local officials to deal with displaced victims, and began to help communities repair problems that exposed them to floods. But FEMA dropped the ball in New Orleans. President George W. Bush had appointed administrators with more experience in politics than in emergency response, and when FEMA became part of the newly created DHS in 2003, it lost its direct line to the president.

The bottom-line judgment of FEMA's handling of Katrina was brutally simple: The agency was unprepared, disorganized, and poorly equipped.[1] Local authorities had tried to evacuate New Orleans, but thousands of residents had ignored a mandatory evacuation order and still others had no means by which to leave the city. Nearly 80 percent of the city was flooded, and emergency transportation was unable to reach many of those left stranded.

The earthquake and tsunami that struck Japan in 2011—devastating towns and triggering a crisis at a nuclear power facility—illustrate how even well-prepared nations can suffer devastating losses from natural disasters. Most governments around the world have programs in place to reduce the human costs of natural disasters, but they are not all equally successful.

A recent estimate is that one million people died as a result of natural disasters worldwide between 1991 and 2005.

Some nations are more successful than others in coping with natural disasters. Cuba, for example, instituted widespread disaster planning after a 1963 hurricane killed 1,000 residents. When a category 5 storm (the most severe level, with winds of 155-plus mph) struck the island in 2004, it suffered *no* storm-related fatalities. By investing heavily in meteorological training and facilities, Cuba improved storm prediction and was able to alert residents at least three days in advance of a hurricane landing.

But Cuba takes other actions as well. Civil protection committees, organized down to the level of a city block, put plans into effect; public transportation supports mass evacuations, moving residents to higher ground. Students learn about hurricanes in school, and local authorities oversee emergency practice drills each year. Evacuees are expected to move to shelters or stay with relatives in safe areas; homes must be secured, windows covered, and debris removed from the streets. Public shelters are well stocked and supported by medical experts and social workers. Military deployments reassure evacuated residents that their personal possessions will be safe from looting. So effective are these plans that during Hurricane Ike in 2008, an estimated 2.6 million residents, nearly a quarter of Cuba's total population, evacuated their homes.[2]

What explains Cuba's effective emergency response? Part of the answer lies in the ruling Communist Party's power to coordinate action. It compels individual citizens to evacuate and commandeers the resources needed to accomplish the task. Nor are Cubans expected to fend for themselves by providing their own transportation, food, and medical care. When Katrina hit New Orleans, some segments of the city's population were unable to cope—the poor and needy (particularly those who were elderly and physically handicapped) suffered most. At worst, if citizens are forced to fend for themselves, economic differences will translate into differential capacities to survive.[3]

FEMA enjoys several assets in the United States—high levels of public literacy and a dense communication network that quickly spreads the word of impending danger. But FEMA must coordinate action across federal, state, and local government jurisdictions—governments that enjoy greater autonomy than those in Cuba. Moreover, Americans resent government intrusion in their lives and are confident that they can meet their own needs.

IN THIS CHAPTER we examine the basic features of all bureaucracies and analyze what makes U.S. government bureaucracies distinctive from others. We also review the factors that have shaped the growth of American bureaucracy, the variety of forms bureaucratic organizations take, and just how large government bureaucracy is in the United States. Finally, we review ways to hold government bureaucrats accountable for their actions. As you read this chapter, keep in mind our two core questions:

WHY ARE WE THE WAY WE ARE?
WHY DOES IT MATTER TO YOU?

In particular, how can we make the need for bureaucracy in a complex social and economic world compatible with our definition of democracy?

DEMOCRACY AND BUREAUCRACY IN THE UNITED STATES

Government does more than make laws, adjudicate disputes, and initiate proposals—the core activities of Congress, the courts, and the president. Government must build roads, deliver mail, patrol borders, inspect food, conduct medical research, protect the environment, collect taxes, protect citizens, and distribute Social Security payments. Indeed, "civilized life within a constitutional democracy like that of the United States would be hard to comprehend without the services of a modern administrative state" (or bureaucracy).[4] These tasks and many more fall to **bureaucrats,** a group of government employees who have been harshly criticized over the past three decades and throughout American history. The federal **bureaucracy** is sometimes called the fourth branch of government, although the Constitution only alludes to its existence. From a fledgling structure that was established under the Articles of Confederation, the administrative arm of the national government now sprawls throughout the country and around the world.

Growth of the government and expansion of its activities have been sources of concern for decades, and the terms "bureaucracy" and "bureaucrat" often imply ineffectiveness, red tape, and the unwelcome expansion of official responsibility into areas better left to the private sector. When Ronald Reagan was inaugurated as president in 1981, he identified bureaucracy as a particularly pressing problem in American life. As Reagan discussed the economic ills then facing the nation, he forcefully argued, "Government is not the solution to our problem; government *is* the problem" [emphasis added].[5] Nor was this skepticism about government action exclusively a Republican attitude. Democrat Jimmy Carter campaigned for the presidency in 1976 by railing against Washington and entered office promising to reorganize government and reduce the national budget, which he, like many of his successors, viewed as full of wasteful spending. And President Bill Clinton, addressing a joint session of Congress on January 23, 1996, delivered a similar message:

> We know big government does not have all the answers. We know there's not a program for every problem. We have worked to give the American people a smaller, less bureaucratic government in Washington. And we have to give the American people one that lives within its means . . . The era of big government is over.[6]

Politicians score political points by denouncing big government and chastising bureaucrats. But there is a larger underlying issue: Is democracy compatible with a powerful and influential government bureaucracy? This question arises more often in the United States than in other modern democracies because of our history and culture. Americans are suspicious that government rules and regulations might represent unwarranted intrusions on their personal liberty, and the number of regulations continues to grow, as shown in Figure 14.1. Yet unhappy citizens cannot vote bureaucrats out of office. In contrast, defenders of government action argue that bureaucrats enhance the liberty of Americans by providing necessary services and controlling the effects of otherwise unchecked private power. Protecting citizens from unsafe drugs, food, air, water, and myriad predatory practices makes liberty possible in a complex economic and social system. But the defense of bureaucrats largely falls on deaf ears.

KEY TO understanding

Bureaucrats accomplish many of the important functions of government, but Americans have always been suspicious of bureaucrats. Presidents and other politicians denounce big government, but others argue that bureaucrats make it possible for Americans to enjoy liberty. Is democracy compatible with a powerful and influential government bureaucracy?

bureaucrat
An employee of a government or corporation, often with the negative connotation of being overly concerned with the application of rules.

bureaucracy
Structure created to achieve complex goals through coordinated action undertaken either by governments (public bureaucracy) or corporations (private bureaucracy).

picture YOURSELF ...

AS A TOURIST IN KENYA

You are enjoying your visit to Kenya, a beautiful East African nation that is ethnically diverse and rich in wildlife but still building its modern communications and transportation infrastructure. Kenya is home to the Great Rift Valley, origin of *homo erectus*, and beautiful beaches near Mombasa on the Indian Ocean. Before heading out from the United States, you had to get lots of vaccinations—for yellow fever, typhoid, Hepatitis A, diphtheria—because health services in Kenya are primitive and diseases run rampant. Taking antimalarial medication during the visit is essential.

You were also warned before you arrived of the high crime rates, with offenses ranging from pickpocketing and "snatch-and-run" street crimes to carjacking, home invasions, and banditry on the highways. You've been careful so far to always travel with a group of friends, and you're surprised at how many police checkpoints you've had to pass through.

You notice many other differences from life at home. For instance, you constantly have to remind yourself not to drink water from the tap, something you have always taken for granted. (Luckily, there are lots of breweries, and beer is readily available.) Making international calls to family and friends back home is frustrating. In most areas of the country you can't use an international calling card or even reach 800 numbers. When you are able to find a way to get through, the long-distance rates are outrageously high. At the other extreme, Internet cafes in Nairobi, the nation's capital, now provide ready access to such things as exquisitely detailed maps that help guide your travels.

Because English is the official language in Kenya, making travel arrangements is easy to do, but actually traveling around the country is difficult. The passenger trains only run a few days a week and are often delayed by derailments. Each car trip is an adventure. In fact, the staff at the American embassy warned you that one American dies in a road-related incident each week in Kenya. The roads are in poor shape, frequently blocked by goats or people, and the local drivers have never finished a driver's education course. For example, when confronted by a traffic jam, Kenyan drivers routinely cross the median and force oncoming traffic to make way for them. Driving conditions are even worse during the rainy seasons, which occur in November and again from late March into May.

Only after you've been in Kenya for a while do you realize how many of the services provided by government agencies back in the States are either unavailable or practically missing. This realization is illuminating to you, making it clear how essential these services are to a smoothly functioning community.*

---

* Country Brief Assessment (Sample) prepared by FAM International Logistics, Inc. July 10, 2008, http://www.faminternational.com/pdf/sample_country_2008.pdf. Also see the travel advice provided by the U.S. Department of State at http://travel.state.gov/travel/cis_pa_tw/cis/cis_1151.html#country.

questions to consider

1. **What are the services you consider "essential"? Which of these are offered by government and which by the private sector? Of those offered privately, which are subject to government regulation?**

2. **Think of places you have traveled, both inside and outside the United States. What significant differences did you notice in conveniences, services, and safety?**

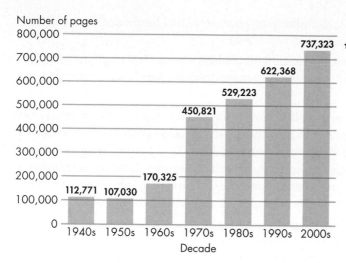

Number of pages

```
800,000 ┐
700,000 ┤                                              737,323
600,000 ┤                                      622,368
500,000 ┤                              529,223
400,000 ┤                      450,821
300,000 ┤
200,000 ┤              170,325
100,000 ┤ 112,771 107,030
      0 ┘
         1940s 1950s 1960s 1970s 1980s 1990s 2000s
                         Decade
```

FIGURE 14.1

★ NEW FEDERAL REGISTER PAGES PER DECADE

Conservative thinkers point to the increase in the number of pages in the *Federal Register*, a book listing government regulations, as an indication of the growth of federal regulations over time. What purposes do these regulations serve? Do they impinge on American democracy?

Source: Office of Federal Register.

As one observer concludes, "The battle between bureaucracy and democracy is written into our history. So is the fact that democracy must win. All we have left to debate is the cost."[7]

FEATURES OF A MODERN BUREAUCRACY

What do we mean by the term *bureaucracy*? What are the key elements that help us to recognize one when we see it? Is a bureaucracy hopelessly inefficient, as much of the public believes? In the next section we look at the classic model of bureaucracy developed by sociologist Max Weber and see how his ideas have shaped our thinking about public bureaucracies.

KEY TO understanding ★

Public officials operate within a distinctive context of cultural values and political relationships. This context is bureaucratic in nature. What is distinctive about the U.S. bureaucracy? To answer this question, we explore sociologist Max Weber's five-part model, which serves as the foundation of modern bureaucracies.

WEBER'S MODEL OF BUREAUCRACY

Many of our modern ideas about bureaucracies originate with the work of Max Weber, a German sociologist who wrote about the historical evolution of administrative systems at the turn of the twentieth century. Weber's bureaucracy accentuated certain features based on characteristics that were displayed by organizations in modern society but would be unlikely to be found in reality—that is, an "ideal type." Five basic qualities characterize Weber's model:

- *Hierarchy of authority.* The structure is usually represented as a pyramid, with an ultimate goal-setter at the apex and those higher up in the structure supervising those below.
- *System of rules.* Rules are typically extensive and used to guide decisions by organization members; ensures that all citizens are treated impartially.
- *Division and specialization of labor.* This feature ensures that those with specific expertise will be responsible for the associated segment of an organization's work.

- *Written records.* Extensive recordkeeping guarantees that future decisions will be consistent with past practices and precedents.
- *Careers are based on merit.* Organization members obtain their positions and are promoted to higher positions based on personal ability rather than on political or family connections.

These key features can be found in both government and private-sector bureaucracies. In political systems, they are central to the ability to accomplish complex collective tasks, ranging from creating irrigation systems in ancient Egypt to providing for national defense in a nuclear age. Weber regarded the five characteristics as *functional features* of bureaucracy—that is, components that contribute to a positive result. Hierarchy creates obedience to direction from above, just as specialization allows the most knowledgeable employees to complete a task, and so on.

Weber and others also identified *dysfunctional features* of bureaucracies—that is, components that might inhibit positive results:

- *Understanding fades up the ladder.* Those at the top of the hierarchy know less about a problem than those who are closer to it, yet those higher up in the organization issue orders.
- *Bureaucrats make decisions based on rules.* People are treated as categories; impartial decisions ignore the unique problems of individuals and make them feel depersonalized.
- *Specialization can blur the big picture.* Those lower in the hierarchy may be more committed to their immediate goals—obtaining the budget and materials required to complete their daily tasks—than to fulfilling the larger mission of the bureaucracy.
- *Written records delay responses to new developments.* This is especially true if the bureaucracy makes decisions based solely on precedents found in written records.
- *Career officials may value future benefits over current productivity.* Individuals may be more interested in putting in their time until they reach retirement age than in doing the work expected of them.

In short, there are plenty of reasons to criticize bureaucracies as well as to appreciate the complex tasks they can accomplish. Inherently, bureaucracy is neither good nor bad, and while the term *bureaucrat* is often used in a derogatory way, the career employees working for the government fill many different types of jobs (see Figure 14.2), all performing assignments that are designed to benefit citizens.

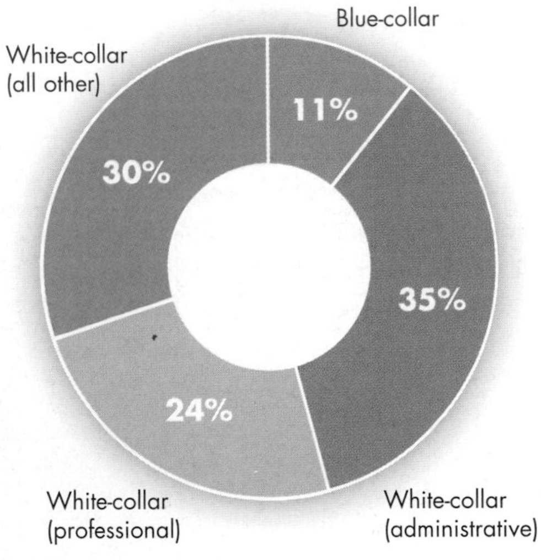

DISTINCTIVE FEATURES OF U.S. BUREAUCRACY

Weber's concept of bureaucracy was intended to help scholars understand bureaucracies around the world and suggested that basic principles of modern organization transcend cultural differences; subsequent scholarship has both explored Weber's model and revealed how one nation's bureaucracies vary from another's. Several factors may have contributed to a distinctly American style of public bureaucracy, namely:

- a cultural distrust of government power
- lack of constitutional standing

Blue-collar — 11%

White-collar (all other) — 30%

White-collar (administrative) — 35%

White-collar (professional) — 24%

FIGURE 14.2

★ OCCUPATIONAL CATEGORIES OF GOVERNMENT WORKERS

The U.S. bureaucracy classifies each job according to blue- and white-collar categories. What kinds of jobs do you suppose are included in white collar?

Source: Office of Personnel Management, Federal Civilian Workforce Statistics, The Fact Book, 2007 Edition

- uncertain guidance
- neutral agents forced to be political
- pragmatic structure

A Cultural Distrust of Government Power

Influential political scientist Harold Laski observed six decades ago that "most Americans . . . tend to feel that what is done by a government institution is bound to be less well done than if it were undertaken by individuals, whether alone or in the form of private corporations."[8] Today, the situation is much the same. With the exception of protecting national security, Americans are skeptical of programs operated by government officials. They frequently use "bureaucratic" as a synonym for slow and inefficient action. Individuals deeply believe that making separate decisions in a marketplace likely improves efficiency and that government wastes money. Figure 14.3 shows that public skepticism toward government is growing. By 2009 Americans believed that half of every tax dollar going to Washington, D.C., was wasted. Most European nations, on the other hand, have long histories of powerful central government structures (bureaucracies) that were essential to their emergence as nation-states. In some nations—France, for example—government administrators have a strong identity separate from politicians. In those nations, citizens are more likely than Americans to respect and support actions taken by government administrators. However, as trust in national governments declines throughout Europe, the distinctive role of administrators may erode.[9]

Lack of Constitutional Standing

Although largely falling within the executive branch, the federal bureaucracy is looked upon as an instrument that accomplishes the legislature's will and has no independent position in the system of checks and balances.[10] In truth, only Congress can create government agencies and departments. So bureaucrats must pay attention to the guidance provided by both elective branches of government.

Uncertain Guidance

If bureaucrats are to accomplish the people's will as expressed by the legislature, but also be subject (in most cases) to direction by the executive, how do they know what to do when Congress and presidents disagree? Because the legislature is internally divided and the president separately elected, *it is often difficult* to determine the people's will. As political scientist Norton Long posed in his classic question, "In case of conflict between any or all of these, who should be supreme as the authentic representative of what the people want?"[11] No such problem afflicts parliamentary systems around the world where legislative and executive powers are merged.

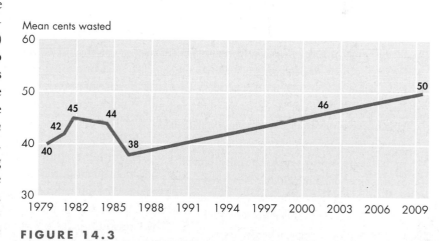

FIGURE 14.3

★ PUBLIC PERCEPTION OF BUREAUCRATIC WASTE

How has the perception of government waste changed over time?

Source: Lydia Saad, "Americans: Uncle Sam Wastes 50 Cents on the Dollar," Gallup website, September 15, 2009, http://www.gallup.com/poll/122951/americans-uncle-sam-wastes-50-cents-dollar.aspx

Neutral Agents Forced to Be "Political"

Bureaucrats require political guidance and support in order to perform their public tasks. When they receive uncertain or conflicting guidance from above, they are forced to generate the political support they need on their own, turning to interest groups and beneficiaries in the public to lobby on behalf of larger budgets for their programs and expanded missions. As Norton Long observed in the mid-twentieth century, "They must supplement the resources available through the hierarchy with those they can muster on their own, or accept the consequences in frustration."[12] Bureaucrats in most other nations need not engage in such openly political efforts to secure the support they need. In parliamentary systems such as India or England, legislative and executive authorities are almost always in agreement and bureaucrats do not need to find their own support.

Pragmatic Structure

Rather than adopting a single set of organizational structures, the United States has willingly experimented with many different ones for public bureaucracies, crafting structures to suit particular circumstances in hopes of making them work. This has resulted in the dizzying array of arrangements discussed below.

These features of American culture and government structure make the U.S. federal bureaucracy distinct from bureaucracies in other nations. Although career government officials operate in many of the same ways that officials in other countries do, the context differs and so do the challenges and constraints they face. In most respects, these factors—a distrustful public, a divided government, and the need to assemble their own supportive coalition in a highly fragmented political environment—make the lives of federal bureaucrats more difficult. Although bureaucrats are often portrayed as too powerful, most of these factors actually weaken the power they could potentially exercise.

THE CHECKERED HISTORY OF BUREAUCRACY IN THE UNITED STATES

KEY to understanding

★ Distrust of the agents of a powerful central government—the bureaucracy—is deeply ingrained in American political culture, dating back to the Revolutionary War. During the nineteenth century, the U.S. federal bureaucracy grew from a small group with limited powers into a powerful force responding to the problems created by rapid population growth, industrialization, and urbanization. International crises stimulated further government growth during the twentieth century. With increased power came a major issue: How much power are Americans willing to cede to experts working in government bureaucracies?

It should come as no surprise that a nation born with a strong sense of outrage at King George III's excessive exercise of power would distrust centralized government and the bureaucrats needed to implement its laws. The king's tax collectors and his army were the instruments of England's tyranny in the eighteenth century, violating basic rights itemized in the Declaration of Independence.[13] The colonists resisted creating a new central authority and distrusted its agents. During the Revolutionary War and immediately after independence, government was treated as a responsibility of the states.

The Constitutional Convention arose because the loose confederation of states, lacking an independent source of revenue and without authority over its citizens, was unable to provide for defense, maintain domestic order, or build a thriving economy. Faced with these same problems, European monarchs in the sixteenth and seventeenth centuries modernized their nations by establishing centralized administrations in France, England, Sweden, Russia, Prussia, Spain, and Portugal. In the case of the United States, constitutional reformers faced the challenge of convincing state leaders that an effective national government, complete with a permanent bureaucracy, would not endanger citizens' hard-won liberty. Under the Articles of Confederation, Congress created three departments of government staffed by permanent officials: Foreign Affairs, Treasury, and War. Benjamin Franklin also organized a postal system.[14]

HAMILTON VERSUS JEFFERSON

With the launch of the new government in 1789, George Washington and John Adams had to create new administrative structures. The Constitution was silent on what this new national bureaucracy would look like, leaving these critical decisions to the first cohort of national leaders.[15] Alexander Hamilton, the first Secretary of the Treasury (pictured on the $10 bill), became the driving force in creating the new agencies of government, providing answers that often provoked contrary responses from Thomas Jefferson, the first Secretary of State. Treasury and State were two of four original government departments that also included War and the Attorney General, the latter a lone legal adviser rather than the head of a large department.

During the Constitutional Convention, Hamilton forcefully advocated for a strong, energetic central government. In the early years of the new republic, his ideas led to an effective central administration based on a sound financial foundation—predictable sources of revenue (tariffs on imports and excise taxes on whiskey), guaranteed repayment of public debts, a central bank, and a plan to help fledgling industries. Hamilton also made important contributions in foreign affairs, helped organize the military, and developed early policies to guide a cadre of civil servants. In short, Hamilton sought to plan and direct the nation's emergence as a world power and endorsed a number of European administrative practices that he believed would further that goal.

Jefferson, in contrast, preferred to rely on the state governments, concerned that a strong central administration would pose a danger to liberty; he also distrusted the powers of both elected and appointed officials. Each leader was partly successful; Jefferson's vision of a weak central government with constrained powers and a small number of permanent officials prevailed throughout most of the nineteenth century, and Hamilton's vision of an active, directive central government came to fruition at the turn of the twentieth century, when the emergence of an interdependent, industrialized society triggered significant growth in the powers and reach of the U.S. government.[16]

Jefferson's vision of government prevailed during most of the nineteenth century. Most programs that touched citizens remained under the auspices of the states. In addition to defense, the national government expanded its territory and promoted economic development through internal improvements—roads, canals, railroads, river and harbor projects, and lighthouses.[17] In most communities, the clearest evidence of the federal government's presence were "land offices, post offices and customhouses," providers of key services to an ever-growing population driven by the desire to make money.[18]

Why did the federal bureaucracy in the United States develop more slowly than it did elsewhere? Beyond the culturally ingrained distrust of centralized power, most observers point to a *different sequence of political development* that unfolded in the United States. In the European nations, a powerful, central administration emerged prior to the establishment of institutions of democracy—elections, political parties, and widespread voting. In the United States, democracy came first and the demand for concentrated national power arose later, especially during the late nineteenth century when millions of Americans moved from the farm to the cities as industrialization spread. This change in the character of American life created new social and economic pressures at the same time that the United States was emerging as a major world power in the Spanish-American War and World War I. In order to deal with these dramatic changes, the nation needed to provide the federal government with expanded powers and the administrative structures to exercise them.[19]

NINETEENTH-CENTURY CHANGES

Although the Constitution called for separated powers and vested executive power in the hands of the president, it was Congress that stood at the center of national government for most of the nineteenth century. Heavily influenced by the powerful, locally based political parties that developed in the 1830s, members of Congress enthusiastically supported patronage—the promise of government jobs and contracts that would come with a presidential victory, and one of the most powerful incentives available to the parties to win voters' support.

spoils system
Practice popular in the nineteenth century that allowed presidents to appoint party loyalists and campaign workers to government jobs as a reward for their support, establishing the adage of "to the victor belongs the spoils."

rotation in office
Principle established by Andrew Jackson that allowed the president to replace persons holding government jobs with loyal supporters.

Andrew Jackson is credited with initiating the **spoils system,** the practice of appointing political supporters to government positions. After his victory in 1828, he established the practice of **rotation in office,** replacing incumbent jobholders in the federal government with new appointees who supported the winner in the election. If all citizens were equally capable of doing the job, of course, it made little difference precisely who held such positions.

Political scientist Matthew Crenson suggests that Jackson's rotation in office determined one requirement for a modern bureaucracy: People in the organization's structure are interchangeable rather than irreplaceable. Jackson's administration also introduced several modern procedures for exercising control over the bureaucracy, including routine audits of spending, reorganizing government structures, explicitly stating an agency's mission, and specializing the jobs performed by employees.[20] These changes made the U.S. government more fully resemble the model of bureaucracy that Weber had in mind.

THE CREATION OF THE U. S. CIVIL SERVICE

By the late nineteenth century government reformers believed that only the most meritorious citizens should be chosen for government jobs, not simply those loyal to the party. Several nations—the United States among them—began to staff government agencies with better qualified professionals. Great Britain introduced competitive written examinations as a way to select government workers in 1870; those earning higher grades got the jobs. Canada adopted a similar system in 1882. Japan began using exams to determine promotions in 1887, and Prussia created a career system for its bureaucrats in 1873.[21] Other keys to the new systems included political neutrality and career security—that is, government workers could not be fired simply for disagreeing with the elected officials of the moment. Establishing a civil service system in the United States was part of an international trend.

In the United States, reform arrived following a presidential assassination, but efforts started with President Ulysses S. Grant (1868–1876) and President Rutherford B. Hayes (1877–1881). Then along came James A. Garfield (1881) who served as president for only 200 days. Shot in July 1881 by Charles J. Guiteau, a man usually described as a "disappointed office seeker" (actually an emotionally unstable campaign supporter of Garfield who was demanding a job), Garfield lingered until September. After Garfield's dramatic shooting and slow death, groups supporting civil service reform sprang up across the nation and coalesced into the National Civil Service Reform League, and journalists and political cartoonists in *Harper's Weekly* and *Puck*, two influential publications of the era, made the assassination into a *cause célèbre*, encouraging the nation to adopt reforms as a way to honor the fallen president. After two years of struggle, Congress adopted the **Pendleton Civil Service Reform Act** in January 1883. This bill mandated that only the best-qualified, not the best-connected,

Pendleton Civil Service Reform Act
Legislation approved in 1883 that created the U.S. civil service system, in which government employees are chosen based on expertise and experience rather than party loyalty.

★ A political cartoon published on the cover of *Puck* from July 13, 1881, depicts Guiteau seeking a federal job.

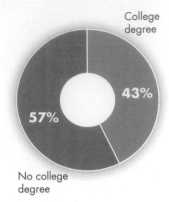

College degree

43%

57%

No college degree

FIGURE 14.4

★ FEDERAL CIVILIAN EMPLOYEES WITH COLLEGE DEGREES

Why is it significant that a large percentage of civilian federal workers have completed college?

Source: Office of Personnel Management, Federal Civilian Workforce Statistics, The Fact Book, 2007 Edition

General Schedule of Classified Positions

Matrix of responsibility and experience that specifies the pay that federal civil service employees should receive—for example, a GS-10.

individuals would be selected for government jobs. All citizens would have an equal chance of competing for a government position, and the prestige of public jobs would grow.

The Senate (38–5 and 33 not voting) and the House (155–47 and 85 not voting) reluctantly passed the civil service reform legislation. The high level of abstentions reflected that the law would weaken legislators' ability to reward campaign supporters. Even after the passage of the Act in 1883, however, most federal jobs were still filled through the spoils system until shortly before World War I.

A provision in the Pendleton Civil Service Reform Act allowed future presidents to fold increasing numbers of positions into the system to expand its coverage. From reform came a system that coordinated the way that government recruits, selects, trains, deploys, compensates, and retains employees. Although far from perfect, the new system was widely regarded as a marked improvement over the earlier patronage system, and most members of the civil service bring strong qualifications to the positions, including education (see Figure 14.4).

State, county, and municipal governments adopted central features of the federal system as well. Shifting government jobs from "who you know" (patronage) to "what you know" (competence) is a broadly embraced principle of good government, as is protecting government employees from undue partisan pressure. Extensive systems of rules and regulations grew up around testing, hiring, firing, transferring, assigning overtime, and so forth, all in the effort to guarantee observance of these principles and protections. The pay system is one example.

To help enforce the goal of "equal pay for equal work," a basic principle of a modern civil service system, the Civil Service Commission and Congress created the **General Schedule of Classified Positions,** which assigned every classified position in the federal government a pay level determined by its tasks and responsibilities. From this emerged a pay schedule in 1949 based on characteristics of the job and an employee's "step" or experience in the position (see Table 14.1). Today, salaries can range from $17,803 (Grade 1, Step 1) to $129,517 (Grade 15, Step 10). Persons in the civil service's most senior pay grades, GS 16–18 (not in the chart), constitute a group known as the Senior Executive Service (SES), created in 1978 as part of a number of other significant reforms intended to enforce the merit system's basic principles. In 2011 SES salaries ranged from $119,554 to $179,700. In addition to the grades in this pay schedule, there are "super" pay grades—Executive Levels I–V—that cover political appointees in the top administrative posts. These salaries range from $145,700 to $199,700.

The complex General Schedule represents incentives for the workforce. Workers earn more by increasing their grade (moving down the grid through promotion or transfer) or remaining in a job over time (moving to the right in the grid). Raises come regardless of performance. Although built on the principle of equal pay for equal work, some pay differences exist across ethnic groups, as shown in Figure 14.5. This structure remained in place for nearly half a century with raises approved by Congress, but it came under heavy attack during the George W. Bush administration as excessively inflexible. Proposed changes were beaten back by federal workers' unions. (See the discussion of personnel on p. 513.)

There are alternative pay systems. Members of the SES, a cadre of high-level career bureaucrats just below the political appointees and found in department and agency leadership positions, are eligible for merit-pay bonuses and can be reassigned to new jobs more easily than the typical government employee. To have such an elite group of

TABLE 14.1
2011 general schedule annual rates by grade and step

For many federal employees, this schedule shapes decisions about how long to stay at a job, where to transfer, or whether to change jobs at all. It also shows what level of compensation one might expect in the future.

GRADE	STEP 1	STEP 2	STEP 3	STEP 4	STEP 5	STEP 6	STEP 7	STEP 8	STEP 9	STEP 10
1	17803	18398	18990	19579	20171	20519	21104	21694	21717	22269
2	20017	20493	21155	21717	21961	22607	23253	23899	24545	25191
3	21840	22568	23296	24024	24752	25480	26208	26936	27664	28392
4	24518	25335	26152	26969	27786	28603	29420	30237	31054	31871
5	27431	28345	29259	30173	31087	32001	32915	33829	34743	35657
6	30577	31596	32615	33634	34653	35672	36691	37710	38729	39748
7	33979	35112	36245	37378	38511	39644	40777	41910	43043	44176
8	37631	38885	40139	41393	42647	43901	45155	46409	47663	48917
9	41563	42948	44333	45718	47103	48488	49873	51258	52643	54028
10	45771	47297	48823	50349	51875	53401	54927	56453	57979	59505
11	50287	51963	53639	55315	56991	58667	60343	62019	63695	65371
12	60274	62283	64292	66301	68310	70319	72328	74337	76346	78355
13	71674	74063	76452	78841	81230	83619	86008	88397	90786	93175
14	84697	87520	90343	93166	95989	98812	101635	104458	107281	110104
15	99628	102949	106270	109591	112912	116233	119554	122875	126196	129517

Source: Office of Personnel Management, http://www.opm.gov/oca/11tables/indexGS.asp

administrators working in the space between political officials and permanent bureaucrats is relatively common. As shown in Figure 14.6, 21 of the 30 nations in the Organization for Economic Cooperation and Development (OECD) maintain such an intermediary group (Australia, Belgium, Canada, Czech Republic, Finland, France, Great Britain, Hungary, Iceland, Italy, Japan, Luxembourg, Netherlands, New Zealand, Norway, Poland, Portugal, Slovak Republic, South Korea, Turkey, United States) while only nine do not (Austria, Denmark, Germany, Ireland, Mexico, Spain, Sweden, Switzerland, Turkey).

FIGURE 14.5

★ AVERAGE SALARY BY WHITE-COLLAR OCCUPATIONAL CATEGORY

Salaries are determined not only by type of profession, but also by education and years on the job. What factors might account for the disparities between ethnic groups shown in the figure?

Source: Office of Personnel Management, Federal Civilian Workforce Statistics, The Fact Book, 2007 Edition, http://www.opm.gov/feddata/factbook/2007/2007FACTBOOK.pdf.

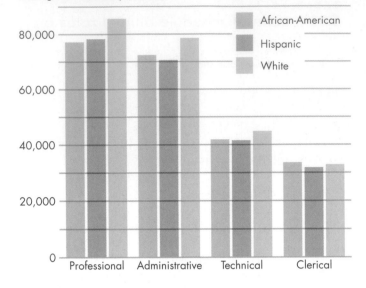

Average annual salary (dollars)

- African-American
- Hispanic
- White

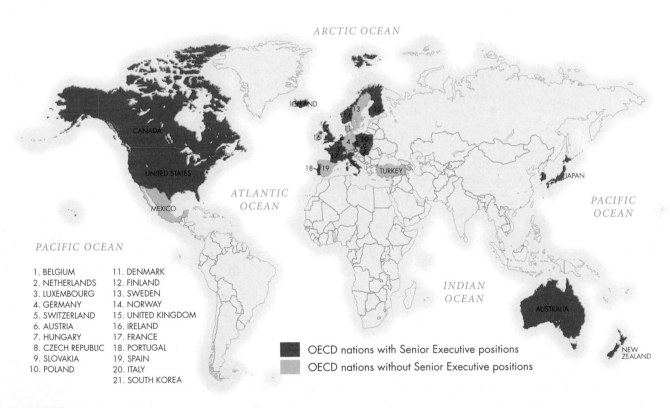

PACIFIC OCEAN

1. BELGIUM
2. NETHERLANDS
3. LUXEMBOURG
4. GERMANY
5. SWITZERLAND
6. AUSTRIA
7. HUNGARY
8. CZECH REPUBLIC
9. SLOVAKIA
10. POLAND
11. DENMARK
12. FINLAND
13. SWEDEN
14. NORWAY
15. UNITED KINGDOM
16. IRELAND
17. FRANCE
18. PORTUGAL
19. SPAIN
20. ITALY
21. SOUTH KOREA

■ OECD nations with Senior Executive positions
■ OECD nations without Senior Executive positions

FIGURE 14.6

★ MAP OF OECD NATIONS WITH AND WITHOUT SENIOR EXECUTIVE POSITIONS

THE STRUCTURE OF THE FEDERAL BUREAUCRACY

People often think of the federal bureaucracy as a single structure with the president at the top of a pyramid issuing orders that subordinates must obey. In reality, it is a collection of separate bureaucracies, each one exhibiting some of the features that Weber described, but each also developing a distinctive culture and set of rules that guide its behavior. Some are under tight presidential control, but others have considerable autonomy, either wholly or in part. Some are larger and some are smaller, and they assume different forms. In this section, we discuss several of the organizational forms that make up the federal bureaucracy, and we note whether they are primarily managed by the president, by Congress, or are independent.[22] Collectively they are called the federal bureaucracy, and most organizations lie within the executive branch, but the president is decidedly not a single controlling figure as one would find in Weber's ideal type.

KEY TO understanding ★

Americans approach bureaucratic structure pragmatically—adopt whatever it takes to get the job done. Creating a department signals a major commitment to a public purpose (for example, Defense) or recognizes the needs of a segment of the public that wants important services from government (for example, Commerce for business and Labor for unions). Independent agencies lie outside departments, and some of these "independent" regulatory agencies that oversee important parts of the economy even lie outside the clear control of either the president or Congress. Is it good to have so many variations, even hybrid structures that combine features of private- and public-sector organizations?

DEPARTMENTS

The most significant building blocks of the federal bureaucracy are the executive departments, often referred to as the cabinet departments because their heads—secretaries—are members of the president's cabinet; these members form a line of succession in the event that the president, vice president, Speaker of the House, and Senate *president pro tempore* are unable to assume the tasks of president.[23] There are currently 15 cabinet-level departments, with the newest one, the Department of Homeland Security, created in 2002 (see the timeline in Figure 14.7).

Creating a new executive department is a big deal. Through this action, Congress and the president signal that the department's programs and policies reflect a major national commitment. This was true for transportation, urban planning, energy, and homeland security, for example, at the time those departments were created. Alternatively, the creation of a department signals that a segment of the population served by the programs is important—farmers, business, organized labor, veterans, or educators, for example, lobbied actively for creation of the departments that address their interests. In some instances, the president and Congress create a department to better

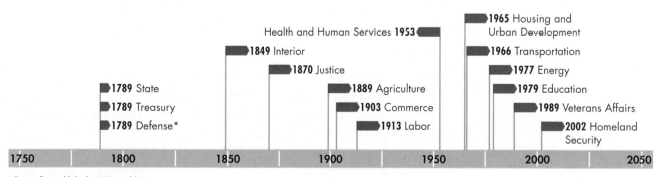

*Originally established as War and Navy.

FIGURE 14.7

★ CABINET DEPARTMENTS OF THE U.S. GOVERNMENT

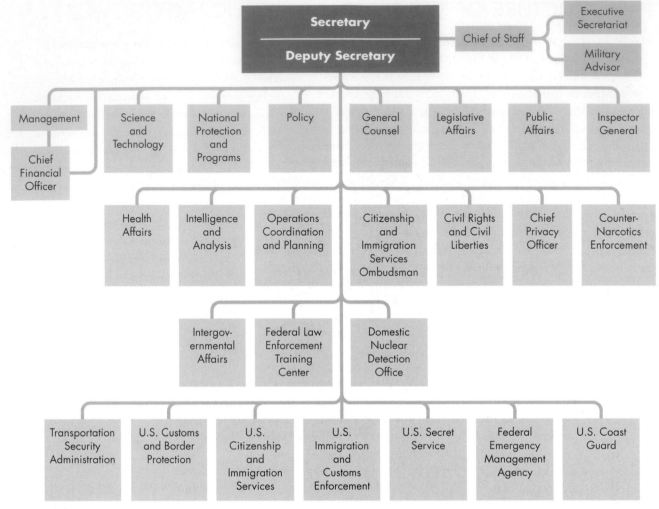

FIGURE 14.8

★ CURRENT STRUCTURE
OF THE DEPARTMENT
OF HOMELAND
SECURITY

address a set of public problems, often by consolidating related agencies under one roof. Consolidation was the principal reason for the creation of the Department of Defense in 1947, when the departments of War and Navy were combined into a single entity. Similarly, President Eisenhower encouraged creating the Department of Health, Education, and Welfare in 1954, later renamed Health and Human Services.[24]

Creating new departments is not easy, as the establishment of the Department of Homeland Security demonstrates. When it was created by Congress in 2002, it was given three primary missions:

• Prevent terrorist attacks within the United States.

• Reduce the vulnerability of the United States to terrorism.

• Minimize the damage caused by, and assist in the recovery from, terrorist attacks that occur within the United States.[25]

To accomplish these goals, however, Congress needed to relocate 22 offices and agencies from other departments throughout the federal government and house them within a single, organized entity; such a structure would allow the DHS to better coordinate their activities.[26] Figure 14.8 illustrates how the new structure houses some of these transferred agencies.

This government-wide reshuffling of responsibilities triggered turf wars within both the bureaucracy and Congress. (Also see the discussion in Chapter 12.) Departments did not want to lose units to the new DHS, and members of congressional committees with longstanding ties to these units wanted them to remain unchanged. The final grouping reflected many compromises and a number of mistakes that required later attention.

INDEPENDENT AGENCIES

In the twentieth century, Congress vastly expanded the number of federal agencies, many of which are not housed inside one of the principal executive departments. Each agency has a specific mission and often exercises authority delegated from Congress to make and enforce regulations. No single, comprehensive list of these independent agencies exists, but the White House website maintains a partial catalog,[27] Most independent agencies are part of the executive branch; familiar examples include the Central Intelligence Agency (CIA), the Environmental Protection Agency (EPA), and the National Aeronautics and Space Administration (NASA). A few agencies are part of the legislative branch, including the **Government Accountability Office (GAO),** the Library of Congress, and the Government Printing Office. Each agency has a list of responsibilities to fulfill; each operates under a separate budget; and each must have leaders to establish a set of relationships with the political masters it serves.

INDEPENDENT REGULATORY COMMISSIONS

A special group of agencies, the so-called **independent regulatory commissions,** have an ambiguous status that makes them part of neither the executive nor the legislative branch. Congress created the Civil Service Commission (1883) and the **Interstate Commerce Commission** (1887) as agencies that would be independent of the president's direct control. The goal was for these agencies to develop and enforce a set of regulations outside normal political channels. As noted earlier, government reformers were convinced that creating a professional civil service in place of patronage appointments would improve government performance and eliminate the corruption rampant in awarding government contracts. This new system was overseen by the Civil Service Commission. The ICC oversaw freight rates charged by railroads.

The **Office of Personnel Management (OPM)** replaced the Civil Service Commission in 1978 and Congress abolished the ICC in 1995 when policy thinking shifted toward deregulating most transportation industries.

Numerous independent regulatory commissions arose in the twentieth century to oversee a segment of the economy or an area of public policy. A group of experts, appointed by the president and subject to Senate confirmation, exercise what are commonly called "quasi-legislative" and "quasi-judicial" powers delegated to them by Congress. In essence, the commissions can develop and enforce regulations directly affecting businesses or individuals under its jurisdiction. Some of the commissions that are still operating are listed in Table 14.2.

The commissions are described as "independent" because they are not part of an executive department, and presidents can only remove commission members from office for specific reasons. They typically range in size from 3 to 11 members and are required to include members from both political parties who serve overlapping terms

Government Accountability Office (GAO)
New name (2004) for the original GAO that reflects the agency's broader role in evaluating whether government programs perform in ways consistent with national needs, not just in the expenditure of funds.

independent regulatory commissions
Type of federal government agency designed to allow experts, not politicians, to oversee and regulate a sector of the economy (for example, railroads) usually to protect consumers from unfair business practices but also to protect the businesses in that sector.

Interstate Commerce Commission
First federal regulatory agency, created in 1887 and abolished in 1995, which was intended to regulate rates charged by railroads and whose responsibilities were later expanded to include oversight of the trucking industry.

Office of Personnel Management
Agency created in 1978 as part of the Civil Service Reform Act to manage the civil service for presidents.

★ Astronaut Stephanie Wilson floats freely in Space Shuttle Discovery. NASA was created in 1958 to research flight within and outside Earth's atmosphere. Since that time, NASA has fueled technological advances and a greater understanding of Earth and the universe.

of office. Over time, presidents gained the power to appoint commission chairpersons, thereby giving them more influence over commission work but not full control. Most academic studies suggest that Congress and the interest groups directly affected by a commission's decisions influence commission members.[28]

For many years, students of comparative politics believed that this heavy reliance on regulatory agencies was a uniquely American approach to exercising government control over economic markets. However, other parts of the world have adopted the same strategy for regulating electricity, financial markets, and telecommunications; this is particularly true in Europe as nations increasingly adopt more market-driven policies.[29]

Ironically, just as other nations began to emulate the U.S. approach to regulating parts of the economy, Washington changed its approach. Deregulation reigned supreme in the 1970s and 1980s—an approach that relies on market forces rather than government regulators to set prices and the conditions of competition. Congress eliminated several regulatory commissions and encouraged competition to influence the price of airline, rail, bus, and truck services.

An especially dramatic example of deregulation involved the airline industry; the 1978 Airline Deregulation Act reduced the power of the Civil Aeronautics Board (CAB) to determine how many airlines served which cities at what prices, powers it had wielded since 1938 when Congress created it to guide development of the airline industry. The CAB was abolished altogether in 1985. Travelers immediately benefited from lower air fares driven by aggressive price competition launched by newly formed, low-cost airlines (like Southwest Airlines), who also added more flights to the most popular destinations. Before deregulation the United States had 36 airlines, but that number grew to 123 by 1984. This proliferation triggered intense competition and forced established companies to go out of business or merge. It also dramatically reduced service to out-of-the-way destinations, reduced the number of nonstop flights, and adversely affected passenger services including baggage charges and food service. Some regulation of airlines remained in place. The Federal Aviation Administration located in the Department of Transportation continues to oversee the safety of aircraft, the professional training of pilots, and the air traffic control system.[30]

GOVERNMENT CORPORATIONS

The British and Dutch governments were the first to establish organizations that mixed public and private resources. The British East India Company, the Plymouth Company, and the Hudson Bay Company were seventeenth-century "corporations" that played roles in establishing colonies in the new world. By the end of the twentieth century,

TABLE 14.2

common independent regulatory commissions

COMMISSION	YEAR ESTABLISHED	ROLE
Federal Reserve Board of Governors	1913	The principal government body regulating banks in the United States, it seeks to fight inflation as a means to maintain economic growth by setting interest rates; serves as the equivalent of a United States central bank.
Federal Trade Commission (FTC)	1914	Protects consumers from business practices that suppress competition and enforces antitrust laws, including reviewing proposed mergers between businesses
Federal Communications Commission (FCC)	1934	Regulates interstate and international communications by radio, television, wire, satellite, and cable
Securities and Exchange Commission	1934	Regulates the stock markets and protects investors from unfair corporate practices
National Labor Relations Board (NLRB)	1935	Protects workers' right to organize, oversees union elections, can intervene in unfair labor practices
Commodity Futures Trading Commission	1974	Originally created to protect against fraud and manipulation in the agricultural commodities and futures markets; it now shares responsibility with the SEC to police increasingly complex investment products
Nuclear Regulatory Commission	1974	Succeeded the Atomic Energy Commission in overseeing the civilian nuclear energy industry in the United States, including safety, non-power use of nuclear materials and managing nuclear waste

there was somewhere between 25 and 50 U.S. federal **government corporations** (depending on how these are defined). Congress created them "to perform a public purpose, provide a market-oriented service and produce revenues to meet or approximate its expenditures."[31] The United States Postal Service, the Federal Deposit Insurance Corporation (FDIC), and AMTRAK (the National Railroad Passenger Corporation) are among the better-known government corporations. Government corporations provide an advantage: They afford greater administrative flexibility because they are not subject to many of the federal regulations that apply to government agencies. For example, the customary budgetary process used in the federal system requires agencies to observe a host of federal guidelines since they are fully funded by taxpayers.

Most government corporations have boards of directors that guide their operations. For example, a majority of AMTRAK's 15-person board is appointed by the president but subject to Senate confirmation, and the remainder represents shareholders of preferred stock (all owned by the federal government) and common stock (owned by participating freight railroads). Its mission is to salvage intercity passenger rail service, particularly between Washington and Boston (see Figure 14.9), which was quickly disappearing in the 1970s. Although there are expectations that such entities will become self-sustaining and phase out their government subsidies, that hope has frequently fallen short, as in the case of AMTRAK, triggering recurrent political crises about the government continuing to subsidize their budgets.[32]

government corporations
Business enterprises wholly or partly owned by the government that Congress created to perform a public purpose or provide a market-oriented service but are designed to meet their costs by generating revenues through operations.

FIGURE 14.9

★ AMTRAK PASSENGER SERVICE IN THE NORTHEASTERN UNITED STATES

Amtrak routes connect the major cities of the northeast corridor. Why might the federal government continue to subsidize this corporation despite its financial losses?

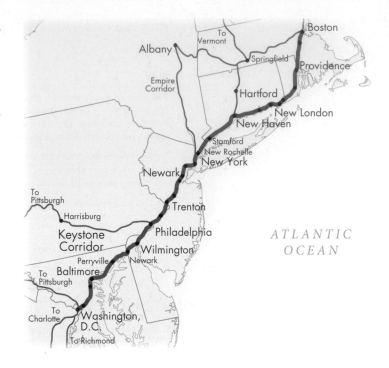

HYBRID ORGANIZATIONS

quasi-governmental organizations (quagos)

Hybrid organizations that share some characteristics of public agencies and some features of private corporations, like the Smithsonian Institution.

Quasi-governmental organizations ("quagos") are sometimes described as hybrid organizations because they share some of the attributes of public- and private-sector bureaucracies.[33] Consider the Smithsonian Institution, for example, whose museums you almost certainly have visited if you have been to Washington, D.C. It is government owned and financially supported, and it is administered by employees working for the federal government, but it has many qualities of a private organization, with a governing board of regents, an endowment, and substantial profits from sales of magazines and gift shop items.

quasi-non-governmental organizations (quangos)

Private-sector organizations that fulfill some of the roles of government agencies, like the disaster recovery activities of the American Red Cross.

The quagos' counterpart in the private sector, the **quasi-non-governmental organizations ("quangos")**, are essentially private-sector entities that exercise some public responsibilities, much as the American Red Cross does when it provides assistance to victims of disasters. They perform services frequently identical to those that government agencies provide, but not through the government. Students of public administration, the study of government management, have recently become more willing to blur the usual distinctions between public-sector and private-sector organizations. As such thinking changes we are likely to see a proliferation of these hybrid examples in the future. Several that we discuss below have been much in the news.

government sponsored enterprises (GSEs)

Financial services corporations created by Congress to provide credit to targeted areas of American life; for example, "Fannie Mae" and "Freddie Mac" specialize in home mortgages.

Government-sponsored enterprises (GSEs)[34] are financing agencies chartered by Congress to provide loans to help farmers, students, and homeowners. In 2008, home loans became newsworthy when the two largest GSEs, Fannie Mae and Freddie Mac, required a $134 billion government bailout. Congress created Fannie Mae (the Federal National Mortgage Association) in 1938 to stabilize the mortgage market as the country was emerging from the Great Depression.[35] Later, in 1968, President Johnson modified Fannie Mae's operations, making it a shareholder-owned business rather than a government agency as part of an effort to reduce the federal deficit. Freddie Mac (the Federal Home Loan Mortgage Corporation) was created as a GSE in 1970 to compete with Fannie Mae. These GSEs helped to stabilize the U.S. housing market by buying the mortgage loans issued by others and then issuing bonds that could be bought and sold on the open market. The bonds were a good investment because the federal government seemed to guarantee their value. In the process, they made fortunes for their shareholders because both businesses were enormously profitable with an implicit guarantee from the federal government that it would not let them fail.

Fannie Mae and Freddie Mac helped provide U.S. homeowners with long-term, fixed-rate mortgages. Most frequently, the same interest rate was paid over the life of a typical 30-year mortgage. Few foreign nations have anything comparable, but that does not mean that the U.S. approach is better. Although Fannie Mae, Freddie Mac, and their congressional defenders argued that these policies produced a much higher percentage of U.S. citizens owning their own homes than anywhere else in the world, the data tell us otherwise. As shown in Figure 14.10, several industrial nations had

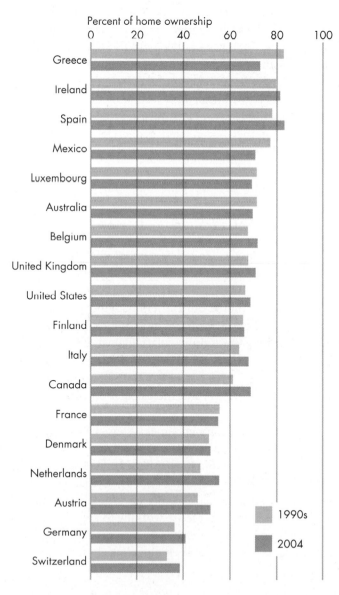

FIGURE 14.10

★ HOME OWNERSHIP IN SELECT INDUSTRIAL NATIONS

In which nations is home ownership surprisingly higher than in the United States? In which ones is it surprisingly lower?

Notes: Rates in the 1990s are 1987 for Austria, 1990 for Spain, 1991 for Italy, 1992 for Denmark and Switzerland, 1994 for Canada, France, Germany, Mexico, and the Netherlands, 1995 for Australia, Belgium, Finland, Greece, and Ireland, 1997 for Luxembourg and the United States. Rates in 2004 are 2003 for Australia, 2007 for Germany and the United States. The data are particularly dated for Belgium (2000), France (2000), Ireland (2000), and the Netherlands (1999).

Sources: OECD, Luxembourg Income Study (LIS), GSOEP and the American Housing Survey. In D. Andrews and A. Caldera Sanchez (2011), "Drivers of Homeownership Rates in Selected OECD Countries," OECD Economics Department Working Papers, No. 849, OECD Publishing. p. 9

and continue to have home ownership rates higher than the United States. In most of these nations, homebuyers borrow money at interest rates that change frequently (often every 12 months in the United Kingdom, every five years in Canada) which makes buying a home much riskier—you cannot be sure what the monthly payment will be in 10 years, let alone next year. After the expensive government bailout of 2008 when the United States government acquired ownership of these two GSEs, the Obama administration proposed dismantling Fannie and Freddie and moving toward a system with features more like those of Denmark or Germany where private lenders bear the risk of mortgage failures instead of placing the burden on the government.

federally funded research and development centers (FFRDCs)
Private, nonprofit corporations that perform contract work for the government, such as the Rand Corporation.

Federally funded research and development centers (FFRDCs) are private, nonprofit corporations that perform contract work for the government. Perhaps the best-known is the RAND Corporation, created by the Air Force after World War II. Congress created many more FFRDCs during the 1950s and 1960s, especially to undertake military research. More recently, the Internal Revenue Service and the Department of Homeland Security created research centers to help them fulfill their responsibilities. There were 37 operating FFRDCs in 2006, and the National Science Foundation maintains an up-to-date listing.[36] Although there are complaints about the cozy relationship between agencies and the centers conducting research for them, FFRDCs are also praised for their ability to transfer new technologies developed by their research efforts into the private sector. However, the most spectacular example of technology transfer—creation of the Internet—originated in the Defense Advanced Research and Projects Agency, a government agency, not an FFRDC.

THE SIZE OF THE FEDERAL BUREAUCRACY

KEY to understanding Although employment in the federal government has been declining since the mid-1990s, does this also mean that government has been shrinking? To appreciate the true size of the federal government, we need to include persons working on government contracts and grants, a total that has risen over the past 15 years. Compared with the size of governments in other advanced industrial democracies in Europe, however, the size of the federal government in the United States is about average.

Most people in the United States consider the bureaucracy to be "too big." Is this the case? To assess the size of the bureaucracy, we start with the number of federal employees. As we pointed out earlier, many people performing public services are *not* employed by the federal government. In fact, if we consider the number of civilian federal civil servants, the American government has been shrinking over the past two decades. In 2005, there were nearly half a million fewer federal employees than there were in 1990. But the calculation is more complicated than it might seem.

Paul Light, a specialist in the federal personnel system, has argued persuasively that in order to gauge the "true size of government" we need to include other categories of workers. Two are very obvious: military personnel (another 1.5 million) and postal workers (about 750,000). But Light also argues that we need to include the full range of people and organizations receiving government grants and contracts to get a full account of just how many people are working to accomplish federal goals. Together, these categories encompass another 10.5 million people. This group of workers has been expanding as direct federal employment declines, thereby constituting a "hidden workforce."[37] Light estimates that 14.6 million Americans worked directly and indirectly for the federal government in 2005, a substantial *increase* over the total in 1990.

Although politicians' rhetoric might make you think that the bureaucracy never stops growing, in fact the number of federal employees declined during a 15-year period before growing slightly in the last few years. This decrease was intentional. The Clinton administration launched an ambitious effort to "reinvent government" under the direction of Vice President Al Gore in 1993. Its proposals included a reduction in the size of the federal workforce, made possible by strategies to "work smarter," as the plan's architects liked to say. Although total federal employment fell by more than 365,000 from 1990 to 2005, the number of jobs supported by federal contracts grew by more than 2.5 million over the same time period and accelerated during the George W. Bush administration.

Although Light's data give us some sense of government size over time, how do his estimates compare with government size elsewhere? Several researchers have sought to answer this question, and they frequently complain of the problems in getting good, comparable data (see the complex Notes). Most nations have arranged

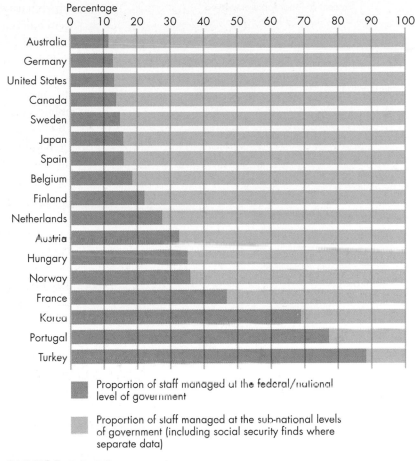

Proportion of staff managed at the federal/national level of government

Proportion of staff managed at the sub-national levels of government (including social security funds where separate data)

FIGURE 14.11

★ EMPLOYMENT IN GOVERNMENT BY LEVEL OF GOVERNMENT, 2005

Why do some nations choose to concentrate workforces at the federal level and others at the local level?

Notes: Data are in number of employees, except for Austria, the Netherlands, and Sweden. Employment in Social Security is not taken into account at the national level in Austria, Belgium, Finland, France, Hungary, Japan, Korea, the Netherlands, Spain, Sweden, and Turkey. Employment in Social Security is not taken into account at other levels of government in Australia, Canada, Germany, Norway, Portugal (for 2005), and the United States. Austria: Data do not include private nonprofit institutions financed by government. Mixed data 2004 and 2005. Data for public corporations are partial and only include universities that have been reclassified. Belgium: Data are for 2004 and not 2005. Finland: Mixed data 2004 and 2005. CEPD survey, OECS.

their public bureaucracies in ways that are just as complex as those in the United States. Nonetheless, the Organization of Economic Cooperation and Development (OECD) collects data on public sector employment among its 30 member states. We discuss some of these findings below.

Notice that nations with federal systems and strong local governments tend to have fewer federal employees than those with more centralized governments. We see this pattern in Figure 14.11, where Australia, Germany, the United States, and Canada—all nations with strong federalism—have far fewer civil servants at the federal level than at the local level. At the other end of the spectrum, Turkey, Portugal, and Korea,

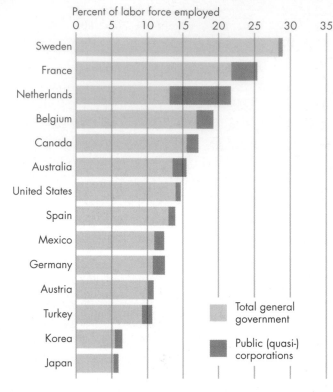

Percent of labor force employed

FIGURE 14.12

★ EMPLOYMENT IN GOVERNMENT AS A PERCENTAGE OF THE LABOR FORCE, 2005

Why do some nations have a higher percentage of the labor force working for government than does the United States?

Notes: Data are in number of employees, except for Austria, the Netherlands, and Sweden where they are in full-time equivalents. Employment numbers for those countries are thus underestimated. Austria: Data do not include private nonprofit institutions financed by government. Mixed data 2004 and 2005; for 1995, data for Social Security are missing but are of minor importance as a percentage of workforce (around 26,000 employees). Data for public corporations are partial and only include universities that have been reclassified. Belgium: Data are for 2004 and not 2005. France: Data exclude some Public Establishments. Data are for 2004. Mexico: Data are for 2000. Poland: 2004 and not 2005.

Source: CEPD survey; Labor Force Survey (OECD).

which have more centralized governments, have more than half of their public employees working at the federal level.

Using data similar to Light's but omitting contract workers, the OECD has calculated the percentage of the national labor force working for government and public corporations. As shown in Figure 14.12, the OECD finds that the United States is in the middle of 14 nations with about 15 percent of the total labor force working for government, about midway between Sweden's 29 percent and Japan's 6 percent.

These figures suggest that the public sector in the United States is not excessively large. State and local government employment is far greater than federal. There has been growth in recent years, especially if we include the "hidden workforce" of people whose jobs depend on government grants or contracts, but relative to other nations, the size of the U.S. public sector seems about average.

But is government larger than it *needs* to be? Given such an extensive enterprise, it seems almost inevitable that there will be some duplication of effort, redundancy of agency assignments, overlapping of programs, waste, fraud, and abuse. Elected officials often cite waste, fraud, and abuse as the targets of their efforts to reduce wasteful spending and improve government performance. A 2011 report from the Government Accountability Office (GAO) provides insight into other structural problems, identifying the following multiple efforts:

- 80 federal programs pursue economic development
- 100 federal programs deal with surface transportation
- 54 federal programs address financial literacy
- 20 federal agencies manage government cars, trucks, and airplanes
- 15 federal agencies deal with food safety[38]

Perhaps multiple public efforts are sometimes necessary, but as the report implies, a starting point for effecting budget savings is to assess whether some of these efforts might be unnecessary. Beginning with this initial analysis, the GAO will report to Congress annually. We will see whether it makes a difference, since much of the blame for redundant programs lies at the feet of Congress, who created the programs in the first place!

THE SEARCH FOR CONTROL

Who controls the bureaucrats? Because bureaucrats lie outside direct citizen control, the only way to make government action accountable to the public is through indirect means—through the actions of elected officials. Exercising control, however, has become a larger problem over time as the bureaucracy expanded and its powers grew. Congress gives government officials responsibility to develop and carry out the many plans required to accomplish its policy goals. Agencies create programs and adopt regulations under this **delegated authority** as a way to accomplish the general purposes stated by Congress. Rather than providing agency officials with highly detailed guidelines on how to proceed, Congress usually allows them considerable flexibility, termed **administrative discretion,** in determining how to achieve the general goals. Thus, agencies exercise considerable power over putting programs in place—**implementation** of policy that translates general goals into concrete action.

With such an extensive structure making so many critical decisions about policies and programs, how is it possible to ensure that bureaucrats will not reinterpret the mandate they have been given? Where are the checks on bureaucratic power? How can the public hope to exercise control? The traditional model for thinking about this issue is shown in Figure 14.13. The officials elected by the public must exercise control over the bureaucrats on behalf of the public. This indirect control can be exercised through many instruments, as discussed below.

Over time, the Congress and the president have devised multiple, parallel means to exercise control (see Table 14.3). These methods include:

- annual budget
- authorization of programs
- oversight of agency performance
- nomination and confirmation of political appointees
- reorganization of the bureaucracy
- management of public employees (members of the civil service)

We discuss each of these control techniques in the section that follows.

ANNUAL BUDGET

Few things are closer to bureaucrats' hearts than the budget resources they need to accomplish their mission. The budget determines the size of an agency's staff, its supplies and equipment, and the extent to which it can embark on new projects as well as complete those already under way. Both Congress and the president pose budget challenges to an agency. Until 1921, Congress dominated budget

How can we exercise control over bureaucrats? Congress and the president use similar techniques to control bureaucrats, emphasizing budgets, personnel, and monitoring. At the same time, bureaucrats are able to generate support from allies in the public to defend their programs, producing relationships that are often referred to as "iron triangles." Ultimately, Americans are reluctant to rely too heavily on the independent judgment of bureaucrats even though their politically neutral policy expertise might be superior to that of elected officials. ★

delegated authority
Power to make decisions enjoyed by an agency or department that was approved by Congress.

administrative discretion
Opportunity granted to bureaucrats by Congress to use their judgment in making decisions between alternative courses of action.

implementation
The process of carrying out the wishes of Congress as expressed in a policy through the creation and enforcement of programs and regulations by bureaucratic agencies.

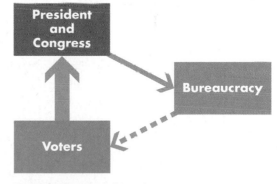

FIGURE 14.13

★ THE AMERICAN MODEL OF ADMINISTRATIVE ACCOUNTABILITY
Voters exercise indirect control over bureaucrats through the activities of their elected officials. Do nonvoters have ways to influence bureaucrats?

TABLE 14.3

techniques to control bureaucrats

PRESIDENT	CONGRESS
BUDGET	BUDGET
• OMB	• CBO
• Annual budget	• Annual appropriations
AUTHORIZATION	AUTHORIZATION
• Legislative clearance	• Statutory review of programs
OVERSIGHT	OVERSIGHT
• Monitoring	• Committee hearings
• Management systems	• Investigations
	• Case work
NOMINATION	CONFIRMATION
• Select nominees	• Review presidential nominees
REORGANIZATION PERSONNEL	REORGANIZATION PERSONNEL
• Managed by OPM	• Determined by civil service policies

Office of Management and Budget (OMB)

Successor agency to the Bureau of the Budget, created in 1970 and designed to perform management oversight that went beyond the traditional budget and central clearance functions performed by the BOB.

decisions. But the Budget and Accounting Act of 1921 required departments and agencies to submit their requests for next year's budget for presidential review before it went to Congress. Presidents now submit a single, unified executive budget assembled by the **Office of Management and Budget (OMB),** known until 1970 as the Bureau of the Budget. At the same time, Congress created the General Accounting Office (GAO) to give its members the capacity to track government spending. The GAO was renamed the Government Accountability Office in 2004.

Assembling the president's budget takes nearly 18 months, starting with preliminary guidelines sent out to the government's many bureaucracies. As the deadline for submitting a budget to Congress approaches, OMB's officials review the projected budgets of all agencies and departments and make a final recommendation that agencies may appeal. Ultimately, an agency's budget becomes part of the president's annual recommended budget submitted to Congress for approval.

Then Congress takes over. Members of the subcommittees within the House and Senate Appropriation Committees play the most important roles in the approval process. These senior legislators have long experience in tracking presidential and agency budgets and receive expert assistance from the Congressional Budget Office (CBO). The full committees rely heavily on the expertise of their colleagues serving on the subcommittees, as they are the most familiar with the programs and services of the agencies they review. Congressional appropriations committees can agree with the president's request, increase it, or reduce it—hence their enormous power over the agencies subject to their review. Rather than review each budget from top to bottom, these committees focus particularly on the changes from the previous year's budget—that is, the incremental adjustments. By the end of September, Congress is supposed to have reviewed and approved the new budget for the fiscal year starting on October 1, but it often misses that deadline, triggering the kind of drama we witnessed in the spring of 2011 when the federal government was on the brink of shutting down nonessential services. (See the expanded budget discussion in Chapter 16.)

AUTHORIZATION OF PROGRAMS

As with the budget, presidents start the process of program authorization, but Congress has the last word. Presidents established a system of **central clearance,** essentially a review of agencies' program ideas and proposals performed by the OMB. Even before a proposal gets to the OMB, however, the department or agency's political appointees (see below) evaluate the proposal to determine whether it conforms to the president's goals. Once the proposal reaches the OMB, its staff determines whether the proposal is in accord with the president's agenda. At this point, bureaucrats might float their ideas past sympathetic interest groups and members of Congress, hoping that their support will influence the president, or they might wait until later in the process to raise the idea again. Ultimately, Congress must approve (or authorize) all programs and they can only be continued if Congress reapproves (or reauthorizes) them.

Most congressional standing committees have permanent jurisdiction over a collection of government programs. Without a committee's approval (the original authorization), an agency cannot establish these programs. During program renewal (reauthorization), legislators assess whether the programs have achieved their stated goals and will make adjustments if needed. Reauthorization, then, marks a critical point in an agency's life as it determines whether existing programs will be renewed, discontinued, or modified.

For example, in 2000, the Department of Education's core programs were scheduled for reauthorization—as they typically are every five to seven years. These programs were created under the Elementary and Secondary Education Act of 1965, which established the principal federal programs in education. Concern about the persistent mediocrity of U.S. schools was widespread, but Congress was unable to come to agreement on the terms of the reauthorization because education reform was the platform centerpiece of Republican candidate George W. Bush. As a result, Congress decided to merely extend the existing programs for an additional year, but later adopted a dramatically refashioned set of guidelines proposed by the new president in January 2002. This came to be known as the No Child Left Behind Act. This Act mandated that each state develop standards in reading and math that all students would achieve by 2014. Progress would be measured by annual tests for students in grades 3 through 8 and results would be reported for many subgroups in the school, district,

and state populations. If students failed to achieve adequate yearly progress in moving toward proficiency, schools were subject to sanctions and federal funding could be reduced.[39] In this instance, Congress used reauthorization to enhance the federal government's ability to force states and school districts across the country to adopt a new set of practices—changes far more extensive than might be expected from the 6 to 7 percent of total education spending that the federal government then controlled. (See a fuller discussion of education policy in Chapter 17.)

OVERSIGHT OF AGENCY PERFORMANCE

Both Congress and the president monitor agency and department performance at times other than during budget review and program reauthorization—part of the many ways that Congress provides **oversight,** or routine review of program performance. In providing case work for their constituents, congressional staff members interact with bureaucrats as they try to determine why the folks back home are not getting the services or level of responsiveness they expect. Presidents, too, have staff members who perform this kind of work, but Congress collectively has larger staff resources. When interactions with the bureaucracy identify problems, they become the focus of further congressional study and potentially the subject of a full-scale investigation.

For example, citizen complaints about the Internal Revenue Service (IRS) triggered congressional hearings and media investigations in 1997–1999. The principal concern was the abuse of power by tax collectors when they audited returns and took action against citizens who allegedly owed taxes. Senator Bill Roth (R-DE), chairman of the Senate Finance Committee that held the hearings, summed up the need for action by saying, "There is no other agency in this country that touches the lives of more Americans, nor strikes more fear into their hearts. The threat of an audit, the awesome power of the IRS, looms like the sword of Damocles over the heads of taxpayers."[40] The push for reform resulted in the creation of a taxpayer bill of rights limiting the agency's authority, together with a restructuring of the IRS.[41]

Part of the job of presidential aides who are part of the Executive Office of the President (see Chapter 13) is to monitor the performance of agencies in their area of responsibility. The OMB has the broadest charge, and its employees maintain close oversight of the agencies in their portfolios. White House aides will also monitor what goes on in the bureaucracy, particularly on high-profile programs that are near and dear to the president's heart. The Obama White House staff, for example, closely monitored progress of implementing the health care reforms adopted in 2010.

The George W. Bush administration tracked how departments improved their effectiveness in reforming their personnel systems, increasing reliance on private-sector resources (outsourcing government jobs), improving financial management, expanding electronic government, and linking budget decisions to the performance of specific agency programs. The OMB published quarterly scorecards on the Web to improve transparency and put pressure on departments to step up their performance. Everyone could read posted success stories.[42] President Obama scrapped the Bush efforts and developed a different set of management goals he wanted to see achieved.[43] Other presidents, notably Presidents Nixon and Reagan, also sought to improve government efficiency, but the standards to judge performance remain both imperfect and controversial.[44]

NOMINATION AND CONFIRMATION OF POLITICAL APPOINTEES

As discussed earlier in this chapter, civil service reforms at the end of the nineteenth century removed a potentially powerful lever from the president's control. Under the spoils system, presidents chose loyalists to fill government positions, making it plain that appointees would follow his direction—or be replaced. Creating a politically neutral career civil service reduced the potential control presidents could exercise over the bureaucracy. Instead of having all federal jobs potentially under presidents' control, they suddenly controlled only a small number of positions that lay outside the civil service system. These still provide the president with political "plums" to distribute to loyal supporters.[45] They also include the most senior positions in departments and agencies, political appointees in policy-making positions, as well as appointments lower in the hierarchy. President Obama had approximately 4,300 positions that he could fill and another 3,700 senior career personnel he could potentially draw upon to help him manage the federal bureaucracy of approximately 2 million civilian employees. That may sound like a lot of help, but it is modest in relation to the number of bureaucrats.

Unlike political appointees in a parliamentary system, the president's political appointees cannot be members of Congress. Separation of powers requires the president to assemble his team rather than simply appoint members of the **shadow government** already serving in parliament to administrative posts, as is done in the UK. For more than 1,000 of these presidential nominations, the Senate has the power to advise and consent. (The Congress determines which positions are subject to Senate review.) Since the mid-1800s, Senate committees have reviewed most of the nominated candidates' qualifications, and since the mid-twentieth century, the committees have customarily held public hearings to grill the candidates before reporting the nomination out to the larger Senate or refusing to do so.[46] On rare occasions, nominations can be reported out of committee to the full Senate without a positive committee vote. Most nominees are confirmed under the general belief that presidents should have the opportunity to assemble their own team.

Political appointees seldom stay in their positions for long; the average tenure of political appointees in federal agencies is two years, so their commitment to the agency's mission is shallower than that of the career bureaucrats with whom they work. Given the pattern of how often congressional incumbents win reelection and how committee leaders are chosen (see Chapter 12), bureaucrats can expect to be dealing with the same cast of congressional characters far longer than they will with the administration's appointees.

REORGANIZATION OF THE BUREAUCRACY

Congress and executive branch officials care a great deal about how the government is structured because it will have a direct bearing on how programs are implemented. It also has a direct bearing on who has influence to shape what issues. Even if the quest for *power* lies at the heart of reorganization efforts, they are usually justified in public as desirable because such efforts will enhance efficiency, produce economies, or solve a pressing national problem.

For most of U.S. history, Congress and the president wrestled over the right to determine the structure of the federal bureaucracy, with Congress coming out on top. Ultimately, Congress must approve the creation of departments and agencies, and it jealously guards its right to manage government resources to achieve its ends. But is Congress or the president better able to determine how the government should be organized to accomplish its purposes? During the 1920s and 1930s Congress and the president adopted many management reforms (for example, the centralized budgeting discussed earlier) designed to make presidents more effective at managing federal

shadow government
A government-in-waiting in parliamentary systems where leading members of the opposition party speak out on specific areas of government policy as they prepare to assume leading roles should they gain control of government.

bureaucrats. In 1932, in the midst of an economic crisis, Congress allowed President Hoover to propose organizational changes that Congress promised they would act upon quickly to save money, but the Democrat-controlled Congress accepted none of the president's recommendations. Although Congress later provided greater flexibility to President Franklin D. Roosevelt, they were still unwilling to grant him a free hand to organize government as he wished.

Post-Depression and post–World War II, Congress gave presidents expanded **reorganization authority,** the power to propose changes in executive branch structures that would go into effect unless one or both houses of Congress used a **legislative veto** to reverse the proposal. Under the statutory authority, the president could transfer an agency from one location to another, consolidate functions from several agencies, abolish all or part of an agency or its functions, and delegate responsibilities. Executive departments, however, were off-limits; presidents could neither create nor abolish them. From 1949 to 1973, presidents submitted 85 proposals, and Congress accepted 65.[47]

But in the 1970s, Congress reasserted its constitutional powers in several areas, including reorganization. Following a series of showdowns with President Nixon over spending and war powers, Congress refused to renew broad reorganization authority given to Nixon's predecessors. And in 1983, in a case that had no direct bearing on reorganization, the Supreme Court declared the use of legislative vetoes unconstitutional because they violated the constitutional provisions that require a presidential signature for acts of Congress to go into effect. Once Congress lost the use of the procedure it had employed for decades to review and potentially reverse presidential reorganization proposals, it no longer even considered giving later presidents such broad authority. Now Congress uses the normal legislative process when considering reorganization proposals as it did in the case of the DHS. Presidents want to reorganize, but Congress refuses to grant this power. Despite repeated efforts by President George W. Bush to restore greater presidential influence over reorganization, for instance, Congress rejected them all. President Obama requested similar powers in 2011, but Congress once again said no.

★ An officer from the Department of Homeland Security inspects baggage at the crossing between Tijuana, Mexico, and San Diego, California. Following 9/11, the federal government formed DHS from 22 offices and agencies that were located in other departments.

reorganization authority
Powers given to presidents by Congress to propose changes in executive branch organization, subject to a legislative veto.

legislative veto
Technique that was used by Congress to reject presidential reorganization proposals until it was ruled unconstitutional by the Supreme Court.

MANAGEMENT OF PUBLIC EMPLOYEES

Congress establishes the broad outlines of personnel policies for government workers. Thus, the Civil Service Reform Act of 1978 replaced the Civil Service Commission and created new policies for the federal Civil Service. Presidents rely on the Office of

Personnel Management to oversee that system. As the twenty-fifth anniversary of that statute approached, evaluations of what the last round had accomplished and proposals for additional reforms were in the air. Many discussions called for providing agency managers with greater flexibility in hiring workers, paying them at levels based on their job performance, and firing the lowest-producing employees. Civil service regulations—the product of decades of practice and precedent—restricted management discretion in all three areas. A behind-the-scenes battle raged during the George W. Bush years over which civil service protections would remain and which ones would disappear.

The terrorist attacks of 9/11 unexpectedly highlighted civil service practices. FEMA, for example, drew praise for its effectiveness; it was one of the few federal agencies to earn plaudits for its performance. Bush argued that unless the civil service personnel system was reformed, the nation could not win the war on terror.[48] As such, FEMA became part of the Department of Homeland Security, which Congress exempted from regulations in hiring (more candidates to choose from), setting pay and job classifications (four or five broad salary ranges instead of 15 grades and raises based on performance), and dismissing employees. These modifications triggered a showdown between the administration and Senate Democrats in the fall of 2002. But when the midterm elections returned a supportive Republican majority to the Senate, Bush's proposed changes were adopted.

The exemptions given to Homeland Security (DHS) were large in scope (170,000 employees); they could have paved the way for establishing a new *pay-for-performance system* throughout the government, compensating people based on their productivity rather than on their years in a position as called for by the General Schedule. But Congress remained only partly convinced that modifications were needed.[49] In 2003, Bush convinced Congress that the new flexibility should also apply to the mammoth (potentially 700,000 people) Department of Defense (DOD) civilian workforce. Federal employee unions, particularly the American Federation of Government Employees and the National Treasury Employees Union, convinced federal district and appeals courts to rule against the administration's reforms in DHS, but a different appeals court panel upheld some of the DOD changes. After Democrats regained control of Congress in 2007, the changes were reversed for DHS. The president and a Republican-controlled Congress had been moving toward a redesign of the civil service system, but court action and a Democrat-controlled Congress halted progress. Changes in the DOD survived into the second year of the Obama administration but then were cancelled.[50]

Battles over the civil service are by no means limited to the United States. Margaret Thatcher's government in Great Britain (1979–1990) sought many of the same reforms in the British civil service system that George W. Bush sought in the United States—introducing performance-based pay systems, making it easier to dismiss low-performing civil servants, exercising greater political control over policy making by long-time civil servants, and increasing government efficiency by contracting out government services to private firms,—in essence introducing competition with the private sector. Thatcher's successors continued many of these efforts.[51] Unlike the American system, the British parliament is relatively compliant in accepting administrative reforms and provides far less assistance to those who resist the changes.

State officials have also launched efforts to expand control over public workers. Three states—Georgia, Texas, and Florida—led the way in giving agency managers more control over whom they could hire and fire. Other states have followed the same path, including Wisconsin, where public employee bargaining rights became the center of a prolonged political drama during the winter of 2011. A new Republican governor had just been elected, and the legislature adopted new work provisions that encountered strong opposition from unionized state employees. Days of public marches and vocal demonstrations in the Wisconsin state capitol building failed to derail the reforms that would give elected officials and their appointees much greater control over public workers. Later, union members failed in their effort to remove Wisconsin's governor from office.

WHEN CONTROL PROVES ELUSIVE

Despite the many instruments of control at the disposal of the president and Congress, it remains unclear who *really* controls the bureaucracy. Exercising control requires effort, and both presidents and members of Congress have limited time, competing priorities, and finite knowledge. In addition, they disagree. Presidents insist they should be in control, but Congress jealously guards its prerogatives. With two masters, to whom should bureaucrats listen? Who speaks for the public in providing bureaucrats with guidance?

The separation of powers system makes it highly likely that differences will arise between the president and Congress as well as between the two houses of Congress. Consequently, the agency may find itself without clear policy guidance. In the absence of a consensus from above, bureaucrats by necessity must become politicians and construct the political support they require on their own. The resulting *bureaucratic politics* of budget and program battles have become the raw material of day-to-day life in the nation's capital, and bureaucrats are often the winners, bringing substantial resources to bear—longevity, expertise, and longstanding alliances.

It is not surprising, then, that bureaucrats form close alliances with the committee members and staffs with whom they work—alliances that also include the principal

★ Public employees do yoga at the Capitol Building in Madison, Wisconsin, after Governor Scott Walker threatened to lay off state personnel.

interest groups concerned with the agency's programs. Who will be more interested in the Department of Agriculture's policies on tobacco, pork, or milk production, for example, than the farmers who grow these products and the members of Congress who have secured seats on the authorizing committee that can help these farmers in their districts? As depicted in Figure 14.14, this **iron triangle** of relationships comprising three parties—an agency, a congressional committee, and an interest group—share a mutual interest to help each other shape policies that will benefit an identifiable group. Iron triangles exist for many agencies and they are so strong that presidents find them difficult to break. The interest groups representing the program beneficiaries provide political support to members of Congress (votes, campaign contributions) *and* bureaucrats (political support when needed). Both elected and career officials see it as their responsibility to maintain and expand existing programs; they are accustomed to working closely with each other in creating policies that meet their own needs if not necessarily the public will.

If neither the Congress nor the president can establish a clear claim to interpreting the public will, perhaps bureaucrats can provide expert, neutral guidance for public policy on their own—that is, become an independent force. When the Senior Executive Service was created in 1978, one of the hopes was that career administrators would receive the respect they deserve for the professionalism and expertise they bring to their jobs. Such a tradition is well established in European systems and gives unelected officials independent standing—one of the aspects of British bureaucracy that Margaret Thatcher sought to reverse.

Europeans with a career in public administration have usually had training at some of the nation's most elite educational institutions and often enjoy more prestige than politicians. Thus, some students of public administration argue that bureaucrats provide government with an institutional memory of policy strategies tried and failed, and they serve as repositories of policy wisdom. If this is the case, should bureaucrats always be subordinate to elected officials? Wouldn't government that relies on expert guidance provide greater continuity and potentially better service to the public than government based on shifting political coalitions? In American political culture, though, it is assumed that if bureaucrats guide elected officials, turning the American model of administrative accountability upside down, they must therefore represent unchecked administrative power and should be feared. This view of democracy is likely to win out in the long run but might sacrifice the benefits to be gained were we to rely more heavily on experts.

iron triangle
The close relationship established and maintained among a trio of actors: the beneficiaries of a government policy (interest groups), the agency responsible for the beneficial programs (bureaucracy) and the congressional committees responsible for authorizing and funding the programs.

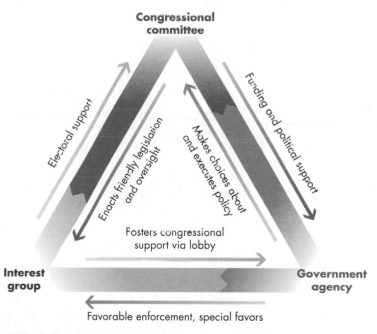

FIGURE 14.14

★ THE IRON TRIANGLE

Interest groups, congressional committees and government bureaucrats establish powerful relationships through their involvement with common policy problems.

Why Are We
THE WAY WE ARE?

The power of government bureaucracy has grown in American life from a presence barely hinted at in the Constitution to a pervasive force in the twenty-first century. That development is widely viewed as dangerous, a perspective often encouraged by contemporary politicians speaking to the hot-button issue of the Revolutionary War—excessive power wielded by government agents invading citizens' rights. But bureaucracy is not always bad; instead, competent, extensive administration of public affairs promotes personal health, safety, and convenience. Admittedly, American bureaucracy is far from perfect, and sometimes the failures can be spectacular, as in the case of FEMA and Hurricane Katrina. More often, successes go virtually unnoticed.

AMERICANS' THEORY OF DEMOCRACY

The position of the bureaucracy in national government has always been a bone of contention between the president and Congress. Both claim authority to direct the activities of federal employees, and both use a wide array of mechanisms to assert control. Under Americans' theory of democracy, the people control bureaucrats through their elected representatives, but often those elected officials disagree over what should be done and how it should be accomplished. Thus, the battle for control rages over how to design government-wide systems (like the civil service) as well as how to implement very specific policies approved by both the legislative and executive branches. One might think that such widespread struggles would limit the discretion of American bureaucrats. But in the midst of such conflict they often find a way to steer a path toward the goal preferred by the professionals, arguably an even better outcome.

THE RESULT OF BEING A NON-PARLIAMENTARY SYSTEM

In other nations, bureaucrats often receive more respect than they do in the United States. In the historical accounts that transmit political culture from one generation to the next, bureaucrats are depicted as building and sustaining the modern nation, earning them greater cultural respect. And the permanent government officialdom provides continuity in political systems where coalition governments come and go rapidly. In Italy, for example, where there have been nearly 60 governments since 1946, administrators provide some measure of stability. Facing a financial crisis in 2011, Italy turned to professionally trained "technocrats" to fill their cabinet positions—not politicians.

In other parliamentary systems, the boundary between the elected government and the bureaucracy is far less distinct than it is in the United States. In the United Kingdom, Canada, and Australia, members of parliament head the principal government agencies; they are political allies of the prime minister who hold legislative and executive positions at the same time. These members of the parliamentary team oversee the permanent bureaucracy, which must be able to serve either party effectively. In these British-patterned democracies, no constitutional divide is built into the relationship between civil servants and the executive branch as one finds in the United States. Thus, different histories and different constitutional structures produce distinctive roles for the government bureaucrats.

. . . AND WHY DOES IT Matter?

Government often appears very distant from us. It seems to be about current and potential military conflicts on the other side of the world or about abstract disagreements over economic policy. But unelected officials at federal, state, and local levels of government have an enormous impact on everyday life. From enforcing the speed limit to ensuring that the water is safe to drink to guaranteeing that there is enough electricity to cool our homes even in the hottest weather, government bureaucrats perform innumerable services that make modern life possible. They also make us angry—when April 15 rolls around each year and we have to pay our federal taxes; when our car fails to pass its safety inspection; when the student loan program that we depend on is changed and benefits are reduced. Numerous citizens feel that faceless bureaucrats are to blame for many of their ills: the government costs too much and taxes are too high; government officials are overpaid; rush hour traffic is ridiculously congested; there is no end in sight for the rising cost of gas. With growing government responsibilities have come growing public expectations of government performance.

More generally, do bureaucrats pose a danger to the American way of life? Or do officials make that quality of life possible? Politically, it has been easier to emphasize the threats posed by big government than the benefits that it might provide. Such attacks play to the nation's self-image—of rugged colonists overcoming hardships and frontiersmen winning the West, carving out a new life on their own with minimal government help or presence. Modern life is very different. It involves increased complexity and many interdependencies—of producers and consumers, suppliers and transporters, health care providers and the sick, banks and savers, emergency responders and potential victims of natural disasters. The list is endless, and government has a potential and often a real role to play in each area, making certain that competition is fair, patients receive safe services, and citizens are protected against catastrophic loss of savings, homes, or lives.

critical thinking questions

1. The Bureau of Labor Statistics reports that "With more than 1.8 million civilian employees, the Federal Government, excluding the Postal Service, is the Nation's largest employer." Does that tell us that government is too large? How do we determine what the "right size" is for the federal government?

2. The credit crisis that plunged the U.S. economy into recession thrust the Federal Reserve Board into the news during 2008. Is it a good idea that the principal responsibility for overseeing the monetary system is separated from the direct control of either the president or Congress? How would the nation benefit by making credit and banking policy more directly responsible to the people's elected representatives?

3. When the United States created a federal civil service system in the last half of the nineteenth century, it was hailed as a major reform of U.S. government. Yet today, the protections provided by that system are often portrayed as impediments to government efficiency and effectiveness. Can the original benefits associated with civil service reform be retained in the twenty-first century, or do government workers need to work in a dramatically redesigned system? Justify your answer.

4. Would the United States be better served by a streamlined bureaucratic structure that answers wholly to the President and far less to the Congress? Or does U.S. government work best when both the president and Congress share control?

key terms

THE JUDICIARY

- Define judicial independence and discuss its importance to the rule of law.
- Explain the development, application, and significance of judicial review.
- Describe the structure of the U.S. court system and identify the advantages and disadvantages of this type of system.
- Examine how a case reaches and gets decided by the Supreme Court.
- Understand the impact of judicial philosophy on how Supreme Court justices decide cases and craft legal opinions.
- Identify the range of limits placed on the Supreme Court to prevent it from overreaching or abusing its power.
- Compare and contrast the criteria used to select judges at the state and federal levels.

PERSPECTIVE
When Do Reactions to Unpopular Court Decisions Threaten Judicial Independence?

Judicial independence is a cornerstone of the American system of government. Specific court rulings and judges have sometimes prompted hostile reactions from politicians, interest groups, the media, and the public, but no matter how upset these opponents may be, official responses are limited to employing legitimate checks on the court. For example, some critics were greatly angered by state court decisions striking down laws banning same-sex marriage. President George W. Bush accused these "activist judges" of arbitrarily redefining marriage, but he worked within constitutional means to respond to these decisions: He called for an amendment to the Constitution to ban same-sex marriage.[1]

At the same time, the Republican-controlled House of Representatives—fearful that the U.S. Supreme Court would extend state court rulings on same-sex marriage—exercised its constitutional power to alter the Supreme Court's *appellate jurisdiction* (that is, its power to review cases from lower courts). It passed H.R. 3313, a bill to withdraw jurisdiction from the U.S. Supreme Court to accept appeals in cases involving challenges to the 1996 Defense of Marriage Act. In so doing, the House relied on Article III, Section 2 of the Constitution, which says that Congress can limit the Supreme Court's appellate jurisdiction. Like most previous attempts by Congress to use this "Exceptions Clause" power to limit the Court, H.R. 3313 stalled in the Senate and never became law.

Some contend that even utilizing these legitimate checks may undermine the independence of the American judiciary. However, in many countries around the world, the idea of judicial independence is hard to fathom. Judges fear official reprisal for unpopular decisions—they might find themselves summarily fired, placed under arrest, or worse.

In 2007, for example, Pakistani president Pervez Musharraf unilaterally fired the Chief Justice of Pakistan's Supreme Court, Iftikhar Muhammad Chaudhry. Musharraf had seized control of the government in a bloodless military coup d'état in October 1999 and declared himself the president of Pakistan in 2001. The following year, he attempted to legitimize his seizure of power by allowing a nationwide referendum to give him a five-year presidential term. According to the official results, the referendum favored Musharraf by 97.5 percent, but there were widespread charges of election fraud.[2] Musharraf then proceeded to suppress civil liberties, detain opponents without charge, and ban public rallies and demonstrations. Nonetheless the Supreme Court, led by Chaudhry, stood up to him. The Court heard cases involving government corruption and "forced disappearances," in which government intelligence agents rounded up people without due process of law.

In 2007, Musharraf announced that he would seek another five-year term as president. But this time, he called for an indirect election by national and provincial assemblies. His action would be equivalent to a U.S. president asking to be reelected by a vote of Congress and state legislatures controlled by his own party, rather than a free election by the people. Opponents questioned the legality of the election and whether Musharraf was eligible for another term.[3]

Fearful that the Supreme Court would rule against him, Musharraf declared a state of emergency, suspended the constitution, fired Chief Justice Chaudhry and 60 other judges, and held Chaudhry and his family under house arrest. His actions precipitated a backlash of opposition. The exiled opposition leader Benazir Bhutto returned to Pakistan in October 2007 to run for office in the parliamentary elections scheduled for January 2008, but she was assassinated on December 27, 2007, throwing the country into even deeper turmoil. Musharraf eventually resigned in August 2008, and Bhutto's husband, Asif Ali Zardari, was elected president the next month.

Despite initial resistance, Zardari finally agreed in March 2009 to the reinstatement of Chaudhry and the other judges, signaling at least a temporary victory for an independent judiciary and the rule of law. Chaudhry has gone on to become one of the most trusted men in Pakistan—a popular hero—and the Court has been willing, and even eager, to take on cases challenging the new president, who was viewed by many in his country as corrupt and inept.[4]

THIS CHAPTER FOCUSES on the centrality of judicial independence to enforcement of the rule of law. It traces the development of judicial review; describes the basic structure of our court system, including how it is staffed and how it operates; examines the factors that influence judicial decision making; explains what "judicial activism" really means and how it compares with "judicial restraint"; and discusses limits on the exercise of judicial power. As you read this chapter, keep in mind our two core questions:

WHY ARE WE THE WAY WE ARE?
WHY DOES IT MATTER TO YOU?

> **In particular, why is judicial independence so important, and what elements are essential to creating and maintaining that independence?**

JUDICIAL INDEPENDENCE

Article III of the U.S. Constitution established the U.S. Supreme Court, gave Congress the power to create lower federal courts (state courts already existed), and established specific provisions to guarantee judicial independence. First, short of impeachment, federal judges have life tenure. They cannot, for example, be fired by the president as in Pakistan. Second, the Constitution guarantees compensation to federal judges "which shall not be diminished during their continuance in office," thereby preventing Congress from using a pay cut to punish judges for their rulings. These constitutional guarantees reinforce the institutional independence of federal courts from the other branches and from threats of retaliation from the people.

KEY TO understanding ▲

Judicial independence is integral to the rule of law, and the U.S. Constitution contains specific guarantees that promote such independence. This is not always the case in other countries. What are these provisions guaranteeing an independent judiciary? Does a written constitution necessarily guarantee the rule of law?

picture YOURSELF ...

AS A JUDGE IN COLOMBIA

judges by holding hearings behind one-way mirrors and using voice-distortion equipment to prevent them from being recognized.* The identities of prosecutors and witnesses are also shielded.

Such danger is not unique to Colombia. Judges in Mexico have become targets of drug violence, prompting the Mexican government to consider following Colombia's example by shielding judges' identities. And in Iraq, where the United States helped to establish an

* Jeremy Schwartz, "Judges Latest Target in Mexico Drug War," Cox News Service, February 2, 2008 (www.coxwashington.com/hp/content/reporters/stories/2008/02/02/MEXICO_JUDGES02_COX.html).

continued

As a judge in the United States, you might expect to lead a comfortable life, with interesting work, decent pay, and the respect of the members of your community. And you probably assume that being a judge is a fairly safe profession. But picture yourself in Colombia, where choosing to be a judge in this South American country makes you vulnerable to assassination. From 1978 to 1991, drug cartels murdered 278 judges there. Starting in 1991, the Colombian government instituted a system of protecting

independent judiciary after ousting Saddam Hussein, more than 30 judges were killed in the line of duty between 2003 and 2007.[†] Violence against judges and other participants in the judicial system is commonplace in some parts of the world, and it constitutes another threat to judicial independence.

[†] Robert H. Reid, "Wave of Attacks Threaten Iraqi Judges," *Associated Press*, June 30, 2008.
[‡] David Aquila Lawrence, "'Faceless' Justice in Drug Wars Faces Scrutiny in Colombia," *Las Vegas Sun*, March 34, 1997 (http://www.lasvegassun.com/news/1997/mar/24/faceless-justice-in-drug-war-faces-scrutiny-in-col/).

questions to consider

1. What is the best way to protect the safety of judges, prosecutors, and witnesses?

2. In what ways, if any, does preventing the accused from knowing the identities of their accusers violate due process?

3. Does anonymity of the judge pose any problem? For example, an anonymous judge in Colombia sentenced two leaders of a major drug cartel to very light sentences: only 10 and 12 years in prison.[‡] Should the judge have been publicly accountable for the sentences by having his identity revealed?

4. What do you think is the greatest threat to judicial independence in the United States? Is protecting the safety of judges a threat?

An independent judiciary protects the rule of law, ensuring that all parts of government are subservient to the Constitution. As Thomas Paine famously put it, "A constitution is a thing *antecedent* to a government, and a government is only the creature of a constitution."[5]

Not all countries that have a written constitution protect the rule of law. China has a written constitution, including guarantees of free speech and religious freedom, but its constitution is subservient to the Communist Party. Article 126 states that the courts shall "exercise judicial power independently and are not subject to interference by administrative organs, public organizations or individuals." Yet involvement by the Chinese Communist Party leadership in court decisions is deemed "leadership" rather than "interference."[6] Moreover, China has neither separation of powers (which allows the judiciary to be independent of the other branches) nor judicial review (which allows the judiciary to enforce the Constitution). Both are key elements of judicial independence that are essential to the rule of law.

judicial review
The power of courts, when confronted with a legitimate case, to review and strike down acts of government that violate the Constitution.

JUDICIAL REVIEW

KEY TO understanding ★

This section focuses on the power of judicial review. What is that power, where does the Supreme Court get it, and why is it so important? What is the difference between judicial review of coequal branches at the national level (justified in *Marbury v. Madison*) and judicial review of state action? Which has a stronger textual justification in the Constitution?

Judicial review is the power of courts to review acts of government and strike down those that violate the Constitution. Judicial review hinges upon both judicial independence and the separation of powers: the Court can strike down an act of Congress or declare other decisions by federal, state, and local governments unconstitutional. In this section, we will trace the development and application of this important judicial power.

THE CREATION OF JUDICIAL REVIEW

The Constitution did not specifically enumerate the power of judicial review. Some of the Framers, including Alexander Hamilton in *Federalist* 78, assumed that the power was implied, but the practice of judicial review was not firmly established until the 1803 Supreme Court case *Marbury v. Madison*.[7] However, precedents for judicial review had emerged long before the Constitution was written.

Precedents for Judicial Review

As early as 1610, a judge in England, Sir Edward Coke, suggested in *Dr. Bonham's Case* that "when an Act of Parliament is against common right and reason, or repugnant, or impossible to be performed, the common law will control it, and adjudge such Act to be void."[8] Coke's bold suggestion never took root in England. Some 150 years later, however, some American colonists—angered by actions of the British Parliament—embraced the concept of judicial review as a tool to check legislative abuse. Nonetheless, scholars are divided not only about how widely the doctrine of judicial review came to be accepted among the colonists but also over how frequently state courts actually exercised judicial review under the Articles of Confederation. Some claim that the practice of state courts using state constitutions to invalidate acts of state legislatures was widespread enough for the framers of the Constitution to simply assume the power without including any specific provision for it at the national level.[9] Others, however, disagree.[10]

The Framers' Intent

Scholars also debate the framers' intent. Notes revealing what went on at the Constitutional Convention are sketchy and incomplete—one reason why some people argue that "original intent" is so difficult to discern. The precise number of delegates who supported or rejected judicial review, and how strongly they held their views on that matter, may always remain unclear. Those who argue that the framers intended judicial review point to two clauses. The first is the "arising under" clause of Article III, Section 2, which states that "The judicial power shall extend to all cases, in law and equity, arising under this Constitution, the Laws of the United States, and Treaties. . . ." The other is the supremacy clause of Article VI, which says that "This Constitution, and the Laws of the United States which shall be made in pursuance thereof . . . shall be the supreme law of the Land. . . ." If federal courts have judicial power in all cases arising under the U.S. Constitution, and the U.S. Constitution is supreme, then surely the courts must enforce the Constitution against inferior laws that run contrary to it. But despite this logic, neither clause explicitly established judicial review, and both clauses could well have been passed without any expectation of judicial review.[11]

Those who argue that the framers assumed an inherent power of judicial review point to *Federalist 78*, where Alexander Hamilton wrote that courts are "the bulwarks of a limited Constitution against legislative encroachments,"[12] and that no legislative act that is contrary to the Constitution can be valid. The Court, Hamilton concluded, is in the best position to enforce the Constitution and police the limits of legislative authority.

MARBURY V. MADISON

Even if Hamilton's position enjoyed widespread support, the fact remains that the United States Supreme Court did not use the power of judicial review to invalidate an act of Congress for another 15 years.[13] This first use of judicial review came in *Marbury v. Madison.*

Marbury v. Madison
The 1803 Supreme Court case that serves as a precedent for the use of judicial review.

The Context of *Marbury v. Madison*

Marbury v. Madison arose out of the great tensions that surrounded the elections of 1800. Federalists fared poorly at both the national and state level in the elections of 1800.

They lost control of the White House and Congress to their rival Democratic-Republicans, and the elections turned out to be the beginning of the end of the Federalist Party. Thomas Jefferson's victory in the presidential election came only after high drama: a tie in the Electoral College that threw the election to the Federalist-controlled House of Representatives.[14]

In the midst of all the turmoil, the lame-duck Federalists passed the Judiciary Act of 1801, creating 16 new federal judgeships with lifetime tenure. They also passed additional legislation that created 42 justices of the peace with fixed terms of office in the District of Columbia. All were to be nominated by the incumbent Federalist president, John Adams, and confirmed by the lame-duck Federalist-controlled Senate. Federalists claimed the new judgeships were necessary, but the Democratic-Republicans cried foul, claiming they were part of a partisan ploy to pack the courts with loyal Federalists.

William Marbury was one of the 42 justices of the peace nominated by President Adams and confirmed by the Senate just before the Democratic-Republicans were due to take power. The last step in the appointment process was to deliver a commission: an official document signed by the president that conferred the post. The responsibility for delivering such commissions belonged to Adams' secretary of state, John Marshall, but Marbury's appointment had come so close to the end of the Adams administration that Marshall did not have time to deliver Marbury's commission. Thus, he left it for his successor to deliver. When President Jefferson took office, however, he forbade his secretary of state, James Madison, from delivering the commission. Marbury then sued Madison to force its delivery. Marbury brought his suit directly to the Supreme Court under its **original jurisdiction.** In his suit, Marbury asked the Court to issue a **writ of mandamus** commanding Secretary of State Madison to perform his official duty of delivering the commission.

Marbury could not have chosen a more favorable court to hear his case. Not only were all six members of the Supreme Court loyal Federalists, but the man who was supposed to deliver the commission in the first place—John Marshall—was now chief justice (having been nominated by President Adams and confirmed by the Senate during the lame-duck session controlled by the Federalists). Rather than **recuse** himself—that is, refuse to participate in the case because of a conflict of interest—Marshall not only participated in the case but wrote the opinion for the Court.

The Court decided *Marbury v. Madison* in the midst of a major power struggle between the federal judiciary, controlled by Federalists, and the other two branches, controlled by the Democratic-Republicans. Convinced that the federal courts had been politicized, the Democratic-Republican Congress repealed the Judiciary Act of 1801, thereby abolishing the federal judgeships it had created, and considered impeaching Federalist judges. In a brazen threat to judicial independence, Congress even cancelled the Supreme Court's 1802 term. When the Court finally heard arguments in *Marbury v. Madison* in 1803, Madison sent no lawyer to argue his side. In not sending a lawyer, he seemed to be casting doubt on the Court's authority and was probably signaling that he would not comply if the Court ruled against him—another threat to judicial independence.

Chief Justice Marshall feared that any ruling in *Marbury v. Madison* could further undermine the power and legitimacy of the Supreme Court.

original jurisdiction
The authority of the Supreme Court to hear a case that originates before it (as opposed to an appeal from a lower court).

writ of mandamus
A court order instructing an official to perform a mandatory duty.

recuse
When a judge does not participate in a case because of a conflict of interest or prejudice.

★ In an interview with Supreme Court Justice Antonin Scalia, *60 Minutes* reporter Leslie Stahl accused the Supreme Court of making a political decision to stop the recount in the close 2000 presidential election. Some believe the decision temporarily damaged the legitimacy of the Supreme Court.

If the Court issued the writ of mandamus but Secretary of State Madison ignored it, the weakness of the Court would be revealed. Madison's noncompliance would send a signal that others need not obey the Supreme Court either. On the other hand, if the Court did not issue the writ of mandamus, everyone would assume that it had simply caved in to pressure, so this decision, too, would seem to weaken the Court.

In the end, Marshall ingeniously crafted a decision in which the Court gave the Jefferson administration what it wanted (no writ of mandamus) but, in so doing, claimed for itself the power of judicial review. Rather than weakening the Court, the ruling in *Marbury v. Madison* actually increased its power, at least in the long run.

The Decision in *Marbury v. Madison*

In his opinion for the Court, Marshall conceded that Marbury had a right to his commission and that the law offered a remedy in the form of a writ of mandamus. However, he concluded that the legislative provision in the **Judiciary Act of 1789** that gave the Supreme Court the authority to issue such a writ was unconstitutional because it expanded the Court's original jurisdiction in violation of Article III, Section 2, paragraph 2 of the Constitution. According to Marshall, the Court's original jurisdiction could only be expanded through constitutional amendment. Therefore, the Court lacked jurisdiction to issue the writ.[15]

Judiciary Act of 1789
The act of Congress that established lower federal courts in the United States and defined the Supreme Court's appellate jurisdiction.

In striking down this portion of the Judiciary Act, the Court exercised the power of judicial review. Although this power is not enumerated in the Constitution, Marshall insisted that it is essential to limited government. The Constitution, he argued, is "the fundamental and paramount law of the nation," and it is "emphatically, the province and duty" of the Court "to say what the law is." If two laws conflict, the Court must choose between them as part of its judicial function. And, if the Court regards the Constitution as "superior to any ordinary act of the legislature, the constitution, and not such ordinary act, must govern the case to which they both apply"[16]

Marshall's argument in support of judicial review is compelling, but it has not gone unchallenged. Critics have argued that it gives too much power to unelected judges and undermines the majoritarian process by eroding the power of duly elected representatives in Congress to legislate. Justice John Bannister Gibson, of the Pennsylvania Supreme Court, responded in 1825 with a classic retort to John Marshall. All branches of government are *equal*, Gibson argued, and the oath to support the constitution is taken by all officers of government, not only judges. "For these reasons," he wrote, "I am of the opinion, that it rests with the people, in whom full and absolute sovereign power resides, to correct abuses in legislation, by instructing their representatives to repeal the obnoxious act."[17]

However, relying on the people to correct unconstitutional acts raises the threat of "tyranny of the majority." A majority can tyrannize just as much as an authoritarian monarch. The majority might not take the necessary steps to reject an unconstitutional law, and it may even embrace such a law. Moreover, voters tend to have short memories and are motivated by many factors. By the time of the next election the electorate might not remember their representative's support for an unconstitutional law, or they might cast their vote on the basis of other factors.

Gibson changed his mind 20 years later and came out in support of courts exercising the power of judicial review.[18] Today the power of judicial review is so entrenched in the United States that doing away with it would probably require a constitutional amendment. But controversy regarding judicial review remains—not over *whether*

★ A federal court of appeals struck down California Proposition 8, a 2008 ballot initiative and amendment to the California constitution banning same-sex marriage, arguing that it violated the due process and equal protection clauses of the U.S. Constitution. As a result, same-sex marriage remains legal in California.

courts have the power of judicial review, but over *when* and *how often* they should use it. We will return to this issue near the end of this chapter when we discuss judicial activism and judicial restraint.

JUDICIAL REVIEW OF STATE ACTION

Marbury v. Madison established the Supreme Court's power to review actions of coequal branches of government, but the supremacy clause affirms the Supreme Court's right to review the constitutionality of state laws. Judicial review of state action is arguably even more important than judicial review of coequal branches. The United States probably could have survived—and survived quite well—without judicial review of coequal branches. England has. But if the Supreme Court did not have judicial review of state action, our nation's success would have been less certain, with conflicting state and federal laws pulling the nation apart and no central authority to rein in disobedience from the states. What if a state refused to follow a treaty or would not comply with a federal law such as the Clean Air Act? What if it enacted laws in violation of due process or the First Amendment? Without judicial review of state action, there would be no judicial enforcement of the supremacy clause and the weaknesses of the Articles of Confederation would have continued under the new Constitution. As discussed in Chapter 4, the twentieth century saw the selective incorporation of the Bill of Rights. This process has left less discretion to individual states and led to controversy because incorporation has expanded the opportunity for judicial review of state laws dealing with contentious topics such as abortion, gay rights, school prayer, and obscenity.

JUDICIAL REVIEW AROUND THE WORLD

The United States was the first country to embrace the use of judicial review, followed by a few countries including Argentina and Canada in the nineteenth century. After World War II, the defeated Axis powers—Italy, Japan, and West Germany—adopted judicial review as part of their new constitutions, and other countries, including Belgium and Spain, followed suit. Another wave came after the collapse of the Berlin Wall in 1989 and the disintegration of the Soviet Union. Eager to protect their newfound freedom, Eastern European countries that had been under the control of the Soviet Union embraced judicial review. By the start of the twenty-first century, some 70 countries had adopted some form of judicial review, including much of Latin America.[19]

The term "judicial review" means different things in different countries (and sometimes even within a country). In the United States, we usually associate judicial review with "constitutional review," that is, with courts imposing constitutional limitations on government power. But some countries that do not give their courts the power to exercise constitutional review (such as England) do allow courts to subject administrative actions to judicial review. This is also a type of judicial review used in the United States. For example, the Supreme Court may review a specific action of the Environmental Protection Agency to see if it complies with the Clean Air Act. If the Court were to strike down the regulation in such a case, it would be doing so because the regulation violated an act of Congress, not because it violated the Constitution. In such a case, Congress could overturn the Court's ruling through simple legislation, thereby maintaining legislative supremacy.

In the United States, the Supreme Court cannot hear a case involving judicial review unless someone has been directly injured. As a result, the U.S. Supreme Court cannot issue *advisory opinions*—that is, rule on the constitutionality of a law before someone is injured. Nor can Congress ask the Supreme Court to offer its judgment on the constitutionality of a law before it is enacted. By contrast, advisory opinions on the constitutionality of proposed legislation are the most common form of constitutional review in western European countries. German law, for example, requires constitutional courts to resolve constitutional questions whenever they are asked to do so by an elected official.

Another big difference is that constitutional courts in some countries, such as Italy, France, Germany, and Spain, can use their power of judicial review not only to strike down laws but also to compel legislative action by issuing directives to the legislature. Their constitutions not only place *limits* on what government can do (negative rights) but also impose *duties* by telling government what it *must* do (positive rights).[20] For example, the German Federal Constitutional Court relied on the constitutional right of human dignity in Article One of the German constitution to declare that the government has a responsibility to rehabilitate criminals, and then the Court ordered legislation to accomplish that goal.[21]

★ Pearse Doherty, a member of the political party Sinn Féin, talks to reporters after he and others went to Ireland's High Court to seek judicial review of the government's failure to hold a special election to fill a vacant seat in the Irish Parliament. The Court ruled that the election must proceed, and Doherty won the seat.

AN OVERVIEW OF THE U.S. COURT SYSTEM

Our system of federalism has led to a complicated network of both federal and state courts, a marked contrast to the court system in countries such as France with a unitary system of government. The division in the United States between a system of federal courts and a system of state courts is sometimes referred to as a **dual court system.** But since each state creates its own system of courts, and since no two states have identical court systems, we really have 51 different court systems in the United States: one at the federal level plus 50 others.

Cases originate in **trial courts.** Thousands of trial courts are spread out across the United States at both the state and federal levels. Different courts have *jurisdiction* to hear different types of cases. *Territorial jurisdiction* involves the power of a court to hear cases within a certain geographic boundary. *Subject matter jurisdiction* involves the ability of a particular court to hear particular types of cases. Thus, Traffic Court would not have jurisdiction to try a murder case, nor would a court in Texas normally have the jurisdiction to hear a case involving a crime committed in Rhode Island.

KEY TO understanding ★

The United States has a complicated "dual system" of both state and federal courts with overlapping jurisdiction. Courts at both levels hear a variety of civil disputes and criminal cases. What are the advantages and disadvantages of this dual system?

dual court system
The existence of separate national and local courts in a federal system.

trial court
Courts where cases originate and trials take place (as opposed to appellate courts).

The U.S. Supreme Court, by contrast, is an **appellate court.** Each state also has appellate courts, and there are lower appellate courts at the federal level, too. Appellate courts review actions of lower courts to make sure that there was no error in their judgments.

Both federal and state courts have the power to hear two basic types of disputes: civil cases and criminal cases. In **civil cases,** one party sues another. These involve legal disputes over such matters as child custody, divorce, money, property, copyright infringement, personal injury, and failure to live up to a contractual obligation. Usually the parties in civil cases are private individuals or businesses. Monetary damages are often involved. But the government, or a government official, can also be a party in a civil case. *Marbury v. Madison* is a good example. In that case, Marbury—a private citizen—was suing a government official to get what he thought was rightfully his: delivery of the commission that would allow him to become a justice of the peace. The party who brings a civil suit against another is called the **plaintiff.** The party being sued is called the **defendant.** Sometimes a group of individuals collectively bring a suit. In such a case, called a **class action,** each participant in the class has suffered the same injury.

Criminal cases are brought by the government against an individual or a business accused of breaking the law. They involve crime and punishment and can result in fines, jail sentences, and even the death penalty, depending upon the seriousness of the crime and the jurisdiction where it is committed.

Criminal justice in the United States is based on the **adversarial system.** In this system, the defendant is presumed to be innocent, and guilt is determined through an adversarial process in which prosecutors face off against defense attorneys in a trial. The adversarial system is also used in Britain.

By contrast, the justice systems of many Latin American and European countries such as France are based on an **inquisitorial system.** The judge, in particular, plays a very different role in an inquisitorial system. Instead of presiding in a relatively passive fashion, as is the case in the adversarial system, the judge (or "magistrate") plays an active role in gathering evidence. It is the judge who decides if there is enough evidence to go to trial. If so, there is a presumption of guilt that the defendant must rebut. In the trial, the judge is primarily responsible for questioning witnesses. The attorneys in the case play a much more limited role than is the case in the adversarial system. The judge then decides the verdict and gives the sentence in the case. There is no jury. Rights of criminal defendants are more carefully protected in an adversarial system than they are in an inquisitorial system.

In the United States, minor criminal offenses, such as trespassing, disorderly conduct, and minor traffic violations, are called **misdemeanors.** Serious criminal offenses, such as murder, rape, and armed robbery, are called **felonies.** There is some variation from state to state both in what constitutes a crime (for example, whether possession of a small amount of marijuana is a crime) and in whether a crime is categorized as a felony or a misdemeanor (for example, the failure of convicted sex offenders to register with law enforcement agencies is categorized as a felony in some states and a misdemeanor in others).

Since states are responsible for creating most criminal laws, most criminal trials take place in state court. But Congress also passes criminal laws, punishing such offenses as counterfeiting, tax evasion, and the murder of government officials. The amount of criminal legislation passed by Congress has increased in recent years and has included legislation in some areas traditionally thought to be the province of the states, such as gun control and labor laws. Congress has accomplished this by relying on broad interpretations of constitutional provisions, such as its power to regulate interstate commerce (see Chapter 3).

Sometimes a single action can result in both a criminal case and a civil case. For example, a barroom brawl could result in criminal charges, such as assault and battery, and also in a civil suit between the parties involved, to recover monetary damages to pay for expenses such as medical treatment for injuries sustained. Thus, a jury famously found O. J. Simpson innocent in a state criminal trial for the murder of his ex-wife and her friend, but the jury in a subsequent civil case ordered Simpson to pay monetary damages to the families of the murder victims. The seemingly contradictory rulings are possible because the standard for guilt in a criminal case—guilty beyond all reasonable doubt—is higher than the preponderance of the evidence standard for guilt in civil suits.

Likewise, a single action can sometimes lead to separate cases in both state court and federal court. For example, officers from the Los Angeles Police Department were tried and acquitted in state court on multiple criminal charges—including assault, using excessive force, and filing a false police report—related to their conduct after stopping an African American named Rodney King for speeding on the night of March 2, 1991. However, a bystander had videotaped the police kicking King and striking him more than 50 times with their batons while King, who appeared to pose no threat, struggled on the ground. Public airings of the videotape led many to conclude that the officers were guilty, and their acquittal, in 1992, triggered riots in Los Angeles. Separate charges were subsequently brought in federal court where the officers were tried for violating federal civil rights laws. This time, two of the officers were found guilty and sentenced to serve 30 months in prison. In addition to the state and federal criminal cases, King also filed a civil suit in Los Angeles court against the officers. He won, and the jury awarded him $3.8 million in damages.

THE FEDERAL COURT SYSTEM

Only state courts existed under the Articles of Confederation, and those courts were free from control by the national government. Thus, courts in each state could interpret federal law differently. The resulting mayhem ensured a general agreement at the Constitutional Convention that there should be one national supreme court to hear appeals from state courts. But states' rights advocates, such as John Rutledge of South Carolina, were wary of a broader system of federal trial and appellate courts that they feared would undermine local control of justice and infringe upon the sovereignty of the states.[22]

The language of Article III of the Constitution, thus, was a compromise between those who wanted a powerful and extensive system of federal courts and those who remained fearful of such a system. Article III created one Supreme Court but postponed a decision about whether to create lower federal courts by leaving the decision to Congress. During the ratification debate, Anti-Federalists argued that even that compromise gave too much power to the national government.[23]

With the Judiciary Act of 1789, however, Congress quickly created a system of lower federal courts. Lower federal courts have been in place ever since, although Congress

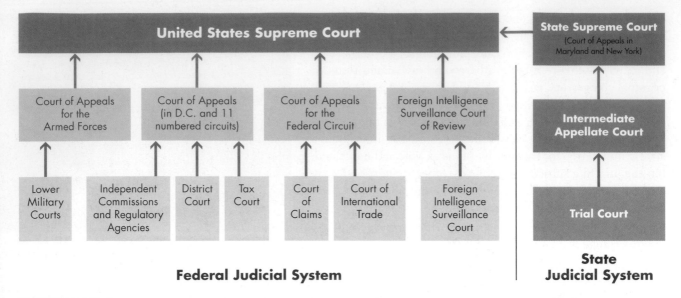

United States Supreme Court

State Supreme Court
(Court of Appeals in
Maryland and New York)

Court of Appeals for the Armed Forces

Court of Appeals (in D.C. and 11 numbered circuits)

Court of Appeals for the Federal Circuit

Foreign Intelligence Surveillance Court of Review

Intermediate Appellate Court

Lower Military Courts

Independent Commissions and Regulatory Agencies

District Court

Tax Court

Court of Claims

Court of International Trade

Foreign Intelligence Surveillance Court

Trial Court

Federal Judicial System

State Judicial System

FIGURE 15.1

★ THE STRUCTURE OF THE FEDERAL COURT SYSTEM

Source: From Harrison, American Democracy Now, 2/e TX ed. Copyright © 2011. Used by permission of McGraw-Hill Companies, Inc.

Article III courts
Federal courts created by Article III of the Constitution. Judges in these courts have life tenure.

Article I courts
Federal courts created by Congress under its power derived from Article I of the Constitution. Judges in these courts serve for fixed terms.

U.S. district courts
Federal trial courts, where most federal cases are initiated.

has changed the precise structure of those courts through legislation. The system comprises three levels of courts that form a sort of pyramid with the Supreme Court at the top (see Figure 15.1). The federal courts discussed below—district courts, courts of appeals, and the Supreme Court—all have *general jurisdiction,* or broad power to hear a wide range of cases. These courts are categorized as **Article III courts,** and their judges, as mandated by the Constitution, have life tenure.

In addition to these courts of general jurisdiction, the federal judicial system also includes a number of more specialized courts. Some of these specialized courts are also Article III courts—for example, the U.S. Court of International Trade, which hears trade cases, such as customs and border protection disputes. Other specialized courts have been created by Congress. These are known as **Article I courts.** Their judges do not have life tenure. An example is the U.S. Tax Court, which has the authority to resolve disputes involving the Internal Revenue Service and federal income tax.

U.S. District Courts

Courts designated as **U.S. district courts** are trial courts. Since this is where most federal cases originate (only a tiny fraction come to the Supreme Court under its original jurisdiction), district courts hear more cases than any other type of court in the federal system. There are also more district courts than any other kind of federal court: currently 94 courts with 678 full-time judgeships. District courts hear federal criminal cases as well as civil cases that meet one of these conditions:

- They are brought against the federal government.
- They involve a claim based on the U.S. Constitution, federal law, or a federal treaty.
- They involve a citizen of one state suing a citizen of another state and more than $75,000 is at issue.

Proceedings in district court are presided over by a single judge. Trials take place there, complete with jury, testimony by witnesses, cross examination, and the introduction of evidence. Each state has at least one district, and those with heavier caseloads have more than one (see Figure 15.2). No district extends beyond the boundary of a single state. In keeping with the concept of local control of justice, district courts are staffed with judges

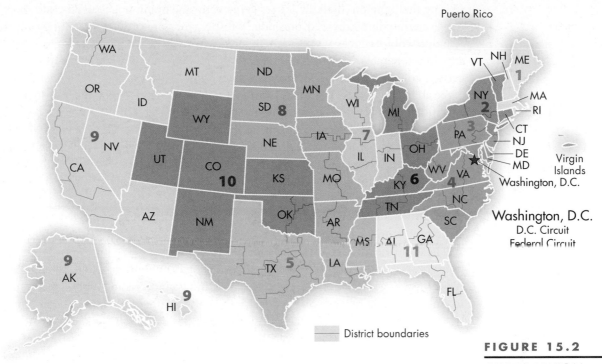

Puerto Rico

District boundaries

FIGURE 15.2

★ GEOGRAPHICAL
BOUNDARIES OF
U.S. COURTS OF
APPEALS AND U.S.
DISTRICT COURTS

who are residents of the state that the district falls within. Like all federal judges, district court judges are nominated by the president and confirmed by the Senate.

U.S. Courts of Appeals

The middle tier of the federal court system consists of the **U.S. courts of appeals.** These were originally called circuit courts (the current name has been in effect since 1948). Courts of appeals fall within a geographic region that is still known as a circuit, with each circuit made up of several districts. Currently, there are 12 regional circuits: one for the District of Columbia and 11 other numbered circuits covering the remainder of the country. In addition, there is a U.S. Court of Appeals for the Federal Circuit, which has nationwide jurisdiction over a variety of specialized subject matters including international trade, government contracts, trademarks, and veterans' benefits. As shown in Figure 15.2, each of the numbered circuits has jurisdiction over several states, although the number of states varies from circuit to circuit. The number of judges also varies across circuits, from 6 for the First Circuit to 28 for the Ninth Circuit, for a current total of 167 full-time judgeships.

The courts of appeals have jurisdiction to hear appeals from the district courts that fall within their particular circuit. As appellate courts, they answer questions of *law* rather than questions of *fact*. In other words, they determine whether the lower court made an error in its application of the law. Appeals are usually heard by a panel of three judges. Since this is not a trial but an appeal, there are no witnesses, no testimony, and no jury. Instead, lawyers representing both sides present legal arguments in the form of written **briefs.**

In many appeals, attorneys also present **oral arguments** in front of the judges. A majority vote of the judges is needed to overturn a lower court ruling, and the court of appeals issues a written opinion explaining its ruling. One judge is responsible for

U.S. courts of appeals
An intermediate level of federal appellate courts.

brief
A written statement of legal arguments submitted by the parties in a case and sometimes by outside groups.

oral arguments
The opportunity for lawyers on both sides of a case to appear before the appellate courts to give a verbal argument and respond to questions from the judges about why their side should prevail.

writing that opinion. If all the judges agree, only one opinion is issued by the court. If, however, the court is divided, one judge is responsible for writing the **majority opinion.** A judge who disagrees with the outcome described in the majority opinion explains why in a separate **dissenting opinion.** Even if the court is unanimous in arriving at a certain conclusion (say, overturning a conviction by a lower court), judges may disagree about some aspect of the reasoning used to arrive at that conclusion (such as the specific reason for overturning the conviction). If that is the case, a judge writes a separate **concurring opinion** to explain the alternate reasoning. All of these opinions are published, and the majority opinion serves as a **precedent** for rulings in subsequent cases decided in that circuit. Sometimes a precedent from one circuit conflicts with a precedent in another. Such disagreements can be resolved by appeal to the Supreme Court. If there is no appeal, or if the Supreme Court refuses to hear the appeal, such disagreements stand. Under such circumstances, a case might be resolved differently in one circuit from the way it would be resolved in another.

The doctrine of precedent, or ***stare decisis*** (Latin for "let the law stand"), has sometimes been compared with a coral reef. Both evolve, but both are solid structures that typically change slowly and thereby offer continuity and predictability. It is important to emphasize that reliance on past decisions is not rigidly mechanical. Precedents may be ignored in subsequent court decisions or—especially in the area of constitutional interpretation—they may be overruled by the Supreme Court. Louis Brandeis, who served as a justice on the Supreme Court from 1916 to 1939, argued that the law is partly a matter of trial and error. Judges learn from their past mistakes and correct them. In such cases, he wrote, courts bow "to the lessons of experience and the force of better reasoning."[24] But precedents may also be jettisoned for more cynical reasons, such as a desire by judges to achieve a particular policy outcome in a case. After all, judges don't just discover the law; they also make it.

The U.S. Supreme Court

The U.S. Supreme Court is the highest appellate court in the federal system. Its size is determined by Congress (another compromise at the Constitutional Convention). Originally set by the Judiciary Act of 1789 at six members, the Court fluctuated in size until after the Civil War, reaching a high of ten members in 1863 before being set at the current number of nine justices in 1869.[25] The nineteenth-century increases in size usually were intended to accommodate the increased caseload brought about by the addition of new states, especially since Supreme Court justices were then responsible for **circuit riding**—each justice was assigned a circuit in which he was required to hear cases (at that time, circuit courts did not have their own judges). Circuit riding was minimized by the creation of separate circuit court judges in the Judiciary Act of 1869, but not completely abolished until 1911.

The vast majority of the cases heard by the Supreme Court are appeals. Litigants can appeal a decision from the U.S. courts of appeals to the Supreme Court. Cases from the highest appellate court in a state can also be appealed to the Supreme Court as long as they involve a **federal question**—that is, a dispute over how to interpret the U.S. Constitution, federal law, or a federal treaty. Such cases would include, for example, appeals from criminal defendants convicted under state law who allege that their constitutional rights were violated by such practices as a coerced confession or the introduction of improperly obtained evidence.

Note that a variety of "gatekeeping rules" limit the types of cases the Court can hear. There must be an injured party with **standing** to bring the case. There must also be a

Civil Court structure

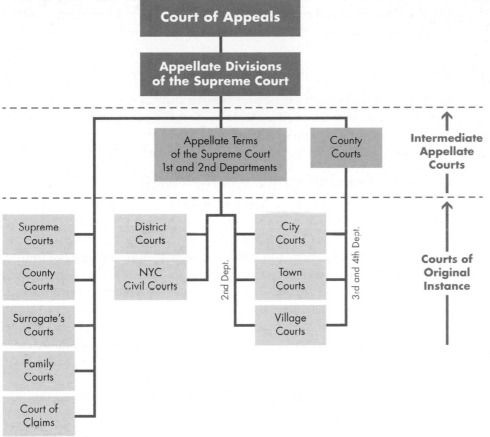

FIGURE 15.3

★ STATE COURT STRUCTURE OF NEW YORK

Source: From New York State Unified Court System, (http://courts.state.ny.us/courts/structure.shtml)

Criminal Court structure

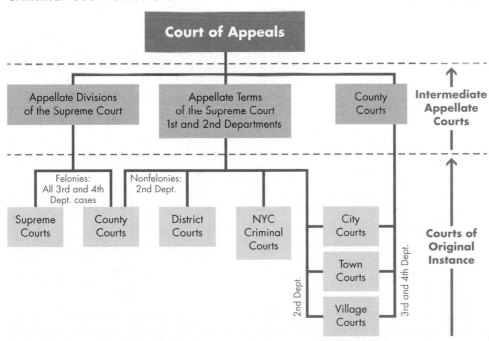

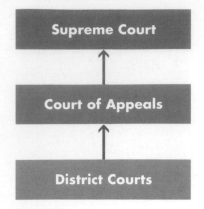

courts of limited jurisdiction
Courts that hear a specialized type
of case (such as Traffic Court).

courts of general jurisdiction
Courts that have broad authority to
hear a wide range of cases.

appellate jurisdiction
The authority of a higher court to
review the judgment of a lower
court.

real, live "case or controversy" that is sufficiently ripe (the case cannot be a hypothetical one in which no one has yet been injured) and the case cannot be moot (a real conflict must still exist). If events have transpired that resolve the conflict, the case is considered moot and the Court will not rule on it.

STATE COURT SYSTEMS

Most cases are not heard in federal court but in a state court system, where the vast majority of cases end. Since each state has its own distinct system of courts, a comprehensive overview is impossible. Some state court systems, such as New York's, are very complicated (see Figure 15.3), while others, such as Minnesota's, are much simpler (see Figure 15.4). Nonetheless, some generalizations about state courts can be made. Like federal courts, state courts are divided between trial courts and appellate courts, although the names of these courts differ from state to state.

In most states, trial courts, the point of entry into the state judicial system, are themselves subdivided into courts of limited jurisdiction, also called "minor trial courts," and courts of general jurisdiction, also called "major trial courts." **Courts of limited jurisdiction** can hear only certain specialized types of cases. Divorce Court, Small Claims Court, and Traffic Court are all examples of courts of limited jurisdiction. They hear cases that are less serious than those heard in courts of general jurisdiction. **Courts of general jurisdiction** have broad authority to hear a wide range of serious cases. These include civil suits involving large sums of money and criminal cases involving serious felonies. In contrast, most misdemeanors and minor civil disputes would be heard in courts of limited jurisdiction.

Most states have an intermediate level of appellate courts, which perform a function similar to the U.S. courts of appeals at the federal level. All states have an appellate court of last resort, which is usually called the state's "supreme court." Although states are bound by the Supremacy Clause to follow the U.S. Constitution, federal law, and federal treaties, it is possible—absent some explicit legal prohibition—for state constitutions and state courts to extend rights further than the federal government. For example, the Supreme Judicial Court of Massachusetts ruled in 2003 that it was unconstitutional under the Massachusetts constitution to ban same-sex marriage, thus paving the way for Massachusetts to become, in 2004, the first state to recognize same-sex marriage.[26]

THE SUPREME COURT IN ACTION

★ **KEY** to understanding

This section examines how cases get to the Supreme Court and, once there, how they are decided. What factors influence whether the Court will "grant cert" in a particular case? Why do so few cases reach the Supreme Court?

The Supreme Court has two types of jurisdiction: original and appellate. Original jurisdiction, which allows a case to originate before the Supreme Court, is spelled out in the Constitution and cannot be altered by Congress. Cases that fall under its original jurisdiction constitute a minuscule portion of the cases currently heard by the Court (usually no more than two or three a year). The vast majority of the cases are appeals heard under its **appellate jurisdiction**, which is regulated by Congress.

Since 1925, the Supreme Court, with rare exceptions, has had the power to decide which appeals it will accept, and today it accepts very few. Currently, some 7,000 cases a year are appealed to the Supreme Court, but on average it accepts only about 100 for review.[27] Most litigants do not even attempt an appeal. As a result, the courts of appeals have the final word in over 99 percent of the cases that come before them.[28] To see the number of cases that have been decided by the Supreme Court from 1970 through 2010, see Figure 15.5.

GETTING TO THE COURT: PETITIONING FOR A WRIT OF *CERTIORARI*

Since 1988, almost all appeals reach the Supreme Court by way of a **writ of certiorari.**[29] *Certiorari* is a Latin term that means "to make more certain." Litigants who petition the Court for a writ of certiorari are asking it to review their case. Most petitions come from the U.S. Courts of Appeals or (as long as there is a federal question) a state court of last resort, but under some circumstances an appeal can come from a special three-judge U.S. District Court. Currently, it takes four of the nine justices on the Supreme Court to **grant cert**—that is, to accept the petition and agree to hear the case. This practice is known as the **rule of four.**

Law clerks—law school graduates who assist the individual justices—are responsible for the initial review of cert petitions. Currently each justice can have up to four clerks. Almost all of the clerks have already held a similar position for a lower federal court judge.[30] One of the first tasks of the law clerks is to prepare "cert memos" for their justices, recommending whether cert should be granted in that case. Justices review these memos to help them decide how to vote. If the Supreme Court does not grant cert in a particular case, the lower court ruling is left undisturbed. The rejection of cert in a particular case is not an endorsement of the lower court ruling; it is simply a decision not to review that ruling.[31]

Cert is far more likely to be granted if the case is brought by the **solicitor general,** a senior member of the Justice Department, appointed by the president with the advice and consent of the Senate, who plays an important role in setting the agenda for the courts of appeals and the Supreme Court. Responsible for handling all appeals on behalf of the U.S. government, the solicitor general decides which of the cases the government loses in lower federal courts will be appealed.[32]

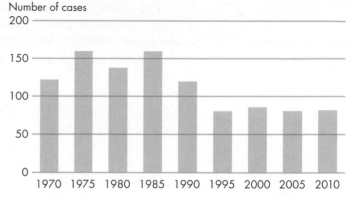

Number of cases

FIGURE 15.5

★ NUMBER OF CASES DECIDED BY THE U.S. SUPREME COURT, 1970–2010 TERMS

Source: Data from http://www.scotusblog.com/reference/stat-pack/

writ of certiorari
An instruction to a lower court to send up the record in a particular case. This is the most common avenue for appeal to the U.S. Supreme Court.

grant cert
The decision by the Supreme Court to issue a writ of certiorari—that is, to agree to review a decision by a lower court.

rule of four
The requirement that four of the nine justices on the Supreme Court vote to grant a writ of certiorari.

solicitor general
A senior member of the Justice Department who is responsible for handling all appeals of cases in which the U.S. government is a party.

★ Does the Mojave Memorial Cross, erected in 1934 by the VFW in the Mojave National Preserve to honor fallen soldiers from World War I and rebuilt in 1998, violate the establishment clause? The Ninth Circuit Court of Appeals said yes, but the U.S. Supreme Court said no because Congress had transferred the land under the cross to the VFW. The Supreme Court's ruling accepted the argument of then-solicitor-general Elena Kagan.

The solicitor general also decides what position the government should take and argues the case before the Court. Such arguments stand a very good chance of being successful. Political scientist Kevin McGuire suggests that this high success rate is largely attributable to the solicitor general's extensive litigation experience before the Court.[33] Solicitors general and members of their staff argue far more cases before the Court than any other party. The solicitor general may also build up credit with the Court by minimizing the number of government appeals and thus helping the justices manage their caseload.

HOW THE COURT DECIDES CASES

docket
A list of cases that a court is scheduled to decide.

Once the Supreme Court grants cert, the case is added to the Court's **docket,** a list of cases that the Court will hear, and assigned a number. Lawyers representing both sides of the case file written briefs with the Court containing detailed legal arguments. In addition, interest groups and other parties with a stake in the outcome of the case may, with the permission of the Court, file separate *amicus curiae* **briefs,** arguing in favor of a particular outcome.

amicus curiae briefs
"Friend of the court" briefs submitted by third parties who are not named in a case but who hope to influence the outcome of a particular case.

Amicus curiae briefs are as close to lobbying the Court as interest groups get, and they are the most common type of interest group involvement in litigation. Interest groups can also sponsor litigation. For example, the NAACP Legal Defense Fund, created in 1939, achieved great success in advancing civil rights by identifying individuals whose civil rights had been violated and offering legal support to bring those cases to court (see Chapter 5). Many other groups, such as the American Civil Liberties Union, have also sponsored cases. Sponsorship by interest groups allows the court to hear cases that litigants might not otherwise have the initiative or financial resources to bring.[34]

After reviewing the written briefs, justices hear oral arguments. Early in our nation's history, there was no limit to how long oral arguments could last, and some went on for days. In 1848, the Court limited oral arguments in a single case to eight hours, with subsequent reductions coming in 1871 and 1911. Since 1925, each side has gotten just 30 minutes to argue its case, although more time is occasionally granted in exceptional cases.[35]

Justices frequently interrupt oral arguments with questions. Such questions are very important—not only as a way for the lawyers to respond to the justices, but as a way for the justices to communicate to each other which issues in the case they deem especially important. It is, after all, the first and only time that the justices gather as a group and concentrate on the single case before them until they meet at conference to vote. Oral arguments are the only public part of the Supreme Court's deliberation. Television cameras are not allowed, but oral arguments have been tape-recorded since 1955. In rare instances, such as *Bush v. Gore* in 2000, the Court released the audio immediately and allowed it to be broadcast. Since 2010, the Court has posted audio files of the oral arguments on its website (www.supremecourt.gov) the Friday of each week in which arguments are heard. Transcripts are posted on the website the same day as the oral argument.

conference
A meeting of Supreme Court justices in which they discuss cases and vote on how those cases should be decided.

After oral arguments, the justices meet privately in their Friday **conference,** where they vote on how the case should be decided. The conference is highly structured. The justices usually come to it having already made up their minds about how to vote. The chief justice summarizes the case. Then each of the justices, starting with the chief and proceeding in order of seniority, announces his or her vote and summarizes the reasoning behind it. By the time the junior justices have their chance to speak, there is usually little left to say.[36] If the chief justice is in the majority, he chooses who will write the opinion. If he is not, the longest serving justice in the majority chooses. Any of the justices may write a separate dissenting or concurring opinion.

Law clerks often play an important role in drafting opinions. One law clerk estimated that "well over half of the text the Court now produces was generated by law clerks."[37] This has led some critics to argue that clerks have become too powerful.[38] Once written, all of the opinions are circulated among the justices, and revisions may ensue. Occasionally, justices will even change their vote. No opinion is considered final or binding until it is officially announced. As soon as the decision is announced in open court, the Supreme Court's public information office makes the full text of the opinions available to the public. They are posted online and also published by the government in volumes called *U.S. Reports.*

THE ROLE OF JUDICIAL PHILOSOPHY IN DECISION MAKING

Scholars have identified three models to explain judicial decision making. The first, called the **legal model,** assumes that judges are impartial and that they simply apply the law by examining relevant legal texts. In other words, judging is a process of discovery. The emphasis is on a close reading of legal texts (sometimes called "strict construction") and a strong reliance on precedent. As suggested in Figure 15.6, this is the approach favored by the public.

The second, called the **attitudinal model,** assumes that judges are policy-makers and that they decide cases based on their personal policy preferences, or "attitudes." According to this approach, judging is a process of creation, with legal precedents being used to justify a particular outcome rather than to dictate that outcome. Thus, proponents of the attitudinal model use the ideology of individual judges, rather than an analysis of precedents and legal texts, to predict how they will vote.

The third, called the **strategic model,** also assumes that judges are policy-makers but recognizes that judges operate under certain constraints. Blindly voting one's preference, as the attitudinal model predicts, may not make much sense if you are on the losing side. Instead, the strategic model assumes that judges are pragmatic, getting as close to their preferences as possible by building winning coalitions. This model explains why justices sometimes change their vote between the conference and the announcement of the court's decision.

Even if judges want to follow the legal model and just "discover" the law, they face some major difficulties because the precise meaning of specific constitutional language and other legal texts is often elusive. The Fourth Amendment bans "unreasonable searches and seizures," but what exactly does that phrase mean? Judges disagree not only about what the word "unreasonable" means, but also about what constitutes a "search" (for instance, is a wiretap a search?). The problem extends to many of the most important clauses of the Constitution. What exactly does "due process" mean? "Equal protection"? "Cruel and unusual punishment"? Even seemingly straightforward clauses, like the First Amendment command that Congress shall make no law abridging

KEY TO understanding ★

What guides Supreme Court justices when they decide a case and write a legal opinion? Their "judicial philosophy"—their choices about how to decipher ambiguous texts and how deferential they should be to the other branches when exercising judicial review—can have a powerful impact on the decisions they make. In particular, we focus on judicial "activism" versus "restraint." What characterizes each approach? How does the test used by each approach affect judicial outcomes?

legal model
A model of judicial decision making that assumes judges will decide cases according to the law (as opposed to the attitudinal model).

attitudinal model
A model of judicial decision making that assumes judges will decide cases according to their ideological preferences (or attitudes).

strategic model
A model of judicial decision making that assumes judges are rational actors who will strategically try to get as close to their preferences as possible by building winning coalitions.

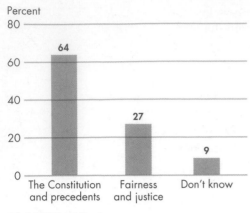

Percent

FIGURE 15.6

★ RULED BY THE CONSTITUTION—OR
FAIRNESS?

The graph shows how people responded to
a pollster's question about what basis the
Supreme Court should use in making decisions.
What problems might occur when people
expect a judge to make a decision based solely
on what is written in the U.S. Constitution?

Source: Data from Matthew J. Franck, "Ruled by the Constitution -or
'Fairness'?" National Review, February 3, 2009, (http://www
.nationalreview.com/bench-memos/50482/ruled-constitution-or-
fairness/matthew-j-franck)

**jurisprudence of original
intent**
An approach to interpreting the
Constitution that relies on the
original intent of its framers to
clarify the meaning of ambiguous
clauses.

judicial restraint
The idea that the Supreme Court
should defer to the actions of other
branches of government as long as
they have a rational basis.

judicial activism
The idea that the Supreme Court
should strictly scrutinize actions of
other branches of government that
restrict fundamental rights, such as
free speech.

freedom of speech, can lead to widely divergent interpretations because people can reasonably disagree about what constitutes "speech" (see Chapter 4). Hence, a judge's own value judgments and ideological predilections may influence how these questions are answered. To the extent that this happens, unelected judges expose themselves to charges that they are "legislating from the bench" and making policy. Concern about judicial policy making has led some to call for ways to limit the opportunity for judicial discretion.

THE JURISPRUDENCE OF ORIGINAL INTENT

One suggestion for limiting judicial discretion is to try to minimize the ambiguity of constitutional language by determining the original intent of those who framed it, but this approach is problematic. First, original intent may be impossible to discern. For one thing, the evidence may be lacking (notes from the convention are notoriously incomplete). For another, the Constitution was a jointly drafted document that required compromise. As a result, language was sometimes purposely ambiguous. Second, whose intent counts? Not only did members of the Constitutional Convention disagree, but so did those who voted on ratification of the Constitution. Third, even if the intent is clear, is it relevant for us today? Some argue that it is anachronistic to allow people who lived generations before us in entirely different societal settings to dictate the current meaning of a phrase like "cruel and unusual punishment." They argue that each generation must apply such language using contemporary standards. Nonetheless, proponents of the **jurisprudence of original intent** argue that the intent of the framers is as good as written into the Constitution if it can be determined.

JUDICIAL RESTRAINT VERSUS JUDICIAL ACTIVISM

Some people suggest that another way to limit judicial discretion is for judges to minimize the opportunity for policy making by using self-restraint and employing judicial review very sparingly. According to this concept of **judicial restraint,** when a range of different interpretations are all plausible, judges should defer to the other branches and the will of the majority in choosing among the interpretations. To do otherwise would result in unelected judges substituting their policy preferences for the policy preferences of those who have been elected by the people.

Judges who use judicial restraint employ the rational basis test to assess laws whose constitutionality has been challenged. A judge who uses the rational basis test would start with the default position of deference to the other branches. For example, if an act of Congress is being challenged, the judge starts out with the assumption that it is constitutional. The burden of proof would then be on the party challenging the law to convince her otherwise. In other words, the judge must be convinced that the law lacks a rational basis—that it is arbitrary and unreasonable. This is difficult to do, so use of the rational basis test usually allows a law to stand.

Not everyone is content with so passive a use of judicial review. Those who favor a more aggressive use of judicial review—**judicial activism**—argue that whenever the Court reviews a case in which a law restricts a fundamental constitutional right, like freedom of speech, the Court must subject the law to strict scrutiny. A judge who uses the strict scrutiny test starts with the assumption that any law that violates a fundamental right must initially be presumed to be unconstitutional. Therefore, the burden of proof shifts away from the party challenging the law to the government. In other words, the government must convince the Court that the law is, in fact, constitutional. To do this, the government must do more than just show that there is a rational basis for the law. It must show that the government has a compelling interest that justifies restricting a fundamental right. The Court must also be convinced that the law is "narrowly tailored." When limiting speech, for example, strict scrutiny only allows government to restrict speech that poses a "clear and present danger." If a law is "overbroad" and limits other speech as well, the presumption of unconstitutionality would be maintained. Strict scrutiny is also triggered by laws that discriminate on the basis of race (see Chapter 5).

The problem, of course, is determining which constitutional rights are fundamental. Activists believe some constitutional rights are more important than others. These include, for example, freedom of speech and the press, and the religious freedoms. In contrast, restraintists reject an "Honor Roll" of rights and insist that all constitutional rights should be treated equally.

Nothing compels a judge to use one test over another, so the decision of which test to use is his or her own choice. Decisions about these and other tests help to form a judge's "judicial philosophy"—an approach to how cases should be decided. But the choice of which test to use is often key to determining how a case will be resolved. That is why the judicial philosophy of a nominee for a federal judicial post, especially the Supreme Court, draws such close attention. Finally, it is essential to remember that the distinguishing characteristic that divides judicial activism from judicial restraint is the degree of deference to other parts of government and to the majoritarian process, *not ideology*. In certain time periods, ideology may be correlated with one or the other approach, but history clearly shows that such ideological links are not consistent over time.

LIMITS ON THE SUPREME COURT

What recourse exists if the Supreme Court abuses its power of judicial review? The Constitution sanctions several limits on the Court's power. Beyond these is the potential for outright resistance to Court decisions through noncompliance.

Judicial independence does not mean that judges are not held accountable for their decisions. There are a variety of limits on the Supreme Court that can be invoked if it overreaches or abuses its power. These range from a variety of constitutional checks to simple noncompliance with Court rulings. Are these limits sufficient?

KEY TO understanding ★

CONSTITUTIONAL CHECKS

There are several limits on the Supreme Court that are sanctioned by the Constitution. These include constitutional amendments to overturn Court rulings; use of Congress's Exceptions Clause power to take away the Court's jurisdiction to hear certain types of appeals; impeachment of judges; and Congress's power to change the size of the Court (and thereby alter its composition).

Constitutional amendments are difficult to enact. Amendments have succeeded in overturning a Supreme Court decision only four times in U.S. history.[39] As we saw at the outset of this chapter, George W. Bush called for a constitutional amendment to ban same-sex marriage, but the amendment failed to get enough support in Congress to be sent to the states for ratification. Likewise, both Ronald Reagan and George H.W. Bush sought unsuccessfully to overturn *Roe v. Wade*, the 1973 abortion rights decision, by constitutional amendment.

Use of Congress's Exceptions Clause power to strip the Supreme Court of its ability to hear appeals in certain types of cases is also extremely rare. It is also controversial because, if abused, it could possibly infringe on basic rights by closing off avenues of appeal. Since the Exceptions Clause contains no precise limit on the number of "exceptions" Congress can make to the Supreme Court's appellate jurisdiction, one can imagine a scenario in which so much appellate jurisdiction is withdrawn that the core function of the Supreme Court—its power to review actions of lower courts—is eviscerated. Would such an extreme use of the Exceptions Clause violate the separation of powers? Some legal scholars say yes. Luckily, we have never had to confront that issue. Most attempts to withdraw jurisdiction fail, but the Supreme Court did uphold the constitutionality of such withdrawals in an 1869 case in which Congress took away the Court's power to review habeas corpus appeals.[40]

Congress can also remove Supreme Court justices and other federal judges through impeachment, but impeachment is a difficult, time-consuming process that is seldom used. The only Supreme Court justice ever impeached by the House of Representatives (Samuel Chase in 1804) was acquitted by the Senate and remained on the bench. Only twelve other federal judges have been impeached by the House in the entire history of the United States, and only seven have been removed after a Senate trial.

Finally, Congress can alter the size of the Supreme Court (thus providing the opportunity to pack it with a new majority of justices who could overturn earlier rulings). Congress has not changed the size of the Supreme Court since 1869. President Franklin Roosevelt encouraged Congress to do so in 1937 because a conservative majority on the Court was striking down major pieces of New Deal legislation, but his suggestion was viewed as politically motivated and Congress did not increase the size of the Court.

Even though they are rarely carried out, the mere threat of these constitutional checks may be enough to influence the Court's decisions.

NONCOMPLIANCE

It is also important to remember that the Supreme Court depends on other institutions to enforce its rulings. When the Court, in an opinion written by Chief Justice John Marshall, ruled that Cherokee Indians in Georgia had tribal sovereignty, President Andrew Jackson supposedly said, "John Marshall has made his decision; now let him enforce it."[41]

The Supreme Court hands down rulings, but the actual implementation of those rulings is left to others. The Court may rule, for example, that state-sponsored prayer in public schools violates the Constitution, but enforcement of that ruling depends upon the support of a wide array of players, including school administrators and teachers.

Whether it be a public act of defiance—like Roy Moore, the former Chief Justice of the Supreme Court of Alabama, defying an order by a federal court to remove a 5,280-pound granite monument to the Ten Commandments that he had installed in the rotunda of the state judicial building, or Governor Orval Faubus of Arkansas standing in the schoolhouse door in Little Rock to block school desegregation ordered by the Supreme Court in *Brown v. Board of Education*—or a more subtle failure to implement

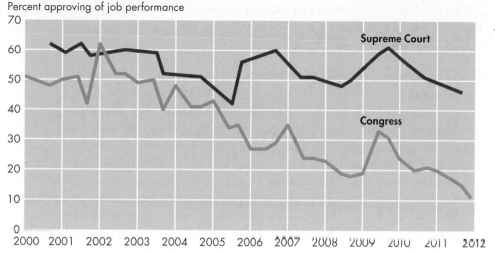

Percent approving of job performance

FIGURE 15.7

★ PUBLIC APPROVAL OF
THE SUPREME COURT
COMPARED WITH THAT
OF CONGRESS

How does public approval
of the Supreme Court
compare with public
approval of Congress? Do
you find it odd that
approval is lower for an
elected branch of
government than it is for the
unelected Court? What role
might judicial
independence play in the
Court's approval ratings?

Source: Data from www.pollingreport.com

some aspect of a judicial decision, noncompliance with Supreme Court rulings happens more often than one might think.[42] Noncompliance can be rectified (Moore was removed from office, and President Eisenhower called out the National Guard to enforce school desegregation), but not by the Supreme Court itself.

The Court's main source of power is its legitimacy. If it loses its legitimacy, compliance becomes much more difficult to achieve. As shown in Figure 15.7, the Supreme Court has maintained a relatively high level of public approval in recent years. A desire to maintain legitimacy is what motivates some to advocate judicial restraint and urge judges to defer to the will of the majority. And even though we sometimes focus on a few key cases in which the Supreme Court, rather than elected parts of government, spurred social change (such as *Brown v. Board of Education* and *Roe v. Wade*), the fact of the matter is that the Supreme Court seldom bucks public opinion for long. As political scientist Robert Dahl famously put it: "Except for short-lived transitional periods when the old alliance is disintegrating and the new one is struggling to take control of political institutions, the Supreme Court is inevitably a part of the dominant national alliance."[43] This is because the dominant national alliance ultimately chooses who sits on the Court.

HOW JUDGES ARE SELECTED

The way judges are selected can have an important impact on just how independent judges really are. The Framers designed the procedure for selecting federal judges to support judicial independence by preventing one part of government from dominating the selection process. We will examine judicial selection at both the federal and the state levels.

The process of selecting judges at the state level is different from the way it is handled at the federal level. Some aspects of lower federal judicial selection vary from the way Supreme Court justices are selected. How do these differences affect judicial independence? What qualities should be considered when selecting judges? How important are representational considerations, such as race, gender, party affiliation, religion, and geographic representation? Doctrinal considerations?

KEY TO understanding ★

THE SELECTION OF SUPREME COURT JUSTICES

Article II, Section 2 of the Constitution gives the president the power to nominate Supreme Court justices, but appointment comes only with the "Advice and Consent of the Senate." The Senate has the power to confirm or reject a president's nominee by a simple majority vote. A filibuster is possible, although there has been lively debate about whether or not filibusters should be used against judicial nominees.

Choosing Supreme Court Nominees

In contrast with its very specific requirements for presidents, senators, and representatives, the Constitution contains no specific requirements for Supreme Court justices—no minimum age requirement, no citizenship requirements, not even a requirement that justices be lawyers. While all Supreme Court justices have been lawyers, many were appointed without any prior experience as a judge. That lack of judicial experience did not seem to handicap justices such as John Marshall, Felix Frankfurter, Earl Warren, and William Rehnquist, none of whom had been a judge before serving on the Supreme Court. In stark contrast, many other nations, such as Japan and most European countries, have a cadre of professional judges. Much like civil servants, they devote their careers to judging and are promoted through the judicial hierarchy.[44]

Lack of formal constitutional or statutory requirements does not mean that unofficial standards are not in place for screening prospective nominees. Since 1853 the Justice Department has identified and recommended potential nominees. Today, the Office of White House Counsel, created as part of the president's personal staff during the administration of Harry S. Truman (1946–1953), also plays an important role in the vetting process, and the FBI conducts background checks of all potential nominees.

In addition to the vetting process that goes on within the government, the American Bar Association (ABA) reviews the professional qualifications of all federal judicial nominees, including Supreme Court nominees, and rates each one. The ABA began this practice in 1946; in 1953, President Dwight D. Eisenhower established a formal relationship with the ABA, agreeing that the president would not nominate anyone without an ABA rating. At the time, the ABA was a conservative organization, but over the years it has become more liberal. Conservatives have alleged that ABA ratings reflect the ideology of the nominee. At least one scholarly study reinforces this allegation.[45] This concern led George W. Bush to sever the White House relationship with the ABA in 2001, but Barack Obama reestablished it in 2009.

High professional standards are a fundamental criterion for selecting Supreme Court nominees. That is not, however, the only criterion. Presidents take into account at least two other factors: representational and doctrinal considerations.

Representational considerations include the partisan affiliation of nominees, the geographic regions that they come from, and other factors such as their race, gender, religion, and ethnicity. With rare exceptions, presidents appoint justices who share their political affiliation. Circuit riding made geographic representation a necessity in the early part of our history, but presidents still make an effort to have geographic diversity on the Court. Sometimes this is done for political reasons. Both Herbert Hoover and Richard Nixon nominated southerners to the Court as part of an effort to build electoral support in the South for their respective reelection bids.

For much of our history, the Court, like the nation's other political institutions, was overwhelmingly white, male, and Protestant. Lyndon Johnson appointed the first African-American justice (Thurgood Marshall) to the Supreme Court in 1967, and Ronald Reagan appointed the first woman (Sandra Day O'Connor) in 1981. A "Catholic seat" on the Court existed by tradition starting in 1836, as did a "Jewish seat" since 1916 (except for 1969 to 1993). With George W. Bush's appointments of John G. Roberts, Jr., and Samuel A. Alito, Jr., in 2006, Catholics made up a majority of the Supreme Court for the first time, and with Barack Obama's appointments of Sonia Sotomayor and Elena Kagan, six Catholics and three Jews sat on the Court. It was the first time in history that no Protestants sat on the Court. Ethnic considerations are also a factor. Both Bill Clinton and George W. Bush seriously considered appointing a Hispanic to the Court, but the distinction went to Obama with his appointment of Sotomayor in 2009.

★ In order to win confirmation, Supreme Court nominees must now engage in grueling televised testimony before the Senate Judiciary Committee. Sonia Sotomayor is shown here during her testimony.

Doctrinal considerations center on a nominee's judicial philosophy and approach to public policy issues, with presidents seeking to choose individuals whose views are similar to their own. In theory, impartial judges who objectively apply the Constitution and other legal texts according to established standards of interpretation should all reach the same "correct" decision in cases that come before them. But, in practice, judges hold very different views about how to interpret such texts. After all, judges are human beings who are influenced, at least in part, by their backgrounds, political and religious beliefs, and personal predilections. Quite simply, different justices will often reach different conclusions when confronted with the same case. Thus, George W. Bush relied on the conservative Federalist Society to help vet nominees.

Doctrinal considerations are important because they can have an impact on how the Supreme Court will rule on important matters of public policy. Since federal judges have life tenure, presidents make Supreme Court appointments (and other federal judicial appointments) knowing that their choices can affect the outcome of cases for years to come. Presidents can never completely guarantee how their appointees will end up voting once they are on the bench, and the degree to which presidents now screen nominees for ideological purity varies from one administration to another. Still, doctrinal considerations continue to be an important factor in selecting judicial nominees.

Confirming Supreme Court Nominees

Once nominated by the president, a candidate to the Supreme Court must be confirmed by the Senate. This requires a simple majority vote unless the nomination faces a filibuster. Some other countries, including Argentina, Latvia, and South Korea, have a similar system in which the legislature confirms judicial nominees submitted by the executive. But in most countries, judges are appointed unilaterally by some part of the executive branch, be it the monarch (as in Belgium and Sweden), the president (as in India and Sri Lanka), or the prime minister (as in Canada, where the prime minister acts on the advice of the governor general).[46] Some countries share the responsibility of appointing judges but without a formal check like Senate confirmation in the U.S. system. For example, the Italian Supreme Constitutional Court (the Corte Suprema Costituzionale) consists of 15 judges. Five are appointed by the president, five are appointed by a joint session of the parliament, and five are chosen by judges from three Italian courts. None, however, are subject to a confirmation vote.[47]

Before the full U.S. Senate debates and votes on a nominee, the Senate Judiciary Committee holds hearings. Until the twentieth century, the deliberation of the Judiciary Committee was usually a very secretive process. Its hearings took place behind closed doors, as did Senate floor debate on judicial nominees, and often there was not even a roll-call vote. Nominees did not testify at the committee hearings, nor did they talk to the press. Presidents also remained publicly silent about their nominees.

The process changed over the course of the twentieth century. The ratification of the Seventeenth Amendment to the Constitution in 1913 led to the direct election of senators (thereby allowing for electoral retaliation), and Senate rule changes in 1929 opened floor debate on a regular basis (allowing interest groups and the public to see where senators stood). Shortly thereafter, the Senate Judiciary Committee opened its hearings to the public. Representatives of organized interest groups first testified at a Supreme Court confirmation hearing in 1930 and have testified at every confirmation hearing since 1971. Nominees have routinely testified at their confirmation hearings since 1955 (although Harlan Fiske Stone testified in 1925, nominee testimony remained unusual for another 30 years). Judiciary Committee hearings have been televised since 1981, and beginning with Ronald Reagan, presidents have routinely offered public support for their nominees during the confirmation process.[48]

Ronald Reagan's unsuccessful nomination of Robert Bork to the Supreme Court in 1987 is sometimes viewed as a watershed event in the modern Supreme Court confirmation process.[49] The Senate ultimately rejected Bork—not because of any lack of qualifications or because of unethical behavior, but simply because of how he would likely vote as a member of the Court. If confirmed, Bork would have become the decisive fifth vote necessary to overturn a variety of precedents, including *Roe v. Wade,* the landmark 1973 abortion rights case.[50]

Interest groups mobilized in an unprecedented manner against the Bork nomination. They moved beyond simply testifying at confirmation hearings and mobilizing their own base to a full-fledged public relations offensive, including television, radio, and print ads, mass mailings, and the use of telephone banks to target the wider public. The Senate ended up rejecting Bork. Fifty-eight senators, including six Republicans, voted against confirmation.

The defeat of Bork's nomination was the culmination of a series of factors that came together to create an epic battle. It generated a new verb: to *bork,* which means unleashing a lobbying and public relations campaign designed to defeat a nominee. It also hardened battle lines for future confirmations and helped to usher in what some have described as a "confirmation mess." But Bork was by no means the first Supreme Court nominee to be defeated, nor was he even the first nominee to be "borked" (John Rutledge, nominated by George Washington in 1795, holds both of those distinctions).[51]

In fact, the failure rate of Supreme Court nominees is the highest for any appointive post requiring Senate confirmation.[52] If we exclude consecutive nominations of the same individual by the same president for the same seat on the Court, which has sometimes happened for technical reasons, and Reagan's 1987 nomination of Douglas Ginsburg, which was announced but never formally submitted to the Senate, presidents submitted 152 Supreme Court nominations to the Senate as of April 2012. Out of these, seven individuals declined after being nominated, one died before taking office, one expected vacancy failed to materialize, and another for an associate justice seat was withdrawn before Senate action and resubmitted to fill the newly vacated chief justice seat. Of the remaining 142 nominations, 116 were confirmed by the Senate. The other 26 may be classified as "failed" nominations because Senate opposition blocked them (see Table 15.1).

TABLE 15.1

failed supreme court nominees

NOMINEE AND YEAR OF NOMINATION	PRESIDENT AND PARTY	COMPOSITION OF SENATE	ACTION
John Rutledge, 1795	Washington (F)	19 F, 13 DR	Rejected 14-10
Alexander Wolcott, 1811	Madison (DR)	28 DR, 6 F	Rejected 24-9
John J. Crittenden, 1828	J. Q. Adams (NR)	28 J, 20 NR	Postponed 23-17
Roger B. Taney, 1835	Jackson (D)	20 D, 20 W	Postponed 24-21
John C. Spencer, 1844	Tyler (W)	28 W, 25 D	Rejected 26-21
Reuben H. Walworth, 1844	Tyler (W)	28 W, 25 D	Postponed 27-20
Edward King, 1844	Tyler (W)	28 W, 25 D	Postponed 29-18
John M. Read, 1845	Tyler (W)	28 W, 25 D	No action
George W. Woodward, 1845	Polk (D)	31 D, 25 W	Rejected 20-19
Edward A. Bradford, 1852	Fillmore (W)	35 D, 24 W	No action
George E. Badger, 1853	Fillmore (W)	35 D, 24 W	Postponed 26-25
William C. Micou, 1853	Fillmore (W)	35 D, 24 W	No action
Jeremiah S. Black, 1861	Buchanan (D)	36 D, 26 R	Rejected 26-25
Henry Stanbery, 1866	A. Johnson (R)	42 U, 10 D	No action
Ebenezer R. Hoar, 1869	Grant (R)	56 R, 11 D	Rejected 33-24
George H. Williams, 1873	Grant (R)	49 R, 19 D	Withdrawn
Caleb Cushing, 1874	Grant (R)	49 R, 19 D	Withdrawn
Stanley Matthews, 1881	Hayes (R)	42 D, 33 R	No action
William Hornblower, 1893	Cleveland (D)	44 D, 38 R	Rejected 30-24
Wheeler H. Peckham, 1894	Cleveland (D)	44 D, 38 R	Rejected 41-32
John J. Parker, 1930	Hoover (R)	56 R, 39 D	Rejected 41-39
Abe Fortas, 1968	Johnson (D)	64 D, 36 R	Withdrawn
Clement Haynsworth, 1969	Nixon (R)	58 D, 42 R	Rejected 55-45
G. Harrold Carswell, 1970	Nixon (R)	58 D, 42 R	Rejected 51-45
Robert H. Bork, 1987	Reagan (R)	55 D, 45 R	Rejected 58-42
Douglas Ginsburg, 1987	Reagan (R)	55 D, 45 R	Withdrawn
Harriet Miers, 2005	G. W. Bush (R)	55 R, 44 D, 1 I	Withdrawn

Source. John Anthony Maltese, *The Selling of Supreme Court Nominees* (Baltimore: Johns Hopkins University Press, 1995), p. 3. Updated by author.

The large number of failed Supreme Court nominees in recent years is partly a reflection of "divided government," the situation in which different political parties control the White House and the Senate. From 1969 through 2012, the same party controlled the White House and the Senate for only 20 out of 44 years. In contrast, the same party controlled the White House and the Senate for 58 out of 68 years from 1901 through 1968. The statistics regarding Supreme Court nominees are striking: confirmation rates are close to 90 percent when the same party controls the White House and the Senate but are only about 55 percent when different parties are in control.

Further compounding the problem was an increase in partisanship since 1969. With conservative southern Democrats being replaced by Republicans, and liberal Republicans being replaced by Democrats, parties in Congress became more polarized and the ideological gap between them widened. The result was a dramatic increase in partisan voting, even on Supreme Court nominees. With rare exceptions, Supreme Court nominees used to be confirmed by bipartisan majorities. For example, Antonin Scalia was confirmed by a vote of 98–0 in 1986 and Anthony Kennedy was confirmed by a vote of 97–0 in 1988. In contrast, John Roberts and Samuel Alito, both George W. Bush nominees, were confirmed by votes of 78–22 and 58–42 in 2005 and 2006, and Sonia Sotomayor and Elena Kagan, both Obama nominees, were confirmed by votes of 68–31 and 63–37 in 2009 and 2010.

The selection process for lower federal court judges, to which we now turn, is similar to that for Supreme Court justices. Not surprisingly, as you will see, divided government and polarized politics have contributed to contentious confirmation battles for lower federal judicial nominees as well.

THE SELECTION OF LOWER FEDERAL COURT JUDGES

Supreme Court appointments usually get more attention, but lower federal court appointments are also very important since over 99 percent of all federal cases end there. Indeed, the power to appoint the more than 800 judges who make up the lower federal judiciary is arguably one of the most important powers of the president. During his eight years in office, George W. Bush appointed 261 judges to the U.S. district courts and 59 judges to the U.S. courts of appeals. These 320 lower federal court judges with life tenure, slightly fewer than were appointed by Clinton or Reagan during the same length of time (see Table 15.2), have the power to affect the outcome of cases for years to come.

TABLE 15.2

appointments to the u.s. district courts and courts of appeals, by president
(Nixon through first two years of Obama)

RESIDENT	TOTAL APPOINTMENTS	MALE	FEMALE	WHITE	AFRICAN AMERICAN	HISPANIC	ASIAN	NATIVE AMERICAN
Nixon (1969–1974)	224	223 (99.6%)	1 (0.4%)	215 (96.0%)	6 (2.6%)	2 (0.9%)	1 (0.4%)	0
Ford (1974–1977)	64	63 (98.4%)	1 (1.6%)	58 (90.6%)	3 (4.7%)	1 (1.6%)	2 (3.1%)	0
Carter (1977–1981)	258	218 (84.5%)	40 (15.5%)	202 (78.3%)	37 (14.3%)	16 (6.2%)	2 (0.8%)	1 (0.4%)
Reagan (1981–1989)	368	340 (92.4%)	28 (7.6%)	344 (93.5%)	7 (1.9%)	15 (4.1%)	2 (0.5%)	0
G. H. W. Bush (1989–1993)	185	148 (80.0%)	37 (20.0%)	165 (89.2%)	12 (6.5%)	8 (4.3%)	0	0
Clinton (1993–2001)	366	259 (70.8%)	107 (29.2%)	274 (74.9%)	61 (16.7%)	25 (6.8%)	5 (1.4%)	1 (0.3%)
G. W. Bush (2001–2009)	320	251 (78.4%)	69 (21.6%)	263 (82.2%)	24 (7.5%)	29 (9.1%)	4 (1.3%)	0
Obama (2009–2010 only)	59	30	29	33	16	4	6	0

Source: Drawn from Tables 2 and 4 in Sheldon Goldman et al., "Picking Judges in a Time of Turmoil: W. Bush's Judiciary During the 109th Congress," *Judicature*, 90 (May–June 2007), p. 272 and p. 282; and from Table 6.1 (for Ford and Nixon) from Sheldon Goldman, *Picking Federal Judges: Lower Court Selection from Roosevelt through Reagan* (New Haven: Yale University Press, 1997), pp. 227–229. Figures for George W. Bush courtesy of Sheldon Goldman. Figures for Obama are drawn from Table 6 of Goldman et al., "Obama's Judiciary at Midterm," *Judicature*, 94 (May–June 2011), p. 301.

Senatorial Courtesy Versus Presidential Prerogative

Lower federal court appointments follow the same basic process as Supreme Court appointments: the president nominates and the Senate, after Judiciary Committee hearings, either confirms or rejects by majority vote. However, a notable difference is that presidents have less control over the selection of lower federal court judges than they do over the selection of Supreme Court justices because of **senatorial courtesy,** an informal rule that has existed since the presidency of George Washington. The Senate will usually refuse to confirm nominees who do not have the support of the senators from the state where the vacancy occurs.

As a result of the threat of senatorial courtesy, presidents traditionally turned to home-state senators for advice about whom to nominate. Senators began to treat lower court appointments as a form of patronage, even though the president technically made the nomination. In 1977, President Jimmy Carter tried to reform the system. He argued that judges should be selected because of merit. Therefore, he issued an executive order that took power away from senators by creating a Circuit Court Nominating Commission for each circuit to develop a short list of nominees for the courts of appeals based on merit. The president would then nominate someone from that list.[53] Carter also urged, but did not require, senators to create their own statewide nominating commissions to develop similar lists for district court vacancies. By 1979, senators from 31 states had complied with that request.[54]

When Ronald Reagan came to office in 1981, however, he abolished Carter's commission system. With Carter having wrested control of the initial screening process from home-state senators, Reagan was more readily able to centralize control of the process in the White House and to use that process to screen for ideology.[55] But while their power to tell the president whom to nominate was significantly diminished, home-state senators could still invoke senatorial courtesy. That power has led to obstruction from both political parties in recent years. Senators can also use a filibuster to block judicial nominations. Whereas a simple majority vote is enough to confirm a nominee, ending a filibuster requires a three-fifths vote of the entire Senate (60 votes).

Diversifying the Bench

The idea that federal courts should reflect the diversity of society at large is a recent one. For many years, courts and the legal profession remained the province of white males. Table 15.3 illustrates the early history of diversifying the bench. The first president to make a concerted effort to appoint women and minorities to the federal judiciary was Jimmy Carter (see Table 15.2). The task was not easy, as these groups were still vastly underrepresented in the legal profession. In fact, segregation had made legal training largely unavailable to African Americans until the 1950s. As late as 1970, African-American, Hispanic, Native American, and Asian-American lawyers combined made up only 2 percent of all lawyers in the United States,[56] and women made up only 3 percent of all lawyers.[57]

During his four years as president (1977–1981), Carter appointed more women, African Americans, and Hispanics than had all of his predecessors combined. In his 258 appointments to the district courts and courts of appeals, Carter named 40 women (15.5 percent of his appointments to those courts), 37 African Americans (14.3 percent), and 16 Hispanics (6.2 percent), as well as two Asian Americans and one Native American (see Table 15.2). As a point of comparison, presidents from Franklin

senatorial courtesy
An informal rule that senators will refuse to confirm nominees to the lower federal courts who do not have the support of the senators from the state where the vacancy occurs.

Roosevelt through Gerald Ford (1933–1977) appointed only 8 women, 22 African Americans, and 8 Hispanics to the district courts and courts of appeals.[58]

As you can see in Table 15.2 (p. 548), Republican presidents in the years following Carter (Reagan, George H. W. Bush, and George W. Bush) placed less emphasis on diversifying the bench. In contrast, Bill Clinton (1993–2001) appointed higher percentages of women and minorities than had Carter, as well as far greater numbers because of his longer time in office (eight years rather than four). Diversity has also been a major emphasis for President Obama. Including his two Supreme Court appointments, a remarkable 70.5 percent of Obama's judicial appointees during his first two years in office (43 out of 61) were "nontraditional" (that is, not white males), and just over half were women—thus making him the first president in American history to preside over the appointment of a majority of nontraditional judges.[59]

JUDICIAL SELECTION IN THE STATES

The manner in which state court judges are selected varies not only from state to state but also within states according to the type of court. So do the requirements for becoming a judge. Nonetheless, a few generalizations can be made. Basically, there are five methods for choosing state court judges: (1) appointment by the governor, (2) appointment by the legislature, (3) partisan election, (4) nonpartisan election, and (5) the Merit Plan (sometimes referred to as the "Missouri Plan" after the state that first used it). State court judges usually serve a fixed term of office rather than having life tenure as federal judges do.[60]

The two oldest methods of judicial selection in the states are appointment by the governor and appointment by the legislature. All of the original 13 states selected

TABLE 15.3
diversifying the bench—significant appointments

PRESIDENT	YEAR	APPOINTMENT
Rutherford Hayes	1873	John A. Moss, an African American, appointed as a justice of the peace in the District of Columbia
Herbert Hoover	1928	Genevieve Cline, first woman appointed to a federal court (the U.S. Customs Court—now the U.S. Court of International Trade)
Franklin Roosevelt	1934	Florence Allen, first woman appointed to the U.S. Court of Appeals
Harry Truman	1945	Irvin C. Mollison, an African American, appointed to the U.S. Customs Court
Harry Truman	1949	Burnita Matthews, first woman appointed to a U.S. District Court
Harry Truman	1950	William H. Hastie, first African American appointed to the U.S. Court of Appeals
John F. Kennedy	1961	James B. Parsons, first African American appointed to a U.S. District Court
Lyndon Baines Johnson	1967	Thurgood Marshall, first African American appointed to the Supreme Court
Ronald Reagan	1981	Sandra Day O'Connor, first woman appointed to the Supreme Court

judges by one of these two methods, but today only 9 of the 50 states use it for at least some of their judges. Over the years, appointment was replaced by other methods as a result of several waves of reforms.

First, a wave of reform spurred by Jacksonian Democracy in the early 1800s led to the rise of partisan elections for judges. By the time of the Civil War, 24 of the 36 states had embraced the *partisan election* of judges, as did every new state until 1912.[61] As a result, judges became more accountable to the public but also less independent. Another wave of reform in the early twentieth century led to a push for the *nonpartisan election* of judges, in which judicial candidates ran without their party affiliation being listed next to their name. Reformers believed this would make judges more removed from political pressure.

The most recent wave of reform, starting in Missouri in 1940, resulted in judicial selection based on the *Merit Plan*. This method was designed to simultaneously minimize the role of politics in judicial selection, increase the emphasis on qualifications, and provide for accountability of judges. Under the Merit Plan, a commission is assigned the task of screening potential judges and providing a short list of names of the most qualified individuals. The governor then appoints one of those on the short list to serve a fixed term, after which the judge goes before the electorate in an uncontested retention election where the voters decide whether the judge will stay in office. If the judge is voted out, the process starts all over again. The Merit Plan is currently the most popular form of judicial selection.

The only exception in our judicial system to the unwritten rule that judges be lawyers occurs at the lowest rung of some state court systems in certain types of courts of limited jurisdiction. These *lay judges* are often justices of the peace who preside over very minor types of civil and criminal cases. Such a post is usually not a full-time job, nor is the salary very good. Lay judges often serve in rural areas, where they are usually elected, and they seldom hear cases in formal courtrooms. They are trusted in their communities, though, and fill an important function in areas where it would be very expensive to maintain formal courthouses staffed by lawyer judges.[62] A quite accurate portrayal of a lay judge is provided by the character Andy Taylor on television's classic *Andy Griffith Show*. Wise and trusted, if not especially well educated, Sheriff Taylor turned his office in the Mayberry jail into a courtroom merely by turning the nameplate on his desk from "Sheriff" to "Justice of the Peace."

Why Are We
THE WAY WE ARE?

Several characteristics of our judicial system help to define why we are the way we are. We have a rather complicated dual court system with overlapping jurisdiction in many areas of the law. Our entire governmental system is based on the rule of law, and our system fosters judicial independence so that courts can enforce the rule of law without fear of retribution.

A DUAL COURT SYSTEM

Our system of federalism is responsible for our dual court system, which consists of both state and federal courts. The precise structure of state courts varies from state to state, as do basic state laws. What is legal in one state (the use of medical marijuana, for example) is not necessarily legal in another, and some laws (such as those involving Sunday alcohol sales) may vary from county to county within a state. This reflects the principle of local control of justice. So does the fact that not only state court judges, but also federal district court judges, are residents of the state where the court operates.

How important is local control of justice? This question brings us back to some of the same questions we addressed in Chapter 3 regarding a federal versus a unitary system of government. Regional differences are reflected in our dual court system, with the assurance that—at least when there is a federal question involved—there is an opportunity for review by the U.S. Supreme Court.

Not all federal systems have a dual court system. Canada, a federal system that consists of ten provinces and three territories, has both federal law (passed by the national parliament) and provincial law (passed by the various provincial assemblies)—much as we have both state and federal law. But rather than establishing a dual court system, Canada has a single court system that interprets and applies both federal law and provincial law.[63]

THE RULE OF LAW

One of the most important distinguishing characteristics of our system of government is the rule of law—the idea that no one, not even the most powerful public official, is above the law. The Constitution serves as our supreme law, and we enforce the rule of law, in part, through judicial review. As we have seen, many countries have constitutional guarantees but do not protect the rule of law. We are the way we are not only because of the written guarantees in the Constitution but because of an underlying acceptance of the principle of the rule of law. Without adherence to that principle, constitutional guarantees would be hollow—worth little more than the paper they are written on.

JUDICIAL INDEPENDENCE

The rule of law could not be enforced without judicial independence. Thus, federal judges are insulated from retaliation for their rulings through such things as life tenure and a guarantee that their pay will not be diminished. Separation of powers also fosters judicial independence.

We opened this chapter with a description of attempts to undermine judicial independence in Pakistan. Although we take judicial independence for granted in the United States, attempts to undermine judicial independence have arisen at various points in our history from both ends of the political spectrum. Recently, several U.S. Supreme Court justices, including Chief Justice John Roberts, have publicly criticized what they perceive to be a rise in the number of threats to judicial independence.[64] Concerned about such threats, the American Judicature Society created a task force to monitor and respond to attacks on the judiciary.[65] Likewise, the American Bar Association has had a Standing Committee on Judicial Independence since 1997.

One aspect of judicial independence is the life tenure accorded to Supreme Court justices. Some reformers have suggested giving justices fixed terms instead. For example, one proposal that has attracted champions at both ends of the political spectrum suggests a constitutional amendment that would create 18-year terms staggered every two years. After completing that term, Supreme Court justices could choose to serve on other federal courts, and their salary would continue for life even if they chose to retire— thus helping to maintain judicial independence. If a justice died or retired early, a replacement would be nominated by the president and confirmed by the Senate to fill out the remainder of the 18-year term, and then would have the same option: continue as a judge on another federal court or retire with full pay. The routine of filling a Supreme Court vacancy every two years, and knowing that justices have fixed terms, might help to diffuse confirmation battles.[66]

. . . AND WHY DOES IT Matter?

All of this matters to you in fundamental ways. Judicial independence and adherence to the rule of law facilitate judicial review. This allows the Supreme Court and other parts of the American court system to protect your civil rights and civil liberties, enforce federalism, and ensure that Congress and the president are not overstepping their constitutional bounds.

In so doing, however, judges influence policy. By interpreting our rights and the powers of government, courts help to determine how we live, how we work, how we vote, and even how we die. Since the stakes are so high, judicial rulings are sometimes the focus of great controversy. Are judges *too* independent? After all, critics complain of "rule from the bench" by unelected, unaccountable, "activist" judges.

Concern about how judges will vote on controversial issues is why federal judicial appointments can be extremely contentious, and why they matter to you. Yet, for all their power, courts in the United States are part of a broad system of checks and balances. Judges are independent, but they are not unchecked. These limits are designed to correct genuine abuses of judicial power. Your awareness of these limits, and the concurrent need for judicial independence, does more than make you an informed citizen. It helps to make the system work.

critical thinking questions

1. Would the United States be better or worse off with a single-court system, as exists in Canada? How would it change the U.S justice system? And why do you think such a system is not in place?

2. Would it be possible to enforce the rule of law without courts having the power of judicial review? Why or why not?

3. How concerned should we be about judicial independence in the United States? What are the greatest threats to that independence?

key terms

THE ECONOMY AND NATIONAL BUDGET

* * *

- Compare and contrast different economic models, and identify specific features of the U.S. model.
- Describe how the U.S. government's role in the economy expanded and the nation became a leading economic power.
- Identify the key people and factors involved in attempting to make coherent and effective U.S. economic policy.
- Analyze how government influences U.S. economic policy, and discuss the potential conflicts and concerns that can result.
- Describe the factors that led to the Great Recession of 2007–2009, and explain how the U.S. political system responded to the crisis.

PERSPECTIVE
How Does a Nation's Past, Ideology, and Politics Shape Its Economic Policy?

On June 26, 2009, German Chancellor Angela Merkel met in Washington with President Barack Obama. They discussed not only two U.S. policies that the German public and politicians had strongly opposed—the U.S. invasion of Iraq and the American position on global warming—but also the urgent economic problems caused by the worldwide recession. Surprisingly, it was on this latter issue that the leaders clashed.

Germans' economic experience following World War I (1914–1918) produced a deeply ingrained fear of inflation, which is a sustained rise in price levels. Salaries and savings can be wiped out overnight by hyperinflation as prices rise by hundreds of percentage points in a year, a month, or even a week. Indeed, in post-World War I Germany, it took a wheelbarrow loaded with Deutsche marks to purchase even small items as the currency became worthless. At fault was the government, which had printed money irresponsibly in order to meet its debts, causing the value of the currency to decline.

Why would events of nine decades earlier disrupt relations between the United States and Germany in 2009? The two countries adopted different strategies in response to the severe economic slowdown that spread globally during the fall of 2008. In the United States, the principal economic concern was unemployment rather than inflation. Memories of the Great Depression of 1929–1939 colored U.S. policy decisions. At that time, about a third of America's workforce became chronically unemployed; families lost their homes and went hungry. American decision makers dealt with the recession of 2007–2009 through massive government intervention, committing trillions of dollars to stave off the job losses. To fund this spending, however, the U.S. Treasury borrowed additional funds from investors around the world to make money available to businesses and consumers.

One lesson for Americans from the 1930s was that government should avoid raising taxes in the midst of an economic slowdown. Putting money into the pockets of consumers, rather than attempting to balance the government's budget, encourages consumer spending, enabling businesses to maintain their workforce. Government must borrow money rather than increase tax revenues. Government should even create public programs to hire the unemployed. The downside to these actions is that spending during a recession increases the nation's debt and eventually the money must be paid back. And it is difficult to know precisely when the government should shift from a policy of pumping more money into the economy to a policy of slowing economic activity before it gets out of control and triggers inflation. Chancellor Merkel and the Germans were worried that American policies would have inflationary effects not just for the United States but also for other major economies, including Germany.[1]

When Obama had attended an April 2009 summit of political leaders from the world's 20 largest economies, known as the G-20, he had encouraged them to stimulate domestic spending as a way to fight the global recession. The French and German leaders not only feared inflation but resented the high levels of government and consumer debt that Americans and Britons had run up over the previous decade and which they felt had triggered a crisis in world banking that had reached a climax in September and October of 2008.[2]

Germans were reluctant to borrow against the future.[3] As the chancellor explained in an interview with *The New York Times*, Germany's hesitation to pump more money into the economy reflected its view of the future as well as its memories of the past. The German public would age dramatically over the next decade, which meant that paying back government loans would be even more difficult than it would be in a nation such as the United States where the population was growing steadily.[4]

Who was right, the U.S. president or the German chancellor? There is no right answer, and national governments must address a range of choices in making economic policies. Those choices reflect historical experiences, perspectives shaped by ideology, and old-fashioned politics, which involves questions of who has power.

IN THIS CHAPTER we first examine several models of the relationship between government and the economy. We then trace the historical evolution of the federal and state governments' relationship to the economy in the United States. We analyze how economic policy is formed, exploring both the federal budget process and the taxation system. Then we assess the various methods that domestic governments use to stabilize the economy. We conclude by evaluating government actions during the Great Recession of 2007–2009. As you read this chapter, keep in mind our two core questions:

WHY ARE WE THE WAY WE ARE?
WHY DOES IT MATTER TO YOU?

In particular, how does the U.S. government use different strategies and policy tools to influence economic conditions?

GOVERNMENT AND THE ECONOMY

Nations not only have different political systems but different economic systems as well. In addition, the relationship between politics and economics differs across countries, developing from distinctive historical experiences, elite and public attitudes, and political outcomes in the competition for control. The mix that has emerged in the United States is just one possibility and not the only mix or the correct one.

COMPARING ECONOMIC SYSTEMS

The famous rallying cry of "no taxation without representation" expressed the colonists' frustration at having the mother country—Great Britain— impose taxes on them without giving them representatives in the British parliament. At issue was the colonists' share of costs for their own defense in the wake of the French and Indian Wars. Also at issue was the right of the colonists to conduct business as they pleased. Under the dominant economic theory of the time, **mercantilism,** the role of the government was to promote a trade surplus. Hence, Great Britain regarded the colonies as an economic asset to enhance the mother country's wealth, a source of raw materials, and a market for British goods. Great Britain thus regulated the colonies' imports and exports.

Eighteenth-century reformers placed individual liberty at the heart of economic relations as well as political relations. An influential group of Scottish writers challenged the traditional role of the government in guiding economic affairs. In particular, Adam Smith's seminal work, *The Wealth of Nations,* published in 1776, called for a free-market system in which the government's role in the economy should be minimal, a policy known as **laissez-faire**—coined from French economists' similar argument for leaving the market alone. Smith's ideas became a central component of **capitalism,** an economic system distinguished by its reliance on the self-interested decisions of producers and consumers exchanging items of value in a market of supply and demand largely free of government direction.

Views of the government's proper degree of involvement in the economy differ, and debates over the best system have spanned the nearly two-and-a-half centuries since the publication of *The Wealth of Nations* (see Figure 16.1). Socialism arose in the twentieth century as the major economic system to challenge free-market capitalism. Rather than rely mainly on private ownership of production and on an unregulated market to allocate goods and services, a **socialist system** views government as both an owner of enterprises and a distributor of goods and services. Socialist theory developed in response to the excesses of industrialization under a system of capitalism, particularly the extreme wealth of a few that contrasted sharply with the poverty and squalid life conditions of most workers. When Social Democratic political parties in Europe came into power in the twentieth century, they enacted policies that held the government responsible for the welfare of its citizens. France, England, and Germany nationalized whole industries, bringing them under public control. When the Labour Party came to power in Britain after World War II, they nationalized the steel and coal industries, most utilities, the railways, and the airlines. By the early 1950s approximately 20 percent of the British economy was owned by the government.

KEY TO understanding

Several models describe government's relationship to the economy, with unfettered free market capitalism at one end of a spectrum and a command economy at the other end. Most nations have mixed economies in which government actions shape the behavior of individuals and firms in markets. In the United States, government seeks to stabilize overall economic conditions, regulate behavior to achieve economic or social goals, provide necessary services, and help both citizens and businesses.

★

mercantilism
Economic policies adopted by European nations (including England) during the seventeenth and eighteenth centuries that treated colonial products, trade, and markets as a way to enrich the mother country.

laissez-faire
View that originated with eighteenth-century French economists that government should play a minimal role in the economy.

capitalism
An economic system distinguished by its reliance on the self-interested decisions of producers and consumers exchanging items of value in a market of supply and demand largely free of government direction.

socialist system
An economic system, developed in the nineteenth century as a way to correct many excesses of capitalism, in which the government acts as both an owner of enterprises and a distributor of goods and services.

Laissez-faire capitalism — Mixed economy — Command economy

Smaller role — Greater role

FIGURE 16.1

★ MODELS OF GOVERNMENT'S ROLE IN THE ECONOMY

command economy
Soviet-style system where government officials exercise broad control to decide the allocation of resources, levels of production, and prices of goods.

mixed economy
An economic system in which government officials share power with markets in deciding or influencing how resources are allocated in the society.

Other nations adopted a **command economy** in which governments embrace central planning and give government officials broad powers to decide the allocation of resources, levels of production, and prices of goods. The Communist Party established a command economy in the Soviet Union following World War I. Under this system of central planning, the government in Moscow launched an ambitious industrialization program designed to achieve in a few decades the social and economic developments experienced by more advanced industrial nations in Western Europe over the prior century. Other nations—China and India, for example—that sought rapid transformations in the period from 1950 to 1980 sometimes adopted the Soviet model. But central planning, at least Soviet style, discouraged innovation, encouraged corruption, and created a black (illegal) market in goods and services that existed outside the government-controlled system. Moreover, Western market economies after World War II outpaced the Soviet Union, raising doubts about the potential success of the Soviet model. In the 1990s, Russia, the successor state to the Soviet Union, shifted to a market economy.

★ India and many other former command economies have adopted a free-market system, including headache-inducing stock exchanges that experience boom and bust cycles.

Most economies in the world are **mixed economies.** Government shares power with markets in influencing how resources are allocated in the economy. In Sweden, for example, policy makers use government power to exercise considerable control over the flow of resources, but they do so within a largely free-market system where 90 percent of industrial output comes from private firms.[5] In Australia, the government owns businesses that compete in communications, transportation, banking, and other sectors, but beginning in the mid-1980s, more of those businesses shifted from public to private ownership. In fact, countries around the world have moved toward the privatization of industries. Even China has moved in this direction, though slowly.

GOVERNMENT AND THE ECONOMY IN THE UNITED STATES

Traditionally, the United States has embraced the free-market system and relied heavily on markets as the way to make economic decisions, but the government has also played a substantial role in the American economy. The U.S. government established a highly favorable environment for creative economic activity by maintaining a system of property rights that gave individuals an incentive to work hard in order to profit from their efforts, by establishing a court system for resolving disputes in a fair and trustworthy

way, and by providing security from the physical destruction and disruption associated with war.[6] American governments also invested in internal improvements. State governments led the way with heavy investments in roads and canals during the nation's first half-century. The national government then assumed the lead, encouraging expansion of the railroad system and technological innovation. As cities grew, urban governments invested in schools, roads, water and sewage systems, and electrical infrastructure. In addition to providing these foundations, the federal government fulfills four crucial roles as an economic stabilizer, regulator, service provider, and social helper.

Economic Stabilizer

Through their policies, government officials seek to steer the economy onto a stable path of economic growth and prosperity. Free markets are not always successful in producing a thriving economy, and American history is full of examples of "boom and bust" cycles—periods when growth proceeds at a rapid if not frenetic pace followed by periods of severe economic slowdowns. The costs of downturns in the business cycle can be devastating. People lose their jobs, their homes, their life savings, and the capacity to provide food and shelter for themselves and their families.

In response to the most severe downturn in American history—the Great Depression that started in 1929 and lasted throughout the next decade—government assumed the role of **economic stabilizer,** taking action to offset the highs and lows of the business cycle. The Employment Act of 1946 gave the president and Congress a mandate to deal with the nation's economy as a whole and to minimize economic disruptions. Since then, the American government has assumed growing responsibility for

economic stabilizer
Role of American government to manage unemployment and inflation in order to prevent the disruption and human costs caused by the boom and bust rhythm of the business cycle.

- maintaining a steady rate of economic growth that produces new jobs and higher productivity to keep pace with population growth;
- preventing unemployment from rising to damaging levels;

economic regulation
Efforts by government to establish and maintain fair competition in markets to help consumers.

antitrust policies
Government legislation and regulations designed to prevent collusion among businesses that would suppress competition in order to produce unnaturally high prices.

social regulation
Laws and rules created to prevent corporations from engaging in practices that result in undesirable outcomes for society, such as air and water pollution or unsafe working conditions.

consumer protection
Laws and rules designed to protect citizens from unsafe products and unfair business practices.

WARNING: Cigarettes are addictive.

1-800-QUIT-NOW

© U.S. HHS

BRAND

20 Class A Cigarettes

★ The Food and Drug Administration requires that one of nine graphic health warnings appears on each pack of cigarettes. Despite this, young people continue to develop the habit. Although the United States was the first to adopt such warnings, many other nations now use them.

- avoiding rising prices that seriously erode the buying power of citizens' earnings and savings—in other words, preventing uncontrolled inflation.

To accomplish these goals, Congress and the president adopt annually a set of spending, taxing, and borrowing policies in the annual federal budget, as will be discussed later in the chapter.

Regulator

Modern governments also establish regulations that restrict the conduct of businesses. In general, political scientists distinguish between economic and social regulation as well as the related area of consumer protection.

Economic regulation seeks to establish and maintain fair competition in markets so that multiple sources of goods and services meet consumer needs rather than having any single producer grow so large and so powerful that it can exercise a monopoly over some valuable item. The first government regulatory agency in the United States was the Interstate Commerce Commission, created in 1887 to prevent railroads from setting unfair freight rates for farmers and manufacturers. By setting the terms of competition, government sought to balance the marketplace. Later, legislation also sought to prevent collusion among businesses who avoided competition by fixing prices and production levels. These so-called **antitrust policies** (opposed to predatory practices among businesses) seek to maintain competition. For example, would consumers get good cell phone service at a fair price if two of the larger companies—AT&T and T-Mobile—combined? The Obama administration said "no" when it opposed the proposed merger in 2011, and the merger ultimately failed.

Social regulation seeks to prevent corporate practices that have undesirable results for society. For instance, the Occupational Safety and Health Administration enforces laws that protect employees from dangerous working conditions, whereas the Environmental Protection Agency enforces regulations that prevent companies from cutting costs by using production or disposal methods that pollute the air or water. **Consumer protection** regulations arose in the early twentieth century as policy makers recognized that citizens need to be protected from tainted food products or untrustworthy drugs, resulting in the establishment of the Food and Drug Administration, now within the Department of Health and Human Services. In the 1970s, the government created the Consumer Product Safety Commission, and most recently, Congress approved creating the Consumer Financial Protection Bureau within the Treasury Department to protect consumers from financial products that have produced widespread losses from 2000 to today.

Service Provider

In the United States, the government rather than the private sector provides many services. Examples include education, defense, justice, police protection, fire protection, highway construction, sanitary services, and mail delivery. In most of these areas, private companies compete with the government to provide the same services—private schools, private security guards, Fed Ex and UPS delivery services, and even privately owned and maintained highways—but government became and remains the principal provider of these services in the United States. Often complaints are raised about the quality of these services—for example, "Why did the post office lose my mail?" or "Why are the roads so poor?" Since the 1980s, policy-makers have reduced government's **service provider** role by turning over activities to private contractors in hopes of improving quality and reducing costs. Nonetheless, most of these services remain primarily in government hands.

Social Helper

The U.S. government also promotes the social welfare of its citizens and intervenes to provide opportunities to the poor and to meet social goals. For example, Social Security and Medicare are federal programs that were created expressly to meet the income and health care needs of retired senior citizens (see Chapter 17). The government also guarantees loans to students who need to borrow money to attend college, to small businesses and farmers, and to home buyers who have only limited money to put into a down payment. Businesses also benefit from technological advances made through government-sponsored research. The National Technology Transfer Center provides a wide range of services to help commercialize scientific advances.

The federal government's multiple economic roles were not set out in the Constitution or even in a single piece of legislation. Rather, they evolved over time as needs and pressures arose. The next section reviews this unfolding story.

GOVERNMENT'S EVOLVING ROLE IN THE U.S. ECONOMY

Conservatives and libertarians argue for limiting government intervention in the economy. For example, in his campaign for the 2012 Republican presidential nomination, Representative Ron Paul (R-TX) argued that the U.S. government had become too large and that one way to counter that trend would be to dissolve the Internal Revenue Service and thereby discontinue the federal income tax, denying the federal government its principal source of revenue. Even if they do not go quite that far, many Americans express concern about the size of government and its intrusiveness into their lives. Yet many Americans also want government to do more for them when they encounter problems and wonder why government did not prevent the problems they experienced in the first place. In other words, Americans crave the services but do not want to pay for them, not unlike the attitude of American colonists on the eve of the Revolutionary War. As a result, the government's role in the economy has grown substantially over the course of American history.

KEY TO understanding ★

England forced the American colonies to be a source of wealth for the home nation. After independence, Alexander Hamilton stabilized the nation's creditworthiness, and politics in Washington often centered on banking policy during the nineteenth century. The Civil War, World Wars I and II, and responses to the Great Depression shifted significant economic powers from the states to the federal government. During the Progressive Era and the New Deal, the federal government assumed significant regulatory powers. Why did the United States emerge as the world's leading economy in the period following World War II?

THE COLONIAL INHERITANCE

North America was originally settled as a profit-making venture. The King of England granted two charters to groups of investors to colonize Virginia (the London Company) and New England (the Plymouth Company). The first permanent English colony settled in Jamestown, Virginia, in 1607. The initial effort in New England failed, followed by the Massachusetts Bay Company in 1630 whose settlers, not the investors, controlled the charter. The British crown encouraged the production of crops and goods necessary for competing globally with the French and the Dutch. England provided protection on sea and land for merchants and farmers as well as guaranteed markets for colonial products. But colonists resented Britain's interference with the natural business of producing and marketing goods as well as the new taxes imposed to help defray the costs of defense.

FROM INDEPENDENCE TO THE CIVIL WAR

Gaining independence proved expensive. Coming out of the Revolutionary War, the 13 newly independent states had accumulated a collective debt of $50 million, including $8 million owed to foreign investors.[7] Emerging from the British mercantile system proved a major challenge. Independence severed 150-year-old trade relations with the mother country and other British colonies. The central government was unable to pay off the nation's debts, could not prevent states from interfering with interstate commerce, and was hampered in negotiating with other nations.

The new Constitution, drafted in 1787 and activated in 1789, did not immediately change economic conditions. In fact, the supremacy of the national government in interstate commerce was not established until after the Civil War and a series of Supreme Court decisions made during the late nineteenth century. Nonetheless, the new Constitution established the preconditions for economic growth and development. Alexander Hamilton, the first Secretary of Treasury, paid off wartime debts, established a national bank (20 percent owned by the federal government) and stabilized the national currency. To provide the new government with revenue, Hamilton's policies created **tariffs** on imported goods and taxes on specific products such as whiskey. By 1803 when the United States paid $15 million to France for the Louisiana Purchase, lenders across Europe had the confidence to buy bonds to cover the massive expenditure.[8] Because the national government leaned so heavily on tariffs as a source of revenue, they became a critical political issue. Tariffs had the potential to encourage the growth of domestic manufacturing industries, primarily favoring New England and Mid-Atlantic states.[9] In contrast, residents of the South and West preferred no tariffs so that they could use their earnings from exporting indigo, rice, tobacco, cotton, and farm produce to purchase cheap imported products. A political fault line developed between these regions. The South's economy, moreover, was based on a system of slave labor that lay at the heart of recurrent political crises.

tariff
A tax levied by the government on goods imported into a nation, applied in order to raise revenue or in order to protect the domestic manufacturers of the same item.

★ Prior to the Civil War, slave labor not only fueled the economy of the South but also lay at the heart of the nation's political crisis.

Through their policies, federal and state governments encouraged industrialization, population growth (immigration), and continental settlement. American governments pursued these goals by

- establishing protective tariffs that peaked in 1828, with rates declining until after the Civil War
- building the transportation infrastructure in the form of canals (the Erie Canal in 1825), public roads (the Cumberland Pike in 1818), navigable rivers, secure harbors, and railroads
- establishing a communication infrastructure, first through a national postal service and later by supporting the telegraph and subsequent broadcast technologies

During the pre-Civil War era, states outspent the federal government nearly nine to one in their expenditures on transportation. What emerged was a large domestic market that also included ways to exploit the rich natural resources of furs, gold, timber, coal, iron ore, and oil. Along the way, the United States developed a modern financial system and invented the prototype for the corporation, an answer to the complex challenges of building railroads. Encouraging growth industries is not a policy that was limited to the nineteenth century, as we see with Brazil today (see Picture Yourself in Brazil).

picture YOURSELF ...
AS A FLEX-FUEL VEHICLE DRIVER IN BRAZIL

Brazil, one of four rapidly developing, large economies commonly referred to as the BRIC nations—Brazil, Russia, India, and China—is on its way to becoming an economic powerhouse. Brazil is the largest and most populous nation in Latin America, with nearly 200 million residents. It is also blazing the path to renewable energy for the world through government programs that encourage the development of targeted industries.

You would have trouble driving your traditional, gas-powered American car in Brazil. Brazil's ethanol and biodiesel programs lead the world, taking advantage of the nation's ideal growing conditions and intense cultivation of sugarcane to produce valuable biofuels that can substitute for petroleum imports. Gas in the United States has typically included about 10 percent ethanol, as noted on the pump. In Brazil you will notice that gas now includes 25 percent ethanol. And Brazil's automobile industry has led the way in producing flex-fuel vehicles capable of operating with any combination of ethanol and gasoline, including 100 percent ethanol. If you rent a flex-fuel car, you will need to make some quick calculations. Unlike U.S. drivers who simply seek out the cheapest price per gallon at the pump, Brazilian drivers must calculate the relative advantages of two fuels by assessing both distance and cost. Because 100 percent ethanol provides only 70 percent of the energy you get from the gasohol blend, it will only be worth buying if it costs 30 percent less per gallon than the blend. But on a longer trip, you might choose the blend, regardless of price, to minimize the number of times you will have to refill your fuel tank.

Brazil's government encouraged the shift toward reducing dependence on foreign oil. Ethanol had been a major

continued

fuel source for Brazil at various times in the twentieth century, but after oil prices rose dramatically in the 1970s, the government (then a military dictatorship) mandated that gas stations install ethanol pumps, encouraged the fuel's use, and continued to do so even when gas prices dropped.* The government offered favorable loans for new factories to produce ethanol, subsidized prices at the pump, and sponsored research to improve sugarcane production. Volkswagen's introduction of a flex-fuel vehicle to the Brazilian market in 2003 encouraged the shift from gas to ethanol. Brazil's annual production of ethanol now stands second only to the United States, and the country is the world's largest ethanol exporter. As scientists and nations assess how to move the world away from gasoline toward renewable energy sources, interest has grown in the relative advantages of Brazil's sugarcane-based alternative fuel compared with the corn-based ethanol system found in the United States. Most of the advantages lie with the sugarcane.** Although sugarcane-based ethanol is cheaper to produce, for 30 years the U.S. government limited imports of Brazilian ethanol by assessing a $.54 per gallon tariff as a way to protect the less-efficient U.S. ethanol industry from foreign competition and encourage its growth. In 2011 Congress removed the tariff and discontinued subsidies for the U.S. ethanol industry—actions that could increase the flow of cheaper Brazilian ethanol into the country.

* Monte Reel, "Brazil's Road to Energy Independence," *Washington Post* (August 20, 2006) A1.

** Don Hofstrand, "Brazil's Ethanol Industry," Iowa State University Extension AgDM Newsletter, January 2009 (http://www.extension.iastate.edu/agdm/articles/hof/HofJan09.html)

questions to consider

1. Should the United States aggressively encourage the production of more flex-fuel vehicles as Brazil has?

2. Was it a good idea for the United States to change its policies that had discouraged importing Brazilian ethanol?

THE EFFECTS OF THREE MAJOR WARS

The Civil War (1861–1865), like World War I and World War II, triggered a major expansion of the national government's political and economic power in the pursuit of victory. During the Civil War, the federal government provided valuable subsidies to the Union Pacific and Central Pacific railroads, enabling them to complete a transcontinental connection.[10] During the war, the federal government consolidated its oversight of immigrants, created the Department of Agriculture to advance the interests of farmers, expanded its production of weapons and ammunition at national armories, and produced both uniforms and food for the troops. The newly created National Academy of Sciences was tasked with applying new technologies to support the war effort, and the federal government found ways to provide support for land-grant colleges also charged with providing instruction in subjects needed for the war effort. Thus, encouraging scientific innovation became a national policy that grew even more rapidly a century later during the Cold War.

Many important financial changes enacted during the Civil War continued into the post-war period. During the war, the federal government established a uniform system of currency (the famous "greenbacks") and created a national banking system that consolidated power in Washington rather than decentralizing it to state-centered banks that had dominated the period from 1832 to 1862. Both changes persisted after the war. Although the income tax established in 1862 was revoked in 1872, it had established a precedent that generated new legislation to create a federal income tax in 1894. That law was struck down by a Supreme Court decision in 1895, but the system resumed in 1913 after ratification of the Sixteenth Amendment. The war also produced a large group of citizens who came to depend on government support—Civil War veterans whose pensions grew during the subsequent decades. During the post-war period, Northern Republicans exercised political control over Southern agricultural interests, and Congress decisively raised tariffs to levels that protected new Northern industries from foreign competition and made imported products very expensive.

World Wars I and II left important legacies that continued to affect the nation long after the wars had concluded. Government spending and revenues ballooned, the federal government began to regulate more aspects of the economy, and government factories directly participated in production.[11] The federal government's entire budget in 1914, on the eve of war in Europe, was about $775 million. By 1919, the total stood at just under $18.5 billion. Similarly, the federal debt was 25 times higher in 1919 than it had been in 1914. Although tax rates increased substantially during the war and the middle class began to pay taxes as well as the wealthy, the government's sale of Liberty bonds to the public financed most of the spending growth. The federal government established agencies to coordinate railroad schedules, control the prices of food and fuel, and plan the use of scarce resources. These experiences provided a foundation for actions taken by the Roosevelt administration (1933–1945) a decade later to combat the Great Depression and fight another global war.

During World War II, government expenditures rose dramatically, increasing tenfold to $92.7 billion by 1945, the final year of conflict. Tax revenues rose sevenfold over the same time period as Congress approved higher tax rates, but the increase was not enough to cover the higher expenditures. Government borrowing covered the resulting deficit, but managing that debt became a permanent issue in post-war politics. Government again exercised vigorous controls over the prices and supplies of food, gasoline, and consumer goods through a system of rationing and diverted resources from consumer products to meet critical war needs. By the end of the war, both the public and political elites had become accustomed to extensive government intervention in the economy.

THE RISE OF GOVERNMENT REGULATION AND RELIEF PROGRAMS

During the period following 1870, the nation's economy underwent rapid change. Steel and oil, industries that proved important for the next century, expanded dramatically. Railroad mileage tripled between 1870 and 1890. The percentage of the population living in towns and cities rose from 26 to 46 percent in the three decades before 1910. Cities expanded sewage, water, electric, telephone, and gas service to the new residents.[12]

Also during this period both state and federal governments intervened to correct market problems. After many states had taken separate action, the Interstate Commerce Commission protected farmers from unfair pricing practices of the railroads, which could set unreasonably high freight charges. In many localities, one rail line served a community, and the railroad charged more for short hauls of freight than long ones. In 1890, Congress passed the Sherman Antitrust Act, the first federal effort to control concentration and collusion within an industry. Overall, governments responded to the strategies pursued by corporations to restrain competition or provide shoddy goods as a way to maximize profits.

During the period known as the Progressive Era (roughly 1895 to 1930), governments adopted an avalanche of political and economic reforms at the federal, state, and local levels. New legislation protected the safety of mine and railroad workers and helped resolve labor-management disputes. The ICC began to regulate the telephone, telegraph, radio, and telegraphic cable (not yet television cable) industries. Railroad workers got an eight-hour day (1916) and many states set minimum wages for women. In 1913, Congress established the Federal Reserve System (discussed later in this chapter) to provide the services of a central bank and regulate the nation's banking system. The nation established an especially unpopular regulation when it prohibited the sale of alcoholic beverages in 1920 (later rescinded in 1933 when the Twenty-First Amendment to the Constitution repealed the Eighteenth Amendment).[13]

As part of the New Deal, Franklin Roosevelt and Congress regulated financial markets, widely viewed as the cause of the Depression. Congress and the president also created federal agencies and programs to help citizens weather future economic downturns. The Federal Deposit Insurance Corporation (1933) and the Federal Savings and Loan Insurance Corporation (1934) provided insurance to protect customers from losing their savings if banks failed. The Social Security program (1935) provided a flow of income from the federal government to those unable to work because they were blind, to children surviving the death of the family's principal breadwinner, and to elderly retirees. To help the nation climb out of the Depression, the federal government created an extensive list of loan programs to help farmers, home buyers, advocates of rural electrification, and businesses. It also hired the unemployed to fill public jobs that ranged from basic maintenance to more skilled tasks. The Tennessee Valley Authority (TVA) constructed a series of hydroelectric dams and sponsored programs to develop the economy of an entire region of the nation.

Wars have had an important and lasting effect on government's role in the economy, but most economic historians would argue that the peacetime economic crisis of the Great Depression had an even greater impact. Although Congress eventually disassembled many of the short-run programs designed to provide relief from the worst problems of the crisis, others have become permanent. The debate after World War II was seldom about whether to keep major federal programs in housing, agriculture, and social insurance but instead focused on ways to improve and expand them. And with the memory of how Roosevelt guided the entire economy out of depression, Congress and the public expected the federal government to actively steer the nation toward a secure economic future.

In subsequent decades, the government's role expanded into social regulation during the 1960s and 1970s. President Johnson's (1963–1969) Great Society programs pushed federal government activity into areas that had previously been reserved to the states, including health care for the elderly (Medicare) and education. Consumer interests, civil rights, and the so-called war on poverty were additional areas of activity that produced new regulatory efforts in the 1970s. Congress partnered with Presidents Nixon (1969–1974) and Ford (1974–1977) to create and fund the Occupational Safety and Health Administration (1970), the Consumer Product Safety Commission (1972), and the Environmental Protection Agency (1970). Each established new social regulations that businesses must observe.

By the end of the 1970s, however, thinking among academics and government officials about the effectiveness of regulating business had changed. Regulated industries also lobbied to lift the government's reins from their activities. What emerged was a concerted effort at **deregulation,** the dismantling of many forms of economic regulation. Market pressures, it was argued, would do a better job of regulating behavior than government officials.

Thus, Congress and the administrations of Carter (1977–1981), Reagan (1981–1989), and Clinton (1993–2001) pushed to remove many of the controls on the airlines as well as the railway and trucking industries. Companies got the right to enter markets more easily and to set prices. Later, deregulation occurred in energy, communications and telecommunications, and banking. Some of the changes removed controls that dated to the New Deal and earlier.

It remains unclear whether market competition has truly been effective in reducing costs and improving the quality of services. For example, after consumers initially benefited from an airline price war, air service declined, with fewer flights serving fewer cities under more crowded conditions. Fingers also point to unregulated activities of the securities industry as a major cause of the recession in 2007–2009. The strict boundaries between commercial banking, investment banking, and insurance that had been created under the New Deal broke down in the late 1990s so that banks could make money through riskier ventures. These changes no doubt contributed to the banking crisis of 2008.

★ The 2010 explosion at the Massey mine in West Virginia killed 29 miners. One year earlier, the Mine Safety and Health Administration from the Department of Labor had investigated hundreds of violations of safety regulations but failed to bring the company into compliance.

deregulation
Efforts during the 1970s, 1980s, and 1990s to remove many forms of economic regulation created earlier in the nation's history to control the business practices of airlines, communications technology, and banking.

RISE OF A GLOBAL ROLE

In the wake of World War II, the United States was the world's most powerful economic system as well as a world military power. The United States and more than 40 other nations established the **Bretton Woods system,** a set of rules and institutions created in 1944 to restore international trade, investment flows, and financial arrangements in the post-war period. The signatory states agreed to maintain a steady value for their currencies based on their holdings of gold reserves or a reserve currency that could be exchanged for gold. The reserve currency was the dollar, thereby giving the United States a privileged position in post-war international economic relations. Moreover, the United States emerged as the key source of money for rebuilding Europe and Japan as well as for assisting newly independent nations throughout the world. When the United States abandoned the gold standard—that is, refused to any longer exchange dollars for gold—in 1971, the dollar became the world's top reserve currency, held by other nations as a way to settle trades between nations. Later in that decade, worldwide oil sales were transacted using dollars, further cementing the dollar's central role.

As the world's largest economy, the United States continues to have a major influence on other nations' decisions. However, not only have European unification and the

Bretton Woods system
System of international agreements created at the end of World War II that created a global financial and trade system dominated by the U.S. dollar.

fiscal year
Period covered by the budget decisions made annually, running from October 1 to September 30 for the federal government and July 1 to June 30 for many state governments.

Office of Management and Budget
Successor agency to the Bureau of the Budget, created in 1970 and designed to perform management oversight that went beyond the traditional budget and central clearance functions performed by the BOB.

discretionary spending
One-third of the annual budget for which funding must be reapproved by Congress each year, subjecting these programs to annual changes.

rise of China eroded American dominance, but so has the growth of free trade and rapid globalization. The World Trade Organization (WTO) is the major institution that facilitates and monitors free trade. The WTO, and its predecessor institution, the General Agreement on Tariffs and Trade (GATT), urge nations to maintain uniform tariff policies on goods traded among all member nations, a way to ensure that everyone is treated equally. In this way, trade policy supersedes domestic economic policies and even two-nation trade agreements. Global finance also has an infrastructure through which vast amounts of capital can flow quickly from one nation to another. Hence, a financial crisis in one country, such as a debt crisis in Greece or a housing crisis in the United States, can trigger international consequences.

Americans' willingness to import foreign products remains an important engine of world trade and therefore has a significant impact on the economic activity in other nations. A slowdown in the American economy or a change in interest rates paid on funds loaned to the United States by non-Americans can have major effects on economies around the globe—hence Chancellor Merkel's concerns about the long-term impact of American economic policies adopted in response to the Great Recession, as seen in the example that opens this chapter.

FRAGMENTED ECONOMIC DECISION MAKING

KEY TO understanding

★

Many different decision makers are involved in formulating economic policy in the United States. The U.S. Congress and president establish an annual budget that reflects both economic and political goals. The tax system also achieves policy goals such as offering tax credits for improved energy efficiency. Different types of taxes, in conjunction with government programs, can also redistribute income in a country. How do decision makers coordinate their efforts in pursuit of coherent policies that achieve national goals?

Economic policy at the national level begins with decisions made jointly by the president and Congress in the annual process of determining the federal budget. (Governors and state legislatures engage in a similar process.) The federal government's budget year—or **fiscal year**—runs from October 1 to September 30. As a shorthand way of referring to these budget years, government officials abbreviate *fiscal year* to *FY* and add the last two numbers of the year in question. *FY13*, for example, refers to the budget covering October 1, 2012, to September 30, 2013—or fiscal year 2013. Only since 1921 has the president been obliged to submit a single federal budget proposal to Congress, which now occurs on or before the first Monday in February of each year.

THE BUDGET PROCESS

Before 1921, each department and agency of the government sought its own budget from Congress. The **Office of Management and Budget** (OMB) assists the president in compiling a budget that meets requirements in law, recommends how much should be spent on public programs, lays out previous budgets and makes projections for the next five to ten years.

Congress then has approximately eight months to work out tax and spending decisions through a process in which legislators—working in subcommittees, committees, and on the floor of the whole chamber—make a series of choices about how to raise revenue and spend money. The president's budget specifies funding requested for **discretionary spending**—spending levels that must be reapproved by Congress each year—as well as **mandatory spending**—spending levels set automatically. Discretionary spending funds the federal government's support for education, transportation, natural resources, environmental protection, foreign aid, homeland security, defense, science, space and technology, and the federal courts. Yet only about one-third of the budget consists of discretionary spending. Mandatory spending funds entitlement programs such as Social Security, Medicare, and Medicaid, as well as smaller programs such as unemployment compensation, Food Stamps, and child nutrition. In all of these cases the government has made a standing commitment to provide benefits to those citizens who qualify. If the president proposes changes in entitlement programs or in the tax code that generates revenue, these must also be specified in the budget. Congress must approve spending levels as well as any statutory changes.

Congress begins by adopting a **budget resolution** that originates in the Budget Committees of both the House and Senate, as shown in Figure 16.2. This resolution sets out broad guidelines on revenue and spending, and it gives specific amounts for the programs that fall within different committees' jurisdictions. Unlike regular legislation, the budget resolution is a concurrent resolution and therefore is not subject to a presidential veto or a Senate filibuster. Only a simple majority vote in both houses is needed to adopt a budget resolution, and although the goal is to have the two houses adopt a common budget resolution by April 15, this process often takes longer. To help them make the many budget decisions they face, legislators in 1973 created the **Congressional Budget Office** (CBO).

After the budget resolution has been approved by both houses, action in Congress then shifts to the standing committees. Almost every committee participates in the budget process. Authorizing committees must consider changes in legislation that establishes programs; House and Senate appropriations committees decide on funding for the next fiscal year; and revenue committees in both the House (the Ways and Means Committee) and Senate (the Finance Committee) make any changes needed in tax laws. Indeed, this decision-making process is so fragmented that it is amazing that a final product ever emerges.

The goal for Congress is to adopt the 12 separate appropriations bills that fund different segments of the federal government by September 30. Each segment,

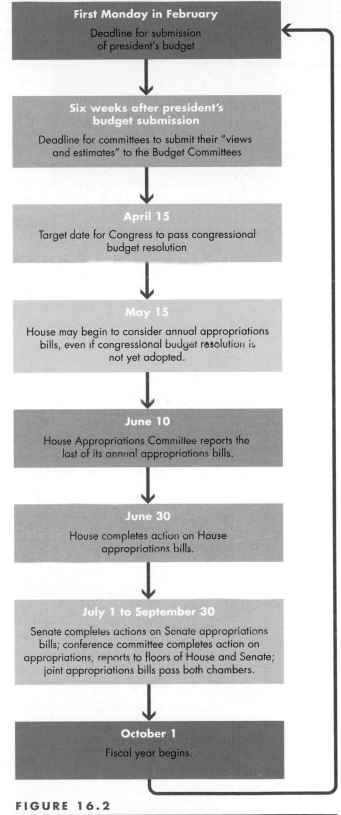

FIGURE 16.2

★ BASIC STEPS IN THE BUDGET PROCESS

Source: Truthandpolitics.org, (http://www.truthandpolitics.org/budget-basics.php)

★ The U.S. Army hopes that the Abrams tanks deployed in Afghanistan will protect soldiers from roadside bombs. High-tech weaponry, like this tank, is expensive. For the first time in the nation's history, the federal government has not raised wartime taxes to pay for combat in Iraq and Afghanistan.

mandatory spending
Two-thirds of the federal budget for which funding decisions are not controlled by annual appropriations, particularly entitlements such as Social Security, Medicare, and Medicaid.

budget resolution
Initial step in the congressional budget process that establishes broad guidelines on government revenue and spending for the next fiscal year and gives specific amounts for the programs that fall within different committees' jurisdictions.

Congressional Budget Office
Specialized staff created in 1973 to assist Congress in making budget decisions.

continuing resolution
When Congress and the president fail to meet the October 1 deadline for approving a new fiscal year budget, they can adopt a temporary action that allows those programs lacking a new annual appropriation to remain in operation.

supplemental appropriation
Spending decisions made by Congress and the President outside the regular budget process.

as well as changes in legislation, must receive a presidential signature in order to become law. Consistent with the Constitution, the House moves first on appropriations decisions. When Congress fails to meet the October 1 deadline (which happens frequently), Congress approves a **continuing resolution,** a temporary action that allows the programs that have not yet received a new annual appropriation to continue to operate.

Disagreements within Congress as well as disagreements between Congress and the president can cause delays. For example, when President Clinton was unable to agree with the Republican-controlled Congress, several continuing resolutions kept the government operating during the fall of 1995, but when the president objected to cuts made by Congress in these temporary funding arrangements, the government partially shut down. As a result of this impasse, nonessential personnel stayed home for one week in November 1995 and nearly three weeks over the holidays in 1995–1996. Much the same nearly happened in 2011 when only a last-minute agreement to cut federal spending prevented a government shutdown.

Congress and the president may also make **supplemental appropriations,** spending decisions outside the regular budget process. Congress funded the wars in Afghanistan and Iraq through such supplemental appropriations from 2001 to 2009. President Obama, however, included these costs as part of his annual budget.

NATIONAL PRIORITIES AND BURDENS

The product of the budget process is an annual budget that establishes priorities among different purposes—the programs the government supports with funding—and allocates the costs according to how revenue is collected. In essence, the budget prioritizes the purposes of government and allocates the burdens to different segments of society. The Concord Coalition, a group dedicated to helping the American public better understand the budget decisions made by the nation's elected officials and their long-term implications, provides an annual analysis of the way government sets priorities and allocates burdens. Figure 16.3 shows the Coalition's analysis of the projected budget for the fiscal year 2011 in terms of broad categories of spending and revenue. Federal spending was expected to be $3.71 trillion, fully $1.48 trillion above expected revenues, producing a deficit budget.

Figure 16.3 shows that combined spending on Medicare and Medicaid, the health care programs for the elderly and poor, respectively, as well as Social Security were larger than the defense budget. Does this mean that Americans place a higher value on social welfare than on defense? Not necessarily. As shown in Figure 16.4, the United States spends more than any other nation for defense—five times more in 2009 than the next closest country, China. Do Americans value defense more than other countries, or does this figure reflect the country's position as a military superpower? Clearly, budgets reflect not only current American values,

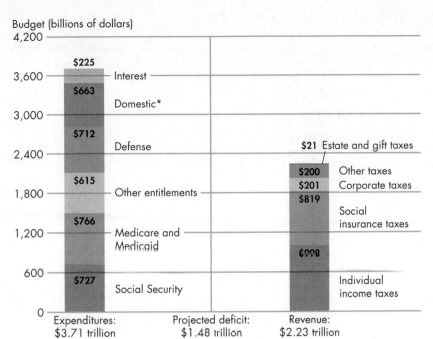

Budget (billions of dollars)

$225 Interest
$663 Domestic*
$712 Defense
$615 Other entitlements
$766 Medicare and Medicaid
$727 Social Security

$21 Estate and gift taxes
$200 Other taxes
$201 Corporate taxes
$819 Social insurance taxes
$992 Individual income taxes

Expenditures: $3.71 trillion
Projected deficit: $1.48 trillion
Revenue: $2.23 trillion

* Includes all appropriated domestic spending such as education, ransportation, security, housing assistance, and foreign aid.

FIGURE 16.3

★ PROJECTED BUDGET FOR FISCAL YEAR 2011

Given this general picture, what is the best way to bring expenditures into better alignment with revenues?

Source: The Concord Coalition, 2011.

but also past decisions and commitments that we continue to support as discussed in Chapter 18.

Another important category, interest paid on the national debt, reflects the cost of running a budget deficit—the government needs to pay interest on the money it borrows to meet its obligations. As it borrows more, the interest total rises. Between 2008 and 2010, the nation's public debt rose dramatically as government spending increased to combat the Great Recession. The sharp rise triggered heated discussions about future policies, as we will discuss later.

TAXATION

Who pays for government? As shown in Figure 16.5, the largest share came from individuals who pay income taxes and have payroll taxes withheld from their paychecks. Corporate income taxes provide a substantially lower portion of overall federal revenues than that paid by individuals. Other fees and excise taxes (for example, federal taxes on alcoholic beverages, tobacco products, and gasoline) generate most of the remainder.

These summaries of revenue sources, however, understate how complex tax policy really is. The federal tax code, the full collection of tax laws, is nearly 6,000 pages long and full of highly technical provisions, the consequence of many different groups lobbying to reduce their tax burden. Such special treatments are often referred to as **tax loopholes,** but policy makers also use tax provisions as a way to encourage or discourage certain individual and business activities. Tax laws can reward certain behaviors (buying a home allows you to deduct interest paid on your home mortgage) or penalize others (cashing in your IRA retirement plan early results in a tax

tax loopholes
Special treatment given to groups of taxpayers in the tax laws that help lower or eliminate their tax burden.

FIGURE 16.4

★ GLOBAL MILITARY
SPENDING IN 2009

Does high U.S. defense
spending allow other
nations to spend less?

Source: Data drawn from the military
expenditure database maintained
by SIPRI, 2011 and reported on
www.GlobalIssues.org.

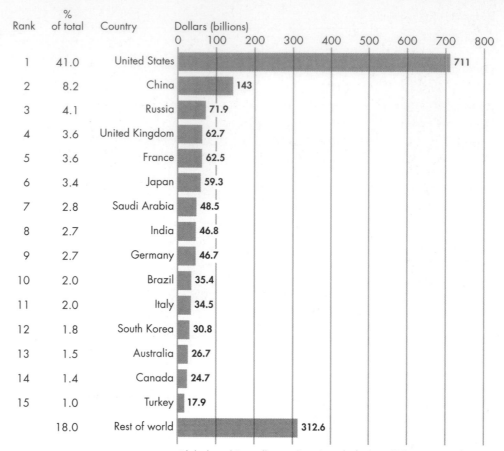

Rank	% of total	Country	Dollars (billions)
1	41.0	United States	711
2	8.2	China	143
3	4.1	Russia	71.9
4	3.6	United Kingdom	62.7
5	3.6	France	62.5
6	3.4	Japan	59.3
7	2.8	Saudi Arabia	48.5
8	2.7	India	46.8
9	2.7	Germany	46.7
10	2.0	Brazil	35.4
11	2.0	Italy	34.5
12	1.8	South Korea	30.8
13	1.5	Australia	26.7
14	1.4	Canada	24.7
15	1.0	Turkey	17.9
	18.0	Rest of world	312.6

Global total (not all countries shown): $1,735 billion.

FIGURE 16.5

★ FEDERAL REVENUES BY
SOURCE, FISCAL YEAR 2011

Individuals contribute the vast
majority of revenues received by
the federal government. What is
the "fair share" that citizens
should pay?

Source: Tax Policy Center, (http://www
.taxpolicycenter.org/taxtopics/currentdistribution
.cfm)

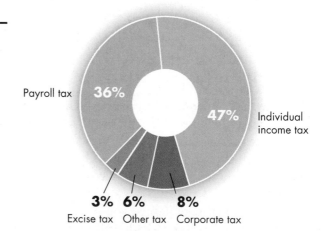

Payroll tax 36%

47% Individual income tax

3% Excise tax 6% Other tax 8% Corporate tax

progressive tax system
Taxation in which citizens with
higher incomes pay a higher
percentage of their income in
taxes than people in lower income
groups.

penalty). In 2011, President Obama proposed to give businesses a tax credit for hiring new workers.

Like the budget, the taxation system also reflects the nation's political values. In general, the American income tax system is described as **progressive,** which means that citizens who have higher incomes and who can therefore afford to pay more for government services pay a higher tax rate on their income than people in lower income groups. In the United States, those families with incomes in the top 25 percent of all families pay a larger share of the nation's revenues and pay higher tax rates on their income than others earning less income, reflecting their greater capacity to pay. Tax rates may also be **regressive,** meaning that the share of income paid in taxes declines as income increases, or **proportional,** in which everyone pays the same flat rate regardless of income differences.

In the United States, some types of taxes are progressive but others are regressive. For example, many states and localities impose sales taxes, which are considered regressive because lower-income families spend a larger portion of their total income on taxable items than higher-income families do. Some states exclude essentials—like food—from the sales tax or sponsor tax holidays at key times, such as the end of the summer when families prepare to send children back to school. Taxes can have effects on society as a whole. A system of progressive taxes in a nation that provides high levels of public services (for example, Sweden) has the effect of reducing income inequalities, or redistributing income, and is therefore described as redistributive.

Are there alternatives to the current U.S. tax system? Different nations employ different systems. Citizens of Monaco pay no tax on the annual income they earn. Instead, the government of Monaco funds itself through relatively high corporate taxes and a value-added tax (VAT), a tax based on the additional value that businesses add to a commodity during stages of production. Unlike a sales tax (assessed by many states in the United States), in which citizens pay taxes on the final value of a product, producers pay the VAT tax on the additional value of a product added at each stage of production.

A major difference across nations is the tax rate levied on incomes. Some nations have a single tax rate applied to all citizens regardless of their personal wealth, a strategy called a "flat tax" by proponents of this policy in the United States. For example, the Czech Republic, Bulgaria, Romania, Latvia, and Russia utilize a single rate. Estonia was the first European country to establish such a system in 1994, and other Eastern European nations have followed suit.[14] Advocates of introducing a flat tax in the United States also point to simplification—a tax return could be written on a postcard. In fact, the United States had a flat tax, established in 1867 at 3 percent as a way to pay for the Civil War. However, recent proposals to establish a flat tax in the United States have been roundly criticized as favoring the wealthy. Herman Cain, candidate for the Republican presidential nomination in 2012, called for a 9 percent national flat tax on income as well as 9 percent on corporations and a 9 percent national sales tax.

Most nations establish multiple rates depending on citizens' incomes. In Sweden, for example, rates range from 0 to 57 percent. Swedish citizens with the highest incomes pay more than half their annual income in taxes. Tax rates in the United States today range from 0 to 35 percent. Large numbers of U.S. citizens—estimated at 46 percent in 2011, an unusually high percentage—pay no federal income taxes. The rates paid by the remainder range from a low of 10 percent to a high of 35 percent. Even those not

★ The gambling casinos in Monaco attract visitors who generate a good portion of the country's revenue.

regressive tax rates
Taxation in which the share of citizens' income paid in taxes declines as income increases.

proportional tax rates
Taxation in which citizens pay the same flat tax rate regardless of income level.

paying income taxes, however, do pay Social Security and other forms of taxes. Of course, it does not always work out that those with higher incomes pay higher rates. Billionaire investor Warren Buffett has famously pointed out that he pays a lower rate of taxes than his secretary because his income is derived from investments while hers comes from a salary, and tax law provides for different treatment of income earned in these ways.[15]

INEQUALITY

The taxation system can reduce or increase income inequality. Does inequality matter and should nations try to reduce it? Inequality, argue some, can be beneficial. Investments made by the wealthy create jobs—the wealth trickles down to help others, but only if there are rewards for taking the additional risks. On the other hand, some social scientists see a link between inequality and social conflict. They argue that the frequent conflicts in Latin America and sub-Saharan Africa result from the extreme differences in income and wealth. Inequality may also reduce a nation's quality of life. As Nobel prize-winning economist Joseph Stiglitz explains, "The rich don't need to rely on government for parks or education or medical care or personal security—they can buy all these things for themselves."[16] Without a need, there is a reluctance to contribute and a resistance to paying a larger share of the costs. On the other hand, inequality seems to be a feature of all societies—it is a question of degree and inequality's likely effects.

Economists have developed a way to measure inequality—the GINI coefficient. At one extreme (0), everyone earns the same income. At the other extreme (1), a single person earns all the income. The higher the coefficient, the greater a nation's income inequality. Using the GINI coefficient for nations around the world, Figure 16.6 reveals that the United States has greater inequality than most other nations. Using a finer measure, Sweden emerges as the nation with the least inequality, and the other Scandinavian nations come close behind.

Today, the Americans with the top 1 percent of incomes take in 25 percent of the nation's total income. Additionally, the top 1 percent control 40 percent of the nation's total wealth. Just 25 years ago, the top 1 percent controlled only 12 percent of income and 33 percent of wealth. In other words, the gap between rich and poor has been growing, a point made by thousands of demonstrators "occupying" downtown areas in major cities during 2011. But the gap is also growing in most other industrialized nations, as the OECD recently reported.[17] It's just that the United States started with greater inequality—greater than all other OECD nations except Mexico and Turkey.

Public policies can aim to reduce income differences. A progressive tax system is one strategy, as are expenditures on social services—transportation, health care, and so forth—and cash transfers to low-income households. These policies effectively redistribute income and wealth from one sector of society—those paying higher tax rates—to another. Across OECD nations, the United States relies more heavily on its tax system to moderate income differences than on the other strategies. Cash transfers in the United States to unemployed workers and low-income families are relatively modest and do little to reduce inequality. The United States also spends less on social services than do most other industrialized nations.

If we start out in poverty, what is the chance that Americans will leave it? Most Americans would be surprised to learn that there is a high probability that their

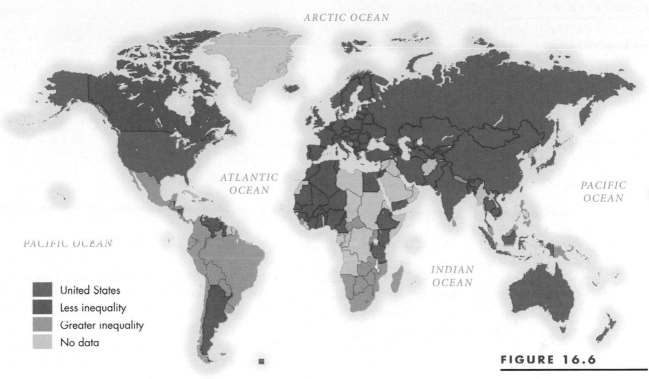

United States
Less inequality
Greater inequality
No data

FIGURE 16.6

★ ECONOMIC
INEQUALITY AROUND
THE WORLD

Source: Data from the CIA World
FactBook

children's earnings and position in society will be much the same as their own. And this is more likely to be true in the United States than in many other industrialized nations.[18] The opportunity to improve one's station in life is better elsewhere. Perhaps surprisingly, it's easier to live "the American dream" of upward mobility in Denmark or Finland.

BUDGET DEFICITS

national debt
Cumulative total of annual budget deficits.

When revenues fall short of expenditures in a given year, the nation runs a budget deficit, and the cumulative total of those annual deficits constitutes the **national debt.** As Figure 16.7 shows, budget deficits in the United States have persisted since 1940.

As noted earlier, one reason that the government runs a budget deficit is to fund wars and national emergencies. World War II triggered a tremendous surge in spending relative to revenues during the period from 1941 to 1945 (see Figure 16.7), a pattern repeated in more modest, barely visible form during the Korean War, 1950–1954, and at the height of the Vietnam War, 1965–1972. But since the 1950s, the federal government has seldom run a balanced budget whether in war or during peacetime. Lyndon Johnson (1963–1969) left office with a budget that was balanced (accomplished by the trick of folding the Social Security surplus into the budget for the first time), but that feat was not repeated until nearly three decades later in 1998–2001 when Bill Clinton sought to make budget discipline a part of his administration's legacy.

FIGURE 16.7

★ FEDERAL EXPENDITURES
AND REVENUES,
1940–2015

Why have Congress and
the president been able to
balance the budget so few
times since 1970?

Source: National Priorities Project, Inc.

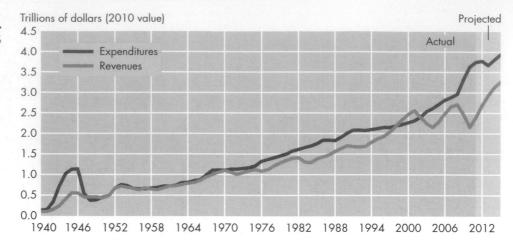

Clinton's legacy, however, was short-lived. Following the terrorist attacks of 9/11, the federal government embarked on a program to improve homeland security and to pursue the planners of the attacks by sending troops to Afghanistan and later to Iraq. And then came the Great Recession and spending to restore economic growth. Congress approved these efforts despite the need to borrow the money to pay for them, which moved the nation from a budget surplus to a budget deficit. Persistent deficit spending has been a source of concern for fiscal conservatives who believe that the government should be held to the same standards as a family, which must find a way to keep expenditures within its means. The Tea Party has demanded that the nation adopt a balanced budget amendment to ensure that government spending does not continue out of control. As others have noted, however, such an amendment would make it impossible for government to intervene to help stabilize the economy, a goal discussed in the next section.

DOMESTIC ECONOMIC POLICIES

KEY TO understanding

Government uses policies—fiscal and monetary—to guide the economy, but these policies are crafted by different institutions with differing interests. In enacting polices that influence the spending, taxing, and borrowing decisions in the annual budget, Congress and the president are most concerned about unemployment. The Federal Reserve Board, independent of both the legislative and executive branches, is most concerned about the threat of inflation. How do different priorities get reconciled?

★

Many different public and private decision makers set economic policies in the United States. Consumers and producers—the key participants in a market economy—collectively shape the most important contours of the economic landscape, but government influences the contexts within which economic decisions are made. For example, when government actions intentionally increase interest rates, both consumers and businesses are less likely to borrow money to pay for new homes, new cars, additional education, or new manufacturing equipment. Likewise, if the government reduces taxes so that both consumers and businesses have more money to spend, then house sales, car sales, and investment are likely to get a boost. By changing these policies, government can influence economic decisions made in the marketplace. Economists divide government economic policy into two broad categories: fiscal policy and monetary policy.

FISCAL POLICY

The federal government enacts **fiscal policy** when the people's elected representatives intentionally adjust taxes, government spending, and government borrowing to stimulate or slow the economy. Although the federal government's fiscal policies have the greatest influence on the overall economy, state and local governments also make tax and spending decisions. Unlike the federal government, however, state and local governments must balance their revenues and expenditures annually. The federal government, by contrast, can run a **budget deficit,** spending more in any given year than it receives in revenues and making up the difference by borrowing money from citizens and non-citizens.

Despite concerns about the national debt, there are economic justifications for running a deficit. Since the 1930s, government has intervened when the nation's economic activity has slowed down and the value of all goods and services, the **gross domestic product** (or GDP), has fallen. Economists call this a **recession** if it persists for at least six months or a **depression** when it becomes even more severe with declines in the GDP of 10 percent and greater. During these downturns workers typically see their earnings diminish or, worse yet, disappear altogether when they lose their jobs as employers reduce production and employment because of declining sales. With fewer workers earning less money, government revenues from income taxes also decline. To maintain a balanced budget during a recession or depression, the government needs to cut back its spending, as many states and cities were forced to do between 2008 and 2012. But such actions by government worsen the economic conditions. Some government workers lose their jobs; government programs to assist the unemployed or to retrain workers are reduced just when citizens need them most; and government's overall impact on the economy as a consumer of goods and services drops.

Since the 1930s, most economists have supported the view that government should play a countercyclical role in the economy in order to stabilize conditions. In their view, the government should increase its spending during economic downturns to help stimulate economic activity and combat unemployment. Today, specialists in the federal government closely monitor the levels of unemployment nationally, regionally, and in different sectors of the economy. They also follow the direction in which prices are moving, carefully monitoring the price of specific products that are important to economic growth, such as the costs of oil, iron ore, food, and other raw materials used in manufacturing. When these multiple indicators show a slowdown in the economy, federal policies are typically put in place to offset this trend.

Keynesian economics, a set of policy actions proposed by British economist John Maynard Keynes at the time of the Great Depression, endorses this countercyclical role of government. According to this approach, government policy during economic declines should stimulate the economy through increased spending, reduced taxes, or both. These actions are likely to produce an even greater deficit that the government must meet by borrowing money through the sale of bonds to investors at home and abroad. This is exactly what happened in the United States in response to the recent recession, leading to a ballooning deficit. The opposite policy also holds true: During times when the economy is expanding at too rapid a pace, when rising wages trigger increased prices for goods and services—inflationary conditions—the government can reduce spending, increase taxes, or both. The resulting surplus can be used to reduce the national debt, but as we have seen, this rarely occurs.

fiscal policy
Efforts made by Congress and the president to stabilize the economy through the taxing, spending, and borrowing decisions made as part of the annual budget process.

budget deficit
Result of government spending more in any given year than it receives in revenues and making up the difference by borrowing money from citizens and noncitizens.

gross domestic product (GDP)
Total value of goods and services produced in the economy.

recession
Decline in economic activity (GDP) for a sustained period, often defined as two consecutive quarters or at least six months.

depression
Decline in economic activity (GDP) over a sustained period that totals 10 percent or more.

Keynesian economics
Set of countercyclical policy prescriptions proposed by British economist John Maynard Keynes at the time of the Great Depression, calling for government to use taxes and expenditures to control economic recessions and expansions.

FIGURE 16.8

★ ACTUAL AND
PROJECTED FEDERAL
EXPENDITURES AS
PERCENT OF GDP,
1969–2019

Source: Congressional Budget Office,
(http://www.cbo.gov/ftpdocs/
100xx/doc10014/Chapter1.5.1
.shtml#1100244)

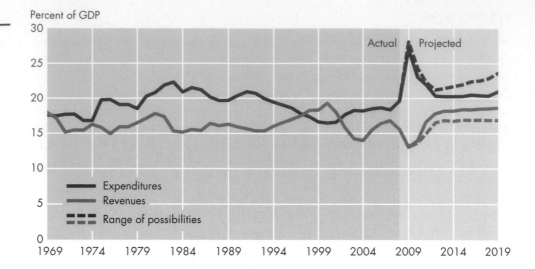

supply-side economics
Policies designed to stimulate
producers' economic activity by
reducing tax rates and removing
the costs of regulation.

There are alternative strategies of government intervention. The most notable has been **supply-side economics** in which the government stimulates the economy by providing incentives to produce goods and services. Lowering income tax rates and reducing regulation, say supply-siders, encourages people to work, save, and invest. The Reagan administration relied heavily on supply-side logic to guide its policies, and defenders point to the sustained growth of the economy during the 1990s as evidence that it works.

One way to evaluate the deficit's magnitude is to compare it to the total value of goods and services produced in the economy—the GDP. By looking at the deficit as a percentage of the GDP (the measure on the vertical axis in Figure 16.8), the CBO projected a dramatic spike in the deficit to 28 percent of GDP that was expected to occur in 2009 and to continue for years afterward in response to the severe economic recession that began in December 2007. The CBO projected the future deficits (dotted line) to be even higher than the OMB had projected (solid lines) for the budget proposed by President Obama.

After he took office in 2009, President Obama and the Congress quickly approved a large economic stimulus package of $789 billion designed to counter the economic slowdown. It included spending for many so-called "shovel ready" construction projects—that is, road, bridge, and public works projects that could be quickly started as a way to provide jobs and pump money into the economy. As it turned out, however, few of these projects could be started quickly. Because this stimulus money would be combined with the funds already spent during the fall and winter of 2008 to 2009 to prevent the failure of banks, financial firms, and auto manufacturers General Motors and Chrysler, fiscal year 2009 (FY09) ended with the largest budget deficit in U.S. history, a staggering $1.42 trillion. President Obama also proposed a $3.55 trillion budget for FY10 that would produce an additional deficit of more than $1 trillion. Figure 16.9 expresses these deficits in terms of the percentage of GDP, showing the trend since 1969. Members of Congress became increasingly uncomfortable with projections of deficits well into the future. These were the same projections that Angela Merkel, Chancellor of Germany, had found so distressing, as seen in our opening example.

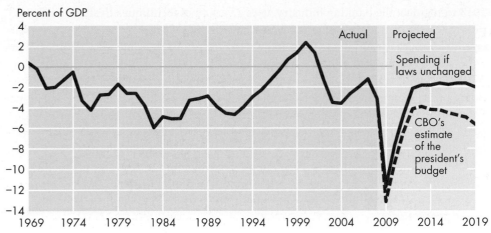

Percent of GDP

FIGURE 16.9

★ TOTAL DEFICITS OR SURPLUSES AS PERCENT OF GDP, 1969–2019

If you had been a policy maker looking at this projection in 2009 of a severe deficit followed by years of continued deficits, what would you have done?

Source: Congressional Budget Office, (http://www.cbo.gov/ftpdocs/ 100xx/doc10014/Chapter1.5.1 .shtml#1100244)

THE NATIONAL DEBT

In October 2008, the National Debt Clock located in midtown Manhattan, a public record of the federal government's total indebtedness, ran out of digits to record the total when it reached $10 trillion. To accommodate the growing total, the clock dropped the dollar sign from the display and added a "1." When the clock was unveiled in 1989, the debt stood at $2.7 trillion. In 20 years the total more than quadrupled, but not inadvertently. Congress must approve government borrowing by setting a **debt ceiling,** the limit up to which the Treasury Department is authorized to borrow money. To combat the economic recession, Congress raised that limit from $11.315 trillion to $12.104 trillion effective February 17, 2009. It continued to climb, rising to more than $15 trillion in August 2011.

A growing debt increases the interest payments that the government must pay to lenders, a mandatory expense. Moreover, it means that current revenues do not cover current spending, so future generations of Americans are responsible for paying off the current generation's debt. Congress established a debt ceiling for the first time in 1917, on the brink of the United States entering World War I. Until then, each time the United States wanted to issue bonds for the public to purchase and thereby loan money to the government, Congress had to approve. A debt ceiling gave the Treasury Department greater financial flexibility. Most congressional votes on raising the debt ceiling (nearly 100) have been routine, but not so in 2011. As the federal government approached the approved ceiling, House Republicans, concerned that government spending was out of control, insisted that current spending be cut before they would approve an additional increase. After months of wrangling, only a last-minute agreement that further delayed the decision on spending cuts until later in the year prevented the wealthiest nation on earth from failing to pay its obligations.

The public was disgusted by the spectacle of their elected representatives unable to resolve such an important issue. The most frequent response in a survey conducted by the Pew Research Center for the People and the Press was "ridiculous" followed by "disgusting," "stupid," "frustrating," "childish," and "terrible."[19]

debt ceiling
The official limit set by Congress and the president on the federal government's ability to borrow funds through the sale of Treasury bonds.

MONETARY POLICY

Government spending and taxes are not the only way to influence economic conditions. The **Federal Reserve Board** (the Fed), an independent federal agency created in

Federal Reserve Board
An independent federal agency created in 1913 to regulate the banking industry and set monetary policy.

monetary policy
Terms under which money and credit are made available to buyers and sellers in the market economy.

1913 to regulate the banking industry, uses a variety of techniques to shape **monetary policy,** the terms under which money and credit are made available to buyers and sellers in the market economy, and so controls the supply of money circulating in the nation. The Fed tries to maintain steady and sustainable economic growth, full employment, and stable prices while ensuring the safety of bank practices. A seven-member Board of Governors based in Washington, D.C., coordinates the activities of 12 regional Federal Reserve Banks and 25 branches located in major cities throughout the nation (see Figure 16.10). Board members and regional bank presidents monitor conditions in their section of the nation's economy and a subgroup (the Federal Open Market Committee) meets monthly to take actions that move interest rates up (called a *contractionary* policy because it reduces the supply of money) or down (an *expansionary* policy) as a way to influence consumer and business spending and borrowing. They can ease, tighten, or maintain the nation's money supply, resulting in interest rates that increase, decrease, or remain the same.

How did the United States end up with the Federal Reserve system? After more than a century of political conflict inside Congress and between presidents and Congress, Woodrow Wilson signed legislation creating the Federal Reserve System on December 23, 1913. This action resolved the long-running question of whether there should be a central authority overseeing the U.S. financial system, a policy first recommended by Alexander Hamilton in 1791.

Farming and local business interests from the West and South defeated the first and second Banks of the United States, which operated from 1791–1811 and 1816–1836, because they believed local banks would be more responsive to the needs of their communities than the distant banks in the East. The decentralized banking system of small, undercapitalized banks could not meet the financial needs of the nation's growing industrial power. A devastating economic depression in 1893 and a financial panic

FIGURE 16.10

★ TWELVE FEDERAL RESERVE DISTRICTS

Source: The Federal Reserve Board, (http://www.federalreserve.gov/otherfrb.htm)

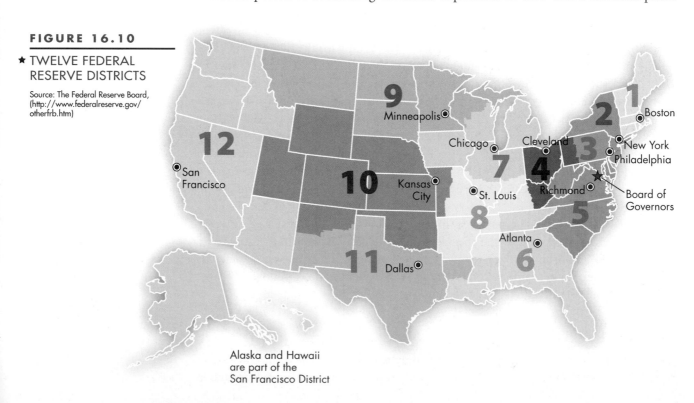

Alaska and Hawaii are part of the San Francisco District

triggered by Wall Street intrigue in 1907 made monetary reform a major national issue, championed by William Jennings Bryan, the Democrats' presidential nominee in three elections from 1896–1908.

Woodrow Wilson, the Democrats' presidential candidate in 1912, took a firm position against creating a privately owned central bank but favored establishing public control over banking. The plan that emerged allowed bankers to control regional reserve banks but also provided for a Federal Reserve Board that would assert centralized public control.[20] Wilson personally guided the legislation creating the Federal Reserve System to victory using a dramatic presidential address to a joint session of Congress—a common political tactic today—and private meetings with critics of his bill to find common ground. Wilson managed to hold his party together in Congress, confronted by the uncompromising opposition of the American Bankers Association, which denounced the effort to establish public control over the banking system as "socialistic" and "un-American."[21] When he prevailed, Wilson had created not just a new financial system but also a new, modern model for how presidents can lead Congress.

The Fed's designers hoped to remove politics from banking activities as much as possible. The Fed is self-financing; that is, Congress does not appropriate funding for it as part of the annual budget process, which insulates the Fed from political pressure. In addition, members of the Board of Governors serve a single 14-year term that spans multiple presidential administrations. The Board's chair and vice-chair serve four-year terms (they usually serve more than one term) and are nominated by the president, subject to Senate confirmation. The result is a highly independent agency whose leaders must coordinate their policies with Congress and the president but are not unduly controlled by politics. Thus, the Fed chair reports to Congress at least twice a year and often more frequently in response to congressional requests for testimony. The chair also participates in meetings with other influential financial leaders in the administration including the secretary of Treasury, members of the Council of Economic Advisers, and the director of OMB. Clearly, then, the Fed's leadership is well aware of the political context in which it must act, but the Fed is buffered from the most direct political pressures.

The regional Federal Reserve Banks perform many services necessary for a modern economy: distribute U.S. currency and coin, process checks, and provide electronic forms of payment between banks within their districts. They also regulate state-chartered commercial banks and serve as clearinghouses for bank-to-bank transfers of funds that make it possible to have direct deposit of payroll checks, electronic bill payment, and direct deposit of government payments such as Social Security checks. During economic crises—for example, in the fall of 2008 when the international financial system was teetering on the edge of collapse—the Fed becomes the "lender of last resort." In this role, the Fed can lend money to banks and other financial institutions to ensure that shortages at one or several banks do not disrupt the flow of funds throughout the financial system. The Fed can pump money into the banking system when no other bank or institution is willing or able to do so.

Just as Congress and the president tend to increase deficits during recessions, so too does the Fed seek to change interest rates in response to changing economic conditions. As shown in Figure 16.12, the Fed can raise the interest rate that banks charge each other for short-term loans—the **federal funds rate**—as it did dramatically in the late 1970s and early 1980s to bring inflation under control, or it can reduce that rate to try to stimulate

federal funds rate
The interest charges that banks collect from each other for loans, which are set by a committee of the Federal Reserve Board in order to influence economic activity through monetary policy.

FIGURE 16.11

★ FEDERAL FUNDS RATE IN RELATION TO RECESSIONS, 1950–2010

What can the Fed do after reducing the funds rate to nearly zero?

Note: Shaded areas indicate U.S. recessions. 2009 research: stlouisfed.org.

Source: Federal Reserve Bank of St. Louis, (http://research.stlouisfed.org/fred2/series/FEDFUNDS)

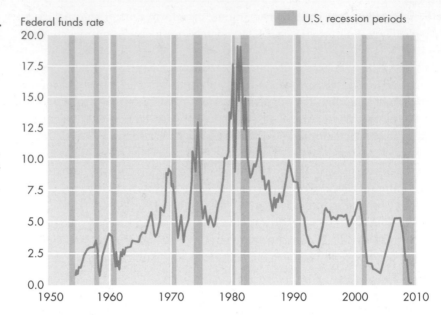

economic activity, as it did during recessionary periods (the tan bars in Figure 16.11). (The interest rates that banks charge to business and individual borrowers roughly parallel the federal funds rate.) Most recently, the Fed reduced effective interest rates to near zero in response to the severe recession beginning in 2008.

Every major industrial nation in the world has a central bank comparable to the Fed. They typically control the national currency, set national interest rates, and buttress the banking industry with loans during times of financial stress—exactly the same actions taken by the Fed. In 2008, many central banks around the world adopted policies similar to those followed in the United States. As Figure 16.12 shows, policy makers in several major economies took actions similar to the Fed's in order to stimulate

FIGURE 16.12

★ OFFICIAL INTEREST RATES IN SELECTED ECONOMIES, 2005–2009

Note: The data are daily and extend through February 18, 2009. The data shown are, for Canada, the overnight rate: for the euro area, the minimum bid rate on main refinancing operations; for Japan, the call money rate; for the United Kingdom, the official bank rate paid on commercial reserves; for the United States, the target federal funds rate.

Source: Federal Reserve Board, (http://www.federalreserve.gov/monetarypolicy/mpr_20090224_part2.htm)

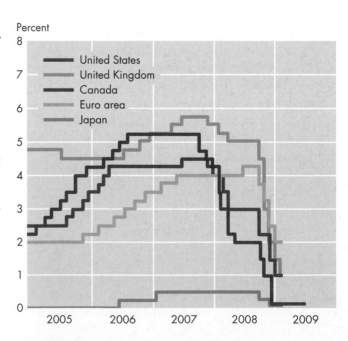

economic activity in the face of the global recession. There were also nations reluctant to adopt such policies, such as Germany.

The Fed is an unlikely but prototypically American construct—a decentralized central bank. The Fed's structure was a compromise between populists who distrusted powerful East Coast bankers and banking interests who wanted a stronger central authority. The new system was unable to stem the tide of the Great Depression, however. Nearly 10,000 banks failed between 1930 and 1933. But a stronger Fed emerged in subsequent decades and, in the opinion of most analysts, proved its worth during the financial crisis of 2008.

REGULATION

Both federal and state authorities regulate economic activity in the United States. The government seeks to prevent monopolies or near-monopolies from charging unfair prices to consumers and also strives to create an infrastructure that fosters economic growth. During its life, from 1887 to 1995, the Interstate Commerce Commission regulated railroads, interstate telephone service (until creation of the Federal Communications Commission in 1934), and trucking companies. In subsequent decades, Congress created similar agencies, including the following:

- Federal Trade Commission (1914) to regulate unfair business practices across a wide range of industries
- Federal Communications Commission (1934) to regulate radio, television, and telecommunications
- Securities and Exchange Commission (1934) to regulate stock trading
- Civil Aeronautics Board (1940) to regulate the airlines
- National Labor Relations Board (1935) to protect labor unions' organizing rights and to investigate unfair labor practices
- Consumer Product Safety Commission (1972) to protect citizens against injury caused by product defects

At the state and local level, public service and public utilities commissions regulate the cost and reliability of electricity, natural gas, telephone, cable, water, and wastewater companies. Originally, municipalities often gave companies exclusive service rights to guarantee the profits they needed for growth. But the commissions controlled these monopolies to prevent unfair pricing practices. AT&T grew to become the largest company in the world by 1970 because other companies could not gain entry into the local phone business dominated by its 18 "baby bells" that operated around the country and its monopoly on long-distance calling. A federal court decision forced AT&T to divest itself of the local phone business. The result has been greater service innovation and reduced prices as competitors jumped into the market.[22] Wireless telephone services are not regulated and operate in a highly competitive market, although service providers use various strategies to lock in their customers.

Those interests affected by regulation have many avenues to secure support from Congress, the president, and the bureaucrats who regulate them. This means that regulators often serve the interests of the businesses rather than the general public who are ostensibly being protected. There are, however, self-appointed public interest groups who claim to represent the best interests of the unorganized public, as discussed in Chapter 10.

THE LIMITS OF DOMESTIC ECONOMIC POLICIES

In today's world, formulating economic policy is complicated by interdependence among nations. Policies in the United States are tightly connected to those of its major trading partners, financial partners, and creditors around the globe. Just as other nations are concerned about the health of the U.S. economy, U.S. business and government policy makers worry about conditions abroad. Financial problems in Ireland, Portugal, Greece, and Italy during 2010–2012 had ripple effects on the U.S. stock markets. A shift in exchange rates has immediate impacts on the price of goods being bought or sold. Speculation over the future supply of oil and other critical commodities can quickly drive up prices for consumers and stress family budgets. The unique role played by the United States in the world economy over the past 65 years has made the nation far more dependent on the policies and actions of others than it had been before.

Under these conditions, international coordination must be the rule of the day—every day. Prime ministers and presidents, finance ministers, and central bankers meet regularly and communicate daily, even more frequently during crises. Global markets respond to each other constantly, operating day and night. American policy makers—already facing the challenge of coordinating decisions across institutions—must now do so internationally as well. But coordination to what ends? Just when decision makers need greater certainty about *what happened, why,* and *how to prevent it from recurring,* economists seem more confused about the answers and their underlying theories. Both Keynesian and monetarist policy were designed to address the problems of national economies. Global markets are different, and our understanding of how they operate remains quite elementary.[23]

RESPONDING TO THE GREAT RECESSION OF 2007–2009 AND BEYOND

KEY to understanding ★

Both the Bush and Obama administrations sought to stimulate the economy with massive combinations of tax cuts and spending increases that produced huge budget deficits. Additionally, the Treasury Department and the Federal Reserve worked to stabilize the banking system and save major corporations that teetered on the brink of bankruptcy. Loans to corporations, dramatically low interest rates, and programs to reduce home mortgage defaults slowed the recession, although unemployment remained stubbornly high.

How does a highly fragmented political system respond to a major economic crisis? The case of the Great Recession which ran from December 2007 to mid-2009 and whose effects continued well afterward offers an illustration of the difficulties involved in crafting a coherent response.

Many factors contributed to the onset of the economic recession that began in the United States and then spread globally. Because it was the largest economic slowdown since the Great Depression of the 1930s, commentators began calling it the Great Recession. Lawrence Summers, director of President Obama's National Economic Council and a noted economist, explained in a March 2009 speech that modern recessions arise for two reasons: either central banks raise interest rates too high in the effort to fight inflation, or markets react to a period of excessive risk-taking and speculation in the chase for easy profits, periods often called "bubbles." Summers viewed the Great Recession as the second type, a "correction of financial excesses."[24] Other economists have pointed out a link between the two types—that Fed policies during 2002 to 2004 encouraged rampant speculation by keeping interest rates too low. Investors took advantage of these low rates to borrow heavily as they chased rising housing prices and risky investments that they expected to produce certain profits. Everyone believed the prices of housing, stocks, and other investment products would just keep rising, encouraging many to borrow more money in hopes of making money.

When overextended homeowners and investors in the United States began to have problems repaying their loans, banks began to call in the debts and reclaim the properties. Banks seized homes with unpaid mortgages. Hedge funds and investment banks, financial institutions different from the traditional commercial banks, had expanded quickly in the deregulated environment of the 1990s and now began to experience problems that caused many to fail. Operating without clear regulatory supervision, these institutions had created many complex investment opportunities that promised high returns without informing investors of the risks involved. Many U.S. home loans, for example, had been repackaged and sold to investors around the world who expected to earn income from the mortgage payments in the United States. When homeowners defaulted on their mortgages, the value of these mortgage-backed securities fell.

The strains on both traditional banks and investment banks set off a chain reaction in the global financial system. Summers reported that over a period of 18 months from September 2007 to March 2009, investors and homeowners lost $50 trillion worldwide, including $7 trillion in the U.S. stock markets and $6 trillion in the housing market. With so much wealth disappearing so quickly, overconfidence and greed suddenly turned into fear: people began to save rather than spend and rushed to sell their investments before the value fell even further. The decline in demand for goods and services as well as the collapse of normal financial services rippled through more and more sectors of the economy, creating a vicious downward cycle. Panic spread quickly.

Policy makers in the Bush administration and around the world had difficulty staying ahead of rapidly deteriorating conditions and often improvised solutions as new problems cropped up. President Bush and Congress approved a $168 billion stimulus plan in early 2008, sending checks to Americans in order to encourage spending. The Fed began reducing interest rates in September 2007, hoping to stave off a recession by stimulating consumer demand and business investment to create new jobs. And the Fed went well beyond monetary policy in its efforts to slow the decline. It provided a loan to prop up one investment bank, reluctantly allowed another to go bankrupt, and encouraged the takeover of two more by large commercial banks. Fed loans to the giant insurance company AIG eventually totaled more than $180 billion, an effort to prevent the company from failing to honor its financial obligations around the world. As was often said during public discussions, AIG (and later the U.S. automakers) was "too big to [be allowed to] fail." Once the Fed had lowered interest rates to almost zero, Fed chairman Ben Bernanke came up with new ways to continue pumping money into the economy, generating almost another $2 trillion in financial assets available for banks and businesses to use.

In addition, the federal government provided a $200 billion loan and virtually took over two giant mortgage-lending

★ The housing crisis during the Great Recession pushed whole families out of their homes and onto the streets. Policy makers struggled to figure out how to reverse this trend.

agencies (Fannie Mae and Freddie Mac) that were on the brink of financial failure. These organizations were technically government-sponsored enterprises (see Chapter 14). When improvised policies could no longer keep up with the crisis and the nation's banking system nearly ground to a halt, unable to make needed loans to consumers and businesses, President Bush's secretary of the Treasury, Henry Paulson, and Fed Chairman Bernanke jointly devised a massive rescue plan (critics called it a "bailout" plan) to buy up the failing mortgages held by financial institutions at a price tag of $700 billion. This infusion of cash was intended to restore normal financial operations. After a costly week of delay (recounted in Chapter 12), which triggered the largest one-day sell-off in stock market history, Congress approved the sweeping package and agreed to immediately provide half the money.

In the face of declining auto sales, the government made loans to General Motors and Chrysler to prevent a massive layoff of workers that would also affect car dealerships and parts suppliers, but in return, government officials in both the Bush and Obama administrations pressured the corporations to embark on a sweeping process of internal restructuring, with the goal of making them more competitive in the future. By the summer of 2009, the U.S. government had provided additional loans to the two companies totaling about $50 billion, and the federal government—really the taxpayers—became a major shareholder in both firms as they went through bankruptcy proceedings. The hope was that Chrysler, with a new major partner in Fiat, and General Motors—with half its previous car brands, fewer dealerships, a reduced workforce, and smaller obligations to its retirees—would be able to compete more effectively with foreign manufacturers. Both companies bounced back.

But these steps, massive as they were, still did not halt the economic slide. After taking office the Obama administration proposed an even larger economic stimulus package—$789 billion composed of $282 billion in tax cuts and $507 billion in additional spending. It was designed to save and create jobs as well as help the states weather the recession, but congressional Republicans lined up against the package—only three Senate Republicans voted in favor—believing that it included many examples of wasteful spending and would prove ineffective. Obama's package invested heavily in health care, energy, and education as well as in the financial industry, committing the second installment of $350 billion to shore up bank assets and proposing new regulatory controls on risky investments. Finally, Obama provided new funding to refinance mortgages as a way to help stabilize the housing market, but it continued to falter.

By the middle of 2009, with the unemployment rate rapidly approaching 10 percent, debate turned to the need for another stimulus bill. But there was also growing concern that the nation lacked an "exit strategy"—a way to return to more restrained government spending and to curtail borrowing after the emergency was over. And additional financial problems loomed on the horizon both domestically and abroad, including the rising cost of programs for retirees as baby boomers leave the workforce and international pressures to restructure the global financial system in the wake of its near-collapse in 2008.[25] There seemed to be a subtle shift from "spend whatever is needed" to "reduce future commitments." This shift in attitude was even more apparent after the Republicans, propelled by the enthusiasm of Tea Party activists, gained control of the House in 2011 and confronted the Obama administration over government spending and ballooning deficits. With the recession lingering longer than expected, policy makers looked for new solutions.

In fashioning policies to combat the recession, there were extensive consultations among officials from the Fed, Treasury Department, Congress, and the White House; among appointees of the incoming Obama and outgoing Bush administrations; between federal and state officials; and among finance ministers and central bankers around the world. Coordinating government efforts was a critical part of the response—sometimes slow and halting, but especially vital in a highly fragmented system such as that of the United States. But this crisis-driven experience has triggered a new debate about the nation's policy priorities—whether the United States can afford Social Security, Medicare, and Medicaid or continue to function as the world's police force—and who should pay how much for the government's services.

Why Are We
THE WAY WE ARE?

Americans believe in free markets, a deeply ingrained part of their self-image and collective historical memory. Yet the U.S. government has played a vital role in economic affairs since the nation's beginning, and as the United States has become a more close-knit economic unit, that role has grown appreciably. Some growth in the government's role has resulted from responses to crises—wars and the Great Depression. But its role has also grown because citizens wanted the protections or assistance that the federal government can most easily provide. Although they now have taxation *with* representation, modern Americans do not like paying for these services any more than did their colonial forebears.

DISTINCTIVE IDEOLOGY OF ECONOMIC FREEDOM

The American experience differs from that of other nations. The American Revolution provided both political freedom and independence from Britain's overbearing economic control, but it did not create an economic unit. Alexander Hamilton's policies moved the nation in that direction, but the transportation and communication systems allowed for only loose national coordination. States dominated internal improvements and banking, resulting in a far more decentralized economy than in any of the major industrializing European nations (England, France, Sweden, Spain), where monarchies had already instituted tight central controls during the seventeenth and eighteenth centuries. Thus, the ideology of economic freedom was well established in the United States before the last third of the nineteenth century, when the federal government's powers grew in response to industrialization and urbanization.

It might surprise many Americans to learn that *The Economist,* a British news magazine heavily committed to free markets, regards the U.S. federal government as far less influential than central governments in other nations. In their view, the United States is "less bureaucratic at the national level than most other countries." But foreign firms seeking to do business in the United States must contend with 50 different tax systems, business registration requirements, and environmental regulations, rather than the single bureaucracy they face in their home country.[26] In short, the tradition of decentralization is alive and well in the twenty-first century even if it is less pronounced now than in the past.

FRAGMENTED CENTRAL AUTHORITY

Economic policy making must also constantly resolve the tensions that arise from the constitutional separation of powers, complicated by the actions of the largely autonomous Federal Reserve Board. Thus, fiscal policy depends upon the decisions of the two elected branches of government, and monetary policy, directed by the Fed, cannot afford to be too far out of alignment lest the economy suffer. In the face of crisis during 2007–2009, the separate centers of decision making found ways to work together, even if inefficiently.

PRAGMATISM + CAPITALISM

The United States clearly has a mixed economy. When the Great Recession required forceful action, the federal government played a highly active role in guiding banks through the financial crisis and taking action to save two-thirds of the domestic auto industry by virtually nationalizing it. Only Ford escaped the new government influence. These newest steps reflect the general thrust of government's role over time—pragmatic actions taken within the context of a strong commitment to capitalism.

. . . AND WHY DOES IT Matter?

Although many Americans would like to shrink government—Texas Governor Rick Perry campaigned for the Republican presidential nomination in 2011 on the promise to make government as "irrelevant" as possible and other candidates echoed a similar message—citizens also want the services that government provides, particularly when calamities befall them, such as hurricanes, unemployment, catastrophic illness, and crime. A different set of complaints focuses on how government allows business to gouge or mislead the public. Where were the regulators when medicines had side-effects, tainted produce spread illness, and airlines began charging outrageous prices for luggage? And those millions of Americans who lost their jobs and homes during the Great Recession are wondering why government was unable to keep their lives intact.

Some patterns appear over and over in American life. The belief that government is interfering with individual liberty has deep roots. Seldom does an election cycle go by without resentment over taxes, complaints about government waste, fraud, and abuse, and distrust of Wall Street bankers.

As this chapter demonstrates, government's impact on the American economy is pervasive. And this is not a new phenomenon. Alexander Hamilton set in motion a plan designed to create a modern economic powerhouse, and that plan, tweaked along the way, has probably succeeded beyond his wildest dreams. Some may wish to roll back the way government guides the economy, but the likelihood of that happening and the United States remaining an economic power are indeed quite slim. It is more likely that citizens and officials will disagree about what the current plan should be—which policy options with which likely consequences should be put into place and when. Did the Bush-Obama stimulus policies work? Did they work fast enough? Were they large enough? Should something else have been done? What should be done now, when the economy is still staggering?

Many detailed issues, beyond the philosophical one of government's reach, are likely to engage Americans in debate: Would a flat tax be fair if all citizens, regardless of whether they were rich or poor, had to pay the same tax rate? Should those Americans who are able to pay more for government services be required to do so? And if so, how much more? Should those who benefit from a program have to pay for it, or should the program's cost be shared by many, even those who do not benefit? Government budgets provide endless details to debate, and the economy touches everyone's life. Understanding its opaque operations empowers citizens to advocate for policies consistent with both their political values and economic interests.

critical thinking questions

1. **What are the differences between how the U.S. government intervenes in the free market and how the government operates in a socialist system?**

2. **Should the government remove controls on transportation and all public utilities—water, sewer, electricity, cable television—as a way to encourage free-market competition? Justify your answer by explaining the possible implications of this measure.**

3. What effect would a progressive income tax system, a proportional system, and a regressive tax system be likely to have on income distribution? Which system is best suited to meet American political and economic goals?

4. Should the federal government be required to balance its budget each year? Why or why not? When is it legitimate to run a budget deficit?

key terms

DOMESTIC POLICY

★ ★ ★

- Summarize the stages of making public policy.
- Analyze the century-long debate surrounding the U.S. health care system and the 2010 health care reform that produced near-universal coverage.
- Explore Social Security's complex financial structure, the pressures it faces as baby boomers begin to retire, and the implications for policy making.
- Compare and contrast U.S. policy goals of energy security and environmental protection.
- Describe federal intervention and strategies to improve U.S. education and discuss the tension such federal policies have created with the states.

PERSPECTIVE
Must Policy Solutions Reflect a Nation's Uniqueness?

Changing public policies is seldom easy. Change is even more difficult if it affects many different interests in society, as was the case for health care reform in the United States. When Barack Obama launched his reform effort in 2009, health care made up one-sixth of the total U.S. economy. Many elected officials and health care specialists agreed that reform was needed but could not agree on specific proposals for change. Legislators exchanged sharp words in Congress, fearful citizens confronted their representatives in public meetings, and television ads and radio talk shows whipped emotions into a frenzy. Confusing claims and counterclaims filled the air.

Those engaged in the debate often referred to health care in other political systems. Critics pointed to shortcomings in Canada and the United Kingdom, where programs described as "socialized medicine" produced long delays for medical care. The Dutch health care system received less attention, although international studies showed it to be the best in Europe following extensive reforms made in 2006. Could a nation as large as the United States learn from the Dutch example? Could the experience of one nation transfer to another, or was it necessary for nations to devise distinctive policy solutions reflecting their unique systems? Studies show that medical care in the Netherlands is better than that in the United States in most respects. In only a few areas does the Dutch system trail the U.S. system—for example, ready access to medical specialists and cancer survival rates.[1]

On New Year's Day 2006, the Dutch instituted the first stages of a multi-year health reform process. This step-by-step strategy ensured that policy makers could make adjustments gradually rather than adopt large changes they might later regret. Unlike the United States, the Netherlands had one major policy piece already in place—the Dutch had established universal medical coverage in 1941, encouraged by the German authorities who occupied their nation during World War II.[2] The Dutch reforms aimed to control rapidly rising costs through competition among private health insurance companies.[3] Dutch citizens can switch insurance companies, and companies cannot deny coverage because of "preexisting conditions"—health problems that affected clients before they purchased insurance.

Earlier attempts at reform in both countries had failed because, once the plan became public, interest groups aroused public fears that changes would reduce quality, threaten their present health care, and trigger higher government spending. When President Bill Clinton developed an earlier reform bill largely in secret in the 1990s, it faced stiff opposition after its content became public. The Netherlands faced a similar situation in 1974. Health care providers opposed the blueprints for a dramatically new system drawn up by policy experts in private, and even after Dutch officials negotiated with affected interests, they were unable to reach agreement.

By 2006, health care costs were rising so sharply in the Netherlands that both public officials and private interests recognized the need for change. A similar consensus emerged in the United States in early 2009. In both cases, the goal was to find a politically viable combination of policy actions. In the Netherlands, legislators agreed to a set of steps that started the process of gradual change. In the United States, everything depended on President Obama's ability to create enough public confidence to effect large-scale change in the face of harsh criticism that had slowed the decision process. After seemingly endless maneuvering, Congress approved reform proposals in mid-March 2010 and the president signed the massive changes into law. Opponents, led by Republicans, pledged to prevent the changes from going into effect.

Different political strategies in the United States and the Netherlands reflect cultural and structural differences. The Dutch have a long tradition of close cooperation between government and organized interests. Building broad agreement through slow bargaining and negotiation is consistent with the Dutch parliamentary system, which requires a coalition of multiple political parties to reach a governing majority. By contrast, the U.S. presidential system hinges much more on the public's trust in the president and the chief executive's ability to build the coalitions needed to get major policy proposals through Congress. Thus, the gradualist strategy adopted in the Netherlands might not have been appropriate for the United States, but the "big change strategy" guaranteed that some U.S. interests would continue to fight the reforms.

THIS CHAPTER opens by considering an ideal model of policy making that scholars use to describe the formal stages of public policy making. Then we proceed to examine four domestic policy areas that have already been major areas of concern and are likely to remain so. We consider health care reform as part of the security net the U.S. government establishes for its citizens. We then turn to the looming problem of maintaining Social Security amid demographic changes. We analyze the balance between the need to increase energy supplies and the need to protect the environment. Finally, we assess problems in our educational system and explore how policy-makers have tried to address them. As you read this chapter, keep in mind our two core questions:

WHY ARE WE THE WAY WE ARE?
WHY DOES IT MATTER TO YOU?

In particular, how does the highly fragmented decision-making system in the United States affect public policies?

MAKING PUBLIC POLICY

Public policies are the products of the political pressures and official decision making we have studied in this book, resulting in government action or inaction that affects the lives of citizens. In setting public policies, governments help the nation perform several activities: solve collective problems such as "provide for the common defense," protect law-abiding citizens from criminal activity, and prevent the rampant spread of diseases; allocate scarce resources; and respond to citizens' needs and demands.

Citizens vary in what they expect government to do. Particularly in the United States where democracy was established well before an integrated system of communication and transportation, there has been a longstanding presumption of self-sufficiency. As they traveled westward, settlers moved into places where government had little capacity to provide much help or assert much control. This reality of the frontier experience created a pervasive outlook that has taken on a reality of its own: Individuals and communities need to provide for themselves and rely on a form of **rugged individualism** to meet their own needs. Later, when government was established, some of this self-sufficiency was surrendered. Sometimes government action was welcomed, but often it was viewed as intrusive. In this sense, many Americans have a **negative view of government:** when government collects resources (taxes) from some citizens to meet the needs of others, it is exceeding its legitimate powers. Also resonating with the negative view of government is the preference for market-based solutions to public problems. Citizens, in this view, can solve problems by exchanging resources with each other and working in conjunction with businesses rather than by relying on government. Moreover, competition should be encouraged in the public realm as well as the private to make government run more effectively. As we will see in the next section, solutions for health care and education often rely on competition.

In contrast, some Americans have a **positive view of government:** government action is necessary for citizens to meet their full potential, and government-run programs are the only way to accomplish some goals. These opposing views of government coexist in U.S. politics today. The positive view of government is more prevalent in Europe and Japan where communal values are stronger than the individualistic orientation so prevalent in the United States (See Chapter 6 for a more in-depth discussion of political culture.)

Public policies seek to solve problems collectively, allocate scarce resources, and respond to citizen and group demands. General attitudes about government shape Americans' policy preferences. Typically, the policy-making process has multiple stages: agenda setting, policy formulation, policy adoption, policy implementation, and policy evaluation. How do different participants contribute and dominate different stages of this process?

public policy
Products of political pressures and governmental decision making that result in governmental action or inaction that affects the lives of citizens.

rugged individualism
Widespread belief in the United States that citizens must provide for their own needs rather than rely on government to do so.

negative view of government
A perception that government actions intrude on the privacy and individual rights of citizens.

positive view of government
A perception that government actions are necessary for citizens to realize their full potential.

AN IDEALIZED MODEL OF POLICY MAKING

Scholars provide a model of policy making that includes four important stages: agenda-setting, policy formulation, policy adoption, and policy implementation.

Agenda Setting

Government officials engage in **agenda-setting** when they identify the areas of public life that require action. Although government officials may make the final determination, many others help identify problems and make suggestions about what to do.

agenda-setting
Stage in the policy-making process where officials identify the problems that government needs to address.

During electoral campaigns, candidates identify problems, propose possible solutions, and evaluate the progress made since the last election. The media and interest groups also identify problems for action. Journalists uncover numerous issues each year and receive national recognition for their efforts. In 2010, for example, Pulitzer Prizes were presented to reporters for uncovering the mismanagement of natural gas payments in Virginia, corrupt narcotics police in Philadelphia, poor regulation of food safety by the Food and Drug Administration, and the dangers of cell phone use while driving.[4]

In addition, unions, businesses and other organized interests press their demands on government. Citizen activists use mass marches to highlight demands with calls for equal treatment regardless of race (civil rights), gender (women's rights), age, disability, and sexual preference (LGBT rights). Other groups carve out a special day each year, such as Earth Day, to highlight their concerns. Finally, events shape the public agenda. Hurricane Katrina, which struck New Orleans and the Gulf Coast in the summer of 2005, shifted the nation's focus away from reforming Social Security, President Bush's top priority, to rebuilding storm-torn areas and assisting displaced residents.

Policy Formulation

policy formulation
Stage in the policy-making process in which government officials and non-government activists identify solutions to address the nation's problems.

Both governmental and non-governmental stakeholders suggest solutions to the nation's problems during the **policy formulation** stage. Career bureaucrats draw on their expertise and institutional knowledge of programs, public needs, and past strategies, as do members of congressional staffs and specialized interest groups. Staffs in other government agencies play important roles, especially the Government Accountability Office (GAO) and the Office of Management and Budget (OMB), units discussed in Chapters 12 and 14. Think tanks with expertise in the budget, defense policy, international relations, and the environment offer ideas as well. Policy alternatives develop in a rich "stew" of ideas and alternatives with groups releasing **issue briefs** (or white papers) that define problems and láy out alternative solutions. Task forces with representatives from within and outside of the government study specific issues and formulate recommendations for action. For example, the National Commission on Fiscal Responsibility and Reform, composed of prominent Democrats and Republicans both inside and outside of the government, reported its recommendations for reducing chronic national budget deficits in December 2010.

issue briefs (or **white papers**)
Discussions of public problems and possible solutions developed and released by non-governmental groups.

★ During legislative consideration of restrictions on cell phone use while driving, the *Seattle Post* reported that the Insurance Institute for Highway Safety found that drivers on cell phones are four times more likely to crash. This is an example of media influence on public policy.

Policy Adoption

Ultimately, public officials decide *whether* action will be taken and *what* that action should be—the **policy adoption** stage. When action is taken through statutes, legislators must share power with executives. The famous checks and balances swing into operation as negotiations unfold between the president and Congress, governors and state legislatures, mayors and city councils, or county executives and county councils.

Americans expect that policies crafted in the legislature will be reached through an open, accessible process that provides all affected parties with the opportunity to have their views heard and thereby participate in the policy making. Frequently, however, negotiations occur behind the scenes, and the media and watchdog groups monitor policy making to ensure that the public's interests have been fully heard.

Policy Implementation

Governments take action by creating programs or drafting regulations designed to achieve the goals identified in statutes—that is, they engage in **policy implementation.** When legislators rely on career officials to provide the details not specified in the legislation, this is called **delegation.** This practice is sometimes challenged as unconstitutional because it allows unelected officials to exercise considerable power as they use their discretion to translate broad purposes into specific actions. At other times, critics fault Congress when it attempts to micromanage details over programs with which the members have only limited familiarity. Should elected officials make all the detailed decisions themselves, or are they justified in delegating the details to experts? There is no right answer to this question.

To protect against excessive administrative discretion, federal career bureaucrats must adhere to a set of standards established in the Administrative Procedure Act to ensure that affected parties can learn what rules are being considered and have the opportunity to comment. Similar guidelines exist in the states. Government agencies must publish pending regulations, thus giving affected interests and the public opportunities to respond before the rules are made final.

Policy Evaluation

After policies are implemented, someone needs to determine whether programs and regulations are achieving policy goals— that is, to engage in **policy evaluation.** How effective are the government's efforts? Do the programs need modification?

Many officials and private citizens evaluate the effectiveness of a policy. Both the legislative and executive branches conduct systematic oversight of programs. In Congress, this occurs when committees reauthorize or renew programs, making adjustments, adopting new strategies, or discontinuing past efforts. Responsible career bureaucrats muster data to demonstrate how they are achieving the original goals or to prove that they need additional resources and strategies to do so. Oversight also occurs when the appropriations committees in both the House and Senate determine the next year's budget. Presidents rely on the OMB to conduct evaluations of effectiveness during the annual budget process, and Congress can call for studies by the Congressional Research Service and the Government Accountability Office.

policy adoption
Stage in the policy-making process in which officials decide whether action will be taken and what that action should be.

policy implementation
Programs or regulations designed to achieve the goals identified in legislative statutes.

delegation
Reliance by elected officials on career bureaucrats to provide the details needed to translate broad policy goals into specific actions.

policy evaluation
Final stage in the policy-making process in which officials determine whether the programs put into place are achieving the desired goals.

★ Former OMB director Jacob Lew testified on President Obama's FY2012 Budget during a House Budget Committee Hearing.

Those affected by government programs seek opportunities to be heard. They lobby in Congress either for or against the programs in place and maintain close ties with the bureaucrats operating the programs, reflecting the tight relationships known as iron triangles discussed in Chapter 14. If they are unable to convince Congress or the executive to adopt policies more to their liking, they can challenge programs in the courts.

To illustrate policy making, we discuss four important areas of government action: health care, Social Security, energy/environment, and education. In each case, we organize the discussion into three parts: a *background* on the policy area; the *problems* and *solutions* identified by decision makers; and the *politics* of decision making.

HEALTH CARE

★ **KEY** TO understanding

After nearly a century of off-and-on debate, the United States created a system that provides near-universal health care for its residents. The national debate that produced health care reform in 2010 reflected an American preference for solutions that are market-based rather than government-based. Nonetheless, the federal government has a much greater impact on health care than most Americans realize.

universal health care
Policies ensuring that all citizens of a nation receive adequate health care.

In 2010, the United States, Mexico, and Turkey were the only members of the Organization for Economic Cooperation and Development (OECD) not to have a **universal health care** system or at least near-universal coverage in place.[5] (The OECD's 34 member nations are commonly considered the world's most advanced industrial nations.) Although the United States lacked a national health care program, creating one had been debated for nearly a century.

BACKGROUND

Since the beginning of the twentieth century, American politicians have debated how to meet the nation's health care needs. At its founding convention in 1901, the Socialist Party of the United States endorsed health care insurance (along with accident, unemployment, and old age insurance) and the issue later entered the political mainstream. Major proposals came from Teddy Roosevelt's Progressive Party in 1912, President Harry Truman in 1948, and President John F. Kennedy in 1960. For a brief time after 1915, the American Medical Association (AMA), the largest professional group representing physicians, even supported a plan for compulsory health insurance but changed its position in 1918 and vigorously opposed subsequent proposals. By contrast, unions have been staunch supporters of national health insurance.[6]

In the absence of national health insurance, the United States developed a system of private health insurance provided by employers. This benefit spread rapidly during World War II when employers, confronted by stringent controls on wages (imposed to prevent inflation during a time of labor shortages), used health insurance and other benefits to attract workers.[7] Thus, the United States constructed a system in which both employers and employees share the cost of

premiums paid to insurance companies. About two-thirds of the U.S. population has been covered by employer-provided health care plans.

In European and other nations, health insurance was one of several government-sponsored social insurance programs provided to everyone. Conservative governments sometimes enacted these programs to stave off more radical reforms. For example, Prussia (the precursor to modern Germany) introduced health insurance in 1883. Sometimes a socialist or social democratic government established the program. Not all universal insurance systems are the same. In Germany and Switzerland, for example, all citizens are required to participate but make payments to private insurance companies. By contrast, England smoothly transitioned from a wartime system of government-provided medical care to a public National Health Service in the years after World War II.[8]

The United States has sought ways to meet the health care needs of those not covered by an employer plan. In 1965, pushed by Lyndon Johnson (1963–1969), Democrats and Republicans approved government health care insurance systems for elderly Americans (Medicare) and for poor Americans (Medicaid). Medicare is health insurance—workers contribute a portion of their paychecks throughout their working lives to a fund that pays for the health care of retirees, and then they become eligible to receive such coverage when they reach age 65. Medicare is an example of an **entitlement program**—the law establishes qualifications for participation, and each citizen who meets these qualifications is entitled to the benefits. Because the system is universal in the United States, those who contributed at some point in the past can expect to benefit later.

By contrast, Medicaid is a **public assistance program**—only those Americans who meet a "means test" are eligible to receive benefits. Americans qualify for Medicaid benefits if they have low family incomes and few financial assets such as a house or car. The government uses tax dollars to pay for these benefits, and thus many who have contributed to Medicaid (by paying state and federal taxes) will never benefit from the program. States share Medicaid costs with the federal government.

Medicaid is one strand of the **social safety net** designed to help the poorest and most vulnerable members of American society. Because these programs are paid for with tax dollars, they represent a transfer of wealth from one sector of society to another. Medicaid was the largest public assistance program in the country and the costliest, providing benefits to children, their parents, pregnant women, and persons with disabilities. Medicaid is a non-cash assistance program, the direction in which U.S. reform moved after 1996 when the principal cash welfare program, Aid to Families with Dependent Children, was redesigned.[9] There is now a five-year, lifetime limit on cash payments that individuals can receive under the Temporary Assistance to Needy Families program (TANF). Many former welfare recipients must now find jobs, but they remain heavily reliant on public help for medical care (Medicaid), food (Food Stamps), and housing (subsidized rent or public housing). Six different federal departments provide assistance programs, and state and local agencies are important partners in these efforts along with private, non-governmental organizations. This patchwork of programs was established over time, producing overlapping services and differing requirements that can be very confusing for potential beneficiaries.[10]

In addition to Medicare and Medicaid, the federal government pays the health care insurance premiums of government employees, maintains an extensive medical system for military families, and allows tax deductions to employers and individuals for insurance premiums and out-of-pocket medical expenses. Depending on how these expenditures are calculated, experts estimate that the federal government covers from 40 to

entitlement program
Programs such as Medicare and Social Security, in which benefits are provided to all citizens who meet eligibility qualifications established by law.

public assistance program
Policy that provides help to beneficiaries who meet a means test—that is, whose incomes are low enough for them to qualify to receive benefits from public sources.

social safety net
The collection of policies designed to meet the needs of poor and disadvantaged citizens in a nation.

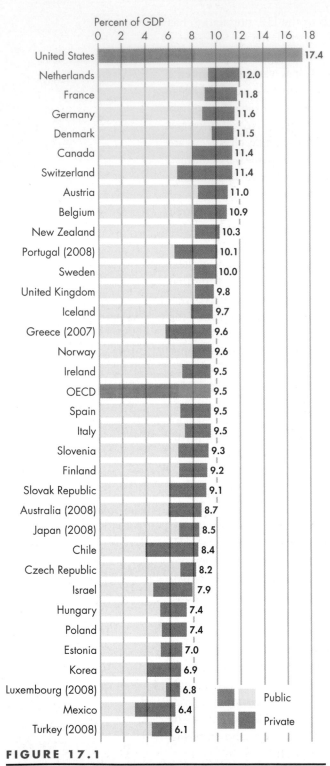

Percent of GDP

Country	Percent of GDP
United States	17.4
Netherlands	12.0
France	11.8
Germany	11.6
Denmark	11.5
Canada	11.4
Switzerland	11.4
Austria	11.0
Belgium	10.9
New Zealand	10.3
Portugal (2008)	10.1
Sweden	10.0
United Kingdom	9.8
Iceland	9.7
Greece (2007)	9.6
Norway	9.6
Ireland	9.5
OECD	9.5
Spain	9.5
Italy	9.5
Slovenia	9.3
Finland	9.2
Slovak Republic	9.1
Australia (2008)	8.7
Japan (2008)	8.5
Chile	8.4
Czech Republic	8.2
Israel	7.9
Hungary	7.4
Poland	7.4
Estonia	7.0
Korea	6.9
Luxembourg (2008)	6.8
Mexico	6.4
Turkey (2008)	6.1

Public
Private

FIGURE 17.1

★ HEALTH EXPENDITURES AS A SHARE OF GDP, OECD COUNTRIES, 2009

Why does the United States lead the OECD by a wide margin in health care spending as a percentage of GDP, the overall value of goods and services produced in the economy?

Source: OECD Health Data 2011 "How does the United States compare," (http://www.oecd.org/dataoecd/46/2/38980580.pdf)

60 percent of the total cost of U.S. health care. As shown in Figure 17.1, the United States spends a larger portion of its gross domestic product on health care than any of the other 34 member states of the OECD (17.4 percent in 2009).[11] Yet more than half the burden of paying for health care in the United States is borne by the citizens themselves from their savings, earnings, and insurance payments.

PROBLEMS AND SOLUTIONS

Reformers sought two goals: guarantee medical care for all Americans and slow the rise in health care costs. Little progress was made on either front during the 1970s and 1980s. President Bill Clinton (1993–2001) advanced a comprehensive proposal in 1993 that met with vigorous opposition. Like Truman's initiative, the Clinton proposals never came to a vote in Congress. George W. Bush (2001–2009) succeeded in convincing Congress to expand Medicare by including a prescription drug plan as part of health coverage for the elderly.

Should health care solutions be national in scope or developed and implemented at the state level? A prevalent view on domestic policy in the United States is that "one size does not fit all." In other words, because problems vary across a nation as large and diverse as the United States, so must strategies and solutions. When Washington decision makers failed to address important health problems such as reducing the number of uninsured, several states took on the problem themselves. Just two years after Massachusetts began connecting individuals and businesses to insurance providers through a state-run website, only 2.4 percent of the state's residents remained uninsured, the lowest percentage in the country. Other states, including Vermont, Illinois, and Washington, pursued somewhat different strategies.

Thus, by 2009, the U.S. health care system reflected a strong preference for private solutions over public, had launched state rather than national solutions, made purchase of insurance coverage voluntary rather than mandatory, and had private companies managing a majority of care, with government handling a significant share. President Obama and his advisors sought comprehensive reform. But Washington lacked the mutual trust between government and private interests found in the Netherlands. Furthermore, the plan did not introduce change gradually, leaving the stakeholders little recourse if mistakes became apparent during the implementation of the reform.

Basic Design

OECD member states have implemented two basic health care system models. Canada and the United Kingdom (UK) established a **single-payer system** in which citizens' taxes pay for services from private or public providers (as in Canada) or from doctors and other professionals who are government employees (as in the United Kingdom). Countries like Germany, France, Japan, and the Netherlands created a **regulated multi-payer system** in which government revenues subsidize insurance for some groups (for example, citizens with severe medical conditions) but a robust private health insurance industry, closely regulated by government, pays for patients' health services. Under either plan, all citizens are required to participate and therefore be covered. As it worked to achieve reform, Congress considered these solutions and others, concentrating on three major problem areas—*access, quality,* and *costs.*

Access

In 2009, more than 15 percent of U.S. residents—an estimated 46 million—had no health care insurance, making them unable to contend with major illnesses and unlikely to seek preventive care. An equivalent number of citizens lost health coverage at some point in the year because they changed jobs or worked for employers who had discontinued health insurance because of rapidly rising premiums. Among those frequently lacking health insurance are workers laid off from a job, college and graduate students, early retirees not yet covered by Medicare, workers in entry-level jobs in a service industry (for example, fast food restaurants) or in a small business, and non-residents. Young workers—ages 19 to 24—are especially unlikely to have health insurance in their part-time or beginning jobs; nearly a third of these young workers lacked insurance in 2004.[12] In addition, health insurance companies make money based on the difference between the amount of money they collect in premiums and the amount they pay out to cover their customers' costs. Thus, companies have a simple incentive: "seek out the healthy and avoid the sick."[13] Denying coverage to those who need it most—persons with severe health conditions—produces maximum profits.

★ The National Health Service provides public health care in the United Kingdom. Today, some employers are offering private insurance as well.

Quality

Despite the large amount of money Americans pay for health care, quality is a major concern. Not only does the United States spend the most on health care among OECD countries but it also leads in per capita spending at $7,290 per person, which is two and one-half times the OECD average ($2,964) and well above the next highest spender, Norway, at $4,763 per person. But "the nation's highest-in-the-world health spending isn't necessarily buying the highest-quality health care."[14] Table 17.1 compares the United States to OECD averages on four measures of health care effectiveness. To compare the U.S. system with that in the Netherlands (highlighted at the beginning of this chapter), 60 percent of the Dutch can get same-day doctor's appointments versus only 26 percent of Americans; Dutch citizens go to urgent care centers instead of waiting for hours in hospital emergency rooms, which the Dutch reserve for only the most serious cases; and the Dutch spend only 10 percent of their gross domestic product (GDP) on health care.

TABLE 17.1
how the united states compares with OECD averages in health care

Are these differences between U.S. health care and that of other nations large enough to be significant?

HEALTH CARE MEASURE	U.S.	OECD AVG.
Physicians per 1,000 residents	2.4	3.1
Acute care hospital beds/1,000	2.7	3.8
Life expectancy	78.1	79.0 years
Infant mortality rate/1,000 births	6.7	4.9

Source: OECD Health Data 2009, "How Does the United States Compare?" (www.oecd.org/dataoecd/46/2/38980580.pdf)

Costs

Health care spending as a portion of the nation's GDP has been rising since the middle of the twentieth century, as shown in Figure 17.2. Earlier, President Nixon (1969–1974) recommended relying on managed care (health maintenance organizations, or HMOs) as a way to control costs. Analysts have identified many potential sources of rising costs:

- The high costs of developing new drugs and new medical technologies
- Heavy reliance on specialists to provide most medical care
- The desire by most Americans to take maximum advantage of their insurance coverage so that they demand all available care, not just necessary care
- The high costs of treating the uninsured, who tend to delay treatment until their medical conditions become serious
- The inability of government or anyone else to hold down costs by negotiating lower prices from health care providers
- Higher prices resulting from health care providers' need for profits, contrasted with nonprofit service providers in other nations
- The possibility that some diseases and conditions are more common in the United States than elsewhere (for example, diabetes, obesity, asthma)
- Higher administrative costs because the U.S. system is highly decentralized with individuals and businesses purchasing care separately
- The high cost of malpractice insurance caused by doctors' and hospitals' need to protect against lawsuits

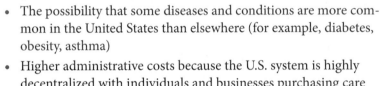

Percent of GDP spent on health care costs

FIGURE 17.2

★ HEALTH-CARE SPENDING AS A PORTION OF THE U.S. GROSS DOMESTIC PRODUCT

What do you believe causes health care costs in the United States to rise so steadily?

Source: Kaiser Family Foundation, "Health Care Costs: A Primer" March 2009 Figure 1, (http://www.kff.org/insurance/upload/7670_02.pdf)

POLITICS

Advocates believe the health care reform of 2010 addressed all three major issues: access, quality, and rising costs. To make coverage universal under the multi-payer plan envisioned, policy makers require that those not covered by an employer's plan purchase coverage on their own, with the government subsidizing the cost for low-income Americans who don't qualify for Medicaid. Coverage is mandatory, a major concern of critics; those who do not sign up will pay a penalty starting in 2016. New regulations require the insurance companies to provide care for high-risk clients—those with preexisting conditions—but not until 2014. Parents' plans provide coverage for children until age 26, a benefit introduced immediately. Workers with employer-provided coverage keep it; large employers (50 workers or more) are required to offer health care. After all these changes are put in place, coverage will become almost universal, including approximately 94 percent of American citizens by 2019. To improve the quality of care, the reform approved in

picture YOURSELF ...
LOOKING FOR A DOCTOR ON THE CANADIAN-U.S. BORDER

If you lived on the American side of the border between the United States and Canada and your friend lived on the Canadian side, who would receive better care?

In many respects, there are few differences between the United States and Canada, particularly when you live close to the border. Workers and goods flow easily from one side to the other; television and radio stations broadcast to citizens of both nations; and citizens share the same professional sports, with baseball and NBA teams in Canada as well as NHL teams in the United States. But some of the ads aired during the health care debate might lead you to suspect that Canadians wait forever to see a doctor or, worse yet, that Canadian bureaucrats stand between patients and their doctors. Ads seldom addressed the principal advantage Canadians enjoy, however: Canadian health care minimizes costs to citizens and makes them more willing to seek medical care.

By some, but not all, measures, Canadians' health care is superior to Americans'. Studies have found that

while Canadian death rates are lower for a large number of serious ailments, outcomes in the U.S. system are better for those who have certain illnesses, especially for people who have heart attacks.* American hospitals are more likely to have cutting-edge technology, so patients will have readier access to the most sophisticated medical tests and have to wait a shorter time to have the tests conducted. And in one survey, while 40 percent of Canadians with chronic medical conditions reported having to wait two months or longer to see a specialist, only 10 percent of Americans had to wait that long.** On the other hand, since no one in

Canada fails to receive medical care because they cannot afford it, Canadians are more likely to visit their family doctor when they first develop symptoms of illness. But if your condition is not critical, you might find that you'll have to live with it longer in Canada before it gets treated.

So where is it better to get sick?

* G. Guyatt et al., "A Systematic Review of Studies Comparing Health Outcomes in Canada and the United States." *Open Medicine*, North America, 1 (April 2007). Retrieved August 10, 2009, from http://www.openmedicine.ca/article/view/8/1.
** Cathy Schoen and Robin Osborn, 2008 Commonwealth Fund International Health Policy Survey of Sicker Adults, November 2008 (http://www.commonwealthfund.org/Surveys/2008/2008-Commonwealth-Fund-International-Health-Policy-Survey-of-Sicker-Adults.aspx).

questions to consider

1. **Does the profit-based medical system in the United States meet its citizens' needs better than the government-administered system in Canada? Why or why not?**

2. **Which is more important, affordability with a possible waiting period or immediate access to sophisticated equipment at a premium cost?**

3. **How can we determine which health care system is better?**

2010 calls for doctors, hospitals, and other health care providers to report extensively on their performance in delivering care. Finally, the reform intends to reduce costs; the Congressional Budget Office estimated that the new plan will reduce the nation's health care costs by more than $100 billion over its first decade.

Several factors contributed to the reform effort's success. Democrats had substantial majorities in both houses of Congress and controlled the White House. The president invested time in lobbying Congress and speaking publicly. Businesses and consumers were concerned about the rising costs of health care, heightened by the economic recession. Furthermore, unlike the Clintons, President Obama started out by securing support from most major interests affected by reform and set out basic principles for Congress to discuss, rather than initiating the process by issuing a comprehensive plan.[15]

A March 2009 White House forum aimed to create consensus among key leaders from Congress and representatives from major health care interests, trade associations, and professional organizations. Congressional party leaders had to reconcile differences among plans produced by two committees in the Senate and three in the House. Think tanks inundated both sides with recommendations. Democrats had to overcome internal party divisions: conservatives worried about limiting costs and controlling the budget deficit; progressives pushed for a strong government-run option; pro-life advocates wanted reassurance that federal funds would not be used to finance abortions. Senate Democrats also negotiated special deals for their states because each of their 60 votes was critical to preventing a Republican filibuster.

The House narrowly approved a reform bill in early November, with only a single Republican voting in favor. The Senate ended 25 days of debate by approving a bill on December 24, 2009, with no Republican votes. While a conference committee tried to resolve differences between House and Senate versions of the bill, Democrats lost their ability to halt a Senate filibuster when a special election in Massachusetts filled Senator Kennedy's now-vacant seat with a Republican. Democrats found a way around the problem. First, the House approved the Senate version of health reform, and it was signed into law by the president. Then the House and Senate approved changes to the reforms through an arcane parliamentary maneuver called "reconciliation." Republicans denounced the Democrats for ignoring their views throughout a process that commentators spent hours trying to explain, but the maneuvers allowed the Democrats to bypass a Senate filibuster.

Yet, public opposition to the health care plan spread and was at least in part responsible for the Republican success during the midterm elections of 2010. As a result, Republicans have challenged the new law in Congress, in the courts, and at the state level. Some Republican governors began planning to implement the new health law, while others refused to accept the federal money allocated to help plan for the launch in 2014.[16] And the push for cuts in government spending will likely include reductions in both Medicare and Medicaid. The Supreme Court heard a case in 2012 challenging whether citizens can be compelled to pay a penalty for not purchasing health insurance. The justices ruled 5-4 that the penalty was a tax that could constitutionally be imposed. But the court also limited provisions of the law compelling states to expand their Medicaid coverage.

SOCIAL SECURITY

On August 14, 2010, the Social Security program in the United States turned 75 years old. Established in 1935, Social Security was a cornerstone of the New Deal, the collection of programs introduced by President Franklin D. Roosevelt (1933–1945) during the 1930s. The original legislation creating the program included not just income for retired persons but also programs providing unemployment benefits and aid to the states for various health and welfare programs, all justified as ways to combat the Great Depression. In 2010, this major entitlement program was poised to undergo a stress test as millions of American baby boomers, about to turn 65, lined up to retire.

KEY TO understanding ★

The largest social insurance program in the United States, Social Security, turned 75 years old in 2010 but faces severe financial pressures as baby boomers retire. Addressing the system's long-term financing challenges is an unavoidable policy problem but one that is full of political danger and therefore especially difficult to resolve. Is it likely that Social Security will still exist when you retire in about 45 years?

BACKGROUND

The basic logic of the U.S. Social Security system is fairly simple: current workers, through contributions made to a national fund, replace a portion of retired workers' income once they are no longer employed. By working and contributing to the Social Security trust fund for a minimum of 10 years, American workers can qualify for benefits. In this "pay as you go" system, current workers' contributions pay for the benefits of current retirees, and any surplus is set aside for future needs. Recipients qualify for Social Security benefits not because their low income makes them "needy" but because they contributed to the program in the past. Social Security, then, is considered a **social insurance program** rather than a public assistance program. Participants meeting the requirements automatically qualify for benefits. Unlike Medicaid (reviewed earlier), there is no means test.

When Social Security was created in 1935, millions of Americans lacked jobs, savings, or help from either family members or the government. Particularly vulnerable were the elderly, who had lost their savings in bank failures and their pension (if they had one) as former employers went out of business. Thirty-five million workers received Social Security cards during 1936 and began paying taxes into a fund from which the first monthly check was issued to Ida May Fuller of Vermont in 1940.

social insurance program
Government program such as Social Security or Medicare that spreads the risk of income loss or illness across a broad population rather than requiring each individual to bear the risk alone.

Her benefits totaled more than $22,000 before she died at age 100 in 1975, far more than she had contributed during the three years before she retired. By 1950, Social Security covered about half of American workers. Later changes to the program extended coverage until it gradually became nearly universal, with 162 million working Americans paying into the fund during 2008.

Because of its complex financial structure and the need to project benefits payments decades into the future, the original law required policy-makers to make 75-year plans for the Social Security program, far longer than virtually any other government program. From 1937 to 2005, Social Security had received more than $10.7 trillion in revenue (tax payments and interest earned on securities) and paid out $8.9 trillion. During its long history, there have been only 12 years when Social Security's current tax receipts did not equal the benefits paid out, with most of these years falling in the mid- to late 1970s.[17] When current revenues do not equal current benefits, the program dips into the surplus revenues from the past to cover the difference.

cost of living adjustment (COLA)
Automatic increase in benefits paid by Social Security to retirees to keep pace with rising prices.

Social Security benefits are determined by Congress and until 1972 were increased only when Congress voted to raise the amount—an irregular process fraught with politics. This practice caused problems because inflation (the increasing cost of rent, health care, electricity, and other essentials over time) eroded the value of the benefit. Congress changed the law—effective in 1975—to provide a **cost of living adjustment (COLA)** in beneficiaries' checks equal to the annual increase in consumer prices. At the same time the initial benefits paid by Social Security were indexed to rising wages. So by the end of the 1970s, Social Security benefits kept pace with increases in both wages and prices.

Social Security affects a remarkably large number of citizens—one of every six Americans (or nearly 51 million persons) receives benefits through one of the Social Security programs. Monthly Social Security benefits are sent to nearly 35 million former workers and spouses, and additional benefits go to more than 15 million others under SSI or survivors insurance (see Figure 17.3).

The program has kept many elderly Americans out of poverty. In 1959, nearly 39 percent of elderly Americans had incomes below the poverty level, as defined by the government. By 1994, that figure had fallen to 11.7 percent, and *CQ Researcher*, a highly respected nonpartisan source of information on policy, estimated that in 2005 nearly 22 million Americans were boosted above the poverty line because of Social Security.[18] Women especially benefit from Social Security because they are less likely than men to have held jobs that provided a retirement pension, and women's pensions pay less than men's. Women are also likely to live longer, surviving husbands if they are married. Finally, the cost of administering Social Security benefits is much lower than the administrative costs of private insurance companies.

★ Ida May Fuller became the first recipient of Social Security in 1940, ultimately receiving over $22,000.

PROBLEMS AND SOLUTIONS

As popular and effective as the Social Security program is, a problem is developing: at some point in the future, the program will need to begin paying out more in benefits than it receives in revenue every year, eventually depleting its surplus. Statements are sometimes made in the media and in public debates suggesting that "Social Security is going broke." To understand this issue, we need to review the mix of demographics, benefits, and expectations that shape Social Security. The search for solutions has focused on ways to reduce costs or enhance revenues.

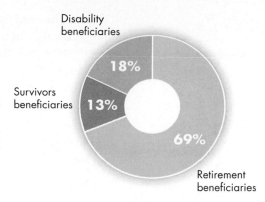

FIGURE 17.3

★ SOCIAL SECURITY IS MORE THAN A RETIREMENT PROGRAM

Source: Social Security Administration, (http://www.ssa.gov/pubs/10055.html)

Changing Demographics

Many members of the **baby boom generation,** those born between 1946 and 1964, are the children of families started after soldiers who had served in World War II returned home. Seventy-seven million children were born during this 18-year period as newly married couples or couples who had been separated during four years of war began to have children. The oldest members of that generation have begun to retire, and they are eligible for early Social Security benefits at 62 and for full benefits at 66. (For those born in 1960 and later, the age at which a worker can retire with full benefits is 67.) Because of the expected number of baby boomer retirees, the financial drain on the Social Security trust fund will grow. And with the help of medical science, baby boomers are likely to live longer than previous generations, collecting benefits for many years after they retire.

baby boom generation
Millions of Americans born between 1946 and 1964 whose approaching retirement poses financial problems for Social Security and Medicare.

As the baby boomers have aged, this large group has had ripple effects throughout society. Their numbers put pressure on school capacity in the 1950s and 1960s, and they will have a growing impact on the health care system as they age. During the period when baby boomers have been working, Social Security benefits could be set at relatively high levels because there were many workers per retiree. That ratio has now dwindled to about 3:1 and is projected to shrink even further, as shown in Figure 17.4. In 1990, the proportion of the population that was elderly was 11 percent. In 2020, this number is projected to be 16 percent.

The Gap Between Benefits and Revenue

Officials responsible for Social Security's solvency—its ability to meet its financial obligations—must set the terms of the program so that contributions will cover future commitments. There is no "right" amount that should be paid to retirees as benefits. Social Security's architects aimed to replace about 40 percent of the income of an average American worker. Retirees would meet remaining needs through personal savings, earnings from a part-time job, or from other sources, such as a pension provided by a former employer (only about half of American workers have such pensions). Nonetheless, many retired persons—nearly a third—depend almost entirely on their Social Security checks, and rising health care costs have severely pinched all retirees' budgets. Reducing the benefits of current recipients would be

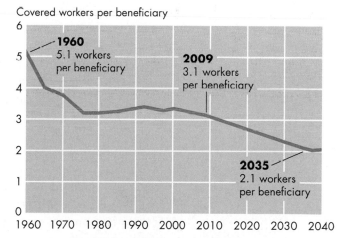

FIGURE 17.4

★ RATIO OF CONTRIBUTING WORKERS TO SOCIAL SECURITY RETIREES

Source: Social Security Administration, (http://www.ssa.gov/pubs/10055.html)

hard-hearted (who wants to make life worse for their grandparents, aunts, uncles, and parents?), not to mention politically unpopular.

The focus, then, has been more on changing the promises made to *future beneficiaries* and the demands placed on *current contributors*. For example, by raising the retirement age, policy makers can delay the point at which the government must begin to pay benefits. By raising the tax paid by current workers, they can increase revenues. Increasingly, younger workers fear that they will never collect from the program they have been paying into, and the principal problem is the looming bill for benefits expected by the many Americans approaching retirement.

Policy Alternatives

As we have seen, by making modest changes like increasing the age at which people receive benefits, Congress could achieve large savings when these changes are applied to many people over a long period of time. Generally, Democrats prefer strategies that increase revenues without cutting benefits. Since the program's creation in 1935, Congress has raised FICA tax rates 20 times, so some ask, why not raise them again? Opponents of higher taxes recoil at the rate that would be needed to meet the program's full obligations over the next 75 years—around 18 percent rather than the current 12.4 percent, divided equally between employer and employee. Ultimately, there is probably a limit on how high taxes can be raised. An alternative would be to make all income taxable instead of capping the amount subject to taxes, a change that would hit those earning high incomes especially hard. Paying Social Security benefits to millionaires or billionaires also makes little sense, so some have suggested making Social Security means-tested, which means that individuals exceeding a certain level of wealth would not receive benefits.

Bipartisan negotiations produced a balanced set of cost and benefit changes in 1983 that were intended to generate a financial surplus to meet the greater needs projected in the future. But the surplus generated by Social Security had become part of the overall national budget in 1969 when Lyndon Johnson wanted to leave office with a balanced budget. Thereafter the surplus was used to help pay for other programs—the Social Security trust fund loaned the money to the federal government and received a set of promises for the future. Those IOUs will soon need to be collected to meet the cost of promised benefits. Current benefit commitments exceeded current tax revenues in 2010 because of the recession (unemployed workers don't contribute, and the tax rate was lowered by 2 percent), and the trust funds—which are actually general government revenues—will have to make up the difference. This change would add to the strain on the national budget. Rather than helping to solve budget problems, as it has done for four decades, Social Security will start to cause budget problems. Moreover, the reserves in the trust fund (the total of $2.4 trillion in government bonds that earned a return of 5.1 percent in 2008) will be exhausted in 2037. At that point, current revenue from FICA payments will cover about 75 percent of the promised benefits.[19]

POLITICS

George W. Bush advocated a major restructuring of Social Security—he wanted to tie the program to the U.S. stock market because stocks would provide higher returns on the money paid into the trust fund. Bush's basic goal was to "pre-fund" benefits—making them dependent on the returns that could be generated from savings rather than on current workers' contributions. Bush's plan was the top domestic priority in his second term, and he campaigned hard for it during 2005. It failed miserably. The

proposal never received a vote in Congress, even though his own party controlled both the House and Senate. Unions were adamantly opposed and Democrats refused to negotiate with the president. Without Democrats meeting them halfway, Republican members of Congress were wary of any proposals for changes in Social Security.

Politicians are aware of the political muscle of the "gray lobby," the mobilized political power of retirees and near-retirees in American politics. Politicians realize that older people are far more likely to vote than younger ones, giving them extra power at the ballot box. In addition, the elderly have a powerful organization lobbying for their interests. The American Association of Retired Persons (AARP) boasts that it has more than 39 million members, making it the largest organization in U.S. politics, and it is able to mobilize its members into a political force aimed at protecting the interests of the elderly. The organization spent nearly $22 million in 2010 lobbying at both the state and national level on issues affecting the elderly.

The severe economic recession has made changing Social Security more difficult than ever. When the stock markets crashed in September and October of 2008, millions of Americans saw large portions of their retirement savings evaporate. Social Security was a foundation that remained untouched, and the lesson was obvious: stock market returns might be greater, but so is market risk. After this experience, the public suddenly began to save more, reflecting a newfound need to put aside resources rather than spend them.

President Obama proposed collecting FICA taxes on the full earnings of workers making $250,000 a year or more as a way to generate additional revenue. But health care reform and the rising costs of Medicare, the health care plan for the elderly, took up more of Obama's attention than Social Security. As the projected costs for health care reform attracted increasing attention—the CBO projected a cost of just under $1 trillion over 10 years—the administration found it difficult to argue that Congress must take action on Social Security. As budget priorities came to dominate the national agenda in 2010 and 2011, Social Security became a potential target for significant savings. What was the nature of the commitment to Americans approaching retirement age? How much would the government require younger, working Americans to contribute to fulfill its promise to the Baby Boomers? These recurrent questions are likely to continue shaping the Social Security debate in the years to come.

ENERGY AND THE ENVIRONMENT

Energy security and environmental protection have been competing policy goals for the past four decades. Energy security came to the forefront of the national agenda in the 1970s and climate change in the 1990s. The nation faces a challenge: to balance the need for ever-expanding energy use with the need to protect the environment, particularly to reduce the emission of greenhouse gases in order to slow climate change. If both goals are equally important, are they compatible or mutually exclusive?

During the second half of the twentieth century, scientists realized not only that technological and industrial development could have a negative impact on the environment, but also that the world would eventually exhaust its supply of oil, natural gas, and other resources. To avert future disasters, presidents and Congress wrestled with how policy alternatives would affect the overall economy. They also considered the relative advantages of several options: developing new sources of power (hydrogen, nuclear, wind); redirecting the nation away from an economy and lifestyle based on the use of fossil fuels (oil, natural gas, gasoline-powered automobiles); and finding new supplies of fossil fuels.

BACKGROUND

We need energy to run our businesses, power the home appliances that free up time for work and leisure, maintain the suburb-centered lifestyle that developed after World War II, and support the United States' role in the world. National policy makers must ensure that energy is readily available, reasonably priced, and efficiently distributed. Consumers want cheap energy, while energy producers need profits to finance exploration, research, and development.

Today's U.S. energy needs are met primarily by carbon-based fossil fuels. These include coal, petroleum, and natural gas, each of which is the basis for a major industry whose growth and development in the late nineteenth and early twentieth centuries helped the United States become an industrial leader in the world. As shown in Figure 17.5, coal began to surpass wood as

FIGURE 17.5

★ U.S. ENERGY CONSUMPTION BY SOURCE, 1775–2010

Can you imagine another significant energy source on the horizon?

Source: Energy Information Administration, "History of Energy in the United States," (http://www.eia.doe.gov/emeu/aer/eh/frame.html)

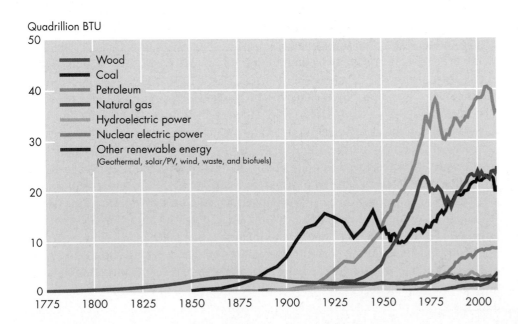

Quadrillion BTU

Wood
Coal
Petroleum
Natural gas
Hydroelectric power
Nuclear electric power
Other renewable energy
(Geothermal, solar/PV, wind, waste, and biofuels)

50
40
30
20
10
0

1775 1800 1825 1850 1875 1900 1925 1950 1975 2000

an energy source around 1885 and was subsequently surpassed by petroleum and natural gas. Each of these fuels can be converted into electricity, which is also generated at hydroelectric and nuclear reactor facilities. But the supply of carbon-based fuels is not inexhaustible—there are finite known oil and natural gas reserves. Coal is the most plentiful of the nonrenewable fuels in the United States, but its mining and burning have serious impacts on the environment.

Ample natural resources fed rapid economic growth, but even in the nineteenth century, conservationists began to question whether all stands of timber should be cut, whether all mountains were fair game for mining operations, and whether all streams should be dammed for hydroelectric power. Yellowstone National Park became the world's first preserved nature area in 1872, but Teddy Roosevelt (1901–1909) is often credited with crafting the first national policies on preserving forests and setting aside large areas of wilderness. Later in the century, public concern grew over a different set of problems: air pollution, water pollution, chemical dumps, and the harmful effects of pesticides. In response, an environmental movement lobbied for important legislation adopted in the 1970s to regulate pollution of air, water, and land. The newly created Environmental Protection Agency consolidated enforcement of the many new regulations affecting the production and consumption of energy. Industry, however, has consistently argued that the new regulations had harmful effects of their own—on the economy.

As the nation's demand for energy has grown, the United States has depleted its domestic supplies of petroleum. Oil companies tapped the readily accessible oil fields in the continental United States, in the Gulf of Mexico, and finally Alaska. Annual petroleum production declined. U.S. companies aggressively sought to develop new deposits around the world. This supply, however, is subject to potential disruption by hostile nations and poses environmental risks of its own. Producers have also pressed for the opportunity to develop new potential in U.S. territory that has been off-limits.

In the 1970s, two events heightened awareness of the nation's **energy security,** the ability of the United States to meet its energy needs. First, the Arab members of the Organization of the Petroleum Exporting Countries (OPEC) refused to export oil to the United States in retaliation for U.S. support of Israel during the 1973 Arab-Israeli war. Gas shortages produced long lines and high prices, seriously disrupting everyday life. Then in 1979, Iranian revolutionaries seized the American embassy staff in Tehran as hostages, and the subsequent international tension severely disrupted global oil supplies, with prices again rising dramatically. Starting with President Ford (1974–1977), successive administrations have purchased and stored oil in the Strategic Petroleum Reserve as insurance against another supply disruption. At the rate of current consumption, however, the reserve can satisfy only about 50 days of the nation's needs.

In response to both disruptions, American officials sought to reduce oil imports by encouraging citizens to conserve energy, by mandating new standards of energy efficiency, and by encouraging the development of alternative sources of energy including solar, geothermal, wind, and coal. The Carter administration (1977–1981) created the Department of Energy in 1977 to oversee initiatives. The nation made modest progress in its efforts at conserving energy during the 1970s and 1980s, but new sources of oil that were developed in Alaska and the North Sea increased world supplies and lowered prices. With oil again cheap, the need to establish energy independence became less urgent. The Reagan administration (1981–1989) promoted two different strategies, developing clean coal technologies and expanding the use of nuclear power.

energy security
The ability of the United States to meet its own energy needs.

During the 1990s, concern shifted from adverse effects on the nation's environment to global climate change. Evidence mounted that the earth was undergoing a dramatic warming because of rising levels of atmospheric carbon dioxide, a byproduct of the use of fossil fuels and a so-called **greenhouse gas** because it retains solar heat that warms the earth rather than allowing it to radiate back into space. Industrial smokestacks, electric generating plants, home chimneys, and internal combustion engines have released carbon dioxide since the start of the Industrial Revolution in 1750. As more and more nations industrialize, the pace of climate change accelerates. To prevent future disasters, many countries have pursued international cooperation on this issue (see Chapter 18), and the American government at all levels has been developing policies to deal with the impact of climate change and to compensate for diminishing levels of resources.

greenhouse gas
Several gases emitted by human consumption of fuels that retain solar heat rather than allowing it to radiate back into space, therefore producing global warming.

★ Mountains of scientific data document the rise of global warming, but sometimes we need to see evidence with our own eyes. These photos show the Athabasca glacier in Jasper National Park, Canada, in 1919 and 2005. They show the shrinking of a once mighty ice sheet over the past century. Similar photos document the same effects in the Alps and the Andes.

Source: http://www.worldviewofglobalwarming.org/pages/glaciers.htm.

PROBLEMS AND SOLUTIONS

There are no easy ways to satisfy the ever-growing demand for energy while also enacting more responsible environmental policies. Several problems seem paramount: the dependence on imported oil, potential problems with coal and nuclear power, an inefficient electrical system, and the public's reluctance to change. Each problem has associated solutions.

Dependence on Imported Oil

As Figure 17.6 shows, the United States relies on imported petroleum to meet about 45 percent of its petroleum needs. As recently as 2007, the Energy Information Administration had predicted that U.S. dependence on imported oil would increase to 64 percent by 2020.[20] Instead, it fell, largely due to the impact of the economic recession, interrupting the nation's steadily growing reliance on imported oil. Surprisingly, Canada is the largest supplier of imported petroleum to the United States accounting for 29 percent of U.S. oil imports, followed by Saudi Arabia (14), Venezuela (11), Nigeria (10) and Mexico (8). About 22 percent of the United States' imported petroleum comes from the Persian Gulf, site of supply disruptions in 1973 and 1979.

Figure 17.7 shows that as consumption has risen since 1950, the United States has come to rely more heavily on imported oil. Domestic production peaked in the late 1960s, although new technologies now make it possible to tap deposits trapped in shale. Imports fill the resulting gap between production and rising consumption.[21]

The Bush administration's energy task force chaired by Vice President Richard Cheney sought to boost domestic oil supplies through oil exploration on federal lands and off the Atlantic and Pacific coasts with deep-water drilling, with wells extending a mile and more beneath the surface. An explosion on such a deep-water oil rig owned by BP (British Petroleum) off the coast of Louisiana in April 2010 dumped millions of gallons of crude oil into the Gulf of Mexico, creating the greatest environmental disaster in U.S. history, damaging marine life, wetlands, birds, and the fishing and tourism industries along the Gulf Coast.

Clean Coal

Like oil, coal is a nonrenewable energy source that required millions of years to create, but it is plentiful. The United States has the world's largest known reserves of coal, enough to last 225 years at current rates of consumption (see Figure 17.8). About two-thirds of U.S. coal is excavated through surface mining and the remainder through underground mining. Coal-fired power plants generate nearly half of the electricity in the United States, but coal is most heavily used in the Midwest and in the South.

Despite its ready availability, coal has negative impacts on the environment. Surface mining leaves behind badly scarred landscapes that producers try to restore. Burning coal produces carbon dioxide, sulfur oxide, coal ash, and other pollutants that contribute to global warming as well as acid rain. Mercury—another product of burning coal—has negative health effects on humans after it enters the food chain through fish. Approximately 300,000 newborns each year may have increased risk of developing learning disabilities due to excessive mercury exposure in utero.[22] The electricity generating industry has sought to develop chimney-scrubbing technology to reduce the most dangerous emissions, but critics argue that "clean coal" does not exist now and never will.

Nuclear Power

Nuclear power is generated from the peaceful use of uranium, an ore mined in the western United States and elsewhere around the world. Britain began operating the first nuclear-powered commercial electric generating plant in 1956, and the United States opened its first plant in 1957 with the promise of clean, cheap, and plentiful power. Today, 65 nuclear power plants operate 104 reactors in 31 U.S. states. Nuclear power now accounts for about 20 percent of the electricity generated in the United States annually, but that constitutes nearly one-third of all the nuclear energy generated in the world. Nuclear-generated power is usually cheaper than that provided by burning fossil fuels and produces no carbon dioxide or other gases associated with global warming.

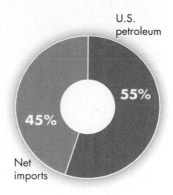

FIGURE 17.6

★ NET IMPORTS AND DOMESTIC PETROLEUM AS SHARES OF U.S. DEMAND, 2011

Source: Energy Information Administration.

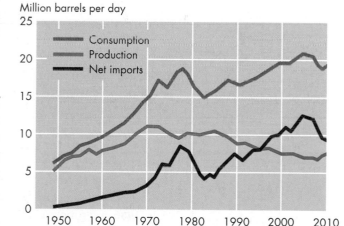

FIGURE 17.7

★ U.S. DAILY OIL CONSUMPTION, PRODUCTION, AND IMPORTS

If production and consumption move in opposite directions, are increased imports the only answer?

Source: Energy Information Administration, *Annual Energy Review*.

FIGURE 17.8

★ MAJOR COAL REGIONS IN THE UNITED STATES

More than 86,000 miners working in 26 states produced 1,085.3 million short tons (2,000 pounds/ton) of coal in 2010. What energy sources are relied upon by states lacking coal deposits?

Source: U.S. Energy Information Administration, *Quarterly Coal Report*, October–December 2010 (April 2010), preliminary 2010 data.

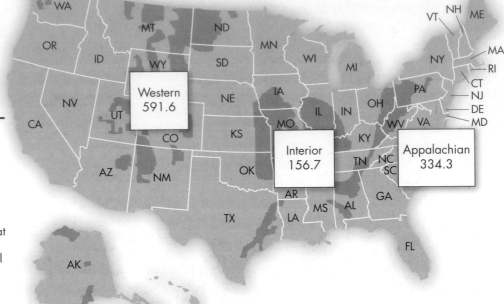

Some nations have invested heavily in nuclear power and use it to meet a large share of their energy needs. In France, 78 percent of electrical power comes from 59 reactors. Also responding to the oil shock of 1973, the French government increased its nuclear generating capacity, and the nation now exports large amounts of electricity to Italy, which has no nuclear reactors of its own. France is now an international leader in nuclear technology and is developing a fourth-generation reactor.[23]

After rapid growth in the 1970s, the number of new U.S. nuclear power plants leveled off in 1980. Rising construction and maintenance costs prevented several decommissioned reactors from being replaced. Natural gas prices dropped so low that it could power new plants more cheaply than uranium. In addition, safety became a major concern after an accident occurred in 1979 at Three Mile Island, a nuclear reactor near Harrisburg, Pennsylvania. Although there was no official order to evacuate, more than 100,000 nearby residents left the area. Americans' fears about the nuclear power industry are personified in the comic figure of Homer Simpson, the clumsy, oafish, incompetent, occasional hero in the long-running animated television comedy *The Simpsons*, who works as a safety inspector in a nuclear power plant.

In 1986, a far more severe accident occurred at the Chernobyl reactor in what was then the Ukrainian Soviet Socialist Republic, with health effects expected to linger for decades. And in March 2011, a 9.0 earthquake triggered a giant tsunami that knocked four reactors out of operation at Japan's Fukushima Daiichi power plant. Teams of workers frantically sought to control the threat of radiation being released from the melted cores either into the air or by the contaminated water used for cooling.[24] In response to Chernobyl and prompted by the Green Party, Germany decided to decommission the nation's reactors after 2022 and shift to heavy reliance on wind energy. But a later German government reversed this decision because of the potential economic

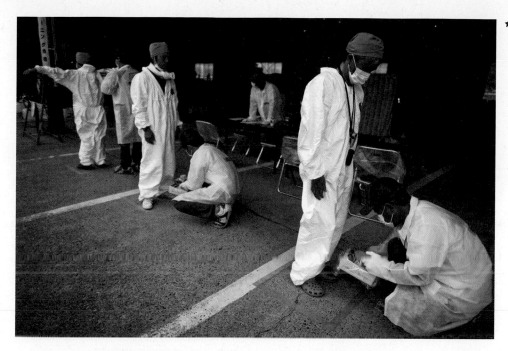

★ Evacuees are screened for radiation contamination following the 2011 tsunami that severely damaged the Fukushima Daiichi nuclear power plant in Japan.

impacts. Then in 2011, the government again announced that all nuclear reactors would be closed by 2022, in response to public concerns about the Japanese nuclear accident.[25]

An even larger problem with nuclear power is the storage of nuclear waste. Plants must store high-level waste after it has been used to generate electricity—spent fuel rods that are highly radioactive are stored in dry or wet storage sites until the Department of Energy completes a permanent national repository to house waste materials that will be radioactive for millions of years. Figure 17.9 shows the 121 temporary storage sites located around the country. Until a permanent disposal plan is developed, the Department of Energy estimates that 161 million Americans will continue to live within 75 miles of nuclear storage facilities. A California law adopted in 1976 prohibits the construction of any new nuclear plants in the state until the long-term waste problem is solved.[26]

Inefficient Electrical Grid

Together, coal and nuclear power generate 61 percent of U.S. electricity (as shown in Figure 17.10), which is consumed in almost equal measures by residential, industrial, and commercial users. Electricity offers numerous advantages—it is clean, flexible, controllable, safe, effortless, and instantly available—but only about a third of the energy used to generate electricity is actually delivered to consumers in the form of usable current. Much energy in the form of heat is lost at the point of generation and then through the transmission process. The demand for electricity grows at an impressive rate despite efforts to improve the efficiency of heating and cooling systems, household appliances, and lighting. Economic growth depends on continued expansion of the supply of electricity.

The U.S. electrical "grid," the complex system of electrical transmission and delivery links that connects consumers with generating plants, uses technology developed in the first half of the twentieth century. This outdated infrastructure based on centralized

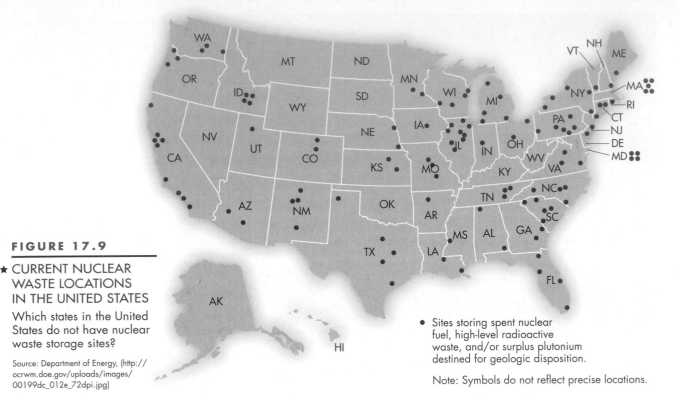

FIGURE 17.9

★ CURRENT NUCLEAR WASTE LOCATIONS IN THE UNITED STATES

Which states in the United States do not have nuclear waste storage sites?

Source: Department of Energy, (http://ocrwm.doe.gov/uploads/images/00199dc_012e_72dpi.jpg)

● Sites storing spent nuclear fuel, high-level radioactive waste, and/or surplus plutonium destined for geologic disposition.

Note: Symbols do not reflect precise locations.

generating stations contributes to power loss and prevents the use of new technologies projected to spread during the twenty-first century. Denmark, by contrast, has replaced a few massive generating plants with scores of generating points in a decentralized system based on wind and other renewable sources. The U.S. Department of Energy and major electricity companies have been working to design a "smart grid" that will meet the nation's needs moving into the future.[27]

Consumer Attitudes

Americans consume an enormous amount of energy per capita compared with other nations. Americans constitute 5 percent of the world's population but account for 25 percent of its energy usage.[28] Americans have become accustomed to cheap gas, cheap electricity, cool houses in the summer and warm houses in the winter, muscular cars capable of transporting large families and towing large boats, and homes far removed from their places of work. Many Americans are unconvinced that their behavior should change and that it has consequences for others. As shown in Figure 17.11, Americans and Chinese, citizens of two of the world's largest polluters, are less concerned about global warming than citizens in many other nations. Yet as the growing scarcity of resources drives energy prices up and as Americans increasingly have to deal with the consequences of climate change, high-energy consumption habits need to change.

42% Coal

25% Natural gas

19% Nuclear

8% Hydroelectric

5% Other renewables

1% Petroleum

FIGURE 17.10

★ ELECTRIC GENERATION BY FUEL, 2009

If you had to expand the nation's electric power generation, which fuel source would you choose?

Source: U.S. Energy Information Administration, *Energy in Brief* June 27, 2012.

POLITICS

The Bush and Obama administrations approached the energy/environment trade-off differently. Bush's energy task force recommended reducing regulations on oil and gas drilling, expanding the use of coal-fired plants with fewer demands for clean emissions, and building more nuclear power plants. High on the administration's priority list was opening the untapped reserves in the Arctic National Wildlife Refuge (ANWR) and making federal lands in the "lower 48" available for new oil and natural gas exploration. The administration placed the push for energy security ahead of the commitment to reduce global warming but was only partly successful. Although Congress approved expanded drilling offshore and on federal lands, it repeatedly rejected opening ANWR.

Obama took more concerted action on global climate change than his predecessor. The economic stimulus package provided funding for starting the kind of smart grid pioneered in Denmark, for weatherizing the houses of low-income families, for reducing energy consumption in federal buildings, and for encouraging the development of renewable energy and energy efficiency at the state and local level. The administration set ambitious goals: the average car and light truck's fuel economy would be 34.1 miles per gallon by 2016 and 25 percent of the nation's energy would be generated by renewable sources by 2025, up from 8.3 percent in 2009. The president also authorized the Environmental Protection Agency to regulate carbon dioxide emissions, a major departure from the past that was later upheld by the Supreme Court.

However, the Senate did not approve Obama's most ambitious initiative, a House-approved plan to control greenhouse gas emissions, a **cap and trade system** similar to one already operating in Europe. To reduce carbon dioxide emissions, the government would set a limit (the *cap*) on the total amount of carbon emissions allowed in the economy, with the goal of steadily reducing that total to a sustainable level by 2050. Businesses could sell their so-called carbon credits (or permits to pollute) to other companies as they discover ways to reduce their pollution levels. Utilities, major manufacturers such as the auto industry, and oil companies were concerned about the cost of such a system. Senators from coal-producing, manufacturing, and farm states sought protection from those costs. Many feared this mammoth change would adversely affect economic growth.[29] Some environmental groups believed the limits proposed by the administration were too low, while others accepted the need for compromise. Ultimately, economic concerns derailed the initiative.

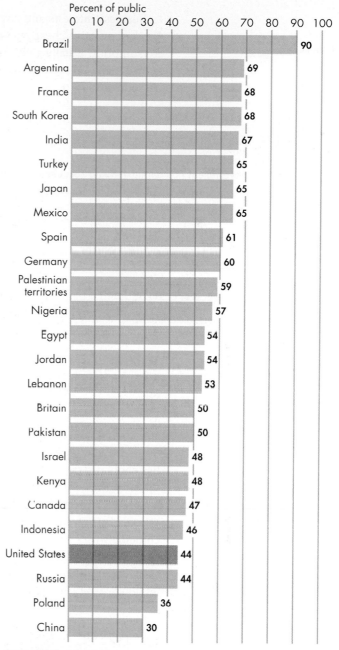

Percent of public

Country	Percent
Brazil	90
Argentina	69
France	68
South Korea	68
India	67
Turkey	65
Japan	65
Mexico	65
Spain	61
Germany	60
Palestinian territories	59
Nigeria	57
Egypt	54
Jordan	54
Lebanon	53
Britain	50
Pakistan	50
Israel	48
Kenya	48
Canada	47
Indonesia	46
United States	44
Russia	44
Poland	36
China	30

FIGURE 17.11

★ PERCENTAGE OF THE PUBLIC THAT VIEWS GLOBAL WARMING AS "VERY SERIOUS," 2009

Do you see any pattern as to which nations regard global warming as a more or less serious problem?

Source: Pew Global Attitudes Project, "Global Warming Seen as a Major Problem around the World" December 2, 2009, (http://pewresearch.org/pubs/1427/global-warming-major-problem-around-world-americans-less-concerned)

cap and trade system
Strategy to reduce greenhouse gas emissions and encourage technological innovation by allowing industries to emit carbon dioxide and to buy and sell pollution permits.

Business interests and environmentalists pose clashing demands to policy makers. On the one hand, cheap energy fuels the economy; on the other hand, increased energy consumption usually soils the environment. How does the nation balance these conflicting demands? Other nations have found their own balance point and so will the United States.

EDUCATION

★ **KEY** TO understanding

The federal government has a longstanding commitment to education. Nonetheless, there is a tradition of local control. The federal government has intervened to enforce equal access and more recently to reduce the achievement gap among different population groups. Great disparities remain in the financing and the effectiveness of education across the United States. Should the nation accept such differences?

How should the citizens of a democracy be educated? In the United States there are thousands of answers to that question as defined by the local communities that control the nation's education policies. The history of education in the United States reflects the differences in what local communities believe the next generation should learn. Nonetheless, as one study concluded, "the federal role in American schools has grown exponentially in the period since the mid-twentieth century,"[30] with the result that presidents, Congress, and the courts have taken steps to provide a more uniform answer to our question.

BACKGROUND

Educational policy making is highly decentralized in the United States. Unlike France, as we saw in Chapter 3, where curriculum decisions are made in a central bureaucracy and apply to the entire nation, each locality in the United States decides *what* (curriculum) and *how* (pedagogy) to teach students. There are more than 13,800 separate public school districts, a surprisingly high number but far fewer than the 117,108 separate districts that existed in 1939–1940.[31] Some districts coincide with counties and are largely run by county governments (Maryland). Hawaii has only a single statewide school district, but in many states (including much of the Northeast), the districts coincide with small towns and townships. In most cases, the school district is governed by a separately elected body, a school board that reflects community values and priorities. There are nearly 100,000 public schools in the United States, along with about 34,000 private schools and a growing number (nearly 4,600 in 2010) of charter schools, publicly funded schools that enjoy considerable freedom from the local district's control.

Every state constitution includes the obligation to provide an education for all citizens, and federal officials have never ignored education. Even under the Articles of Confederation, Congress set aside federal land whose sale was used to support schools in the Northwest Territories (now the upper Midwest). During the Civil War, Congress set aside land to provide financial support for higher education in the Morrill Act, which led to the establishment of "land grant colleges" such as Kansas State University and Michigan State University.

Following the Civil War, Congress established the U.S. Office of Education and monitored new federal programs designed to educate former slaves. Federal assistance for education grew over time: for job training during World War I, for educating veterans following that war, for teaching disabled students during the 1920s and 1930s, and for providing free and reduced-price school lunches during the late 1930s. During World War II, federal funds helped build schools for families who relocated to work in the war effort and supported preschool programs for children whose mothers were working full-time in war industries. After the war, hundreds of thousands of veterans attended college under the **G.I. Bill,** which provided former servicemen and women with up to 48 months of tuition and living expenses—one month for each month spent in the military. Education became a central responsibility of the Department of Health, Education, and Welfare when it was created in 1953 and for the Department of Education in 1979.

G.I. Bill
Federal education program following World War II that paid the college tuition fees of former servicemen and women.

By the beginning of the twentieth century, the United States led the world in delivering education to its citizens. The United States achieved near-universal literacy during the first half of the nineteenth century. As the twentieth century began, it became increasingly important for American workers to complete schooling beyond a basic, elementary level. As a result, high school and then college education became the norm in the United States well before it became common elsewhere.

President Lyndon Johnson substantially enlarged the federal role in American education through passage of the Elementary and Secondary Education Act (ESEA) of 1965, which provided substantial funding for students attending schools in economically depressed urban and rural areas. Each time Congress reauthorized the act (1981, 1994, 2001) the federal role grew, including funding for students with limited English proficiency. Congress took separate action in 1975 to help fund the education of disabled children after a series of federal court decisions forced states to do so. When this law was reauthorized in 1990, it was renamed the Individuals with Disabilities Education Act, or IDEA for short.

When President George W. Bush signed the most recent ESEA reauthorization in January 2002, he established federal guidelines that states would need to meet in order to receive federal funding. Popularly known as **No Child Left Behind (NCLB),** the new requirements drew on reform strategies that Bush had championed as governor of Texas: using standardized tests to chart student progress toward mastering state-established standards; meeting annual targets on the road to 100 percent student proficiency in reading and math by 2014; reporting student progress by subgroups, such as African-American, Hispanic, Native American, low-income, and disabled students.

No Child Left Behind
Bush education reforms adopted by Congress in 2001 that monitored student progress toward mastery of state-defined math, reading, and science standards.

Reformers believed that NCLB had established a system of **accountability (educational policy),** holding educators responsible for the progress made by their students. Schools that consistently fell short of meeting their goals would face sanctions, including loss of federal funding. As the full implications of NCLB sank in, states, local school boards, and educators objected vociferously to this heavy federal intervention and the implication that there is one best way to deliver education across a diverse nation. As a result, Congress failed to reauthorize NCLB on schedule.

accountability (educational policy)
Education policies that hold educators individually or collectively responsible (or "accountable") for the progress made by their students.

PROBLEMS AND SOLUTIONS

NCLB has helped to highlight three major problem areas in education: gaps in student achievement, unequal access to education, and unequal education funding.

Gaps in Achievement

Two achievement gaps have drawn attention. The first exists among different groups of students within U.S. schools. African-American and Hispanic students trail white students; low-income students trail higher-income; disabled students trail non-disabled. However, U.S. students as a whole also trail the performance of other nations' students in math and science. In the long run, these gaps mean that the United States will be less able to compete effectively in a global economy because its workers are not as well prepared as those in other nations.

Some researchers find that families have the greatest impact on student learning,[32] suggesting that the nation can best improve education by reducing income differences between families. Much research indicates that next to the influence of family, teachers have the greatest effect on student achievement. Teachers with stronger content knowledge—those who completed undergraduate majors in the fields they teach or who hold advanced degrees—are more likely to be assigned to schools serving high-income families than to schools in disadvantaged areas. Special programs can assist children from especially needy groups. For example, the Head Start and Early-Start Programs help low-income and minority children develop pre-reading and counting skills needed in school.

Are there ways to give teachers incentives to improve their performance in the classroom? Some reformers believe that establishing **pay for performance** is the answer so that teachers who produce measurable student improvement will earn more. Teachers' unions have generally resisted such proposals, arguing that encouraging cooperation among teachers in a school is more likely to enhance student learning than creating the competition associated with pay for performance.

Many reformers believe that encouraging competition in education will produce a market-like environment that triggers improvements. If families are allowed to choose where their children will attend school, parents and students can select the most successful and engaging schools. Charter schools use innovative instructional strategies and work with student populations that have been ill-served by traditional schools, perhaps pressuring traditional schools to become more innovative in order to retain students. The KIPP Network of Charter Schools, for example, garnered favorable national attention and foundation funding in 2011 to expand its 109 schools enrolling 32,000 students in 20 states.[33] Both the Bush and Obama administrations were strong advocates of charter schools despite inconclusive evidence about whether students in charter schools generally perform better than those in traditional schools. Finally, education vouchers would allow students to use public money to pay for tuition in nonpublic schools that might better meet their needs. Vouchers were first proposed as a strategy to make it possible for Catholic students to receive federal benefits, but they have been strongly opposed by most teachers' unions and Democrats. Several local districts have launched voucher experiments, including Milwaukee, Wisconsin, and Washington, D.C.

Equal Access

Despite the strong cultural support for education found in the United States, access to education has never been equal. Not until the Supreme Court's decision in *Brown v. Board*

pay for performance
Education reform that links teachers' pay to the academic progress of students in their classrooms.

of *Education of Topeka, KS* in 1954 was there clear recognition that providing separate schools for black citizens produced inherently unequal educational results. School integration was intended to ensure that all public schools would have a diverse mix of students, overcoming not only official policies of racial separation (so-called ***de jure segregation***) but also the segregation resulting from residential patterns (so-called ***de facto segregation***). Policy debates about how best to achieve integrated schools consumed much of the 1960s, 1970s, and 1980s, although studies show that racial integration has since declined.

Within the past two decades, federal policy makers have decided that placing students with learning and physical disabilities in separate programs, as was the case for many decades, deprives them of the opportunity to learn. And as the number of Hispanic-speaking students grows across the United States, policy makers have devoted increased attention to the needs of students who are learning English. Much debate has centered on whether their instruction should be in bilingual programs that combine both Spanish and English or primarily in English.

de jure segregation
Racial separation in the schools that results from official policies of states or localities.

de facto segregation
Racial separation in the schools that results from the private decisions of citizens on where to live.

Unequal Funding

Funding for education reflects the complex structure of local control described earlier in this section. Money comes from local sources (usually property taxes), state tax revenues, and federal tax revenues. The federal share of education spending is by far the smallest, now about 9.5 percent of the total amount of money spent on education each year, although that percentage varies by district. As a result of this funding hodgepodge, education expenditures per pupil vary tremendously. Figure 17.12 shows that nationally, local and state sources of revenue were almost equal at 43.8 percent and 46.7 percent in 2008–2009, with federal sources a distant third. But these statistics hide the state-by-state variations; in Hawaii, the state contributed 89.8 percent of education revenues, but in Nebraska the state share was only 31.7 percent.[34] Where the state's contribution is low, property taxes tend to be higher.

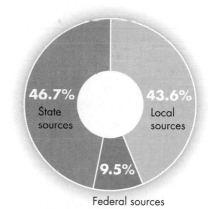

FIGURE 17.12

★ SOURCES OF REVENUE FOR PUBLIC ELEMENTARY AND SECONDARY SCHOOLS, 2008–2009

Does it matter whether education funding comes from state, local, or federal sources?

Source: U.S. Census Bureau, 2009 Annual Survey of Local Government Finances—School Systems.

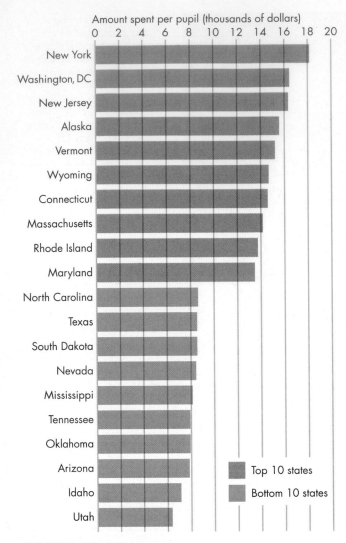

Amount spent per pupil (thousands of dollars)

New York	
Washington, DC	
New Jersey	
Alaska	
Vermont	
Wyoming	
Connecticut	
Massachusetts	
Rhode Island	
Maryland	
North Carolina	
Texas	
South Dakota	
Nevada	
Mississippi	
Tennessee	
Oklahoma	
Arizona	
Idaho	
Utah	

Top 10 states
Bottom 10 states

FIGURE 17.13

★ ELEMENTARY AND SECONDARY PER-PUPIL SPENDING AMOUNTS BY STATE, 2008–2009 (TOP 10 AND BOTTOM 10 STATES)

Do students attending school in high-spending states have an advantage?

Source: U.S. Census Bureau "Public Education Finances: 2009," released May 2011.

The result of different revenue mixes is large differences in spending per pupil, as shown in Figure 17.13. On average, spending per pupil in the United States was just over $10,000 in 2008–2009, with the highest-spending states concentrated in the North and East and the lowest-spending states in the South and West.

Research shows that higher spending does not necessarily translate into a better education, but over the past 30 years court challenges have been filed in 44 states contending that unequal education funding violates students' rights to a good education. By 2000, state supreme courts had required 19 states to restructure their systems for financing public education to reduce the disparity in per-pupil expenditures across districts.[35] Efforts to equalize spending have been contained within single states, and significant cross-state disparities remain.

POLITICS

Federal funding for education grew dramatically under the economic stimulus package adopted in early 2009—providing an additional $48.6 billion—as a way to discourage states from cutting their education budgets in the face of reduced revenues caused by the recession (see Chapter 16). About $4 billion were set aside for President Obama's special program—Race to the Top—which placed greater emphasis on finding ways to improve the performance of schools whose students were lagging.

Many education groups praised the new proposals, but the two largest teachers' unions—the National Education Association with 3.2 million members and the American Federation of Teachers with 1.2 million—were critical of proposals to link teacher pay to student performance. Even before they won the 2010 midterm elections, Republicans made it known that they preferred modest changes to a major overhaul of the Bush-era program.[36] In many ways, then, the situation had returned to the pre-NCLB pattern: deep partisan divisions over what to do delayed congressional action. Facing such a prospect, Obama's Department of Education announced in 2011 that it would accept requests from states to waive the requirements of NCLB if they embraced the administration's reform goals. Thus, the administration used competition for federal funding and regulation, not legislation, as ways to pursue its goals.

Why Are We
THE WAY WE ARE?

Domestic policies reflect a nation's politics—its decision-making structures, political culture, and historical experiences. Policies also reflect current thinking on how best to address the nation's needs: put more power into the hands of Washington decision makers or decentralize them to state capitals; rely on markets to allocate resources or provide services from the government; help citizens meet their needs or depend on citizens to do so on their own. In general, several factors shape U.S. domestic policies.

FRAGMENTED DECISION MAKING

Policy making in the United States is highly fragmented. State and federal governments share responsibilities; few areas of public policy are exclusively the concern of one or the other, and the precise mix of government responsibility varies along a spectrum from *predominantly state* to *predominantly federal*. In the cases we have examined, educa-

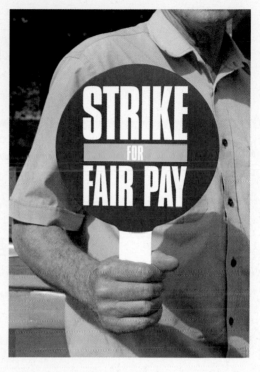

tion, originally an overwhelmingly state responsibility, has gradually become a greater concern for federal officials, although it remains predominantly state-centered; responsibilities for health care, energy, and the environment are fairly evenly shared; Social Security is a federal program. Frequently, when officials at one level of government prove unresponsive to a problem, those at another level will take action. For example, the federal government stepped in to enforce integration in the 1950s; California established rigorous state regulations for automobile emissions after the federal government failed to act; and several states (including Massachusetts) created universal health care coverage when the federal government failed to meet the needs of the uninsured.

Nor does fragmentation stop with federalism. Officials in different branches of government typically share influence over agenda setting, policy formulation, adoption, and evaluation, and within those branches, there are sometimes multiple centers of decision making—for example, subcommittees and committees. Policy making in the United States could scarcely be better structured to ensure that organized interests have maximum influence on public policy. With multiple centers of authority, groups seek to influence policy at local, state, and federal levels, among a wide range of elected and unelected officials.

Similar situations arise in other nations. For example, the provinces are especially important centers for policy making in Canada, as are the Laender in Germany. But in most other political systems, state officials are either significantly less influential or the federal government is less internally fragmented. A more unified central government changes the dynamics of decision making. If leaders in parliamentary systems are confident of majority support, there is less need to build coalitions across party or ideological lines. The U.S. system, on the other hand, necessitates compromise and coalition building across party, ideological, and regional lines in order to create policies. During periods when such compromise is difficult to achieve, national policy is frozen in place.

PREFERENCE FOR MARKET SOLUTIONS

Americans prefer market solutions. This is particularly evident in the policies that have been proposed to deal with education and health care. When a solution seems to create a larger role for government or to shift influence from state to national control, resistance is virtually guaranteed. This pervasive distrust of government power is more widespread in the United States than in other political systems.

A related difference can be found in the balance between individual rights and responsibilities. If citizens are ultimately responsible for providing their own health care in a market setting, for example, they will be less willing to assume shared responsibility to ensure that all citizens enjoy such benefits. Most other developed nations in the world treat health care similarly to the way Americans treat education—access to basic services is available to everyone, although the quality of those services might vary.

DIFFICULTY OF LONG-RANGE PLANNING

Finally, long-range planning is difficult for public officials, whether in the United States or elsewhere. Decisions that apply to a time frame that extends well beyond the time horizon of legislators' terms in office have less urgency. Social Security requires officials to adopt a 75-year time horizon in making program decisions. No comparable requirement to adopt the long view exists in any of the other policy areas we have examined, although it also makes sense in approaches to global warming. Why has there been resistance to taking the long view? Do U.S. officials find it more difficult than policy makers in other nations to engage in long-term thinking? Or are there structural features that make the U.S. system different?

Not every advanced industrial nation needs to provide identical policies. There is more pressure among European nations to standardize policies because they are now part of a common economic system. But the United States has been an outlier in a number of respects, differing not only from Europe but also from Canada, New Zealand, and Australia. Thus, cross-national comparisons can reveal a great deal about why we make the decisions we do.

. . . AND WHY DOES IT Matter?

Schools vary in quality. Hospital services are better and more accessible in some communities than in others. Energy is cheaper in Texas than in Maine. Are citizens living in communities with poor schools, subpar hospitals, and expensive energy being shortchanged? Do citizens deserve equal services regardless of where they live?

Diversity has always been a central feature of American life. So has freedom of movement. The assumption is that persons upset with the schools, health care, or cost of living in one area can move someplace else—across town, elsewhere in the state, or elsewhere in the nation. For example, millions have moved from states in the Northeast to states in the rapidly growing Sun Belt to escape snowy winters and expensive heating costs. But not everyone can move, especially during an economic recession.

Which policies should become standardized regardless of where people live? There is no "right" answer. Your list is likely to differ from the list of the student sitting next to you. If for example, we said that a minimum quality of education, health care, and housing should prevail regardless of where you live, why not include other services such as police and fire protection? And do you have an obligation to provide persons less fortunate than yourself with housing, health care, or food? Where do we draw the line?

Questions of quality inevitably raise questions of money. Who pays, and how much do they pay for what services? Americans have accepted varying payment plans—federal taxes, state taxes, local taxes paid for different services or mixed in different proportions to pay for services. No one answer fits all times and all policies.

Ultimately, Americans hope that public policies reflect their long-term preferences at the local level, the state level, and the national level.

critical thinking questions

1. In your view, what public services, if any, should be standardized for the entire nation?

2. Should most policy decisions be left to government and non-government experts rather than politicians? Why or why not?

3. What responsibility do the citizens of a nation collectively have for the well-being of its less fortunate citizens suffering from disability, ill health, old age, and other difficulties?

4. Do citizens have a right to receive minimum levels of health care, education, and income security? Justify your answer.

5. Should the United States look abroad for solutions to its health care, energy/environment, education, and Social Security problems, or do solutions need to be distinctive to each nation?

key terms

FOREIGN AND NATIONAL
SECURITY POLICY

* ★ ★ ★

- Trace the events that helped to shape contemporary U.S. foreign policy.
- Examine the factors that favor presidents over Congress in shaping U.S. foreign affairs.
- Evaluate how and to what extent the media, think tanks, and interest groups influence U.S. foreign policy.
- Explain some of the twenty-first century challenges faced by the United States.

PERSPECTIVE
How Can Nations Contend with Failed States and Protect Against the Security Threats They Pose?

On September 11, 2001, the terrorist organization al Qaeda hijacked four airliners. Two attacked targets in New York City and one attacked the Pentagon in Washington, D.C. A fourth crashed in Pennsylvania after passengers fought the hijackers and detoured the plane. About 3,000 people were killed in all. Osama bin Laden and al Qaeda, his terrorist group, took credit for the attacks, which came as a rude awakening to the American public after a decade dominated by domestic issues. Only Japan's 1941 assault on Pearl Harbor had so dramatically and suddenly focused Americans' attention on international dangers.

In the wake of 9/11, the United States and its allies stepped up anti-terrorism efforts world-wide. A coalition of international forces intervened in Afghanistan in October 2001, where a fundamentalist Islamic militia group known as the Taliban controlled the capitol city and had permitted al Qaeda to set up training bases. After two decades of foreign intervention and civil war, Afghanistan had become an ideal breeding ground for international terrorism—it was a so-called "failed state" that had no central government and easily fell prey to terrorist influence.

Despite early military success against Taliban and al Qaeda forces, the U.S.-led international coalition found it difficult to rebuild an entire society while constructing a democracy where one had never existed. Free elections were a foreign concept in a nation accustomed to operating on the basis of clan loyalties and bribed officials. In addition, the U.S. focus quickly shifted to Iraq, where it launched an invasion in 2003 that involved more troops and more dollars. The Taliban began a steady comeback in Afghanistan and reestablished their control of large areas. In 2009, President Obama increased U.S. military commitments in Afghanistan in an effort to turn the tide.

Australia similarly sought to stabilize a failed state when it led a multinational intervention in the Solomon Islands, a Pacific Island nation that had gained independence from Great Britain in 1978. With just over a half-million residents living on 900 islands covering an area smaller than the state of Maryland, these islands are home mostly to Melanesians and a smaller minority population of Polynesians, Micronesians, Chinese, and others. The population is overwhelmingly Christian. Police and troops from 15 nations, Australia in the lead, established the Regional Assistance Mission to the Solomon Islands (RAMSI)[1] in July 2003 at the request of the elected government to reestablish law and order, disarm battling militias, and help restore government effectiveness.[2]

Australia's efforts in the Solomon Islands went better than those of the United States in Afghanistan, perhaps as a result of several important differences:

- The Solomons, though spread out geographically, presented a smaller challenge than Afghanistan with its population of 30 million spread over an area nearly the size of Texas.
- The Solomon Islands' government invited the RAMSI forces to enter the country.
- Armed political dissidents in the Solomons did not have a nearby sanctuary to hide in as the Taliban and al Qaeda leadership did when they fled to Pakistan.
- Religious beliefs were neither central to the conflict in the Solomons nor a source of conflict with the intervening forces.
- RAMSI was a regional response by multiple neighboring nations, not a distant nation helped by other distant allies.
- And the effort in the Solomons was police-led, not military-led.

As the experiences of the United States and Australia demonstrate, foreign policy is no longer limited to relations among states—terrorist organizations are real and potential dangers. One of the greatest challenges facing the United States and other nations today is the need to uncover new strategies to deal effectively with new threats in a world where security cannot be guaranteed by weapons races and traditional balances of power.

IN THIS CHAPTER, we first explore the historical context of U.S. foreign and security policy, its idealistic desire to spread democracy by example, the emergence of the United States as a world power, engagement in the Cold War, and the expansion of free trade during a period of rapid globalization. We review how presidents, the Congress, and non-governmental influences help to shape foreign policy. Finally, we examine the U.S. role as world leader and discuss the rising challenges it faces, including economic rivals, illegal immigration, nuclear proliferation, global warming, terrorism, and excessive commitments. As you read this chapter, keep in mind our two core questions:

WHY ARE WE THE WAY WE ARE?
WHY DOES IT MATTER TO YOU?

In particular, how do American values and goals continue to guide U.S. policies toward the world?

U.S. FOREIGN POLICY IN HISTORICAL CONTEXT

Foreign policy encompasses the many ways a nation interacts with other countries and non-state organizations (such as corporations) in the global system. A nation may employ nonviolent tactics like diplomacy, foreign aid, economic incentives, and embargoes, or it may rely on forms of coercion and military force. Traditionally, national governments were the main or only actors in the international arena, but the twenty-first century world is more complex with large multinational corporations, international organizations, and even paramilitary or terrorist groups taking on roles in international relations and complicating the interactions among nations. **National security policy** centers on efforts to ensure a state's political and economic safety. The 9/11 attacks on the Twin Towers in New York City gave rise to a focus on "homeland security" that goes well beyond traditional concerns with defending the nation's borders and interests.

Over the course of U.S. history, both foreign and national security policy have evolved in response to changes in the world and at home, producing shifts in how the United States defined itself as a nation and in what it valued. As a result, there are differing views of what the nation's foreign policy should be, as is evident when public officials clash in addressing the nation's current challenges.

Two enduring traditions characterize American foreign policy: idealism and realism. The United States abandoned its general policy of isolationism late in the nineteenth century; internationalism has predominated since World War II. The United States became the world's lone superpower when the Soviet Union collapsed, encouraging the spread of free trade and democracy. Should it be the responsibility of the United States to teach other countries how to set up and operate democracies?

foreign policy
The wide range of ways in which one nation interacts with other nations and with non-governmental organizations in the international and global systems.

national security policy
A policy centered on the possible and actual use of force in international affairs.

IDEALISM AND REALISM

America was born with global aspirations. The founders believed they were constructing a new model of relationships between a government and its citizens that other countries would want to emulate—a government based on the consent of the governed, a universal truth that should apply to all persons. On the forty-fifth anniversary of the signing of the Declaration of Independence, former President John Quincy Adams praised the document's enduring importance: "It stands forever, a light of admonition to the rulers of men, a light of salvation and redemption to the oppressed."

★ Susan Rice, U.S. Ambassador to the United Nations, speaking at a UN Security Council meeting. The UN, housed in New York City, was one way to demonstrate that unlike the U.S. retreat from the world following the First World War, the United States would remain engaged following World War II.

What did it mean for the United States to be a global role model? Adams urged caution, believing that the United States should support the efforts of others to gain independence but not go "abroad in search of monsters to destroy." Becoming directly involved in the wars of others would endanger liberty at home.[3] Thus, from the outset, U.S. foreign policy reflected a deep strand of **idealism,** the view that the nation has a historic mission to serve as the world's messenger of universal truths—democracy and self-determination. It also later became a justification for the United States to project its military might.

In addition to idealism, self-interest has played an important role in guiding U.S. foreign policy. Early in American history, it was *not* in the nation's self-interest to convert the world to democracy. Rather, with the major exception of trade, the guiding principle was **isolationism**—the policy of limited involvement in international relations—lest more powerful nations threaten U.S. independence. But even isolationism did not prevent the United States from asserting its interest in the affairs of neighboring nations. The **Monroe Doctrine** of 1823 established the policy that the United States would refrain from becoming involved in the affairs of Europe and that the Europeans in turn should remain uninvolved in the affairs of the Western Hemisphere.

Although U.S. foreign policy makers kept the promise to remain uninvolved in the affairs of more powerful states, they showed no hesitation in meddling in the affairs of Mexico, Panama, Argentina, Chile, Nicaragua, and other nations in the Western Hemisphere. Indeed, to consolidate U.S. control of the territory from the Atlantic to the Pacific in the nineteenth century, the United States acquired land from France in the Louisiana Purchase of 1803, aggressively advanced boundary claims against Spain and Great Britain, fought a war with Mexico (1848), and overran the Native Americans. In these instances, self-interest demanded that the United States behave much like the nations of the European "Old World" by pursuing a policy of *realpolitik* or **realism**—that is, a foreign policy based on projecting and deploying power when it served the country's best interests, not in the service of ideals. Advocates of these two traditions—idealism and realism—continue to wrestle over the direction of U.S. foreign policy today.

U.S. ENTRY ONTO THE WORLD STAGE AND TWO WORLD WARS

Developments in the twentieth century seemed to confirm Americans' belief that the United States was destined to play a special role in world history. As President Bill Clinton summarized in his second inaugural address, "America became the world's mightiest industrial power; saved the world from tyranny in two world wars and a long cold war; and time and again reached out across the globe to millions who, like us, longed for the blessings of liberty." In Clinton's words, *"America stands alone as the world's indispensable nation."*[4]

America boldly abandoned isolationism in the Spanish-American War in 1898. In just 109 days, the United States helped Cuban rebels gain independence from Spain and simultaneously seized for itself Puerto Rico, Guam, and the Philippines, where the United States waged a long and ugly guerrilla war against nationalists.[5] A decade later, President Woodrow Wilson went to great lengths to maintain U.S. neutrality from European conflict during World War I (1914–1918) until a German submarine sank

idealism
The view that American foreign policy should reflect the universal truths contained in the Declaration of Independence.

isolationism
The policy of limited involvement in international matters that prevailed in the United States throughout most of the nineteenth century and between the two world wars.

Monroe Doctrine
(1823) Proclamation of U.S. primacy in the western hemisphere and a warning that European nations should remain uninvolved.

realism or *realpolitik*
The view that U.S. foreign policy should serve the nation's self-interest regardless of the tactics used or the nature of the states enlisted as partners.

the *Lusitania*, a passenger ship carrying many Americans, an outrage that propelled the United States into intervening in 1917. Nearly three million men were drafted into military service and more than 300,000 were killed or wounded.

After the war, government policy reverted to isolationism. The Senate rejected the United States' entry into the **League of Nations**—President Wilson's brainchild to promote peace and cooperation through a permanent international organization. The U.S. government also demobilized all but a small professional military force and sought to avoid entanglements in other European conflicts through a series of Neutrality Acts passed in the 1930s that severely restricted national policy.

During the 1930s, however, Japan aggressively pursued expansionist goals in China and the Pacific, while Germany, led by the Nationalist Socialist (Nazi) Party, provoked another European War in September 1939 when it invaded Poland after taking control of Austria and part of Czechoslovakia. The American public and most policy makers feared another costly foreign war. Operating within these limits, President Franklin D. Roosevelt provided as much help as he dared to Great Britain and France. Then on December 7, 1941, Japan attacked U.S. naval forces at Pearl Harbor, Hawaii, and a few days later Germany and Italy, allied to Japan, declared war on the United States, decisively resolving the nation's internal policy debate.

In contrast to World War I when America's military contribution came too late to make much difference, in World War II the United States carried most of the military effort in the Pacific theater of war and assumed increasing responsibilities on the western front in Europe. The Russians, then organized as the communist U.S.S.R. (Union of Soviet Socialist Republics), fought Germany alone on the eastern front and absorbed

League of Nations
The international organization established after World War I under the encouragement of Woodrow Wilson.

★ Provocative news coverage highlighting Spanish atrocities toward the Cubans and "treachery" toward the United States helped trigger the Spanish American War.

devastating civilian and military losses. To assist the other nations resisting German and Japanese aggression, the United States provided supplies, weapons, and materiel to all its allies, serving as the "arsenal of democracy" (as President Franklin D. Roosevelt termed the effort).

The grand alliance of the United States, Great Britain, France, the Soviet Union, and China (then non-Communist) emerged victorious from World War II, but only the Americans and the Soviets were not completely exhausted by the war effort. These two countries thus emerged as the world's two great powers, so dominant that they were called **superpowers.** For U.S. policy makers, one question in particular loomed large: Should the United States return to its prewar isolationist policy or remain engaged in the world?

THE COLD WAR AND ITS AFTERMATH

Unlike isolationism, **internationalism** is the idea that the United States should participate actively in global affairs by engaging politically, militarily, and economically with other countries. This emerged as the United States' dominant postwar policy, largely in response to continuing international threats. As the war in Europe came to a close, the Western allies became increasingly concerned with Soviet attempts to spread communism to Europe and the rest of the world. The **Cold War** (1947–1991), a period of heightened tensions and a fierce arms race between the two surviving powers from the wartime coalition, erupted. The positions where Soviet troops had come to rest at the war's end hardened into the geographic foundation for many subsequent confrontations.

Cold War Battle Lines

Initially, U.S. policy makers aimed to rebuild war-torn Europe and to take the lead in preventing future wars through the creation of the **United Nations (UN),** an international organization dedicated to world peace and security and international cooperation in solving world problems. As a symbol of Americans' ongoing commitment, policy makers located the United Nations headquarters in New York City in 1945. With support from key Republican internationalists in Congress, the Truman administration launched in 1947 an extensive program of European economic assistance, named the **Marshall Plan.** That same year, the United States took several bold steps to counter what many experts perceived as a growing Soviet threat. Poland, Czechoslovakia,

superpower
A dominant nation in the international system able to project its influence, either economic or military, far beyond its boundaries in order to pursue its interests.

internationalism
The idea that a country should participate actively in global affairs by cooperating politically and economically with other countries.

Cold War
(1947–1991) The period of heightened tensions and competition (economic, ideological, and arms) between the United States and the Soviet Union.

United Nations (UN)
The international organization created following World War II to promote world peace and mutual security through international cooperation in solving world problems.

Marshall Plan
The program of economic assistance provided by the United States to the nations of Europe following the devastation of World War II.

★ Some of the surviving shreds of the Iron Curtain, the physical symbol of the ideological divide between Eastern and Western Europe for almost half a century.

Hungary, Romania, Bulgaria, Yugoslavia, and the eastern half of Germany fell under the Soviets' control. Former British Prime Minister Winston Churchill described these lands as lying behind an **iron curtain** extending across Europe from the Baltic to the Adriatic. The Soviets installed communist governments in each of these nations and exerted political and military pressure on Austria, Greece, and Turkey. Meanwhile, communist parties in France and Italy sought to control the governments through elections rather than through the use of arms.

In Asia, Soviet forces had occupied the northern half of Korea at the war's end and established a dividing line that separates North and South Korea even today. When communist-inspired guerrillas forced the Nationalist Chinese government to flee the Chinese mainland in 1949 and seek asylum on the island of Taiwan, it seemed to be another victory for the ideology of **Marxism-Leninism,** which was seeking to export its successful Russian revolution. Washington policy-makers viewed these developments as part of a centralized plot to expand communist influence around the world and largely ignored important differences that separated communist states based on culture and national aspirations.

U.S. policy makers adopted a strategy of **containment**—that is, limiting the spread of communism—whereby government officials would apply sustained pressure to block further Soviet expansion. The United States rebuilt its military forces and established a ring of alliances with democracies and friendly non-democracies in regions considered ripe for Soviet expansion. These alliances included the **North Atlantic Treaty Organization,** or **NATO** (covering Western Europe), SEATO (South-East Asia) and CENTO (the Middle East). Signatory nations received U.S. military and financial assistance and benefited from the presence of the large numbers of U.S. forces that were stationed abroad to help protect them (see Figure 18.1).

To confront the Americans' alliances, Moscow created the **Warsaw Pact** (or alliance) in Eastern Europe and formed close ties with China, North Korea, and, later, Cuba and North Vietnam, which were widely viewed as USSR "satellites." Both superpowers assisted their allies and adopted some states as "clients," providing extensive military and economic assistance in exchange for their loyalty. Cuba switched patrons in 1959 when rebels led by Fidel Castro overthrew the U.S.-supported dictator and then looked to the U.S.S.R. for economic and military assistance. Cuban-American relations remain strained today.

An Escalating Arms Race and Intensifying Conflict

The Cold War involved a struggle short of military conflict ("hot war"). The United States fought two major and costly **proxy wars**—military conflicts

iron curtain
Winston Churchill's description of the division of Europe into a free West and Soviet-dominated East.

Marxism-Leninism
Policies established by Vladimir Lenin in Soviet Russia following the 1917 revolution that rested loosely on Karl Marx's philosophical foundations of communism.

containment
United States policy following World War II of using military alliances to prevent the expansion of Soviet influence.

North Atlantic Treaty Organization or **NATO**
The military alliance formed by the United States, Canada, and Western European nations to combat Soviet expansion following World War II.

Warsaw Pact
The collective security alliance formed by the Soviet Union with its satellite nations in Eastern Europe to combat NATO and maintain communist governments.

proxy wars
Conflicts fought during the Cold War between one of the superpowers and the allies of the other.

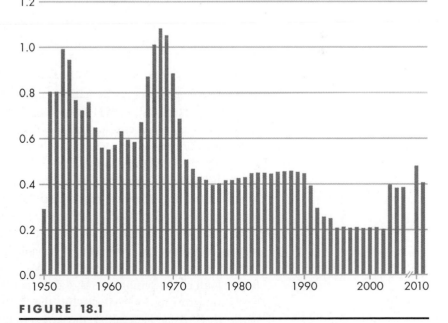

Number of troops (millions)

FIGURE 18.1

★ U.S. TROOPS ABROAD

In what regions of the world were U.S. force levels highest?

Source: Data from U.S. Department of Defense (1951, 1952 estimated).

with Soviet allies—in Korea (1950–1953) and Vietnam (1964–1973) as well as less costly conflicts throughout Africa, Asia, and South America. The superpowers also engaged in an **arms race,** aggressively expanding their atomic and nuclear stockpile of bombs and warheads with the necessary delivery systems—bombers and missiles—to threaten the other side. A system of **mutual assured destruction (MAD)** emerged—both nations could unleash so many nuclear weapons on the other, even after absorbing an initial attack, that neither would survive a first strike. Critics stressed that this system of mutual **deterrence**—preventing the opponent from making a move out of fear of the consequences—was indeed a *mad* foundation for national security because it risked the deaths of millions of citizens. In October 1962, the United States and the Soviet Union nervously navigated through a nuclear showdown over Soviet installation of nuclear weapons in Cuba, the closest the world has come to the unthinkable.

Superpower conflict occasionally erupted into open warfare. The Soviets provided military supplies to the communist forces with whom the United States fought. In Korea, U.S. and Chinese forces fought each other directly, and China also supported the Vietnamese in their later struggle for independence. In turn, the United States sought to drain Soviet power whenever it could. For example, after the Soviets invaded Afghanistan in 1980, the United States provided extensive support to the tribal forces seeking to oust the Soviet military, including the Taliban whom you read about earlier.

Détente, Human Rights, and Dissolution

Freezes and thaws—periods that were more and less tense—marked the Cold War. The 1970s saw a period of **détente,** a relaxing of superpower tensions, brought about through astute maneuvering by President Richard Nixon (1969–1974) and his principal foreign policy advisor, Henry Kissinger. Nixon's visits to Beijing and Moscow in 1972 were followed by a negotiated end to the U.S. combat involvement in Vietnam (January 1973). The United States and the Soviet Union also negotiated two Strategic Arms Limitation Treaties (**SALT I** and **II**), which slowed the growth of the superpowers' nuclear arsenals. Two more rounds of negotiations begun during the presidency of Ronald Reagan and continued by George H. W. Bush produced the Strategic Arms Reduction Treaties (**START I** and **II**) in 1991 and 1993 that began the process of reducing nuclear arsenals.

Most of these steps were considered examples of realism—a willingness to negotiate with enemies if it was in the nation's self-interest. Idealism was also plainly at work. President Carter (1977–1981) shifted the emphasis to **human rights**—the promotion of basic, unalienable entitlements such as the freedoms of speech and religion—pushing undemocratic governments to extend privileges to their citizens and to reduce state controls on religion and the press. The administration of Ronald Reagan (1981–1989) shifted back to realism but eventually established a dialogue through three summits with the Soviet leaders that brought about a rapprochement with the U.S.S.R. As Soviet leader Mikhail Gorbachev took steps to reform his nation, the Soviet Union stood by as protesters tore down the Berlin Wall and East and West Germany reunified into a single state in 1990. Then Lithuania, a Baltic nation, became the first Soviet republic to declare full independence. Many analysts viewed the tearing down of the Berlin Wall as the symbolic end of the Cold War. Finally, in 1991, beset by economic woes and growing internal dissent, the Soviet Union dissolved into its constituent parts. The Russian Federation, the largest of those old republics, inherited most of the territory and military weaponry of the old U.S.S.R. Today it is still the world's largest country geographically, even without the other former republics.

---

arms race
A competition between nations to exceed each other's military arsenals.

mutual assured destruction (MAD)
The strategic policy adopted by both the United States and the Soviet Union that deterred an opponent's attack by ensuring a devastating retaliatory attack.

deterrence
A military strategy designed to prevent an opponent from launching an attack because of the damage that the other country will in turn suffer.

détente
A relaxing of superpower tensions during the Cold War in the 1970s resulting from efforts of President Richard Nixon and Henry Kissinger, his National Security Adviser.

SALT I and **II (Strategic Arms Limitation Treaties)**
Treaties established between the United States and the Soviet Union in the 1970s to slow the nuclear arms race and control its most dangerous features.

START I and **II (Strategic Arms Reduction Treaties)**
Treaties established between the United States and the Soviet Union in the 1990s to reverse the growth of nuclear weapons and produce some disarmament.

human rights
United States pressure on undemocratic governments to extend basic, unalienable freedoms of speech, religion, and the press.

A UNIPOLAR SYSTEM

A single military superpower remained—the United States—and the bipolar dynamics that had dominated world politics for nearly 50 years starkly changed. Some features of the international landscape continue to look much the same as they did during the Cold War. Korea is still divided between North and South. (For a view of the DMZ, the strip of land that divides North and South Korea, see this chapter's Picture Yourself feature.) NATO survives, although it is seeking to redefine its purpose after the disappearance of the Soviet threat—the reason for its creation. In place of the old Soviet government, Russia seeks to consolidate a new political and economic system based on democracy and capitalism, although more recent policies have reversed some of the early reforms.

As change unfolded in the former Soviet bloc, the world witnessed the new stresses that proliferated in the post-Cold War era. On August 2, 1990, Iraqi President Saddam Hussein invaded Kuwait, an oil-rich ally of the United States. President George H. W. Bush sent a large force of U.S. troops at the request of Saudi Arabia, but he did not take action until the United Nations and Congress had approved a resolution authorizing the use of force in the event that Iraq did not respond to sanctions. Other Middle Eastern countries joined the multinational coalition that quickly defeated the Iraqi army in January 1991. Multilateral action had been successful, although Saddam Hussein remained in power.

★ During the 1950s, U.S. school children routinely practiced what to do in the event of an attack by long-range Soviet bombers, but the exercise was discontinued with the emergence of intercontinental nuclear missiles that reduced warning time and minimized the likelihood of surviving.

picture YOURSELF ...
ONE HOUR FROM SEOUL, SOUTH KOREA, STANDING AT THE DMZ

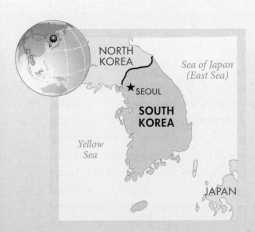

The Cold War is alive and well on the Korean Peninsula, which has become a "destination" of sorts for tourists, including you. The armistice that ended fighting in Korea in 1953 established a 2,000-meter-wide (about 1-1/4 mile-wide) strip that cuts more than 150 miles across the entire Korean peninsula from west to east. The Korean demilitarized zone (DMZ) stands as testimony to the Cold War and the continued animosities between a communist North and democratic South Korea.

You have taken the bus from Seoul, South Korea's capital—barely an hour's ride away—and have visited museums commemorating the military clashes that have sustained southern independence. Now, from observation posts, you can observe the watchtowers, anti-tank barriers, and razor-wire fences that keep North Korean military forces at bay. Later, you even visit several tunnels

continued

dug by North Koreans in an effort to infiltrate the southern defense lines by going under the heavy-duty defenses.

Back in Seoul, you learned that approximately 20,000 U.S. troops are stationed in Korea, down from about 37,000 as recently as 2004. (Between 1950 and 1953, the number of U.S. servicemen and women who served in the Korean theater totaled 1,789,000.) The troops serve as a "trip-wire" in the event of a Northern attack; American deaths will ensure that the United States will intervene in support of the South Korean forces, approximately 600,000

* Bill Clinton as quoted in CNN.com, February 22, 2002 (http://edition.cnn.com/2002/WORLD/ asiapcf/east/02/19/koreas.dmz/).

strong, in an effort to defend this staunch U.S. ally. Tensions along the DMZ are palpable, leading former president Bill Clinton to describe the sector as "the scariest place on earth."* North Korea's governmental instability makes the situation even scarier, as illustrated by the alarms that went off around the world in December 2011 when its dictator, Kim Jong-Il, died.

questions to consider

1. Should U.S. forces guarantee the security of other nations around the world?

2. What kinds of strains does permanent stationing of U.S. forces in foreign nations create with citizens of those nations?

3. Is it good or bad that nations with large contingents of U.S. forces become "Americanized" to the point of playing favorite U.S. Christmas carols during the holiday season?

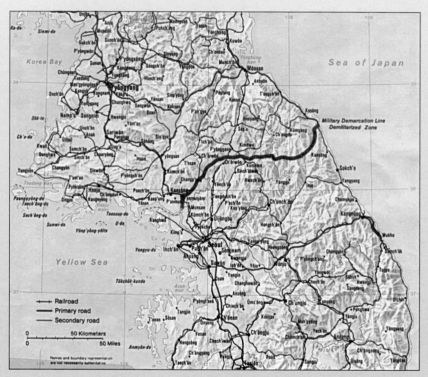

TRADE POLICY AND ENLARGEMENT

The same Marshall Plan that contained the spread of communism also bolstered war-torn Europe economically. Many believed that protectionism—economic policies aimed at protecting domestic producers from foreign competition—had prolonged the Great Depression of the 1930s. They hoped that war could be averted in the future by establishing an international free trade system, a series of international agreements and institutions that would lower the barriers to trade and economic cooperation. Many saw free trade as mutually advantageous. If Nation A produces wine more cheaply than Nation B, for instance, while Nation B produces cheese more cheaply than Nation A, both nations benefit by trading the products they produce more cheaply.

After the conclusion of World War II, American factories met not just U.S. demand for manufactured goods but as much as 40 percent of the world's demand because so many European and Asian factories had been destroyed by the war. For decades, the United States ran substantial trade surpluses, exporting more products and services than it imported. With American assistance and investment, however, nations damaged during the war rebuilt their industries and became competitors. During the 1970s, both Germany and Japan became industrial powers whose factories used more modern equipment than comparable industries in the United States. Foreign-made products often performed better, as well—Nikon cameras, Honda cars, and Sony electronics were highly desirable in the American market.

Although it increased competition with domestically produced goods, U.S. officials encouraged the expansion of free trade by lowering taxes (tariffs) on goods imported into the United States. They used bilateral (nation-to-nation) agreements to lower tariffs. Officials believed that participation in an open global economy was the key not only to national prosperity but also to international peace. During Bill Clinton's presidency (1993–2000), the United States actively pursued **enlargement,** a policy aimed at encouraging the democratization and economic liberalization of the many new independent states emerging after the fall of the U.S.S.R. Meanwhile, President Clinton pushed through the North American Free Trade Agreement (NAFTA), which promoted free trade among Mexico, Canada, and the United States. Clinton also helped initiate the Asia-Pacific Economic Cooperation agreement, the Free Trade Area of the Americas, and the World Trade Organization (WTO), which along with the International Monetary Fund (IMF) and the World Bank helps facilitate the growth of free trade. The newly independent nations were required to adopt democratic practices and free trade policies in order to join these economically beneficial organizations. Research showed that democratic states tend not to go to war with each other, so enlargement advanced the goals of both idealism and realism.

enlargement
Clinton-era policy encouraging nations to adopt democracy and market economies as the way to overcome uncertainties in a post-Cold War world.

FAILED STATES AND MULTILATERAL INTERVENTION

Once the iron fist of communist rule relaxed over Eastern Europe, some of the states found themselves in the throes of violent ethnic conflict. A bipolar world was orderly—the Cold War froze many political conflicts in place. Ethnic and religious animosities that had been suppressed for decades broke loose in region after region, creating a

★ China's production of yarn for export to the United States and Europe has contributed to its status as an economic powerhouse.

★ Genocidal violence ravaged Bosnia, Rwanda, Sudan, and elsewhere in the mid-1990s. Shown here are child victims of the brutal civil war in Rwanda.

failed states
Nations in danger of collapse because their governments are unable to protect citizens from violence and terrorism or to provide essential services (health, transportation, communication).

disorder that posed new challenges to American policy makers. As John Ikenberry, a professor of politics and international affairs at Princeton University, has noted, "In the twenty-first century, the game of American grand strategy is not a game of chess but a Rubik's cube puzzle where a lot of different pieces have to be put together."[6] Bosnia, Somalia, Ethiopia, and many other states have experienced the kind of internal collapse of law, finance, and public services associated with **failed states.** Neighboring states fear the instability that a failing state might bring into the region.

At times the world succeeded in responding to threats to peace, but at other times the effort failed or did not occur. When Yugoslavia broke apart into nations with mixed ethnic backgrounds, the United States and its NATO allies intervened against the Serbs who terrorized populations in Slovenia, Croatia, Bosnia, and later Kosovo. Although NATO's actions were often halting and poorly coordinated, the alliance sought to prevent war crimes and atrocities committed against civilians in these brutal conflicts. But the international community failed to intervene in 1994 to halt the genocidal violence in Rwanda, a small East African nation where ethnic violence claimed the lives of nearly a million civilians. In Somalia, a U.S. effort to ease the deaths from famine came to a sudden halt; the United States withdrew after American forces were massacred in a 1993 firefight chronicled in the book and film *Black Hawk Down*.

CONTROLLING U.S. FOREIGN POLICY

★ **KEY** to understanding

The Constitution divides control of U.S. foreign policy between the president and Congress. Congress periodically asserts its powers in foreign and national security policy and officials in the foreign policy bureaucracies are also important decision makers. Why did presidents come to dominate, particularly during the Cold War era?

Decisions about foreign and national security policies are made by multiple officials of the U.S. government, both elected and appointed. Although presidents exercise enormous influence in this process, they are not the sole determiners of U.S. relations with the world. Instead, the Constitution makes it clear that Congress, in particular, will share these responsibilities.

INVITATION TO STRUGGLE

Edward S. Corwin, a distinguished expert in constitutional law, famously argued that the constitutional provisions governing who controls foreign affairs amounted to "an invitation to struggle for the privilege of directing American foreign policy."[7] Indeed, Articles I and II of the Constitution give foreign policy powers to both Congress—to provide for the common defense, regulate commerce, declare war, raise and support a militia—and the president—to serve as commander-in-chief of the army and navy, make treaties, and receive ambassadors. Over time, a third force also emerged as a powerful influence on the decision-making process: the foreign policy and national security bureaucracies.

Constitutional ambiguity surrounds the respective powers of the president and Congress. If the Constitution provides no clear answer as to who guides foreign affairs, control over policy will result from political struggles and institutional confrontations, making these issues part of the domestic partisan debate. In hopes of producing a unified front toward the world, especially during periods of international conflict, political leaders since World War II have often sought to forge a **bipartisan consensus** on basic foreign policy principles. Thus, Democratic president Harry Truman sought and received support from internationalist-leaning Republicans for the Marshall Plan and containing Soviet expansion.

bipartisan consensus
Agreement between Democrats and Republicans on the basic direction of U.S. foreign policy.

But sometimes agreement cannot be reached, especially when the Congress and the presidency are controlled by different political parties. During periods of policy disagreement, presidents may encounter intense congressional opposition to their policies that sometimes spreads to the public. For example,

- Presidents Richard Nixon and George W. Bush encountered strong congressional and public opposition to their wartime policies in Vietnam and Iraq, respectively, mostly from Democrats but also from prominent members of their own party.
- The Reagan administration's policies in Central America ultimately triggered a constitutional crisis when it was revealed in 1986 that the administration had sold weapons to Iran in order to free U.S. hostages from Middle East terrorists and to generate funding for anti-government rebels in Nicaragua; these actions violated an explicit congressional prohibition against trying to overthrow the legitimately elected Nicaraguan government and the administration's own policy against dealing with terrorists.
- A Republican-controlled Congress explicitly voted against Bill Clinton's policies in Kosovo, upset at the president's unwillingness to secure congressional approval before U.S. forces joined a NATO bombing campaign, followed by a peacekeeping mission on the ground.[8]
- Republicans criticized Barack Obama over his policies toward Libya in 2011 when he authorized U.S. strikes on targets without obtaining congressional authorization. Opposition also grew toward the administration's strategy in Afghanistan, some seeing troop withdrawals as happening too soon and others believing they needed to follow a faster timetable.

To understand these showdowns, we need to review the larger policy-making landscape.

PRESIDENTIAL PROMINENCE

Over the course of American history, successive presidents have asserted their powers as chief diplomat and commander-in-chief, roles examined in Chapter 13, to such a degree that the constitutional ambiguity described by Corwin has been partially resolved in the executive's favor. There is little doubt that at the outset of the twenty-first century, presidents are the principal shapers of foreign and national security policies. As the United States became ever more engaged with the world and war became a constant possibility, presidential power grew. Stationing U.S. forces in Europe and Asia placed many Americans in precarious positions (like the Korean DMZ) and raised the possibility of military crises. In fact, crisis situations arose frequently during the Cold War, requiring rapid decisions in Washington, and presidents enjoy institutional advantages in dealing with such immediate problems.

The need for decisiveness tilted the institutional balance toward presidents rather than Congress. Unlike the bicameral, multi-member Congress, where power and influence are highly fragmented, as explained in Chapter 12, presidents have the advantage of *unity*. Presidents can reach final decisions on foreign and security problems wholly on their own or after consulting with whomever they wish. Making a presidential decision is far easier than reaching one in Congress, where decisions require extensive coordination and consultation. With a single "decider," as George W. Bush once famously described himself, or a small circle of advisors, presidents also enjoy a level of *secrecy* that is unavailable to Congress, where leaks of important information are inevitable. With these advantages, presidents can also act with *dispatch*—the ability to take action rapidly. Finally, presidents enjoy an advantage in the *information* that is available to them; it is the full-time job of the vast foreign policy bureaucracy to gather and analyze information collected from satellites, electronic eavesdropping, spies, and public sources. Congress, in fact, must rely heavily on communications from experts in the intelligence agencies, the military, and the Foreign Service to reach its own decisions, and all of these sources are supervised by the president.

Modern presidents claim the right to decide when the United States should initiate the use of force. In effect, this claim is the result of positioning American forces in exposed locations around the world, a mainstay of the U.S. defense strategy in the post–World War II period. The advent of nuclear weapons also established pressure to shift decision making to the executive. In the event of a surprise missile attack on the U.S. mainland, a president might have a window of as little as 30 minutes to decide

★ Members of the U.S. military transfer the briefcase containing the codes needed to launch U.S. nuclear forces—the "football."

whether to retaliate. During the nuclear era, presidents are accompanied at all times by military aides carrying "the football," a briefcase containing the codes required to authorize a U.S. nuclear response. Of course, not all national security situations are so time-sensitive that an immediate response is required.

Presidents have also sought to be the sole voice of American foreign policy. In deciding whether to receive ambassadors, presidents may recognize the legitimacy of other governments or refuse to do so. For example, unlike most other nations in the world, the United States refused to establish diplomatic relations with the communist government in China from 1949 until 1979 when Jimmy Carter extended official recognition. Presidents also make, implement, or terminate international agreements, sometimes through treaties that require Senate approval and even more often through executive agreements that do not. Through the appointment of officials to conduct foreign and military policy (subject to Senate confirmation) presidents are able to exercise considerable (though not total, as we saw in Chapter 14) control over the day-to-day operations of the departments of State and Defense.

Both Congress and the courts have deferred to presidential leadership during wartime. The public provides support for strong presidential leadership during times of international crisis. Students of public opinion have repeatedly found that the public "rallies 'round the flag," or responds with heightened patriotism, during crisis situations. In the wake of the terrorist attacks of 9/11, public approval of George W. Bush soared and remained at high levels for most of the following year (see the discussion in Chapter 13). Under these conditions, presidents have the advantage of strong and broad public support for their actions, providing further reason for Congress and the courts to defer to their leadership. Barack Obama experienced a similar surge in support after the assassination of Osama bin Laden in 2011. These rallying events, however, can be short-lived, as was Obama's. So presidents must realize that the best way to proceed is to shape a common policy with their institutional partners rather than trying to fashion policy unilaterally.

CONGRESS'S FOREIGN POLICY PREROGATIVES

Congress sometimes asserts its institutional prerogatives in foreign policy. Declaring war is one of the constitutional powers the framers granted to Congress, an open acknowledgement of the founders' concern that monarchs (and executives) are less reluctant to engage in war than the people's representatives assembled in Congress. In U.S. history, Congress and the president have agreed to wage war on 11 foreign nations, the combatants identified in five formal declarations of war: the War of 1812 (Great Britain), Mexican-American War (Mexico, 1846), Spanish-American War (Spain, 1898), World War I (Germany and Austria-Hungary, 1917), and World War II (Japan, Germany, Italy, Bulgaria, Hungary, Romania, 1941).

In addition, several extended military engagements have occurred that critics have called **undeclared wars**—conflicts for which the government did not formally declare war. In these instances, Congress provided necessary funding and sometimes explicitly approved the use of force through means other than a formal declaration of war. These conflicts include a naval war with France (1798–1800), the Barbary Pirates (1801–1805, 1815), the Korean War (1950–1953), the Vietnam War (1964–1973), the Persian Gulf War (1991), the Bosnia conflict (1995–1996), the war against the Taliban and terrorists in Afghanistan (2001–present) and the Iraq War (2003–present). As Table 18.1 shows, these major conflicts that have taken place since 1950 have resulted in a varying number of combat deaths, with the largest number occurring in the Korean and Vietnam Wars. Further, there have been hundreds of other instances in which U.S. forces have been deployed at the president's direction and without explicit congressional approval.[9]

Following the withdrawal of U.S. combat forces from Vietnam, Congress sought to avoid repeating what war critics widely regarded as a "presidential war." Over President Nixon's veto, Congress passed the **War Powers Resolution,** a statute that legislators hoped would guarantee that Congress would be fully consulted before presidents made military commitments and would give Congress the option of forcing future presidents to withdraw the military from combat operations.

Yet the War Powers Resolution has failed to live up to expectations. Presidents regard it as an infringement on their constitutional powers and adhere to the letter of the law when meeting

undeclared wars
Conflicts for which the U.S. government did not formally declare war as specified in the Constitution.

War Powers Resolution
Passed by Congress over Nixon's veto in 1973, this law establishes a framework for Congress to participate in presidential decisions to use force—short of a formal declaration of war—and to halt such a military deployment.

TABLE 18.1
U.S. combat deaths in major conflicts since 1950

CONFLICT	HOSTILE DEATHS	NON-HOSTILE DEATHS
Korea	33,739	2,835
Vietnam	47,434	10,786
Persian Gulf	147	235
Afghanistan	1,660	339 (10/7/01–10/1/12)
Iraq	3,488	934 (3/19/03–8/31/10)

Sources: U.S. Department of Defense, Defense Manpower Data Center, Statistical Information Analysis Center (http://siadapp.dmdc.osd.mil/personnel/CASUALTY/WCPRINCIPAL.pdf and http://www.defense.gov/news/casualty.pdf). Also see the discussion in Anne Leland and Mari-Jana Oboroceanu, CRS Report RL32492 "American War and Military Operations Casualties: Lists and Statistics" (February 26, 2010).

reporting requirements while denouncing its constitutionality. Congress continues to feel bypassed by presidents who use military forces when they deem it necessary to do so. In 2011, President Barack Obama used American forces to support the military operations of NATO allies against Libya, but because there were no U.S. personnel involved in "hostilities"—there were no land forces involved and air combat was conducted by unmanned drone aircraft—he argued that he did not need authorization from Congress after the 60 days granted under the War Powers Resolution ran out. Angry House Republicans refused to adopt a resolution supporting U.S. action in Libya but also defeated a proposal to cut off funding for the effort.

Congressional assertiveness in the 1970s did not stop with war powers. Senator Frank Church (D-Idaho) chaired the Senate Select Committee on Intelligence, which extensively investigated the activities of U.S. intelligence agencies. The committee's work revealed, for example, that the Central Intelligence Agency (CIA) had conducted surveillance on U.S. citizens who opposed the Vietnam War on the possibility that foreign powers were financing their activities. The agency had also plotted to assassinate at least five foreign leaders (although officials reported never having been successful) and had successfully overthrown several constitutionally elected governments (Guatemala and Iran, 1954; Greece, 1967; and Chile, 1973) regarded as too radical for the safety of American interests. (Presidents Gerald Ford and Ronald Reagan later issued executive orders that forbade government-sponsored assassination attempts.)

As a result of the Church committee's findings, Congress replaced the weak and informal oversight that it had been exercising over intelligence activities for decades with new and permanent intelligence committees having oversight responsibilities. These committees played an important role in the investigation of intelligence failures that followed the terrorist attacks of 9/11, although most public and media attention focused on the 9/11 Commission, officially the National Commission on Terrorist Attacks upon the United States. Its final report, issued August 2004, also recommended establishing a new position to coordinate the collection and analysis of intelligence throughout the government.

Congressional clout in foreign policy reached a high point in the 1970s, and that decade serves as a reminder to future presidents that it is better to reach agreement with Congress on major foreign policy initiatives than to struggle with an energized legislature. Each administration since Johnson has had to engage in at least one major foreign policy struggle over legislative-executive powers.

THE NATIONAL SECURITY APPARATUS

Bureaucrats are actively engaged in determining foreign and defense policy. Two events have deeply shaped that government apparatus—the emergence of the Cold War and the terrorist attacks of 9/11. The growing post–World War II tensions with the Soviet Union prompted Congress to pass the National Security Act of 1947, which formalized a number of policy-making arrangements that had been created on the fly during World War II.[10]

Joint Chiefs of Staff
A structure created in 1947 to coordinate action among the separate military services and provide military advice to the president and the Secretary of Defense.

- Established the **Joint Chiefs of Staff,** a permanent structure to coordinate military action and strategy among the senior officers of the Army, Navy, Marines, and Air Force (1947).

★ President Obama and Vice President Biden meet with their civilian and military advisors in the White House Situation Room, including the secretaries of defense and state, director of the CIA, and chairman of the Joint Chiefs of Staff.

- Created the Central Intelligence Agency (CIA), a permanent intelligence agency to replace the wartime Office of Strategic Services (1947).
- Merged the departments of War and Navy (1947) into a single National Military Establishment renamed the Department of Defense (DOD) two years later (1949).
- Created the National Security Council (NSC) to assist presidents in coordinating the activities of the many foreign policy advisors including the Departments of State and Treasury, longstanding bureaucracies (1947).

Harry Truman came to rely on the NSC as a policy making forum during the Korean War. Truman's successor, President Dwight Eisenhower (1953–1961), created the position of National Security Advisor to oversee this new advisory arrangement. Presidents have modified and refined these structures along the way. Then, in 2001, the terrorist attacks of 9/11 produced a flurry of new organizational changes.

- President Bush created the Homeland Security Council, and Congress pushed for creation of the Department of Homeland Security, a step endorsed by President Bush and put in place (2002).
- Congress insisted on creating a Director of National Intelligence (DNI) who has responsibility for coordinating the activities of the government's 16 intelligence agencies and for overcoming the divisions and traditional jealousies that prevail among them (2005).[11]

Table 18.2 provides a list of the national security agencies and the officials who headed them in 2011.

As the international agenda shifts toward non-security issues, many other U.S. government agencies find themselves dealing with aspects of foreign affairs. Predominantly "domestic" agencies such as Education, Agriculture, Commerce, Labor, Interior, and Health and Human Services all have international components. Combating world health contagions (such as avian flu), food shortages, and refugee crises requires coordinated global action; education and cultural exchanges and financial transactions continue to expand. Other issues are inherently international; for example, many U.S. government agencies conduct research that has a bearing on global climate change. This reality inspired the creation in 1990 of the U.S. Global Change Research Program, which integrates findings generated through research sponsored by more than a dozen agencies, including the Agency for International Development, the Environmental Protection Agency, and the National Science Foundation.[12]

TABLE 18.2

principal national security structures and officials in U.S. government, 2012

AGENCY	YEAR CREATED	CURRENT HEAD
Department of State	1789	Hillary Clinton
Department of Treasury	1789	Timothy Geithner
Department of Defense	1947	Leon Panetta
Central Intelligence Agency	1947	Gen. David Petraeus
National Security Council	1947	Thomas Donilon
Joint Chiefs of Staff (Chair)	1947	Gen. Martin Dempsey
Office of U.S. Trade Representative	1961	Ronald Kirk
Dept. of Homeland Security	2002	Janet Napolitano
Director of National Intelligence	2005	James Clapper

NONGOVERNMENTAL INFLUENCES ON FOREIGN POLICY

★ **KEY** TO understanding

Foreign and national security policies are not exclusively the province of elected and appointed government officials. Members of the media, think tanks, and interest groups play an important but uneven role in shaping American foreign policy. Why has our understanding of the role played by public opinion evolved from dismissing it as a valuable influence to now recognizing it as important but potentially subject to manipulation?

Foreign policy is the product not only of government officials but also of an extensive cast of domestic interests outside government. Indeed, the media, think tanks, and interest groups monitor developments in foreign affairs and seek to influence public opinion—and ultimately, government policy.

THE MEDIA

Print and electronic media have played important roles in U.S. foreign policy through their influence on public opinion. The United States' entry into the Spanish-American War in 1898 is often attributed to the war hysteria generated by influential newspapers of the time who took up the cause of Cubans battling Spanish authority as a way to sell newspapers. By contrast, dramatic television news coverage of American battlefield deaths and casualties suffered in Vietnam probably increased anti-war opinion at home and generated pressure on decision makers to change U.S. policy. Battlefield coverage can also generate public support. During the opening month of the U.S. invasion of Iraq in 2003, journalists traveling with U.S. forces helped Americans follow the steady progress toward Baghdad in real time—that is, without the delays associated with transporting film or eyewitness reports from the battlefield.

Journalists and opinion commentators are part of the policy-making world in Washington and other capitals around the world. Government officials read, watch, and listen to their coverage of world events and their discussion of what those events mean. Revelations made by major newspapers or networks such as *The New York Times,* the *Washington Post, Wall Street Journal,* and CBS News often shape the agendas of policy makers. Thus, when the *Times* published portions of a top-secret history of the Vietnam War completed by the Department of Defense in 1971, the so-called *Pentagon Papers,* many of the basic documents and private conversations among policy makers were revealed for the public to see for the first time and helped turn public opinion against the war. Reports in 2004 presented on the CBS News program *60 Minutes II* and published in *The New Yorker* magazine revealed how U.S. military personnel were abusing prisoners housed in Abu Ghraib prison in Iraq. The powerful photos produced revulsion in the American public and triggered a major public discussion of U.S. methods in the war on terror.

With readership declining, most newspapers have decreased the coverage given to international news and reduced the resources devoted to it.[13] Coverage of foreign affairs was once a major focus of television news and the investment in overseas news bureaus reached a high point in the 1980s. But the number of stories shown on network television with a foreign dateline began to decline after 1989—the perceived end of the Cold War—and then rose in 2001–2003, only to decline again despite the ongoing wars in Iraq and Afghanistan (see Figure 18.2). In addition, networks could acquire feeds from other sources, but their commitment to international developments was clearly weakening. Cable news has also lost viewers but regains audience during international crises when their 24/7 coverage attracts substantially more viewers.

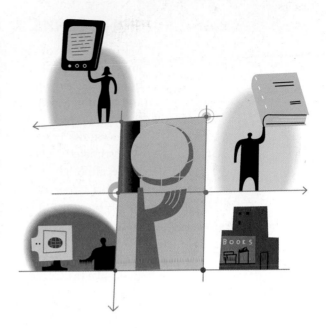

Other sources of information on foreign affairs and policy are available to the interested public. *Harper's* and *Atlantic Monthly* have long provided extensive coverage of international issues and news, but both have small circulations, as do political opinion magazines such as *National Review* and *The New Republic*—none rank within the top 200 in magazine circulation. Unlike other magazines whose influence is measured by circulation totals, *Foreign Affairs,* published by the Council on Foreign Relations, gauges its impact on **opinion leaders,** persons in positions of authority and influence over policy and opinion in both the public and private sectors. A media marketing and advertising firm polled such a group of 483,000 persons in 2006 and found that *Foreign Affairs* was ranked as the nation's most influential publication, even though its circulation was a mere 145,000.[14] *Who* read it was more important than *how many* read it.

opinion leaders
Persons in positions of authority and influence over foreign policy who are more likely to have their voices heard than the average citizen.

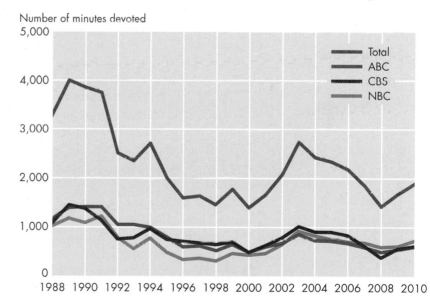

FIGURE 18.2

★ NUMBER OF MINUTES DEVOTED TO STORIES FILED BY REPORTERS WITH A FOREIGN DATELINE, 1988–2010

Why do major TV news organizations devote less and less time to international stories?

Source: Andrew Tyndall, http://tyndallreport.com, posted as part of the Pew Research Center's *The State of the News Media* annual report.

THINK TANKS

think tanks
Organizations whose specialists conduct research and exchange their views with other experts from government and the media.

Many activities of the Council on Foreign Relations are akin to those of **think tanks,** nongovernmental organizations whose staffs conduct research and exchange information and ideas within a community of specialists that includes government officials and opinion leaders. The earliest U.S. think tanks arose during the first decades of the twentieth century, and think tanks proliferated at the end of the two World Wars as well as in the 1980s, with the intent to generate ideas that would guide public policy.[15] An estimated 2,000-plus such organizations are operating today in the United States alone, although by no means do all focus on foreign affairs.

Think tanks have become part of the "revolving door" in Washington, providing a supply of new minds eager to take on the nation's problems with each new administration and a convenient place for former government officials to continue to reflect on the nation's challenges. Think tanks compete with one another for influence in government as well as for media attention that might shape public thinking.[16] Older think tanks like the Carnegie Endowment for International Peace (founded in 1910) and the Council on Foreign Relations (1921) have been joined by newer organizations such as the Hudson Institute (1961), the Heritage Foundation (1973), and the Cato Institute (1977), which include foreign policy among the topics they address.[17]

INTEREST GROUPS

In the United States today, many interest groups actively seek to shape foreign policy. Some represent the interests of émigré or ethnic communities, such as Cuban exiles living in Florida who have consistently demanded that the United States continue its trade embargo with Cuba, in place since 1962, or American Jews who lobby in support of Israel. The greatest pressure, however, may be exerted by domestic industries that lobby both for and against free trade.

Congress has traditionally exercised considerable influence over U.S. trade policy rather than deferring to the executive branch. Free trade policies, however, drew criticism from workers in industries and sectors of the economy unable to compete with cheaper, non-unionized foreign labor. When corporations shifted production offshore, workers were left behind. Entire industries disappeared from the United States—shoes from New England, textiles from South Carolina, steel from the Midwest—as they proved unable to keep up with foreign-produced goods. The American automobile industry came under intense pressure from imports—Japanese imports constituted 13 percent of motor vehicle sales in 1979 and Asian manufacturers (including the Koreans) garnered 32.5 percent of sales in 2003. (Today jobs are returning to the United States.)

Meanwhile, non-manufacturing sectors of the economy prospered (especially services such as finance) and advocates of free trade argued that all consumers benefited from the lower prices and resulting lower inflation. As Americans perceived that more and more U.S. jobs were moving overseas, trade policy became a major political issue in Pennsylvania, Ohio, and Michigan, where many manufacturing jobs had been lost. Labor unions insisted that "fair trade" should be the nation's goal. In 2002, in response to pressures from American steelmakers, the Bush administration imposed a 30 percent tariff on imported steel. In 2003, the WTO ruled that these tariffs were illegal.

The same pressures arise elsewhere in the world. For example, French and German farmers wielded enormous political clout both at home and throughout the European Community, successfully defending expensive subsidies for their members and

★ Farmers and manufacturers might support either a protectionist or a free trade stance. Corn growers benefitted for 30 years from the tariff on imported ethanol and were eager to maintain it.

forcing concessions in international trade negotiations to protect their products from foreign competition.[18]

Scholars often point to the American Israel Public Affairs Committee (AIPAC) as the preeminent example of an interest group exercising powerful influence over U.S. foreign policy—in this case, policy toward Israel. Founded in 1953, the organization generates funding through its mass membership (claimed to be 100,000 strong), which includes Democrats, Republicans, and Independents.[19] AIPAC's influence has been enormously controversial, described by some as wielding unmatched power, particularly in contrast with weak pro-Arab groups.[20] AIPAC, critics point out, seeks to control the public conversation about policy toward Israel by influencing the media and minimizing debate in Congress. Other research suggests that AIPAC's claim to influence is exaggerated, helped by the fact that it can readily lobby Congress as well as the executive branch.[21] As non-security policy issues gain prominence, it is reasonable to expect that foreign policy making will become more like domestic policy making in that business, labor, and farming interest groups will increasingly seek to shape the wide array of trade and economic policies. Environmental groups, for example, have already worked hard on global warming and related issues.

PUBLIC OPINION

During the years before and after World War II, experts in international relations viewed the making of foreign policy as the proper domain of experts on little-known parts of the world who would be able to address problems unfamiliar to the public. If the broad public had little knowledge of world affairs and tended to react emotionally to events, they could not be trusted to guide the United States' role in the world.

Realists believed that successful policy required secrecy and flexibility, conditions impossible to maintain if decisions involved extensive public debate and disclosure.[22] Woodrow Wilson and other idealists made a different argument: an enlightened public could serve as a check on leaders who might otherwise be overly anxious to engage in war. But the question persisted: Could the public understand issues far from their everyday lives? Early public opinion surveys provided evidence that the public was ill-informed about the details of foreign affairs and had few coherent beliefs. In contrast, surveys found that elites had greater knowledge and attitudes that were more consistent. These findings suggested that elites should be given great flexibility in making international decisions.

The Vietnam War inflamed opposition and greatly stimulated research on public opinion and foreign policy. New polls conducted during the Vietnam War years showed that public attitudes about foreign affairs were more consistent than had earlier been believed. In addition, it became clear that although the public was content to leave many aspects of foreign policy to elites, at times the American public became engaged and intent on influencing these decisions.

Most scholars now view public opinion as an important factor in shaping U.S. foreign policy, but they also question whether public opinion can be manipulated. During the Korean and Vietnam wars, initial public support for the conflicts declined as casualties mounted and victory was not achieved. Policy makers were well aware of the American public's "strong aversion to embarking on such ventures again."[23] More recently, public support for the war in Iraq eroded even more rapidly than during the two earlier wars, partly because the administration's principal justifications for war were undermined: congressional investigations found no evidence that Iraq's government was involved in the terrorist attacks of 9/11, and military reconnaissance found no evidence on the battlefield of an active Iraqi program to develop a nuclear capability to supplement chemical and biological weapons of mass destruction. Nonetheless, the public had been convinced to support the war at its outset, possibly because it is easier to manipulate public opinion during an international crisis.[24] Thus, while the influence of public opinion on foreign policy has grown, the research does not indicate that it is always well-informed.

★ During wartime, the public shows its supports for the troops with various paraphernalia, including placards, bumper stickers, yellow ribbons, bracelets, and lapel pins.

globalization
The increasing volume in the flow of information, people, ideas, and goods around the globe as improvements in transportation and communication expand links among nations and their populations.

CHALLENGES FOR U.S. POLICY MAKERS TODAY

KEY TO understanding ★

There is no single agenda of foreign policy goals and menu of means to achieve those goals, but there is surprising agreement on what challenges the United States is likely to face. There is concern that the United States' influence in the world is declining. More nations now challenge U.S. dominance in aspects of "soft power," and non-security issues have grown increasingly important during the post–Cold War era.

Ultimately, policies must address the major issues confronting the nation. What significant foreign policy challenges does the United States face as the twenty-first century unfolds? There is no single agenda. Military power remains a crucial option available to American leaders, but there is growing consensus that military might is less important today than in the past. The world is changing. There is a heightened "flow of information, people, ideas and goods around the globe," a development broadly termed **globalization**.[25] And for these relationships, nonmilitary sources of influence are more important.

Although the United States remains the world's preeminent military power, there are distinct limits to the use of that power, and the waning of its power in other areas presents a challenge to its position as a global leader. Power in the global system not only rests on military might but also on the ability to effectively encourage the cooperation of other members of the international community. Other countries enjoy growing clout because they *control scarce resources;* for example, oil gives Middle Eastern nations such as Saudi Arabia and the United Arab Emirates far greater significance than they otherwise would have. American policy makers also face competition with respect to the *conduct of diplomacy;* indeed, a rise in multilateral undertakings has made France and other nations in the European Union powerful international players. The worldwide response to the U.S. invasion of Iraq illustrates the importance of *moral authority,* an area where the United States lost credibility. Other countries either have already challenged the United States' influence over the nonmilitary dimensions of foreign affairs—that is, **soft power**—or will soon do so.

The National Intelligence Council, a group of U.S. government officials that provides strategic advice on long-term trends to the Director of National Intelligence, has suggested that U.S. power is declining and anticipates a world with multiple powers— not just the United States but also China, India, Russia, and others. In this section, we explore some of the challenges that the United States faces as the current leader of a unipolar international system

soft power
Increasingly important forms of nonmilitary influence that a state can exercise in international relations, including economic importance, diplomacy, the control of scarce resources, and moral authority.

THE RISE OF ECONOMIC RIVALS

While still the world's largest economy, the United States confronts *new economic powerhouses,* particularly in the European Union and China, the latter now the world's second-largest and fastest-growing economy, projected to surpass the United States within two decades. Russia, Brazil, and India have enormous economic potential. The global financial crisis of 2008 further eroded the United States' economic position as nations around the world questioned the reliance on free, largely unregulated markets that the United States had championed.

balance of payments deficit
The deficit that arises when the total value of goods and services sold by Americans to non-Americans is less than the total value of goods and services purchased by Americans from abroad.

Trade Deficit

China, with its cheap labor and favorable government policies, now leads the world's economics in producing manufactured goods, trailed by Germany and the United States. Only the combined exports of the 27 members of the European Union exceed China, as seen in Figure 18.3.

Although the United States sells more *services* abroad than it buys, it imports far more *goods* from abroad than it sells. The surplus in services sold abroad is offset by the large deficit in merchandise, creating a chronic **balance of payments deficit** (see Figure 18.4). Today, the United States is a heavy importer of necessary resources (crude oil), equipment needed for its own businesses (computers, auto parts, telecommunications and office equipment) and many consumer goods— cars, clothing, furniture, toys. Its principal import partners in 2009 were China (19.3 percent of imports), Canada (14.2 percent), and Mexico (11.1 percent). Its principal export partners were Canada (19.4 percent), Mexico (12.2 percent), and China (6.6 percent).

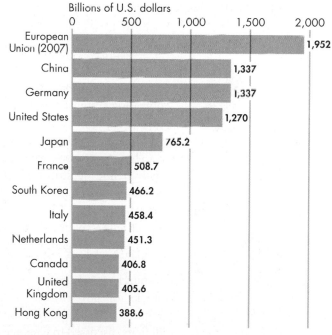

Billions of U.S. dollars

European Union (2007)	1,952
China	1,337
Germany	1,337
United States	1,270
Japan	765.2
France	508.7
South Korea	466.2
Italy	458.4
Netherlands	451.3
Canada	406.8
United Kingdom	405.6
Hong Kong	388.6

FIGURE 18.3

★ TOP 12 WORLD TRADE PARTNERS IN EXPORTS
What factors make a nation's products desirable?

Source: CIA World Factbook, (https://www.cia.gov/library/publications/the-world-factbook/index.html)

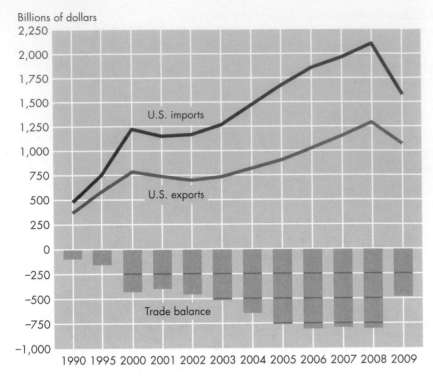

Billions of dollars

FIGURE 18.4

★ U.S. IMPORTS, EXPORTS, AND TRADE BALANCES, 1990–2009 (IN BILLIONS)

Why does the United States today import so much more than it exports? This has not always been the case.

Source: Congressional Research Service based on data from U.S. Department of Commerce; Dick K. Nanto and J. Michael Donnelly, "U.S. International Trade: Trends and Forecasts," CRS Report RL33577 (December 10, 2010), Figure 4.

U.S. exports include agricultural products, industrial supplies like chemicals, goods that other countries use for their own manufacturing (transistors, aircraft, computers), and consumer goods (cars, medicines).

By far, the greatest portion of the merchandise trade imbalance arises from U.S. trade with China (see Figure 18.5), whose exports to the United States exceeded its imports from the United States by $227 billion in 2009, a giant leap up from just $32 billion in 1995. In fact, the trade imbalance with China even exceeded the cost of foreign oil imported into the United States in 2009—a total of $192.573 billion.

China opened its domestic economy in the 1990s to the global market, and the United States opened its markets to Chinese goods in hopes of selling U.S. products and of encouraging both capitalism and democracy to flourish in this communist nation. American firms recognized the advantages of shifting operations to nations like China where labor costs were lower and environmental laws weaker.

Goods were produced more cheaply there, and global telecommunication and transportation systems made it possible to import these goods to the United States at lower prices. As Chinese workers begin to earn higher salaries, however, some of these cost advantages have begun to shift back to the United States.

There were also problems in pricing; the American dollar fluctuated in value, initially being too strong relative to other currencies and thereby raising the prices of American-made goods while making foreign goods cheaper. By contrast, many analysts believe that China intentionally depresses the value of its currency in order to increase the volume of goods sold abroad. Hence, U.S. consumers began to purchase more and more goods made in China. Buying so many imported goods and services has the effect of flooding the world with U.S. dollars. Foreign citizens use those dollars to purchase U.S. goods or invest those dollars back in the United States in the form of stocks or government bonds. More often than not, they choose investing (see Figure 18.5). In fact, one way the United States was able to finance the chronic budget deficits discussed in Chapter 16 was to sell U.S. treasury bonds to non-citizens. Eventually, those have to be paid back and will become a drain on U.S. wealth.

Running a chronic trade deficit can have both economic and political implications. A trade deficit can discourage foreign citizens from investing in U.S. government securities. Indeed, if the dollar seems to be losing value and purchasing power, why would a trade partner or nation hold on to an asset of shrinking value? This problem could pressure the Federal Reserve Board to raise interest rates as a way to stimulate foreign investors to retain U.S. dollars, which would have an impact on the domestic economy. Trade deficits can also affect a country's economic growth. Expanding U.S. exports helped to stimulate economic activity and job growth between 1990 and 2009—but the pace of growth did not offset imports.

The Declining Importance of the Dollar

Running large trade deficits can produce a steep decline in the value of a nation's currency relative to other currencies around the world. But because other nations hold dollars in reserve as a way to transact business, the impact was less than it might have been. Instead, other factors like the budget deficit and the rise of the euro (the common currency used in countries that belong to the European Economic Union) led to the declining importance of the dollar. Americans traveling to other nations discovered how expensive it had become to purchase food, lodging, and tickets to local attractions overseas because the dollar was able to purchase fewer units of the local currency than it had in the past, losing about one-third of its value against major international currencies between 2002 and 2007. Cheap foreign travel, one advantage Americans enjoyed during the heyday of U.S. economic dominance,

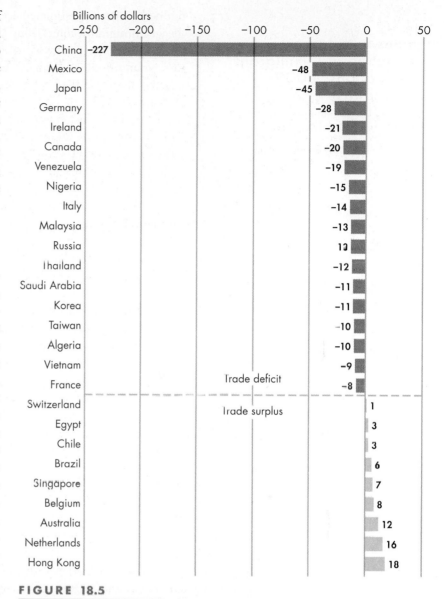

FIGURE 18.5

★ U.S. MERCHANDISE TRADE BALANCES WITH SELECTED NATIONS, 2009

Source: Congressional Research Service based on data from U.S. Department of Commerce; Dick K. Nanto and J. Michael Donnelly, "U.S. International Trade: Trends and Forecasts," CRS Report RL33577 (December 10, 2010) Figure 7.

nance, disappeared even as the nation remained a military superpower. However, the main implication for U.S. standing in the world is an unwillingness of other countries to hold dollars for fear of further declines in the value of their assets. Fewer countries holding dollars causes U.S. borrowing to become more expensive and hinders trade.

ILLEGAL IMMIGRATION

In 2010, the Pew Research Center estimated that 11.1 million illegal immigrants were living in the United States. This was a decline of nearly 1 million from two years earlier

TABLE 18.3
states with largest unauthorized immigrant populations, 2009 (thousands)

Why do illegal immigrants cluster in some states more than others?

ESTIMATED POPULATION	
U.S. Total	**11,100**
California	2,550
Texas	1,600
Florida	675
New York	650
Illinois	525
New Jersey	475
Georgia	425
Arizona	375
North Carolina	275
Maryland	250
Virginia	240
Colorado	210

Source: Jeffrey S. Passel and D'Vera Cohn, "U.S. Unauthorized Immigration Flows Are Down Sharply Since Mid-Decade," The Pew Hispanic Center of the Pew Research Center (September 1, 2010), Table 4, p. 3.

but three times the estimated 3.5 million in 1990.[26] About 80 percent of illegal immigrants come from Latin America, with nearly 60 percent from Mexico. Four states were home to nearly half of the nation's illegal immigrants in 2009—California, Texas, Florida, and New York—and nearly a quarter of the total reside in California (see Table 18.3).

Many illegal immigrants enter the United States to gain employment or escape political persecution in their home countries. Their cheap labor is important to agriculture, landscaping, building services/construction, restaurant work, and cleaning services.

Illegal immigrants are heavy consumers of health, housing, and education services. Disgruntled voters in California and Arizona approved propositions in the 1990s that forbade granting public services to illegal immigrants, although later federal court decisions mandated that the states had to provide most services. As the U.S. economy moved into recession in 2008 and jobs became scarce, substantial numbers of illegal immigrants returned to their native lands and fewer entered the United States.

The federal government also stepped up enforcement efforts. Both Presidents Bush and Obama sought congressional approval of proposals to legalize most immigrants already in the United States, but to win support they needed to prove that the federal government would do a better job of policing the border. Federal officials extended the border fence between Mexico and the United States to 652 miles, hired additional border patrol agents, and enlisted local law enforcement officials to support efforts to apprehend and deport illegal immigrants.[27] Even so, research shows that more than 90 percent of attempts to enter the United States illegally are successful. The Department of Homeland Security also increased deportations to a record 400,000 in 2010.[28]

But state officials had lost confidence in federal efforts and began to take their own actions against illegal immigration. In 2010, Arizona police were required by state law to check the immigration status of anyone suspected of being in the United States illegally and were authorized to arrest anyone suspected of committing a deportable offense. Immigrants had to carry their federal immigration card in order to prove their status and could not work in Arizona if they were in the country illegally. Other states (including Alabama and Georgia) considered or adopted similar provisions. Immigrant rights groups objected, and the federal government challenged the Arizona law in court. A federal circuit court declared in 2011 that four of the Arizona law's provisions (those noted above) undercut federal immigration law, damaged the nation's foreign policy, and could not be enforced.[29] Immigration resurfaced as a hot-button issue during the 2012 national elections.

Many nations must cope with migration pressures. Worldwide, there were 214 million migrants in 2010, and the United Nations projects an increase to 405 million by 2050.[30] The United States is the top destination for immigrants and has the largest foreign-born population of any country in the world (42.8 million in 2009). Nations in Western Europe (Germany, France, and Great Britain) are also highly desirable destinations. Not surprisingly, nations that are in high demand as destinations want to control entry rather than be overrun.[31] Others encourage immigration. This was true of the United States, Canada, Australia, and New Zealand during the nineteenth and early twentieth centuries, although all were interested in limiting the country of origin of potential immigrants. In terms of losing population, Russia, Mexico, India, and Bangladesh were the nations with the largest numbers of emigrants in 2000, the last year that official data are available. But these patterns change according to push and pull forces. When jobs are plentiful at home, democracy flourishing, and population growth under control, one finds smaller numbers seeking to emigrate.[32]

GLOBAL WARMING

Energy is both a domestic and a foreign policy issue. Late in the twentieth century, scientists began to suspect that human activity might be affecting the earth's environment. During the 1970s, research indicated that the release of chlorofluorocarbons (CFCs) into the atmosphere from products such as aerosol sprays was creating a hole in the ozone layer. Data also clearly indicated that global surface temperatures were rising (see Figure 18.6) as a result of humans burning fossil fuels that release gases like carbon dioxide into Earth's atmosphere. Increasingly sophisticated scientific models raised concerns about potential effects—melting of the polar ice caps, rising sea levels, and changing global climate patterns that are likely to cause more severe weather patterns.

The dangers posed by these environmental threats and questions about how to respond to them sparked a heated political debate. Conservatives feared that additional environmental restrictions would dampen the U.S. economy, and they believed that warnings of environmental threats were exaggerated. As discussed in Chapter 17, new sources of energy were sorely needed for economic growth. Global climate change attracted renewed public attention in 2007 when former vice president Al Gore received two Academy Awards and shared the Nobel Peace Prize for his documentary film *An Inconvenient Truth.*

Most scientists agree that global warming will have pervasive and long-term adverse effects on the world. It will affect plant, animal, and human habitats; encourage the spread of diseases into new areas; and disrupt food supplies. Political instability is bound to follow. Further, global climate change is likely to affect the international balance of power in ways large and small—ways that are difficult to predict. For example, the Joint Chiefs of Staff have expressed concern that the United States has fallen behind the Russians in a critical area of competition: heavy ice breakers. As shipping lanes that have been frozen for centuries open across the northern passage, concern grows that the United

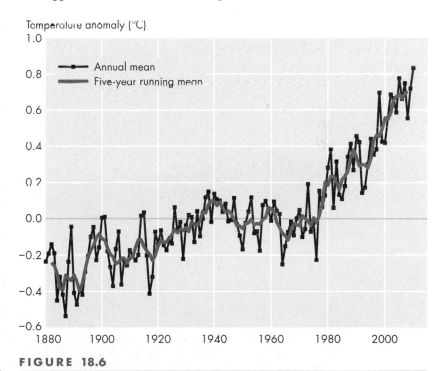

FIGURE 18.6

★ GLOBAL TEMPERATURE RISES

The graph shows rising global annual-mean surface air temperature change, in comparison with the base period 1951–1980, from data collected from a meteorological station network.

Source: NASA website, (http://data.giss.nasa.gov/gistemp/graphs).

States has only two heavy ice breakers to assist in protecting the shipping lanes, while the Russians have aggressively expanded their fleet to 14, including seven nuclear-powered vessels. The fear is that Russia will dominate the new unfrozen north with its large potential energy deposits.[33]

The Kyoto Protocol

The United States has been less proactive than other Western nations in pursuing green initiatives. Foreign publics believed that the Bush administration retreated from the U.S. commitment, made in the Kyoto Protocol in 1997, to join with most of the world's other nations to reduce carbon emissions through 2012. In truth, both the Clinton and Bush administrations shared reservations about the protocol, which once ratified would commit nations to meet targets designed to reduce emissions of CO_2 and other greenhouse gases linked to global warming. Clinton never submitted the protocol to Congress for ratification, and Bush explicitly rejected the agreement in 2001. The source of their concern was simple: the treaty did not require developing nations to also reduce emissions. Critics argued that China, India, and other recently industrializing nations (among them Brazil) were getting free rein to emit as many climate-altering gases as they wanted while the older industrial nations would bear the brunt of reductions. Both administrations also worried about the economic impact of forcing U.S. industries to install tougher pollution-reducing devices.

Figure 18.7 illustrates that the United States and the most industrialized members of the European Union bear heavy responsibility for carbon dioxide emissions during the period from 1850 to 2007. Recently, however, the picture has changed. Although the United States and the European Union remained among the top polluters, other nations have joined the list of problem states, most prominently China and India, both of which have huge populations and are rapidly industrializing. As long as these countries were excluded from obligations, the United States refused to approve the Kyoto treaty.

President Obama campaigned on the promise to pass legislation that would cap greenhouse gases, but the effort stalled in the Democrat-controlled Senate and lost all hope for passage after Republicans, who oppose expanded government regulation, gained control of the House in 2011. Instead, the administration implemented Bush-era regulations requiring better fuel economy for domestic automobiles, encouraged renewable energy projects, and sought to reduce pollution under existing law. In a dramatic round of last-minute negotiations, Obama was credited with salvaging the Copenhagen global summit meeting held in December 2009 and brokering an agreement with some of the world's most rapidly industrializing nations—Brazil, China, India, and South Africa—to limit warming by 2050 and monitor their progress toward achieving goals.[34] Finding ways to encourage cooperation among the nations of the world on this common problem remains one of the great challenges facing world leaders.

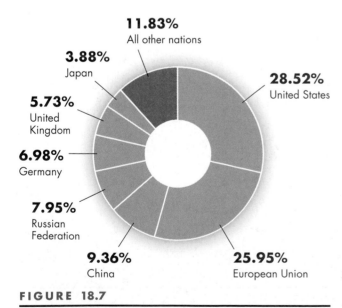

11.83%
All other nations

3.88%
Japan

5.73%
United Kingdom

6.98%
Germany

7.95%
Russian Federation

9.36%
China

28.52%
United States

25.95%
European Union

FIGURE 18.7

★ PERCENTAGE OF CUMULATIVE CO_2 EMISSIONS, 1850–2007

Source: Climate Analysis Indicators Tool, World Resources Institute (http://cait.wri.org/)

NUCLEAR PROLIFERATION

Nuclear weapons pose a special threat to the world. The best public estimate is that nine nations have more than 20,000 nuclear warheads in their arsenals, as shown in Table 18.4. Secrecy shrouds several of these nuclear programs, but North Korea probably has not deployed its weapons or missiles, and Israel's stockpile is top secret. Thousands if not millions of casualties would result from a war involving nuclear weapons. Thus, there is great concern when intense enemies are both armed with nuclear weapons, such as India and Pakistan, as well as fear of the potential outcome if Israel confronted a nuclear-armed Syria or Iran.

Fears abound that the nuclear club will grow. One hundred eighty-nine nations have signed the Nuclear Non-Proliferation Treaty that went into effect in 1970. Five of those nations with nuclear weapons pledge not to spread the weapons to other nations, to limit their use, and to work toward disarmament: the United States, the Russian Federation (successor to the USSR), the United Kingdom, France, and China. Other signatory nations have the right to use nuclear energy for peaceful purposes, as in generating electricity. But some activities necessary for peaceful nuclear energy programs—the enrichment of uranium—are also important steps toward developing a weapons program.

Since the signing of the NPT, four additional states have acquired nuclear weapons: India, Pakistan, North Korea, and probably Israel. Neither India nor Pakistan had signed the NPT; North Korea had signed, was openly charged with violating it, and then withdrew from the agreement; Israel, never a signatory, will neither confirm nor deny its nuclear capability. On the other hand, during the same period South Africa and Libya have abandoned nuclear weapons programs.

Will other nations decide to acquire nuclear weapons? Worldwide, there are 440 nuclear reactors in 29 nations, and the International Atomic Energy Agency has

TABLE 18.4
world nuclear forces by number of deployed warheads, january 2012

Why would a nation want to join this list by obtaining nuclear weapons?

COUNTRY	YEAR OF FIRST NUCLEAR TESTING	WARHEADS ON LAUNCHERS	OTHER WARHEADS	TOTAL
United States	1945	2,150	5,850	~8,000
Russia	1949	1,800	8,200	~10,000
United Kingdom	1952	160	65	225
France	1960	290	10	300
China	1964	–	200	240
India	1974	–	80–100	80–100
Pakistan	1998	–	70–90	70–90
Israel	–	–	80	80
North Korea	2006	–	–	–
Total		**~4,400**	**~14,600**	**~19,000**

Source: Stockholm International Peace Research Institute, SIPRI Yearbook 2012 (http://www.sipri.org/research/armaments/nbc/nuclear)

estimated that all could develop nuclear weapons in a fairly short time.[35] Of foremost concern is Iran, whose declared animosity toward Israel would make the Middle East an even more dangerous region. The international community is using diplomatic and economic sanctions to pressure Iran against developing nuclear weapons. Current nuclear states might also share technology or weaponry with another nation. Pakistan's chief nuclear scientist confessed to transferring important uranium enrichment technology to Libya, Iran, and North Korea during the 1990s, possibly after a bribe was paid to Pakistani military officials. There is similar concern that North Korea, desperate for financial resources, might sell the technology to others.

Could a non-state group, specifically terrorists, steal or purchase a nuclear weapon? President Obama warned the world of al Qaeda's efforts to obtain weapons of mass destruction during the Nuclear Security Summit convened in Washington, D.C., in April 2010.[36] Unstable governments pose a special danger—"loose nukes." When NATO-supported rebels defeated Moammar Gadhafi's Libyan military in 2011, Western nations hastened to make sure that nuclear and chemical materials were placed under control. Pakistan presents an even larger danger. Its government is unstable, the nation has large supplies of nuclear material, and there are strong fundamentalist Islamic influences inside the military and intelligence agencies. If the Pakistani government were to collapse, who would control the weapons?[37] Similarly, when North Korea's longtime dictator died in December 2011 without leaving a clear successor, fears grew that the nation's nuclear weapons might suddenly become available on the international arms market.

The collapse of the U.S.S.R. posed a proliferation nightmare, with nuclear weapons and nuclear facilities scattered across Central Europe and much of Asia. Bipartisan congressional legislation helped former parts of the Soviet empire to decommission their nuclear arsenals. Ukraine, Kazakhstan, and Belarus are now free of nuclear weapons.[38] There is great concern about the potential for theft—the IAEA has received 1,500 reports of incidents related to nuclear security and is concerned that these reported incidents may be just the tip of the iceberg.

TERRORISM

The U.S. arsenal of nuclear weapons has little practical utility in confronting the threats posed by al Qaeda and other international terrorist groups, and fears of another 9/11 weigh heavily on Americans' collective mind. The Commission on the Prevention of Weapons of Mass Destruction Proliferation and Terrorism predicted in December 2008 that a biological terrorist attack would be launched somewhere in the world by 2013.[39] Preventing another terrorist strike on U.S. soil requires action both at home and abroad—designing effective policies for homeland security, suppressing the activities of the principal terrorist groups, removing the sources of their appeal to new recruits, and encouraging forces of moderation in the Muslim world and elsewhere.

In response to the events of 9/11 and as part of a new "War on Terror," U.S. policy makers took several unprecedented steps in the ensuing months. The United States led a coalition of indigenous and international forces to overthrow the fundamentalist Islamic Taliban regime. Congress and President Bush passed the U.S.A. PATRIOT

Act, which gave new powers to the federal government to pursue terrorists at home. Congress and the Bush administration established the Department of Homeland Security, the largest government reorganization since the creation of the Department of Defense at the onset of the Cold War, to protect the nation from future attacks. In 2003, President George W. Bush convinced Congress to support an invasion of Iraq. This act represented a significant departure from the multilateral approach to foreign policy adopted by both President Bill Clinton and Bush's father, President George H. W. Bush.

Iraq and Afghanistan

Initially, bipartisan unity advanced the "war on terror," but domestic criticism mounted after the Bush administration invaded Iraq in 2003 because of alleged ties between Iraq and al Qaeda. This action drove a wedge between the United States and many of its allies. In contrast to the international support given to the earlier U.S. efforts in the region, France, Germany, and Russia led opposition to the U.S. action against Iraq in the United Nations. In response, the administration formed a "coalition of the willing" comprising those nations willing to follow the U.S. lead in Iraq.

The wars dragged on for more than a decade. By April 2011, the American military commitment in Afghanistan and Iraq had cost a staggering $1.283 trillion, and 145,000 military personnel were still deployed on active duty that year.[40] But the real cost of the war was even greater—somewhere between $3.2 and $4 trillion, including the interest on funds borrowed to pay for the war and health care costs for the two million Americans who had served in the field.[41] Future expenditures will be even greater as veterans' need for medical care grows over the years.

However, money was not the war's only cost. Through the end of 2011, more than 6,000 American servicemen and women had died, along with another 2,300 private Pentagon contractors who provided security services in the war areas. Almost 1,200 coalition forces and more than 3,500 Pakistani forces had also died.[42] A Brown University study estimated that in 10 years of warfare, 137,000 civilians had been killed in Iraq and Afghanistan with perhaps just as many more in Pakistan. Additionally, nearly 8 million civilians had either fled Iraq and Afghanistan or been displaced within their countries. In June 2010, Afghanistan surpassed Vietnam as the longest war in U.S. history.[43]

In August 2010, the Obama administration ended U.S. combat operations in Iraq. Most American soldiers immediately left Iraq. A substantial force remained behind to assist Iraqi security forces until December 2011 when they also departed. And the president announced in mid-2011 that 10,000 troops would withdraw from Afghanistan by the end of the year and another 23,000 by the summer of 2012. This followed the surge in force levels that had occurred in late 2009 and early 2010.

SUPERPOWER FATIGUE

Both Congress and the public had grown weary of these lingering conflicts as well as the decades-long American effort around the globe. Tracing the number of U.S. troops deployed outside the country provides a graphic portrait of U.S. conflicts over the past half-century. Fighting in Korea, Vietnam, and Iraq/Afghanistan triggered dramatic increases in the number of forces sent overseas. At no time during this 55-year period did the total number of forces stationed abroad fall below about 200,000. This was true even during the post-Cold War period of the 1990s when the United States emerged victorious from its long conflict with the Soviet Union and presumably faced fewer

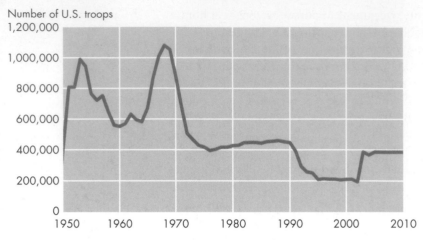

Number of U.S. troops

FIGURE 18.8

★ NUMBER OF U.S.
TROOPS IN FOREIGN
COUNTRIES

Why did the United States
keep so many troops
abroad even in peacetime?

Source: Heritage Foundation calculations
based on annual records from U.S.
Department of Defense, Directorate for
Information Operations and Records.

threats. The Persian Gulf War stands out from the other wars because it did not trigger a large increase in U.S. military forces (they were repositioned), and after the fall of the Soviet Union, there was a corresponding reduction in U.S. forces abroad during the 1990s, as Figure 18.8 shows.

Such a sustained effort takes a toll. In 2006, Graham E. Fuller, a former senior CIA official, wrote an essay exploring whether the United States had begun to display "superpower fatigue." Published in a conservative-leaning journal, Fuller's article noted that after establishing an ambitious international agenda that included unilateral action—that is, acting without consulting other countries—to suppress international threats and to expand freedom in the world, the Bush administration was experiencing problems at home and abroad. Foreign nations were resisting U.S. leadership, and many voices at home were criticizing the administration's efforts. Foreign publics now believed that the United States was primarily motivated by naked self-interest rather than its traditional idealism.[44] Whereas foreign public opinion had been broadly favorable toward the United States in 2002, it had turned substantially negative by 2007.

Most countries viewed the invasion of Iraq as a violation of international law, and leaders feared that it might encourage other nations to take similar unilateral action. In short, the global superpower seemed to be out of control, seeking to remake the world according to its wishes. And the United States was doing a poor job of explaining its policies. After the fall of the Soviet Union, the United States had dismantled most of its *public diplomacy* programs—that is, efforts to explain American policy to foreign publics through print, radio, and television outlets. These programs resumed following 9/11, but not before international support had badly eroded.

Part of the United States' problem was being overcommitted. Everyone saw the U.S. military capability as stretched very thin, making it difficult to respond to other problems around the world such as the civil war in Libya when it arose in 2011. And while the United States struggled in both Iraq and Afghanistan, the U.S. economy went into a tailspin (see Chapter 16). Budget deficits grew to all-time highs, economic growth slowed, the housing market collapsed, and energy prices spiked. Nor were the economic problems felt only in the United States; the world complained that the U.S. housing crisis had triggered a global financial crisis that slowed economic growth and reduced international trade.

The historic American mission in foreign policy—to spread democracy by example and through sympathetic support—came to be viewed in many parts of the world as no more than a justification for replacing governments that resist American control. John Quincy Adams, quoted at the beginning of this chapter, might understandably view the current situation as a realization of his fears that the United States, once engaged in the battles of the globe, "might become the dictatress of the world."[45]

Why Are We
THE WAY WE ARE **?**

Many factors influence how the United States approaches the world:

- historical perspectives on the world and the nation's place in it;
- a general outlook based on whether conflict is inevitable (realism) or the product of misunderstandings and miscommunications (idealism);
- the geopolitical situation confronting the nation;
- the public's understanding of international problems and how those views translate into political appeals and pressures;
- world views held by elected and appointed officials.

At times in U.S. history, there have been high levels of agreement on what the nation's principal foreign policy objectives are (the ends) and how to achieve them (the means). At other times, policy makers have disagreed over both ends and means.

GLOBAL LEADERSHIP

The United States became the world's leading power about midway through the twentieth century. Although some politicians had encouraged these aspirations, global leadership would not have happened if the United States had returned to its long tradition of isolationism. Instead, internationalism won out following World War II when the United States emerged as the most powerful member of the winning coalition. For more than four decades, American foreign policy was then oriented around the global competition with the Soviet Union. When the United States' great Cold War adversary—the U.S.S.R.—disintegrated, the United States became the world's lone superpower. With that role came responsibilities for dealing with disruptions around the globe and for encouraging free trade and the spread of democracy and peace, not merely within its own region, as Australia is able to do, but in many regions.

U.S. foreign policy makers suddenly had to deal with regional and ethnic conflicts that had been latent for decades. These included problems in Africa (Somalia), the Middle East (Persian Gulf, Iraq, Israel, Egypt, Libya), and West Asia (Afghanistan, Pakistan). At the same time, policy experts recognized the importance of non-security issues in an increasingly integrated, dangerously warming world. Thus, new security threats—such as terrorism, nuclear proliferation, access to weapons of mass destruction, and the rise of regional (Iran) and global (China) powers—coexisted with the problems of immigration, trade, and global warming. In almost every way, today's world is more complex and less readily understandable than it was during the Cold War, but America's responsibilities are even greater.

FRAGMENTED INFLUENCE

"Solving" these foreign policy problems is an unrealistic expectation. Solutions will always remain elusive; problems constantly morph into new shapes, much like the pieces of colored glass in a kaleidoscope. Coping with these challenges is the task of the nation's executive and legislative leaders, but the Constitution is unclear as to who takes the lead. In general, practice and precedent have enhanced the president's powers, but Congress intermittently asserts its own foreign policy prerogatives.

As globalization becomes an ever-larger factor in American life, the role of Congress will rise, as will that of states, the courts, and non-governmental organizations like think tanks and interest groups. Thus, fashioning policies to cope with change will continue to be a challenge that many other nations with less robust media and interest group systems do not face. China, for example, does not have formal government divisions that fragment policy making, nor does it have a flourishing public debate about policy. Even parliamentary democracies like Australia and the United Kingdom do not need to contend with an assertive legislature.

. . . AND WHY DOES IT Matter?

Each week brings an avalanche of daily headlines from around the globe that might make Americans want to escape their responsibilities: famine, genocide, civil wars, spreading nuclear weapons, terrorist attacks, and tsunamis. But escaping the world is not an option, especially now that technology has so radically reduced distances and increased connections. But how do Americans engage with the rest of the world? By pursuing naked self-interest or by serving some larger purpose?

At heart, the realist urges self-interest because there is danger lurking in every corner—in the nations that envy the United States and want to supplant it as the global superpower; in the nations able to charge outrageous prices for a barrel of oil; in the shadowy terrorist organizations planning to unleash mayhem; in the poverty that threatens the internal stability of friendly governments. To the idealist, the world is a less frightening place because mankind can use reason to find shared interests and resolve disputes while solving common problems faced by the global community, such as global warming. Moreover, idealists believe that all humans share the desire to live in freedom, a prominent goal in America's own national story, and that more and more of the world's interactions will not involve security.

Each generation faces its own agenda of foreign and national security challenges. Decision makers can anticipate some of those challenges, but others will arrive on the nation's doorstep unanticipated. And disagreements about goals and means are encouraged by the nation's constitutional structure and the openness of political debate. Foreign and national security policy will remain vital problems for the nation to resolve and the job will never be "finished."

critical thinking questions

1. Should Congress simply accept the view that presidents are institutionally better equipped than the legislature to decide whether to use force and cede to the president the power to wage war?

2. Who has the more accurate outlook on the international challenges faced by the United States, realists or idealists?

3. In view of the enormous cost in dollars and lives of serving as the global superpower, should the United States step aside and allow other nations to take the lead—for example, China?

4. Should the costs of reducing global warming be allocated exclusively to the nations who caused the problem over the past century or shared by those who are now adding to the problem?

key terms

★

THE DECLARATION of INDEPENDENCE

In Congress, July 4, 1776

THE UNANIMOUS DECLARATION OF THE THIRTEEN UNITED STATES OF AMERICA

When, in the course of human events, it becomes necessary for one people to dissolve the political bands which have connected them with another, and to assume, among the powers of the earth, the separate and equal station to which the laws of nature and of nature's God entitle them, a decent respect to the opinions of mankind requires that they should declare the causes which impel them to the separation.

We hold these truths to be self-evident, that all men are created equal; that they are endowed by their Creator with certain unalienable rights; that among these, are life, liberty, and the pursuit of happiness. That, to secure these rights, governments are instituted among men, deriving their just powers from the consent of the governed; that, whenever any form of government becomes destructive of these ends, it is the right of the people to alter or to abolish it, and to institute a new government, laying its foundation on such principles, and organizing its powers in such form, as to them shall seem most likely to effect their safety and happiness. Prudence, indeed, will dictate that governments long established, should not be changed for light and transient causes; and, accordingly, all experience hath shown, that mankind are more disposed to suffer, while evils are sufferable, than to right themselves by abolishing the forms to which they are accustomed. But, when a long train of abuses and usurpations, pursuing invariably the same object, evinces a design to reduce them under absolute despotism, it is their right, it is their duty, to throw off such government and to provide new guards for their future security. Such has been the patient sufferance of these colonies, and such is now the necessity which constrains them to alter their former systems of government. The history of the present King of Great Britain is a history of repeated injuries and usurpations, all having, in direct object, the establishment of an absolute tyranny over these States. To prove this, let facts be submitted to a candid world:

He has refused his assent to laws the most wholesome and necessary for the public good.

He has forbidden his governors to pass laws of immediate and pressing importance, unless suspended in their operation till his assent should be obtained; and, when so suspended, he has utterly neglected to attend to them.

He has refused to pass other laws for the accommodation of large districts of people, unless those people would relinquish the right of representation in the legislature; a right inestimable to them, and formidable to tyrants only.

He has called together legislative bodies at places unusual, uncomfortable, and distant from the depository of their public records, for the sole purpose of fatiguing them into compliance with his measures.

He has dissolved representative houses repeatedly for opposing, with manly firmness, his invasions on the rights of the people.

He has refused, for a long time after such dissolutions, to cause others to be elected; whereby the legislative powers, incapable of annihilation, have returned to the people at large for their exercise; the state remaining, in the meantime, exposed to all the danger of invasion from without, and convulsions within.

He has endeavored to prevent the population of these States; for that purpose, obstructing the laws for naturalization of foreigners, refusing to pass others to encourage their migration hither, and raising the conditions of new appropriations of lands.

He has obstructed the administration of justice, by refusing his assent to laws for establishing judiciary powers.

He has made judges dependent on his will alone, for the tenure of their offices, and the amount and payment of their salaries.

He has erected a multitude of new offices, and sent hither swarms of officers to harass our people, and eat out their substance.

He has kept among us, in time of peace, standing armies, without the consent of our legislatures.

He has affected to render the military independent of, and superior to, the civil power.

He has combined, with others, to subject us to a jurisdiction foreign to our Constitution, and unacknowledged by our laws; giving his assent to their acts of pretended legislation:

For quartering large bodies of armed troops among us:

For protecting them by a mock trial, from punishment, for any murders which they should commit on the inhabitants of these States:

For cutting off our trade with all parts of the world:

For imposing taxes on us without our consent:

For depriving us, in many cases, of the benefit of trial by jury:

For transporting us beyond seas to be tried for pretended offences:

For abolishing the free system of English laws in a neighboring province, establishing therein an arbitrary government, and enlarging its boundaries, so as to render it at once an example and fit instrument for introducing the same absolute rule into these colonies:

For taking away our charters, abolishing our most valuable laws, and altering, fundamentally, the powers of our governments:

For suspending our own legislatures, and declaring themselves invested with power to legislate for us in all cases whatsoever.

He has abdicated government here, by declaring us out of his protection, and waging war against us.

He has plundered our seas, ravaged our coasts, burnt our towns, and destroyed the lives of our people.

He is, at this time, transporting large armies of foreign mercenaries to complete the works of death, desolation, and tyranny, already begun, with circumstances of cruelty and perfidy scarcely paralleled in the most barbarous ages, and totally unworthy of the head of a civilized nation.

He has constrained our fellow citizens, taken captive on the high seas, to bear arms against their country, to become the executioners of their friends, and brethren, or to fall themselves by their hands.

He has excited domestic insurrections amongst us, and has endeavored to bring on the inhabitants of our frontiers, the merciless Indian savages, whose known rule of warfare is an undistinguished destruction of all ages, sexes, and conditions.

In every stage of these oppressions, we have petitioned for redress, in the most humble terms; our repeated petitions have been answered only by repeated injury. A prince, whose character is thus marked by every act which may define a tyrant, is unfit to be the ruler of a free people.

Nor have we been wanting in attention to our British brethren. We have warned them, from time to time, of attempts made by their legislature to extend an unwarrantable jurisdiction over us. We have reminded them of the circumstances of our emigration and settlement here. We have appealed to their native justice and magnanimity, and we have conjured them, by the ties of our common kindred, to disavow these usurpations, which would inevitably interrupt our connections and correspondence. They, too, have been deaf to the voice of justice and of consanguinity. We must, therefore, acquiesce in the necessity which denounces our separation, and hold them as we hold the rest of mankind, enemies in war, in peace, friends.

We, therefore, the representatives of the United States of America, in general Congress assembled, appealing to the Supreme Judge of the world for the rectitude of our intentions, do, in the name, and by the authority of the good people of these colonies, solemnly publish and declare, that these united colonies are, and of right ought to be, free and independent states: that they are absolved from all allegiance to the British Crown, and that all political connection between them and the state of Great Britain is, and ought to be, totally dissolved; and that, as free and independent states, they have full power to levy war, conclude peace, contract alliances, establish commerce, and to do all other acts and things which independent states may of right do. And, for the support of this declaration, with a firm reliance on the protection of Divine Providence, we mutually pledge to each other our lives, our fortunes, and our sacred honor.

The foregoing Declaration was, by order of Congress, engrossed, and signed by the following members:

John Hancock

NEW HAMPSHIRE	MASSACHUSETTS BAY	RHODE ISLAND	CONNECTICUT
Josiah Bartlett	*Samuel Adams*	*Stephen Hopkins*	*Roger Sherman*
William Whipple	*John Adams*	*William Ellery*	*Samuel Huntington*
Matthew Thornton	*Robert Treat Paine*		*William Williams*
	Elbridge Gerry		*Oliver Wolcott*

NEW YORK
William Floyd
Philip Livingston
Francis Lewis
Lewis Morris

NEW JERSEY
Richard Stockton
John Witherspoon
Francis Hopkinson
John Hart
Abraham Clark

PENNSYLVANIA
Robert Morris
Benjamin Rush
Benjamin Franklin

John Morton
George Clymer
James Smith
George Taylor
James Wilson
George Ross

DELAWARE
Caesar Rodney
George Reed
Thomas M'Kean

MARYLAND
Samuel Chase
William Paca
Thomas Stone
Charles Carroll, of Carrollton

VIRGINIA
George Wythe
Richard Henry Lee
Thomas Jefferson
Benjamin Harrison
Thomas Nelson, Jr.
Francis Lightfoot Lee
Carter Braxton

NORTH CAROLINA
William Hooper
Joseph Hewes
John Penn

SOUTH CAROLINA
Edward Rutledge
Thomas Heyward, Jr.
Thomas Lynch, Jr.
Arthur Middleton

GEORGIA
Button Gwinnett
Lyman Hall
George Walton

Resolved, That copies of the Declaration be sent to the several assemblies, conventions, and committees, or councils of safety, and to the several commanding officers of the continental troops; that it be proclaimed in each of the United States, at the head of the army.

★

THE CONSTITUTION of the UNITED STATES of AMERICA[1]

We the People of the United States, in Order to form a more perfect Union, establish Justice, insure domestic Tranquility, provide for the common defence, promote the general Welfare, and secure the Blessings of Liberty to ourselves and our Posterity, do ordain and establish this CONSTITUTION for the United States of America.

Article I

SECTION 1

All legislative Powers herein granted shall be vested in a Congress of the United States, which shall consist of a Senate and House of Representatives.

SECTION 2

The House of Representatives shall be composed of Members chosen every second Year by the People of the several States, and the Electors in each State shall have the Qualifications requisite for Electors of the most numerous Branch of the State Legislature.

No Person shall be a Representative who shall not have attained to the Age of twenty-five Years, and been seven Years a Citizen of the United States, and who shall not, when elected, be an Inhabitant of that State in which he shall be chosen.

[Representatives and direct Taxes[2] shall be apportioned among the several States which may be included within this Union, according to their respective Numbers, which shall be determined by adding to the whole Number of free Persons, including those bound to Service for a Term of Years, and excluding Indians not taxed, three fifths of all other Persons.][3] The actual Enumeration shall be made within three Years after the first Meeting of the Congress of the United States, and within every subsequent Term of ten Years, in such Manner as they shall by Law direct. The Number of Representatives shall not exceed one for every thirty Thousand, but each State shall have at Least one Representative; and until such enumeration shall be made, the State of New Hampshire shall be entitled to chuse three, Massachusetts eight, Rhode Island and Providence Plantations one, Connecticut five, New York six, New Jersey four, Pennsylvania eight, Delaware one, Maryland six, Virginia ten, North Carolina five, South Carolina five, and Georgia three.

When vacancies happen in the Representation from any State, the Executive Authority thereof shall issue Writs of Election to fill such Vacancies.

The House of Representatives shall chuse their Speaker and other Officers; and shall have the sole Power of Impeachment.

SECTION 3

The Senate of the United States shall be composed of two Senators from each State, chosen by the Legislature thereof, for six Years; and each Senator shall have one Vote.

Immediately after they shall be assembled in Consequence of the first Election, they shall be divided as equally as may be into three Classes. The Seats of the Senators of the first Class shall be vacated at the Expiration of the second Year, of the second Class at the Expiration of the fourth Year, and of the third Class at the Expiration of the sixth Year, so

---

[1] This version, which follows the original Constitution in capitalization and spelling, was published by the United States Department of the Interior, Office of Education, in 1935.
[2] Altered by the Sixteenth Amendment.
[3] Negated by the Fourteenth Amendment.

that one-third may be chosen every second Year; and if Vacancies happen by Resignation, or otherwise, during the Recess of the Legislature of any State, the Executive thereof may make temporary Appointments until the next Meeting of the Legislature, which shall then fill such Vacancies.

No Person shall be a Senator who shall not have attained to the Age of thirty Years, and been nine Years a Citizen of the United States, and who shall not, when elected, be an Inhabitant of that State for which he shall be chosen.

The Vice President of the United States shall be President of the Senate, but shall have no vote, unless they be equally divided.

The Senate shall chuse their other Officers, and also a President pro tempore, in the absence of the Vice President, or when he shall exercise the Office of President of the United States.

The Senate shall have the sole Power to try all Impeachments. When sitting for that purpose they shall be on Oath or Affirmation. When the President of the United States is tried, the Chief Justice shall preside: And no person shall be convicted without the Concurrence of two thirds of the Members present.

Judgment in Cases of Impeachment shall not extend further than to removal from Office, and disqualification to hold and enjoy any Office of honor, Trust, or Profit under the United States: but the Party convicted shall nevertheless be liable and subject to Indictment, Trial, Judgment and Punishment, according to Law.

SECTION 4

The Times, Place and Manner of holding Elections for Senators and Representatives, shall be prescribed in each State by the Legislature thereof; but the Congress may at any time by Law make or alter such Regulations, except as to the Places of Chusing Senators.

The Congress shall assemble at least once in every Year, and such Meeting shall be on the first Monday in December, unless they shall by Law appoint a different Day.

SECTION 5

Each House shall be the Judge of the Elections, Returns and Qualifications of its own Members, and a Majority of each shall constitute a Quorum to do Business; but a smaller number may adjourn from day to day, and may be authorized to compel the Attendance of absent Members, in such Manner, and under such Penalties, as each House may provide.

Each House may determine the Rules of its Proceedings, punish its Members for disorderly Behaviour, and, with the Concurrence of two thirds, expel a Member.

Each House shall keep a Journal of its Proceedings, and from time to time publish the same, excepting such Parts as may in their Judgment require Secrecy; and the Yeas and Nays of the Members of either House on any question shall, at the Desire of one fifth of those Present, be entered on the Journal.

Neither House, during the Session of Congress, shall, without the Consent of the other, adjourn for more than three days, nor to any other Place than that in which the two Houses shall be sitting.

SECTION 6

The Senators and Representatives shall receive a Compensation for their Services, to be ascertained by Law, and paid out of the Treasury of the United States. They shall in all Cases, except Treason, Felony, and Breach of the Peace, be privileged from Arrest during their Attendance at the Session of their respective Houses, and in going to and returning from the same; and for any Speech or Debate in either House, they shall not be questioned in any other Place.

No Senator or Representative shall, during the Time for which he was elected, be appointed to any civil Office under the Authority of the United States, which shall have been created, or the Emoluments whereof shall have been increased, during such time; and no Person holding any Office under the United States shall be a Member of either House during his continuance in Office.

SECTION 7

All Bills for raising Revenue shall originate in the House of Representatives; but the Senate may propose or concur with Amendments as on other bills.

Every Bill which shall have passed the House of Representatives and the Senate, shall, before it becomes a Law, be presented to the President of the United States; if he approve he shall sign it, but if not he shall return it, with his Objections, to that House in which it shall have originated, who shall enter the Objections at large on their Journal, and proceed to reconsider it. If after such Reconsideration two thirds of that House shall agree to pass the bill, it shall be sent, together with the objections, to the other House, by which it shall likewise be reconsidered, and if approved by two thirds of that House, it shall become a Law. But in all such Cases the Votes of both Houses shall be determined by Yeas and Nays, and the Names of the Persons voting for and against the Bill shall be entered on the Journal of each House respectively. If any Bill shall not be returned by the President within ten Days (Sundays excepted) after it shall have been presented to him, the Same shall be a Law, in like Manner as if he had signed it, unless the Congress by their Adjournment prevent its Return, in which Case it shall not be a Law.

Every Order, Resolution, or Vote to which the Concurrence of the Senate and House of Representatives may be necessary (except on a question of Adjournment) shall be presented to the President of the United States; and before the Same shall take Effect, shall be approved by him, or being disapproved by him, shall be repassed by two thirds of the Senate and House of Representatives, according to the Rules and Limitations prescribed in the Case of a Bill.

SECTION 8

The Congress shall have Power To lay and collect Taxes, Duties, Imposts and Excises, to pay the Debts and provide for the common Defence and general Welfare of the United States; but all Duties, Imposts and Excises shall be uniform throughout the United States;

To borrow money on the credit of the United States;

To regulate Commerce with foreign Nations, and among the several States, and with the Indian Tribes;

To establish a uniform rule of Naturalization, and uniform Laws on the subject of Bankruptcies throughout the United States;

To coin Money, regulate the Value thereof, and of foreign Coin, and fix the Standard of Weights and Measures;

To provide for the Punishment of counterfeiting the Securities and current Coin of the United States;

To establish Post Offices and post Roads;

To promote the Progress of Science and useful Arts, by securing for limited Times to Authors and Inventors the exclusive Right to their respective Writings and Discoveries;

To constitute Tribunals inferior to the Supreme Court;

To define and punish Piracies and Felonies committed on the high Seas, and Offenses against the Law of Nations;

To declare War, grant Letters of Marque and Reprisal, and make Rules concerning Captures on Land and Water;

To raise and support Armies, but no Appropriation of Money to that Use shall be for a longer Term than two Years;

To provide and maintain a Navy;

To make Rules for the Government and Regulation of the land and naval forces;

To provide for calling forth the Militia to execute the Laws of the Union, suppress Insurrections and repel Invasions;

To provide for organizing, arming, and disciplining the Militia, and for governing such Part of them as may be employed in the Service of the United States, reserving to the States respectively, the Appointment of the Officers, and the Authority of training the Militia according to the discipline prescribed by Congress;

To exercise exclusive Legislation in all Cases whatsoever, over such District (not exceeding ten Miles square) as may, by Cession of particular States, and the acceptance of Congress, become the Seat of the Government of the United States, and to exercise like Authority over all Places purchased by the Consent of the Legislature of the State in which the Same shall be, for the Erection of Forts, Magazines, Arsenals, Dock-yards, and other needful Buildings;—And

To make all Laws which shall be necessary and proper for carrying into Execution the foregoing Powers, and all other Powers vested by this Constitution in the Government of the United States, or in any Department or Officer thereof.

SECTION 9

The Migration or Importation of such Persons as any of the States now existing shall think proper to admit, shall not be prohibited by the Congress prior The Constitution of the United States of America to the Year one thousand eight hundred and eight, but a tax or duty may be imposed on such Importation, not exceeding ten dollars for each Person.

The privilege of the Writ of Habeas Corpus shall not be suspended, unless when in Cases of Rebellion or Invasion the public Safety may require it.

No bill of Attainder or ex post facto Law shall be passed.

No capitation, or other direct, Tax shall be laid unless in Proportion to the Census or Enumeration herein before directed to be taken.

No Tax or Duty shall be laid on Articles exported from any State.

No Preference shall be given by any Regulation of Commerce or Revenue to the Ports of one State over those of another: nor shall Vessels bound to, or from, one State, be obliged to enter, clear, or pay Duties in another.

No Money shall be drawn from the Treasury, but in Consequence of Appropriations made by Law; and a regular Statement and Account of the Receipts and Expenditures of all public Money shall be published from time to time.

No Title of Nobility shall be granted by the United States: And no Person holding any Office of Profit or Trust under them, shall, without the Consent of the Congress, accept of any present, Emolument, Office, or Title, of any kind whatever, from any King, Prince, or foreign State.

SECTION 10

No State shall enter into any Treaty, Alliance, or Confederation; grant Letters of Marque and Reprisal; coin Money; emit Bills of Credit; make any Thing but gold and silver Coin a Tender in Payment of Debts; pass any Bill of Attainder, ex post facto Law, or Law impairing the Obligation of Contracts, or grant any Title of Nobility.

No State shall, without the Consent of the Congress, lay any Imposts or Duties on Imports or Exports, except what may be absolutely necessary for executing its inspection Laws; and the net Produce of all Duties and Imposts, laid by any State on Imports or Exports, shall be for the use of the Treasury of the United States; and all such Laws shall be subject to the Revision and Control of the Congress.

No state shall, without the Consent of Congress, lay any duty of Tonnage, keep Troops, or Ships of War in time of Peace, enter into any Agreement or Compact with another State, or with a foreign Power, or engage in War, unless actually invaded, or in such imminent Danger as will not admit of delay.

Article II

SECTION 1

The executive Power shall be vested in a President of the United States of America. He shall hold his Office during the Term of four years, and, together with the Vice President, chosen for the same Term, be elected, as follows:

Each State shall appoint, in such Manner as the Legislature thereof may direct, a Number of Electors, equal to the whole Number of Senators and Representatives to which the State may be entitled in the Congress: but no Senator or Representative, or Person holding an Office of Trust or Profit under the United States, shall be appointed an Elector.

[The Electors shall meet in their respective States, and vote by Ballot for two persons, of whom one at least shall not be an Inhabitant of the same State with themselves. And they shall make a List of all the Persons voted for, and of the Number of Votes for each; which List they shall sign and certify, and transmit sealed to the Seat of the Government of the United States, directed to the President of the Senate. The President of the Senate shall, in the Presence of the Senate and House of Representatives, open all the Certificates, and the Votes shall then be counted. The Person having the greatest Number of Votes shall be the President, if such Number be a Majority of the whole Number of Electors appointed; and if there be more than one who have such Majority, and have an equal Number of Votes, then the House of Representatives shall immediately chuse by Ballot one of them for President; and if no Person have a Majority, then from the five highest on the List the said House shall in like Manner chuse the President. But in chusing the President, the Votes shall be taken by States, the Representation from each State having one Vote; a quorum for this Purpose shall consist of a Member or Members from two-thirds of the States, and a Majority of all the States shall be necessary to a Choice. In every Case, after the Choice of the President, the Person having the greatest Number of Votes of the Electors shall be the Vice President. But if there should remain two or more who have equal votes, the Senate shall chuse from them by Ballot the Vice President.][4]

The Congress may determine the Time of chusing the Electors, and the Day on which they shall give their Votes; which Day shall be the same throughout the United States.

[4] Revised by the Twelfth Amendment.

No person except a natural-born Citizen, or a Citizen of the United States, at the time of the Adoption of this Constitution, shall be eligible to the Office of President; neither shall any Person be eligible to that Office who shall not have attained to the Age of thirty-five years, and been fourteen Years a Resident within the United States.

In Case of the Removal of the President from Office, or of his Death, Resignation, or Inability to discharge the Powers and Duties of the said Office, the same shall devolve on the Vice President, and the Congress may by Law provide for the Case of Removal, Death, Resignation, or Inability, both of the President and Vice President, declaring what Officer shall then act as President, and such Officer shall act accordingly, until the disability be removed, or a President shall be elected.

The President shall, at stated Times, receive for his Services a Compensation, which shall neither be increased nor diminished during the Period for which he shall have been elected, and he shall not receive within that Period any other Emolument from the United States, or any of them.

Before he enter on the execution of his Office, he shall take the following Oath or Affirmation:—"I do solemnly swear (or affirm) that I will faithfully execute the Office of President of the United States, and will, to the best of my Ability, preserve, protect, and defend the Constitution of the United States."

SECTION 2

The President shall be Commander in Chief of the Army and Navy of the United States, and of the Militia of the several States, when called into the actual Service of the United States; he may require the Opinion, in writing, of the principal Officer in each of the executive Departments, upon any subject relating to the Duties of their respective Offices, and he shall have Power to Grant Reprieves and Pardons for Offenses against the United States, except in Cases of Impeachment.

He shall have Power, by and with the Advice and Consent of the Senate, to make Treaties, provided two-thirds of the Senators present concur; and he shall nominate, and by and with the Advice and Consent of the Senate, shall appoint Ambassadors, other public Ministers and Consuls, Judges of the supreme Court, and all other Officers of the United States, whose Appointments are not herein otherwise provided for, and which shall be established by Law: but the Congress may by Law vest the Appointment of such inferior Officers, as they think proper, in the President alone, in the Courts of Law, or in the Heads of Departments.

The President shall have Power to fill up all Vacancies that may happen during the Recess of the Senate, by granting Commissions which shall expire at the End of their next Session.

SECTION 3

He shall from time to time give to the Congress Information of the State of the Union, and recommend to their Consideration such Measures as he shall judge necessary and expedient; he may, on extraordinary occasions, convene both Houses, or either of them, and in Case of Disagreement between them, with respect to the Time of Adjournment, he may adjourn them to such Time as he shall think proper; he shall receive Ambassadors and other public Ministers; he shall take care that the Laws be faithfully executed, and shall Commission all the Officers of the United States.

SECTION 4

The President, Vice President and all civil Officers of the United States, shall be removed from Office on Impeachment for, and Conviction of, Treason, Bribery, or other high Crimes and Misdemeanors.

Article III

SECTION 1

The judicial Power of the United States, shall be vested in one supreme Court, and in such inferior Courts as the Congress may from time to time ordain and establish. The Judges, both of the supreme and inferior Courts, shall hold their Offices during good Behaviour, and shall, at stated Times, receive for their Services, a Compensation, which shall not be diminished during their Continuance in Office.

SECTION 2

The judicial Power shall extend to all Cases, in Law and Equity, arising under this Constitution, the Laws of the United States, and Treaties made, or which shall be made, under their Authority;—to all Cases affecting ambassadors, other public ministers and consuls;—to all cases of admiralty and maritime Jurisdiction; –to Controversies to which the United States shall be a Party;—to Controversies between two or more states;—between a State and Citizens of another State;[5] —between Citizens of different States—between Citizens of the same State claiming Lands under Grants of different States, and between a State, or the Citizens thereof, and foreign States, Citizens, or Subjects.

In all Cases affecting Ambassadors, other public Ministers and Consuls, and those in which a State shall be Party, the supreme Court shall have original Jurisdiction. In all the other Cases before mentioned, the supreme Court shall have appellate Jurisdiction, both as to Law and Fact, with such Exceptions, and under such Regulations as the Congress shall make.

The trial of all Crimes, except in Cases of Impeachment, shall be by Jury; and such Trial shall be held in the State where the said Crimes shall have been committed; but when

[5] Qualified by the Eleventh Amendment.

not committed within any State, the Trial shall be at such Place or Places as the Congress may by Law have directed.

SECTION 3

Treason against the United States, shall consist only in levying War against them, or in adhering to their Enemies, giving them Aid and Comfort. No Person shall be convicted of Treason unless on the Testimony of two Witnesses to the same overt Act, or on Confession in open Court.

The Congress shall have power to declare the Punishment of Treason, but no Attainder of Treason shall work Corruption of Blood, or Forfeiture except during the Life of the Person attainted.

Article IV

SECTION 1

Full Faith and Credit shall be given in each State to the public Acts, Records, and judicial Proceedings of every other State. And the Congress may by general Laws prescribe the Manner in which such Acts, Records and Proceedings shall be proved, and the Effect thereof.

SECTION 2

The Citizens of each State shall be entitled to all Privileges and Immunities of Citizens in the several States.

A Person charged in any State with Treason, Felony, or other Crime, who shall flee from Justice, and be found in another State, shall on demand of the executive Authority of the State from which he fled, be delivered up, to be removed to the State having Jurisdiction of the crime.

No Person held to Service or Labour in one State, under the Laws thereof, escaping into another, shall, in Consequence of any Law or Regulation therein, be discharged from such Service or Labour, but shall be delivered up on Claim of the Party to whom such Service or Labour may be due.

SECTION 3

New States may be admitted by the Congress into this Union; but no new State shall be formed or erected within the Jurisdiction of any other State; nor any State be formed by the Junction of two or more States, or parts of States, without the Consent of the Legislatures of the States concerned as well as of the Congress.

The Congress shall have Power to dispose of and make all needful Rules and Regulations respecting the Territory or other Property belonging to the United States; and nothing in this Constitution shall be so construed as to Prejudice any Claims of the United States, or of any particular State.

SECTION 4

The United States shall guarantee to every State in this Union a Republican Form of Government, and shall protect each of them against Invasion; and on Application of the Legislature, or of the Executive (when the Legislature cannot be convened) against domestic Violence.

Article V

The Congress, whenever two-thirds of both Houses shall deem it necessary, shall propose Amendments to this Constitution, or, on the Application of the Legislatures of two-thirds of the several States, shall call a Convention for proposing Amendments, which, in either Case, shall be valid to all Intents and Purposes, as part of this Constitution, when ratified by the Legislatures of three-fourths of the several States, or by Conventions in three-fourths thereof, as the one or the other Mode of Ratification may be proposed by the Congress; Provided that no Amendment which may be made prior to the Year One thousand eight hundred and eight shall in any Manner affect the first and fourth Clauses in the Ninth Section of the first Article; and that no State, without its Consent, shall be deprived of its equal Suffrage in the Senate.

Article VI

All Debts contracted and Engagements entered into, before the Adoption of this Constitution, shall be as valid against the United States under this Constitution, as under the Confederation.

This Constitution, and the Laws of the United States which shall be made in Pursuance thereof; and all Treaties made, or which shall be made, under the Authority of the United States, shall be the supreme Law of the Land; and the Judges in every State shall be bound thereby, any Thing in the Constitution or Laws of any State to the Contrary notwithstanding.

The Senators and Representatives before mentioned, and the Members of the several State Legislatures, and all executive and judicial Officers, both of the United States and of the several States, shall be bound by Oath or Affirmation to support this Constitution; but no religious Tests shall ever be required as a qualification to any Office or public Trust under the United States.

Article VII

The Ratification of the Conventions of nine States shall be sufficient for the Establishment of this Constitution between the States so ratifying the same.

Done in Convention by the Unanimous Consent of the States present the Seventeenth Day of September in the Year of our Lord one thousand seven hundred and Eighty seven, and of the Independence of the United States of America the Twelfth. In Witness whereof We have hereunto subscribed our Names.[6]

[6] These are the full names of the signers, which in some cases are not the signatures on the document.

GEORGE WASHINGTON
President and deputy from Virginia

NEW HAMPSHIRE
John Langdon
Nicholas Gilman

MASSACHUSETTS
Nathaniel Gorham
Rufus King

CONNECTICUT
William Samuel Johnson
Roger Sherman

NEW YORK
Alexander Hamilton

NEW JERSEY
William Livingston
David Brearley
William Paterson
Jonathan Dayton

PENNSYLVANIA
Benjamin Franklin
Thomas Mifflin
Robert Morris
George Clymer
Thomas FitzSimmons
Jared Ingersoll
James Wilson
Gouverneur Morris

DELAWARE
George Read
Gunning Bedford, Jr.
John Dickinson
Richard Bassett
Jacob Broom

MARYLAND
James McHenry
Daniel of St. Thomas Jenifer
Daniel Carroll

VIRGINIA
John Blair
James Madison, Jr.

NORTH CAROLINA
William Blount
Richard Dobbs Spaight
Hugh Williamson

SOUTH CAROLINA
John Rutledge
Charles Cotesworth Pinckney
Charles Pinckney
Pierce Butler

GEORGIA
William Few
Abraham Baldwin

Articles in Addition to, and Amendment of, the Constitution of the United States of America, Proposed by Congress, and Ratified by the Legislatures of the Several States, Pursuant to the Fifth Article of the Original Constitution[7]

Amendment I

Congress shall make no law respecting an establishment of religion, or prohibiting the free exercise thereof; or abridging the freedom of speech, or of the press; or the right of the people peaceably to assemble, and to petition the Government for a redress of grievances.

Amendment II

A well regulated Militia, being necessary to the security of a free State, the right of the people to keep and bear Arms shall not be infringed.

[7] This heading appears only in the joint resolution submitting the first ten amendments, which are collectively known as the Bill of Rights. They were ratified on December 15, 1791.

Amendment III

No Soldier shall, in time of peace, be quartered in any house, without the consent of the Owner, nor in time of war, but in a manner to be prescribed by law.

Amendment IV

The right of the people to be secure in their persons, houses, papers, and effects, against unreasonable searches and seizures, shall not be violated, and no Warrants shall issue, but upon probable cause, supported by Oath or affirmation, and particularly describing the place to be searched, and the persons or things to be seized.

Amendment V

No person shall be held to answer for a capital or otherwise infamous crime, unless on a presentment or indictment of a Grand Jury, except in cases arising in the land or naval forces, or in the Militia, when in actual service in time of War or public danger; nor shall any person be subject for the same offence to be twice put in jeopardy of life or limb; nor shall be compelled in any criminal case to be a witness against himself, nor be deprived of life, liberty, or property, without due process of law; nor shall private property be taken for public use, without just compensation.

Amendment VI

In all criminal prosecutions, the accused shall enjoy the right to a speedy and public trial, by an impartial jury of the State and district wherein the crime shall have been committed, which district shall have been previously ascertained by law, and to be informed of the nature and cause of the accusation; to be confronted with the witnesses against him; to have compulsory process for obtaining witnesses in his favour, and to have the Assistance of Counsel for his defence.

Amendment VII

In suits at common law, where the value in controversy shall exceed twenty dollars, the right of trial by jury shall be preserved, and no fact tried by a jury, shall be otherwise reexamined in any Court of the United States, than according to the rules of the common law.

Amendment VIII

Excessive bail shall not be required, nor excessive fines imposed, nor cruel and unusual punishments inflicted.

Amendment IX

The enumeration of the Constitution, of certain rights, shall not be construed to deny or disparage others retained by the people.

Amendment X

The powers not delegated to the United States by the Constitution, nor prohibited by it to the States, are reserved to the States respectively, or to the people.

Amendment XI [1795]

The Judicial power of the United States shall not be construed to extend to any suit in law or equity, commenced or prosecuted against one of the United States by Citizens of another State, or by Citizens or Subjects of any Foreign State.

Amendment XII [1804]

The Electors shall meet in their respective States and vote by ballot for President and Vice-President, one of whom, at least, shall not be an inhabitant of the same State with themselves; they shall name in their ballots the person voted for as President, and in distinct ballots the person voted for as Vice-President, and they shall make distinct lists of all persons voted for as President, and of all persons voted for as Vice-President, and of the number of votes for each, which lists they shall sign and certify, and transmit sealed to the seat of the government of the United States, directed to the President of the Senate;—The President of the Senate shall, in the presence of the Senate and House of Representatives, open all the certificates and the votes shall then be counted;—The person having the greatest number of votes for President, shall be the President, if such number be a majority of the whole number of Electors appointed; and if no person have such majority, then from the persons having the highest numbers not exceeding three on the list of those voted for as President, the House of Representatives shall choose immediately, by ballot, the President. But in choosing the President, the votes shall be taken by states, the representation from each state having one vote; a quorum for this purpose shall consist of a member or members from two-thirds of the states, and a majority of all the states shall be necessary to a choice. And if the House of Representatives shall not choose a President whenever the right of choice shall devolve upon them, before the fourth day of March next following, then the Vice-President shall act as President, as in the case of the death or other constitutional disability of the President—The person having the greatest number of votes as Vice-President, shall be the Vice-President, if such number be a majority of the whole number of Electors appointed, and if no person have a majority, then from the two highest numbers on the list, the Senate shall choose the Vice-President; a quorum for the purpose shall consist of two-thirds of the whole number of Senators, and majority of the whole number shall be necessary to a choice. But no person constitutionally ineligible to the office of President shall be eligible to that of Vice-President of the United States.

Amendment XIII [1865]

SECTION 1

Neither slavery nor involuntary servitude, except as a punishment for crime whereof the party shall have been duly convicted, shall exist within the United States, or any place subject to their jurisdiction.

SECTION 2

Congress shall have power to enforce this article by appropriate legislation.

Amendment XIV [1868]

SECTION 1

All persons born or naturalized in the United States, and subject to the jurisdiction thereof, are citizens of the United States and of the State wherein they reside. No State shall abridge the privileges or immunities of citizens of the United States; nor shall any State deprive any person of life, liberty, or property, without due process of law; nor deny to any person within its jurisdiction the equal protection of the laws.

SECTION 2

Representatives shall be apportioned among the several States according to their respective numbers, counting the whole number of persons in each State, excluding Indians not taxed. But when the right to vote at any election for the choice of electors for President and Vice-President of the United States, Representatives in Congress, the Executive and Judicial officers of a State, or the members of the Legislature thereof, is denied to any of the male inhabitants of such State, being twenty-one years of age, and citizens of the United States, or in any way abridged, except for participation in rebellion, or other crime, the basis of representation therein shall be reduced in the proportion which the number of such male citizens shall bear to the whole number of male citizens twenty-one years of age in such State.

SECTION 3

No person shall be a Senator or Representative in Congress, or elector of President and Vice-President, or hold any office, civil or military, under the United States, or under any State, who, having previously taken an oath, as a member of Congress, or as an officer of the United States, or as a member of any State legislature, or as an executive or judicial officer of any State, to support the Constitution of the United States, shall have engaged in insurrection or rebellion against the same, or given aid or comfort to the enemies thereof. But Congress may by a vote of two-thirds of each House, remove such disability.

SECTION 4

The validity of the public debt of the United States, authorized by law, including debts incurred for payment of pensions and bounties for services in suppressing insurrection or rebellion, shall not be questioned. But neither the United States nor any State shall assume or pay any debts or obligation incurred in aid of insurrection or rebellion against the United States, or any claim for the loss or emancipation of any slave; but all such debts, obligations, and claims shall be held illegal and void.

SECTION 5

The Congress shall have the power to enforce, by appropriate legislation, the provisions of this article.

Amendment XV [1870]

SECTION 1

The right of citizens of the United States to vote shall not be denied or abridged by the United States or by any State on account of race, color, or previous condition of servitude.

SECTION 2

The Congress shall have power to enforce this article by appropriate legislation.

Amendment XVI [1913]

The Congress shall have power to lay and collect taxes on incomes, from whatever source derived, without apportionment among the several States, and without regard to any census or enumeration.

Amendment XVII [1913]

The Senate of the United States shall be composed of two Senators from each State, elected by the people thereof, for six years; and each Senator shall have one vote. The electors in each State shall have the qualifications requisite for electors of the most numerous branch of the State legislatures.

When vacancies happen in the representation of any State in the Senate, the executive authority of such State shall issue writs of election to fill such vacancies: Provided, That the legislature of any State may empower the executive thereof to make temporary appointments until the people fill the vacancies by election as the legislature may direct.

This amendment shall not be so construed as to affect the election or term of any Senator chosen before it becomes valid as part of the Constitution.

Amendment XVIII [1919]

SECTION 1

After one year from the ratification of this article the manufacture, sale, or transportation of intoxicating liquors within, the importation thereof into, or the exportation thereof from the United States and all territory subject to the jurisdiction thereof for beverage purposes is hereby prohibited.

SECTION 2

The Congress and the several States shall have concurrent power to enforce this article by appropriate legislation.

SECTION 3

This article shall be inoperative unless it shall have been ratified as an amendment to the Constitution by the legislatures of the several States, as provided in the Constitution, within seven years from the date of the submission hereof to the States by the Congress.

Amendment XIX [1920]

The right of citizens of the United States to vote shall not be denied or abridged by the United States or by any State on account of sex.

Congress shall have power to enforce this article by appropriate legislation.

Amendment XX [1933]

SECTION 1

The terms of the President and Vice-President shall end at noon on the 20th day of January, and the terms of Senators and Representatives at noon on the 3d day of January, of the years in which such terms would have ended if this article had not been ratified; and the terms of their successors shall then begin.

SECTION 2

The Congress shall assemble at least once in every year, and such meeting shall begin at noon on the 3d day of January, unless they shall by law appoint a different day.

SECTION 3

If, at the time fixed for the beginning of the term of the President, the President elect shall have died, the Vice-President elect shall become President. If a President shall not have been chosen before the time fixed for the beginning of his term or if the President elect shall have failed to qualify, then the Vice-President elect shall act as President until a President shall have qualified; and the Congress may by law provide for the case wherein neither a President elect nor a Vice-President elect shall have qualified, declaring who shall then act as President, or the manner in which one who is to act shall be selected, and such person shall act accordingly until a President or Vice-President shall have qualified.

SECTION 4

The Congress may by law provide for the case of the death of any of the persons from whom the House of Representatives may choose a President whenever the right of choice shall have devolved upon them, and for the case of the death of any of the persons from whom the Senate may choose a Vice-President whenever the right of choice shall have devolved upon them.

SECTION 5

Sections 1 and 2 shall take effect on the 15th day of October following the ratification of this article.

SECTION 6

This article shall be inoperative unless it shall have been ratified as an amendment to the Constitution by the legislatures of three-fourths of the several States within seven years from the date of its submission.

Amendment XXI [1933]

SECTION 1

The eighteenth article of amendment to the Constitution of the United States is hereby repealed.

SECTION 2

The transportation or importation into any State, Territory, or possession of the United States for delivery or use therein of intoxicating liquors, in violation of the laws thereof, is hereby prohibited.

SECTION 3

This article shall be inoperative unless it shall have been ratified as an amendment to the Constitution by conventions in the several States, as provided in the Constitution, within seven years from the date of the submission hereof to the States by the Congress.

Amendment XXII [1951]

No person shall be elected to the office of the President more than twice, and no person who has held the office of President, or acted as President, for more than two years of a term to which some other person was elected President shall be elected to the office of the President more than once.

But this Article shall not apply to any person holding the office of President when this Article was proposed by the Congress, and shall not prevent any person who may be holding the office of President, or acting as President, during the term within which this Article becomes operative from holding the office of President or acting as President during the remainder of such term.

This article shall be inoperative unless it shall have been ratified as an amendment to the Constitution by the legislatures of three-fourths of the several states within seven years from the date of its submission to the states by the Congress.

Amendment XXIII [1961]

SECTION 1

The District constituting the seat of Government of the United States shall appoint in such manner as the Congress may direct:

A number of electors of President and Vice-President equal to the whole number of Senators and Representatives in Congress to which the District would be entitled if it were a State, but in no event more than the least populous State; they shall be in addition to those appointed by the States, but they shall be considered, for the purposes of the election of President and Vice-President, to be electors appointed by a State; and they shall meet in the District and perform such duties as provided by the twelfth article of amendment.

SECTION 2

The Congress shall have power to enforce this article by appropriate legislation.

Amendment XXIV [1964]

SECTION 1

The right of citizens of the United States to vote in any primary or other election for President or Vice President, for electors for President or Vice President, or for Senator or Representative in Congress, shall not be denied or abridged by the United States or any state by reason of failure to pay any poll tax or other tax.

SECTION 2

The Congress shall have the power to enforce this article by appropriate legislation.

Amendment XXV [1967]

SECTION 1

In case of the removal of the President from office or of his death or resignation, the Vice President shall become President.

SECTION 2

Whenever there is a vacancy in the office of the Vice President, the President shall nominate a Vice President who shall take office upon confirmation by a majority vote of both Houses of Congress.

SECTION 3

Whenever the President transmits to the President Pro Tempore of the Senate and the Speaker of the House of Representatives his written declaration that he is unable to discharge the powers and duties of his office, and until he transmits to them a written declaration to the contrary, such powers and duties shall be discharged by the Vice President as Acting President.

SECTION 4

Whenever the Vice President and a majority of either the principal officers of the executive departments or of such other body as Congress may by law provide, transmit to the President Pro Tempore of the Senate and the Speaker of the House of Representatives their written declaration that the President is unable to discharge the powers and duties of his office, the Vice President shall immediately assume the powers and duties of the office as Acting President.

Thereafter, when the President transmits to the President Pro Tempore of the Senate and the Speaker of the House of Representatives his written declaration that no inability exists, he shall resume the powers and duties of his office unless the Vice President and a majority of either the principal officers of the executive departments or of such other body as Congress may by law provide, transmit within four days to the President Pro Tempore of the Senate and the Speaker of the House of Representatives their written declaration that the President is unable to discharge the powers and duties of his office. Thereupon Congress shall decide the issue, assembling within forty-eight hours for that purpose if not in session. If the Congress, within twenty-one days after receipt of the latter written declaration, or, if Congress is not in session, within twenty-one days after Congress is required to assemble, determines by two-thirds vote of both Houses that the President is unable to discharge the powers and duties of his office, the Vice President shall continue to discharge the same as Acting President; otherwise, the President shall resume the powers and duties of his office.

Amendment XXVI [1971]

SECTION 1

The right of citizens of the United States, who are eighteen years of age or older, to vote shall not be denied or abridged by the United States or by any State on account of age.

SECTION 2

The Congress shall have the power to enforce this article by appropriate legislation.

Amendment XXVII [1992]

No law varying the compensation for the service of Senators and Representatives shall take effect until an election of Representatives shall have intervened.

★

FEDERALIST NO. 10 (JAMES MADISON)

Among the numerous advantages promised by a well-constructed union, none deserves to be more accurately developed than its tendency to break and control the violence of faction. The friend of popular governments never finds himself so much alarmed for their character and fate as when he contemplates their propensity to this dangerous vice. He will not fail, therefore, to set a due value on any plan which, without violating the principles to which he is attached, provides a proper cure for it. The instability, injustice, and confusion introduced into the public councils have, in truth, been the mortal diseases under which popular governments have everywhere perished, as they continue to be the favorite and fruitful topics from which the adversaries to liberty derive their most specious declamations. The valuable improvements made by the American constitutions on the popular models, both ancient and modern, cannot certainly be too much admired; but it would be an unwarrantable partiality to contend that they have as effectually obviated the danger on this side, as was wished and expected. Complaints are everywhere heard from our most considerate and virtuous citizens, equally the friends of public and private faith and of public and personal liberty, that our governments are too unstable, that the public good is disregarded in the conflicts of rival parties, and that measures are too often decided, not according to the rules of justice and the rights of the minor party, but by the superior force of an interested and overbearing majority. However anxiously we may wish that these complaints had no foundation, the evidence of known facts will not permit us to deny that they are in some degree true. It will be found, indeed, on a candid review of our situation, that some of the distresses under which we labor have been erroneously charged on the operation of our governments; but it will be found, at the same time, that other causes will not alone account for many of our heaviest misfortunes; and, particularly, for that prevailing and increasing distrust of public engagements and alarm for private rights which are echoed from one end of the confinent to the other. These must be chiefly, if not wholly, effects of the unsteadiness and injustice with which a factious spirit has tainted our public administration.

By a faction I understand a number of citizens, whether amounting to a majority or minority of the whole, who are united and actuated by some common impulse of passion, or of interest, adverse to the rights of other citizens, or to the permanent and aggregate interests of the community.

There are two methods of curing the mischiefs of faction: the one, by removing its causes; the other, by controlling its effects.

There are again two methods of removing the causes of faction: the one, by destroying the liberty which is essential to its existence; the other, by giving to every citizen the same opinions, the same passions, and the same interests.

It could never be more truly said than of the first remedy that it was worse than the disease. Liberty is to faction what air is to fire, an aliment without which it instantly expires. But it could not be a less folly to abolish liberty, which is essential to political life, because it nourishes faction than it would be to wish the annihilation of air, which is essential to animal life, because it imparts to fire its destructive agency.

The second expedient is as impracticable as the first would be unwise. As long as the reason of man continues fallible, and he is at liberty to exercise it, different opinions will be formed. As long as the connection subsists between his reason and his self-love, his opinions and his passions will have a reciprocal influence on each other; and the former will be objects to which the latter will attach themselves. The diversity in the faculties of men, from which the rights of property originate, is not less an insuperable obstacle to a uniformity of interest. The protection of these faculties is the first object of government. From the protection of different and unequal faculties of acquiring property, the possession of different degrees and kinds of property immediately results; and from the influence of these on the sentiments and views of the respective proprietors ensues a division of the society into different interests and parties.

The latent causes of faction are thus sown in the nature of man; and we see them everywhere brought into different degrees of activity, according to the different circumstances of civil society. A zeal for different opinions concerning religion, concerning government, and many other points, as well of speculation as of practice; an attachment to different leaders ambitiously contending for pre-eminence and power; or to persons of other descriptions whose fortunes have been interesting to the human passions, have, in turn, divided mankind into parties, inflamed them with mutual animosity, and rendered them much more disposed to vex and oppress each other than to co-operate for their common good. So strong is this propensity of mankind to fall into mutual animosities that where no substantial occasion presents itself the most frivolous and fanciful distinctions have been sufficient to kindle their unfriendly passions and excite their most violent conflicts. But the most common and durable source of factions has been the various and unequal distribution of property. Those who hold and those who are without property have ever formed distinct interests in society. Those who are creditors, and those who are debtors, fall under a like discrimination. A landed interest, a manufacturing interest, a mercantile interest, a moneyed interest, with many lesser interests, grow up of necessity in civilized nations, and divide them into different classes, actuated by different sentiments and views. The regulation of these various and interfering interests forms the principal task of modern legislation and involves the spirit of party and faction in the necessary and ordinary operations of government.

No man is allowed to be a judge in his own cause, because his interest would certainly bias his judgment, and, not improbably, corrupt his integrity. With equal, nay with greater reason, a body of men are unfit to be both judges and parties at the same time; yet what are many of the most important acts of legislation but so many judicial determinations, not indeed concerning the rights of single persons, but concerning the rights of large bodies of citizens? And what are the different classes of legislators but advocates and parties to the causes which they determine? Is a law proposed concerning private debts? It is a question to which the creditors are parties on one side and the debtors on the other. Justice ought to hold the balance between them. Yet the parties are, and must be, themselves the judges; and the most numerous party, or in other words, the most powerful faction must be expected to prevail. Shall domestic manufacturers be encouraged, and in what degree, by restrictions on foreign manufacturers? [These] are questions which would be differently decided by the landed and the manufacturing classes, and probably by neither with a sole regard to justice and the public good. The apportionment of taxes on the various descriptions of property is an act which

seems to require the most exact impartiality; yet there is, perhaps, no legislative act in which greater opportunity and temptation are given to a predominant party to trample on the rules of justice. Every shilling with which they overburden the inferior number is a shilling saved to their own pockets.

It is in vain to say that enlightened statesmen will be able to adjust these clashing interests and render them all subservient to the public good. Enlightened statesmen will not always be at the helm. Nor, in many cases, can such an adjustment be made at all without taking into view indirect and remote considerations, which will rarely prevail over the immediate interest which one party may find in disregarding the rights of another or the good of the whole.

The inference to which we are brought is that the *causes* of faction cannot be removed and that relief is only to be sought in the means of controlling its *effects*.

If a faction consists of less than a majority, relief is supplied by the republican principle, which enables the majority to defeat its sinister views by regular vote. It may clog the administration, it may convulse the society; but it will be unable to execute and mask its violence under the forms of the Constitution. When a majority is included in a faction, the form of popular government, on the other hand, enables it to sacrifice to its ruling passion or interest both the public good and the rights of other citizens. To secure the public good and private rights against the danger of such a faction, and at the same time to preserve the spirit and the form of popular government, is then the great object to which our inquiries are directed. Let me add that it is the great desideratum by which alone this form of government can be rescued from the opprobrium under which it has so long labored and be recommended to the esteem and adoption of mankind.

By what means is this object attainable? Evidently by one of two only. Either the existence of the same passion or interest in a majority at the same time must be prevented, or the majority, having such coexistent passion or interest, must be rendered, by their number and local situation, unable to concert and carry into effect schemes of oppression. If the impulse and the opportunity be suffered to coincide, we well know that neither moral nor religious motives can be relied on as an adequate control. They are not found to be such on the injustice and violence of individuals, and lose their efficacy in proportion to the number combined together, that is, in proportion as their efficacy becomes needful.

From this view of the subject it may be concluded that a pure democracy, by which I mean a society consisting of a small number of citizens, who assemble and administer the government in person, can admit of no cure for the mischiefs of faction. A common passion or interest will, in almost every case, be felt by a majority of the whole, a communication and concert result from the form of government itself; and there is nothing to check the inducements to sacrifice the weaker party or an obnoxious individual. Hence it is that such democracies have ever been spectacles of turbulence and contention; have ever been found incompatible with personal security or the rights of property; and have in general been as short in their lives as they have been violent in their deaths. Theoretic politicians, who have patronized this species of government, have erroneously supposed that by reducing mankind to a perfect equality in their political rights, they would at the same time be perfectly equalized and assimilated in their possessions, their opinions, and their passions.

A republic, by which I mean a government in which the scheme of representation takes place, opens a different prospect and promises the cure for which we are seeking. Let us examine the points in which it varies from pure democracy, and we shall comprehend both the nature of the cure and the efficacy which it must derive from the Union.

The two great points of difference between a democracy and a republic are: first, the delegation of the government, in the latter, to a small number of citizens elected by the rest; secondly, the greater number of citizens and greater sphere of country over which the latter may be extended.

The effect of the first difference is, on the one hand, to refine and enlarge the public views by passing them through the medium of a chosen body of citizens, whose wisdom may best discern the true interest of their country and whose patriotism and love of justice will be least likely to sacrifice it to temporary or partial considerations. Under such a regulation it may well happen that the public voice, pronounced by the representatives of the people, will be more consonant to the public good than if pronounced by the people themselves, convened for the purpose. On the other hand, the effect may be inverted. Men of factious tempers, of local prejudices, or of sinister designs, may, by intrigue, by corruption, or by other means, first obtain the suffrages, and then betray the interests of the people. The question resulting is, whether small or extensive republics are most favorable to the election of proper guardians of the public weal; and it is clearly decided in favor of the latter by two obvious considerations.

In the first place it is to be remarked that however small the republic may be the representatives must be raised to a certain number in order to guard against the cabals of a few; and that however large it may be they must be limited to a certain number in order to guard against the confusion of a multitude. Hence, the number of representatives in the two cases not being in proportion to that of the constituents, and being proportionally greatest in the small republic, it follows that if the proportion of fit characters be not less in the large than in the small republic, the former will present a greater option, and consequently a greater probability of a fit choice.

In the next place, as each representative will be chosen by a greater number of citizens in the large than in the small republic, it will be more difficult for unworthy candidates to practice with success the vicious arts by which elections are too often carried; and the suffrages of the people being more free, will be more likely to center on men who possess the most attractive merit and the most diffusive and established characters.

It must be confessed that in this, as in most other cases, there is a mean, on both sides of which inconveniencies will be found to lie. By enlarging too much the number of electors, you render the representative too little acquainted with all their local circumstances and lesser interests; as by reducing it too much, you render him unduly attached to these, and too little fit to comprehend and pursue great and national objects. The federal Constitution forms a happy combination in this respect; the great and aggregate interests being referred to the national, the local and particular to the State legislatures.

The other point of difference is the greater number of citizens and extent of territory which may be brought within the compass of republican than of democratic government; and it is this circumstance principally which renders factious combinations less to be dreaded in the former than in the latter. The smaller the society, the fewer probably will be the distinct parties and interests composing it; the fewer the distinct parties and interests, the more frequently will a majority be found of the same party; and the smaller the number of individuals composing a majority, and the smaller the compass within which they are placed, the more easily will they concert and execute their plans of oppression. Extend the sphere and you take in a greater variety of parties and interests; you make it less probable that a majority of the whole will have a common motive to invade the rights of other citizens; or if such a common motive exists, it will be more difficult for all who feel it to discover their own strength and to act in unison with each other. Besides other impediments, it may be remarked that, where there is a consciousness of unjust or dishonorable purposes, communication is always checked by distrust in proportion to the number whose concurrence is necessary.

Hence, it clearly appears that the same advantage which a republic has over a democracy in controlling the effects of faction is enjoyed by a large over a small republic—is enjoyed by the Union over the States composing it. Does this advantage consist in the substitution of representatives whose enlightened views and virtuous sentiments render them superior to local prejudices and to schemes of injustice? It will not be denied that the representation of the Union will be most likely to possess these requisite endowments.

Does it consist in the greater security afforded by a greater variety of parties, against the event of any one party being able to outnumber and oppress the rest? In an equal degree does the increased variety of parties comprised within the Union increase this security. Does it, in fine, consist in the greater obstacles opposed to the concert and accomplishment of the secret wishes of an unjust and interested majority? Here again the extent of the Union gives it the most palpable advantage.

The influence of factious leaders may kindle a flame within their particular States but will be unable to spread a general conflagration through the other States. A religious sect may degenerate into a political faction in a part of the Confederacy; but the variety of sects dispersed over the entire face of it must secure the national councils against any danger from that source. A rage for paper money, for an abolition of debts, for an equal division of property, or for any other improper or wicked project, will be less apt to pervade the whole body of the Union than a particular member of it, in the same proportion as such a malady is more likely to taint a particular county or district than an entire State.

In the extent and proper structure of the Union, therefore, we behold a republican remedy for the diseases most incident to republican government. And according to the degree of pleasure and pride we feel in being republicans ought to be our zeal in cherishing the spirit and supporting the character of Federalists.

FEDERALIST NO. 51 (JAMES MADISON)

To what expedient, then, shall we finally resort, for maintaining in practice the necessary partition of power among the several departments as laid down in the Constitution? The only answer that can be given is that as all these exterior provisions are found to be inadequate, the defect must be supplied, by so contriving the interior structure of the government as that its several constituent parts may, by their mutual relations, be the means of keeping each other in their proper places. Without presuming to undertake a full development of this important idea I will hazard a few general observations which may perhaps place it in a clearer light, and enable us to form a more correct judgment of the principles and structure of the government planned by the convention.

In order to lay a due foundation for that separate and distinct exercise of the different powers of government, which to a certain extent is admitted on all hands to be essential to the preservation of liberty, it is evident that each department should have a will of its own; and consequently should be so constituted that the members of each should have as little agency as possible in the appointment of the members of the others. Were this principle rigorously adhered to, it would require that all the appointments for the supreme executive, legislative, and judiciary magistracies should be drawn from the same fountain of authority, the people, through channels having no communication whatever with one another. Perhaps such a plan of constructing the several departments would be less difficult in practice than it may be in contemplation appear. Some difficulties, however, and some additional expense would attend the execution of it. Some deviations, therefore, from the principle must be admitted. In the constitution of the judiciary department in particular, it might be inexpedient to insist rigorously on the principle; first, because peculiar qualifications being essential in the members, the primary consideration ought to be to select that mode of choice which best secures these qualifications; second, because the permanent tenure by which the appointments are held in that department must soon destroy all sense of dependence on the authority conferring them.

It is equally evident that the members of each department should be as little dependent as possible on those of the others for the emoluments annexed to their offices. Were the executive magistrate, or the judges, not independent of the legislature in this particular, their independence in every other would be merely nominal.

But the great security against a gradual concentration of the several powers in the same department consists in giving to those who administer each department the necessary constitutional means and personal motives to resist encroachments of the others. The provision for defense must in this, as in all other cases, be made commensurate to the danger of attack. Ambition must be made to counteract ambition. The interest of the man must be connected with the constitutional rights of the place. It may be a reflection on human nature that such devices should be necessary to control the abuses of government. But what is government itself but the greatest of all reflections on human nature? If men were angels no government would be necessary. If angels were to govern men, neither external nor internal controls on government would be necessary. In framing a government which is to be administered by men over men, the great difficulty lies in this: you must first enable the government to control the governed; and in the next place oblige it to control itself. A dependence on the people is, no doubt, the primary control on the government; but experience has taught mankind the necessity of auxiliary precautions.

This policy of supplying, by opposite and rival interests, the defect of better motives, might be traced through the whole system of human affairs, private as well as public. We see it particularly displayed in all the subordinate distributions of power, where the constant aim is to divide and arrange the several offices in such a manner as that each may be a check on the other—that the private interest of every individual may be a sentinel over the public rights. These inventions of prudence cannot be less requisite in the distribution of the supreme powers of the State.

But it is not possible to give to each department an equal power of self-defense. In republican government, the legislative authority necessarily predominates. The remedy for this inconveniency is to divide the legislature into different branches; and to render them, by different modes of election and different principles of action, as little connected with each other as the nature of their common functions and their common dependence on the society will admit. It may even be necessary to guard against dangerous encroachments by still further precautions. As the weight of the legislative authority requires that it should be thus divided, the weakness of the executive may require, on the other hand, that it should be fortified. An absolute negative on the legislature appears, at first view, to be the natural defense with which the executive magistrate should be armed. But perhaps it would be neither altogether safe nor alone sufficient. On ordinary occasions it might not be exerted with the requisite firmness, and on extraordinary occasions it might be perfidiously abused. May not this defect of an absolute negative be supplied by some qualified connection between this weaker department and the weaker branch of the stronger department, by which the latter may be led to support the constitutional rights of the former, without being too much detached from the rights of its own department?

If the principles on which these observations are founded be just, as I persuade myself they are, and they be applied as a criterion to the several State constitutions, and to the federal Constitution, it will be found that if the latter does not perfectly correspond with them, the former are infinitely less able to bear such a test.

There are, moreover, two considerations particularly applicable to the federal system of America, which place that system in a very interesting point of view.

First. In a single republic, all the power surrendered by the people is submitted to the administration of a single government; and the usurpations are guarded against by a division of the government into distinct and separate departments. In the compound republic of America, the power surrendered by the people is first divided between two distinct governments, and then the portion allotted to each subdivided among distinct and separate departments. Hence a double security arises to the rights of the people. The different governments will control each other, at the same time that each will be controlled by itself.

Second. It is of great importance in a republic not only to guard the society against the oppression of its rulers, but to guard one part of the society against the injustice of the other part. Different interests necessarily exist in different classes of citizens. If a majority be united by a common interest, the rights of the minority will be insecure. There are but two methods of providing against this evil: the one by creating a will in the community independent of the majority—that is, of the society itself; the other, by comprehending in the society so many separate descriptions of citizens as will render an unjust combination of a majority of the whole very improbable, if not impracticable. The first method prevails in all governments possessing an hereditary or self-appointed authority. This, at best, is but a precarious security; because a power independent of the society may as well espouse the unjust views of the major as the rightful interests of the minor party, and may possibly be turned against both parties. The second method will be exemplified in the federal republic of the United States. Whilst all authority in it will be derived from and dependent on the society, the society itself will be broken into so many parts, interests and classes of citizens, that the rights of individuals, or of the minority, will be in little danger from interested combinations of the majority. In a free government the security for civil rights must be the same as that for religious rights. It consists in the one case in the multiplicity of interests, and in the other in the multiplicity of sects. The degree of security in both cases will depend on the number of interests and sects; and this may be presumed to depend on the extent of country and number of people comprehended under the same government. This view of the subject must particularly recommend a proper federal system to all the sincere and considerate friends of republican government, since it shows that in exact proportion as the territory of the Union may be formed into more circumscribed Confederacies, or States, oppressive combinations of a majority will be facilitated; the best security, under the republican forms, for the rights of every class of citizen, will be diminished; and consequently the stability and independence of some member of the government, the only other security, must be proportionately increased. Justice is the end of government. It is the end of civil society. It ever has been and ever will be pursued until it be obtained, or until liberty be lost in the pursuit. In a society under the forms of which the stronger faction can readily unite and oppress the weaker, anarchy may as truly be said to reign as in a state of nature, where the weaker individual is not secured against the violence of the stronger; and as, in the latter state, even the stronger individuals are prompted, by the uncertainty of their condition, to submit to a government which may protect the weak as well as themselves; so, in the former state, will the more powerful factions or parties be gradually induced, by a like motive, to wish for a government which will protect all parties, the weaker as well as the more powerful. It can be little doubted that if the State of Rhode Island was separated from the Confederacy and left to itself, the insecurity of rights under the popular form of government within such narrow limits would be displayed by such reiterated oppressions of factious majorities that some power altogether independent of the people would soon be called for by the voice of the very factions whose misrule had proved the necessity of it.

In the extended republic of the United States, and among the great variety of interests, parties, and sects which it embraces, a coalition of a majority of the whole society could seldom take place on any other principles than those of justice and the general good; whilst there being thus less danger to a minor from the will of a major party, there must be less pretext, also, to provide for the security of the former, by introducing into the government a will not dependent on the latter, or, in other words, a will independent of the society itself. It is no less certain than it is important, notwithstanding the contrary opinions which have been entertained, that the larger the society, provided it lie within a practicable sphere, the more duly capable it will be of self-government. And happily for the republican cause, the practicable sphere may be carried to a very great extent by a judicious modification and mixture of the federal principle.

GLOSSARY

527 committees Advocacy groups that are allowed to advertise on political issues and are not subject to regulation by the Federal Election Commission.

A

accountability The capacity to impose consequences on officials for their actions, including removal from office.

accountability (educational policy) Education policies that hold educators individually or collectively responsible (or "accountable") for the progress made by their students.

administrative discretion Opportunity granted to bureaucrats by Congress to use their judgment in making decisions between alternative courses of action.

administrative strategy Strategy to achieve the administration's goals by using the president's budget, personnel, reorganization, and regulatory powers.

adversarial system Criminal justice system in which defendants are presumed innocent, and guilt is determined when prosecutors face off against defense attorneys in a trial.

affirmative action A policy intended to promote equal opportunities for members of previously disadvantaged groups in education and employment.

agenda-setting Stage in the policy-making process where officials identify the problems that government needs to address.

agents of political socialization The people and institutions from whom we learn about politics.

agricultural association An organization either of farmers in general, or of a particular kind of farmer.

American exceptionalism The idea that the political culture of the United States is distinctive in the world and that the United States has a special role to build democracy in the world.

amicus curiae **briefs** "Friend of the court" briefs submitted by third parties who are not named in a case but who hope to influence the outcome of a particular case.

Anti-Federalists States' rights advocates who opposed the ratification of the Constitution.

antitrust policies Government legislation and regulations designed to prevent collusion among businesses that would suppress competition in order to produce unnaturally high prices.

appellate court A court that hears appeals from lower courts. Appeals involve questions of law rather than questions of fact.

appellate jurisdiction The authority of a higher court to review the judgment of a lower court.

arms race A competition between nations to exceed each other's military arsenals.

Article I courts Federal courts created by Congress under its power derived from Article I of the Constitution. Judges in these courts serve for fixed terms.

Article III courts Federal courts created by Article III of the Constitution. Judges in these courts have life tenure.

Articles of Confederation The first constitution of the United States (1781–1788), under which states retained sovereignty over all issues not specifically delegated to the weak central government, comprising a unicameral (one-house) legislature and no independent executive or judiciary.

attack ads Television ads criticizing the opponent, usually in terms of the opponent's positions on issues and his or her record in office.

attitudinal model A model of judicial decision making that assumes judges will decide cases according to their ideological preferences (or attitudes).

Australian ballot A set of reforms introduced in the 1880s and 1890s to make elections more fair and secret.

automatic registration Enrollment of voters done by the government automatically, without requiring the individual to take any particular action to be eligible to vote.

B

baby boom generation Millions of Americans born between 1946 and 1964 whose approaching retirement poses financial problems for Social Security and Medicare.

bad tendency test The least protective free speech test, which allows government to restrict speech that merely poses a tendency or possibility to do harm (as opposed to a clear and present danger).

balance of payments deficit The deficit that arises when the total value of goods and services sold by Americans to non-Americans is less than the total value of goods and services purchased by Americans from abroad.

bicameral legislature A legislature that has two chambers, with each chamber typically reflecting a different part of society or political grouping.

Bill of Rights The first 10 amendments of the U.S. Constitution, which form the basis of civil liberties.

bill Proposal for government action that is introduced in either the House or Senate and may result in a law.

bipartisan consensus Agreement between Democrats and Republicans on the basic direction of U.S. foreign policy.

bipartisanship Broad agreement on policy across the membership of both major U.S. parties, as in the containment of Soviet expansion following World War II.

Black Codes Post-Civil War laws that perpetuated discrimination against African Americans.

block grants Funds from the national government to state and local governments that are earmarked for some general policy area, such as education, while giving the recipients flexibility to spend those funds within that policy area as they see fit.

Bretton Woods system System of international agreements created at the end of World War II that created a global financial and trade system dominated by the U.S. dollar.

brief A written statement of legal arguments submitted by the parties in a case and sometimes by outside groups.

Brown v. Board of Education (1954) Supreme Court decision that overturned the "separate but equal" doctrine and declared racially segregated schools to be unconstitutional.

budget deficit Result of government spending more in any given year than it receives in revenues and making up the difference by borrowing money from citizens and noncitizens.

budget resolution Initial step in the congressional budget process that establishes broad guidelines on government revenue and spending for the next fiscal year and gives specific amounts for the programs that fall within different committees' jurisdictions.

bureaucracy Structure created to achieve complex goals through coordinated action undertaken either by governments (public bureaucracy) or corporations (private bureaucracy).

bureaucrat An employee of a government or corporation, often with the negative connotation of being overly concerned with the application of rules.

C

cabinet Group of senior advisors to either a president or prime minister who head a major department and meet collectively to discuss policy and political issues.

cap and trade system Strategy to reduce greenhouse gas emissions and encourage technological innovation by allowing industries to emit carbon dioxide and to buy and sell pollution permits.

capitalism An economic system distinguished by its reliance on the self-interested decisions of producers and consumers exchanging items of value in a market of supply and demand largely free of government direction.

categorical grants Funds from the national government to state and local governments that must be used to implement a specific federal regulation in a particular way, leaving recipients no flexibility regarding how to spend the money.

caucus A gathering of party supporters at the neighborhood level who select delegates to a state nominating convention, which in turn selects delegates to the national nominating convention.

central clearance Central coordinating practice established in the 1930s to review all legislative proposals arising from executive branch agencies in light of the president's agenda to determine whether they were consistent or inconsistent with those goals.

champion A member of Congress or the legislature who personally believes strongly in the goals of an interest group and is willing to work hard to help the group achieve its goals.

checks and balances A method to protect against unrestrained governmental power by dividing and sharing powers among the legislative, executive, and judicial branches.

chief administrator Role established in Article II of the Constitution, the wording of which suggests the president's responsibilities to direct the national administrative apparatus.

chief budgeter Presidential role established by the Budget and Accounting Act of 1921, which instituted more regular procedures for creating and overseeing a unified federal budget.

chief communicator Informal role that presidents have come to play by being the focal point of media coverage and the public's attention on major matters of national policy.

chief diplomat Role established in Article II of the Constitution regarding the president's powers to conduct foreign affairs.

chief economist Presidential role that emerged from the aggressive economic leadership of Franklin D. Roosevelt during the Great Depression of the 1930s and was codified by

the Employment Act of 1946, which requires that the president submit an annual economic report dealing with macroeconomic policy (employment, production, and investment).

chief legislator Role established in Article II of the Constitution that outlines the president's checks on Congress.

chief magistrate Implied role established in Article II of the Constitution dealing with the president's responsibilities in enforcing the laws and ensuring effective operation of the courts.

circuit riding The burdensome practice, minimized in 1869 but not completely abolished until 1911, of Supreme Court justices traveling to ("riding") an assigned circuit to decide cases.

citizen A member of a country's population who is legally recognized as a subject or national of the country.

citizen group A membership organization based on a shared set of policy goals; the group is open to all who agree with the policy goals of the organization.

citizen journalist A non-professional who reports news via alternative outlets such as the Internet or other social media.

civil case A case in which one party sues another, often for monetary damages.

civil liberties The basic freedoms that citizens enjoy from governmental interference, such as the freedoms of speech, press, assembly, and religion, and the guarantees of due process and other specific protections accorded to criminal defendants.

Civil Rights Act of 1964 The most sweeping civil rights legislation since the 1870s, which expanded civil rights and increased protections against various forms of discrimination.

Civil Rights Cases (1883) Cases wherein the Supreme Court ruled that Congress did not have the authority to outlaw private discrimination in business establishments.

civil rights Freedom from governmental discrimination (unequal treatment) based on age, gender, race, or other personal characteristics.

civil service laws Laws requiring that public jobs be filled on the basis of competitive examinations.

class action A lawsuit brought by one or more plaintiffs on behalf of a larger group that shares a common legal claim.

classical liberalism The doctrine that a society is good only to the extent that all of its members are able to develop their capacities to the fullest, and that to encourage this result, government should intervene as little as possible in people's lives.

clear and present danger test A free speech test that allows government to restrict only speech that poses a clear and present danger of substantive evil; over time it has become increasingly protective of speech.

closed primary A primary election in which only those who have registered with a party designation may vote; they may vote only in that party's primary.

closed rule Restrictive guidelines provided by the House Rules Committee that preclude amendments made from the floor during consideration of a bill.

cloture Senate rules provision that allows 60 votes to conclude debate on a bill and bring it to a vote on the floor.

cluster sample An approximation of a true random sample, in which a sample of localities is randomly drawn and then a small random sample of individuals are interviewed in each locality.

Cold War (1947–1991) The period of heightened tensions and competition (economic, ideological, and arms) between the United States and the Soviet Union.

command economy Soviet-style system where government officials exercise broad control to decide the allocation of resources, levels of production, and prices of goods.

Commander-in-Chief Role established in Article II of the Constitution regarding the president's oversight of the nation's military forces.

commerce clause Article I, Section 8 of the Constitution, which gives Congress the authority to "regulate Commerce

with foreign Nations, and among the several States, and with the Indian Tribes."

committee government Period during the mid-twentieth century when chairs of the standing committees were the most powerful figures in the Congress.

committee jurisdiction Defined areas of standing committee responsibilities, comprising the policy areas, programs, and agencies that each committee oversees.

committee of the whole Situation in which the whole House or whole Senate considers business rather than delegating work to committees.

comparison Comparing aspects of a country's government and politics to those aspects in other countries, to better understand their causes.

competitive bipartisanship Agreement between the president and the opposing party's congressional leaders in selected policy areas while they continue to disagree in others.

concurrent powers Powers shared by the national government and the states (both, for example, have the power to tax).

concurring opinion A written opinion by a judge who agrees with the outcome of a case but not with its legal reasoning.

confederal system A system of government in which power rests primarily with regional entities that have banded together to form a league of independent governments.

confederation A union of independent, sovereign states whose central government is charged with defense and foreign affairs, but where the primary power—especially with regard to domestic politics—rests with the individual states.

conference A meeting of Supreme Court justices in which they discuss cases and vote on how those cases should be decided.

conference committee Temporary committee, consisting of both House and Senate members, formed to resolve differences in versions of a bill approved by both chambers before it can be sent to the president.

Congressional Budget Office Specialized staff created in 1973 to assist Congress in making budget decisions.

congressional campaign committees Four committees, two for each party in the Senate and the House of Representatives, that recruit able candidates for Senate or House seats and raise money for congressional campaigns.

conservatism In the United States, the ideology that supports government intervention on behalf of religious values but opposes intervention in the economic sphere.

conservative coalition The voting alliance of a majority of Republicans with conservative Southern Democrats (a minority of Democrats) that frequently frustrated the efforts of liberal reformers from 1940 to 1964 and after.

constituency service Assistance provided by representatives and senators to help residents of their districts or states resolve problems involving government programs and agencies.

constitutional theory View of the president's powers, elaborated by William Howard Taft, as strictly limited to those enumerated in the Constitution or conferred by congressional statutes.

consumer interest A group of people consuming a product.

consumer protection Laws and rules designed to protect citizens from unsafe products and unfair business practices.

containment United States policy following World War II of using military alliances to prevent the expansion of Soviet influence.

continuing resolution When Congress and the president fail to meet the October 1 deadline for approving a new fiscal year budget, they can adopt a temporary action that allows those programs lacking a new annual appropriation to remain in operation.

conventional participation Routine behavior that occurs within the formal governmental process of a democracy, such as voting in elections, working for a candidate or party, putting a bumper sticker on your car, or contacting a member of Congress.

cooperative federalism An interpretation of federalism that favors national supremacy and assumes that states will cooperate in the enforcement of federal regulations.

coordinate construction Refers to constitutional interpretation by Congress or the president. Proponents of coordinate construction believe that all three branches of government (not just the judiciary) have the power and duty to interpret the Constitution.

cost of living adjustment (COLA) Automatic increase in benefits paid by Social Security to retirees to keep pace with rising prices.

courts of general jurisdiction Courts that have broad authority to hear a wide range of cases.

courts of limited jurisdiction Courts that hear a specialized type of case (such as Traffic Court).

criminal case A case brought by the government against a party accused of breaking the law.

critical election An election that causes the bases of support for the two main parties to change fairly suddenly.

cross-partisanship A president's efforts to find selected members of the opposing party who will vote for certain policy proposals, often in exchange for the president's support for a goal of their own.

crossover voting Voting in a primary election for a party other than the one with which you are registered.

D

de facto **segregation** Racial separation in the schools that results from the private decisions of citizens on where to live.

de jure **segregation** Racial separation in the schools that results from official policies of states or localities.

debt ceiling The official limit set by Congress and the president on the federal government's ability to borrow funds through the sale of Treasury bonds.

Declaration of Independence A statement written by Thomas Jefferson and approved by the Second Continental Congress on July 4, 1776, that asserted

the independence of the American colonies from Great Britain.

defendant The party against whom a legal action is brought.

delegate model A form of representation in which legislators closely reflect the preferences and opinions of constituents in discharging their representative responsibilities—for example, voting the way constituents prefer on an issue.

delegated authority Power to make decisions enjoyed by an agency or department that was approved by Congress.

delegation Reliance by elected officials on career bureaucrats to provide the details needed to translate broad policy goals into specific actions.

democracy Rule by the people.

depression Decline in economic activity (GDP) over a sustained period that totals 10 percent or more.

deregulation Efforts during the 1970s, 1980s, and 1990s to remove many forms of economic regulation created earlier in the nation's history to control the business practices of airlines, communications technology, and banking.

descriptive representation Belief that the extent to which a legislature reflects the demographic composition of the larger population is vitally important in determining the legislature's responsiveness to group needs.

détente A relaxing of superpower tensions during the Cold War in the 1970s resulting from efforts of President Richard Nixon and Henry Kissinger, his National Security Adviser.

deterrence A military strategy designed to prevent an opponent from launching an attack because of the damage that the other country will in turn suffer.

direct democracy Democracy in which all of the people of a community gather to decide policies for the community.

direct primary An election to determine a party's nominee for a general election.

discharge petition Parliamentary maneuver that allows a majority of House members to bring a bill up for a vote on the floor even though the

responsible committee has not provided a final report.

discretionary spending One-third of the annual budget for which funding must be reapproved by Congress each year, subjecting these programs to annual changes.

dissenting opinion A written opinion by a judge who disagrees with the outcome of a case.

divided government When political systems elect the president and legislature independently, conflict can easily arise if Congress is controlled by a party other than that of the presidency.

docket A list of cases that a court is scheduled to decide.

dual court system The existence of separate national and local courts in a federal system.

dual federalism An interpretation of federalism that favors states' rights and regards states and the national government as "dual sovereigns" (two relative equals).

due process clauses Clauses in the Fifth and Fourteenth Amendments that prevent the federal government (in the case of the Fifth) and states (in the case of the Fourteenth) from depriving people of life, liberty, or property without fair proceedings.

E

earmark Provision in a bill that provides a benefit to a specific organization or for a specific project, either through direct spending or a tax break.

economic regulation Efforts by government to establish and maintain fair competition in markets to help consumers.

economic stabilizer Role of American government to manage unemployment and inflation in order to prevent the disruption and human costs caused by the boom and bust rhythm of the business cycle.

elastic clause (necessary and proper clause) This constitutional provision provided Congress with flexibility, allowing it to determine which new areas of national need it would address and which areas of government activity it would move into to fulfill its responsibilities.

Electoral College The system by which presidents are elected in the United States. Voters vote for a set of electors, and the set that wins casts its vote for the candidate to which it is pledged.

electoral mobilization Energizing of large numbers of people to act together.

electoral realignment A new and lasting rearrangement of the geographic and social bases of support for the parties, ushered in by a critical election.

electoral system A set of rules to determine, based on the outcome of an election, which individuals will hold office.

energy security The ability of the United States to meet its own energy needs.

enlargement Clinton-era policy encouraging nations to adopt democracy and market economies as the way to overcome uncertainties in a post–Cold War world.

enrolled bill Final version of a bill that has survived the legislative process and is sent to the president for his signature or veto.

entitlement program Programs such as Medicare and Social Security, in which benefits are provided to all citizens who meet eligibility qualifications established by law.

enumerated powers Powers specifically listed in the Constitution, such as congressional powers outlined in Article I, Section 8.

Equal Pay Act (1963) Legislation that prohibits wage discrimination based on sex.

Equal Rights Amendment (ERA) A proposed constitutional amendment that would have guaranteed that the government could not deny or abridge the rights of women on account of their sex. It was not ratified.

equal time rule An FCC regulation that requires a broadcast outlet that sells air time for a political advertisement for one candidate to provide equal time for any other candidate who wishes to purchase it.

Era of Good Feelings A brief period centering on the election of 1820 when the Federalists were in sharp decline and there was no organized opposition to the dominant Democratic-Republican Party.

establishment clause First Amendment provision that prevents government from imposing religion on citizens and is used to justify the separation of church and state.

exclusionary rule Principle, created by the Supreme Court, that illegally seized evidence may not be introduced in criminal trials.

Executive Office of the President Bureaucratic structure created in 1939 to house the personal staff and professional staff units created to help the president discharge a growing range of responsibilities.

executive orders Unilateral decrees issued by presidents to deal with policy or procedural matters that fall under their authority.

exit polls Polls conducted on Election Day at the voting places to provide television news stations with instantaneous analysis of what was moving the voters on that day.

extradition clause A provision of Article IV, Section 2 of the Constitution that requires states to return (extradite), upon request, a fugitive who has fled the law to the state that has jurisdiction over the crime.

F

failed states Nations in danger of collapse because their governments are unable to protect citizens from violence and terrorism or to provide essential services (health, transportation, communication).

Fairness Doctrine An FCC regulation in place from 1949 to 1987 that required broadcast licensees to devote a reasonable percentage of their broadcast time to conveying a balanced discussion of public issues of interest and importance to the community.

fairness The belief that everyone should be treated in the way that they deserve.

fascism A nationalist, racist ideology of the 1930s that centered power on a single charismatic leader.

fast-track legislation Expedited procedures used to speed up the ordinary legislative process, usually through bypassing a time-consuming stage such as committee consideration.

Federal Communications Commission (FCC) An independent U.S. government agency created by the Communications Act of 1934 to oversee and regulate the broadcast industry.

federal funds rate The interest charges that banks collect from each other for loans, which are set by a committee of the Federal Reserve Board in order to influence economic activity through monetary policy.

federal question A dispute over how to interpret the U.S. Constitution, acts of Congress, or a federal treaty. Cases involving a federal question can move from state court to federal court.

Federal Reserve Board An independent federal agency created in 1913 to regulate the banking industry and set monetary policy.

federal system A system in which power is formally divided between the national government and regional entities such as states.

Federalist Papers Essays by James Madison, Alexander Hamilton, and John Jay. Supporting ratification of the Constitution. Originally published in newspapers under the pseudonym "Publius" (Latin for "the people"), they were gathered together in 1788 and published in two volumes as *The Federalist*.

Federalists Those who supported ratification of the Constitution and the stronger national government that it created.

federally funded research and development centers (FFRDCs) Private, nonprofit corporations that perform contract work for the government, such as the Rand Corporation.

felony A serious criminal offense, such as murder.

Fifteenth Amendment (1870) Constitutional amendment guaranteeing that the right to vote will not be denied based on race, color, or previous condition of servitude.

filibuster Delay tactic used in the Senate that rests on members' right to speak as long as they desire on a topic, thereby preventing a vote from being taken.

filtering The process by which the media decide what constitutes "news"—what to cover and what not to cover.

First Party System The period from 1800 to 1820, which was marked by the appearance of the new Democratic-Republican Party and the gradual decline of their opponents, the Federalists.

fiscal policy Efforts made by Congress and the president to stabilize the economy through the taxing, spending, and borrowing decisions made as part of the annual budget process.

fiscal year Period covered by the budget decisions made annually, running from October 1 to September 30 for the federal government and July 1 to June 30 for many state governments.

focus group A small group of people who meet with campaign workers to discuss issues and a candidate.

foreign policy The wide range of ways in which one nation interacts with other nations and with non-governmental organizations in the international and global systems.

Fourteenth Amendment (1868) Constitutional amendment containing the guarantee that no state shall deprive any person of the equal protection of the laws.

Fourth Estate A term used to describe the press as a social and political force independent of government.

framing The way the media interpret, or present, the news that they have decided to cover.

free exercise clause First Amendment provision that protects the right of citizens to practice their religion without governmental interference.

free riders Those who take advantage of the fact that a public good cannot possibly be denied to anyone, by refusing to pay their share of the cost of providing the public good.

frontload To move a state's primary or caucuses to the earliest date that the party's rules will permit.

fugitive slave clause A provision of Article IV, Section 2 of the Constitution that required the return of escaped slaves to their owners even if they fled to a state where slavery was outlawed. Repealed by the Thirteenth Amendment (1865).

full faith and credit clause The requirement of Article IV, Section 1 of the Constitution that requires states to recognize "the public Acts, Records, and judicial Proceedings of every other state."

G

G.I. Bill Federal education program following World War II that paid the college tuition fees of former servicemen and women.

gatekeeping The role played by reporters in vetting and verifying information and news sources in order to prevent publication of inaccurate information.

gender gap The difference between the percent of women and the percent of men voting for a candidate, which has been significant since about 1980.

general election A regularly scheduled election at which voters make their final choices of public officials.

General Schedule of Classified Positions Matrix of responsibility and experience that specifies the pay that federal civil service employees should receive—for example, a GS-10.

generational effect A change in a whole generation's political viewpoint brought about by an event.

generational replacement Change in overall attitudes caused by differences of opinion between young and old that gradually lead to a shift in overall opinion as older citizens pass from the scene.

gerrymandering Drawing the boundaries of congressional or legislative districts with the deliberate intent to affect the outcomes of elections.

globalization The increasing volume in the flow of information, people, ideas, and goods around the globe as improvements in transportation and communication expand links among nations and their populations.

going public A presidential strategy designed to influence Congress by appealing directly to the public, asking them to pressure legislators for passage of the president's proposals.

government The set of people who make decisions that are binding for all people in the country and have the right to use force and coercion to implement their choices.

Government Accountability Office (GAO) New name (2004) for the original GAO that reflects the agency's broader role in evaluating whether government programs perform in ways consistent with national needs, not just in the expenditure of funds.

government corporations Business enterprises wholly or partly owned by the government that Congress created to perform a public purpose or provide a market-oriented service but are designed to meet their costs by generating revenues through operations.

government sponsored enterprises (GSEs) Financial services corporations created by Congress to provide credit to targeted areas of American life; for example, "Fannie Mae" and "Freddie Mac" specialize in home mortgages.

grandfather clauses Exempted voters from literacy tests and poll taxes if they could prove that their grandfathers had voted before the end of the Civil War.

grant cert The decision by the Supreme Court to issue a writ of certiorari—that is, to agree to review a decision by a lower court.

grassroots lobbying Activities by an interest group to influence a decision by a member of Congress indirectly by mobilizing their supporters in the member's district to bring pressure to bear on the member.

Great Compromise The decision by the Constitutional Convention to resolve the debate over equal versus proportional representation by establishing a bicameral (two-house) legislature with proportional representation in the lower house, equal representation in the upper house, and different methods of selecting representatives for each house.

Great Society Name given to the comprehensive program of action proposed and enacted under the leadership of Lyndon B. Johnson in the mid-1960s, which focused on eliminating poverty and racial injustice in areas such as employment, health care, and education.

greenhouse gas Several gases emitted by human consumption of fuels that retain solar heat rather than allowing it to radiate back into space, therefore producing global warming.

gross domestic product (GDP) Total value of goods and services produced in the economy.

group ratings Scores measuring how often a member of Congress has voted in accordance with an interest group's wishes.

groupthink The tendency within a small group of presidential advisors to agree with one another because finding consensus on policy matters and maintaining group loyalty is more important to them than critically evaluating policy options.

H

head of state Role usually played by an elected president or a monarch who symbolizes the entire nation, is above politics, and therefore exercises very limited political powers, usually in only the most fundamental issues such as forming a new cabinet.

historical analysis Examining the way politics has developed over time in a country, in order to understand how its development has helped to shape its current form.

Honest Leadership and Open Government Act A bill regulating and limiting contacts between lobbyists and members of Congress.

human rights United States pressure on undemocratic governments to extend basic, unalienable freedoms of speech, religion, and the press.

I

idealism The view that American foreign policy should reflect the universal truths contained in the Declaration of Independence.

ideology An interconnected set of ideas.

impeachment Power of the Congress to remove a president from office

before the elected term has expired. Technically, the House impeaches ("charges") a president with "high crimes and misdemeanors" and the Senate may find the president guilty or not guilty of the charges.

implementation The process of carrying out the wishes of Congress as expressed in a policy through the creation and enforcement of programs and regulations by bureaucratic agencies.

implied powers Powers not specifically enumerated in the Constitution, but which are considered "necessary and proper" to carry out the enumerated powers.

incorporation The process by the which the Supreme Court has made specific provisions of the Bill of Rights applicable to state and local governments as well as the federal government.

independent regulatory commissions Type of federal government agency designed to allow experts, not politicians, to oversee and regulate a sector of the economy (for example, railroads) usually to protect consumers from unfair business practices but also to protect the businesses in that sector.

indirect democracy Democracy in which the people do not decide policies for the community themselves, but elect representatives to decide the policies.

individualism The belief that people should have freedom to make decisions and act, with as little government intervention or other control as possible.

initiative A procedure by which a sufficient number of voters, by petition, can place a proposition on the ballot to be decided in a referendum.

inquisitorial system Criminal justice system in which defendants are presumed guilty until proven innocent and guilt is determined by the judge (rather than a jury) who plays an active role in gathering evidence and questioning witnesses.

inside tactics Tactics that involve working directly with government officials.

institutional presidency Term applied to the staff support enjoyed by modern

presidents, especially those staff units with relatively continuous operation such as the Office of Management and Budget, the National Security Council, and the cabinet.

interest group A group of people organized to influence government policies.

internationalism The idea that a country should participate actively in global affairs by cooperating politically and economically with other countries.

Internet polling Drawing a truly random sample and getting the people in the sample to agree (in return for an incentive) to take part in surveys administered online.

Interstate Commerce Commission First federal regulatory agency, created in 1887 and abolished in 1995, which was intended to regulate rates charged by railroads and whose responsibilities were later expanded to include oversight of the trucking industry.

interstate compacts Contracts between two or more states that create an agreement on a particular policy issue.

"introduce" ads Upbeat television ads, usually appearing early in a campaign, that are designed to create a positive first impression of a candidate.

iron curtain Winston Churchill's description of the division of Europe into a free West and Soviet-dominated East.

iron triangle The close relationship established and maintained among a trio of actors: the beneficiaries of a government policy (interest groups), the agency responsible for the beneficial programs (bureaucracy) and the congressional committees responsible for authorizing and funding the programs.

isolationism The policy of limited involvement in international matters that prevailed in the United States throughout most of the nineteenth century and between the two world wars.

issue briefs (or white papers) Discussions of public problems and possible solutions developed and released by non-governmental groups.

J

Jim Crow laws State and local laws requiring the segregation of the races, including prohibition of interracial marriage and mandating of racially segregated schools.

Joint Chiefs of Staff A structure created in 1947 to coordinate action among the separate military services and provide military advice to the president and the Secretary of Defense.

joint committee Congressional committee that includes members from both the Senate and House.

judicial activism The idea that the Supreme Court should strictly scrutinize actions of other branches of government that restrict fundamental rights, such as free speech.

judicial restraint The idea that the Supreme Court should defer to the actions of other branches of government as long as they have a rational basis.

judicial review The power of courts, when confronted with a legitimate case, to review and strike down acts of government that violate the Constitution.

judicial strategy A presidential strategy designed to achieve the administration's goals through the appointment of like-minded judges to the federal judiciary and the establishment of clear priorities for federal law enforcement.

Judiciary Act of 1789 The act of Congress that established lower federal courts in the United States and defined the Supreme Court's appellate jurisdiction.

jurisprudence of original intent An approach to interpreting the Constitution that relies on the original intent of its framers to clarify the meaning of ambiguous clauses.

K

Keynesian economics Set of countercyclical policy prescriptions proposed by British economist John Maynard Keynes at the time of the Great Depression, calling for government to use taxes and expenditures to control economic recessions and expansions.

L

laissez-faire View that originated with eighteenth-century French economists that government should play a minimal role in the economy.

lame duck Description of presidents nearing the end of their fixed term in office who have little remaining leverage to accomplish their policy goals.

League of Nations The international organization established after World War I under the encouragement of Woodrow Wilson.

legal model A model of judicial decision making that assumes judges will decide cases according to the law (as opposed to the attitudinal model).

legislative liaison White House and agency officials whose job is to lobby Congress on behalf of the president or an agency.

legislative strategy Presidential strategy to achieve goals based on proposals presented to Congress for statutory action.

legislative veto Technique that was used by Congress to reject presidential reorganization proposals until it was ruled unconstitutional by the Supreme Court.

libel Written defamation of character, which is not accorded First Amendment protection.

liberalism In the United States, the ideology that opposes government intervention on behalf of religious values but supports intervention in the economic sphere to reduce inequality.

libertarianism In the United States, the ideology that opposes government intervention in any area of people's lives.

literacy tests A precondition for voting in some states, purportedly to verify a voter's ability to read or write, but designed to prevent blacks from voting.

lobbying Attempting to persuade officials to enact a policy.

M

majority opinion A written opinion that expresses the legal reasoning used to justify an appellate court's ruling in a particular case.

majority rule The principle that 50 percent plus one of the people should

be able to elect a majority of elected officials and thereby determine the direction of policy.

majority-minority district A congressional district in which a majority of the electorate are of an ethnic minority. Sometimes these are deliberately created through gerrymandering.

mandatory spending Two-thirds of the federal budget for which funding decisions are not controlled by annual appropriations, particularly entitlements such as Social Security, Medicare, and Medicaid.

***Marbury v. Madison* (1803)** The Supreme Court case that serves as a precedent for the use of judicial review.

margin of error (in polling) Statistical measure of how much the sample estimate from a poll is likely to deviate from the true amount in the full population.

mark up A committee's line-by-line, word-by-word review of a bill's text prior to a final vote on the modified version.

Marshall Plan The program of economic assistance provided by the United States to the nations of Europe following the devastation of World War II.

Martin Luther King, Jr. Prominent civil rights leader who embraced Gandhi's nonviolent civil protest and formed the Southern Christian Leadership Conference in 1957.

Marxism-Leninism Policies established by Vladimir Lenin in Soviet Russia following the 1917 revolution that rested loosely on Karl Marx's philosophical foundations of communism.

mass media The wide array of organizations and outlets that collect and distribute information to the people.

media effects Changes in public opinion based on the influence of the media.

mercantilism Economic policies adopted by European nations (including England) during the seventeenth and eighteenth centuries that treated colonial products, trade, and markets as a way to enrich the mother country.

midterm election Elections held two years after a presidential election, in which all members of the House of Representatives and one-third of Senators are elected, and many states hold elections for governor and other state offices.

minority rights Basic human rights that are considered important to guarantee for minorities in a democracy.

Miranda **warnings** The list of rights that police must read to suspects at the time of arrest, including the right to remain silent and the right to request a lawyer. Absent such warnings, information obtained from suspects is inadmissible in court.

misdemeanor A lesser criminal offense (such as driving over the speed limit).

mixed economy An economic system in which government officials share power with markets in deciding or influencing how resources are allocated in the society.

mobilization An election strategy that relies on getting a candidate's supporters to the polls.

modern presidency Shaped heavily by FDR's 12 years in office, modern presidents are distinguished from earlier executives by the expanded roles they play, the additional staffs they have to help them, and the greater expectations held by the public.

monetary policy Terms under which money and credit are made available to buyers and sellers in the market economy.

Monroe Doctrine (1823) Proclamation of U.S. primacy in the western hemisphere and a warning that European nations should remain uninvolved.

muckraking A type of journalism prevalent in the early part of the twentieth century that exposed corruption in business and government in order to promote reform.

multiparty system A party system in which three or more parties regularly have a significant chance of gaining office.

mutual assured destruction (MAD) The strategic policy adopted by both the United States and the Soviet Union that deterred an opponent's attack by ensuring a devastating retaliatory attack.

N

NAACP National Association for the Advancement of Colored People, an organization devoted to promoting the civil rights of African Americans.

narrowcasting Programming designed to appeal to a particular segment of the population (as opposed to broadcasting, which is designed to appeal to as many people as possible).

national committee A committe that oversees the day-to-day business of the political parties at the national level.

national debt Cumulative total of annual budget deficits.

national nominating convention A national gathering of delegates to choose a political party's presidential nominee, write a platform of policy positions, and transact other national party business.

National Security Council Group created in 1947 to coordinate foreign, defense, financial, and intelligence policies for the president.

national security policy A policy centered on the possible and actual use of force in international affairs.

natural rights Basic rights that all human beings are entitled to, whether or not they are formally recognized by government.

necessary and proper (or "elastic") clause The last clause of Article I, Section 8 of the Constitution, which authorizes Congress to make "all laws which shall be necessary and proper" for executing the Constitution's enumerated powers; sometimes called the elastic clause because it allows congressional powers to expand.

negative view of government A perception that government actions intrude on the privacy and individual rights of citizens.

net neutrality The unhindered flow of information over the Internet without interference by those who run or own the service providers.

New Deal The title given by Franklin D. Roosevelt to characterize the many reform proposals offered during the 1930s to move the United States out of the Great Depression. Teddy Roosevelt had proposed a "Square Deal" and Harry Truman later offered a "Fair Deal"—additional examples of slogans used by presidents to characterize their programs.

New Jersey Plan A plan, favored by small states, to amend (rather than replace) the Articles of Confederation. It would have retained the one-state/one-vote system of voting in the national legislature, with representatives chosen by state legislatures.

new media Media, such as cable television and the Internet, that that led to a vast increase in the amount of information available to the people and allowed targeting of particular segments of the population via specialized channels and Web pages.

Nineteenth Amendment (1920) Constitutional amendment that guaranteed women the right to vote.

No Child Left Behind Bush education reforms adopted by Congress in 2001 that monitored student progress toward mastery of state-defined math, reading, and science standards.

nomination The designation of candidates among whom voters will choose in an election.

North Atlantic Treaty Organization or NATO The military alliance formed by the United States, Canada, and Western European nations to combat Soviet expansion following World War II.

nullification The concept that states can invalidate federal laws that they believe to be unconstitutional.

O

objective journalism A type of journalism that embraces the idea that newspapers should report news in a fair and neutral manner, devoid of partisanship and sensationalism (as opposed to yellow journalism).

Office of Management and Budget (OMB) Successor agency to the Bureau of the Budget, created in 1970 and designed to perform management oversight that went beyond the traditional budget and central clearance functions performed by the BOB.

Office of Personnel Management Agency created in 1978 as part of the Civil Service Reform Act to manage the civil service for presidents.

open primary A primary election in which all voters may participate and may choose which party's primary they wish to vote in.

open rule Guidelines provided by the House Rules Committee that allow germane amendments to be made from the floor during consideration of a bill.

open seat A congressional seat whose sitting member retires, runs for some other office, or dies.

opinion leaders Persons in positions of authority and influence over foreign policy who are more likely to have their voices heard than the average citizen.

oral arguments The opportunity for lawyers on both sides of a case to appear before the appellate courts to give a verbal argument and respond to questions from the judges about why their side should prevail.

original jurisdiction The authority of the Supreme Court to hear a case that originates before it (as opposed to an appeal from a lower court).

outside tactics Tactics that seek to influence officials indirectly, such as working in elections and mobilizing supporters to bring pressure on decision makers.

oversight Review and monitoring by Congress, particularly the relevant authorizing and appropriations committees, of executive branch activities to ensure that they are consistent with legislative intent.

P

pack journalism A type of journalism conducted by groups (or "packs") of reporters who are assigned to cover the same institution, and which is characterized by uniform coverage of issues, reliance on official channels of information, and lack of original research.

paradox of voting The fact that one person's vote is highly unlikely to change the outcome of an election, so there is no concrete benefit for an individual who chooses to vote.

parliamentary system Political system in which the legislature (parliament) selects the executive either through a single party majority or a majority coalition, providing for closer institutional coordination.

partisan press A type of journalism associated with the late 1700s through the early 1800s when newspapers were affiliated with and controlled by a particular political party or emerging political party.

party caucus Term used by House Democrats referring to the meeting of all party members.

party conference Term used by House Republicans and both Democrats and Republicans in the Senate referring to the meeting of all party members.

party identification A sense of belonging to one or another of the political parties.

party in government The elected officials of a party, who organize themselves along party lines.

party in the electorate The party's supporters in the electorate, including those who identify with the party and vote for it and activists who campaign for it.

party organization A formal structure that conducts managerial and legal tasks for the party.

party platform A set of policy positions adopted by a party at its national nominating convention.

party polarization Increased feelings among partisans that their party is right and the other is wrong.

party unity A measure of how often a majority of Republican legislators vote against a majority of Democrat legislators.

patronage Financial rewards (especially public jobs) given to people in return for their political support.

pay for performance Education reform that links teachers' pay to the academic progress of students in their classrooms.

peer groups Groups of friends and acquaintances that can strongly influence our choices and values.

Pendleton Civil Service Reform Act Legislation approved in 1883 that created the U.S. civil service system, in which government employees are chosen based on expertise and experience rather than party loyalty.

penny press Newspapers that emerged in 1830 and that, due to technological advances, sold for one penny—a sixth of what papers had previously sold for. This development made newspapers accessible to a wide array of people from all economic classes.

photo opportunity A time period reserved for the media to photograph a public official, usually staged to reinforce a particular frame or theme that the official wishes to convey to the public.

plaintiff The party that initiates a civil lawsuit.

***Plessy v. Ferguson* (1896)** A Supreme Court ruling that established the "separate but equal" doctrine, upholding state segregation laws.

pocket veto A bill does not become law if the president fails to sign it within the required 10-day period and Congress has adjourned during that time.

police powers The powers reserved to the states under the Tenth Amendment dealing with health, safety, public welfare, and morality.

policy adoption Stage in the policy-making process in which officials decide whether action will be taken and what that action should be.

policy evaluation Final stage in the policy-making process in which officials determine whether the programs put into place are achieving the desired goals.

policy formulation Stage in the policy-making process in which government officials and non-government activists identify solutions to address the nation's problems.

policy implementation Programs or regulations designed to achieve the goals identified in legislative statutes.

political action committee (PAC) An organization that donates money to political candidates and officeholders.

political campaign The period during which candidates try to convince voters to support them.

political consultant Professional political strategist who advises candidates on broad strategy as well as specific logistics.

political culture A people's attitudes, beliefs, and factual assumptions about the basic nature of society and basic principles of politics.

political identity An image of who you are, to the extent that your identity carries political content, such as your religion or your membership in a political party.

political leader Role played by the U.S. president and in parliamentary systems by the prime minister in mobilizing political support behind major policy initiatives, requiring that the leader engage in explicitly political efforts.

political machine A party organization providing its supporters with benefits such as city jobs and other favors, and in return controlling them politically.

political participation All of the various ways that citizens can influence the government.

political party An organization combining activists and potential officeholders, whose purpose is to determine who will hold office.

political socialization The process of learning political values and factual assumptions about politics.

politico model A form of representation in which legislators play different roles depending on whether constituents have strong views on an issue and the nature of that issue.

politics The process by which decisions that are binding for everyone in the country are made, such as a law, a system of taxes, or a social program.

poll A set of questions asked of a carefully constructed sampling of a population, selected in such a way that the people in the sample are likely to mirror the total population fairly accurately.

poll taxes Tax payments required prior to voting; revived by states in the late nineteenth century as a way to prevent poor blacks from voting.

popular legitimacy Belief among the citizens of a political system that the government's actions deserve to be obeyed because they reflect the will of the people.

pork barrel The traditional way to preserve pork for gradual consumption, it refers more recently to public money used to meet local needs that lack a sound public purpose.

position papers Documents prepared by candidates describing in detail their stands on various issues.

positive view of government A perception that government actions are necessary for citizens to realize their full potential.

power of the purse Congressional authority to set the national budget, which provides legislators with enormous influence in the checks and balances system.

precedent A previous court decision that is used to determine the outcome of subsequent cases involving a similar legal question.

prerogative theory View that justifies an executive using discretionary power to act in areas without congressional approval or even to violate the law if such action is in the public good and consistent with the national interest.

presidential system Political system distinguished by having an executive selected separately by the public rather than by the legislature; frequently characterized by fewer parties but higher levels of legislative-executive conflict.

prime minister Executive officer in a parliamentary system who is supported in the legislature by a majority of his or her own party or a majority based on a coalition.

prior restraint Censorship before publication (such as government prohibition against future publication).

privileges and immunities clause A provision of Article IV, Section 2 of the Constitution that forbids a state from depriving citizens of other states the rights it confers upon its own citizens.

producer interest A group of people involved in producing a product.

professional association An organization of members of a profession.

Progressive movement A movement of mostly middle-class reformers in the early twentieth century who worked to eliminate machine politics.

progressive tax system Taxation in which citizens with higher incomes pay a higher percentage of their income in taxes than people in lower income groups.

proportional representation (PR) electoral system An electoral system in which seats are allocated to parties in proportion to their shares of the vote.

proportional tax rates Taxation in which citizens pay the same flat tax rate regardless of income level.

proxy wars Conflicts fought during the Cold War between one of the superpowers and the allies of the other.

public assistance program Policy that provides help to beneficiaries who meet a means test—that is, whose incomes are low enough for them to qualify to receive benefits from public sources.

public good Something that benefits all members of the community and that no one can possibly be prevented from using.

public opinion The collective opinion of citizens on a policy issue or a principle of politics.

public policy Products of political pressures and governmental decision making that result in governmental action or inaction that affects the lives of citizens.

push polls Sets of questions used by political campaigns to present negative information about an opposing candidate by taking advantage of the trust people feel for pollsters.

Q

quasi-governmental organizations (quagos) Hybrid organizations that share some characteristics of public agencies and some features of private corporations, like the Smithsonian Institution.

quasi-non-governmental organizations (quangos) Private-sector organizations that fulfill some of the roles of government agencies, like the disaster recovery activities of the American Red Cross.

R

random digit dialing Drawing a roughly random sample by randomly dialing telephone numbers.

random sample A sample drawn from the full population in such a way that every member of the population has an equal probability of belonging to the sample.

realism or *realpolitik* The view that U.S. foreign policy should serve the nation's self-interest regardless of the tactics used or the nature of the states enlisted as partners.

recession Decline in economic activity (GDP) for a sustained period, often defined as two consecutive quarters or at least six months

recuse When a judge does not participate in a case because of a conflict of interest or prejudice.

redistricting Redrawing the boundaries of congressional or legislative districts because of population shifts that show up every 10 years after the U.S. Census has been conducted.

referendum A provision of elections allowing citizens to vote directly on constitutional amendments or changes in law.

registration A requirement by almost all states that citizens who wish to vote enroll prior to the election.

regressive tax rates Taxation in which the share of citizens' income paid in taxes declines as income increases.

regulated multi-payer system Health care systems where government regulates private health insurance companies that reimburse for medical services provided to citizens.

reorganization authority Powers given to presidents by Congress to propose changes in executive branch organization, subject to a legislative veto.

republic A country that is not ruled by a monarch but by the people through its representatives.

republicanism A form of government in which power rests with the people, but where the people rule only indirectly through elected representatives bound by the rule of law.

responsible party government Doctrine stating that parties should present clear alternative programs and enact them faithfully once in office.

retrospective voting Voting to reelect an official if your life and the lives of those around you have gone well over the years that the person has been in office; if not, voting to oust the official.

rider Amendment to a bill that is usually unrelated to the central subject of the bill; allowed in the Senate but usually not allowed in the House.

rotation in office Principle established by Andrew Jackson that allowed the president to replace persons holding government jobs with loyal supporters.

rugged individualism Widespread belief in the United States that citizens must provide for their own needs rather than rely on government to do so.

rule of four The requirement that four of the nine justices on the Supreme Court vote to grant a writ of certiorari.

rule of law The idea that laws, rather than the whims or personal interests of officials, should determine the government's actions.

Rules Committee Powerful committee in the House of Representatives that reviews all bills to determine the guidelines for debate and amendment under which they will be considered on the floor.

S

safe seats Members of Congress who, election after election, win by large margins.

SALT I and II (Strategic Arms Limitation Treaties) Treaties established between the United States and the Soviet Union in the 1970s to slow the nuclear arms race and control its most dangerous features.

secession The act of withdrawing from membership in a federation.

Second Party System The period from the early 1830s until just before the Civil War, which was marked by rivalry between the Democratic Party and the Whigs.

select committee Congressional committee formed for a specific purpose and limited period of time.

selective benefits Benefits that can be given to some people but withheld from others; they are the opposite of public goods.

Senate Majority Leader Leader of the majority party in the Senate, who plays an important role in managing the business of the chamber.

senatorial courtesy An informal rule that senators will refuse to confirm nominees to the lower federal courts who do not have the support of the senators from the state where the vacancy occurs.

seniority rule Long-running practice followed in Congress in which the member of the majority party with the longest continuous service on a standing committee automatically becomes its chair.

separate but equal doctrine Based on the *Plessy v. Ferguson* ruling that claimed the equal protection clause of the Fourteenth Amendment allows the segregation of races.

separation of powers The division of governmental powers among three separate and co-equal branches: legislative, executive, and judicial.

service provider Government's role in meeting public needs (for example, by providing education, police protection, trash collection, and mail delivery) even when there may be private firms that provide competing services.

shadow government A government-in-waiting in parliamentary systems where leading members of the opposition party speak out on specific areas of government policy as they prepare to assume leading roles should they gain control of government.

Shays' Rebellion An armed rebellion by farmers in Massachusetts who, facing foreclosure, tried using force to shut down courthouses where the foreclosures were issued. The national government's inability to quell the rebellion made the event a potent symbol of the weakness of the Articles of Confederation.

single-member-district, plurality (SMDP) electoral system An electoral system in which the country is divided into districts, each of which elects a single member to the Congress or parliament. The candidate receiving a plurality of votes wins the seat.

single-payer system Health care system in which the government collects revenues and pays the providers for services delivered to citizens, as in Canada and the United Kingdom.

slander Spoken defamation of character, which is not accorded First Amendment protection.

social contract The idea, drawn from the writings of John Locke and others, that government is accountable to the people and bound to protect the natural rights of its citizens. If government breaks this contract, the people have the right to rebel and replace the government with one that will enforce it.

social insurance program Government program such as Social Security or Medicare that spreads the risk of income loss or illness across a broad population rather than requiring each individual to bear the risk alone.

social media Technologies such as blogs, texting, video file sharing, and other Internet resources that enable people to exchange information. These technologies have helped to blur the line between news consumer and news producer.

social movement An informally organized, often temporary group that springs up around an issue or an event to advance a specific point of view.

social regulation Laws and rules created to prevent corporations from engaging in practices that result in undesirable outcomes for society, such as air and water pollution or unsafe working conditions.

social safety net The collection of policies designed to meet the needs of poor and disadvantaged citizens in a nation.

socialism An ideology that favors having the government take over most businesses and run them in the interest of social and economic equality.

socialist system An economic system, developed in the nineteenth century as a way to correct many excesses of capitalism, in which the government acts as both an owner of enterprises and a distributor of goods and services.

soft power Increasingly important forms of nonmilitary influence that a state can exercise in international relations, including economic importance, diplomacy, the control of scarce resources, and moral authority.

solicitor general A senior member of the Justice Department who is responsible for handling all appeals of cases in which the U.S. government is a party.

Speaker of the House of Representatives Constitutionally prescribed position of the presiding officer in the House, which became more partisan and more program-focused in the nineteenth century.

spin Attempts by government officials to influence how the media will report an event by suggesting how a story should be framed.

split-ticket voting When several candidates for different offices appear on a ballot, the practice of voting for a candidate of one party for one office and a candidate of another party for another office.

spoils system Practice popular in the nineteenth century that allowed presidents to appoint party loyalists and campaign workers to government jobs as a reward for their support, establishing the adage of "to the victor belongs the spoils."

Stamp Act Congress The first national meeting of representatives from the colonies in 1765. In response to duties (taxes) imposed by Parliament on the colonies through the Stamp Act, this Congress passed a Declaration of Rights that denounced taxation without representation—an important step toward the American Revolution.

standing A party who has been injured by some law or action and thus has the legal authority to bring a lawsuit.

standing committee A permanent committee in the House or Senate whose responsibilities carry over from one Congress to the next, as does much of its membership.

stare decisis Latin for "let the law stand," this is the practice of relying on precedent to decide cases.

START I and II (Strategic Arms Reduction Treaties) Treaties established between the United States and the Soviet Union in the 1990s to reverse the growth of nuclear weapons and produce some disarmament.

State of the Union Address Annual address delivered by the president in person to a joint session of Congress and other government leaders. Today this address is broadcast to a primetime television audience.

stewardship theory View of the president's role as a "steward" of the people who serves their interests because of the president's unique role as the representative of the entire nation and who is therefore empowered to define the position as broadly as necessary.

strategic model A model of judicial decision making that assumes judges are rational actors who will strategically try to get as close to their preferences as possible by building winning coalitions.

substantive due process A judicially created concept whereby the due process clauses of the Fifth and Fourteenth Amendments can be used to strike down laws that are deemed to be arbitrary or unfair.

substantive representation The capacity of a legislator or a legislature to represent the interests of groups despite not sharing the demographic characteristics of that group.

Super PAC Independent campaign organization that may raise unlimited funds, and spend them on overt attacks or support for candidates; it may not coordinate its strategy with campaigns.

Super Tuesday The first Tuesday in a primary season on which parties allow states (except for early contests like New Hampshire or Iowa) to schedule primaries or caucuses; large numbers of states usually schedule their contests for this day, which makes it "super."

superdelegates Delegates to the Democratic Party's national nominating convention who are not selected through a primary or caucus procedure but go to the convention because of the office they hold in the party or the government.

superpower A dominant nation in the international system able to project its influence, either economic or military, far beyond its boundaries in order to pursue its interests.

supplemental appropriation Spending decisions made by Congress and the President outside the regular budget process.

supply-side economics Policies designed to stimulate producers' economic activity by reducing tax rates and removing the costs of regulation.

supremacy clause Article VI, Clause 2 of the Constitution specifying that federal laws and treaties passed pursuant to the Constitution trump contradictory state laws dealing with the same topic.

symbolic speech Communication that is neither spoken nor written but is nonetheless accorded free speech protection under the First Amendment.

T

talk radio A radio forum that opens the lines to listeners to discuss various topics of interest.

targeted marketing Using consumer research to divide voters into tiny segments based on a wide variety of indicators so that different messages can be sent to various groups of voters.

tariff A tax levied by the government on goods imported into a nation, applied in order to raise revenue or in order to protect the domestic manufacturers of the same item.

tax loopholes Special treatment given to groups of taxpayers in the tax laws that help lower or eliminate their tax burden.

Tenth Amendment The amendment to the Constitution that says: "The powers not delegated to the United States by the Constitution, nor prohibited by it to the States, are reserved to the States respectively, or to the people."

think tanks Organizations whose specialists conduct research and exchange their views with other experts from government and the media.

third parties Small political parties that are so greatly handicapped by the single-member, plurality electoral system in the United States and other obstacles that they have a low probability of winning office.

Thirteenth Amendment (1865) Constitutional amendment that abolished slavery and other forms of involuntary servitude.

Three-Fifths Compromise The decision by the Constitutional Convention to count slaves as three-fifths of a person for purposes of representation.

time, place, and manner restrictions Stipulation that the freedoms of speech and assembly do not mean that people can assemble anytime, anywhere, and say whatever they want, however they want.

Title IX One of the Education Amendments of 1972 designed to abolish all forms of sex discrimination in public education.

tracking polls Short, simple polls that are repeated day after day to allow a candidate to track exactly how a campaign is going on a daily basis.

trade association An organization of businesses who share the same trade.

trial court Courts where cases originate and trials take place (as opposed to appellate courts).

trustee model A form of representation in which legislators are not required to reflect the preferences and opinions of their constituents because voters expect them to use their own knowledge and good judgment.

Twenty-Second Amendment Advanced in 1946 by the first Republican-controlled Congress since 1930, limits presidents to two terms and ensures that their final months or years in office will be less productive.

two-party system A party system with two, and only two, parties that regularly nominate candidates with a serious chance of winning office.

U

U.S. courts of appeals An intermediate level of federal appellate courts.

U.S. district courts Federal trial courts, where most federal cases are initiated.

unconventional participation Behavior that challenges the normal workings of government by disrupting it or by making people uncomfortable.

undeclared wars Conflicts for which the U.S. government did not formally declare war as specified in the Constitution.

unfunded mandate A legal requirement imposed on states by Congress to administer a program that comes with no federal money to pay for it.

unified government Distinct from divided government, a situation in which the presidency and the two houses of Congress are controlled by the same political party, providing the basis for joint action.

unitary executive doctrine Controversial view of the president's constitutional authority, espoused by the George W. Bush administration, that rejects congressional or judicial encroachments on executive authority and asserts the right of presidents to take actions that might even violate the law.

unitary system A system of government in which the national government has ultimate control over all areas of policy.

United Nations (UN) The international organization created following World War II to promote world peace and mutual security through international cooperation in solving world problems.

universal health care Policies ensuring that all citizens of a nation receive adequate health care.

unpledged delegates Delegates to the Republican Party's national nominating convention who are not selected through a primary or caucus procedure but go to the convention by right of the office they hold in the party or the government.

V

veto Constitutional power of a president to reject legislation passed by the legislature. In the United States, presidents have 10 days to act on legislation, which may be signed or returned with objections to the house in which it originated. Congress may override the veto and pass the bill by means of a two-thirds majority in both houses.

Virginia Plan A plan, favored by large states, to replace (rather than amend) the Articles of Confederation and create a strong national government consisting of three branches. It also called for replacing the one-state/one-vote system used under the Articles of Confederation with proportional voting power in the legislature.

Voting Rights Act of 1965 Landmark legislation that outlawed literacy tests and took other steps to guarantee the voting rights of African Americans.

W

War Powers Resolution Passed by Congress over Nixon's veto in 1973, this law establishes a framework for Congress to participate in presidential decisions to use force—short of a formal declaration of war—and to halt such a military deployment.

Warsaw Pact The collective security alliance formed by the Soviet Union with its satellite nations in Eastern Europe to combat NATO and maintain communist governments.

Watergate The political scandals associated with Richard Nixon, triggered by the judicial, congressional, and media investigations into the illegal break-in at the Democratic National Committee's offices in the Watergate office complex in Washington, D.C.

Whig Party A party active from 1830 to the verge of the Civil War; it opposed the extension of presidential power and supported development of transportation and infrastructure.

whip The member of the party leadership team charged with keeping the members in line—that is, getting them to cast votes in the way the party leaders would like.

white primaries A Southern strategy for minimizing black voter influence that allowed only white voters to vote in the primary elections (the only ones that really mattered).

women's suffrage movement The drive to grant women the right to vote.

writ of certiorari An instruction to a lower court to send up the record in a particular case. This is the most common avenue for appeal to the U.S. Supreme Court.

writ of *habeas corpus* A judicial order requiring that a prisoner be brought before a judge to determine whether there is a lawful justification for incarceration.

writ of mandamus A court order instructing an official to perform a mandatory duty.

Y

yellow journalism A type of journalism that emerged in the late 1800s, characterized by scandal-mongering and sensationalistic reporting.

Chapter 1

1. World Values Survey, fourth wave (http://www.worldvaluessurvey.org/).

2. Technically, we can speak of politics for any group of people—that is, making collective decisions for that group. We can speak of office politics or church politics, for example. For the sake of simplicity, we will confine ourselves here to the most usual kind of politics, the politics of an entire country.

3. Max Weber, "Politics as a Vocation." In H. H. Gerth and C. Wright Mills (Transl. and Eds.), *From Max Weber: Essays in Sociology* (New York: Oxford University Press, 1958), pp. 77–128. The essay was first written in 1919.

4. Though all male citizens could participate in a city-state like Athens, actually that was a small fraction of the people living in Athens. Aside from female citizens, there were also large numbers of slaves and other non-citizens who were unable to participate.

5. Although, as we have noted, "democracy" is a matter of degree, here for convenience we are dichotomizing the concept, treating all countries as being either democracies or not democracies.

6. Larry Diamond, *The Spirit of Democracy* (New York: Times Books, 2008), Chapter 3.

7. In 2009 and 2010 support for stricter gun controls dropped sharply, so that a majority in Gallup polls no longer support the position.

8. "Public good" is a technical term that is defined and discussed on page 12.

9. Actually, this is a partial definition of the term. In economics, from which political scientists have borrowed the term, a public good is a good that is non-rival and non-excludable. Non-rivalry means that one person enjoying the good does not reduce the enjoyment of others. Non-excludability means that no one can be denied the good. We have left the first part out of our definition here, because we are interested in public goods in relation to the problem of free ridership, which often requires the intervention of government. The full definition is too complicated for an introductory course and is not necessary for our purposes here.

10. The basic statement on the problem of public goods and free riders is Mancur Olson's *Logic of Collective Action* (Cambridge, MA: Harvard University Press, 1965).

11. Author's observation.

12. International Monetary Fund, *Government Finance Statistics Yearbook 2007*.

13. International Monetary Fund, *Finance Statistics Yearbook 2008*. The figures refer to combined national and local governmental expenditures.

14. World Values Survey, 2005/2006 Wave (http://www.worldvaluessurvey.org/).

15. Frederick Jackson Turner, "The Significance of the Frontier in American History," paper presented to the American History Association meetings in Chicago, July 12, 1893. The essay is reprinted in Frederick Jackson Turner, *The Frontier in American History* (New York: Holt, 1920).

16. Classical liberalism is obviously different from what we call "liberalism" today. As we will see later in this chapter, today's liberalism argues for considerable central control in some areas such as the economy, while arguing for individual freedom in others, such as abortion and free speech.

17. John Locke (1632–1704) is often considered the father of liberalism. He argued in *Two Treatises of Government* that government is based on humans' natural, individual rights and that an unjust government that did not honor those rights should be overthrown. He also argued for the separation of church and state.

18. World Values Survey, 1990 Wave (http://www.worldvaluessurvey.org).

19. Geert Hofstede, *Culture's Consequences*, 2nd ed. (Thousand Oaks, CA: Sage, 2001), pp. 214–216.

20. World Values Survey, fourth wave, 1999/2000. Retrieved February 1, 2010, from http://www.worldvaluessurvey.org.

21. Friedrich Engels, "Why There Is no Large Socialist Party in America," letter to Friedrich A. Sorge, December 2, 1893. In Frank Mecklenburg and Manfred Stassen (Eds.), *German Essays on Socialism in the Nineteenth Century* (New York: Continuum, 1990), pp. 75–76.

22. OECD, "Society at a Glance 2011", Retrieved January 12, 2012, from http://www.oecd.org/document/24/0,3746,en_2649_37419_2671576_1_1_1_37419,00.html.

23. W. Phillips Shively, *Power and Choice: An Introduction to Political Science*, 12th ed. (New York: McGraw-Hill, 2011), p. 160.

24. Angus Maddison, "A Comparison of Levels of GDP per Capita in Developed and Developing Countries, 1700–1980," *Journal of Economic History*, 43(1), (March 1983), p. 30.

25. A good example is Adam Przeworski et al., *Democracy and Development: Political Institutions and Well-being in the World, 1950–1990* (New York: Cambridge University Press, 2000).

26. Ibid., p. 230.

27. World Values Survey, fifth wave, 2006 (http://www.worldvaluessurvey.org).

Chapter 2

1. Joseph J. Ellis, *Founding Brothers: The Revolutionary Generation* (New York: Alfred A. Knopf, 2000), p. 9.

2. Jennifer Widner, "Constitution Writing in Post-Conflict Settings: An Overview," *William and Mary Law Review*, 49 (March 2008), p. 1513.

3. Several websites offer detailed guidelines for drafting a constitution (see, for example, the Public International Law & Policy Group's "Post-Conflict Constitution Drafter's Handbook" at http://www.publicinternationallaw.org/areas/peacebuilding/consthandbook/).

4. Joseph J. Ellis, *American Creation* (New York: Random House, 2007), p. 3.

5. This section is drawn from material in Paul Soifer and Abraham Hoffman, *U.S. History I* (Hoboken, NJ: Wiley, 1998), pp. 19–29.

6. Edmund S. Morgan, *The Birth of the Republic, 1763–89*, 3rd ed. (Chicago: University of Chicago Press, 1992), pp. 5–6.

7. Morgan, *The Birth of the Republic*, pp. 6–8.

8. Morgan, *The Birth of the Republic*, p. 9.

9. Text of the Magna Carta (http://www.fordham.edu/halsall/ngc.asp?page=source/magnacarta.html). Translations from the Latin vary slightly.

10. Quoted in Morgan, *The Birth of the Republic*, p. 18.

11. The full text of the Virginia Stamp Act Resolutions can be found at http://www.ushistory.org/declaration/related/vsa65.htm.

12. The Massachusetts legislature issued the invitation in June 1765 for all colonies to send representatives to the Congress. The four colonies that did not send representatives were Georgia, New Hampshire, North Carolina, and Virginia.

13. The full text of the Declaration of Rights can be found at http://www.constitution.org/bcp/dor_sac.htm.

14. The full text of the Declaratory Act can be found at http://www.constitution.org/bcp/decl_act.htm.

15. None other than the young John Adams defended the British soldiers at trial. The British captain was found not guilty, as were six of the remaining eight soldiers. Two were found guilty of manslaughter. As punishment, they were branded on their thumbs. David McCullough, *John Adams* (New York: Simon and Schuster, 2001), pp. 67–68.

16. Morgan, *The Birth of the Republic*, pp. 58–59.

17. Merrill Jensen, *The Articles of Confederation: An Interpretation of the Social-Constitutional History of the American Revolution, 1774–1781* (Madison: University of Wisconsin Press, 1940), p. 56.

18. The full text of the Declaration and Resolves from the First Continental Congress can be found at http://www.historywiz.com/primarysources/declarationandresolves.htm.

19. Ellis, *American Creation*, p. 41.

20. Ellis, *American Creation*, p. 42.

21. This is the figure provided at http://www.census.gov/Press-Release/www/releases/archives/facts_for_features_special_editions/004772.html.

22. When *Common Sense* was first published, 1 out of 5 people bought a copy, which is equivalent to 2/10, or 1/5. To determine that 62 million copies would need to be sold today to reach a proportionate number of Americans, we would have to multiply the population figure from 2010 Census, 308,745,538, by 0.2 (or divide it by 5).

23. Willi Paul Adams, *The First American Constitutions: Republican Ideology and the*

Making of the State Constitutions in the Revolutionary Era (Rita and Robert Kimber, Ttansl.) (Lanham, MD: Rowman & Littlefield, 2001), p. 3.

24. Joseph J. Ellis, *American Sphinx: The Character of Thomas Jefferson* (New York: Vintage Books, 1998), p. 57.

25. Jefferson originally wrote "certain inherent and inalienable rights." Congress deleted "inherent" and later printed versions changed "inalienable" to "unalienable." Both words mean the same thing, but there continues to be some debate about which is correct (http://www.ushistory.org/Declaration/unalienable.htm).

26. For an extended discussion of all of these debates, see Jensen, *The Articles of Confederation*, Chapter 6.

27. Morgan, *The Birth of the Republic*, pp. 104–112.

28. Keith L. Dougherty, *Collective Action under the Articles of Confederation* (Cambridge: Cambridge University Press, 2001), p. 29.

29. Morgan, *The Birth of the Republic*, p. 126.

30. This requisition system was spelled out in Article VIII of the Articles of Confederation. For a detailed discussion of this and the collective action problems associated with such a system, see Dougherty, *Collective Action under the Articles of Confederation*.

31. Jensen, *The Articles of Confederation*, p. 132.

32. David O. Stewart, *The Summer of 1787* (New York: Simon & Schuster, 2007), p. 23.

33. Charles C. Thach, Jr., *The Creation of the Presidency, 1775–1789: A Study in Constitutional History* (Baltimore: Johns Hopkins University Press, 1923), Chapter 3.

34. Stewart, *The Summer of 1787*, p. 19.

35. Morgan, *The Birth of the Republic*, p. 125.

36. For the full text of Madison's critique, see http://memory.loc.gov/cgi-bin/query/r?ammem/mjmtext:@field(DOCID+@lit(jm020120)).

37. This paragraph is based on Stewart, *The Summer of 1787*, Chapter 4.

38. Charles A. Beard, *An Economic Interpretation of the Constitution* (New York: Macmillan, 1913).

39. Stewart, *The Summer of 1787*, pp. 25, 68, 41, and 44.

40. Robert E. Brown, *Charles Beard and the Constitution: A Critical Analysis of "An Economic Interpretation of the Constitution"* (Princeton: Princeton University Press, 1956); Forrest McDonald, *We the People: The Economic Origins of the Constitution* (Chicago: University of Chicago Press, 1958).

41. Stewart, *The Summer of 1787*, pp. 49–51.

42. Ellis, *American Creation*, p. 103.

43. Stewart, *The Summer of 1787*, p. 57.

44. Stewart, *The Summer of 1787*, p. 65.

45. Stewart, *The Summer of 1787*, pp. 66–78.

46. Forrest McDonald, *The American Presidency: An Intellectual History* (Lawrence, KS: University Press of Kansas, 1994), pp. 132–133.

47. Thomas Jefferson, *Notes on the State of Virginia*, quoted in Richard J. Ellis, Ed., *Founding the American Presidency* (Lanham, MD: Rowman and Littlefield, 1999), p. 4.

48. McDonald, *The American Presidency*, p. 157.

49. Quoted in Ellis, *Founding the American Presidency*, p. 63.

50. Ellis, *Founding the American Presidency*, p. 64.

51. Quoted in Ellis, *Founding the American Presidency*, p. 64.

52. http://www.law.umkc.edu/faculty/projects/ftrials/conlaw/convention1787.html

53. Ellis, *American Creation*, p. 114. The remainder of this section relies on pages 115–117.

54. For example, the seven-volume set: *The Complete Anti-Federalist*, Ed. Herbert Storing and Murray Dry (Chicago: University of Chicago Press, 1981).

55. Ellis, *American Creation*, p. 120.

56. John R. Vile, *Encyclopedia of Constitutional Amendments, Proposed Amendments, and Amending Issues, 1789–2002*, 2nd ed. (Santa Barbara, CA: ABC-CLIO, 2003), p. xx.

57. Six Failed Amendments (http://www.usconstitution.net/constamfail.html).

58. *Marbury v. Madison*, 5 U.S. (1 Cranch) 137 (1803).

59. *Brown v. Board of Education*, 347 U.S. 483 (1954), which overturned the "separate but equal" doctrine of *Plessy v. Ferguson*, 163 U.S. 537 (1896).

60. Louis Fisher, *Constitutional Dialogues* (Princeton: Princeton University Press, 1988), Chapter 7.

61. Letter from Jefferson to Abigail Adams, July 22, 1804, quoted in Fisher, *Constitutional Dialogues*, p. 238.

62. Charlie Savage, "Bush challenges hundreds of laws, President cites his powers of office," *Boston Globe*, April 30, 2006, A1. Although this article brought public attention to Bush's use of signing statements, political scientist Christopher S. Kelley had already written a doctoral dissertation on the topic: Christopher S. Kelley, "The Unitary Executive and the Presidential Signing Statement" (Ph.D. dissertation, Miami University, 2003).

63. American Bar Association Task Force on Presidential Signing Statements, "Report," August 2006, p. 32. The full text of the report is available at http://www.abanet.org/media/docs/signstatereport.pdf.

64. Charlie Savage, "Obama Looks to Limit Impact of Tactic Bush Used to Sidestep New Laws," *New York Times*, March 10, 2009, p. A12.

65. Anne Flaherty, "Democrats irked by Obama's signing statement," *Washington Examiner*, July 20, 2009 (http://washingtonexaminer.com/politics/2009/07/democrats-irked-obama-signing-statement).

66. Learned Hand, *The Spirit of Liberty* 144 (Irving Dillard, Ed., 1959) [quoted in William Van Alstyne, "Quintessential Elements of Meaningful Constitutions in Post-Conflict States," *William and Mary Law Review*, 49 (March 2008), p. 1511.

Chapter 3

1. "How to Fix No Child Left Behind," *Time*, May 24, 2007 (http://www.time.com/time/magazine/article/0,9171,1625192,00.html).

2. Patrik Jonsson, "America's Biggest Teacher and Principal Cheating Scandal Unfolds in Atlanta," *Christian Science Monitor*, July 5, 2011 (http://www.csmonitor.com/USA/Education/2011/0705/America-s-biggest-teacher-and-principal-cheating-scandal-unfolds-in-Atlanta).

3. Alistair Cole, "Education and Educational Governance." In Alistair Cole, Patrick Le Galès, and Jonah Levy (Eds.), *Developments in French Politics 3* (New York: Palgrave Macmillan, 2005), p. 196.

4. Peter Gumbel, "France Scores an F in Education," *Time*, October 4, 2010 (http://www.time.com/time/magazine/article/0,9171,2021009-2,00.html).

5. Cole, "Education and Educational Governance," p. 201.

6. Jane Marshall, "How Sarkozy Is Forcing Reform on a Reluctant Establishment," *The Independent*, July 1, 2010 (http://www.independent.co.uk/news/education/schools/how-sarkozy-is-forcing-reform-on-a-reluctant-establishment-2014821.html); "Teachers and Students March Against Education Reforms," *France 24*, November 2, 2009 (http://www.france24.com/en/20090210-teachers-students-march-against-education-reform-).

7. *New York State Ice Company v. Liebmann*, 285 U.S. 262 (1932), dissent by Justice Brandeis at 311.

8. Wendy Koch, "Biggest U.S. Tax Hike on Tobacco Takes Effect," *USA Today*, April 3, 2009 (http://www.usatoday.com/money/perfi/taxes/2009-03-31-cigarettetax_N.htm).

9. For a state-by-state comparison of excise taxes on cigarettes, see http://www.tobaccofreekids.org/research/factsheets/pdf/0097.pdf.

10. *Milwaukee County v. M.E. White Co.*, 296 U.S. 268 (1935), 277.

11. Council of State Governments—National Center for Interstate Compacts, "Understanding Interstate Compacts," 1 (http://www.cglg.org/projects/water/compacteducation/understanding_interstate_compacts—csgncic.pdf).

12. Council of State Governments—National Center for Interstate Compacts, "Understanding Interstate Compacts," 2 (http://www.cglg.org/projects/water/compacteducation/understanding_interstate_compacts—csgncic.pdf).

13. For a history of the Port Authority, see http://www.panynj.gov/about/history-port-authority.html.

14. For a similar, expansive use of the term "cooperative federalism," see Ducat, *Constitutional Interpretation*, 9th ed., pp. 270–272.

15. Justice Harlan Fiske Stone introduced this term to describe the Tenth Amendment in his opinion for a unanimous Supreme Court in *U.S. v. Darby*, 312 U.S. 100 (1941) at 124: "The Tenth Amendment states but a truism that all is retained which has not been surrendered."

16. To read Hamilton's opinion of the constitutionality of the First Bank of the United States, go to http://avalon.law.yale.edu/18th_century/bank-ah.asp.

17. *McCulloch v. Maryland*, 17 U.S. 316, at 431.

18. *McCulloch v. Maryland*, 17 U.S. 316, at 436.

19. *Gibbons v. Ogden*, 22 U.S. 1, at 196 and 197.

20. "South Carolina Ordinance of Nullification," November 24, 1832 (http://avalon.law.yale.edu/19th_century/ordnull.asp).

21. To view the text of the Force Act, go to http://memory.loc.gov/cgi-bin/ampage?collId=llsl&fileName=004/llsl004.db&recNum=679.

22. *Texas v. White*, 74 U.S. 700 (1869).

23. To view the organization's website, go to: http://www.texasnationalist.com/.

24. Paul Starobin, "Divided We Stand," *Wall Street Journal*, June 13, 2009 (http://online.wsj.com/article/SB10001424052970204482304574219813708759806.html).

25. http://vermontrepublic.org/

26. http://www.akip.org/

27. *Kohlhaas v. State of Alaska,* 147 P.3d 714 (2006), (http://caselaw.findlaw.com/ak-supreme-court/1497483.html).

28. *The Slaughterhouse Cases,* 83 U.S. 36 (1873).

29. *Civil Rights Cases,* 109 U.S. 3 (1883).

30. *Plessy v. Ferguson,* 163 U.S. 537 (1896).

31. *U.S. v. E.C. Knight,* 156 U.S. 1 (1895).

32. For example, *Hammer v. Dagenhart,* 247 U.S. 251 (1918).

33. *Schechter Poultry Corp. v. United States,* 295 U.S. 495 (1935).

34. *Carter v. Carter Coal Company,* 298 U.S. 238 (1936).

35. Peter H. Irons, *A People's History of the Supreme Court* (New York: Viking, 1999), pp. 303–304.

36. The "Four Horsemen" were Justices Pierce Butler, Willis Van Devanter, James Clark McReynolds, and George Sutherland.

37. The "Three Musketeers" were Justices Louis Brandeis, Benjamin Cardozo, and Harlan Fiske Stone.

38. Chief Justice Charles Evans Hughes and Justice Owen Roberts.

39. One, Harlan Fiske Stone, was initially appointed as an associate justice by President Calvin Coolidge in 1925, but Roosevelt elevated him to the post of chief justice in 1941 to replace Charles Evans Hughes.

40. *National Labor Relations Board v. Jones & Laughlin Steel Corp.,* 301 U.S. 1 (1937).

41. *U.S. v. Darby,* 312 U.S. 100 (1941).

42. Kenneth Finegold, Laura Wherry, and Stephanie Schardin, "Block Grants: Historical Overview and Lessons Learned," *Urban Institute,* April 21, 2004 (http://www.urban.org/publications/310991.html).

43. President Bill Clinton, "State of the Union Address," January 23, 1996 (http://clinton4.nara.gov/WH/New/other/sotu.html).

44. "History of the Violence Against Women Act," *Legal Momentum: The Women's Legal Defense and Education Fund* (http://www.legalmomentum.org/our-work/vaw/history-of-vawa.html).

45. Devlin Barrett, "New Medical Marijuana Policy: Obama Administration Will Not Seek Arrests for People Following State Laws," *Huffington Post,* October 18, 2009 (http://www.huffingtonpost.com/2009/10/19/new-medical-marijuana-pol_n_325426.html).

46. Charlie Savage and Sheryl Gay Stolberg, "In Shift, U.S. Says Marriage Act Blocks Gay Rights," *New York Times,* February 23, 2011 (http://www.nytimes.com/2011/02/24/us/24marriage.html).

47. *National Federation of Independent Business v. Sebelius,* 567 U.S.___(2012).

48. James C. McKinley, Jr., "Texas Conservative Win Curriculum Change," *The New York Times,* March 12, 2010, (http://www.nytimes.com/2010/03/13/education/13texas.html); Katherine Mangan, "Ignoring Experts' Pleas, Texas Board Approves Controversial Curriculum Standards," *The Chronicle of Higher Education,* May 23, 2010 (http://chronicle.com/article/Texas-Board-Approves/65661/).

49. This happened in 2005. See Jodi Wilgoren, "Kansas School Board Approves Controversial Science Standards," *The New York Times,* November 8, 2005 (http://www.nytimes.com/2005/11/08/national/08cnd-kansas.html).

Chapter 4

1. Sharon LaFraniere, Michael Wines, and Edward Wong, "China Reins in Entertainment and Blogging," *The New York Times,* October 26, 2011 (http://www.nytimes.com/2011/10/27/world/asia/china-imposes-new-limits-on-entertainment-and-bloggers.html?hpw).

2. This section is based on an interactive website, "China and Internet Censorship," hosted by CNN.com at http://www.cnn.com/interactive/world/0603/explainer.china.internet/frameset.exclude.html. See also "Chinese Government Cracks Down on Internet Free Speech," PBS NewsHour with Jim Lehrer, October 19, 2005 (http://www.pbs.org/newshour/extra/features/july-dec05/china_10-19.html).

3. See, for example, the website of the Congressional-Executive Commission on China, created by Congress in October 2000 to monitor human rights and the development of the rule of law in China: http://www.cecc.gov/pages/virtualAcad/exp/.

4. "China Defends Internet Regulation," BBC News, February 15, 2006 (http://news.bbc.co.uk/2/hi/asia-pacific/4715044.stm). A copy of the official Chinese press release on this matter can be found at http://losangeles.china-consulate.org/eng/news/topnews/t235553.htm.

5. *Terminello v. Chicago,* 337 U.S. 1 (1949), Justice Jackson's dissent at 37.

6. The text of the Virginia Declaration of Rights can be found in Gordon Lloyd and Margie Lloyd, (Eds.), *The Essential Bill of Rights: Original Arguments and Fundamental Documents* (Lanham, MD: University Press of America, 1998), pp. 188–196.

7. Delaware, Maryland, Massachusetts, New Hampshire, North Carolina, Pennsylvania, and Virginia.

8. Robert Scigliano (Ed.), *The Federalist: A Commentary on the Constitution of the United States* (New York: The Modern Library, 2001), p. 550.

9. Richard Labunski, *James Madison and the Struggle for the Bill of Rights* (New York: Oxford University Press, 2006), p. 8.

10. Labunski, *James Madison,* p. 8.

11. Labunski, *James Madison,* p. 62. See *Federalist 38, 44,* and 66.

12. Letter from James Madison to George Eve, January 2, 1789, quoted in Labunski, *James Madison,* p. 164.

13. The text of Madison's speech introducing his proposed amendments on June 8, 1789, along with the text of the 17 amendments initially approved by the House on August 24, 1789 and the final 12 amendments approved by the First Congress on September 25, 1789, can be found in Lloyd and Lloyd (Eds.), *The Essential Bill of Rights,* pp. 331–357.

14. Michael Kent Curtis, *No State Shall Abridge: The Fourteenth Amendment and the Bill of Rights* (Durham, NC: Duke University Press, 1986), p. 21.

15. In *Barron v. Baltimore,* 32 U.S. 243 (1833), Chief Justice John Marshall explained why this was so. In the original Constitution, whenever state action was limited (as in Article I, Section 10), there was unambiguous language that said: "No state shall. . . ." In contrast, the more general prohibitions of Article I, Section 9 (e.g., "No Bill of Attainder or ex post facto Law shall be passed") were clearly aimed at Congress and not the states. If the Bill of Rights was meant to limit the states, Marshall concluded, it would have explicitly said "No state shall. . . ."

16. *Barron v. Baltimore,* 32 U.S. 243 (1833), 243.

17. Curtis, *No State Shall Abridge,* p. 19.

18. Curtis, *No State Shall Abridge,* p. 30.

19. Curtis, *No State Shall Abridge,* p. 23.

20. This paragraph is drawn from Curtis, *No State Shall Abridge,* pp. 28–32.

21. Justice Hugo Black was a leading exponent of this position on the Supreme Court. See his dissent in *Adamson v. California,* 332 U.S. 46 (1947), at 68–123. See also W. W. Crosskey, "Charles Fairman, 'Legislative History,' and the Constitutional Limitations on State Authority," *University of Chicago Law Review,* 22(1), (1954), and Curtis, *No State Shall Abridge.*

22. Charles Fairman, "Does the Fourteenth Amendment Incorporate the Bill of Rights?" *Stanford Law Review,* 2(5), (1949). See also Raoul Berger, *Government by Judiciary* (Cambridge: Harvard University Press, 1977).

23. Curtis, *No State Shall Abridge,* pp. 64–65.

24. *Butchers' Benevolent Association v. Crescent City Livestock Landing & Slaughterhouse Co.* [The Slaughterhouse Cases], 83 U.S. 36 (1873).

25. *Palko v. Connecticut,* 302 U.S. 319 (1937).

26. *Adamson v. California,* 332 U.S. 46 (1947), Black dissent, 89.

27. *McDonald v. Chicago,* 561 U.S. 3025 (2010).

28. *U.S. v. Cruikshank,* 92 U.S. 542 (1875); *Presser v. Illinois,* 116 U.S. 252 (1886); *U.S. v. Miller,* 307 U.S. 174 (1939).

29. *District of Columbia v. Heller,* 554 U.S. 570 (2008).

30. *Near v. Minnesota,* 283 U.S. 697 (1931).

31. *New York Times v. United States,* 403 U.S. 713 (1971).

32. Thomas Varela and David Gauthier-Villars, "France Urges Restraint From Media, Politicians," *Wall Street Journal,* May 18, 2011 (http://online.wsj.com/article/SB10001424052748703421204576328982375553362.html); François Quintard-Morénas, "The French Have a Legal Point," *The New York Times,* May 26, 2011 (http://www.nytimes.com/roomfordebate/2011/05/26/can-strauss-kahn-get-a-fair-trial/the-french-have-a-legal-point).

33. Leonard W. Levy, *Emergence of a Free Press* (New Haven, CT: Yale University Press, 1985), pp. 3–15.

34. Leonard Levy, *Origins of the Bill of Rights* (New Haven, CT: Yale University Press, 1999), p. 22.

35. Those convicted of conspiracy under the act could be fined $5,000 and sentenced to up to five years in prison.

36. Labunski, *James Madison,* p. 257.

37. Adjusted for inflation, $10,000 in 1917 would equal $176,502 in 2011.

38. The names of such men were routinely published in newspapers at that time.

39. *Schenck v. United States,* 249 U.S. 47 (1919).

40. *Schenck v. United States,* 249 U.S. 47 (1919), at 52.

41. *Abrams v. United States,* 250 U.S. 616 (1919).

42. Ibid., Holmes dissent at 629.

43. *Gitlow v. New York,* 268 U.S. 652 (1925), at 669.

44. *Whitney v. California,* 274 U.S. 357 (1927), Brandeis concurrence, at 376 and 378 (emphasis added).

45. *U.S. v. Dennis,* 341 U.S. 494 (1951).

46. *Brandenburg v. Ohio,* 395 U.S. 444 (1969).

47. *Stromberg v. People of State of California,* 283 U.S. 359 (1931).

48. *Tinker v. Des Moines Independent Community School District,* 393 U.S. 503 (1969).

49. *Morse v. Frederick,* 551 U.S. 393 (2007).

50. *Texas v. Johnson,* 491 U.S. 397 (1989).

51. *Texas v. Johnson,* 491 U.S. 397 (1989), at 403 (quoting *United States v. O'Brien,* 391 U.S. 367 (1968) at 376 and 409.

52. *Near v. Minnesota,* 283 U.S. 697 (1931).

53. *Jacobellis v. Ohio,* 378 U.S. 184 (1964), Justice Stewart's concurring opinion at 197.

54. *Regina v. Hicklin,* 3 Queen's Bench 360 (1868).

55. *Ex Parte Jackson,* 96 U.S. 727 (1877).

56. For a full discussion of this, see Lee Epstein and Thomas G. Walker, *Constitutional Law for a Changing America: Rights, Liberties, and Justice,* 5th ed. (Washington, DC: CQ Press, 2004), pp. 363–367.

57. *New York Times v. Sullivan,* 376 U.S. 254 (1964), at 280.

58. Epstein and Walker, *Constitutional Law,* 396.

59. *New York Times v. Sullivan,* 376 U.S. 254 (1964), at 271.

60. *Valentine v. Chrestensen,* 316 U.S. 52 (1942).

61. *Bates v. State Bar of Arizona,* 433 U.S. 350 (1977); *Bigelow v. Virginia,* 421 U.S. 809 (1975).

62. *Bolger v. Youngs Drugs Products Corp.,* 463 U.S. 60 (1983), at 74.

63. Quoted in Mary Beth Marklein, "On Campus: Free Speech for You but Not for Me?" *USA Today,* November 3, 2003, online edition: http://www.usatoday.com/news/washington/2003-11-02-free-speech-cover_x.htm.

64. *Doe v. Michigan,* 721 F.Supp. 852 (E.D. Mich 1989).

65. *Adderley v. Florida,* 385 U.S. 39 (1966).

66. *Edwards v. South Carolina,* 372 U.S. 229 (1963).

67. *Smith v. Collin,* 439 U.S. 916 (1978).

68. *Chaplinsky v. New Hampshire,* 315 U.S. 568 (1942).

69. Josh Belzman, "Behind Their Hate, a Constitutional Debate: Anti-gay Group Targeting Military Funerals Sparks Free Speech Debate," MSNBC, January 24, 2008 (http://www.msnbc.msn.com/id/12071434/).

70. *Snyder v. Phelps,* Docket No. 09-751.

71. *Engel v. Vitale,* 370 U.S. 421 (1962).

72. Ducat, *Constitutional Interpretation,* p. 1049.

73. Anthony Lewis, "Mr. Meese's Freedom," *The New York Times* (September 30, 1985), p. A15.

74. Epstein and Walker, *Rights, Liberties, and Justice,* p. 202.

75. *Everson v. Board of Education,* 330 U.S. 1 (1947).

76. *Lemon v. Kurtzman,* 403 U.S. 602 (1971).

77. *Wallace v. Jaffree,* 472 U.S. 38 (1985).

78. *Edwards v. Aguillard,* 482 U.S. 578 (1987).

79. *Glassroth v. Moore,* 335 F.3d 1282 (2003).

80. *Loi du 9 décembre 1905 concernant la separation des Églises et de l'État.*

81. *Loi n° 2004-228 du 15 mars 2004 encadrant, en application du principe de laïcité, le port de signes ou de tenues manifestant une appartenance religieuse dans les écoles, collèges et lycées publics.*

82. *Annual Report of the United States Commission on International Religious Freedom,* May 2007, pp. 94–95.

83. Epstein and Walker, *Rights, Liberties, and Justice,* p. 114.

84. Tony Mauro, "Thank Jehovah's Witnesses for Speech Freedoms," *USA Today,* May 30, 2000. See also Shawn Francis Peters, *Judging Jehovah's Witnesses* (Lawrence, KS: University Press of Kansas, 2000).

85. *Reynolds v. United States,* 98 U.S. 145 (1879).

86. *West Virginia State Board of Education v. Barnette,* 319 U.S. 624 (1943); *Minersville School District v. Gobitis,* 310 U.S. 586 (1940).

87. Epstein and Walker, *Rights, Liberties, and Justice,* p. 114.

88. *Employment Division, Department of Human Resources v. Smith,* 484 U.S. 872 (1990).

89. *Griswold v. Connecticut,* 381 U.S. 479 (1965).

90. *Eisenstadt v. Baird,* 405 U.S. 438 (1972).

91. *Griswold v. Connecticut,* 381 U.S. 479 (1965), Justice Black's dissent, at 507.

92. *Griswold v. Connecticut,* 381 U.S. 479 (1965), Justice Black's dissent, at 510.

93. *Roe v. Wade,* 410 U.S. 113 (1973).

94. *City of Akron v. Akron Center for Reproductive Health,* 462 U.S. 416 (1983), Justice O'Connor's dissent.

95. *Planned Parenthood of Southeastern Pennsylvania v. Casey,* 505 U.S. 833 (1992).

96. Ronald Dworkin, *Life's Dominion: An Argument About Abortion, Euthanasia, and Individual Freedom* (New York: Vintage Books, 1993), p. 6.

97. *Bowers v. Hardwick,* 478 U.S. 186 (1986).

98. *Lawrence v. Texas,* 539 U.S. 558 (2003).

99. *Lawrence v. Texas,* 539 U.S. 558 (2003), Justice Scalia's dissent, at 605.

100. *Goodridge v. Department of Public Health,* 440 Mass. 309, at 344.

101. *Cruzan v. Director, Missouri Department of Health,* 497 U.S. 261 (1990).

102. *Gonzales v. Oregon,* 546 U.S. 243 (2006).

103. Derek Humphry, "Assisted Suicide Laws Around the World" (http://www.assistedsuicide.org/suicide_laws.html).

104. *Palko v. Connecticut,* 302 U.S. 319 (1937); *Adamson v. California,* 332 U.S. 46 (1947).

105. *Duncan v. Louisiana,* 391 U.S. 145 (1968).

106. *Williams v. Florida,* 399 U.S. 78 (1970); *Apodaca v. Oregon,* 406 U.S. 404 (1972).

107. *Ballew v. Georgia,* 435 U.S. 223 (1978).

108. *Burch v. Louisiana,* 441 U.S. 130 (1979).

109. *Gideon v. Wainwright,* 372 U.S. 335 (1963).

110. *Miranda v. Arizona,* 384 U.S. 436 (1966).

111. *Dickerson v. United States,* 530 U.S. 428 (2000).

112. *Weeks v. United States,* 232 U.S. 383 (1914).

113. *Wolf v. Colorado,* 338 U.S. 25 (1949).

114. *Mapp v. Ohio,* 367 U.S. 643 (1961).

115. *United States v. Leon,* 468 U.S. 897 (1984).

116. *Baze v. Rees,* 553 U.S. 35 (2008).

117. Amnesty International, "Death Sentences and Executions in 2010" (http://www.amnesty.org.au/images/uploads/adp/Death%20Sentences%20and%20Executions%202010.pdf).

118. http://www.gallup.com/poll/1606/death-penalty.aspx

119. *Furman v. Georgia,* 408 U.S. 238 (1972).

120. *Coker v. Georgia,* 433 U.S. 584 (1977).

121. *Atkins v. Virginia,* 536 U.S. 304 (2002).

122. *Roper v. Simmons,* 543 U.S. 551 (2005).

123. James Risen and Eric Lichtblau, "Bush Lets U.S. Spy on Callers Without Courts," *The New York Times,* December 16, 2005, p. A1.

124. Paul Kane and Felicia Somnez, "Patriot Act Extension Signed into Law Despite Bipartisan Resistance in Congress," *Washington Post,* May 27, 2011 (http://www.washingtonpost.com/politics/patriot-act-extension-signed-into-law-despite-bipartisan-resistance-in-congress/2011/05/27/AGbVlsCH_story.html).

125. *Hamdi v. Rumsfeld,* 542 U.S. 507 (2004).

126. *Hamdan v. Rumsfeld,* 126 S.Ct. 2749 (2006).

127. Richard M. Pious, "Obama's Use of Prerogative Powers in the War on Terrorism." In James A. Thurber (Ed.), *Obama in Office* (Boulder, CO: Paradigm Publishers, 2011), p. 258.

128. Pious, "Obama's Use of Prerogative Powers in the War on Terrorism," pp. 255–268.

Chapter 5

1. "Presidential Memorandum—International Initiatives to Advance the Human Rights of Lesbian, Gay, Bisexual, and Transgender Persons," December 6, 2011 (http://www.whitehouse.gov/the-press-office/2011/12/06/presidential-memorandum-international-initiatives-advance-human-rights-l).

2. Farouk Chothia, "Gay rights: Africa, the new frontier," *BBC News,* December 7, 2011.

3. "Nigeria moves ahead with anti-gay bill," *News24,* December 8, 2011 (http://www.news24.com/Africa/News/Nigeria-moves-ahead-with-anti-gay-bill-20111107).

4. "Nigeria pushes ahead with anti-gay bill despite US moves," *Angola Press,* December 9, 2011 (http://www.portalangop.co.ao/motix/en_us/noticias/africa/2011/11/49/Nigeria-pushes-ahead-with-anti-gay-bill-despite-moves,46032859-2aef-4cb4-b47d-d53ea91f10a0.html).

5. Ibid.

6. For the full text of the speech, see http://www.state.gov/secretary/rm/2011/12/178368.htm.

7. *Bowers v. Hardwick,* 478 U.S. 186 (1986).

8. *Lawrence v. Texas,* 539 U.S. 558 (2003).

9. *Prigg v. Pennsylvania,* 41 U.S. 539 (1842), 625.

10. *U.S. v. Amistad,* 40 U.S. 518 (1841).

11. *Dred Scott v. Sandford,* 60 U.S. 393, 405.

12. *Dred Scott v. Sandford,* 60 U.S. 393, 452.

13. Donald Lively, *The Constitution, Race, and Renewed Relevance of Original Intent* (Amherst, NY: Cambria Press, 2008), p. 45.

14. http://www.civilwarhome.com/blackcodes.htm

15. Lively, *The Constitution, Race, and Renewed Relevance of Original Intent,* p. 44.

16. *Civil Rights Cases,* 109 U.S. 3 (1883).

17. John Anthony Maltese, *The Selling of Supreme Court Nominees* (Baltimore: Johns Hopkins University Press, 1995), pp. 95–97.

18. *Plessy v. Ferguson,* 163 U.S. 537 (1897), Justice Harlan's dissent, 559, 562.

19. *Breedlove v. Suttles,* 302 U.S. 277 (1937); *Harper v. Virginia State Board of Elections,* 383 U.S. 663 (1966).

20. *Guinn v. United States,* 238 U.S. 347 (1915).

21. Maltese, *The Selling of Supreme Court Nominees,* pp. 101–104.

22. *Buchanan v. Warley,* 245 U.S. 60 (1917).

23. *Sweatt v. Painter,* 339 U.S. 629 (1950), 634, 635.

24. These included Felix Frankfurter and Robert Jackson.

25. *Brown v. Board of Education I,* 347 U.S. 483 (1954), 493–495.

26. Gerald N. Rosenberg, *The Hollow Hope: Can Courts Bring About Social Change?* (Chicago: University of Chicago Press, 1991), p. 50 (Table 2.1).

27. *Boynton v. Virginia,* 364 U.S. 454 (1960).

28. Raymond Arsenault, *Freedom Riders: 1961 and the Struggle for Racial Justice* (New York: Oxford University Press, 2006).

29. Thomas E. Patterson, *The Vanishing Voter: Public Involvement in an Age of Uncertainty* (New York: Alfred A. Knopf, 2002), pp. 5 and 6.

30. Jerry Markon, "Justice Department Rejects South Carolina Voter ID law, Calling It Discriminatory," *Washington Post,* December 21, 2011 (http://www.washingtonpost.com/politics/justice-dept-rejects-south-carolina-voter id-law-calling-it-discriminatory/2011/12/23/gIQAhLJAEP_story.html)

31. Pia Katarina Jakobsson, "Daughters of Liberty: Women and the American Revolution." In Crista DeLuzio and Peter C. Mancall (Eds.), *Women's Rights: People and Perspectives* (Santa Barbara, CA: ABC CLIO, 2010), p. 36.

32. Susan Gluck Mezey, *In Pursuit of Equality: Women, Public Policy, and the Federal Courts* (New York: St. Martin's Press, 1992), p. 9.

33. Sharon Hartman Strom, *Women's Rights* (Westport, CT: Greenwood Press, 2003), p. 55.

34. Kathleen S. Sullivan, *Constitutional Context: Women and Rights Discourse in Nineteenth-Century America* (Baltimore: Johns Hopkins University Press, 2007), p. 9.

35. Strom, *Women's Rights,* pp. 34–36.

36. Mezey, *In Pursuit of Equality,* p. 9.

37. For the full text of the Declaration of Sentiments, see Strom, *Women's Rights,* pp. 66–68.

38. Charles E. Euchner and John Anthony Maltese, *Selecting the President: From Washington to Bush* (Washington, DC: CQ Press, 1992), pp. 4–5.

39. The Supreme Court created intermediate scrutiny for gender classifications in *Craig v. Boren,* 429 U.S. 190 (1976).

40. *Rostker v. Golberg,* 453 U.S. 57 (1981).

41. *Williams v. Saxbe,* 413 F. Supp. 654 (D.D.C. 1976).

42. *Meritor Savings Bank v. Vinson,* 477 U.S. 57 (1986).

43. *Oncale v. Sundowner Offshore Services,* 523 U.S. 75 (1998).

44. *Wal-Mart Stores, Inc. v. Duke,* 564 U.S. (2011).

45. Felicia Sonmez, "Democrats React to Supreme Court Ruling on Wal-Mart," *Washington Post,* June 20, 2011 (http://www.washingtonpost.com/blogs/2chambers/post/congresswoman-reacts-to-supreme-court-ruling-on-wal-mart/2011/06/20/AGyHFzcH_blog.html).

46. Cynthia Fuchs Epstein, *Women in Law,* 2nd ed. (Urbana, IL: University of Illinois Press, 1993), p. 5.

47. *United States v. Virginia,* 518 U.S. 515 (1996).

48. *Employment Division, Department of Human Resources of Oregon v. Smith,* 494 U.S. 872 (1990).

49. John D. McKinnon, "U.S. Offers an Official Apology to Native Americans," *Wall Street Journal,* December 22, 2009 (http://blogs.wsj.com/washwire/2009/12/22/us-offers-an-official-apology-to-native-americans/).

50. *Korematsu v. U.S.,* 323 U.S. 214 (1944).

51. http://www.loc.gov/teachers/classroommaterials/presentationsandactivities/presentations/immigration/italian8.html

52. Jerry Markon and Michael D. Shear, "Justice Department Sues Arizona over Immigration Law," *Washington Post,* July 7, 2010 (http://www.washingtonpost.com/wp-dyn/content/article/2010/07/06/AR2010070601928.html).

53. Markon and Shear, "Justice Department Sues Arizona over Immigration Law"; Adam Liptak, "Court to Weigh Arizona Statute on Immigration," *New York Times,* December 12, 2011 (http://www.nytimes.com/2011/12/13/us/supreme-court-to-rule-on-immigration-law-in-arizona.html?_r=1&scp=1&sq=Supreme%20Court%20Arizona%20law&st=cse).

54. Stephen Caeser, "Federal Court Blocks Parts of Alabama Immigration Law," *Los Angeles Times,* October 14, 2011 (http://articles.latimes.com/2011/oct/14/nation/la-na-alabama-immigration-20111015). For an overview of the status of other court challenges to other state immigration laws, see Patrik Jonsson, "Alabama Immigration Law Faces Legal Challenge: Can It Survive?" *Christian Science Monitor* (http://www.csmonitor.com/USA/Politics/2011/0708/Alabama-immigration-law-faces-legal-challenge-Can-it-survive/Arizona).

55. *Mendez v. Westminster,* 64 F. Supp. 544 (1946). For more information about the *Mendez* case, see http://www.mendezvwestminster.com/.

56. *Westminster School District of Orange County v. Mendez,* 161 F.2d 774 (1947).

57. *Hernandez v. Texas,* 347 U.S. 475 (1954).

58. http://www.maldef.org/about/mission/index.html

59. Liz Halloran, "With Repeal of 'Don't Ask, Don't Tell,' An Era Ends," *NPR,* September 20, 2011 (http://www.npr.org/2011/09/20/140605121/with-repeal-of-dont-ask-dont-tell-an-era-ends).

60. Sheryl Gay Stolberg, "Obama Widens Medical Rights for Gay Partners," *New York Times,* April 15, 2010 (http://www.nytimes.com/2010/04/16/us/politics/16webhosp.html).

61. *Romer v. Evans,* 517 U.S. 620 (1996), 635–36, 632.

62. *Boy Scouts of America v. Dale,* 530 U.S. 640 (2000).

63. *Adarand Constructor's, Inc. v. Pena,* 515 U.S. 200 (1995).

64. *Grutter v. Bolling,* 539 U.S. 306 (2003).

65. Adam Liptak, "Justice Take Up Race as a Factor in College Entry," *New York Times,* February 21, 2012, http://www.nytimes.com/2012/02/22/us/justices-to-hear-case-on-affirmative-action-in-higher-education.html.

66. Alfred L. Brophy, *Reparations Pro and Con* (New York: Oxford University Press, 2006), p. 74.

67. Brophy, *Reparations Pro and Con,* pp. 76–77.

68. Juan Williams, "What Obama's Victory Means for Racial Politics," *Wall Street Journal,* November 10, 2008 (http://online.wsj.com/article/SB122628263723412543.html).

69. Charlie Savage, "Holder Signals Tough Review of New State Laws on Voting," *The New York Times,* December 13, 2011 (http://www.nytimes.com/2011/12/14/us/politics/in-speech-holder-to-critique-new-voting-laws.html?_r=1&scp=3&sq=eric%20holder&st=cse).

Chapter 6

1. International Monetary Fund, *Government Finance Statistics Yearbook.*

2. World Values Study, 2005–2008 sample (http://www.worldvaluessurvey.org).

3. Gordon S. Wood, "The Democratization of Mind in the American Revolution." In Robert H. Howitz (Ed.), *The Moral Foundations of the American Republic,* 3rd ed. (Charlottesville, VA.: University of Virginia Press, 1986), p. 129.

4. Alexis deTocqueville, *Democracy in America.* (New York: Knopf, 1980).

5. United States General Social Survey, 1972–2010 (http://www3.norc.org/GSS+Website/).

6. John L. Sullivan, Pat Walsh, Michal Shamir, David G. Barnum, and James I. Gibson, "Why Politicians Are More Tolerant: Selective Recruitment and Socialization Among Political Elites in Britain, Israel, New Zealand, and the United States," *British Journal of Political Science, 23* (January 1993), pp. 51–76.

7. Samuel A. Stouffer, *Communism, Conformity, and Civil Liberties* (New York: Doubleday, 1995), for the 1954 figure; for the figures after 1954, James Allan Davis, Tom W. Smith, and Peter V. Marsden, *General Social Surveys, 1972–2010. Cumulative Codebook,* Principal Investigator, James A. Davis; Director and Co-Principal Investigator, Tom W. Smith (Chicago: National Opinion Research Center, 2010).

8. National Election Studies (http://www.electionstudies.org/nesguide).

9. National Election Studies (http://www.electionstudies.org/nesguide). In fact, this difference understates the decrease in efficacy somewhat, because the National Election Studies changed their question wording on this question from 1988 on, to make it possible for people to reply more easily that they did not have an opinion on the question. Presumably some people who in 2008 would have replied that they believed people do not have a say replied instead that they were unsure.

10. World Values Surveys, 1990 wave. The two countries closest to the United States were India and South Korea. To compare a couple of other countries, in Great Britain, 42 percent thought they could change an unjust law, in France only 22 percent.

11. The gizzard is an organ in birds that grinds up food for digestion. It is one of the entrails that is thrown out before eating a chicken or turkey, and is tough, gristly, and generally unpleasant.

12. John R. Hibbing and Elizabeth Theiss-Morse, *Stealth Democracy: Americans' Belief About How Government Should Work* (New York: Cambridge University Press, 2002).

13. Thomas Patterson, *The Vanishing Voter* (New York: Alfred P. Knopf, 2003).

14. Ibid., p. 125.

15. Gordon Wood, *The Idea of America: Reflections on the Birth of the United States* (New York: Penguin Press, 2011), pp. 2–3.

16. William H. McNeill, "Epilogue: Fundamentalism and the World of the 1990s." In Martin R. Marty and R. Scott Appleby (Eds.), *Fundamentalisms and Society* (Chicago: University of Chicago Press, 1993), p. 569; quoted in Samuel P. Huntington, *The Clash of Civilizations and the Remaking of World Order* (New York: Simon & Schuster, 1996), p. 213.

17. George W. Bush, *Address to a Joint Session of Congress, September 20, 2001.* President Bush made clear in the speech, however, that he was referring to Islamic terrorists, not to Islam in general.

18. Calculated from Table 2 of Richard G. Niemi and M. Kent Jennings, "Issues and Inheritance in the Formation of Party Identification," *American Journal of Political Science, 35* (November 1991), pp. 970–988.

19. M. Kent Jennings and Richard G. Niemi, *The Political Character of Adolescence* (Princeton, NJ: Princeton University Press, 1974).

20. U.S. Department of Education, Institute of Education Sciences, National Center for Education Statistics, *The Nation's Report Card: Civics 2006* (figures from calculator on the National Center's website, http://nces .ed.gov/nationsreportcard/nde/).

21. Ernest L. Boyer and May Jean Whitelaw, *The Condition of the Professoriate: Attitudes and Trends, 1989* (New York: Harper and Row, 1989), cited in Robert S. Erikson and Kent L. Tedin, *American Public Opinion,* 5th ed. (Boston: Allyn and Bacon, 1995), p. 134.

22. Mark D. Mariani and Gordon J. Hewitt, "Indoctrination U.? Faculty Ideology and Changes in Student Political Orientation," *PS: Political Science and Politics,* 41(4), (October 2008), pp. 773-783.

23. Stephen Kull, Clay Ramsay, and Evan Lewis, "Misperceptions, the Media, and the Iraq War," *Political Science Quarterly, 118* (Winter, 2003–2004), pp. 569–598. Cited in Gary C. Jacobson, *A Divider Not a Uniter: George W. Bush and the American People* (New York: Pearson Longman, 2007), p. 251.

24. Diana C. Mutz and Byron Reeves, "The New Videomalaise: Effects of Televised Incivility on Political Trust," *American Political Science Review,* 99(1), (2005), pp. 1–15.

25. Robert S. Erikson and Kent L. Tedin, *American Public Opinion,* updated 7th ed. (New York: Pearson Longman, 2007), p. 152.

26. Exit polls.

27. Jeffrey S. Passel and D'Vera Cohn, "U.S. Population Projections: 2005–2050," Pew Research Center. *Social and Demographic Trends Report,* 2008.

28. National Election Studies, 2008 presidential election survey.

29. Christine Fong, "Social Preferences, Self-Interest, and the Demand for Redistribution," *Journal of Public Economics,* 88 (2001), pp. 225–246.

30. Exit polls.

31. Darryl Fears, "Black Opinion on Simpson Shifts," *Washington Post,* September 27, 2007, p. A03.

32. Exit polls.

33. World Values Study, 2005–2008 sample (http://www.worldvaluessurvey.org).

34. Calculated from exit polls.

35. John C. Green, *The American Religious Landscape and Political Attitudes: A Baseline for 2004* (Washington, DC: The Pew Forum on Religion and Public Life, 2004).

36. Pew Research Center. *Muslim Americans: Middle Class and Mostly Mainstream* (Washington, DC: Pew Research Center, 2007), p. 41

37. Ibid., pp. 41–46.

38. Ibid., p. 52.

39. United Nations, *Human Development Report 2010.*

40. Evidence that there were no class differences before 1932 is offered by W. Phillips Shively, "A Reinterpretation of the New Deal Realignment," *Public Opinion Quarterly, 35*(4), (1971), pp. 621–624.

41. National Election Studies, 2008 presidential election study.

42. National Women's Law Center report on the 2010 Census (http://www.nwlc.org/ analysis-new-2010-census-poverty-data--- september-2011).

43. The Pew Research Center for the People and the Press, Survey Reports, *September 4, 2003: Two Years Later, the Fear Lingers.*

44. The Pew Research Center for the People and the Press, Survey Reports, *September 22, 2005: Katrina Has Only Modest Impact on Basic Public Values.*

45. National Election Studies.

46. Anne Hendershott, "How Support for Abortion Became Kennedy Dogma," *The Wall Street Journal,* January 2, 2009, p. W11.

47. More systematic evidence for the parties' role in defining liberalism and conservatism— beyond anecdotes such as this—is offered in Paul Goren, "Party Identification and Core Values," *American Journal of Political Science, 49* (October 2005), pp. 882–897. In a causal analysis, Goren finds that voters' party identifications shape their ideologies, but *not* vice-versa. See also Paul Goren, Christopher M. Federico, and Miki Caul Kittilson, "Source Cues, Partisan Identities, and Political Value Expression," *American Journal of Political Science, 53* (October 2009), pp. 805–820, and Matthew Levendusky, *The Partisan Sort* (Chicago: University of Chicago Press, 2009), chapter 6, esp. pp. 113-114.

48. Richard H. Davis, "The Anatomy of a Smear Campaign," *The Boston Globe,* March 21, 2004.

49. Jonathon P. Schuldt, Sara H. Konrath, and Norbert Schwarz. "'Global Warming' or 'Climate Change'? Whether the Planet Is Warming Depends on Question Wording," *Public Opinion Quarterly* (Spring 2011), pp. 115–124.

50. ABC News/Washington Post polls from 1999 through 2011 (http://www.pollingreport.com/ guns.htm).

51. Larry M. Bartels, "Constituency Opinion and Congressional Policy: The Reagan Defense Build Up," *The American Political Science Review,* 85 (2), (June 1991), pp. 457–474. The next two paragraphs summarize his study.

52. Ibid.

53. Bartels had available poll data from more than100 congressional districts, allowing him to measure public opinion on the question in each of those districts.

54. Martin Gilens, "Inequality and Democratic Responsiveness," *Public Opinion Quarterly,* 69(5, Special Issue 2005), pp. 778–796. Gilens also found that there was a relatively small, but systematic, bias in favor of wealthier Americans. If the poor and the well-off disagreed on an issue, government policy followed the well-off more than the poor.

Chapter 7

1. Press release of the Xinhua News Agency, June 28, 2010.

2. We will present interest groups in detail in Chapter 10.

3. Mark P. Jones, "Explaining the High Level of Party Discipline in the Argentine Congress," in Scott Morgenstern and Benito Nacif (Eds.), *Legislative Politics in Latin America* (New York: Cambridge University Press, 2002), pp. 147–184.

4. This example is taken from W. Phillips Shively, *Power and Choice,* 13th ed. (New York: McGraw-Hill, 2012), p. 258.

5. John Aldrich (*Why Parties?* Chicago: University of Chicago Press, 1995) argues that the main impetus for the formation of parties came from elected officials. Marty Cohen, David Carol, Hans Noel, and John Zaller (*The Party Decides: Presidential Nominations Before and After Reform,* Chicago: University of Chicago Press, 2008) argue that the impetus came partly from elected officials, but also largely from activists in the electorate.

6. Cohen, Carol, Noel, and Zaller, p. 57.

7. William L. Riordon, *Plunkitt of Tammany Hall* (1905), edited by Terrence J. McDonald (Boston: Bedford St. Martins, 1994), p. 64.

8. Good evidence that those of differing economic circumstances were not distinctly Republican or Democratic before 1932–1936 is offered by the *Literary Digest* poll. The *Literary Digest* was an important national magazine that ran an unscientific poll in the 1920s and 1930s, before statisticians had learned how to poll accurately. Their "poll" was limited to their subscribers and to names drawn from automobile registration lists and telephone books—sources that in the 1920s and 1930s consisted primarily of the upper class and upper middle class. In 1924, 1928, and 1932 the poll was almost exactly correct in predicting the presidential vote, which means that the upper class and upper middle class were not voting differently from other voters. In 1936, by which time the Republican and Democratic parties were realigned along New Deal lines, the poll proved disastrously wrong. It predicted that Roosevelt would lose in a landslide. What had happened is that between 1932 and 1936 the party sympathies of the upper class and upper middle class had shifted to the Republicans. See W. Phillips Shively, "A Reinterpretation of the New Deal Realignment," *Public Opinion Quarterly, 35* (1971), pp. 621–624.

9. The Progressives stood especially for opening up government by making more decisions directly accessible to voters, but they also favored greatly expanded regulation of business corporations to prevent abuses.

10. The demise of the machines was also caused partly by the development of welfare programs, Social Security, and other measures of the New Deal. With the government now helping to ensure people's economic security, the poor were not as dependent on political machines as they once had been.

11. The one exception after 1964 is the election of 1972, when southerner Jimmy Carter ran on the Democratic ticket.

12. Ironically, the Civil Rights Act of 1964 was strongly supported by Republicans. In the House of Representatives, for instance, the vote among Democrats was 152 for the bill, 96 against; but among Republicans the vote was 138 for, 34 against. However, Barry Goldwater was the Republican presidential candidate in 1964. He was one of only six Republican Senators who had voted against the bill, but he made his opposition to it a major part of his campaign. His visible opposition permanently established the Republican Party in the public's mind as the defender of the interests of the white South. Though Goldwater lost the election badly, he succeeded in ripping the South from its Democratic allegiance, to which it never returned.

13. California, Connecticut, Maine, Massachusetts, New Hampshire, New York, Oregon, Rhode Island, Vermont, and Washington

14. We will examine the conventions and their platforms in the section titled "The Party Organization."

15. Exit polls, CBS News, http://www.cbsnews.com/election2010/exit.shtml?state=US&jurisdiction=0&race=H, accessed March 28, 2011.

16. *The Economist*/YouGov poll, July 23–26, 2011. Cited in "Glum and Glummer," *The Economist*, July 30, 2011, p. 25.

17. Paul S. Herrnson, "National Party Organizations at the Dawn of the Twenty-First Century," in L. Sandy Maisel, *The Parties Respond*, 4th ed. (Boulder, CO: Westview, 2002), p. 51.

18. See Figure 6.11, page 206.

19. An example of an instance in which state and county party officials did involve themselves in a nomination fight was the attempt in 2010 of Harold Ford to replace incumbent Senator Kirsten E. Gillibrand of New York. Ford charged that county Democratic leaders were organizing early endorsements of Gillibrand to forestall his efforts to be nominated at the state party convention. (Michael Barbaro, "As a Senator Gathers Endorsements, Her Rival Calls It 'Underhanded.'" *New York Times*, Feb. 8, 2010, p. A16).

20. Adam Nagourney, "G.O.P. Adopts 'Purity' Pledge After Revisions," *New York Times*, January 30, 2010, p. A11.

21. Paul S. Herrnson, "National Party Organizations at the Dawn of the Twenty-first Century," in L. Sandy Maisel (Ed.), *The Parties Respond*, 4th ed. (Cambridge, MA: Westview Press, 2002), p. 55; Federal Election Commission press releases.

22. For an interesting argument that the 2000 picture is not as clean as we have presented it here, read Gary Langer's blog, "The Numbers," at http://blogs.abcnews.com/thenumbers/2008/02/spoilage.html.

23. The distinction is found in many sources but is presented well in John Aldrich, *Why Parties?* (Chicago: University of Chicago Press, 1995), pp. 7–12.

24. Austin Ranney, *Curing the Mischiefs of Faction: Party Reform in America* (Berkeley, CA: University of California Press, 1975), p. 43.

25. Matthew Levendusky, *The Partisan Sort: How Liberals Became Democrats and Conservatives Became Republicans* (Chicago: University of Chicago Press, 2009).

Chapter 8

1. *Bush v. Gore*, 531 U.S. 98 (2000).

2. Pamela Paxton, "Women's Suffrage in the Measurement of Democracy: Problems of Operationalization," *Studies in Comparative International Development, 35*(3), appendix.

3. http://www.fec.gov/hava/hava.htm

4. Adam Przeworski, Susan C. Stokes, and Bernard Manin (Eds.), *Democracy, Accountability, and Representation* (New York: Cambridge University Press, 1999). There are other ways officials can be held accountable, including, for example, judicial review of their actions. But the vote is the one tool by which a citizen can directly hold officials accountable for their decisions.

5. A small number of delegates are selected from United States territories like Guam and Puerto Rico.

6. There are numerous variants of the open primary, allowing voters to move between parties in varying ways.

7. Michael P. McDonald, United States Election Project, 2012 Presidential Nomination Contest Rates. Online at http://elections.gmu.edu/Turnout_2012P.html (accessed March 1, 2012). There is a question about whether the eligible voting population is the proper base for considering turnout in primary elections (David P. Redlawsk, Caroline J. Tolbert, and Todd Donovan, *Why Iowa?* Chicago: University of Chicago Press, 2001, p. 123), since the primaries or caucuses are intended solely for partisan voters but the eligible electorate includes independents as well. However, in both Iowa and New Hampshire independents are free to participate if they choose, so considering turnout based just on the registered voters for either party could lead to misleading results. In New Hampshire in 2008, for instance, the number of voters in the Democratic primary equaled 110 percent of the registered Democratic voters, presumably because a large number of independents voted in that primary along with registered Democrats.

8. Ibid.

9. *Des Moines Register*, archives. We have only counted here contests in which there was open competition among candidates. That eliminates contests in which a party had an incumbent president, such as the Republican contest in 1984 when Ronald Reagan ran unopposed. And it also eliminates the Democratic contest in 1992 when Iowa's Democratic Senator Tom Harkin ran for president and no other Democratic candidates mounted campaigns in his home state.

10. David P. Redlawsk, Caroline J. Tolbert, and Todd Donovan, *Why Iowa?* (Chicago: University of Chicago Press, 2011), p. 131.

11. Alan Abramowitz, "Don't Blame Primary Voters for Polarization," *The Forum. 5*(4)(http://www.bepress.com/forum/vol5/iss4/art4).

12. Several other democracies use primary elections to choose their candidates, so the United States is not unique in this regard. Venezuela, for instance, uses primary elections. However, the majority of democracies keep nominations under the control of the party organization.

13. RealClearPolitics tracking polls (http://www.realclearpolitics.com/epolls/2008/president/US/general_election_mccain_vs_obama).

14. There was also a debate between the vice-presidential candidates on October 11.

15. RealClearPolitics tracking polls.

16. Bruce I. Oppenheimer, "Deep Red and Blue Congressional Districts." In Lawrence Dodd and Bruce I. Oppenheimer (Eds.), *Congress Reconsidered,* 8th ed. (Washington, DC: CQ Press, 2005), p. 140.

17. This is necessary because the size of the House of Representatives was fixed by law in 1911 at 435 (including new states added since then).

18. Members of the House from states like Wyoming or Delaware, which are small enough to have one House seat, are the exception to this. The boundaries of the state are the boundaries of the sole district in the state, and they never change. So for these members, boundaries cannot be manipulated. But these are only 7 members in a House of 435.

19. Ron Lieber, "When to Call Your Elected Representative for Help." *The New York Times* October 20, 2012, p. B1.

20. Federal Election Commission press release, December 29, 2009.

21. United Kingdom Electoral Commission, "Election 2005: Constituencies, Candidates, and Results" (March 2006). Turnover was no higher than this because many districts are very safe for one district or another, even without gerrymandering.

22. This is how elections for the House of Representatives are set up in the United States. Elections for the Senate are a variant of SMDP. There are two senators from each state, not one, so a senator is not quite a "single member"; however, only one senator runs at a time, so effectively the races are "single member." A more important difference is that since states obviously have different populations, senate "districts" do not have "roughly equal populations."

23. This may be why, as we noted earlier in this chapter, since 1864 third parties have won a limited number of seats in the House of Representatives (about 1 percent of seats, on the average), but have *never* won the presidency.

24. Source: International IDEA Table of Electoral Systems Worldwide (www.idea.int); Elections Worldwide project, now administered by Wikipedia (http://en.wikipedia.org/wiki/Wikipedia:WikiProject_Elections_and_Referenda/Overview_of_results). Two-party systems are defined as countries in which the two largest parties hold at least 95 percent of the seats in Parliament or Congress; the electoral systems are as defined by International IDEA. Countries were included if they were identified by Freedom House as electoral democracies.

25. Two other elections, 1824 and 1876, also produced a winner with less than a plurality of the popular vote, but the 1824 election was determined in a number of states by the legislature rather than by voters, and the 1876 election was determined by a bargain to end Reconstruction in return for a distorted outcome in the presidential election. Neither provides a "clean" case of a winner who received fewer votes than the loser because of the Electoral College.

26. White House scheduling (http://www.whitehouse.gov/schedule/president).

27. Cited on the website of National Popular Vote (http://www.nationalpopularvote.com/).

28. Inter-parliamentary Union, "Women in National Parliaments," May 31, 2010 (http://www.ipu.org/wmn-e/world.htm).

29. Pippa Norris, "Women's Representation and Electoral Systems." In Richard Rose (Ed.),

Encyclopedia of Electoral Systems (Washington, DC: CQ Press, 2000).

30. "Majority-minority" districts can also occur naturally, of course. An inner-city area might be heavily populated by a minority, so that any district, no matter how its boundaries were drawn, would have a majority from among the minority. In our discussion here we are looking only at deliberate gerrymandering to create majority-minority districts.

31. United Kingdom Electoral Commission, *2010 UK General Election: Party Finance.*

32. Peter Ferdinand, "Party Funding and Political Corruption in East Asia: The Cases of Japan, South Korea and Taiwan." In Reginald Austin and Maja Tjernström (Eds.), *Funding of Political Parties and Election Campaigns* (Stockholm, Sweden: International IDEA, 2003), p. 64.

33. Calculated from estimates in "Assessment of US Senate Campaign Expenditure in 2000, 2002 and 2004, with Predictions for 2006," Center for Communication and Civic Engagement Working Paper #2005-2, Department of Communication, University of Washington, Seattle, Washington.

34. *Buckley v. Valeo,* 424 U.S. 1 (1976).

35. Robert G. Boatwright, "Campaign Financing in the 2008 Election." In Janet M. Box-Steffensmeier and Steven E. Schier (Eds.), *The American Elections of 2008* (New York: Rowman & Littlefield, 2009), p. 145.

36. *Citizens United v. Federal Election Commission,* 130 S.Ct. 876 (2010).

37. US Court of Appeals for the District of Columbia: *SpeechNow.org v. Federal Election Commission.* No. 08-5223.

38. In practice, 527 committees and Super PACs have skirted very close to the line in coordinating with campaigns. "Independent" ads for Democrat Ben Nelson included an interview with the candidate (*The New York Times,* October 13, 2011, p. A17), and the website for Republican presidential candidate Rick Perry used some video that also appeared on the website of "Make Us Great Again," a Super PAC supporting his candidacy (*Politico* November 26, 2011, http://www.politico.com/blogs/bensmith/1111/Perry_ad_features_SuprPAC_footage.html?showall).

39. Nicholas Confessore, "Super PAC Plans Major Primary Campaign for Perry," *The New York Times,* Sept. 7, 2011, p. A21.

40. Jeremy W. Peters, "'Super PACs', Not Campaigns, Do Bulk of Ad Spending", *The New York Times* March 3, 2012, p. A10.

41. Mike McIntire and Michael Luo, "Fine Line Between 'Super PACs' and Campaigns", *The New York Times* February 26, 2012, p. A1.

42. Torsten Persson and Guido Tabellini, "Electoral Systems and Economic Policy." In Barry Weingast and Donald Wittman (Eds.). *Oxford Handbook of Political Economy* (Oxford: Oxford University Press, 2008).

Chapter 9

1. Rafael López Pintor and Maria Gratschew, *Voter Turnout Since 1945* (Stockholm: International IDEA, 2002), pp. 83, 84, 168.

2. World Values Surveys from 1990 to 2006, averaging results across several surveys. Retrieved July 5, 2011, from http://www.wvsevsdb.com/wvs/.

3. 2005 World Values Survey. Retrieved July 5, 2011, from http://www.wvsevsdb.com/wvs/.

4. "percent voted" is based on data from the U.S. Census Bureau, Current Population Survey, "Voting and Registration in the Election of November 2008." These statistics indicate the percent of citizens voting but do not take into account citizens who could not vote because they were disqualified as felons or for other reasons. Throughout this chapter, unless otherwise indicated the United States Census reports will be our basic source on turnout. Figures for all other forms of participation in this table are from the National Election Studies, 2008 Presidential Election Survey.

5. 2005 World Values Survey. Retrieved July 5, 2011, from http://www.wvsevsdb.com/wvs/.

6. Rafael López Pintor and Maria Gratschew, *Voter Turnout Since 1945: A Global Report* (Stockholm: International IDEA, 2002), pp. 83, 158.

7. Also, of course, this suggests that some portion of the apparently high turnout before the 1890s might have consisted of fraudulent ballots.

8. United States Census Bureau.

9. United States Census Bureau reports, *Voting and Registration in the Election of 2008.*

10. Several states, however, allow citizens to register at the polls on Election Day if they have not registered beforehand.

11. G. Bingham Powell, Jr., "American Voter Turnout in Comparative Perspective," *American Political Science Review, 80* (March 1986), pp. 17–43.

12. Michael P. McDonald, "The Return of the Voter: Voter Turnout in the 2008 Presidential Election," *The Forum, 6*(4), (2008) (http://www.bepress.com/forum/vol6/iss4/art4).

13. B. F. Skinner, *Walden Two* (New York: Macmillan, 1948), pp. 220–221.

14. Calculated from Table 5.11 of Michael S. Lewis-Beck, William G. Jacoby, Helmut Norpoth, and Herbert F. Weisberg, *The American Voter Revisited* (Ann Arbor: University of Michigan Press, 2008).

15. Estimated based on somewhat incomplete returns on November 8, 2012, using citizens over 18 as the base. One should bear in mind that high turnout in battleground states could also have been caused by greater efforts and spending invested in these close states by the candidates.

16. United States Census Bureau, *Statistical Abstract of the United States;* Corporation for National and Community Service, *Volunteering in America.* Retrieved March 27, 2009, from http://www.volunteeringinamerica.gov.

17. Source for percent voting: United States Census Bureau, *Statistical Abstract of the United States 2008.* Source for percent volunteering: Corporation for National and Community Service, *Volunteering in America.* (http://www.volunteeringinamerica.gov). Utah was eliminated from the graph because the volunteerism score for the state was idiosyncratically raised by the preponderance of members of the Mormon Church in its population.

18. U. S. Census Bureau, Current Population Studies.

19. The exception was the 1992 election, but it is likely that this was a statistical quirk in the survey.

20. National Election Studies, 2008 Presidential Election Study, ANES Guide to Public Opinion and Electoral Behavior (http://electionstudies.org/nesguide).

21. Kristen Oshyn and Tova Andrea Wang, *Youth Vote 2008,* Issue Brief of the Century Foundation, p. 9.

22. http://www.census.gov/hhes/www/socdemo/voting/publications/p20/2010/tables.html

23. U.S. Census Bureau, Current Population Survey, "Voting and Registration in the Election of November 2010" (http://www.census.gov/hhes/www/socdemo/voting/publications/p20/2010/tables.html).

24. Information on the United States, France, and Italy from Jens Alber and Ulrich Kohler, "The Inequality of Electoral Participation in Europe and America and the Politically Integrative Functions of the Welfare State," in Jens Alber and Neil Gilbert (Eds.), *United in Diversity? Comparing Social Models in Europe and America* (New York: Oxford University Press, 2008), p. 75. Information on India from Juan Linz, Alfred Stepan, and Yogendra Yadav, *Democracy and Diversity* (New York, Oxford University Press, 2007), p. 99.

25. Sidney Verba, Norman H. Nie, and Jae-on Kim argue in *Participation and Political Equality* (Chicago: University of Chicago Press, 1987) that there is less difference between participation rates of the poor and well-off in European countries than in the United States because in Europe there are explicitly labor union-based socialist parties that directly mobilize workers to vote.

26. There are no fines for failing to vote, but a notation is made on the legal books that the person who did not vote has broken the law.

27. United States Census Bureau, *Voting and Registration in the Election of November 2010.*

28. For this comparison the source is *National Election Studies, 2008 Presidential Election Study.* Available at ANES Guide to Public Opinion and Electoral Behavior (http://electionstudies.org/nesguide), since the Census does not report party affiliation.

29. United States Census Bureau, *Statistical Abstract of the United States.*

30. United States Census Bureau, *Voting and Registration in the Elections of November 2008, 2010.*

31. Pew Research Center Publications, "Public Knows Basic Facts about Politics, Economics, but Struggles with Specifics," November 18, 2010 (http://pewresearch.org/ppubs/1804/political-news-quiz-iq-deficit-spending-tarp-inflation-boehner).

32. Thomas Patterson, *The Vanishing Voter* (New York: Alfred P. Knopf, 2003).

33. Ibid., p. 125.

34. Michael S. Lewis-Beck, William G. Jacoby, Helmut Norpoth, and Herbert F. Weisberg, *The American Voter Revisited* (Ann Arbor: University of Michigan Press, 2008), pp. 55–56. This study looks at presidential elections, but the four factors apply in races of all sorts.

35. Robert S. Erikson, "Economic Conditions and the Presidential Vote," *The American Political Science Review, 83* (June 1989), pp. 567–573.

36. Michael S. Lewis-Beck, *Economics and Elections: The Major Western Democracies* (Ann Arbor: University of Michigan Press, 1988).

37. Christopher H. Achen and Larry M. Bartels, "Blind Retrospection: Electoral Responses to Drought, Flu and Shark Attacks." Paper presented at the 2002 Annual Meeting of the American Political Science Association.

38. Gallup press release January 5, 2011: "Democratic Party ID Drops in 2010, Tying 22-Year Low."

39. Gary C. Jacobson, *A Divider, Not a Uniter: George W. Bush and the American People* (New York: Pearson Longman, 2007), Figure 6.3.

40. Calculated from Michael S. Lewis-Beck, William G. Jacoby, Helmut Norpoth, and Herbert F. Weisberg, *The American Voter Revisited* (Ann Arbor: University of Michigan Press, 2008), Table 7.6. Only those who identify with a party are included in the figure.

41. Exit polls.

42. 2008 Exit Polls, CNN ElectionCenter2008 (http://www.cnn.com/ELECTION/2008/results/polls/#val=USP00p1).

43. Calculated from 2000, 2012 exit polls.

44. Donald E. Stokes and Gudmund R. Iversen, "On the Existence of Forces Restoring Party Competition," *Public Opinion Quarterly*, 26 (1962), pp. 159–171.

45. Dennis W. Johnson, *No Place for Amateurs* (New York: Routledge, 2001), p. xiii.

46. Ashley Parker, "An Unconventional Strategist Reshaping Romney," *The New York Times*, September 20, 2011.

47. See John Geer, *In Defense of Negativity: Attack Advertising in Presidential Campaigns* (Chicago: University of Chicago Press, 2006).

48. Noam Cohen, "Is Obama a Mac and Clinton a PC?" *The New York Times*, February 4, 2008.

49. Jim Rutenberg and Jeff Zeleny, "Obama Mines for Voters with High-Tech Tools," *The New York Times*, March 8, 2012, p. A1.

50. W. Phillips Shively, "From Differential Abstention to Conversion: A Change in Electoral Change, 1864–1988." *American Journal of Political Science*, 36 (May 1992), pp. 309–330.

51. Katharine Q. Seelye, "Obama Backers Mobilize in Bid to Wrest State from Republican Grip," *The New York Times*, August 17, 2008, p. A13.

52. Exit polls (www.cnn.com/ELECTION/2008/results/polls/#val=USP00p1).

53. Much has been written on this topic, but see particularly Morris P. Fiorina, Samuel J. Abrams, and Jeremy C. Pope, *Culture War?: The Myth of a Polarized America*, 2nd ed. (New York: Pearson Longman, 2006); Barbara Sinclair, *Party Wars: Polarization and the Politics of the National Policy-Making Process* (Norman, OK: University of Oklahoma Press, 2006); and Gary C. Jacobson, *A Divider Not a Uniter: George W. Bush and the American People* (New York: Pearson Longman, 2007), Chapter 1.

54. National Election Surveys, Guide to Public Opinion.

55. Ibid.

56. Ibid.

57. Ibid.

58. "Political Segregation: The Big Sort," *The Economist*, June 21, 2008, page 41.

59. See, for instance, Michael S. Lewis-Beck and Martin Paldam (Eds.), special issue of *Electoral Studies*, 19 (2000), nos. 2–3.

60. Martin Gilens, "Policy Consequences of Representational Inequality." In Peter K. Enns and Christopher Wlezien (Eds.), *Who Gets Represented?* (New York: Russell Sage Foundation, 2011), pp. 247–284.

Chapter 10

1. Abdul Maleque, *Pressure Groups: Dynamics of Bangladesh Politics* (Dhaka, Bangladesh: Academic Press and Publishers Library, 2007), pp. 359–362.

2. *Government Affairs Yellow Book: Who's Who in Government Affairs* (New York: Leadership Directories, Inc., Winter 2010).

3. Ibid.

4. Frank R. Baumgartner, Jeffrey M. Berry, Marie Hojnacki, David C. Kimball, and Beth L. Leech, *Lobbying and Policy Change: Who Wins, Who Loses, and Why.* (Chicago: University of Chicago Press, 2009), p. 9.

5. Alexis de Tocqueville, *Democracy in America* (1832), edited by Bruce Frohnen (Washington, DC: Regnery Publishing, 2002), p. 148.

6. Jocelyn Elise Crowley and Theda Skocpol, "The Rush to Organize: Explaining Associational Formation in the United States, 1860s–1920s," *American Journal of Political Science*, 45(4), (October 2001), pp. 813–829.

7. Daniel J. Tichenor and Richard A. Harris, "The Development of Interest Group Politics in America: Beyond the Conceits of Modern Times," *Annual Review of Political Science*, 8, (2005), pp. 251–270, Figure 1.

8. Terry M. Moe, *The Organization of Interests* (Chicago: University of Chicago Press, 1980).

9. "Right to work" laws in 22 states, however, ban such agreements in contracts.

10. Frank R. Baumgartner, Jeffrey M. Berry, Marie Hojnacki, David C. Kimball, and Beth L. Leech, *Lobbying and Policy Change: Who Wins, Who Loses, and Why* (Chicago: University of Chicago Press, 2009), p.199, Table 10.3.

11. Estimate of the NRA in 2010. http://www.nraila.org/Issues/Faq/?s=27.

12. Frank R. Baumgartner, Jeffrey M. Berry, Marie Hojnacki, David C. Kimball, and Beth L. Leech, *Lobbying and Policy Change: Who Wins, Who Loses, and Why* (Chicago: University of Chicago Press, 2009), p.199, Table 10.3.

13. Binyamin Appelbaum, "Auto Dealers Could Be Exempt from Proposed Regulator's Oversight," *New York Times*, June 23, 2010, p. B3.

14. Quoted in Bertram J. Levine, *The Art of Lobbying: Building Trust and Selling Policy* (Washington, DC: CQ Press, 2009), p. 100.

15. William Safire, *Safire's Political Dictionary*, 5th ed. (New York: Oxford University Press, 2008).

16. Marie Hojnacki and David C. Kimball, "Organized Interests and the Decision of Whom to Lobby in Congress," *American Political Science Review*, 92(4), (December 1998), pp. 775–790; Richard L. Hall and Alan V. Deardorff, "Lobbying as Legislative Subsidy," *American Political Science Review*, 100(1), (February, 2006), pp. 69–84.

17. Richard L. Hall and Alan V. Deardorff, op. cit.

18. Ken Kollman, *Outside Lobbying: Public Opinion and Interest Group Strategies* (Princeton, NJ: Princeton University Press, 1998), p. 5.

19. David White, "Wholesale Robbery in Liquor Sales," *The New York Times*, April 4, 2011, p. A19.

20. Laurie Goodstein, "Obama Wins Unlikely Allies in Immigration," *The New York Times*, July 19, 2010, p. A1.

21. Adapted from Anthony J. Nownes and Patricia Freeman, "Interest Group Activity in the States," *The Journal of Politics*, 60(1), (February 1998), p. 92. The results here are for activity in the states, but similar, older surveys of activities of national groups give similar results. The one figure that would probably be significantly different nationally in comparison with the state level is the use of advertisements, which is probably lower at the state level than nationally

because it is often inefficient to run a TV or radio ad for a single state.

22. The bill eventually failed in the Senate, however, because it could not attract 60 votes to prevent a filibuster and was withdrawn.

23. Rick VanderKnyff, "Bush Signs Big Fat Tax Bill," MSN Money. Retrieved January 1, 2011, from http://moneycentral.msn.com/content/taxes/p96971.asp.

24. This issue is dealt with especially in Frank R. Baumgartner, Jeffrey M. Berry, Marie Hojnacki, David C. Kimball, and Beth L. Leech, *Lobbying and Policy Change: Who Wins, Who Loses, and Why* (Chicago: University of Chicago Press, 2009), pp. 70–77.

25. Ibid., pp. 70–71.

26. Ibid., p. 74.

27. Ibid., pp. 190–191.

28. Calculated from O. Gokcekus, J. Knowles, and F. Tower, "Sweetening the Pot: How American Sugar Buys Protection." In Devashish Mitra and Arvind Panagariya (Eds.), *The Political Economy of Trade, Aid and Foreign Investment Policies* (Amsterdam: Elsevier, 2004), p. 178. (Calculated for a family of four in 1998.)

29. Martin Sebaldt, *Organisierter Pluralismus* (Opladen, Germany: Westdeutscher Verlag GmbH, 1997), pp. 79–82.

30. This is not to say that there are *no* interest groups consisting of students or other young people. Public Interest Research Groups (PIRGs) often draw their membership primarily from students, for instance.

31. David K. Kirkpatrick, "Intended to Rein in Lobbyists, Law Sends Them Underground," *The New York Times*, January 18, 2010, p. A1.

32. The transition of women's groups is analyzed in Anne N. Costain, "Representing Women: The Transition from Social Movement to Interest Group," *The Western Political Quarterly*, 34(1), (March 1981), pp. 100–113.

33. United Nations Development Programme. *Human Development Report 2009.* (http://hdr.undp.org/).

34. Ibid.

35. World Values Survey, fourth wave. (http://www.worldvaluessurvey.org/)

Chapter 11

1. "The Story of Mohamed Bouazizi, the man who toppled Tunisia," *International Business Times*, January 14, 2011 (http://www.ibtimes.com/articles/101313/20110114/the-story-of-mohamed-bouazizi-the-man-who-toppled tunisia.htm); Bob Simon, "How a Slap Sparked Tunisia's Revolution," *60 Minutes*, February 20, 2011 (http://www.cbsnews.com/stories/2011/02/20/60minutes/main20033404.shtml).

2. Cameron Joseph, "Tea Party Triumphs on Twitter, Facebook," *National Journal*, September 24, 2010 (http://hotlineoncall.nationaljournal.com/archives/2010/09/tea_party_trium.php).

3. Brian Deagon, "Tea Party Movement a Political Tsunami, Thanks to Internet," *Investor's Business Daily*, September 22, 2010 (http://www.investors.com/NewsAndAnalysis/Article/548152/201009221919/Tea-Party-Movement-A-Political-Tsunami-Thanks-To-Internet.aspx) (full text at http://texasteapartypac.ning.com/profiles/blogs/tea-party-movement-a-political).

4. Robert M. Entman, "Foreword." In Karen Callaghan and Frauke Schnell (Eds.), *Framing*

American Politics (Pittsburgh: University of Pittsburgh Press, 2005), p. viii.

5. Bill Carter and Brian Stelter, "In 'Daily Show' Role on 9/11 Bill, Echoes of Murrow," *The New York Times,* December 26, 2010 (http://www.nytimes.com/2010/12/27/business/media/27stewart.html).

6. David L. Paletz, *The Media in American Politics: Contents and Consequences* (New York: Longman, 1999), p. 141.

7. "Media Watchdog Criticizes Coverage of Famine in Ethiopia," *IJNET,* May 24, 2001 (http://ijnet.org/opportunities/media-watchdog-criticizes-coverage-famine-ethiopia).

8. Rick Hampson, "Ethiopia's New Fame: 'A Ticking Time Bomb,'" *USA Today,* August 17, 2008 (http://www.usatoday.com/news/world/2008-08-17-ethiopia_N.htm).

9. Paletz, *The Media in American Politics,* p. 119.

10. "ACORN Officials Videotaped Telling 'Pimp,' 'Prostitute' How to Lie to IRS," Fox News.com, September 10, 2009 (http://www.foxnews.com/us/2009/09/10/acorn-officials-videotaped-telling-pimp-prostitute-lie-irs/#).

11. WikiLeaks can be found at www.wikileaks.org.

12. Scott Shane and Andrew W. Lehren, "Leaked Cables Offer Raw Look at U.S. Diplomacy," *The New York Times,* November 28, 2010 (http://www.nytimes.com/2010/11/29/world/29cables.html).

13. Andrew P. Thomas, "The CSI Effect: Fact or Fiction," *The Yale Law Journal Online,* January 31, 2006 (http://yalelawjournal.org/the-yale-law-journal-pocket-part/criminal-law-and-sentencing/the-csi-effect:-fact-or-fiction/).

14. Frank Luther Mott, *American Journalism,* (New York: Macmillan, 1960), p. 251.

15. The first successful trans-Atlantic cable took place on August 5, 1858, between President James Buchanan of the United States and Queen Victoria of England, but that cable soon failed.

16. Eric Burns, *Infamous Scribblers: The Founding Fathers and the Rowdy Beginnings of American Journalism* (New York: Public Affairs, 2006), pp. 31–32.

17. Mott, *American Journalism,* p. 43.

18. Burns, *Infamous Scribblers,* p. 239.

19. Mott, *American Journalism,* p. 108.

20. Richard L. Rubin, *Press, Party, and Presidency* (New York: Norton, 1981), p. 11.

21. Culver H. Smith, *The Press, Politics, and Patronage: The American Government's Use of Newspapers, 1789–1875* (Athens, GA: The University of Georgia Press, 1977), p. 13; Burns, *Infamous Scribblers,* pp. 262–266.

22. Martin Mayes, *An Historical-Sociological Inquiry into Certain Phases of the Development of the Press in the United States* (Richmond: Missourian Press, 1935), p. 48.

23. Mark Wahlgren Summers, *The Press Gang: Newspapers and Politics, 1865–1878* (Chapel Hill: The University of North Carolina Press, 1994), p. 12.

24. Mott, *American Journalism,* pp. 525–526.

25. All of these figures are drawn from https://umdrive.memphis.edu/mbensman/public/history1.html.

26. http://www.museum.tv/exhibitionssection.php?page=79.

27. The Gallup Poll, "Media Use and Evaluation" (http://www.gallup.com/poll/1663/media-use-evaluation.aspx).

28. Rodney Ho, "Rush Limbaugh Tops Talk Radio Rankings as Usual, Glenn Beck Moves Up," *Access Atlanta,* March 3, 2010 (http://blogs.ajc.com/radio-tv-talk/2010/03/03/rush-limbaugh-tops-talk-radio-rankings-as-usual-glenn-beck-moves-up/).

29. John P. Robinson and Leo W. Jeffres, "The Changing Role of Newspapers in the Age of Television," *Journalism Monographs,* No. 63 (September 1979), p. 2.

30. National Institute of Mental Health, *Television and Behavior, Vol. 1* (Washington, DC: Government Printing Office, 1982), p. 1.

31. Steve M. Barkin, *American Television News: The Media Marketplace and the Public Interest* (Armonk, NY: M. E. Sharpe, 2003), p. 37. See also http://www.museum.tv/eotvsection.php?entrycode=kennedyjf.

32. Charles Franklin, "Walter Cronkite, Most Trusted Man in America," *Pollster.com,* July 17, 2009 (http://www.pollster.com/blogs/walter_cronkite_most_trusted_m.php?nr=1).

33. White House press secretary George Christian used the term "shock waves" to describe the Johnson administration's reaction to Cronkite's report. See John Anthony Maltese, *Spin Control: The White House Office of Communications and the Management of Presidential News* (Chapel Hill: The University of North Carolina Press, 1992), p. 14.

34. http://www.ncta.com/About/About/HistoryofCableTelevision.aspx

35. Associated Press, "And Now the News: For Many Young Viewers, It's Jon Stewart," March 4, 2004 (http://today.msnbc.msn.com/id/4400644/ns/today-entertainment/).

36. Kenneth C. Creech, *Electronic Media Law and Regulation,* 3rd ed. (Boston: Focal Press, 2000), pp. 54–56.

37. Creech, *Electronic Media Law and Regulation,* p. 67.

38. Katy Bachman, "Media Ownership Rules in Limbo: Court Hears Arguments in Fight Over FCC Regulations," *Adweek,* February 25, 2011 (http://www.adweek.com/aw/content_display/news/media/e3i86c9ad1856395199a85ab287617b0493#).

39. Edward Wyatt, "A Clash Over the Airwaves," *The New York Times,* April 21, 2011 (http://www.nytimes.com/2011/04/22/business/media/22spectrum.html?ref=federalcommunicationscommission).

40. Edward Wyatt, "House Passes Measure Against 'Net Neutrality,'" *The New York Times,* April 8, 2011 (http://www.nytimes.com/2011/04/09/business/media/09broadband.html?scp=3&sq=FCC&st=cse); Edward Wyatt, "Court Rejects Suit on Net Neutrality Rules," *The New York Times,* April 4, 2011 (http://www.nytimes.com/2011/04/05/technology/05net.html?scp=5&sq=FCC&st=cse).

41. Kevin J. O'Brien, "E.U. to Review Mobile Operators' Policies on Web Access," *The New York Times,* April 18, 2011 (http://www.nytimes.com/2011/04/19/technology/19data.html?scp=6&sq=net%20neutrality&st=cse).

42. Quoted in Creech, *Electronic Media Law and Regulation,* p. 72.

43. *Red Lion Broadcasting Co. v. Federal Communications Commission,* 395 U.S. 367 (1969).

44. Todd S. Purdum, "Terror in Oklahoma: The President; Shifting Debate to the Political Climate, Clinton Condemns 'Promoters of Paranoia,'" *The New York Times,* April 25, 1995 (http://www.nytimes.com/1995/04/25/us/terror-oklahoma-president-shifting-debate-political-climate-clinton-condemns.html?pagewanted=1).

45. "Clinton Wants 'More Balance' on Airwaves," *Politico,* February 12, 2009 (http://www.politico.com/blogs/michaelcalderone/0209/Clinton_wants_more_balance_on_the_airwaves.htm).

46. Creech, *Electronic Media Law and Regulation,* p. 118.

47. *Federal Communication Commission v. Pacifica Foundation,* 438 U.S. 726 (1978).

48. Amy Schatz, "Crying Foul: Supreme Court to Hear Challenge to FCC Cussing Crackdown," *Wall Street Journal,* January 9, 2012, http://online.wsj.com/article/SB10001424052970203436904577148731524813906.html

49. *Reno v. American Civil Liberties Union,* 521 U.S. 844 (1997).

50. *ACLU v.. Mukasey,* 534 F.3d 181 (2008), cert. denied 129 S.Ct. 1032 (2009).

51. *United States v. American Library Association,* 539 U.S. 194 (2003).

52. W. Lance Bennett, *News: The Politics of Illusion,* 2nd ed. (New York: Longman, 1988), p. xi.

53. Leon V. Sigal, *Reporters and Officials: The Organization and Politics of Newsmaking* (Lexington, MA: D. C. Heath and Company, 1973), p. 120.

54. Sigal, *Reporters and Officials,* p. 121 (Table 6–1).

55. Samuel Kernell, *Going Public: New Strategies of Presidential Leadership* (Washington, DC: CQ Press, 1986).

56. Jeffrey K. Tulis, *The Rhetorical Presidency* (Princeton: Princeton University Press, 1987); see especially 64 (Table 3–1). Cf. Mel Laracey, *Presidents and the People: The Partisan Story of Going Public* (College Station: Texas A&M University Press, 2002).

57. Elmer J. Cornwell, Jr., *Presidential Leadership of Public Opinion* (Bloomington: Indiana University Press, 1965), p. 17.

58. Mark Knoller, "Obama's First Year: By the Numbers," *CBS News,* January 20, 2010 (http://www.cbsnews.com/8301-503544_162-6119525-503544.html#).

59. Martha Joynt Kumar, *Managing the President's Message: The White House Communications Operation* (Baltimore: Johns Hopkins University Press, 2007); John Anthony Maltese, *Spin Control: The White House Office of Communications and the Management of Presidential News* (Chapel Hill: The University of North Carolina Press, 1992).

60. Devin Dwyer, "Obama's Media Machine: State Run Media 2.0?", *ABC News,* February 15, 2011 (http://abcnews.go.com/Politics/president-obama-white-house-media-operation-state-run/story?id=12913319).

61. Summers, *The Press Gang,* p. 81.

62. http://www.museum.tv/eotvsection.php?entrycode=uscongress

63. http://legacy.c-span.org/international/links.asp?Cat=Issue&Code=I

64. David R. Mayhew, *Congress: The Electoral Connection* (New Haven: Yale University Press, 1974).

65. David A. Fahrenthold, "27% of Communication by Members of Congress Is Taunting, Professor Concludes," *Washington Post,* April 6, 2011 (http://www.washingtonpost.com/politics/27percent-of-communication-by-members-of-congress-is-taunting-professor-concludes/2011/04/06/AF1no2qC_story.html).

66. Jennifer Steinhauer, "The G.O.P.'s Very Rapid Response Team," *The New York Times*, October 25, 2011, p. A14.

67. Elliot E. Slotnick and Jennifer A. Segal, "'The Supreme Court Decided Today. . . ,' or Did It?" In Elliot E. Slotnick (Ed.), *Judicial Politics: Readings from Judicature*, 2nd ed. (Lanham, MD: Rowman & Littlefield, 1999), p. 449.

68. David L. Paletz and Robert M. Entman, *Media Power Politics* (New York: The Free Press, 1981), p. 48.

69. Paletz and Entman, *Media Power Politics*, p. 47.

70. Paletz and Entman, *Media Power Politics*, p. 45.

71. Michael D. Shear, "Romney Appears to Waver on Ohio Anti-Union Rules," *The New York Times*, October 27, 2011, p. A17.

72. http://people-press.org/2008/03/17/section-iii-the-state-of-journalism-and-views-on-performance/

73. http://people-press.org/2009/09/13/press-accuracy-rating-hits-two-decade-low/

74. Michael Parenti, "Inventing Reality: The Politics of News Media." In Lewis S. Rangel (Ed.), *The Lanahan Readings in Media and Politics* (Baltimore: Lanahan Publishers, 2009), pp. 166, 171–172.

75. Bennett, *News*, p. 45.

76. Bennett, *News*, p. 46.

77. Bennett, *News*, p. 47.

78. Bennett, *News*, p. 47.

79. Arthur Conan Doyle, *The Adventure of the Six Napoleons*, quoted in Paletz and Entman, *Media Power Politics*, p. 79.

Chapter 12

1. DPA News Agency, "Chronology: Financial Crisis Spreads from U.S. to World Markets," *Deutsche Welle*, Oct. 4, 2008 (http://www.dw-world.de/dw/article/0,2144,3689713,00.html).

2. Massimo Calabresi, "Congress and the Bailout Plan: Business as Usual," *Time*, Sept. 23, 2008 (http://www.time.com/time/politics/article/0,8599,1843642,00.html).

3. Michael L. Mezey, "The Functions of Legislatures in the Third World," *Legislative Studies Quarterly*, 8(4), (1983), pp. 511–550.

4. By that time, 29 states were already using a form of popular participation in selecting senators, rather than relying completely on state legislators. See the discussion on the Art and History website of the United States Senate (http://www.senate.gov/artandhistory/history/common/briefing/Direct_Election_Senators.htm).

5. Research in Arizona has shown that in the House, where multi-member districts are used, legislators are more ideological in their voting, while in the Senate, where a single-member district is used, constituency factors are more pronounced.

6. Heinz Eulau, John C. Wahlke, William Buchanan, and Leroy C. Ferguson, "The Role of Representation: Some Empirical Observations on the Theory of Edmund Burke." *The American Political Science Review*, 53(3), (1959), 742–756.

7. Citizens Against Government Waste, "Pork Barrel Report" (http://www.cagw.org/reports/pig-book/#trends).

8. Scott A. Frisch and Sean Q. Kelly, *Cheese Factories on the Moon: Why Earmarks Are Good for American Democracy* (Boulder: Paradigm Publishers, 2011); Jason Iuliano, "Eliminating Earmarks: Why the Congressional Line Item Veto Can Succeed Where the Presidential Line

Item Veto Failed," *West Virginia Law Review*, 112 (2010).

9. Kerr L. Haynie "African Americans and the New Politics of Inclusion." In Lawrence D. Dodd and Bruce L. Oppenheimer (Eds), *Congress Reconsidered*, 8th ed. (Washington, DC: CQ Press, 2005), pp. 395–409.

10. Inter-Parliamentary Union, "Women in National Parliaments." Retrieved April 30, 2011, from http://www.ipu.org/wmn-e/classif.htm).

11. See David R. Mayhew, *Congress: The Electoral Connection* (New Haven, CT: Yale University Press, 1975).

12. Richard F. Fenno, "US House Members in Their Constituencies: An Exploration," *The American Political Science Review*, 71(3), (1977), pp. 883–917.

13. Gary Fields and John R. Emshwiller, "As Criminal Laws Proliferate, More Are Ensnared," *Wall Street Journal*, July 23, 2011 (http://online.wsj.com/article/SB10001424052748703749504576172714184601654.html?mod=djem_jiewr_PS_domainid#project%3DCRIMES_FEDOFFENSES_1107%26articleTabs%3Darticle).

14. Human Rights Watch, 2009 (http://www.hrw.org/en/news/2009/07/24/united-states-ratification-international-human-rights-treaties); Human Rights Index, 2011, *International Accents*, University of Iowa (http://accents.international.uiowa.edu/worldviews/human-rights-index-united-nations-convention-on-the-elimination-of-all-forms-of-discrimination-against-women-spring-2011-30/),

15. http://www.senate.gov/artandhistory/history/common/briefing/Nominations.htm

16. Robert Jay Dilger, "Congressional Member Organizations: Their Purpose and Activities, History, and Formation," Congressional Research Service, July 1, 2009, CRS-R40683 (http://assets.opencrs.com/rpts/R40683_20090701.pdf)

17. "Boren's Announcement Leaves Plenty of Dry Eyes in the House" *CQ Weekly*, June 13, 2011, p. 1243.

18. Shawn Zeller, "2010 Vote Studies: Party Unity," *CQ Weekly*, Jan. 3, 2011, pp. 30–35 (http://library.cqpress.com/cqweekly/weeklyreport112-000003788817).

19. http://www.senate.gov/artandhistory/history/common/briefing/Party_Whips.htm

20. Richard A. Smith, "Advocacy, Interpretation, and Influence in the U.S. Congress," *The American Political Science Review*, 78(1), (1984), pp. 44–63.

21. Kathryn Pearson, "Party Discipline in the Contemporary Congress: Rewarding Loyalty with Legislative Preference." Paper presented at the annual meeting of the American Political Science Association, August 28–31, 2003, in Philadelphia, PA.

22. Gebe Martinez, "DeLay's Conservatism Solidifies GOP Base for Bush," *CQ Weekly Online*, July 12, 2003, pp. 1726–1733 (http://library.cqpress.com/cqweekly/weeklyreport108-000000760850).

23. Ben Pershing, "Pelosi, Harman Have Long History," Capital Briefing, *Washington Post*, April 23, 2009 (http://voices.washingtonpost.com/capitol-briefing/2009/04/pelosi_harman_have_long_histor.html?hpid=news-col-blog).

24. Richard F. Fenno, *Congressmen in Committees* (Boston: Little Brown, 1973).

25. John H. Aldrich and David W. Rohde, "Congressional Committees in a Partisan Era." In Lawrence C. Dodd and Bruce I.

Oppenheimer (Eds.), *Congress Reconsidered*, 8th ed. (Washington, DC: CQ Press, 2005), pp. 249–270.

26. Rebecca Kimitch, "CQ Guide to the Committees: Democrats Opt to Spread the Power," *CQ Weekly Online*, April 16, 2007, pp. 1080–1083.

27. James W. Endersby and Karen M. McCurdy, "Committee Assignments in the U.S. Senate," *Legislative Studies Quarterly*, 21(2), (1996), pp. 219–233.

28. Ida A. Brudnick, "Congressional Salaries and Allowances," Congressional Research Service. Retrieved Jan. 4, 2011, from (http://www.senate.gov/CRSReports/crs-publish.cfm?pid='0E%2C*PL%5B%3D%23P%20%20%0A).

29. Eric Petersen, "Legislative Branch Staffing, 1954–2007," Congressional Research Service, Oct. 15, 2008, CRS-R40056 (http://assets.opencrs.com/rpts/R40056_20081015.pdf); Eric Petersen, Parker H. Reynolds, and Amber Hope Wilhelm, "House of Representatives and Senate Staff Levels in Member, Committee, Leadership and Other Offices, 1977–2010," Congressional Research Service, Aug. 10, 2010, CRS-R41366 (http://assets.opencrs.com/rpts/R41366_20100810.pdf).

30. For a brief history of the filibuster, see the United States Senate Art and History website at http://www.senate.gov/artandhistory/history/common/briefing/Filibuster_Cloture.htm

31. John H. Aldrich and David W. Rohde, "Congressional Committees in a Partisan Era" in Lawrence C. Dodd and Bruce I. Oppenheimer (Eds.), *Congress Reconsidered*, 8th ed. (Washington, DC: CQ Press, 2005), pp. 249–270; Barbara Sinclair, "New World of US Senators" in Lawrence C. Dodd and Bruce I. Oppenheimer (Eds.), *Congress Reconsidered*, 8th ed. (Washington, DC: CQ Press, 2005), pp. 1–22.

32. Daniel Diermeier and Roger B. Myerson, "Bicameralism and Its Consequences for the International Organization of Legislatures," *The American Economic Review*, 89(5): 1182–1196.

33. David C. King, "The Nature of Congressional Committee Jurisdictions," *The American Political Science Review*, 88(1), pp. 48–62.

34. Jena Baker McNeill, "Congressional Oversight of Homeland Security in Dire Need of Overhaul," *The Heritage Foundation*, Backgrounder 2161 (http://www.heritage.org/research/HomelandDefense/bg2161.cfm#_ftn11). Also see "Untangling the Web," White Paper of the Center for Strategic and International Studies and the Business Executives for National Security, Dec. 10, 2004 (http://www.csis.org/media/csis/events/041210_dhs_tf_whitepaper.pdf).

35. Kady II, Martin "Three Years On, Homeland Security Turf Wars Persist," *CQ Weekly Online*, June 26, 2006, pp. 1776–1777 (http://library.cqpress.com/cqweekly/weeklyreport109-000002312160).

36. "Senate Eliminates 42 Committees," U.S. Senate, *Historical Minutes* (http://www.senate.gov/artandhistory/history/minute/Senate_Eliminates_42_Committees.htm); Valerie Heitshusen, "Committee Types and Roles," CRS Report for Congress, updated Nov. 10, 2010 (http://assets.opencrs.com/rpts/98-241_20101110.pdf).

37. Elaine K. Swift, "The Start of Something New: Clay, Stevenson, Polk and the Development of the Speakership, 1789–1869," in Roger

H. Davidson, Susan Webb Hammond, and Raymond Smock (Eds.), *Masters of the House: Congressional Leaders Over Two Centuries* (Boulder, CO: Westview Press, 1998).

38. Major Garrett, "Being Boehner: The Speaker Is Running the House His Way, Not the Way of His Recent Predecessors," *National Journal,* June 7, 2011 (http://www.nationaljournal.com/magazine/being-boehner-20110602?page=1).

39. John Stanton, "Boehner's Style Weakened Hand in Negotiations," *Roll Call,* July 20, 2011 (http://www.rollcall.com/issues/57_10/John-Boehner-Weakened-Hand-Negotiations-207474-1.html).

40. Joseph J. Schatz and Steven Sloan "Tax Deal Sets Stage for Late Action," *CQ Weekly* (Dec. 27, 2010), pp. 2940–2942 (http://library.cqpress.com/cqweekly/weeklyreport111-000003786958); Joseph J. Schatz "2010 Vote Studies: Presidential Support," *CQ Weekly,* Jan. 3, 2011, pp. 18–24 (http://library.cqpress.com/cqweekly/weeklyreport112-000003788814).

41. Peter Katel (July 22, 2005), "Lobbying Boom," *CQ Researcher,* July 22, 2005, pp. 613–636.

42. Kevin M. Esterling, "Buying Expertise: Campaign Contributions and Attention to Policy Analysis in Congressional Committees," *American Political Science Review, 101*(1), (February 2007), pp. 93–109.

43. http://www.senate.gov/reference/resources/pdf/howourlawsaremade.pdf

44. Lee Hamilton, "What I Wish Political Scientists Would Teach about Congress," *PS: Political Science and Politics, 33*(4), pp. 757–764.

Chapter 13

1. Clive Crook, "Foreign Affairs: Essay—Tony Blair's Downfall," *National Journal,* May 25, 2007.

2. Giovani Sartori, *Comparative Constitutional Engineering: An Inquiry Into Structures, Incentives and Outcomes,* 2nd ed. (New York: New York University Press, 1997), pp. 83–86. Elijah Ben-Zion Kaminsky also stresses the need for policy agreement between legislature and executive in a parliamentary system. Elijah Ben-Zion Kaminsky, "On the Comparison of Presidential and Parliamentary Governments," *Presidential Studies Quarterly, 27* (Spring 1997), pp. 221–229.

3. Alfred Stepan and Cindy Skach, "Constitutional Frameworks and Democratic Consolidation: Parliamentarism versus Presidentialism," *World Politics, 46*(1), (October 1993), pp. 1–22.

4. Note that this includes Canada, which was a member of the British Commonwealth until recently and never made a sharp break with Britain

5. Parts of this section are adapted, with permission, from W. Phillips Shively, *Power and Choice,* 11th ed. (New York: McGraw-Hill, 2008).

6. "Anne Burford, 62; Embattled EPA Chief for President Reagan," *Los Angeles Times,* July 22, 2004 (http://articles.latimes.com/2004/jul/22/local/me-burford22).

7. Fred I. Greenstein, *The Hidden Hand Presidency: Eisenhower as Leader* (New York: Basic Books, 1981).

8. Interview with Richard Nixon by David Frost, televised May 19, 1977; quoted in Craig Ducat, *Constitutional Interpretation,* 7th ed. (Belmont, CA: West, 2000), p. 206.

9. Joseph A. Pika and John Anthony Maltese, *Politics of the Presidency,* 7th ed. (Washington: CQ Press, 2008), p. 16.

10. Jeffrey Rosen, "Bush's Leviathan State: Power of One," *The New Republic,* July 24, 2006; Joel D. Aberbach, "Supplying the Defect of Better Motives? The Bush II Administration and the Constitutional System." In Colin Campbell, Bert A. Rockman, and Andrew Rudalevige (Eds.), *The George W. Bush Legacy* (Washington: CQ Press, 2008), pp. 112–133.

11. Richard E. Neustadt, *Presidential Power and the Modern Presidents: The Politics of Leadership from Roosevelt to Reagan* (New York: The Free Press, 1990), p. 11.

12. Kenneth Mayer, *With the Stroke of a Pen: Executive Orders and Presidential Power* (Princeton: Princeton University Press, 2002); Samuel Kernell, *Going Public,* 4th ed. (Washington, DC: CQ Press, 2006).

13. Pew Global Attitudes Project (May 17, 2011), "Arab Spring Fails to Improve U.S. Image" (http://pewglobal.org/2011/05/17/arab-spring-fails-to-improve-us-image/2/), and "Obama More Popular Abroad Than At Home, Global Image of U.S. Continues to Benefit" (June 17, 2010), (http://pewglobal.org/2010/06/17/obama-more-popular-abroad-than-at-home/).

14. Matthew J. Dickinson, "Neustadt, New Institutionalism, and Presidential Decision Making: A Theory and Test," *Presidential Studies Quarterly, 35* (June 2005), pp. 259–288.

15. See the four-part series on Vice President Cheney that ran from June 24 to June 27, 2007, starting with Barton Gelman and Jo Becker, "'A Different Understanding with the President,'" *Washington Post* (June 24, 2007), p. A1.

16. "Court politics" refers to politics in a situation where a single leader is isolated and very powerful. This can lead to flattery, attempts to monopolize time with the single powerful leader, unwillingness to bring bad news to the leader, and special power to those—such as spouses, barbers, and so on—who unavoidably have hours of contact with the leader that others would give anything for. The term derives from the politics of the great royal courts of eighteenth-century Europe.

17. "Groupthink" refers to a psychological drive for consensus that suppresses dissent within decision-making groups. See Irving Janis, *Victims of Groupthink* (Boston: Houghton Mifflin, 1972).

18. Fred I. Greenstein, *The Presidential Difference: Leadership Style From FDR to Barack Obama,* 3rd ed. (Princeton University Press, 2009) 217–223.

19. When Nixon's vice president, Spiro T. Agnew, resigned in 1973 under charges of accepting bribes while he was governor of Maryland, Ford was nominated by Nixon and confirmed by Congress under the terms of the Twenty-Fifth Amendment. Ford became the nation's first unelected president in 1974 and in turn named Nelson Rockefeller to fill the vice-presidential vacancy.

20. Paul Light, *The President's Agenda: Domestic Policy Choice from Kennedy to Carter* (Baltimore: The Johns Hopkins University Press, 1982).

21. Charles O. Jones, *The Presidency in a Separated System,* 2nd ed. (Washington: Brookings Institution Press, 2005), p. 24.

22. See the discussion of partisan variation in Jones (2005), *The Presidency in a Separated System,* 2nd ed., pp. 25–31.

23. Andrea Chandler, "Presidential Veto Power in Post-Communist Russia, 1994–1998," *Canadian Journal of Political Science, 34*(3), (September 2001), pp. 487–516.

24. Jeffrey K. Tulis, *The Rhetorical Presidency* (Princeton: Princeton University Press, 1987).

25. Martin P. Wattenberg, "The Changing Presidential Media Environment," *Presidential Studies Quarterly, 34,* (September 2004), pp. 557–558.

26. Reed L. Welch, "Was Reagan Really a Great Communicator? The Influence of Televised Addresses on Public Opinion," *Presidential Studies Quarterly, 33* (December 2003), pp. 853–876.

27. Rebecca Adams, "Lame Duck or Leap Frog?" *CQ Weekly Online* (February 12, 2007), pp. 450–457. Retrieved July 31, 2007, from http://library.cqpress.com/cqweekly/weeklyreport110-000002449623.

28. Ibid.

29. Bush's regulatory record has been analyzed by a number of scholars. Not surprisingly, one study attributed much of the Bush administration's increased regulatory activity in spending and staff increases to expanded efforts in security. Jonathan Rauch, "Social Studies—Flying Blind in a Red-Tape Blizzard," *National Journal* (July 14, 2007).

30. Kenneth R. Mayer, *With the Stroke of a Pen: Executive Orders and Presidential Power* (p. 4) (Princeton: Princeton University Press, 2002).

31. Ibid., 75. Also see the larger discussion, pp. 39–80.

32. Sheldon Goldman (April–May 1989), "Reagan's Judicial Legacy: Completing the Puzzle and Summing Up," *Judicature, 72* (April–May 1981), pp. 319–320.

33. Personal communication to the authors from Susan Smelcer, an analyst on the federal judiciary at the Congressional Research Service, Library of Congress, May 19, 2011.

34. Joseph A. Pika and John Anthony Maltese, *The Politics of the Presidency,* 7th ed., (Washington: CQ Press, 2008), p. 313. Total adjusted for Obama nominations.

35. U.S. Department of Justice, "Matters of Justice: An Overview of Major Issues and Trends," *Strategic Plan, Fiscal Years 2007–2012,* p. 1. http://www.usdoj.gov/jmd/mps/strategic2007-2012/matters_of_justice.pdf.

36. B. Dan Wood and James E. Anderson, "The Politics of U.S. Antitrust Regulation," *American Journal of Political Science, 37* (February 1993), p. 36.

Chapter 14

1. David E. Lewis, "FEMA's Politicization and the Road to Katrina," working paper later published as a chapter in *The Politics of Presidential Appointments: Political Control and Bureaucratic Performance* (p. 42) (Princeton: Princeton University Press, 2008). Also see Rebecca Adams, "FEMA Failure a Perfect Storm of Bureaucracy." *CQ Weekly Online* (Sept. 12, 2005), pp. 2378–2379 Retrieved July 28, 2008, from http://library.cqpress.com/cqweekly/weeklyreport109-000001853459.

2. International Federation of Red Cross and Red Crescent Societies, *World Disasters Report 2005* (Chapter 2), http://www.ifrc.org/publicat/wdr2005/chapter2.asp; Anita Snow, "Lesson from Ike: Nobody Does Evacuations Like Cuba," *Associated Press,* Sept. 10, 2008. (http://news.yahoo.com/s/ap/20080911/ap_on_re_la_am_ca/cuba_evacuations); Martha Thompson with Izaskun Gaviria, *Cuba, Weathering the Storm: Lessons in Risk Reduction from Cuba*

(Boston: Oxfam America, 2004) (http://www.oxfamamerica.org/newsandpublications/publications/research_reports/art7111.html/OA-Cuba_Weathering_the_Storm-2004.pdf).

3. August Nimtz, "Cuba and the Lessons of Katrina," *Monthly Review*, Nov. 18, 2005 (http://mrzine.monthlyreview.org/nimtz181105.html).

4. Richard J. Stillman, II, "The Constitutional Bicentennial and the Centennial of the American Administrative State," *Public Administration Review* 47(1), (Jan./Feb. 1987), p. 6.

5. First Inaugural Address of Ronald Reagan (Jan. 20, 1981) (http://www.reaganlibrary.com/reagan/speeches/first.asp).

6. State of the Union Message, William Jefferson Clinton (Jan. 23, 1996) (http://clinton2.nara.gov/WH/New/other/sotu.html).

7. Barry Karl, "The American Bureaucrat: A History of a Sheep in Wolves' Clothing," *Public Administration Review* 47(1), (Jan/Feb 1987), p. 34.

8. Harold J. Laski (1948). *The American Democracy* (p. 167) (New York: Viking Press), as quoted in Harold Seidman and Robert Gilmour, *Politics, Position and Power: From the Positive to the Regulatory State* 4 ed. (New York: Oxford University Press, 1986), p. 259.

9. Directorate General for Communication, *Eurobarometer 73: Public Opinion in the European Union*, August 2010 (http://ec.europa.eu/public_opinion/archives/eb/eb73/eb73_first_en.pdf).

10. Norton Long, "Bureaucracy and Constitutionalism," *American Political Science Review*, Sept. 1952, pp. 808–818.

11. Ibid., 809.

12. Norton Long, "Power and Administration" *Public Administration Review*, Autumn 1949, p. 258.

13. Ralph Clark Chandler, "Public Administration Under the Articles of Confederation," *Public Administration Quarterly*, 13(4), (Winter 1990), pp. 440–441.

14. Chandler, pp. 443–448.

15. Lynton K. Caldwell, "The Administrative Republic: The Contrasting Legacies of Hamilton and Jefferson," *Public Administration Quarterly*, 13(4), (Winter 1990), pp. 470–493.

16. Richard T. Green, "Alexander Hamilton and the Study of Public Administration," *Public Administration Quarterly*, 13(4), (Winter 1990), pp. 494–519.

17. Stephen Minicucci, "Internal Improvements and the Union, 1790–1860," *Studies in American Political Development*, 18, (Fall 2004), p. 160.

18. Stephen Skowronek, *Building a New American State: The Expansion of National Administrative Capacities, 1877–1920* (Cambridge: Cambridge University Press, 1982), p. 23.

19. Ibid., 9–12.

20. Matthew Crenson, *The Federal Machine* (Baltimore: Johns Hopkins University Press, 1975).

21. Skowronek, *Building a New American State*, 47.

22. There is no simple typology of government organizations. One influential classification scheme was suggested by Harold Seidman and Robert Gilmour, *Politics, Position and Power: From the Positive to the Regulatory State* (4th ed., pp. 254–259) (New York: Oxford University Press, 1986).

23. Harold C. Relyea, "Homeland Security: Department Organization and Management," CRS Report RL31493, Aug. 7, 2002 (http://fpc.state.gov/documents/organization/13385.pdf).

24. Ibid., 3–4.

25. Homeland Security Act of 2002 (http://www.dhs.gov/xabout/laws/law_regulation_rule_0011.shtm).

26. For a list of these units, see http://www.dhs.gov/xabout/history/editorial_0133.shtm.

27. http://www.whitehouse.gov/government/independent-agencies.html

28. Seidman and Gilmour, 276.

29. Fabrizio Gilardi, "The Institutional Foundation of Regulatory Capitalism: The Diffusion of Independent Regulatory Agencies in Western Europe," *The Annals of the American Academy of Political and Social Science*, 598 (March 2005), pp. 84–101.

30. Peter Katel, "Future of the Airlines," *CQ Researcher*, 18, (March 7, 2008), pp. 217–240 (http://library.cqpress.com/cqresearcher/).

31. Ronald C. Moe (Nov. 24, 1998), "Federal Government Corporations: An Overview," CRS Report 98–954: 1 (http://www.jhu.edu/~ccss/toolsworkbooks/pdfbook5/part1/a2.pdf).

32. For example, through 2005, AMTRAK had received $29 billion in federal subsidies for its operating budget but had never turned a profit. See Adriel Bettelheim, "Amtrak: A Limping Iron Horse Lives Year to Year." *CQ Weekly Online*, Dec. 12, 2005, pp. 3308–3315. Retrieved July 27, 2008, from http://library.cqpress.com/cqweekly/weeklyreport109-000001998153

33. Kevin R. Kosar, "The Quasi-Government: Hybrid Organizations with Both Government and Private Sector Legal Characteristics," CRS Report, Feb. 13, 2007 (http://www.fas.org/sgp/crs/misc/RL30533.pdf). Also see Ronald C. Moe, "The Emerging Federal Quasi-Government: Issues of Management and Accountability," *Public Administration Review*, 61(3), (May/June 2001), pp. 290–312.

34. There are at least five such entities, with more in the wings (Kosar, p. 9). The government definition of a GSE is found in Title 2, Chapter 17A, section 8 of the 2 US Code Sec 622. 8). The term "government-sponsored enterprise" means a corporate entity created by a law of the United States that (A)(i) has a Federal charter authorized by law; (ii) is privately owned, as evidenced by capital stock owned by private entities or individuals; (iii) is under the direction of a board of directors, a majority of which is elected by private owners; (iv) is a financial institution with power to - (I) make loans or loan guarantees for limited purposes such as to provide credit for specific borrowers or one sector; and (II) raise funds by borrowing (which does not carry the full faith and credit of the Federal Government) or to guarantee the debt of others in unlimited amounts; and (B)(i) does not exercise powers that are reserved to the Government as sovereign (such as the power to tax or to regulate interstate commerce); (ii) does not have the power to commit the Government financially (but it may be a recipient of a loan guarantee commitment made by the Government); and (iii) has employees whose salaries and expenses are paid by the enterprise and are not Federal employees subject to title 5.

35. http://business.timesonline.co.uk/tol/business/industry_sectors/banking_and_finance/article4345872.ece

36. http://www.nsf.gov/statistics/nsf06316/

37. Paul Light, "The New True Size of Government," Research Brief No. 2 (Aug. 2006), Wagner School, NYU, p. 10.

38. Paul Light, "Light on Leadership" blog (http://views.washingtonpost.com/leadership/light/2011/03/fog-of-government-bureaucratic-overlap.html), Government Accountability Office, *Opportunities to Reduce Potential Duplication in Government Programs, Save Tax Dollars, and Enhance Revenue*, March 2011.

39. Jason Mycoff and Joseph A. Pika, *Confrontation and Compromise: Presidential and Congressional Leadership, 2001–2006* (Chapter 2) (Lanham, MD: Rowman & Littlefield, 2007).

40. As quoted in Mary H. Cooper, "IRS Reform," *CQ Researcher*, 8 (Jan. 16, 1998), pp. 25–48.

41. The Report of the National Commission on the Restructuring of the Internal Revenue Service (http://www.house.gov/natcommirs/final.htm).

42. http://www.whitehouse.gov/results/agenda/FY08Q2-SCORECARD.pdf

43. Philip Joyce, "Obama's Performance Management Agenda," *Governing* (March 23, 2011) (http://www.governing.com/columns/mgmt-insights/obama-performance-measurement-agenda.html).

44. Brittany Ballenstedt, Robert Brodsky, Gautham Nagesh, Elizabeth Newell and Alyssa Rosenberg), "Running the Light," *Government Executive*, Dec. 1, 2007 (http://www.govexec.com/story_page.cfm?filepath=/features/1207-01/1207-01s1.htm).

45. The published list of positions in the federal government subject to noncompetitive appointment is referred to as the "plum book," officially known as *United States Government Policy and Supporting Positions* and published just after a presidential election so that everyone knows the potential spoils from the campaign.

46. Official Senate History (http://www.senate.gov/artandhistory/history/common/briefing/Nominations.htm).

47. Clifford L. Berg, "Lapse of Reorganization Authority," *Public Administration Review*, 35(2) (March/April 1975), pp. 195–199.

48. Brian Friel, "Unshackled," *Government Executive*, Nov. 15, 2002 (http://www.govexec.com/story_page.cfm?filepath=/features/1102/1102s3.htm).

49. Tanya N. Ballard, "Back to the Future," *Government Executive*, Oct. 16, 2003 (http://www.govexec.com/story_page.cfm?filepath=/dailyfed/1003/101603pb.htm); Shawn Zeller, "Smashing the System," *Government Executive* (Nov. 15, 2003) (http://www.govexec.com/story_page.cfm?filepath=/features/1103/1103s2.htm).

50. J. Edward Kellough, Lloyd G. Nigro and Gene A. Brewer, "Civil Service Reform Under George W. Bush: Ideology, Politics and Public Personnel Administration," *Review of Public Personnel Administration*, 30 (Dec. 2010), p. 4.

51. David L. Dillman, "Enduring Values in the British Civil Service," *Administration and Society*, 39(7), (Nov. 2007), pp. 883–900.

Chapter 15

1. Remarks by President George W. Bush in the Roosevelt Room, February 24, 2004 (http://www.cnn.com/2004/ALLPOLITICS/02/24/elec04.prez.bush.transcript/index.html).

2. "Pakistan: Entire Election Process 'Deeply Flawed,'" *Human Rights Watch Background Briefing*, October 9, 2002 (http://www.hrw.org).

3. Salman Masood, "Furor Over Musharraf's Suspension of Pakistan's Chief Justice," *International Herald Tribune*, March 15, 2007.

4. "Pakistan's Populist Judges: Courting Trouble," *The Economist*, February 11, 2011 (http://www.economist.com/node/18114729).

5. Thomas Paine, *Rights of Man* (New York: Everyman's Library/Knopf, 1994), p. 41.

6. Andrew J. Nathan, "China's Constitutionalist Option." In Lowell Dittmer and Guoli Liu (Eds.), *China's Deep Reform: Domestic Politics in Transition* (Lanham, MD: Rowman & Littlefield, 2006), p. 184.

7. *Marbury v. Madison,* 5 U.S. (1 Cranch) 137 (1803).

8. *Dr. Bonham's Case,* 77 Eng. Rep. 646 (1610), 652.

9. Leonard W. Levy, *Original Intent and the Framers' Constitution* (New York: Macmillen, 1988), p. 91; Edward S. Corwin, *Doctrine of Judicial Review* (Princeton, NJ: Princeton University Press, 1914); Charles Warren, *Making of the Constitution* (Boston: Little, Brown, 1928); Raoul Berger, *Congress v. the Supreme Court* (Cambridge, MA: Harvard University Press, 1969).

10. Levy, *Original Intent,* p. 99; Louis B. Boudin, *Government by Judiciary* (New York: William Godwin, 1932); William W. Crosskey, *Politics and the Constitution in the History of the United States* (Chicago: University of Chicago Press, 1953).

11. For a more thorough discussion of this topic, see Levy, *Original Intent,* pp. 108–110.

12. Alexander Hamilton, "Federalist No. 78," in *The Federalist: A Commentary on the Constitution of the United States,* ed. Robert Scigliano (New York: The Modern Library, 2000), p. 500.

13. Arguably, the Court engaged in a form of judicial review of congressional action in *Hylton v. United States,* 3 U.S. (3 Dall.) 171 (1796), when the Court upheld a federal tax on carriages, but unlike *Marbury,* that case invalidated nothing.

14. At that time, there was no separate ticket for president and vice president; electors simply cast two votes. As a result, Thomas Jefferson and Aaron Burr (unofficially recognized as the vice presidential candidate for the Democratic-Republicans) tied. After 36 ballots, the House elected Jefferson president and Burr vice president.

15. Some have suggested that the Court may have misinterpreted the relevant portion of the Judiciary Act and argued that the Act was not, in fact, unconstitutional. See, for example, William Van Alstyne, "A Critical Guide to *Marbury v. Madison,*" 1969 *Duke Law Journal* (1969), p. 1.

16. *Marbury v. Madison,* 5 U.S. (1 Cranch) 137 (1803).

17. *Eakin v. Raub,* Supreme Court of Pennsylvania, 12 S. & R. 330 (1825), Justice Gibson's dissent.

18. Craig R. Ducat, *Constitutional Interpretation,* 9th ed. (Boston: Wadsworth, 2009), p. 14; see *Norris v. Clymer,* 2 Pa. 277 (1845) at p. 281.

19. Walter F. Murphy, C. Herman Pritchett, Lee Epstein, and Jack Knight (Eds.), *Courts, Judges, and Politics: An Introduction to the Judicial Process,* 6th ed. (New York: McGraw Hill, 2006), pp. 48–49.

20. Alec Stone Sweet, *Governing with Judges: Constitutional Politics in Europe* (Oxford: Oxford University Press, 2000), p. 94.

21. Stone Sweet, *Governing with Judges,* p. 113.

22. Harry P. Stumpf, *American Judicial Politics,* 2nd ed. (Upper Saddle River, NJ: Prentice-Hall, 1998), p. 94.

23. Saul Cornell, *The Other Founders: Anti-Federalism and the Dissenting Tradition in America, 1788–1828* (Chapel Hill, NC: University of North Carolina Press, 1999), pp. 31, 90.

24. Henry J. Abraham, *The Judicial Process,* 7th ed. (New York: Oxford University Press, 1998), p. 360, quoting Justice Brandeis in *Barnet v. Coronado Oil & Gas Co.,* 2285 U.S. 293 (1932).

25. Since justices have life tenure, no justice was removed when the size of the Court was reduced; rather, when a justice left, he was not replaced.

26. *Goodridge v. Department of Public Health,* 798 N.E.2d 941 (Mass., 2003).

27. Lawrence Baum, *American Courts: Process and Policy,* 6th ed. (Boston: Houghton Mifflin, 2008), p. 34. For the 2001–2005 terms, the average was less than 80 cases per term; in earlier years it had been closer to 150 per term.

28. G. Alan Tarr, *Judicial Process and Policymaking,* 2nd ed. (New York: West/Wadsworth, 1999), p. 40.

29. Prior to legislation passed by Congress in 1988 (102 Stat. 662), cases reached the Supreme Court in one of three ways: by appeal, by certification, and by certiorari. Since 1988, the Court has become an almost all certiorari tribunal. See Ducat, *Constitutional Interpretation,* 9th ed., p. 27.

30. For more on the history and function of law clerks, see: Todd C. Peppers, *Courtiers of the Marble Palace: The Rise and Influence of the Supreme Court Law Clerk* (Stanford: Stanford University Press, 2006), and Artemus Ward and David Weiden, *Sorcerers' Apprentices: 100 Years of Law Clerks at the United States Supreme Court* (New York: New York University Press, 2006).

31. Ducat, *Constitutional Interpretation,* 9th ed., p. 31.

32. Rebecca Mae Salokar, *The Solicitor General: The Politics of Law* (Philadelphia: Temple University Press, 1992), p. 3.

33. Kevin T. McGuire, "Explaining Executive Success in the U.S. Supreme Court," *Political Research Quarterly 51* (June 1998), p. 522.

34. Baum, *American Courts,* pp. 256–257.

35. Stephen L. Wasby, *The Supreme Court in the Federal Judicial System,* 3rd ed. (Chicago: Nelson-Hall, 1988), pp. 223–224.

36. Lawrence Baum, *The Supreme Court,* 6th ed. (Washington, DC: CQ Press, 1998), p. 136.

37. Quoted in Baum, *The Supreme Court,* p. 21.

38. For example, Stuart Taylor, Jr., and Benjamin Wittes, "Of Clerks and Perks," *Atlantic* (July/August 2006), (http://www.theatlantic.com/doc/200607/supreme-court-clerks).

39. The Eleventh, Thirteenth, Sixteenth, and Twenty-Seventh Amendments.

40. *Ex Parte McCardle,* 74 U.S. 506 (1869).

41. The case in question was *Worcester v. Georgia,* 31 U.S. (6 Pet.) 515 (1832).

42. Baum, *American Courts,* p. 295.

43. Robert A. Dahl, "Decision Making in a Democracy: The Supreme Court as a National Policy Maker." In Walter F. Murphy, C. Herman Pritchett, Lee Epstein, and Jack Knight (Eds.), *Courts, Judges, and Politics,* 6th ed. (New York: McGraw Hill, 2006), p. 69.

44. Allan Ashman and Malia Reddick, "Methods of Judicial Selection." In Herbert M. Kritzer (Ed.),

Legal Systems of the World (Santa Barbara, CA: ABC Clio, 2002), p. 800.

45. Richard L. Vining, Jr., Amy Steigerwalt, and Susan Navarro Smelcer, "Bias and the Bar: Evaluating the ABA Ratings of Federal Judicial Nominees," Paper presented at the annual meeting of the Midwest Political Science Association, Chicago, Illinois, April 2009.

46. Ashman and Reddick, "Methods of Judicial Selection" In Herbert M. Kritzer (Ed.), *Legal Systems of the World* (Santa Barbara, CA: ABC Clio, 2002), p. 799.

47. Ottavio Campanella, "The Italian Legal Profession," *The Journal of the Legal Profession, 19* (1995), p. 81.

48. For a more complete account of these developments, see John Anthony Maltese, *The Selling of Supreme Court Nominees* (Baltimore: Johns Hopkins University Press, 1995), especially Chapter 6.

49. Lee Epstein, René Lindstädt, Jeffrey A. Segal, and Chad Westerland, "The Changing Dynamics of Senate Voting on Supreme Court Nominees," *The Journal of Politics, 68*(May 2006), pp. 296ff.

50. *Roe v. Wade,* 410 U.S. 113 (1973).

51. For a detailed discussion of the Rutledge nomination, see Maltese, *The Selling of Supreme Court Nominees,* pp. 26–31.

52. P.S. Ruckman, Jr., "The Supreme Court, Critical Nominations, and the Senate Confirmation Process," *The Journal of Politics, 55* (August 1993), p. 794.

53. Larry C. Berkson and Susan B. Carbon, *The United States Circuit Court Nominating Commissions: Their Members, Procedures, and Candidates* (Chicago: American Judicature Society, 1980).

54. Alan Neff, *The United States District Court Nominating Commissions: Their Members, Procedures, and Candidates* (Chicago: American Judicature Society, 1981).

55. Sheldon Goldman, "Reagan's Judicial Legacy: Completing the Puzzle and Summing Up," *Judicature, 72* (April-May 1989), pp. 319–320.

56. Edward M. Chen, "The Judiciary, Diversity, and Justice for All," *California Law Review, 91* (July 2003), p. 1112.

57. "How Women Lawyers Fare," *U.S. News & World Report* (January 15, 1996), p. 14.

58. Based on Tables 9.1 and 9.2 in Sheldon Goldman, *Picking Federal Judges: Lower Court Selection from Roosevelt through Reagan* (New Haven: Yale University Press, 1997), pp. 350 and 356.

59. Sheldon Goldman, Elliot Slotnick, and Sara Schiavoni, "Obama's Judiciary at Midterm," *Judicature,* May-June 2011, p. 262.

60. Rhode Island is one state that gives its judges life tenure.

61. Tarr, *Judicial Process and Judicial Policymaking,* p. 63.

62. For a sympathetic treatment of lay judges, see Doris Marie Provine, *Judging Credentials: Nonlawyer Judges and the Politics of Professionalism* (Chicago: University of Chicago Press, 1986). Not surprisingly, professional organizations, such as the American Bar Association, are more critical of non-lawyer judges.

63. Frederick Lee Morton, *Law, Politics, and the Judicial Process in Canada,* 3rd ed. (Calgary: University of Calgary Press, 2002), p. 93.

64. Tony Mauro, "Roberts, Gonzales Speak on Judicial Independence," *Legal Times*

(October 2, 2006), (http://www.law.com/jsp/article.jsp?id=1159567621347). See also Tony Mauro, "O'Connor Fires Back on Judicial Independence," *Legal Times* (November 28, 2005), (http://www.law.com/jsp/article.jsp?id=1132740311603), and the transcript of a PBS NewsHour interview with O'Connor and Breyer discussing judicial independence on September 26, 2006 (http://www.pbs.org/newshour/bb/law/july-dec06/independence_09-26.html).

65. See http://www.ajs.org/cji/cji_task_force.asp.

66. Hendrik Hertzberg, "Perry's Good Idea," *New Yorker*, January 30, 2012, p. 18. For a full exposition of the proposal, see Steven G. Calabresi and James Lindgren, "Term Limits for the Supreme Court: Life Tenure Reconsidered," *Harvard Journal of Law & Public Policy, 29* (2006), p. 769.

Chapter 16

1. David Kestenbaum, "Will Overstimulating Economy Bring Inflation?" Report broadcast on National Public Radio, June 26, 2009 (http://www.npr.org/templates/story/story.php?storyId=105924913&ft=1&f=94427042).

2. "Germany's Economy: The Export Model Sputters," *The Economist*, May 7, 2009 (http://www.economist.com/opinion/displaystory.cfm?story_id=13611300); "Europe's Economies: A New Pecking Order," *The Economist*, May 7, 2009 (http://www.economist.com/opinion/displaystory.cfm?story_id=13610767).

3. Deutsche Welle, DW-World.DE, June 26, 2009 (http://www.dw-world.de/popups/popup_single_mediaplayer/0,,4434679_type_video_struct_1432_contentId_4433963,00.html).

4. Nicholas Kulish and Judy Dempsey, "Merkel is Set to Greet, and Then Resist, Obama," *New York Times*, March 29, 2009 (http://www.nytimes.com/2009/03/30/world/europe/30merkel.html?_r=1).

5. CIA World Factbook (https://www.cia.gov/library/publications/the-world-factbook/geos/SW.html).

6. Price Fishback, "Government and the Economy." In Price V. Fishback, *Government and the American Economy: A New History* (Chicago. University of Chicago Press, 2007).

7. Robert A. McGuire, "The Founding Era, 1774–1791." In Fishback, *Government and the American Economy*, p. 62.

8. Richard Sylla, "Reversing Financial Reversals." In Fishback, *Government and the American Economy*, pp. 121–122.

9. John Joseph Wallis, "The National Era." In Fishback, *Government and the American Economy*, p. 157.

10. Jeffrey Rogers Hummel, "The Civil War and Reconstruction." In Fishback, *Government and the American Economy*, p. 207.

11. Robert Higgs, "The World Wars." In Fishback, *Government and the American Economy*.

12. Mark Guglielmo and Werner Troesken, "The Gilded Age." In Fishback, *Government and the American Economy*, p. 265.

13. Price Fishback, "The Progressive Era." In Fishback, *Government and the American Economy*, especially Table 10.1 on pp. 291–292.

14. "Simpler Taxes: the flat-tax revolution," *The Economist* (April 14, 2005) http://www.economist.com/printedition/displayStory.cfm?Story_ID=3861190&source=login_payBarrier).

15. Warren Buffett, "Stop Coddling the Super-Rich," *The New York Times*, August 14, 2011.

16. Joseph E. Stiglitz, "Of the 1%, by the 1%, for the 1%," *Vanity Fair* (May 2011) (http://www.vanityfair.com/society/features/2011/05/top-one-percent-201105).

17. OECD, "Growing Income Inequality in OECD Countries: What Drives It and How Can Policy Tackle It?" *Policy Forum*, May 2, 2011.(http://www.oecd.org/dataoecd/32/20/47723414.pdf).

18. Markus Jantti, "Mobility in the United States in Comparative Perspective," *Focus 26*(2), (Fall 2009). Also see Dylan Matthews, "How Great is American Income Mobility?" *Washington Post*, August 3, 2010

19. Bill McInturff, "A Pivot Point in American Opinion," *Public Opinion Strategies*, August 2011 (http://pos.org/documents/a_pivot_point_in_american_opinion_the_debt_ceiling_negotiation_and_its_consequences.pdf).

20. For a more conspiratorial interpretation of how bankers manipulated the 1912 presidential election and Wilson to achieve their goals, see Henry C. K. Liu, "Banking Bunkum: The U.S. Experience," *Asia Times* (November 16, 2002) (http://www.atimes.com/atimes/Global_Economy/DK16Dj02.html).

21. Roger T. Johnson, "Historical Beginnings . . . The Federal Reserve," *Federal Reserve Bank of Boston*, 2010 (http://www.bos.frb.org/about/pubs/begin.pdf).

22. See the fascinating discussion of regulation on a site maintained by the Smithsonian Institution (http://americanhistory.si.edu/powering/).

23. Jim Tankersley and Michael Hirsh, "Neo Voodoo Economics," *National Journal*, May 21, 2011, pp. 20–26.

24. Lawrence Summers, text of prepared remarks delivered at the Brookings Institution, March 13, 2009 (http://www.brookings.edu/~/media/Files/events/2009/0313_summers/0313_summers_remarks.pdf).

25. "Caveat Creditor," *The Economist*, July 2, 2009 (http://www.economist.com/businessfinance/displaystory.cfm?story_id=13952950).

26. "Country Views Wire on the United States," *The Economist* (http://www.economist.com/countries/usa/profile.cfm?folder=Profile%2DPolitical%20Forces).

Chapter 17

1. Jonathan Cohn, "Healthy Examples: Plenty of Countries Get Health Care Right," *Boston Globe*, July 5, 2009 (http://www.boston.com/bostonglobe/ideas/articles/2009/07/05/healthy_examples_plenty_of_countries_get_health_care_right/).

2. Frederik T. Schut, "Health Care Reform in the Netherlands: Balancing Corporatism, Etatism and Market Mechanisms," *Journal of Health Politics, Policy and Law, 20*(3), (Fall 1995), pp. 615–652.

3. Ab Klink, "Experiences Abroad: Health Care Reform in the Netherlands," AARP International (http://www.aarpinternational.org/resourcelibrary/resourcelibrary_show.htm?doc_id=705282).

4. http://www.pulitzer.org/awards/2010

5. Mexico had set the goal for a universal system by 2012, but its performance on virtually all service indicators lagged well below the OECD average (http://www.oecd.org/dataoecd/46/9/38980018.pdf).

6. Anne-Emanuelle Birn, Sc.D., Theodore M. Brown, Ph.D., Elizabeth Fee, Ph.D., and Walter J. Lear, M.D., "Struggles for National Health Reform in the United States," *American Journal of Public Health, 93*(1), (January 2003), pp. 86–91.

7. Atul Gawande, "Getting There from Here: How Should Obama Reform health care?" *The New Yorker*, January 26, 2009.

8. Ibid.

9. Stephen Ohlemacher, "Welfare State Growing Despite Overhauls," Associated Press, February 26, 2007.

10. U.S. Government Accountability Office, "Human Services Programs: Opportunities to Reduce Inefficiencies." Testimony of Kay E. Brown before House Subcommittee on Human Resources Committee on Ways and Means, April 5, 2011.

11. OECD Health Data 2011, "How Does the United States Compare?" (http://www.oecd.org/dataoecd/46/2/38980580.pdf).

12. Jeffrey A. Rhoades, "The Uninsured in America, 2004: Estimates for the U.S. Civilian Noninstitutionalized Population Under Age 65," *Medical Expenditure Panel Survey Statistical Brief #83*, June 2005, Agency for Health Care Research and Quality.

13. Marilyn Moon, "The Future of Medicare as an Entitlement Program," *The Elder Law Journal, 12*(1), p. 228.

14. Marcia Clemmitt, "Rising Health Costs," *CQ Researcher, 16*(13), (April 7, 2006).

15. http://www.whitehouse.gov/issues/health_care/

16. Jonathan Weisman, "Health Law Puts Governors in Pickle," *Wall Street Journal*, August 26, 2011.

17. http://www.ssa.gov/history/tftable.html

18. Peter Katel, "Straining the Safety Net," *CQ Researcher, 19*(July 31, 2009), pp. 645–668. Retrieved August 7, 2009, from CQ Researcher Online (http://library.cqpress.com/cqresearcher/cqresrre2009073100).

19. The Trustees of the Old Age and Survivors Insurance and Federal Disability Trust Fund report annually to Congress with their 75-year projections. For the report made in May 2009, see http://www.ssa.gov/OACT/TR/2009/tr09.pdf.

20. "History of Energy in the United States, 1635–2000," Energy Information Administration (http://www.eia.doe.gov/emeu/aer/eh/frame.html).

21. Energy Information Administration, "How Dependent Are We on Foreign Oil?" (http://tonto.eia.doe.gov/energy_in_brief/print_pages/foreign_oil_dependence.pdf).

22. "Mercury: Human Exposure," U.S. Environmental Protection Agency website, accessed September 18, 2011.

23. World Nuclear Association, country briefing on France, July 20, 2009 (http://www.world-nuclear.org/info/inf40.html).

24. For a detailed report, see the World Nuclear Association's posting on the Fukushima Accident at http://www.world-nuclear.org/info/fukushima_accident_inf129.html.

25. For a summary of these developments, see the World Nuclear Association's report on "Nuclear Power in Germany" at http://www.world-nuclear.org/info/inf43.html.

26. World Nuclear Association, country briefing on "US Nuclear Power Policy," July 2009 (http://www.world-nuclear.org/info/inf41_US_nuclear_power_policy.html).

27. U.S. Department of Energy, *The Smart Grid: An Introduction* (http://www.oe.energy.gov/DocumentsandMedia/DOE_SG_Book_Single_Pages(1).pdf).

28. "China Overtakes U.S. as Top Energy Consumer," *Huffington Post,* June 8, 2011 (http://www.huffingtonpost.com/2011/06/08/china-top-energy-consumer_n_873007.html).

29. Coral Davenport, Benton Ives, and Phil Mattingly, "Carbon, From the Ground Up," *CQ Weekly Online* (August 3, 2009), pp. 1836–1844, retrieved March 30, 2010, from http://library.cqpress.com/cqweekly/weeklyreport111-000003184508; Coral Davenport, "2009 Legislative Summary: Climate Change Mitigation," *CQ Weekly Online* (January 4, 2010), pp. 42–42, retrieved March 30, 2010, from http://library.cqpress.com/cqweekly/weeklyreport111-000003274891; Coral Davenport, "No Senate Sequel for Influential Climate Group," *CQ Weekly Online* (March 29, 2010), pp. 735–736, retrieved March 30, 2010, from http://library.cqpress.com/cqweekly/weeklyreport111-000003634201.

30. New York State Education Department, *States' Impact on Federal Education Policy* (http://www.archives.nysed.gov/edpolicy/research/res_essay_intro_fedrole.shtml).

31. Digest of Education Statistics 2010, Table 90 (http://nces.ed.gov/programs/digest/d10/tables/dt10_090.asp).

32. James S. Coleman, *Equality of Educational Opportunity Study* (Washington, DC: U.S. Department of Health, Education, and Welfare, Office of Education/National Center for Education Statistics, 1966).

33. Christina Samuels, "KIPP Charter Network Receives $25.5 Million From Walton Family Foundation," *Education Week,* November 15, 2011.

34. U.S. Census Bureau News Release, July 27, 2009 (http://news.prnewswire.com/DisplayReleaseContent.aspx?ACCT=104&STORY=/www/story/07-27-2009/0005066568&EDATE).

35. Michael Lind and Ted Halstead, "The National Debate Over School Funding Needs a Federal Focus," *Los Angeles Times,* October 7, 2000 (http://www.newamerica.net/publications/articles/2000/the_national_debate_over_school_funding_needs_a_federal_focus).

36. Alyson Klein, "Administration Unveils ESEA Renewal Blueprint," *Education Week* (published online March 13, 2010); Seth Stern, "Obama Seeks Many Changes in 'No Child,' But Critics Look for Slower Approach," *CQ Weekly Online,* March 22, 2010 (http://library.cqpress.com/cqweekly/weeklyreport111-000003618143).

Chapter 18

1. http://www.ramsi.org/

2. Elsina Wainwright, "Responding to State Failure—The Case of Australia and Solomon Islands," *Australian Journal of International Affairs, 57*(3), (November 2003).

3. John Quincy Adams, address delivered to the House of Representatives on July 4, 1821 (http://www.teachingamericanhistory.org/library/index/asp?document=2336).

4. Second Inaugural Address of William Jefferson Clinton, January 20, 1997 (http://www.yale.edu/lawweb/avalon/presiden/inaug/clinton2.htm).

5. The U.S. recognized Philippine independence on July 4, 1946, but Filipinos celebrate their Independence Day as June 12, 1898. The Philippines became a "commonwealth" in 1934. For a rich account of this history, see http://www.pbs.org/frontlineworld/stories/philippines/tl01.html. Also see the Library of Congress history at http://memory.loc.gov/frd/cs/phtoc.html. The American military also occupied Cuba, another focus of the war, until 1902 when Cuban independence was recognized. The United States insisted that the Cubans continue to extend special privileges inconsistent with full sovereignty (for example, the rights to a naval base at Guantanamo Bay) and again dispatched troops from 1917–1933.

6. As quoted in Kenneth Jost, "Rethinking Foreign Policy: Should President Bush's Approach Be Abandoned?" *CQ Researcher, 5*(17), (February 2, 2007), pp. 97–120 . Retrieved August 23, 2008, from CQ Researcher Online, http://library.cqpress.com/cqresearcher/cqresrre2007020200.

7. Edward S. Corwin, *The President: Office and Powers, 1787–1984,* 5th ed., p. 201.

8. Alison Mitchell, "Crisis in the Balkans: In Congress; Kosovo Is Causing Breaks and Shifts in the Two Parties," *The New York Times,* April 8, 1999.

9. For a comprehensive review, see Richard F. Grimmett, "Instances of Use of United States Armed Forces Abroad, 1798–2010," CRS Report R41677 (March 10, 2011).

10. Text of the National Security Act of 1947 can be found at http://www.intelligence.gov/0-natsecact_1947.shtml.

11. Office of the Director of National Intelligence (http://www.odni.gov/who.htm); for an overview of the "intelligence community, also see http://www.intelligence.gov/1-members.shtml.

12. http://www.climatescience.gov/

13. Pew Research Center, Project for Excellence in Journalism, "The Changing Newsroom," July 21, 2008. This study was based on a survey of executives at 259 newspapers and interviews with executives in 15 cities (http://journalism.org/node/11963). Also see Jodi Enda, "Retreating from the World," *American Journalism Review* (December/January 2011) (http://www.ajr.org/article.asp?id=4985).

14. Results of the survey by Erdos and Morgan as reported in *Foreign Affairs* (November 30, 2006) (http://www.cfr.org/publication/12277/).

15. Alan Raucher, "The First Foreign Affairs Think Tanks," *American Quarterly, 30*(4), (Autumn 1978) p. 493.

16. Andrew Rich and R. Kent Weaver, "Think Tanks in the U.S. Media," *The Harvard International Journal of Press/Politics, 5*(4), (Fall 2000), pp. 81–103.

17. For a general discussion of major foreign policy think tanks, see *U.S. Foreign Policy Agenda, November 2002* (http://usinfo.state.gov/journals/itps/1102/ijpe/pj73fact2.htm).

18. John T. S. Keeler, "Agricultural Power in the European Community: Explaining the Fate of CAP and GATT Negotiations," *Comparative Politics, 28*(2), (January 1996), pp. 127–149.

19. http://www.aipac.org/about_AIPAC/default.asp

20. John J. Mearsheimer and Stephen M. Walt, "The Israel Lobby and U.S. Foreign Policy," Working Paper 14 (March 2006), p. 1 (http://ksgnotes1.harvard.edu/Research/wpaper.nsf/rwp/RWP06-011/$File/rwp_06_011_walt.pdf), later published in the *London Review of Books, 28*(6), (March 23, 2006).

21. David Howard Goldberg, *Foreign Policy and Ethnic Interest Groups* (Westport, CT: Greenwood Publishing Group, 1990). Goldberg compared AIPAC's activities in the United States with those of the Canada-Israel Committee (CIC) during the 15-year period from 1973 to 1988 and concluded that AIPAC was not as influential as is often assumed but was *more* influential than the CIC because it had better funding and could seek to influence either the legislative or executive branch, depending on which was more receptive, whereas the CIC focused only on the executive branch. American political culture also makes U.S. officials more receptive to the efforts of groups to influence policy.

22. Ole R. Holsti, "Public Opinion and Foreign Policy: Challenges to the Almond-Lippmann Consensus," *International Studies Quarterly, 36* (1992), pp. 439–466.

23. John Mueller, "The Iraq Syndrome," *Foreign Affairs, 84*(6), (Nov-Dec 2005), p. 44.

24. Holsti, p. 461. Also see Jon Western, *Selling Intervention and War: The Presidency, the Media, and the American Public* (Baltimore: Johns Hopkins University Press, 2005).

25. The Chicago Council on Foreign Relations, *Global Views 2004: American Public Opinion and Foreign Policy* (Chicago, 2004), p. 4 (http://www.thechicagocouncil.org/UserFiles/File/POS_Topline percent20Reports/POS percent202004/US percent20Public percent20Opinion percent20Global_Views_2004_US.pdf).

26. Jeffrey S. Passel and D'Vera Cohn, "U.S. Unauthorized Immigration Flows Are Down Sharply Since Mid-Decade," The Pew Hispanic Center of the Pew Research Center (September 1, 2010).

27. Steven A. Camarota and Karen Jensenius, "Homeward Bound: Recent Immigration Enforcement and the Decline in the Illegal Alien Population," Center for Immigration Studies (July 2008) (http://www.cis.org/trends_and_enforcement).

28. Hans Nichols and Kate Andersen Brower, "Obama Says Overhauling U.S. Immigration Laws Is an Economic Imperative," (May 11, 2011), *Bloomberg News* (http://www.bloomberg.com/news/2011-05-10/obama-says-immigration-law-overhaul-an-economic-imperative-1-.html). Also see Amanda Paulson, "Obama to Lay Out New Immigration Reform Blueprint in El Paso," *Christian Science Monitor* (May 10, 2011) (http://www.csmonitor.com/USA/2011/0510/Obama-to-lay-out-new-immigration-reform-blueprint-in-El-Paso).

29. Warren Richey, "Arizona May Not Enforce Key Parts of Immigration Law, Court Rules," *Christian Science Monitor* (April 11, 2011) (http://www.csmonitor.com/USA/Justice/2011/0411/Arizona-may-not-enforce-key-parts-of-immigration-law-court-rules).

30. International Organization for Migration, World Migration Report 2010, *The Future of Migration: Building Capacities for Change* (2010) (http://publications.iom.int/bookstore/free/WMR_2010_ENGLISH.pdf).

31. Eytan Meyers, "Theories of International Immigration Policy—A Comparative Analysis," *International Migration Review* (Winter 2000), pp. 1245–1282.

32. Damien Cave, "Better Lives for Mexicans Cut Allure of Going North," *The New York Times,* July 6, 2011 (http://www.nytimes.

com/interactive/2011/07/06/world/americas/immigration.html?hp).

33. Andrew C. Revkin, "A Push to Increase Icebreakers in the Arctic," *The New York Times,* August 16, 2008 (http://www.nytimes.com/2008/08/17/world/europe/17arctic.html?_r=1&oref=slogin).

34. John M. Broder, "Many Goals Remain Unmet in Five Nations' Climate Deal," *The New York Times,* December 18, 2009 (http://www.nytimes.com/2009/12/19/science/earth/19climate.html?pagewanted=all).

35. Frederik Dahl, "IAEA Seeks Safety Checks in All Atomic Energy States," Reuters (August 23, 2011); Mohamed El-Baradei, "Nuclear Weapons: A Relic of the Past," op ed written by IAEA Director (February 4, 2009) (http://iaea.org/newscenter/transcripts/2009/sz040209.html).

36. Alex Spillius, "Al Qaeda Trying to Secure Nuclear Weapons, says Barack Obama," *The Telegraph* (April 12, 2010) (http://www.telegraph.co.uk/news/worldnews/barackobama/7583173/Al-Qaeda-trying-to-secure-nuclear-weapons-says-Barack-Obama.html.

37. Ibid.

38. http://lugar.senate.gov/nunnlugar/scorecard.html

39. Bob Graham, Jim Talent, et al., *World at Risk: The Report of the Commission on the Prevention of WMD Proliferation and Terrorism* (authorized version) (New York: Vintage Books, 2008) (http://clipsandcomment.com/wp-content/uploads/2008/12/world-at-risk-study.pdf).

40. Amy Belasco, "The Cost of Iraq, Afghanistan, and Other Global War on Terror Operations Since 9/11," CRS Report RL 33110 (March 29, 2011) (http://www.fas.org/sgp/crs/natsec/RL33110.pdf).

41. "Costs of War," Watson Institute for International Studies, Neta Crawford and Catherine Lutz, project directors (http://costsofwar.org/).

42. Ibid.

43. Tom Nagorski, "Editor's Notebook"(June 7, 2010) (http://abcnews.go.com/Politics/afghan-war-now-longest-war-us-history/story?id=10849303).

44. Graham E. Fuller, "Strategic Fatigue," *The National Interest, 84* (Summer 2006), pp. 37–43.

45. Supra, Note 3, John Quincy Adams, address delivered to the House of Representatives on July 4, 1821 (http://www.teachingamericanhistory.org/library/index/asp?document=2336).

CREDITS

Photos

Table of Contents

Page vi (top): K Armstrong Photography/ Flickr/ Getty Images; p. vi (bottom): Antenna/Getty Images; p. vii: plainpicture/apply pictures; p. viii (top): Jan Stromme/Stone Getty Images; p. viii (bottom): © Flip Schulke/Corbis; p. ix: © Jose Luis Pelaez Inc/Blend Images, LLC RF; p. x (top): Karen D'Silva/The Image Bank /Getty Images; p. x (bottom): Mark Wilson/Reportage/ Getty Images; p. xi: iStockphoto; p. xii: Chris Maddaloni/CQ-Roll Call/Getty Images; p. xiii (top): © T.J. Kirkpatrick/Corbis; p. xiii (bottom): VisionsofAmerica/Joe Sohm/Digital Vision/Getty Images; p. xiv (top): © The McGraw-Hill Companies, Inc.; p. xiv (bottom): © Mark Weiss/ Corbis; p. xv: Isham Ibrahim/Photographers Choice/Getty Images; p. xvi (top): © Brooks Kraft/Corbis; p. xvi (bottom): © Mike Kemp/Tetra Images/Corbis; p. xvii: © Philip Cheung/Corbis.

About the Authors:

Photo courtesy Meredith Grant.

Chapter 1

Opener: K Armstrong Photography/Flickr/Getty Images; p. 5: © Dana Nalbandian/PhotoEdit; p. 6: Blend Images RF; p. 8: The McGraw-Hill Companies, Inc./Jill Braaten, Photographer; p. 10: © Dinno Kovic/Southcreek Global/Corbis; p. 11: Rob Crandall/Alamy; p. 13: © Mike Segar/Reuters/ Corbis; p. 16: Susan See Photography RF; p. 17: © Jonathan Ernst/Reuters/Corbis; p. 18: © Joseph Sohm/Visions of America/Corbis; p. 19: Al Behrman/AP Images; p. 20: The McGraw-Hill Companies/John Flournoy, Photographer; p. 22: Jimmy Lopes/Alamy; p. 24: Michael Probst/AP Images; p. 29: Punchstock RF.

Chapter 2

Opener: Antenna/Getty Images; p. 37 Andy Sacks/ Getty Images; p. 41 Library of Congress RF; p. 42: Library of Congress RF; p. 43: AP Photo/© Paul Sakuma/Corbis; p. 45: Library of Congress RF; p. 46: Mahmud Hams/AFP/Getty Images; p. 49: The Granger Collection, New York; p. 54: David Mbiyu / Demotix/Corbis; p. 72: © Kevin Lamarque/ Corbis; p. 73: Photodisc/Getty Images RF.

Chapter 3

Opener: plainpicture/apply pictures; p. 83: U.S. Coast Guard RF; p. 88:Mike Derer/AP Images; p. 93; Library of Congress RF; p. 94 (top): OE Jaszweski/MCT/Landov; p. 94 (bottom): Kirby Franze/Bell Newspaper/Mary Hardin-Baylor University; p. 95: Samir Delic/AP Images; p. 97: Library of Congress RF; p. 98: FDR Library ; p. 99: Library of Congress RF; p. 101: © Don Hammond/ Design Pics/Corbis RF; p. 103: Nik Taylor/Flickr Open/ Getty Images.

Chapter 4

Opener: Jan Stromme/Stone/Getty Images; p. 112: ©Ocean/Corbis RF; p. 113: Historicus, Inc. RF;

p. 114: ©Suzanne DeChillo/The New York Times/ Redux Pictures; p. 119: Ted Benson/AP Images; p. 123: © Clay Good/Zuma Press; p. 125: © Tanushree Punwani/Reuters/Corbis; p. 127: © David Butow/ Corbis SABA; p. 129: Punchstock RF; p. 130: © Peter Marshall/Demotix/Corbis; p. 140: Koji Sasahara/AP Images; p. 146: Punchstock RF.

Chapter 5

Opener: © Flip Schulke/Corbis; p. 154: Library of Congress; p. 156: © Bettmann/Corbis; p. 158: © Brian Cahn/Zuma Press/Corbis; p. 159 (top): © Anthony S. Karen; p. 159 (bottom): Igor Studenkov/Flickr/Getty Images; p. 161: Historicus, Inc. RF; p. 162: AP Images; p. 164: Historicus, Inc. RF; p. 166: Mark Duncan/AP Images; p. 167: George Doyle/Getty Images RF; p. 168: Thomas Cockrem/Alamy; p. 171: Jacquelyn Martin/AP Images; p. 173: Mark Wilson/Getty Images; p. 174: © Richard van der AA / Demotix/Corbis; p. 177: © White House/Handout/CNP/Corbis; p. 178: Laverrue was here/Flickr/Getty Images RF; p. 179: Stan Honda/AFP/Getty Images; p. 180: John A Rizzo/Getty Images RF; p. 183: John Bazemore/AP Images.

Chapter 6

Opener: © Jose Luis Pelaez Inc/Blend Images, LLC RF; p. 189: Sean MacDonald/SportsRoadTrips.com; p. 190: Carson Ganci/Design Pics RF; p. 195: © Hill Street Studios/Blend Images/Corbis; p. 196: © Hill Street Studios/Blend RF; p. 197: © Tony Kurdsuk/ Star Ledger/Corbis; p. 199: blue jean images/Getty Images RF; p. 202: Design Pics/Don Hammond RF; p. 208: © Zhu Wei/Xinhua Press/Corbis; p. 213: W. Eugene Smith/Time & Life Pictures/Getty Images; p. 215: Jae C. Hong/AP Image; p. 216: The McGraw-Hill Companies, Inc./Jill Braaten, Photographer.

Chapter 7

Opener: Karen D'Silva/The Image Bank/Getty Images; p. 226: Comstock Image/Alamy RF; p. 227: Julian Finney/Getty images; p. 228: LM Otero/AP Images; p. 231: Photodisc/Getty Images RF; p. 234: Tim Boyle/Getty Images; p. 240: Chris Maddaloni/ CQ-Roll Call/Getty Images; p. 245: © Tristan Spinski/Corbis; p. 247: © Kevin Kolczynski/Reuters/ Corbis; p. 252: © Paul J. Richards/Getty Images; p. 256: Vstock LLC/Getty Images.

Chapter 8

Opener: Mark Wilson/Reportage/Getty Images; p. 262: © Rick Wilking/Reuters/Corbis; p. 263: Milwaukee Journal-Sentinel, Gary Porter/AP Images; p. 264: Mike Carlson/AP Images; p. 272: Pius Utomi Ekpei/AFP/Getty Images; p. 276: Library of Congress; p. 290: © Tannen Maury/ Corbis; p. 291 © Jewel Samad/AFP/Getty Images.

Chapter 9

Opener: iStockphoto; p. 299 (top): Susan See Photography RF;P. 299 (bottom): © Diego Azubel/ Corbis; p. 300: © Ron Haviv/Corbis; p. 303: Mike Simons/Getty Images; p. 307: The McGraw-Hill Companies, Inc./ Jill Braaten, Photographer; p. 310: Dana Edelson/NBC/AP Images; p. 312: © Joel Stettenheim/Corbis; p. 313: VStock, LLC/Getty

Images; p. 314: The McGraw-Hill Companies, Inc./ Barry Barker, Photographer; p. 316: © Sajeed Taji Farouky/Demotix/Corbis; p. 319: Fuse/Getty Images; p. 320: Scott Dunlap/Getty Images RF; p. 322: Visions of America, LLC/Alamy RF; p. 326: © Andrew Gombert/Reuters/Corbis.

Chapter 10

Opener: Chris Maddaloni/CQ-Roll Call/Getty Images; p. 334: © Image Source/Corbis; p. 335: © Kevin Sullivan/Zuma Press/Corbis; p. 336: Dave Moyer/Alamy; p. 337: Library of Congress RF; p. 342: © Ingram Publishing/SuperStock; p. 343: Aaron Roeth Photography RF; p. 345: © Andersen Ross/Blend Images/Corbis RF; p. 353: © Simon Wedege Petersen/Demotix/Corbis; p. 358: Ingram Publishing RF; p. 362: © Marco Salustro/Corbis; p. 363: Daniel Sheehan/Liaison Agency/Getty Images; p. 364: Comstock Images/Getty Images.

Chapter 11

Opener: © T.J. Kirkpatrick/Corbis; p. 371: © Digital Vision Ltd./SuperStock RF; p. 373:© Jasna Hodzic; p. 375: Photofest; p. 377: SuperStock/Getty Images; p. 386: © Mark Peterson/Corbis; p. 388: Eric Vandeville/Gamma-Rapho/Getty Images; p. 391: Pablo Martinez Monsivais/AP Images; p. 397: Chris Jobs/Alamy.

Chapter 12

Opener: VisionsofAmerica/Joe Sohm/Digital Vision/Getty Images; p. 406: Reed Saxon/AP Images; p. 408: © 2011 Hall Anderson/ AlaskaStock.com; p. 410 (top), (center): © Bettmann/Corbis; p. 410 (bottom): Historicus, Inc. RF; p. 414: Haraz N. Ghanbari/AP Images; p. 417: © Brooks Kraft/Corbis; p. 418: © Michael Reynolds/epa/Corbis; p. 420: Bethany Thomas/ NBC NewsWires/AP Images; p. 421: The McGraw-Hill Companies, Inc./Jill Braaten, Photographer; p. 428: © Amit Bhargava/Corbis; p. 432 (left): The Granger Collection, New York; p. 432 (right): © Mark Cornelison/Zuma Press/Corbis; p. 439: Punchstock RF.

Chapter 13

Opener: © The McGraw-Hill Companies, Inc.; p. 447: Mark Wilson/Getty Images; p. 450: US Department of Defense RF; p. 451: Historicus, Inc. RF; p. 453: Stocktrek Images/Getty Images RF; p. 455 (top left): Library of Congress RF; p. 445 (top right): Marie Hansen/Time & Life Pictures/Getty Images; p. 458: © Shawn Baldwin/Corbis; p. 462 (left): Universal History Archive/Getty Images; p. 462 (right): Jim Spellman/Getty Images; p. 464: © Keskue E. Kossoff/Pool/Polaris Images/Corbis; p. 466 (top): Historicus RF; p. 466 (bottom): Arnold Sachs/Getty Images; p. 469: Graphic Leftovers; p. 471: The McGraw-Hill Companies, Inc./Jill Braaten, Photographer; p. 478: PhotoDisc RF.

Chapter 14

Opener: © Mark Weiss/Corbis; p. 486 Punchstock RF; p. 491: Image Source/Getty Images RF; p. 493: Library of Congress; p. 500: NASA RF ; p. 509: Image 100 RF; p. 512: David R. Frazier Photo Library RF; p. 514: Jeffrey Phelps/AP Images; p. 516: Photosdisc/Getty Images RF.

Chapter 15

Opener: Isham Ibrahim/Photographers Choice/Getty Images; p. 523: Christina Escobar Mora/AP Images; p. 526: Stephan Savola/AP Images; p. 528: © Kim Kulish/Corbis; p. 529: Julien Behal/AP Images; p. 531: The Agency Collection/Getty Images RF; p. 537: Liberty Legal Institute/Henry and Wanda Sandoz/AP Images; p. 545: Alex Wong/Getty Images; p. 552:Comstock/Jupiterimages RF.

Chapter 16

Opener: © Brooks Kraft/Corbis; p. 560: Indranil Mukherjee/AFP/Getty Images;

p. 561: Stacy Bengs/The Minnesota Daily/AP Images; p. 562: FDA/Getty Images

p. 564: Library of Congress RF; p. 566: Andrew Harrer/Getty Images

p. 569: © Davis Turner/epa/Corbis; p. 570: Mike Kemp/Rubberball/Getty Images RF; p. 572: Purestock/SuperStock RF; p. 575: Purcell Team/Alamy; p. 577: Brand X Pictures RF; p. 587: Ted Foxx/Alamy; p. 588: Glow Images RF; p. 590: Emmanuel Dunand/SFP/Getty Images.

Chapter 17

Opener: © Mike Kemp/Tetra Images/Corbis; p. 598: Elaine Thompson/AP Images; p. 599: Mark Wilson/Getty Images; p. 600: © Najlah Feanny/Corbis SABA; p. 603: © Mike Kemp/Corbis; p. 605: Image Source/Veer RF; p. 606: Robert Giroux/Getty Images; p. 608 (top): PhotoDisc/Getty Images RF; p. 608 (bottom): AP Images; p. 611: J.D. Pooley/Getty Images; p. 612: Livio Sinibaldi/Digital Vision/Getty Images RF; p. 614: William O. Field/National Snow and Ice Data Center/USGS; p. 617: Athit Perawongmetha/Getty Images; p. 620: Hill Street Studios/Blend Images RF; p. 623: Noah Berger/AP Images; p. 625: © Chris Cooper-Smith/Alamy RF.

Chapter 18

Opener: © Philip Cheung/Corbis; p. 633: Emmanuel Dunand/AFP/Getty Images;

p. 635: The Granger Collection, New York; p. 636: © Greg Chandler; p. 639: American Stock/Getty Images; p. 640: Greg Mathieson/Time & Life Pictures/Getty Images; p. 641: Bloomberg/Getty Images; p. 642: © David Turnley/Corbis; p. 644: © Wally McNamee/Corbis; p. 647: Pete Souza/White House/Getty Images; p. 649: Doug Ross/Getty Images; p. 651: Ed Lallo/Photolibrary/Getty Images; p. 652: The McGraw-Hill Companies, Inc./John Flournoy, Photographer; p. 660: Library of Congress RF; p. 663: © Mark Karass/Corbis RF.

Text/Illustrations

Chapter 1

Figure 1.1: From Freedom House, *Map of Freedom*, 2009. Used with permission.; Figure 1.3: U.S. Department of Commerce, Historical Statistics of the United States; Peter Flora, ed., State, Economy, and Society in Western Europe, 1815-1975 (London: MacMillan, 1983): International Monetary Fund, Government Finance Statistics Yearbook; Footnote 14: Copyright © 2006 World Values Survey. World Values Survey, 2005/2006 Wave; Figure 1.5: from OECD (2011), Society at a Glance 2011: OECD Social Indicators, OECD Publishing., http://dx.doi.org/10.1787/soc_glance-2011-en. Used with permission.

Chapter 2

Footnote 1: Joseph Ellis quote, Joseph J. Ellis, *Founding Brothers: The Revolutionary Generation*

Copyright © 2000, Alfred A. Knopf, a division of Random House, Inc.; Footnote 4: Joseph Ellis quote, Joseph Ellis, *American Creation*. Copyright © 2007 Random House, Inc.; p. 38: Edmund Morgan quote from Edmund S. Morgan, *The Birth of the Republic, 1763-89*, 3rd ed. Copyright © 1992 University of Chicago Press, pp. 5-5, 6-8; Footnote 17, Merrill Jensen quote, Merrill Jensen, *The Articles of Confederation: An Interpretation of the Social-Constitutional History of the American Revolution, 1774-1781* Copyright 1940 University of Wisconsin Press, p. 56; Footnote 19: Joseph Ellis quote, from Joseph Ellis, American Creation. Copyright © 2007 Vintage Books, a division of Random House, Inc.; Footnote 32: David Stewart quote, from Joseph Ellis, American Creation. Copyright © 2007 Vintage Books, a division of Random House, Inc.; Figure 2.6: Copyright © 2007 Shelly Nelson. Used with permission.; Figure 2.7: Data from Gallup Poll, March 25-27, 2011, http://www.pollingreport.com/institut.htm; Figure 2.8: Data from Gallup Poll, March 25-27, 2011, http://www.pollingreport.com/institut.htm; Figure 2.9: Source: http://www.columbia.edu/itc/law/witt/images/lect8/fx12_states_fight_over_ratification_of_the_constitution.jpg; Figure 2.10: From University of Texas, Austin. Copyright © James R. Henson.

Chapter 3

Figure 3.1: From Harrison, *American Democracy Now*, 2/e TX ed. Copyright © 2011. Used by permission of McGraw-Hill Companies, Inc.; Figure 3.2: Federations of the world map, Intergovernmental Affairs Department, 2009. Reproduced with the permission of the Minister of Public Works and Government Services Canada, 2012; Footnote 11: Council of State Governments quote, Council of State Governments—National Center for Interstate Compacts, "Understanding Interstate Compacts," 1, http://www.cglg.org/projects/water/compacteducation/understanding interstate_compacts—csgncic.pdf; Footnote 12: Description of three broad types of interstate contracts, Council of State Governments—National Center for Interstate Compacts, "Understanding Interstate Compacts," 2, http://www.cglg.org/projects/water/compacteducation/understanding_interstate_compacts—csgncic.pdf; Figure 3.3: Map found at http://www.lawrencevilleweather.com/blog/2007/10/where-exactly-is-the-lake-lanier-drainage-basin.html; Figure 3.4: Gallup, May 20, 2011 www.gallup.com/poll/147662/First-Time-Majority-Americans-Favor-Legal-Gay-Marriage.aspx Copyright © 2011 Gallup, Inc. Used with permission.

Chapter 4

Footnote 2: Keywords for blocking Internet access in China, based on material from http://www.cnn.com/interactive/world/0603/explainer.china.internet/frameset.exclude.html; Figure 4.1: http://www.gallup.com/poll/105721/public-believes-americans-right-own-guns.aspx Copyright © 2008 Gallup, Inc. Used with permission.; Table 4.1: from Craig Ducat, *Constitutional Interpretation*, 9E. © 2009 Wadsworth, a part of Cengage Learning, Inc. Reproduced by permission. www.cengage.com/permissions; Table 4.2: From Craig Ducat, *Constitutional Interpretation*, 9E,© 2009 Wadsworth, a part of Cengage Learning, Inc. Reproduced by permission. www.cengage.com/permissions; Footnote 34: Leonard Levy quote, Leonard Levy, *Origins of the Bill of Rights*. Copyright © 1999 Yale University Press; Footnote 63: Jason Mattera quote, Copyright © 2003 Jason Mattera; Figure 4.2: Data from State of the First Amendment Survey, 2010 http://www.firstamendmentcenter.com/pdf/SOFA.Sept.2010data.pdf; Footnote 87:

Epstein and Walker, Constitutional Law for a Changing America: *Rights, Liberties, and Justice*, 114. CQ Press, 7/e. Copyright © 2009 CQ Press; Figure 4.3: Copyright © 2007 Center for Reproductive Rights. Used with permission.; Footnote 109: Norimitsu Onishi, "Japan Learns Dreaded Task of Jury Duty," *New York Times*, July 16, 2007.

Copyright © 2007 The New York Times Company, Inc. Used with permission.; Figure 4.4: From http://www.deathpenaltyinfo.org/FactSheet.pdf (page 3); Figure 4.5: Data from http://blog.amnestyusa.org/deathpenalty/u-s-in-top-5-for-executions-worldwide/attachment/execleaders010/; Figure 4.6: From http://www.gallup.com/poll/1606/death-penalty.aspx, Copyright © 2011 Gallup, Inc. Used with permission.; Figure 4.7: From http://pewforum.org/docs/?DocID=272

Copyright © 2008 Gallup, Inc. and Pew Forum on Religion and Public Life. Used with permission

Chapter 5

Footnote 13: Donald Lively quote, From Donald Lively, *The Constitution, Race, and Renewed Relevance of Original Intent* (Amherst, NY: Cambria Press, 2008), p. 45; Figure 5.1: Copyright © 2012 Ashbrook Center. http://teachingamericanhistory.org; Table 5.2: Data from Inter-Parliamentary Union at http://www.ipu.org/wmn-e/suffrage.htm; Figure 5.5: Copyright © 2012, U.S. English, Inc. all rights reserved. http://www.us-english.org/view/13; Figure 5.6: © 2007 Pew Research Center, Social & Demographic Trends Project. Blacks See Growing Gap Between Poor and Middle Class, http://pewsocialtrends.org/files/2010/10/Race-2007.pdf; Footnote 83: Juan Williams quote, Juan Williams, "What Obama's Victory Means for Racial Politics," *Wall Street Journal*, November 10, 2008.

Chapter 6

Footnote 7: Is Intolerance Decreasing in America?, data from Samuel A. Stouffer, *Communism, Conformity, and Civil Liberties* (New York: Doubleday, 1995), for the 1954 figure; for the figures after 1954, James Allan Davis, Tom W. Smith, and Peter V. Marsden, *General Social Surveys, 1972 2010: Cumulative Codebook/Principal Investigator*, James A. Davis; Director and Co-Principal Investigator, Tom W. Smith – Chicago: National Opinion Research Center, 2010; Footnote 8: Trust in Government, data from National Election Studies, http://www.electionstudies.org/nesguide/toptable/tab5a_1.htm; Footnote 15: Excerpt from Gordon Wood, Gordon Wood, *The Idea of America: Reflections on the Birth of the United States*. Copyright © 2011 Penguin Group USA; Footnote 16: Quote from William H. McNeill, "Epilogue: Fundamentalism and the World of the 1990s," in Martin R. Marty and R. Scott Appleby, eds. Fundamentalisms and Society (Chicago: University of Chicago Press, 1993), p. 569. Copyright © 1993 University of Chicago Press. Used with permission.; Table 6.2: From Robert S. Erikson and Kent L. Tedin, *American Public Opinion*, updated 7th ed. Copyright © 2007. Reprinted by permission of Pearson Education.; Footnote 25: From Robert S. Erikson and Kent L. Tedin, *American Public Opinion*, updated 7th ed. Copyright © 2007. Reprinted by permission of Pearson Education.; Footnote 28: Data from Jeffrey S. Passel and D'Vera Cohn, "U.S. Population Projections: 2005-2050," Pew Research Center. Social and Demographic Trends Report, 2008; Footnote 34: Importance of Religion in America, data from World Values Study, 2005-2008 sample, http://www.worldvaluessurvey.org; Footnote 40: Widening Income Differences, data from United

Nations, Human Development Report 2010; Footnote 42: Attitude Differences by Social Class, data from National Election Studies, 2008, Presidential Election Study; Figure 6.10: Data from National Election Study 2008, Presidential Election Study; Figure 6.11: Data from National Election Studies, 2008, Presidential Election Study; Figure 6.12: Data from National Election Studies, 2008, Presidential Election Study; Footnote 44: Excerpts on Hurricane Katrina, *Katrina has Only Modest Impact on Basic Public Values in Spite of Political Fallout . . .* " September 22, 2005, Pew Research Center for the People and the Press, a project of the Pew Research Center; Footnote 45: Excerpts on Hurricane Katrina, "Two Years Later, the Fear Lingers: 75% Say It's a More Dangerous World," September 4 2003, Pew Research Center for the People and the Press, a project of the Pew Research Center; Figure 6.14: Data from National Election Studies; Footnote 48: Poll question, from Richard H. Davis, "The Anatomy of a Smear Campaign," *The Boston Globe*, March 21, 2004. Copyright © 2004 The Boston Globe.

Chapter 7

Figure 7.1: From W. Phillips Shively, Power and Choice, 13e, figure 11.1

Credit: from W. Phillips Shively, Power and Choice, 13e. Copyright © 2012 McGraw-Hill Companies, Inc. Used with permission.; Table 7.2: Data from Exit polls, CBS News http://www.cbsnews.com/election2010/exit.shtml?state=US&jurisdiction=0&race=H, accessed March 28, 2011; Figure 7.6: Based on New York Times CBS News "2008 Republican National Delegate Survey" and "2008 Democratic National Delegate Survey," http://graphics8.nytimes.com/packages/pdf/politics/20080901-poll.pdf and http://graphics8.nytimes.com/packages/pdf/politics/demdel20080824.pdf.

Chapter 8

Figure 8.1: From Phillip's Atlas of World History. http://qed.princeton.edu/index.php/User:Student/Women_and_the_right_to_vote,_20th_Century; Figure 8.5: Data from David P. Redlawsk, Caroline J. Tolbert, and Todd Donovan, *Why Iowa?* (Chicago: University of Chicago Press, 2011), p. 131; Figure 8.6: Data from www.opensecrets.org/bigpicture/reelect_img.php?chamb=H; Figure 8.9: Data from Federal Election Commission press release, December 29, 2009, table "Historical Comparison for General Election Campaigns 1992-2008; Figure 8.10: Data from National Election Studies, ANES Guide to Public Opinion and Voting Behavior; Figure 8.11: Data from Office of the Clerk of the U.S. House of Representatives; Table 8.1: Data from International IDEA Table of Electoral Systems Worldwide (www.idea.int), Elections Worldwide project; Figure 8.12: Data from International Institute for Democracy and Electoral Assistance, www.idea.int.; Figure 8.13: Data from www.house.gov; Figure 8.14: From www.nationalatlas.gov.

Chapter 9

Figure 9.1: Data from U.S. Census Bureau, Historical Statistics of the United States and Statistical Central Bureau, Statistics Norway; Table 9.1: Data from U.S. Census Bureau, Current Population Survey; Figure 9.2: Data from http://www.idea.int/vt/; Figure 9.3: Data from U.S. Census Bureau; p. 304: Editorial cartoon, Dana Summers, Orlando Sentinel, March 9, 2010. © Tribune Media Services, Inc. All Rights Reserved. Reprinted with permission.; Footnote 13: Skinner quote, from *Walden Two*, Macmillan (NY) 1948, pp. 220, 221. Courtesy of the B.F. Skinner Foundation; Figure 9.5: Data from U.S. Census Bureau, Current Population

Statistics; Figure 9.6: Data from U.S. Census Bureau (http://www.census.gov/hhes/www/socdemo/voting/publications/p20/2010/tables.htm); Figure 9.7: Data from U.S. Census Bureau, Statistical Abstract of the US; Table 9.6: From Thomas Patterson, The Vanishing Voter. Copyright © 2002, 2003 Thomas E. Patterson. Reprinted with the permission of Alfred P. Knopf, a division of Random House, Inc, p. 125; Figure 9.8: Data from Michael S. Lewis-Beck, William G. Jacoby, Helmut Norpoth, and Herbert F. Weisberg, *The American Voter Revisited* (Ann Arbor: University of Michigan Press, 2008), Table 7.6; Table 9.7: Data from National Election Studies; Figure 9.9: Data from 2008 Exit Polls, CNN Election Center 2008; Figure 9.10: Data from National Election Studies, Guide to Public Opinion (http://www.electionstudies.org/nesguide/nesguide.htm); Figure 9.11: Data from National Election Studies, Guide to Public Opinion (http://www.electionstudies.org/nesguide/nesguide.htm); Figure 9.12: Data from National Election Studies, Guide to Public Opinion (http://www.electionstudies.org/nesguide/nesguide.htm).

Chapter 10

Table 10.2: United Nations Development Programme. *Human Development Report 2009.* (http://hdr.undp.org/)d, Table M of Statistical Annex; Footnote 5: Alexis de Tocqueville quote, from Alexis de Tocqueville, *Democracy in America* (1832), edited by Bruce Frohnen (Washington D. C.: Regnery Publishing, 2002), p. 148; Figure 10.1: Data from *Washington Representatives,* serial (Washington, D.C.: Columbia Books), various annual volumes; Table 10.3: From Frank R. Baumgartner, Jeffrey M. Berry, Marie Hojnacki, David C. Kimball, and Beth L. Leech, *Lobbying and Policy Change: Who Wins, Who Loses, and Why,* table 10.3, p.199. Copyright © 2009 University of Chicago Press. Used with permission.; Figure 10.3: Data from http://www.bls.gov/news.release/union2.t05.htm; Figure 10.4: Based on data from www.aclu.org/aclu-history; Figure 10.5: Data from Open Secrets website, http://www.opensecrets.org/bigpicture/blio.php; p. 348: Harry and Louise, used courtesy of Goddard Gunster; Table 10.4: Adapted from Anthony J. Nownes and Patricia Freeman, "Interest Group Activity in the States", *The Journal of Politics* 60:1 (February, 1998), p. 92. Copyright © 1998 Cambridge University Press. Used with permission.; Footnote 25: Lobbyist quote, from Frank R. Baumgartner, Jeffrey M. Berry, Marie Hojnacki, David C. Kimball, and Beth L. Leech, *Lobbying and Policy Change: Who Wins, Who Loses, and Why*, pp. 70-77. Copyright © 2009 University of Chicago Press. Used with permission.; Footnote 26: Lobbyist quote, from Frank R. Baumgartner, Jeffrey M. Berry, Marie Hojnacki, David C. Kimball, and Beth L. Leech, *Lobbying and Policy Change: Who Wins, Who Loses, and Why*, p. 74. Copyright © 2009, University of Chicago Press. Used with permission.; p. 356: Courtesy of Public Citizen. www.citizen.org; Figure 10.6: from W. Shively, Power and Choice: An Introduction to Political Science, 12e. Copyright © McGraw-Hill Companies, Inc. Used with permission.

Chapter 11

p. 372: Poll question, "What is the most important issue facing the country?" Copyright © 2011 Gallup, Inc.; Figure 11.2: From Harrison, American Democracy Now, 2/e, figure. 10.3, p. 317. data from The Gallup Poll. *Media Use and Evaluation.* http://www.gallup.com/poll/1663/media-use-evaluation.aspx; Figure 11.3: Data from Steve M. Barkin, *American Television News: The Media Marketplace and the Public Interest* (Armonk, NY: M. E. Sharpe, 2003), p. 37; Figure 11.4: From Harrison, *American*

Democracy Now, 2/e, Figure. 10.4, p. 318. Data from The Gallup Poll. *Media Use and Evaluation*; Figure 11.5: http://stateofthemedia.org/2011/overview-2/key-findings/ from Pew Research Center's Project for Excellence in Journalism, State of the News Media, 2011. Used with permission.; Figure 11.6: Data from: http://people-press.org/2009/09/13/press-accuracy-rating-hits-two-decade-low/; Figure 11.7: From http://stateofthemedia.org/2011/overview-2/key-findings/from Pew Research Center's Project for Excellence in Journalism, State of the News Media, 2011. Used with permission.; p. 388: Excerpt from Stille, from Alexander Stille, *The Sack of Rome.* Copyright © 2006 by Alexander Stille. Used by permission of The Penguin Press, a division of Penguin Group (USA) Inc., p. 10; Figure 11.9: Lymari Morales, "Majority in U.S. Continues to Distrust the Media, Perceive Bias," Gallup Web site, September 22, 2011, http://www.gallup.com/poll/149624/majority-continue-distrust-media-perceive-bias.aspx, Copyright © 2011 Gallup, Inc. Used with permission.; Figure 11.10: Data from Susan Holmberg, http://www.freepress.net/ownership/chart/main.

Chapter 12

Figure 12.1: Copyright © 2011 Citizens Against Government Waste. Used with permission.; Figure 12.4: Map originally by Aris Katsaris made available by Wikipedia Commons http://commons.wikimedia.org/wiki/File:Unibicameral_Map.png; Figure 12.5: Zeller, Shawn. "2010 Vote Studies: Party Unity." *CQ Weekly* (January 3, 2011): 30-35. Copyright © 2011 CQ-Roll Call, Inc.; p. 426: Filibuster U.S. Senate image located at Word Info site, http://wordinfo.info/unit/4430/ip:3/il:F titled, "Filibuster" (from pirates to American politics) or "Filibuster, Pirates in the U.S. Congress". Copyright © John G. Robertson. Used with permission.; Figure 12.7: Reprinted with permission from Untangling the Web: Congressional Oversight and the Department of Homeland Security, A White Paper of the CSIS-BENS Task Force on Congressional Oversight of the Department of Homeland Security (Washing, DC: CSIS< December 2004_.; Figure 12.8: Chart found at: http://lib.lbcc.edu/handouts/images/polsci/billtolaw-sm.jpg.

Chapter 13

Footnote 5: Parts of this section are adapted, with permission, from W. Phillips Shively, *Power & Choice*, 11th edition (New York: McGraw-Hill, 2008.) Copyright © 2008 McGraw-Hill Companies, Inc.; p. 448: Obama lame duck, © Marian Kamensky. www.cartoonstock.com; p. 448: Bush lame duck, © Gary Locke www.garyartgood.com; Footnote 9: from Joseph A. Pika and John Anthony Maltese, *Politics of the Presidency* 7th ed. (Washington: CQ Press, 2008) XX.; Footnote 12: Neustadt quote: Richard E. Neustadt, *Presidential Power and the Modern Presidents: The Politics of Leadership from Roosevelt To Reagan* (New York: The Free Press, 1990) 11. Copyright © 1990 the Free Press; Footnote 14: From Pew Global Attitudes Project, "Arab Spring Fails to Improve U.S. Image," May 17, 2011 http://pewglobal.org/2011/05/17/arab-spring-fails-to-improve-us-image/2/; Figure 13.1: Copyright © 2011 Dow Jones Co. Inc. Used with permission from The Wall Street Journal; Footnote 18: Six personality traits, from Fred I. Greenstein *The Presidential Difference: Leadership Style from Roosevelt to Clinton* (Princeton University Press, 2001). Copyright © 2001 Princeton University Press; Footnote 21: Excerpt from Charles O. Jones, from Charles O. Jones, *The Presidency in a Separated System 2nd ed.* (Washington: Brookings Institution; Figure 13.4: Gerhard Peters and John T. Woolley. "Presidential Job Approval." *The American*

Presidency Project. Santa Barbara, CA: University of California. 1999-2012. Available from the World Wide Web: http://www.presidency.ucsb .edu/data/popularity.php; Footnote 27: from Rebecca Adams, "Lame Duck or Leap Frog?," *CQ Weekly Online* (February 12, 2007): 450-457. http://library.cqpress.com/cqweekly/weeklyreport 110-000002449623 (accessed July 31, 2007); Figure 13.5: National Archives and Records Administration Feb. 12, 2007 CQ Weekly, p. 453; Figure 13.7: Data drawn from Table 1, p 13 of *Justice Held Hostage: Politics and Selecting Federal Judges* updated 2006, The Constitution Project (http://www.constitution project.org/pdf/JusticeHeldHostageUpdated.pdf) and from Russell Wheeler, *Judicial Nominations and Confirmations in the 111th Senate and What to Look for in the 112th*, Brookings Governance Studies, January 4, 2011.

Chapter 14

Footnote 4: From Richard J. Stillman II "The Constitutional Bicentennial and the Centennial of the American Administrative State," *Public Administration Review* 47:1 (January/February 1987) 6; p. 487: Weber's Model of Bureaucracy, adapted with permission of The Free Press, a division of Simon & Schuster, Inc. from *The Theory of Social and Economic Organization* by Max Weber, translated by A.M. Henderson and Talcott Parsons. Edited by Talcott Parsons. Copyright 1947 by Talcott Parsons. Copyright renewed © 1975 by Talcott Parsons. All rights reserved.; Footnote 8: from Harold J. Laski *The American Democracy* (Viking Press, 1948) p. 167 as quoted in Seidman and Gilmour, op. cit., 259, Figure 14.3: Copyright © 2009 Gallup, Inc. Used with permission.; Footnote 11: Norton Long quote, Norton Long, ""Bureaucracy and Constitutionalism" *American Political Science Review* (September 1952); Footnote 12: Norton Long quote, Norton Long, ""Power and Administration" *Public Administration Review* (Autumn 1949) 258; Footnote 18: Stephen Skowronek. *Building A New American State: The Expansion of National Administrative Capacities 1877-1920*. (Cambridge: Cambridge University Press, 1982) 9-12; Footnote 31: Cited in Ronald C. Moe, "Federal Government Corporations: An Overview," CRS Report 98-954 (November 24, 1998) 1. http://www.jhu.edu/~ccss/toolsworkbooks/ pdfbook5/part1/a2.pdf; Figure 14.10: Figure 1 "Homeownership rates by age group" from "Andrews, D. and A. Caldera Sánchez (2011), "Drivers of Homeownership Rates in Selected OECD Countries", OECD Economics Department Working Papers, No. 849, OECD Publishing. http:// dx.doi.org/10.1787/5kgg9mcwc7jf-en; Figure 14.11: Figure 13 "Employment in government by level of government (2005)" from Pilichowski, E. and E. Turkisch (2008), "Employment in Government in the Perspective of the Production Costs of Goods and Services in the Public Domain", OECD Working Papers on Public Governance, No. 8, OECD Publishing. http://dx.doi.org/10.1787/245160338300;

Figure 14.12: Figure 10 "Employment in government and public corporations as a % of the labour force (2005)" from Pilichowski, E. and E. Turkisch (2008), "Employment in Government in the Perspective of the Production Costs of Goods and Services in the Public Domain", OECD Working Papers on Public Governance, No. 8, OECD Publishing, http://dx.doi. org/10.1787/245160338300; Footnote 38: Excerpt from GAO Report

Government Accountability Office, *Opportunities to Reduce Potential Duplication in Government Programs, Save Tax Dollars, and Enhance Revenue*, March 2011; Footnote 40: As quoted in Mary H. Cooper (1998, January 16). IRS reform. *CQ Researcher*, 8, 25-48; Figure 14.14: Harrison et al., *American Democracy Now*, 1/e. Copyright © 2009 McGraw-Hill Companies, Inc. Used with permission.

Chapter 15

Figure 15.1: From Harrison, *American Democracy Now*, 2/e TX ed. Copyright © 2011. Used by permission of McGraw-Hill Companies, Inc.; Figure 15.2: Taken from http://www.supremecourt. gov/about/Circuit%20Map.pdf; Figure 15.3: From http://courts.state.ny.us/courts/structure.shtml; Figure 15.5: Data from http://www.scotusblog.com/ reference/stat-pack/; Figure 15.6: Data from Matthew J. Franck, "Ruled by the Constitution–or 'Fairness'?" National Review, February 3, 2009, http://www. nationalreview.com/bench-memos/50482/ruled-constitution-or-fairness/matthew-j-franck; Figure 15.7: Data from www.pollingreport.com; Table 15.1: Maltese, John Anthony. The Selling of Supreme Court Nominees. pp. 3, Table 1. © 1995, 1998 The Johns Hopkins University Press. Adapted and reprinted with permission of The Johns Hopkins University Press.

Chapter 16

Figure 16.2: From http://www.truthandpolitics.org/ budget-basics.php, Table 4. Copyright © Truth and Politics. Used with permission ; Figure 16.3: The Concord Coalition, 2011, from http://www. concordcoalition.org/files/uploaded_for_nodes/ concord_chart_talk_oct_2011.pdf; Figure 16.5: From http://www.taxpolicycenter.org/taxtopics/ currentdistribution.cfm

Used courtesy of Tax Policy Center; Footnote 16: Joseph E. Stiglitz quote, from Joseph E. Stiglitz, "Of the 1%, by the 1%, for the 1%," Vanity Fair (May 2011). Copyright © 2011 Conde Nast; Figure 16.7: From http://nationalpriorities.org/en/resources/ federal-budget-101/charts/general/federal-outlays-and-revenues-1940-2015/ Copyright © 2010 National Priorities, Inc. Used with permission.; Table 16.10: "Public Sees Budget Negotiations at 'ridiculous,' 'disgusting,' 'stupid,;" Leaders' images tarnished," August 1, 2011, Pew Research Center for the People and the Press, a project of the Pew Research Center; Figure 16.11: From Federal Reserve Bank of St. Louis.

http://research.stlouisfed.org/fred2/series/ FEDFUNDS; Footnote 26: From The Economist Country Views Wire on The United States http:// www.economist.com/countries/usa/profile. cfm?folder=Profile%2DPolitical%20Forces.

Chapter 17

Figure 17.1: from OECD (2011), "OECD Health Data: Health status", OECD Health Statistics (database). Copyright © 2011 OECD. Used with permission. http://dx.doi.org/10.1787/data-00540-en; Footnote 13: Marilyn Moon quote, from Marilyn Moon, "The Future of Medicare as an Entitlement Program," *The Elder Law Journal* 12:1, p. 228. Copyright © 2004 The Elder Law Journal. Used with permission.; Figyre 17.2: Data from Kaiser Family Foundation, "Health Care Costs: A Primer" March 2009 Figure 1 http://www.kff.org/ insurance/upload/7692_02.pdf; Figure 17.11: From Pew Global Attitudes Project, "Global Warming Seen as a Major Problem Around the World: Less Concern in the U.S., Canada, and Russia" December 2, 2009 http://pewresearch.org/pubs/1427/ global-warming-major-problem-around-world-americans-less-concerned.

Chapter 18

Figure 18.1: Data from U.S. Department of Defense (1951, 1952 estimated); p. 642: John Ikenberry quote, Copyright © 2007 John Ikenberry. Used with permission.; p. 642: Edward S. Corwin quote, from Edward S. Corwin, *The President: Office and Powers, 1787-1984* 5th ed. Copyright © 1984 New York University Press. Used with permission.; Figure 18.2: Data from http://tydallreport.com as compiled by Pew Research Center's The State of the News Media 2007 annual report; p. 652: John Mueller quote, reprinted with permission from John Mueller, "The Iraq Syndrome," *Foreign Affairs* 84.6 (Nov-Dec 2005) p. 44. Copyright © 2005 by the Council on Foreign Relations, Inc. www.ForeignAffairs.com; Table 18.3: Jeffrey S. Passel and D'Vera Cohn, "U.S. Unauthorized Immigration Flows are Down Sharply Since Mid-Decade," The Pew Hispanic Center of the Pew Research Center (September 1, 2010), Table 4, p. 3, http://www.pewhispanic.org/2010/09/01/ us-unauthorized-immigration-flows-are-down-sharply-since-mid-decade/; Figure 18.7: From Climate Analysis Indicators Tool, World Resources Institute http://cait.wri.org/ Used with permission.; Table 18.4: Stockholm International Peace Research Institute, SIPRI Yearbook 2010 http://www.sipri.org/ research/armaments/nbc/nuclear

Shannon N. Kile, Vitaly Fedchenko, Bharath Gopalaswamy and Hans M. Kristensen, 'World nuclear forces', *SIPRI Yearbook 2011: Armaments, Disarmament and International Security* (Oxford University Press: Oxford, 2011), Table 7.1. World nuclear forces, January 2011, pp. 319-359; Figure 18.8: From Tim Kane, "Global U.S. Troop Deployment, 1950–2005," Center for Data Analysis, CDA06-02, The Heritage Foundation (May 24, 2006), p. 3.

INDEX

Chinese Exclusion Acts, 174
civil rights of, 174–175, 174f
congressional representation of, 286f
as federal court judge appointees, 548t, 549
population of, 201, 201f
voter turnout by, 306f
Assange, Julian, 374
assembly, freedom of, 4, 111, 126–128, 127f
Association of Community Organizations for Reform Now (ACORN), 374
AT&T, 562, 585
Atlantic Monthly, 649
attacks ads, 319
attitudinal model, 539
attorney general, 260
Audubon Society, 342
Australia
economic system in, 560
federal system in, 82
nominations systems in, 271
in Solomon Islands, 631–632
Australian ballot, 262, 302
authority-disorder bias, media, 396
automatic voter registration, 303
automobile industry
economic bailout of, 588
flex-fuel vehicles, 565–566, 566f
foreign imports and American, 650

B

baby boom generation, 609
Bachmann, Michele, 271, 321
bad tendency test, 121, 122
bailout plan of 2008, economic, 403–404, 588
balance of payments deficit, 653, 654f
balanced budget, 577–578, 578f
ballots, Australian, 262, 302
Bangladesh, 331–332, 361
banks
creation of national banking system, 91, 567
and Great Recession, 586–588
monetary policy and, 581–585, 582f, 584f
securities industry and Great Recession, 569
2009 bail out aid to, 16, 588
Barbour, Haley, 318
Barr, Bob, 250
Barron v. Baltimore, 113
Bartels, Larry M., 312
battleground states, 284, 304, 314
BBC News, 109
Beard, Charles A., 51–52, 53
behavior, regulating, 14
Belgium, 138
belief-action distinction, 132
Bell Laboratories, 380
Bennett, W. Lance, 389, 395–396
Berlin Wall, 638
Berlusconi, Silvio, 387–388, 388f
Bernanke, Ben, 403, 587, 588

Bernstein, Carl, 378
Bhutto, Benazir, 522
bicameral legislature, 54, 55f, 415–417, 416f
Biden, Joseph, 463, 647f
bilateral agreements, 641
Bill of Rights
amendment summary, 67, 67t
vs. civil liberties, 111
in Federalist-Anti-Federalist debate, 66–67
historical basis for, 111–112, 119
incorporation by states, 96, 112–114, 113f
incorporation of the, 114–116, 116f, 116t–117t, 121, 146
Locke's influence on, 18
powers in, 60
protections in, 18
slavery and, 153
Bill of Rights, English, 40, 41
bills, 411, 412f. *See also* legislative process
bills of attainder, 86, 138
bin Laden, Osama, 450, 455, 460, 631, 645
Bingham, John, 114
Bipartisan Campaign Reform Act of 2002 (McCain-Feingold Act)
campaign ads in, 289
passage of, 288
bipartisan consensus, 643
bipartisanship, 469
Bismarck, Otto von, 411
Black Americans. *See* African Americans
Black Codes, 155–156
Black, Justice Hugo, 115, 122, 123, 134, 158
black market, 560
Blackmun, Justice Harry, 135
Blair, Tony, 445, 446, 447f
block grants, 100
blogs
in campaigns, 320
as forum for political views, 373
as narrowcasting venue, 382
Bloomberg, Michael, 251
Blue Dog Coalition, 418
Boehner, John, 392, 432f, 433
Bond, Carol, 413
border compacts, 87
Boren, Dan, 419
Bork, Robert, 546
Bosnia, 642
Bosnian conflict, 645
Boston Globe, 71
Boston Massacre, 42, 42f
Boston *News-Letter*, 376
Boston Tea Party, 43, 300
Bouazizi, Mohamed, 369
Bowers v. Hardwick, 137
Boy Scouts of America, 179
Boynton v. Virginia, 161
Boys Nation, 466f, 467
BP Oil Company, Gulf oil spill of 2010, 83f, 343, 343f, 396, 615
Brandeis, Justice Louis, 83–84, 121, 534

Brandenburg v. Ohio, 122
Brazil
federal system in, 82
flex-fuel vehicles in, 565–566, 566f
multiparty system in, 248, 281
breach of peace, 132
Breedlove v. Suttles, 157
Brennan, Justice William J., 124, 125
Bretton Woods system, 569
bribes and gifts, 435
briefs, 533
British Broadcasting Corporation (BBC), 384
Brown, Gordon, 445–446
Brown, Robert E., 52
Brown v. Board of Education of Topeka, 70, 160–161, 176, 349, 542, 543, 622–623
Brown v. Board of Education of Topeka (II), 160
Brownbeck, Sam, 173
Bryan, William Jennings, 234, 252, 583
Buchanan, James, 459
budget. *See* federal budget
Budget and Accounting Act (1921), 508
budget deficits, 577–578, 578f, 579
budget resolution, 571
Buffett, Warren, 576
Bureau of the Budget, 462, 508
bureaucracy, 482–515
accountability to Congress, 489
accountability to the president, 510
annual budget, 507–508
and authorization of programs, 509–510
Civil Service Reform Act and, 512
control over, 507–515, 507f, 508t
creation of civil service system, 492–495, 493f, 494f, 495t
definition of, 485
democracy and, 485, 487, 487f
departments in, 497–499, 497f, 498f
Executive Office of the President and, 510
features of, 487–490, 488f, 489f
government corporations, 500–501, 502f
history of, 490–496, 493f
hybrid organizations, 502–504
independent agencies, 499
independent regulatory commissions, 499–500, 501t
management of public employees, 512–514, 514f
occupational categories, 488f
oversight of agency performance, 510
political appointees, nomination and confirmation of, 510–555
presidents and the, 472–475, 474f, 475f
public skepticism toward, 489, 489f
quasi-legislative and quasi-judicial roles of, 499
reorganization of the, 511–512

size of, 504–506, 505f, 506f
Weber's model of, 487–488
bureaucrats
civil servants, 492–495, 493f, 494f, 495t, 496f
control over, 507–515, 507f, 508t
definition of, 485
Burford, Anne Gorsuch, 451
Burger, Warren, 124
Burr, Aaron, 231
Bush, George H. W.
executive orders of, 475f
federal court judge appointees by, 548t
flag burning and, 123
judicial selections under, 476f
and *Roe v. Wade*, 542
START treaties under, 638
war with Iraq over Kuwait, 639
Bush, George W.
ABA relationship and, 544
bureaucratic accountability and, 510
campaign efforts on behalf of party, 468
as charter school advocate, 622
civil service protections under, 513
divided government under, 445–446, 447, 469
domestic surveillance under, 143–144
economic bailout plan of, 403, 588
educational reform under, 79, 81
in election of 2000, 79, 192, 252, 259, 310, 310t, 311, 393, 538
in election of 2004, 304
and election of 2008, 322
energy task force, 615, 619
enforcement of Controlled Substances Act, 102
executive orders of, 475f
federal court judge appointees by, 548, 548t
foreign policy of, 447f, 643, 644
free trade agreements by, 449
on global warming legislation, 658
Homeland Security Department creation, 430, 647
Hurricane Katrina response by, 483
immigration reform efforts of, 175, 656
increase of national power under, 101
Internet use by, 456
judicial selections under, 476f
as lame duck, 448f
Medicare prescription drug plan of, 101, 602
No Child Left Behind Act, 79, 80, 101, 451, 509, 621
on Obama, 183
party identification under, 208
party policies under, 254
presidential powers under, 457, 459
public approval of, 460, 461, 461f, 644–645

MoveOn.org, 287, 331, 335*f*
MSNBC, 5, 25
muckraking, 378
multilateral intervention, 641–642
multiparty systems, 248–249, 249*f*, 281, 281*t*
Murrow, Edward R., 379
Musharraf, Pervez, 521–522
Muslim Americans, 203–204
Muslims
    headscarves ban in France, 130, 130*f*
    in Kosovo, 95–96, 95*f*
Mussolini, Benito, 23
mutual assured destruction (MAD), 638

N

NAACP. *See* National Association for the Advancement of Colored People (NAACP)
NAACP Legal Defense and Education Fund, 159, 538
Nader, Ralph, 252, 356, 378
NAFTA (North American Free Trade Agreement), 469, 641
narrowcasting, 382
National Academy of Sciences, 566
National Aeronautics and Space Administration (NASA), 499, 500*f*
National Association for the Advancement of Colored People (NAACP), 363
    Brown v. Board of Education of Topeka and, 349–350
    catalyst for civil rights movement, 161
    formation of, 159–160
    Montgomery bus boycott and, 161
    school desegregation and, 159–160, 161
National Association of Homebuyers, 356
National Association of Manufacturers, 335
National Association of Realtors, 288
National Automobile Dealers Association (NADA), 335, 339, 342
national bank, 91, 567
National Beer Wholesalers Association, 347
National Civil Service Reform League, 493
National Commission on Fiscal Responsibility and Reform, 598
National Commission on Terrorist Attacks upon the United States, 646
national committees, 244–245
national conventions, 243, 243*f*, 245*f*
National Council of Churches of Christ, 129
National Council of La Raza (NCLR), 334
national debt, 573, 577, 579, 581
National Debt Clock, 581

National Democratic Congress (NDC), Ghana, 272–273, 272*f*
National Economic Council, 586
National Education Association (NEA), 624
National Farmers' Union, 356
National Gazette, 377
National Health Service (NHS), 606*f*
National Industrial Recovery Act (1933), 98
National Intelligence Council, 653
National Labor Relations Act (1935), 99
National Labor Relations Board, 585
national nominating convention, 244
National Organization for Women (NOW), 166, 167, 363
National Railroad Passenger Corporation, 501, 502*f*
National Recovery Administration, 98
National Review, 649
National Rifle Association (NRA), 115, 287, 334, 340, 341, 342, 347, 351
National Right to Life, 334, 342
National Science Foundation, 504, 647
national security. *See also* Homeland Security, Department of (DHS); war on terror
    Central Intelligence Agency, 499, 646, 647
    Federal Bureau of Investigation, 451, 477, 544
    Joint Chiefs of Staff, 646, 647*f*
    National Security Agency, 143
    national security apparatus, 646–647
    National Security Council, 110, 462, 647
    presidents role in, 452
    structures and officials, 648*t*
National Security Act (1947), 646
national security advisor, 647
National Security Agency (NSA), 143
National Security Council (NSC), 110, 462, 647
national security policy, 633
National Society of Accountants, 334
National Summit on Education Reform, 623
National Technology Transfer Center, 563
National Woman Suffrage Association, 165
Native American Rights Fund (NARF), 173
Native Americans
    Abramoff scandal and, 359
    Articles of Confederation and, 48
    civil rights of, 172–173, 173*f*
    congressional representation of, 286*f*
    as federal court judge appointees, 548*t*, 549
    formal apology to, 173, 173*f*, 181, 182
    sovereignty issues of, 542
nativism, 174
NATO (North Atlantic Treaty Organization), 449, 452, 637, 639, 642

natural disasters, 483–484
    Hurricane Katrina, 207, 311, 483, 484
    2008 earthquake in China, 299, 299*f*
    2011 earthquake and tsunami in Japan, 483, 616, 617*f*
natural rights, 133–134
Nazis, 127, 127*f*, 131
NCLR (National Council of La Raza), 334
NEA (National Education Association), 624
Near v. Minnesota, 118
Nebraska, 283, 623
necessary and proper clause (elastic clause), 62, 84, 90, 91, 92, 413
negative advertising, 394
negative view of government, 597
net neutrality, 385
Netherlands
    doctor-assisted suicide in, 138
    health care in, 595, 596, 603
Neustadt, Richard, 460, 466
Neutrality Acts, 635
Nevada, 314
Nevada primaries, 267, 268, 269*f*
New Deal
    cooperative federalism and, 90, 97–100, 98*f*, 99*f*
    and Democratic dominance, 235–236
    legislative strategy of, 468
    New Deal coalition, 203, 235–236
    New Deal generation, 198, 198*f*, 209
    New Deal realignment, 241, 324–325
    program, 204, 213, 234, 253, 542, 568
    securities industry under, 569
    Social Security program under, 607
new federalism, 100–101
New Hampshire primaries, 266, 267, 268, 269*f*
New Jersey Plan, 55, 56*f*, 57
new media, 382, 383*f*. *See also* media
New Orleans
    government response to Hurricane Katrina, 207, 311, 483, 484
    mass lynchings in, 175
New Republic, The, 649
New Voters Project, 306
New York, 535*f*
New York Associated Press, 375
New York Daily News, 374
New York Journal, 378
New York Post, 119*f*
New York Times
    civil liberties revelations by, 143
    claims of bias in, 395
    gatekeeping role of, 373
    and German economic policies, 558
    objective journalistic approach of, 378
    publication of the *Pentagon Papers* by, 118–119, 648

publication of WikiLeaks cables by, 374
    stories based on enterprise in, 390
New York Times v. Sullivan, 125
New York Times v. United States, 119
New York Tribune, 113
New York World, 377–378
New Yorker magazine, 649
New Zealand, 190
news, television, 381*f*, 649, 649*f*
newspapers
    declining readership of, 380, 382, 649
    early newspaper correspondents, 391–392
    first colonial, 376
    ideological bias in, 395
    muckraking, 378
    objective journalism, 378
    partisan press, 376–377
    penny press, 377
    rise of, 376*f*
    yellow journalism, 377–378
Nigeria, 151–152, 447
9/11 Commission, 646
9/11 terrorist attacks
    Afghanistan invasion after, 193, 631
    Bush's increases in national power and, 101
    Bush's public approval after, 644–645
    civil liberties after, 143–144, 147
    civil services practices and, 513
    deficit spending after, 578
    generational effect from, 198
    national security policy and, 633
    public opinion after, 207, 208*f*
    trust in government and, 191
Nineteenth Amendment, 166
Ninth Amendment, 133, 134
Nixon, Richard M.
    on biased media, 394
    block grants by, 100
    budgeting techniques of, 454
    bureaucratic accountability and, 510
    communication techniques of, 455–456
    divided government under, 469
    executive orders of, 475*f*
    federal court judge appointees by, 548*t*
    foreign policy of, 638, 643
    HMOs and health care costs, 604
    impeachment charges against, 414, 459
    in 1960 election, 229, 229*f*
    Pentagon Papers and, 118–119
    personal qualities of, 466
    speeches given by, 472
    Supreme Court nominees by, 101, 124, 544
    Vietnam War and, 452, 645
    visit to China, 381
    Watergate scandal, 378, 380, 456, 457, 466, 466*f*
    White House communication strategy of, 390

No Child Left Behind Act (NCLB), 79, 80, 101, 104, 451, 468, 509, 621
nomination process, 264
non-democracies, 3–4, 6, 9
North American Free Trade Agreement (NAFTA), 469, 641
North Atlantic Treaty Organization (NATO), 449, 452, 637, 639, 642
North Carolina
  slavery in, 113–114
  voting issues in, 309, 323
North Korea, 659, 660
Northrop Grumman, 351
Norway
  health care in, 603
  multiparty system in, 248–249, 281
  voter turnout in, 297–298, 297f, 303
NOW (National Organization for Women), 166, 167, 363
NRA (National Rifle Association), 115, 287, 334, 340, 341, 342, 347, 351
NSA (National Security Agency), 143
NSC (National Security Council), 110, 462, 647
nuclear arms limitation treaties, 638
Nuclear Non-Proliferation Treaty, 659
nuclear power, 615–617, 617f
nuclear power plants, 616
Nuclear Security Summit (2011), 660
nuclear waste, 617, 618f
nuclear weapons
  arms limitation treaties, 638
  Cuban missile crisis, 638
  nuclear proliferation, 659–660, 659t
  U.S. response to attack by, 644, 644f
nullification, 93–94

O

Obama, Barack, 234f
  ABA relationship and, 544
  and Afghanistan, 631, 661
  African American support of, 306, 315, 323
  antitrust policies and, 562
  bureaucratic accountability and, 510, 511
  Bush free trade agreements and, 449
  Bush income tax cuts and, 434
  cabinet of, 464, 464f
  campaign efforts on behalf of party, 469
  as charter school advocate, 622
  communication techniques of, 455, 455f
  congressional elections of 2010 and, 274
  and Controlled Substances Act, 102
  and Defense of Marriage Act, 102
  Democratic Party and, 223
  divided government under, 469

  on domestic surveillance, 144
  economic stimulus package of, 580, 588
  education agenda of, 451, 624
  in election of 2008, 206, 247f, 250, 254, 271, 273–274, 283, 289, 317, 322, 323, 433, 466
  in election of 2012, 264, 266, 284
  energy policy under, 619
  on enhanced interrogation, 145
  EOP of, 461, 463t
  executive orders of, 475f
  federal court judge appointees by, 548t, 550
  fiscal policy of, 580, 581f
  foreign policy of, 643
  formal apology to Native Americans, 173, 173f, 181
  on gay and lesbian citizens, 151, 179
  on global warming legislation, 658
  health care reform of, 5, 102, 313, 331, 348, 450, 468, 510, 595, 596, 602, 606, 606f
  immigration reform under, 175, 656
  Internet use by, 320, 455f, 456
  and Iraq War, 445, 661
  judicial selections under, 476f
  as lame duck, 448f
  legislative agenda of, 470
  Libya, U.S. involvement in and, 449, 452, 646
  Lilly Ledbetter Fair Pay Act and, 169
  media use by, 390, 391, 391f
  on military tribunals, 145
  and national security, 647f
  on nuclear weapons, 660
  Osama bin Laden and, 450f, 455, 460
  Pakistan and, 460
  party policies under, 254
  public approval of, 460, 461f, 472, 472f, 645
  and public financing for 2008 election, 289
  race and election of, 183, 285, 306, 315, 323
  reorganization proposal of, 512
  restrictions on lobbyists, 359
  signing statements by, 72
  social networking use by, 391, 391f
  on Social Security, 611
  Somali pirates incident and, 453
  Super PAC, 290
  Supreme Court nominees by, 177, 477, 545, 548, 550
  tax credit proposal by, 574
  under War Powers Resolution, 646
  and U.S. economic policy, 557, 558
  on veto of bills with earmarks, 408
  voter appeal of, 315
  on voter ID laws, 163
  voter turnout for, 306, 308
  youth vote for, 196
objective journalism, 378, 394

obscenity, 123–125, 125f
Occupational Safety and Health Administration, 562, 568–569
Occupy Wall Street movement, 300, 335, 336f, 347, 373–374, 373f
Ochs, Arthur, 378
O'Connor, Justice Sandra Day, 135, 544
O'Donnell, Christine, 271, 420
OECD (Organization for Economic Cooperation and Development), 495, 496f, 505, 506, 506f, 576
Office of Management and Budget (OMB), 462, 473, 508, 509, 510, 570, 580, 598
Office of National Drug Control Policy, 462
Office of Personnel Management (OPM), 499, 512–513
Office of Science and Technology, 462
Ogden, Aaron, 92–93
Ohio, 314
Ohio State Bar Association, 375
oil
  control of, 653
  dependence on imported, 614–615, 615f
  new sources of, 613
  OPEC embargo, 613
  Persian Gulf oil supply disruptions, 613, 614
O'Keefe, James, 374
Oklahoma City, 386
older Americans. See also Medicare; Social Security
  aging of population, 200–201, 200f
OMB (Office of Management and Budget), 462, 473, 508, 509, 510, 570, 580, 598
one-party systems, 248
online retargeting, 321
OPEC (Organization of the Petroleum Exporting Countries), 613
open primaries, 266
open rule, 436
open seat (congressional seat), 275
opinion leaders, 649
opinion polls. See public opinion polls
OPM (Office of Personnel Management), 499, 512–513
oral arguments, 533
order and safety, government's role in maintaining, 11–12
Oregon, 138
Organization for Economic Cooperation and Development (OECD), 495, 496f, 505, 506, 506f, 576
  health care in OECD countries, 600, 602, 602f, 603, 604f
Organization of the Petroleum Exporting Countries (OPEC), 613
original jurisdiction, 526
Oswald, Lee Harvey, 380
Otter, C. L. "Butch," 94f
outside tactics, interest group, 343, 346–349, 347f, 348f

oversight
  of bureaucratic agency performance, 510
  of Department of Homeland Security, 430, 430f, 431
  of executive branch by Congress, 412, 440–441

P

pack journalism, 389–390
PACs. see political action committees
Paine, Thomas, 45, 45f, 376, 524
Pakistan
  democracy in, 9
  judicial independence in, 521–522
  nuclear weapons in, 659, 660
  on Obama, 460
Palin, Sarah, 310
Palko v. Connecticut, 115
paradox of voting, 304
pardons, 452
Parenti, Michael, 395
Parks, Rosa, 161
Parliament, British, 40, 41–43
parliamentary sovereignty, 40
parliamentary systems, 447–448
partially mediated messages, 393
parties, political. See political parties
partisan press, 376–377
partisan realignment, 97
party accountability, in congressional elections, 278–280, 279f
party caucus, 420
party conference, 420
party identification
  campaigns and, 321–322
  political parties and, 229, 229f
  polls and, 213
  public opinion and changes in, 208–209, 209f
  socialization and, 194, 198
  voting preferences and, 313–314, 314f, 327
party in government, 241, 242f, 246–248, 247f
party in the electorate, 241, 242–243, 242f, 243f
party organization, 241, 242f, 243–246
party platform, 244, 270
party polarization, 323–325, 324f, 325f
party unity, 419, 419f
paternalism, 167
Patient Protection and Affordable Care Act (2010), 102
patriotism, 191
patronage, 233, 492, 494
Patterson, John, 162
Patterson, William, 55
Paul, Rand, 22
Paul, Ron, 22, 128, 196, 201, 266, 268
Paulson, Henry, 403, 588
pay-for-performance system, 513, 622
peer groups, 195–196
Pelosi, Nancy
  as Speaker of the House, 410, 423, 432f, 433
  on women's equality, 171

Pendleton Civil Service Reform Act, 493–494
penny press, 377
Pentagon Papers, 118–119
Pentagon Papers, 648–649
People for the American Way, 25
People's Action Party (Singapore), 3–4, 7
Perot, H. Ross, 248, 251
Perry, Rick
    campaign of, 394
    Romney and, 311
    Super PAC, 290
Persian Gulf War (1991), 460, 645, 645t, 662
Peterson, Scott, 119f
Pew Global Attitudes Project, 460
Pew Research Center, 382, 394, 395, 581, 655
peyote, 173
photo identification, state-issued, 163, 262
photo opportunities (photo-op), 390, 471
physician-assisted suicide, 138
Pike, John, 373
Pilgrims, 37
pirates, 453
plaintiff, 530
Planned Parenthood, 300, 347
Planned Parenthood of Southeastern Pennsylvania v. Casey, 135
Plessy, Homer, 157
Plessy v. Ferguson, 96, 157, 159, 160, 184
Plunkitt, George Washington, 233–234, 235, 332
Plymouth Company, 500
pocket veto, 438, 470
police enforcement, 12, 14
police powers, state, 85–86
policy adoption, 599
policy evaluation, 599
policy formulation, 598
policy implementation, 599
policy issues, in voting, 314–315, 315f
political action committees (PACs)
    formation of, 240
    interest groups and, 347, 347f
    regulation of contributions by, 288
    Super PACs, 290
political appointees, nomination and confirmation of, 510–555
political broadcasts, 289–290
political campaigns. *See* campaigns
political consultant, 318
political correctness, 126
political culture, 189–190, 189f
political efficacy, 190, 192
political events, 198
political freedom, 4
political identity, 194
political ideology
    in American politics, 25
    conservatism, 21, 25, 210–211
    definition of, 20
    facism, 23
    in Germany, 24–25, 24f
    liberalism, 21, 25, 210–211

libertarianism, 22–23, 210
    public opinion and, 210–211
    socialism, 23, 210
    value conflicts and, 20–21, 20f, 21f
political issues, 190, 192
political leader, 456, 456f
political machines, 233–234, 235
political participation, 4, 298
    conventional participation, 299, 300–301, 301t
    talk radio and, 379, 379f
    unconventional participation, 298, 299–300, 299f, 300f
political parties, 192, 222–254. *See also* party identification
    characteristics of, 225–226
    in Congress, 245, 246–247, 422–423, 422f, 427
    critical elections and, 240–241
    definition of, 225
    democracy and, 8
    early party formation, 230–232, 230f
    in economic systems, 559
    electoral realignment of, 241
    in the electorate, 241, 242–243, 242f, 243f
    First Party System, 231–232, 232f
    functions of, 227–230
    Golden Age of, 233–234, 239, 240
    in government, 241, 242f, 246–248, 247f
    ideological parties, 251
    leaders of, 230
    minor parties, 250
    national committees, 244–245
    national conventions, 243, 243f
    New Deal and Democratic dominance, 235–236
    organization of, 241–246
    platforms of, 237, 238f, 244, 270
    political machines, 233–234
    in present day, 237–241, 238t
    presidential leadership of, 247, 247f, 468–470, 470f
    realignment in, 241
    red and blue designation, 324
    Republican dominance and recovery, 234–235, 236–237
    responsible party model, 253–254
    resurgence of national party organizations, 245–246, 246f
    Second Party System, 232
    single-issue parties, 251
    state and local party organizations, 244
    in state government, 247–248
    third parties, 250–253, 251f, 252f
    ticket splitting between, 240, 279, 279f
    two-party system, 233, 248–250, 249f, 278
    winner-take-all electoral system, 280–281, 282, 283
political socialization
    agents of, 195
    by churches, 203, 203f

by colleges, 196–197
    definition of, 194, 229
    by families, 194, 195, 195f
    gender and, 205–206, 205f
    generational effects on, 198
    geographic region and, 206, 206f
    by media, 197–198, 197f, 372
    party identification, 194
    by peer groups, 195–196
    political identities, 194
    process of, 195
    public opinion as, 188
    race and ethnicity and, 201–202, 201f
    religion and, 202–205, 202f, 203f
    by schools, 196–197
    socioeconomic class and, 204–205, 204f, 205f
political tolerance, 189–190, 190f
politico model of representation, 407
politics
    aging of population and, 200–201, 200f
    definition of, 5
    energy and, 619–620
    gender and, 205–206, 205f
    health care system and, 604, 606–607, 606f
    interest groups and political information, 342–343
    race and ethnic groups and, 201–202, 201f
    religion and, 202–205, 202f, 203f
    social movements impact on, 361–362, 361f, 362f
    Social Security and, 610–611, 611f
poll taxes, 157, 176, 301
polls. *See* public opinion polls
polygamy, 132
popular legitimacy, 405
popular vs. electoral votes, 283
population, aging of, 200–201, 200f
Populist Party, 234, 248, 251, 252
pork barrel, 277, 407–408, 408f
pornography, broadcast media and, 124–125
Port Authority of New York and New Jersey, 87–88, 88f
Porteous, G. Thomas, Jr., 414, 414f
Portugal, 447
position papers, 321
positive view of government, 597
Postal Service, 501
Potter, Justice Stewart, 124
power of the purse, 405
precedent, 534
prerogative theory, 457
presidency/presidents, 444–477. *See also* executive branch
    administrative role of, 451
    aging of, 462f
    approval ratings of, 459–461, 461f, 467
    Article II on, 63, 71, 449, 457, 543–544, 642
    budget of, 507–508
    budget process and, 572, 599
    bureaucracy and, 472–475, 474f, 475f

bureaucratic accountability to, 510–511
    cabinet of, 415, 464–465, 464f, 497, 497f
    as chief budgeter, 454
    as chief magistrate, 451–452
    as commander-in-chief, 449, 452–453
    communication role of, 455–456, 455f, 465
    Congress and, 433–435, 450–451, 468–472
    as diplomat, 449–450
    economic role of, 454–455
    election of, 57–58, 282–284
    enforcement of federal laws, 477
    Executive Office of the President, 461–463, 463t, 510
    executive orders of, 145, 180, 474–475, 475f
    first-term presidents, 467
    foreign policy role of, 642, 643–645, 644f
    going public strategy and, 471–472, 471f, 472f
    honeymoon period of, 467–468
    interpretation of Constitution, 71–72
    judicial strategy of, 475–477, 476f
    legislative role of, 450–451, 453, 468–472, 470f, 471f, 472f
    media use by, 379, 390–391, 391f, 468
    order of succession, 497
    pardons by, 452
    as party leader, 247, 247f
    presidential powers theories, 457, 459
    public support of, 471–472, 471f, 472f
    qualifications for, 465–467, 466f
    reorganization and, 512
    second-term presidents, 467
    speeches given by, 472
    State of the Union address by, 390, 453
    Supreme Court nominees by, 99, 101, 121, 124, 158, 543–545
    terms of, 467
    veto power of, 71, 438, 470–471, 471f
    War Powers Resolution and, 452
president pro tempore, 421
presidential campaigns, 264, 264f
    expenditures for, 287, 288–289
    general election, 273–274
    nomination process, 267–270, 269f, 271–272
    primaries and caucuses, 265–267, 267f, 270–271, 271f
    public financing for candidates, 288–289
    selecting delegates, 264–265, 265f
presidential elections
    candidates in, 310–311, 310f
    Electoral College and, 282–284
    two-party system and, 250
    voter turnout in, 307–308, 308f
presidential interpretation, 71–72
Presidential Medal of Freedom, 175

Presidential Power (Neustadt), 460
presidential primaries. *See also*
    primary elections
    2012, 22, 201, 264, 264f
presidential signing statements,
    71–72, 72f
presidential systems, 447
press. *See* media; newspapers
press conferences, 390
primary elections
    caucuses and, 265–267, 267f,
      270–271, 271f
    closed, 266
    crossover voting in, 266
    direct primaries, 235
    national conventions, 243, 243f,
      245f, 268–270
    national primaries, 265–267,
      267f, 270–271
    nomination process from, 262,
      267–270, 269f, 271–272
    open, 266
    polls and, 213
    presidential, 22, 201, 264f,
      265–267, 267f
    timeline of, 269f
    in 2000, 215
    in 2008, 213, 265–266, 267–268
    in 2012, 22, 201, 266
    white primaries, 158
prime ministers, 446, 447
Princeton University, 166
Printing Industries of America, 335
prior restraint, 118–119
Priorities USA Action (Super
    PAC), 290
privacy. *See* right to privacy
Privacy International, 110
privileges and immunities clause,
    87, 114
Pro-Life Campaign Committee, 288
procedural due process, 115, 138–139
producer interest groups, 356
production of goods and services, 97,
    98, 99
professional associations, 333t,
    334–335, 336t, 339
Professional Golfers Association
    (PGA), 351
Profiles in Courage (Kennedy), 17
Progressive Change Campaign
    Committee, 25
Progressive movement, 234–235, 251,
    337–338, 378, 568
Progressive Party, 235, 248, 251, 252,
    253, 600
progressive tax system, 574–575
prohibited powers, 86
Prohibition, 252–253, 337, 337f
Prohibition Party, 248, 250, 251, 252
property rights
    of African Americans, 156
    of women, 164, 165, 168
proportional representation (PR)
    electoral system, 281–282,
      281t, 282f, 285
proportional tax rates, 575
Proposition 8 (California), 528f
prosecutorial discretion, 477
protectionism, 640

protective tariffs, 49
proxy wars, 637–638
Prussia, 493, 601
public assistance programs, 601
Public Citizen, 356
public employees. *See* bureaucrats
public goods, 11, 12, 14, 338, 339, 340
public opinion
    approval ratings of the president,
      459–461, 461f, 467, 472, 472f,
      644–645
    on the death penalty, 144f
    definition of, 188
    on foreign policy, 651–652, 652f
    gender gap in, 205–206, 205f
    generational effect on, 198
    generational replacement,
      207–208, 207f, 209f
    on gun control, 115, 116f
    on the Iraq War, 197
    measurement of, 188–189,
      211–215
    origin of polls on, 188–189
    party identification and,
      208–209, 209f
    political culture and, 189–190, 189f
    on political ideology, 210–211
    on same-sex marriage, 102, 102f
public opinion polls
    cell phones and, 214
    definition of, 211
    Internet, 214
    limitations of, 215
    margin of error in, 212, 215
    origins of, 212–213
    in political campaigns,
      214–215, 319
    population in, 211, 212
    random sample in, 211–212
    sampling error in, 215
    sampling in, 213–214
    types of, 214–215
    wording of questions in, 215
public policy
    adoption of, 599
    agenda setting, 597–598
    changing, 595–596
    definition of, 597
    evaluation of, 599–600
    formulation of, 598
    fragmentation in, 625–626
    implementation of, 599
    long-range planning in, 626–627
    market solutions in, 626
    model of policy making, 597–600
public property, displays of religious
    symbols on, 129, 130
public schools. *See* education
public servants. *See* bureaucrats
public service broadcasts, 384
public television, 12
Public Works Administration, 98
Puck, 493, 493f
Pulitzer, Joseph, 377, 378
Pulitzer Prizes, 378, 598
punishments, acts of, 3
Pure Food and Drug Act (1906),
    372, 378
Puritans, 37
push polls, 214–215

Q

Quakers, 164
quasi-governmental organizations
    (quagos), 502
quasi-non-governmental
    organizations (quangos), 502
quid pro quo sexual harassment, 168

R

race and ethnicity. *See also* minorities;
    specific groups
    majority-minority districts and,
      286–287, 286f
    Obama's election and, 183, 285,
      306, 315, 323
    party identification and, 198
    race and ethnic groups, 201–202,
      201f
    voter turnout and, 306, 306f
    voting rights and, 10, 96,
      157–158, 162–163, 260, 301
racially gerrymandered majority-
    minority districts, 286–287,
    286f
radio
    development of, 378–380, 379f
    presidential use of, 390, 471
    satellite, 387
    talk radio, 379, 379f, 386, 386f
Ramstad, James, 352
RAND Corporation, 504
Randolph, Edmund, 54
random digit dialing telephone poll,
    213–214
random sampling, 211–212
rational basis test, 167
Rayburn, Sam, 230, 469
Reagan, Ronald
    block grants by, 100
    budget cut proposals of, 470
    on bureaucracy, 485
    bureaucratic accountability
      and, 510
    criticisms for lack of experience
      of, 271
    deregulation of transportation
      and, 569
    divided government under, 469
    energy policies of, 613
    environmental policies under, 451
    executive orders of, 475f, 646
    federal court judge appointees by,
      548t, 549, 550t
    flag burning against policies
      of, 123
    foreign policy of, 643
    formal apology to Japanese
      Americans, 175, 181–182
    judicial selections under, 476, 476f
    new federalism under, 100
    party identification under, 208
    personal qualities of, 466
    public approval of, 472
    and *Roe v. Wade*, 542
    and school prayer, 129
    signing statements by, 71
    Soviet Union collapse and, 638
    staged events by, 390
    START treaties under, 638

student conservatism
    under, 196
Supreme Court nominees by,
    544, 546
realism or *realpolitik*, 634, 641
recall elections, 235, 262, 263, 263f
recessions, 579
reconciliation, 606
Reconstruction, 158
recuse, 526
Reddit, 347
redistricting, 275
    gerrymandering, 275–276, 276f,
      279, 286
Reed, Thomas B., 432
referendum, 235, 308–309
Regina v. Hicklin, 124
registration, voter, 303
regressive tax rates, 575
regulated multi-payer system, 603
regulatory compacts, 87–88
regulatory policy, 585
Rehabilitation Act (1973), 179
Rehnquist, Chief Justice William,
    141, 544
Reid, Harry, 421f
religion. *See also* freedom of religion
    in American values, 19, 19f
    displays on public property, 129,
      130, 542, 543
    politics and, 202–205, 202f, 203f
    in public schools, 129–130, 129f
    separation of church and state,
      128–129, 130–131, 131f
    volunteerism and religiosity, 26
    wearing of religious symbols,
      130, 130f
religious leaders, government by, 6
religious separatists and nonseparat-
    ists, 37
reorganization authority, 512
reparations, apologies and, 173, 173f,
    175, 181–182, 475
representation
    in Articles of Confederation, 406
    congressional representation of
      minorities, 286f, 287
    in the Constitution, 85–86, 87
    delegate model of, 406–407
    descriptive, 410, 411
    function of Congress, 405–407,
      406f
    politico model of, 407
    pork barrel and earmarks, 277,
      407–408, 408f
    proportional, 281–282, 281t,
      282f, 285
    substantive, 410, 411
    taxation without, 40–43
    trustee model of, 406
    of women and minorities,
      285–287, 286f
representative democracies, 7, 9
Republican National Committee
    (RNC), 244, 245, 249, 265
Republican Party
    church attendance by supporters
      of, 203, 203f
    conservatives and, 25, 210–211
    Contract with America, 254, 433